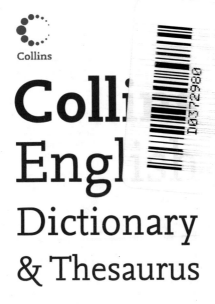

Collins

Colli
Engl
Dictionary
& Thesaurus

HarperCollins Publishers
Westerhill Road
Bishopbriggs
Glasgow
G64 2QT
Great Britain

First Edition 2004

Latest Reprint 2006

© HarperCollins Publishers 2004

ISBN-13 978-0-00-720880-7
ISBN-10 0-00-720880-4

Collins® and Bank of English®
are registered trademarks of
HarperCollins Publishers
Limited

www.collins.co.uk

A catalogue record for this book
is available from the British
Library

Typeset by Morton Word
Processing Ltd, Scarborough

Printed in Italy by Legoprint
S.P.A.

Acknowledgements
We would like to thank those
authors and publishers who
kindly gave permission for
copyright material to be used in
the Collins Word Web. We would
also like to thank Times
Newspapers Ltd for providing
valuable data.

CONTENTS

Adam Lamoureux
7322 - 118A Street N.W.
Edmonton, Alberta Canada
T6G 1V2

©NHL/LNH©

BANK *of* ENGLISH

This dictionary and thesaurus has been compiled with constant reference to the Bank of English, a unique database containing over 524 million words of written and spoken English, enabling Collins lexicographers to analyse how the language is actually used and how it is changing. The Bank of English was set up to be a resource for language research and lexicography. It contains a very wide range of material from books, newspapers, radio, TV, magazines, letters and talks, thereby reflecting the whole spectrum of English today. Its size and range make it an unequalled resource, and the purpose-built software for its analysis is unique to Collins dictionaries.

This ensures that Collins dictionaries accurately reflect English as it is used today in a way that is most helpful to the dictionary and thesaurus user.

FEATURES OF THE DICTIONARY AND THESAURUS

Short, clear definitions

Spelling help with changes in form of entry word

❶ symbol directs you to the thesaurus entry

Key synonyms highlighted

Generous choice of synonyms

tide ❶ *n* rise and fall of sea happening twice each day. **tidal** *adj* **tidal wave** great wave, esp. produced by earthquake. **tide over** help someone for a while.

tidings *pl n* news.

tidy ❶ *adj* **–dier, –diest 1** orderly, neat. ♦ *v* **2** put in order.

tie ❶ *v* **tying, tied 1** fasten, bind. **2** restrict. **3** equal (score of). ♦ *n* **4** that with which anything is bound. **5** restraint. **6** piece of material worn knotted round neck. **7** connecting link. **8** contest with equal scores. **9** match, game in eliminating competition. **tied** *adj* **1** (of public house) selling beer etc. of only one brewer. **2** (of cottage etc.) rented to tenant employed by owner.

tier ❶ *n* row, rank, layer.

tiff *n* petty quarrel.

tiger *n* large carnivorous feline

————————— THES

sticker, card

tide *n* = **current**, flow, stream, ebb, undertow

tidy *adj* = **neat**, orderly, clean, spruce, well-kept ≠ **untidy**; = (*Inf*) **considerable**, large, substantial, goodly, healthy ≠ **small** ♦ *v* = **neaten**, straighten, order, clean, groom ≠ **disorder**

tie *v* = **fasten**, bind, join, link, connect ≠ **unfasten**; = **tether**, secure; = **restrict**, limit, confine, bind, restrain ≠ **free** ♦ *n* = **fastening**, binding, link, bond, knot; = **bond**, relationship, connection, commitment, liaison; = **draw**, dead heat, deadlock,

FEATURES OF THE DICTIONARY AND THESAURUS

animal.

tight ❶ *adj* 1 taut, tense. 2 closely fitting. 3 secure, firm. 4 not allowing passage of water etc. 5 cramped. 6 *Inf* mean. 7 *Inf* drunk.

tighten *v* **tights** *pl n* one-piece clinging garment covering body from waist to feet. **tightrope** *n* taut rope on which acrobats perform.

● Restrictive labels show the context of use

tile *n* 1 flat piece of ceramic, plastic etc. used for roofs, floors etc. ◆ *v* 2 cover with tiles.

● Parts of speech

till¹ ❶ *v* cultivate.

till² ❶ *n* 1 drawer for money in shop counter. 2 cash register.

tiller *n* lever to move rudder of boat.

● Subject labels

tilt ❶ *v* 1 slope, slant. 2 take part in medieval combat with lances. 3 thrust (at). ◆ *n* 4 slope. 5 *Hist* combat for mounted men with lances.

● Parts of speech

stalemate

tier *n* = **row**, bank, layer, line, level

tight *adj* = **close–fitting**, narrow, cramped, snug, constricted ≠ **loose**; = **secure**, firm, fast, fixed; = **taut**, stretched, rigid ≠ **slack**; = **close**, even, well–matched, hard–fought, evenly–balanced ≠ **uneven**; = (*Inf*) **miserly**, mean, stingy, grasping, parsimonious ≠ **generous**; = (*Inf*) **drunk**, intoxicated, plastered (*Sl*), under the influence (*Inf*), tipsy ≠ **sober**

● Restrictive labels show the context of use

till¹ *v* = **cultivate**, dig, plough, work

till² *n* = **cash register**, cash box

vii

ABBREVIATIONS USED IN THE TEXT

abbrev	abbreviation	Lit	Literary
adj	adjective	masc	masculine
adv	adverb	Maths	Mathematics
Afr	African	Med	Medicine
Amer	American	Mil	Military
Anat	Anatomy	Mus	Music
Arch	Archaic	Myth	Mythology
Aust	Australian	n	noun
Bot	Botany	N	North(ern)
Brit	Britain, British	Naut	Nautical
Canad	Canadian	NZ	New Zealand
cap.	capital	Obs	Obsolete
Chem	Chemistry	Offens	Offensive
comb.	combining	oft.	often
conj	conjuction	orig.	originally
Dial	Dialect	Pathol	Pathology
E	East(ern)	pert.	pertaining
Eng	England, English	Photog	Photography
e.g.	for example	pl	plural
esp.	especially	Poet	Poetic
etc.	et cetera	prep	preposition
fem	feminine	pron	pronoun
Fig	Figurative	S	South(ern)
Fr	French	Scot	Scottish
Geog	Geography	sing.	singular
Hist	History	SI	Slang
Inf	Informal	US(A)	United States
interj	interjection		(of America)
kg	kilogram(s)	usu.	usually
km	kilometre(s)	v	verb
Lat	Latin	Vulg	Vulgar
lb(s)	pound(s)	W	West(ern)

A a

a, an adj 1 the indefinite article meaning one. 2 an is used before vowels.

AA 1 Alcoholics Anonymous. **2** Automobile Association.

aardvark n S Afr. anteater.

aback adv **taken aback** startled.

abandon ❶ v **1** desert. **2** give up. ♦ n **3** freedom from inhibitions etc. **abandoned** adj **1** deserted. **2** uninhibited. **3** wicked.

abase v humiliate, degrade.

abashed adj ashamed.

abate v make or become less.

abattoir n slaughterhouse.

abbey ❶ n **1** community of monks or nuns. **2** abbey church.

abbot n head of monastery.

abbreviate v shorten.

abbreviation n shortened word or phrase.

abdicate v give up (throne etc.).

abdomen n belly. **abdominal** adj

abduct ❶ v carry off, kidnap.

aberration n **1** deviation from normal. **2** lapse.

abet v **abetting, abetted** help, esp. in doing wrong.

abeyance n **in abeyance** not in use.

abhor v **–horring, –horred** loathe. **abhorrence** n **abhorrent** adj

abide ❶ v **1** endure **2** Obs reside. **abide by** obey.

ability ❶ n, pl **–ties** competence, power.

abject adj **1** wretched. **2** servile.

ablaze adj burning.

able ❶ adj capable, competent, or talented. **ably** adv

abnormal ❶ adj **1** not usual or typical. **2** odd. **abnormally** adv **abnormality** n

aboard adv on, onto ship, train, or aircraft.

abolish ❶ v do away with.

abolition n

Aborigine n original inhabitant of

THESAURUS

---

abandon v = **leave**, strand, ditch, forsake, run out on; = **stop**, give up, halt, pack in (Brit inf), discontinue ≠ **continue** ♦ n = **recklessness**, wildness ≠ **restraint**

abbey n = **monastery**, convent, priory, nunnery, friary

abduct v = **kidnap**, seize, carry off, snatch (Sl)

abide v = **tolerate**, suffer, accept, bear, endure

ability n = **capability**, potential, competence, proficiency ≠ **inability**; = **skill**, talent, expertise, competence, aptitude

able adj = **capable**, qualified, efficient, accomplished, competent ≠ **incapable**

abnormal adj = **unusual**, different, odd, strange, extraordinary ◆ ≠ **normal**

A

Australia.

abort ❶ v 1 terminate (a pregnancy) prematurely. 2 end prematurely and unsuccessfully.

abortion n **abortive** adj unsuccessful.

abound ❶ v be plentiful.

about ❶ adv 1 on all sides. 2 nearly. 3 astir. ♦ prep 4 round. 5 near. 6 concerning. **about–turn** n turn to the opposite direction.

above ❶ adv 1 higher up. ♦ prep 2 over. 3 higher than, more than. 4 beyond.

abrasion n 1 place scraped (e.g. on skin). 2 a wearing down.

abrasive n 1 substance for grinding, polishing etc. ♦ adj 2 causing abrasion. 3 grating.

abreast adv side by side.

abridge v shorten.

abroad ❶ adv 1 to or in a foreign country. 2 at large.

abrupt ❶ adj 1 sudden. 2 blunt. 3 steep. **abruptly** adv

abscess n gathering of pus.

abscond v leave secretly.

absent ❶ adj 1 away. 2 missing. ♦ v 3 keep away. **absence** n

absentee n one who stays away.

absently adv

absolute ❶ adj 1 complete. 2 unrestricted. 3 pure. **absolutely** adv 1 completely. ♦ interj 2 certainly.

absolve v free from, pardon.

absorb ❶ v 1 suck up. 2 engross. 3 take in. **absorption** n **absorbent** adj

abstain v refrain. **abstention** n **abstinence** n

abstemious adj sparing in eating and drinking.

abstract ❶ adj 1 existing only in the mind. 2 not concrete. ♦ n 3 summary. ♦ v 4 remove. 5

abolish v = **do away with**, end, destroy, eliminate, cancel ≠ **establish**

abort v = **terminate** (a pregnancy), miscarry; = **stop**, end, finish, check, arrest

abound v = **be plentiful**, thrive, flourish, be numerous, proliferate

about prep = **regarding**, on, concerning, dealing with, referring to; = **near**, around, close to, nearby, beside ♦ adv = **approximately**, around, almost, nearly, approaching

above prep = **over**, upon, beyond, on top of, exceeding ≠ **under**; = **senior to**, over, ahead of, in

charge of, higher than

abroad adv = **overseas**, out of the country, in foreign lands, everywhere, here and there

abrupt adj = **sudden**, unexpected, rapid, surprising, quick ≠ **slow**; = **curt**, brief, short, rude, impatient ≠ **polite**

absent adj = **away**, missing, gone, elsewhere, unavailable ≠ **present**; = **absent–minded**, blank, vague, distracted, vacant ≠ **alert**

absolute adj = **complete**, total, perfect, pure, sheer; = **supreme**, sovereign, unlimited, ultimate, full

absorb v = **soak up**, suck up, receive, digest, imbibe; = **engross**,

summarize. **abstracted** *adj* preoccupied. **abstraction** *n*
abstruse *adj* hard to understand.
absurd ❶ *adj* ridiculous.
absurdity *n*
abundant ❶ *adj* plentiful.
abundantly *adv* **abundance** *n* great amount.
abuse ❶ *v* 1 misuse. 2 address rudely. ♦ *n* 3 wrong treatment. 4 insulting comments. **abusive** *adj*
abusively *adv*
abut *v* **abutting, abutted** adjoin.
abysmal *adj* 1 immeasurable, very great 2 *Inf* extremely bad.
abysmally *adv*
abyss *n* very deep gulf or pit.
AC alternating current.
acacia *n* gum–yielding tree or shrub.
academy *n, pl*–**mies** 1 society to advance arts or sciences. 2 institution for specialized training. 3 *Scot* secondary school. **academic** *adj* 1 of a place of learning. 2

theoretical. ♦ *n* 3 member of college or university.
accede *v* 1 agree. 2 attain (office etc.).
accelerate ❶ *v* (cause to) increase speed. **acceleration** *n* **accelerator** *n* mechanism to increase speed.
accent ❶ *n* 1 stress or pitch in speaking. 2 mark to show this. 3 style of pronunciation. ♦ *v* 4 emphasize.
accentuate *v* stress, emphasize.
accept ❶ *v* 1 take, receive. 2 admit, believe. 3 agree to.
acceptable *adj* **acceptance** *n*
access ❶ *n* 1 right or means of entry. ♦ *v* 2 *Comp* obtain (data).
accessible *adj* easy to approach.
accessibility *n*
accession *n* 1 attaining of office, right etc. 2 addition.
accessory ❶ *n, pl*–**ries** 1 supplementary part of car, woman's dress etc. 2 person assisting crime.

———————— THESAURUS ————————

involve, engage, fascinate, rivet
abstract *adj* = **theoretical**, general, academic, speculative, indefinite ≠ **actual** ♦ *n* = **summary**, résumé, outline, digest, epitome ≠ **expansion** ♦ *v* = **extract**, draw, pull, remove, separate ≠ **add**
absurd *adj* = **ridiculous**, crazy (*Inf*), silly, foolish, ludicrous ≠ **sensible**
abundant *adj* = **plentiful**, full, rich, liberal, generous ≠ **scarce**
abuse *n* = **maltreatment**, damage, injury, hurt, harm; = **insults**, blame, slights, put–downs,

censure; = **misuse**, misapplication ♦ *v* = **ill-treat**, damage, hurt, injure, harm ≠ **care for**; = **insult**, offend, curse, put down, malign ≠ **praise**
accelerate *v* = **increase**, grow, advance, extend, expand ≠ **fall**
accent *n* = **pronunciation**, tone, articulation, inflection, brogue ♦ *v* = **emphasize**, stress, highlight, underline, underscore
accept *v* = **receive**, take, gain, pick up, secure ≠ **reject**
access *n* = **admission**, entry, passage

A

accident ❶ n 1 event happening by chance. 2 mishap, esp. causing injury. **accidental** adj **accidentally** adv

acclaim ❶ v 1 applaud, praise. ♦ n 2 applause. **acclamation** n

acclimatize v accustom to new climate or environment.

accolade n 1 public approval. 2 honour. 3 token of knighthood.

accommodate ❶ v 1 supply, esp. with lodging. 2 oblige. 3 adapt. **accommodating** adj obliging. **accommodation** n lodgings.

accompany ❶ v –nying, –nied 1 go with. 2 supplement. 3 occur with. 4 play music to support a soloist. **accompaniment** n

accomplice n one assisting another in crime.

accomplish v 1 carry out. 2 finish. **accomplished** adj 1 complete. 2 proficient.

accord ❶ n 1 agreement, harmony. ♦ v 2 (cause to) be in accord with. 3 grant. **according to** 1 as stated by. 2 in conformity with. **accordingly** adv 1 as the circumstances suggest. 2 therefore.

accordion n musical instrument with bellows and reeds.

accost v approach and speak to.

account ❶ n 1 report. 2 importance. 3 statement of moneys received, paid, or owed. 4 person's money held in bank. ♦ v 5 regard as. 6 give reason, answer (for). **accountable** adj responsible.

accountancy n keeping, preparation of business accounts.

accountant n **accounting** n

accoutrements pl n 1 equipment, esp. military. 2 trappings.

accredited adj authorized, officially recognized.

accrue v –cruing, –crued 1 be added. 2 result.

accumulate ❶ v 1 gather. 2 collect. **accumulation** n

———— THESAURUS ————

accessory n = **extra**, addition, supplement, attachment, adjunct; = **accomplice**, partner, ally, associate (in crime), assistant

accident n = **crash**, smash, wreck, collision; = **misfortune**, disaster, tragedy, setback, calamity

acclaim v = **praise**, celebrate, honour, cheer, admire ♦ n = **praise**, honour, celebration, approval, tribute ≠ **criticism**

accommodate v = **house**, put up, take in, lodge, shelter; = **help**, support, aid, assist, cooperate with; = **adapt**, fit, settle, alter, adjust

accompany v = **go with**, lead, partner, guide, attend; = **occur with**, belong to, come with, supplement, go together with

accord n = **treaty**, contract, agreement, arrangement, settlement

account n = **description**, report, story, statement, version; = **importance**, standing, concern, value, note ♦ v = **consider**, rate, value, judge, estimate

accumulate v = **build up**, increase, be stored, collect, gather

accurate ❶ *adj* exact, correct.
accurately *adv* **accuracy** *n*
accursed *adj* **1** under a curse. **2**
detestable.
accuse ❶ *v* **1** charge with
wrongdoing. **2** blame.
accusation *n*
accustom ❶ *v* make used to,
familiarize. **accustomed** *adj* **1**
usual. **2** used (to). **3** in the habit
(of).
ace ❶ *n* **1** one at dice, cards,
dominoes. **2** *Tennis* winning serve.
3 *Inf* expert.
acetylene *n* colourless, flammable
gas.
ache ❶ *n* **1** continuous pain. ◆ *v* **2**
to be in pain. **aching** *adj*
achieve ❶ *v* accomplish, gain.
achievement *n*
acid ❶ *adj* **1** sharp, sour. ◆ *n* **2**
Chem compound which combines
with bases to form salts. **acidic** *adj*
acidity *n*

acknowledge ❶ *v* **1** admit,
recognize. **2** say one has received.
acknowledgment *n*
acme *n* highest point.
acne *n* pimply skin disease.
acorn *n* fruit of the oak tree.
acoustic *adj* of sound and
hearing. **acoustics** *pl n* **1** science of
sounds. **2** features of room or
building as regards sounds heard
in it.
acquaint *v* make familiar, inform.
acquaintance *n* **1** person known. **2**
personal knowledge.
acquiesce *v* agree, consent.
acquiescence *n*
acquire ❶ *v* gain, get. **acquisition**
n **1** act of getting. **2** material gain.
acquit ❶ *v* –**quitting,** –**quitted 1**
declare innocent. **2** settle (a debt).
3 behave (oneself). **acquittal** *n*
acre *n* measure of land, 4840
square yards.
acrid *adj* pungent, sharp.

———————— THESAURUS ————————

≠ **disperse**
accurate *adj* = **precise**, close,
correct, careful, strict ≠ **inaccurate**
accuse *v* = **charge with**, indict for,
impeach for, censure with,
incriminate for ≠ **absolve**
accustom *v* = **familiarize**, train,
discipline, adapt, instruct
ace *n* = (*Cards, dice, etc.*) **one**,
single point; = (*Inf*) **expert**, star,
champion, authority, professional
◆ *adj* = (*Inf*) **great**, brilliant, fine,
wonderful, excellent
ache *v* = **hurt**, suffer, burn, pain,
smart ◆ *n* = **pain**, discomfort,
suffering, hurt, throbbing (*Inf*)

achieve *v* = **accomplish**, fulfil,
complete, gain, perform
acid *adj* = **sour**, tart, pungent,
acerbic, acid ≠ **sweet**; = **sharp**,
cutting, biting, bitter, harsh
≠ **kindly**
acknowledge *v* = **admit**, own up,
allow, accept, reveal ≠ **deny**;
= **greet**, address, notice,
recognize, salute ≠ **snub**; = **reply
to**, answer, notice, recognize,
respond to ≠ **ignore**
acquire *v* = **get**, win, buy, receive,
gain ≠ **lose**
acquit *v* = **clear**, free, release,
excuse, discharge ≠ **find guilty**

acrobat *n* one skilled in gymnastic feats, esp. in circus etc. **acrobatic** *adj* **acrobatics** *pl n*

acronym *n* word formed from initial letters of other words.

across *adv/prep* **1** crosswise. **2** from side to side. **3** on or to the other side.

acrylic *n* synthetic fibre.

ACT Australian Capital Territory.

act ❶ *n* **1** thing done, deed. **2** doing. **3** law or decree. **4** section of a play. ♦ *v* **5** perform, as in a play. **6** exert force, work, as mechanism. **7** behave. **acting** *n/adj* temporary. **action** *n* **1** operation. **2** deed. **3** gesture. **4** expenditure of energy. **5** battle. **6** lawsuit. **active** *adj* **1** in operation. **2** busy, occupied. **3** brisk, energetic. **activate** *v* **actively** *adv* **activity** *n* **actor, actress** *n* one who acts in a play, film etc.

actual ❶ *adj* **1** existing in the present. **2** real. **actuality** *n* **actually** *adv* really, indeed.

actuary *n, pl* **–aries** expert in insurance statistics.

actuate *v* activate.

acumen *n* keen discernment.

acupuncture *n* medical treatment by insertion of needles into the body.

acute ❶ *adj* **1** shrewd. **2** sharp. **3** severe. ♦ *n* **4** accent (´) over letter. **acutely** *adv*

AD anno Domini.

ad *n* abbrev. of ADVERTISEMENT.

adage *n* proverb.

adagio *adj/n Mus* slow (passage).

adamant ❶ *adj* unyielding.

Adam's apple projecting part at front of throat.

adapt ❶ *v* **1** alter for new use. **2** modify. **3** change. **adaptable** *adj* **adaptation** *n* **adaptor, –er** *n* device for connecting two electrical appliances to a single socket.

add ❶ *v* **1** join. **2** increase by. **3** say further. **addition** *n* **additional** *adj* **additionally** *adv* **additive** *n* something added, esp. to foodstuffs.

addendum *n, pl* **–da** thing to be

————— THESAURUS —————

act *v* = **do something**, perform, function, pretend to be, impersonate; = **perform**, mimic ♦ *n* = **deed**, action, performance, achievement, undertaking; = **pretence**, show, front, performance, display; = **law**, bill, measure, resolution, decree; = **performance**, show, turn, production, routine
actual *adj* = **real**, substantial, concrete, definite, tangible ≠ **theoretical**

acute *adj* = **serious**, important, dangerous, critical, crucial; = **sharp**, shooting, powerful, violent, severe
adamant *adj* = **determined**, firm, fixed, stubborn, uncompromising ≠ **flexible**
adapt *v* = **adjust**, change, alter, modify, accommodate
add *v* = **count up**, total, reckon, compute, add up ≠ **take away**; = **include**, attach, supplement, adjoin, augment

added.

adder *n* small poisonous snake.

addict ⊕ *n* one who has become dependent on something.

addicted *adj* **addiction** *n*

address ⊕ *n* **1** direction on letter. **2** place where one lives. **3** speech. ♦ *v* **4** mark destination. **5** speak to. **6** direct.

adenoids *pl n* tissue at back of nose.

adept ⊕ *adj* **1** skilled. ♦ *n* **2** expert.

adequate ⊕ *adj* **1** sufficient, suitable. **2** not outstanding. **adequacy** *n* **adequately** *adv*

adhere *v* **1** stick to. **2** be firm in opinion etc. **adherence** *n* **adherent** *n* **adhesion** *n* **adhesive** *adj/n*

ad hoc *adj/adv* for a particular occasion only.

adieu *interj* farewell.

adjacent ⊕ *adj* lying near, next (to).

adjective *n* word which qualifies a noun.

adjoin ⊕ *v* **1** be next to. **2** join.

adjourn ⊕ *v* **1** close (meeting etc.) temporarily. **2** *Inf* move elsewhere. **adjournment** *n*

adjudge *v* **1** declare. **2** decide.

adjudicate *v* **1** judge. **2** sit in judgment. **adjudication** *n* **adjudicator** *n*

adjunct *n* person or thing added or subordinate.

adjure *v* earnestly entreat.

adjust ⊕ *v* **1** adapt. **2** alter slightly, regulate. **adjustable** *adj* **adjustment** *n*

adjutant *n* military officer who assists superiors.

ad-lib *v* **-libbing, -libbed 1** improvise. ♦ *n* **2** improvised remark.

administer ⊕ *v* **1** manage. **2** dispense, as justice etc.

administrate *v* manage (an organization). **administration** *n* **1** management, supervision. **2** governing body. **administrative** *adj* **administrator** *n*

—————————— THESAURUS ——————————

addict *n* = **junkie** (*Inf*), freak (*Inf*), fiend (*Inf*); = **fan**, lover, nut (*Sl*), follower, enthusiast

address *n* = **location**, home, place, house, point; = **speech**, talk, lecture, discourse, sermon ♦ *v* = **speak to**, talk to, greet, hail, approach

adept *adj* = **skilful**, able, skilled, expert, practised ≠ **unskilled** ♦ *n* = **expert**, master, genius, hotshot (*Inf*), dab hand (*Brit inf*)

adequate *adj* = **sufficient**, enough ≠ **insufficient**

adjacent *adj* = **adjoining**, neighbouring, nearby ≠ **far away**

adjoin *v* = **connect with** or **to**, join, link with, touch on, border on

adjourn *v* = **postpone**, delay, suspend, interrupt, put off ≠ **continue**

adjust *v* = **adapt**, change, alter, accustom, conform; = **change**, reform, alter, adapt, revise

administer *v* = **manage**, run, control, direct, handle; = **dispense**, give, share, provide, apply

admiral *n* naval officer of highest rank.

admire ❶ *v* regard with approval, respect, or wonder. **admirable** *adj* **admirably** *adv* **admiration** *n* **admirer** *n* **admiring** *adj*

admit ❶ *v* –mitting, –mitted 1 confess. 2 accept as true. 3 allow. 4 let in. **admissible** *adj* **admission** *n* 1 permission to enter. 2 entrance fee. 3 confession. **admittance** *n* permission to enter. **admittedly** *adv*

admonish *v* 1 reprove. 2 exhort. **admonition** *n*

ad nauseam *Lat* to a boring or disgusting extent.

ado *n* fuss.

adolescence ❶ *n* period of life just before maturity. **adolescent** *n/adj* young (person).

adopt ❶ *v* 1 take as one's child. 2 take up, as principle, resolution. **adoption** *n*

adore ❶ *v* 1 love intensely. 2 worship. **adorable** *adj* **adoration** *n* **adoring** *adj*

adorn ❶ *v* decorate.

adrenal *adj* near the kidney.

adrenalin *n* hormone secreted by adrenal glands.

adrift ❶ *adj/adv* 1 drifting 2 *Inf* detached 3 *Inf* off course.

adroit *adj* 1 skilful. 2 clever. **adroitly** *adv*

adulation *n* flattery.

adult ❶ *adj* 1 grown-up. 2 mature. ♦ *n* 3 mature person, animal or plant.

adulterate *v* make impure by addition. **adulteration** *n*

adultery *n, pl* –teries sexual unfaithfulness of a husband or wife. **adulterer** *n* **adulterous** *adj*

advance ❶ *v* 1 bring forward. 2 suggest. 3 lend (money). 4 go forward. 5 improve in position or value. ♦ *n* 6 progress. 7 movement forward. 8 improvement. 9 a loan. ♦ *adj* 10 ahead in time or position. **advanced** *adj* 1 at a late stage. 2 not elementary. 3 ahead of the times. **advancement** *n*

admire *v* = **respect**, value, prize, honoured, praise ≠ **despise**
admit *v* = **confess**, confide, own up, come clean (*Inf*); = **allow**, agree, accept, reveal, grant ≠ **deny**; = **let in**, allow, receive, accept, introduce ≠ **keep out**
adolescence *n* = **teens**, youth, minority, boyhood, girlhood
adopt *v* = **take in**, raise, nurse, mother, rear ≠ **abandon**
adore *v* = **love**, honour, admire, worship, esteem ≠ **hate**

adorn *v* = **decorate**, array, embellish, festoon
adrift *adj* = **drifting**, afloat, unmoored, unanchored; = **aimless**, goalless, directionless, purposeless
adult *n* = **grown-up**, mature person, person of mature age, grown or grown-up person, man or woman ♦ *adj* = **fully grown**, mature, grown-up, of age, ripe
advance *v* = **progress**, proceed, come forward, make inroads,

advantage ❶ n more favourable position or state. **advantageous** adj

advent n 1 arrival, coming. 2 (with cap.) the four weeks before Christmas.

adventure ❶ n exciting undertaking or happening. **adventurous** adj

adverb n word added to verb etc. to modify meaning.

adverse ❶ adj 1 hostile. 2 unfavourable. **adversary** n enemy. **adversely** adv **adversity** n distress, misfortune.

advert ❶ n Inf advertisement.

advertise ❶ v 1 publicize. 2 give notice of, esp. in newspapers etc. 3 make public request (for). **advertisement** n **advertising** adj/n

advice ❶ n 1 counsel. 2 notification.

advocate ❶ n 1 one who pleads the cause of another, esp. in court of law. 2 Scot barrister. ♦ v 3 recommend. **advocacy** n

aeon n long period of time.

aerate v 1 charge liquid with gas. 2 expose to air.

aerial adj 1 operating in the air. 2 pertaining to aircraft. ♦ n 3 part of radio etc. receiving or sending radio waves.

aerobatics pl n stunt flying.

aerobics pl n exercise system designed to increase oxygen in the blood. **aerobic** adj

aerodrome n airfield.

aerodynamics pl n study of air flow, esp. round moving solid bodies. **aerodynamic** adj

aeronautics pl n science of air navigation and flying in general. **aeronautical** adj

———————— THESAURUS ————————

make headway ≠ retreat; = **accelerate**, speed, promote, hasten, bring forward; = **improve**, rise, develop, pick up, progress; = **suggest**, offer, present, propose, advocate ≠ withhold ♦ n = **down payment**, credit, loan, fee, deposit; = **attack**, charge, strike, assault, raid; = **improvement**, development, gain, growth, breakthrough ♦ adj = **prior**, early, beforehand

advantage n = **benefit**, help, profit, favour ≠ disadvantage; = **lead**, sway, dominance, precedence

adventure n = **venture**, experience, incident, enterprise, undertaking

adverse adj = **unfavourable**, hostile, unlucky; opposing, hostile

advert n = (Brit inf) **advertisement**, notice, commercial, ad (Inf), announcement

advertise v = **publicize**, promote, plug (Inf), announce, inform

advice n = **guidance**, help, opinion, direction, suggestion

advocate v = **recommend**, support, champion, encourage, propose ≠ oppose ♦ n = **supporter**, spokesman, champion, defender, campaigner; = (Law) **lawyer**, attorney, solicitor, counsel, barrister

aeroplane n heavier–than–air flying machine.

aerosol n (substance dispensed from) pressurized can.

aerospace n earth's atmosphere and space beyond.

aesthetic adj relating to principles of beauty. **aesthetics** pl n study of beauty. **aesthetically** adv **aesthete** n

afar adv from, at, or to, a great distance.

affable adj polite and friendly.

affair ❶ n 1 thing done or attended to. 2 business. 3 happening. 4 sexual liaison. ♦ pl 5 personal or business interests. 6 matters of public interest.

affect ❶ v 1 act on. 2 move feelings. 3 make show of.

affectation n show, pretence.

affected adj 1 making a pretence. 2 moved. 3 acted upon. **affection** n fondness, love. **affectionate** adj **affectionately** adv

affidavit n written statement on oath.

affiliate ❶ v/n (join as an) associate. **affiliation** n

affinity ❶ n, pl –ties 1 natural liking. 2 resemblance. 3 chemical attraction.

affirm ❶ v 1 assert positively. 2 make solemn declaration. **affirmation** n **affirmative** adj/n positive (statement).

affix v fasten (to).

afflict ❶ v cause to suffer. **affliction** n

affluent ❶ adj wealthy. **affluence** n

afford ❶ v 1 to be able to (buy, do). 2 provide. **affordable** adj

affront v/n insult.

afield adv far afield far away.

aflame adv/adj burning.

afloat adv 1 floating. 2 at sea.

afoot adv 1 astir. 2 on foot.

aforesaid, aforementioned adj previously mentioned.

afraid ❶ adj 1 frightened. 2 regretful.

——————— THESAURUS ———————

affair n = **matter**, business, happening, event, activity; = **relationship**, romance, intrigue, fling, liaison

affect v = **influence**, concern, alter, change, manipulate; = **emotionally move**, touch, upset, overcome, stir

affiliate v = **associate**, unite, join, link, ally

affinity n = **attraction**, liking, leaning, sympathy, inclination ≠ **hostility**; = **similarity**, relationship, connection,

correspondence, analogy ≠ **difference**

affirm v = **declare**, state, maintain, swear, assert ≠ **deny**; = **confirm**, prove, endorse, ratify, verify ≠ **refute**

afflict v = **torment**, trouble, pain, hurt, distress

affluent adj = **wealthy**, rich, prosperous, loaded (Sl), well–off ≠ **poor**

afford v = **have the money for**, manage, bear, pay for, spare; = **bear**, stand, sustain, allow

A

afresh *adv* again, anew.

African *adj* of Africa. **African violet** house plant with pink or purple flowers.

aft *adv* towards stern of ship.

after 𝕋 *adv* 1 later. 2 behind. ♦ *prep* 3 behind. 4 later than. 5 on the model of. 6 pursuing. ♦ *conj* 7 later than. **afters** *pl n* dessert.

afterbirth *n* membrane expelled after a birth.

aftermath 𝕋 *n* result, consequence.

afternoon *n* time from noon to evening.

aftershave *n* lotion applied to face after shaving.

afterwards, afterward *adv* later.

again 𝕋 *adv* 1 once more. 2 in addition.

against 𝕋 *prep* 1 in opposition to. 2 in contact with. 3 opposite.

agape *adj/adv* open-mouthed.

agate *n* semiprecious quartz.

age 𝕋 *n* 1 length of time person or thing has existed. 2 time of life. 3 period of history. 4 long time. 5 maturity, old age. ♦ *v* 6 make or grow old. **aged** *adj* 1 old. ♦ *pl n* 2 old people. **ageing** *n/adj*

agenda 𝕋 *pl n* list of things to be attended to.

agent 𝕋 *n* 1 one authorized to act for another. 2 person or thing producing effect. **agency** *n* 1 organization providing service. 2 business, premises of agent.

aggrandize *v* make greater in size, power, or rank.

aggravate 𝕋 *v* 1 make worse or more severe 2 *Inf* annoy. **aggravation** *n*

aggregate 𝕋 *v* 1 gather into mass. ♦ *adj* 2 gathered thus. ♦ *n* 3

——————— THESAURUS ———————

yourself

afraid *adj* = **scared**, frightened, nervous, terrified, shaken ≠ **unafraid**; = **reluctant**, frightened, scared, unwilling, hesitant

after *adv* = **following** later, next, succeeding, afterwards

aftermath *n* = **effects**, results, wake, consequences, outcome

again *adv* = **once more**, another time, anew, afresh; = **also**, in addition, moreover, besides, furthermore

against *prep* = **beside**, on, up against, in contact with, abutting; = **opposed to**, anti (*Inf*), hostile to, in opposition to, averse to; = **in**

opposition to, resisting, versus, counter to, in the opposite direction of

age *n* = **years**, days, generation, lifetime, length of existence; = **old age**, maturity, experience, seniority, majority ≠ **youth**

agenda *n* = **programme**, list, plan, schedule, diary

agent *n* = **representative**, rep (*Inf*), negotiator, envoy, surrogate; = **author**, worker, vehicle, instrument, operator

aggravate *v* = **make worse**, exaggerate, intensify, worsen, exacerbate ≠ **improve**; = (*Inf*) **annoy**, bother, provoke, irritate, nettle ≠ **please**

mass, sum total. **4** gravel etc. for concrete.

aggression ❶ *n* **1** unprovoked attack. **2** hostile activity.

aggressive *adj* **aggressively** *adv*

aggrieved *adj* upset, angry.

aghast *adj* appalled.

agile *adj* **1** nimble. **2** quick. **agility** *n*

agitate ❶ *v* **1** stir, shake up. **2** trouble. **3** stir up public opinion (for or against). **agitation** *n* **agitator** *n*

aglow *adj* glowing.

AGM Annual General Meeting.

agnostic *n* one who believes that we cannot know whether God exists.

ago *adv* in the past.

agog *adj/adv* eager, astir.

agony ❶ *n, pl* **-nies** extreme suffering. **agonize** *v* **1** suffer agony. **2** worry greatly. **agonizing** *adj*

agoraphobia *n* fear of open spaces. **agoraphobic** *adj/n*

agree ❶ *v* **agreeing, agreed 1** be of same opinion. **2** consent. **3** harmonize. **4** approve. **agreeable** *adj* **1** willing. **2** pleasant. **agreeably** *adv* **agreement** *n*

agriculture ❶ *n* (science of) farming. **agricultural** *adj*

aground *adv* (of boat) touching bottom.

ahead ❶ *adv* **1** in front. **2** onwards.

ahoy *interj* ship's hailing cry.

aid ❶ *v/n* help, support.

aide ❶ *n* assistant.

AIDS *n* disease that destroys the body's immune system.

ail *v* **1** trouble. **2** be ill. **ailing** *adj* **ailment** *n* illness.

aim ❶ *v* **1** direct (weapon etc.). **2** intend. ♦ *n* **3** aiming. **4** intention.

aimless *adj* without purpose. **aimlessly** *adv*

ain't *Nonstandard* **1** am not. **2** is not. **3** are not. **4** has not. **5** have not.

———— THESAURUS ————

aggregate *n* = **total**, body, whole, amount, collection ♦ *v* = **combine**, mix, collect, assemble, heap

aggression *n* = **hostility**, malice, antagonism, antipathy, aggressiveness; = **attack**, campaign, injury, assault, raid

agitate *v* = **stir**, beat, shake, disturb, toss; = **upset**, worry, trouble, excite, distract ≠ **calm**

agony *n* = **suffering**, pain, distress, misery, torture

agree *v* = **concur**, be as one, sympathize, assent, see eye to eye

≠ **disagree**; = **correspond**, match, coincide, tally, conform

agriculture *n* = **farming**, culture, cultivation, husbandry, tillage

ahead *adv* = **in front**, in advance, towards the front, frontwards

aid *n* = **help**, backing, support, benefit, favour ≠ **hindrance** ♦ *v* = **help**, support, serve, sustain, assist ≠ **hinder**

aide *n* = **assistant**, supporter, attendant, helper, right-hand man

aim *v* = **try for**, seek, work for, plan for, strive ♦ *n* = **intention**, point, plan, goal, design

air ❶ *n* 1 (gases of) earth's atmosphere. 2 breeze. 3 tune. 4 manner. ◆ *pl* 5 affected manners. ◆ *v* 6 expose to air. 7 communicate, make known. **airless** *adj* stuffy. **airy** *adj* 1 well–ventilated. 2 jaunty, nonchalant. **air bed** inflatable mattress. **air conditioning** control of temperature and humidity in building. **aircraft** *n* flying machines generally. **airplane** 2 aeroplane. **airfield** *n* landing and taking–off area for aircraft. **air force** armed force using aircraft. **air gun** gun discharged by compressed air. **airline** *n* company operating aircraft. **airliner** *n* large passenger aircraft. **air mail** mail sent by aircraft. **airman** *n* member of air force. **airplay** *n* performances of a record on radio. **airport** *n* station for civilian aircraft. **air raid** attack by aircraft. **airship** *n* lighter–than–air flying machine with means of propulsion. **airstrip** *n* strip of ground where aircraft can take off and land. **airtight** *adj* not allowing passage of air. **airworthy** *adj* fit to fly.
aisle ❶ *n* passage between rows of seats.

ajar *adv* partly open.
akimbo *adv* with hands on hips.
akin *adj* 1 related by blood. 2 alike.
alabaster *n* white, decorative stone.
à la carte *Fr* selected freely from the menu.
alacrity *n* eager willingness.
alarm ❶ *n* 1 fright. 2 apprehension. 3 danger signal. ◆ *v* 4 frighten. 5 alert. **alarming** *adj*
alas *interj* cry of grief.
albatross *n* large sea bird.
albino *n*, *pl* –nos individual lacking pigmentation.
album *n* 1 book for photographs, stamps etc. 2 collection of items in book or record form.
alchemy *n* medieval form of chemistry. **alchemist** *n*
alcohol *n* 1 intoxicating fermented liquor. 2 class of organic chemical substances. **alcoholic** *adj* 1 of alcohol. ◆ *n* 2 person addicted to alcoholic drink. **alcoholism** *n*
alcove *n* recess.
alder *n* tree related to the birch.
alderman *n* formerly, senior local councillor.
ale *n* kind of beer.

———————— THESAURUS ————————

air *n* = **wind**, breeze, draught, gust, zephyr; = **atmosphere**, sky, heavens, aerosphere; = **tune**, song, theme, melody, strain; = **manner**, appearance, look, aspect, atmosphere ◆ *v* = **publicize**, reveal, exhibit, voice, express; = **ventilate**, expose, freshen, aerate
aisle *n* = **passageway**, path, lane, passage, corridor
alarm *n* = **fear**, panic, anxiety, fright, apprehension ≠ **calmness**; = **danger signal**, warning, bell, alert, siren ◆ *v* = **frighten**, scare, panic, distress, startle ≠ **calm**

alert ❶ *adj* 1 watchful. 2 brisk. ◆ *n* 3 warning. ◆ *v* 4 warn. 5 draw attention to. **alertness** *n*

alfresco *adv/adj* in the open air.

algae *pl n* (*sing*) various water plants.

algebra *n* method of calculating, using symbols to represent quantities.

Algonquin, Algonkin *n* 1 a member of a North American Indian people formerly living along the St Lawrence and Ottawa Rivers in Canada. 2 the language of this people, a dialect of Ojibwa.

alias *adv* 1 otherwise. ◆ *n* 2 assumed name.

alibi *n* plea of being elsewhere at time of crime.

alien ❶ *adj* 1 foreign. 2 different in nature. 3 repugnant (to). ◆ *n* 4 foreigner. **alienate** *v* 1 estrange. 2 transfer. **alienation** *n*

alight¹ ❶ *v* 1 get down. 2 land.

alight² ❶ *adj* 1 burning. 2 lit up.

align ❶ *v* 1 bring into line or agreement. 2 ally, side (with). **alignment** *n*

alike ❶ *adj/adv* similar(ly).

alimony *n* allowance paid to separated or divorced spouse.

alive ❶ *adj* 1 living. 2 active. 3 aware. 4 swarming.

alkali *n* substance which combines with acid and neutralizes it, forming a salt. **alkaline** *adj*

all ❶ *adj* 1 the whole of, every one of. ◆ *adv* 2 entirely. ◆ *n* 3 the whole. 4 everything, everyone. **all right** *adj* 1 adequate, satisfactory. 2 unharmed. ◆ *interj* 3 expression of approval.

allay *v* relieve, soothe.

allege ❶ *v* state without proof. **allegation** *n* **allegedly** *adv*

allegiance ❶ *n* loyalty, esp. to one's country.

——————— THESAURUS ———————

alert *adj* = **attentive**, awake, vigilant, watchful, on the lookout ≠ **careless** ◆ *n* = **warning**, signal, alarm, siren ≠ **all clear** ◆ *v* = **warn**, signal, inform, alarm, notify ≠ **lull**

alien *adj* = **foreign**, strange, imported, unknown, exotic ◆ *n* = **foreigner**, incomer, immigrant, stranger, outsider ≠ **citizen**

alight¹ *v* = **get off**, descend, get down, disembark, dismount; = **land**, light, settle, come down, descend ≠ **take off**

alight² *adj* = **lit up**, bright, brilliant, shining, illuminated

align *v* = **ally**, side, join, associate,

affiliate; = **line up**, order, range, regulate, straighten

alike *adj* = **similar**, close, the same, parallel, resembling ≠ **different** ◆ *adv* = **similarly**, identically, equally, uniformly, correspondingly ≠ **differently**

alive *adj* = **living**, breathing, animate, subsisting, existing ≠ **dead**; = **in existence**, existing, functioning, active, operative ≠ **inoperative**

all *adj* = **complete**, greatest, full, total, perfect ◆ *adv* = **completely**, totally, fully, entirely, absolutely

allege *v* = **claim**, charge,

allegory *n, pl* **-ries** symbolic story, poem. **allegorical** *adj*

allegro *adv/adj/n, pl* **-gros,** *Mus* fast (passage).

allergy ❶ *n, pl* **-gies** abnormal sensitivity to a specific substance. **allergic** *adj*

alleviate ❶ *v* ease, lessen.

alley ❶ *n* **1** narrow street. **2** enclosure for skittles.

alliance ❶ *n* union, e.g. by treaty, agreement, or marriage.

alligator *n* animal of crocodile family found in America.

alliteration *n* beginning of successive words with same sound.

allocate ❶ *v* assign as a share. **allocation** *n*

allot *v* **-lotting, -lotted** allocate. **allotment** *n* **1** distribution. **2** portion of land rented for cultivation. **3** portion allotted.

allow ❶ *v* **1** permit. **2** set aside. **3** acknowledge. **allowable** *adj* **allowance** *n*

alloy *n* metallic mixture.

allude *v* refer (to). **allusion** *n*

allure *v* **1** entice. ♦ *n* **2** attractiveness. **alluring** *adj*

ally ❶ *v, pl* **-lies 1** join by treaty, friendship etc. ♦ *n* **2** friend. **allied** *adj*

almanac *n* calendar of tides, events etc.

almighty *adj* **1** all–powerful. **2** *Inf* very great.

almond *n* **1** tree of peach family. **2** its edible seed.

almost ❶ *adv* very nearly.

alms *pl n* gifts to the poor.

aloft *adv* **1** on high. **2** overhead.

alone ❶ *adj/adv* **1** by oneself, by itself. **2** without equal, unique.

along *adv* **1** lengthwise. **2** together (with). **3** forward. ♦ *prep* **4** over the length of. **alongside** *adv/prep* beside.

aloof *adj* **1** indifferent. **2** at a distance.

aloud ❶ *adv* **1** loudly. **2** audibly.

alphabet *n* set of letters used in

———————— THESAURUS ————————

challenge, state, maintain ≠ deny

allegiance *n* = **loyalty**, devotion, fidelity, obedience, constancy ≠ **disloyalty**

allergy *n* = **sensitivity**, reaction, susceptibility, antipathy, hypersensitivity

alleviate *v* = **ease**, reduce, relieve, moderate, soothe

alley *n* = **passage**, walk, lane, pathway, alleyway

alliance *n* = **union**, league, association, agreement, marriage ≠ **division**

allocate *v* = **assign**, grant, distribute, designate, set aside

allow *v* = **permit**, approve, enable, sanction, endure ≠ **prohibit**; = **let**, permit, sanction, authorize, license ≠ **forbid**; = **give**, provide, grant, spare, devote

ally *n* = **partner**, friend, colleague, associate, mate ≠ **opponent**

almost *adv* = **nearly**, about, close to, virtually, practically

alone *adj* = **solitary**, isolated, separate, apart, by yourself ≠ **accompanied**

writing a language.

already ⊕ *adv* 1 previously. 2 sooner than expected.

Alsatian *n* large wolflike dog.

also ⊕ *adv* besides, moreover.

also-ran *n* loser in a contest.

altar *n* 1 Communion table. 2 sacrificial table.

alter ⊕ *v* change, make or become different. **alterable** *adj* **alteration** *n*

altercation *n* quarrel.

alternate ⊕ *v* 1 (cause to) occur by turns. ♦ *adj* 2 in turn. 3 every second. **alternately** *adv* **alternative** *n* 1 one of two choices. ♦ *adj* 2 replacing. **alternatively** *adv*

although ⊕ *conj* despite the fact that.

altitude *n* height, elevation.

alto *n, pl* **-tos** 1 *Mus* male singing voice or instrument above tenor. 2 contralto.

altogether ⊕ *adv* 1 entirely. 2 in total.

altruism *n* unselfish concern for others.

aluminium *n* light nonrusting silvery metal.

always ⊕ *adv* 1 at all times. 2 for ever.

am first person sing. of BE.

a.m. before noon.

amalgamate *v* mix, (cause to) combine. **amalgamation** *n*

amass ⊕ *v* collect in quantity.

amateur ⊕ *n* 1 one who does something for interest not money. 2 unskilled practitioner. **amateurish** *adj*

amaut, amowt *n* Canad a hood on an Eskimo woman's parka for carrying a child.

amaze ⊕ *v* surprise greatly, astound. **amazing** *adj* **amazement** *n*

ambassador ⊕ *n* senior diplomatic representative

——————— THESAURUS ———————

aloud *adv* = **out loud**, clearly, plainly, distinctly, audibly

already *adv* = **before now**, before, previously, at present, by now

also *adv* = **and**, too, further, in addition, as well

alter *v* = **modify**, change, reform, vary, transform

alternate *v* = **interchange**, change, fluctuate, take turns, oscillate ♦ *adj* = **alternating**, interchanging, every other, rotating, every second

although *conj* = **though**, while, even if, even though, whilst

altogether *adv* = **absolutely**, quite, completely, totally, perfectly; = **completely**, fully, entirely, thoroughly, wholly ≠ **partially**; = **on the whole**, generally, mostly, in general, collectively

always *adv* = **habitually**, regularly, every time, consistently, invariably ≠ **seldom**; = **forever**, for keeps, eternally, for all time, evermore

amass *v* = **collect**, gather, assemble, compile, accumulate

amateur *n* = **nonprofessional**, outsider, layman, dilettante, layperson

amaze *v* = **astonish**, surprise,

overseas.

amber *n* yellow fossil resin.

ambidextrous *adj* able to use both hands with equal ease.

ambience *n* atmosphere of a place.

ambiguous ❶ *adj* **1** having more than one meaning. **2** obscure. **ambiguity** *n*

ambition ❶ *n* **1** desire for success. **2** goal, aim. **ambitious** *adj*

ambivalence *n* simultaneous existence of conflicting emotions.

amble *v/n* (move at an) easy pace.

ambulance *n* conveyance for sick or injured people.

ambush ❶ *v/n* attack from hiding.

ameliorate *v* improve.

amen *interj* so be it.

amenable *adj* **1** easily controlled. **2** answerable.

amend ❶ *v* **1** correct. **2** alter. **amendment** *n*

amenity ❶ *n*, *pl* **–ties** (*oft. pl*) useful or pleasant facility or

service.

amiable *adj* friendly, kindly.

amicable *adj* friendly. **amicably** *adv*

amid ❶ amidst *prep* among.

amiss *adj* **1** wrong. ♦ *adv* **2** faultily.

ammonia *n* pungent alkaline gas.

ammunition ❶ *n* **1** projectiles that can be discharged from weapon. **2** facts that can be used in argument.

amnesia *n* loss of memory.

amnesty ❶ *n*, *pl* **–ties** general pardon.

amoeba *n*, *pl* **–bae**, **–bas** microscopic single–celled animal.

amok *adv* **run amok** run about in a violent frenzy.

among ❶, **amongst** *prep* **1** in the midst of. **2** of the number of. **3** between. **4** with one another.

amoral *adj* having no moral standards.

amorous *adj* inclined to love.

——————— THESAURUS ———————

shock, stun, alarm

ambassador *n* = **representative**, minister, agent, deputy, diplomat

ambiguous *adj* = **unclear**, obscure, vague, dubious, enigmatic ≠ **clear**

ambition *n* = **goal**, hope, dream, target, aim; = **enterprise**, longing, drive, spirit, desire

ambush *v* = **trap**, attack, surprise, deceive, dupe ♦ *n* = **trap**, snare, lure, waylaying

amend *v* = **change**, improve, reform, fix, correct

amenity *n* = **facility**, service,

advantage, comfort, convenience

amid, amidst *prep* = **during**, among, at a time of, in an atmosphere of

ammunition *n* = **munitions**, rounds, shot, shells, powder

amnesty *n* = **general pardon**, mercy, pardoning, immunity, forgiveness

among, amongst *prep* = **in the midst of**, with, together with, in the middle of, amid; = **in the group of**, one of, part of, included in, in the company of; = **between**, to

amorphous *adj* without distinct shape.

amount ❶ *v* 1 come, be equal (to). ◆ *n* 2 quantity. 3 sum total.

amp *n* 1 ampere 2 *Inf* amplifier.

ampere *n* unit of electric current.

ampersand *n* sign (&) meaning *and*.

amphetamine *n* synthetic medicinal stimulant.

amphibian *n* 1 animal that lives first in water then on land. 2 vehicle, plane adapted to land and water. **amphibious** *adj*

amphitheatre *n* arena surrounded by rising tiers of seats.

ample ❶ *adj* 1 big enough. 2 large, spacious. **amply** *adv*

amplify *v*–**fying**, –**fied** 1 increase. 2 make bigger, louder etc. **amplification** *n* **amplifier** *n*

amplitude *n* spaciousness, width.

amputate *v* cut off (limb etc.). **amputation** *n*

amulet *n* thing worn as a charm against evil.

amuse ❶ *v* 1 entertain. 2 cause to laugh or smile. **amusing** *adj* **amusement** *n*

an see A.

anachronism *n* something put in wrong historical period.

anaconda *n* large snake which kills by constriction.

anaemia *n* deficiency of red blood cells. **anaemic** *adj* pale, sickly.

anaesthetic ❶ *n*/*adj* (drug) causing loss of sensation. **anaesthetist** *n* **anaesthetize** *v*

anagram *n* word(s) whose letters can be rearranged to make new word(s).

anal see ANUS.

analgesic *adj*/*n* (drug) relieving pain.

analogy ❶ *n*, *pl*–**gies** likeness in certain respects. **analogous** *adj* similar.

analysis ❶ *n*, *pl*–**ses** 1 separation into elements or components. 2 evaluation, study. **analyse** *v* 1 examine critically. 2 determine constituent parts. **analyst** *n* **analytical** *adj*

anarchy ❶ *n* 1 absence of government and law. 2 disorder. **anarchic** *adj* **anarchist** *n* one who opposes all forms of government.

anathema *n* 1 anything detested. 2 curse of excommunication or

——— THESAURUS ———

amount *n* = **quantity**, measure, size, supply, mass

ample *adj* = **plenty of**, generous, lavish, abundant, plentiful ≠ **insufficient**

amuse *v* = **entertain**, please, delight, charm, cheer ≠ **bore**

anaesthetic *n* = **painkiller**, narcotic, sedative, opiate, anodyne ◆ *adj* = **pain-killing**,

dulling, numbing, sedative, deadening

analogy *n* = **similarity**, relation, comparison, parallel, correspondence

analysis *n* = **examination**, test, inquiry, investigation, interpretation

anarchy *n* = **lawlessness**, revolution, riot, disorder,

denunciation.

anatomy ❶ *n, pl* –**mies 1** (study of) bodily structure. **2** detailed analysis. **anatomical** *adj* **anatomist** *n*

ancestor ❶ *n* **1** person from whom another is descended. **2** forerunner. **ancestral** *adj* **ancestry** *n*

anchor *n* **1** heavy implement dropped to stop vessel drifting. **2** any similar device. ♦ *v* **3** secure with anchor. **anchorage** *n* act, place of anchoring.

anchovy *n, pl* –**vies** small savoury fish of herring family.

ancient ❶ *adj* **1** belonging to former age. **2** very old.

ancillary *adj* subordinate, auxiliary.

and ❶ *conj* word used to join words and sentences, introduce a consequence etc.

andante *adv/adj/n Mus* moderately slow (passage).

androgynous *adj* having male and female characteristics.

android *n* robot resembling a human.

anecdote ❶ *n* short account of a single incident. **anecdotal** *adj*

anemone *n* flower related to buttercup.

anew *adv* afresh, again.

angel ❶ *n* **1** divine messenger. **2** guardian spirit. **3** very kind person. **angelic** *adj*

anger ❶ *n* **1** extreme annoyance. **2** wrath. ♦ *v* **3** make angry. **angry** *adj* **angrily** *adv*

angina *n* severe pain accompanying heart disease.

angle ❶ *n* **1** meeting of two lines or surfaces. **2** point of view. ♦ *v* **3** bend at an angle. **4** fish. **angler** *n* one who fishes for sport. **angling** *n*

Anglican *adj/n* (member) of the Church of England.

Anglo– *comb. form* English or British, as in *Anglo–German*.

angora *n* **1** goat with long silky hair. **2** cloth or wool of this.

anguish ❶ *n* great mental or bodily pain. **anguished** *adj*

————————— THESAURUS —————————

confusion ≠ **order**

anatomy *n* = **structure**, build, make-up, frame, framework; = **examination**, study, division, inquiry, investigation

ancestor *n* = **forefather**, predecessor, precursor, forerunner, forebear ≠ **descendant**

ancient *adj* = **classical**, old, former, past, bygone

and *conj* = **also**, including, along with, together with, in addition to

anecdote *n* = **story**, tale, sketch,

short story, yarn

angel *n* = **divine messenger**, cherub, archangel, seraph; = (*Inf*) **dear**, beauty, saint, treasure, darling

anger *n* = **rage**, outrage, temper, fury, resentment ≠ **calmness** ♦ *v* = **enrage**, outrage, annoy, infuriate, incense ≠ **soothe**

angle *n* = **gradient**, bank, slope, incline, inclination; = **intersection**, point, edge, corner, bend; = **point of view**, position, approach,

angular *adj* **1** (of people) bony. **2** having angles. **3** measured by an angle.

animal ❶ *n* **1** living creature that can move at will. **2** beast. ♦ *adj* **3** of animals. **4** sensual.

animate ❶ *v* **1** give life to. **2** enliven. **3** inspire. **4** actuate. **5** make cartoon film of. **animated** *adj*

animation *n* **animator** *n*

animosity *n, pl* **-ties** hostility, enmity.

animus *n* **1** hatred. **2** animosity.

aniseed *n* liquorice–flavoured seed of plant.

ankle *n* joint between foot and leg.

annals *pl n* yearly records.

annex *v* **1** append, attach. **2** take possession of. **annexation** *n*

annexe *n* **1** extension to a building. **2** nearby building used as an extension.

annihilate *v* reduce to nothing, destroy utterly. **annihilation** *n*

anniversary *n, pl* **-ries 1** yearly return of a date. **2** celebration of this.

anno Domini *Lat* in the year of our Lord.

annotate *v* make notes upon. **annotation** *n*

announce ❶ *v* make known, proclaim. **announcement** *n*

announcer *n*

annoy ❶ *v* **1** vex. **2** irritate. **annoyance** *n*

annual ❶ *adj* **1** yearly. ♦ *n* **2** plant which completes its life cycle in a year. **3** book published each year. **annually** *adv*

annul *v* **-nulling, -nulled** make void, cancel. **annulment** *n*

anodyne *n* **1** thing that relieves pain or distress. ♦ *adj* **2** relieving pain or distress.

anoint *v* **1** smear with oil or ointment. **2** consecrate with oil.

anomaly ❶ *n, pl* **-lies** irregular or abnormal thing. **anomalous** *adj*

anon. anonymous.

anonymous ❶ *adj* without (author's) name. **anonymously** *adv* **anonymity** *n*

anorak *n* waterproof hooded jacket.

————— THESAURUS —————

direction, aspect

anguish *n* = **suffering**, pain, distress, grief, misery

animal *n* = **creature**, beast, brute ♦ *adj* = **physical**, gross, bodily, sensual, carnal

animate *adj* = **living**, live, moving, alive, breathing ♦ *v* = **enliven**, excite, inspire, move, fire ≠ **inhibit**

announce *v* = **make known**, tell, report, reveal, declare ≠ **keep secret**

annoy *v* = **irritate**, trouble, anger, bother, disturb ≠ **soothe**

annual *adj* = **once a year**, yearly; = **yearlong**, yearly

anomaly *n* = **irregularity**, exception, abnormality, inconsistency, eccentricity

anonymous *adj* = **unnamed**, unknown, unidentified, nameless, unacknowledged ≠ **identified**; = **unsigned**, uncredited, unattributed ≠ **signed** impersonal,

anorexia *n* loss of appetite.
anorexic *adj/n*
another *pron/adj* **1** one other. **2** a different one. **3** one more.
answer ❶ *v* **1** reply (to). **2** be accountable (for, to). **3** match. **4** suit. ♦ *n* **5** reply. **6** solution.
answerable *adj*
ant *n* small social insect. **anteater** *n* animal which feeds on ants.
antagonist *n* opponent.
antagonism *n* **antagonistic** *adj*
antagonize *v* arouse hostility in.
Antarctic *adj/n* (of) south polar regions.
ante– *comb. form* before, as in *antechamber*.
antecedent *adj/n* (thing) going before.
antelope *n* deerlike animal.
antenatal *adj* of care etc. during pregnancy.
antenna *n* **1** insect's feeler. **2** aerial.
anterior *adj* **1** to the front. **2** before.
anthem ❶ *n* **1** song of loyalty. **2** sacred choral piece.
anther *n* pollen sac of flower.
anthology ❶ *n, pl* **–gies** collection of poems.

anthracite *n* slow–burning coal.
anthrax *n* infectious disease of cattle and sheep.
anthropoid *adj/n* manlike (ape).
anthropology *n* study of origins, development of human race.
anti– *comb. form* against, as in *anti-aircraft*.
antibiotic *n/adj* (of) substance used against bacterial infection.
antibody *n, pl* **–bodies** substance which counteracts bacteria.
anticipate ❶ *v* **1** expect. **2** look forward to. **3** foresee.
anticipation *n*
anticlimax *n* sudden descent to the trivial or ludicrous.
anticlockwise *adv/adj* in the opposite direction to the rotation of the hands of a clock.
antics ❶ *pl n* absurd behaviour.
anticyclone *n* high–pressure area and associated winds.
antidote *n* counteracting remedy.
antifreeze *n* liquid added to water to prevent freezing.
antihistamine *n* drug used esp. to treat allergies.
antimony *n* brittle, bluish–white metal.
antipathy *n* dislike, aversion.

——————— THESAURUS ———————

faceless
answer *v* = **reply**, explain, respond, resolve, react ≠ **ask** ♦ *n* = **reply**, response, reaction, explanation, comeback ≠ **question**; = **solution**, resolution, explanation; = **remedy**, solution
anthem *n* = **song of praise**, carol, chant, hymn, psalm

anthology *n* = **collection**, selection, treasury, compilation, compendium
anticipate *v* = **expect**, predict, prepare for, hope for, envisage; = **await**, look forward to, count the hours until
antics *pl n* = **clowning**, tricks, mischief, pranks, escapades

antiperspirant n substance used to reduce sweating.
antipodes pl n regions on opposite side of the globe.
antipodean adj
antique ❶ n **1** object valued because of its age. ♦ adj **2** ancient. **3** old-fashioned. **antiquarian** n collector of antiques. **antiquated** adj out-of-date. **antiquity** n **1** great age. **2** former times.
antiseptic n/adj **1** (substance) preventing infection. ♦ adj **2** free from infection.
antisocial adj **1** avoiding company. **2** (of behaviour) harmful to society.
antithesis n, pl **-ses 1** direct opposite. **2** contrast.
antler n branching horn of certain deer.
antonym n word of opposite meaning to another.
anus n open end of rectum. **anal** adj
anvil n heavy iron block on which a smith hammers metal.
anxious ❶ adj **1** uneasy. **2** concerned. **anxiety** n

anxiously adv
any adj/pron **1** one indefinitely. **2** some. **3** every. **anybody** n **anyhow** adv **anyone** n **anything** n **anyway** adv **anywhere** adv
aorta n main artery carrying blood from the heart.
apace adv swiftly.
apart ❶ adv **1** separately, aside. **2** in pieces.
apartheid n (esp. formerly in S Africa) official policy of segregation.
apartment ❶ n **1** room. **2** flat.
apathy ❶ n **1** indifference. **2** lack of emotion. **apathetic** adj
ape n **1** tailless monkey. **2** imitator. ♦ v **3** imitate.
aperitif n alcoholic appetizer.
aperture n opening, hole.
apex n **1** top, peak. **2** vertex.
aphid, aphis n small insect which sucks the sap from plants.
aphorism n maxim, clever saying.
aphrodisiac adj/n (substance) exciting sexual desire.
apiece ❶ adv for each.
aplomb n assurance.
apocalypse n prophetic

————————— THESAURUS —————————

antique n = **period piece**, relic, bygone, heirloom, collector's item ♦ adj = **vintage**, classic, antiquarian, olden; = **old-fashioned**, outdated, obsolete, archaic
anxious adj = **eager**, keen, intent, yearning, impatient ≠ **reluctant**; = **uneasy**, concerned, worried, troubled, nervous ≠ **confident**
apart adv = **to pieces**, to bits,

asunder; = **away from each other**, distant from each other
apartment (US) n = **flat**, room, suite, penthouse, crib; = **rooms**, quarters, accommodation, living quarters
apathy n = **lack of interest**, indifference, inertia, coolness, passivity ≠ **interest**
apiece adv = **each**, individually, separately, for each, to each ≠ **all**

revelation, esp. of the end of the world. **apocalyptic** *adj*

apocryphal *adj* of questionable authenticity.

apology 🛈 *n, pl* **–gies 1** expression of regret for a fault. **2** poor substitute (for). **apologetic** *adj* **apologetically** *adv* **apologize** *v*

apoplexy *n* paralysis caused by broken or blocked blood vessel in the brain. **apoplectic** *adj* **1** of apoplexy **2** *Inf* furious.

Apostle *n* **1** one of the first disciples of Jesus **2** (*without cap.*) enthusiastic supporter of a cause.

apostrophe *n* mark (') showing omission of letter(s).

appal 🛈 *v* **–palling, –palled** dismay, terrify. **appalling** *adj Inf* terrible.

apparatus 🛈 *n* equipment for performing experiment, operation etc.

apparel *n* clothing.

apparent 🛈 *adj* **1** seeming. **2** obvious. **3** acknowledged. **apparently** *adv*

apparition *n* ghost.

appeal 🛈 *v* **1** make earnest request. **2** be attractive. **3** apply to higher court. ♦ *n* **4** request. **5** attractiveness. **appealing** *adj*

appear 🛈 *v* **1** become visible or present. **2** seem, be plain. **3** be seen in public. **4** perform. **appearance** *n* **1** an appearing. **2** aspect. **3** pretence.

appease 🛈 *v* pacify, satisfy. **appeasement** *n*

append *v* join on, add.

appendicitis *n* inflammation of the appendix.

appendix 🛈 *n, pl* **–dices, –dixes 1** supplement **2** *Anat* small worm-shaped part of the intestine.

appertain *v* belong, relate to.

appetite 🛈 *n* desire, inclination, esp. for food. **appetizer** *n*

————————————— THESAURUS —————————————

together

apology *n* = **regret**, explanation, excuse, confession; **apology for something** *or* **someone** = **mockery of**, excuse for, imitation of, caricature of, travesty of

appal *v* = **horrify**, shock, alarm, frighten, outrage

apparatus *n* = **organization**, system, network, structure, bureaucracy

apparent *adj* = **seeming**, outward, superficial, ostensible ≠ **actual**; = **obvious**, marked, visible, evident, distinct ≠ **unclear**

appeal *v* = **plead**, ask, request,

pray, beg ≠ **refuse** ♦ *n* = **plea**, call, application, request, prayer ≠ **refusal**; = **attraction**, charm, fascination, beauty, allure ≠ **repulsiveness**

appear *v* = **look (like** *or* **as if)** seem, occur, look to be, come across as; = **come into view**, emerge, occur, surface, come out ≠ **disappear**

appease *v* = **pacify**, satisfy, calm, soothe, quiet ≠ **anger**; = **ease**, calm, relieve, soothe, alleviate

appendix *n* = **supplement**, postscript, adjunct, appendage, addendum

something stimulating appetite.
appetizing *adj*

applaud ❶ *v* **1** praise by clapping. **2** praise loudly. **applause** *n*

apple *n* **1** round, firm fleshy fruit. **2** tree bearing it.

appliance ❶ *n* piece of equipment, esp. electrical.

apply ❶ *v* **–plying, –plied** **1** utilize. **2** lay or place on. **3** devote. **4** have reference (to). **5** make request (to). **applicable** *adj* relevant. **applicant** *n* **application** *n* **1** request for a job etc. **2** diligence. **3** use, function. **applied** *adj* put to practical use.

appoint ❶ *v* **1** assign to a job or position. **2** fix, equip. **appointment** *n* **1** engagement to meet. **2** (selection for a) job.

apportion *v* divide out in shares.

apposite *adj* appropriate.

appraise *v* estimate value of. **appraisal** *n*

appreciate ❶ *v* **1** value at true worth. **2** be grateful for. **3** understand. **4** rise in value. **appreciable** *adj* noticeable. **appreciably** *adv* **appreciation** *n* **appreciative** *adj*

apprehend *v* **1** arrest. **2** understand. **3** dread. **apprehension** *n* anxiety. **apprehensive** *adj*

apprentice ❶ *n* **1** person learning a trade. **2** novice.

apprise *v* inform.

approach ❶ *v* **1** draw near (to). **2** set about. **3** address request to. **4** approximate to. ◆ *n* **5** a drawing near. **6** means of reaching or doing. **7** approximation. **approachable** *adj*

approbation *n* approval.

appetite *n* = **desire**, liking, longing, demand, taste ≠ **distaste**

applaud *v* = **clap**, encourage, praise, cheer, acclaim ≠ **boo**; = **praise**, celebrate, approve, acclaim, compliment ≠ **criticize**

appliance *n* = **device**, machine, tool, instrument, implement

apply *v* = **request**, appeal, put in, petition, inquire; = **be relevant**, relate, refer, be fitting, be appropriate; = **use**, exercise, carry out, employ, implement; = **put on**, work in, cover with, lay on, paint on

appoint *v* = **assign**, name, choose, commission, select ≠ **fire**; = **decide**, set, choose, establish, fix

≠ **cancel**

appreciate *v* = **enjoy**, like, value, respect, prize ≠ **scorn**; = **be aware of**, understand, realize, recognize, perceive ≠ **be unaware of**; = **be grateful**, be obliged, be thankful, give thanks, be indebted ≠ **be ungrateful for**; = **increase**, rise, grow, gain, improve ≠ **fall**

apprentice *n* = **trainee**, student, pupil, novice, beginner ≠ **master**

approach *v* = **move towards**, reach, near, come close, come near; = **make a proposal to**, speak to, apply to, appeal to, proposition; = **set about**, tackle, undertake, embark on, get down to ◆ *n* = **advance**, coming,

appropriate ❶ *adj* **1** suitable, fitting. ♦ *v* **2** take for oneself. **3** allocate. **appropriately** *adv*

approve ❶ *v* **1** think well of, commend. **2** authorize. **approval** *n*

approx. approximate(ly).

approximate *adj* **1** nearly correct. **2** inexact. ♦ *v* **3** come or bring close. **4** be almost the same as. **approximately** *adv* **approximation** *n*

Apr. April.

après–ski *n* social activities after skiing.

apricot *n* orange–coloured fruit related to plum.

April *n* fourth month.

apron *n* **1** covering worn in front to protect clothes. **2** in theatre, strip of stage before curtain. **3** on airfield, tarmac area where aircraft stand, are loaded etc.

apropos *adv* **1** with reference to. ♦ *adj* **2** appropriate.

apt ❶ *adj* **1** suitable. **2** likely. **3** quick–witted. **aptitude** *n* **aptly** *adv*

aqualung *n* breathing apparatus used in underwater swimming.

aquamarine *n* **1** precious stone. ♦

adj **2** greenish–blue.

aquarium *n, pl* **aquariums, aquaria** tank for water animals or plants.

aquatic *adj* living, growing, done in or on water.

aqueduct *n* artificial channel for water, esp. one like a bridge.

aquiline *adj* like an eagle.

arable *adj* suitable for growing crops.

arbiter *n* judge, umpire. **arbitrary** *adj* **1** despotic. **2** random.

arbitrate *v* settle (dispute) impartially. **arbitration** *n* **arbitrator** *n*

arboreal *adj* of or living in trees.

arc ❶ *n* part of circumference of circle or similar curve.

arcade ❶ *n* **1** row of arches on pillars. **2** covered walk or avenue.

arcane *adj* secret.

arch¹ ❶ *n* **1** curved structure spanning an opening. **2** a curved shape. **3** curved part of the sole of the foot. ♦ *v* **4** form, make into, an arch.

arch² ❶ *adj* knowingly playful.

arch– *comb. form* chief, as in *archangel, archenemy.*

————— THESAURUS —————

nearing, appearance, arrival; **= access**, way, drive, road, passage; (*often plural*) **= proposal**, offer, appeal, advance, application

appropriate *adj* **= suitable**, fitting, relevant, to the point, apt ≠ **unsuitable** ♦ *v* **= seize**, claim, acquire, confiscate, usurp ≠ **relinquish**; **= allocate**, allow, budget, devote, assign ≠ **withhold**

approve *v* **= agree to**, allow, pass,

recommend, permit ≠ **veto**

apt *adj* **= appropriate**, fitting, suitable, relevant, to the point ≠ **inappropriate**; **= inclined**, likely, ready, disposed, prone; **= gifted**, skilled, quick, talented, sharp ≠ **slow**

arc *n* **= curve**, bend, bow, arch, crescent

arcade *n* **= gallery**, cloister, portico, colonnade

archaeology n study of ancient times from remains.

archaeologist n

archaic adj old, primitive.

archaism n word no longer in use.

archbishop n chief bishop.

archetype n 1 prototype. 2 perfect specimen. **archetypal** adj

archipelago n, pl **-gos** group of islands.

architect ❶ n 1 person qualified to design buildings. 2 contriver.

architecture n

Arctic ❶ adj 1 of north polar region 2 (without cap.) very cold. ♦ n 3 north polar region.

ardent ❶ adj 1 intensely enthusiastic. 2 passionate.

ardently adv

arduous adj hard to accomplish.

are pres. tense of BE (used with you, we and they).

area ❶ n 1 surface extent. 2 two-dimensional expanse enclosed by boundary. 3 region. 4 part. 5 field of activity.

arena ❶ n 1 space in middle of amphitheatre or stadium. 2 sphere, territory.

argon n gas found in the air.

argue ❶ v **-guing, -gued** 1 quarrel, offer reasons (for). 2 debate. **arguable** adj **arguably** adv

argument n argumentative adj

aria n song in opera etc.

arid adj 1 dry. 2 dull.

arise ❶ v arising, arose, arisen 1 get up. 2 rise (up). 3 come about.

aristocracy n, pl **-cies** upper classes. **aristocrat** n **aristocratic** adj

arithmetic n science of numbers.

ark n Noah's vessel.

arm¹ ❶ n 1 upper limb from shoulder to wrist. 2 anything similar, as branch of sea, supporting rail of chair etc. 3 sleeve. **armful** n **armhole** n **armpit** n hollow under arm at shoulder.

arm² ❶ v 1 supply with weapons. 2 take up arms. ♦ pl n 3 weapons. 4 war. 5 heraldic emblem. **armada** n large fleet.

——— THESAURUS ———

arch¹ n = **archway**, curve, dome, span, vault; = **curve**, bend, bow, crook, arc ♦ v = **curve**, bridge, bend, bow, span

arch² adj = **playful**, sly, mischievous, saucy, pert

architect n = **designer**, planner, draughtsman, master builder, father

Arctic adj = **polar**, far-northern, hyperborean

ardent adj = **enthusiastic**, keen, eager, avid, zealous ≠ **indifferent**; = **passionate**, intense,

impassioned, lusty, amorous ≠ **cold**

area n = **region**, quarter, district, zone, neighbourhood; = **part**, section, sector, portion, reach

arena n = **ring**, ground, field, theatre, bowl

argue v = **quarrel**, fight, row, clash, dispute; = **discuss**, debate, dispute; = **claim**, reason, challenge, insist, maintain

arise v = **happen**, start, begin, follow, result; = (Old-fashioned) **get to your feet**, get up, rise, stand

armadillo n, pl **-los** S Amer. animal protected by bony plates.

armistice n truce.

armour ⊕ n 1 defensive covering. 2 plating of tanks, warships etc. 3 armoured fighting vehicles.

armoury n

army ⊕ n, pl **armies** 1 military land force. 2 great number.

aroma ⊕ n sweet smell. **aromatic** adj

around ⊕ prep/adv 1 on all sides (of). 2 somewhere in or near. 3 approximately. 4 in a circle. 5 here and there.

arouse ⊕ v awaken, stimulate.

arraign v accuse, indict.

arrange ⊕ v 1 set in proper order. 2 make agreement. 3 plan. 4 adapt music. **arrangement** n

array ⊕ n 1 order, esp. military. 2 dress. 3 imposing show. ◆ v 4 set out. 5 dress richly.

arrears pl n money owed.

arrest ⊕ v 1 detain by legal authority. 2 stop. 3 catch attention. ◆ n 4 seizure by warrant. **arresting** adj striking.

arrive ⊕ v 1 reach destination. 2 (with **at**) reach, attain. 3 Inf succeed. **arrival** n

arrow ⊕ n shaft shot from bow.

——————————— THESAURUS ———————————

up, spring up

arm[1] n = **upper limb**, limb, appendage, part, office

arm[2] v = **equip**, provide, supply, array, furnish

armour n = **protection**, covering, shield, sheathing, armour plate

army n = **soldiers**, military, troops, armed force, legions; = **vast number**, host, gang, mob, flock

aroma n = **scent**, smell, perfume, fragrance, bouquet

around prep = **surrounding**, about, enclosing, encompassing, framing; = **approximately**, about, nearly, close to, roughly ◆ adv = **everywhere**, about, throughout, all over, here and there; = **near**, close, nearby, at hand, close at hand

arouse v = **stimulate**, encourage, inspire, prompt, spur ≠ **quell**; = **awaken**, wake up, rouse, waken

arrange v = **plan**, agree, prepare, determine, organize; = **put in order**, group, order, sort, position ≠ **disorganize**; = **adapt**, score, orchestrate, harmonize, instrument

array n = **arrangement**, show, supply, display, collection; = (Poet) **clothing**, dress, clothes, garments, apparel ◆ v = **arrange**, show, group, present, range; = **dress**, clothe, deck, decorate, adorn

arrest v = **capture**, catch, nick (slang, chiefly Brit.), seize, detain ≠ **release**; = **stop**, end, limit, block, slow ≠ **speed up**; = **fascinate**, hold, occupy, engage, grip ◆ = **capture**, bust (Inf), detention, seizure ≠ **release**; = **stoppage**, suppression, obstruction, blockage, hindrance ≠ **acceleration**

arrive v = **come**, appear, turn up, show up (Inf), draw near ≠ **depart**;

arsenal *n* stores for guns etc.

arsenic *n* soft, grey, very poisonous metallic element.

arson *n* crime of intentionally setting property on fire.

art *n* 1 human skill as opposed to nature. 2 creative skill in painting, poetry, music etc. 3 any of the works produced thus. 4 craft. 5 knack. ◆ *pl* 6 branches of learning other than science. 7 wiles. **artful** *adj* wily. **artfully** *adv*

artist *n* one who practises fine art, esp. painting. **artiste** *n* professional entertainer. **artistic** *adj* **artistry** *n* **artless** *adj* natural, frank. **arty** *adj* **artier, artiest** ostentatiously artistic.

artefact *n* something made by man.

artery *n, pl* **–teries** 1 tube carrying blood from heart. 2 any main channel of communications. **arthritis** *n* painful inflammation of joint(s). **arthritic** *adj/n*

artichoke *n* thistle–like plant with edible flower.

article *n* 1 item, object. 2 short written piece 3 *Grammar* words *the, a, an*. 4 clause in a contract. **articled** *adj* bound as an apprentice.

articulate *adj* 1 fluent. 2 clear, distinct. ◆ *v* 3 utter distinctly. **articulated** *adj* jointed.

artifice *n* contrivance, trick. **artificial** *adj* 1 synthetic. 2 insincere. **artificially** *adv*

artillery *n* 1 large guns on wheels. 2 troops who use them. **artisan** *n* craftsman.

as *adv/conj* 1 denoting: comparison. 2 similarity. 3 equality. 4 identity. 5 concurrence. 6 reason.

asbestos *n* fibrous mineral which does not burn.

ascend *v* 1 go, come up. 2 climb. **ascendancy** *n* dominance. **ascent** *n*

ascertain *v* find out.

ascetic *n/adj* (person) practising severe self–denial.

——————— THESAURUS ———————

= (*Inf*) **succeed**, make it (*Inf*), triumph, do well, thrive

arrow *n* = **dart**, flight, bolt, shaft (*Arch*), quarrel; = **pointer**, indicator, marker

arsenal *n* = **armoury**, supply, store, stockpile, storehouse

art *n* = **artwork**, style of art, fine art, creativity

article *n* = **feature**, story, paper, piece, item; = **thing**, piece, unit, item, object; = **clause**, point, part, section, item

articulate *adj* = **expressive**, clear, coherent, fluent, eloquent ≠ **incoherent** ◆ *v* = **express**, say, state, word, declare

artillery *n* = **big guns**, battery, cannon, ordnance, gunnery

as *conj* = **when**, while, just as, at the time that, during the time that ◆ *prep* = **in the role of**, being, under the name of, in the character of ◆ *conj* = **in the way that**, like, in the manner that; = **since**, because, seeing that, considering that, on account of the fact that

A

ascribe v attribute, assign.

asexual adj without sex.

ash[1] n remains of anything burnt.

ashen adj pale.

ash[2] n 1 deciduous timber tree. 2 its wood.

ashamed ❶ adj feeling shame.

ashore ❶ adv on shore.

aside ❶ adv 1 to, on one side. 2 privately. ♦ n 3 words spoken so as not to be heard by all.

asinine adj stupid, silly.

ask ❶ v 1 make request or inquiry. 2 invite. 3 require.

askance adv with mistrust.

askew adv awry.

asleep ❶ adj/adv sleeping.

asp n small poisonous snake.

asparagus n plant with edible young shoots.

aspect ❶ n 1 appearance. 2 outlook. 3 side.

aspen n type of poplar tree.

aspersion n (usu. pl) malicious remark.

asphalt n covering for road surfaces etc.

aspic n jelly used to coat meat, eggs, fish etc.

aspidistra n plant with long tapered leaves.

aspire v have great ambition.

aspiration n aspiring adj

aspirin n (tablet of) drug used to relieve pain and fever.

ass ❶ n 1 donkey. 2 fool.

assail ❶ v 1 attack, assault. 2 criticize. **assailable** adj **assailant** n

assassin ❶ n one who kills for money or political reasons. **assassinate** v **assassination** n

assault ❶ n/v attack.

assemble ❶ v 1 meet, bring together. 2 put together. **assembly** n

assent v 1 agree. ♦ n 2

─────────── THESAURUS ───────────

ashamed adj = **embarrassed**, sorry, guilty, distressed, humiliated ≠ **proud**

ashore adv = **on land**, on the beach, on the shore, aground, to the shore

aside adv = **to one side**, separately, apart, beside, out of the way ♦ n = **interpolation**, parenthesis

ask v = **inquire**, question, quiz, query, interrogate ≠ **answer**; = **request**, appeal to, plead with, demand, beg; = **invite**, bid, summon

asleep adj = **sleeping**, napping, dormant, dozing, slumbering

aspect n = **feature**, side, factor, angle, characteristic; = **position**, view, situation, scene, prospect; = **appearance**, look, air, condition, quality

ass n = **donkey**, moke (Sl); = **fool**, idiot, twit (Inf, chiefly Brit), oaf, jackass

assassin n = **murderer**, killer, slayer, liquidator, executioner

assault n = **attack**, raid, invasion, charge, offensive ≠ **defence** ♦ v = **strike**, attack, beat, knock, bang

assemble v = **gather**, meet, collect, rally, come together ≠ **scatter**; = **bring together**, collect, gather, rally, come

A

agreement.

assert *v* declare strongly, insist upon. **assertion** *n* **assertive** *adj* **assertively** *adv*

assess *v* 1 fix value or amount of. 2 evaluate. **assessment** *n* **assessor** *n*

asset *n* 1 valuable or useful person, thing. ◆ *pl* 2 things that can be used to raise money.

assiduous *adj* persevering. **assiduously** *adv*

assign *v* 1 appoint. 2 allot. 3 transfer. **assignation** *n* secret meeting. **assignment** *n*

assimilate *v* 1 take in. 2 incorporate. 3 (cause to) become similar. **assimilation** *n*

assist *v* give help to. **assistance** *n* **assistant** *n*

associate *v* 1 link, connect. 2 join. 3 keep company. 4 combine,

unite. ◆ *n* 5 partner. 6 friend. 7 subordinate member. ◆ *adj* 8 affiliated. **association** *n*

assonance *n* rhyming of vowel sounds but not consonants.

assorted *adj* mixed.

assortment *n* mixture.

assume *v* 1 take for granted. 2 pretend. 3 take on. **assumption** *n*

assure *v* 1 tell positively, promise. 2 make sure. 3 insure against loss, esp. of life. **assurance** *n* **assured** *adj* 1 sure. 2 confident, self–possessed.

aster *n* plant with starlike flowers.

asterisk *n* star (*) used in printing.

astern *adv* 1 in, behind the stern. 2 backwards.

asteroid *n* small planet.

asthma *n* illness in which one has difficulty breathing. **asthmatic**

——————— THESAURUS ———————

together

assert *v* = **state**, argue, maintain, declare, swear ≠ **deny**; = **insist upon**, stress, defend, uphold, put forward ≠ **retract**

assess *v* = **judge**, estimate, analyse, evaluate, rate; = **evaluate**, rate, tax, value, estimate

asset *n* = **benefit**, help, service, aid, advantage ≠ **disadvantage**

assign *v* = **give**, set, grant, allocate, give out; = **select for**, post, commission, elect, appoint; = **attribute**, credit, put down, set down, ascribe

assist *v* = **help**, support, aid, cooperate with, abet

associate *v* = **connect**, link, ally,

identify, join ≠ **separate**; = **socialize**, mix, accompany, mingle, consort ≠ **avoid** ◆ *n* = **partner**, friend, ally, colleague, mate (*Inf*)

assorted *adj* = **various**, different, mixed, varied, diverse ≠ **similar**

assume *v* = **presume**, think, believe, expect, suppose ≠ **know**; = **take on**, accept, shoulder, take over, put on; = **simulate**, affect, adopt, put on, imitate

assure *v* = **convince**, encourage, persuade, satisfy, comfort; = **make certain**, ensure, confirm, guarantee, secure; = **promise to**, pledge to, vow to, guarantee to, swear to

adj/n

astigmatism *n* inability of lens (esp. of eye) to focus properly.

astir *adv* on the move.

astonish 🟊 *v* amaze, surprise, stun. **astonishment** *n*

astound *v* astonish greatly. **astounding** *adj*

astral *adj* of the stars.

astray *adv/adj* 1 off the right path. 2 into error or sin.

astride *adv* with legs apart.

astringent *adj* 1 sharp. 2 stopping bleeding. ♦ *n* 3 astringent substance.

astrology *n* foretelling of events by stars. **astrologer** *n* **astrological** *adj*

astronaut *n* one trained for travel in space.

astronomy *n* scientific study of heavenly bodies. **astronomer** *n* **astronomical** *adj* 1 very large. 2 of astronomy. **astronomically** *adv*

astute 🟊 *adj* perceptive, shrewd. **astutely** *adv*

asunder *adv* 1 apart. 2 in pieces.

asylum 🟊 *n* 1 refuge, place of safety 2 *Obs* mental hospital.

asymmetry *n* lack of symmetry. **asymmetrical** *adj*

at *prep/adv* 1 denoting: location in space or time. 2 rate. 3 condition or state. 4 amount. 5 direction. 6 cause.

atheism *n* belief that there is no God. **atheist** *n*

atigi *n* a type of parka worn by the Inuit in Canada.

atlas *n* book of maps.

atmosphere 🟊 *n* 1 gases surrounding earth etc. 2 prevailing mood. **atmospheric** *adj* **atmospherics** *pl n* radio interference.

atoll *n* ring-shaped coral island enclosing lagoon.

atom 🟊 *n* 1 smallest unit of matter which can enter into chemical combination. 2 any very small particle. **atomic** *adj* **atomizer** *n* instrument for discharging liquids in a fine spray. **atomic bomb** bomb with immense power derived from nuclear fission or fusion. **atomic energy** nuclear energy.

atonal *adj* (of music) not in an established key.

atone *v* make amends (for). **atonement** *n*

atop *prep* on top of.

atrocious *adj* 1 extremely cruel. 2 horrifying 3 *Inf* very bad. **atrociously** *adv* **atrocity** *n*

atrophy *n, pl* –phies 1 wasting

—————————— THESAURUS ——————————

astonish *v* = **amaze**, surprise, stun, stagger, bewilder

astute *adj* = **intelligent**, sharp, clever, subtle, shrewd ≠ **stupid**

asylum *n* = (*Old–fashioned*) **mental hospital**, hospital, institution, psychiatric hospital, madhouse

(*Inf*); = **refuge**, haven, safety, protection, preserve

atmosphere *n* = **air**, sky, heavens, aerosphere; = **feeling**, character, environment, spirit, surroundings

atom *n* = **particle**, bit, spot, trace, molecule

away. ♦ v 2 waste away.
attach ➊ v 1 join, fasten. 2
attribute. **attached** adj (with) fond
of. **attachment** n
attaché n specialist attached to
diplomatic mission. **attaché case**
flat rectangular briefcase.
attack ➊ v 1 take action against. 2
criticize. 3 set about with vigour. 4
affect adversely. ♦ n 5 attacking
action. 6 bout. **attacker** n
attain ➊ v 1 arrive at. 2 achieve.
attainable adj **attainment** n
attempt ➊ v/n try.
attend ➊ v 1 be present at. 2
accompany 3 take care of. 4 pay
attention to. **attendance** n 1 an
attending. 2 persons attending.
attendant n/adj **attention** n 1
notice. 2 heed. 3 care. 4 courtesy.
attentive adj 1 giving attention. 2
considerately helpful.
attest v bear witness to.
attic ➊ n space within roof.
attire v/n dress, array.

attitude ➊ n 1 mental view,
opinion. 2 posture, pose. 3
disposition, behaviour.
attorney n person legally
appointed to act for another, esp.
a lawyer.
attract ➊ v 1 draw (attention
etc.). 2 arouse interest of. 3 cause
to come closer (as magnet etc.).
attraction n **attractive** adj
attribute ➊ v 1 regard as
belonging to or produced by. ♦ n
2 quality or characteristic.
attributable adj **attribution** n
attrition n wearing away.
attune v 1 tune. 2 adjust.
atypical adj not typical.
aubergine n purple fruit eaten as
vegetable.
auburn adj/n reddish brown.
auction n 1 public sale in which
goods are sold to the highest
bidder. ♦ v 2 sell by auction.
auctioneer n
audacious adj 1 bold. 2

attach v = **ascribe**, connect,
attribute, assign, associate
attack v = **assault**, strike (at),
mug, ambush, tear into ≠ **defend**;
= **invade**, occupy, raid, infringe,
storm ♦ n = **assault**, charge,
campaign, strike, raid ≠ **defence**;
= **criticism**, censure, disapproval,
abuse, bad press; = **bout**, fit,
stroke, seizure, spasm
attain v = **obtain**, get, reach,
complete, gain
attempt v = **try**, seek, aim,
struggle, venture ♦ n = **try**, go
(Inf), shot (Inf), effort, trial

attend v = **be present**, go to,
visit, frequent, haunt ≠ **be absent**;
= **pay attention**, listen, hear, mark,
note ≠ **ignore**
attic n = **loft**, garret, roof space
attitude n = **opinion**, view,
position, approach, mood;
= **position**, bearing, pose, stance,
carriage
attract v = **allure**, draw, persuade,
charm, appeal to ≠ **repel**; = **pull**,
draw, magnetize
attribute v = **ascribe**, credit, refer,
trace, assign ♦ n = **quality**, feature,
property, character, element

impudent. **audaciously** adv
audacity n
audible adj able to be heard.
audibly adv
audience ❶ n 1 people assembled to listen to or watch. 2 formal interview.
audit n 1 formal examination of accounts. ♦ v 2 examine accounts. **auditor** n
audition n 1 test of prospective performer. ♦ v 2 set, perform such a test. **auditorium** n place where audience sits.
Aug. August.
augment v increase, enlarge.
augur v foretell.
August n eighth month.
auk n northern sea bird.
aunt n 1 father's or mother's sister. 2 uncle's wife. **auntie** n Inf aunt.
au pair n young foreigner who receives board and lodging in return for housework etc.
aura ❶ n atmosphere considered distinctive of person or thing.
aural adj of, by ear.
auricle n 1 outside ear. 2 an upper cavity of heart.
aurora n, pl –ras, –rae 1 lights in the sky radiating from polar regions. 2 dawn.
auspices pl n patronage.
auspicious adj giving hope of future success. **auspiciously** adv
austere adj 1 severe. 2 without luxury. **austerity** n
authentic ❶ adj genuine.
authentically adv **authenticate** v make valid. **authenticity** n
author ❶ n 1 writer. 2 originator.
authority ❶ n, pl –ties 1 legal power or right. 2 delegated power. 3 influence. 4 permission. 5 expert. 6 board in control.
authoritarian n/adj (person) insisting on strict obedience.
authoritative adj **authorize** v 1 empower. 2 permit.
authorization n
autism n disorder causing children to become withdrawn and divorced from reality. **autistic** adj
auto– comb. form self, as in autosuggestion.
autobiography n, pl –phies life of person written by himself.
autobiographical adj
autocrat n 1 absolute ruler. 2 despotic person. **autocratic** adj
autocracy n

————— THESAURUS —————

audience n = **spectators**, company, crowd, gathering, gallery; = **interview**, meeting, hearing, exchange, reception
aura n = **air**, feeling, quality, atmosphere, tone
authentic adj = **real**, pure, genuine, valid, undisputed ≠ fake
author n = **writer**, composer,
novelist, hack, creator; = **creator**, father, producer, designer, founder
authority n usually plural = **powers that be**, government, police, officials, the state; = **expert**, specialist, professional, master, guru; = **command**, power, control, rule, management (Inf)

Autocue ® *n* electronic television device displaying speaker's script unseen by audience.

autogiro, autogyro *n, pl* **–ros** self-propelled aircraft with unpowered rotor.

autograph *n* 1 signature. ♦ *v* 2 sign.

automatic 𝕋 *adj* 1 operated or controlled mechanically. 2 done without conscious thought. ♦ *adj/n* 3 self-loading (weapon). **automatically** *adv* **automation** *n* introduction of automatic devices in industry. **automaton** *n* 1 robot. 2 person who acts mechanically.

automobile *n* motorcar.

autonomy 𝕋 *n* self-government. **autonomous** *adj*

autopsy *n, pl* **–sies** postmortem.

autumn *n* season after summer. **autumnal** *adj*

auxiliary *adj/n* (person) helping, subsidiary.

avail *v* 1 be of use, advantage. ♦ *n* 2 benefit. **available** *adj* 1 obtainable. 2 accessible. **availability** *n*

avalanche 𝕋 *n* 1 mass of snow, ice, sliding down mountain. 2 any great quantity.

avant-garde 𝕋 *adj* innovative and progressive.

avarice *n* greed for wealth. **avaricious** *adj*

avenge *v* take vengeance for.

avenue 𝕋 *n* 1 wide street. 2 approach. 3 double row of trees.

aver *v* averring, averred affirm, assert.

average 𝕋 *n* 1 middle or usual value. ♦ *adj* 2 ordinary. ♦ *v* 3 calculate an average. 4 form an average.

averse *adj* disinclined. **aversion** *n* (object of) dislike.

avert 𝕋 *v* 1 turn away. 2 ward off.

aviary *n, pl* **aviaries** enclosure for birds.

——————— THESAURUS ———————

automatic *adj* = **mechanical**, automated, mechanized, push-button, self-propelling ≠ **done by hand**; = **involuntary**, natural, unconscious, mechanical, spontaneous ≠ **conscious**

autonomy *n* = **independence**, freedom, sovereignty, self-determination, self-government ≠ **dependency**

avalanche *n* = **snow-slide**, landslide, landslip; = **large amount**, barrage, torrent, deluge, inundation

avant-garde *adj* = **progressive**,

pioneering, experimental, innovative, unconventional ≠ **conservative**

avenue *n* = **street**, way, course, drive, road

average *n* = **standard**, normal, usual, par, mode ♦ *adj* = **usual**, standard, general, normal, regular ≠ **unusual**; = **mean**, middle, medium, intermediate, median ≠ **minimum** ♦ *v* = **make on average**, be on average, even out to, do on average, balance out to

avert *v* = **ward off**, avoid, prevent, frustrate, fend off; = **turn**

aviation n art of flying aircraft.

aviator n

avid adj 1 keen. 2 greedy (for).

avidly adv

avocado n, pl **–dos** tropical pear–shaped fruit.

avoid ⊕ v 1 keep away from. 2 refrain from. 3 not allow to happen. **avoidable** adj **avoidance** n

avow v 1 declare. 2 admit. **avowal** n **avowed** adj

await ⊕ v 1 wait or stay for. 2 be in store for.

awake ⊕ v awaking, awoke, awoken 1 emerge or rouse from sleep. 2 (cause to) become alert. ◆ adj 3 not sleeping. 4 alert. **awaken** v awake. **awakening** n

award ⊕ v 1 give formally. ◆ n 2 thing awarded.

aware ⊕ adj informed, conscious.

awareness n

awash adv covered by water.

away ⊕ adv 1 absent, apart, at a distance, out of the way. ◆ adj 2 not present.

awe ⊕ n 1 dread mingled with reverence. ◆ v 2 astonish, frighten.

awesome adj

awful ⊕ adj 1 dreadful. 2 Inf very great. **awfully** adv 1 in an unpleasant way. 2 Inf very much.

awhile adv for a time.

awkward ⊕ adj 1 clumsy. 2 difficult. 3 inconvenient. 4 embarrassed. **awkwardly** adv

awkwardness n

awl n tool for boring wood etc.

— THESAURUS —

away, turn aside

avoid v = **prevent**, stop, frustrate, hamper, foil; = **refrain from**, bypass, dodge, eschew, escape; = **keep away from**, dodge, shun, evade, steer clear of

await v = **wait for**, expect, look for, look forward to, anticipate; = **be in store for**, wait for, be ready for, lie in wait for, be in readiness for

awake adj = **not sleeping**, sleepless, wide–awake, aware, conscious ≠ **asleep** ◆ v = **wake up**, come to, wake, stir, awaken; = **alert**, stimulate, provoke, revive, arouse

award n = **prize**, gift, trophy, decoration, grant ◆ v = **present with**, give, grant, hand out, confer

aware adj = **informed**, enlightened, knowledgeable, learned, expert ≠ **ignorant**

away adj = **absent**, out, gone, elsewhere, abroad ◆ adv = **off**, elsewhere, abroad, hence, from here; = **aside**, out of the way, to one side; = **at a distance**, far, apart, remote, isolated

awe n = **wonder**, fear, respect, reverence, horror ≠ **contempt** ◆ v = **impress**, amaze, stun, frighten, terrify

awful adj = **bad**, poor, terrible, appalling, foul ≠ **wonderful**; = **unwell**, poorly (Inf), ill, terrible, sick

awkward adj = **embarrassing**, difficult, sensitive, delicate, uncomfortable ≠ **comfortable**; = **inconvenient**, difficult, troublesome, cumbersome,

awning n (canvas) roof to protect from weather.

AWOL adj Mil absent without leave.

awry adv 1 crookedly. 2 amiss. ◆ adj 3 crooked. 4 wrong.

axe ❶ n 1 tool for chopping. 2 Inf dismissal from employment. ◆ v 3 Inf dismiss from employment.

axiom n accepted principle.

axiomatic adj

axis ❶ n, pl **axes** (imaginary) line round which body spins.

axle n shaft on which wheels turn.

aye, ay interj 1 yes. ◆ n 2 affirmative answer or vote.

azalea n genus of shrubby flowering plants.

azure adj sky–blue.

——————— THESAURUS ———————

unwieldy ≠ **convenient**; = **clumsy**, lumbering, bumbling, unwieldy, ponderous ≠ **graceful**

axe n = **hatchet**, chopper, tomahawk, cleaver, adze ◆ v

= (Inf) **abandon**, end, eliminate, cancel, scrap

axis n = **pivot**, shaft, axle, spindle, centre line

B b

BA Bachelor of Arts.

baas *n* S Afr boss.

babble *v/n* (make) foolish, incoherent speech.

babe *n* baby.

babiche *n* Canad thongs or lacings of rawhide.

baboon *n* large monkey.

baby 🆃 *n, pl* –**bies** infant. **baby–sitter** *n* one who cares for children when parents are out. **baby–sit** *v*

bach *n* NZ small holiday cottage.

bachelor *n* unmarried man.

bacillus *n, pl* –**li** minute organism sometimes causing disease.

back 🆃 *n* 1 hind part of anything, e.g. human body. 2 part opposite front. 3 part further away or less used. 4 (position of) player in ball games. ◆ *adj* 5 situated behind. 6 earlier. ◆ *adv* 7 at, to the back. 8 in, into the past. 9 in return. ◆ *v* 10 move backwards. 11 support. 12 put wager on. 13 provide with back. 14 provide with musical accompaniment. **backer** *n*

backward *adj* behind in education. **backwardness** *n* **backwards** *adv* to rear, past, worse state. **backbite** *v* slander absent person. **backbone** *n* 1 spinal column. 2 strength of character. **backcloth, backdrop** *n* painted cloth at back of stage. **backdate** *v* make effective from earlier date. **backfire** *v* 1 (of plan, scheme, etc.) fail to work. 2 ignite wrongly. **backgammon** *n* game played with draughtsmen and dice. **background** *n* 1 space behind chief figures of picture etc. 2 past history of person. **backhand** *n* stroke made with hand turned backwards. **backlash** *n* sudden adverse reaction. **backside** *n* rump.

bacon *n* cured pig's flesh.

bacteria 🆃 *pl n, sing* –**rium** microscopic organisms. **bacterial** *adj* **bacteriology** *n*

bad 🆃 *adj* **worse, worst** 1 faulty. 2 harmful. 3 evil. 4 severe. 5 rotten 6 Sl very good. **badly** *adv*

─────── THESAURUS ───────

baby *n* = **child**, infant, babe, bairn (*Scot*), newborn child ◆ *adj* = **small**, little, minute, tiny, mini

back *n* = **spine**, backbone, vertebrae, spinal column, vertebral column ◆ *adj* = **rearmost**, hind, hindmost ◆ *v* = **support**, help, aid, champion, defend ≠ **oppose**

bacteria *pl n* = **microorganisms**,

viruses, bugs (*Sl*), germs, microbes

bad *adj* = **harmful**, damaging, dangerous, destructive, unhealthy ≠ **beneficial**; = **unfavourable**, distressing, unfortunate, grim, unpleasant; = **inferior**, poor, inadequate, faulty, unsatisfactory ≠ **satisfactory**; = **incompetent**, poor, useless, incapable, unfit;

badge ✪ n distinguishing emblem.

badger ✪ n 1 burrowing night animal. ◆ v 2 pester, worry.

badminton n game played with rackets and shuttlecocks.

baffle ✪ v 1 check, frustrate, bewilder. ◆ n 2 device to regulate flow of liquid etc.

bag ✪ n 1 sack. 2 measure of quantity. 3 woman's handbag. ◆ v 4 bulge. 5 sag. 6 put in bag. 7 kill as game, etc. **baggy** adj loose.

bagatelle n 1 trifle. 2 game like pinball.

baggage ✪ n suitcases, luggage.

bagpipes pl n musical wind instrument.

bail¹ ✪ n 1 Law security given for person's reappearance in court. ◆ v 2 (obtain) release on security.

bail² n Cricket crosspiece on wicket.

bail³, **bale** v empty water from

boat. **bail out** parachute.

bailiff n land steward, agent.

bait ✪ n 1 food to entice fish. 2 any lure. ◆ v 3 lure. 4 persecute.

baize n smooth woollen cloth.

bake v 1 cook or harden by dry heat. ◆ v 2 make bread, cakes etc.

baker n **bakery** n, pl **–eries**. **baking powder** raising agent used in cooking.

bakeapple n cloudberry.

bakkie n S Afr small truck.

balalaika n Russian musical instrument, like guitar.

balance ✪ n 1 pair of scales. 2 equilibrium. 3 surplus. 4 sum due on an account. 5 difference between two sums. ◆ v 6 weigh. 7 bring to equilibrium.

balcony ✪ n, pl **–nies** 1 platform outside window. 2 upper seats in theatre.

bald ✪ adj 1 hairless. 2 plain. 3 bare. **balding** adj

———— THESAURUS ————

= **grim**, severe, hard, tough; = **wicked**, criminal, evil, corrupt, immoral ≠ **virtuous**

badge n = **image**, brand, stamp, identification, crest

badger v = **pester**, harry, bother, bug (Inf), bully

baffle v = **puzzle**, confuse, stump, bewilder, confound ≠ **explain**

bag n = **sack**, container, sac, receptacle ◆ v = **catch**, kill, shoot, capture, acquire

baggage n = **luggage**, things, cases, bags, equipment

bail¹ n = (Law) **security**, bond, guarantee, pledge, warranty

bait n = **lure**, attraction, incentive, carrot (Inf), temptation ◆ v = **tease**, annoy, irritate, bother, mock

balance v = **stabilize**, level, steady ≠ **overbalance** = **offset**, match, square, even up; = **weigh**, consider, compare, estimate, contrast; = (Finance) **calculate**, total, determine, estimate, settle ◆ n = **equilibrium**, stability, steadiness, evenness ≠ **instability**; = **stability**, equanimity, steadiness; = **parity**, equity, fairness, impartiality, equality

balcony n = **terrace**, veranda;

bale n/v bundle or package.

baleful adj menacing.

balk, baulk v **1** swerve, pull up. **2** thwart. **3** shirk. ♦ n **4** hindrance.

ball¹ ❶ n **1** anything round. **2** globe, sphere, esp. as used in games. ♦ v **3** gather into a mass.

ball bearings steel balls used to lessen friction.

ball² n assembly for dancing. **ballroom** n

ballad n **1** narrative poem. **2** simple song.

ballast n heavy material put in ship to steady it.

ballet n theatrical presentation of dancing and miming. **ballerina** n

ballistics pl n scientific study of motion of projectiles.

balloon ❶ n **1** large bag filled with air or gas. ♦ v **2** puff out.

ballot ❶ n **1** voting, usually by paper. ♦ v **2** vote.

balm n healing or soothing (ointment).

balmy adj **balmier, balmiest** (of weather) mild and pleasant.

balsa n Amer. tree with light but strong wood.

balsam n resinous aromatic substance.

bamboo n large tropical treelike reed.

bamboozle v mystify, hoax.

ban ❶ v **banning, banned 1** prohibit, forbid, outlaw. ♦ n **2** prohibition. **3** proclamation.

banal adj commonplace, trite. **banality** n

banana n **1** tropical treelike plant. **2** its fruit.

band¹ ❶ n **1** strip used to bind. **2** range of frequencies. **bandage** n/v (apply) strip of cloth for binding wound.

band² ❶ n **1** company. **2** company of musicians. ♦ v **3** bind together.

bandanna, bandana n handkerchief.

bandit ❶ n **1** outlaw. **2** robber.

bandwagon n **jump on the bandwagon** join something that seems assured of success.

bandy v **-dier, -diest** toss from one to another. **bandy-legged** adj curving outwards.

bane n person or thing causing misery or distress. **baneful** adj

bang ❶ n **1** sudden loud noise. **2**

———————— THESAURUS ————————

= **upper circle**, gods, gallery

bald adj = **hairless**, depilated, baldheaded; = **plain**, direct, frank, straightforward, blunt

ball¹ n = **sphere**, drop, globe, pellet, orb

balloon v = **expand**, rise, increase, swell, blow up

ballot n = **vote**, election, voting, poll, polling

ban v = **prohibit**, bar, block, veto, forbid ≠ **permit** ♦ n = **prohibition**, restriction, veto, boycott, embargo ≠ **permission**

band¹ n = **headband**, strip, ribbon; strip, belt

band² n = **ensemble**, group, orchestra, combo; = **gang**, company, group, party, team

bandit n = **robber**, outlaw, raider,

heavy blow. ♦ v **3** make loud noise. **4** beat. **5** slam.

banger n **1** Sl sausage. **2** Inf old car. **3** loud firework.

bangle n ring worn on arm or leg.

banish ⊕ v **1** exile. **2** drive away.

banisters pl n railing on staircase.

banjo n, pl **–jos, –joes** musical instrument like guitar.

bank¹ ⊕ n **1** mound of earth. **2** edge of river etc. ♦ v **3** enclose with ridge. **4** pile up.

bank² ⊕ n **1** establishment for keeping, lending, exchanging etc. money. ♦ v **2** put in bank. **3** keep with bank. **banker** n **banking** n **banknote** n written promise of payment. **bank on** rely on.

bankrupt ⊕ n **1** one who fails in business, insolvent debtor. ♦ adj **2** financially ruined. ♦ v **3** make bankrupt. **bankruptcy** n

banner ⊕ n **1** placard. **2** flag.

banns pl n public declaration of intended marriage.

banquet ⊕ n/v feast.

banshee n spirit whose wailing warns of death.

bantam n **1** small chicken. **2** very light boxing weight.

banter v make fun of. ♦ n **2** light, teasing language.

bar ⊕ n **1** rod or block of any substance. **2** obstacle. **3** rail in law court. **4** body of lawyers. **5** counter where drinks are served. **6** unit of music. ♦ v **7** fasten. **8** obstruct. **9** exclude. ♦ prep **10** except. **barman** n

barachois n (in the Atlantic Provinces of Canada) a shallow lagoon formed by a sand bar.

barb n **1** sharp point curving backwards. **2** cutting remark. **barbed** adj

barbecue n **1** meal cooked

plunderer, mugger (Inf)

bang n = **explosion**, pop, clash, crack, blast; = **blow**, knock, stroke, punch, bump ♦ v = **resound**, boom, explode, thunder, thump ♦ adv = **exactly**, straight, square, squarely, precisely

banish v = **expel**, exile, outlaw, deport ≠ admit; = **get rid of**, remove

bank¹ n = **side**, edge, margin, shore, brink; = **mound**, banking, rise, hill, mass ♦ v = **tilt**, tip, pitch, heel, slope

bank² n = **financial institution**, repository, depository; = **store**, fund, stock, source, supply ♦ v

= **deposit**, keep, save

bankrupt adj = **insolvent**, broke (Inf), ruined, wiped out (Inf), impoverished ≠ solvent

banner n = **flag**, standard, colours, placard, pennant

banquet n = **feast**, spread (Inf), dinner, meal, revel

bar n = **public house**, pub (Inf, chiefly Brit), counter, inn, saloon; = **rod**, staff, stick, stake, rail; = **obstacle**, block, barrier, hurdle, hitch ≠ aid ♦ v = **lock**, block, secure, attach, bolt; = **block**, restrict, restrain, hamper, thwart; = **exclude**, ban, forbid, prohibit, keep out of ≠ admit

outdoors over open fire. ◆ *v* **2** cook thus.

barber *n* person who shaves beards and cuts hair.

barbiturate *n* derivative of barbituric acid used as drug.

bard *n* poet.

bare ❶ *adj* **1** uncovered. **2** naked. **3** plain. **4** scanty. ◆ *v* **5** make bare. **barely** *adv* only just. **barefaced** *adj* shameless.

bargain ❶ *n* **1** something bought at favourable price. **2** agreement. ◆ *v* **3** haggle, negotiate.

barge ❶ *n* **1** flat–bottomed freight boat. ◆ *v* **2** *Inf* bump (into), push.

baritone *n* **1** (singer with) second lowest adult male voice. ◆ *adj* **2** of, for this voice.

barium *n* white metallic element.

bark¹ ❶ *n/v* (utter) sharp loud cry of dog etc.

bark² ❶ *n* outer layer of tree.

barley *n* grain used for food and making malt.

barmy *adj* **–mier, –miest** *Sl* insane.

barn *n* building to store grain, hay etc. **barnyard** *n*

barnacle *n* shellfish which sticks to rocks and ships.

barometer *n* instrument to measure pressure of atmosphere. **barometric** *adj*

baron *n* **1** member of lowest rank of peerage. **2** powerful businessman. **baronial** *adj* **baronet** *n* lowest British hereditary title.

baroque *adj* extravagantly ornamented.

barque *n* sailing ship.

barracks ❶ *pl n* building for lodging soldiers.

barrage ❶ *n* **1** heavy artillery fire. **2** continuous heavy delivery of questions etc. **3** dam across river.

barrel *n* **1** round wooden vessel. **2** tube of gun etc.

barren ❶ *adj* **1** sterile. **2** unprofitable.

barricade ❶ *n* **1** improvised barrier. ◆ *v* **2** block.

——————————————— THESAURUS ———————————————

bare *adj* = **naked**, nude, stripped, uncovered, undressed ≠ **dressed**; = **simple**, spare, stark, austere, spartan ≠ **adorned**

bargain *n* = **good buy**, discount purchase, good deal, steal (*Inf*), snip (*Inf*); = **agreement**, deal (*Inf*), promise, contract, arrangement ◆ *v* = **negotiate**, deal, contract, mediate, covenant

barge *n* = **canal boat**, lighter, narrow boat, flatboat, impose yourself (on)

bark¹ *v* = **yap**, bay, howl, snarl,

growl ◆ *n* = **yap**, bay, howl, snarl, growl

bark² *n* = **covering**, casing, cover, skin, layer

barracks *pl n* = **camp**, quarters, garrison, encampment, billet

barrage *n* = **bombardment**, attack, bombing, assault, shelling; = **torrent**, mass, burst, stream, hail

barren *adj* = **desolate**, empty, desert, waste, unfruitful ≠ **fertile**; = **unproductive**, dry, arid, unfruitful tedious

barricade *n* = **barrier**, wall, fence,

barrier ✪ *n* fence, obstruction.

barrister *n* advocate in the higher law courts.

barrow *n* 1 small wheeled handcart. 2 wheelbarrow.

barter *v/n* (trade by) exchange of goods.

base¹ ✪ *n* 1 bottom, foundation. 2 starting point. 3 centre of operations. ♦ *v* 4 found, establish.

baseless *adj* **basement** *n* lowest storey of building.

base² ✪ *adj* 1 low, mean. 2 despicable.

baseball *n* game played with bat and ball.

bash ✪ *Inf* ♦ *v* 1 strike violently. ♦ *n* 2 blow. 3 attempt.

bashful *adj* shy, modest.

basic ✪ *adj* 1 relating to, serving as base. 2 fundamental. 3 necessary. **basically** *adv* **basics** *pl n* fundamental principles, facts etc.

basil *n* aromatic herb.

basin *n* 1 deep circular dish. 2 harbour. 3 land drained by river.

basis ✪ *n*, *pl* **–ses** 1 foundation. 2 principal constituent.

bask ✪ *v* lie in warmth and sunshine.

basket *n* vessel made of woven cane, straw etc. **basketball** *n* ball game played by two teams.

bass¹ ✪ *n* 1 lowest part in music. 2 bass singer or voice. ♦ *adj* 3 of bass.

bass² *n* sea fish.

bassoon *n* woodwind instrument of low tone.

bastard *n* 1 child born of unmarried parents. 2 *Inf* unpleasant person. ♦ *adj* 3 illegitimate. 4 spurious.

bastion *n* 1 projecting part of fortification. 2 defence.

bat¹ *n* 1 club used to hit ball in cricket etc. ♦ *v* 2 strike with bat.

bat² *n* nocturnal mouselike flying animal.

batch ✪ *n* group or set of similar objects.

bated *adj* with bated breath

blockade, obstruction ♦ *v* = **bar**, block, defend, secure, lock

barrier *n* = **barricade**, wall, bar, fence, boundary

base¹ *n* = **bottom**, floor, lowest part ≠ **top**; = **support**, stand, foot, rest, bed; = **foundation**, institution, organization, establishment ♦ *v* = **ground**, found, build, establish, depend; = **place**, set, post, station, establish

base² *adj* = **dishonourable**, evil, disgraceful, shameful, immoral

≠ **honourable**

bash *v* (*Inf*) = **hit**, beat, strike, knock, smash

basic *adj* = **fundamental**, main, essential, primary, vital; = **vital**, needed, important, key, necessary

basis *n* = **arrangement**, way, system, footing, agreement

bask *v* = **lie**, relax, lounge, sprawl, loaf

bass¹ *adj* = **deep**, low, resonant, sonorous, low–pitched

batch *n* = **group**, set, lot, crowd, pack

anxiously.

bath ❶ n **1** vessel or place to bathe in. **2** water for bathing. **3** act of bathing. ♦ v **4** wash.

bathroom n

bathe ❶ v **1** swim. **2** apply liquid. **3** wash. **4** immerse in water. ♦ n **5** swim. **6** wash. **bather** n

baton ❶ n stick, esp. of policeman, conductor, marshal.

battalion n military unit of three companies.

batten n **1** strip of wood. ♦ v **2** fasten.

batter ❶ v **1** strike continuously. ♦ n **2** mixture of flour, eggs, milk, used in cooking.

battery ❶ n, pl **-teries 1** connected group of electrical cells. **2** accumulator. **3** number of similar things occurring together **4** Law assault by beating. **5** number of guns.

battle ❶ n **1** fight between armies. ♦ v **2** fight. **battle–axe** n **1** large heavy axe **2** Inf domineering

woman.

battlement n wall with openings for shooting.

battleship n heavily armed and armoured fighting ship.

batty ❶ adj **-tier, -tiest** Inf crazy, silly.

bauble n showy trinket.

bawdy adj **bawdier, bawdiest** obscene, lewd.

bawl v/n **1** cry. **2** shout.

bay¹ ❶ n wide inlet of sea.

bay² ❶ n **1** space between two columns. **2** recess.

bay³ ❶ n/v bark. **at bay 1** cornered. **2** at a distance.

bayonet n **1** stabbing weapon fixed to rifle. ♦ v **2** stab with this.

bazaar ❶ n **1** market (esp. in the East). **2** sale for charity.

bazooka n powerful rocket launcher.

B & B bed and breakfast.

BBC British Broadcasting Corporation.

BC before Christ.

———————— THESAURUS ————————

bath n = **wash**, cleaning, shower, soak, cleansing ♦ v = **clean**, wash, shower, soak, cleanse

bathe v = **wash**, clean, bath, shower, soak; = **cleanse**, clean, wash, soak, rinse

baton n = **stick**, club, staff, pole, rod

batter v = **beat**, hit, strike, knock, bang

battery n = **artillery**, ordnance, gunnery, gun emplacement, cannonry

battle n = **fight**, attack, action,

struggle, conflict ≠ **peace**; = **conflict**, campaign, struggle, dispute, contest ♦ v = **wrestle**, war, fight, argue, dispute

batty adj = **crazy**, odd, mad, eccentric, peculiar

bay¹ n = **inlet**, sound, gulf, creek, cove

bay² n = **recess**, opening, corner, niche, compartment

bay³ v = **howl**, cry, roar, bark, wail ♦ n = **cry**, roar, bark, howl, wail

bazaar n = **market**, exchange, fair, marketplace; = **fair**, fête, gala,

be ⊕ v, present sing 1st person **am**. 2nd person **are**. 3rd person **is**. present pl **are**. past sing 1st person **was**. 2nd person **were**. 3rd person **was**. past pl **were**. present participle **being**. past participle **been 1** live. **2** exist. **3** have a state or quality.

beach ⊕ n **1** shore of sea. ♦ v **2** run boat on shore.

beacon ⊕ n **1** fire used to give signal. **2** lighthouse, buoy.

bead ⊕ n **1** little ball pierced for threading. **2** drop of liquid. **beaded** adj **beady** adj small and glittering.

beagle n small hound.

beak n **1** projecting horny jaws of bird. **2** anything similar **3** SI magistrate.

beaker n **1** large drinking cup. **2** glass vessel used by chemists.

beam ⊕ n **1** long thick piece of wood. **2** ray of light etc. ♦ v **3** aim light, radio waves etc. (to). **4** shine. **5** smile broadly.

bean n edible seed of various leguminous plants.

beanie n Brit, Aust & NZ close–fitting woollen hat.

bear¹ ⊕ v **bearing, bore, borne 1** carry. **2** support. **3** produce. **4** endure. **5** press (upon). **bearer** n

bear² n heavy carnivorous animal.

beard n **1** hair on chin. ♦ v **2** oppose boldly.

bearing ⊕ n **1** support for mechanical part. **2** relevance. **3** behaviour. **4** direction. **5** relative position.

beast ⊕ n **1** four–footed animal. **2** brutal man. **beastly** adj

beat ⊕ v **beating, beat, beaten 1** strike repeatedly. **2** overcome. **3** surpass. **4** stir vigorously. **5** flap (wings). **6** make, wear (path). **7** throb. ♦ n **8** stroke. **9** pulsation. **10** appointed course. **11** basic rhythmic unit of music. ♦ adj **12** SI exhausted. **beater** n

beau n, pl **beaux, beaus** suitor.

——————— THESAURUS ———————

bring–and–buy

be v = **be alive**, live, exist, survive, breathe

beach n = **shore**, coast, sands, seaside, water's edge

beacon n = **signal**, sign, beam, flare, lighthouse

bead n = **drop**, tear, bubble, pearl, dot

beam v = **smile**, grin; = **transmit**, show, air, broadcast, cable ♦ n = **ray**, flash, stream, glow, streak; = **rafter**, support, timber, spar, plank; = **smile**, grin

bear¹ v = **carry**, take, move, bring,

transfer ≠ **put down**; = **support**, shoulder, sustain, endure, uphold ≠ **give up**; = **display**, have, show, hold, carry; = **suffer**, experience, go through, sustain, stomach

bearing n (usually with on or **upon**) = **relevance**, relation, application, connection, import ≠ **irrelevance**; = **manner**, attitude, conduct, aspect, behaviour

beast n = **animal**, creature, brute; = **brute**, monster, savage, barbarian, fiend

beat v = **batter**, hit, strike, knock, pound (Inf); = **pound**, strike,

beauty ❶ *n, pl* **-ties 1** loveliness, grace. **2** beautiful person or thing. **beautiful** *adj* **beautifully** *adv* **beautician** *n* person who gives beauty treatments.

beaver *n* **1** amphibious rodent. **2** its fur. ◆ *v* **3** work industriously.

becalmed *adj* (of ship) motionless through lack of wind.

because ❶ *adv/conj* by reason of, since.

beckon ❶ *v* summon by signal.

become ❶ *v* **-coming, -came, -come 1** come to be. **2** suit. **becoming** *adj* suitable.

bed ❶ *n* **1** piece of furniture for sleeping on. **2** garden plot. **3** bottom of river. **4** layer, stratum. ◆ *v* **5** lay in a bed. **6** plant. **bedding** *n* **bedpan** *n* container used as lavatory by bedridden people. **bedridden** *adj* confined to bed. **bedroom** *n* **bedsit** *n* one-roomed flat. **bedstead** *n*

bedevil *v* **-illing, -illed** harass or torment.

bedlam *n* noisy confused scene.

bedraggled *adj* messy and wet.

bee *n* insect that makes honey.

beech *n* European tree with smooth greyish bark and small nuts.

beef *n* **1** flesh of cattle for eating. **2** *Inf* complaint. ◆ *v* **3** *Inf* complain. **beefy** *adj* muscular. **beefburger** *n* flat grilled or fried cake of minced beef.

beer *n* fermented alcoholic drink made from hops and malt. **beer parlour** *Canad* licensed place where beer is sold to the public.

beet *n* any of various plants with root used for food. **beetroot** *n* type of beet plant with a dark red root.

beetle *n* class of insect with hard upper-wing cases.

befall *v* happen (to).

befit *v* be suitable to.

before ❶ *prep* **1** in front of. **2** in presence of. **3** in preference to. **4** earlier than. ◆ *adv* **5** earlier. **6** in front. ◆ *conj* **7** sooner than. **beforehand** *adv* previously.

———————— THESAURUS ————————

hammer, batter, thrash; **= throb**, thump, pound, quake, vibrate; **= hit**, strike, bang ◆ *n* **= throb**, pounding, pulse, thumping, vibration; **= route**, way, course, rounds, path

beauty *n* **= attractiveness**, charm, grace, glamour, elegance ≠ **ugliness**; **= good-looker**, lovely (*SI*), belle, stunner (*Inf*), good

because *conj* **= since**, as, in that

beckon *v* **= gesture**, sign, wave, indicate, signal

become *v* **= come to be**, develop into, be transformed into, grow into, change into; **= suit**, fit, enhance, flatter, embellish

bed *n* **= bedstead**, couch, berth, cot, bunk; **= plot**, area, row, strip, patch; **= bottom**, ground, floor

before *prep* **= earlier than**, ahead of, prior to, in advance of ≠ **after**; **= in front of**, ahead of, in advance of ◆ *adv* **= previously**, earlier, sooner, in advance, formerly ≠ **after**; **= in the past**, earlier,

befriend v become a friend to.

beg ❶ v **begging, begged 1** ask earnestly. **2** ask for money or food. **beggar** n

begin ❶ v –**ginning, –gan, –gun** (cause to) start. **beginner** n **beginning** n

begonia n tropical plant.

begrudge v grudge, envy anyone the possession of.

beguile v **1** charm, fascinate. **2** amuse. **3** deceive.

behalf n **on behalf of** in the interest of.

behave ❶ v **1** act in particular way. **2** act properly. **behaviour** n conduct.

behead v cut off the head of.

behest n charge, command.

behind ❶ prep **1** further back or earlier than. ♦ adv **2** in the rear.

behold v –**holding, –held** watch, see.

beholden adj bound in gratitude.

beige n **1** undyed woollen cloth. **2** its colour.

being ❶ n **1** existence. **2** that which exists. **3** creature. ♦ v present participle of BE.

belated adj **1** late. **2** too late.

belch v **1** expel wind by mouth. **2** eject violently. ♦ n **3** this act.

beleaguered ❶ adj **1** besieged. **2** surrounded or beset.

belfry n, pl –**fries** bell tower.

belie v show to be untrue.

believe v regard as true or real have faith. **belief** n **believable** adj **believer** n

belittle v regard, speak of, as having little worth.

bell n **1** hollow metal instrument giving ringing sound when struck. **2** electrical device emitting ring.

——————— THESAURUS ———————

once, previously, formerly

beg v = **implore**, plead with, beseech, request, petition; = **scrounge**, bum (Inf), touch (someone) for (SI), cadge, sponge on (someone) for ≠ **give**

begin v = **start**, commence, proceed ≠ **stop**; = **commence**, start, initiate, embark on, set about

behave v (often reflexive) = **be well-behaved**, mind your manners, keep your nose clean, act correctly, conduct yourself properly ≠ **misbehave**

behind prep = **at the rear of**, at the back of, at the heels of; = **after**, following ♦ adv = **after**,

next, following, afterwards, subsequently ≠ **in advance of**; = **behind schedule**, delayed, running late, behind time ≠ **ahead**

being n = **individual**, creature, human being, living thing; = **life**, reality ≠ **nonexistence**; = **soul**, spirit, substance, creature, essence

beleaguered adj = **harassed**, troubled, plagued, hassled (Inf), badgered; = **besieged**, surrounded, blockaded, beset, encircled

belief n = **trust**, confidence, conviction ≠ **disbelief**; = **faith**, principles, doctrine, ideology, creed; = **opinion**, feeling, idea, impression, assessment

belle n beautiful woman.

bellicose adj warlike.

belligerent adj 1 hostile, aggressive. 2 making war. **belligerence** n

bellow ⊕ v/n 1 roar. 2 shout.

bellows pl n instrument for creating stream of air.

belly ⊕ n, pl –lies 1 stomach. ◆ v 2 swell out.

belong v 1 be property of. 2 be member of. 3 have an allotted place. 4 pertain to. **belongings** pl n personal possessions.

beloved ⊕ adj 1 much loved. ◆ n 2 dear one.

below ⊕ adv 1 beneath. ◆ prep 2 lower than.

belt ⊕ n 1 band. 2 girdle. 3 zone. ◆ v 4 Inf thrash.

bemoan v grieve over.

bench ⊕ n 1 long seat. 2 seat or body of judges etc.

bend ⊕ v bending, bent (cause to) form a curve.

beneath ⊕ prep 1 under, lower than. ◆ adv 2 below.

benefit ⊕ n 1 advantage, profit. 2 money paid to unemployed etc. ◆ v 3 do good to. 4 receive good. **benefactor** n 1 one who helps or does good to others. 2 patron. **beneficial** adj

benign ⊕ adj kindly, favourable.

bent ⊕ adj 1 curved. 2 resolved (on). 3 Inf corrupt. 4 Inf deviant. ◆ n 5 inclination.

benzene n one of group of flammable liquids used as solvents etc.

bequeath v leave property etc. by will. **bequest** n 1 bequeathing. 2 legacy.

berate v scold harshly.

——————————————— THESAURUS ———————————————

bellow v = **shout**, cry (out), scream, roar, yell ◆ n = **shout**, cry, scream, roar, yell

belly n = **stomach**, insides (Inf), gut, abdomen, tummy

beloved adj = **dear**, loved, valued, prized, admired

below prep = **under**, underneath, lower than ◆ adv = **lower**, down, under, beneath, underneath

belt n = **waistband**, band, sash, girdle, girth; = **conveyor belt**, band, loop, fan belt, drive belt

bench n = **seat**, stall, pew; = **worktable**, stand, table, counter, trestle table

bend v = **twist**, turn, wind, lean, hook ◆ n = **curve**, turn, corner, twist, angle

beneath prep = **under**, below, underneath, lower than ≠ **over**; = **inferior to**, below ◆ adv = **underneath**, below, in a lower place

benefit n = **good**, help, profit, favour ≠ **harm** ◆ v = **profit from**, make the most of, gain from, do well out of, reap benefits from

benign adj = **benevolent**, kind, kindly, warm, friendly ≠ **unkind**; = (Med) **harmless**, innocent, innocuous, curable, inoffensive ≠ **malignant**

bent adj = **misshapen**, twisted, angled, bowed, curved ≠ **straight** ◆ n = **inclination**, ability, leaning,

beret n round, close-fitting hat.

berg n S Afr mountain.

berm n NZ narrow grass strip between the road and the footpath in a residential area.

berry n, pl **-ries** small juicy stoneless fruit.

berserk adj **go berserk** become violent or destructive.

berth ❶ n **1** ship's mooring place. **2** place to sleep in ship. ♦ v **3** moor.

beryl n variety of crystalline mineral, e.g. aquamarine, emerald.

beseech v **-seeching, -sought** entreat, implore.

beset v surround with danger, problems.

beside ❶ prep **1** by the side of, near. **2** distinct from. **besides** adv/prep in addition (to).

besiege ❶ v surround.

besotted adj **1** drunk. **2** foolish. **3** infatuated.

best ❶ adj/adv superlative of GOOD and WELL. ♦ v defeat. **best man** groom's attendant at wedding. **bestseller** n book sold in great numbers.

bestial adj like a beast, brutish.

bestir v rouse to activity.

bestow ❶ v give, confer.

bet ❶ v **1** agree to pay money if wrong in guessing result of contest. ♦ n **2** money so risked.

bête noire n particular dislike.

betray ❶ v **1** be disloyal to. **2** reveal, divulge. **3** show signs of. **betrayal** n

better ❶ adj/adv comparative of GOOD and WELL. ♦ v improve.

between ❶ prep/adv **1** in the intermediate part, in space or

———— THESAURUS ————

tendency, preference

berth n = **bunk**, bed, hammock, billet; = (Naut) **anchorage**, haven, port, harbour, dock ♦ v = (Naut) **anchor**, land, dock, moor, tie up

beside prep = **next to**, near, close to, neighbouring, alongside

beside yourself

besiege v = **harass**, harry, plague, hound, hassle (Inf); = **surround**, enclose, blockade, encircle, hem in

best adj = **finest**, leading, supreme, principal, foremost ♦ n = **finest**, top, prime, pick, flower ♦ adv = **most highly**, most fully, most deeply

bestow v = **present**, give, award, grant, commit ≠ **obtain**

bet v = **gamble**, chance, stake, venture, hazard ♦ n = **gamble**, risk, stake, venture, speculation

betray v = **be disloyal to**, double-cross (Inf), stab in the back, be unfaithful to, inform on or against; = **give away**, reveal, expose, disclose, uncover

better adv = **to a greater degree**, more completely, more thoroughly; = **in a more excellent manner**, more effectively, more attractively, more advantageously, more competently ≠ **worse** ♦ adj = **well**, stronger, recovering, cured, fully recovered ≠ **worse**; = **superior**, finer, higher-quality,

time. **2** indicating reciprocal relation or comparison.

bevel *n* **1** angled surface. ◆ *v* **2** slope, slant.

beverage ❶ *n* drink.

beverage room *n* Canadian tavern.

bevy *n, pl* **bevies** flock or group.

bewail *v* lament.

beware ❶ *v* be on one's guard.

bewilder ❶ *v* puzzle, confuse.

bewitch *v* charm, fascinate.

beyond ❶ *adv* **1** farther away. ◆ *prep* **2** on the farther side of. **3** out of reach of.

bias ❶ *n* **1** slant. **2** inclination. ◆ *v* **3** influence, affect. **biased** *adj* prejudiced.

bib *n* **1** cloth put under child's chin when eating. **2** top of apron.

Bible *n* sacred writings of the Christian religion. **biblical** *adj*

bibliography *n, pl* **-phies** list of books on a subject.

bicentenary *n* 200th anniversary.

biceps *n* two-headed muscle, esp. of upper arm.

bicker *v/n* quarrel over petty things.

bicycle *n* vehicle with two wheels. **bicyclist** *n*

bid ❶ *v* **bidding, bade, bidden** **1** offer. **2** say. **3** command. **4** invite. ◆ *n* **5** offer, esp. of price. **6** try. **7** *Card games* call. **bidder** *n* **bidding** *n* command.

bide *v* **1** remain. **2** dwell. **3** await.

bier *n* frame for coffin.

big ❶ *adj* **bigger, biggest** of great size, height, number, power etc.

bighead *n Inf* conceited person. **big-headed** *adj*

bigamy *n* crime of marrying a person while one is still legally married to someone else.

bigamist *n*

bigot *n* person intolerant of ideas of others. **bigoted** *adj* **bigotry** *n*

bike *n* short for BICYCLE or MOTORBIKE.

surpassing, preferable ≠ **inferior**

between *prep* = **amidst**, among, mid, in the middle of, betwixt

beverage *n* = **drink**, liquid, liquor, refreshment

beware *v* = **be careful**, look out, watch out, be wary, be cautious

bewilder *v* = **confound**, confuse, puzzle, baffle, perplex

beyond *prep* = **after**, over, past, above

bias *n* = **prejudice**, leaning, tendency, inclination, favouritism ≠ **impartiality** ◆ *v* = **influence**, colour, weight, prejudice, distort

bid *n* = **attempt**, try, effort, go (*Inf*), shot (*Inf*); = **offer**, price, amount, advance, proposal ◆ *v* = **make an offer**, offer, propose, submit, tender; = **wish**, say, call, tell, greet; = **tell**, ask, order, require, direct

big *adj* = **large**, great, huge, massive, vast ≠ **small**; = **important**, significant, urgent, far-reaching ≠ **unimportant**; = **powerful**, important, prominent, dominant, influential, skookum (*US & Canad*); = **grown-up**, adult, grown, mature, elder ≠ **young**

bikini n woman's two-piece swimming costume.

bilberry n small moorland plant with edible blue berries.

bile n 1 fluid secreted by the liver. 2 ill temper. **bilious** adj nauseous, nauseating.

bilge n 1 bottom of ship's hull. 2 dirty water collecting there. 3 Inf nonsense.

bilingual adj speaking, or written in, two languages.

bill¹ ❶ n 1 written account of charges. 2 draft of Act of Parliament. 3 poster. 4 commercial document. 5 US and Canad banknote. ♦ v 6 present account of charges. 7 announce by advertisement.

bill² ❷ n bird's beak.

billet n/v –leting, –leted (provide) civilian quarters for troops.

billiards n game played on table with balls and cues.

billion n 1 thousand million, 10⁹. 2 Obs million million, 10¹².

billow n 1 swelling wave. ♦ v 2 swell.

biltong n S Afr strips of dried meat.

bin n receptacle for corn, refuse etc.

binary adj 1 composed of, characterized by, two. 2 dual.

bind ❶ v binding, bound 1 tie fast. 2 tie round. 3 oblige. 4 seal. 5 constrain. 6 bandage. 7 cohere. 8 put (book) into cover. **binder** n

binding n 1 cover of book. 2 tape for hem etc.

binge ❶ n Inf spree.

bingo n game of chance in which numbers drawn are matched with those on a card.

binoculars pl n telescope made for both eyes.

bio– comb. form life, living, as in biochemistry.

biodegradable adj capable of decomposition by natural means.

biography ❶ n, pl –phies story of one person's life. **biographer** n **biographical** adj

biology n study of living organisms. **biological** adj **biologist** n

bionic adj having physical functions aided by electronic

———— THESAURUS ————

bill¹ n = **charges**, rate, costs, score, account; = **act of parliament**, measure, proposal, piece of legislation, projected law; = **list**, listing, programme, card, schedule; = **advertisement**, notice, poster, leaflet, bulletin ♦ v = **charge**, debit, invoice, send a statement to, send an invoice to; = **advertise**, post, announce, promote, plug (Inf)

bill² n = **beak**, nib, neb (archaic or dialect), mandible

bind v = **oblige**, make, force, require, engage; = **tie**, join, stick, secure, wrap ≠ **untie** ♦ n = (Inf) **nuisance**, inconvenience, hassle (Inf), drag (Inf), spot (Inf)

binge n = (Inf) **bout**, spell, fling, feast, stint

biography n = **life story**, life, record, account, profile

equipment.

biopsy *n, pl* **–sies** examination of tissue from a living body.

biped *n* two–footed animal.

birch *n* 1 tree with silvery bark. 2 rod for punishment. ◆ *v* 3 flog.

bird *n* feathered animal.

birdie *n* *Golf* score of one stroke under par.

Biro ® *n* ballpoint pen.

birth ⊕ *n* 1 bearing, or the being born, of offspring. 2 parentage, origin. **birthday** *n* **birthmark** *n* blemish on the skin.

biscuit *n* dry, small, thin variety of cake.

bisect *v* divide into two equal parts.

bisexual *adj* sexually attracted to both men and women.

bishop *n* 1 clergyman governing diocese. 2 chess piece.

bison *n, pl* **–son** 1 large wild ox. 2 Amer. buffalo.

bistro *n, pl* **–tros** small restaurant.

bit¹ ⊕ *n* fragment, piece.

bit² *n* 1 biting, cutting part of tool. 2 mouthpiece of horse's bridle.

bit³ *n* *Comp* smallest unit of information.

bitch *n* 1 female dog, fox, or wolf. 2 *Offens* spiteful woman. **bitchy** *adj*

bite ⊕ *v* **biting, bit, bitten** 1 cut into, esp. with teeth. 2 grip. 3 rise to the bait. 4 corrode. ◆ *n* 5 act of biting. 6 wound so made. 7 mouthful. **biting** *adj* 1 piercing or keen. 2 sarcastic.

bitter ⊕ *adj* 1 sour tasting. 2 (of person) resentful. 3 sarcastic. **bitterly** *adv* **bitterness** *n*

bittern *n* wading bird.

bitumen *n* viscous substance occurring in asphalt, tar etc.

bivouac *n* 1 temporary encampment of soldiers, hikers etc. ◆ *v* 2 camp.

bizarre ⊕ *adj* unusual, weird.

blab *v* **blabbing, blabbed** 1 reveal secrets. 2 chatter idly.

black ⊕ *adj* 1 of the darkest colour. 2 without light. 3 dark. 4 evil. ◆ *n* 5 darkest colour. 6 black dye, clothing etc. 7 (*with cap.*) person of dark–skinned race. ◆ *v* 8 boycott in industrial dispute.

blacken *v* 1 make black. 2 defame.

blackball *v* vote against, exclude.

blackberry *n* plant with dark juicy berries, bramble. **blackbird** *n* common European songbird.

blackboard *n* dark surface for writing on with chalk. **black box** Inf. name for FLIGHT RECORDER.

——————— THESAURUS ———————

birth *n* = **childbirth**, delivery, nativity, parturition ≠ **death** start; = **ancestry**, stock, blood, background, breeding

bit¹ *n* = **piece**, scrap

bite *v* = **nip**, cut, tear, wound, snap ◆ *n* = **snack**, food, piece, taste, refreshment; = **wound**, sting, pinch, nip, prick

bitter *adj* = **resentful**, angry, offended, sour, sore ≠ **happy**; = **freezing**, biting, severe, intense, raw ≠ **mild**; = **sour**, sharp, acid, harsh, tart ≠ **sweet**

bizarre *adj* = **strange**, unusual, extraordinary, fantastic, weird

blackhead n small dark spot on skin. **blackleg** n strikebreaker.
blacklist n 1 list of people considered suspicious. ◆ v 2 put on such a list. **black market** illegal buying and selling of goods. **black spot** dangerous place, esp. on a road.

blackguard n scoundrel.

blackmail 🟊 v 1 extort money by threats. ◆ n 2 extortion. **blackmailer** n

blackout n 1 complete failure of electricity supply. 2 state of temporary unconsciousness. 3 obscuring of lights as precaution against night air attack.

blacksmith n person who works in iron.

bladder n membranous bag to contain liquid.

blade n 1 edge, cutting part of knife or tool. 2 leaf of grass etc. 3 sword.

blame 🟊 v 1 censure. 2 culpability. ◆ v 3 find fault with. 4 censure. **blameless** adj

blameworthy adj

blanch v 1 whiten, bleach. 2 turn pale.

blancmange n pudding made from milk.

bland 🟊 adj 1 devoid of distinctive characteristics. 2 smooth in manner. **blandly** adv

blank 🟊 adj 1 without marks or writing. 2 empty. 3 vacant, confused. ◆ n 4 empty space. 5 cartridge containing no bullet. **blankly** adv

blanket 🟊 n 1 thick bed cover. 2 concealing cover. ◆ v 3 cover, stifle.

blare v 1 sound loudly and harshly. ◆ n 2 such sound.

blarney n flattering talk.

blasé adj 1 indifferent through familiarity. 2 bored.

blaspheme v show contempt for God, esp. in speech. **blasphemous** adj **blasphemy** n

blast 🟊 n 1 explosion. 2 shock wave. 3 gust of wind. 4 loud sound. ◆ v 5 blow up. 6 blight.

——— THESAURUS ———

≠ **normal**
black adj = **dark**, raven, ebony, sable, jet ≠ **light**; = **gloomy**, sad, depressing, grim, bleak ≠ **happy**; = **terrible**, bad, devastating, tragic, fatal
blackmail n = **threat**, intimidation, ransom, extortion, hush money (SI) ◆ v = **threaten**, squeeze, compel, intimidate, coerce
blame v = **hold responsible**, accuse, denounce, indict, impeach

≠ **absolute** ◆ n = **responsibility**, liability, accountability, onus, culpability ≠ **praise**
bland adj = **dull**, boring, plain, flat, dreary ≠ **exciting**
blank adj = **unmarked**, white, clear, clean, empty ≠ **marked**; = **expressionless**, empty, vague, vacant, deadpan ≠ **expressive** ◆ n = **empty space**, space, gap
blanket n = **cover**, rug, coverlet; = **covering**, sheet, coat, layer, carpet ◆ v = **coat**, cover, hide,

blatant ⊕ *adj* obvious. **blatantly** *adv*

blaze¹ ⊕ *n* 1 strong fire or flame. 2 brightness. 3 outburst. ♦ *v* 4 burn strongly. 5 be very angry.

blaze² *v* 1 establish trail. ♦ *n* 2 white mark on horse's face.

blazer *n* type of jacket worn esp. for sports.

bleach ⊕ *v* 1 make or become white. ♦ *n* 2 bleaching substance.

bleak ⊕ *adj* 1 cold, exposed. 2 dismal. **bleakness** *n*

bleary *adj* **–rier, –riest** with eyes dimmed, as with tears, sleep.

bleat *v* 1 cry, as sheep. 2 say plaintively. ♦ *n* 3 sheep's cry.

bleed ⊕ *v* **bleeding, bled** 1 lose blood. 2 draw blood from.

bleep *n* short high–pitched sound. **bleeper** *n*

blemish *n* 1 defect. ♦ *v* 2 make defective. **blemished** *adj*

blend ⊕ *v* 1 mix. ♦ *n* 2 mixture.

blender *n* electrical appliance for mixing food.

bless ⊕ *v* 1 consecrate. 2 ask God's favour for. 3 make happy. **blessed** *adj* **blessing** *n*

blether *v* 1 speak at length, esp. foolishly. ♦ *n* 2 foolish or babbling talk.

blight ⊕ *n* 1 plant disease. 2 harmful influence. ♦ *v* 3 injure.

blighter *n Inf* irritating person.

blind ⊕ *adj* 1 unable to see. 2 heedless. 3 closed at one end. ♦ *v* 4 deprive of sight. ♦ *n* 5 window screen. 6 pretext. **blindly** *adv* **blindness** *n* **blindfold** *v/n* (cloth used to) cover the eyes.

blink ⊕ *v* 1 wink. 2 twinkle. ♦ *n* 3

——————————————— THESAURUS ———————————————

mask, conceal

blast *n* = **explosion**, crash, burst, discharge, eruption; = **gust**, rush, storm, breeze, puff; = **blare**, blow, scream, trumpet, wail ♦ *v* = **blow up**, bomb, destroy, burst, ruin

blatant *adj* = **obvious**, clear, plain, evident, glaring ≠ **subtle**

blaze¹ *v* = **burn**, glow, flare, be on fire, go up in flames ♦ *n* = **inferno**, fire, flames, bonfire, combustion; = **flash**, glow, glitter, flare, glare

bleach *v* = **lighten**, wash out, blanch, whiten

bleak *adj* = **dismal**, dark, depressing, grim, discouraging ≠ **cheerful**; = **exposed**, empty, bare, barren, desolate ≠ **sheltered**

bleed *v* = **lose blood**, flow, gush,

spurt, shed blood; = **blend**, run, meet, unite, mix; = (*Inf*) **extort**, milk, squeeze, drain, exhaust

blend *v* = **mix**, join, combine, compound, merge; = **go well**, match, fit, suit, go with ♦ *n* = **mixture**, mix, combination, compound, brew

bless *v* = **sanctify**, dedicate, ordain, exalt, anoint ≠ **curse**; = **endow**, give to, provide for, grant for, favour ≠ **afflict**

blight *n* = **curse**, suffering, evil, corruption, pollution ≠ **blessing**; = **disease**, pest, fungus, mildew, infestation ♦ *v* = **frustrate**, destroy, ruin, crush, mar

blind *adj* = **sightless**, unsighted, unseeing, eyeless, visionless

gleam. **blink at** ignore. **on the blink** Inf not working.

blip n repetitive sound or visible pulse, e.g. on radar screen.

bliss ① n perfect happiness. **blissful** adj **blissfully** adv

blister ① n 1 bubble on skin. 2 surface swelling. ♦ v 3 form blisters (on). **blistering** adj 1 very hot. 2 extremely harsh.

blithe adj happy. **blithely** adv

blitz ① n concentrated attack.

blizzard n blinding storm of wind and snow.

blob n soft mass or drop.

block ① n 1 solid (rectangular) piece of wood, stone etc. 2 obstacle. 3 pulley with frame. 4 large building of offices, flats etc. ♦ v 5 obstruct, stop up. 6 shape. **blockage** n **blockhead** n stupid person. **block letter** plain capital letter.

blockade ① n 1 physical prevention of access, esp. to port. ♦ v 2 prevent access.

bloke ① n Inf fellow, chap.

blood ① n 1 red fluid in veins. 2 kindred. ♦ v 3 initiate (into hunting, war etc.). **bloodless** adj **bloody** adj 1 covered in blood. 2 savage. 3 extreme. ♦ adv 4 Sl extremely. ♦ v 5 make bloody. **blood bath** massacre. **bloodhound** n large dog used for tracking. **bloodshed** n slaughter. **bloodshot** adj (of eyes) inflamed. **bloodthirsty** adj cruel. **bloody-minded** adj deliberately unhelpful.

bloom ① n 1 flower. 2 prime. 3 glow. ♦ v 4 be in flower. 5 flourish.

bloomer n Inf mistake.

bloomers pl n wide, baggy

——— THESAURUS ———

≠ sighted; often with **to** = unaware of, unconscious of, ignorant of, indifferent to, insensitive to **≠ aware**; = **unquestioning**, prejudiced, wholesale, indiscriminate, uncritical

blink v = **flutter**, wink, bat; = **flash**, flicker, wink, shimmer, twinkle; **on the blink** = (Sl) **not working (properly)**, faulty, defective, playing up, out of action

bliss n = **joy**, ecstasy, euphoria, rapture, nirvana **≠ misery**

blister n = **sore**, boil, swelling, cyst, pimple

blitz n = **attack**, strike, assault, raid, offensive

block n = **piece**, bar, mass, brick, lump; = **obstruction**, bar, barrier, obstacle, impediment ♦ v = **obstruct**, close, stop, plug, choke **≠ clear**

blockade n = **stoppage**, block, barrier, restriction, obstacle

bloke n = (Inf) **man**, person, individual, character (Inf), guy (Inf)

blood n = **lifeblood**, gore, vital fluid; = **family**, relations, birth, descent, extraction

bloom n = **flower**, bud, blossom; = **prime**, flower, beauty, height, peak; = **glow**, freshness, lustre, radiance **≠ pallor** ♦ v = **flower**, blossom, open, bud **≠ wither**; = **grow**, develop, wax

knickers.

blossom ❶ n 1 flower. ♦ v 2 flower. 3 flourish.

blot n 1 spot, stain. ♦ v 2 spot, stain. 3 obliterate. 4 soak up ink.

blotter n

blotch n 1 dark spot. ♦ v 2 make spotted.

blouse n light, loose upper garment.

blow¹ ❶ v blowing, blew, blown 1 make a current of air. 2 pant. 3 drive air upon or into. 4 drive by current of air. 5 make sound 6 Sl squander. ♦ n 7 blast. 8 gale.

blower n **blowfly** n fly which infects food etc. **blowlamp** n small burner with very hot flame.

blowout n 1 sudden puncture in tyre. 2 uncontrolled escape of oil, gas, from well 3 Sl large meal.

blow up 1 explode. 2 fill with air 3 Inf enlarge photograph 4 Inf lose one's temper.

blow² ❶ n 1 stroke, knock. 2 sudden misfortune.

blubber v 1 weep. ♦ n 2 whale fat.

bludge v 1 Aust & NZ inf to scrounge from (someone). 2 evade work. **bludger** n person who scrounges.

bludgeon n 1 short thick club. ♦ v 2 strike with one. 3 coerce.

blue ❶ adj 1 of the colour of sky. 2 depressed. 3 indecent. ♦ n 4 colour of sky. 5 dye or pigment. ♦ pl 6 Inf depression. 7 form of jazz music. ♦ v 8 make blue. **bluish** adj

bluebell n wild spring flower.

bluebottle n blowfly. **blueprint** n 1 copy of drawing. 2 original plan.

bluff¹ ❶ n 1 cliff, steep bank 2 Canad clump of trees. ♦ adj 3 hearty. 4 blunt.

bluff² ❶ v/n (deceive by) pretence.

blunder ❶ n/v (make) clumsy mistake.

blunt ❶ adj 1 not sharp. 2 (of speech) abrupt. ♦ v 3 make blunt. **bluntly** adv

blossom n = **flower**, bloom, bud, efflorescence, floret ♦ v = **bloom**, grow, develop, mature; = **succeed**, progress, thrive, flourish, prosper

blow¹ v = **move**, carry, drive, sweep, fling; = **be carried**, flutter; = **exhale**, breathe, pant, puff

blow² n = **knock**, stroke, punch, bang, sock (Sl); = **setback**, shock, disaster, reverse, disappointment

blue adj = **depressed**, low, sad, unhappy, melancholy ≠ **happy**; = **smutty**, obscene, indecent,

lewd, risqué ≠ **respectable**

bluff¹ n = **precipice**, bank, peak, cliff, ridge ♦ adj = **hearty**, open, blunt, outspoken, genial ≠ **tactful**

bluff² n = **deception**, fraud, sham, pretence, deceit ♦ v = **deceive**, trick, fool, pretend, cheat

blunder n = **mistake**, slip, fault, error, oversight ≠ **correctness** ♦ v = **make a mistake**, blow it (Sl), err, slip up (Inf), foul up ≠ **be correct**; = **stumble**, fall, reel, stagger, lurch

blunt adj = **frank**, forthright, straightforward, rude, outspoken

B

blur ❶ v blurring, blurred 1 make, become less distinct. ◆ n 2 something indistinct.
blurb n statement recommending book etc.
blurt v utter suddenly.
blush ❶ v 1 become red in face. 2 be ashamed. ◆ n 3 this effect.
blusher n cosmetic to give rosy colour to face.
bluster v/n (indulge in) noisy, aggressive behaviour. **blustery** adj (of wind) gusty.
BO Inf body odour.
boa n 1 large, nonpoisonous snake. 2 long scarf of fur or feathers.
boar n 1 male pig. 2 wild pig.
board ❶ n 1 broad, flat piece of wood, card etc. 2 table. 3 meals. 4 group of people who administer company. ◆ v 5 cover with planks. 6 supply food daily. 7 enter ship etc. 8 take daily meals. **boarder** n
boardroom n
boast ❶ v 1 speak too much in praise of oneself. 2 brag of. 3 have to show. ◆ n 4 thing boasted (of).

boastful adj
boat n 1 small open vessel. 2 ship. ◆ v 3 sail about in boat. **boater** n flat straw hat. **boatswain** n ship's officer in charge of equipment.
bob ❶ v bobbing, bobbed 1 move up and down. 2 move jerkily. 3 cut (women's) hair short. ◆ n 4 jerking motion. 5 short hairstyle. 6 weight on pendulum etc.
bobbin n reel for thread.
bobble n small, tufted ball.
bobby n, pl –bies Inf police officer.
bobotie n S Afr dish of curried mince.
bobsleigh n 1 sledge for racing. ◆ v 2 ride on this.
bode v be an omen of.
bodice n upper part of woman's dress.
bodkin n large blunt needle.
body ❶ n, pl bodies 1 whole frame of man or animal. 2 corpse. 3 main part. 4 substance. 5 group regarded as single entity. **bodily** adj/adv **bodyguard** n escort to protect important person. **bodywork** n outer shell of motor

———— THESAURUS ————

≠ **tactful**; = **dull**, rounded, dulled, edgeless, unsharpened ≠ **sharp** ◆ v = **dull**, weaken, soften, numb, dampen ≠ **stimulate**
blur n = **haze**, confusion, fog, obscurity, indistinctness ◆ v = **become indistinct**, become vague, become hazy, become fuzzy
blush v = **turn red**, colour, glow, flush, redden ≠ **turn pale** ◆ n = **reddening**, colour, glow, flush, pink tinge

board n = **plank**, panel, timber, slat, piece of timber; = **council**, directors, committee, congress, advisers; = **meals**, provisions, victuals, daily meals ◆ v = **get on**, enter, mount, embark ≠ **get off**
boast v = **brag**, crow, vaunt, talk big (SI), blow your own trumpet ≠ **cover up**; = **possess**, exhibit
bob v = **bounce**, duck, hop, wobble, oscillate

vehicle.

boffin n Inf scientist.

bog n wet, soft ground. **boggy** adj **bog down** bogging, bogged stick as in a bog.

bogan n Aust dated & NZ slang youth who dresses and behaves rebelliously.

bogey n **bogy** n 1 thing that causes fear. 2 Golf score of one stroke over par.

boggle v stare, be surprised.

bogus n adj sham, false.

bohemian n/adj (person) leading unconventional life.

boil¹ n v 1 (cause to) change from liquid to gas, esp. by heating. 2 cook or become cooked by boiling. 3 Inf be hot. 4 Inf be angry. ◆ n 5 boiling state. **boiler** n equipment providing hot water.

boil² n n inflamed swelling on skin.

boisterous adj 1 wild. 2 noisy.

bold n adj 1 daring,

presumptuous. 2 prominent.

boldly adv **boldness** n

bole n tree trunk.

bolero n, pl –ros 1 Spanish dance. 2 short loose jacket.

bollard n 1 post to secure mooring lines. 2 post in road as barrier.

bolster n v 1 support, uphold. ◆ n 2 long pillow. 3 pad, support.

bolt n n 1 bar or pin (esp. with thread for nut). 2 rush. 3 lightning. 4 roll of cloth. ◆ v 5 fasten. 6 swallow hastily. 7 rush away.

bomb n n 1 explosive projectile. 2 any explosive device. ◆ v 3 attack with bombs. **bomber** n 1 aircraft that drops bombs. 2 person who throws or plants a bomb. **bombard** v 1 shell. 2 attack (verbally). **bombshell** n shocking surprise.

bona fide Lat genuine.

bonanza n sudden wealth.

——— THESAURUS ———

body n = **physique**, build, form, figure, shape; = **torso**, trunk; = **corpse**, dead body, remains, stiff (Sl), carcass; = **organization**, company, group, society, association; = **main part**, matter, material, mass, substance

bog n = **marsh**, swamp, slough, wetlands, fen

bogey n = **bugbear**, bête noire, horror, nightmare, bugaboo

bogus adj = **fake**, false, artificial, forged, imitation ≠ **genuine**

boil¹ v = **simmer**, bubble, foam, seethe, fizz

boil² n = **pustule**, gathering, swelling, blister, carbuncle

bold adj = **fearless**, enterprising, brave, daring, heroic ≠ **timid**; = **impudent**, forward, confident, rude, cheeky ≠ **shy**

bolster v = **support**, help, boost, strengthen, reinforce

bolt n = **pin**, rod, peg, rivet; = **bar**, catch, lock, latch, fastener ◆ v = **lock**, close, bar, secure, fasten; = **dash**, fly; = **gobble**, stuff, wolf, cram, gorge

bomb n = **explosive**, mine, shell, missile, device ◆ v = **blow up**,

bond ❶ *n* 1 thing which binds. 2 link. 3 written promise. ◆ *v* 4 bind.

bondage *n* slavery.

bone *n* 1 hard substance forming skeleton. 2 piece of this. ◆ *v* 3 take out bone. **bony** *adj* **bone-idle** *adj* extremely lazy.

bonfire *n* large outdoor fire.

bongo *n*, *pl* **-gos, -goes** small drum played with fingers.

bonk *v* 1 *Inf* hit. 2 have sexual intercourse (with).

bonnet *n* 1 hat with strings. 2 cap. 3 cover of motor vehicle engine.

bonny *adj* **-nier, -niest** beautiful, handsome.

bonsai *n*, *pl* **-sai** (art of growing) dwarf trees, shrubs.

bonus ❶ *n* extra (unexpected) payment or gift.

boo *interj* 1 expression of disapproval. 2 exclamation to surprise esp. child. ◆ *v* 3 make this sound.

boob *n* 1 *Sl* foolish mistake. 2 female breast.

boogie *v Inf* dance quickly to pop music.

book ❶ *n* 1 sheets of paper bound together. 2 literary work. ◆ *v* 3 reserve room, ticket etc. 4 charge with legal offence. 5 enter name in book. **booklet** *n* **book-keeping** *n* systematic recording of business transactions. **bookmaker** *n* one who takes bets. **bookworm** *n* person devoted to reading.

boom¹ ❶ *n* 1 sudden commercial activity. 2 prosperity. ◆ *v* 3 prosper.

boom² *v/n* (make) deep sound.

boom³ *n* long spar for bottom of sail.

boomerang *n* curved wooden missile of Aust. Aborigines, which returns to the thrower.

boon ❶ *n* something helpful, favour.

boor *n* rude person. **boorish** *adj*

boost ❶ *n* 1 encouragement. 2 upward push. 3 increase. ◆ *v* 4 encourage. 5 push. **booster** *n*

boot ❶ *n* 1 covering for the foot and ankle. 2 luggage space in car 3 *Inf* kick. ◆ *v* 4 *Inf* kick.

————— THESAURUS —————

attack, destroy, assault, shell

bond *n* = **tie**, union, coupling, link, association; = **fastening**, tie, chain, cord, shackle; = **agreement**, word, promise, contract, guarantee ◆ *v* = **form friendships**, connect

bonus *n* = **extra**, prize, gift, reward, premium

book *n* = **work**, title, volume, publication, tract; = **notebook**, album, journal, diary, pad ◆ *v*

= **reserve**, schedule, engage, organize, charter

boom¹ *n* = **expansion**, increase, development, growth, jump ≠ **decline**

boon *n* = **benefit**, blessing, godsend, gift

boost *v* = **increase**, develop, raise, expand, add to ≠ **decrease** ◆ *n* = **rise**, increase, jump, addition, improvement ≠ **fall**;

= **encouragement**, help

booth n 1 stall. 2 cubicle.

bootleg v 1 make, carry, sell illicit goods, esp. alcohol. ♦ adj 2 produced, sold illicitly. **bootlegger** n

booty n, pl **-ties** plunder, spoil.

booze n/v Inf (consume) alcoholic drink.

border 🔂 n 1 margin. 2 frontier. 3 limit. 4 strip of garden. ♦ v 5 provide with border. 6 adjoin.

bore¹ 🔂 v 1 pierce hole. ♦ n 2 hole. 3 calibre of gun.

bore² 🔂 v 1 make weary by repetition. ♦ n 2 tiresome person or thing. **boredom** n **boring** adj

boron n chemical element used in hardening steel etc.

borough n town.

borrow 🔂 v 1 obtain on loan. 2 copy, steal. **borrower** n

borstal n formerly, prison for young criminals.

borzoi n tall dog with long, silky coat.

bosom n human breast.

boss 🔂 n 1 person in charge of or employing others. ♦ v 2 be in charge of. 3 be domineering over.

bossy adj **bossier, bossiest** overbearing.

botany n study of plants. **botanical** adj **botanist** n

botch v 1 spoil by clumsiness. ♦ n 2 blunder.

both adj/pron the two.

bother 🔂 v 1 pester. 2 perplex. 3 trouble. ♦ n 4 fuss, trouble.

bottle n 1 vessel for holding liquid. 2 its contents. ♦ v 3 put into bottle. 4 restrain. **bottleneck** n narrow outlet which impedes smooth flow.

bottom 🔂 n 1 lowest part. 2 bed of sea etc. 3 buttocks. ♦ adj 4 lowest. ♦ v 5 put bottom to. 6 base (upon). 7 get to bottom of. **bottomless** adj

bough n branch of tree.

boulder n large rock.

boulevard n broad street or promenade.

———— THESAURUS ————

boot v = **kick**, punt, put the boot in(to) (Sl), drop-kick

border n = **frontier**, line, limit, bounds, boundary; = **edge**, margin, verge, rim ♦ v = **edge**, bound, decorate, trim, fringe

bore¹ v = **drill**, mine, sink, tunnel, pierce

bore² v = **tire**, fatigue, weary, wear out, jade ≠ **excite** ♦ n = **nuisance**, pain (Inf), yawn (Inf), anorak (Inf)

borrow v = **take on loan**, touch (someone) for (Sl), scrounge (Inf),

cadge, use temporarily ≠ **lend**; = **steal**, take, copy, adopt, pinch (Inf)

boss n = **manager**, head, leader, director, chief

bother v = **trouble**, concern, worry, alarm, disturb ♦ n = **trouble**, problem, worry, difficulty, fuss ≠ **help**

bottom n = **lowest part**, base, foot, bed, floor ≠ **top**; = **underside**, sole, underneath, lower side ♦ adj = **lowest**, last ≠ **higher**

bounce ⊕ v 1 (cause to) rebound on impact. ◆ n 2 rebounding. 3 quality causing this. 4 Inf vitality. **bouncer** n person who removes unwanted people from nightclub etc. **bouncing** adj vigorous.

bound¹ ⊕ n (usu. pl) 1 limit. ◆ v 2 restrict. **boundary** n **boundless** adj

bound² ⊕ v/n spring, leap.

bound³ adj on a specified course.

bound⁴ adj 1 committed. 2 certain. 3 tied.

bounty n, pl **-ties** 1 liberality. 2 gift. 3 premium. **bounteous, bountiful** adj

bouquet ⊕ n 1 bunch of flowers. 2 aroma. 3 compliment.

bourbon n US whisky made from maize.

bourgeois ⊕ n/adj middle class.

bout ⊕ n 1 period of time spent doing something. 2 contest, fight.

boutique n small shop, esp. one selling clothes.

bow¹ ⊕ v 1 bend body in respect, assent etc. 2 submit. 3 bend downwards. 4 crush. ◆ n 5 bowing.

bow² n 1 weapon for shooting arrows. 2 implement for playing violin etc. 3 ornamental knot. 4 bend. ◆ v 5 bend.

bow³ n fore end of ship.

bowel n (oft. pl) 1 part of intestine. 2 inside of anything.

bowl¹ ⊕ n 1 round vessel, deep basin. 2 drinking cup. 3 hollow.

bowl² ⊕ n 1 wooden ball. ◆ pl 2 game played with such balls. ◆ v 3 roll or throw ball in various ways. **bowler** n **bowling** n

bowler n man's low-crowned stiff felt hat.

box¹ ⊕ n 1 (wooden) container, usu. rectangular. 2 its contents. 3 any boxlike cubicle or receptacle. ◆ v 4 put in box. 5 confine. **box office** place where tickets are sold.

box² ⊕ v 1 fight with fists, esp. with padded gloves on. 2 strike. ◆ n 3 blow. **boxer** n 1 one who boxes. 2 large dog resembling bulldog. **boxing** n

box³ n evergreen shrub used for

———— THESAURUS ————

bounce v = **rebound**, recoil, ricochet ◆ n = **springiness**, give, spring, resilience, elasticity; = (Inf) **life**, go (Inf), energy, zip (Inf), vigour

bound¹ v = **surround**, confine, enclose, encircle, hem in; = **limit**, restrict, confine, restrain, circumscribe

bound² n = **leap**, bob, spring, jump, bounce

bouquet n = **bunch of flowers**, spray, garland, wreath, posy;

= **aroma**, smell, scent, perfume, fragrance

bourgeois adj = **middle-class**, traditional, conventional, materialistic, hidebound

bout n = **period**, term, fit, spell, turn; = **fight**, match, competition, struggle, contest

bow¹ v = **bend**, bob, nod, stoop, droop ◆ n = **bending**, bob, nod, obeisance, kowtow

bowl¹ n = **basin**, plate, dish, vessel

bowl² v = **throw**, hurl, launch,

hedges.

boy 𝕆 n **1** male child. **2** young man. **boyish** adj **boyfriend** n woman's male companion.

boycott 𝕆 v **1** refuse to deal with or participate in. ◆ n **2** such refusal.

bra n woman's undergarment, supporting breasts.

braaivlies, braai S Afr ◆ n **1** grill on which food is cooked over hot charcoal, usu. outdoors. ◆ v **2** cook (food) in this way.

brace 𝕆 n **1** tool for boring. **2** clamp. **3** pair. **4** support. ◆ pl **5** straps to hold up trousers. ◆ v **6** steady (oneself) as before a blow. **7** support. **bracelet** n ornament for the arm. **bracing** adj invigorating.

bracken n large fern.

bracket n **1** support for shelf etc. **2** group. ◆ pl **3** marks, () used to enclose words etc. ◆ v **4** enclose in brackets. **5** connect.

brackish adj (of water) slightly salty.

brag v **bragging, bragged 1** boast. ◆ n **2** boastful talk.

braggart n

braid v **1** interweave. **2** trim with braid. ◆ n **3** anything plaited. **4** ornamental tape.

Braille n system of printing for blind, with raised dots.

brain n **1** mass of nerve tissue in head. **2** intellect. ◆ v **3** kill by hitting on head. **brainy** adj
brainchild n creative idea of a person. **brainwash** v force someone to change beliefs.
brainwave n sudden, clever idea.

braise v stew in covered pan.

brake 𝕆 n **1** instrument for slowing motion of wheel on vehicle. ◆ v **2** apply brake to.

bramble n prickly shrub.

bran n sifted husks of corn.

branch n **1** limb of tree. **2** local office. ◆ v **3** bear branches. **4** diverge. **5** spread.

brand 𝕆 n **1** trademark. **2** class of goods. **3** particular kind. **4** mark made by hot iron. **5** burning piece of wood. ◆ v **6** burn with iron. **7** mark. **8** stigmatize. **brand–new** adj absolutely new.

brandish v flourish, wave.

brandy n, pl **–dies** spirit distilled

———— THESAURUS ————

cast, pitch

box¹ n = **container**, case, chest, trunk, pack ◆ v = **pack**, package, wrap, encase, bundle up

box² v = **fight**, spar, exchange blows

boy n = **lad**, kid (Inf), youth, fellow, youngster

boycott v ≠ **embargo**, reject, snub, black ≠ **support**

brace v = **steady**, support, secure,

stabilize ◆ n = **support**, stay, prop, bolster, bracket

brake n = **control**, check, curb, restraint, constraint ◆ v = **slow**, decelerate, reduce speed

branch n = **bough**, shoot, arm, spray, limb; = **office**, department, unit, wing, chapter

brand n = **label**, mark, sign, stamp, symbol ◆ v = **stigmatize**, mark, expose, denounce, disgrace;

from wine.
brash ⊕ *adj* bold, impudent.
brass *n* 1 alloy of copper and zinc.
2 group of brass wind
instruments. 3 *Inf* money. 4 *Inf*
(army) officers. ♦ *adj* 5 made of
brass.
brassiere *n* bra.
brat *n* unruly child.
bravado *n* showy display of
boldness.
brave ⊕ *adj* 1 courageous. 2
splendid. ♦ *n* 3 warrior. ♦ *v* 4 defy,
meet boldly. **bravery** *n*
bravo *interj* well done!
brawl ⊕ *v/n* (take part in) noisy
fight.
brawn *n* 1 muscle. 2 strength. 3
pickled pork. **brawny** *adj*
bray *n/v* (make) donkey's cry.
brazen *adj* 1 of, like brass. 2
shameless. ♦ *v* 3 face, carry
through with impudence.
brazier *n* pan for burning coals.
breach ⊕ *n* 1 opening. 2 breaking
of rule etc. ♦ *v* 3 make a gap in.
bread ⊕ *n* 1 food make of flour

baked. 2 food 3 *Sl* money.
breadwinner *n* main earner in
family.
breadth ⊕ *n* 1 extent across,
width. 2 largeness of view, mind.
break ⊕ *v* breaking, broke,
broken 1 part by force. 2 shatter.
3 burst, destroy. 4 become
broken. 5 fail to observe. 6
disclose. 7 interrupt. 8 surpass. 9
weaken. 10 accustom (horse) to
being ridden. 11 decipher (code).
12 open, appear. 13 come
suddenly. ♦ *n* 14 fracture. 15 gap.
16 opening. 17 separation. 18
interruption. 19 respite. 20
interval. 21 *Inf* opportunity.
breakable *adj* **breakage** *n* **breaker**
n 1 one that breaks. 2 wave
beating on shore. **breakdown** *n* 1
collapse. 2 failure to function. 3
analysis. **breakfast** *n* first meal of
the day. **break-in** *n* illegal entering
of building. **breakneck** *adj* fast and
dangerous. **breakthrough** *n*
important advance.
bream *n* broad, thin fish.

————————— THESAURUS —————————

= **mark**, burn, label, stamp, scar
brash *adj* = **bold**, rude, cocky,
pushy (*Inf*), brazen ≠ **timid**
brave *adj* = **courageous**, daring,
bold, heroic, adventurous ≠ **timid**
♦ *v* = **confront**, face, suffer, tackle,
endure ≠ **give in to**
brawl *n* = **fight**, clash, fray,
skirmish, scuffle ♦ *v* = **fight**, scrap
(*Inf*), wrestle, tussle, scuffle
breach *n* = **nonobservance**,
abuse, violation, infringement,
trespass ≠ **compliance**; = **opening**,

crack, split, gap, rift
bread *n* = **food**, fare,
nourishment, sustenance
breadth *n* = **width**, spread, span,
latitude, broadness; = **extent**,
range, scale, scope, compass
break *v* = **shatter**, separate,
destroy, crack, snap ≠ **repair**;
= **fracture**, crack, smash; = **burst**,
tear, split; = **disobey**, breach, defy,
violate, disregard ≠ **obey**; = **stop**,
cut, suspend, interrupt, cut short;
= **disturb**, interrupt ♦ *n* = **fracture**,

breast *n* **1** human chest. **2** milk-secreting gland on woman's chest. **3** seat of the affections. ♦ *v* **4** face, oppose. **5** reach summit of.
breaststroke *n* stroke in swimming.
breath 🔊 *n* **1** air used by lungs. **2** life. **3** respiration. **4** slight breeze. **breathe** *v* **2** inhale and exhale (air). **2** live. **3** rest. **4** whisper. **breather** *n* short rest. **breathing** *n*
breathless *adj* **breathtaking** *adj* causing awe or excitement.
Breathalyser ® *n* device that estimates amount of alcohol in breath. **breathalyse** *v*
breech *n* **1** buttocks. **2** hind part of anything. **breeches** *pl n* trousers.
breed 🔊 *v* **breeding, bred 1** generate. **2** rear. **3** be produced. **4** be with young. ♦ *n* **5** offspring produced. **6** race, kind. **breeder** *n* **breeding** *n* result of good upbringing.
breeze 🔊 *n* gentle wind. **breezy** *adj* **1** windy. **2** lively.

brethren *pl n* brothers.
brevity *n* **1** conciseness of expression. **2** short duration.
brew 🔊 *v* **1** prepare liquor, as beer. **2** make drink, as tea. **3** plot. **4** be in preparation. ♦ *n* **5** beverage produced by brewing. **brewer** *n* **brewery** *n, pl* **–eries**
bribe 🔊 *n* **1** anything offered or given to gain favour. ♦ *v* **2** influence by bribe. **bribery** *n*
bric–a–brac *n* small ornamental objects.
brick *n* **1** oblong mass of hardened clay used in building. ♦ *v* **2** build, block etc. with bricks.
bride *n* woman about to be, or just, married. **bridal** *adj* **bridesmaid** *n*
bridge[1] 🔊 *n* **1** structure for crossing river etc. **2** something joining or supporting other parts. **3** raised narrow platform on ship. **4** upper part of nose. ♦ *v* **5** make bridge over, span.
bridge[2] *n* card game.
bridle *n* **1** headgear of horse. **2**

———— THESAURUS ————

opening, tear, hole, split; = **interval**, pause, interlude, intermission; = **holiday**, leave, vacation, time off, recess
breath *n* = **inhalation**, breathing, pant, gasp, gulp
breed *n* = **variety**, race, stock, type, species; = **kind**, sort, type, variety, brand ♦ *v* = **rear**, tend, keep, raise, maintain; = **reproduce**, multiply, propagate, procreate, produce offspring; = **produce**, cause, create,

generate, bring about
breeze *n* = **light wind**, air, draught, gust, waft ♦ *v* = **sweep**, move briskly, pass, sail, hurry
brew *v* = **boil**, make, soak, steep, stew; = **make**, ferment ♦ *n* = **drink**, preparation, mixture, blend, liquor
bribe *n* = **inducement**, pay-off (*Inf*), sweetener (*Sl*), kickback (*US*), backhander (*Sl*) ♦ *v* = **buy off**, reward, pay off (*Inf*), corrupt, suborn

curb. ♦ v **3** put on bridle. **4** restrain. **5** show resentment.

brief ❶ adj **1** short in duration. **2** concise. **3** scanty. ♦ n **4** document containing facts of legal case. **5** summary. ♦ pl **6** underpants. **7** panties. ♦ v **8** give instructions.

briefly adv **briefcase** n flat case for carrying papers, books etc.

brier, briar n wild rose with long thorny stems.

brier see BRIAR.

brigade ❶ n **1** subdivision of army. **2** organized band. **brigadier** n high–ranking army officer.

brigand n bandit.

bright ❶ adj **1** shining. **2** full of light. **3** cheerful. **4** clever. **brighten** v **brightly** adv **brightness** n

brilliant ❶ adj **1** shining. **2** sparkling. **3** splendid. **4** very clever. **5** distinguished. **brilliance, brilliancy** n

brim ❶ n margin, edge, esp. of river, cup, hat. **brimful** adj

brine n **1** salt water. **2** pickle.

bring ❶ v **bringing, brought 1** fetch. **2** carry with one. **3** cause to happen.

brinjal n S Afr dark purple tropical fruit, cooked and eaten as a vegetable.

brink ❶ n edge of steep place.

brisk ❶ adj active, vigorous. **briskly** adv

brisket n meat from breast.

bristle ❶ n **1** short stiff hair. ♦ v **2** stand erect. **3** show temper. **bristly** adv

brittle ❶ adj **1** easily broken. **2** curt.

broach v **1** introduce (subject). **2** open.

broad ❶ adj **1** wide, spacious, open. **2** obvious. **3** coarse. **4** general. **broaden** v **broadly** adv

—— THESAURUS ——

bridge¹ n = **arch**, span, viaduct, flyover, overpass

brief adj = **short**, quick, fleeting, swift, short–lived ≠ **long** ♦ v = **inform**, prime, prepare, advise, fill in (Inf) ♦ n = **summary**, résumé, outline, sketch, abstract

brigade n = **corps**, company, force, unit, division

bright adj = **vivid**, rich, brilliant, glowing, colourful; = **shining**, glowing, dazzling, gleaming, shimmering

brilliant adj = **intelligent**, sharp, intellectual, clever, profound ≠ **stupid**; = **expert**, masterly, talented, gifted, accomplished

≠ **untalented**; = **splendid**, famous, celebrated, outstanding, superb

brim n = **rim**, edge, border, lip, margin ♦ v = **be full**, spill, well over, run over

bring v = **fetch**, take, carry, bear, transfer; = **take**, guide, conduct, escort

brink n = **edge**, limit, border, lip, margin

brisk adj = **quick**, lively, energetic, active, vigorous ≠ **slow**

bristle n = **hair**, spine, thorn, whisker, barb ♦ v = **stand up**, rise, stand on end; = **be angry**, rage, seethe, flare up, bridle

brittle adj = **fragile**, delicate,

B

broadcast v 1 transmit by radio or television. 2 make widely known. ♦ n 3 radio or television programme. **broadcaster** n **broadcasting** n **broad-minded** adj tolerant. **broadside** n 1 discharge of guns. 2 strong (verbal) attack.

brocade n rich woven fabric with raised design.

broccoli n type of cabbage.

brochure ❶ n pamphlet.

broekies [**brook**-eez] pl n S Afr informal underpants.

brogue n 1 stout shoe. 2 dialect, esp. Irish accent.

broil v US and Canad grill.

broke ❶ adj Inf having no money.

broker ❶ n one employed to buy and sell for others.

bromide n chemical compound used in medicine and photography.

bromine n liquid element used in production of chemicals.

bronco n, pl –cos US wild pony.

brontosaurus n large plant-eating dinosaur.

bronze ❶ n 1 alloy of copper and tin. ♦ adj 2 made of, or coloured

like, bronze. ♦ v 3 give appearance of bronze to.

brooch n ornamental pin.

brood ❶ n 1 family of young, esp. of birds. ♦ v 2 sit, as hen on eggs. 3 fret over. **broody** adj

brook¹ ❶ n small stream.

brook² v put up with.

broom n 1 brush for sweeping. 2 yellow-flowered shrub.

broomstick n handle of broom.

broth n thick soup.

brothel n house of prostitution.

brother ❶ n 1 son of same parents. 2 one closely united with another. **brotherly** adj **brotherhood** n 1 fellowship. 2 association. **brother-in-law** n, pl **brothers-in-law** 1 brother of husband or wife. 2 husband of sister.

brow n 1 ridge over eyes. 2 forehead. 3 eyebrow. 4 edge of hill. **browbeat** v frighten with threats.

brown ❶ adj 1 of dark colour inclining to red or yellow. ♦ n 2 the colour. ♦ v 3 make, become brown.

———————— THESAURUS ————————

crisp, crumbling, frail ≠ tough

broad adj = **wide**, large, ample, generous, expansive; = **large**, huge, vast, extensive, ample ≠ **narrow**

brochure n = **booklet**, advertisement, leaflet, hand-out, circular

broke adj = (Inf) **penniless**, short, ruined, bust (Inf), bankrupt ≠ **rich**

broker n = **dealer**, agent, trader,

supplier, merchant

bronze adj = **reddish-brown**, copper, tan, rust, chestnut

brood n = **offspring**, issue, clutch, litter, progeny ♦ v = **think**, obsess, muse, ponder, agonize

brook¹ n = **stream**, burn (Scot & Northern English), rivulet, beck, watercourse

brother n = **monk**, cleric, friar, religious

browse ⓥ v 1 look through (book etc.) in a casual manner. 2 feed on shoots and leaves.

bruise ⓥ v 1 injure without breaking skin. ♦ n 2 contusion, discoloration caused by blow.

bruiser n tough person.

brumby n Aust 1 wild horse. 2 unruly person.

brunch n breakfast and lunch combined.

brunette n 1 woman of dark complexion and hair. ♦ adj 2 dark brown.

brunt n chief shock of attack.

brush¹ ⓥ n 1 device with bristles, hairs etc. used for cleaning, painting etc. 2 act of brushing. 3 brief contact. 4 skirmish. 5 bushy tail. ♦ v 6 apply, remove, clean, with brush. 7 touch lightly.

brush² n thick shrubbery.

brusque adj curt.

Brussels sprout vegetable like a tiny cabbage.

brute n 1 any animal except man. 2 crude, vicious person. ♦ adj 3 animal. 4 sensual. 5 stupid. 6 physical. **brutal** adj **brutality** n **brutally** adv

BSc Bachelor of Science.

BST British Summer Time.

bubble ⓝ n 1 hollow globe of liquid, blown out with air. 2 something insubstantial. ♦ v 3 rise in bubbles. **bubbly** adj

bubonic plague acute infectious disease characterized by swellings.

buccaneer n pirate.

buck n 1 male deer, or other male animal. 2 act of bucking. 3 US & Aust SI dollar. ♦ v 4 (of horse) attempt to throw rider. **buckshot** n lead shot in shotgun shell.

bucket n vessel, round with arched handle, for water etc. **bucketful** n

buckle ⓥ n 1 metal clasp for fastening belt, strap etc. ♦ v 2 fasten with buckle. 3 warp, bend.

bud ⓝ n 1 shoot containing unopened leaf, flower etc. ♦ v 2 begin to grow.

budge ⓥ v move, stir.

brown adj = brunette, bay, coffee, chocolate, chestnut ♦ v = fry, cook, grill, sear, sauté

browse v = skim, scan, glance at, survey, look through; = graze, eat, feed, nibble

bruise n = discoloration, mark, injury, blemish, black mark ♦ v = hurt, injure, mark

brush¹ n = broom, sweeper, besom; = conflict, clash, confrontation, skirmish, tussle; = encounter, meeting, confrontation, rendezvous ♦ v = clean, wash, polish, buff; = touch, sweep, kiss, stroke, glance

bubble n = air ball, drop, bead, blister, blob ♦ v = boil, seethe; = foam, fizz, froth, percolate, effervesce

buckle n = fastener, catch, clip, clasp, hasp ♦ v = fasten, close, secure, hook, clasp; = distort, bend, warp, crumple, contort

bud n = shoot, branch, sprout,

budgerigar, budgie n small Aust. parakeet.

budget 🛈 n 1 annual financial statement. 2 plan of systematic spending. ◆ v 3 make financial plan.

buff¹ 🛈 n 1 leather from buffalo hide. 2 light yellow colour. 3 polishing pad. ◆ v 4 polish.

buff² 🛈 n expert.

buffalo n type of cattle.

buffer 🛈 n device to lessen impact.

buffet¹ 🛈 n 1 refreshment bar. 2 meal at which guests serve themselves. 3 sideboard.

buffet² n 1 blow, slap. ◆ v 2 strike with blows. 3 contend against.

buffoon n 1 clown. 2 fool.

bug 🛈 n 1 any small insect. 2 Inf disease, infection. 3 concealed listening device. ◆ v 4 annoy. 5 listen secretly.

bugbear n 1 object of needless terror. 2 nuisance.

bugger n Sl unpleasant person or thing.

bugle n instrument like trumpet.

build 🛈 v **building, built** 1 construct by putting together parts. 2 develop. ◆ n 3 make, form. **builder** n **building** n **building society** organization where money can be borrowed or invested.

bulb n 1 modified leaf bud emitting roots from base, e.g. onion. 2 globe surrounding filament of electric light. **bulbous** adj

bulge 🛈 n 1 swelling. 2 temporary increase. ◆ v 3 swell.

bulk 🛈 n 1 size. 2 volume. 3 greater part. 4 cargo. ◆ v 5 be of weight or importance. **bulky** adj

─────────── THESAURUS ───────────

sprig, offshoot ◆ v = **develop**, grow, shoot, sprout, burgeon

budge v = **move**, stir

budget n = **allowance**, means, funds, income, finances ◆ v = **plan**, estimate, allocate, cost, ration

buff¹ v = **polish**, smooth, brush, shine, rub

buff² n = (Inf) **expert**, fan, addict, enthusiast, admirer

buffer n = **safeguard**, screen, shield, cushion, intermediary

buffet¹ n = **snack bar**, café, cafeteria, brasserie, refreshment counter

bug n = (Inf) **illness**, disease, virus, infection, disorder; = **fault**, error,

defect, flaw, glitch (Inf) ◆ v = **tap**, eavesdrop, listen in on; = (Inf) **annoy**, bother, disturb, irritate, hassle (Inf)

build v = **construct**, make, raise, put up, assemble ≠ **demolish** ◆ n = **physique**, form, body, figure, shape

bulge v = **swell out**, project, expand, stick out, protrude ◆ n = **lump**, swelling, bump, projection, hump ≠ **hollow**; = **increase**, rise, boost, surge, intensification

bulk n = **size**, volume, dimensions, magnitude, substance; = **weight**, size, mass, heaviness, poundage

bull n **1** male of cattle. **2** male of various other animals. **bulldog** n thickset breed of dog. **bulldozer** n powerful tractor for excavating etc. **bullfight** n public show in which bull is killed. **bullock** n castrated bull. **bull's-eye** n centre of target.

bullet ➊ n projectile discharged from rifle, pistol etc.

bulletin ➊ n official report.

bullion n gold or silver in mass.

bully ➊ n, pl **-lies** one who hurts or intimidates weaker people.

bulrush n tall reedlike marsh plant.

bulwark n **1** rampart. **2** any defence.

bum n Sl buttocks, anus.

bumble v perform clumsily.

bumblebee n large hairy bee.

bumf, bumph, bumph n Inf official papers.

bump ➊ n **1** knock. **2** thud. **3** swelling. ♦ v **4** strike or push against. **bumper** n **1** horizontal bar on motor vehicle to protect against damage. ♦ adj **2** abundant.

bumpkin n simple country person.

bumptious adj self-assertive.

bun n **1** small, round cake. **2** round knot of hair.

bunch ➊ n **1** number of things tied or growing together. **2** group, party. ♦ v **3** gather together.

bundle ➊ n **1** package. **2** number of things tied together. ♦ v **3** tie in bundle. **4** send (off) without ceremony.

bung n **1** stopper for cask. ♦ v **2** stop up **3** Sl sling.

bungalow n one-storeyed house.

bungle ➊ v/n botch.

bunion n inflamed swelling on foot or toe.

bunk n narrow shelflike bed.

bunker n **1** large storage container for coal etc. **2** sandy hollow on golf course. **3** underground defensive position.

bunny n, pl **-nies** Inf rabbit.

bunting n material for flags.

bunyip n Aust legendary monster said to live in swamps and lakes.

buoy ➊ n **1** floating marker anchored in sea. ♦ v **2** prevent from sinking. **buoyancy** n **buoyant** adj

——————— THESAURUS ———————

bullet n = **projectile**, ball, shot, missile, slug

bulletin n = **report**, account, statement, message, communication

bully n = **persecutor**, tough, oppressor, tormentor, bully boy ♦ v = **persecute**, intimidate, torment, oppress, pick on

bump v = **knock**, hit, strike, crash,

smash; = **jerk**, shake, bounce, rattle, jog ♦ n = **knock**, blow, impact, collision, thump; = **thud**, crash, knock, bang, smack

bunch n = **group**, band, crowd, party, team; = **cluster**, clump

bundle n = **bunch**, group, collection, mass, pile ♦ v = **push**, thrust, shove, throw, rush

bungle v = **mess up**, blow (Sl),

burden ⊕ n 1 load. 2 weight, cargo. 3 anything difficult to bear. ♦ v 4 load, encumber.

burdensome adj

bureau ⊕ n, pl –reaus, –reaux 1 writing desk. 2 office. 3 government department.

bureaucracy n 1 government by officials. 2 body of officials.

bureaucrat n

burgeon v 1 bud. 2 flourish.

burglar ⊕ n one who enters building to commit crime esp. theft. **burglary** n **burgle** v

burgundy n name of various wines, white and red.

burlesque n/v caricature.

burly adj –lier, –liest sturdy, stout, robust.

burn ⊕ v burning, burnt 1 destroy or injure by fire. 2 be on fire. 3 be consumed by fire. ♦ n 4 injury, mark caused by fire. **burning** adj 1 intense. 2 urgent.

burnish v/n polish.

burp v/n Inf belch.

burrow ⊕ n 1 hole dug by rabbit etc. ♦ v 2 dig.

bursar n official managing finances of college etc. **bursary** n scholarship.

burst ⊕ v bursting, burst 1 break into pieces. 2 break suddenly into some expression of feeling. 3 shatter, break violently. ♦ n 4 bursting. 5 explosion. 6 outbreak. 7 spurt.

bury ⊕ v burying, buried 1 put underground. 2 inter. 3 conceal.

burial n/adj

bus n large motor vehicle for passengers.

bush ⊕ n 1 shrub. 2 uncleared country. **bushy** adj shaggy.

bushbaby n tree-living, nocturnal Afr. animal.

——————————— THESAURUS ———————————

ruin, spoil, blunder ≠ **accomplish**

buoy n = **float**, guide, signal, marker, beacon

burden n = **trouble**, worry, weight, responsibility, strain; = **load**, weight, cargo, freight, consignment ♦ v = **weigh down**, worry, load, tax, bother

bureau n = **office**, department, section, branch, station

burglar n = **housebreaker**, thief, robber, pilferer, filcher

burn v = **be on fire**, blaze, be ablaze, smoke, flame; = **set on fire**, light, ignite, kindle, incinerate; = **scorch**, toast, sear, char, singe

burrow n = **hole**, shelter, tunnel, den, lair ♦ v = **dig**, tunnel, excavate

burst v = **explode**, blow up, break, split, crack; = **rush**, run, break, break out, erupt ♦ n = **rush**, surge, outbreak, outburst, spate; = **explosion**, crack, blast, bang, discharge

bury v = **inter**, lay to rest, entomb, consign to the grave, inhume ≠ **dig up**; = **hide**, cover, conceal, stash (Inf), secrete ≠ **uncover**; = **sink**, embed, immerse, enfold

bush n = **shrub**, plant, hedge, thicket, shrubbery

bushel *n* dry measure of eight gallons.

business ⊕ *n* 1 occupation. 2 commercial or industrial establishment. 3 trade. 4 responsibility. 5 work. **businesslike** *adj*

busker *n* street entertainer. **busk** *v*

bust¹ ⊕ *n* 1 sculpture of head and shoulders. 2 woman's breasts.

bust² *Inf* ♦ *v* 1 burst. 2 make, become bankrupt. 3 raid. 4 arrest. ♦ *adj* 5 broken. 6 bankrupt.

bustle ⊕ *v* 1 be noisily busy. ♦ *n* 2 fuss, commotion.

busy ⊕ *adj* busier, busiest 1 actively employed. 2 full of activity. ♦ *v* 3 occupy. **busily** *adv* **busybody** *n* nosy person.

but ⊕ *conj* 1 without. 2 except. 3 yet. 4 still. 5 besides. ♦ *adv* 6 only.

butane *n* gas used for fuel.

butch *adj Inf* aggressively masculine.

butcher ⊕ *n* 1 one who kills animals for food, or sells meat. 2 savage man. ♦ *v* 3 slaughter. **butchery** *n*

butler *n* chief male servant.

butt¹ ⊕ *n* 1 thick end. 2 unused end.

butt² ⊕ *n* 1 target. 2 object of ridicule.

butt³ ⊕ *v* 1 strike with head. 2 interrupt. ♦ *n* 3 blow made with head.

butter *n* 1 fatty substance got from cream by churning. ♦ *v* 2 spread with butter. 3 flatter.

buttercup *n* plant with glossy, yellow flowers.

butterfly *n* insect with large wings.

butterscotch *n* kind of hard,

———— THESAURUS ————

business *n* = **trade**, selling, industry, manufacturing, commerce; = **establishment**, company, firm, concern, organization; = **profession**, work, job, line, trade; = **concern**, affair

bust¹ *n* = **bosom**, breasts, chest, front

bust² (*Inf*) *v* = **break**, smash, split, burst, shatter; = **arrest**, catch, raid **go bust** = **go bankrupt**, fail, be ruined, become insolvent

bustle *v* = **hurry**, rush, fuss, hasten, scuttle ≠ **idle** ♦ *n* = **activity**, to-do, stir, excitement, fuss ≠ **inactivity**

busy *adj* = **active**, industrious, rushed off your feet ≠ **idle**;

= **occupied with**, working, engaged in, on duty, employed in ≠ **unoccupied**

but *conj* = **however**, still, yet, nevertheless ♦ *prep* = **except (for)**, save, bar, barring, excepting ♦ *adv* = **only**, just, simply, merely

butcher *n* = **murderer**, killer, slaughterer, slayer, destroyer ♦ *v* = **slaughter**, prepare, carve, cut up, dress; = **kill**, slaughter, massacre, destroy, cut down

butt¹ *n* = **end**, handle, shaft, stock, shank; = **stub**, tip, leftover, fag end (*Inf*)

butt² *n* = **target**, victim, dupe, laughing stock, Aunt Sally

butt³ *v* = **knock**, push, bump,

brittle toffee.

buttock n (usu. pl) rump, protruding hind part.

button n 1 knob, stud for fastening dress. 2 knob that operates doorbell, machine etc. ◆ v 3 fasten with buttons.

buttonhole n 1 slit in garment to pass button through. 2 flower worn on lapel etc. ◆ v 3 detain (unwilling) person in conversation.

buttress n 1 structure to support wall. 2 prop. ◆ v 3 support.

buxom adj full of health, plump.

buy 🛈 v buying, bought 1 get by payment, purchase. 2 bribe. ◆ n 3 thing purchased. **buyer** n

buzz v/n (make) humming sound. **buzzer** n **buzzword** n fashionable word.

buzzard n bird of prey.

by 🛈 prep 1 near. 2 along. 3 past. 4 during. 5 not later than. 6 through use or agency of. 7 in units of. ◆ adv 8 near. 9 aside. 10 past. **by and by** soon. **by and large** on the whole.

bye-bye n interj Inf goodbye.

by-election n election to fill vacant seat.

bygone adj 1 past, former. ◆ n (oft. pl) 2 past occurrence. 3 small antique.

bylaw, bye-law n law, regulation made by local authority.

bypass 🛈 n road for diversion of traffic from overcrowded centres. ◆ v make detour round.

byre n cowshed.

byte n Comp sequence of bits processed as single unit of information.

byway n secondary or side road.

byword n well-known name or saying.

——————————— THESAURUS ———————————

thrust, ram

buy v = **purchase**, get, pay for, obtain, acquire ≠ sell ◆ n = **purchase**, deal, bargain, acquisition, steal (Inf)

by prep = **through**, through the agency of; = **via**, over, by way of; = **near**, past, along, close to, closest to ◆ adv = **nearby**, close, handy, at hand, within reach

bypass v = **get round**, avoid

C c

C 1 *Chem* carbon. 2 Celsius. 3 Centigrade.

c. circa.

cab ⓘ *n* 1 taxi. 2 driver's compartment on lorry etc.

cabal *n* 1 small group of intriguers. 2 secret plot.

cabaret *n* floor show at a nightclub.

cabbage *n* green vegetable.

cabin ⓘ *n* 1 hut, shed. 2 small room, esp. in ship.

cabinet ⓘ *n* 1 piece of furniture with drawers or shelves. 2 outer case of television, radio etc. 3 committee of politicians.

cable *n* 1 strong rope. 2 wires conveying electric power, television signals etc. 3 telegraph. ◆ *v* 4 telegraph by cable. **cable car** vehicle pulled up slope on cable.

cache *n* 1 secret hiding place. 2 store of food etc.

cackle *v/n* (make) chattering noise, as of hen.

cacophony *n* 1 disagreeable sound. 2 discord of sounds.

cactus *n, pl* **–tuses**, **–ti** spiny succulent plant.

cad *n* unchivalrous person.

cadaver *n* corpse. **cadaverous** *adj*

caddie, **caddy** *n, pl* **–dies** golfer's attendant.

caddy *n, pl* **–dies** small box for tea.

cadence *n* fall or modulation of voice in music or verse.

cadenza *n Mus* elaborate solo passage.

cadet *n* youth in training, esp. for armed forces.

cadge *v* get (food, money etc.) by begging.

cadmium *n* metallic element.

caecum *n, pl* **–ca** part of large intestine.

Caesarean section surgical operation to deliver a baby.

caesium *n* metallic element.

café *n* small restaurant serving light refreshments. **cafeteria** *n* self-service restaurant.

caffeine *n* stimulating chemical found in tea and coffee.

caftan *n* see KAFTAN.

cage ⓘ *n* 1 enclosure, box with bars or wires, esp. for keeping animals or birds. ◆ *v* 2 put in cage, confine. **cagey** *adj* wary.

cagoule *n* lightweight anorak.

THESAURUS

---

cab *n* = **taxi**, minicab, taxicab, hackney carriage

cabin *n* = **room**, berth, quarters, compartment; = **hut**, shed, cottage, lodge, shack

cabinet *n* = **cupboard**, case, locker, dresser, closet; = **council**, committee, administration, ministry, assembly

café *n* = **snack bar**, restaurant,

cairn n heap of stones, esp. as monument or landmark.

cajole v persuade by flattery, wheedle.

cake ⊕ n 1 baked, sweet, bread-like food. 2 compact mass. ♦ v 3 harden (as of mud).

calamine n soothing ointment.

calamity n, pl **–ties** disaster. **calamitous** adj

calcium n metallic element, the basis of lime.

calculate ⊕ v 1 estimate. 2 compute. 3 make reckonings. **calculable** adj **calculating** adj 1 shrewd. 2 scheming. **calculation** n **calculator** n electronic device for making calculations.

calendar n 1 table of months and days in the year. 2 list of events.

calf¹ pl **calves** n 1 young of cow and other animals. 2 leather of calf's skin.

calf² n fleshy back of leg below knee.

calibre ⊕ n 1 size of bore of gun. 2 capacity, character. **calibrate** v

calico n, pl **–coes** cotton cloth.

call ⊕ v 1 speak loudly to attract attention. 2 summon. 3 telephone. 4 name. 5 shout. 6 pay visit. ♦ n 7 shout. 8 animal's cry. 9 visit. 10 inner urge. 11 demand. **caller** n **calling** n vocation, profession. **call up 1** summon to serve in army. 2 imagine.

calligraphy n handwriting.

callous adj hardened, unfeeling.

callow adj inexperienced.

callus n, pl **–luses** area of hardened skin.

calm ⊕ adj/v 1 (make, become) still, tranquil. 2 (make) composed. ♦ n 3 absence of wind. **calmly** adv **calmness** n

calorie n 1 unit of heat. 2 unit of energy from foods.

calypso n, pl **–sos** (West Indies) improvised song.

cam n device to change rotary to

——————— THESAURUS ———————

cafeteria, coffee shop, brasserie

cage n = **enclosure**, pen, coop, hutch, pound

cake n = **block**, bar, slab, lump, cube

calculate v = **work out**, determine, estimate, count, reckon; = **plan**, design, aim, intend, arrange

calibre, US **caliber** n = **worth**, quality, ability, talent, capacity; = **standard**, level, quality, grade

call v = **name**, entitle, dub, designate, term; = **cry**, shout, scream, yell, whoop ≠ **whisper**;

= **phone**, telephone, ring (up) (Inf, chiefly Brit); summon; = **summon**, gather, rally, assemble, muster ≠ **dismiss**; = **waken**, arouse, rouse ♦ n = **request**, order, demand, appeal, notice; usually used in a negative construction = **need**, cause, reason, grounds, occasion

calm adj = **cool**, relaxed, composed, sedate, collected ≠ **excited**; = **still**, quiet, smooth, mild, serene ≠ **rough** ♦ n = **peacefulness**, peace, serenity ♦ v = **soothe**, quiet, relax, appease, still ≠ **excite**

reciprocating motion.

camaraderie *n* spirit of comradeship, trust.

camber *n* curve on road surface.

cambric *n* fine white linen or cotton cloth.

camcorder *n* portable video camera and recorder.

camel *n* animal of Asia and Africa, with humped back.

camellia *n* ornamental shrub.

cameo *n, pl* **cameos 1** medallion, brooch etc. with design in relief. **2** small part in film etc.

camera *n* apparatus used to make photographs. **cameraman** *n*

camisole *n* underbodice.

camouflage **❶** *n* **1** disguise, means of avoiding enemy observation. ◆ *v* **2** disguise.

camp[1] **❶** *n* **1** (place for) tents of hikers, army etc. **2** group supporting political party etc. ◆ *v* **3** form or lodge in camp.

camp[2] **❶** *adj* **1** *Inf* homosexual. **2** consciously artificial.

campaign **❶** *n/v* (organize) series of coordinated activities for some purpose, e.g. political, military.

camphor *n* solid essential oil with aromatic taste and smell.

campus *n, pl* **-puses** grounds of university.

can[1] *past* **could** *v* **1** be able. **2** have the power. **3** be allowed.

can[2] *n* **1** container, usu. metal, for liquids, foods. ◆ *v* **2** put in can.

canned *adj* **1** preserved in can. **2** (of music) previously recorded.

cannery *n*

Canada Day *n* July 1, the anniversary of the day when Canada became the first British colony to receive dominion status.

Canada goose *n* large greyish-brown N American goose with a black neck and head and a white throat patch.

Canada jay *n* a large common jay of North America with a grey body, and a white–and–black crestless head.

canal **❶** *n* **1** artificial watercourse. **2** duct in body.

canary *n, pl* **-ries** yellow singing bird.

canasta *n* card game played with two packs.

cancan *n* high–kicking dance.

cancel **❶** *v* **-celling, -celled 1** cross out. **2** annul. **3** call off.

cancellation *n*

cancer **❶** *n* malignant growth or tumour. **cancerous** *adj*

camouflage *n* = **disguise**, cover, screen, blind, mask ◆ *v* = **disguise**, cover, screen, hide, mask ≠ **reveal**

camp[1] *n* = **camp site**, tents, encampment, bivouac, camping ground

camp[2] *adj* = (*Inf*) **affected**, mannered, artificial, posturing, ostentatious

campaign *n* = **drive**, appeal, movement, push (*Inf*), offensive; = **operation**, drive, attack, movement, push

canal *n* = **waterway**, channel, passage, conduit, duct

cancel *v* = **call off**, drop, forget

candid *adj* frank, impartial. **candour** *n*

candidate ❶ *n* 1 one who seeks office etc. 2 person taking examination. **candidacy**, **candidature** *n*

candle *n* 1 stick of wax with wick. 2 light. **candelabrum** *n* large, branched candle holder. **candlestick** *n*

candy *n, pl* **–dies** 1 crystallized sugar 2 *US* confectionery in general. ♦ *v* 3 preserve with sugar. **candyfloss** *n* fluffy mass of spun sugar.

cane *n* 1 stem of small palm or large grass. 2 walking stick. ♦ *v* 3 beat with cane.

canine *adj* 1 like, pert. to, dog. ♦ *n* 2 sharp pointed tooth.

canister *n* container, usu. of metal, for storing dry food.

canker *n* 1 eating sore. 2 thing that destroys, corrupts.

cannabis *n* 1 hemp plant. 2 drug derived from this.

cannelloni *pl n* tubular pieces of pasta filled with meat etc.

cannibal *n* one who eats human flesh. **cannibalism** *n*

cannon¹ ❶ *n* large gun.

cannonball *n* heavy metal ball.

cannon² *n* 1 billiard stroke. ♦ *v* 2

make this stroke. 3 rebound, collide.

cannot negative form of CAN¹.

canny *adj* **–nier, –niest** 1 shrewd. 2 cautious.

canoe *n* 1 very light boat propelled with paddle. ♦ *v* 2 travel by canoe.

canon ❶ *n* 1 law or rule, esp. of church. 2 standard. 3 list of saints. **canonize** *v* enrol in list of saints.

canopy ❶ *n, pl* **–pies** 1 covering over throne, bed etc. ♦ *v* 2 cover with canopy.

cant *n* 1 hypocritical speech. 2 technical jargon. 3 slang, esp. of thieves. ♦ *v* 4 use cant.

cantankerous *adj* quarrelsome.

cantata *n* choral work.

canteen *n* place in factory, school etc. where meals are provided.

canter *n*/*v* (move at) easy gallop.

cantilever *n* beam, girder etc. fixed at one end only.

Canuck *n*/*adj Informal* Canadian.

canvas *n* coarse cloth used for sails, painting on etc.

canvass *v* 1 solicit votes, contributions etc. 2 discuss.

canyon *n* deep gorge.

cap ❶ *n* 1 covering for head. 2 lid, top. ♦ *v* 3 put a cap on. 4 outdo.

capable ❶ *adj* 1 able. 2

———————— THESAURUS ————————

about

cancer *n* = **growth**, tumour, malignancy; corruption, sickness

candidate *n* = **contender**, competitor, applicant, nominee, entrant

cannon¹ *n* = **gun**, big gun, field

gun, mortar

canon *n* = **rule**, standard, principle, regulation, formula; = **list**, index, catalogue, roll

canopy *n* = **awning**, covering, shade, sunshade

cap *v* = (*Inf*) **beat**, top, better,

competent. **3** having the power.
capability n, pl
capacity ❶ n, pl **–ties 1** power of
holding. **2** room. **3** volume. **4**
function, role. **5** ability.
cape¹ ❶ n headland.
cape² n covering for shoulders.
caper n **1** skip. **2** frolic. **3**
escapade. ♦ v **4** skip, dance.
capillary n, pl **–laries** small blood
vessel.
capital ❶ n **1** chief town. **2**
money. **3** large–sized letter. ♦ adj
4 involving or punishable by
death. **5** chief. **6** excellent.
capitalism n economic system
based on private ownership of
industry. **capitalist** n/adj **capitalize**
v **1** convert into capital **2** turn to
advantage.
capitulate v surrender.
capon n castrated cock fowl
fattened for eating.
cappuccino n, pl **–nos** coffee with
steamed milk.

caprice n whim, freak. **capricious**
adj
capsize v (of boat) overturn
accidentally.
capstan n machine to wind cable.
capsule ❶ n case for dose of
medicine.
captain ❶ n **1** commander of
vessel or company of soldiers. **2**
leader. ♦ v **3** be captain of.
captaincy n
caption n heading, title of article,
picture etc.
captive ❶ n **1** prisoner. ♦ adj **2**
taken, imprisoned. **captivate** v
fascinate. **captivity** n
capture ❶ v **1** seize, make
prisoner. ♦ n **2** seizure, taking.
captor n
car ❶ n **1** road vehicle. **2**
passenger compartment.
carafe n glass water bottle for the
table, decanter.
caramel n **1** burnt sugar for
cooking. **2** chewy sweet.

———— THESAURUS ————

exceed, eclipse
capable adj = **accomplished**,
qualified, talented, gifted, efficient
≠ incompetent
capacity n = **ability**, facility, gift,
genius, capability; = **size**, room,
range, space, volume; = **function**,
position, role, post, province
cape¹ n = **headland**, point, head,
peninsula, promontory
capital n = **money**, funds,
investment(s), cash, finances ♦ adj
= (Old–fashioned) **first–rate**, fine,
excellent, superb, sterling
capsule n = **pill**, tablet, lozenge;

= (Bot) **pod**, case, shell, vessel,
sheath
captain n = **leader**, boss, master,
skipper, head
captive adj = **confined**, caged,
imprisoned, locked up, enslaved ♦
n = **prisoner**, hostage, convict,
prisoner of war, detainee
capture v = **catch**, arrest, take,
bag, secure **≠ release** ♦ n = **arrest**,
catching, trapping, imprisonment,
seizure
car n = **vehicle**, motor, wheels
(Inf), auto (US), automobile; = (US
& Canad) **(railway) carriage**, coach,

carat *n* 1 weight used for gold, diamonds etc. 2 measure used to state fineness of gold.

caravan *n* 1 large vehicle for living in, pulled by car etc. 2 company of merchants travelling together.

caraway *n* plant with spicy seeds used in cakes etc.

carbohydrate *n* any compound containing carbon, hydrogen and oxygen, esp. sugars and starches.

carbon *n* nonmetallic element, substance of pure charcoal, found in all organic matter. **carbonate** *n* salt of carbonic acid. **carbon copy** 1 copy made with carbon paper. 2 very similar person or thing.

carbon dioxide colourless gas exhaled in respiration.

carbuncle *n* inflamed ulcer, boil or tumour.

carburettor *n* device for mixing petrol with air in engine.

carcass, carcase *n* dead animal body.

card *n* 1 thick, stiff paper. 2 piece of this giving identification etc. 3 illustrated card sending greetings etc. 4 playing card. ◆ *pl* 5 any card game. **cardboard** *n* thin, stiff board made of paper pulp.

cardsharp *n* cheating card player.

cardiac *adj* pert. to the heart.

cardiograph *n* instrument which records movements of the heart.

cardiology *n* study of heart diseases.

cardigan *n* knitted jacket.

cardinal ❶ *adj* 1 chief, principal. ◆ *n* 2 rank next to the Pope in R.C. church. **cardinal numbers** 1,2,3 etc.

care ❶ *v* 1 be anxious. 2 have regard or liking (for). 3 look after. 4 be disposed to. ◆ *n* 5 attention. 6 protection. 7 anxiety. 8 caution. **careful** *adj* **careless** *adj* **carefree** *adj*

caretaker *n* person in charge of premises.

career ❶ *n* 1 course through life. 2 profession. 3 rapid motion. ◆ *v* 4 run or move at full speed.

caress *v* 1 fondle, embrace, treat with affection. ◆ *n* 2 affectionate embrace or touch.

caret *n* mark (⟨) showing where to insert word etc.

cargo ❶ *n*, *pl* –**goes** load, freight, carried by ship, plane etc.

caribou *n*, *pl* –**bou** N American reindeer.

caricature ❶ *n* 1 likeness exaggerated to appear ridiculous. ◆ *v* 2 portray in this way.

C

———————— THESAURUS ————————

cable car, dining car, sleeping car
cardinal *adj* = **principal**, first, leading, chief, main ≠ **secondary**
care *v* = **be concerned**, mind, bother, be interested, be bothered ◆ *n* = **custody**, keeping, control, charge, management; = **caution**, attention, pains, consideration,

heed ≠ **carelessness**; = **worry**, concern, pressure, trouble, responsibility ≠ **pleasure**
career *n* = **occupation**, calling, employment, pursuit, vocation ◆ *v* = **rush**, race, speed, tear, dash
cargo *n* = **load**, goods, contents, shipment, freight

cark v Aust & NZ slang die.

carnage ❶ n slaughter.

carnal adj fleshly, sensual.

carnation n cultivated flower.

carnival ❶ n 1 festive occasion. 2 travelling fair.

carol ❶ n/v (sing) song or hymn of joy.

carouse v have merry drinking spree. **carousal** n

carousel n 1 US merry-go-round. 2 rotating device for holding slides.

carp¹ ❶ v 1 find fault. 2 nag.

carp² n freshwater fish.

carpenter ❶ n worker in timber. **carpentry** n

carpet n heavy fabric for covering floor.

carriage ❶ n 1 railway coach. 2 bearing. 3 horse-drawn vehicle.

carriageway n part of road along which traffic passes in a single line.

carrion n rotting dead flesh.

carrot n 1 plant with orange-red edible root. 2 inducement.

carry ❶ v -rying, -ried 1 convey, transport. 2 capture, win. 3 effect. 4 behave. 5 (of projectile, sound) reach. **carrier** n

cart n 1 open (two-wheeled) vehicle. ♦ v 2 carry in cart. 3 carry with effort. **carthorse** n heavily built horse. **cartwheel** n sideways somersault.

carte blanche Fr complete authority.

cartel n industrial alliance for fixing prices etc.

cartilage n 1 firm elastic tissue in the body. 2 gristle.

cartography n map making.

carton ❶ n cardboard or plastic container.

cartoon ❶ n 1 drawing, esp. humorous or satirical. 2 sequence of drawings telling story. **cartoonist** n

cartridge n 1 case containing charge for gun. 2 container for film etc.

carve ❶ v 1 cut. 2 hew. 3 sculpture. 4 engrave. 5 cut (meat) in pieces or slices. **carving** n

———————— THESAURUS ————————

caricature n = **parody**, cartoon, distortion, satire, send-up (Brit inf) ♦ v = **parody**, take off (Inf), mock, distort, ridicule

carnage n = **slaughter**, murder, massacre, holocaust, havoc

carnival n = **festival**, fair, fête, celebration, gala

carol n = **song**, hymn, Christmas song

carp¹ v = **find fault**, complain, criticize, reproach, quibble ≠ **praise**

carpenter n = **joiner**, cabinet-maker, woodworker

carriage n = **vehicle**, coach, trap, gig, cab; = **bearing**, posture, gait, deportment, air

carry v = **convey**, take, move, bring, bear; = **transport**, take, transfer

carton n = **box**, case, pack, package, container

cartoon n = **drawing**, parody, satire, caricature, comic strip; = **animation**, animated film,

cascade *n* waterfall.

case¹ *n* 1 instance. 2 circumstance. 3 question at issue. 4 arguments supporting particular action etc. 5 *Med* patient. 6 lawsuit. **in case** so as to allow for eventualities.

case² *n* 1 box, sheath, covering. 2 receptacle. 3 box and contents. ◆ *v* 4 put in a case.

cash *n* 1 money, banknotes and coins. ◆ *v* 2 turn into or exchange for money. **cashier** *n* one in charge of receiving and paying of money.

cashier *v* dismiss from office.

cashmere *n* fine soft fabric made from goat's wool.

casino *n, pl* **–nos** building, institution for gambling.

cask *n* barrel.

casket *n* small case for jewels etc.

casserole *n* 1 fireproof cooking dish. 2 stew.

cassette *n* plastic container for film, magnetic tape etc.

cassock *n* clergyman's long tunic.

cast *n* 1 throw or fling. 2 shed. 3 deposit (a vote). 4 allot, as parts in play. 5 mould. ◆ *n* 6 throw. 7 squint. 8 mould. 9 that which is shed or ejected. 10 set of actors. 11 type or quality. **castaway** *n* shipwrecked person. **cast-iron** *adj* 1 made of hard, brittle type of iron. 2 rigid or unchallengeable. **cast-off** *adj/n* discarded (garment).

castanets *pl n* two small curved pieces of wood clicked together in hand.

caste *n* 1 section of society in India. 2 social rank.

caster sugar, castor sugar *n* finely powdered sugar.

castigate *v* rebuke severely.

castle *n* fortress.

castor *n* 1 bottle with perforated top. 2 small swivelled wheel on table leg etc.

castor oil *n* vegetable medicinal oil.

castrate *v* remove testicles.

———————————— THESAURUS ————————————

animated cartoon

carve *v* = **sculpt**, cut, chip, whittle, chisel; = **etch**, engrave

cascade *n* = **waterfall**, falls, torrent, flood, shower ◆ *v* = **flow**, fall, flood, pour, plunge

case¹ *n* = **situation**, event, circumstance(s), state, position; = **instance**, example, occasion, specimen, occurrence; = (*Law*) **lawsuit**, trial, suit, proceedings, dispute

case² *n* = **cabinet**, box, chest, holder

cash *n* = **money**, funds, notes, currency, silver

cast *n* = **actors**, company, players, characters, troupe; = **type**, sort, kind, style, stamp ◆ *v* = **choose**, name, pick, select, appoint; = **bestow**, give, level, direct; = **give out**, spread, deposit, shed, distribute; = **throw**, launch, pitch, toss, thrust

caste *n* = **class**, order, rank, status, stratum

castle *n* = **fortress**, keep, palace, tower, chateau

castration n

casual ⓘ adj 1 accidental. 2 unforeseen. 3 occasional. 4 unconcerned. 5 informal. **casually** adv **casualty** n person killed or injured in accident, war etc.

cat ⓘ n any of various feline animals, esp. small domesticated furred animal. **catty** adj spiteful.

catcall n derisive cry. **catkin** n drooping flower spike. **catnap** v/n doze. **Catseye** ® n glass reflector set in road to indicate traffic lanes.

catwalk n narrow platform.

cataclysm n 1 (disastrous) upheaval. 2 deluge.

catalogue ⓘ n 1 descriptive list. ♦ v 2 make such list.

catalyst n substance causing or assisting a chemical reaction without taking part in it.

catamaran n type of sailing boat with twin hulls.

catapult n 1 small forked stick with sling for throwing stones. 2 launching device. ♦ v 3 launch with force.

cataract n 1 waterfall. 2

downpour. 3 disease of eye.

catarrh n inflammation of mucous membrane.

catastrophe ⓘ n great disaster. **catastrophic** adj

catch ⓘ v catching, caught 1 take hold of. 2 hear. 3 contract disease. 4 be in time for. 5 detect. 6 be contagious. 7 get entangled. 8 begin to burn. ♦ n 9 seizure. 10 thing that holds, stops etc. 11 what is caught. 12 Inf snag, disadvantage. **catcher** n **catching** adj **catchy** adj (of tune) easily remembered.

catechism n instruction by questions and answers.

category ⓘ n, pl –ries class, order. **categorize** v **categorical** adj positive.

cater v provide, esp. food. **caterer** n

caterpillar n hairy grub of moth or butterfly.

catharsis n, pl –ses relief of strong suppressed emotions. **cathartic** adj

cathedral n principal church of diocese.

————————— THESAURUS —————————

casual adj = **careless**, relaxed, unconcerned, blasé, offhand ≠ **serious**; = **chance**, unexpected, random, accidental, incidental ≠ **planned**; = **informal**, leisure, sporty, non–dressy ≠ **formal**
cat n = **feline**, pussy (Inf), moggy (Sl), puss (Inf), tabby
catalogue, US **catalog** n = **list**, record, schedule, index, register ♦ v = **list**, file, index, register, classify
catastrophe n = **disaster**,

tragedy, calamity, cataclysm, trouble
catch v = **capture**, arrest, trap, seize, snare ≠ **free**; = **trap**, capture, snare, ensnare, entrap; = **seize**, get, grab, snatch; = **grab**, take, grip, seize, grasp ≠ **release** ♦ n = **fastener**, clip, bolt, latch, clasp; = (Inf) **drawback**, trick, trap, disadvantage, hitch ≠ **advantage**
category n = **class**, grouping, heading, sort, department

Catherine wheel n rotating firework producing sparks.

catholic adj 1 universal. 2 including whole body of Christians. 3 (with cap.) relating to R.C. church. ♦ n 4 (with cap.) adherent of R.C. church. **Catholicism** n

cattle ❶ pl n pasture animals, esp. oxen, cows. **cattleman** n

cauldron n large pot used for boiling.

cauliflower n variety of cabbage with edible white flowering head.

cause ❶ n 1 that which produces an effect. 2 reason. 3 motive. 4 charity, movement. 5 lawsuit. ♦ v 6 bring about, make happen.

causeway n raised path over marsh etc.

caustic adj 1 burning. 2 bitter. ♦ n 3 corrosive substance.

cauterize v burn with caustic or hot iron.

caution ❶ n 1 heedfulness, care. 2 warning. ♦ v 3 warn. **cautious** adj **cavalcade** n procession.

cavalier adj 1 careless, disdainful. ♦ n 2 courtly gentleman. 3 Obs horseman 4 (with cap.) supporter

of Charles I.

cavalry ❶ n, pl –ries mounted troops.

cave ❶ n 1 hollow place in the earth. 2 den. **cavern** n deep cave. **cavernous** adj cavity n hollow. **caveman** n prehistoric cave dweller.

caviar, caviare n salted sturgeon roe.

cavil v –illing, –illed make trifling objections.

cavort v prance, frisk.

CBE Commander of the British Empire.

cc cubic centimetre.

CD compact disc. **CD–ROM** compact disc storing written information, displayed on VDU.

cease ❶ v bring or come to an end. **ceaseless** adj **ceasefire** n temporary truce.

cedar n large evergreen tree.

cede v yield, give up, transfer.

cedilla n accent (͵) below letter.

ceilidh n informal social gathering for dancing.

ceiling n inner, upper surface of a room.

celebrate ❶ v 1 have festivities to

——————— THESAURUS ———————

cattle pl n = **cows**, stock, beasts, livestock, bovines

cause n = **origin**, source, spring, agent, maker ≠ **result**; = **reason**, call, need, grounds, basis; = **aim**, movement, principle, ideal, enterprise ♦ v = **produce**, create, lead to, result in, generate ≠ **prevent**

caution n = **care**, discretion, heed,

prudence, vigilance ≠ **carelessness**; = **reprimand**, warning, injunction, admonition ♦ v = **warn**, urge, advise, alert, tip off

cavalry n = **horsemen**, horse, mounted troops ≠ **infantrymen**

cave n = **hollow**, cavern, grotto, den, cavity

cease v = **stop**, end, finish, come to an end ≠ **start**

mark (happy day, event etc.). **2** observe (birthday etc.). **3** perform (religious ceremony etc.). **4** praise publicly. **celebrated** *adj* famous. **celebration** *n* **celebrity** *n, pl* **–rities 1** famous person. **2** fame.

celery *n* vegetable with long juicy edible stalks.

celestial *adj* heavenly, divine.

cell ❶ *n* **1** small room in prison. **2** small cavity. **3** minute, basic unit of living matter. **4** device converting chemical into electrical energy. **cellular** *adj*

cellar *n* **1** underground room for storage. **2** stock of wine.

cello *n, pl* **–los** stringed instrument of violin family.

Cellophane ® *n* transparent wrapping.

cellulose *n* fibrous carbohydrate.

Celsius *adj/n* (of) scale of temperature from 0° to 100°.

cement ❶ *n* **1** fine mortar. **2** glue. ♦ *v* **3** unite as with cement.

cemetery ❶ *n, pl* **–teries** burial ground.

cenotaph *n* monument to one

buried elsewhere.

censor ❶ *n* **1** one authorized to examine films, books etc. and suppress parts considered unacceptable. ♦ *v* **2** suppress. **censorious** *adj* fault-finding. **censorship** *n*

censure ❶ *n/v* blame.

census *n, pl* **–suses** official counting of people, things etc.

cent *n* hundredth part of dollar etc.

centaur *n* mythical creature, half man, half horse.

centenary *n, pl* **–naries 1** 100 years. **2** celebration of hundredth anniversary. ♦ *adj* **3** pert. to a hundred.

centigrade *adj/n* another name for CELSIUS.

centimetre *n* hundredth part of metre.

centipede *n* small segmented animal with many legs.

centre ❶ *n* **1** midpoint. **2** pivot. **3** place for specific organization or activity. **central** *adj* **centralize** *v* **centrally** *adv*

———— THESAURUS ————

celebrate *v* = **rejoice**, party, enjoy yourself, carouse, live it up (*Inf*); = **commemorate**, honour, observe, toast, drink to

cell *n* = **room**, chamber, lock-up, compartment, cavity; = **unit**, group, section, core, nucleus

cement *n* = **mortar**, plaster, paste; = **sealant**, glue, gum, adhesive ♦ *v* = **stick**, join, bond, attach, seal

cemetery *n* = **graveyard**, churchyard, burial ground,

necropolis, God's acre

censor *v* = **expurgate**, cut, blue–pencil, bowdlerize

censure *v* = **criticize**, blame, condemn, denounce, rebuke ≠ **applaud** ♦ *n* = **disapproval**, criticism, blame, condemnation, rebuke ≠ **approval**

centre *n* = **middle**, heart, focus, core, nucleus ≠ **edge** ♦ *v* = **focus**, concentrate, cluster, revolve, converge

centurion n Roman commander of 100 men.

century n, pl **–ries** 1 100 years. 2 any set of 100.

cereal n 1 any edible grain. 2 (breakfast) food.

cerebral adj pert. to brain.

ceremony ⊕ n, pl **–nies** 1 formal observance. 2 sacred rite. 3 courteous act. **ceremonial** adj/n

certain ⊕ adj 1 sure. 2 inevitable. 3 some, one. 4 moderate (in quantity, degree etc.). **certainly** adv **certainty** n

certify ⊕ v **–fying, –fied** 1 declare formally. 2 guarantee. **certificate** n written declaration.

cervix n, pl **cervixes, cervices** neck, esp. of womb. **cervical** adj

cessation n stop, pause.

chafe v 1 make sore or worn by rubbing. 2 warm. 3 vex.

chaff n 1 husks of corn. 2 worthless matter. ♦ v 3 tease.

chaffinch n small songbird.

chagrin n 1 vexation, disappointment. ♦ v 2 embarrass.

chain ⊕ n 1 series of connected rings. 2 thing that binds. 3 connected series of things or events. 4 surveyor's measure. ♦ v 5 fasten with a chain. 6 restrain.

chair n 1 movable seat, with back, for one person. 2 seat of authority. ♦ v 3 preside over. 4 carry in triumph. **chairman** n one who presides over meeting.

chairperson n **chairwoman** n

chalet n Swiss wooden house.

chalice n Poet cup.

chalk n 1 white substance, carbonate of lime. 2 crayon. ♦ v 3 mark with chalk. **chalky** adj

challenge ⊕ v 1 call to fight or account. 2 dispute. 3 stimulate. ♦ n 4 challenging. **challenger** n

chamber ⊕ n 1 (room for) assembly. 2 compartment. 3 cavity. ♦ pl 4 office or apartment of barrister. **chambermaid** n woman who cleans bedrooms.

chameleon n lizard with power of changing colour.

chamois n, pl **–ois** 1 goatlike mountain antelope. 2 soft pliable leather.

———————— THESAURUS ————————

ceremony n = **ritual**, service, rite, observance, commemoration; = **formality**, ceremonial, propriety, decorum

certain adj = **sure**, convinced, positive, confident, satisfied ≠ **unsure**; = **bound**, sure, fated, destined ≠ **unlikely**

certify v = **confirm**, declare, guarantee, assure, testified

chain n = **tether**, coupling, link, bond, shackle; = **series**, set, train, string, sequence ♦ v = **bind**, confine, restrain, handcuff, shackle

challenge n = **dare**, provocation; = **test**, trial, opposition, confrontation, ultimatum ♦ v = **dispute**, question, tackle, confront, defy

chamber n = **hall**, room; = **council**, assembly, legislature, legislative body; = **room**, bedroom, apartment, enclosure, cubicle

champ n 1 munch noisily. 2 be impatient.

champagne n light, sparkling white wine.

champion ❶ n 1 one that excels all others. 2 defender of a cause. ♦ v 3 fight for. **championship** n

chance ❶ n 1 unpredictable course of events. 2 luck. 3 opportunity. 4 possibility. 5 risk. 6 probability. ♦ v 7 risk. 8 happen. ♦ adj 9 casual, unexpected. **chancy** adj

chancel n part of a church where altar is.

chancellor n 1 high officer of state. 2 head of university.

chandelier n hanging frame with branches for lights.

change ❶ v 1 alter, make or become different. 2 put on (different clothes, fresh coverings). 3 put or give for another. 4

exchange. ♦ n 5 alteration. 6 variety. 7 coins. 8 balance received on payment. **changeable** adj

channel ❶ n 1 bed of stream. 2 strait. 3 deeper part of strait. 4 groove. 5 means of conveying. 6 band of radio frequencies. 7 television broadcasting station. ♦ v 8 groove. 9 guide.

chant ❶ n 1 simple song or melody. 2 rhythmic slogan. ♦ v 3 utter chant. 4 speak monotonously.

chaos ❶ n disorder, confusion. **chaotic** adj

chap¹ ❶ n Inf fellow, man.

chap² v (of skin) become raw and cracked.

chapati, chapatti n thin unleavened bread used in Indian cookery.

chapel n 1 place of worship. 2 division of church with its own

champion n = **winner**, hero, victor, conqueror, title holder; = **defender**, guardian, patron, backer, protector ♦ v = **support**, back, defend, promote, advocate

chance n = **probability**, odds, possibility, prospect, likelihood ≠ **certainty**; = **opportunity**, opening, occasion, time; = **accident**, fortune, luck, fate, destiny ≠ **design**; = **risk**, speculation, gamble, hazard ♦ v = **risk**, try, stake, venture, gamble

change n = **alteration**, innovation, transformation, modification, mutation; = **variety**, break (Inf), departure, variation, novelty

≠ **monotony** ♦ v = **alter**, reform, transform, adjust, revise ≠ **keep**; = **shift**, vary, transform, alter, modify ≠ **stay**

channel n = **means**, way, course, approach, medium; = **strait**, sound, route, passage, canal; = **duct**, artery, groove, gutter, furrow ♦ v = **direct**, guide, conduct, transmit, convey

chant n = **song**, carol, chorus, melody, psalm ♦ v = **sing**, chorus, recite, intone, carol

chaos n = **disorder**, confusion, mayhem, anarchy, lawlessness ≠ **orderliness**

chap¹ n = (Inf) **fellow**, man,

altar.

chaplain n clergyman attached to prison, college etc.

chapter ❶ n 1 division of book. 2 assembly of clergy. 3 organized branch of society.

char v charring, charred scorch.

character ❶ n 1 nature. 2 qualities making up individuality. 3 moral qualities. 4 eccentric person. 5 fictional person.

characteristic adj 1 typical. ◆ n 2 distinguishing feature.

characterize v 1 mark out. 2 describe.

charade n 1 absurd act. ◆ pl 2 word–guessing game.

charcoal n charred wood.

charge ❶ v 1 ask as price. 2 bring accusation against. 3 lay task on. 4 attack. 5 fill (with electricity). 6 make onrush, attack. ◆ n 7 price. 8 accusation. 9 attack. 10 command. 11 accumulation of electricity. **chargeable** adj **charger** n 1 that which charges, esp. electrically. 2 warhorse.

chargé d'affaires pl **chargés d'affaires** head of small diplomatic mission.

chariot n 1 two–wheeled vehicle used in ancient fighting. 2 state carriage. **charioteer** n

charisma ❶ n special power of individual to inspire fascination, loyalty etc. **charismatic** adj

charity ❶ n, pl –ties 1 giving of help, money to needy. 2 organization for this. 3 love, kindness. **charitable** adj

charlatan n impostor.

charm ❶ n 1 attractiveness. 2 anything that fascinates. 3 amulet. 4 magic spell. ◆ v 5 bewitch. 6

——————— THESAURUS ———————

chapter n = **section**, part, stage, division, episode; = **period**, time, stage, phase

character n = **personality**, nature, attributes, temperament, complexion; = **nature**, kind, quality, calibre; = **reputation**, honour, integrity, good name, rectitude; = **role**, part, persona; = **eccentric**, card (Inf), original, oddball (Inf)

charge v = **accuse**, indict, impeach, incriminate, arraign ≠ **acquit**; = **attack**, assault, assail ≠ **retreat**; = **rush**, storm, stampede; = **fill**, load ◆ n = **price**, rate, cost, amount, payment; = **accusation**, allegation, indictment, imputation ≠ **acquittal**; = **care**, trust, responsibility, custody, safekeeping; = **duty**, office, responsibility, remit; = **ward**, pupil, protégé, dependant; = **attack**, rush, assault, onset, onslaught ≠ **retreat**

charisma n = **charm**, appeal, personality, attraction, lure

charity n = **charitable organization**, fund, movement, trust, endowment; = **donations**, help, relief, gift, contributions ≠ **meanness**; = **kindness**, humanity, goodwill, compassion, generosity ≠ **ill will**

delight. **charmer** n **charming** adj

chart ❶ n **1** map of sea. **2** tabulated statement. ♦ v **3** map.

charter ❶ n **1** document granting privileges etc. ♦ v **2** let or hire. **3** establish by charter. **chartered** adj officially qualified.

charwoman n woman paid to clean office, house etc.

chary adj **–rier, –riest** cautious, sparing.

chase ❶ v **1** hunt, pursue. **2** drive from, away, into etc. ♦ n **3** pursuit, hunting.

chasm n deep cleft.

chassis n, pl **–sis** framework of motor vehicle.

chaste adj **1** virginal. **2** pure. **3** modest. **4** virtuous. **chastity** n.

chasten v **1** correct by punishment. **2** subdue. **chastise** v inflict punishment on.

chat ❶ v **1** talk idly or familiarly. ♦

n **2** such talk. **chatty** adj

chateau n, pl **–teaux, –teaus** (esp. in France) castle, country house.

chauffeur n paid driver of motorcar.

chauvinism n irrational feeling of superiority. **chauvinist** n/adj

cheap ❶ adj **1** low in price. **2** of little value. **3** inferior. **cheaply** adv **cheapen** v **cheapskate** n Inf miserly person.

cheat ❶ v **1** deceive. **2** practise deceit to gain advantage. ♦ n **3** fraud.

check ❶ v **1** stop. **2** control. **3** examine. ♦ n **4** stoppage. **5** restraint. **6** brief examination. **7** pattern of squares. **8** threat to king at chess. **checkmate** n/v (make) final winning move. **checkout** n counter in supermarket where customers pay. **check–up** n examination (esp. medical) to see

———————— THESAURUS ————————

charm n = **attraction**, appeal, fascination, allure, magnetism ≠ **repulsiveness**; = **talisman**, trinket, amulet, fetish; = **spell**, magic, enchantment, sorcery ♦ v = **attract**, delight, fascinate, entrance, win over ≠ **repel**; = **persuade**, seduce, coax, beguile, sweet–talk (Inf)

chart n = **table**, diagram, blueprint, graph, plan ♦ v = **plot**, map out, delineate, sketch, draft; = **monitor**, follow, record, note, document

charter n = **document**, contract, permit, licence, deed ♦ v = **hire**, commission, employ, rent, lease;

= **authorize**, permit, sanction, entitle, license

chase v = **pursue**, follow, track, hunt, run after ♦ n = **pursuit**, race, hunt, hunting

chat v = **talk**, gossip, jaw (Sl), natter, blather ♦ n = **talk**, tête-à-tête, conversation, gossip, heart-to-heart

cheap adj = **inexpensive**, reduced, keen, reasonable, bargain ≠ **expensive**; = **inferior**, poor, worthless, second–rate, shoddy ≠ **good**; = (Inf) **despicable**, mean, contemptible ≠ **decent**

cheat v = **deceive**, trick, fool, con (Inf), mislead ♦ n = **deceiver**,

if all is in order.

Cheddar n smooth hard cheese.

cheek ❶ n 1 side of face below eye 2 Inf impudence. **cheeky** adj

cheep v/n (utter) high–pitched cry, as of young bird.

cheer ❶ v 1 comfort. 2 gladden. 3 encourage by shouts. 4 shout applause. ♦ n 5 shout of approval. 6 happiness. 7 mood. **cheerful** adj **cheerless** adj **cheery** adj

cheerio interj Inf goodbye.

cheese n food made from solidified curd of milk. **cheesy** adj

cheesecake n dessert made from biscuits and cream cheese.

cheetah n large, swift, spotted feline animal.

chef n head cook.

chemistry n science concerned with properties of substances and their combinations and reactions. **chemical** n/adj **chemically** adv **chemist** n 1 dispenser of medicines. 2 shop that sells medicines etc. 3 one trained in chemistry.

chemotherapy n treatment of disease by chemicals.

chenille n soft cord, fabric of silk

or worsted.

cheque n 1 written order to banker to pay money from one's account. 2 printed slip of paper used for this. **chequebook** n

cheque card banker's card.

chequer n 1 marking as on chessboard. 2 marble, peg etc. used in games. ♦ v 3 mark in squares. 4 variegate. **chequered** adj

cherish ❶ v treat tenderly.

cherry n, pl –ries 1 small red fruit with stone. 2 tree bearing it.

cherub n, pl –ubs, –ubim 1 winged creature with human face. 2 angel. **cherubic** adj

chess n game played on chequered board. **chessman** n piece used in chess.

chest ❶ n 1 upper part of trunk of body. 2 large, strong box. **chest of drawers** piece of furniture containing drawers.

chestnut n 1 tree bearing large nut in prickly husk 2 Inf old joke. ♦ adj 3 reddish–brown.

chevron n Mil V–shaped braid designating rank.

chew ❶ v 1 grind with teeth. ♦ n

—————————— THESAURUS ——————————

sharper, shark, charlatan, trickster

check v often with **out** = examine, test, study, look at, research ≠ **overlook**; = **stop**, limit, delay, halt, restrain ≠ **further** ♦ n = **examination**, test, research, investigation, inspection

cheek n = (Inf) **impudence**, nerve, disrespect, audacity, lip (Sl)

cheer v = **applaud**, hail, acclaim,

clap ≠ **boo**; = **hearten**, encourage, comfort, uplift, brighten ≠ **dishearten** ♦ n = **applause**, ovation, plaudits, acclamation

cherish v = **cling to**, prize, treasure, hold dear, cleave to ≠ **despise**; = **care for**, love, support, comfort, look after ≠ **neglect**

chest n = **breast**, front

2 chewing. **chewy** adj **chewing gum** flavoured gum.

chianti n red Italian wine.

chic 🛈 adj 1 stylish. ◆ n 2 stylishness.

chicane n obstacle on racing circuit. **chicanery** n trickery.

chick n 1 young of birds, esp. of hen. 2 Sl girl, young woman.

chickpea n edible pealike seed.

chicken n 1 domestic fowl. 2 Sl coward. ◆ adj 3 cowardly.

chickenpox n infectious disease.

chicory n, pl –ries salad plant whose root is used instead of coffee.

chide v chiding, chided scold.

chief 🛈 n 1 head or principal person. ◆ adj 2 principal, foremost. **chiefly** adv **chieftain** n leader of tribe.

chiffon n gauzy material.

chilblain n inflamed sore on hands, legs etc. due to cold.

child 🛈 n, pl **children** 1 young human being. 2 offspring. **childish** adj silly. **childlike** adj 1 of or like a child. 2 innocent. **childhood** n

chill 🛈 n 1 coldness. 2 cold with shivering. 3 anything that discourages. ◆ v 4 make, become cold. **chilly** adj 1 cold. 2 unfriendly.

chilli, chili n small red hot-tasting seed pod.

chime n 1 sound of bell. ◆ v 2 ring harmoniously. 3 agree. 4 strike (bells).

chimney n vertical passage for smoke.

chimpanzee n ape of Africa.

chin n part of face below mouth. **chinwag** n Inf chat.

china 🛈 n 1 fine earthenware, porcelain. 2 cups, saucers etc.

chinchilla n S Amer. rodent with soft, grey fur.

chink n cleft, crack.

chintz n cotton cloth printed in coloured designs.

chip 🛈 n 1 splinter. 2 place where piece has been broken off. 3 thin strip of potato, fried. 4 tiny wafer of silicon forming integrated circuit. ◆ v 5 chop into small pieces. 6 break small pieces from. 7 break off. **chip in 1** interrupt. **2** contribute.

chipmunk n small, striped N

——————— THESAURUS ———————

chew v = **munch**, bite, grind, champ, crunch

chic adj = **stylish**, smart, elegant, fashionable, trendy (Brit inf) ≠ **unfashionable**

chief n = **head**, leader, director, manager, boss (Inf) ≠ **subordinate** ◆ adj = **primary**, highest, leading, main, prime ≠ **minor**

child n = **youngster**, baby, kid (Inf), infant, babe

chill v = **cool**, refrigerate, freeze; = **dishearten**, depress, discourage, dismay, dampen ◆ n = **coldness**, bite, nip, sharpness, coolness; ◆ adj = **chilly**, biting, sharp, freezing, raw

china n = **pottery**, ceramics, ware, porcelain, crockery

chip n = **fragment**, shaving, wafer, sliver, shard ◆ v = **nick**, damage, gash

Amer. squirrel.

chiropodist n one who treats disorders of feet. **chiropody** n

chirp n/v (make) short, sharp cry. **chirpy** adj Inf happy.

chisel n 1 cutting tool. ◆ v 2 cut with chisel. 3 Sl cheat.

chit n informal note.

chitchat n gossip.

chivalry n 1 bravery and courtesy. 2 medieval system of knighthood. **chivalrous** adj

chlorine n nonmetallic element, yellowish–green poison gas. **chloride** n bleaching agent. **chlorinate** v disinfect.

chloroform n volatile liquid formerly used as anaesthetic.

chlorophyll n green colouring matter in plants.

chock n block or wedge.

chocolate n confectionery, drink made from ground cacao beans.

choice ❶ n 1 act or power of choosing. 2 alternative. 3 thing or person chosen. ◆ adj 4 select, fine.

choir n band of singers.

choke ❶ v 1 hinder, stop the breathing of. 2 smother, stifle. 3 obstruct. 4 suffer choking. ◆ n 5 act, noise of choking. 6 device to increase richness of petrol–air mixture. **choker** n tight–fitting necklace.

cholera n deadly infectious disease.

choleric adj bad–tempered.

cholesterol n substance found in animal tissue and fat.

chook n Aust & NZ hen or chicken.

choose ❶ v **choosing, chose, chosen** 1 pick out, select. 2 take by preference. 3 decide, think fit. **choosy** adj

chop ❶ v **chopping, chopped** 1 cut with blow. 2 hack. ◆ n 3 cutting blow. 4 cut of meat with bone. **chopper** n 1 short axe. 2 Inf helicopter. **choppy** adj **–pier, –piest** (of sea) having short, broken waves.

chopsticks pl n implements used by Chinese for eating food.

choral adj of, for a choir.

chorale n slow, stately hymn tune.

chord n simultaneous sounding of musical notes.

chore ❶ n (unpleasant) task.

choreography n art of arranging dances, esp. ballet.

choreographer n

chorister n singer in choir.

chortle v/n (make) happy chuckling sound.

chorus ❶ n, pl **–ruses** 1 (music for) band of singers. 2 refrain. ◆ v 3 sing or say together.

———————— THESAURUS ————————

choice n = **range**, variety, selection, assortment; = **selection**, preference, pick ◆ adj = **best**, prime, select, excellent, exclusive

choke v = **suffocate**, stifle, smother, overpower, asphyxiate;

= **strangle**, throttle, asphyxiate

choose v = **pick**, prefer, select, elect, adopt ≠ **reject**

chop v = **cut**, fell, hack, sever, cleave

chore n = **task**, job, duty, burden,

chow[1] *n Inf* food.

chow[2] *n* thick–coated dog with curled tail, orig. from China.

Christian *n/adj* (person) following, believing in Christ.

christen *v* baptize, give name to.

christening *n* **Christianity** *n*

Christmas ❶ *n* festival of birth of Christ.

chromosome *n* microscopic gene–carrying body in the tissue of a cell.

chronic *adj* **1** lasting a long time. **2** habitual. **3** *Inf* serious. **4** *Inf* of bad quality.

chronicle ❶ *n/v* (write) record of historical events.

chrysalis *n* **1** resting state of insect. **2** case enclosing it.

chrysanthemum *n* garden flower of various colours.

chub *n* freshwater fish.

chubby *adj* **–bier, –biest** plump.

chuck ❶ *v* **1** *Inf* throw. **2** pat affectionately (under chin). **3** give up.

chuckle ❶ *v/n* (make) soft laugh.

chuffed *adj Inf* pleased, delighted.

chum ❶ *n Inf* close friend. **chummy** *adj*

chunk ❶ *n* thick, solid piece. **chunky** *adj*

church *n* **1** building for Christian worship. **2** (*with cap.*) whole body or sect of Christians. **3** clergy.

churlish *adj* rude or surly.

churn ❶ *n* **1** large container for milk. **2** vessel for making butter. ◆ *v* **3** shake up, stir **4** produce rapidly.

chute *n* slide for sending down parcels, coal etc.

chutney *n* pickle of fruit, spices etc.

CIA *US* Central Intelligence Agency.

CID Criminal Investigation Department.

cider *n* fermented drink made from apples.

cigar *n* roll of tobacco leaves for smoking. **cigarette** *n* finely–cut tobacco rolled in paper for smoking.

cinch *n Inf* easy task.

cinder *n* remains of burned coal.

cinema ❶ *n* **1** building used for showing of films. **2** films generally.

hassle (*Inf*)

chorus *n* = **refrain**, response, strain, burden; = **choir**, singers, ensemble, vocalists, choristers

Christmas *n* = **festive season**, Noël, Xmas (*Inf*), Yule (*Arch*), Yuletide (*Arch*)

chronicle *v* = **record**, tell, report, enter, relate ◆ *n* = **record**, story, history, account, register

chuck *v* (*Inf*) = **throw**, cast, pitch,

toss, hurl

chuckle *v* = **laugh**, giggle, snigger, chortle, titter

chum *n* = (*Inf*) **friend**, mate (*Inf*), pal (*Inf*), companion, comrade

chunk *n* = **piece**, block, mass, portion, lump

churn *v* = **stir up**, beat, disturb, swirl, agitate

cinema *n* = **pictures**, movies, picture–house, flicks (*Sl*); = **films**,

cinnamon *n* spice from bark of Asian tree.

cipher *n* **1** secret writing. **2** arithmetical symbol. **3** person of no importance.

circa *Lat* about, approximately.

circle ❶ *n* **1** perfectly round figure. **2** ring. **3** *Theatre* section of seats above main level of auditorium. **4** group, society with common interest. ♦ *v* **5** surround. **6** move round. **circular** *adj* **1** round. ♦ *n* **2** letter sent to several persons. **circulate** *v* **1** move round. **2** pass round. **3** send round. **circulation** *n* **1** flow of blood. **2** act of moving round. **3** extent of sale of newspaper etc.

circuit ❶ *n* **1** complete round or course. **2** area. **3** path of electric current. **4** round of visitation. **circuitous** *adj* indirect.

circumcise *v* cut off foreskin of. **circumcision** *n*

circumference *n* boundary line, esp. of circle.

circumflex *n* accent (^) over a letter.

circumnavigate *v* sail right round.

circumscribe *v* confine, bound, limit.

circumspect *adj* cautious.

circumstance ❶ *n* **1** detail. **2** event. ♦ *pl* **3** state of affairs. **4** condition in life, esp. financial. **5** surroundings or things accompanying an action. **circumstantial** *adj*

circumvent *v* outwit, evade, get round.

circus *n*, *pl* **-cuses** (performance of) acrobats, clowns, performing animals etc.

cirrhosis *n* disease of liver.

cirrus *n*, *pl* **-ri** high wispy cloud.

cistern *n* water tank.

citadel *n* city fortress.

cite ❶ *v* **1** quote. **2** bring forward as proof. **citation** *n* **1** quoting. **2** commendation for bravery etc.

citizen ❶ *n* **1** member of state, nation etc. **2** inhabitant of city. **citizenship** *n*

citrus fruit lemons, oranges etc.

city ❶ *n*, *pl* **-ties** large town.

civic ❶ *adj* pert. to city or citizen.

civil ❶ *adj* **1** relating to citizens. **2** not military. **3** refined, polite **4** *Law*

———————— THESAURUS ————————

pictures, movies, big screen (*Inf*), motion pictures

circle *n* = **ring**, disc, hoop, halo; = **group**, company, set, club, society ♦ *v* = **go round**, ring, surround, enclose, envelop; = **wheel**, spiral

circuit *n* = **course**, tour, track, route, journey, = **racetrack**, course, track, racecourse

circumstance *n* usually plural

= **situation**, condition, contingency, state of affairs, lie of the land

cite *v* = **quote**, name, advance, mention, extract

citizen *n* = **inhabitant**, resident, dweller, denizen, subject

city *n* = **town**, metropolis, municipality, conurbation

civic *adj* = **public**, municipal, communal, local

not criminal. **civilian** *n* nonmilitary person. **civility** *n*

civilize ⊙ *v* 1 bring out of barbarism. 2 refine. **civilization** *n* 1 refinement. 2 cultured society. **civilized** *adj*

claim ⊙ *v* 1 demand as right. 2 assert. 3 call for. ♦ *n* 4 demand for thing supposed due. 5 right. 6 thing claimed. **claimant** *n*

clairvoyance *n* power of seeing things not present to senses. **clairvoyant** *n/adj*

clam *n* edible mollusc.

clamber *v* to climb awkwardly.

clammy *adj* –mier, –miest moist and sticky.

clamour ⊙ *n/v* (make) loud outcry. **clamorous** *adj*

clamp ⊙ *n* 1 tool for holding. ♦ *v* 2 fasten with or as with clamp. 3 (*with* **down**) become stricter.

clan ⊙ *n* 1 collection of families of common ancestry. 2 group.

clandestine *adj* 1 secret. 2 sly.

clang *v* 1 (cause to) make loud ringing sound. ♦ *n* 2 this sound.

clap ⊙ *v* **clapping, clapped** 1 (cause to) strike with noise. 2 strike (hands) together. 3 applaud. 4 pat. 5 place or put quickly. ♦ *n* 6 hard, explosive sound. 7 slap.

claret *n* dry red wine.

clarify ⊙ *v* –fying, –fied make or become clear. **clarification** *n* **clarity** *n*

clarinet *n* woodwind instrument.

clash ⊙ *n* 1 loud noise. 2 conflict, collision. ♦ *v* 3 make clash. 4 come into conflict. 5 strike together.

clasp ⊙ *n* 1 hook or fastening. 2 embrace. ♦ *v* 3 fasten. 4 embrace, grasp.

class ⊙ *n* 1 any division, order, kind, sort. 2 rank. 3 group of school pupils. 4 division by merit. 5 quality. ♦ *v* 6 assign to proper division. **classy** *adj Inf* stylish,

———— THESAURUS ————

civil *adj* = **civic**, political, domestic, municipal ≠ **state**; = **polite**, obliging, courteous, considerate, affable ≠ **rude**

civilize *v* = **cultivate**, educate, refine, tame, enlighten

claim *v* = **assert**, insist, maintain, allege, uphold; = **demand**, call for, ask for, insist on ♦ *n* = **assertion**, statement, allegation, declaration, pretension; = **demand**, application, request, petition, call

clamour *n* = **noise**, shouting, racket, outcry, din

clamp *n* = **vice**, press, grip, bracket, fastener ♦ *v* = **fasten**, fix,

secure, brace, make fast

clan *n* = **family**, group, society, tribe, fraternity; = **group**, set, circle, gang, faction

clap *v* = **applaud**, cheer, acclaim ≠ **boo**

clarify *v* = **explain**, interpret, illuminate, clear up, simplify

clash *v* = **conflict**, grapple, wrangle, lock horns, cross swords; = **disagree**, conflict, vary, counter, differ; ♦ *n* = **conflict**, fight, brush, confrontation, collision

clasp *v* = **grasp**, hold, press, grip, seize ♦ *n* = **grasp**, hold, grip, embrace, hug; = **fastening**, catch,

elegant. **classify** v arrange methodically in classes. **classification** n

classic ⊕ adj 1 of highest rank, esp. of art. 2 typical. 3 famous. ◆ n 4 (literary) work of recognized excellence. ◆ pl 5 ancient Greek and Latin literature. **classical** adj 1 refined, elegant. 2 of ancient Greek and Latin culture.

clatter n 1 rattling noise. ◆ v 2 (cause to) make clatter.

clause ⊕ n 1 part of sentence. 2 article in formal document.

claustrophobia n abnormal fear of confined spaces. **claustrophobic** adj

clavicle n collarbone.

claw ⊕ n 1 sharp hooked nail of animal. ◆ v 2 tear with claws.

clay n 1 fine-grained earth, plastic when wet, hardening when

baked. 2 earth. **clayey** adj

clean ⊕ adj 1 free from dirt. 2 pure. 3 guiltless. 4 trim. ◆ adv 5 so as to leave no dirt. 6 entirely. ◆ v 7 free from dirt. **cleaner** n

cleanliness n **cleanly** adv **cleanse** v make clean.

clear ⊕ adj 1 pure, bright. 2 free from cloud. 3 transparent. 4 plain, distinct. 5 without defect. 6 unimpeded. ◆ adv 7 brightly. 8 wholly, quite. ◆ v 9 make clear. 10 acquit. 11 pass over. 12 make as profit. 13 free from obstruction, difficulty. 14 become clear, bright, free, transparent. **clearly** adv **clearance** n **clearing** n land cleared of trees.

cleave¹ cleaving, cleft, cleaved, v (cause to) split. **cleavage** n **cleaver** n short chopper.

cleave² v 1 stick, adhere. 2 be

—————————— THESAURUS ——————————

grip, hook, pin

class n = **group**, set, division, rank ◆ v = **classify**, group, rate, rank, brand

classic adj = **typical**, standard, model, regular, usual; = **masterly**, best, finest, world-class, consummate ≠ **second-rate** ◆ n = **standard**, masterpiece, prototype, paradigm, exemplar

clause n = **section**, condition, article, chapter, passage

claw n = **nail**, talon ◆ v = **scratch**, tear, dig, rip, scrape

clean adj = **hygienic**, fresh, sterile, pure, purified ≠ **contaminated**; = **spotless**, fresh, immaculate, impeccable, flawless ≠ **dirty**;

= **moral**, good, pure, decent, innocent ≠ **immoral** ◆ v = **cleanse**, wash, scrub, rinse, launder ≠ **dirty**

clear adj = **comprehensible**, explicit, understandable ≠ **confused**; = **obvious**, plain, apparent, evident, distinct ≠ **ambiguous**; = **certain**, sure, convinced, positive, satisfied ≠ **confused**; = **transparent**, see-through, translucent, crystalline, glassy ≠ **opaque**; = **unobstructed**, open, free, empty, unhindered ≠ **blocked** ◆ v = **unblock**, free, loosen, extricate, open; = **remove**, clean, wipe, cleanse, tidy (up); = **brighten**, break up, lighten; = **pass over**, jump, leap, vault,

loyal.

clef n Mus mark to show pitch.

cleft n crack, fissure, chasm.

clematis n climbing plant.

clement adj 1 merciful. 2 gentle. 3 mild. **clemency** n

clench v 1 set firmly together. 2 grasp, close (fist).

clergy ✆ n body of ministers of Christian church. **clergyman** n

clerical adj 1 of clergy. 2 of office work. **cleric** n clergyman.

clerk n 1 subordinate who keeps files etc. 2 officer in charge of records, correspondence etc.

clever ✆ adj 1 intelligent. 2 able, skilful, adroit. **cleverly** adv

cliché ✆ n stereotyped hackneyed phrase.

click n/v (make) short, sharp sound.

client ✆ n customer. **clientele** n clients.

cliff ✆ n steep rock face.

cliffhanger n thing which is exciting and full of suspense.

climate ✆ n condition of country with regard to weather. **climatic** adj

climax ✆ n highest point, culmination. **climactic** adj

climb ✆ v go up or ascend. **climber** n

clinch ✆ v conclude (agreement).

cling ✆ v clinging, clung 1 adhere. 2 be firmly attached to. **clingfilm** n thin polythene wrapping material.

clinic n place for medical examination, advice or treatment. **clinical** adj

clink n 1 sharp metallic sound. ♦ v 2 (cause to) make this sound.

clip¹ ✆ v clipping, clipped 1 cut with scissors. 2 cut short. ♦ n 3 Inf sharp blow. **clipping** n thing cut out, esp. newspaper article.

clip² ✆ v (attach with) gripping device.

———— THESAURUS ————

miss

clergy n = **priesthood**, ministry, clerics, clergymen, churchmen

clever adj = **intelligent**, bright, talented, gifted, smart ≠ **stupid**; = **shrewd**, bright, ingenious, resourceful, canny ≠ **unimaginative**

cliché n = **platitude**, stereotype, commonplace, banality, truism

client n = **customer**, consumer, buyer, patron, shopper

cliff n = **rock face**, overhang, crag, precipice, escarpment

climate n = **weather**, temperature, environment, spirit,

surroundings

climax n = **culmination**, top, summit, height, highlight

climb v = **ascend**, scale, mount, go up, clamber

clinch v = **secure**, close, confirm, conclude, seal

cling v = **clutch**, grip, embrace, grasp, hug

clip¹ v = **trim**, cut, crop, prune, shorten; = (Inf) **smack**, strike, knock, punch, thump ♦ n = (Inf) **smack**, strike, knock, punch, thump

clip² v = **attach**, fix, secure, connect, pin

clipper n fast sailing ship.

clique n 1 small exclusive set. 2 faction, group of people.

clitoris n part of female genitals. **clitoral** adj

cloak 🛈 n/v 1 (cover with) loose outer garment. 2 disguise. **cloakroom** n

clobber v Inf beat, batter.

clock n instrument for measuring time. **clockwise** adv/adj in the direction that the hands of a clock rotate. **clockwork** n wind–up mechanism for clocks, toys etc.

clod n lump of earth.

clog 🛈 v clogging, clogged 1 hamper, impede, choke up. ◆ n 2 wooden–soled shoe.

cloister n 1 covered pillared arcade. 2 monastery or convent. **cloistered** adj secluded.

clone n 1 cells of same genetic constitution as another, derived by asexual reproduction. 2 Inf lookalike. ◆ v 3 replicate.

close¹ 🛈 v 1 shut. 2 stop up. 3 prevent access to. 4 finish. 5 come together. 6 grapple. ◆ v 7 end. 8 shut–in place. 9 precinct of cathedral. **closure** n

close² 🛈 adj 1 near. 2 compact. 3 crowded. 4 intimate. 5 almost equal. 6 careful, searching. 7 confined. 8 secret. 9 unventilated. 10 niggardly. 11 restricted. ◆ adv 12 nearly. 13 tightly. **closely** adv **close–up** n close view.

closet n 1 small private room. 2 US cupboard. ◆ adj 3 secret. ◆ v 4 shut away in private.

clot n 1 mass or lump (of blood). 2 Inf fool. ◆ v 3 (cause to) form into lumps.

cloth 🛈 n woven fabric. **clothe** v put clothes on. **clothes** pl n 1 dress. 2 bed coverings. **clothing** n

cloud 🛈 n 1 vapour floating in air. 2 state of gloom. ◆ v 3 darken. 4 become cloudy. **cloudy** adj

clout 🛈 n 1 Inf blow. 2 influence, power. ◆ v 3 strike.

clove n pungent spice.

——— THESAURUS ———

cloak n = cape, coat, wrap, mantle; ◆ v = cover, coat, wrap, blanket, shroud

clog v = obstruct, block, jam, hinder, impede

close¹ v = shut, lock, fasten, secure ≠ open; = shut down, finish, cease; = wind up, finish, shut down, terminate; ◆ n = end, ending, finish, conclusion, completion

close² adj = near, neighbouring, nearby, handy, adjacent ≠ far; = intimate, loving, familiar, thick

(Inf), attached ≠ distant; = noticeable, marked, strong, distinct, pronounced; = careful, detailed, intense, minute, thorough; = even, level, neck and neck, fifty–fifty (Inf), evenly matched; = imminent, near, impending, at hand, nigh ≠ far away

cloth n = fabric, material, textiles

cloud n = mist, haze, vapour, murk, gloom ◆ v = confuse, distort, impair, muddle, disorient; = darken, dim, be overshadowed

clover n forage plant.
clown ⊕ n circus comic.
club ⊕ n 1 thick stick. 2 bat. 3 association. 4 suit at cards. ◆ v 5 strike. 6 join.
cluck v/n (make) noise of hen.
clue ⊕ n indication, esp. of solution of mystery or puzzle.
clueless adj stupid.
clump¹ ⊕ n cluster of plants.
clump² v/n (move with) heavy tread.
clumsy ⊕ adj –sier, –siest awkward. **clumsily** adv **clumsiness** n
cluster ⊕ n/v group, bunch.
clutch ⊕ v 1 grasp eagerly. 2 snatch (at). ◆ n 3 grasp, tight grip. 4 device enabling two revolving shafts to be (dis)connected at will.

clutter ⊕ v 1 cause obstruction, disorder. ◆ v n 2 disordered mass. 3 state of untidiness.
cm centimetre.
Co. 1 Company. 2 County.
co– comb. form together, jointly, as in coproduction.
c/o 1 care of. 2 carried over.
coach ⊕ n 1 long–distance bus. 2 large four–wheeled carriage. 3 railway carriage. 4 tutor, instructor. ◆ v 5 instruct.
coagulate v curdle, clot.
coal n 1 mineral used as fuel. 2 glowing ember.
coalesce v unite.
coalition ⊕ n alliance.
coarse ⊕ adj 1 rough. 2 unrefined. 3 indecent. **coarsely** adv **coarseness** n

———————————— THESAURUS ————————————

clout (Inf) v = **hit**, strike, punch, slap, sock (Sl) ◆ n = **thump**, blow, punch, slap, sock (Sl)
clown n = **comedian**, fool, comic, harlequin, joker; = **fool**, idiot, twit (Inf, chiefly Brit), imbecile (Inf), ignoramus ◆ v (usually with **around**) = **play the fool**, mess about, jest, act the fool
club n = **association**, company, group, union, society; = **stick**, bat, bludgeon, truncheon, cosh (Brit) ◆ v = **beat**, strike, hammer, batter, bash
clue n = **indication**, lead, sign, evidence, suggestion
clump¹ n = **cluster**, group, bunch, bundle ◆ v = **stomp**, thump, lumber, tramp, plod
clumsy adj = **awkward**,

lumbering, bumbling, ponderous, ungainly ≠ skilful
cluster n = **gathering**, group, collection, bunch, knot ◆ v = **gather**, group, collect, bunch, assemble
clutch v = **hold**, grip, embrace, grasp, cling to
clutter n = **untidiness**, mess, disorder, confusion, litter ≠ order ◆ v = **litter**, scatter, strew, mess up ≠ tidy
coach n = **instructor**, teacher, trainer, tutor, handler; = **bus**, charabanc ◆ v = **instruct**, train, prepare, exercise, drill
coalition n = **alliance**, union, association, combination, merger
coarse adj = **rough**, crude, unfinished, homespun, impure

coast ① *n* **1** sea shore. ♦ *v* **2** move under momentum. **coastal** *adj* **coaster** *n* **1** small ship. **2** small mat.

coat ① *n* **1** sleeved outer garment. **2** animal's fur. **3** covering layer. ♦ *v* **4** cover. **coating** *n* covering layer.

coax ① *v* persuade.

cob *n* **1** short-legged stout horse. **2** male swan. **3** head of corn.

cobalt *n* **1** metallic element. **2** blue pigment from it.

cobber *n Aust or NZ informal* friend.

cobble *v* **1** patch roughly. **2** mend shoes. ♦ *n* **3** round stone. **cobbler** *n*

cobra *n* poisonous, hooded snake.

cobweb *n* spider's web.

cocaine *n* addictive narcotic drug used medicinally.

cochineal *n* scarlet dye.

cock *n* **1** male bird, esp. of domestic fowl. **2** tap. **3** hammer of gun. ♦ *v* **4** draw back to firing position. **5** raise, turn. **cockerel** *n* young cock.

cockatoo *n* crested parrot.

cockie, cocky *n, pl* **-kies** *Aust & NZ informal* farmer.

cockle *n* shellfish.

cockpit *n* pilot's seat, compartment in small aircraft.

cockroach *n* insect pest.

cocktail *n* **1** mixed drink of spirits. **2** appetizer.

cocky *adj* **cockier, cockiest** conceited, pert.

cocoa *n* **1** powdered seed of cacao tree. **2** drink made from this.

coconut *n* large, hard nut.

cocoon *n* sheath of insect in chrysalis stage.

COD cash on delivery.

cod *n* large sea fish.

coda *n Mus* final part of musical composition.

code ① *n* **1** system of letters, symbols to transmit messages secretly. **2** scheme of conduct. **3** collection of laws. **codify** *v*

codeine *n* pain-killing drug.

coerce *v* compel, force. **coercion** *n*

coexist *v* exist together. **coexistence** *n*

C of E Church of England.

coffee *n* **1** seeds of tropical shrub. **2** drink made from these.

coffer *n* chest for valuables.

coffin *n* box for corpse.

cog *n* one of series of teeth on rim of wheel. **cogwheel** *n*

cogent *adj* convincing.

cogitate *v* think, reflect, ponder.

THESAURUS

≠ **smooth**; = **vulgar**, rude, indecent, improper, earthy; ≠ **well-mannered**

coast *n* = **shore**, border, beach, seaside, coastline ♦ *v* = **cruise**, sail, drift, taxi, glide

coat *n* = **fur**, hair, skin, hide, wool;

= **layer**, covering, coating, overlay ♦ *v* = **cover**, spread, plaster, smear

coax *v* = **persuade**, cajole, talk into, wheedle, sweet-talk (*Inf*) ≠ **bully**

code *n* = **principles**, rules, manners, custom, convention;

cogitation n

cognac n French brandy.

cognizance n knowledge.

cognizant adj

cohabit v live together as husband and wife.

cohere v stick together, be consistent. coherent adj 1 capable of logical speech, thought. 2 connected, making sense.

cohesion n tendency to unite. cohesive adj

cohort n 1 troop. 2 associate.

coiffure n hairstyle.

coil ❶ v 1 twist into winding shape. ♦ n 2 series of rings. 3 anything coiled.

coin ❶ n 1 piece of money. 2 money. ♦ v 3 stamp. 4 invent. coinage n

coincide ❶ v happen together. coincidence n chance happening. coincidental adj

coke[1] n residue left from distillation of coal, used as fuel.

coke[2] n 1 Coca-Cola 2 Sl cocaine.

cola n flavoured soft drink.

colander n strainer for food.

cold ❶ adj 1 lacking heat. 2 indifferent, unmoved. 3 unfriendly. ♦ n 4 lack of heat. 5 illness, marked by runny nose etc.

coldly adv cold-blooded adj lacking pity.

coleslaw n cabbage salad.

colic n severe pains in the intestines.

collaborate ❶ v work with another. collaboration n collaborator n

collage n (artistic) composition of bits and pieces stuck together on background.

collapse ❶ v 1 fall. 2 fail. ♦ n 3 act of collapsing. 4 breakdown. collapsible adj

collar ❶ n 1 band, part of garment, worn round neck. ♦ v 2 seize. collarbone n bone joining shoulder blade to breast bone.

collate v compare carefully.

collateral n security pledged for

——— THESAURUS ———

= cipher, cryptograph

coil v = wind, twist, curl, loop, spiral

coin n = money, change, cash, silver, copper ♦ v = invent, create, make up, forge, originate

coincide v = occur simultaneously, coexist, synchronize, be concurrent; = agree, match, accord, square, correspond ≠ disagree

cold adj = chilly, freezing, bleak, arctic, icy ≠ hot; = distant, reserved, indifferent, aloof, frigid

≠ emotional ♦ n = coldness, chill, frigidity, frostiness, iciness

collaborate v = work together, team up, join forces, cooperate, play ball (Inf); = conspire, cooperate, collude, fraternize

collapse v = fall down, fall, give way, subside, cave in; = fail, fold, founder, break down, fall through (Inf) ♦ n = falling down, ruin, falling apart, cave-in, disintegration; = failure, slump, breakdown, flop, downfall

collar v = (Inf) seize, catch, arrest,

loan.

colleague *n* fellow worker.

collect *v* gather, bring, come together. **collected** *adj* calm.

collection *n* **collective** *n* 1 factory, farm etc. owned by its workers. ◆ *adj* 2 shared. **collectively** *adv* **collector** *n*

college *n* place of higher education. **collegiate** *adj*

collide *v* crash together. **collision** *n*

collie *n* breed of sheepdog.

colliery *n, pl* **-lieries** coal mine.

colloquial *adj* pert. to, or used in, informal conversation. **colloquialism** *n*

collusion *n* secret agreement for a fraudulent purpose. **collude** *v*

cologne *n* perfumed liquid.

colon[1] *n* mark (:) indicating break in a sentence.

colon[2] *n* part of large intestine.

colonel *n* commander of regiment or battalion.

colonnade *n* row of columns.

colony *n, pl* **-nies** 1 body of people who settle in new country.

2 country so settled. **colonial** *adj* **colonist** *n* **colonize** *v* **colonization** *n*

colossal *adj* huge, gigantic.

colour *n* 1 hue, tint. 2 complexion. 3 paint. 4 pigment. 5 *Fig* semblance, pretext. 6 timbre, quality. ◆ *pl* 7 flag. 8 *Sport* distinguishing badge, symbol. ◆ *v* 9 stain, paint. 10 disguise. 11 influence or distort. 12 blush. **colourful** *adj* 1 bright. 2 interesting. **colourless** *adj* **colour-blind** *adj* unable to distinguish between certain colours.

colt *n* young male horse.

columbine *n* garden flower.

column *n* 1 long vertical pillar. 2 division of page. 3 body of troops. **columnist** *n* journalist writing regular feature.

coma *n* unconsciousness. **comatose** *adj*

comb *n* 1 toothed instrument for tidying hair. 2 cock's crest. 3 mass of honey cells. ◆ *v* 4 use comb on. 5 search.

combat *v/n* **-bating, -bated** fight, contest. **combatant** *n*

—————— THESAURUS ——————

grab, capture

colleague *n* = **fellow worker**, partner, ally, associate, assistant

collect *v* = **gather**, save, assemble, heap, accumulate ≠ **scatter**; = **assemble**, meet, rally, cluster, come together ≠ **disperse**

collide *v* = **crash**, clash, meet head-on, come into collision; = **conflict**, clash, be incompatible, be at variance

colony *n* = **settlement**, territory,

province, possession, dependency

colour, *U.S.* **color** *n* = **hue**, tone, shade, tint, colourway; = **paint**, stain, dye, tint, pigment ◆ *v* = **blush**, flush, redden

column *n* = **pillar**, support, post, shaft, upright; = **line**, row, file, rank, procession

coma *n* = **unconsciousness**, trance, oblivion, stupor

comb *v* = **untangle**, arrange, groom, dress; = **search**, hunt

combative *adj*
combine ⊕ *v* 1 join together. ◆ *n* 2 syndicate, esp. of businesses. **combination** *n* **combine harvester** machine to harvest and thresh grain.
combustion *n* process of burning. **combustible** *adj*
come ⊕ *v* coming, came 1 approach, arrive, move towards. 2 reach. 3 occur. 4 originate (from). 5 become. **comeback** *n* 1 *Inf* return to active life. 2 retort. **comedown** *n* 1 decline in status. 2 disappointment. **comeuppance** *n Inf* deserved punishment.
comedy ⊕ *n, pl* **–dies** 1 light, amusing play. 2 humour. **comedian** *n* entertainer who tells jokes.
comely *adj* **–lier, –liest** good–looking.

comet *n* luminous heavenly body.
comfort ⊕ *n* 1 ease. 2 (means of) consolation. ◆ *v* 3 soothe. 4 console. **comfortable** *adj* 1 giving comfort. 2 well–off. **comfortably** *adv* **comforter** *n*
comic ⊕ *adj* 1 relating to comedy. 2 funny. ◆ *n* 3 comedian. 4 magazine of strip cartoons. **comical** *adj*
comma *n* punctuation mark (,).
command ⊕ *v* 1 order. 2 rule. 3 compel. 4 have in one's power. ◆ *n* 5 order. 6 power of controlling. 7 mastery. 8 post of one commanding. 9 jurisdiction. **commandant** *n* **commandeer** *v* seize for military use. **commander** *n* **commandment** *n*
commando *n, pl* **–dos, –does** (member of) special military unit.
commemorate ⊕ *v* keep in

through, rake, sift, scour
combat *n* = **fight**, war, action, battle, conflict ≠ **peace** ◆ *v* = **fight**, oppose, resist, defy, withstand ≠ **support**
combine *v* = **amalgamate**, mix, blend, integrate, merge ≠ **separate**
come *v* = **approach**, near, advance, move towards, draw near; = **reach**, extend, come up to, come as far as; = **happen**, fall, occur, take place, arise
comedy *n* = **light entertainment** ≠ **tragedy** soapie or soapie; = **humour**, fun, joking, farce, jesting ≠ **seriousness**
comfort *n* = **ease**, luxury,

wellbeing, opulence; = **consolation**, succour, help, support, relief ≠ **annoyance** ◆ *v* = **console**, reassure, soothe, hearten, commiserate with ≠ **distress**
comic *adj* = **funny**, amusing, witty, humorous, farcical ≠ **sad** ◆ *n* = **comedian**, funny man, humorist, wit, clown
command *v* = **order**, tell, charge, demand, require ≠ **beg**; = **have authority over**, lead, head, control, rule ≠ **be subordinate to** ◆ *n* = **order**, demand, instruction, requirement, decree; = **domination**, control, rule, mastery, power

memory by ceremony.
commemorative *adj*
commence ⊕ *v* begin.
commend ⊕ *v* 1 praise. 2 entrust.
commendable *adj*
commensurate *adj* 1 equal. 2 in proportion.
comment ⊕ *n/v* 1 remark. 2 gossip. 3 note. **commentary** *n, pl* -taries 1 explanatory notes. 2 spoken accompaniment to film etc. **commentate** *v* **commentator** *n*
commerce ⊕ *n* trade. **commercial** *adj* 1 of business, trade etc. ♦ *n* 2 advertisement, esp. on radio or television.
commiserate *v* sympathize with. **commiseration** *n*
commission ⊕ *n* 1 authority. 2 (body entrusted with) some special duty. 3 agent's payment by percentage. 4 document appointing to officer's rank. 5 committing. ♦ *v* 6 charge with duty. 7 *Mil* confer a rank. 8 give order for. **commissioner** *n*

commissionaire *n* uniformed doorman.
commit ⊕ *v* –mitting, –mitted 1 give in charge. 2 be guilty of. 3 pledge. 4 send for trial.
commitment *n* **committal** *n*
committee *n* body appointed, elected for special business.
commode *n* 1 chest of drawers. 2 stool containing chamber pot.
commodity *n, pl* -ities article of trade.
commodore *n* 1 senior naval or air officer. 2 president of yacht club.
common ⊕ *adj* 1 shared by all. 2 public. 3 ordinary. 4 inferior. ♦ *n* 5 land belonging to community. ♦ *pl* 6 ordinary people. 7 (*with cap.*) House of Commons. **commoner** *n* one not of the nobility. **commonly** *adv* **commonplace** *adj* 1 ordinary. ♦ *n* 2 trite remark. **commonwealth** *n* 1 republic. 2 (*with cap.*) federation of self–governing states.

C

———————— THESAURUS ————————

commemorate *v* = **celebrate**, remember, honour, recognize, salute ≠ **ignore**
commence *v* = **embark on**, start, open, begin, initiate ≠ **stop**
commend *v* = **praise**, acclaim, applaud, compliment, extol ≠ **criticize**; = **recommend**, suggest, approve, advocate, endorse
comment *v* = **remark**, say, note, mention, point out ♦ *n* = **remark**, statement, observation; = **note**, explanation, illustration, commentary, exposition

commission *v* = **appoint**, order, contract, select, engage ♦ *n* = **duty**, task, mission, mandate, errand; = **fee**, cut, percentage, royalties, rake–off (*SI*); = **committee**, board, representatives, commissioners, delegation
commit *v* = **do**, perform, carry out, execute, enact; = **put in custody**, confine, imprison ≠ **release**
common *adj* = **usual**, standard, regular, ordinary, familiar ≠ **rare**;

commotion *n* stir, disturbance.

commune[1] **ⓘ** *v* converse intimately. **communion** *n* 1 sharing of thoughts, feelings etc. 2 (*with cap.*) (participation in) sacrament of the Lord's Supper.

commune[2] **ⓘ** *n* group living together and sharing property, responsibility etc. **communal** *adj* for common use.

communicate **ⓘ** *v* 1 impart, convey. 2 reveal. ◆ *v* 3 give or exchange information. 4 have connecting door. **communicable** *adj* **communication** *n* 1 giving information. 2 message. 3 (*usu. pl*) means of exchanging messages. **communicative** *adj* willing to talk. **communiqué** *n* official announcement.

communism **ⓘ** *n* doctrine that all means of production etc. should be property of community. **communist** *n/adj*

community **ⓘ** *n, pl* **-ties** 1 body of people living in one district. 2 the public. 3 joint ownership. 4 similarity.

commute *v* 1 travel daily some distance to work. 2 exchange. 3 reduce (punishment). **commuter** *n*

compact[1] **ⓘ** *adj* 1 closely packed. 2 solid. 3 terse. ◆ *v* 4 make, become compact. **compact disc** small audio disc played by laser.

compact[2] **ⓘ** *n* agreement.

compact[3] *n* small case to hold face powder etc.

companion **ⓘ** *n* comrade.

company **ⓘ** *n, pl* **-nies** 1 gathering of persons. 2 companionship. 3 guests. 4 business firm. 5 division of regiment.

compare **ⓘ** *v* 1 notice likenesses and differences. 2 liken. 3 be like. 4 compete with. **comparability** *n* **comparable** *adj* **comparative** *adj* 1

———— THESAURUS ————

= **popular**, general, accepted, standard, routine; = **shared**, collective; = **ordinary**, average, typical ≠ **important**

commune[1] *n* = **community**, collective, cooperative, kibbutz

communicate *v* = **contact**, talk, speak, make contact, get in contact

communism *n* = **socialism**, Marxism, collectivism, Bolshevism, state socialism

community *n* = **society**, people, public, residents, commonwealth

compact[1] *adj* = **closely packed**, solid, thick, dense, compressed

≠ **loose**; = **concise**, brief, to the point, succinct, terse ≠ **lengthy** ◆ *v* = **pack closely**, stuff, cram, compress, condense ≠ **loosen**

compact[2] *n* = **agreement**, deal, understanding, contract, bond

companion *n* = **friend**, partner, ally, colleague, associate;

= **assistant**, aide, escort, attendant

company *n* = **business**, firm, association, corporation, partnership; = **group**, set, community, band, crowd;

= **troop**, unit, squad, team;

= **companionship**, society, presence, fellowship

relative. **2** *Grammar* denoting form of adjective, adverb meaning *more*. **comparison** *n* act of comparing.

compartment ❶ *n* part divided off.

compass ❶ *n* **1** instrument for showing north. **2** (*usu. pl*) instrument for drawing circles. **3** scope. ♦ *v* **4** surround. **5** comprehend. **6** attain.

compassion ❶ *n* pity, sympathy. **compassionate** *adj*

compatible ❶ *adj* agreeing with. **compatibility** *n*

compatriot *n* fellow countryman.

compel ❶ *v* **–pelling, –pelled** force.

compendium *n, pl* **–diums, –dia 1** collection of different games. **2** summary. **compendious** *adj* brief but inclusive.

compensate ❶ *v* **1** make up for. **2**

recompense. **compensation** *n*

compere *n* **1** one who introduces cabaret, television shows etc. ♦ *v* **2** act as compere.

compete ❶ *v* strive in rivalry, contend for. **competition** *n* **1** rivalry. **2** contest. **competitive** *adj* **competitor** *n*

competent ❶ *adj* **1** able. **2** properly qualified. **3** sufficient. **competence** *n*

compile ❶ *v* make up from various sources. **compilation** *n*

complacent ❶ *adj* self–satisfied. **complacency** *n*

complain ❶ *v* **1** grumble. **2** make known a grievance **3** make known that one is suffering from.

complaint *n* **1** grievance. **2** illness.

complement ❶ *n* **1** something making up a whole. **2** complete amount. ♦ *v* **3** add to, make complete. **complementary** *adj*

—————— THESAURUS ——————

compare *v* = **contrast**, balance, weigh, set against, juxtapose

compartment *n* = **section**, carriage, berth; = **bay**, booth, locker, niche, cubicle

compass *n* = **range**, field, area, reach, scope

compassion *n* = **sympathy**, understanding, pity, humanity, mercy ≠ **indifference**

compatible *adj* = **consistent**, in keeping, congruous ≠ **inappropriate**

compel *v* = **force**, make, railroad (*Inf*), oblige, constrain

compensate *v* = **recompense**, repay, refund, reimburse,

remunerate; = **make amends**, make up for, atone, make it up to someone, pay for

compete *v* = **contend**, fight, vie, challenge, struggle

competent *adj* = **able**, skilled, capable, proficient ≠ **incompetent**

compile *v* = **put together**, collect, gather, organize, accumulate

complacent *adj* = **smug**, self–satisfied, pleased with yourself, resting on your laurels, contented ≠ **insecure**

complain *v* = **find fault**, moan, grumble, whinge (*Inf*), carp

complement *v* = **enhance**, complete, improve, boost, crown

complete *adj* **1** perfect. **2** ended. **3** entire. **4** thorough. ◆ *v* **5** make whole. **6** finish. **completely** *adv* **completion** *n*

complex *adj* **1** intricate, compound, involved. ◆ *n* **2** group of related buildings. **3** obsession. **complexity** *n*

complexion *n* **1** look, colour of skin, esp. of face. **2** aspect, character.

complicate *v* make involved, difficult. **complication** *n*

complicity *n* partnership in wrongdoing.

compliment *n/v* praise. **complimentary** *adj* **1** expressing praise. **2** free of charge.

comply *v* **–plying, –plied** do as asked. **compliance** *n* **compliant** *adj*

component *n* part, constituent of whole.

compose *v* **1** put in order. **2** write, invent. **3** make up. **4** calm. **composer** *n* one who composes, esp. music. **composite** *adj* made up of distinct parts. **composition** *n* **composure** *n* calmness.

compos mentis *Lat* sane.

compost *n* decayed vegetable matter for fertilizing soil.

compound¹ *n* **1** substance, word, made up of parts. ◆ *adj* **2** not simple. **3** composite. ◆ *v* **4** mix, make up. **5** make worse. **6** compromise.

compound² *n* enclosure containing houses etc.

——— THESAURUS ———

◆ *n* = **accompaniment**, companion, accessory, completion, finishing touch; = **total**, capacity, quota, aggregate, contingent

complete *adj* = **total**, perfect, absolute, utter, outright; = **whole**, full, entire ≠ **partial**; = **entire**, full, whole, intact, unbroken ≠ **incomplete** ◆ *v* = **finish**, conclude, end, close, settle ≠ **start**

complex *adj* = **compound**, multiple, composite, manifold, heterogeneous; = **complicated**, difficult, involved, elaborate, tangled ≠ **simple** ◆ *n* = **structure**, system, scheme, network, organization; = (*Inf*) **obsession**, preoccupation, phobia, fixation, fixed idea

complexion *n* = **skin**, colour, colouring, hue, skin tone; = **nature**, character, make–up

complicate *v* = **make difficult**, confuse, muddle, entangle, involve ≠ **simplify**

compliment *n* = **praise**, honour, tribute, bouquet, flattery ≠ **criticism** ◆ *v* = **praise**, flatter, salute, congratulate, pay tribute to ≠ **criticize**

comply *v* = **obey**, follow, observe, submit to, conform to ≠ **defy**

component *n* = **part**, piece, unit, item, element ◆ *adj* = **constituent**, inherent, intrinsic

compose *v* = **put together**, make up, constitute, comprise, make ≠ **destroy**; = **create**, write, produce, invent, devise; = **arrange**, make up, construct, put together, order

comprehend ⊕ v **1** understand. **2** include. **comprehensible** adj
comprehension n **comprehensive** adj **1** taking in much. **2** pert. to education of children of all abilities.
compress ⊕ v **1** squeeze together. **2** make smaller. ◆ n **3** pad of lint applied to wound, inflamed part etc. **compressible** adj **compression** n **compressor** n
comprise ⊕ v include, contain.
compromise ⊕ n **1** coming to terms by giving up part of claim. ◆ v **2** settle by making concessions. **3** expose to suspicion.
compulsion n **1** act of compelling. **2** urge. **compulsive**

adj **compulsory** adj not optional.
compunction n regret.
compute ⊕ v calculate.
computation n **computer** n electronic machine for processing information. **computerize** v
comrade ⊕ n friend.
con[1] ⊕ v Inf swindle.
con[2] n vote against.
concave adj rounded inwards.
conceal ⊕ v hide. **concealment** n
concede ⊕ v **1** admit truth of. **2** give up.
conceit n vanity. **conceited** adj
conceive ⊕ v **1** believe. **2** become pregnant. **3** devise. **conceivable** adj
concentrate ⊕ v **1** focus (one's efforts etc.). **2** increase in strength.

——————— THESAURUS ———————

compound[1] n = **combination**, mixture, blend, composite, fusion ≠ **element** ◆ v = **intensify**, add to, complicate, worsen, heighten ≠ **lessen**; = **combine**, unite, mix, blend, synthesize ≠ **divide**
comprehend v = **understand**, see, take in, perceive, grasp ≠ **misunderstand**
compress v = **squeeze**, crush, squash, press; = **condense**, contract, concentrate, shorten, abbreviate
comprise v = **be composed of**, include, contain, consist of, take in
compromise n = **give-and-take**, agreement, settlement, accommodation, concession ≠ **disagreement** ◆ v = **meet halfway**, concede, make concessions, give and take, strike a

balance ≠ **disagree**; = **undermine**, expose, embarrass, weaken, prejudice ≠ **support**
compute v = **calculate**, total, count, reckon, figure out
comrade n = **companion**, friend, partner, ally, colleague
con[1] (Inf) v = **swindle**, trick, cheat, rip off (Sl), deceive ◆ n = **swindle**, trick, fraud, deception, scam (Sl)
conceal v = **hide**, bury, cover, screen, disguise ≠ **reveal**
concede v = **admit**, allow, accept, acknowledge, own ≠ **deny**; = **give up**, yield, hand over, surrender, relinquish ≠ **conquer**
conceive v = **imagine**, envisage, comprehend, visualize, think; = **think up**, create, design, devise, formulate; = **become pregnant**, get pregnant, become

3 devote all attention. ♦ n 4 concentrated substance. **concentration** n

concentric adj having the same centre.

concept 🛈 n abstract idea. **conceptual** adj

conception 🛈 n 1 idea, notion. 2 act of conceiving.

concern 🛈 v 1 relate to. 2 worry. 3 involve (oneself). ♦ n 4 affair. 5 worry. 6 business, enterprise. **concerned** adj 1 worried. 2 involved. **concerning** prep about.

concert n 1 musical entertainment. 2 agreement. **concerted** adj mutually planned. **concertina** n musical instrument with bellows. **concerto** n composition for solo instrument and orchestra.

concession 🛈 n 1 act of conceding. 2 thing conceded.

concession road n Canad one of a series of roads separating concessions in a township.

conch n seashell.

conciliate v win over from hostility. **conciliation** n **conciliatory** adj

concise adj brief, terse.

conclave n private meeting.

conclude 🛈 v 1 finish. 2 deduce. 3 settle. 4 decide. **conclusion** n **conclusive** adj decisive.

concoct v 1 make mixture. 2 contrive. **concoction** n

concord n 1 agreement. 2 harmony.

concourse n 1 crowd. 2 large, open place in public area.

concrete 🛈 n 1 mixture of sand, cement etc. ♦ adj 2 specific. 3 actual. 4 solid.

concubine n 1 woman cohabiting with man. 2 secondary wife.

———— THESAURUS ————

impregnated

concentrate v = **focus your attention on**, focus on, pay attention to, be engrossed in, put your mind to ≠ **pay no attention to**; = **focus**, centre, converge, bring to bear

concept n = **idea**, view, image, theory, notion

conception n = **idea**, plan, design, image, concept; = **impregnation**, insemination, fertilization, germination

concern n = **anxiety**, fear, worry, distress, unease; = **worry**, care, anxiety; = **affair**, issue, matter, consideration ♦ v = **worry**,

trouble, bother, disturb, distress; = **be about**, cover, deal with, go into, relate to

concession n = **compromise**, agreement, settlement, accommodation, adjustment; = **privilege**, right, permit, licence, entitlement

conclude v = **decide**, judge, assume, gather, work out; = **come to an end**, end, close, finish, wind up ≠ **begin**; = **bring to an end**, end, close, finish, complete ≠ **begin**

concrete adj = **specific**, precise, explicit, definite, clear–cut ≠ **vague**; = **real**, material, actual,

concur *v* **-curring, -curred 1** agree. **2** happen together.

concurrent *adj* **concurrently** *adv*

concussion *n* brain injury.

condemn ✪ *v* **1** blame. **2** find guilty. **3** doom. **4** declare unfit.

condemnation *n*

condense *v* **1** concentrate. **2** turn from gas to liquid. **condensation** *n*

condescend *v* **1** treat graciously one regarded as inferior. **2** stoop.

condescension *n*

condiment *n* seasoning for food.

condition ✪ *n* **1** state or circumstances. **2** thing on which something else depends. **3** prerequisite. **4** physical fitness. ◆ *v* **5** accustom. **6** regulate. **7** make fit.

conditional *adj* dependent on events. **conditioner** *n* liquid to make hair or clothes feel softer.

condolence *n* sympathy.

condom *n* sheathlike rubber contraceptive worn by man.

condone ✪ *v* overlook, forgive.

conducive *adj* leading (to).

conduct ✪ *n* **1** behaviour. **2** management. ◆ *v* **3** guide. **4** direct. **5** manage. **6** transmit (heat etc.). **conduction** *n* **conductor** *n* **1** person in charge of bus etc. **2** director of orchestra. **3** substance capable of transmitting heat etc.

conduit *n* channel or pipe for water, cables etc.

cone *n* **1** tapering figure with circular base. **2** fruit of pine, fir etc.

conical *adj*

confederate *n* **1** ally. **2** accomplice. ◆ *v* **3** unite.

confederation *n* alliance of political units.

confer ✪ *v* **-ferring, -ferred 1** grant. **2** talk with. **conference** *n* meeting for consultation.

confess ✪ *v* **1** admit. **2** declare one's sins orally to priest.

confession *n* **confessional** *n* confessor's box. **confessor** *n* priest who hears confessions.

——————— THESAURUS ———————

substantial, sensible ≠ **abstract**

condemn *v* = **denounce**, damn, criticize, disapprove, censure ≠ **approve**; = **sentence**, convict, damn, doom, pass sentence on ≠ **acquit**

condition *n* = **state**, order, shape, nick (*Brit inf*), trim; = **situation**, state, position, status, circumstances; = **requirement**, terms, rider, restriction, qualification; = **health**, shape, fitness, trim, form ◆ *v* = **train**, teach, adapt, accustom

condone *v* = **overlook**, excuse,

forgive, pardon, turn a blind eye to ≠ **condemn**

conduct *v* = **carry out**, run, control, manage, direct; = **accompany**, lead, escort, guide, steer ◆ *n* = **management**, running, control, handling, administration; = **behaviour**, ways, bearing, attitude, manners

confer *v* = **discuss**, talk, consult, deliberate, discourse; = **grant**, give, present, accord, award

confess *v* = **admit**, acknowledge, disclose, confide, own up ≠ **cover up**; = **declare**, allow, reveal,

confetti *pl n* bits of coloured paper thrown at weddings.
confide ⊕ *v* 1 tell secrets. 2 entrust. **confidence** *n* 1 trust. 2 assurance. 3 intimacy. 4 secret.
confident *adj* 1 certain. 2 self–assured. **confidential** *adj* 1 private. 2 secret.
configuration *n* shape.
confine ⊕ *v* 1 keep within bounds. 2 shut up. **confines** *pl n* limits. **confinement** *n* 1 being confined. 2 childbirth.
confirm ⊕ *v* 1 make sure. 2 strengthen. 3 make valid. 4 admit as member of church. **confirmation** *n* **confirmed** *adj* long–established.
confiscate ⊕ *v* seize by authority. **confiscation** *n*
conflict ⊕ *n* 1 struggle. 2 disagreement. ♦ *v* 3 be at odds with. 4 clash.
conform ⊕ *v* 1 comply with accepted standards etc. 2 adapt to

rule, pattern, custom etc.
conformist *n* **conformity** *n*
confound ⊕ *v* 1 perplex. 2 confuse. **confounded** *adj Inf* damned.
confront ⊕ *v* 1 face. 2 bring face to face with. **confrontation** *n*
confuse ⊕ *v* 1 bewilder. 2 jumble. 3 make unclear. 4 mistake. **confusion** *n*
conga *n* 1 dance by people in single file. 2 large drum.
congeal *v* solidify.
congenial *adj* pleasant.
congenital *adj* 1 existing at birth. 2 dating from birth.
conger *n* sea eel.
conglomerate *n* 1 substance composed of smaller elements. 2 business organization comprising many companies.
congratulate ⊕ *v* express pleasure at good fortune, success etc. **congratulations** *pl n*
congregate *v* 1 assemble. 2 flock

———— THESAURUS ————

confirm, concede
confide *v* = **tell**, admit, reveal, confess, whisper
confine *v* = **imprison**, enclose, shut up, intern, incarcerate; = **restrict**, limit
confirm *v* = **prove**, support, establish, back up, verify; = **ratify**, establish, sanction, endorse, authorize
confiscate *v* = **seize**, appropriate, impound, commandeer, sequester ≠ **give back**
conflict *n* = **dispute**, difference, opposition, hostility, disagreement

≠ **agreement**; = **struggle**, battle, clash, strife ♦ *v* = **be incompatible**, clash, differ, disagree, collide ≠ **agree**
conform *v* = **fit in**, follow, adjust, adapt, comply; = **fulfil**, meet, match, suit, satisfy
confound *v* = **bewilder**, baffle, confuse, astound, perplex
confront *v* = **tackle**, deal with, cope with, meet head–on
confuse *v* = **mix up with**, take for, muddle with; = **bewilder**, puzzle, baffle, perplex, mystify
congratulate *v* = **compliment**, pat

together. **congregation** n
assembly, esp. for worship.
congress 🛈 n 1 formal assembly.
2 legislative body.
conifer n cone-bearing tree.
coniferous adj
conjecture n/v guess. **conjectural**
adj
conjugal adj of marriage.
conjugate v Grammar inflect verb
in its various forms. **conjugation** n
conjunction n 1 union. 2
simultaneous happening. 3 part of
speech joining words, phrases etc.
conjunctive adj
conjunctivitis n inflammation of
membrane of eye.
conjure 🛈 v 1 produce magic
effects. 2 perform tricks. **conjuror,
-er** n
conker n Inf horse chestnut.
connect 🛈 v 1 join together,
unite. 2 associate in the mind.
connection, connexion n 1

association. 2 connecting thing. 3
relation.
connive v conspire.
connoisseur n expert in fine arts.
conquer 🛈 v 1 overcome. 2
defeat. 3 be victorious. **conqueror**
n **conquest** n
conscience 🛈 n sense of right or
wrong. **conscientious** adj
conscious 🛈 adj 1 aware. 2
awake. 3 intentional.
consciousness n
conscript n one compulsorily
enlisted for military service. ♦ v 2
enlist thus. **conscription** n
consecrate v make sacred.
consecration n
consecutive 🛈 adj in unbroken
succession. **consecutively** adv
consensus 🛈 n widespread
agreement.
consent 🛈 v 1 agree to. ♦ n 2
permission. 3 agreement.
consequence 🛈 n 1 result,

———— THESAURUS ————

on the back, wish joy to
congress n = **meeting**, council,
conference, assembly, convention
conjure v = **produce**, generate,
bring about, give rise to, make
connect v = **link**, join, couple,
attach, fasten ≠ **separate**
conquer v = **seize**, obtain,
acquire, occupy, overrun;
= **defeat**, overcome, overthrow,
beat, master ≠ **lose to**
conscience n = **principles**,
scruples, moral sense, sense of
right and wrong, still small voice
conscious adj (often with **of**)
= **aware of**, alert to, responsive to,

sensible of ≠ **unaware**;
= **deliberate**, knowing, studied,
calculated, self-conscious
≠ **unintentional**; = **awake**, wide-
awake, sentient, alive ≠ **asleep**
consecutive adj = **successive**,
running, succeeding, in turn,
uninterrupted
consensus n = **agreement**,
general agreement, unanimity,
common consent, unity
consent n = **agreement**, sanction,
approval, go-ahead (Inf),
permission ≠ **refusal** ♦ v = **agree**,
approve, permit, concur, assent
≠ **refuse**

outcome. **2** importance.
consequent *adj* **consequential** *adj* important. **consequently** *adv* therefore.
conserve 🛈 *v* **1** keep from change etc. **2** preserve. ♦ *n* **3** jam.
conservation *n* protection of environment. **conservationist** *n*
conservative *adj/n* **1** (person) tending to avoid change. **2** moderate (person). **conservatory** *n* greenhouse.
consider 🛈 *v* **1** think over. **2** examine. **3** make allowance for. **4** be of opinion that. **considerable** *adj* **1** important. **2** large.
considerably *adv* **considerate** *adj* thoughtful towards others.
consideration *n* **1** act of considering. **2** recompense.
considering *prep* taking into account.
consign *v* **1** hand over. **2** entrust.
consignment *n* goods consigned.
consignor *n*
consist *v* be composed of.
consistency *n* **1** agreement. **2**

degree of firmness. **consistent** *adj*
consistently *adv*
console[1] 🛈 *v* comfort, cheer in distress. **consolation** *n*
console[2] *n* **1** bracket. **2** keyboard etc. of organ. **3** cabinet for television, radio etc.
consolidate 🛈 *v* **1** combine. **2** make firm. **consolidation** *n*
consommé *n* clear meat soup.
consonant *n* **1** sound, letter other than a vowel. ♦ *adj* **2** agreeing with, in accord. **consonance** *n*
consort *v* **1** associate. ♦ *n* **2** husband, wife, esp. of ruler.
consortium *n* association of banks, companies etc.
conspicuous 🛈 *adj* noticeable.
conspire 🛈 *v* plot together.
conspiracy *n* **conspirator** *n*
constable *n* policeman.
constabulary *n, pl* **-laries** police force.
constant 🛈 *adj* **1** unchanging. **2** steadfast. **3** continual. ♦ *n* **4** quantity that does not vary.
constancy *n* loyalty. **constantly** *adv*

———— THESAURUS ————

consequence *n* = **result**, effect, outcome, repercussion, issue; = **importance**, concern, moment, value, account
conserve *v* = **save**, husband, take care of, hoard, store up ≠ **waste**
consider *v* = **think**, see, believe, rate, judge; = **think about**, reflect on, weigh, contemplate, deliberate; = **bear in mind**, remember, respect, think about, take into account
console[1] *v* = **comfort**, cheer,

soothe, support, encourage
≠ **distress**
consolidate *v* = **strengthen**, secure, reinforce, fortify, stabilize; = **combine**, unite, join, merge, unify
conspicuous *adj* = **obvious**, clear, patent, evident, noticeable
≠ **inconspicuous**
conspire *v* = **plot**, scheme, intrigue, manoeuvre, contrive; = **work together**, combine, contribute, cooperate, concur

constellation n group of stars.
consternation n alarm, dismay.
constipation n difficulty in
emptying bowels. **constipated** adj
constituent ⓘ adj 1 making up
whole. ♦ n 2 component part. 3
elector. **constituency** n, pl –cies 1
body of electors. 2 parliamentary
division.
constitute ⓘ v 1 form. 2 found.
constitution n 1 composition. 2
health. 3 principles on which state
is governed. **constitutional** adj 1
inborn. 2 statutory. ♦ n 3 walk for
good of health.
constrain ⓘ v force. **constraint** n 1
compulsion. 2 restriction.
construct ⓘ v 1 build. 2 put
together. **construction** n
constructive adj positive.
construe v –struing, –strued

interpret.
consul n government
representative in a foreign
country. **consulate** n consul's
office.
consult ⓘ v seek advice,
information from. **consultancy** n, pl
–cies. **consultant** n specialist,
expert. **consultation** n **consultative**
adj
consume ⓘ v 1 eat or drink. 2
engross. 3 use up. 4 destroy.
consumer n **consumption** n
consummate v/adj 1 perfect. 2
complete. **consummation** n
cont. continued.
contact ⓘ n 1 touching. 2 being
in touch. 3 useful acquaintance. ♦
v 4 get in touch with. **contact lens**
lens fitting over the eyeball.
contain ⓘ v 1 hold. 2 have room

——————— THESAURUS ———————

constant adj = **continuous**,
sustained, perpetual, interminable,
unrelenting ≠ **occasional**;
= **unchanging**, even, fixed,
permanent, stable ≠ **changing**;
= **faithful**, true, devoted, loyal,
stalwart ≠ **undependable**
constituent n = **voter**, elector,
member of the electorate;
= **component**, element,
ingredient, part, unit ♦ adj
= **component**, basic, essential,
integral, elemental
constitute v = **represent**, be,
consist of, embody, exemplify
constrain v = **restrict**, confine,
curb, restrain, constrict; = **force**,
bind, compel, oblige, necessitate
construct v = **build**, make, form,

create, fashion ≠ **demolish**
consult v = **ask**, refer to, turn to,
take counsel, pick (someone's)
brains
consume v = **eat**, swallow,
devour, put away, gobble (up);
= **use up**, spend, waste, absorb,
exhaust; = **destroy**, devastate,
demolish, ravage, annihilate;
= **obsess**, dominate, absorb,
preoccupy, eat up
contact n = **communication**, link,
association, connection,
correspondence; = **touch**,
contiguity; = **connection**,
colleague, associate, liaison,
acquaintance ♦ v = **get** or **be in**
touch with, call, reach, approach,
write to

for. **3** comprise. **4** restrain.
container *n*
contaminate ⊕ *v* pollute.
contamination *n*
contemplate ⊕ *v* **1** meditate on.
2 gaze upon. **3** intend.
contemplation *n*
contemporary ⊕ *adj* **1** existing at
same time. **2** modern. ◆ *n* **3** one
of same age. **contemporaneous**
adj
contempt ⊕ *n* **1** scorn, disgrace.
2 wilful disrespect of authority.
contemptible *adj* **contemptuous**
adj showing contempt.
contend ⊕ *v* **1** strive, dispute. **2**
maintain (that). **contender** *n*
competitor. **contention** *n*
contentious *adj*
content[1] ⊕ *adj* **1** satisfied. **2**

willing (to). ◆ *v* **3** satisfy. ◆ *n* **4**
satisfaction. **contented** *adj*
contentment *n*
content[2] ⊕ *n* **1** thing contained. ◆
pl **2** index of topics.
contest ⊕ *n* **1** competition. ◆ *v* **2**
dispute. **3** compete for.
contestant *n*
context ⊕ *n* words coming before
and after a word or passage.
continent[1] *n* large continuous
mass of land. **continental** *adj*
continent[2] *adj* in control of bodily
functions.
contingent *adj* **1** depending (on).
◆ *n* **2** group part of larger group.
contingency *n*, *pl* **-cies**
continue ⊕ *v* **-tinuing, -tinued 1**
remain. **2** carry on. **3** resume. **4**
prolong. **continual** *adj* **continually**

——— THESAURUS ———

contain *v* = **hold**, incorporate,
accommodate, enclose, have
capacity for; = **include**, consist of,
embrace, comprise, embody;
= **restrain**, control, hold in, curb,
suppress
contaminate *v* = **pollute**, infect,
stain, corrupt, taint ≠ **purify**
contemplate *v* = **consider**, plan,
think of, intend, envisage; = **think
about**, consider, ponder, reflect
upon, ruminate (upon); = **look at**,
examine, inspect, gaze at, eye up
contemporary *adj* = **modern**,
recent, current, up–to–date,
present–day ≠ **old–fashioned**;
= **coexisting**, concurrent,
contemporaneous ◆ *n* = **peer**,
fellow, equal
contempt *n* = **scorn**, disdain,

mockery, derision, disrespect
≠ **respect**
contend *v* = **argue**, hold,
maintain, allege, assert;
= **compete**, fight, struggle, clash,
contest
content[1] *adj* = **satisfied**, happy,
pleased, contented, comfortable
content[2] *n* = **subject matter**,
material, theme, substance,
essence; = **amount**, measure, size,
load, volume
contest *n* = **competition**, game,
match, trial, tournament ◆ *v*
= **compete in**, take part in, fight
in, go in for, contend for;
= **oppose**, question, challenge,
argue, debate
context *n* = **circumstances**,
conditions, situation, ambience

adv **continuation** *n* **continuity** *n, pl*
logical sequence. **continuous** *adj*
contort *v* twist out of normal
shape. **contortion** *n*
contour *n* outline, shape, esp.
mountains, coast etc.
contra– *comb. form* against.
contraband *n/adj* smuggled
(goods).
contraception *n* prevention of
conception. **contraceptive** *adj/n*
contract ⊕ *v* **1** make or become
smaller. **2** enter into agreement. **3**
incur. ◆ *n* **4** agreement.
contraction *n* **contractor** *n* one
making contract, esp. builder.
contractual *adj*
contradict ⊕ *v* **1** deny. **2** be
inconsistent with. **contradiction** *n*
contradictory *adj*
contraflow *n* flow of traffic in
opposite direction.

contralto *n, pl* **–tos** lowest female
voice.
contraption *n* **1** gadget. **2** device.
contrary ⊕ *adj* **1** opposed. **2**
perverse. ◆ *n* **3** the exact opposite.
◆ *adv* **4** in opposition.
contrast ⊕ *v* **1** bring out, show
difference. ◆ *n* **2** striking
difference.
contravene *v* infringe.
contribute ⊕ *v* **1** give, pay to
common fund. **2** help to occur. **3**
write for the press. **contribution** *n*
contributor *n*
contrite *adj* remorseful.
contrition *n*
contrive ⊕ *v* **1** arrange. **2** devise,
invent. **contrivance** *n*
control ⊕ *v* **1** command. **2**
regulate. **3** direct, check. ◆ *n* **4**
power to direct or determine. **5**
curb, check. ◆ *pl* **6** instruments to

———————— THESAURUS ————————

continue *v* = **keep on**, go on,
maintain, sustain, carry on ≠ **stop**;
= **go on**, progress, proceed, carry
on, keep going; = **resume**, return
to, take up again, proceed, carry
on ≠ **stop**
contract *n* = **agreement**,
commitment, arrangement,
settlement, bargain ◆ *v* = **agree**,
negotiate, pledge, bargain,
undertake ≠ **refuse**; = **constrict**,
confine, tighten, shorten,
compress; = **tighten**, narrow,
shorten ≠ **stretch**
contradict *v* = **deny**, challenge,
belie, fly in the face of, be at
variance with; = **deny**, negate,
rebut, controvert ≠ **confirm**

contrary *adj* = **opposite**, different,
opposed, clashing, counter ≠ **in
agreement**; = **perverse**, difficult,
awkward, intractable, obstinate
≠ **cooperative** ◆ *n* = **opposite**,
reverse, converse, antithesis
contrast *n* = **difference**,
opposition, comparison,
distinction, foil ◆ *v* = **differentiate**,
compare, oppose, distinguish, set
in opposition; = **differ**, be
contrary, be at variance, be
dissimilar
contribute *v* = **give**, provide,
supply, donate, subscribe
contrive *v* = **devise**, plan,
fabricate, create, design;
= **manage**, succeed, arrange,

control car, aircraft etc.

controller n

controversy ❶ n, pl **–sies** debate.
controversial adj

contusion n bruise.

conundrum n riddle.

conurbation n large built–up
area.

convalesce v recover health after
illness, operation etc.

convalescence n **convalescent**
adj/n

convection n transmission of heat
by currents.

convene ❶ v call together,
assemble. **convenor, –er** n

convention n 1 assembly. 2 treaty.
3 accepted usage. **conventional**
adj 1 (slavishly) observing customs
of society. 2 customary. 3 (of
weapons, war etc.) not nuclear.

convenient ❶ adj 1 handy. 2
favourable to needs, comfort.

convenience n 1 ease, comfort,

suitability. 2 public toilet. ◆ adj 3
(of food) quick to prepare.
conveniently adv

convent n religious community,
esp. of nuns.

convention ❶ see CONVENE.

converge ❶ v tend to meet.

conversant adj familiar (with),
versed in.

converse[1] v 1 talk (with). ◆ n 2
talk. **conversation** n **conversational**
adj

converse[2] adj 1 opposite,
reversed. ◆ n 2 the opposite.
conversely adv

convert ❶ v 1 apply to another
purpose. 2 change. 3 transform. 4
cause to adopt (another) religion,
opinion. ◆ n 5 converted person.
conversion n **convertible** n 1 car
with folding roof. ◆ adj 2 capable
of being converted.

convex adj curved outwards.

convey ❶ v 1 transport. 2 impart.

————————— THESAURUS —————————

manoeuvre

control n = **power**, authority,
management, command,
guidance; = **restraint**, check,
regulation, brake, limitation ◆ v
= **have power over**, manage,
direct, handle, command; = **limit**,
restrict, curb

controversy n = **argument**,
debate, row, dispute, quarrel

convene v = **call**, gather,
assemble, summon, bring
together

convenient adj = **suitable**, fit,
handy, satisfactory; = **useful**,
practical, handy, serviceable,

labour–saving ≠ **useless**; = **nearby**,
available, accessible, handy, at
hand ≠ **inaccessible**

convention n = **custom**, practice,
tradition, code, usage;
= **agreement**, contract, treaty,
bargain, pact; = **assembly**,
meeting, council, conference,
congress

converge v = **come together**,
meet, join, combine, gather

convert v = **change**, turn,
transform, alter, transpose;
= **adapt**, modify, remodel,
reorganize, customize ◆ n
= **neophyte**, disciple, proselyte

3 *Law* transfer. **conveyance** *n*
conveyancer *n* one skilled in legal
forms of transferring property.
conveyancing *n* **conveyor belt**
continuous moving belt.
convict ⊕ *v* 1 prove or declare
guilty. ◆ *n* 2 criminal serving
prison sentence. **conviction** *n* 1
verdict of guilty. 2 being
convinced, firm belief.
convince ⊕ *v* persuade by
evidence or argument. **convincing**
adj
convivial *adj* sociable.
convoluted *adj* 1 involved. 2
coiled. **convolution** *n*
convoy *n* 1 party (of ships etc.)
travelling together for protection.
◆ *v* 2 escort.
convulse *v* 1 shake violently. 2
affect with spasms. **convulsion** *n*
coo *n* cooing, cooed, *v* (make) cry
of doves.
cook *v* 1 prepare food, esp. by
heat. 2 undergo cooking. ◆ *n* 3
one who prepares food. **cooker** *n*
apparatus for cooking. **cookery** *n*
cookie *n* US biscuit.
cool ⊕ *adj* 1 moderately cold. 2

calm. 3 lacking friendliness. ◆ *v* 4
make, become cool. **coolly** *adv*
coop[1] *n/v* (shut up in) cage.
coop[2], **co-op** *n* cooperative
society or shop run by one.
cooperate ⊕ *v* work together.
cooperation *n* **cooperative** *adj* 1
willing to cooperate. 2 (of an
enterprise) owned collectively. ◆ *n*
3 collectively owned enterprise.
coordinate *v* 1 bring into order,
harmony. ◆ *adj* 2 equal in degree,
status etc. **coordination** *n*
coordinator *n*
coot *n* small black water bird.
cop *n* Sl policeman.
cope ⊕ *v* 1 deal successfully
(with). 2 manage.
coping *n* sloping top course of
wall.
copious *adj* abundant.
copper[1] *n* 1 reddish–brown metal.
2 coin.
copper[2] *n* Inf policeman.
coppice, copse *n* small wood.
copulate *v* unite sexually.
copulation *n*
copy ⊕ *n*, *pl* **copies** 1 imitation. 2
single specimen of book. ◆ *v* 3

——————— THESAURUS ———————

convey *v* = **communicate**, impart,
reveal, relate, disclose; = **carry**,
transport, move, bring, bear
convict *v* = **find guilty**, sentence,
condemn, imprison, pronounce
guilty ◆ *n* = **prisoner**, criminal, lag
(*Sl*), felon, jailbird
convince *v* = **assure**, persuade,
satisfy, reassure
cool *adj* = **cold**, chilled, refreshing,
chilly, nippy ≠ **warm**; = **calm**,

collected, relaxed, composed,
sedate ≠ **agitated**; = **unfriendly**,
distant, indifferent, aloof,
lukewarm ≠ **friendly**; ◆ *v* = **lose
heat**, cool off ≠ **warm (up)** ◆ *n*
= **coldness**, chill, coolness
cooperate *v* = **work together**,
collaborate, coordinate, join
forces, conspire ≠ **conflict**
≠ **oppose**
cope *v* = **manage**, get by (*Inf*),

make copy of, imitate. **copyright** n
1 legal exclusive right to print and
publish book, work of art etc. ♦ v
2 protect by copyright.

coquette n flirt.

coracle n small round boat.

coral n hard substance made by
sea polyps.

cord ⊕ n **1** thin rope or thick
string. **2** ribbed fabric.

cordial adj **1** sincere, warm. ♦ n **2**
fruit–flavoured drink.

cordon ⊕ n **1** chain of troops or
police. ♦ v **2** form barrier round.
cordon bleu (of cookery) of the
highest standard.

corduroy n cotton fabric with
velvety, ribbed surface.

core ⊕ n **1** seed case of apple. **2**
innermost part. ♦ v **3** take out
core.

corgi n small Welsh dog.

coriander n herb.

cork n **1** bark of an evergreen
Mediterranean oak tree. **2** stopper
for bottle etc. ♦ v **3** stop up with
cork. **corkscrew** n tool for pulling
out corks.

corm n underground stem like a
bulb.

cormorant n large voracious sea
bird.

corn[1] n grain, fruit of cereals.
corny adj Inf trite, oversentimental.
corned beef beef preserved in salt.

cornflakes pl n breakfast cereal.

cornflour n finely ground maize.

cornflower n blue flower growing
in cornfields.

corn[2] n horny growth on foot.

cornea n, pl **–neas**, **–neae**
transparent membrane covering
front of eye.

corner ⊕ n **1** part where two sides
meet. **2** remote or humble place. **3**
Business monopoly. ♦ v **4** drive into
position of no escape. **5** establish
monopoly. **6** move round corner.
cornerstone n indispensable part.

cornet n **1** trumpet with valves. **2**
cone–shaped ice cream wafer.

cornice n moulding below ceiling.

cornucopia n horn overflowing
with fruit and flowers.

corollary n, pl **–laries 1** inference
from a preceding statement. **2**
deduction.

coronary adj **1** of blood vessels
surrounding heart. ♦ n **2** coronary
thrombosis. **coronary thrombosis**
disease of the heart.

coronation n ceremony of
crowning a sovereign.

coroner n officer who holds

——————— THESAURUS ———————

struggle through, survive, carry on

copy n = **reproduction**, duplicate,
replica, imitation, forgery
≠ original ♦ v = **reproduce**,
replicate, duplicate, transcribe,
counterfeit **≠ create**; = **imitate**, act
like, emulate, behave like, follow

cord n = **rope**, line, string, twine

cordon n = **chain**, line, ring,
barrier, picket line

core n = **heart**, essence, nucleus,
kernel, crux

corner n = **angle**, joint, crook;
= **bend**, curve ♦ v = **trap**, catch,
run to earth; = **monopolize**, take
over, dominate, control, hog (Sl)

inquests on unnatural deaths.
coronet n small crown.
corporal¹ adj of the body.
corporal² n noncommissioned
officer below sergeant.
corporation ⊕ n body of persons
legally authorized to act as an
individual. **corporate** adj
corps ⊕ n, pl **corps 1** military
force. **2** any organized body of
persons.
corpse ⊕ n dead body.
corpulent adj fat. **corpulence** n
corpus n, pl **corpora** main part or
body of something.
corpuscle n minute particle, esp.
of blood.
corral n US enclosure for cattle.
correct ⊕ v 1 set right. **2** indicate
errors in. **3** punish. ♦ adj **4** right,
accurate. **correctly** adv **correction**
n **corrective** n/adj
correlate v bring into reciprocal
relation. **correlation** n
correspond ⊕ v 1 be similar (to).

2 exchange letters.
correspondence n **correspondent**
n **1** writer of letters. **2** one
employed by newspaper etc. to
report on particular topic.
corridor ⊕ n passage.
corroborate v confirm.
corroboree n Aust Aboriginal
gathering or dance.
corrode v eat into. **corrosion** n
corrosive adj
corrupt ⊕ adj **1** lacking integrity.
2 involving bribery. **3** wicked. ♦ v
4 make evil. **5** bribe. **6** make
rotten. **corruption** n
corsage n (flower worn on)
bodice of woman's dress.
corset n close-fitting
undergarment to support the
body.
cortege n formal (funeral)
procession.
cortex n, pl **–tices** outer layer of
brain etc.
cortisone n synthetic hormone

———— THESAURUS ————

corporation n = **business**,
company, concern, firm, society;
= **town council**, council, municipal
authorities, civic authorities
corps n = **team**, unit, regiment,
detachment, company
corpse n = **body**, remains,
carcass, cadaver, stiff (Sl)
correct adj = **accurate**, right, true,
exact, precise ≠ **inaccurate**;
= **right**, standard, appropriate,
acceptable, proper ♦ v = **rectify**,
remedy, redress, right, reform
≠ **spoil**; = **rebuke**, discipline,
reprimand, chide, admonish

≠ **praise**
correspond v = **be consistent**,
match, agree, accord, fit ≠ **differ**;
= **communicate**, write, keep in
touch, exchange letters
corridor n = **passage**, alley, aisle,
hallway, passageway
corrupt adj bent (Sl), crooked
(Inf), fraudulent, unscrupulous
≠ **honest**; = **depraved**, vicious,
degenerate, debased, profligate;
= **distorted**, doctored, altered,
falsified ♦ v = **bribe**, fix (Inf), buy
off, suborn, grease (someone's)
palm (Sl); = **deprave**, pervert,

used medically.

cosh n 1 blunt weapon. ♦ v 2 strike with one.

cosine n in a right-angled triangle, ratio of adjacent side to hypotenuse.

cosmetic 🛈 n/adj (preparation) to improve appearance only.

cosmic 🛈 adj 1 relating to the universe. 2 vast.

cosmopolitan 🛈 adj/n (person) familiar with many countries.

cosmos n the universe considered as an ordered system.

cosset v cosseting, cosseted pamper, pet.

cost 🛈 n 1 price. 2 expenditure of time, labour etc. 3 damage. ♦ v 4 have as price. 5 entail payment, or loss of. **costly** adj 1 valuable. 2 expensive.

costume 🛈 n style of dress of particular place or time.

cosy 🛈 adj –sier, –siest snug, comfortable.

cot n child's bed.

cote n shelter for animals or birds.

coterie n social clique.

cottage 🛈 n small house. **cottage cheese** mild, soft cheese. **cottage pie** dish of minced meat and potato.

cotton n 1 plant with white downy fibres. 2 cloth of this.

couch n 1 piece of furniture for reclining on. ♦ v 2 put into (words).

cougar n puma.

cough 🛈 v 1 expel air from lungs with sudden effort and noise. ♦ n 2 act of coughing.

could past tense of CAN¹.

coulomb n unit of electric charge.

council 🛈 n 1 deliberative or administrative body. 2 local governing authority of town etc. **councillor** n

counsel 🛈 n 1 advice. 2 barrister(s). ♦ v 3 advise, recommend. **counsellor** n

———— THESAURUS ————

subvert, debauch ≠ **reform**

cosmetic adj = **superficial**, surface, nonessential

cosmic adj = **extraterrestrial**, stellar

cosmopolitan adj = **sophisticated**, cultured, refined, cultivated, urbane ≠ **unsophisticated**

cost n = **price**, worth, expense, charge, damage (Inf) ♦ v = **sell at**, come to, set (someone) back (Inf), be priced at, command a price of; = **lose**, deprive of, cheat of

costume n = **outfit**, dress,

clothing, uniform, ensemble

cosy adj = **comfortable**, homely, warm, intimate, snug; = **snug**, warm, comfortable, sheltered, comfy (Inf)

cottage n = **cabin**, lodge, hut, shack, chalet

cough v = **clear your throat**, bark, hack ♦ n = **frog** or **tickle in your throat**, bark, hack

council n = **committee**, governing body, board

counsel n = **advice**, information, warning, direction, suggestion; = **legal adviser**, lawyer, attorney,

count[1] **①** v **1** reckon, number. **2** consider to be. **3** be reckoned in. **4** depend (on). **5** be of importance. ◆ n **6** reckoning. **7** total number. **8** act of counting. **countless** adj too many to be counted. **countdown** n counting of the seconds before an event.

count[2] n nobleman. **countess** n noblewoman.

countenance n **1** face, its expression. ◆ v **2** support, approve.

counter[1] n horizontal surface in bank, shop etc., on which business is transacted.

counter[2] **①** adv **1** in opposite direction. **2** in direct contrast. ◆ v **3** oppose.

counter– comb. form reversed, opposite, rival, retaliatory, as in counterclaim, counterproductive.

counteract v neutralize.

counterattack v/n attack in response to attack.

counterbalance n **1** weight balancing another. ◆ v **2** act as balance.

counterfeit adj **1** sham, forged. ◆ n **2** imitation, forgery. ◆ v **3** imitate with intent to deceive. **4** forge.

counterfoil n part of cheque, receipt etc. kept as record.

countermand v cancel (previous order).

counterpane n bed covering.

counterpart **①** n something complementary to another.

counterpoint n melody added as accompaniment to given melody.

countersign v sign document already signed by another.

countersink v enlarge top of hole to take head of screw, bolt etc. below surface.

countertenor n male alto.

country **①** n, pl –**tries 1** region. **2** nation. **3** people of nation. **4** land of birth. **5** rural districts.

countryman n **countryside** n

county **①** n, pl –**ties** division of country.

coup **①** n **1** successful stroke. **2**

——————— THESAURUS ———————

solicitor, advocate ◆ v = **advise**, recommend, advocate, warn, urge

count[1] v often with **up** = **add (up)**, total, reckon (up), tot up, calculate; = **matter**, be important, carry weight, tell, rate; = **consider**, judge, regard, deem, think of; = **include**, number among, take into account or consideration ◆ n = **calculation**, poll, reckoning, sum, tally

counter[2] v = **oppose**, meet, block, resist, parry ◆ adv = **opposite to**,

against, versus, conversely, in defiance of ≠ **in accordance with**

counterpart n = **opposite number**, equal, twin, equivalent, match

country n = **nation**, state, land, commonwealth, kingdom; = **people**, community, nation, society, citizens; = **countryside**, provinces, sticks (Inf), farmland, outback (Aust & NZ) ≠ **town**; = **territory**, land, region, terrain

county n = **province**, district, shire

sudden, violent seizure of government.

coup de grace *Fr* decisive action.

coupé *n* sporty style of motorcar.

couple ① *n* **1** two, pair. **2** husband and wife. ◆ *v* **3** connect, fasten together. **4** join, associate. **couplet** *n* two lines of verse. **coupling** *n* connecting device.

coupon ① *n* ticket entitling holder to discount, gift etc.

courage ① *n* bravery, boldness. **courageous** *adj* **courageously** *adv*

courgette *n* type of small vegetable marrow.

courier ① *n* **1** messenger. **2** person who guides travellers.

course ① *n* **1** movement in space or time. **2** direction. **3** sequence. **4** line of action. **5** series of lectures etc. **6** any of successive parts of meal. **7** area where golf is played.

8 racetrack. ◆ *v* **9** hunt. **10** run swiftly. **11** (of blood) circulate.

court ① *n* **1** space enclosed by buildings, yard. **2** area for playing various games. **3** royal household. **4** body with judicial powers, place where it meets, one of its sittings. ◆ *v* **5** woo. **6** seek, invite. **courtier** *n* one who frequents royal court. **courtly** *adj* **1** ceremonially polite. **2** characteristic of a court. **court card** king, queen or jack at cards. **court martial** *pl* **courts martial** court for trying naval or military offences. **courtship** *n* wooing. **courtyard** *n* enclosed paved area.

courtesy ① *n* politeness. **courteous** *adj*

cousin *n* son or daughter of uncle or aunt.

cove ① *n* small inlet of coast. **coven** *n* gathering of witches.

—— THESAURUS ——

coup *n* = **masterstroke**, feat, stunt, action, exploit

couple *n* = **pair**, two, brace, duo, twosome

coupon *n* = **slip**, ticket, certificate, token, voucher

courage *n* = **bravery**, nerve, resolution, daring, pluck ≠ **cowardice**

courier *n* = **messenger**, runner, carrier, bearer, envoy; = **guide**, representative, escort, conductor

course *n* = **route**, way, line, road, track; = **procedure**, plan, policy, programme, method;

= **progression**, order, unfolding, development, movement;

= **classes**, programme, schedule,

lectures, curriculum; = **racecourse**, circuit, cinder track; = **period**, time, duration, term, passing ◆ *v* = **run**, flow, stream, gush, race; = **hunt**, follow, chase, pursue

court *n* = **law court**, bar, bench, tribunal; = **palace**, hall, castle, manor; = **royal household**, train, suite, attendants, entourage ◆ *v* = **cultivate**, seek, flatter, solicit, pander to; = **invite**, seek, attract, prompt, provoke; = **woo**, go (out) with, date, take out, run after

courtesy *n* = **politeness**, good manners, civility, gallantry, graciousness; = **favour**, kindness, indulgence

cove *n* = **bay**, sound, inlet,

covenant ⊕ *n* 1 agreement. 2 compact. ◆ *v* 3 agree to a covenant.

cover ⊕ *v* 1 place over. 2 extend, spread. 3 bring upon (oneself). 4 protect. 5 travel over. 6 include. 7 be sufficient. 8 report. ◆ *n* 9 covering thing. 10 shelter. 11 insurance. **coverage** *n* **coverlet** *n* top covering of bed.

covert *adj* secret, sly.

covet ⊕ *v* **coveting, coveted** long to possess, esp. what belongs to another. **covetous** *adj*

cow¹ *n* female of bovine and other animals. **cowboy** *n* 1 ranch worker who herds cattle. 2 *Inf* irresponsible worker.

cow² *v* frighten, overawe.

coward ⊕ *n* one who lacks courage. **cowardice** *n* **cowardly** *adj*

cower *v* crouch in fear.

cowl *n* 1 monk's hooded cloak. 2 hooded top for chimney.

cowslip *n* wild primrose.

coxswain *n* steersman of boat.

coy *adj* (pretending to be) shy, modest. **coyly** *adv*

coyote *n* prairie wolf.

coypu *n* aquatic rodent.

crab *n* edible crustacean. **crabbed** *adj* (of handwriting) hard to read. **crabby** *adj* bad-tempered.

crab apple wild sour apple.

crack ⊕ *v* 1 split partially. 2 break with sharp noise. 3 break down, yield. 4 *Inf* tell (joke). 5 solve, decipher. 6 make sharp noise. ◆ *n* 7 sharp explosive noise. 8 split. 9 flaw. 10 *Inf* joke. 11 chat. 12 *Sl* highly addictive form of cocaine. ◆ *adj* 13 *Inf* very skilful. **cracker** *n* 1 decorated paper tube, pulled apart with a bang, containing toy etc. 2 explosive firework. 3 thin dry biscuit. **crackers** *adj Sl* crazy. **cracking** *adj* very good. **crackle** *n/v* (make) sound of repeated small cracks. **crackpot** *n Inf* eccentric person.

————— THESAURUS —————

anchorage

covenant *n* = **promise**, contract, agreement, commitment, arrangement

cover *v* = **conceal**, hide, mask, disguise, obscure ≠ **reveal**; = **clothe**, dress, wrap, envelop ≠ **uncover**; = **overlay**, blanket; = **coat**, cake, plaster, smear, envelop ◆ *n* = **protection**, shelter, shield, defence, guard; = **insurance**, protection, compensation, indemnity, reimbursement; = **covering**, case, top, coating, envelope;

= **bedclothes**, bedding, sheets, blankets, quilt

covet *v* = **long for**, desire, envy, crave, aspire to

coward *n* = **wimp**, chicken (*Sl*), scaredy-cat (*Inf*), yellow-belly (*Sl*)

crack *v* = **break**, split, burst, snap, fracture; = **snap**, ring, crash, burst, explode; = (*Inf*) **hit**, clip (*Inf*), smack, clout (*Inf*); = **break**, cleave; = **solve**, work out, resolve, clear up, fathom ◆ *n* = **break**, chink, gap, fracture, rift; = **split**, break, fracture; = **snap**, pop, crash, burst, explosion; = (*Inf*) **blow**, slap,

cradle ① *n* **1** infant's bed. ♦ *v* **2** hold or rock as in a cradle. **3** cherish.

craft ① *n* **1** skilled trade. **2** skill, ability. **3** cunning. **crafty** *adj* cunning, shrewd. **craftsman** *n* **craftsmanship** *n*

crag *n* steep rugged rock.

cram ① *v* **cramming, crammed 1** stuff. **2** prepare quickly for examination.

cramp¹ ① *n* painful muscular contraction.

cramp² ① *v* hinder.

cranberry *n* edible red berry.

crane *n* **1** wading bird with long legs. **2** machine for moving heavy weights. ♦ *v* **3** stretch neck. **crane fly** long-legged insect.

cranium *n, pl* **-niums, -nia** skull. **cranial** *adj*

crank *n* **1** arm at right angles to axis, for turning main shaft **2** *Inf*

eccentric person. ♦ *v* **3** start (engine) by turning crank. **cranky** *adj* eccentric.

cranny *n, pl* **-nies** small opening.

crash ① *v* **1** (cause to) make loud noise. **2** (cause to) fall with crash. **3** smash. **4** collapse. **5** cause (aircraft) to hit land or water. **6** collide with. **7** move noisily. ♦ *n* **8** loud, violent fall or impact. **9** collision. **10** uncontrolled descent of aircraft. **11** sudden collapse. **12** bankruptcy. **crash helmet** protective helmet.

crass *adj* grossly stupid.

crate ① *n* large (usu. wooden) container for packing goods.

crater ① *n* **1** mouth of volcano. **2** bowl-shaped cavity.

cravat *n* man's neckcloth.

crave ① *v* **1** have very strong desire for. **2** beg. **craving** *n* **craven** *adj* cowardly.

smack, clout (*Inf*), cuff ♦ *adj* = (*Sl*) **first-class**, choice, excellent, ace, elite

cradle *n* = crib, cot, Moses basket, bassinet; = **birthplace**, beginning, source, spring, origin ♦ *v* = **hold**, support, rock, nurse, nestle

craft *n* = **occupation**, work, business, trade, employment; = **skill**, art, ability, technique, know-how (*Inf*)

cram *v* = **stuff**, force, jam, shove, compress; = **pack**, fill, stuff

cramp¹ *n* = **spasm**, pain, ache, contraction, pang

cramp² *v* = **restrict**, hamper, inhibit, hinder, handicap

crash *n* = **collision**, accident, smash, wreck, prang (*Inf*); = **smash**, clash, boom, bang, thunder; = **collapse**, failure, depression, ruin, downfall ♦ *v* = **fall**, plunge, topple, lurch, hurtle; = **plunge**, hurtle; = **collapse**, fail, go under, be ruined, go bust (*Inf*)

crate *n* = **container**, case, box, packing case, tea chest

crater *n* = **hollow**, hole, depression, dip, cavity

crave *v* = **long for**, yearn for, hanker after, want, desire; = (*Inf*) **beg**, ask for, seek, petition, pray for

crawl ⊙ v 1 move on hands and knees. 2 move very slowly. 3 ingratiate oneself. 4 swim with crawl stroke. 5 be overrun (with). ◆ n 6 crawling motion. 7 racing stroke at swimming.

crayfish n edible freshwater crustacean.

crayon n stick or pencil of coloured wax etc.

craze ⊙ n 1 short-lived fashion. 2 strong desire. 3 madness. **crazed** adj crazy adj 1 insane. 2 very foolish. 3 madly eager (for).

creak n/v (make) grating noise.

cream ⊙ n 1 fatty part of milk. 2 food like this. 3 cosmetic like this. 4 yellowish-white colour. 5 best part. ◆ v 6 take cream from. 7 take best part from. 8 beat to creamy consistency. **creamy** adj

crease ⊙ n 1 line made by folding. 2 wrinkle. ◆ v 3 make, develop creases.

create ⊙ v 1 bring into being. 2 make 3 Inf make a fuss. **creation** n **creative** adj imaginative, inventive. **creativity** n **creator** n

creature ⊙ n living being.

crèche n day nursery for very young children.

credentials ⊙ pl n 1 testimonials. 2 letters of introduction.

credible ⊙ adj worthy of belief. **credibility** n

credit ⊙ n 1 commendation. 2 source of honour. 3 trust. 4 good name. 5 system of allowing customers to pay later. 6 money at one's disposal in bank etc. ◆ v 7 attribute, believe. 8 put on credit side of account. **creditable** adj bringing honour. **creditor** n one to whom debt is due.

——— THESAURUS ———

crawl v = **creep**, slither, inch, wriggle, writhe ≠ **destroy** **be crawling with something** = **be full of**, teem with, be alive with, swarm with, be overrun with (Sl)

craze n = **fad**, fashion, trend, rage, enthusiasm

cream n = **lotion**, ointment, oil, essence, cosmetic; = **best**, elite, prime, pick, flower ◆ adj = **off-white**, ivory, yellowish-white

crease n = **fold**, line, ridge, groove, corrugation ◆ v = **crumple**, rumple, fold, double up, corrugate

create v = **cause**, lead to, occasion, bring about; = **make**, produce, invent, compose, devise

≠ **destroy**

creature n = **living thing**, being, animal, beast, brute

credentials pl n = **qualifications**, ability, skill, fitness, attribute

credible adj = **believable**, possible, likely, reasonable, probable ≠ **unbelievable**; = **reliable**, honest, dependable, trustworthy, sincere ≠ **unreliable**

credit n = **praise**, honour, recognition, approval, tribute; = **source of satisfaction** or **pride**, asset, honour, feather in your cap; = **prestige**, reputation, standing, position, influence; = **belief**, trust, confidence, faith, reliance ◆ v = **believe**, rely on, have faith in,

credulous *adj* too easy of belief, gullible. credulity *n*

creed ❶ *n* statement of belief.

creek ❶ *n* narrow inlet on coast.

creep ❶ *v* creeping, crept 1 move slowly, stealthily. 2 crawl. 3 act in servile way. 4 (of flesh) feel shrinking sensation. ♦ *n* 5 creeping. 6 *Sl* repulsive person. ♦ *pl* 7 feeling of fear or repugnance. creeper *n* creeping or climbing plant. creepy *adj*

creole *n* language developed from mixture of languages.

creosote *n* oily liquid used for preserving wood.

crepe *n* fabric with crimped surface.

crescendo *n, pl* -dos *Mus* gradual increase of loudness.

crescent ❶ *n* (shape of) moon seen in first or last quarter.

cress *n* various plants with edible pungent leaves.

crest ❶ *n* 1 tuft on bird's or animal's head. 2 top of mountain, wave etc. 3 badge above shield of

coat of arms. crestfallen *adj* disheartened.

cretin *n* 1 person afflicted by retardation. 2 *Inf* stupid person. cretinous *adj*

crevasse *n* deep open chasm.

crevice *n* cleft, fissure.

crew ❶ *n* 1 ship's, aircraft's company 2 *Inf* gang.

crib *n* 1 child's cot. 2 rack for fodder. 3 plagiarism. ♦ *v* 4 copy dishonestly.

cribbage *n* card game.

crick *n* cramp esp. in neck.

cricket¹ *n* chirping insect.

cricket² *n* game played with bats, ball and wickets. cricketer *n*

crime ❶ *n* 1 violation of law. 2 wicked act. criminal *adj/n*

crimson *adj/n* (of) rich deep red.

cringe *v* 1 shrink, cower. 2 behave obsequiously.

crinkle *v/n* wrinkle.

crinoline *n* hooped petticoat or skirt.

cripple ❶ *n* 1 disabled person. ♦ *v* 2 disable.

——— THESAURUS ———

trust, accept

creed *n* = belief, principles, doctrine, dogma, credo

creek *n* = inlet, bay, cove, bight, firth *or* frith (*Scot*); = (*US, Canad, Aust & NZ*) stream, brook, tributary, bayou, rivulet

creep *v* = sneak, steal, tiptoe, slink, skulk ♦ *n* = (*Inf*) bootlicker (*Sl*) sneak, sycophant, crawler (*Sl*), toady

crescent *n* = meniscus, sickle, new moon

crest *n* = top, summit, peak, ridge, highest point; = tuft, crown, comb, plume, mane; = emblem, badge, symbol, insignia, bearings

crew *n* = (ship's) company, hands, (ship's) complement; = team, squad, gang, corps, posse; = (*Inf*) crowd, set, bunch (*Inf*), band, pack

crime *n* = offence, violation, trespass, felony, misdemeanour; = lawbreaking, corruption,

crisis ⊙ n, pl **-ses 1** turning point. **2** time of acute danger.

crisp ⊙ adj **1** brittle. **2** brisk. **3** clear-cut. **4** fresh. ♦ n **5** very thin, fried slice of potato. **crispy** adj

crispbread n thin dry biscuit.

crisscross v **1** go in crosswise pattern. ♦ adj **2** crossing in different directions.

criterion ⊙ n, pl **-ria** standard of judgment.

critic n **1** professional judge of any of the arts. **2** person who finds fault.

critical adj **1** fault-finding. **2** discerning. **3** skilled in judging.

croak v/n (utter) deep hoarse cry.

crochet n **-cheting, -cheted**, v (do) handicraft like knitting.

crock n earthenware pot.

crockery n earthenware dishes etc.

crocodile n large amphibious reptile.

crocus n, pl **-cuses** small bulbous plant.

croft n small farm.

croissant n crescent-shaped bread roll.

crone n witchlike old woman.

crony n, pl **-nies** intimate friend.

crook ⊙ n **1** hooked staff **2** Inf swindler, criminal. **crooked** adj **1** twisted. **2** deformed. **3** dishonest.

croon v sing in soft tone.

crop ⊙ n **1** produce of cultivated plants. **2** harvest. **3** pouch in bird's gullet. **4** whip. **5** short haircut. ♦ v **6** cut short. **7** produce crop. **8** (of animals) bite, eat down. **cropper** n **1** Inf heavy fall. **2** disastrous failure. **crop up** Inf happen unexpectedly.

croquet n lawn game played with balls and hoops.

croquette n fried ball of minced meat, fish etc.

cross ⊙ n **1** structure or symbol of two intersecting lines or pieces. **2** such a structure as means of execution. **3** symbol of Christian faith. **4** any thing in shape of cross. **5** affliction. **6** hybrid. ♦ v **7** move or go across (something). **8** intersect. **9** meet and pass. **10** mark with lines across. **11** delete. **12** place in form of cross. **13** make sign of cross. **14** breed by

———— THESAURUS ————

illegality, vice, misconduct
cripple v = **disable**, paralyse, lame, maim, incapacitate; = **damage**, destroy, ruin, spoil, impair ≠ **help**
crisis n = **emergency**, plight, predicament, trouble, deep water; = **critical point**, climax, height, crunch (Inf), turning point
crisp adj = **firm**, crunchy, crispy, crumbly, fresh ≠ **soft**; = **bracing**, fresh, refreshing, brisk,

invigorating ≠ **warm**; = **clean**, smart, trim, neat, tidy
criterion n = **standard**, test, rule, measure, principle
critic n = **judge**, authority, expert, analyst, commentator
crook n = (Inf) **criminal**, rogue, cheat, thief, shark
crop n = **yield**, produce, gathering, fruits, harvest ♦ v = **graze**, eat, browse, feed on, nibble; = **cut**, trim, clip, prune,

intermixture. **15** thwart. ◆ *adj* **16** angry. **17** transverse. **18** contrary. **crossing** *n* **1** intersection of roads, rails etc. **2** part of street where pedestrians are expected to cross. **cross-country** *adj/adv* by way of open fields. **cross-examine** *v* examine witness already examined by other side. **cross-examination** *n* **cross-eyed** *adj* having eyes turning inward. **cross-ply** *adj* (of tyre) having fabric cords in outer casing running diagonally. **cross-reference** *n* reference within text to another part of text. **crossroads** *n* **crossword puzzle** puzzle built up of intersecting words, indicated by clues. **The Cross** cross on which Jesus Christ was executed. **crosswalk** *n* Canad place marked where pedestrians may cross a road. **crotch** *n* angle between legs. **crotchet** *n* musical note.

crotchety *adj Inf* bad-tempered. **crouch** ❶ *v* **1** bend low. **2** huddle down close to ground. **3** stoop. **croupier** *n* person dealing cards, collecting money etc. at gambling table. **crouton** *n* piece of toasted bread served in soup. **crow**¹ *n* large black carrion-eating bird. **crow**² ❶ *v* **1** utter cock's cry. **2** boast. ◆ *n* **3** cock's cry. **crowbar** *n* iron bar. **crowd** ❶ *n* **1** throng, mass. ◆ *v* **2** flock together. **3** cram, pack. **4** fill with people. **crown** ❶ *n* **1** monarch's headdress. **2** royal power. **3** various coins. **4** top of head. **5** summit, top. **6** perfection of thing. ◆ *v* **7** put crown on. **8** occur as culmination **9** *Inf* hit on head. **crucial** ❶ *adj* **1** decisive, critical. **2** *Inf* very important. **crucially** *adv*

———— THESAURUS ————

shear

cross *v* = **go across**, pass over, traverse, cut across, move across; = **span**, bridge, go across, extend over; = **intersect**, intertwine, crisscross; = **oppose**, interfere with, obstruct, block, resist; = **interbreed**, mix, blend, cross-pollinate, crossbreed ◆ *n* = **trouble**, worry, trial, load, burden; = **mixture**, combination, blend, amalgam, amalgamation ◆ *adj* = **angry**, annoyed, put out, grumpy, short ≠ **good-humoured** **crouch** *v* = **bend down**, kneel, squat, stoop, bow

crow² *v* = **gloat**, triumph, boast, swagger, brag **crowd** *n* = **multitude**, mass, throng, army, host; = **group**, set, lot, circle, gang ◆ *v* = **flock**, mass, collect, gather, stream; = **squeeze**, pack, pile, bundle, cram **crown** *n* = **coronet**, tiara, diadem, circlet; = **laurel wreath**, trophy, prize, honour, garland; = **high point**, top, tip, summit, crest ◆ *v* = **top**, cap, be on top of, surmount; = **cap**, finish, complete, perfect, round off; = (*Sl*) **strike**, belt (*Inf*), bash, hit over the head, box

C

crucible *n* small melting pot.

crude 🛈 *adj* 1 vulgar. 2 in natural or raw state. 3 rough. **crudely** *adv* **crudity** *n*

cruel *adj* causing pain or suffering. **cruelly** *adv* **cruelty** *n*

cruet *n* small container for salt, pepper etc.

cruise 🛈 *v* 1 travel about in a ship. ◆ *n* 2 voyage. **cruiser** *n* 1 ship that cruises. 2 warship.

crumb 🛈 *n* fragment of bread.

crumble 🛈 *v* 1 break into small fragments. 2 collapse. **crumbly** *adj*

crumpet *n* 1 flat, soft cake eaten with butter. 2 *Sl* sexually desirable woman or women.

crumple 🛈 *v* 1 (cause to) collapse. 2 make or become creased.

crunch 🛈 *n* 1 sound made by chewing crisp food, treading on gravel etc. 2 *Inf* critical situation. ◆

v 3 make crunching sound. **crunchy** *adj*

crusade 🛈 *n* 1 medieval Christian war. 2 concerted action to further a cause. ◆ *v* 3 take part in crusade. **crusader** *n*

crush 🛈 *v* 1 compress so as to break. 2 break to small pieces. 3 defeat utterly. ◆ *n* 4 act of crushing. 5 crowd of people etc.

crust 🛈 *n* 1 hard outer part of bread. 2 similar casing. **crusty** *adj* 1 having crust. 2 bad-tempered.

crustacean *n* hard-shelled animal, e.g. crab, lobster.

crutch *n* 1 staff with crosspiece to go under armpit of lame person. 2 support. 3 crotch.

crux *n, pl* **cruxes** that on which a decision turns.

cry 🛈 *v* **crying, cried** 1 weep. 2 utter call. 3 shout. 4 beg (for). 5

—————— THESAURUS ——————

crucial *adj* = (*Inf*) **vital**, important, pressing, essential, urgent

crude *adj* = **rough**, basic, makeshift; = **simple**, rudimentary, basic, primitive, coarse; = **vulgar**, dirty, rude, obscene, coarse ≠ **tasteful**

cruel *adj* = **brutal**, ruthless, callous, sadistic, inhumane ≠ **kind**

cruise *n* = **sail**, voyage, boat trip, sea trip ◆ *v* = **sail**, coast, voyage; = **travel along**, coast, drift, keep a steady pace

crumb *n* = **bit**, grain, fragment, shred, morsel

crumble *v* = **disintegrate**, collapse, deteriorate, decay, fall apart; = **crush**, fragment,

pulverize, pound, grind

crumple *v* = **crush**, squash, screw up, scrumple; = **crease**, wrinkle, rumple, ruffle, pucker

crunch *v* = **chomp**, champ, munch, chew noisily, grind ◆ *n* = (*Inf*) **critical point**, test, crisis, emergency, crux

crusade *n* = **campaign**, drive, movement, cause, push

crush *v* = **squash**, break, squeeze, compress, press; = **overcome**, overwhelm, put down, subdue, overpower; = **demoralize**, depress, devastate, discourage, humble ◆ *n* = **crowd**, mob, horde, throng, pack

crust *n* = **layer**, covering, coating,

proclaim. ♦ n **6** loud utterance. **7** call of animal. **8** fit of weeping.

crypt n vault, esp. under church.

cryptic adj secret, mysterious.

crystal n **1** transparent mineral. **2** very clear glass. **3** cut-glass ware. **4** form with symmetrically arranged plane surfaces. **crystalline** adj **crystallize** v **1** form into crystals. **2** become definite.

cu. cubic.

cub ⊕ n **1** young of fox and other animals. **2** (with cap.) junior Scout.

cubbyhole n small enclosed space.

cube n **1** solid figure with six equal square sides. **2** cube-shaped block. **3** product obtained by multiplying number by itself twice. ♦ v **4** multiply thus. **cubic** adj

cubicle n enclosed section of room.

cuckoo n **1** migratory bird. **2** its call.

cucumber n long fleshy green fruit used in salad.

cud n food which ruminant animal brings back into mouth to chew again.

cuddle ⊕ v **1** hug. **2** lie close and snug, nestle. ♦ n **3** hug. **cuddly** adj

cudgel n **1** short thick stick. ♦ v **2** beat with cudgel.

cue¹ ⊕ n **1** signal to act or speak. **2** hint.

cue² n long tapering rod used in billiards.

cuff¹ n ending of sleeve.

cuff² v **1** strike with open hand. ♦ n **2** blow with hand.

cuisine n **1** style of cooking. **2** food cooked.

cul-de-sac n street open only at one end.

culinary adj of, for, suitable for, cooking or kitchen.

cull v **1** select. **2** take out animals from herd.

culminate ⊕ v **1** reach highest point. **2** come to a head. **culmination** n

culottes pl n women's trousers flared like skirt.

culpable adj blameworthy.

culprit ⊕ n one guilty of offence.

cult ⊕ n **1** system of worship. **2** devotion to some person, thing.

cultivate ⊕ v **1** till and prepare (ground). **2** develop, improve. **3** devote attention to. **cultivated** adj

——————— THESAURUS ———————

skin, surface

cry v = **weep**, sob, shed tears, blubber, snivel ≠ **laugh**; = **shout**, scream, roar, yell, howl ≠ **whisper** ♦ n = **weep**, sob, bawl, blubber; = **shout**, call, scream, roar, yell; = **appeal**, plea

cub n = **young**, baby, offspring, whelp

cuddle v = **hug**, embrace, fondle, cosset

cue¹ n = **signal**, sign, hint, prompt, reminder

culminate v = **end up**, close, finish, conclude, wind up

culprit n = **offender**, criminal, felon, guilty party, wrongdoer

cult n = **sect**, faction, school, religion, clique; = **craze**, fashion, trend, fad

cultured. **cultivation** n

culture ❶ n 1 state of manners, taste and intellectual development. 2 cultivating.

cultural adj **cultured** adj

culvert n drain under road.

cumbersome adj unwieldy.

cummerbund n sash worn round waist.

cumulative adj becoming greater by successive additions.

cumulus n, pl –li round billowing cloud.

cunning ❶ adj 1 crafty, sly. ◆ n 2 skill in deceit or evasion.

cup ❶ n 1 small drinking vessel with handle. 2 various cup-shaped formations. 3 cup-shaped trophy as prize. ◆ v 4 shape as cup (hands etc.). ◆ **cupful** n **cupboard** n piece of furniture with door, for storage.

cur n 1 dog of mixed breed. 2 contemptible person.

curate n parish priest's appointed assistant.

curator n custodian, esp. of museum.

curb ❶ n 1 check, restraint. ◆ v 2 restrain. 3 apply curb to.

curd n coagulated milk. **curdle** v turn into curd, coagulate.

cure ❶ v 1 heal, restore to health. 2 remedy. 3 preserve (fish, skins etc.). ◆ n 4 remedy. 5 course of medical treatment. 6 restoration to health. **curable** adj

curfew n 1 official regulation prohibiting movement of people, esp. at night. 2 deadline for this.

curio n, pl –rios rare or curious thing bought for collections.

curious ❶ adj 1 eager to know, inquisitive. 2 puzzling, odd. **curiosity** n **curiously** adv

curl ❶ v 1 take, bend into spiral or curved shape. ◆ n 2 spiral lock of hair. 3 spiral. **curly** adj

curlew n large long-billed wading bird.

curmudgeon n bad-tempered

———— THESAURUS ————

cultivate v = **farm**, work, plant, tend, till; = **develop**, establish, foster; = **court**, seek out, run after, dance attendance upon

culture n = **civilization**, society, customs, way of life; = **lifestyle**, habit, way of life, mores

cunning adj = **crafty**, sly, devious, artful, sharp ≠ **frank**; = **ingenious**, imaginative, sly, devious, artful; ◆ n = **craftiness**, guile, trickery, deviousness, artfulness ≠ **candour**; = **skill**, subtlety, ingenuity, artifice, cleverness ≠ **clumsiness**

cup n = **mug**, goblet, chalice,

teacup, beaker

curb v = **restrain**, control, check, restrict, suppress ◆ n = **restraint**, control, check, brake, limitation

cure v = **make better**, correct, heal, relieve, remedy; = **preserve**, smoke, dry, salt, pickle ◆ n = **remedy**, treatment, antidote, panacea, nostrum

curious adj = **inquisitive**, interested, questioning, searching, inquiring ≠ **uninterested**; = **strange**, unusual, bizarre, odd, novel

curl n = **ringlet**, lock ◆ v = **twirl**,

person.

currant n 1 dried type of grape. 2 fruit of various plants allied to gooseberry.

current ⊕ adj 1 of immediate present. 2 in general use. ♦ n 3 body of water or air in motion. 4 transmission of electricity.

currently adv **currency** n, pl –cies 1 money in use. 2 state of being in use.

curriculum n, pl –la, –lums specified course of study.

curriculum vitae outline of career.

curry n, pl –ries 1 highly-flavoured, pungent condiment. 2 dish flavoured with it. ♦ v 3 prepare, flavour dish with curry.

curse ⊕ n 1 profane or obscene expression of anger etc. 2 magic spell. 3 affliction. ♦ v 4 utter curse, swear (at). 5 afflict.

cursor n movable point showing position on computer screen.

cursory adj hasty, superficial.

curt adj rudely brief, abrupt.

curtail ⊕ v cut short.

curtain ⊕ n 1 hanging drapery at window etc. ♦ v 2 provide, cover with curtain.

curtsy, curtsey n, pl –sies, –seys, v (perform) woman's bow.

curve ⊕ n 1 line of which no part is straight. ♦ v 2 bend into curve.

cushion ⊕ n 1 bag filled with soft stuffing or air, to support or ease body. ♦ v 2 provide, protect with cushion. 3 lessen effects of.

cushy adj **cushier, cushiest** Inf easy.

custard n 1 dish made of eggs and milk. 2 sweet sauce of milk and cornflour.

custody ⊕ n guardianship, imprisonment. **custodian** n keeper, curator.

custom ⊕ n 1 habit. 2 practice. 3 usage. 4 business patronage. ♦ pl

——— THESAURUS ———

turn, bend, twist, curve

current n = **flow**, course, undertow, jet, stream; = **draught**, flow, breeze, puff ♦ adj = **present**, fashionable, up-to-date, contemporary, trendy (Brit inf) ≠ **out-of-date**; = **prevalent**, common, accepted, popular, widespread

curse v = **swear**, cuss (Inf), blaspheme, take the Lord's name in vain; = **abuse**, damn, scold, vilify ♦ n = **oath**, obscenity, blasphemy, expletive, profanity; = **malediction**, anathema, jinx, hoodoo (Inf), excommunication;

= **affliction**, plague, scourge, trouble, torment

curtail v = **reduce**, diminish, decrease, dock, cut back

curtain n = **hanging**, drape (Chiefly US), portière

curve n = **bend**, turn, loop, arc, curvature ♦ v = **bend**, turn, wind, twist, arch

cushion n = **pillow**, pad, bolster, headrest, beanbag ♦ v = **soften**, dampen, muffle, mitigate, deaden

custody n = **care**, charge, protection, supervision, safekeeping; = **imprisonment**, detention, confinement,

5 taxes levied on imports.
customary *adj* usual, habitual.
customer *n* **1** one who enters shop to buy, esp. regularly. **2** purchaser.
cut ⓣ *v* **cutting, cut 1** sever, wound, divide. **2** pare, detach, trim. **3** intersect. **4** reduce, decrease. **5** abridge. **6** *Inf* ignore (person). ♦ *n* **7** act of cutting. **8** stroke. **9** blow, wound. **10** reduction. **11** fashion, shape. **12** *Inf* share. **cutter** *n* **cutting** *n* **1** piece cut from plant. **2** article from newspaper. **3** passage for railway. ♦ *adj* **4** keen, piercing. **5** hurtful.
cutthroat *n* **1** killer. ♦ *adj* **2** murderous. **3** fiercely competitive.
cute ⓣ *adj* appealing, pretty.
cuticle *n* dead skin, esp. at base of fingernail.
cutlass *n* curved sword.
cutlery *n* knives, forks etc.
cutlet *n* small piece of meat.
cuttlefish *n* sea mollusc like squid.
CV curriculum vitae.
cyanide *n* extremely poisonous

chemical compound.
cybernetics *pl n* comparative study of control mechanisms of electronic and biological systems.
cyclamen *n* plant with flowers having turned–back petals.
cycle ⓣ *n* **1** recurrent, complete series or period. **2** bicycle. ♦ *v* **3** ride bicycle. **cyclical** *adj* **cyclist** *n* bicycle rider.
cyclone *n* circular storm.
cygnet *n* young swan.
cylinder *n* roller-shaped body, of uniform diameter. **cylindrical** *adj*
cymbal *n* one of two brass plates struck together to produce clashing sound.
cynic ⓣ *n* one who believes the worst about people or outcome of events. **cynical** *adj* **cynicism** *n* being cynical.
cypress *n* coniferous tree with very dark foliage.
cyst *n* sac containing liquid secretion or pus. **cystitis** *n* inflammation of bladder.

————— THESAURUS —————

incarceration
custom *n* = **tradition**, practice, convention, ritual, policy; = **habit**, way, practice, procedure, routine; = **customers**, business, trade, patronage
cut *v* = **slit**, score, slice, slash, pierce; = **chop**, split, slice, dissect; = **carve**, slice; = **sever**, cut in two; = **shape**, carve, engrave, chisel, form; = **slash**, wound; = **clip**, mow, trim, prune, snip ♦ *n* = **incision**, nick, stroke, slash, slit;

= **gash**, nick, wound, slash, laceration; = **reduction**, fall, lowering, slash, decrease; = (*Inf*) **share**, piece, slice, percentage, portion
cute *adj* = **appealing**, sweet, attractive, engaging, charming
cycle *n* = **series of events**, circle, revolution, rotation
cynic *n* = **sceptic**, doubter, pessimist, misanthrope, misanthropist

D d

dab ⊙ *v* dabbing, dabbed 1 apply with momentary pressure. ♦ *n* 2 small mass.

dabble *v* 1 splash about. 2 be amateur (in).

dachshund *n* short–legged long–bodied dog.

dad, daddy *n Inf* father. **daddy–longlegs** *n Inf* fly with long thin legs.

daffodil *n* yellow spring flower.

daft ⊙ *adj* foolish, crazy.

dagga *n S Afr informal* cannabis.

dagger *n* short stabbing weapon.

dahlia *n* garden plant of various colours.

daily ⊙ *adj/adv* 1 (done) every day. ♦ *n* 2 daily newspaper. 3 charwoman.

dainty *adj* –tier, –tiest 1 delicate. 2 choice. 3 fastidious. ♦ *n* 4 delicacy. **daintiness** *n*

dairy *n, pl* dairies place for processing milk and its products.

dais *n* raised platform.

daisy *n, pl* –sies flower with yellow centre and white petals.

dale *n* valley.

dally *v* –lying, –lied 1 trifle. 2 loiter.

Dalmatian *n* white dog with black spots.

dam ⊙ *n/v* (barrier to) hold back flow of waters.

damage ⊙ *n* 1 injury, harm. ♦ *pl* 2 compensation for injury. ♦ *v* 3 harm.

damask *n* 1 patterned woven material. 2 velvety red.

dame ⊙ *n* 1 *Obs* lady. 2 (with cap.) title of lady in Order of the British Empire. 3 *Sl* woman.

damn ⊙ *v* 1 condemn. 2 curse. ♦ *interj* 3 expression of annoyance etc. **damnable** *adj* **damnation** *n*

damp ⊙ *adj* 1 moist. ♦ *n* 2 moisture. ♦ *v* 3 make damp. 4 deaden. **dampen** *v* damp. **damper**

THESAURUS

---

dab *v* = pat, touch, tap; = apply, daub, stipple ♦ *n* = spot, bit, drop, pat, smudge; = touch, stroke, flick

daft *adj* (*Inf, chiefly Brit*) = stupid, crazy, silly, absurd, foolish

daily *adv* = every day, day by day, once a day ♦ *adj* = everyday, diurnal, quotidian

dam *n* = barrier, wall, barrage, obstruction, embankment ♦ *v* = block up, restrict, hold back, barricade, obstruct

damage *v* = spoil, hurt, injure, harm, ruin ≠ fix ♦ *n* = destruction, harm, loss, injury, suffering ≠ improvement; = (*Inf*) cost, price, charge, bill, amount

dame *n* = lady, baroness, dowager, grande dame (*Fr*), noblewoman

damn *v* = criticize, condemn, blast, denounce, put down

n **1** anything that discourages. **2** plate in flue.

damson n small dark–purple plum.

dance ⊕ v **1** move with rhythmic steps, to music. **2** bob up and down. **3** perform (dance). ◆ n **4** rhythmical movement. **5** social gathering. **dancer** n

dandelion n yellow–flowered wild plant.

dandruff n dead skin in small scales among the hair.

dandy n, pl **–dies 1** man excessively concerned with smartness of dress. ◆ adj **2** Inf excellent.

danger ⊕ n **1** exposure to harm. **2** peril. **dangerous** adj **dangerously** adv

dangle ⊕ v hang loosely.

dank adj damp and chilly.

dapper adj neat, spruce.

dappled adj marked with spots.

dare ⊕ v **1** have courage (to). **2** challenge. ◆ n **3** challenge. **daring** adj/n **daredevil** adj/n reckless (person).

dark ⊕ adj **1** without light. **2** gloomy. **3** deep in tint. **4** unenlightened. ◆ n **5** absence of light. **darken** v **darkly** adv **darkness** n **dark horse** person, thing about whom little is known.

darling ⊕ adj/n beloved (person).

darn v mend (hole) by sewing.

dart ⊕ n **1** small pointed missile. **2** darting motion. **3** small seam. ◆ pl **4** indoor game played with numbered target. ◆ v **5** throw, go rapidly.

dash ⊕ v **1** move hastily. **2** throw, strike violently. **3** frustrate. ◆ n **4** rush. **5** small amount. **6** smartness. **7** punctuation mark (–) showing change of subject. **dashing** adj lively, stylish. **dashboard** n instrument panel.

———— THESAURUS ————

≠ **praise**

damp adj = **moist**, wet, soggy, humid, dank ≠ **dry** ◆ n = **moisture**, liquid, drizzle, dampness, wetness ≠ **dryness** ◆ v = **moisten**, wet, soak, dampen, moisturize

dance v = **prance**, trip, hop, skip, sway; = **caper**, trip, spring, jump, bound ◆ n = **ball**, social, hop (Inf), disco, knees–up (Brit inf)

danger n = **jeopardy**, vulnerability

dangle v = **hang**, swing, trail, sway, flap

dare v = **risk doing**, venture, presume, make bold, hazard

doing; = **challenge**, provoke, defy, taunt, goad

dark adj = **dim**, murky, shady, shadowy, grey; = **black**, brunette, ebony, dark–skinned, sable ≠ **fair**; = **evil**, foul, sinister, vile, wicked; = **secret**, hidden, mysterious, concealed; = **gloomy**, sad, grim, miserable, bleak ≠ **cheerful** ◆ n = **darkness**, shadows, gloom, dusk, obscurity; = **night**, twilight, evening, dusk, night–time

darling n = **beloved**, love, dear, dearest, angel ◆ adj = **beloved**, dear, treasured, precious, adored

dart v = **dash**, run, race, shoot, fly

dastardly adj mean.
data ⊕ pl n (oft. with sing v) **1** series of facts. **2** information.
database n store of information.
date¹ ⊕ n **1** day of the month. **2** time of occurrence. **3** appointment. ♦ v **4** mark with date. **5** reveal age of. **6** exist (from). **7** become old–fashioned.
dated adj
date² n fruit of palm.
daub v paint roughly.
daughter n one's female child.
daughter-in-law n, pl **daughters-in-law** son's wife.
dawdle v idle, loiter.
dawn ⊕ n **1** daybreak. **2** beginning. ♦ v **3** begin to grow light. **4** (begin to) be understood.
day ⊕ n **1** period of 24 hours. **2** time when sun is above horizon. **3** time period. **daybreak** n dawn.
daydream n **1** idle fancy. ♦ v **2**

have such fancies. **daydreamer** n
daylight n **1** natural light. **2** dawn.
daze ⊕ v **1** stun, bewilder. ♦ n **2** bewildered state. **dazed** adj
dazzle ⊕ v **1** blind, confuse with brightness. **2** impress greatly.
dazzling adj
DC direct current.
de– comb. form **1** removal of, from, reversal of, as in delouse. **2** removal of, from, reversal of desegregate.
deacon n one who assists in a church.
dead ⊕ adj **1** no longer alive. **2** obsolete. **3** numb. **4** lacking vigour. **5** complete. ♦ n (oft. pl) **6** dead person(s). ♦ adv **7** utterly.
deaden v **deadly** adj **1** fatal. **2** deathlike. ♦ adv **3** as if dead. **4** extremely. **deadline** n limit of time allowed. **deadlock** n standstill.
deadpan adj expressionless.
deaf ⊕ adj **1** without hearing. **2**

dash v = **rush**, run, race, shoot, fly ≠ **dawdle**; = **throw**, cast, pitch, slam, toss; = **crash**, break, smash, shatter, splinter ♦ n = **rush**, run, race, sprint, dart; = **drop**, little, bit, shot (Inf), touch ≠ **lot**; = **style**, spirit, flair, flourish, verve
data n = **information**, facts, figures, details, intelligence
date¹ n = **time**, stage, period; = **appointment**, meeting, arrangement, commitment, engagement ♦ v = **put a date on**, assign a date to, fix the period of; = **become dated**, become old–fashioned
dawn n = **daybreak**, morning,

sunrise, daylight, aurora (Poet); = (Lit) **beginning**, start, birth, rise, origin ♦ v = **begin**, start, rise, develop, emerge; = **grow light**, break, brighten, lighten
day n = **daytime**, daylight
daze v = **stun**, shock, paralyse, numb, stupefy ♦ n = **shock**, confusion, distraction, trance, bewilderment
dazzle v = **impress**, amaze, overwhelm, astonish, overpower; = **blind**, confuse, daze, bedazzle ♦ n = **splendour**, sparkle, glitter, brilliance, magnificence
dead adj = **deceased**, departed, late, perished, extinct ≠ **alive**;

unwilling to listen. **deafen** v make deaf. **deafness** n

deal¹ ❶ v 1 distribute. 2 act. 3 treat. 4 do business (with, in). ◆ n 5 agreement. 6 treatment. 7 share. **dealer** n

deal² n (plank of) pine wood.

dean n 1 university official. 2 head of cathedral chapter.

dear ❶ adj 1 beloved. 2 precious. 3 expensive. ◆ n 4 beloved one. **dearly** adv

dearth n scarcity.

death ❶ n 1 dying. 2 end of life. 3 end. **deathly** adj/adv

debacle ❶ n utter collapse, rout, disaster.

debase v lower in value.

debate ❶ v 1 argue, esp. formally.

◆ n 2 formal discussion. **debatable** adj **debater** n

debilitate v weaken.

debit Finance ◆ n 1 entry in account of sum owed. ◆ v 2 enter as due.

debonair adj suave, genial.

debrief v report result of mission.

debris ❶ n rubbish.

debt ❶ n 1 what is owed. 2 state of owing. **debtor** n

debunk v expose falseness of, esp. by ridicule.

debut ❶ n first appearance in public. **debutante** n girl making society debut.

Dec. December.

decade n period of ten years.

decaffeinated adj (of tea, coffee)

————— THESAURUS —————

= **boring**, dull, dreary, flat, plain; = **not working**, useless, inactive, inoperative ≠ **working**; old; = **numb**, frozen, paralysed, insensitive, inert; = **total**, complete, absolute, utter, outright; = (Inf) **exhausted**, tired, worn out, spent, done in (Inf) ◆ n = **middle**, heart, depth, midst ◆ adv = (Inf) **exactly**, completely, totally, directly, fully

deaf adj = **hard of hearing**, without hearing, stone deaf; = **oblivious**, indifferent, unmoved, unconcerned, unsympathetic

deal¹ n = (Inf) **agreement**, understanding, contract, arrangement, bargain; = **amount**, quantity, measure, degree, mass

dear adj = **beloved**, close, valued, favourite, prized ≠ **hated**; = (Brit

inf) **expensive**, costly, high-priced, pricey (Inf), at a premium ≠ **cheap** ◆ n = **darling**, love, dearest, angel, treasure

death n = **dying**, demise, end, passing, departure ≠ **birth**; = **destruction**, finish, ruin, undoing, extinction ≠ **beginning**

debacle n = **disaster**, catastrophe, fiasco

debate n = **discussion**, talk, argument, dispute, analysis ◆ v = **discuss**, question, talk about, argue about, dispute; = **consider**, reflect, think about, weigh, contemplate

debris n = **remains**, bits, waste, ruins, fragments

debt n = **debit**, commitment, obligation, liability

debut n = **entrance**, beginning,

with caffeine removed.
decant v pour off (wine).
decanter n stoppered bottle.
decapitate v behead.
decathlon n athletic contest with ten events.
decay ❶ v 1 rot. 2 decline. ◆ n 3 rotting.
decease n 1 death. ◆ v 2 die.
deceased adj/n dead (person).
deceive ❶ v mislead, delude.
deceit n 1 fraud. 2 duplicity.
deceitful adj
decelerate v slow down.
December n twelfth month.
decent ❶ adj 1 respectable. 2 fitting. 3 adequate. 4 Inf kind.
decency n
deception ❶ n 1 deceiving. 2 trick. **deceptive** adj misleading.
decibel n unit for measuring intensity of sound.
decide ❶ v 1 (cause to) reach a decision. 2 settle (a contest or

question). **decision** n judgment, conclusion or resolution.
deciduous adj (of trees) losing leaves annually.
decimal adj 1 relating to tenths. ◆ n 2 decimal fraction.
decimalization n decimal point dot between unit and fraction.
decimate v destroy or kill a tenth of, large proportion of.
decipher v 1 make out meaning of. 2 decode.
deck n 1 floor, esp. one covering ship's hull. 2 turntable of record player. ◆ v 3 decorate. **deck chair** folding canvas chair.
declaim v speak rhetorically.
declare ❶ v 1 announce formally. 2 state emphatically. **declaration** n
decline ❶ v 1 refuse. 2 slope downwards. 3 deteriorate. 4 diminish. ◆ n 5 deterioration. 6 diminution. 7 downward slope.
decode v convert from code into

———— THESAURUS ————

launch, coming out, introduction
decay v = **rot**, spoil, crumble, deteriorate, perish; = **decline**, diminish, crumble, deteriorate, fall off ≠ **grow** ◆ n = **rot**, corruption, mould, blight, decomposition; = **decline**, collapse, deterioration, failing, fading ≠ **growth**
deceive v = **take in**, trick, fool (Inf), cheat, con (Inf)
decent adj = **satisfactory**, fair, all right, reasonable, sufficient ≠ **unsatisfactory**; = **proper**, becoming, seemly, fitting, appropriate ≠ **improper**; = **respectable**, pure, proper,

modest, chaste
deception n = **trickery**, fraud, deceit, cunning, treachery ≠ **honesty**; = **trick**, lie, bluff, hoax, decoy
decide v = **resolve**, answer, determine, conclude, clear up; = **settle**, determine, resolve
declare v = **state**, claim, announce, voice, express
decline v = **deteriorate**, weaken, pine, decay, worsen ≠ **improve**; = **refuse**, reject, turn down, avoid, spurn ≠ **accept** ◆ n = **depression**, recession, slump, falling off, downturn ≠ **rise**

ordinary language. **decoder** n

decompose v rot.

decongestant adj/n (drug) relieving (esp. nasal) congestion.

decontaminate v render harmless.

decor n decorative scheme.

decorate 🟊 v 1 beautify. 2 paint room etc. 3 invest (with medal etc.). **decoration** n **decorative** adj **decorator** n

decorum n propriety, decency. **decorous** adj

decoy n 1 bait, lure. ◆ v 2 lure, be lured as with decoy.

decrease 🟊 v 1 diminish, lessen. ◆ n 2 diminishing.

decree 🟊 n/v (give) order having the force of law.

decrepit adj 1 old. 2 worn out.

decry v –crying, –cried disparage.

dedicate 🟊 v 1 commit wholly to special purpose. 2 inscribe or address. 3 devote. **dedicated** adj **dedication** n

deduce v draw as conclusion.

deduct 🟊 v subtract. **deductible** adj **deduction** n 1 deducting. 2 amount subtracted. 3 conclusion.

deed 🟊 n 1 action. 2 exploit. 3 legal document.

deem v judge, consider, regard.

deep 🟊 adj 1 extending far down. 2 at, of given depth. 3 profound. 4 hard to fathom. 5 (of colour) dark. 6 (of sound) low. ◆ n 7 deep place. 8 the sea. ◆ adv 9 far down etc. **deeply** adv **deepen** v

deer n, pl **deer** ruminant animal typically with antlers in male.

deface v spoil or mar surface.

defame v speak ill of. **defamation** n **defamatory** adj

default 🟊 n 1 failure to act, appear or pay. ◆ v 2 fail (to pay).

defeat 🟊 v 1 vanquish. 2 thwart.

—————————————— THESAURUS ——————————————

decorate v = **adorn**, trim, embroider, ornament, embellish; = **do up**, paper, paint, wallpaper, renovate (Inf); = **pin a medal on**, cite, confer an honour in or upon

decrease v = **drop**, decline, lessen, lower, shrink ◆ n = **lessening**, decline, reduction, loss, falling off ≠ **growth**

decree n = **law**, order, ruling, act, command ◆ v = **order**, rule, command, demand, proclaim

dedicate v = **devote**, give, apply, commit, pledge; = **offer**, address, inscribe

deduct v = **subtract**, remove, take off, take away, reduce by ≠ **add**

deed n = **action**, act, performance, achievement, exploit; = (Law) **document**, title, contract

deep adj = **big**, wide, broad, profound, yawning ≠ **shallow**; = **intense**, great, serious (Inf), acute, extreme ≠ **superficial**; = **sound**, profound, unbroken, undisturbed, untroubled; = **absorbed**, lost, gripped, preoccupied, immersed; = **dark**, strong, rich, intense, vivid ≠ **light**; = **low**, booming, bass, resonant, sonorous ≠ **high** ◆ n = **middle**, heart, midst, dead

default v = **fail to pay**, dodge,

♦ n 3 overthrow.
defecate v empty the bowels.
defect ❶ n 1 lack, blemish. ♦ v 2 desert. **defection** n **defective** adj **defector** n
defend ❶ v 1 protect, ward off attack. 2 support by argument. **defence** n 1 protection. 2 justification. 3 statement by accused person in court. **defenceless** adj **defendant** n person accused in court. **defender** n **defensible** adj **defensive** adj 1 serving for defence. ♦ n 2 attitude of defence.
defer¹ ❶ v postpone.
defer² v –ferring, –ferred, submit to opinion or judgement of another. **deference** n 1 obedience. 2 respect. **deferential** adj
deficient adj lacking in something. **deficiency** n **deficit** n amount by which sum of money is too small.
defile v 1 soil. 2 sully.
define ❶ v 1 state meaning of. 2 mark out. **definite** adj 1 exact. 2

clear. 3 certain. **definitely** adv
definition n statement of the meaning of a word or phrase.
definitive adj conclusive.
deflate v (cause to) collapse by release of gas from. **deflation** n Economics reduction of economic and industrial activity.
deflect ❶ v (cause to) turn from straight course. **deflection** n
deform v 1 spoil shape of. 2 disfigure. **deformity** n
defraud v cheat, swindle.
defrost v 1 make, become free of frost, ice. 2 thaw.
deft adj skilful, adroit.
defunct adj dead, obsolete.
defuse v 1 remove fuse of bomb etc. 2 remove tension.
defy ❶ v –fying, –fied challenge, resist successfully. **defiance** n resistance. **defiant** adj openly and aggressively hostile.
degenerate ❶ v 1 deteriorate to lower level. ♦ adj 2 fallen away in quality. ♦ n 3 degenerate person. **degeneration** n **degenerative** adj

————— THESAURUS —————

evade, neglect ♦ n = **failure**, neglect, deficiency, lapse, omission
defeat v = **beat**, crush, overwhelm, conquer, master ≠ **surrender**; = **frustrate**, foil, thwart, ruin, baffle ♦ n = **conquest**, beating, overthrow, rout ≠ **victory**
defect n failing ♦ v = **desert**, rebel, quit, revolt, change sides
defend v = **protect**, cover, guard, screen, preserve; = **support**,

champion, justify, endorse, uphold
defer¹ v = **postpone**, delay, put off, suspend, shelve
define v = **mark out**, outline, limit, bound, delineate; = **describe**, interpret, characterize, explain, spell out
deflect v = **turn aside**, bend
defy v = **resist**, oppose, confront, brave, disregard
degenerate v = **decline**, slip, sink, decrease, deteriorate ♦ adj = **depraved**, corrupt, low,

degrade ❶ v 1 dishonour. 2 debase. 3 reduce. 4 decompose chemically. **degradable** adj
degradation n
degree n 1 step, stage in process. 2 university rank. 3 unit of measurement.
dehydrate v remove moisture from.
deify v –fying, –fied make a god of. **deity** n god.
deign v condescend.
déjà vu Fr feeling of having experienced something before.
dejected adj miserable.
dejection n
delay ❶ v 1 postpone. 2 linger. ♦ n 3 delaying.
delectable adj delightful.
delegate ❶ n 1 representative. ♦ v 2 send as deputy. 3 entrust.

delegation n
delete ❶ v remove, erase.
deletion n
deliberate ❶ adj 1 intentional. 2 well-considered. 3 slow. ♦ v 4 consider. **deliberately** adv
deliberation n
delicate ❶ adj 1 exquisite. 2 fragile. 3 requiring tact. **delicacy** n 1 elegance. 2 delicious food.
delicatessen n shop selling esp. imported or unusual foods.
delicious ❶ adj delightful, pleasing to taste.
delight ❶ v 1 please greatly. 2 take great pleasure (in). ♦ n 3 great pleasure. **delightful** adj charming.
delinquent n/adj (one) guilty of delinquency. **delinquency** n (minor) offence or misdeed.

———————— THESAURUS ————————

perverted, immoral
degrade v = **demean**, disgrace, humiliate, shame, humble ≠ **ennoble**; = **demote**, lower, downgrade ≠ **promote**
delay v = **put off**, suspend, postpone, shelve, defer; = **hold up**, detain, hold back, hinder, obstruct ≠ **speed (up)** ♦ n = **hold-up**, wait, setback, interruption, stoppage
delegate n = **representative**, agent, deputy, ambassador, commissioner ♦ v = **entrust**, transfer, hand over, give, pass on; = **appoint**, commission, select, contract, engage
delete v = **remove**, cancel, erase, strike out, obliterate
deliberate adj = **intentional**,

meant, planned, intended, conscious ≠ **accidental**; = **careful**, measured, slow, cautious, thoughtful ≠ **hurried** ♦ v = **consider**, think, ponder, discuss, debate
delicate adj = **fine**, elegant, exquisite, graceful; = **subtle**, fine, delicious, faint, refined ≠ **bright**; = **fragile**, weak, frail, brittle, tender; = **skilled**, precise, deft, Victorian, proper (Inf)
delicious adj = **delectable**, tasty, choice, savoury, dainty ≠ **unpleasant**
delight n = **pleasure**, joy, satisfaction, happiness, ecstasy ≠ **displeasure** ♦ v = **please**, satisfy, thrill, charm, cheer ≠ **displease**

D

delirium n **1** disorder of mind, esp. in feverish illness. **2** violent excitement. **delirious** adj

deliver ⊕ v **1** carry to destination. **2** hand over. **3** release. **4** give birth or assist in birth (of). **5** utter.

deliverance n rescue. **delivery** n, pl **-eries**

dell n wooded hollow.

delta n alluvial tract at river mouth.

delude v **1** deceive. **2** mislead. **delusion** n

deluge n **1** flood, downpour. ♦ v **2** flood, overwhelm.

de luxe 1 rich, sumptuous. **2** superior in quality.

delve v **1** search intensively. **2** dig.

demagogue n mob leader or agitator.

demand ⊕ v **1** ask as giving an order. **2** call for as due, necessary. ♦ n **3** urgent request. **4** call for.

demanding adj requiring effort.

demean v degrade, lower.

demeanour n conduct, bearing.

demented adj mad, crazy.

dementia n mental deterioration.

demerit n undesirable quality.

demi- comb. form half, as in demigod.

demijohn n large bottle.

demilitarize v prohibit military presence.

demise ⊕ n **1** death. **2** conveyance by will or lease.

demobilize v **1** disband (troops). **2** discharge (soldier).

democracy ⊕ n, pl **-cies 1** government by the people or their elected representatives. **2** state so governed. **democrat** n advocate of democracy. **democratic** adj

demolish ⊕ v **1** knock to pieces. **2** destroy utterly. **demolition** n

demon ⊕ n devil, evil spirit.

demonstrate ⊕ v **1** show by reasoning, prove. **2** describe, explain. **3** make exhibition of support, protest etc.

demonstrable adj **demonstration** n

demonstrative adj **1** expressing feelings. **2** pointing out. **3** conclusive. **demonstrator** n **1** one who takes part in a public demonstration. **2** assistant in

——— THESAURUS ———

deliver v = **bring**, carry, bear, transport, distribute; = **hand over**, commit, give up, yield, surrender; = **give**, read, present, announce, declare; = **strike**, give, deal, launch, direct; = (Dated) **release**, free, save, rescue, loose

demand v = **request**, ask (for), order, expect, claim; = **challenge**, ask, question, inquire; = **require**, want, need, involve, call for ≠ **provide** ♦ n = **request**, order;

= **need**, want, call, market, claim

demise n = **failure**, end, fall, defeat, collapse; = (Euphemistic) **death**, end, dying, passing, departure

democracy n = **self-government**, republic, commonwealth

demolish v = **knock down**, level, destroy, dismantle, flatten ≠ **build**

demon n = **evil spirit**, devil, fiend, goblin, ghoul; = **wizard**, master, ace (Inf), fiend, beast

laboratory etc.

demoralize v 1 deprive of courage. 2 undermine morally.

demote v reduce in rank. **demotion** n

demur v **-murring, -murred 1** make difficulties, object. ♦ n 2 demurring.

demure adj reserved.

den ❶ n 1 hole of wild beast. 2 small room, esp. study.

denigrate v belittle.

denim n strong cotton fabric.

denizen n inhabitant.

denote v 1 stand for. 2 show.

denouement n unravelling of plot.

denounce ❶ v 1 speak violently against. 2 accuse. **denunciation** n

dense ❶ adj 1 thick, compact. 2 stupid. **density** n, pl **-ties**

dent ❶ n/v (make) hollow or mark

by blow or pressure.

dental adj of teeth or dentistry.

dentist n surgeon who attends to teeth. **dentistry** n art of dentist.

denture n (usu. pl) set of false teeth.

denude v strip, make bare.

deny ❶ v **-nying, -nied 1** declare untrue. 2 contradict. 3 reject. 4 refuse to give. **denial** n

depart ❶ v 1 go away. 2 start out. 3 vary. 4 die. **departure** n

department ❶ n 1 division. 2 branch. **departmental** adj

depend ❶ v 1 rely entirely. 2 live. 3 be contingent. **dependable** adj reliable. **dependant** n one who relies on another. **dependent** adj depending on. **dependence, dependency** n

depict ❶ v 1 give picture of. 2 describe. **depiction** n

——————— THESAURUS ———————

demonstrate v = **prove**, show, indicate, make clear, manifest; = **show**, express, display, indicate, exhibit; = **march**, protest, rally, object, parade

den n = **lair**, hole, shelter, cave, haunt; = (Chiefly US) **study**, retreat, sanctuary, hideaway, sanctum

denounce v = **condemn**, attack, censure, revile, vilify

dense adj = **thick**, heavy, solid, compact, condensed ≠ **thin**; = **heavy**, thick, opaque, impenetrable; = (Inf) **stupid**, thick, dull, dumb (Inf), dozy (Brit inf) ≠ **bright**

dent v = **make a dent in**, press in, gouge, hollow, push in ♦ n

= **hollow**, chip, indentation, depression, impression

deny v = **contradict**, disagree with, rebuff, negate, rebut ≠ **admit**; = **renounce**, reject, retract, repudiate, disown; = **refuse**, forbid, reject, rule out, turn down ≠ **permit**

depart v = **leave**, go, withdraw, retire, disappear ≠ **arrive**; = **deviate**, vary, differ, stray, veer

department n = **section**, office, unit, station, division

depend v = **be determined by**, be based on, be subject to, hang on, rest on; = **count on**, turn to, trust in, bank on, lean on

depict v = **illustrate**, portray,

deplete ⓣ *v* 1 empty. 2 reduce. **depletion** *n*

deplore ⓣ *v* 1 lament, regret. 2 denounce. **deplorable** *adj*

deploy ⓣ *v* organize (troops) in battle formation. **deployment** *n*

depopulate *v* (cause to) be reduced in population. **depopulation** *n*

deport ⓣ *v* expel, banish. **deportation** *n*

deportment *n* behaviour.

depose ⓣ *v* 1 remove from office. 2 make statement on oath.

deposit ⓣ *v* 1 set down. 2 give into safe keeping. 3 let fall. ♦ *n* 4 thing deposited. 5 money given in part payment. 6 sediment.

deposition *n* 1 statement written and attested. 2 act of deposing or depositing. **depositor** *n*

depository *n*

depot ⓣ *n* storehouse.

deprecate *v* express disapproval of.

depreciate *v* 1 (cause to) fall in value, price. 2 belittle. **depreciation** *n*

depress ⓣ *v* 1 affect with low spirits. 2 lower. **depression** *n* 1 hollow. 2 low spirits. 3 low state of trade.

deprive *v* dispossess. **deprivation** *n* **deprived** *adj* lacking adequate food, care, amenities etc.

depth ⓣ *n* 1 (degree of) deepness. 2 deep place. 3 intensity.

deregulate *v* remove regulations or controls from.

derelict ⓣ *adj* 1 abandoned. 2 falling into ruins. **dereliction** *n* 1 neglect of duty. 2 abandonment.

deride *v* treat with contempt, ridicule. **derision** *n* **derisive** *adj* **derisory** *adj*

———————— THESAURUS ————————

picture, paint, outline; = **describe**, present, represent, outline, characterize

deplete *v* = **use up**, reduce, drain, exhaust, consume ≠ **increase**

deplore *v* = **disapprove of**, condemn, object to, denounce, censure

deploy *v* = **use**, station, position, arrange, set out

deport *v* = **expel**, exile, throw out, oust, banish

depose *v* = **oust**, dismiss, displace, demote, dethrone

deposit *v* = **down payment**, security, stake, pledge, instalment; = **accumulation**, mass, build–up,

layer; ♦ *v* = **put**, place, lay, drop; = **store**, keep, put, bank, lodge

depot *n* = **bus station**, station, garage, terminus

depress *v* = **sadden**, upset, distress, discourage, grieve ≠ **cheer**; = **lower**, cut, reduce, diminish, decrease ≠ **raise**; = **devalue**, depreciate, cheapen

depth *n* = **deepness**, drop, measure, extent; = **insight**, wisdom, penetration, profundity, discernment ≠ **superficiality**

derelict *adj* = **abandoned**, deserted, ruined, neglected, discarded ♦ *n* = **tramp**, outcast, drifter, down–and–out, vagrant

derive v get, come from.
derivation n **derivative** adj
dermatitis n inflammation of skin.
derogatory adj belittling.
derv n diesel oil for road vehicles.
descant n Mus decorative variation to basic melody.
descend ❶ v 1 come or go down. 2 spring from. 3 be transmitted. 4 attack. **descendant** n person descended from an ancestor.
descent n
describe ❶ v give detailed account of. **description** n
descriptive adj
desecrate v 1 violate sanctity of. 2 profane.
desert¹ ❶ n uninhabited and barren region.
desert² ❶ v 1 abandon, leave. 2 run away from service. **deserter** n
desertion n
desert³ n (usu. pl) what is due as reward or punishment.

deserve ❶ v show oneself worthy of.
design ❶ v 1 sketch. 2 plan. 3 intend. ♦ n 4 sketch. 5 plan. 6 decorative pattern. 7 project.
designer n/adj
designate ❶ v 1 name, appoint. ♦ adj 2 appointed but not yet installed.
desire ❶ v 1 wish, long for. 2 ask for. ♦ n 3 longing. 4 expressed wish. 5 sexual appetite. **desirable** n 1 worth having. 2 attractive. **desirability** n **desirous** adj
desist v cease, stop.
desk n writing table.
desolate adj 1 uninhabited. 2 neglected. 3 solitary. 4 forlorn. ♦ v 5 lay waste. 6 overwhelm with grief. **desolation** n
despair ❶ v 1 lose hope. ♦ n 2 loss of all hope. 3 cause of this.
desperate ❶ adj 1 reckless from despair. 2 hopelessly bad.

——————— THESAURUS ———————

descend v = **fall**, drop, sink, go down, plunge ≠ **rise**; = **go down**, come down, walk down, move down, climb down; = **slope**, dip, incline, slant
describe v = **relate**, tell, report, explain, express; = **portray**, depict
desert¹ n = **wilderness**, waste, wilds, wasteland, dry
desert² v = **abandon**, leave, quit, forsake
deserve v = **merit**, warrant, be entitled to, have a right to, rate
design v = **plan**, draw, draft, trace, outline; = **create**, plan, fashion, propose, invent; = **intend**,

mean, plan, aim, purpose ♦ n = **pattern**, form, style, shape, organization; = **plan**, drawing, model, scheme, draft; = **intention**, end, aim, goal, target
designate v = **name**, call, term, style, label; = **choose**, reserve, select, label, flag
desire n = **wish**, want, longing, hope, urge; = **lust**, passion, libido, appetite, lasciviousness ♦ v = **want**, long for, crave, hope for, ache for
despair n = **despondency**, depression, misery, gloom, desperation ♦ v = **lose hope**, give

desperately *adv* **desperation** *n*
desperado *n* reckless, lawless person.
despise 🟊 *v* look down on as inferior. **despicable** *adj* base, contemptible, vile.
despite 🟊 *prep* in spite of.
despoil *v* plunder, rob.
despondent *adj* dejected, depressed.
despot *n* tyrant, oppressor.
despotic *adj* **despotism** *n*
dessert *n* sweet course, or fruit, served at end of meal.
destination 🟊 *n* place one is bound for.
destitute *adj* in absolute want.
destroy 🟊 *v* **1** ruin. **2** put an end to. **3** demolish. **destroyer** *n* small, swift warship. **destructible** *adj* **destruction** *n* ruin. **destructive** *adj*
desultory *adj* **1** aimless. **2** unmethodical.
detach 🟊 *v* unfasten, separate.

detachable *adj* **detached** *adj* **1** standing apart. **2** disinterested.
detachment *n* **1** aloofness. **2** detaching. **3** body of troops on special duty.
detail 🟊 *n* **1** particular. **2** small or unimportant part. **3** treatment of anything item by item. **4** soldier assigned for duty. ♦ *v* **5** relate in full. **6** appoint.
detain 🟊 *v* **1** keep under restraint. **2** keep waiting. **detention** *n*
detect 🟊 *v* find out or discover.
detection *n* **detective** *n* policeman detecting crime. **detector** *n*
deter 🟊 *v* **-terring, -terred 1** discourage. **2** prevent. **deterrent** *adj/n*
detergent *n/adj* cleaning (substance).
deteriorate 🟊 *v* become or make worse. **deterioration** *n*
determine 🟊 *v* **1** decide. **2** fix. **3** be deciding factor in. **4** come to

up, lose heart
desperate *adj* = **grave**, pressing, serious, severe, extreme; = **last-ditch**, daring, furious, risky, frantic
despise *v* = **look down on**, loathe, scorn, detest, revile ≠ admire
despite *prep* = **in spite of**, in the face of, regardless of, even with, notwithstanding
destination *n* = **stop**, station, haven, resting-place, terminus
destroy *v* = **ruin**, crush, devastate, wreck, shatter
detach *v* = **separate**, remove, divide, cut off, sever ≠ attach
detail *n* = **point**, fact, feature,

particular, respect; = **fine point**, particular, nicety, triviality; = (*Mil*) **party**, force, body, duty, squad ♦ *v* = **list**, relate, catalogue, recount, rehearse; = **appoint**, name, choose, commission, select
detain *v* = **hold**, arrest, confine, restrain, imprison; = **delay**, hold up, hamper, hinder, retard
detect *v* = **discover**, find, uncover, track down, unmask; = **notice**, see, spot, note, identify
deter *v* = **discourage**, inhibit, put off, frighten, intimidate
deteriorate *v* = **decline**, worsen, degenerate, slump, go downhill

an end. **5** come to a decision.
determination *n* **1** determining. **2**
resolute conduct. **3** resolve.
determined *adj* resolute.
detest *v* hate, loathe. **detestable**
adj
dethrone *v* remove from position
of authority.
detonate *v* (cause to) explode.
detonation *n* **detonator** *n*
detour *n* roundabout way.
detract *v* take away (a part) from,
diminish. **detractor** *n*
detriment *n* harm done, loss,
damage. **detrimental** *adj*
deuce *n* **1** card with two spots. **2**
Tennis forty all. **3** in exclamatory
phrases, the devil.
devalue *v* **–valuing, –valued**
reduce in value. **devaluation** *n*
devastate ❶ *v* **1** lay waste. **2**
ravage. **devastated** *adj* extremely
shocked. **devastation** *n*
develop ❶ *v* **1** bring to maturity.
2 elaborate. **3** evolve. **4** treat
photographic film to bring out
image. **5** improve or change use of

(land). **6** grow to maturer state.
developer *n* **development** *n*
deviate *v* diverge. **deviant** *n*/*adj*
(person) deviating from normal,
esp. in sexual practices. **deviation**
n **devious** *adj* **1** deceitful. **2**
roundabout. **deviousness** *n*
device ❶ *n* **1** contrivance. **2**
scheme.
devil ❶ *n* **1** personified spirit of
evil. **2** person of great wickedness,
cruelty etc. **3** *Inf* fellow. **4** *Inf*
something difficult or annoying.
devilish *adj* **devilment** *n* **devilry** *n*
devil-may-care *adj* happy-go-
lucky.
devise ❶ *v* plan.
devoid ❶ *adj* empty.
devolve *v* (cause to) pass on to
another. **devolution** *n* devolving.
devote ❶ *v* give up exclusively (to
person, purpose etc.). **devoted** *adj*
loving. **devotee** *n* ardent
enthusiast. **devotion** *n* **1** deep
affection. **2** dedication. ◆ *pl* **3**
prayers.
devour ❶ *v* eat greedily.

————————— THESAURUS —————————

(*Inf*) ≠ **improve**
determine *v* = **settle**, learn,
establish, discover, find out;
= **decide on**, choose, elect,
resolve; = **decide**, conclude,
resolve, make up your mind
devastate *v* = **destroy**, ruin, sack,
wreck, demolish
develop *v* = **grow**, advance,
progress, mature, evolve;
= **establish**, set up, promote,
generate, undertake
device *n* = **gadget**, machine, tool,

instrument, implement; = **ploy**,
scheme, plan, trick, manoeuvre
devil *n* = **evil spirit**, demon, fiend;
= **brute**, monster, beast,
barbarian, fiend; = **person**,
individual, soul, creature, thing;
= **scamp**, rogue, rascal, scoundrel,
scallywag (*Inf*)
devise *v* = **work out**, design,
construct, invent, conceive
devoid *adj* with **of** = **lacking in**,
without, free from, wanting in,
bereft of

devout ⊕ *adj* deeply religious.

dew *n* moisture from air deposited as small drops at night.

dexterity *n* manual skill.
dexterous *adj*

diabetes *n* various disorders characterized by excretion of abnormal amount of urine.
diabetic *n/adj*

diabolic *adj* devilish. **diabolical** *adj Inf* extremely bad.

diadem *n* crown.

diagnosis ⊕ *n, pl* –ses identification of disease from symptoms. **diagnose** *v*

diagonal *adj/n* (line) from corner to corner.

diagram ⊕ *n* drawing, figure, to illustrate something.

dial *n* 1 face of clock etc. 2 plate marked with graduations on which pointer moves. 3 numbered disc on front of telephone. ♦ *v* 4 operate telephone.

dialect *n* characteristic speech of district.

dialogue ⊕ *n* conversation.

dialysis *n Med* filtering of blood through membrane to remove waste products.

diameter *n* (length of) straight line through centre of circle.

diametrically *adv* completely.

diamond *n* 1 very hard and brilliant precious stone. 2 rhomboid figure. 3 suit at cards.

diaper *n US and Canad* towelling cloth to absorb baby's excrement.

diaphragm *n* muscle between abdomen and chest.

diarrhoea *n* excessive looseness of the bowels.

diary ⊕ *n, pl* –ries 1 daily record of events. 2 book for this.

diatribe *n* violently bitter verbal attack, denunciation.

dice *pl n* **dice** (*sing*) 1 cubes each with six sides marked one to six for games of chance. ♦ *v* 2 gamble with dice. 3 *Cookery* cut vegetables into small cubes.

dichotomy *n, pl* –mies division into two parts.

dictate ⊕ *v* 1 say or read for another to transcribe. 2 prescribe. 3 impose. ♦ *n* 4 bidding. **dictation** *n* **dictator** *n* absolute ruler. **dictatorial** *adj* **dictatorship** *n*

—————— THESAURUS ——————

devote *v* = **dedicate**, give, commit, apply, reserve

devour *v* = **eat**, consume, swallow, wolf, gulp; = **enjoy**, take in, read compulsively or voraciously

devout *adj* = **religious**, godly, pious, pure, holy ≠ **irreverent**

diagnosis *n* = **identification**, discovery, recognition, detection

diagram *n* = **plan**, figure,

drawing, chart, representation

dialogue *n* = **discussion**, conference, exchange, debate; = **conversation**, discussion, communication, discourse

diary *n* = **journal**, chronicle

dictate *v* = **speak**, say, utter, read out ♦ *n* = **command**, order, decree, demand, direction; = **principle**, law, rule, standard, code

diction n 1 choice and use of words. 2 enunciation.

dictionary ⊕ n, pl -aries book listing, alphabetically, words with meanings etc.

did past tense of DO.

die[1] ⊕ v dying, died 1 cease to live. 2 end. 3 Inf look forward (to).

die-hard n/adj (person) resisting change.

die[2] n shaped block to form metal in forge, press etc.

diesel adj 1 pert. to internal-combustion engine using oil as fuel. ♦ n 2 this engine. 3 the fuel.

diet ⊕ n 1 restricted or regulated course of feeding. 2 kind of food lived on. ♦ v 3 follow a diet, as to lose weight. **dietary** adj

differ ⊕ v 1 be unlike. 2 disagree. **difference** n 1 unlikeness. 2 point of unlikeness. 3 disagreement. 4 remainder left after subtraction. **different** adj **differently** adv **differential** adj 1 varying with circumstances. ♦ n 2 mechanism in car etc. allowing back wheels to revolve at different speeds. 3 difference between two rates of pay. **differentiate** v 1 serve to distinguish between, make different. 2 discriminate.

difficult ⊕ adj 1 requiring effort, skill etc. 2 not easy. 3 obscure. **difficulty** n 1 difficult task, problem. 2 embarrassment. 3 hindrance. 4 trouble.

diffident adj lacking confidence.

diffuse v 1 spread slowly. ♦ adj 2 widely spread. 3 loose, wordy. **diffusion** n

dig ⊕ v digging, dug 1 work with spade. 2 turn up with spade. 3 excavate. 4 thrust into. ♦ n 5 piece of digging. 6 thrust. 7 jibe. ♦ pl 8 Inf lodgings.

digest ⊕ v 1 prepare (food) in stomach etc. for assimilation. 2 bring into handy form by summarizing. ♦ n 3 methodical

———————— THESAURUS ————————

dictionary n = wordbook, vocabulary, glossary, lexicon

die[1] v = pass away, expire, perish, croak (Sl), give up the ghost ≠ **live**; = **stop**, fail, halt, break down, run down; = **dwindle**, decline, sink, fade, diminish ≠ **increase**

diet n = food, provisions, fare, rations, nourishment; = **fast**, regime, abstinence, regimen ♦ v = **slim**, fast, lose weight, abstain, eat sparingly ≠ **overindulge**

differ v = be dissimilar, contradict, contrast with, vary, belie ≠ **accord**; = disagree, clash, dispute, dissent ≠ **agree**

difficult adj = hard, tough, taxing, demanding, challenging ≠ **easy**; = **problematical**, involved, complex, complicated, obscure ≠ **simple**; = **troublesome**, demanding, perverse, fussy, fastidious ≠ **cooperative**

dig v = hollow out, mine, quarry, excavate, scoop out; = **delve**, tunnel, burrow; = **search**, hunt, root, delve, forage ♦ n = **cutting remark**, crack (Sl), insult, taunt, sneer; = **poke**, thrust, nudge,

summary. **digestible** adj **digestion** n **digestive** adj

digit n **1** finger or toe. **2** numeral. **digital** adj

dignity ① n, pl **–ties 1** stateliness, gravity. **2** worthiness. **dignify** v give dignity to. **dignitary** n holder of high office.

digress v deviate from subject. **digression** n

dike n see DYKE.

dilapidated adj in ruins.

dilate v widen, expand. **dilation** n

dilemma ① n position offering choice only between unwelcome alternatives.

dilettante n, pl **–tantes, –tanti 1** person who enjoys fine arts as pastime. **2** dabbler.

diligent adj hard-working. **diligently** adv **diligence** n

dill n herb with medicinal seeds.

dilute ① v reduce (liquid) in strength, esp. by adding water. **dilution** n

dim ① adj **dimmer, dimmest 1** faint, not bright. **2** mentally dull. **3** unfavourable. ♦ v **4** make, grow dim. **dimly** adv

dime n US 10-cent piece.

dimension ① n measurement, size.

diminish ① v lessen. **diminutive** adj very small.

diminuendo adj/adv Mus (of sound) dying away.

dimple n small hollow in surface of skin, esp. of cheek.

din ① n **1** continuous roar of confused noises. ♦ v **2** ram (fact, opinion etc.) into.

dine ① v eat dinner. **diner** n

dinghy n, pl **–ghies 1** small open boat. **2** collapsible rubber boat.

dingo n, pl **–goes** Aust. wild dog.

dingy adj **–gier, –giest** dirty-looking, dull.

dinner ① n **1** chief meal of the day. **2** official banquet.

dinosaur n extinct reptile, often of

—————— THESAURUS ——————

prod, jab

digest v = **ingest**, absorb, incorporate, dissolve, assimilate; = **take in**, absorb, grasp, soak up ♦ n = **summary**, résumé, abstract, epitome, synopsis

dignity n = **decorum**, gravity, majesty, grandeur, respectability; = **self-importance**, pride, self-esteem, self-respect

dilemma n = **predicament**, problem, difficulty, spot (Inf), mess

dilute v = **water down**, thin (out), weaken, adulterate, make thinner ≠ **condense**; = **reduce**, weaken,

diminish, temper, decrease ≠ **intensify**

dim adj = **poorly lit**, dark, gloomy, murky, shady; = **cloudy**, grey, gloomy, dismal, overcast ≠ **bright**; = **unclear**, obscured, faint, blurred, fuzzy ≠ **distinct** ♦ v = **turn down**, fade, dull; = **grow** or become faint fade, dull, grow or become dim

dimension n = **aspect**, side, feature, angle, facet

diminish v = **decrease**, decline, lessen, shrink, dwindle ≠ **grow**

din n = **noise**, row, racket, crash, clamour ≠ **silence**

D

gigantic size.

dint n **by dint of** by means of.

diocese n district, jurisdiction of bishop.

diode n *Electronics* device for converting alternating current to direct current.

dip 🕈 v **dipping, dipped 1** plunge or be plunged partly or for a moment into liquid. **2** take up in ladle, bucket etc. **3** direct headlights of vehicle downwards. **4** go down. **5** slope downwards. ◆ n **6** act of dipping. **7** bathe. **8** downward slope. **9** hollow.

diphtheria n infectious disease causing breathing difficulties.

diphthong n union of two vowel sounds.

diploma n document vouching for person's proficiency.

diplomacy 🕈 n **1** management of international relations. **2** tactful dealing. **diplomat** n **diplomatic** adj

dipper n **1** ladle, scoop. **2** bird (water ouzel).

dipsomania n uncontrollable craving for alcohol. **dipsomaniac** n/adj

dire 🕈 adj **1** terrible. **2** urgent.

direct 🕈 v **1** control, manage, order. **2** point out the way. **3** aim. ◆ adj **4** frank. **5** straight. **6** immediate. **7** lineal. **direction** n **1** directing. **2** aim. **3** instruction. **directive** adj/n **directly** adj **directness** n **director** n **1** one who directs, esp. a film. **2** member of board managing company. **directorial** adj **directorship** n **directory** n book of names, addresses, streets etc.

dirge n song of mourning.

dirk n short dagger.

dirt 🕈 n **1** filth. **2** soil. **3** obscene material. **dirty** adj **1** unclean. **2** obscene. **3** unfair. **4** dishonest.

dis– comb. form **1** negation,

——————— THESAURUS ———————

dine v = **eat**, lunch, feast, sup

dinner n = **meal**, main meal, spread (*Inf*), repast

dip v = **plunge**, immerse, bathe, duck, douse; = **drop (down)**, fall, lower, sink, descend ◆ n = **plunge**, ducking, soaking, drenching, immersion; = **nod**, drop, lowering, slump, sag; = **hollow**, hole, depression, pit, basin

diplomacy n = **statesmanship**, statecraft, international negotiation; = **tact**, skill, sensitivity, craft, discretion ≠ **tactlessness**

dire adj = **desperate**, pressing,

critical, terrible, crucial

direct adj = **quickest**, shortest; = **first-hand**, personal, immediate ≠ **indirect** ◆ v = **aim**, point, level, train, focus; = **guide**, show, lead, point the way, point in the direction of; = **control**, run, manage, lead, guide; = **order**, command, instruct, charge, demand

direction n = **way**, course, line, road, track; = **management**, control, charge, administration, leadership

dirt n = **filth**, muck, grime, dust, mud; = **soil**, ground, earth, clay,

opposition, deprivation. **2** in many verbs indicates undoing of the action of simple verb.

disable ❶ v **1** make unable. **2** cripple, maim. **disabled** adj

disability n, pl –ties

disabuse v **1** undeceive, disillusion. **2** free from error.

disadvantage ❶ n **1** drawback. **2** hindrance. ♦ **3** handicap.

disadvantaged adj deprived, discriminated against.

disadvantageous adj

disaffected adj ill-disposed.

disaffection n

disagree ❶ v –greeing, –greed **1** be at variance. **2** conflict. **3** (of food etc.) have bad effect on.

disagreeable adj **disagreement** n

disallow v reject as invalid.

disappear ❶ v **1** cease to be visible. **2** cease to exist.

disappearance n

disappoint ❶ v fail to fulfil (hope). **disappointment** n

disarm ❶ v **1** deprive of weapons. **2** win over. **disarming** adj removing hostility, suspicion.

disarmament n

disarray ❶ v **1** throw into disorder. ♦ n **2** disorderliness.

disaster ❶ n sudden or great misfortune. **disastrous** adj

disband v (cause to) cease to function as a group.

disbelieve v reject as false.

disburse v pay out money.

disc n **1** thin, flat, circular object. **2** record. **disc jockey** announcer playing records.

discard ❶ v **1** reject. **2** cast off.

discern v **1** make out. **2** distinguish. **discernible** adj **discerning** adj discriminating.

discharge ❶ v **1** release. **2** dismiss. **3** emit. **4** perform (duties), fulfil (obligations). **5** fire off. **6** unload. **7** pay. ♦ n **8** discharging. **9** being discharged.

disciple n follower of a teacher.

———— THESAURUS ————

turf

disable v = **handicap**, cripple, damage, paralyse, impair

disadvantage n = **drawback**, trouble, handicap, nuisance, snag ≠ **advantage**

disagree v = **differ (in opinion)**, argue, clash, dispute, dissent ≠ **agree**; = **make ill**, upset, sicken, trouble, hurt

disappear v = **vanish**, recede, evanesce ≠ **appear**; = **pass**, fade away, bolt, run away, take off (Inf) (Brit sl)

disappoint v = **let down**, dismay,

fail, disillusion, dishearten

disarm v = **demilitarize**, disband, demobilize, deactivate; = **win over**, persuade

disarray n = **confusion**, disorder, indiscipline, disunity, disorganization ≠ **order**; = **untidiness**, mess, chaos, muddle, clutter ≠ **tidiness**

disaster n = **catastrophe**, trouble, tragedy, ruin, misfortune

discard v = **get rid of**, drop, throw away or out reject, abandon ≠ **keep**

discharge v = **release**, free, clear,

discipline ● n 1 training that produces orderliness, obedience, self-control. 2 system of rules etc. 3 punishment. ♦ v 4 train. 5 punish. **disciplinarian** n person practising strict discipline. **disciplinary** adj

disclaim v deny, renounce. **disclaimer** n

disclose ● v make known. **disclosure** n

disco n, pl –cos club etc. for dancing to recorded music.

discolour v stain.

discomfit v embarrass.

discomfort ● n inconvenience.

disconcert v ruffle, upset.

disconnect v 1 break connection. 2 stop supply of electricity, gas etc.

disconsolate adj very unhappy.

discontent ● n lack of contentment.

discontinue v bring to an end.

discord n 1 strife. 2 disagreement of sounds. **discordant** adj

discount ● v 1 reject as unsuitable. 2 deduct from usual price. ♦ n 3 amount deducted from cost.

discourse ● n 1 conversation. 2 speech. ♦ v 3 speak, converse.

discourteous adj showing bad manners.

discover ● v 1 (be the first to) find. 2 learn about for first time. **discovery** n, pl –eries

discredit ● v 1 damage

——————— THESAURUS ———————

liberate, pardon; **= dismiss**, sack (Inf), fire (Inf), remove, expel; **= carry out**, perform, fulfil, accomplish, do; **= pay**, meet, clear, settle, square (up); **= pour forth**, release, leak, emit, dispense; **= fire**, shoot, set off, explode, let off ♦ n **= release**, liberation, clearance, pardon, acquittal; **= dismissal**, notice, removal, the boot (Sl), expulsion; ooze, secretion, excretion, pus; **= firing**, report, shot, blast, burst

discipline n **= control**, authority, regulation, supervision, orderliness; **= punishment**, penalty, correction, chastening, chastisement ♦ v **= punish**, correct, reprimand, castigate, chastise; **= train**, educate

disclose v **= make known**, reveal,

publish, relate, broadcast ≠ keep secret; **= show**, reveal, expose, unveil, uncover ≠ hide

discomfort n **= pain**, hurt, ache, throbbing, irritation ≠ comfort; **= uneasiness**, worry, anxiety, doubt, distress ≠ reassurance

discontent n **= dissatisfaction**, unhappiness, displeasure, regret, envy

discount n **= deduction**, cut, reduction, concession, rebate ♦ v **= mark down**, reduce, lower; **= disregard**, reject, ignore, overlook, discard

discourse n **= conversation**, talk, discussion, speech, communication; **= speech**, essay, lecture, sermon, treatise

discover v **= find out**, learn, notice, realize, recognize; **= find**,

reputation of. **2** cast doubt on. **3** reject as untrue. ♦ *n* **4** disgrace. **5** doubt.

discreet ⓘ *adj* prudent, circumspect.

discrepancy ⓘ *n, pl* **-cies** variation, as between figures.

discrete *adj* separate, distinct.

discretion ⓘ *n* **1** quality of being discreet. **2** freedom to act as one chooses. **discretionary** *adj*

discriminate ⓘ *v* **1** show prejudice. **2** distinguish between. **discriminating** *adj* showing good taste. **discrimination** *n*

discursive *adj* rambling.

discus *n* disc-shaped object thrown in athletic competition.

discuss ⓘ *v* **1** exchange opinions about. **2** debate. **discussion** *n*

disdain ⓘ *n/v* scorn. **disdainful** *adj*

disease ⓘ *n* illness.

disembark *v* land from ship etc.

disembodied *adj* (of spirit) released from bodily form.

disembowel *v* **-elling, -elled** remove the entrails of.

disenchanted *adj* disillusioned. **disenchantment** *n*

disengage *v* release.

disfavour *n* disapproval.

disfigure *v* mar appearance of.

disgrace ⓘ *n* **1** shame, dishonour. ♦ *v* **2** bring shame upon.

disgraceful *adj* **disgracefully** *adv*

disgruntled ⓘ *adj* **1** vexed. **2** put out.

disguise ⓘ *v* **1** change appearance of, make unrecognizable. **2** conceal. ♦ *n* **3** device to conceal identity.

disgust ⓘ *n/v* (affect with) violent

———————— THESAURUS ————————

come across, uncover, unearth, turn up

discredit *v* = **disgrace**, shame, smear, humiliate, taint ≠ **honour**; = **dispute**, question, challenge, deny, reject ♦ *n* = **disgrace**, scandal, shame, disrepute, stigma ≠ **honour**

discreet *adj* = **tactful**, diplomatic, guarded, careful, cautious ≠ **tactless**

discrepancy *n* = **disagreement**, difference, variation, conflict, contradiction

discretion *n* = **tact**, consideration, caution, diplomacy, prudence ≠ **tactlessness**; = **choice**, will, pleasure, preference, inclination

discriminate *v* = **differentiate**,

distinguish, separate, tell the difference, draw a distinction

discuss *v* = **talk about**, consider, debate, examine, argue about

disdain *n* = **contempt**, scorn, arrogance, derision, haughtiness ♦ *v* = **scorn**, reject, slight, disregard, spurn

disease *n* = **illness**, condition, complaint, infection, disorder

disgrace *n* = **shame**, degradation, disrepute, ignominy, dishonour ≠ **honour**; = **scandal**, stain, stigma, blot, blemish ♦ *v* = **shame**, humiliate, discredit, degrade, taint ≠ **honour**

disgruntled *adj* = **discontented**, dissatisfied, annoyed, irritated, put out

distaste, loathing.

dish ❶ n 1 shallow vessel for food. 2 portion or variety of food. ♦ v 3 serve (up).

dishearten v weaken hope, enthusiasm etc.

dishevelled adj untidy.

dishonest adj not honest or fair. **dishonesty** n

dishonour v 1 treat with disrespect. ♦ n 2 lack of respect. 3 shame, disgrace. **dishonourable** adj

disillusion v 1 destroy ideals of. ♦ n 2 disenchantment.

disinformation n false information intended to mislead.

disingenuous adj not sincere.

disinherit v deprive of inheritance.

disintegrate ❶ v fall to pieces.

disinterested adj free from bias or partiality.

disk n computer storage device.

dislike ❶ v 1 consider unpleasant or disagreeable. ♦ n 2 feeling of not liking.

dislocate v put out of joint. **dislocation** n

dislodge v drive out from previous position.

disloyal adj deserting one's allegiance. **disloyalty** n

dismal ❶ adj depressing.

dismantle ❶ v take apart.

dismay ❶ v 1 dishearten, daunt. ♦ n 2 consternation.

dismember v tear limb from limb.

dismiss ❶ v 1 discharge from employment. 2 send away. 3 reject. **dismissal** n **dismissive** adj scornful.

dismount v get off horse, bicycle.

disobey v refuse or fail to obey.

disobedience n **disobedient** adj

disorder ❶ n 1 confusion. 2 ailment. **disorderly** adj 1 disorganized. 2 unruly.

——————— THESAURUS ———————

disguise n = **costume**, mask, camouflage ♦ v = **hide**, cover, conceal, screen, mask

disgust n = **loathing**, revulsion, hatred, dislike, nausea ≠ **liking**; ♦ v = **sicken**, offend, revolt, put off, repel ≠ **delight**

dish n = **bowl**, plate, platter, salver; = **food**, fare, recipe, assign, designate

disintegrate v = **break up**, crumble, fall apart, separate, shatter

dislike v = **hate**, object to, loathe, despise, disapprove of ≠ **like**

dismal adj = **bad**, awful, dreadful,

rotten (Inf), terrible

dismantle v = **take apart**, strip, demolish, disassemble, take to pieces or bits

dismay n = **alarm**, fear, horror, anxiety, dread ♦ v = **alarm**, frighten, scare, panic, distress

dismiss v = **reject**, disregard; = **banish**, dispel, discard, set aside, cast out; = **sack**, fire (Inf), remove (Inf), axe (Inf), discharge

disorder n = **illness**, disease, complaint, condition, sickness; = **untidiness**, mess, confusion, chaos, muddle; = **disturbance**, riot, turmoil, unrest, uproar

disorientate, disorient v cause (someone) to lose his bearings, confuse. **disorientation** n

disown v refuse to acknowledge.

disparage v belittle.

dispassionate adj impartial.

dispatch ⊕ v 1 send off promptly. 2 finish off. ♦ n 3 speed. 4 official message.

dispel ⊕ v –pelling, –pelled drive away.

dispense ⊕ v 1 deal out. 2 make up (medicine). 3 administer (justice). **dispensable** adj **dispensary** n, pl –saries place where medicine is made up. **dispensation** n dispense with 1 do away with. 2 manage without.

disperse ⊕ v scatter. **dispersal** n

displace ⊕ v 1 move from its place. 2 take place of.

displacement n

display ⊕ v/n show.

displease v 1 offend. 2 annoy. **displeasure** n

dispose ⊕ v 1 arrange. 2 distribute. 3 deal with. **disposable** adj designed to be thrown away after use. **disposal** n **disposition** n 1 temperament. 2 arrangement. **dispose of** sell, get rid of.

disprove v show to be incorrect.

dispute ⊕ v 1 debate, discuss. 2 call into question. 3 contest. ♦ n 4 disagreement. **disputable** adj

disqualify v make ineligible. **disqualification** n

disquiet n anxiety, uneasiness.

disregard ⊕ v 1 ignore. ♦ n 2 lack of attention, respect.

disrepair n state of bad repair, neglect.

———— THESAURUS ————

dispatch v = **send**, consign; = **kill**, murder, destroy, execute, slaughter; = **carry out**, perform, fulfil, effect, finish ♦ n = **message**, news, report, story, account

dispel v = **drive away**, dismiss, eliminate, expel, disperse

dispense v = **distribute**, assign, allocate, allot, dole out; = **prepare**, measure, supply, mix; = **administer**, operate, carry out, implement, enforce

disperse v = **scatter**, spread, distribute, strew, diffuse; = **break up**, separate, scatter, dissolve, disband ≠ gather

displace v = **replace**, succeed, supersede, oust, usurp (Inf); = **move**, shift, disturb, budge,

misplace

display v = **show**, present, exhibit, put on view ≠ conceal ♦ n = **proof**, exhibition, demonstration, evidence, expression; = **exhibition**, show, demonstration, presentation, array

dispose v = **arrange**, put, place, group, order

dispute n = **disagreement**, conflict, argument, dissent, altercation ♦ v = **contest**, question, challenge, deny, doubt; = **argue**, fight, clash, disagree, fall out (Inf)

disqualify v = **ban**, rule out, prohibit, preclude, debar

disregard v = **ignore**, discount, overlook, neglect, pass over ≠ pay

disrepute n bad reputation.
disreputable adj
disrespect n lack of respect.
disrespectful adj
disrupt ⊕ v throw into disorder.
disruption n **disruptive** adj
dissatisfied ⊕ adj not pleased,
disappointed. **dissatisfaction** n
dissect v cut up (body) for
detailed examination.
dissemble v pretend, disguise.
disseminate v spread abroad.
dissent ⊕ v 1 differ in opinion. ♦
n 2 such difference. **dissension** n
dissertation n written thesis.
disservice n ill turn, wrong.
dissident ⊕ n/adj (one) not in
agreement, esp. with government.
dissimilar adj not alike, different.
dissipate v 1 scatter. 2 waste,
squander. **dissipated** adj
dissipation n
dissociate v separate, sever.
dissolute adj lax in morals.
dissolution n 1 break up. 2
termination.
dissolve ⊕ v 1 absorb or melt in

fluid. 2 annul. 3 disappear. 4
scatter. **dissolvable, dissoluble** adj
dissuade v advise to refrain,
persuade not to.
distance ⊕ n 1 amount of space
between two things. 2
remoteness. 3 aloofness. **distant**
adj
distaste n dislike. **distasteful** adj
distemper n 1 disease of dogs. 2
paint.
distend v swell out. **distension** n
distil v -tilling, -tilled 1 vaporize
and recondense a liquid. 2 purify.
distillation n **distiller** n maker of
alcoholic drinks. **distillery** n
distinct ⊕ adj 1 easily seen. 2
definite. 3 separate. **distinctly** adv
distinction n 1 point of difference.
2 act of distinguishing. 3 repute,
high honour. **distinctive** adj
characteristic.
distinguish ⊕ v 1 make difference
in. 2 recognize. 3 honour. 4 draw
distinction, grasp difference.
distinguishable adj **distinguished**
adj

——————— THESAURUS ———————

attention to
disrupt v = **interrupt**, stop, upset,
hold up, interfere with
dissatisfied adj = **discontented**,
frustrated, unhappy, disappointed,
fed up ≠ **satisfied**
dissent n = **disagreement**,
opposition, protest, resistance,
refusal ≠ **assent**
dissident n = **protester**, rebel,
dissenter, demonstrator, agitator
♦ adj = **dissenting**, disagreeing,
nonconformist, heterodox

dissolve v = **melt**, soften, thaw,
liquefy, deliquesce; = **end**,
suspend, break up, wind up,
terminate
distance n = **space**, length,
extent, range, stretch;
= **aloofness**, reserve, detachment,
restraint, stiffness **in the distance**
distinct adj = **different**, individual,
separate, discrete, unconnected
≠ **similar**; = **striking**, dramatic,
outstanding, noticeable, well-
defined

distort ❶ v 1 put out of shape. 2 misrepresent. **distortion** n

distract ❶ v 1 draw attention away. 2 divert. 3 perplex, drive mad. **distraction** n 1 agitation. 2 amusement.

distraught ❶ adj frantic, distracted.

distress ❶ n 1 trouble, pain. ♦ v 2 afflict.

distribute ❶ v 1 deal out. 2 spread. **distribution** n **distributor** n

district ❶ n 1 region, locality. 2 portion of territory.

distrust ❶ v 1 regard as untrustworthy. ♦ n 2 suspicion, doubt.

disturb ❶ v 1 intrude on. 2 trouble, agitate, unsettle. **disturbance** n

disuse n state of being no longer used. **disused** adj

ditch ❶ n 1 long narrow hollow dug in ground for drainage etc. ♦ v 2 Inf abandon.

dither v 1 be uncertain or indecisive. ♦ n 2 this state.

ditto n, pl **-tos** the same.

ditty n, pl **-ties** simple song.

divan n bed, couch without back or head.

dive ❶ v diving, dived 1 plunge under surface of water. 2 descend suddenly. 3 go deep down into. ♦ n 4 act of diving 5 Sl disreputable bar or club. **diver** n

diverge v 1 get farther apart. 2 separate.

diverse ❶ adj different, varied. **diversify** v **-fying, -fied** make

———————— THESAURUS ————————

distinguish v = differentiate, determine, separate, discriminate, decide; = **characterize**, mark, separate, single out, set apart; = **make out**, recognize, perceive, know, see

distort v = misrepresent, twist, bias, disguise, pervert; = **deform**, bend, twist, warp, buckle

distract v = divert, sidetrack, draw away, turn aside, lead astray; = **amuse**, occupy, entertain, beguile, engross

distraught adj = frantic, desperate, distressed, distracted, worked-up

distress n = suffering, pain, worry, grief, misery; = **need**, trouble, difficulties, poverty, hard times ♦ v = **upset**, worry, trouble,

disturb, grieve

distribute v = hand out, pass round; = **circulate**, deliver, convey

district n = area, region, sector, quarter, parish

distrust v = suspect, doubt, be wary of, mistrust, disbelieve ≠ trust ♦ n = **suspicion**, question, doubt, disbelief, scepticism ≠ trust

disturb v = interrupt, trouble, bother, plague, disrupt; = **upset**, concern, worry, trouble, alarm ≠ calm; = **muddle**, disorder, mix up, mess up, jumble up

ditch n = channel, drain, trench, dyke, furrow ♦ v = (Sl) **get rid of**, dump (Inf), scrap, discard, dispose of

dive v = plunge, drop, duck, dip, descend ♦ n = **plunge**, spring,

D

varied. **diversity** n, pl **–ties**

divert ⊕ v **1** turn aside. **2** amuse. **diversion** n

divide ⊕ v **1** make into parts, split up. **2** distribute, share. **3** become separated. ◆ n **4** watershed.

dividend n share of profits.

divine ⊕ adj **1** of, pert. to God. **2** sacred. ◆ v **3** guess. **4** predict.

divinity n **1** being divine. **2** study of theology.

division ⊕ n **1** act of dividing. **2** part of whole. **3** barrier. **4** section. **5** difference in opinion etc. **6** *Maths* method of finding how many times one number is contained in another. **7** army unit. **divisible** adj **divisive** adj causing disagreement.

divorce ⊕ n/v **1** (make) legal dissolution of marriage. **2** split.

divorcé n divorced person.

divulge v reveal.

DIY do-it-yourself.

dizzy ⊕ adj **–zier, –ziest** feeling dazed, unsteady. **dizziness** n

DJ disc jockey.

DNA n abbrev. for deoxyribonucleic acid, main constituent of the chromosomes of all organisms.

do v **does, doing, did, done 1** perform, effect, finish. **2** work at. **3** solve. **4** suit. **5** provide. **6** *Sl* cheat. **7** act. **8** fare. **9** suffice. **10** makes negative and interrogative sentences and expresses emphasis. ◆ n **11** *Inf* celebration. **do away with** destroy. **do up 1** fasten. **2** renovate.

Doberman pinscher, Doberman large black-and-tan dog.

dob in v **dobbing, dobbed** *Aust & NZ* **1** *informal* **2** inform against. **3 4** contribute to a fund.

docile adj willing to obey,

———— THESAURUS ————

jump, leap, lunge

diverse adj = **various**, mixed, varied, assorted, miscellaneous; = **different**, unlike, varying, separate, distinct

divert v = **redirect**, switch, avert, deflect, deviate; = **distract**, sidetrack, lead astray, draw or lead away from; = **entertain**, delight, amuse, please, charm

divide v = **share**, distribute, allocate, dispense, allot; = **split**, break up, come between, estrange, cause to disagree

divine adj = **heavenly**, spiritual, holy, immortal, supernatural; = **sacred**, religious, holy, spiritual,

blessed ◆ v = **guess**, suppose, perceive, discern, infer

division n = **separation**, dividing, splitting up, partition, cutting up; = **sharing**, sharing, distribution, assignment, rationing; = **disagreement**, split, rift, rupture, abyss ≠ **unity**; = **department**, group, branch

divorce n = **separation**, split, break-up, parting, split-up ◆ v = **separate**, split up, part company, dissolve your marriage

dizzy adj = **giddy**, faint, light-headed, swimming, reeling; = **confused**, dazzled, at sea, bewildered, muddled

submissive. **docility** n

dock¹ ❶ n 1 artificial enclosure for loading or repairing ships. ◆ v 2 put or go into dock. **docker** n **dockyard** n

dock² ❶ n 1 solid part of tail. 2 stump. ◆ v 3 cut short. 4 deduct (an amount) from.

dock³ n enclosure in criminal court for prisoner.

dock⁴ n coarse weed.

docket n piece of paper sent with package etc.

doctor ❶ n 1 medical practitioner. 2 one holding university's highest degree. ◆ v 3 treat medically. 4 repair. 5 falsify (accounts etc.).

doctrine ❶ n 1 what is taught. 2 belief, dogma. **doctrinaire** adj stubbornly insistent about applying theories.

document ❶ n 1 piece of paper etc. providing information. ◆ v 2 furnish with proofs.

documentary adj, pl **-ries**, n type of film dealing with real life.

dodder v totter, as with age.

dodge ❶ v 1 (attempt to) avoid by moving quickly. 2 evade. ◆ n 3 trick, act of dodging. **dodgy** adj **dodgier, dodgiest** Inf untrustworthy.

Dodgem ® n car used for bumping other cars in rink at funfair.

dodo n, pl **dodos, dodoes** large extinct bird.

doe n female of deer, hare, rabbit.

does third person sing. of DO.

doff v take off.

dog ❶ n 1 domesticated carnivorous four-legged mammal. 2 male of wolf, fox and other animals. 3 person (in contempt, abuse or playfully). ◆ v 4 follow closely. **dogged** adj persistent, tenacious. **dog-ear** n turned-down corner of page in book.

dog-end n 1 Inf cigarette end. 2 rejected piece of anything.

dogfight n 1 close combat between fighter aircraft. 2 rough fight. **dogleg** n sharp bend.

dogsbody n Inf one carrying out menial tasks.

doggerel n trivial verse.

—— THESAURUS ——

dock¹ n = **port**, haven, harbour, pier, wharf ◆ v = **moor**, land, anchor, put in, tie up; **link up**, unite, join, couple, rendezvous

dock² v = **cut**, reduce, decrease, diminish, lessen ≠ **increase**; = **deduct**, subtract

doctor n = **physician**, medic (Inf), general practitioner, medical practitioner, G.P. ◆ v = **change**, alter, interfere with, disguise, pervert; = **add to**, spike, cut, mix

something with something, dilute

doctrine n = **teaching**, principle, belief, opinion, conviction

document n = **paper**, form, certificate, report, record ◆ v = **support**, certify, verify, detail, validate

dodge v = **duck**, dart, swerve, sidestep, shoot; = **evade**, avoid, escape, get away from, elude ◆ n = **trick**, scheme, ploy, trap, device

dog n = **hound**, canine, pooch

dogma n article of belief.

dogmatic adj asserting opinions with arrogance.

doily n, pl **-lies** small lacy mat to place under cake, dish etc.

doldrums pl n **1** state of depression. **2** region of light winds and calms near the equator.

dole n **1** Inf payment made to unemployed. ◆ v **2** distribute.

doleful adj dreary, mournful.

doll n child's toy image of human being.

dollar n standard monetary unit of many countries, esp. USA.

dollop n Inf semisolid lump.

dolly n, pl **-lies 1** doll. **2** wheeled support for film, TV camera.

dolphin n sea mammal with beaklike snout.

domain n **1** lands held or ruled over. **2** sphere of influence.

dome n **1** rounded roof. **2** something of this shape.

domestic ❶ adj **1** of, in the home. **2** home-loving. **3** (of animals) tamed. **4** of, in one's own country.

◆ n **5** house servant. **domesticate** v tame.

domicile n person's regular place of abode.

dominate ❶ v rule, control. **2** (of heights) overlook. **3** be most influential. **dominance** n **dominant** adj **domination** n **domineering** adj imperious.

dominion n **1** sovereignty. **2** rule. **3** territory of government.

don¹ ❶ v **donning, donned** put on (clothes).

don² n **1** fellow or tutor of college. **2** Spanish title, Sir.

donate ❶ v give. **donation** n **donor** n

done past participle of DO.

donkey n ass.

doodle v/n scribble.

doom ❶ n **1** fate. **2** ruin. **3** judicial sentence. ◆ v **4** condemn. **5** destine. **doomsday** n **1** day of Last Judgment. **2** dreaded day.

door ❶ n hinged barrier to close entrance. **doorway** n

dope ❶ n **1** narcotic drug **2** Inf

———————— THESAURUS ————————

(SI), cur, man's best friend ◆ v = **plague**, follow, trouble, haunt, hound; = **pursue**, follow, track, chase, trail

domestic adj = **home**, internal, native, indigenous; = **household**, home, family, private; = **home-loving**, homely, housewifely, stay-at-home, domesticated; = **domesticated**, trained, tame, pet, house-trained ◆ n = **servant**, help, maid, daily, char (Inf)

dominate v = **control**, rule, direct, govern, monopolize; = **tower above**, overlook, survey, stand over, loom over

don¹ v = **put on**, get into, dress in, pull on, change into

donate v = **give**, present, contribute, grant, subscribe

doom n = **destruction**, ruin, catastrophe, downfall ◆ v = **condemn**, sentence, consign, destine

door n = **opening**, entry, entrance, exit, doorway

stupid person. ♦ v 3 drug. **dopey,
dopy** adj

dormant adj 1 not active. 2
sleeping.

dormitory n, pl **-ries** sleeping
room with many beds.

dormouse n, pl **-mice** small
hibernating mouselike rodent.

dorp n S Afr small town.

dorsal adj of, on back.

dose ⊕ n 1 amount (of drug etc.).
♦ v 2 give doses to. **dosage** n

dossier n set of papers on
particular subject.

dot ⊕ n 1 small spot, mark. ♦ v 2
mark with dots. 3 sprinkle.

dote v **dote on** love to an
excessive degree. **dotage** n
senility.

double ⊕ adj 1 of two parts,
layers etc. 2 twice as much or
many. 3 designed for two users. ♦
adv 4 twice. 5 to twice the amount
or extent. 6 in a pair. ♦ n 7 person
or thing exactly like another. 8
quantity twice as much as
another. 9 sharp turn. 10 running
pace. ♦ v 11 make, become

double. 12 increase twofold. 13
fold in two. 14 turn sharply.
doubly adv **double bass** lowest
member of violin family. **double–
cross** v betray.

doubt ⊕ v 1 suspect. 2 hesitate to
believe. 3 call in question. ♦ n 4
(state of) uncertainty. **doubtful** adj
doubtless adv 1 certainly. 2
presumably.

dough n 1 flour or meal kneaded
with water 2 Sl money. **doughnut**
n sweetened and fried piece of
dough.

doughty adj **-tier, -tiest** hardy,
resolute.

dour adj grim, severe.

douse v 1 thrust into water. 2
extinguish (light).

dove n bird of pigeon family.

dovetail v fit closely, neatly
together.

dowager n widow with title or
property from husband.

dowdy adj **-dier, -diest** shabbily
dressed.

dowel n wooden, metal peg.

down¹ ⊕ adv 1 to, in, or towards,

——————— THESAURUS ———————

dope n = (Sl) **drugs**, narcotics,
opiates; = (Inf) **idiot**, fool, twit (Inf,
chiefly Brit), dunce, simpleton (Inf)
♦ v = **drug**, knock out, sedate,
stupefy, anaesthetize

dose n = **measure**, amount,
allowance, portion, prescription

dot n = **spot**, point, mark, fleck,
jot ♦ v = **spot**, stud, fleck, speckle
on the dot = **on time**, promptly,
precisely, exactly (Inf), to the
minute

double adj = **dual**, enigmatic,
twofold ♦ v = **multiply by two**,
duplicate, increase twofold,
enlarge, increase twofold ♦ n
= **twin**, lookalike, spitting image,
clone, replica (Inf) **at** or **on the
double**

doubt n = **uncertainty**, confusion,
hesitation, suspense, indecision
≠ **certainty** ♦ v = **be uncertain**, be
sceptical, be dubious; = **waver**,
hesitate, vacillate, fluctuate

lower position. **2** (of payment) on the spot. ◆ *prep* **3** from higher to lower part of. **4** along. ◆ *adj* **5** depressed. ◆ *v* **6** knock, pull, push down. **7** *Inf* drink. **downward** *adj/adv* **downwards** *adv* **downbeat** *adj Inf* gloomy. **downcast** *adj* **1** dejected. **2** looking down. **downfall** *n* sudden loss of position. **downpour** *n* heavy fall of rain. **downright** *adj* **1** straightforward. ◆ *adv* **2** quite, thoroughly. **down-and-out** *adj/n* destitute, homeless (person).

down² *n* **1** soft underfeathers, hair. **2** fluff. **downy** *adj*

downs *pl n* open high land.

downtown *US, Canad and NZ* *n* **1** the central or lower part of a city, especially the main commercial area. ◆ *adv* **2** towards, to, or into this area.

dowry *n, pl* **-ries** property wife brings to husband.

doyen *n* senior, respected member of group.

doze *v/n* sleep, nap. **dozy** *adj* **dozier, doziest**

dozen *n* (set of) twelve.

drab *adj* **drabber, drabbest** dull, monotonous.

draconian *adj* very harsh, cruel.

draft¹ ❶ *n* **1** sketch. **2** rough copy of document. **3** order for money. **4** detachment of troops. ◆ *v* **5** make sketch of. **6** make rough copy of. **7** send detached party.

draft² *n US* select for compulsory military service.

drag ❶ *v* **dragging, dragged 1** pull along with difficulty. **2** trail. **3** sweep with net. **4** protract. **5** lag, trail. **6** be tediously protracted. ◆ *n* **7** check on progress. **8** checked motion.

dragon *n* mythical fire–breathing monster. **dragonfly** *n* long–bodied insect with gauzy wings.

dragoon *n* **1** cavalryman. ◆ *v* **2** coerce.

drain ❶ *v* **1** draw off (liquid) by pipes, ditches etc. **2** dry. **3** empty, exhaust. **4** flow off or away. ◆ *n* **5** channel. **6** sewer. **7** depletion. **8** strain. **drainage** *n*

drake *n* male duck.

dram *n* small draught of strong drink.

drama ❶ *n* **1** stage play. **2** art or literature of plays. **3** playlike series of events. **dramatic** *adj* **1** of drama. **2** striking or effective. **dramatist** *n*

———————— THESAURUS ————————

down¹ *adj* = **depressed**, low, sad, unhappy, discouraged ◆ *v* = (*Inf*) **swallow**, drink (down), drain, gulp (down), put away

draft¹ *n* = **outline**, plan, sketch, version, rough; = **money order**, bill (of exchange), cheque, postal order ◆ *v* = **outline**, write, plan, produce, create

drag *v* = **pull**, draw, haul, trail, tow ◆ *n* = (*Sl*) **nuisance**, pain (*Inf*), bore, bother, pest

drain *v* = **remove**, draw, empty, withdraw, tap; = **flow out**, leak, trickle, ooze, seep; = **drink up**, swallow, finish, put away, quaff ◆ *n* = **sewer**, channel, pipe, sink, ditch; = **reduction**, strain, drag,

writer of plays. **dramatize** v adapt for acting.

drape ❶ v cover, adorn with cloth. **draper** n dealer in cloth, linen etc. **drapery** n, pl **–peries**

drastic ❶ adj 1 extreme. 2 severe.

draught ❶ n 1 current of air. 2 act of drawing. 3 act of drinking. 4 quantity drunk at once. ♦ pl 5 game played on chessboard with flat round pieces. ♦ adj 6 for drawing. 7 drawn. **draughty** adj full of air currents. **draughtsman** n one who makes drawings, plans etc. **draughtsmanship** n

draw ❶ v drawing, drew, drawn 1 portray with pencil etc. 2 pull, haul. 3 attract. 4 come (near). 5 entice. 6 take from (well, barrel etc.). 7 receive (money). 8 get by lot. 9 make, admit current of air. 10 (of game) tie. ♦ n 11 act of drawing. 12 casting of lots. 13 tie.

drawer n 1 one who or that which draws. 2 sliding box in table or chest. **drawing** n 1 art of depicting in line. 2 sketch so done.

drawback n snag. **drawbridge** n hinged bridge to pull up. **drawing room** living room, sitting room. **draw up** 1 arrange in order. 2 stop.

drawl v 1 speak slowly. ♦ n 2 such speech.

drawn ❶ adj haggard.

dread ❶ v 1 fear greatly. ♦ n 2 awe, terror. ♦ adj 3 feared, awful. **dreadful** adj disagreeable, shocking or bad. **dreadfully** adv

dream ❶ n 1 vision during sleep. 2 fancy, reverie, aspiration. ♦ v 3 have dreams. 4 see, imagine in dreams. 5 think of as possible. **dreamer** n **dreamy** adj

dreary ❶ adj drearier, dreariest dismal, dull. **drearily** adv

————————— THESAURUS —————————

exhaustion, sapping

drama n = **play**, show, stage show, dramatization; = **theatre**, acting, stagecraft, dramaturgy; = **excitement**, crisis, spectacle, turmoil, histrionics

drape v = **cover**, wrap, fold, swathe

drastic adj = **extreme**, strong, radical, desperate, severe

draught n = **breeze**, current, movement, flow, puff

draw v = **sketch**, design, outline, trace, portray; = **pull**, drag, haul, tow, tug; = **extract**, take, remove; = **deduce**, make, take, derive, infer ♦ n = **tie**, deadlock, stalemate,

impasse, dead heat; = (Inf) **appeal**, pull (Inf), charm, attraction, lure

drawn adj = **tense**, worn, stressed, tired, pinched

dread v = **fear**, shrink from, cringe at the thought of, quail from, shudder to think about ♦ n = **fear**, alarm, horror, terror, dismay

dream n = **vision**, illusion, delusion, hallucination; = **ambition**, wish, fantasy, desire, pipe dream; = **delight**, pleasure, joy, beauty, treasure ♦ v = **have dreams**, hallucinate

dreary adj = **dull**, boring, tedious, drab, tiresome ≠ **exciting**

dredge v **1** bring up mud etc. from sea bottom. ♦ n **2** scoop.

dredger n boat with machinery for dredging.

dregs pl n sediment, grounds.

drench ⊕ v wet thoroughly, soak.

dress ⊕ v **1** put on clothes. **2** array for show. **3** prepare. **4** put dressing on (wound). ♦ n **5** one-piece garment for woman. **6** clothing. **7** evening wear. **dresser** n **1** one who dresses. **2** kitchen sideboard. **dressing** n something applied, as sauce to food, ointment to wound etc. **dressing-down** n Inf severe scolding. **dressing gown** robe worn before dressing. **dressy** adj stylish.

dressage n method of training horse.

drey n squirrel's nest.

dribble ⊕ v **1** flow in drops, trickle. **2** run at the mouth. ♦ n **3** trickle, drop.

drift ⊕ v **1** be carried as by current of air, water. ♦ n **2** process of being driven by current. **3** tendency. **4** meaning. **5** wind-heaped mass of snow, sand etc.

drifter n driftwood n wood washed ashore by sea.

drill¹ ⊕ n **1** boring tool. **2** exercise of soldiers. **3** routine teaching. ♦ v **4** bore hole. **5** exercise in routine. **6** practise routine.

drill² v/n (machine to) sow seed in furrows.

drink ⊕ v drinking, drank, drunk **1** swallow liquid. ♦ n **2** liquid for drinking. **3** intoxicating liquor. **drinkable** adj **drinker** n

drip ⊕ v dripping, dripped **1** fall or let fall in drops. ♦ n **2** Med intravenous administration of solution **3** Inf insipid person. **dripping** n **1** melted fat from roasting meat. ♦ adj **2** very wet. **drip-dry** adj (of fabric) drying free of creases if hung up while wet.

drive ⊕ v driving, drove, driven **1**

————————— THESAURUS —————————

drench v = **soak**, flood, wet, drown, steep

dress n = **frock**, gown, robe; = **clothing**, clothes, costume, garments, apparel ♦ v = **put on clothes**, don clothes, slip on or into something ≠ **undress**; = **bandage**, treat, plaster, bind up

dribble v = **run**, drip, trickle, drop, leak; = **drool**, drivel, slaver, slobber

drift v = **float**, go (aimlessly), bob, coast, slip; = **wander**, stroll, stray, roam, meander ♦ n = **pile**, bank, mass, heap, mound; = **meaning**, point, gist, direction, import

drill¹ n = **bit**, borer, gimlet, boring tool; = **training**, exercise, discipline, instruction, preparation ♦ v = **bore**, pierce, penetrate, sink in, puncture; = **train**, coach, teach, exercise, discipline

drink v = **swallow**, sip, suck, gulp, sup; = **booze** (Inf), tipple, tope, hit the bottle (Inf) ♦ n = **glass**, cup, draught; = **beverage**, refreshment, potion, liquid; hooch or hootch (informal, chiefly U.S. & Canad.)

drip v = **drop**, splash, sprinkle, trickle, dribble ♦ n = **drop**, bead, trickle, dribble, droplet; = (Inf)

urge in some direction. **2** make
move and steer (vehicle, animal
etc.). **3** be conveyed in vehicle. **4**
hit with force. ♦ *n* **5** act, action of
driving. **6** journey in vehicle. **7**
united effort, campaign. **8** energy.
9 forceful stroke. **driver** *n*

drivel *v* **1** run at the mouth. **2** talk
nonsense. ♦ *n* **3** silly nonsense.

drizzle *v/n* rain in fine drops.

droll *adj* funny, odd.

dromedary *n, pl* **–daries** one–
humped camel.

drone *n* **1** male bee. **2** lazy idler. **3**
deep humming. ♦ *v* **4** hum. **5** talk
in monotonous tone.

drool *v* slaver, drivel.

droop *v* **1** hang down. **2** wilt, flag.
♦ *n* **droopy** *adj*

drop ⊕ *n* **dropping, dropped 1**
globule of liquid. **2** very small
quantity. **3** fall, descent. **4** distance
to fall. ♦ *v* **5** (let) fall. **6** utter
casually. **7** set down. **8**

discontinue. **9** come or go
casually. **droplet** *n* **dropout** *n*
person who fails to complete
course of study or one who rejects
conventional society. **droppings** *pl*
n dung of rabbits, sheep, birds etc.

dropsy *n* disease causing watery
fluid to collect in the body.

dross *n* **1** scum of molten metal. **2**
impurity, refuse.

drought ⊕ *n* long spell of dry
weather.

drove ⊕ *n* herd, flock, esp. in
motion. **drover** *n* driver of cattle
etc.

drown ⊕ *v* **1** die or be killed by
immersion in liquid. **2** make sound
inaudible by louder sound.

drudge *v* **1** work at menial or
distasteful tasks. ♦ *n* **2** one who
drudges. **drudgery** *n*

drug ⊕ *n* **1** medical substance. **2**
narcotic. ♦ *v* **3** mix drugs with. **4**
administer drug to.

———— THESAURUS ————

weakling, wet (*Brit inf*), weed (*Inf*),
softie (*Inf*), mummy's boy (*Inf*)

drive *v* = **operate**, manage,
direct, guide, handle; = **push**,
propel; = **thrust**, push, hammer,
ram; = **herd**, urge, impel ♦ *n*
= **run**, ride, trip, journey, spin (*Inf*);
= **initiative**, energy, enterprise,
ambition, motivation; = **campaign**,
push (*Inf*), crusade, action, effort

drop *v* = **fall**, decline, diminish;
often with **away** = **decline**, fall,
sink; = **plunge**, fall, tumble,
descend, plummet ♦ *v*
= **decrease**, fall, cut, lowering,
decline; = **droplet**, bead, globule,

bubble, pearl; = **dash**, shot (*Inf*),
spot, trace, sip; = **fall**, plunge,
descent

drought *n* = **water shortage**,
dryness, dry spell, aridity ≠ **flood**

drove *n* (*often plural*) = **herd**,
company, crowds, collection, mob

drown *v* = **drench**, flood, soak,
steep, swamp; = **overwhelm**,
overcome, wipe out, overpower,
obliterate

drug *n* = **medication**, medicine,
remedy, physic, medicament;
= **dope** (*Sl*), narcotic (*Sl*),
stimulant, opiate ♦ *v* = **knock out**,
dope (*Sl*), numb, deaden, stupefy

drum ❶ n 1 percussion instrument of skin stretched over round hollow frame. 2 thing shaped like drum. ♦ v 3 play drum. 4 tap, thump continuously. **drummer** n **drum major** leader of military band. **drumstick** n 1 stick for beating drum. 2 lower joint of cooked fowl's leg.

drunk ❶ adj/n (person) overcome by strong drink. **drunkard** n **drunken** adj **drunkenness** n

dry ❶ adj **drier, driest** 1 without moisture. 2 not yielding liquid. 3 unfriendly. 4 caustically witty. 5 uninteresting. 6 lacking sweetness. ♦ v 7 remove water, moisture. 8 become dry. 9 evaporate. **dryer, drier** n 1 person or thing that dries. 2 apparatus for removing moisture. **dryly, drily** adv **dry–clean** v clean clothes with solvent. **dry–cleaner** n **dry–cleaning** n

dual ❶ adj twofold.

dub v **dubbing, dubbed** 1 confer knighthood on. 2 give title to. 3 provide film with soundtrack.

dubious ❶ adj causing doubt.

duchess n duke's wife or widow.

duck ❶ n 1 common swimming bird. ♦ v 2 plunge (someone) under water. 3 bob down. 4 Inf avoid. **duckling** n young duck.

duct n channel, tube.

dud n 1 futile, worthless person or thing. ♦ adj 2 worthless.

due ❶ adj 1 owing. 2 proper, expected. 3 timed for. ♦ adv 4 (with points of compass) exactly. ♦ n 5 person's right. 6 charge, fee etc. **duly** adj 1 properly. 2 punctually. **due to 1** attributable to. 2 caused by.

duel ❶ n 1 arranged fight with deadly weapons, between two persons. ♦ v 2 fight in duel.

———————— THESAURUS ————————

drum v = **pound**, beat, tap, rap, thrash

drunk adj = **intoxicated**, plastered (Sl), drunken, merry (Brit inf), under the influence (Inf) ♦ n = **drunkard**, alcoholic, lush (Sl), boozer (Inf), wino (Inf)

dry adj = **dehydrated**, dried–up, arid, parched, desiccated ≠ **wet**; = **thirsty**, parched; = **sarcastic**, cynical, low–key, sly, sardonic ♦ v = **drain**, make dry

dual adj = **twofold**, double, twin, matched, paired

dubious adj = **suspect**, suspicious, crooked, dodgy (Brit, Aust & NZ inf), questionable ≠ **trustworthy**;

= **unsure**, uncertain, suspicious, hesitating, doubtful ≠ **sure**

duck v = **bob**, drop, lower, bend, bow; = (Inf) **dodge**, avoid, escape, evade, elude; = **dunk**, wet, plunge, dip, submerge

due adj = **expected**, scheduled; = **fitting**, deserved, appropriate, justified, suitable; = **payable**, outstanding, owed, owing, unpaid ♦ adv = **directly**, dead, straight, exactly, undeviatingly ♦ n = **right(s)**, privilege, deserts, merits, comeuppance (Inf)

duel n = **single combat**, affair of honour ♦ v = **fight**, struggle, clash, compete, contest

duet n piece of music for two performers.

duffel, duffle n 1 coarse woollen cloth. 2 coat of this.

duffer n stupid inefficient person.

dugout n 1 covered excavation to provide shelter. 2 canoe of hollowed–out tree. 3 *Sport* covered bench for players when not on the field.

duke n peer of rank next below prince. **dukedom** n

dulcet adj (of sounds) sweet, melodious.

dulcimer n stringed instrument played with hammers.

dull ⓣ adj 1 stupid. 2 sluggish. 3 tedious. 4 overcast. ◆ v 5 make or become dull. **dullard** n **dully** adv

dumb ⓣ adj 1 incapable of speech. 2 silent. 3 *Inf* stupid.

dumbbell n weight for exercises.

dumbfound v confound into silence.

dummy ⓣ n, pl **–mies** 1 tailor's or dressmaker's model. 2 imitation object. 3 baby's dummy teat. ◆

adj 4 sham, bogus.

dump ⓣ v 1 throw down in mass. 2 deposit. 3 unload. ◆ n 4 rubbish heap. 5 temporary depot of stores 6 *Inf* squalid place. ◆ pl 7 low spirits. **dumpling** n small round pudding of dough. **dumpy** adj short, stout.

dunce n stupid pupil.

dune n sandhill.

dung n excrement of animals.

dungarees pl n overalls made of coarse cotton fabric.

dungeon n underground cell for prisoners.

dunk v dip bread etc. into liquid before eating it.

duo n, pl **duos** pair of performers.

duodenum n, pl **–na, –nums** upper part of small intestine. **duodenal** adj

dupe n 1 victim of delusion or sharp practice. ◆ v 2 deceive.

duplex n US and Canad an apartment on two floors.

duplicate ⓣ v 1 make exact copy of. ◆ adj 2 double. ◆ n 3 exact

———— THESAURUS ————

dull adj = boring, tedious, dreary, flat, plain ≠ **exciting**; = lifeless, indifferent, apathetic, listless, unresponsive ≠ **lively**; = cloudy, dim, gloomy, dismal, overcast ≠ **bright**; = blunt, blunted, unsharpened ≠ **sharp** ◆ v = relieve, blunt, lessen, moderate, soften

dumb adj = unable to speak, mute ≠ **articulate**; = silent, mute, speechless, tongue–tied, wordless

dummy n = model, figure,

mannequin, form, manikin; = imitation, copy, duplicate, sham, counterfeit; = (*SI*) fool, idiot, dunce, oaf, simpleton ◆ adj = imitation, false, fake, artificial, mock

dump v = drop, deposit, throw down, let fall, fling down; = get rid of, tip, dispose of, unload, jettison ◆ n = rubbish tip, tip, junkyard, rubbish heap, refuse heap; = (*Inf*) pigsty, hole (*Inf*), slum, hovel

copy. **duplication** n **duplicator** n **duplicity** n deceitfulness, double-dealing.

durable ⊕ adj lasting, resisting wear. **durability** n.

duration ⊕ n time things last.

duress n compulsion.

during prep throughout, in the time of, in the course of.

dusk ⊕ n darker stage of twilight. **dusky** adj

dust ⊕ n 1 fine particles, powder of earth or other matter. 2 ashes of the dead. ♦ v 3 sprinkle with powder. 4 rid of dust. **duster** n cloth for removing dust. **dusty** adj covered with dust. **dustbin** n container for household rubbish.

Dutch adj pert. to the Netherlands, its inhabitants, its language.

duty ⊕ n, pl **-ties** 1 moral or legal obligation. 2 that which is due. 3 tax on goods. **duteous** adj **dutiful** adj

duvet n quilt filled with down or artificial fibre.

dwarf ⊕ n, pl **dwarfs**, **dwarves** 1 very undersized person. 2 mythological, small, manlike creature. ♦ adj 3 unusually small. ♦ v 4 make seem small. 5 make stunted.

dwell ⊕ v **dwelling**, **dwelt** 1 live, make one's home (in). 2 think, speak at length (on). **dwelling** n house.

dwindle ⊕ v waste away.

dye ⊕ v 1 impregnate (cloth etc.) with colouring matter. 2 colour thus. ♦ n 3 colouring matter in solution.

dyke n 1 embankment to prevent flooding. 2 ditch.

dynamic adj full of energy, ambition, and new ideas.

dynamics pl n branch of physics dealing with force as producing or

——————— THESAURUS ———————

duplicate v = **repeat**, reproduce, copy, clone, replicate ♦ adj = **identical**, matched, matching, twin, corresponding ♦ n = **copy**, facsimile

durable adj = **hard-wearing**, strong, tough, reliable, resistant ≠ **fragile**

duration n = **length**, time, period, term, stretch

dusk n = **twilight**, evening, nightfall, sunset, dark ≠ **dawn**

dust n = **grime**, grit, powder ♦ v = **sprinkle**, cover, powder, spread, spray

duty n = **responsibility**, job, task, work, role; = **tax**, toll, levy, tariff, excise

dwarf v = **tower above** or over dominate, overlook, stand over, loom over ♦ adj = **miniature**, small, baby, tiny, diminutive

dwell v = (Formal, literary) **live**, reside, lodge, abide

dwindle v = **lessen**, decline, fade, shrink, diminish ≠ **increase**

dye v = **colour**, stain, tint, tinge, pigment ♦ n = **colouring**, colour, pigment, stain, tint

dynamic adj = **energetic**, powerful, vital, go-ahead, lively ≠ **apathetic**

affecting motion. **dynamic** *adj* energetic and forceful.

dynamite *n* **1** high explosive mixture. ♦ *v* **2** blow up with this.

dynamo *n, pl* **-mos** machine to convert mechanical into electrical energy, generator of electricity.

dynasty ❶ *n, pl* **-ties** line, family of hereditary rulers.

dysentery *n* infection of intestine causing severe diarrhoea.

dysfunction *n* abnormal, impaired functioning.

dyslexia *n* impaired ability to read. **dyslexic** *adj*

dyspepsia *n* indigestion.

dyspeptic *adj/n*

dystrophy *n* wasting of bodily tissues, esp. muscles.

———— THESAURUS ————

dynasty *n* = **empire**, house, rule, regime, sovereignty

E e

E 1 East. **2** Eastern. **3** English.
each ⊕ *adj/pron* every one taken
separately.
eager ⊕ *adj* **1** having a strong
wish. **2** keen, impatient.
eagle *n* large bird of prey.
ear¹ ⊕ *n* **1** organ of hearing. **2**
sense of hearing. **3** sensitiveness to
sounds. **4** attention. **earache** *n*
pain in ear. **eardrum** *n* thin piece
of skin inside the ear. **earmark** *v*
assign for definite purpose.
earphone *n* receiver for radio etc.
held or put in ear. **earring** *n*
ornament for lobe of the ear.
earshot *n* hearing distance. **earwig**
n small insect with pincer–like tail.
ear² *n* spike, head of corn.
earl *n* British nobleman.
early ⊕ *adj/adv* **–lier, –liest 1**
before expected or usual time. **2** in
first part, near beginning.

earn ⊕ *v* **1** obtain by work or
merit. **2** gain. **earnings** *pl n*
earnest ⊕ *adj* serious, sincere.
earth ⊕ *n* **1** planet we live on. **2**
ground. **3** soil. **4** electrical
connection to earth. ♦ *v* **5** cover,
connect with earth. **earthly** *adj*
possible. **earthy** *adj* **1** of earth. **2**
uninhibited. **earthenware** *n*
(vessels of) baked clay. **earthquake**
n convulsion of earth's surface.
earthworm *n*
ease ⊕ *n* **1** comfort. **2** freedom
from constraint, awkwardness or
trouble. **3** idleness. ♦ *v* **4** reduce
burden. **5** give ease to. **6** slacken.
7 (cause to) move carefully. **easily**
adv **easy** *adj* **1** not difficult. **2** free
from pain, care, or anxiety. **3**
compliant. **4** comfortable. **easy–**
going *adj* **1** not fussy. **2** indolent.
easel *n* frame to support picture

─────── THESAURUS ───────

each *pron* = **every one**, all, each
one, each and every one, one and
all
eager *adj* = **anxious**, keen,
hungry, impatient, itching
≠ **unenthusiastic**
ear¹ *n* = **sensitivity**, taste,
discrimination, appreciation,
observation
early *adv* = **in good time**,
beforehand, ahead of schedule, in
advance, with time to spare
≠ **late**; ♦ *adj* = **first**, opening,

initial, introductory; = **premature**,
forward, advanced, untimely,
unseasonable ≠ **belated**
earn *v* = **be paid**, make, get,
receive, gain; = **deserve**, win,
gain, attain, justify
earnest *adj* = **serious**, grave,
intense, dedicated, sincere
≠ **frivolous**; = **determined**,
dogged, intent, persistent,
persevering
earth *n* = **world**, planet, globe,
sphere, orb; = **ground**, land, dry

etc.

east n 1 part of horizon where sun rises. 2 eastern lands, orient. ◆ adj 3 on, in, or near, east. 4 coming from east. ◆ adv 5 from, or to, east. **easterly** adj/adv **eastern** adj **eastward** adj/adv **eastwards** adv

Easter n festival of the Resurrection of Christ.

easy 🛈 adj 1 not difficult. 2 free from pain, care, or anxiety. 3 tolerant and understanding.

eat 🛈 v eating, ate, eaten 1 chew and swallow. 2 destroy. 3 gnaw. 4 wear away. **eatable** adj

eau de Cologne Fr light perfume.

eaves pl n overhanging edges of roof. **eavesdrop** v listen secretly.

ebb 🛈 v 1 flow back. 2 decay. ◆ n 3 flowing back of tide. 4 decline, decay.

ebony adj/n, pl –onies (made of) hard black wood.

ebullient adj exuberant.

ebullience n

eccentric 🛈 adj 1 odd, unconventional. 2 irregular. 3 not placed centrally. ◆ n 4 odd, unconventional person.

eccentricity n

echo 🛈 n, pl –oes 1 repetition of sounds by reflection. 2 imitation. ◆ v 3 repeat as echo. 4 imitate. 5 resound. 6 be repeated.

éclair n finger–shaped iced cake filled with cream.

eclectic adj selecting from various sources.

eclipse 🛈 n 1 blotting out of sun, moon etc. by another heavenly body. 2 obscurity. ◆ v 3 obscure. 4 surpass.

——— THESAURUS ———

land, terra firma

ease n = **straightforwardness**, simplicity, readiness; = **comfort**, luxury, leisure, relaxation, prosperity ≠ **hardship**; = **peace of mind**, peace, content, quiet, comfort ◆ v = **agitation** ◆ v = **relieve**, calm, soothe, lessen, alleviate ≠ **aggravate**; = **reduce**, diminish, lessen, slacken; = **move carefully**, edge, slip, inch, slide

easy adj = **simple**, straightforward, no trouble, not difficult, effortless ≠ **hard**; = **untroubled**, relaxed, peaceful, serene, tranquil; = **carefree**, comfortable, leisurely, trouble-free, untroubled ≠ **difficult**

eat v = **consume**, swallow, chew, scoff (Sl), devour; = **have a meal**, lunch, breakfast, dine, snack

ebb v = **flow back**, go out, withdraw, retreat, wane; = **decline**, flag, diminish, decrease, dwindle ◆ n = **flowing back**, going out, withdrawal, retreat, wane

eccentric adj = **odd**, strange, peculiar, irregular, quirky ≠ **normal** ◆ n = **crank** (Inf), character (Inf), oddball (Inf), nonconformist, weirdo or weirdie (Inf)

echo n = **reverberation**, ringing, repetition, answer, resonance; = **copy**, reflection, clone, reproduction, imitation ◆ v = **reverberate**, repeat, resound, ring, resonate; = **recall**, reflect, copy, mirror, resemble

economy 𝟏 *n, pl* **–mies 1** careful management of resources to avoid unnecessary expenditure. **2** system of interrelationship of money, industry and employment. **economic** *adj* **economical** *adj* frugal. **economics** *pl n* **1** study of economies of nations (*used as pl*) **2** financial aspects. **economist** *n* **economize** *v*

ecstasy 𝟏 *n* exalted state of feeling. **ecstatic** *adj*

eczema *n* skin disease.

eddy *n, pl* **eddies 1** small whirl in water, smoke etc. ♦ *v* **2** move in whirls.

edge 𝟏 *n* **1** border, boundary. **2** cutting side of blade. **3** sharpness. **4** advantage. ♦ *v* **5** sharpen. **6** give edge or border to. **7** move gradually. **edgy** *adj* irritable. **on edge 1** nervy. **2** excited.

edible *adj* eatable.

edict *n* order, decree.

edifice *n* building.

edify *v* **–fying, –fied** improve morally, instruct.

edit 𝟏 *v* prepare book, film, tape etc. **edition** *n* **1** form in which something is published. **2** number of copies. **editor** *n* **editorial** *adj/n* article stating opinion of newspaper etc.

educate 𝟏 *v* **1** provide schooling for, teach. **2** train. **education** *n* **educational** *adj*

eel *n* snakelike fish.

eerie 𝟏 *adj* **eerier, eeriest** weird, uncanny.

efface *v* wipe or rub out.

effect 𝟏 *n* **1** result. **2** impression. **3** condition of being operative. ♦ *pl* **4** property. **5** lighting, sounds etc. ♦ *v* **6** bring about. **effective** *adj* **1** useful. **2** in force. **effectual** *adj*

effeminate *adj* womanish, unmanly.

efficient 𝟏 *adj* capable, competent. **efficiency** *n*

effigy *n, pl* **–gies** image, likeness.

effluent *n* liquid discharged as

———————— THESAURUS ————————

eclipse *n* = **obscuring**, covering, blocking, shading, dimming ♦ *v* = **surpass**, exceed, overshadow, excel, transcend

economy *n* = **financial system**, financial state

ecstasy *n* = **rapture**, delight, joy, bliss, euphoria ≠ **agony**

edge *n* = **border**, side, limit, outline, boundary ♦ *v* = **inch**, ease, creep, slink, steal; = **border**, fringe, hem, pipe

edit *v* = **revise**, improve, correct, polish, adapt

educate *v* = **teach**, school, train, develop, improve

eerie *adj* = **uncanny**, strange, frightening, ghostly, weird

effect *n* = **result**, consequence, conclusion, outcome, event; = **impression**, feeling, impact, influence; = **purpose**, impression, sense, intent, essence ♦ *v* = **bring about**, produce, complete, achieve, perform

efficient *adj* = **effective**, successful, structured, productive, systematic ≠ **inefficient**

waste.

effort 🛈 *n* exertion, endeavour, attempt or something achieved. **effortless** *adj*

effrontery *n* impudence.

e.g. for example.

egalitarian *adj* believing that all people should be equal.

egg¹ *n* oval or round object from which young emerge.

egg² *v* **egg on** urge.

ego *n, pl* **egos** the self. **egotism, egoism** 1 selfishness. 2 self-conceit. **egotist, egoist** *n* **egotistic, –ical** *adj* **egocentric** *adj* self-centred.

egregious *adj* blatant.

eider *n* Arctic duck. **eiderdown** *n* 1 its breast feathers. 2 quilt.

eight *adj/n* cardinal number one above seven. **eighteen** *adj/n* eight more than ten. **eighteenth** *adj/n* **eighth** *adj/n* **eightieth** *adj/n* **eighty** *adj/n* ten times eight.

either *adj/n* 1 one or the other. 2 one of two. 3 each. ♦ *adv/conj* 4 bringing in first of alternatives.

ejaculate *v* 1 eject (semen). 2 exclaim. **ejaculation** *n*

eject 🛈 *v* 1 throw out. 2 expel.

ejection *n* **ejector** *n*

eke out make (supply) last.

elaborate 🛈 *adj* 1 detailed. 2 complicated. ♦ *v* 3 expand (upon). 4 work out in detail. **elaboration** *n*

élan *n* style and vigour.

elapse *v* (of time) pass.

elastic 🛈 *adj* 1 springy. 2 flexible. ♦ *n* 3 tape containing strands of rubber. **elasticity** *n*

elbow 🛈 *n* 1 joint between fore and upper parts of arm. 2 part of sleeve covering this. ♦ *v* 3 shove with elbow. **elbow room** *n* room to move.

elder¹ 🛈 *adj* 1 older, senior. ♦ *n* 2 person of greater age. 3 official of certain churches. **elderly** *adj* **eldest** *adj* oldest.

elder² *n* tree with black berries.

elect 🛈 *v* 1 choose by vote. 2 choose. ♦ *adj* 3 appointed but not yet in office. 4 chosen. **election** *n* **elective** *adj* appointed by election. **elector** *n* **electoral** *adj* **electorate** *n* body of electors.

electricity *n* 1 form of energy. 2 electric current. **electric** *adj* of, transmitting or powered by

——— THESAURUS ———

effort *n* = **attempt**, try, endeavour, shot (*Inf*), bid; = **exertion**, work, trouble, energy, struggle

eject *v* = **throw out**, remove, turn out, expel, oust

elaborate *adj* = **complicated**, detailed, studied, complex, precise ♦ *v* = **develop**, flesh out

elastic *adj* = **flexible**, supple,

rubbery, pliable, plastic ≠ **rigid**; = **adaptable**, yielding, variable, flexible, accommodating ≠ **inflexible**

elbow *n* = **joint**, angle, curve

elder¹ *adj* = **older**, first, senior, first–born ♦ *n* = **older person**, senior, leader

elect *v* = **vote for**, choose, pick, determine, select

electricity. **electrical** *adj* using or concerning electricity. **electrician** *n* one trained in installation etc. of electrical devices. **electrify** *v* **electrification** *n*

electro- *comb. form* by, caused by electricity, as in *electrotherapy*.
electrocute *v* kill by electricity. **electrocution** *n*
electrode *n* conductor of electric current.

electron *n* one of fundamental components of atom, charged with negative electricity.
electronics *pl n* technology of electronic devices and circuits.
electronic *adj* **1** (of a device) dependent on the action of electrons. **2** (of a process) using electronic devices.

elegant **①** *adj* **1** graceful, tasteful. **2** refined. **elegance** *n*
elegy *n, pl* **-egies** lament for the dead in poem. **elegiac** *adj*
element **①** *n* **1** substance which cannot be separated by ordinary chemical techniques. **2** component part. **3** trace. **4** heating wire in electric kettle etc. **5** proper sphere. ◆ *pl* **6** powers of atmosphere. **7** rudiments.

elemental *adj* **elementary** *adj* rudimentary, simple.
elephant *n* huge animal with ivory tusks and long trunk.
elevate **①** *v* raise, exalt. **elevation** *n* **1** raising. **2** height, esp. above sea level. **3** drawing of one side of building etc. **elevator** *n US* lift.
eleven *adj/n* number next above 10. **eleventh** *adj*
elf *n, pl* **elves** fairy. **elfin, elvish** *adj*
elicit **①** *v* draw out.
eligible **①** *adj* **1** qualified. **2** desirable. **eligibility** *n*
eliminate **①** *v* remove, get rid of, set aside. **elimination** *n*
elite **①** *n* the pick or best part of society.
elixir *n* remedy.
elk *n* large deer.
ellipse *n* oval. **elliptical** *adj*
elm *n* tree with serrated leaves.
elocution *n* art of public speaking.
elongate *v* lengthen.
elope *v* run away from home with lover. **elopement** *n*
eloquence *n* fluent, powerful use of language. **eloquent** *adj* **eloquently** *adv*
else *adv* **1** besides, instead. **2** otherwise. **elsewhere** *adv* in or to

——————————————— THESAURUS ———————————————

elegant *adj* = **stylish**, fine, sophisticated, delicate, handsome ≠ **inelegant**
element *n* = **component**, part, unit, section, factor
elevate *v* = **promote**, raise, advance, upgrade, exalt; = **increase**, lift, raise, step up, intensify

elicit *v* = **bring about**, cause, derive, bring out, evoke; = **obtain**, extract, exact, evoke, wrest
eligible *adj* = **entitled**, fit, qualified, suitable ≠ **ineligible**
eliminate *v* = **remove**, end, stop, withdraw, get rid of (*Sl*)
elite *n* = **aristocracy**, best, pick, cream, upper class ≠ **rabble**

some other place.

elucidate v explain.

elude ❶ v 1 escape. 2 baffle.

elusive adj difficult to catch.

emaciated adj abnormally thin.

emanate ❶ v issue, proceed from.

emanation n

emancipate v set free.

emancipation n

emasculate v 1 castrate. 2 enfeeble, weaken. **emasculation** n

embalm v preserve corpse.

embankment n artificial mound carrying road, railway, or to dam water.

embargo ❶ n, pl –goes 1 order stopping movement of ships. 2 ban. ♦ v 3 put under embargo. 4 requisition.

embark ❶ v 1 board ship, aircraft etc. 2 (with on) commence new project etc.

embarrass ❶ v 1 disconcert. 2 abash. 3 confuse.

embarrassment n

embassy n, pl –sies office or official residence of ambassador.

embattled adj having many difficulties.

embed v –bedding, –bedded fix fast (in).

embellish v adorn, enrich.

embellishment n

ember n glowing cinder.

embezzle v misappropriate (money in trust etc.).

embezzlement n **embezzler** n

emblem n 1 symbol. 2 badge.

emblematic adj

embody ❶ v –bodying, –bodied represent, include, be expression of. **embodiment** n

embolism n Med obstruction of artery.

embrace ❶ v 1 clasp in arms, hug. 2 accept. 3 comprise. ♦ n 4 hug.

embrocation n lotion for rubbing limbs etc. to relieve pain.

embroider v ornament with needlework. **embroidery** n

embroil ❶ v involve (someone) in problems.

embryo ❶ n, pl –bryos

——— THESAURUS ———

elude v = **evade**, escape, lose, avoid, flee; = **escape**, baffle, frustrate, puzzle, stump

emanate v = **flow**, emerge, spring, proceed, arise

embargo n = **ban**, bar, restriction, boycott, restraint ♦ v = **block**, stop, bar, ban, restrict

embark v = **go aboard**, climb aboard, board ship, step aboard, go on board ≠ **get off**

embarrass v = **shame**, distress, show up (Inf), humiliate,

disconcert

embody v = **personify**, represent, stand for, manifest, exemplify; = **incorporate**, include, contain, combine, collect

embrace v = **hug**, hold, cuddle, seize, squeeze; = **accept**, support, welcome, adopt, take up; = **include**, involve, cover, contain, take in ♦ n = **hug**, hold, cuddle, squeeze, clinch (Sl)

embroil v = **involve**, mix up, implicate, entangle, mire

**undeveloped offspring, germ.
embryonic** adj

emend v to remove errors from, correct. **emendation** n

emerald n bright green gem.

emerge *v* **1** come up, out. **2** rise to notice. **emergence** n

emergency *v n, pl* **–cies** sudden unforeseen event needing prompt action.

emery n hard mineral used for polishing.

emigrate *v* go and settle in another country. **emigrant** n **emigration** n

eminent *adj* distinguished. **eminently** adv **eminence** n

emissary n, pl **–saries** agent, representative sent on mission.

emit *v* emitting, emitted give out, put forth. **emission** n

emollient adj **1** softening, soothing. ◆ *n* **2** ointment.

emotion *n* excited state of feeling, as joy, fear etc. **emotional** adj **emotive** adj arousing emotion.

empathy n understanding of another's feelings.

emperor n ruler of an empire.

emphasis *n, pl* **–ses 1** importance attached. **2** stress on words. **emphasize** v **emphatic** adj forceful.

emphysema n disease of lungs, causing breathlessness.

empire *n* group of states under supreme leader.

empirical *adj* relying on experiment or experience.

emplacement n position for gun.

employ *v* **1** provide work for in return for money. **2** keep busy. **3** use. **employee** n **employer** n **employment** n **1** employing, being employed. **2** work. **3** occupation.

empower *v* authorize.

——————— THESAURUS ———————

embryo n = **foetus**, unborn child, fertilized egg

emerge v = **come out**, appear, surface, rise, arise ≠ **withdraw**; = **become apparent**, come out, become known, come to light, crop up

emergency n = **crisis**, danger, difficulty, accident, disaster

emigrate v = **move abroad**, move, relocate, migrate, resettle

eminent adj = **prominent**, noted, respected, famous, celebrated ≠ **unknown**

emit v = **give off**, release, leak, transmit, discharge ≠ **absorb**

emotion n = **feeling**, spirit, soul, passion, excitement

emphasis n = **importance**, attention, weight, significance, stress; = **stress**, accent, force, weight

empire n = **kingdom**, territory, province, federation, commonwealth

empirical adj = **first-hand**, direct, observed, practical, actual ≠ **hypothetical**

employ v = **hire**, commission, appoint, take on, retain; = **use**, apply, exercise, exert, make use of; = **spend**, fill, occupy, involve, engage

empower v = **authorize**, allow,

empty ⓘ *adj* **–tier, –tiest 1** containing nothing. **2** unoccupied. **3** senseless. ♦ *v* **4** make, become devoid of content. **5** discharge (contents) into. **empties** *pl n* empty bottles etc. **emptiness** *n*

emu *n* large Aust. flightless bird.

emulate ⓘ *v* **1** strive to equal or excel. **2** imitate. **emulation** *n*

emulsion *n* **1** light–sensitive coating of film. **2** liquid with oily particles in suspension. **3** paint in this form. **emulsifier** *n*

enable ⓘ *v* make able.

enact ⓘ *v* **1** make law. **2** act part.

enamel *n* **1** glasslike coating applied to metal etc. **2** coating of teeth. **3** any hard coating. ♦ *v* **4** cover with this.

encapsulate *v* **1** summarize. **2** enclose.

enchant ⓘ *v* bewitch, delight. **enchantment** *n*

encircle *v* **1** surround. **2** enfold.

enclave *n* part of country entirely surrounded by foreign territory.

enclose ⓘ *v* **1** shut in. **2** surround. **3** place in with letter. **enclosure** *n*

encompass ⓘ *v* surround, contain.

encore *interj* **1** again. ♦ *n* **2** (call for) repetition of song etc.

encounter ⓘ *v* **1** meet unexpectedly. **2** meet in conflict. ♦ *n* **3** encountering.

encourage ⓘ *v* **1** inspire with hope. **2** embolden. **encouragement** *n*

encroach *v* intrude (on). **encroachment** *n*

encrust *v* cover with layer.

encumber *v* **1** hamper. **2** burden.

———— THESAURUS ————

commission, qualify, permit

empty *adj* = **bare**, clear, abandoned, deserted, vacant ≠ **full**; = **meaningless**, cheap, hollow, vain, idle; = **worthless**, meaningless, hollow, pointless, futile ≠ **meaningful** ♦ *v* = **clear**, drain, void, unload, pour out ≠ **fill**

emulate *v* = **imitate**, follow, copy, mirror, echo

enable *v* = **allow**, permit, empower, give someone the opportunity, give someone the means ≠ **prevent**

enact *v* = **establish**, order, command, approve, sanction; = **perform**, play, present, stage, represent

enchant *v* = **fascinate**, delight,

charm, entrance, dazzle

enclose *v* = **surround**, circle, bound, fence, confine; = **send with**, include, put in, insert

encompass *v* = **include**, hold, cover, admit, deal with; = **surround**, circle, enclose, close in, envelop

encounter *v* = **experience**, meet, face, suffer, have; = **meet**, confront, come across, bump into (*Inf*), run across ♦ *n* = **meeting**, brush, confrontation, rendezvous, chance meeting; = **battle**, conflict, clash, contest, run–in (*Inf*)

encourage *v* = **inspire**, comfort, cheer, reassure, console ≠ **discourage**; = **urge**, persuade, prompt, spur, coax ≠ **dissuade**

encumbrance *n*

encyclopedia, encyclopaedia *n* book, set of books of information on one or all subjects.

encyclopedic, –paedic *adj*

end ① *n* 1 limit. 2 extremity. 3 conclusion. 4 fragment. 5 latter part. 6 death. 7 event. 8 aim. ◆ *v* 9 put an end to. 10 come to an end, finish. **ending** *n* **endless** *adj*

endanger ① *v* put in danger.

endear *v* make beloved. **endearment** *n* loving word.

endeavour ① *v* 1 try, strive after. ◆ *n* 2 attempt.

endorse ① *v* 1 sanction. 2 confirm. 3 sign back of. 4 record conviction on driving licence. **endorsement** *n*

endow ① *v* 1 provide permanent income for. 2 furnish (with). **endowment** *n*

endure ① *v* 1 undergo. 2 tolerate, bear. 3 last. **endurable** *adj* **endurance** *n*

enema *n* medicine, liquid injected into rectum.

enemy ① *n*, *pl* **–mies** 1 hostile person. 2 opponent. 3 armed foe.

energy ① *n*, *pl* **–gies** 1 vigour, force, activity. 2 source of power, as oil, coal etc. 3 capacity of machine, battery etc. for work. **energetic** *adj* **energize** *v*

enervate *v* weaken.

enfeeble *v* weaken.

enfold *v* cover by wrapping something around.

enforce ① *v* 1 compel obedience to. 2 impose (action) upon. **enforceable** *adj* **enforcement** *n*

enfranchise *v* 1 give right of voting to. 2 give parliamentary representation to. 3 set free.

engage ① *v* 1 participate. 2 involve. 3 employ. 4 bring into operation. 5 begin conflict. **engaged** *adj* 1 pledged to be married. 2 in use. **engagement** *n* 1 appointment. 2 pledge of

———————— THESAURUS ————————

end *n* = **close**, ending, finish, expiry, expiration ≠ **beginning**; = **conclusion**, ending, climax, completion, finale ≠ **start**; = **finish**, close, stop, resolution, conclusion; = **extremity**, limit, edge, border, extent; = **tip**, point, head, peak, extremity ◆ *v* = **stop**, finish, halt, cease, wind up ≠ **start**

endanger *v* = **put at risk**, risk, threaten, compromise, jeopardize ≠ **save**

endeavour (*Formal*) *v* = **try**, labour, attempt, aim, struggle ◆ *n* = **attempt**, try, effort, trial, bid

endorse *v* = **approve**, back, support, champion, promote; = **sign**, initial, countersign, sign on the back of

endow *v* = **provide**, favour, grace, bless, supply

endure *v* = **experience**, suffer, bear, meet, encounter; = **last**, continue, remain, stay, stand

enemy *n* = **foe**, rival, opponent, the opposition, competitor ≠ **friend**

energy *n* = **strength**, might, stamina, forcefulness

enforce *v* = **carry out**, apply,

marriage. **engaging** adj charming.
engender v give rise to.
engine ❶ n 1 any machine to convert energy into mechanical work. 2 railway locomotive.
engineer n 1 one who is in charge of engines, machinery etc. 2 one who originates, organizes. ♦ v 3 construct as engineer. 4 contrive.
engineering n
engrave v 1 cut in lines on metal for printing. 2 carve, incise. 3 impress deeply. **engraving** n
engross v 1 absorb (attention). 2 occupy wholly.
engulf v swallow up.
enhance ❶ v intensify value or attractiveness of. **enhancement** n
enigma n puzzling thing or person. **enigmatic** adj
enjoy ❶ v 1 delight in. 2 have

benefit of. **enjoy oneself** be happy. **enjoyable** adj **enjoyment** n
enlarge ❶ v 1 make bigger. 2 grow bigger. 3 talk in greater detail. **enlargement** n
enlighten ❶ v give information to. **enlightenment** n
enlist ❶ v engage as soldier or helper.
enliven v animate.
enmity n, pl **-ties** ill will, hostility.
enormous ❶ adj very big, vast.
enormity n, pl **-ties** gross offence.
enough ❶ adj/n/adv as much as need be.
enquire SEE INQUIRE.
enrich ❶ v 1 make rich. 2 add to.
enrol ❶ v **-rolling, -rolled** 1 write name of on roll. 2 enlist. 3 become member.
en route ❶ Fr on the way.

——— THESAURUS ———

implement, fulfil, execute
engage v (with **in**) = **participate in**, join in, take part in, undertake, embark on; = **captivate**, catch, arrest, fix, capture; = **occupy**, involve, draw, grip, absorb; = **employ**, appoint, take on, hire, retain ≠ **dismiss**; = **set going**, apply, trigger, activate, switch on
engine n = **machine**, motor, mechanism, generator, dynamo
engineer v = **design**, plan, create, construct, devise
enhance v = **improve**, better, increase, lift, boost ≠ **reduce**
enjoy v = **take pleasure in** or from like, love, appreciate, relish ≠ **hate**; = **have**, use, own, experience, possess

enlarge v = **expand**, increase, extend, add to, build up ≠ **reduce**; = **grow**, increase, extend, expand, swell
enlighten v = **inform**, tell, teach, advise, counsel
enlist v = **join up**, join, enter (into), register, volunteer; = **recruit**, take on, hire, sign up, call up
enormous adj = **huge**, massive, vast, extensive, tremendous ≠ **tiny**
enough adv = **sufficiently**, amply, reasonably, adequately, satisfactorily
enrich v = **enhance**, develop, improve, boost, supplement; = **make rich**, make wealthy, make affluent, make prosperous, make

ensemble ⊕ *n* 1 all parts taken together. 2 woman's complete outfit 3 *Mus* group of soloists performing together.
enshrine *v* preserve with sacred affection.
ensign *n* 1 naval or military flag. 2 badge.
enslave *v* make into slave.
ensnare *v* 1 trap. 2 entangle.
ensue ⊕ *v* follow, happen after.
ensure ⊕ *v* make certain.
entail ⊕ *v* necessitate.
entangle *v* 1 ensnare. 2 perplex.
entente *n* friendly understanding between nations.
enter ⊕ *v* 1 go, come into. 2 penetrate. 3 join. 4 write in 5

begin. **entrance** *n* 1 going, coming in. 2 door, passage. 3 right to enter. 4 fee. **entrant** *n* one who enters. **entry** *n, pl* –tries
enterprise ⊕ *n* 1 bold undertaking. 2 bold spirit. 3 business. **enterprising** *adj*
entertain ⊕ *v* 1 amuse, receive as guest. 2 consider. **entertainer** *n* **entertainment** *n*
enthral *v* –thralling, –thralled captivate.
enthusiasm ⊕ *n* ardent eagerness. **enthuse** *v* **enthusiast** *n* **enthusiastic** *adj*
entice ⊕ *v* allure, attract.
entire ⊕ *adj* whole, complete.
entirely *adv* **entirety** *n*

——————— THESAURUS ———————

well-off
enrol *v* = **enlist**, register, be accepted, be admitted, join up
en route *adv* = **on** or **along the way**, travelling, on the road, in transit, on the journey
ensemble *n* = **group**, company, band, troupe, cast; = **collection**, set, body, whole, total; = **outfit**, suit, get-up (*Inf*) costume
ensue *v* = **follow**, result, develop, proceed, arise ≠ **come first**
ensure *v* = **make certain**, guarantee, secure, make sure, confirm; = **protect**, defend, secure, safeguard, guard
entail *v* = **involve**, require, produce, demand, call for
enter *v* = **come**, arrive, set foot in somewhere, cross the threshold of somewhere, make an entrance ≠ **exit**; = **penetrate**, get in, pierce,

pass into, perforate; = **join**, start work at, begin work at, enrol in, enlist in ≠ **leave**; = **participate in**, join (in), be involved in, get involved in, play a part in
enterprise *n* = **firm**, company, business, concern, operation; = **venture**, operation, project, adventure, undertaking; = **initiative**, energy, daring, enthusiasm, imagination
entertain *v* = **amuse**, interest, please, delight, charm; = **show hospitality to**, receive, accommodate, treat, put up; = **consider**, imagine, think about, contemplate, conceive of
enthusiasm *n* = **keenness**, interest, passion, motivation, relish
entice *v* = **lure**, attract, invite, persuade, tempt
entire *adj* = **whole**, full, complete,

entitle 𝟏 v 1 qualify. 2 name.
entitlement n

entity 𝟏 n, pl –ties 1 thing's being or existence. 2 reality.

entomology n study of insects.

entourage n group of people assisting important person.

entrails pl n intestines.

entrance¹ 𝟏 see ENTER.

entrance² 𝟏 v delight.

entreat v 1 ask earnestly. 2 beg, implore. **entreaty** n, pl –ties

entrench v establish firmly.

entrepreneur 𝟏 n businessman who attempts to profit by risk and initiative.

entrust 𝟏 v commit, charge with.

entwine v plait, interweave.

enumerate v mention one by one.

enunciate v state clearly.

envelop v enveloping, enveloped wrap up, surround.

envelope 𝟏 n cover of letter.

environment 𝟏 n 1 surroundings. 2 conditions of life or growth.

environmental adj **environs** pl n outskirts.

envisage 𝟏 v visualize.

envoy 𝟏 n diplomat.

envy 𝟏 v 1 grudge another's good fortune. ♦ n 2 (object of) this feeling. **enviable** adj **envious** adj

enzyme n any of group of proteins produced by living cells and acting as catalysts.

epaulette n shoulder ornament on uniform.

ephemeral adj short-lived.

epic n 1 long poem telling of achievements of hero. ♦ adj 2 on grand scale.

epicentre n point immediately

total, gross

entitle v = **give the right to**, allow, enable, permit, sanction; = **call**, name, title, term, label

entity n = **thing**, being, individual, object, substance

entrance¹ n = **way in**, opening, door, approach, access ≠ exit; = **appearance**, coming in, entry, arrival, introduction ≠ exit; = **admission**, access, entry, entrée, admittance

entrance² v = **enchant**, delight, charm, fascinate, dazzle ≠ bore; = **mesmerize**, bewitch, hypnotize, put a spell on, cast a spell on

entrepreneur n = **businessman** or **businesswoman**, tycoon,

executive, industrialist, speculator

entrust v = **give custody of**, deliver, commit, delegate, hand over

envelope n = **wrapping**, casing, case, covering, cover

environment n = **surroundings**, setting, conditions, situation, medium

envisage v = **imagine**, contemplate, conceive (of), visualize, picture

envoy n = **ambassador**, diplomat, emissary; = **messenger**, agent, representative, delegate, courier

envy n = **covetousness**, resentment, jealousy, bitterness, resentfulness ♦ v = **be jealous (of)**,

above origin of earthquake.

epicure n one delighting in eating and drinking. **epicurean** adj/n

epidemic ❶ adj 1 (esp. of disease) prevalent and spreading rapidly. ◆ n 2 serious outbreak.

epidermis n outer skin.

epidural n spinal anaesthetic.

epigram n witty saying.

epigraph n 1 quotation at start of book. 2 inscription.

epilepsy n disorder of nervous system causing fits. **epileptic** n/adj

epilogue n closing speech.

episcopal adj of, ruled by bishop.

episode ❶ n 1 incident. 2 section of (serialized) book etc. **episodic** adj

epistle n letter.

epitaph n inscription on tomb.

epithet n descriptive word.

epitome n typical example. **epitomize** v

epoch n period, era.

equable adj even–tempered, placid.

equal ❶ adj 1 the same in number, size, merit etc. 2 fit. ◆ n 3 one equal to another. ◆ v 4 be equal to. **equally** adv **equality** n **equalize** v

equanimity n composure.

equate ❶ v make equal. **equation** n equating of two mathematical expressions.

equator n imaginary circle round earth equidistant from the poles.

equestrian adj of horse–riding.

equilateral adj having equal sides.

equilibrium ❶ n, pl –ria state of steadiness.

equinox n time when sun crosses equator and day and night are equal.

equip ❶ v equipping, equipped supply, fit out. **equipment** n

equivalent ❶ adj equal in value. **equivocal** adj of double or doubtful meaning. **equivocate** v

era ❶ n period of time.

———————— THESAURUS ————————

resent, begrudge, be envious (of)

epidemic n = **outbreak**, plague, growth, spread, scourge; = **spate**, plague, outbreak, wave, rash

episode n = **event**, experience, happening, matter, affair; = **instalment**, part, act, scene, section

equal adj = **identical**, the same, matching, equivalent, uniform ≠ **unequal**; = **fair**, just, impartial, egalitarian, unbiased ≠ **unfair**; = **even**, balanced, fifty–fifty (Inf), evenly matched ≠ **uneven** ◆ n = **match**, equivalent, twin,

counterpart ◆ v = **amount to**, make, come to, total, level ≠ **be unequal to**

equate v = **identify**, associate, connect, compare, relate

equilibrium n = **stability**, balance, symmetry, steadiness, evenness

equip v = **supply**, provide for, stock, arm, array

equivalent n = **equal**, counterpart, twin, parallel, match ◆ adj = **equal**, same, comparable, parallel, identical ≠ **different**

era n = **age**, time, period, date, generation

eradicate ❶ *v* wipe out.

erase ❶ *v* **1** rub out. **2** remove.

ere *prep/conj Poet* before.

erect ❶ *adj* **1** upright. ◆ *v* **2** set up. **3** build. **erection** *n*

ermine *n* stoat in northern regions.

erode ❶ *v* **1** wear away. **2** eat into. **erosion** *n*

erotic ❶ *adj* of sexual pleasure.

err *v* **1** make mistakes. **2** be wrong. **3** sin. **erratic** *adj* irregular or unpredictable. **erratum** *n*, *pl* **-ta** error, esp. in printing. **erroneous** *adj* wrong or incorrect. **error** *n* mistake.

errand *n* short journey for simple business.

errant *adj* wandering.

erstwhile *adj* former.

erudite *adj* learned.

erupt ❶ *v* burst out. **eruption** *n*

escalate ❶ *v* increase, be increased, in extent, intensity etc.

escalation *n*

escalator *n* moving staircase.

escape ❶ *v* **1** get free. **2** get off safely. **3** find way out. **4** elude. **5** leak. ◆ *n* **6** escaping. **escapade** *n* wild adventure. **escapism** *n* taking refuge in fantasy.

escarpment *n* steep hillside.

eschew *v* avoid, shun.

escort ❶ *n* **1** person accompanying another to guard, guide etc. ◆ *v* **2** accompany.

Eskimo *n* **1** a member of a group of peoples inhabiting N Canada, Greenland, Alaska, and E Siberia, having a culture adapted to an extremely cold climate. **2** the language of these peoples. see INUIT.

esoteric *adj* obscure.

ESP extrasensory perception.

especial *adj* **1** pre-eminent. **2** particular. **especially** *adv*

espionage ❶ *n* spying.

——————— THESAURUS ———————

eradicate *v* = **wipe out**, eliminate, remove, destroy, get rid of

erase *v* = **delete**, cancel out, wipe out, remove, eradicate; = **rub out**, remove, wipe out, delete

erect *v* = **build**, raise, set up, construct, put up ≠ **demolish**; = **found**, establish, form, create, set up ◆ *adj* = **upright**, straight, stiff, vertical, elevated ≠ **bent**

erode *v* = **disintegrate**, crumble, deteriorate, corrode, break up

erotic *adj* = **sexual**, sexy (*Inf*), crude, explicit, sensual

erupt *v* = **explode**, blow up, emit lava; = **discharge**, expel, emit,

eject, spout

escalate *v* = **grow**, increase, extend, intensify, expand ≠ **decrease**

escape *v* = **get away**, flee, take off, fly, bolt; = **avoid**, miss, evade, dodge, shun; = **leak out**, flow out, gush out, emanate, seep out ◆ *n* = **getaway**, break, flight, break-out; = **avoidance**, evasion, circumvention

escort *n* = **guard**, bodyguard, train, convoy, entourage; = **companion**, partner, attendant, guide, beau ◆ *v* = **accompany**, lead, partner, conduct, guide

esplanade n promenade.

espouse v 1 support. 2 Obs marry. **espousal** n

espy v espying, espied catch sight of.

Esq. Esquire, title used on letters.

essay ⊕ n 1 prose composition. 2 attempt. ♦ v 3 try.

essence ⊕ n 1 all that makes thing what it is. 2 extract got by distillation. **essential** adj 1 vitally important. 2 basic. ♦ n 3 essential thing.

establish ⊕ v 1 set up. 2 settle. 3 prove. **establishment** n

estate ⊕ n 1 landed property. 2 person's property. 3 area of property development. **estate agent** one who values, leases and sells property.

esteem ⊕ v/n regard, respect.

ester n Chem organic compound.

estimate ⊕ v/n (form) approximate idea of (amounts, measurements etc.). **estimable** adj worthy of regard. **estimation** n opinion.

estranged adj no longer living with one's spouse.

estuary ⊕ n, pl –aries mouth of river.

etc. et cetera.

et cetera Lat and the rest, and others, and so on.

etch ⊕ v make engraving on metal plate with acids etc. **etching** n

eternal ⊕ adj everlasting. **eternity** n

ether n 1 colourless liquid used as anaesthetic. 2 clear sky. **ethereal** adj 1 airy. 2 heavenly.

——————— THESAURUS ———————

espionage n = **spying**, intelligence, surveillance, counter-intelligence, undercover work

essay n = **composition**, study, paper, article, piece ♦ v = (Formal) **attempt**, try, undertake, endeavour

essence n = **fundamental nature**, nature, being, heart, spirit; = **concentrate**, spirits, extract, tincture, distillate

establish v = **set up**, found, create, institute, constitute; = **prove**, confirm, demonstrate, certify, verify

estate n = **lands**, property, area, grounds, domain; = **area**, centre, park, development, site

esteem n = **respect**, regard, honour, admiration, reverence ♦ v = **respect**, admire, think highly of, love, value

estimate v = **calculate roughly**, value, guess, judge, reckon; = **think**, believe, consider, rate, judge ♦ n = **approximate calculation**, guess, assessment, judgment, valuation; = **assessment**, opinion, belief, appraisal, evaluation

estuary n = **inlet**, mouth, creek, firth, fjord

etch v = **engrave**, cut, impress, stamp, carve

eternal adj = **interminable**, endless, infinite, continual, immortal ≠ **occasional**

ethnic ❶ *adj* of race or relating to classification of humans into different groups.

ethos *n* distinctive spirit of people, culture etc.

etiquette *n* conventional code of conduct.

étude *n* short musical composition, exercise.

etymology *n, pl* **–gies** tracing, account of word's origin, development.

eucalyptus, eucalypt *n* Aust. tree, providing timber and gum.

Eucharist *n* Christian sacrament of the Lord's Supper.

eugenics *pl n* science of improving the human race by selective breeding.

eulogy *n, pl* **–gies** praise. **eulogize** *v*

eunuch *n* castrated man.

euphemism *n* substitution of mild term for offensive one. **euphemistic** *adj*

euphoria ❶ *n* sense of elation.

euphoric *adj*

eureka *interj* exclamation of triumph.

euthanasia *n* painless putting to death to relieve suffering.

evacuate ❶ *v* **1** empty. **2** withdraw from. **evacuation** *n* **evacuee** *n*

evade ❶ *v* **1** avoid. **2** elude. **evasion** *n* **evasive** *adj*

evaluate ❶ *v* find or judge value of. **evaluation** *n*

evangelical *adj* of, or according to, gospel teaching. **evangelism** *n* **evangelist** *n*

evaporate ❶ *v* turn into vapour. **evaporation** *n*

eve ❶ *n* **1** evening before. **2** time just before. **evensong** *n* evening service.

even ❶ *adj* **1** flat, smooth. **2** uniform, equal. **3** divisible by two. **4** impartial. ♦ *v* **5** smooth. **6** equalize. ♦ *adv* **7** equally. **8** simply. **9** notwithstanding.

evening ❶ *n* close of day.

——————— THESAURUS ———————

ethnic *adj* = **cultural**, national, traditional, native, folk

euphoria *n* = **elation**, joy, ecstasy, rapture, exhilaration ≠ **despondency**

evacuate *v* = **remove**, clear, withdraw, expel, move out

evade *v* = **avoid**, escape, dodge, get away from, elude ≠ **face**; = **avoid answering**, parry, fend off, fudge, hedge

evaluate *v* = **assess**, rate, judge, estimate, reckon

evaporate *v* = **disappear**, vaporize, dematerialize, vanish, dissolve; = **dry up**, dry, dehydrate, vaporize, desiccate

eve *n* = **night before**, day before, vigil; = **brink**, point, edge, verge, threshold

even *adj* = **regular**, stable, constant, steady, smooth ≠ **variable**; = **level**, straight, flat, smooth, true ≠ **uneven**; = **equal**, like, matching, similar, identical ≠ **unequal**; = **equally matched**, level, tied, on a par, neck and neck ≠ **ill-matched**

event ❶ *n* **1** happening. **2** notable occurrence. **3** result. **4** any one contest in sporting programme. **eventful** *adj* full of exciting events. **eventual** *adj* resulting in the end. **eventuality** *n* possible event.

ever ❶ *adv* **1** always. **2** at any time. **evergreen** *n/adj* (tree or shrub) bearing foliage throughout the year. **evermore** *adv* for all time to come.

every *adj* **1** each of all. **2** all possible. **everybody** *n* **everyday** *adj* usual, ordinary. **everyone** *n* **everything** *n* **everywhere** *adv* in all places.

evict *v* expel by legal process, turn out. **eviction** *n*

evidence ❶ *n* **1** ground of belief. **2** sign. **3** testimony. ◆ *v* **4** indicate, prove. **evident** *adj* plain, obvious.

evil ❶ *adj/n* (what is) bad or harmful.

evoke ❶ *v* **1** call to mind. **2** bring about. **evocation** *n* **evocative** *adj*

evolve ❶ *v* **1** (cause to) develop gradually. **2** undergo slow changes. **evolution** *n* development of species from earlier forms.

ewe *n* female sheep.

ex– *comb. form* **1** out from, from, out of or outside, as in *exclaim, exodus*. **2** former, as in *ex–wife, ex–boss*.

exacerbate *v* aggravate, make worse.

exact ❶ *adj* **1** precise, strictly correct. ◆ *v* **2** demand, extort. **exacting** *adj* making rigorous demands. **exactly** *adv*

exaggerate ❶ *v* magnify beyond truth, overstate. **exaggeration** *n*

exalt *v* **1** raise up. **2** praise.

exam *n* examination.

examine ❶ *v* **1** investigate. **2** look at closely. **3** ask questions of. **4** test knowledge of. **examination** *n* **examiner** *n*

E

———————— THESAURUS ————————

evening *n* = **dusk**, night, sunset, twilight, sundown

event *n* = **incident**, happening, experience, affair, occasion; = **competition**, game, tournament, contest, bout

ever *adv* = **at any time**, at all, in any case, at any point, by any chance; = **always**, for ever, at all times, evermore

evidence *n* = **proof**, grounds, demonstration, confirmation, verification; = **sign(s)**, suggestion, trace, indication; ◆ *v* = **show**, prove, reveal, display, indicate

evil *n* = **wickedness**, bad, vice, sin, wrongdoing; = **harm**, suffering, hurt, woe ◆ *adj* = **wicked**, bad, malicious, immoral, sinful; = **harmful**, disastrous, destructive, dire, catastrophic; = **demonic**, satanic, diabolical, hellish, devilish

evoke *v* = **arouse**, cause, induce, awaken, give rise to ≠ **suppress**

evolve *v* = **develop**, metamorphose, adapt yourself

exact *adj* = **accurate**, correct, true, right, specific ≠ **approximate** ◆ *v* = **demand**, claim, force, command, extract

exaggerate *v* = **overstate**, enlarge, embroider, amplify,

example ⊕ n 1 specimen. 2 model.

exasperate v irritate. **exasperation** n

excavate v 1 hollow out. 2 dig. 3 unearth. **excavator** n

exceed ⊕ v 1 be greater than. 2 go beyond. **exceedingly** adv very.

excel v –celling, –celled 1 surpass. 2 be very good. **excellence** n **excellent** adj very good.

except ⊕ prep 1 not including. ♦ v 2 exclude. **exception** n 1 thing not included in a rule. 2 objection. **exceptional** adj above average.

excerpt ⊕ n passage from book etc.

excess ⊕ n 1 too great amount. 2 intemperance. **excessive** adj

exchange ⊕ v 1 give (something) in return for something else. 2 barter. ♦ n 3 giving one thing and receiving another. 4 thing given. 5 building where merchants meet for business. 6 central telephone office. **exchangeable** adj

excise[1] n duty charged on home goods.

excise[2] v cut away.

excite ⊕ v 1 arouse to strong emotion, stimulate. 2 set in motion. **excitable** adj **excitement** n **exciting** adj

exclaim ⊕ v speak suddenly, cry out. **exclamation** n **exclamation mark** punctuation mark (!), used after exclamations.

exclude ⊕ v 1 shut out. 2 debar from. 3 reject, not consider. **exclusion** n **exclusive** adj 1 excluding. 2 select. **exclusiveness, exclusivity** n

excommunicate v cut off from

———— THESAURUS ————

embellish

examine v = **inspect**, study, survey, investigate, explore; = **test**, question, assess, quiz, evaluate; = **question**, quiz, interrogate, cross–examine, grill (Inf)

example n = **instance**, specimen, case, sample, illustration; = **warning**, lesson, caution, deterrent, like

exceed v = **surpass**, better, pass, eclipse, beat; = **go over the limit of**, go beyond, overstep

excel v = **be superior**, eclipse, beat, surpass, transcend

except prep = **apart from**, but for, saving, barring, excepting ♦ v

= **exclude**, leave out, omit, disregard, pass over

excerpt n = **extract**, part, piece, section, selection

excess n = **surfeit**, surplus, overload, glut, superabundance ≠ **shortage**; = **overindulgence**, extravagance, profligacy, debauchery, dissipation ≠ **moderation**

exchange v = **interchange**, change, trade, switch, swap ♦ n = **conversation**, talk, word, discussion, chat

excite v = **thrill**, inspire, stir, provoke, animate; = **arouse**, provoke, rouse, stir up

exclaim v = **cry out**, declare,

sacraments of the Church.
excommunication n

excrement n waste matter from
bowels. **excrete** v discharge from
the system. **excretion** n **excretory**
adj

excruciating adj unbearably
painful.

excursion ① n trip for pleasure.

excuse ① v **1** overlook. **2** try to
clear from blame. **3** gain
exemption. **4** set free. ♦ n **5** that
which serves to excuse. **6** apology.
excusable adj

execrable adj hatefully bad.

execute ① v **1** inflict capital
punishment on, kill. **2** carry out,
perform. **3** make. **execution** n
executioner n/adj **1**
(of) person in administrative
position. **2** (of) branch of

government enforcing laws.

executor n person appointed to
carry out provisions of a will.

exemplify ① v –fying, –fied serve
as example of.

exempt ① v **1** free from. **2** excuse.
♦ adj **3** freed from, not liable for.
exemption n

exercise ① n **1** use of limbs for
health. **2** practice. **3** task. **4** use. ♦
v **5** use. **6** carry out. **7** take
exercise.

exert ① v make effort. **exertion** n

exhale v breathe out.

exhaust ① v **1** tire out. **2** use up. **3**
empty. ♦ n **4** waste gases from
engine. **5** passage for this.
exhaustible adj **exhaustion** n state
of extreme fatigue. **exhaustive** adj
comprehensive.

exhibit ① v **1** show, display. ♦ n **2**

———— THESAURUS ————

shout, proclaim, yell

exclude v = **keep out**, bar, ban,
refuse, forbid ≠ **let in**; = **omit**,
reject, eliminate, rule out, miss out
≠ **include**

excursion n = **trip**, tour, journey,
outing, expedition

excuse n = **justification**, reason,
explanation, defence, grounds
≠ **accusation** ♦ v = **justify**, explain,
defend, vindicate, mitigate
≠ **blame**; = **forgive**, pardon,
overlook, tolerate, acquit; = **free**,
relieve, exempt, release, spare
≠ **convict**

execute v = **put to death**, kill,
shoot, hang, behead; = **carry out**,
effect, implement, accomplish,
discharge

exemplify v = **show**, represent,
display, demonstrate, illustrate

exempt adj = **immune**, free,
excepted, excused, released
≠ **liable** ♦ v = **grant immunity**,
free, excuse, release, spare

exercise v = **put to use**, use,
apply, employ, exert; = **train**, work
out, practise, keep fit, do exercises
♦ n = **use**, practice, application,
operation, discharge; = **exertion**,
training, activity, work, labour;
= **manoeuvre**, campaign,
operation, movement,
deployment

exert v = **apply**, use, exercise,
employ, wield

exhaust v = **tire out**, fatigue,
drain, weaken, weary; = **use up**,

thing shown. **exhibition** n **1** display. **2** public show.
exhibitionist n one with compulsive desire to attract attention. **exhibitor** n
exhilarate v enliven, gladden. **exhilaration** n
exhort v urge.
exhume v dig up (corpse etc.).
exigency n, pl **-cies** urgent need.
exile ① n **1** banishment, expulsion from one's own country. **2** one banished. ◆ v **3** banish.
exist ① v be, have being, live. **existence** n **existent** adj
exit ① n **1** way out. **2** going out. ◆ v **3** go out.
exodus ① n departure.
exonerate v free, declare free,

from blame.
exorbitant adj excessive.
exorcize v cast out (evil spirits) by invocation. **exorcism** n **exorcist** n
exotic ① adj **1** foreign. **2** unusual.
expand ① v increase, spread out.
expandable adj **expanse** n wide space. **expansion** n **expansive** adj **1** extensive. **2** friendly.
expatiate v speak or write at great length (on).
expatriate ① adj/n (one) living in exile.
expect ① v **1** regard as probable. **2** look forward to. **expectant** adj **expectation** n
expedient adj **1** fitting. **2** politic. **3** convenient. ◆ n **4** something suitable, useful. **expediency** n

———— THESAURUS ————

spend, consume, waste, go through
exhibit v = **show**, reveal, display, demonstrate, express; = **display**, show, set out, parade, unveil
exile n = **banishment**, expulsion, deportation, eviction, expatriation; = **expatriate**, refugee, outcast, émigré, deportee ◆ v = **banish**, expel, throw out, deport, drive out
exist v = **live**, be present, survive, endure, be in existence; = **occur**, be present; = **survive**, stay alive, make ends meet, subsist, eke out a living
exit n = **way out**, door, gate, outlet, doorway ≠ **entry**; = **departure**, withdrawal, retreat, farewell, going ◆ v = **depart**, leave, go out, withdraw, retire ≠ **enter**

exodus n = **departure**, withdrawal, retreat, leaving, flight
exotic adj = **unusual**, striking, strange, fascinating, mysterious ≠ **ordinary**; = **foreign**, alien, tropical, external, naturalized
expand v = **get bigger**, increase, grow, extend, swell ≠ **contract**; = **make bigger**, increase, develop, extend, widen ≠ **reduce**; = **spread (out)**, stretch (out), unfold, unravel, diffuse
expatriate n = **exile**, refugee, emigrant, émigré ◆ adj = **exiled**, refugee, banished, emigrant, émigré
expect v = **think**, believe, suppose, assume, trust; = **anticipate**, look forward to, predict, envisage, await; = **require**, demand, want, call for, ask for

expedite v help on, hasten.
expedition n 1 journey for definite purpose. 2 people, equipment comprising expedition.
expel 🕕 v –pelling, –pelled 1 drive out. 2 exclude. **expulsion** n
expend v 1 spend, pay out. 2 use up. **expendable** adj likely to be used up. **expenditure** n **expense** n 1 cost. 2 pl charges incurred. **expensive** adj
experience 🕕 n 1 observation of facts as source of knowledge. 2 being affected by event. 3 the event. 4 knowledge, skill gained. ♦ v 5 undergo, suffer, meet with. **experienced** adj
experiment 🕕 n/v test to discover or prove something. **experimental** adj
expert 🕕 n/adj (one) skilful,

knowledgeable, in something. **expertise** n
expiate v make amends for.
expire 🕕 v 1 come to an end. 2 die. 3 breathe out. **expiry** n end.
explain 🕕 v 1 make clear, intelligible. 2 account for. **explanation** n **explanatory** adj
expletive n 1 exclamation. 2 oath.
explicable adj explainable.
explicit 🕕 adj clearly stated.
explode 🕕 v 1 (make) burst violently. 2 (of population) increase rapidly. 3 discredit. **explosion** n. **explosive** adj/n
exploit 🕕 n 1 brilliant feat, deed. ♦ v 2 turn to advantage. 3 make use of for one's own ends. **exploitation** n
explore 🕕 v 1 investigate. 2

—————————— THESAURUS ——————————

expel v = throw out, exclude, ban, dismiss, kick out (Inf) ≠ **let in**; = **banish**, exile, deport, evict, force to leave ≠ **take in**
experience n = **knowledge**, practice, skill, contact, expertise; = **event**, affair, incident, happening, encounter ♦ v = **undergo**, feel, face, taste, go through
experiment n = **test**, trial, investigation, examination, procedure; = **research**, investigation, analysis, observation, research and development ♦ v = **test**, investigate, trial, research, try
expert n = **specialist**, authority, professional, master, genius

≠ **amateur** ♦ adj = **skilful**, experienced, professional, masterly, qualified ≠ **unskilled**
expire v = **become invalid**, end, finish, conclude, close; = **die**, depart, perish, kick the bucket (Inf), depart this life
explain v = **make clear** or **plain**, describe, teach, define, resolve; = **account for**, excuse, justify, give a reason for
explicit adj = **clear**, obvious, specific, direct, precise ≠ **vague**
explode v = **blow up**, erupt, burst, go off, shatter; = **detonate**, set off, discharge, let off
exploit v = **take advantage of**, abuse, use, manipulate, milk; = **make the best use of**, use, make

examine (country etc.) by going through it. **exploration** n
exploratory adj **explorer** n
exponent see EXPOUND.
export v 1 send (goods) out of the country. ♦ n 2 exporting. 3 product sold abroad.
expose ⊕ v 1 display. 2 reveal (scandalous) truth. 3 leave unprotected. **exposure** n
exposé n bringing of scandal, crime etc, to public notice.
expound v explain, interpret.
exponent n 1 one who expounds or promotes (idea, cause etc.). 2 performer. **exposition** n 1 explanation. 2 exhibition of goods etc.
express ⊕ v 1 put into words. 2 make known or understood. ♦ adj 3 definitely stated. 4 specially designed. 5 speedy. ♦ adv 6 with speed. ♦ n 7 express train. 8 rapid parcel delivery service. **expression**

n 1 expressing. 2 word, phrase. 3 look. **expressive** adj
expropriate v dispossess.
expunge v delete, blot out.
expurgate v remove objectionable parts (from book etc.).
exquisite ⊕ adj of extreme beauty or delicacy.
extend ⊕ v 1 stretch out. 2 prolong. 3 widen. 4 accord, grant. 5 reach. 6 cover area. 7 have range or scope. **extension** n 1 extending. 2 additional part.
extensive adj wide. **extent** n 1 space. 2 scope. 3 size.
extenuate v 1 make less blameworthy. 2 lessen. 3 mitigate.
exterior ⊕ n 1 outside. ♦ adj 2 outer, external.
exterminate v destroy completely. **extermination** n
external ⊕ adj outside, outward.
externally adv

——————— THESAURUS ———————

use of, utilize, cash in on (*Inf*) ♦ n
= **feat**, act, achievement, enterprise, adventure
explore v = **travel around**, tour, survey, scout, reconnoitre;
= **investigate**, consider, research, survey, search
expose v = **uncover**, show, reveal, display, exhibit ≠ **hide**; = **make vulnerable**, subject, endanger, leave open, jeopardize
express v = **state**, communicate, convey, articulate, say; = **show**, indicate, exhibit, demonstrate, reveal ♦ adj = **explicit**, clear, plain, distinct, definite; = **specific**,

exclusive, particular, sole, special;
= **fast**, direct, rapid, priority, prompt
exquisite adj = **beautiful**, elegant, graceful, pleasing, attractive
≠ **unattractive**; = **fine**, beautiful, lovely, elegant, precious
extend v = **spread out**, reach, stretch; = **stretch**, stretch out, spread out, straighten out; = **last**, continue, go on, stretch, carry on;
= **protrude**, project, stand out, bulge, stick out
exterior n = **outside**, face, surface, covering, skin ♦ adj
= **outer**, outside, external, surface,

extinct 🛈 *adj* 1 having died out. 2 quenched. **extinction** *n*

extinguish *v* 1 put out, quench. 2 wipe out.

extol *v* **-tolling, -tolled** praise highly.

extort *v* get by force or threats. **extortion** *n* **extortionate** *adj* excessive.

extra 🛈 *adj* 1 additional. 2 more than usual. ♦ *adv* 3 additionally. 4 more than usually. ♦ *n* 5 extra person or thing. 6 something charged as additional.

extra– *comb. form* beyond, as in *extradition, extramural.*

extract 🛈 *v* 1 take out, esp. by force. 2 get by distillation etc. 3 derive. 4 quote. ♦ *n* 5 passage from book, film etc. 6 concentrated solution. **extraction** *n* 1 extracting. 2 ancestry.

extramural *adj* outside normal courses etc. of university or college.

extraneous *adj* 1 not essential. 2 added from without.

extraordinary 🛈 *adj* very unusual. **extraordinarily** *adv*

extrapolate *v* make inference from known facts.

extrasensory *adj* of perception apparently gained without use of known senses.

extravagant 🛈 *adj* 1 wasteful. 2 exorbitant. **extravagance** *n* **extravaganza** *n* elaborate entertainment.

extreme 🛈 *adj* 1 of high or highest degree. 2 severe. 3 going beyond moderation. 4 outermost. ♦ *n* 5 utmost degree. 6 thing at either end. **extremely** *adv* **extremist** *n/adj* (one) favouring immoderate methods. **extremity** *n*, *pl* **-ties** 1 end. ♦ *pl* 2 hands and feet.

extricate *v* disentangle.

——————— THESAURUS ———————

outward ≠ **inner**

external *adj* = **outer**, outside, surface, outward, exterior ≠ **internal**

extinct *adj* = **dead**, lost, gone, vanished, defunct ≠ **living**

extra *adj* = **additional**, more, added, further, supplementary ≠ **vital**; = **surplus**, excess, spare, redundant, unused ♦ *n* = **addition**, bonus, supplement, accessory ≠ **necessity** ♦ *adv* = **in addition**, additionally, over and above

extract *v* = **take out**, draw, pull, remove, withdraw; = **pull out**, remove, take out, draw, uproot ♦

n = **passage**, selection, excerpt, cutting, clipping; = **essence**, solution, concentrate, juice, distillation

extraordinary *adj* = **remarkable**, outstanding, amazing, fantastic, astonishing ≠ **unremarkable**

extravagant *adj* = **wasteful**, lavish, prodigal, profligate, spendthrift ≠ **economical**; = **excessive**, outrageous, over the top (*Sl*), unreasonable, preposterous ≠ **moderate**

extreme *adj* = **great**, highest, supreme, acute, severe ≠ **mild**; = **severe**, radical, strict, harsh,

extrovert n lively, outgoing person.

extrude v squeeze, force out.

exuberant adj high-spirited. **exuberance** n

exude v **1** ooze out. **2** give off.

exult v rejoice, triumph. **exultant** adj **exultation** n

eye ① n **1** organ of sight. **2** look, glance. **3** attention. **4** aperture. **5** thing resembling eye. ◆ v **6** look

at. **7** observe. **eyebrow** n fringe of hair above eye. **eyelash** n hair fringing eyelid. **eyelet** n small hole. **eyelid** n **eye shadow** coloured cosmetic worn on upper eyelids. **eyesore** n ugly object. **eyetooth** n canine tooth. **eyewitness** n one who was present at an event. **eyrie** n nest of bird of prey, esp. eagle.

————————— THESAURUS —————————

rigid; **= radical**, excessive, fanatical, immoderate ≠ **moderate**; **= farthest**, furthest, far, remotest, far–off ≠ **nearest** ◆ n **= limit**, end, edge, opposite, pole **eye** n **= eyeball**, optic (Inf), organ

of vision, organ of sight; (often plural) **= eyesight**, sight, vision, perception, ability to see ◆ v **= look at**, view, study, watch, survey

F f

F Fahrenheit.

fable n short story with moral.

fabulous adj 1 amazing 2 Inf extremely good.

fabric ❶ n 1 cloth. 2 structure.

fabricate v 1 construct. 2 invent (lie etc.).

face ❶ n 1 front of head. 2 distorted expression. 3 outward appearance. 4 chief side of anything. 5 dignity. ◆ v 6 look or front towards. 7 meet (boldly). 8 give a covering surface. 9 turn.

faceless adj anonymous. **face–lift** n operation to remove wrinkles.

face–saving adj maintaining dignity. **facet** n 1 one side of cut gem. 2 one aspect. **face value** apparent worth. **facial** n 1 cosmetic treatment for face. ◆ adj 2 of face.

facetious adj given to joking.

facia pl **–ciae** see FASCIA.

facile adj 1 easy. 2 superficial.

facilitate v make easy. **facility** n 1 easiness. 2 dexterity. ◆ pl 3 opportunities, good conditions. 4 means, equipment for doing something.

facsimile n exact copy.

fact ❶ n 1 thing known to be true. 2 reality. **factual** adj

faction ❶ n 1 (dissenting) minority group. 2 dissension.

factor ❶ n 1 something contributing to a result. 2 one of numbers which multiplied together give a given number. 3 agent.

factory ❶ n, pl **–ries** building where things are manufactured.

faculty ❶ n, pl **–ties** 1 inherent power. 2 ability. 3 aptitude. 4 department of university.

— THESAURUS —

fabric n = **cloth**, material, stuff, textile, web; = **framework**, structure, make–up, organization, frame

face n = **countenance**, features, profile, mug (Sl), visage; = **expression**, look, air, appearance, aspect; = **side**, front, outside, surface, exterior ◆ v = **look onto**, overlook, be opposite, look out on, front onto; = **confront**, meet, encounter, deal with, oppose; = **accept**, deal with,

tackle, acknowledge, cope with

fact n = **truth**, reality, certainty, verity ≠ fiction; = **event**, happening, act, performance, incident

faction n = **group**, set, party, gang, bloc; = **dissension**, division, conflict, rebellion, disagreement ≠ agreement

factor n = **element**, part, cause, influence, item

factory n = **works**, plant, mill, workshop, assembly line

fad ⊕ *n* short–lived fashion.

fade ⊕ *v* **1** lose colour, strength. **2** cause to fade.

faeces *pl n* excrement.

fag *n* **1** *Inf* boring task. **2** *Sl* cigarette.

faggot *n* **1** ball of chopped liver. **2** bundle of sticks.

Fahrenheit *adj* measured by thermometric scale with freezing point of water 32°, boiling point 212°.

fail ⊕ *v* **1** be unsuccessful. **2** stop working. **3** (judge to) be below the required standard. **4** disappoint, give no help to. **5** be insufficient. **6** become bankrupt. **7** neglect, forget to do. **failing** *n* **1** deficiency. **2** fault. ◆ *prep* **3** in

default of. **failure** *n* **without fail** certainly.

faint ⊕ *adj* **1** feeble, dim, pale. **2** weak. **3** dizzy. ◆ *v* **4** lose consciousness temporarily.

fair¹ ⊕ *adj* **1** just. **2** according to rules. **3** blond. **4** beautiful. **5** of moderate quality or amount. **6** favourable. ◆ *adv* **7** honestly. **fairly** *adv* fairness **n fairway** *n* smooth area on golf course between tee and green.

fair² ⊕ *n* **1** travelling entertainment with sideshows etc. **2** trade exhibition. **fairground** *n*

fairy ⊕ *n, pl* **fairies 1** imaginary small creature with powers of magic. ◆ *adj* **2** of fairies. **3** delicate, imaginary.

————— THESAURUS —————

faculty *n* = **ability**, power, skill, facility, capacity ≠ **failing**; = **department**, school; staff, teachers, professors

fad *n* = **craze**, fashion, trend, rage, vogue

fade *v* = **become pale**, bleach, wash out, discolour, lose colour; = **make pale**, dim, bleach, wash out, blanch

fail *v* = **be unsuccessful**, founder, fall, break down, flop (*Inf*) ≠ **succeed**; = **disappoint**, abandon, desert, neglect, omit; = **stop working**, stop, die, break down, stall; = **wither**, perish, sag, waste away, shrivel up; = **go bankrupt**, collapse, fold (*Inf*), close down, go under

faint *adj* = **dim**, low, soft, faded, distant ≠ **clear**; = **slight**, weak,

feeble, unenthusiastic, remote; = **dizzy**, giddy, light–headed, weak, exhausted ≠ **energetic** ◆ *v* = **pass out**, black out, lose consciousness, keel over (*Inf*), go out ◆ *n* = **blackout**, collapse, coma, swoon (*Lit*), unconsciousness

fair¹ *adj* = **unbiased**, impartial, even–handed, unprejudiced, just ≠ **unfair**; = **respectable**, average, reasonable, decent, acceptable; = **light**, golden, blonde, blond, yellowish; = **fine**, clear, dry, bright, pleasant; = **beautiful**, pretty, attractive, lovely, handsome ≠ **ugly**

fair² *n* = **carnival**, show, fête, festival, exhibition

fairy *n* = **sprite**, elf, brownie, pixie, puck

faith ⊕ n 1 trust. 2 belief (without proof). 3 religion. 4 loyalty.
faithful adj constant, true.
faithfully adv **faithless** adj
fake ⊕ v 1 touch up. 2 counterfeit. ♦ n/adj 3 fraudulent (thing or person).
falcon n small bird of prey.
fall ⊕ v **falling, fell, fallen** 1 drop. 2 become lower. 3 hang down. 4 cease to stand. 5 perish. 6 collapse. 7 be captured. 8 become. 9 happen. ♦ n 10 falling. 11 amount that falls. 12 decrease. 13 collapse. 14 drop. 15 (oft. pl) cascade. 16 yielding to temptation. 17 US autumn. **fallout** n radioactive particles spread as result of nuclear explosion.
fallacy n, pl **-cies** incorrect

opinion or argument. **fallacious** adj
fallible adj liable to error.
fallow adj ploughed but left without crop.
false ⊕ adj 1 wrong. 2 deceptive. 3 faithless. 4 artificial. **falsely** adv
falsehood n **falsify** v alter fraudulently.
falsetto n, pl **-tos** forced voice above natural range.
falter ⊕ v 1 hesitate. 2 waver. 3 stumble.
fame ⊕ n renown. **famed** adj
famous adj widely known.
famously adv Inf excellently.
familiar ⊕ adj 1 well-known. 2 customary. 3 intimate. 4 acquainted. 5 impertinent. ♦ n 6 friend. 7 demon. **familiarity** n
familiarize v

F

—————————— THESAURUS ——————————

faith n = **confidence**, trust, credit, conviction, assurance ≠ **distrust**; = **religion**, church, belief, persuasion, creed ≠ **agnosticism**
fake adj = **artificial**, false, forged, counterfeit, put-on ≠ **genuine** ♦ n = **forgery**, copy, fraud, reproduction, dummy ♦ v = **forge**, copy, reproduce, fabricate, counterfeit; = **sham**, put on, pretend, simulate, feign
fall v = **drop**, plunge, tumble, plummet, collapse ≠ **rise**; = **decrease**, drop, decline, go down, slump ≠ **increase**; = **be overthrown**, surrender, succumb, submit, capitulate ≠ **triumph**; = **be killed**, die, perish, meet your end ≠ **survive**; = **occur**, happen, come about, chance, take place ♦ n

= **drop**, slip, plunge, dive, tumble; = **decrease**, drop, lowering, decline, reduction; = **collapse**, defeat, downfall, ruin, destruction
false adj = **incorrect**, wrong, mistaken, misleading, faulty ≠ **correct**; = **untrue**, fraudulent, trumped up, fallacious, untruthful ≠ **true**; = **artificial**, forged, fake, reproduction, replica ≠ **real** (Inf)
falter v = **hesitate**, delay, waver, vacillate ≠ **persevere**; = **tumble**, totter; = **stutter**, pause, stumble, hesitate, stammer
fame n = **prominence**, glory, celebrity, stardom, reputation ≠ **obscurity**
familiar adj = **well-known**, recognized, common, ordinary, routine ≠ **unfamiliar**; = **friendly**,

family ● *n, pl* **–lies 1** parents and children, relatives. **2** group of allied objects.

famine ● *n* **1** extreme scarcity of food. **2** starvation. **famished** *adj* very hungry.

fan¹ ● *n* **1** instrument for producing current of air. **2** folding object of paper etc., for cooling the face. ◆ *v* **3** blow or cool with fan. **4** spread out.

fan² ● *n Inf* devoted admirer.

fanatic ● *adj/n* (person) filled with abnormal enthusiasm. **fanatical** *adj* **fanaticism** *n*

fancy ● *adj* **–cier, –ciest 1** ornamental. ◆ *n* **2** whim. **3** liking. **4** imagination. **5** mental image. ◆ *v* **6** imagine. **7** be inclined to believe. **8** *Inf* have a liking for.

fancier *n* one with special interest in something. **fanciful** *adj*

fanfare *n* **1** flourish of trumpets. **2** ostentatious display.

fang *n* **1** snake's tooth, injecting poison. **2** long, pointed tooth.

fantasy ● *n, pl* **–sies 1** power of imagination. **2** mental image. **3** fanciful invention. **fantasize** *v*

fantastic *adj* **1** quaint, extremely fanciful, wild. **2** *Inf* very good. **3** *Inf* very large.

far ● *adv* **farther 1** at or to a great distance or a remote time. **2** by very much. ◆ *adj* **3** distant. **4** more distant. **far–fetched** *adj* incredible.

farce ● *n* **1** comedy of boisterous humour. **2** absurd and futile proceeding. **farcical** *adj*

fare ● *n* **1** charge for transport. **2**

———— THESAURUS ————

close, dear, intimate, amicable ≠ **formal**; = **relaxed**, easy, friendly, comfortable, intimate;
= **disrespectful**, forward, bold, intrusive, presumptuous
family *n* = **relations**, relatives, household, folk (*Inf*),
= **children**, kids (*Inf*), offspring, little ones; = **ancestors**, house, race, tribe, clan
famine *n* = **hunger**, want, starvation, deprivation, scarcity
fan¹ *n* = **blower**, ventilator, air conditioner ◆ *v* = **blow**, cool, refresh, air–condition, ventilate
fan² *n* = **supporter**, lover, follower, enthusiast, admirer
fanatic *n* = **extremist**, activist, militant, bigot, zealot
fancy *adj* = **elaborate**, decorative,

extravagant, intricate, baroque ≠ **plain**; ◆ *n* = **whim**, thought, idea, desire, urge; = **delusion**, dream, vision, fantasy, daydream ◆ *v* = **wish for**, want, desire, hope for, long for; = (*Inf*) **be attracted to**, find attractive, lust after, like, take to; = **suppose**, think, believe, imagine, reckon
fantasy *n* = **daydream**, dream, wish, reverie, flight of fancy;
= **imagination**, fancy, invention, creativity, originality
far *adv* = **a long way**, miles, deep, a good way, afar; = **much**, greatly, very much, extremely, significantly ◆ *adj* (*often with* **off**) = **remote**, distant, far–flung, faraway, out–of–the–way ≠ **near**
farce *n* = **comedy**, satire, slapstick,

passenger. **3** food. ♦ v **4** get on. **5** happen. **farewell** interj **1** goodbye. ♦ n **2** leave-taking.

farm ❶ n **1** tract of land for cultivation or rearing livestock. ♦ v **2** cultivate (land). **3** rear livestock (on farm). **farmer** n **farmhouse** n **farmyard** n

fart Vulgar ♦ n **1** (audible) emission of gas from anus. ♦ v **2** break wind.

farther, farthest adv/adj further: comparative of FAR. **farthest** adv/adj furthest: superlative of FAR.

farthing n formerly, coin worth a quarter of a penny.

fascia n, pl **-ciae, -cias 1** flat surface above shop window. **2** dashboard.

fascinate ❶ v attract and delight. **fascination** n

fascism n authoritarian political system opposed to democracy and liberalism. **fascist** adj/n

fashion ❶ n **1** (latest) style, esp. of dress etc. **2** manner. **3** type. ♦ v **4** shape, make. **fashionable** adj

fast¹ ❶ adj **1** (capable of) moving quickly. **2** ahead of true time **3** Obs dissipated. **4** firm, steady. ♦ adv **5** rapidly. **6** tightly. **fast food** food, esp. hamburgers etc., served very quickly.

fast² ❶ v **1** go without food. ♦ n **2** fasting. **fasting** n

fasten ❶ v **1** attach, fix, secure. **2** become joined. **fastener, fastening** n

fastidious adj hard to please.

fat ❶ n **fatter, fattest 1** oily animal substance. **2** fat part. ♦ adj **3** having too much fat. **4** greasy. **5** profitable. **fatten** v **fatty** adj

fate ❶ n **1** power supposed to

———— THESAURUS ————

burlesque, buffoonery; = **mockery**, joke, nonsense, parody, shambles

fare n = **charge**, price, ticket price, ticket money; = **food**, provisions, board, rations, nourishment ♦ v = **get on**, do, manage, make out, prosper

farm n = **smallholding**, ranch (Chiefly US & Canad), farmstead, vineyard, plantation ♦ v = **cultivate**, work, plant, grow crops on, keep animals on

fascinate v = **entrance**, absorb, intrigue, rivet, captivate ≠ **bore**

fashion n = **style**, look, trend, rage, custom; = **method**, way, style, manner, mode ♦ v = **make**, shape, cast, construct, form

fast¹ adj = **quick**, flying, rapid, fleet, swift ≠ **slow**; = **fixed**, firm, sound, stuck, secure ≠ **unstable**; = **dissipated**, wild, exciting, loose, extravagant ♦ adv = **quickly**, rapidly, swiftly, hastily, hurriedly ≠ **slowly**; = **firmly**, staunchly, resolutely, steadfastly, unwaveringly

fast² v = **go hungry**, abstain, go without food, deny yourself ♦ n = **fasting**, diet, abstinence

fasten v = **secure**, close, do up

fat adj = **overweight**, large, heavy, plump, stout ≠ **thin** = **large**, substantial, profitable ♦ n = **fatness**, flesh, bulk, obesity, flab **fat chance**

predetermine events. **2** destiny. **3** person's appointed lot. **4** death or destruction. **fatal** adj ending in death. **fatality** n death. **fatally** adv

fated adj destined. **fateful** adj

father ⊕ n **1** male parent. **2** ancestor. **3** (with cap.) God. **4** originator. **5** priest. ◆ v **6** beget. **7** originate. **fatherhood** n **father-in-law** n, pl **fathers-in-law** husband's or wife's father. **fatherland** n native country.

fathom n **1** measure of six feet of water. ◆ v **2** sound (water). **3** understand.

fatigue ⊕ v **1** tire. ◆ n **2** weariness. **3** toil. **4** weakness of metals etc.

fatuous adj very silly, idiotic.

faucet n US and Canad valve with handle, plug etc. to regulate or stop flow of fluid.

fault ⊕ n **1** defect. **2** misdeed. **3** blame. ◆ v **4** find fault in. **5** (cause to) commit fault. **faultily** adv **faultless** adj **faulty** adj

faun n mythological woodland being with tail and horns.

fauna n, pl **-nas, -nae** animals of region collectively.

faux pas n, pl **faux pas** social blunder or indiscretion.

favour ⊕ n **1** goodwill. **2** approval. **3** especial kindness. **4** partiality. ◆ v **5** regard or treat with favour. **6** oblige. **7** treat with partiality. **8** support. **favourable** adj **favourite** n **1** favoured person or thing. ◆ adj **2** chosen, preferred. **favouritism** n practice of showing undue preference.

fawn¹ n **1** young deer. ◆ adj **2**

fate n = **destiny**, chance, fortune, luck, the stars; = **fortune**, destiny, lot, portion, cup

father n = **daddy** (Inf), dad (Inf), male parent, pop (US inf), old man (Brit inf); = **founder**, author, maker, architect, creator; (usually cap.) = **priest**, minister, vicar, parson, pastor; (usually plural) = **forefather**, predecessor, ancestor, forebear, progenitor ◆ v = **sire**, parent, conceive, bring to life, beget

fatigue n = **tiredness**, lethargy, weariness, heaviness, languor ≠ **freshness** ◆ v = **tire**, exhaust, weaken, weary, drain ≠ **refresh**

fault n = **responsibility**, liability, guilt, accountability, culpability; = **mistake**, slip, error, blunder,

lapse; = **failing**, weakness, defect, deficiency, flaw ≠ **strength** ◆ v = **criticize**, blame, complain, condemn, moan about, = **guilty**, responsible, to blame, accountable, in the wrong; **find fault with something or someone** = **criticize**, complain about, whinge about (Inf), whine about (Inf), quibble **to a fault** = **excessively**, unduly, in the extreme, overmuch, immoderately

favour n = **approval**, goodwill, commendation, approbation ≠ **disapproval**; = **favouritism**, preferential treatment ◆ v = **prefer**, opt for, like better, incline towards, choose ≠ **object to**; = **indulge**, reward, side with,

light yellowish brown.

fawn² v cringe, court favour servilely.

fax n 1 facsimile. ♦ v 2 send by telegraphic facsimile system.

FBI US Federal Bureau of Investigation.

fear ❶ n 1 unpleasant emotion caused by coming danger. ♦ v 2 be afraid. 3 regard with fear. **fearful** adj **fearless** adj

feasible ❶ adj able to be done. **feasibility** n

feast ❶ n 1 banquet. 2 religious anniversary. ♦ v 3 eat banquet. 4 entertain with feast. 5 delight.

feat ❶ n notable deed.

feather n 1 one of the barbed shafts which form covering of birds. 2 anything resembling this. ♦ v 3 provide with feathers. 4 grow feathers. **feathery** adj

feature ❶ n 1 (usu. pl) part of face. 2 notable part of anything. 3 main or special item. ♦ v 4 portray. 5 be prominent (in).

featureless adj without striking features.

Feb. February.

February n second month.

feckless adj ineffectual, irresponsible.

federal adj of the government of states which are united but retain internal independence. **federalism** n **federalist** n **federate** v form into, become, a federation. **federation** n 1 league. 2 federal union.

fee ❶ n payment for services.

feeble ❶ adj 1 weak. 2 not effective or convincing.

feed ❶ v feeding, fed 1 give food to. 2 supply, support. 3 take food. ♦ n 4 feeding. 5 fodder. **feedback** n response. **fed up** Inf bored, dissatisfied.

———————— THESAURUS ————————

smile upon

fear n = **dread**, horror, panic, terror, fright; = **bugbear**, bête noire, horror, nightmare, anxiety (Inf) ♦ v = **be afraid of**, dread, shudder at, be fearful of, tremble at, = **worry**, expect

feasible adj = **practicable**, possible, reasonable, viable, workable ≠ **impracticable**

feast n = **banquet**, repast, spread (Inf), dinner, treat; = **festival**, holiday, fête, celebration, holy day; = **treat**, delight, pleasure, enjoyment, gratification ♦ v = **eat your fill**, wine and dine, overindulge, consume, indulge

feat n = **accomplishment**, act, performance, achievement, enterprise

feature n = **aspect**, quality, characteristic, property, factor; = **article**, report, story, piece, item; = **highlight**, attraction, speciality, main item ♦ v = **spotlight**, present, emphasize, play up, foreground

fee n = **charge**, price, cost, bill, payment

feeble adj = **weak**, frail, debilitated, sickly, puny ≠ **strong**; = **inadequate**, pathetic, insufficient, lame

feed v = **cater for**, provide for,

feel ❶ v feeling, felt 1 touch. 2 experience. 3 find (one's way) cautiously. 4 be sensitive to. 5 show emotion (for). 6 believe, consider. ◆ n 7 feeling. 8 impression perceived by feeling. 9 sense of touch. **feeler** n **feeling** n 1 sense of touch. 2 sensation. 3 emotion. 4 sympathy. 5 opinion. ◆ pl 6 susceptibilities. **feel like** have an inclination for.

feet see FOOT.

feign v pretend, sham.

feint n 1 sham attack. 2 pretence. ◆ v 3 make feint.

feisty adj 1 Inf lively, resilient, and self-reliant. 2 US and Canad frisky. 3 US and Canad irritable.

felicity n 1 great happiness. 2 apt wording. **felicitations** pl n congratulations. **felicitous** adj

feline adj 1 of cats. 2 catlike.

fell[1] ❶ v 1 knock down. 2 cut down (tree). **feller** n

fell[2] n mountain, moor.

fellow ❶ n 1 Inf man, boy. 2 associate. 3 counterpart. 4 member (of society, college etc.).

◆ adj 5 of the same class, associated. **fellowship** n

felon n one guilty of felony.

felony n, pl **-nies** serious crime.

felt[1] n 1 soft, matted fabric. ◆ v 2 make into, or cover with, felt. 3 become matted. **felt-tip pen** pen with writing point of pressed fibres.

female adj 1 of sex which bears offspring. 2 relating to this sex. ◆ n 3 one of this sex.

feminine ❶ adj 1 of women. 2 womanly. **feminism** n advocacy of equal rights for women. **feminist** n/adj **femininity** n

fen n tract of marshy land.

fence ❶ n 1 structure of wire, wood etc. enclosing an area 2 Sl dealer in stolen property. ◆ v 3 erect fence. 4 fight with swords 5 Sl deal in stolen property. **fencing** n art of swordplay.

fend v 1 ward off. 2 repel. 3 provide (for oneself etc.). **fender** n low metal frame in front of fireplace.

fender n US and Canad the part of

nourish, provide with food, supply; **= graze**, eat, browse, pasture ◆ n **= food**, fodder, provender, pasturage; **=** (Inf) **meal**, spread (Inf), dinner, lunch, tea **feel** v **= experience**, bear; **= touch**, handle, manipulate, finger, stroke; detect, discern, experience, notice, **= grope**, explore ◆ n **= texture**, finish, touch, surface, surface quality; **= impression**, feeling, air, sense, quality

fell[1] v **= cut down**, cut, level, demolish, knock down

fellow n = (Old-fashioned) **man**, person, individual, character, guy (Inf); **= associate**, colleague, peer, partner, companion

feminine adj **= womanly**, pretty, soft, gentle, tender ≠ masculine

fence n **= barrier**, wall, defence, railings, hedge ◆ v (often with **in** or **off**) **= enclose**, surround, bound, protect, pen

a car body that surrounds the wheels.

fennel n fragrant plant.

feral adj wild.

ferment n 1 substance causing thing to ferment. 2 excitement. ◆ v 3 (cause to) undergo chemical change with effervescence and alteration of properties. **fermentation** n

fern n plant with feathery fronds.

ferocious ❶ adj fierce, savage, cruel. **ferocity** n

ferret n 1 tamed animal like weasel. ◆ v 2 drive out with ferrets. 3 search about.

ferric, ferrous adj pert. to, containing, iron.

ferry ❶ n, pl **-ries** 1 boat etc. for transporting people, vehicles, across water. ◆ v 2 carry, travel, by ferry.

fertile ❶ adj 1 (capable of) producing offspring, bearing crops etc. 2 producing abundantly. **fertility** n **fertilize** v make fertile. **fertilization** n **fertilizer** n

fervent, fervid adj ardent, intense. **fervour** n

fester v 1 (cause to) form pus. 2 rankle. 3 become embittered.

festival ❶ n 1 day, period of celebration. 2 organized series of events, performances etc. **festive** adj joyous, merry. **festivity** n, pl **-ties** 1 gaiety. 2 rejoicing. ◆ pl 3 festive proceedings.

festoon n 1 loop of flowers, ribbons etc. ◆ v 2 form, adorn with festoons.

fete n 1 gala, bazaar etc., esp. one held out of doors. ◆ v 2 honour with festive entertainment.

fetid adj stinking.

fetish n 1 object believed to have magical powers. 2 object, activity, to which excessive devotion is paid.

fetter n 1 chain for feet. 2 check. ◆ pl 3 captivity. ◆ v 4 chain up. 5 restrain.

fettle n state of health.

fetus, foetus n, pl **-tuses** fully developed embryo. **fetal, foetal** adj

feud ❶ n 1 long bitter hostility. ◆ v 2 carry on feud.

fever ❶ n 1 condition of illness with high body temperature. 2 intense nervous excitement. **fevered** adj **feverish** adj

few adj 1 not many. ◆ pron 2

ferocious adj = **fierce**, violent, savage, ravening, predatory ≠ **gentle**

ferry n = **ferry boat**, boat, ship, passenger boat, packet boat ◆ v = **transport**, bring, carry, ship, take

fertile adj = **productive**, rich, lush, prolific, abundant ≠ **barren**

festival n = **celebration**, fair, carnival, gala, fête; = **holy day**, holiday, feast, commemoration, feast day

feud n = **hostility**, row, conflict, argument, disagreement ◆ v = **quarrel**, row, clash, dispute, fall out

fever n = **excitement**, frenzy,

small number.

fez n, pl **fezzes** red, brimless cap with tassel.

fiancé n person engaged to be married.

fiasco ⊕ n, pl **-cos, -coes** breakdown, total failure.

fib n/v (tell) trivial lie.

fibre ⊕ n 1 filament forming part of animal or plant tissue. 2 substance that can be spun. **fibrous** adj **fibreglass** n material made of fine glass fibres.

fickle adj changeable.

fiction ⊕ n literary works of the imagination. **fictional** adj **fictitious** adj 1 false. 2 imaginary.

fiddle ⊕ n 1 violin 2 Inf fraudulent arrangement. ♦ v 3 play fiddle. 4 fidget 5 Sl cheat. **fiddling** adj trivial. **fiddly** adj small, awkward to handle.

fidelity ⊕ n faithfulness.

fidget v 1 move restlessly. ♦ n 2 (oft. pl) restless mood. 3 one who fidgets. **fidgety** adj

field ⊕ n 1 area of (farming) land. 2 tract of land rich in specified product. 3 players in a game or sport collectively. 4 battlefield. 5 sphere of knowledge. ♦ v 6 Cricket stop and return ball. 7 send player, team, on to sports field. **fielder** n **field day** exciting occasion. **fieldwork** n investigation made away from classroom or laboratory.

fiend n 1 devil. 2 person addicted to something. **fiendish** adj

fierce ⊕ adj 1 savage, wild, violent. 2 intense. **fiercely** adv

fiery ⊕ adj **fierier, fieriest** 1 consisting of, or like, fire. 2 irritable. **fierily** adv

———— THESAURUS ————

ferment, agitation, fervour

fiasco n = **flop**, failure, disaster, mess (Inf), catastrophe

fibre n = **thread**, strand, filament, tendril, pile **moral fibre** = **strength of character**, strength, resolution, resolve, stamina

fiction n = **tale**, story, novel, legend, myth; = **lie**, invention, fabrication, falsehood, untruth

fiddle v (usually with **with**) = **fidget**, play, finger, tamper, mess about or around with; = **tinker**, adjust, interfere, mess about or around ♦ n = (Brit inf) **fraud**, racket, scam (Sl), fix, swindle

fidelity n = **loyalty**, devotion, allegiance, constancy, faithfulness

≠ **disloyalty**; = **accuracy**, precision, correspondence, closeness, faithfulness ≠ **inaccuracy**

field n = **meadow**, land, green, lea (Poet), pasture; = **speciality**, line, area, department, territory; = **line**, reach, sweep ♦ v = (Inf) **deal with**, answer, handle, respond to, reply to; = (Sport) **retrieve**, return, stop, catch, pick up

fierce adj = **ferocious**, wild, dangerous, cruel, savage ≠ **gentle**; = **intense**, strong, keen, relentless, cut-throat

fiery adj = **burning**, flaming, blazing, on fire, ablaze; = **excitable**, fierce, passionate, irritable, impetuous

fiesta n carnival.

fifteen see FIVE.

fig n 1 soft, pear-shaped fruit. 2 tree bearing this.

fight ⊕ v **fighting, fought** 1 contend with in battle. 2 maintain against opponent. 3 settle by combat. ♦ n 4 fighting. **fighter** n person or aircraft that fights.

figment n imaginary thing.

figure ⊕ n 1 numerical symbol. 2 amount, number. 3 (bodily) shape. 4 (conspicuous) appearance. 5 space enclosed by lines. 6 diagram, illustration. ♦ v 7 calculate. 8 show. **figurative** adj (of language) symbolic. **figurine** n statuette. **figurehead** n nominal leader.

filament n 1 fine wire. 2 threadlike body.

filch v steal, pilfer.

file¹ n 1 (box, folder etc. holding) papers for reference. 2 orderly line. ♦ v 3 arrange (papers etc.) and put them away for reference.

4 march in file. **filing** n

file² ⊕ n/v (use) roughened tool for smoothing or shaping. **filing** n scrap of metal removed by file.

filial adj of, befitting, son or daughter.

filibuster v 1 obstruct legislation by making long speeches. ♦ n 2 filibustering.

filigree n fine tracery or openwork of metal.

fill ⊕ v 1 make full. 2 occupy completely. 3 discharge duties of. 4 stop up. 5 satisfy. 6 fulfil. 7 become full. ♦ n 8 full supply. 9 as much as desired. **filling** n/adj

fillet n 1 boneless slice of meat, fish. 2 narrow strip. ♦ v 3 cut into fillets, bone. **filleted** adj

fillip n stimulus.

filly n, pl –**lies** young female horse.

film ⊕ n 1 sequence of images projected on screen, creating illusion of movement. 2 sensitized celluloid roll used in photography, cinematography. 3 thin skin or

fight v = **oppose**, campaign against, dispute, contest, resist; = **battle**, combat, do battle; = **engage in**, conduct, wage, pursue, carry on ♦ n = **battle**, campaign, movement, struggle; = **conflict**, clash, contest, encounter; confrontation

figure n = **digit**, character, symbol, number, numeral; = **shape**, build, body, frame, proportions; = **personage**, person, individual, character, personality; = **diagram**, drawing, picture,

illustration, representation; = **design**, shape, pattern ♦ v (usually with **in**) = **feature**, act, appear, contribute to, play a part; = **calculate**, work out, compute, tot up, total

file² v = **smooth**, shape, polish, rub, scrape

fill v = **swell**, expand, become bloated, extend, balloon; = **pack**, crowd, squeeze, cram, throng; = **stock**, supply, pack, load; = **plug**, close, stop, seal, cork; = **saturate**, charge, pervade,

layer. ♦ adj 4 connected with cinema. ♦ v 5 photograph with cine camera. 6 make cine film of. 7 cover, become covered, with film. **filmy** adj gauzy.

filth n 1 disgusting dirt. 2 obscenity. **filthiness** n **filthy** adj

fin n 1 propelling organ of fish. 2 anything like this.

final ⊙ adj 1 at the end. 2 conclusive. ♦ n 3 game, heat, examination etc., coming at end of series. **finale** n closing part of musical composition. **finalist** n competitor in a final. **finalize** v **finally** adv

finance ⊙ n 1 management of money. 2 (also pl) money resources. ♦ v 3 find capital for. **financial** adj **financier** n

finch n, pl **finches** one of family of small singing birds.

find ⊙ v **finding, found** 1 come across. 2 experience, discover 3

Law give verdict. ♦ n 4 (valuable) thing found. **finding** n conclusion from investigation.

fine¹ ⊙ adj 1 of high quality. 2 not rainy. 3 delicate. 4 subtle. 5 pure. 6 in small particles. 7 Inf healthy, at ease. 8 satisfactory. **finery** n showy dress. **finesse** n skilful management. **fine art** art produced for its aesthetic value. **fine-tune** v make small adjustments.

fine² ⊙ n 1 sum fixed as penalty. ♦ v 2 punish by fine.

finger ⊙ n 1 one of the jointed branches of the hand. 2 various things like this. ♦ v 3 touch with fingers. **fingerprint** n impression of tip of finger.

finicky adj fussy.

finish ⊙ v 1 bring, come to an end, conclude. 2 complete. 3 perfect. ♦ n 4 end. 5 way in which thing is finished. 6 final

——————— THESAURUS ———————

permeate, imbue

film n = **movie**, picture, flick (Sl), motion picture; = **cinema**, the movies ♦ v = **photograph**, record, shoot, video, videotape

final adj = **last**, latest, closing, finishing, concluding ≠ **first**; = **irrevocable**, absolute, definitive, decided, settled

finance v = **fund**, back, support, pay for, guarantee ♦ n = **economics**, business, money, banking, accounts

find v = **discover**, uncover, spot, locate, detect ≠ **lose** = **obtain**, get, come by ♦ n = **discovery**, catch,

asset, bargain, acquisition

fine¹ adj = **excellent**, good, striking, masterly, very good ≠ **poor**; = **satisfactory**, good, all right, suitable, acceptable; = **thin**, light, narrow, wispy; light ≠ **coarse**; = **stylish**, expensive, elegant, refined, tasteful; = **exquisite**, delicate, fragile, dainty; = **minute**, exact, precise, nice

fine² n = **penalty**, damages, punishment, forfeit, financial penalty ♦ v = **penalize**, charge, punish

finger v = **touch**, feel, handle, play

appearance.

finite *adj* bounded, limited.

fiord see FJORD.

fir *n* coniferous tree.

fire ❶ *n* 1 state of burning. 2 mass of burning fuel. 3 destructive burning. 4 device for heating a room etc. 5 shooting of guns. 6 ardour. ◆ *v* 7 discharge (firearm). 8 *Inf* dismiss from employment. 9 bake. 10 make burn. 11 inspire. 12 explode. 13 begin to burn. 14 become excited. **firearm** *n* gun, rifle, pistol etc. **fire brigade** organized body to put out fires. **fire engine** vehicle with apparatus for extinguishing fires. **fire escape** means, esp. stairs, for escaping from burning buildings. **fireman** *n* member of fire brigade. **fireplace** *n* recess in room for fire. **fire station** building housing fire-fighting vehicles and equipment. **firework** *n* 1 device to give spectacular effects by explosions and coloured sparks. ◆ *pl* 2 outburst of temper. **firing squad** group of soldiers ordered to execute offender.

firm ❶ *adj* 1 solid, fixed, stable. ◆ *v* 2 make, become firm. ◆ *n* 3 commercial enterprise.

first *adj* 1 earlier in time or order. 2 foremost in rank or position. **First Nations** *pl n Canad* Canadian aboriginal communities. **First Peoples** *pl n Canad* a collective term for the Native Canadian peoples, the Inuit, and the Métis.

fiscal *adj* of government finances.

fish *n, pl* **fish, fishes** 1 vertebrate cold-blooded animal with gills, living in water. ◆ *v* 2 (attempt to) catch fish. 3 try to get information indirectly. **fishy** *adj* 1 of, like, or full of fish. 2 *Inf* suspicious. **fisherman** *n* **fishmonger** *n* seller of fish.

fissure *n* cleft, split. **fission** *n* 1 splitting. 2 reproduction by

———————— THESAURUS ————————

finish *v* = **stop**, close, complete, conclude, cease ≠ **start**; = **end**, stop, conclude, wind up, terminate; = **consume**, dispose of, devour, polish off, eat; = **use up**, empty, exhaust; = **coat**, polish, stain, texture, wax ◆ *n* = **end**, close, conclusion, run-in, completion ≠ **beginning**; = **surface**, polish, shine, texture, glaze

fire *n* = **flames**, blaze, combustion, inferno, conflagration; = **passion**, energy, spirit, enthusiasm, excitement; = **bombardment**, shooting, firing, shelling, hail ◆ *v* = **let off**, shoot, shell, set off, discharge; = **shoot**, explode, discharge, detonate, pull the trigger; = (*Inf*) **dismiss**, sack, (*Inf*) get rid of, discharge, lay off

firm *adj* = **hard**, solid, dense, set, stiff ≠ **soft**; = **secure**, fixed, rooted, stable, steady ≠ **unstable**; = **strong**, close, tight, steady; unshakeable; = **determined**, resolved, definite, set on, adamant

division of living cells. **3** splitting of atomic nucleus.

fist n clenched hand. **fisticuffs** pl n fighting.

fit¹ ① v fitting, fitted 1 be suited to. **2** be properly adjusted. **3** adjust. **4** supply. ◆ adj **5** well-suited. **6** proper. **7** in good health. ◆ n **8** way anything fits. **fitness** n **fitter** n **fitting** adj appropriate. ◆ n **2** attachment. **3** action of fitting.

fit² ① n 1 seizure with convulsions. **2** passing state, mood. **fitful** adj spasmodic.

five adj/n cardinal number after four. **fifth** adj ordinal number. **fifteen** adj/n ten plus five. **fifteenth** adj **fiftieth** adj **fifty** adj/n five tens.

fix ① v 1 fasten, make firm. **2** determine. **3** repair. **4** Inf influence unfairly. ◆ n **5** difficult situation. **6** position of ship, aircraft ascertained by radar, observation etc. **7** Sl dose of narcotic drug.

fixation n obsession. **fixed** adj

fixture n **1** thing fixed in position. **2** (date for) sporting event.

fizz ① v 1 hiss. ◆ n **2** hissing noise. **3** effervescent liquid. **fizzy** adj

fizzle v splutter weakly. **fizzle out** Inf fail.

fjord n (esp. in Norway) long, narrow inlet of sea.

flabby adj **–bier, –biest 1** limp. **2** too fat. **3** weak and lacking purpose. **flabbiness** n

flag¹ ① n 1 banner, piece of bunting as standard or signal. ◆ v **2** inform by flag signals. **flagpole, flagstaff** n pole for flag. **flagship** n **1** admiral's ship. **2** most important item.

flag² ① v lose vigour.

flagon n large bottle.

flagrant adj blatant.

flail n **1** instrument for threshing corn by hand. ◆ v **2** beat with, move as, flail.

flair ① n 1 natural ability. **2**

≠ **wavering**

fit¹ v = **adapt**, shape, arrange, alter, adjust; = **place**, insert, connect; = **suit**, meet, match, belong to, conform to ◆ adj = **appropriate**, suitable, right, becoming, seemly ≠ **inappropriate**; = **healthy**, strong, robust, sturdy, well ≠ **unfit**

fit² n = **seizure**, attack, bout, spasm, convulsion; = **bout**, burst, outbreak, outburst, spell

fix v = **place**, join, stick, attach, set; = **decide**, set, choose, establish, determine; = **arrange**,

organize, sort out, see to, fix up; = **repair**, mend, service, correct, restore; = **focus**, direct at, fasten on; = (Inf) **rig**, set up (Inf), influence, manipulate, fiddle (Inf) ◆ n = (Inf) **mess**, corner, difficulty, dilemma, embarrassment

fizz v = **bubble**, froth, fizzle, effervesce, produce bubbles

flag¹ n = **banner**, standard, colours, pennant, ensign ◆ v = **mark**, identify, indicate, label, pick out

flag² v = **weaken**, fade, weary, falter, wilt

elegant style.

flak n 1 anti–aircraft fire. 2 Inf adverse criticism.

flake ❶ n 1 small, thin piece. 2 piece chipped off. ◆ v 3 (cause to) peel off in flakes. **flaky** adj

flambé v flambéing, flambéed cook in flaming brandy.

flamboyant ❶ adj showy. **flamboyance** n

flame ❶ n 1 burning gas, esp. above fire. ◆ v 2 give out flames.

flamenco n, pl –cos rhythmical Spanish dance.

flamingo n, pl –gos, –goes large pink bird with long neck and legs.

flammable adj liable to catch fire.

flan n open sweet or savoury tart.

flange n projecting rim.

flank ❶ n 1 part of side between hips and ribs. 2 side of anything. ◆ v 3 be at, move along either side of.

flannel n 1 soft woollen fabric. 2 small piece of cloth for washing face.

flap ❶ v flapping, flapped 1 move (wings, arms etc.) as bird flying. ◆ n 2 act of flapping. 3 broad piece of anything hanging from one side. 4 Inf state of panic.

flapjack n chewy biscuit.

flare ❶ v 1 blaze with unsteady flame. 2 spread outwards. ◆ n 3 instance of flaring. 4 signal light.

flash ❶ n 1 sudden burst of light or flame. 2 very short time. ◆ v 3 break into sudden flame. 4 move very fast. 5 (cause to) gleam. **flash, flashy** adj showy, sham. **flashback** n break in narrative to introduce what has taken place previously.

flask n type of bottle.

flat¹ ❶ adj flatter, flattest 1 level. 2 at full length. 3 smooth. 4 downright. 5 dull. 6 Mus below true pitch. 7 (of tyre) deflated. 8 (of battery) dead. ◆ n 9 what is flat. 10 Mus note half tone below natural pitch. **flatly** adv **flatten** v

———————— THESAURUS ————————

flair n = **ability**, feel, talent, gift, genius; = **style**, taste, dash, chic, elegance

flake n = **chip**, scale, layer, peeling, shaving ◆ v = **chip**, peel (off), blister

flamboyant adj dashing, theatrical; = **showy**, elaborate, extravagant, ornate, ostentatious; = **colourful**, striking, brilliant, glamorous, stylish

flame n = **fire**, light, spark, glow, blaze ◆ v = **burn**, flash, shine, glow, blaze

flank n = **side**, hip, thigh, loin

flap v = **flutter**, wave, flail ◆ n = **flutter**, beating, waving, shaking, swinging; = (Inf) **panic**, state (Inf), agitation, commotion, sweat (Inf)

flare n = **flame**, burst, flash, blaze, glare ◆ v = **blaze**, flame, glare, flicker, burn up

flash n = **blaze**, burst, spark, beam, streak ◆ v = **blaze**, shine, beam, sparkle, flare; = **speed**, race, shoot, fly, tear; = (Inf) **show quickly**, display, expose, exhibit, flourish ◆ adj = (Inf) **ostentatious**, smart, trendy, showy

flatfish n type of fish with broad, flat body. **flat rate** the same in all cases. **flat out** at, with maximum speed or effort.

flat² ⓘ n suite of rooms in larger building.

flatter ⓘ v 1 praise insincerely. 2 gratify. **flatterer** n **flattery** n

flattie n NZ & S Afr informal flat tyre.

flatulent adj suffering from, generating (excess) gases from intestines. **flatulence** n

flaunt v show off.

flavour ⓘ n 1 distinctive taste, savour. ◆ v 2 give flavour to. **flavouring** n

flaw ⓘ n defect, blemish. **flawless** adj

flax n plant grown for its fibres, spun into linen thread. **flaxen** adj 1 of flax. 2 light yellow.

flay v 1 strip skin off. 2 criticize severely.

flea n small, wingless, jumping, blood–sucking insect.

fleck n/v (make) small mark(s).

flee ⓘ v fleeing, fled run away from.

fleece n 1 sheep's wool. ◆ v 2 rob. **fleecy** adj

fleet¹ ⓘ n 1 number of warships organized as unit. 2 number of ships, cars etc.

fleet² adj 1 swift. 2 nimble.

fleeting adj passing quickly.

flesh ⓘ n 1 soft part, muscular substance, between skin and bone. 2 in plants, pulp. 3 fat. 4 sensual appetites. **fleshy** adj plump, pulpy. **in the flesh** in person, actually present.

flex n 1 flexible insulated electric cable. ◆ v 2 bend, be bent.

flexible adj 1 easily bent. 2 manageable. 3 adaptable.

flat¹ adj = **even**, level, levelled, smooth, horizontal ≠ **uneven**; = **punctured**, collapsed, burst, blown out, deflated; = **used up**, finished, empty, drained, expired; = **absolute**, firm, positive, explicit, definite ◆ adv = **completely**, directly, absolutely, categorically, precisely; **flat out** = (Inf) at full speed, all out, to the full, hell for leather (Inf), as hard as possible

flat² n = **apartment**, rooms, quarters, digs, suite

flatter v = **praise**, compliment, pander to, sweet-talk (Inf), wheedle; = **suit**, become, enhance, set off, embellish

flavour n = **taste**, seasoning, flavouring, savour, relish ≠ **blandness**; = **quality**, feeling, feel, style, character ◆ v = **season**, spice, add flavour to, enrich, infuse

flaw n = **weakness**, failing, defect, weak spot, fault

flee v = **run away**, escape, bolt, fly, take off (Inf)

fleet n = **navy**, task force, flotilla, armada

flesh n = **fat**, muscle, tissue, brawn; = **fatness**, fat, adipose tissue, corpulence, weight; = **physical nature**, carnality, human nature, flesh and blood,

flexibility n

flick ⊕ v 1 strike lightly, jerk. ♦ n 2 light blow. 3 jerk. ♦ pl 4 Sl cinema.

flicker ⊕ v 1 burn, shine, unsteadily. ♦ n 2 unsteady light or movement. 3 slight trace.

flight[1] ⊕ n 1 act or manner of flying through air. 2 group of flying birds or aircraft. 3 power of flying. 4 stairs between two landings. **flighty** adj frivolous.

flight recorder electronic device in aircraft storing information about its flight.

flight[2] ⊕ n running away.

flimsy adj –sier, –siest 1 delicate. 2 weak, thin.

flinch v draw back, wince.

fling ⊕ v flinging, flung 1 throw, send, move with force. ♦ n 2 throw. 3 spell of indulgence. 4 vigorous dance.

flint n hard steel–grey stone.

flip ⊕ v flipping, flipped 1 flick lightly. 2 turn over. **flippant** adj treating serious things lightly.

flipper n limb, fin for swimming.

flirt ⊕ v 1 play with another's affections. ♦ n 2 person who flirts. **flirtation** n **flirtatious** adj

flit v flitting, flitted pass lightly and rapidly.

float ⊕ v 1 rest on surface of liquid. 2 be suspended freely. 3 in commerce, get (company) started. 4 obtain loan. ♦ n 5 anything small that floats. 6 small delivery vehicle. 7 motor vehicle carrying tableau etc. 8 sum of money used to provide change. **floating** adj moving about, changing. **flotation** n

flock ⊕ n 1 number of animals of one kind together. 2 religious congregation. ♦ v 3 gather in a crowd.

sinful nature

flick v = jerk, pull, tug, lurch, jolt; = strike, tap, remove quickly, hit, touch

flicker v = twinkle, flash, sparkle, flare, shimmer; = flutter, waver, quiver, vibrate ♦ n = glimmer, flash, spark, flare, gleam; = trace, breath, spark, glimmer, iota

flight[1] n = journey, trip, voyage; = aviation, flying, aeronautics, ability to fly; = flock, group, unit, cloud, formation

flight[2] n = escape, fleeing, departure, retreat, exit

fling v = throw, toss, hurl, launch, cast ♦ n = binge, good time, bash,

party, spree (Inf)

flip v = flick, switch, snap, slick ♦ n = toss, throw, spin, snap, flick

flirt v = chat up, lead on (Inf), make advances at, make eyes at, philander; = toy with, consider, entertain, play with, dabble in ♦ n = tease, philanderer, coquette, heart–breaker

float v = glide, sail, drift, move gently, bob; = be buoyant, hang, hover ≠ sink; = launch, offer, sell, set up, promote ≠ dissolve

flock n = herd, group, flight, drove, colony; = crowd, company, group, host, collection ♦ v = stream, crowd, mass, swarm,

floe n floating ice.

flog ⊕ v **flogging, flogged 1** beat with whip, stick etc. **2** Sl sell.

flood ⊕ n **1** inundation, overflow of water. **2** rising of tide. **3** outpouring. ◆ v **4** inundate. **5** cover, fill with water. **6** arrive, move etc. in great numbers.

floodlight n broad, intense beam of artificial light. **floodlit** adj

floor ⊕ n **1** lower surface of room. **2** set of rooms on one level. **3** (right to speak in) legislative hall. ◆ v **4** supply with floor. **5** knock down. **6** confound. **flooring** n material for floors.

flop ⊕ v **flopping, flopped 1** bend, fall, collapse loosely. **2** fall flat on water etc. **3** Inf fail. ◆ n **4** flopping movement or sound. **5** Inf failure. **floppy** adj **floppy disk** Comp flexible magnetic disk that stores information.

flora n plants of a region. **floral** adj of flowers. **florist** n dealer in flowers.

floret n small flower.

florid adj red with red, flushed complexion. **2** ornate.

floss n mass of fine, silky fibres.

flotilla n **1** fleet of small vessels. **2** group of destroyers.

flotsam n floating wreckage.

flounce[1] v **1** go, move abruptly and impatiently. ◆ n **2** fling, jerk of body or limb.

flounce[2] n ornamental gathered strip on woman's garment.

flounder[1] ⊕ v plunge and struggle, esp. in water or mud.

flounder[2] n flatfish.

flour n powder prepared by sifting and grinding wheat etc.

flourish ⊕ v **1** thrive. **2** brandish. **3** wave about. ◆ n **4** ornamental curve. **5** showy gesture. **6** fanfare.

flow ⊕ v **1** glide along as stream. **2** circulate, as the blood. **3** hang loose. **4** be present in abundance. ◆ n **5** act, instance of flowing. **6** quantity that flows. **7** rise of tide.

flower ⊕ n **1** brightly coloured

———— THESAURUS ————

throng

flog v = **beat**, whip, lash, thrash, whack

flood n = **deluge**, downpour, inundation, tide, overflow; = **torrent**, flow, rush, stream, tide; = **series**, stream, avalanche, barrage, spate ◆ v = **immerse**, swamp, submerge, inundate, drown; = **pour over**, swamp, run over, overflow, inundate

floor v = (Inf) **disconcert**, stump, baffle, confound, throw (Inf); = **knock down**, fell, knock over,

prostrate, deck (Sl)

flop v = **slump**, fall, drop, collapse, sink; = **hang down**, hang, dangle, sag, droop ◆ n = (Inf) **failure**, disaster, fiasco, debacle, washout (Inf) ≠ **success**

flounder[1] v = **falter**, struggle, stall, slow down, run into trouble

flourish v = **thrive**, increase, advance, progress, boom ≠ **fail**; = **succeed**, move ahead, go places (Inf) ◆ n = **wave**, sweep, brandish, swish, swing; = **show**, display, parade, fanfare

part of plant from which fruit is developed. **2** bloom, blossom. **3** choicest part. ♦ v **4** produce flowers. **5** come to prime condition. **flowery** adj **flowerbed** n ground for growing flowers.

fl. oz. fluid ounce.

flu n short for INFLUENZA.

fluctuate 🔊 v vary, rise and fall, undulate. **fluctuation** n

flue n chimney.

fluent 🔊 adj speaking, writing easily and well. **fluency** n

fluff n **1** soft, feathery stuff. ♦ v **2** make or become soft, light **3** Inf make mistake. **fluffy** adj

fluid 🔊 adj **1** flowing easily. **2** flexible. ♦ n **3** gas or liquid. **fluid ounce** unit of capacity 1/20 of pint.

fluke n stroke of luck.

flummox v bewilder, perplex.

flunky, flunkey 1 liveried manservant. **2** servile person.

fluoride n salt containing fluorine.

fluorine n nonmetallic element, yellowish gas.

flurry 🔊 n, pl **-ries 1** gust. **2** bustle. **3** fluttering. ♦ v **4** agitate.

flush¹ 🔊 v **1** blush. **2** flow suddenly or violently. **3** be excited. **4** cleanse (e.g. toilet) by rush of water. **5** excite. ♦ n **6** blush. **7** rush of water. **8** excitement. **9** freshness.

flush² 🔊 adj **1** level with surrounding surface. **2** overflowing.

fluster v **1** make or become nervous, agitated. ♦ n **2** agitation.

flute n **1** wind instrument with blowhole in side. **2** groove. ♦ v **3** play on flute. **4** make grooves in.

flutter 🔊 v **1** flap (as wings) rapidly. **2** quiver. **3** be or make agitated. ♦ n **4** flapping movement. **5** agitation. **6** Inf modest wager.

flux n **1** discharge. **2** constant

———— THESAURUS ————

flow v = **run**, course, rush, sweep, move; = **pour**, move, sweep, flood, stream; = **issue**, follow, result, emerge, spring ♦ n = **stream**, current, movement, motion, course

flower n = **bloom**, blossom, efflorescence; = **elite**, best, prime, finest, pick ♦ v = **bloom**, open, mature, flourish, unfold; = **blossom**, grow, develop, progress, mature

fluctuate v = **change**, swing, vary, alternate, waver

fluent adj = **effortless**, natural, articulate, well-versed, voluble

fluid n = **liquid**, solution, juice, liquor, sap ♦ adj = **liquid**, flowing, watery, molten, melted ≠ **solid**

flurry n = **commotion**, stir, bustle, flutter, excitement; = **gust**, shower, gale, swirl, squall

flush¹ v = **blush**, colour, glow, redden, turn red; (often with **out**) = **cleanse**, wash out, rinse out, flood, swill ♦ n = **blush**, colour, glow, reddening, redness

flush² adj = **level**, even, true, flat, square; = (Inf) **wealthy**, rich, well-off, in the money (Inf), well-heeled (Inf)

flutter v = **beat**, flap, tremble,

succession of changes. **3** substance mixed with metal in soldering etc.

fly¹ ❶ v flying, flew, flown. pl flies **1** move through air on wings or in aircraft. **2** pass quickly. **3** float loosely. **4** run away. **5** operate aircraft. **6** cause to fly. **7** set flying. ◆ n **8** (zip or buttons fastening) opening in trousers. **flyer, flier** n **1** small advertising leaflet. **2** aviator. **flying** adj hurried, brief. **flying colours** conspicuous success. **flying saucer** unidentified disc–shaped flying object. **flying squad** special detachment of police, soldiers etc., ready to act quickly. **flying start** very good start. **flyover** n road passing over another by bridge. **flywheel** n heavy wheel regulating speed of machine.

fly² n, pl flies two–winged insect, esp. common housefly.

foal n young of horse.

foam ❶ n **1** collection of small bubbles on liquid. **2** light cellular solid. ◆ v **3** (cause to) produce foam. **foamy** adj

fob v (with off) ignore, dismiss in offhand manner.

focus ❶ n, pl –cuses, –ci **1** point at which rays meet. **2** state of optical image when it is clearly defined. **3** point on which interest, activity is centred. ◆ v **4** bring to focus. **5** concentrate. **focal** adj

fodder n bulk food for livestock.

foe ❶ n enemy.

fog ❶ n **1** thick mist. ◆ v **2** cover in fog. **3** puzzle. **foggy** adj **foghorn** n large horn to warn ships.

fogey, fogy n, pl –geys, –gies old–fashioned person.

foible n minor weakness, slight peculiarity of character.

foil¹ ❶ v **1** baffle, frustrate. ◆ n **2** blunt sword for fencing.

foil² ❶ n **1** metal in thin sheet. **2** anything which sets off another thing to advantage.

foist v (usually with upon) force,

———— THESAURUS ————

ripple, waver ◆ n = **tremor**, tremble, shiver, shudder, palpitation; = **vibration**, twitching, quiver; = **agitation**, state (Inf), confusion, excitement, flap (Inf)

fly¹ v = **take wing**, soar, glide, wing, sail; = **pilot**, control, operate, steer, manoeuvre; = **airlift**, send by plane, take by plane, take in an aircraft; = **flutter**, wave, float, flap; = **display**, show, flourish, brandish; = **rush**, race, shoot, career, speed

foam n = **froth**, spray, bubbles,

lather, suds ◆ v = **bubble**, boil, fizz, froth, lather

focus v = **concentrate**, centre, spotlight, direct, aim ◆ n = **centre**, focal point, central point; heart, target

foe n = **enemy**, rival, opponent, adversary, antagonist ≠ friend

fog n = **mist**, gloom, haze, smog, murk

foil¹ v = **thwart**, stop, defeat, disappoint, counter

foil² n = **complement**, relief, contrast, antithesis

impose on.

fold¹ ⓣ v 1 double up, bend part of. 2 interlace (arms). 3 clasp (in arms) 4 *Cookery* mix gently. 5 become folded. 6 admit of being folded. 7 *Inf* fail. ♦ n 8 folding. 9 line made by folding. **folder** n binder, file for loose papers.

fold² n enclosure for sheep.

foliage n leaves collectively.

folio n, pl **–lios** 1 sheet of paper folded in half to make two leaves of book. 2 book of largest common size.

folk ⓣ n 1 people in general. 2 family, relative. 3 race of people. **folksy** adj simple, unpretentious. **folklore** n tradition, customs, beliefs popularly held.

follicle n small sac.

follow ⓣ v 1 go or come after. 2 accompany. 3 keep to. 4 be a consequence of. 5 take as guide. 6 grasp meaning of. 7 have keen interest in. **follower** n disciple, supporter. **following** adj 1 about to

be mentioned. ♦ n 2 body of supporters.

folly ⓣ n, pl **–lies** foolishness.

foment v foster, stir up.

fond ⓣ adj tender, loving. **fondness** n **fond of** having liking for.

fondant n flavoured paste of sugar and water.

fondle v caress.

font n bowl for baptismal water.

fontanelle n soft, membraneous gap between bones of baby's skull.

food ⓣ n 1 solid nourishment. 2 what one eats.

fool¹ ⓣ n 1 silly, empty-headed person 2 *Hist* jester. ♦ v 3 delude. 4 dupe. 5 act as fool. **foolhardy** adj foolishly adventurous. **foolish** adj 1 silly, stupid. 2 unwise. **foolishness** n **foolproof** adj unable to fail. **foolscap** n size of paper.

fool² n dessert made from fruit and cream.

foot n, pl **feet** 1 lowest part of leg,

——————— THESAURUS ———————

fold¹ v = **bend**, crease, double over; = (*Inf*) **go bankrupt**, fail, crash, collapse, founder ♦ n = **crease**, gather, bend, overlap, wrinkle

folk n = **people**, persons, individuals, men and women, humanity; (*usually plural*) = **family**, parents, relations, relatives, tribe

follow v = **accompany**, attend, escort, go behind, tag along behind; = **pursue**, track, dog, hunt, chase ≠ *avoid*; = **come after**, go after, come next ≠ *precede*;

= **result**, issue, develop, spring, flow; = **obey**, observe, adhere to, stick to, heed ≠ *ignore*; = **succeed**, replace, come after, take over from, come next; = **understand**, realize, appreciate, take in, grasp

folly n = **foolishness**, nonsense, madness, stupidity, indiscretion ≠ *wisdom*

fond adj = **loving**, caring, warm, devoted, tender ≠ *indifferent*; = **unrealistic**, empty, naive, vain, foolish ≠ *sensible*

food n = **nourishment**, fare, diet,

from ankle down. **2** lower part of anything, base, stand. **3** end of bed etc. **4** measure of twelve inches. ♦ v **5** pay cost of. **footage** n amount of film used. **footing** n basis, foundation. **football** n **1** game played with large blown-up ball. **2** the ball. **footballer** n **foothills** pl n hills at foot of mountain. **foothold** n place giving secure grip for the foot. **footlights** pl n lights across front of stage. **footloose** adj free from ties. **footman** n male servant in livery. **footnote** n note of reference or explanation printed at foot of page. **footprint** n mark left by foot. **footstep** n **1** step in walking. **2** sound made by walking. **footwear** n anything worn to cover feet. **footwork** n skilful use of the feet in football etc. **footle** v Inf loiter aimlessly. **footling** adj trivial. **for** prep **1** directed to. **2** because of. **3** instead of. **4** towards. **5** on account of. **6** in favour of. **7** respecting. **8** during. **9** in search

of. **10** in payment of. **11** in the character of. **12** in spite of. ♦ conj **13** because.

forage n **1** food for cattle and horses. ♦ v **2** collect forage. **3** make roving search.

foray ❶ n raid, inroad.

forbear v **1** cease. **2** refrain (from). **3** be patient. **forbearance** n

forbid ❶ v **1** prohibit. **2** refuse to allow. **forbidden** adj **forbidding** adj uninviting, threatening.

force ❶ n **1** strength, power. **2** compulsion. **3** that which tends to produce a change in a physical system. **4** body of troops, police etc. **5** group of people organized for particular task. **6** validity. **7** vigour. ♦ v **8** compel. **9** produce by effort, strength. **10** break open. **11** hasten maturity of. **forced** adj **1** compulsory. **2** unnatural. **forceful** adj powerful, persuasive. **forcible** adj done by force.

forceps pl n surgical pincers.

ford n **1** shallow place where river may be crossed. ♦ v **2** cross river.

rations, nutrition

fool¹ n = **simpleton**, idiot, mug (Brit sl), dummy (Sl), git (Brit sl) ≠ **genius**; = **dupe**, mug (Brit sl), sucker (Sl), stooge (Sl), laughing stock; = **jester**, clown, harlequin, buffoon, court jester ♦ v = **deceive**, mislead, delude, trick, take in

foray n = **raid**, sally, incursion, inroad, attack

forbid v = **prohibit**, ban, disallow,

exclude, rule out ≠ **permit**

force v = **compel**, make, drive, press, oblige; = **push**, thrust, propel; = **break open**, blast, wrench, prise, wrest ♦ n = **compulsion**, pressure, violence, constraint, oppression; = **power**, might, pressure, energy, strength ≠ **weakness**; = **intensity**, vigour, vehemence, fierceness, emphasis; = **army**, unit, company, host, troop

fore adj 1 in front. ♦ n 2 front part.

forearm n 1 arm between wrist and elbow. ♦ v 2 arm beforehand.

forebear n ancestor.

forecast ⊕ v –casting, –cast 1 estimate beforehand (esp. weather). ♦ n 2 prediction.

forecastle n forward raised part of ship.

foreclose v take away power of redeeming (mortgage).

forecourt n open space in front of building.

forefather n ancestor.

forefinger n finger next to thumb.

forefront ⊕ n most active prominent position.

foregoing adj going before, preceding. **foregone** adj determined beforehand.

foreground n part of view nearest observer.

forehand adj (of stroke in racket games) made with inner side of wrist leading.

forehead n part of face above eyebrows and between temples.

foreign ⊕ adj 1 not of, or in, one's own country. 2 relating to other

countries. 3 strange. **foreigner** n

foreman n 1 one in charge of work. 2 leader of jury.

foremost ⊕ adj/adv first in time, place, importance etc.

forensic adj connected with a court of law. **forensic medicine** application of medical knowledge in legal matters.

forerunner n one who goes before, precursor.

foresee ⊕ v see beforehand.

foreshadow v show, suggest beforehand.

foresight n 1 foreseeing. 2 care for future.

foreskin n skin that covers the tip of the penis.

forest n area with heavy growth of trees. **forestry** n

forestall v prevent, guard against in advance.

foretaste n experience of something to come.

foretell v prophesy.

forethought n thoughtful consideration of future events.

forever ⊕, **for ever** adv 1 always. 2 eternally. 3 Inf for a long time.

forewarn v warn, caution in advance.

——————— THESAURUS ———————

forecast n = **prediction**, prognosis, guess, prophecy, conjecture ♦ v = **predict**, anticipate, foresee, foretell, divine

forefront n = **lead**, centre, front, fore, spearhead

foreign adj = **alien**, exotic, unknown, strange, imported ≠ **native** = **uncharacteristic**,

inappropriate, inapposite

foremost adj = **leading**, best, highest, chief, prime

foresee v = **predict**, forecast, anticipate, envisage, prophesy

forever adv = **evermore**, always, ever, for good, for keeps; = **constantly**, always, all the time, continually, endlessly

foreword n preface.

forfeit ❶ n 1 thing lost by crime or fault. 2 penalty, fine. ♦ adj 3 lost by crime or fault. ♦ v 4 lose by penalty.

forge¹ ❶ v advance steadily.

forge² ❶ n 1 place where metal is worked, smithy. ♦ v 2 shape (metal) by heating and hammering. 3 counterfeit. **forger** n **forgery** n 1 counterfeiting. 2 counterfeit thing.

forget ❶ v **-getting, -got, -gotten** lose memory of, neglect, overlook. **forgetful** adj liable to forget. **forget-me-not** n plant with small blue flowers.

forgive ❶ v **-giving, -gave, -given** 1 cease to blame or hold resentment against. 2 pardon. **forgiveness** n

forgo v 1 go without. 2 give up.

fork ❶ n 1 pronged instrument for eating food. 2 pronged tool for digging or lifting. 3 division into branches. ♦ v 4 branch. 5 dig, lift, throw, with fork. 6 make fork–shaped.

forlorn adj 1 forsaken. 2 desperate.

form ❶ n 1 shape, visible appearance. 2 structure. 3 nature. 4 species, kind. 5 regularly drawn up document. 6 condition. 7 class in school. 8 customary way of doing things. 9 bench. ♦ v 10 shape, organize. 11 conceive. 12 make part of. 13 come into existence or shape. **formation** n 1 forming. 2 thing formed. **formative** adj

formal ❶ adj 1 ceremonial, according to rule. 2 of outward form. 3 stiff. **formality** n, pl **-ties** 1 observance required by custom. 2 condition of being formal.

———————— THESAURUS ————————

forfeit v = **relinquish**, lose, give up, surrender, renounce ♦ n = **penalty**, fine, damages, forfeiture, loss

forge¹ v = **form**, build, create, establish, set up; = **fake**, copy, reproduce, imitate, counterfeit; = **create**, make, work, found, form

forget v = **neglect**, overlook, omit, not remember, be remiss ≠ **remember**; = **leave behind**, lose, lose sight of, mislay, ignore

forgive v = **excuse**, pardon, not hold something against, understand, acquit ≠ **blame**

fork v = **branch**, part, separate, split, divide

form n = **type**, sort, kind, variety, class; = **shape**, formation, configuration, structure, pattern; = **condition**, health, shape, nick (Inf), fitness; = **document**, paper, sheet, questionnaire, application; = **procedure**, etiquette, use, custom, convention; = **class**, year, set, rank, grade ♦ v = **arrange**, combine, line up, organize, assemble; = **make**, produce, fashion, build, create; = **constitute**, make up, compose, comprise; start; = **take shape**, grow, develop, materialize, rise; = **draw up**, devise, formulate, organize

formalize v make official. **formally** adv

format ⚊ n size and shape of book etc.

former ⚊ adj **1** earlier in time. **2** of past times. **3** first named. ♦ pron **4** first named thing or person or fact. **formerly** adv previously.

Formica ® n material used for heat–resistant surfaces.

formidable ⚊ adj **1** to be feared. **2** overwhelming. **3** likely to be difficult.

formula ⚊ n, pl **–las, –lae 1** set form of words, rule **2** Maths rule, fact expressed in symbols and figures. **formulate** v

forsake v **–saking, –sook, –saken 1** abandon, desert. **2** give up.

forswear v **–swearing, –swore,** **–sworn 1** renounce, deny. **2** perjure.

fort ⚊ n stronghold.

forte[1] ⚊ n one's strong point, that in which one excels.

forte[2] adv Mus loudly.

forth ⚊ adv onwards, into view.

forthcoming adj **1** about to come. **2** ready when wanted. **3** willing to talk. **forthwith** adv at once.

forthright adj outspoken.

fortify ⚊ v **–fying, –fied** strengthen. **fortification** n

fortitude ⚊ n endurance.

fortnight n two weeks.

fortress ⚊ n fortified place.

fortuitous adj accidental.

fortune ⚊ n **1** good luck. **2** wealth. **3** chance. **fortunate** adj **fortunately** adv

——————— THESAURUS ———————

formal adj = **serious**, stiff, detached, official, correct ≠ **informal**; = **official**, authorized, endorsed, certified, solemn; = **ceremonial**, traditional, solemn, ritualistic, dressy

format n = **arrangement**, form, style, make–up, look

former adj = **previous**, one–time, erstwhile, earlier, prior ≠ **current**

formidable adj = **impressive**, great, powerful, tremendous, mighty; = **intimidating**, threatening, terrifying, menacing, dismaying ≠ **encouraging**

formula n = **method**, plan, policy, rule, principle

fort n = **fortress**, keep, camp, tower, castle; **hold the fort** = (Inf) **take responsibility**, cover, stand

in, carry on, take over the reins

forte[1] n = **speciality**, strength, talent, strong point, métier ≠ **weak point**

forth adv = (Formal or old– fashioned) **forward**, out, away, ahead, onward

fortify v = **protect**, defend, strengthen, reinforce, support; = **strengthen**, add alcohol to

fortitude n = **courage**, strength, resolution, grit, bravery

fortress n = **castle**, fort, stronghold, citadel, redoubt

fortune n = **wealth**, means, property, riches, resources ≠ **poverty**; = **luck**, fluke (Inf), stroke of luck, serendipity, twist of fate; = **chance**, fate, destiny, providence, the stars

forty pl **–ties** see FOUR.
forum n (place or medium for) meeting, discussion or debate.
forward ⊕ adj 1 lying in front of. 2 onward. 3 presumptuous. 4 advanced. 5 relating to the future. ♦ n 6 player in various team games. ♦ adv 7 towards the future. 8 towards the front, to the front, into view. ♦ v 9 help forward. 10 send, dispatch.
forwards adv
fossick v Aust & NZ search, esp. for gold or precious stones.
fossil n remnant or impression of animal or plant, preserved in earth. **fossilize** v 1 turn into fossil. 2 petrify.
foster ⊕ v 1 promote development of. 2 bring up child, esp. not one's own.
foul ⊕ adj 1 loathsome, offensive. 2 stinking. 3 dirty. 4 unfair. 5 obscene. ♦ n 6 act of unfair play. 7

breaking of a rule. ♦ v 8 make, become foul. 9 jam. 10 collide with.
found¹ ⊕ v 1 establish. 2 lay base of. 3 base. **foundation** n 1 basis. 2 lowest part of building. 3 founding. 4 endowed institution etc. **founder** n
found² v 1 melt and run into mould. 2 cast. **foundry** n place for casting.
founder ⊕ v 1 collapse. 2 sink.
foundling n deserted infant.
fount n 1 fountain. 2 source.
fountain ⊕ n 1 jet of water, esp. ornamental one. 2 spring. 3 source.
four n/adj cardinal number next after three. **fourth** adj ordinal number. **fourteen** n/adj four plus ten. **fourteenth** adj **fortieth** n/adj four tens. **fortieth** adj **foursome** n group of four people.
fowl n 1 domestic cock or hen. 2

——————— THESAURUS ———————

forward adv = **forth**, on, ahead, onwards ≠ **backward(s)** ♦ adj = **leading**, first, head, front, advance; = **future**, advanced, premature, prospective; = **presumptuous**, familiar, bold, cheeky, brash ≠ **shy** ♦ v = **further**, advance, promote, assist, hurry; = **send on**, send, post, pass on, dispatch
foster v = **bring up**, mother, raise, nurse, look after; = **develop**, support, further, encourage, feed ≠ **suppress**
foul adj = **dirty**, unpleasant, stinking, filthy, grubby ≠ **clean**;

= **obscene**, crude, indecent, blue, abusive; = **unfair**, illegal, crooked, shady (Inf), fraudulent; = **offensive**, bad, wrong, evil, corrupt ≠ **admirable** ♦ v = **dirty**, stain, contaminate, pollute, taint ≠ **clean**
found¹ v = **establish**, start, set up, begin, create
founder v = **fail**, collapse, break down, fall through, be unsuccessful; = **sink**, go down, be lost, submerge, capsize
fountain n = **font**, spring, reservoir, spout, fount; = **jet**, stream, spray, gush; = **source**,

bird, its flesh.

fox n 1 red bushy–tailed animal. 2 its fur. 3 cunning person. ♦ v 4 perplex. 5 act craftily. **foxy** adj

foxglove n tall flowering plant.

foxtrot n (music for) ballroom dance.

foyer ⊙ n entrance hall in theatres, hotels etc.

fracas n, pl **–cas** noisy quarrel.

fraction ⊙ n 1 numerical quantity not an integer. 2 fragment.

fracture ⊙ n 1 breakage. 2 breaking of bone. ♦ v 3 break.

fragile ⊙ adj 1 breakable. 2 delicate. **fragility** n

fragrant ⊙ adj sweet–smelling. **fragrance** n

frail adj 1 fragile. 2 in weak health. **frailty** n, pl **–ties**

frame ⊙ n 1 that in which thing is set, as square of wood round picture etc. 2 structure. 3 build of body. ♦ v 4 make. 5 put into words. 6 put into frame. 7 bring false charge against. **framework** n supporting structure.

franc n monetary unit in France, Switzerland etc.

franchise n 1 right of voting. 2 citizenship. 3 privilege or right.

frank ⊙ adj 1 candid, outspoken. 2 sincere. ♦ n 3 official mark on letter either cancelling stamp or ensuring delivery without stamp. ♦ v 4 mark letter thus.

frankfurter n smoked sausage.

frankincense n aromatic gum resin burned as incense.

frantic ⊙ adj 1 distracted with rage, grief, joy etc. 2 frenzied. **frantically** adv

fraternal adj of brother, brotherly. **fraternity** n 1 brotherliness. 2 brotherhood. **fraternize** v 1 associate. 2 make friends.

fraud ⊙ n 1 criminal deception. 2 impostor. **fraudulent** adj

————— THESAURUS —————

fount, wellspring, cause, origin

foyer n = **entrance hall**, lobby, reception area, vestibule, anteroom

fraction n = **percentage**, share, section, slice, portion

fracture n = **break**, split, crack ♦ v = **break**, crack

fragile adj = **unstable**, weak, vulnerable, delicate, uncertain; = **fine**, weak, delicate, frail, brittle ≠ **durable**

fragrant adj = **aromatic**, perfumed, balmy, redolent, sweet–smelling ≠ **stinking**

frail adj = **feeble**, weak, puny, infirm ≠ **strong**; = **flimsy**, weak, vulnerable, delicate, fragile

frame n = **casing**, framework, structure, shell, construction; = **physique**, build, form, body, figure ♦ v = **mount**, case, enclose; = **surround**, ring, enclose, encompass, envelop; = **devise**, draft, compose, sketch, put together; **frame of mind** = **mood**, state, attitude, humour, temper

frank adj = **candid**, open, direct, straightforward, blunt ≠ **secretive**

frantic adj = **frenzied**, wild, furious, distracted, distraught ≠ **calm**; = **hectic**, desperate,

F

fraught *adj* filled (with), involving.

fray¹ ❶ *v* make, become ragged at edge.

fray² *n* **1** fight. **2** noisy quarrel.

frazzle *Inf* ♦ *v* **1** make or become exhausted. ♦ *n* **2** exhausted state.

freak ❶ *n/adj* abnormal (person or thing).

freckle *n* light brown spot on skin, esp. caused by sun.

free ❶ *adj* **freer, freest 1** able to act at will, not under compulsion or restraint. **2** self-ruling. **3** not restricted or affected by. **4** not subject to cost or tax. **5** not in use. **6** (of person) not occupied. **7** loose, not fixed. ♦ *v* **8** set at liberty. **9** remove (obstacles, pain etc.). **10** rid (of). **freedom** *n* **free-for-all** *n* brawl. **freehold** *n* tenure of land without obligation of service or rent. **freelance** *adj/n* (of) self-employed person. **freeloader** *n Sl* scrounger. **free-range** *adj*

kept, produced in natural, nonintensive conditions. **free speech** right to express opinions publicly. **freewheel** *v* travel downhill on bicycle without pedalling.

freeze ❶ *v* **freezing, froze, frozen 1** change (by reduction of temperature) from liquid to solid, as water to ice. **2** preserve (food etc.) by extreme cold. **3** fix (prices etc.). **4** feel very cold. **5** become rigid. **freezer** *n* insulated cabinet for long-term storage of perishable foodstuffs.

freight ❶ *n* **1** commercial transport (esp. by railway, ship). **2** cost of this. **3** goods so carried. ♦ *v* **4** send as or by freight.

freighter *n*

frenetic *adj* frenzied.

frenzy ❶ *n*, *pl* **-zies 1** violent mental derangement. **2** wild excitement. **frenzied** *adj*

——— THESAURUS ———

frenzied, fraught (*Inf*), frenetic

fraud *n* = **deception**, deceit, treachery, swindling, trickery ≠ honesty; = **scam**, deception

fray¹ *v* = **wear thin**, wear, rub, wear out, chafe

freak *adj* = **abnormal**, chance, unusual, exceptional, unparalleled ♦ *n* = (*Inf*) **enthusiast**, fan, nut (*Sl*), addict, buff (*Inf*); = **aberration**, eccentric, anomaly, oddity, monstrosity

free *adj* = **complimentary**, for free (*Inf*), for nothing, unpaid, for love; = **allowed**, permitted, unrestricted, unimpeded, clear;

= **at liberty**, loose, liberated, at large, on the loose ≠ confined; = **independent**, unfettered, footloose, = **non-working**, leisure, unemployed, idle, unoccupied; = **available**, empty, spare, vacant, unused ♦ *v* = **clear**, disengage, cut loose, release, rescue; = **release**, liberate, let out, set free, deliver ≠ confine

freeze *v* = **ice over** *or* **up**, harden, stiffen, solidify, become solid; = **fix**, hold, limit, hold up

freight *n* = **transportation**, traffic, delivery, carriage, shipment; = **cargo**, goods, load, delivery,

frequent ⓸ *adj* 1 happening often. 2 common. 3 numerous. ◆ *v* 4 go often to. **frequency** *n*, *pl* **–cies** 1 rate of occurrence. 2 in radio etc., cycles per second of alternating current.

fresco *n*, *pl* **-coes, -cos** (method of) painting on wet plaster.

fresh ⓸ *adj* 1 not stale. 2 new. 3 additional. 4 different. 5 recent. 6 inexperienced. 7 pure. 8 not pickled, frozen etc. 9 not faded. 10 not tired. 11 (of wind) strong. **freshen** *v* **freshman, fresher** *n* first-year student.

fret[1] ⓸ *v* **fretting, fretted** 1 be irritated, worry. ◆ *n* 2 irritation. **fretful** *adj*

fret[2] *n* 1 repetitive geometrical pattern. ◆ *v* 2 ornament with carved pattern. **fretwork** *n*

friable *adj* easily crumbled.

friar *n* member of religious order.

fricassee *n* dish of stewed pieces of meat.

friction ⓸ *n* 1 rubbing. 2 resistance met with by body moving over another. 3 clash of wills etc.

Friday *n* sixth day of the week.

fridge *n* *Inf* refrigerator.

friend ⓸ *n* one well known to another and regarded with affection and loyalty. **friendly** *adj* 1 kind. 2 favourable. **friendship** *n*

frieze *n* ornamental band, strip (on wall).

frigate *n* fast warship.

fright ⓸ *n* 1 sudden fear. 2 shock. 3 alarm. 4 grotesque or ludicrous person or thing. **frighten** *v* cause fear, fright in. **frightening** *adj* **frightful** *adj* 1 terrible, calamitous. 2 shocking. 3 *Inf* very great, very large. **frightfully** *adv*

frigid *adj* 1 formal. 2 (sexually) unfeeling. 3 cold.

frill *n* 1 strip of fabric gathered at

——————— THESAURUS ———————

burden

frenzy *n* = fury, passion, rage, seizure, hysteria ≠ calm

frequent *adj* = common, repeated, usual, familiar, everyday ≠ infrequent ◆ *v* = visit, attend, haunt, be found at, patronize ≠ keep away

fresh *adj* = additional, more, new, other, added; = natural, unprocessed, unpreserved ≠ preserved; = new, original, novel, different, recent ≠ old; = invigorating, clean, pure, crisp, bracing ≠ stale; = cool, cold, refreshing, brisk, chilly; = lively,

keen, alert, refreshed, vigorous, feisty (*US & Canad*) ≠ weary; = (*Inf*) cheeky, impertinent, forward, familiar, audacious ≠ well-mannered

fret[1] *v* = worry, brood, agonize, obsess, lose sleep

friction *n* = conflict, hostility, resentment, disagreement, animosity; = resistance, rubbing, scraping, grating, rasping

friend *n* = companion, pal, mate (*Inf*), buddy (*Inf*), best friend ≠ foe; = supporter, ally, associate, sponsor, patron

fright *n* = fear, shock, alarm,

one edge. **2** ruff of hair, feathers around neck of dog, bird etc. **3** unnecessary words. **4** superfluous thing. **5** adornment. **frilly** *adj*

fringe ❶ *n* **1** ornamental edge of hanging threads, tassels etc. **2** hair cut in front and falling over brow. **3** edge. ◆ *adj* **4** (of theatre etc.) unofficial.

frisk *v* **1** move, leap, playfully **2** *Inf* search (person). **frisky** *adj*

frisson *n* shiver of excitement.

fritter[1] *n* waste.

fritter[2] *n* piece of food fried in batter.

frivolous *adj* **1** not serious, unimportant. **2** flippant. **frivolity** *n*

frizz *v* **1** crisp, curl into small curls. ◆ *n* **2** frizzed hair. **frizzy** *adj*

frock *n* **1** woman's dress. **2** various similar garments.

frog *n* tailless amphibious animal developed from tadpole. **frogman** *n* underwater swimmer with rubber suit.

frolic *n* **–icking, –icked 1** merrymaking. ◆ *v* **2** behave playfully.

from *prep* expressing point of departure, source, distance, cause, change of state etc.

frond *n* plant organ consisting of stem and foliage.

front ❶ *n* **1** fore part. **2** position directly before or ahead. **3** seaside promenade. **4** outward aspect **5** *Inf* thing serving as respectable cover. ◆ *v* **6** look, face. **7** *Inf* be a cover for. ◆ *adj* **8** of, at the front. **frontal** *adj* **frontage** *n* **1** façade of building. **2** extent of front. **frontier** *n* part of country which borders on another. **frontispiece** *n* illustration facing title page of book.

frost ❶ *n* **1** frozen dew or mist. **2** act or state of freezing. ◆ *v* **3** cover, be covered with frost or something similar in appearance. **frosted** *adj* (of glass) opaque. **frosty** *adj* **1** accompanied by frost. **2** cold. **3** unfriendly. **frostbite** *n* destruction of tissue by cold. **froth** *n* **1** collection of small bubbles, foam. ◆ *v* **2** (cause to) foam. **frothy** *adj*

frown ❶ *v* **1** wrinkle brows. **2** (*with* **upon**) disapprove of. ◆ *n* **3** expression of disapproval.

frugal *adj* **1** sparing. **2** thrifty, economical. **3** meagre.

fruit ❶ *n* **1** seed and its envelope,

——— THESAURUS ———

horror, panic ≠ **courage**

fringe *n* = **border**, edging, edge, trimming, hem; = **edge**, limits, border, margin, outskirts ◆ *adj* = **unofficial**, alternative, radical, innovative, avant–garde

front *n* = **head**, start, lead, forefront; = **exterior**, face, façade, frontage; = **foreground**, fore,

forefront, nearest part; = **front line**, trenches, vanguard, firing line; = (*Inf*) **disguise**, cover, blind, mask, cover–up ◆ *adj* = **foremost**, at the front ≠ **back** ◆ *v* = **face onto**, overlook, look out on, have a view of, look over or onto

frost *n* = **hoarfrost**, freeze, rime

frown *v* = **glare**, scowl, glower,

esp. edible one. **2** vegetable product (*usu. pl*) **3** result, benefit. ♦ *v* **4** bear fruit. **fruitful** *adj* **fruition** *n* **1** enjoyment. **2** realization of hopes. **fruitless** *adj* **fruity** *adj*

frump *n* dowdy woman. **frumpy** *adj*

frustrate ❶ *v* **1** thwart. **2** disappoint. **frustration** *n*

fry¹ *v* **1** cook with fat. **2** be cooked thus.

fry² *pl n* young fishes.

ft. 1 feet. **2** foot.

fuchsia *n* shrub with purple–red flowers.

fuddle *v* (cause to) be intoxicated, confused.

fuddy–duddy *n*, *pl* **–dies** *Inf* (elderly) dull person.

fudge¹ *n* soft, variously flavoured sweet.

fudge² *v* avoid definite decision.

fuel ❶ *n* **1** material for burning as source of heat or power. ♦ *v* **2** provide with fuel.

fugitive ❶ *n* **1** one who flees, esp. from arrest. ♦ *adj* **2** elusive.

fugue *n* musical composition in which themes are repeated in different parts.

fulcrum *n*, *pl* **–crums**, **–cra** point on which a lever is placed for support.

fulfil ❶ *v* **–filling**, **–filled 1** satisfy. **2** carry out. **fulfilment** *n*

full ❶ *adj* **1** containing as much as possible. **2** abundant. **3** complete. **4** ample. **5** plump. ♦ *adv* **6** very. **7** quite. **8** exactly. **fully** *adv* **full–blooded** *adj* vigorous, enthusiastic. **full–blown** *adj* fully developed. **full stop** punctuation mark (.) at end of sentence.

fulminate *v* (*esp. with* **against**) criticize harshly.

fulsome *adj* insincerely excessive.

fumble ❶ *v* **1** grope about. **2** handle awkwardly. ♦ *n* **3** awkward

———— THESAURUS ————

make a face, look daggers

fruit *n* = **produce**, crop, yield, harvest; (*often plural*) = **result**, reward, outcome, end result, return

frustrate *v* = **thwart**, stop, check, block, defeat ≠ **further**

fuel *n* = **incitement**, ammunition, provocation, incentive, power

fugitive *n* = **runaway**, refugee, deserter, escapee

fulfil *v* = **carry out**, perform, complete, achieve, accomplish ≠ **neglect**; = **achieve**, realize, satisfy, attain, consummate; = **satisfy**, please, content, cheer,

refresh

full *adj* = **filled**, stocked, brimming, replete, complete ≠ **empty**; = **satiated**, having had enough, replete; = **extensive**, complete, generous, adequate, ample ≠ **incomplete**; = **comprehensive**, complete, exhaustive, all–embracing; = **rounded**, strong, rich, powerful, intense; = **plump**, rounded, voluptuous, shapely, well–rounded; = **voluminous**, large, loose, baggy, billowing ≠ **tight**; = **rich**, strong, deep, loud, distinct ≠ **thin**

attempt.

fume ⓘ v 1 be angry. 2 emit smoke or vapour. ♦ n 3 smoke. 4 vapour. **fumigate** v apply fumes or smoke to, esp. for disinfection.

fun ⓘ n anything enjoyable, amusing etc. **funny** adj 1 comical. 2 odd. **funnily** adv **funfair** n entertainment with rides and stalls.

function ⓘ n 1 work a thing is designed to do. 2 (large) social event. 3 duty. 4 profession. ♦ v 5 operate, work. **functional** adj

fund ⓘ n 1 stock or sum of money. 2 supply. ♦ pl 3 money resources. ♦ v 4 provide or obtain funds.

fundamental ⓘ adj 1 of, affecting, or serving as, the base. 2 essential, primary. ♦ n 3 basic rule or fact. **fundamentalism** n strict interpretation of religion. **fundamentalist** n/adj

fundi n S Afr expert or boffin.

funeral ⓘ n (ceremony associated with) burial or cremation of dead. **funereal** adj 1 like a funeral. 2 dark. 3 gloomy.

fungus n, pl **–gi, –guses** plant without leaves, flowers, or roots, as mushroom, mould. **fungicide** n substance that destroys fungi.

funk n style of dance music. **funky** adj **funkier, funkiest**

funnel n 1 cone–shaped vessel or tube. 2 chimney of locomotive or ship. ♦ v 3 (cause to) move as through funnel.

fur n 1 soft hair of animal. 2 garment of this. **furry** adj

furious ⓘ adj 1 extremely angry. 2 violent.

furl v roll up and bind.

furlong n eighth of mile.

furnace n apparatus for applying great heat to metals.

furnish ⓘ v 1 fit up house with furniture. 2 supply. **furnishings** pl n **furniture** n

——————— THESAURUS ———————

fumble v = **grope**, flounder, scrabble, feel around

fume v = **rage**, seethe, see red (Inf), storm, rant ♦ pl n = **smoke**, gas, exhaust, pollution, vapour (Brit inf)

fun n = **amusement**, sport, pleasure, entertainment, recreation; = **enjoyment**, pleasure, mirth ≠ gloom

function n = **purpose**, business, job, use, role; = **reception**, party, affair, gathering, bash (Inf) ♦ v = **work**, run, operate, perform, go; = **act**, operate, perform, behave,

do duty

fund n = **reserve**, stock, supply, store, collection ♦ v = **finance**, back, support, pay for, subsidize

fundamental adj = **central**, key, basic, essential, primary ≠ incidental; = **basic**, essential, underlying, profound, elementary

funeral n = **burial**, committal, laying to rest, cremation, interment

furious adj = **angry**, raging, fuming, infuriated, incensed ≠ pleased; = **violent**, intense, fierce, savage, turbulent

furore ⊕ n very angry or excited reaction to something.
furrow n 1 trench. 2 groove. ◆ v 3 make furrows in.
further ⊕ adv 1 more. 2 in addition. 3 at or to a greater distance or extent. ◆ adj 4 more distant. 5 additional: comparative of FAR. ◆ v 6 promote. **furthermore** adv besides. **furthermost** adj
furthest adj/adv superlative of FAR.
furtive adj stealthy, sly, secret.
fury ⊕ n, pl –ries wild rage, violence.
fuse v 1 blend by melting. 2 melt with heat. 3 (cause to) fail as a result of blown fuse. ◆ n 4 soft wire used as safety device in electrical systems. 5 device for

igniting bomb etc. **fusion** n
fuselage n body of aircraft.
fuss ⊕ n 1 needless bustle or concern. 2 complaint. 3 objection. ◆ v 4 make fuss. **fussy** adj
fusty adj –tier, –tiest 1 mouldy. 2 smelling of damp. 3 old–fashioned.
futile ⊕ adj useless, ineffectual, trifling. **futility** n
futon n Japanese padded quilt.
future ⊕ n 1 time to come. 2 what will happen. ◆ adj 3 that will be. 4 of, relating to, time to come.
futuristic adj appearing to belong to some future time.
fuzz n 1 fluff. 2 frizzed hair. 3 blur 4 Sl police. **fuzzy** adj **fuzzier, fuzziest**

———— THESAURUS ————

furnish v = **decorate**, fit out, stock, equip; = **supply**, give, offer, provide, present
furore n = **commotion**, to-do, stir, disturbance, outcry
further adv = **in addition**, moreover, besides, furthermore, also ◆ adj = **additional**, more, new, other, extra ◆ v = **promote**, help, develop, forward, encourage ≠ **hinder**
fury n = **anger**, passion, rage, madness, frenzy ≠ **calmness**; = **violence**, force, intensity, severity, ferocity ≠ **peace**

fuss n = **commotion**, to-do, bother, stir, excitement; = **bother**, trouble, struggle, hassle (Inf), nuisance ◆ v = **worry**, flap (Inf), fret, fidget, take pains
futile adj = **useless**, vain, unsuccessful, pointless, worthless ≠ **useful**
future n = **time to come**, hereafter, what lies ahead; = **prospect**, expectation, outlook ◆ adj = **forthcoming**, coming, later, approaching, to come ≠ **past**

G g

g gram.

gabardine, gaberdine n fine twill cloth like serge.

gabble v talk, utter inarticulately or too fast.

gable n triangular upper part of wall at end of ridged roof.

gad v gadding, gadded (esp. with **about**) go around in search of pleasure.

gadget ⊕ n small mechanical device.

gaffe n tactless remark.

gaffer n 1 old man. 2 Inf foreman, boss.

gag¹ ⊕ v gagging, gagged 1 stop up (person's mouth). 2 Sl retch, choke. ◆ n 3 cloth etc. tied across mouth.

gag² n joke, funny story.

gaggle n flock of geese.

gain ⊕ v 1 obtain (as profit). 2 earn. 3 reach. 4 increase, improve. 5 get nearer. ◆ n 6 profit. 7 increase, improvement.

gainsay v –saying, –said deny, contradict.

gait n manner of walking.

gala ⊕ n 1 festive occasion. 2 show. 3 sporting event.

galaxy n, pl –axies system of stars. **galactic** adj

gale ⊕ n 1 strong wind 2 Inf outburst, esp. of laughter.

gall¹ ⊕ v 1 make sore by rubbing. 2 irritate.

gall² ⊕ n 1 Inf impudence. 2 bitterness. **gall bladder** sac for bile.

gallant adj 1 fine, stately, brave. 2 chivalrous. **gallantry** n

galleon n large sailing ship.

gallery n, pl –ries 1 projecting upper floor in church, theatre etc. 2 place for showing works of art.

galley n 1 one–decked vessel with sails and oars. 2 kitchen of ship or aircraft.

gallivant v gad about.

gallon n liquid measure of eight pints (4.55 litres).

gallop ⊕ n 1 horse's fastest pace.

THESAURUS

---

gadget n = **device**, thing, appliance, machine, tool

gag¹ n = **muzzle**, tie, restraint ◆ v = **suppress**, silence, muffle, curb, stifle; = **retch**, heave

gain v = **acquire**, get, receive, pick up, secure; = **profit**, get, land, secure, collect ≠ **lose**; = **put on**, increase in, gather, build up ◆ n

= **rise**, increase, growth, advance, improvement; = **profit**, return, benefit, advantage, yield ≠ **loss**

gala n = **festival**, fête, celebration, carnival, festivity

gale n = **storm**, hurricane, tornado, cyclone, blast; = (Inf) **outburst**, scream, roar, fit, storm

gall¹ v = **annoy**, provoke, irritate,

2 ride at this pace. ♦ *v* **3** go, ride at gallop. **4** move fast.

gallows *n* structure for hanging criminals.

galore *adv* in plenty.

galoshes *pl n* waterproof overshoes.

gambit *n* opening move, comment etc. intended to secure an advantage.

gamble ❶ *v* **1** play games of chance to win money. **2** act on expectation of amusement. ♦ *n* **3** risky undertaking. **4** bet. **gambler** *n* **gambling** *n*

gambol *v* **–bolling, –bolled** skip, jump playfully.

game ❶ *n* **1** pastime. **2** jest. **3** contest for amusement. **4** scheme. **5** animals or birds hunted. **6** their flesh. ♦ *adj* **7** brave. **8** willing.

gaming *n* gambling. **gamekeeper** *n* man employed to breed game, prevent poaching.

gammon *n* cured or smoked ham.

gamut *n* whole range or scale.

gander *n* male goose.

gang ❶ *n* **1** (criminal) group. **2** organized group of workmen. ♦ *v* **3** form gang.

gangling *adj* lanky.

gangplank *n* portable bridge for boarding or leaving vessel.

gangrene *n* death or decay of body tissue as a result of disease or injury.

gangster ❶ *n* member of criminal gang.

gangway *n* **1** bridge from ship to shore. **2** anything similar. **3** passage between rows of seats.

gannet *n* predatory sea bird.

gantry *n, pl* **–tries** structure to support crane, railway signals etc.

gaol *n see* JAIL.

gap ❶ *n* opening, interval.

gape ❶ *v* **1** stare in wonder. **2** open mouth wide. **3** be, become wide open.

garage *n* **1** (part of) building to

———— THESAURUS ————

gallop *v* = **run**, race, career, speed, bolt

gamble *n* = **risk**, chance, venture, lottery, speculation ≠ **certainty**; = **bet**, flutter (*Inf*), punt (*Chiefly Brit*), wager ♦ *v* = **take a chance**, speculate, stick your neck out (*Inf*); = **risk**, chance, hazard, wager

game *n* = **pastime**, sport, activity, entertainment, recreation ≠ **job**; = **match**, meeting, event, competition, tournament; = **amusement**, joke, entertainment, diversion; = **wild**

animals *or* birds prey, quarry ♦ *adj* = **willing**, prepared, ready, keen, eager; = **brave**, courageous, spirited, daring, persistent ≠ **cowardly**

gang *n* = **group**, crowd, pack, company, band

gangster *n* = **hoodlum** (*Chiefly US*), crook (*Inf*), bandit, hood (*US sl*), robber

gap *n* = **opening**, space, hole, break, crack; = **interval**, pause, interruption, respite, lull; = **difference**, gulf, contrast, disagreement, discrepancy

house cars. **2** refuelling and repair centre for cars.

garb n/v dress.

garbage n US and Canad rubbish.

garden n **1** ground for cultivation. ◆ v **2** cultivate garden. **gardener** n **gardening** n

gargantuan adj immense.

gargle v **1** wash throat with liquid kept moving by the breath. ◆ n **2** gargling. **3** preparation for this purpose.

gargoyle n grotesque carving on church etc.

garish adj **1** showy. **2** gaudy.

garland ❶ n wreath of flowers as decoration.

garlic n (bulb of) plant with strong smell and taste, used in cooking and seasoning.

garment n article of clothing.

garner v store up, collect.

garnet n red semiprecious stone.

garnish ❶ v **1** decorate (esp. food). ◆ n **2** material for this.

garret n attic.

garrison ❶ n **1** troops stationed in town, fort etc. **2** fortified place. ◆ v **3** occupy with garrison.

garrotte, garotte v execute by strangling.

garrulous adj talkative.

garter n band worn round leg to hold up sock or stocking.

gas n, pl **gases, gasses 1** airlike substance. **2** fossil fuel in form of gas. **3** gaseous anaesthetic. **4** gaseous poison or irritant Inf US and Canad **5** petrol. ◆ v **6** poison with gas. **7** talk idly, boastfully. **gaseous** adj of, like gas.

gash n **1** gaping wound, slash. ◆ v **2** cut deeply.

gasket n seal between metal faces, esp. in engines.

gasp ❶ v **1** catch breath as in exhaustion or surprise. ◆ n **2** gasping.

gastric adj of stomach.

gastroenteritis n inflammation of stomach and intestines.

gastronomy n art of good eating.

gate ❶ n **1** opening in wall, fence etc. **2** barrier for closing it. **3** any entrance or way out. **gate-crash** v enter social function etc. uninvited. **gateway** n **1** entrance with gate. **2** means of access.

gâteau n, pl **-teaux** elaborate, rich cake.

———— THESAURUS ————

gape v = **stare**, wonder, goggle, gawp (Brit sl), gawk; = **open**, split, crack, yawn

garland n = **wreath**, band, bays, crown, honours ◆ v = **adorn**, crown, deck, festoon, wreathe

garnish n = **decoration**, embellishment, adornment, ornamentation, trimming ◆ v = **decorate**, adorn, ornament,

embellish, trim ≠ **strip**

garrison n = **troops**, group, unit, section, command; = **fort**, fortress, camp, base, post ◆ v = **station**, position, post, install, assign

gasp v = **pant**, blow, puff, choke, gulp ◆ n = **pant**, puff, gulp, sharp intake of breath

gate n = **barrier**, opening, door, entrance, exit

gather ⊕ v 1 (cause to) assemble.
2 increase gradually. 3 draw
together. 4 collect. 5 learn,
understand. **gathering** n assembly.

gaudy adj **gaudier, gaudiest**
showy in tasteless way.

gauge ⊕ n 1 standard measure, as
of diameter of wire etc. 2 distance
between rails of railway. 3
instrument for measuring. ♦ v 4
measure. 5 estimate.

gaunt adj lean, haggard.

gauntlet n (armoured) glove
covering part of arm.

gauze n thin transparent fabric of
silk, wire etc.

gavel n auctioneer's mallet.

gay ⊕ adj 1 homosexual. 2 merry.
3 bright. **gaiety** n **gaily** adv

gaze ⊕ v 1 look fixedly. ♦ n 2
fixed look.

gazebo n, pl **–bos, –boes**
summerhouse.

gazelle n small graceful antelope.

gazette ⊕ n official newspaper for
announcements. **gazetteer** n
geographical dictionary.

GB Great Britain.

GBH grievous bodily harm.

GCE General Certificate of
Education.

GCSE General Certificate of
Secondary Education.

gear ⊕ n 1 set of wheels working
together, esp. by engaging cogs.
2 equipment. 3 clothing. 4 Sl
drugs. ♦ v 5 adapt (one thing) so
as to conform with another.

gearbox n case protecting gearing
of bicycle, car etc.

geese pl of GOOSE.

geezer n Inf (old or eccentric)
man.

geisha n, pl **–sha, –shas** in Japan,
professional female companion for
men.

gel n jelly–like substance.

gelatine, gelatin n substance

———— THESAURUS ————

gather v = **congregate**, assemble,
collect, meet, mass ≠ **scatter**;
= **assemble**, collect, bring
together, muster, stack together
≠ **disperse**; = **collect**, assemble,
accumulate, mass, muster; = **pick**,
harvest, pluck, reap, garner;
= **build up**, rise, increase, grow,
expand

gauge v = **measure**, calculate,
evaluate, value, determine;
= **judge**, estimate, guess, assess,
evaluate ♦ n = **meter**, dial,
measuring instrument

gay adj = **homosexual**, lesbian;
= **cheerful**, lively, sparkling, merry,

upbeat (Inf) ≠ **sad**; = **colourful**,
rich, bright, brilliant, vivid ≠ **drab**
♦ n = **homosexual**, lesbian
≠ **heterosexual**

gaze v = **stare**, look, view, watch,
regard ♦ n = **stare**, look, fixed look

gazette n = **newspaper**, paper,
journal, periodical, news–sheet

gear n = **mechanism**, works,
machinery, cogs, cogwheels;
= **equipment**, supplies, tackle,
tools, instruments; = **possessions**,
paraphernalia, personal property,
chattels; = **clothing**, wear, dress,
clothes, outfit ♦ v (with **to** or
towards) = **equip**, fit, adjust

prepared from animal bones etc.,
producing edible jelly.
geld v castrate. **gelding** n
castrated horse.
gelignite n powerful explosive
consisting of dynamite in gelatine
form.
gem ❶ n precious stone, esp.
when cut and polished.
gen n Inf information.
gender n sex, male or female.
gene n biological factor
determining inherited
characteristics.
genealogy n, pl **–gies** study or
account of descent from
ancestors.
general ❶ adj 1 widespread. 2 not
particular or specific. 3 usual. 4
miscellaneous. ♦ n 5 army officer
of rank above colonel. **generally**
adv **generalize** v draw general
conclusions. **general practitioner**
doctor serving local area.
generate ❶ v 1 bring into being.
2 produce. **generation** n 1
bringing into being. 2 all persons
born about same time. 3 time

between generations (about 30
years). **generator** n apparatus for
producing (steam, electricity etc.).
generous ❶ adj 1 free in giving. 2
abundant. **generosity** n
genesis ❶ n, pl **–eses** 1 origin. 2
mode of formation.
genial adj 1 cheerful. 2 mild.
genie n in fairy tales, servant
appearing by, and working,
magic.
genital adj relating to sexual
organs or reproduction. **genitals** pl
n sexual organs.
genius ❶ n (person with)
exceptional power or ability.
genocide n murder of entire race
of people.
genre ❶ n style of literary work.
gent Inf ♦ n gentleman. **gents** n
men's public lavatory.
genteel adj 1 well-bred. 2
affectedly proper. **gentility** n
respectability.
gentile adj/n (person) of race
other than Jewish.
gentle ❶ adj 1 mild, not rough or
severe. 2 moderate. 3 well-born.

———— THESAURUS ————

gem n = **precious stone**, jewel,
stone; = **treasure**, prize, jewel,
pearl, masterpiece
general adj = **widespread**,
accepted, popular, public,
common ≠ **individual**; = **overall**,
complete, total, global,
comprehensive ≠ **restricted**;
= **universal**, overall, widespread,
collective, across–the–board
≠ **exceptional**
generate v = **produce**, create,

make, cause, give rise to ≠ **end**
generous adj = **liberal**, lavish,
charitable, hospitable, bountiful
≠ **mean**; = **magnanimous**, kind,
noble, good, high–minded;
= **plentiful**, lavish, ample,
abundant, full ≠ **meagre**
genesis n = **beginning**, origin,
start, birth, creation ≠ **end**
genius n = **brilliance**, ability,
talent, capacity, gift
genre n = **type**, group, order,

gently adv **gentleness** n quality of being gentle. **gentleman** n 1 chivalrous well-bred man. 2 man (used as a mark of politeness).

gentry n people just below nobility in social rank.

genuine ⊕ adj 1 real. 2 sincere.

genus n, pl **genera** class, order, group (esp. of insects, animals etc.) with common characteristics.

geography n science of earth's form, physical features, climate, population etc. **geographer** n **geographical** adj

geology n science of earth's crust, rocks, strata etc. **geological** adj **geologist** n

geometry n science of properties and relations of lines, surfaces etc. **geometrical, –metric** adj

geranium n plant with red, pink or white flowers.

gerbil n desert rodent of Asia and Africa.

geriatrics n science of old age

and its diseases. **geriatric** adj/n old (person).

germ ⊕ n 1 microbe, esp. causing disease. 2 rudiment.

germinate v (cause to) sprout or begin to grow.

gestation n carrying of young in womb.

gesticulate v use expressive movements of hands and arms when speaking.

gesture ⊕ n/v (make) movement to convey meaning.

get ⊕ v **getting, got** 1 obtain. 2 catch. 3 cause to go or come. 4 bring into position or state. 5 induce. 6 be in possession of, have (to do). 7 become.

geyser n 1 hot spring throwing up spout of water. 2 water heater.

ghastly ⊕ adj **–lier, –liest** 1 deathlike. 2 Inf horrible. ♦ adv 3 sickly.

gherkin n small pickled cucumber.

—————— THESAURUS ——————

sort, kind

gentle adj **= kind**, kindly, tender, mild, humane ≠ **unkind**; **= slow**, easy, slight, moderate, gradual; **= moderate**, light, soft, slight, mild ≠ **violent**

genuine adj **= authentic**, real, actual, true, valid ≠ **counterfeit**; **= heartfelt**, sincere, honest, earnest, real ≠ **affected**; dinkum (Aust & NZ inf)

germ n **= microbe**, virus, bug (Inf), bacterium, bacillus; **= beginning**, root, seed, origin, spark

gesture n **= sign**, action, signal,

motion, indication ♦ v **= signal**, sign, wave, indicate, motion

get v **= become**, grow, turn, come to be; **= persuade**, convince, induce, influence, entice; **=** (Inf) annoy, upset, anger, disturb, trouble; **= obtain**, receive, gain, acquire, win; **= fetch**, bring, collect; **= understand**, follow, catch, see, realize; **= catch**, develop, contract, succumb to, fall victim to; **= arrest**, catch, grab, capture, seize

ghastly adj **= horrible**, shocking, terrible, awful, dreadful ≠ **lovely**

ghetto n, pl **–tos, –toes** densely populated (esp. by one racial group) slum area. **ghetto blaster** Inf large portable cassette recorder.

ghost ⊕ n **1** dead person appearing again. **2** spectre. **3** faint trace. **ghostly** adj

ghoul n **1** malevolent spirit. **2** person with morbid interests. **ghoulish** adj

giant ⊕ n **1** mythical being of superhuman size. **2** very tall person, plant etc. ♦ adj **3** huge. **gigantic ⊕** adj enormous, huge.

gibber v make meaningless sounds with mouth. **gibberish** n meaningless speech or words.

gibbon n type of ape.

gibe, jibe v/n jeer.

giblets pl n internal edible parts of fowl.

gidday, g'day interj Aust & NZ expression of greeting.

giddy adj **–dier, –diest 1** dizzy. **2** liable to cause dizziness. **3** flighty.

gift ⊕ n **1** thing given, present. **2** faculty, power. **gifted** adj talented.

gig n performance by pop or jazz musicians.

gigantic ⊕ see GIANT.

giggle ⊕ v **1** laugh nervously, foolishly. ♦ n **2** such a laugh.

gild v **gilding, gilded** put thin layer of gold on. **gilt** n thin layer of gold put on. **gilt-edged** adj guaranteed.

gill¹ n (usu. pl) breathing organ in fish.

gill² n liquid measure, quarter of pint (0.142 litres).

gimmick n stratagem etc., esp. designed to attract attention or publicity.

gin n spirit flavoured with juniper berries.

ginger n **1** plant with hot-tasting spicy root. **2** the root. ♦ v **3** stimulate. **gingerbread** n cake flavoured with ginger.

gingerly adv cautiously.

gingham n cotton cloth, usu. checked.

gingivitis n inflammation of gums.

ginseng n plant root used as tonic.

Gipsy pl **–sies** see GYPSY.

giraffe n Afr. animal with very long neck.

gird v **girding, girded 1** put belt round. **2** prepare (oneself). **girder** n large beam.

girdle n **1** corset. **2** waistband.

girl ⊕ n **1** female child. **2** young (unmarried) woman. **girlfriend** n

——————— THESAURUS ———————

ghost n = **spirit**, soul, phantom, spectre, spook (Inf); = **trace**, shadow, suggestion, hint, suspicion

giant adj = **huge**, vast, enormous, tremendous, immense ≠ tiny ♦ n = **ogre**, monster, titan, colossus

gift n = **donation**, offering, present, contribution, grant; = **talent**, ability, capacity, genius, power

gigantic adj = **huge**, large, giant, massive, enormous ≠ tiny

giggle n = **laugh**, chuckle,

man's female companion.

giro n, pl **–ros** system operated by banks and post offices for the transfer of money.

girth n 1 measurement round thing. 2 band put round horse to hold saddle etc.

gist n substance, main point (of remarks etc.).

give ⊕ n giving, gave, given 1 make present of. 2 deliver. 3 assign. 4 utter. 5 yield, give way. ◆ n 6 yielding, elasticity.

glacé adj 1 crystallized. 2 iced.

glacier n slow-moving river of ice. **glacial** adj

glad ⊕ adj gladder, gladdest 1 pleased. 2 happy. **gladden** v make glad. **gladly** adv

glade n grassy space in forest.

gladiator n trained fighter in Roman arena.

gladiolus n, pl **–lus, –li, –luses** kind of iris, with sword-shaped leaves.

glamour ⊕ n alluring charm, fascination. **glamorous** adj

glance ⊕ v 1 look rapidly or briefly. 2 glide off something struck. ◆ n 3 brief look.

gland n organ controlling different bodily functions by chemical means. **glandular** adj

glare ⊕ v 1 look fiercely. 2 shine intensely. ◆ n 3 glaring. **glaring** adj conspicuous.

glass n 1 hard transparent substance. 2 things made of it. 3 tumbler. 4 its contents. ◆ pl 5 spectacles. **glassy** adj 1 like glass. 2 expressionless.

glaucoma n eye disease.

glaze ⊕ v 1 furnish with glass. 2 cover with glassy substance. 3 become glassy. ◆ n 4 transparent coating. 5 substance used for this.

glazier n one who glazes windows.

gleam ⊕ n/v (give out) slight or

———————— THESAURUS ————————

snigger, chortle, titter

girl n = **female child**, lass, lassie (Inf), miss, maiden (Arch)

give v = **perform**, do, carry out, execute; = **communicate**, announce, transmit, pronounce, utter; = **produce**, make, cause, occasion, engender; = **present**, contribute, donate, provide, supply ≠ **take**; = **concede**, allow, grant; = **surrender**, yield, devote, hand over, relinquish

glad adj = **happy**, pleased, delighted, contented, gratified ≠ **unhappy**; = (Arch) **pleasing**, happy, cheering, pleasant,

cheerful

glamour n = **charm**, appeal, beauty, attraction, fascination

glance v = **peek**, look, view, glimpse, peep ≠ **scrutinize** ◆ n = **peek**, look, glimpse, peep, dekko (Sl) ≠ **good look**

glare v = **scowl**, frown, glower, look daggers, lour or lower; = **dazzle**, blaze, flare, flame ◆ n = **scowl**, frown, glower, dirty look, black look; = **dazzle**, glow, blaze, flame, brilliance

glaze n = **coat**, finish, polish, shine, gloss ◆ v = **coat**, polish, gloss, varnish, enamel

passing beam of light.

glean v 1 pick up. 2 gather.

glee n mirth, merriment. **gleeful** adj

glen n narrow valley.

glib adj **glibber**, **glibbest** fluent but insincere or superficial.

glide v 1 pass smoothly and continuously. ♦ n 2 smooth, silent movement. **glider** n aircraft without engine.

glimmer v 1 shine faintly. ♦ n 2 faint light.

glimpse ❶ n 1 brief view. ♦ v 2 catch glimpse of.

glint v/n flash.

glisten v gleam by reflecting light.

glitter ❶ v 1 shine with bright quivering light, sparkle. ♦ n 2 lustre. 3 sparkle.

gloat v regard with smugness or malicious satisfaction.

globe ❶ n 1 sphere with map of earth or stars. 2 ball. **global** adj 1 relating to whole world. 2 total, comprehensive.

globule n small round drop.

glockenspiel n percussion instrument played with hammers.

gloom ❶ n 1 darkness. 2 melancholy. **gloomy** adj **gloomier**, **gloomiest**

glory ❶ n, pl **-ries** 1 renown. 2 splendour. 3 heavenly bliss. ♦ v 4 take pride (in). **glorify** v 1 make glorious. 2 praise. **glorious** adj 1 illustrious. 2 splendid. 3 Inf delightful. **gloriously** adv

gloss¹ ❶ n 1 surface shine, lustre. ♦ v 2 put gloss on 3 (esp. with **over**) (try to) cover up, pass over (fault, error). **glossy** adj **-sier**, **-siest** smooth, shiny.

gloss² ❶ n 1 interpretation of word. 2 comment. ♦ v 3 interpret. 4 comment. **glossary** n dictionary of special words.

glove n 1 covering for the hand.

——————— THESAURUS ———————

gleam v = **shine**, flash, glow, sparkle, glitter ♦ n = **glimmer**, flash, beam, glow, sparkle; = **trace**, suggestion, hint, flicker, glimmer

glide v = **slip**, sail, slide

glimpse n = **look**, sighting, sight, glance, peep ♦ v = **catch sight of**, spot, sight, view, spy

glitter v = **shine**, flash, sparkle, glare, gleam ♦ n = **glamour**, show, display, splendour, tinsel; = **sparkle**, flash, shine, glare, gleam

globe n = **planet**, world, earth, sphere, orb

gloom n = **darkness**, dark, shadow, shade, twilight ≠ **light**; = **depression**, sorrow, woe, melancholy, unhappiness ≠ **happiness**

glory n = **honour**, praise, fame, distinction, acclaim ≠ **shame**; = **splendour**, majesty, greatness, grandeur, nobility ♦ v = **triumph**, boast, relish, revel, exult

gloss¹ n = **shine**, gleam, sheen, polish, brightness

gloss² n = **interpretation**, comment, note, explanation, commentary ♦ v = **interpret**, explain, comment, translate,

♦ *v* **2** cover as with glove.

glow ❂ *v* **1** give out light and heat without flames. **2** be or look hot.
♦ *n* **3** shining heat. **glow-worm** *n* insect giving out light.

glower *v/n* scowl.

glucose *n* type of sugar found in fruit etc.

glue *n/v* (fasten with) sticky substance. **gluey** *adj*

glum *adj* **glummer, glummest** sullen, gloomy.

glut *n* **1** surfeit, excessive amount.
♦ *v* **2** feed, gratify to the full or to excess.

glutton *n* **1** greedy person. **2** one with great liking or capacity for something. **gluttonous** *adj* **gluttony** *n*

glycerine, glycerin *n* colourless sweet liquid.

GMT Greenwich Mean Time.

gnarled *adj* knobby, twisted.

gnash *v* grind (teeth) together as in anger or pain.

gnat *n* small, biting fly.

gnaw *v* **gnawing, gnawed,** **gnawed** bite or chew steadily.

gnome *n* legendary creature like small old man.

gnu *n* oxlike antelope.

go ❂ *v* **going, went, gone 1** move along. **2** depart. **3** function. **4** fare. **5** fail. **6** elapse. **7** be able to be put. **8** become. ♦ *n* **9** going. **10** energy. **11** attempt. **12** turn. **go-between** *n* intermediary.

goad *n* **1** spiked stick for driving cattle. **2** anything that urges to action. ♦ *v* **3** urge on. **4** torment.

goal ❂ *n* **1** end of race. **2** object of effort. **3** posts through which ball is to be driven in football etc. **4** the score so made.

goat *n* animal with long hair, horns and beard. **goatee** *n* small pointed beard.

gobble¹ *v* eat hastily, noisily or greedily.

gobble² *n/v* (make) cry of turkey. **gobbledegook, gobbledygook** *n* unintelligible language.

goblet *n* drinking cup.

goblin *n Folklore* small, usu. malevolent being.

god *n* **1** superhuman being worshipped as having supernatural power. **2** object of worship, idol. **3** (*with cap.*) the Supreme Being, creator and ruler

——————— THESAURUS ———————

annotate

glow *n* = **light**, gleam, splendour, glimmer, brilliance ≠ **dullness** ♦ *v* = **shine**, burn, gleam, brighten, glimmer

glue *n* = **adhesive**, cement, gum, paste

go *v* = **move**, travel, advance, journey, proceed ≠ **stay**; = **leave**, withdraw, depart, move out, slope

off; = **elapse**, pass, flow, fly by, expire; = **be given**, be spent, be awarded, be allotted; = **function**, work, run, move, operate ≠ **fail**; = **match**, blend, correspond, fit, suit ♦ *n* = **attempt**, try, effort, bid, shot (*Inf*); = **turn**, shot (*Inf*), stint; fossick through (*Aust & NZ*)

goal *n* = **aim**, end, target, purpose, object

of universe. **godly** adj devout, pious. **godfather** n sponsor at baptism. **godforsaken** adj desolate, dismal. **godsend** n something unexpected but welcome.

gogga n S Afr informal any small insect.

goggle v 1 (of eyes) bulge. 2 stare. ♦ pl n 3 protective spectacles.

go-kart, go-cart n miniature, low-powered racing car.

gold n 1 yellow precious metal. 2 coins of this. 3 colour of gold. ♦ adj 4 of, like gold. **golden** adj **golden wedding** fiftieth wedding anniversary. **goldfinch** n bird with yellow feathers. **goldfish** n any of various ornamental pond or aquarium fish.

golf n outdoor game in which small ball is struck into holes. **golfer** n

gondola n Venetian canal boat.

gondolier n rower of gondola.

gong n metal plate which sounds when struck with soft mallet.

good ⊕ adj better, best 1 commendable. 2 right. 3 beneficial. 4 well-behaved. 5 virtuous. 6 sound. 7 valid. ♦ n 8 benefit. 9 wellbeing. 10 profit. ♦ pl 11 property. 12 wares. **goodly** adj large, considerable. **goodness** n **goodwill** n kindly feeling.

goodbye ⊕ interj/n form of address on parting.

gooey adj gooier, gooiest Inf sticky, soft.

goose n, pl geese 1 web-footed bird. 2 its flesh. 3 simpleton. **gooseberry** n 1 thorny shrub. 2 its hairy fruit.

gore¹ ⊕ n (dried) blood from wound. **gory** adj

gore² ⊕ v pierce with horns.

gorge ⊕ n 1 ravine. 2 disgust, resentment. ♦ v 3 feed greedily.

gorgeous ⊕ adj splendid, showy.

——————— THESAURUS ———————

good adj = **excellent**, great, fine, pleasing, acceptable ≠ **bad**; = **proficient**, able, skilled, expert, talented ≠ **bad**; = **beneficial**, useful, healthy, favourable, wholesome ≠ **harmful**; = **honourable**, moral, worthy, ethical, upright ≠ **bad**; = **well-behaved**, polite, orderly, obedient, dutiful ≠ **naughty**; = **kind**, kindly, friendly, obliging, charitable ≠ **unkind**; = **true**, real, genuine, proper; = **full**, complete, extensive ≠ **scant** ♦ n = **benefit**, interest, gain, advantage, use

≠ **disadvantage**; = **virtue**, goodness, righteousness, worth, merit ≠ **evil**

goodbye n = **farewell**, parting, leave-taking ♦ interj = **farewell**, see you, see you later, ciao (Italian), cheerio

gore¹ n = **blood**, slaughter, bloodshed, carnage, butchery

gore² v = **pierce**, wound, transfix, impale

gorge n = **ravine**, canyon, pass, chasm, cleft ♦ v = **overeat**, devour, gobble, wolf, gulp

gorgeous adj = **magnificent**,

gorilla n largest anthropoid ape, found in Africa.

gormless adj Inf stupid.

gorse n prickly shrub.

gosling n young goose.

gospel ❶ n 1 unquestionable truth. 2 (with cap.) any of first four books of New Testament.

gossamer n filmy substance like spider's web.

gossip ❶ n 1 idle (malicious) talk about other persons. 2 one who talks thus. ◆ v 3 engage in gossip.

gouge v 1 scoop out. 2 force out. ◆ n 3 chisel with curved cutting edge.

goulash n stew seasoned with paprika.

gourd n 1 large fleshy fruit. 2 its rind as vessel.

gourmand n glutton.

gourmet ❶ n 1 connoisseur of wine, food. 2 epicure.

gout n disease with inflammation, esp. of joints.

govern ❶ v 1 rule, control. 2 determine. **governess** n woman teacher, esp. in private household.

government n 1 exercise of political authority in directing a people, state etc. 2 system by which community is ruled. 3 governing group. 4 control.

governor n 1 one who governs. 2 chief administrator of an institution. 3 member of committee responsible for an organization or institution.

gown ❶ n 1 loose flowing outer garment. 2 woman's (long) dress. 3 official robe.

GP General Practitioner.

grab ❶ v grabbing, grabbed 1 grasp suddenly. 2 snatch. ◆ n 3 sudden clutch. 4 quick attempt to seize.

grace ❶ n 1 charm, elegance. 2 goodwill, favour. 3 sense of propriety. 4 postponement granted. 5 short thanksgiving for meal. ◆ v 6 add grace to, honour. **graceful** adj **gracious** adj 1 kind. 2 condescending.

grade ❶ n 1 step, stage. 2 class. 3

——————— THESAURUS ———————

beautiful, superb, spectacular, splendid ≠ shabby; = **delightful**, good, great, wonderful, excellent ≠ **awful**

gospel n = **doctrine**, news, teachings, message, revelation; = **truth**, fact, certainty, the last word

gossip n = **idle talk**, scandal, hearsay, tittle-tattle, small talk; = **busybody**, chatterbox (Inf), chatterer, scandalmonger, gossipmonger ◆ v = **chat**, chatter,

jaw (Sl), blether

gourmet n = **connoisseur**, foodie (Inf), bon vivant (Fr), epicure, gastronome

govern v = **rule**, lead, control, command, manage; = **restrain**, control, check, master, discipline

gown n = **dress**, costume, garment, robe, frock

grab v = **snatch**, catch, seize, capture, grip

grace n = **elegance**, poise, ease, polish, refinement ≠ **ungainliness**;

rating. **4** slope. ♦ *v* **5** arrange in classes. **6** assign grade to.

gradation *n* **1** series of steps. **2** each of them.

gradient *n* (degree of) slope.

gradual ⊙ *adj* **1** taking place by degrees. **2** slow and steady. **3** not steep. **gradually** *adv*

graduate ⊙ *v* **1** take university degree. **2** divide into degrees. ♦ *n* **3** holder of university degree.

graduation *n*

graffiti *pl n* (oft. obscene) writing, drawing on walls.

graft¹ ⊙ *n* **1** shoot of plant set in stalk of another. **2** the process. **3** surgical transplant of skin, tissue. ♦ *v* **4** insert (shoot) in another stalk. **5** transplant (living tissue in surgery).

graft² *n* **1** *Inf* hard work. **2** self-advancement, profit by unfair means.

grain ⊙ *n* **1** (seed, fruit of) cereal plant. **2** small hard particle. **3** very small unit of weight. **4**

arrangement of fibres. **5** any very small amount.

gram, gramme *n* one thousandth of a kilogram.

grammar *n* **1** science of structure and usages of language. **2** use of words. **grammatical** *adj* **grammar school** state-maintained secondary school providing academic education.

gramophone *n* record player.

gran *n Inf* grandmother.

granary *n, pl* **–ries** storehouse for grain.

grand ⊙ *adj* **1** magnificent. **2** noble. **3** splendid. **4** eminent.

grandeur *n* **1** nobility. **2** magnificence. **3** dignity. **grandiose** *adj* **1** imposing. **2** affectedly grand.

grandchild *n* child of one's child.

grandson, granddaughter *n*

grandparent *n* parent of parent.

grandfather, grandmother *n*

grandstand *n* structure with tiered seats for spectators.

granite *n* hard crystalline rock.

———————— THESAURUS ————————

= **manners**, decency, etiquette, consideration, propriety ≠ **bad manners**; = **indulgence**, mercy, pardon, reprieve; = **benevolence**, favour, goodness, goodwill, generosity ≠ **ill will**; = **prayer**, thanks, blessing, thanksgiving, benediction ♦ *v* = **adorn**, enhance, decorate, enrich, set off; = **honour**, favour, dignify ≠ **insult**

grade *v* = **classify**, rate, order, class, group ♦ *v* = **degree**

gradual *adj* = **steady**, slow, regular, gentle, progressive

≠ **sudden**

graduate *v* = **mark off**, grade, proportion, regulate, gauge; = **classify**, rank, grade, group, order

graft¹ *n* = **shoot**, bud, implant, sprout, splice ♦ *v* = **join**, insert, transplant, implant, splice

grain *n* = **seed**, kernel, grist; = **cereal**, corn; = **bit**, piece, trace, scrap, particle; = **texture**, pattern, surface, fibre, weave

grand *adj* = **impressive**, great, large, magnificent, imposing

grant ❶ v **1** consent to fulfil (request). **2** permit. **3** admit. ◆ n **4** sum of money provided for specific purpose, esp. education. **5** gift. **6** allowance, concession.

granule n small grain.

grape n small fruit, used to make wine. **grapevine** n **1** grape–bearing plant. **2** Inf unofficial way of spreading news.

grapefruit n subtropical citrus fruit.

graph n drawing depicting relation of different numbers, quantities etc.

graphic ❶ adj **1** vividly descriptive. **2** of writing, drawing, painting etc. ◆ pl n **3** diagrams etc. used on television, computer screen etc.

graphite n form of carbon (used in pencils).

grapple ❶ v **1** wrestle. **2** struggle.

grasp ❶ v **1** (try, struggle to) seize hold. **2** understand. ◆ n **3** grip. **4** comprehension. **grasping** adj greedy, avaricious.

grass n **1** common type of plant with jointed stems and long narrow leaves. **2** such plants grown as lawn. **3** pasture. **4** Sl marijuana. **5** Sl informer. **grassy** adj **–sier, –siest. grasshopper** n jumping, chirping insect. **grass roots** ordinary members of group.

grate¹ n framework of metal bars for holding fuel in fireplace. **grating** n framework of bars covering opening.

grate² v **1** rub into small bits on rough surface. **2** rub with harsh noise. **3** irritate. **grater** n utensil with rough surface for reducing substance to small particles. **grating** adj **1** harsh. **2** irritating. **grate on** to annoy.

grateful ❶ adj **1** thankful. **2** appreciative. **3** pleasing. **gratefully** adv **gratitude** n sense of being thankful.

gratify v **–fying, –fied 1** satisfy. **2** please. **gratification** n

gratis adv/adj free, for nothing.

gratuitous adj **1** given free. **2**

——————— THESAURUS ———————

≠ **unimposing**; = **ambitious**, great, grandiose

grant n = **award**, allowance, donation, endowment, gift ◆ v = **give**, allow, present, award, permit; = **accept**, allow, admit, acknowledge, concede

graphic adj = **vivid**, clear, detailed, striking, explicit ≠ **vague**; = **pictorial**, visual, diagrammatic ≠ **impressionistic**

grapple v = **deal**, tackle, struggle, take on, confront; = **struggle**,

fight, combat, wrestle, battle

grasp v = **grip**, hold, catch, grab, seize; = **understand**, realize, take in, get, see ◆ n = **grip**, hold, possession, embrace, clutches; = **understanding**, knowledge, grip, awareness, mastery; = **reach**, power, control, scope

grateful adj = **thankful**, obliged, in (someone's) debt, indebted, appreciative

gratitude n = **thankfulness**, thanks, recognition, obligation,

uncalled for. **gratuity** n gift of money for services rendered, tip.

grave¹ ❶ n hole dug to bury corpse. **graveyard** n

grave² ❶ adj 1 serious. 2 solemn.

grave³ adj 1 accent (') over letter.

gravel n 1 small stones. 2 coarse sand. **gravelly** adj

graven adj carved, engraved.

gravitate v 1 move by gravity. 2 tend (towards) centre of attraction. 3 sink, settle down.

gravity ❶ n, pl **-ties** 1 force of attraction of one body for another, esp. of objects to the earth. 2 heaviness. 3 importance. 4 seriousness.

gravy n, pl **-vies** 1 juices from meat in cooking. 2 sauce made from these.

graze¹ ❶ v feed on grass, pasture.

graze² ❶ v 1 touch lightly in passing, scratch, scrape. ◆ n 2 grazing. 3 abrasion.

grease n 1 soft melted fat of animals. 2 thick oil as lubricant. ◆ v 3 apply grease to. **greasy** adj **greasier, greasiest. greasepaint** n theatrical make-up.

great ❶ adj 1 large. 2 important. 3 pre-eminent 4 Inf excellent. ◆ comb. form 5 one degree further removed in relationship, as in great-grandfather. 6 one degree further removed in relationship. **greatly** adv

greed ❶ n excessive consumption of, desire for, food, wealth. **greedy** adj

green ❶ adj 1 of colour between blue and yellow. 2 grass-coloured. 3 unripe. 4 inexperienced. 5 envious. ◆ n 6 colour. 7 area of grass, esp. for playing bowls etc. ◆ pl 8 green vegetables. **greenery** n vegetation. **greenfly** n aphid, small green garden pest. **greengrocer** n dealer in vegetables and fruit. **greenhouse** n glass building for rearing plants.

———— THESAURUS ————

appreciation ≠ ingratitude

grave¹ n = **tomb**, vault, crypt, mausoleum, sepulchre

grave² adj = **serious**, important, critical, pressing, threatening ≠ **trifling**; = **solemn**, sober, sombre, dour, unsmiling ≠ **carefree**

gravity n = **seriousness**, importance, significance, urgency, severity ≠ **triviality**; = **solemnity**, seriousness, gravitas ≠ **frivolity**

graze¹ v = **feed**, crop, browse, pasture

graze² v = **scratch**, skin, scrape, chafe, abrade; = **touch**, brush, rub, scrape, shave ◆ n = **scratch**, scrape, abrasion

great adj = **large**, big, huge, vast, enormous ≠ **small**; = **important**, serious, significant, critical, crucial ≠ **unimportant**; = **famous**, outstanding, remarkable, prominent, renowned; = (Inf) **excellent**, fine, wonderful, superb, fantastic (Inf) ≠ **poor**

greed n = **gluttony**, voracity

green adj = **verdant**, leafy, grassy; = **ecological**, conservationist, environment-friendly, ozone-

greet ⓥ v 1 meet with expressions of welcome. 2 salute. 3 receive.
greeting n
gregarious adj sociable.
gremlin n imaginary being blamed for mechanical malfunctions.
grenade n bomb thrown by hand or shot from rifle. **grenadier** n soldier of Grenadier Guards.
grenadine n syrup made from pomegranate juice, for sweetening and colouring drinks.
grey ⓥ adj 1 between black and white. 2 clouded. 3 turning white. 4 aged. 5 intermediate, indeterminate. ♦ n 6 grey colour.
greyhound n swift slender dog.
grid n 1 network of horizontal and vertical lines, bars etc. 2 any interconnecting system of links.
griddle n flat iron plate for cooking.
gridiron n frame of metal bars for grilling.
grief ⓥ n deep sorrow. **grievance** n real or imaginary cause for complaint. **grieve** v 1 feel grief. 2 cause grief to. **grievous** adj 1 painful, oppressive. 2 very serious.
grill n 1 device on cooker to radiate heat downwards. 2 food cooked under grill. 3 gridiron. ♦ v 4 cook (food) under grill. 5 subject to severe questioning.
grille, grill n grating.
grim ⓥ adj grimmer, grimmest 1 stern. 2 relentless. 3 joyless.
grimace n/v (pull) wry face.
grime n ingrained dirt, soot. **grimy** n
grin v grinning, grinned, n (give) broad smile.
grind ⓥ v grinding, ground 1 crush to powder. 2 make sharp, smooth. 3 grate. ♦ n 4 Inf hard work. 5 action of grinding.
grip ⓥ n 1 firm hold. 2 mastery. 3 handle. 4 travelling bag. ♦ v 5 hold tightly. 6 hold attention of.
gripe v 1 Inf complain (persistently). ♦ n 2 intestinal pain (esp. in infants) 3 Inf complaint.
grisly adj –lier, –liest causing terror.
grist n corn to be ground.

———— THESAURUS ————

friendly, non–polluting;
= **inexperienced**, new, raw, naive, immature; = **jealous**, grudging, resentful, envious, covetous; with capital ♦ n = **lawn**, common, turf, sward
greet v = **salute**, hail, say hello to, address, accost
grey adj = **dull**, dark, dim, gloomy, drab; = **boring**, dull, anonymous, faceless, colourless
grief n = **sadness**, suffering, regret, distress, misery ≠ **joy**
grim adj = **terrible**, severe, harsh, forbidding, formidable
grind v = **crush**, mill, powder, grate, pulverize; = **press**, push, crush, jam, mash; = **grate**, scrape, gnash ♦ n = (Inf) **hard work**, labour, sweat, (Inf) chore, toil
grip v = **grasp**, hold, catch, seize, clutch; = **engross**, fascinate, absorb, entrance, hold ♦ n
= **clasp**, hold, grasp; = **control**,

gristle n cartilage, tough flexible tissue.

grit ① n 1 rough particles of sand. 2 courage. ◆ v 3 clench (teeth).

grizzle v Inf whine.

grizzled adj grey (haired).

grizzly n, pl **-zlies** large Amer. bear.

groan ① v/n (make) low, deep sound of grief or pain.

grocer n dealer in foodstuffs.

groceries pl n commodities sold by a grocer. **grocery** n, pl **-ceries** trade, premises of grocer.

grog n spirit (esp. rum) and water. **groggy** adj Inf shaky, weak.

groin n fold where legs meet abdomen.

groom ① n 1 person caring for horses. 2 bridegroom. ◆ v 3 tend or look after. 4 brush or clean (esp. horse). 5 train.

groove ① n 1 narrow channel. 2 routine. ◆ v 3 cut groove in.

grope ① v feel about, search blindly.

gross ① adj 1 very fat. 2 total, not net. 3 coarse. 4 flagrant. ◆ n 5 twelve dozen.

grotesque ① adj 1 (horribly) distorted. 2 ugly or repulsive.

grotto n, pl **-toes, -tos** cave.

grotty adj **-tier, -tiest** Inf nasty, in bad condition.

grouch Inf ◆ n 1 persistent grumbler. 2 discontented mood. ◆ v 3 grumble.

ground ① n 1 surface of earth. 2 soil, earth. 3 reason. 4 special area. ◆ pl 5 dregs. 6 enclosed land round house. ◆ v 7 establish. 8 instruct. 9 place on ground. 10 run ashore. **grounded** adj (of aircraft) unable or not permitted to fly. **grounding** n basic knowledge of subject. **groundless** adj without reason. **groundwork** n preliminary work.

——————— THESAURUS ———————

rule, influence, command, power

grit n = **gravel**, sand, dust, pebbles; = **courage**, spirit, resolution, determination, guts (Inf) ◆ v = **clench**, grind, grate, gnash

groan v = **moan**, cry, sigh; = (Inf) **complain**, object, moan, grumble, gripe (Inf) ◆ n = **moan**, cry, sigh, whine; = (Inf) **complain**, protest, objection, grumble, grouse

groom n = **stableman**, stableboy, hostler or ostler (Arch) ◆ v = **brush**, clean, tend, rub down, curry; = **smarten up**, clean, tidy, preen, spruce up; = **train**, prime, prepare,

coach, ready

groove n = **indentation**, cut, hollow, channel, trench

grope v = **feel**, search, fumble, flounder, fish

gross adj = **flagrant**, blatant, rank, sheer, utter ≠ **qualified**; = **vulgar**, offensive, crude, obscene, coarse ≠ **decent**; = **fat**, overweight, hulking, corpulent ≠ **slim**; = **total**, whole, entire, aggregate, before tax ≠ **net** ◆ v = **earn**, make, take, bring in, rake in (Inf)

grotesque adj = **unnatural**, bizarre, strange, fantastic, distorted ≠ **natural**; = **absurd**,

group 🛈 n 1 number of persons or things together. 2 small musical band. 3 class. ◆ v 4 place, fall into group.

grouse¹ n 1 game bird. 2 its flesh.

grouse² v 1 grumble, complain. ◆ n 2 complaint.

grout n 1 thin fluid mortar. ◆ v 2 fill up with grout.

grove 🛈 n small group of trees.

grovel v –elling, –elled 1 abase oneself. 2 lie face down.

grow 🛈 v growing, grew, grown 1 develop naturally. 2 increase. 3 be produced. 4 become by degrees. 5 produce by cultivation.

growth n 1 growing. 2 increase. 3 what has grown or is growing.

grown-up adj/n adult.

growl v/n (make) low guttural sound of anger.

grub v 1 dig. 2 root up. 3 rummage. ◆ n 4 short, legless larva of certain insects 5 Sl food.

grubby adj –bier, –biest dirty.

grudge 🛈 v 1 be unwilling to give, allow. ◆ n 2 ill will.

gruel n food of oatmeal etc., boiled in milk or water.

gruelling 🛈 adj exhausting.

gruesome 🛈 adj horrible, grisly.

gruff adj rough-voiced, surly.

grumble 🛈 v 1 complain. 2 rumble. ◆ n 3 complaint.

grumpy adj grumpier, grumpiest ill-tempered, surly.

grunt v/n (make) sound characteristic of pig.

G-string n very small covering for genitals.

guarantee 🛈 n 1 formal assurance (esp. in writing) that product etc. will meet certain standards. ◆ v 2 give guarantee. 3 secure (against

———— THESAURUS ————

preposterous ≠ **natural**

ground n = **earth**, land, dry land, terra firma; = **arena**, pitch, stadium, park (Inf), field ◆ v = **base**, found, establish, set, settle; = **instruct**, train, teach, initiate, tutor

group n = **crowd**, party, band, pack, gang; ◆ v = **arrange**, order, sort, class, classify

grove n = **wood**, plantation, covert, thicket, copse

grow v = **develop**, get bigger ≠ **shrink**; = **get bigger**, spread, swell, stretch, expand; = **cultivate**, produce, raise, farm, breed; = **become**, get, turn, come to be; = **originate**, spring, arise, stem,

issue

grudge n = **resentment**, bitterness, grievance, dislike, animosity ≠ **goodwill** ◆ v = **resent**, mind, envy, covet, begrudge ≠ **welcome**

gruelling adj = **exhausting**, demanding, tiring, taxing, severe ≠ **easy**

gruesome adj = **horrific**, shocking, terrible, horrible, grim ≠ **pleasant**

grumble v = **complain**, moan, gripe (Inf), whinge (Inf), carp; = **rumble**, growl, gurgle ◆ n = **complaint**, protest, objection, moan, grievance; = **rumble**, growl, gurgle

risk etc.). **guarantor** n
guard ⊕ v 1 protect, defend. 2
take precautions (against). ◆ n 3
person, group that protects. 4
sentry. 5 official in charge of train.
6 protection. **guarded** adj
cautious, noncommittal. **guardian**
n 1 keeper, protector. 2 person
having custody of infant etc.
guava n tropical tree with fruit
used to make jelly.
guerrilla ⊕ **guerilla** n member of
irregular armed force.
guess ⊕ v 1 estimate. 2
conjecture US and Canad 3 think. ◆
n 4 conclusion reached by
guessing.
guest ⊕ n 1 one entertained at
another's house. 2 one living in
hotel.
guffaw n/v (make) burst of
boisterous laughter.

guide ⊕ n 1 one who shows the
way. 2 adviser. 3 book of
instruction or information. ◆ v 4
lead, act as guide to. **guidance** n
guideline n set principle.
guild ⊕ n organization for mutual
help, or with common object.
guile ⊕ n cunning, deceit.
guillotine n 1 machine for
beheading. 2 machine for cutting
paper. ◆ v 3 use guillotine on.
guilt ⊕ n 1 fact, state of having
done wrong. 2 responsibility for
offence. **guiltless** adj innocent.
guilty adj having committed an
offence.
guinea n formerly, sum of 21
shillings. **guinea pig 1** rodent
originating in S Amer 2 Inf person
or animal used in experiments.
guise ⊕ n external appearance,
esp. one assumed.

——————— THESAURUS ———————

guarantee v = **ensure**, secure,
assure, warrant, make certain ◆ n
= **promise**, pledge, assurance,
certainty, word of honour
guard v = **protect**, defend, secure,
mind, preserve ◆ n = **sentry**,
warder, warden, custodian, watch;
= **shield**, security, defence, screen,
protection
guerrilla n = **freedom fighter**,
partisan, underground fighter
guess v = **estimate**, predict, work
out, speculate, conjecture ≠ **know**;
= **suppose**, think, believe, suspect,
judge ◆ n = **estimate**, speculation,
judgment, hypothesis, conjecture
≠ **certainty**
guest n = **visitor**, company, caller

guide n = **handbook**, manual,
guidebook, instructions,
catalogue; = **directory**, street
map; = **escort**, leader, usher;
= **pointer**, sign, landmark, marker,
beacon ◆ v = **lead**, direct, escort,
conduct, accompany; = **steer**,
control, manage, direct, handle
guild n = **society**, union, league,
association, company
guilt n = **shame**, regret, remorse,
contrition, guilty conscience
≠ **pride**; = **culpability**, blame,
responsibility, misconduct,
wickedness ≠ **innocence**
guise n = **form**, appearance,
shape, aspect, mode; = **pretence**,
disguise, aspect, semblance

guitar n stringed instrument played by plucking or strumming. **guitarist** n

gulch n US and Canad a narrow ravine cut by a fast stream.

gulf ❶ n 1 large inlet of the sea. 2 chasm. 3 large gap.

gull n long–winged web–footed sea bird.

gullet n food passage from mouth to stomach.

gullible adj easily imposed on, credulous.

gully n, pl **–lies** channel or ravine worn by action of water.

gulp v/n 1 swallow. 2 gasp.

gum¹ ❶ n 1 sticky substance issuing from certain trees. 2 adhesive. 3 chewing gum. ♦ v 4 stick with gum. **gumboots** pl n boots of rubber. **gumtree** n any species of eucalypt.

gum² n firm flesh in which teeth are set.

gumption n 1 resourcefulness. 2 shrewdness, sense.

gun ❶ n 1 weapon with metal tube from which missiles are discharged by explosion. 2 cannon, pistol etc. ♦ v 3 shoot. 4

pursue vigorously. **gunner** n

gunpowder n explosive mixture of saltpetre, sulphur, charcoal.

gunshot n 1 shot or range of gun. ♦ adj 2 caused by missile from gun.

gunge n Inf any sticky, unpleasant substance.

gunwale, gunnel n upper edge of ship's side.

guppy n, pl **–pies** small colourful aquarium fish.

gurgle n/v (make) bubbling noise.

guru ❶ n spiritual teacher, esp. in India.

gush ❶ v 1 flow out suddenly and copiously, spurt. ♦ n 2 sudden and copious flow.

gusset n triangle or diamond–shaped piece of material let into garment.

gust n 1 sudden blast of wind. 2 burst of rain, anger, passion etc.

gusto n enjoyment, zest.

gut ❶ n (oft. pl) 1 intestines. 2 material made from guts of animals, e.g. for violin strings etc. ♦ pl 3 Inf courage. ♦ v 4 remove guts from (fish etc.). 5 remove, destroy contents of (house).

———————— THESAURUS ————————

gulf n = **bay**, bight, sea inlet; = **chasm**, opening, split, gap, separation

gum n = **glue**, adhesive, resin, cement, paste ♦ v = **stick**, glue, affix, cement, paste

gun n = **firearm**, shooter (Sl), piece (Sl), handgun

guru n = **authority**, expert, leader, master, pundit

gush v = **flow**, run, rush, flood, pour; = **enthuse**, rave, spout, overstate, effuse ♦ n = **stream**, flow, rush, flood, jet

gut n = (Inf) **paunch**, belly, spare tyre (Brit sl), potbelly ♦ v = **disembowel**, clean; = **ravage**, empty, clean out, despoil ♦ adj = **instinctive**, natural, basic, spontaneous, intuitive

gutter ❶ *n* shallow trough for carrying off water from roof or side of street.

guttural *adj* harsh–sounding, as if produced in the throat.

guy[1] ❶ *n* **1** effigy of Guy Fawkes burnt on Nov. 5th **2** *Inf* person (usu. male). ◆ *v* **3** make fun of. **4** ridicule.

guy[2] *n* rope, chain to steady, secure something, e.g. tent.

guzzle *v* eat or drink greedily.

gym *n* short for GYMNASIUM *or* GYMNASTICS.

gymkhana *n* competition or display of horse riding.

gymnasium *n* place equipped for muscular exercises, athletic training. **gymnastics** *pl n* muscular exercises. **gymnast** *n*

gynaecology *n* branch of medicine dealing with functions and diseases of women. **gynaecologist** *n*

gypsum *n* chalklike mineral, used for making plaster.

Gypsy ❶ *n, pl* –**sies** one of wandering race orig. from NW India.

gyrate *v* move in circle, spiral.

gyroscope *n* disc rotating on axis that can turn in any direction.

———— THESAURUS ————

gutter *n* = **drain**, channel, ditch, trench, trough

guy[1] *n* = (*Inf*) **man**, person, fellow, lad, bloke (*Brit inf*)

Gypsy *n* = **traveller**, roamer, wanderer, Bohemian, rover

H h

haberdasher *n* dealer in articles of dress, ribbons, pins, needles etc. **haberdashery** *n*

habit ❶ *n* 1 settled tendency or practice. 2 customary apparel, esp. of nun or monk. **habitual** *adj* 1 formed or acquired by habit. 2 usual, customary.

habitable *adj* fit to live in. **habitat** *n* natural home (of animal etc.).

habitation *n* abode.

hack¹ ❶ *v* 1 cut, chop (at) violently. 2 *Inf* utter harsh, dry cough. ♦ *n* 3 violent blow. **hacker** *n Sl* computer enthusiast who breaks into computer system of company or government.

hack² ❶ *n* 1 horse for ordinary riding. 2 inferior writer.

hackles *pl n* hairs on back of neck of dog and other animals which are raised in anger.

hackneyed *adj* (of words etc.) stale, trite because of overuse.

hacksaw *n* handsaw for cutting metal.

haddock *n* large, edible sea fish.

haemoglobin *n* colouring and oxygen–bearing matter of red blood corpuscles.

haemophilia *n* illness in which blood does not clot.

haemophiliac *n*

haemorrhage *n* profuse bleeding.

haemorrhoids *pl n* swollen veins in rectum.

hag *n* 1 ugly old woman. 2 witch.

haggard *adj* anxious, careworn.

haggis *n* Scottish dish made from sheep's offal, oatmeal etc.

haggle *v* bargain over price.

hail¹ ❶ *v* 1 greet. 2 acclaim. 3 call. 4 come (from).

hail² ❶ *n* 1 (shower of) pellets of ice. 2 barrage. ♦ *v* 3 pour down as shower of hail. **hailstone** *n*

hair ❶ *n* 1 filament growing from skin of animal, as covering of man's head. 2 such filaments collectively. **hairy** *adj* **hairdo** *n* way of dressing hair. **hairdresser** *n* one who cuts and styles hair. **hairgrip**

THESAURUS

habit *n* = **mannerism**, custom, way, practice, characteristic; = **addiction**, dependence, compulsion

hack¹ *v* = **cut**, chop, slash, mutilate, mangle

hack² *n* = **reporter**, writer, correspondent, journalist, scribbler

hail¹ *v* = **acclaim**, honour,

acknowledge, cheer, applaud ≠ **condemn**; = **salute**, greet, address, welcome, say hello to ≠ **snub**; = **flag down**, summon, signal to, wave down

hail² *n* = **hailstones**, sleet, hailstorm, frozen rain; = **shower**, rain, storm, battery, volley ♦ *v* = **rain**, shower, pelt

n small, tightly bent metal hairpin. **hairpin** *n* pin for keeping hair in place. **hairpin bend** U–shaped turn of road.

hale 🛈 *adj* robust, healthy.

half 🛈 *n, pl* **halves 1** either of two equal parts of thing. ♦ *adj* **2** forming half. ♦ *adv* **3** to the extent of half. **half–baked** *adj Inf* poorly planned. **half–breed, half–caste** *n* person with parents of different races. **half–brother, –sister** *n* brother, sister by one parent only. **half–hearted** *adj* unenthusiastic. **halfwit** *n* feeble–minded person. **halibut** *n* large edible flatfish. **halitosis** *n* bad–smelling breath. **hall** 🛈 *n* **1** (entrance) passage. **2** large room or building used for esp. public assembly.

hallelujah *n/interj* exclamation of praise to God.

hallmark 🛈 *n* **1** mark used to indicate standard of tested gold and silver. **2** mark of excellence. **3** distinguishing feature.

hallo *interj* see HELLO.

hallowed *adj* holy.

hallucinate *v* suffer illusions. **hallucination** *n* **hallucinatory** *adj*

halo *n, pl* **–loes, –los** circle of light.

halt 🛈 *n* **1** interruption or end to progress etc. (esp. as command to stop marching). ♦ *v* **2** (cause to) stop. **halting** *adj* hesitant, lame.

halter *n* **1** rope with headgear to fasten horse. **2** low–cut dress style with strap passing behind neck. **3** noose for hanging person.

halve 🛈 *v* **1** cut in half. **2** reduce to half. **3** share.

ham *n* **1** meat (esp. salted or smoked) from thigh of pig. **2** actor adopting exaggerated style. **3** amateur radio enthusiast. **ham-fisted** *adj* clumsy.

hamburger *n* fried cake of minced beef.

hamlet *n* small village.

hammer 🛈 *n* **1** tool usu. with heavy head at end of handle, for beating, driving nails etc. ♦ *v* **2** strike as with hammer.

hammock *n* bed of canvas etc.,

———————— THESAURUS ————————

hair *n* = **locks**, mane, tresses, shock, mop

hale *adj* = (*Old–fashioned*) **healthy**, well, strong, sound, fit

half *n* = **fifty per cent**, equal part ♦ *adj* = **partial**, limited, moderate, halved ♦ *adv* = **partially**, partly, in part

hall *n* = **passage**, lobby, corridor, hallway, foyer; = **meeting place**, chamber, auditorium, concert hall, assembly room

hallmark *n* = **trademark**, sure

sign, telltale sign; = (*Brit*) **mark**, sign, device, stamp, seal

halt *v* = **stop**, break off, stand still, wait, rest ≠ **continue**; = **come to an end**, stop, cease ♦ *n* = **stop**, end, close, pause, standstill ≠ **continuation**

halve *v* = **cut in half**, reduce by fifty per cent, decrease by fifty per cent, lessen by fifty per cent

hammer *v* = **hit**, drive, knock, beat, strike; = (*Inf*) **defeat**, beat, thrash, trounce, run rings around

hung on cords.

hamper[1] *n* large covered basket.

hamper[2] **ⓣ** *v* impede, obstruct.

hamster *n* type of rodent, sometimes kept as pet.

hamstring *n* tendon at back of knee.

hand ⓣ *n* 1 extremity of arm beyond wrist. 2 side. 3 style of writing. 4 cards dealt to player. 5 manual worker. 6 help. 7 pointer of dial. 8 applause. ♦ *v* 9 pass. 10 deliver. 11 hold out. **handful** *n* 1 small quantity. 2 *Inf* person, thing causing problems. **handiness** *n* 1 dexterity. 2 state of being near, available. **handy** *adj* 1 convenient. 2 clever with hands. **handbag** *n* woman's bag. **handbook** *n* small instruction book. **handcuff** *n* 1 fetter for wrist, usu. joined in pair. ♦ *v* 2 secure thus. **handicraft** *n* manual occupation or skill. **handiwork** *n* thing done by particular person. **handkerchief** *n* small square of fabric for wiping nose etc. **hand-out** *n* 1 thing given

free. 2 written information given out at talk etc. **handwriting** *n* way person writes. **handyman** *n* man employed to do various tasks.

handicap ⓣ *n* 1 something that hampers or hinders. 2 race, contest in which chances are equalized. 3 any physical disability. ♦ *v* 4 hamper, impose handicaps on.

handle ⓣ *n* 1 part of thing to hold it by. ♦ *v* 2 touch, feel with hands. 3 manage. 4 deal with. 5 trade. **handler** *n* person who controls animal. **handlebars** *pl n* curved metal bar to steer cycle.

handsome ⓣ *adj* 1 of fine appearance. 2 generous. 3 ample.

hang ⓣ *v* hanging, hung 1 suspend. 2 attach, set up (wallpaper, doors etc.). 3 be suspended, cling. 4 kill by suspension by neck. **hanger** *n* frame on which clothes etc. can be hung. **hangdog** *adj* sullen, dejected. **hang-glider** *n* glider with light frame from which pilot

——————— THESAURUS ———————

(*Inf*)

hamper[2] *v* = **hinder**, handicap, prevent, restrict, frustrate ≠ **help**

hand *n* = **palm**, fist, paw (*Inf*), mitt (*Sl*); = **worker**, employee, labourer, workman, operative; = **round of applause**, clap, ovation, big hand; = **writing**, script, handwriting, calligraphy ♦ *v* = **give**, pass, hand over, present to, deliver; = **within reach**, nearby, handy, close, available

handicap *n* = **disability**, defect,

impairment, physical abnormality; = **disadvantage**, barrier, restriction, obstacle, limitation ≠ **advantage**; = **advantage**, head start ♦ *v* = **hinder**, limit, restrict, burden, hamstring ≠ **help**

handle *n* = **grip**, hilt, haft, stock ♦ *v* = **manage**, deal with, tackle, cope with; = **deal with**, manage

handsome *adj* = **good-looking**, attractive, gorgeous, elegant, personable ≠ **ugly**; = **generous**, large, princely, liberal,

hangs in harness. **hangman** n person who executes people by hanging. **hangover** n aftereffects of too much drinking. **hang-up** n Inf emotional or psychological problem.

hangar n large shed for aircraft.

hanker v crave.

hanky, hankie n, pl **hankies** Inf handkerchief.

haphazard adj random, careless.

hapless adj unlucky.

happen ❶ v 1 come about, occur. 2 chance to do. **happening** n occurrence, event.

happy ❶ adj –pier, –piest 1 glad, content. 2 lucky. **happily** adv **happiness** n

harangue n 1 vehement speech. 2 tirade. ◆ v 3 address vehemently.

harass ❶ v worry, torment. **harassment** n

harbour ❶ n 1 shelter for ships. ◆ v 2 give shelter. 3 maintain

(secretly).

hard ❶ adj 1 firm, resisting pressure. 2 solid. 3 difficult to do, understand. 4 unfeeling. 5 heavy. ◆ adv 6 vigorously. 7 persistently. 8 close. **harden** v **hardly** adv 1 unkindly, harshly. 2 scarcely, not quite. 3 only just. **hardship** n 1 ill luck. 2 severe toil, suffering. 3 instance of this. **hard–headed** adj shrewd. **hard–hearted** adj unfeeling. **hard shoulder** motorway verge for emergency stops. **hardware** n 1 tools, implements. 2 Comp mechanical and electronic parts. **hardwood** n wood from deciduous trees.

hardy ❶ adj hardier, hardiest 1 robust, vigorous. 2 bold. 3 (of plants) able to grow in the open all the year round.

hare n animal like large rabbit. **harebell** n round–leaved bell–shaped flower. **harebrained** adj

————————— THESAURUS —————————

considerable ≠ **mean**

hang v = **dangle**, swing, suspend; = **execute**, lynch, string up (Inf); = **lower**, suspend, dangle, let down, let droop; = **lean**, incline

happen v = **occur**, take place, come about, result, develop; = **chance**, turn out

happy adj = **pleased**, delighted, content, thrilled, glad; = **fortunate**, lucky, timely, favourable, auspicious ≠ **unfortunate**

harass v = **annoy**, trouble, bother, harry, plague

harbour n = **port**, haven, dock,

mooring, marina ◆ v = **hold**, bear, maintain, nurse, retain; = **shelter**, protect, hide, shield, provide refuge

hard adj = **tough**, strong, firm, solid, stiff ≠ **soft**; = **difficult**, involved, complicated, puzzling, intricate ≠ **easy**; = **exhausting**, tough, exacting, rigorous, gruelling ≠ **easy**; = **harsh**, cold, cruel, stern, callous ≠ **kind**; = **grim**, painful, distressing, harsh, unpleasant ◆ adv = **intently**, closely, carefully, sharply, keenly

hardy adj = **strong**, tough, robust, sound, rugged ≠ **frail**

rash, wild. **harelip** n fissure of upper lip.

harem n **1** women's part of Muslim dwelling. **2** one man's wives.

hark v listen.

harlequin n masked clown in diamond–patterned costume.

harlot n whore, prostitute.

harm 🛈 n/v damage. **harmful** adj **harmless** adj unable or unlikely to hurt.

harmony 🛈 n, pl **–nies 1** agreement. **2** combination of notes to make chords. **3** melodious sound. **harmonic** adj of harmony. **harmonica** n mouth organ. **harmonious** adj **harmonium** n small organ. **harmonize** v **1** bring into harmony. **2** cause to agree. **3** reconcile. **4** be in harmony.

harness 🛈 n **1** equipment for attaching horse to cart, plough etc. ◆ v **2** put on, in harness. **3** utilize energy or power of.

harp n **1** musical instrument of strings played by hand. ◆ v **2** play on harp. **3** dwell on continuously.

harpsichord n stringed instrument like piano.

harpoon n/v (use) barbed spear for catching whales.

harrier n **1** hound used in hunting hares. **2** falcon.

harrow n **1** implement for smoothing, levelling or stirring up soil. ◆ v **2** draw harrow over. **3** distress greatly. **harrowing** adj distressful.

harry 🛈 v **–rying, –ried 1** harass. **2** ravage.

harsh 🛈 adj **1** rough, discordant. **2** severe. **3** unfeeling. **harshly** adv

harvest 🛈 n **1** (season for) gathering grain. **2** gathering of crop. ◆ v **4** reap and gather in. **harvester** n

has third person sing. of HAVE.

has–been n Inf one who is no longer successful.

hash n **1** dish of chopped meat etc. **2** mess. ◆ v **3** cut up small, chop. **4** mix up.

hashish n resinous extract of Indian hemp, esp. used as hallucinogen.

hassle 🛈 n **1** Inf quarrel. **2** a lot of bother, trouble. ◆ v **3** bother.

——————— THESAURUS ———————

harm v = **injure**, hurt, wound, abuse, ill–treat ≠ **heal** ◆ n = **injury**, suffering, damage, ill, hurt

harmony n = **accord**, peace, agreement, friendship, sympathy ≠ **conflict**; = **tune**, melody, unison, tunefulness, euphony ≠ **discord**

harness v = **exploit**, control, channel, employ, utilize ◆ n = **equipment**, tackle, gear, tack

harry v = **pester**, bother, plague, harass, hassle (Inf)

harsh adj = **severe**, hard, tough, stark, austere; = **bleak**, freezing, severe, icy

harvest n = **harvesting**, picking, gathering, collecting, reaping; = **crop**, yield, year's growth, produce ◆ v = **gather**, pick, collect, bring in, pluck

hassle (Inf) n = **trouble**, problem, difficulty, bother, grief (Inf) ◆ v

hassock n kneeling cushion.
haste n 1 speed, hurry. ♦ v 2
hasten. **hasten** v (cause to) hurry.
hastily adv **hasty** adj
hat n head covering usu. with
brim. **hat trick** set of three
achievements.
hatch¹ ❶ v 1 (of young birds etc.)
(cause to) emerge from egg. 2
contrive, devise. **hatchery** n
hatch² n 1 hatchway. 2 trapdoor
over it. 3 opening in wall, to
facilitate service of meals etc.
hatchback n car with lifting rear
door. **hatchway** n opening in deck
of ship etc.
hatchet n small axe.
hate ❶ v 1 dislike strongly. 2 bear
malice towards. ♦ n 3 this feeling.
4 that which is hated. **hateful** adj
detestable. **hatred** n
haughty adj –**tier**, –**tiest** proud,
arrogant. **haughtily** adv
haul ❶ v 1 pull, drag with effort. ♦
n 2 hauling. 3 what is hauled.

haulage n **haulier** n
haunch n human hip or fleshy
hindquarter of animal.
haunt ❶ v 1 visit regularly. 2 visit
in form of ghost. 3 recur to. ♦ n 4
place frequently visited. **haunted**
adj 1 frequented by ghosts. 2
worried. **haunting** adj extremely
beautiful or sad.
have ❶ v (present tense: I, we, you,
they **have**; he, she **has**; present
participle **having**; past tense and
past participle **had**) 1 hold,
possess. 2 be affected with. 3 be
obliged (to do). 4 cheat. 5 obtain.
6 contain. 7 allow. 8 cause to be
done. 9 give birth to. 10 as
auxiliary, forms perfect and other
tenses.
haven ❶ n place of safety.
haversack n canvas bag for
provisions etc. carried on back.
havoc ❶ n 1 devastation, ruin 2 Inf
confusion, chaos.
hawk¹ n bird of prey smaller

——— THESAURUS ———

= **bother**, bug (Inf), annoy, hound,
harass
hatch¹ v = **incubate**, breed, sit on,
brood, bring forth; = **devise**,
design, invent, put together,
conceive
hate v = **detest**, loathe, despise,
dislike, abhor ≠ love; = **dislike**,
detest, shrink from, recoil from,
not be able to bear ≠ like ♦ n
= **dislike**, hostility, hatred,
loathing, animosity ≠ love
haul v = **drag**, draw, pull, heave ♦
n = **yield**, gain, spoils, catch,
harvest

haunt v = **plague**, trouble, obsess,
torment, possess ♦ n = **meeting
place**, hangout (Inf), rendezvous,
stamping ground
have v = **own**, keep, possess, hold,
retain; = **get**, obtain, take, receive,
accept; = **suffer**, experience,
undergo, sustain, endure; = **give
birth to**, bear, deliver, bring forth,
beget; = **experience**, go through,
undergo, meet with, come across
haven n = **sanctuary**, shelter,
retreat, asylum, refuge
havoc n = (Inf) **disorder**,
confusion, chaos, disruption,

than eagle. **2** advocate of warlike policies.

hawk² n offer (goods) for sale, esp. in street. **hawker** n person who travels and sells goods.

hawthorn n thorny shrub or tree.

hay n grass mown and dried. **hay fever** allergic reaction to pollen, dust etc. **haystack** n large pile of hay. **haywire** adj **1** crazy. **2** disorganized.

hazard ❶ n **1** chance. **2** risk, danger. ♦ v **3** expose to risk. **4** run risk of. **hazardous** adj risky.

haze ❶ n **1** mist. **2** obscurity. **hazy** adj **1** misty. **2** vague.

hazel n **1** bush bearing nuts. ♦ adj **2** light brown.

he pron (third person masc) **1** person, animal already referred to. ♦ comb. form **2** male, as in he-goat.

head ❶ n **1** upper part of body, containing mouth, sense organs and brain. **2** upper part of anything. **3** chief of organization, school etc. **4** chief part. **5** aptitude, capacity. **6** crisis. **7** person, animal considered as unit. ♦ adj **8** chief, principal. **9** (of wind) contrary. ♦ v **10** be at the top. **11** lead. **12** provide with head. **13** hit (ball) with head. **14** make for. **15** form a head. **heading** n title. **heady** adj apt to intoxicate or excite. **headache** n continuous pain in head. **headland** n area of land jutting into sea. **headlight** n powerful lamp on front of vehicle etc. **headline** n news summary, in large type in newspaper. **headlong** adv in rush. **headphones** pl n two small loudspeakers strapped against ears. **headquarters** pl n centre of operations. **head start** advantage. **headstrong** adj self-willed. **headway** n progress.

heal ❶ v make or become well. **health** n **1** soundness of body. **2** condition of body. **3** toast drunk in person's honour. **healthy** adj **healthier, healthiest. health food** vegetarian food etc., eaten for dietary value.

heap ❶ n **1** pile. **2** great quantity.

━━━━━━━━ THESAURUS ━━━━━━━━

mayhem

hazard n = **danger**, risk, threat, problem, menace ♦ v = **jeopardize**, risk, endanger, threaten, expose; **hazard a guess** = **guess**, conjecture, presume, take a guess

haze n = **mist**, cloud, fog, obscurity, vapour

head n = **skull**, crown, pate, nut (Sl), loaf (Sl); = **mind**, reasoning, understanding, thought, sense; = **top**, crown, summit, peak, crest; = **leader**, president, director, manager, chief ♦ adj = **chief**, main, leading, first, prime ♦ v = **lead**, precede, be the leader of, be or go first, be or go at the front of; = **top**, lead, crown, cap; = **be in charge of**, run, manage, lead, control; **go to someone's head**; = **make someone conceited**, puff someone up, make someone full of themselves

heal v (sometimes with **up**) = **mend**, get better, get well, cure,

♦ v 3 pile, load with.
hear ❶ v **hearing, heard 1**
perceive sound by ear. **2** listen to
3 Law try (case). **4** heed. **5** learn.
hearing n **1** ability to hear. **2**
earshot. **3** judicial examination.
hearsay n rumour.
hearken v listen.
hearse n funeral carriage for
coffin.
heart ❶ n **1** organ which makes
blood circulate. **2** seat of emotions
and affections. **3** mind, soul,
courage. **4** central part. **5** suit at
cards. **hearten** v make, become
cheerful. **heartless** adj unfeeling.
hearty adj **1** friendly. **2** vigorous. **3**
in good health. **4** satisfying. **heart
attack** sudden severe malfunction
of heart. **heartbeat** n single
pulsation of heart. **heartbreak** n
intense grief. **heartfelt** adj felt
sincerely. **heart-rending** adj
agonizing. **by heart** by memory.
hearth n **1** part of room where fire

is made. **2** home.
heat ❶ n **1** hotness. **2** sensation of
this. **3** hot weather. **4** warmth of
feeling, anger etc. **5** sexual
excitement in female animals. **6**
one of many eliminating races etc.
♦ v **7** make, become hot. **heated**
adj angry. **heater** n
heath n tract of waste land.
heathen adj/n **1** (one) not
adhering to a religious system. **2**
pagan.
heather n shrub growing on
heaths and mountains.
heave v **1** lift (and throw) with
effort. **2** utter (sigh). **3** swell, rise. **4**
feel nausea. ♦ n **5** act of heaving.
heaven ❶ n **1** abode of God. **2**
place of bliss. **3** (also pl) sky.
heavenly adj
heavy ❶ adj **heavier, heaviest 1**
weighty. **2** dense. **3** sluggish. **4**
severe. **5** sorrowful. **6** serious. **7**
dull. **heavily** adv
heckle v interrupt (speaker) by

——— THESAURUS ———

regenerate
health n = **condition**, state, shape,
constitution, fettle; = **wellbeing**,
strength, fitness, vigour, good
condition ≠ **illness**
heap n = **pile**, lot, collection,
mass, stack; (often plural) = (Inf) **a
lot**, lots (Inf), plenty, masses,
load(s) (Inf) ♦ v (sometimes with **up**)
= **pile**, collect, gather, stack,
accumulate
hear v = **overhear**, catch, detect;
= (Law) **try**, judge, examine,
investigate; = **learn**, discover, find
out, pick up, gather

heart n = **nature**, character, soul,
constitution, essence; = **courage**,
will, spirit, purpose, bottle (Brit inf)
heat v sometimes with **up** = **warm
(up)**, cook, boil, roast, reheat
≠ **chill** ♦ n = **warmth**, hotness,
temperature ≠ **cold**; = **hot
weather**, warmth, closeness, high
temperature, heatwave
heaven n = **paradise**, next world,
hereafter, nirvana (Buddhism,
Hinduism), bliss; = (Inf) **happiness**,
paradise, ecstasy, bliss, utopia
heavy adj = **weighty**, large,
massive, hefty, bulky ≠ **light**;

questions, taunts etc.

hectare *n* one hundred ares or 10 000 square metres (2,471 acres).

hectic 𝕠 *adj* rushed, busy.

hedge 𝕠 *v* **1** fence of bushes. ♦ *v* **2** surround with hedge. **3** be evasive. **4** secure against loss.

hedgehog *n* small animal covered with spines.

hedonism *n* pursuit of pleasure. **hedonist** *n*

heed 𝕠 *v* take notice of. **heedless** *adj* careless.

heel[1] *n* **1** hind part of foot. **2** part of shoe supporting this. **3** *Sl* undesirable person. ♦ *v* **4** supply with heel.

heel[2] *v* lean to one side.

hefty 𝕠 *adj* **heftier, heftiest 1** bulky. **2** weighty. **3** strong.

heifer *n* young cow.

height 𝕠 *n* **1** measure from base to top. **2** quality of being high. **3**

elevation. **4** highest degree (*oft. pl*) **5** hilltop. **heighten** *v* **1** make higher. **2** intensify.

heinous *adj* atrocious, extremely wicked, detestable.

heir 𝕠 *n* person entitled to inherit property or rank. **heirloom** *n* thing that has been in family for generations.

helicopter *n* aircraft lifted by rotating blades.

helium *n* very light, nonflammable gaseous element.

helix *n, pl* **helices, helixes** spiral.

hell 𝕠 *n* **1** abode of the damned. **2** abode of the dead generally. **3** place of torture. **hellish** *adj* **hell–bent** *adj* intent.

hello 𝕠 *hallo interj* expression of greeting.

helm 𝕠 *n* tiller, wheel for turning ship's rudder.

helmet *n* defensive or protective

———— THESAURUS ————

= **intensive**, severe, serious, concentrated, fierce

hectic *adj* = **frantic**, chaotic, heated, animated, turbulent ≠ **peaceful**

hedge *v* = **prevaricate**, evade, sidestep, duck, dodge

heed (*Formal*) *v* = **pay attention to**, listen to, take notice of, follow, consider ≠ **ignore** ♦ *n* = **thought**, care, mind, attention, regard ≠ **disregard**

heel[1] *n* = (*Sl*) **swine**, cad (*Brit inf*), bounder (*old–fashioned Brit. slang*), rotter (*slang, chiefly Brit.*)

hefty *adj* (*Inf*) = **big**, strong, massive, strapping, robust ≠ **small**

height *n* = **tallness**, stature, highness, loftiness ≠ **shortness**; = **altitude**, measurement, highness, elevation, tallness ≠ **depth**; = **peak**, top, crown, summit, crest ≠ **valley**

heir *n* = **successor**, beneficiary, inheritor, heiress (*fem.*), next in line

hell *n* = **the underworld**, the abyss, Hades (*Greek myth*), hellfire, the inferno; = (*Inf*) **torment**, suffering, agony, nightmare, misery

hello *interj* = **hi** (*Inf*), greetings, how do you do?, good morning, good evening

covering for head.

help ① v/n 1 aid. 2 support. 3 remedy. **helper** n **helpful** adj

helping n single portion of food.

helpless adj 1 incompetent. 2 unaided. 3 unable to help.

helter-skelter adv/adj/n 1 (in) hurry and confusion. ◆ n 2 high spiral slide at fairground.

hem ① n 1 edge of cloth, folded and sewn down. ◆ v 2 sew thus. 3 confine, shut in.

hemisphere n 1 half sphere. 2 half of the earth.

hemlock n poisonous plant.

hemp n 1 Indian plant. 2 its fibre used for rope etc. 3 any of several narcotic drugs.

hen n female of domestic fowl and others. **henpecked** adj (of man) dominated by wife.

hence ① adv 1 from this point. 2 for this reason. **henceforward, henceforth** adv from now onwards.

henchman n trusty follower.

henna n 1 flowering shrub. 2 reddish dye made from it.

hepatitis n inflammation of the liver.

heptagon n figure with seven angles.

her pron object of SHE. ◆ adj of, belonging to her. **hers** pron of her. **herself** pron emphatic or reflexive form of SHE.

herald ① n 1 messenger, envoy. ◆ v 2 announce. **heraldic** adj

heraldry n study of (right to have) heraldic bearings.

herb n plant used in cookery or medicine. **herbaceous** adj 1 of, like herbs. 2 permanently flowering. **herbal** adj **herbicide** n chemical which destroys plants. **herbivore** n animal that feeds on plants. **herbivorous** adj

herd ① n 1 company of animals feeding together. ◆ v 2 crowd together. 3 tend (herd). **herdsman** n

here adv 1 in this place. 2 at or to this point. **hereabouts** adv near here. **hereafter** adv 1 in time to come. ◆ n 2 future existence. **hereby** adv as a result of this.

——— THESAURUS ———

helm n = (Naut) tiller, wheel, rudder; **at the helm** = in charge, in control, in command, at the wheel, in the saddle

help v (sometimes with **out**) = aid, support, assist, cooperate with, abet ≠ hinder; = improve, ease, relieve, facilitate, alleviate ≠ make worse; = assist, aid, support ◆ n = assistance, aid, support, advice, guidance ≠ hindrance

hem n = edge, border, margin, trimming, fringe

hence conj = therefore, thus, consequently, for this reason, in consequence

herald v = indicate, promise, usher in, presage, portend ◆ n = (Often lit) forerunner, sign, signal, indication, token; = messenger, courier, proclaimer, announcer, crier

herd n = flock, crowd, collection, mass, drove

herein adv in this place. **herewith** adv with this.

heredity n tendency of organism to transmit its nature to its descendants. **hereditary** adj descending by inheritance or heredity.

heresy n, pl **-sies** unorthodox opinion or belief. **heretic** n **heretical** adj

heritage 🛈 n what may be or is inherited.

hermaphrodite n person or animal with characteristics, or reproductive organs, of both sexes.

hermetic adj sealed so as to be airtight. **hermetically** adv

hermit n one living in solitude. **hermitage** n hermit's dwelling.

hernia n projection of organ through lining.

hero 🛈 n, pl **heroes** 1 one greatly regarded for achievements or qualities. 2 principal character in story. **heroic** adj **heroism** n

heroin n highly addictive drug.

heron n long-legged wading bird.

herring n important food fish.

hertz n, pl **hertz** SI unit of frequency.

hesitate 🛈 v 1 hold back. 2 feel, or show indecision. 3 be reluctant. **hesitancy, hesitation** n **hesitant** adj

hessian n coarse jute cloth.

heterogeneous adj composed of diverse elements. **heterogeneity** n

heterosexual n/adj (person) sexually attracted to members of the opposite sex.

hew v hewing, hewed 1 chop, cut with axe. 2 carve.

hexagon n figure with six angles. **hexagonal** adj

hey interj expression of surprise or for catching attention.

heyday n bloom, prime.

hiatus n, pl **-tuses, -tus** break or gap.

hibernate v pass the winter, esp. in a torpid state. **hibernation** n

hiccup, hiccough n/v (have) spasm of the breathing organs with an abrupt sound.

hickory n, pl **-ries** 1 N Amer. nut-bearing tree. 2 its tough wood.

hide¹ 🛈 v hiding, hid, hidden 1 put, keep out of sight. 2 conceal oneself.

hide² 🛈 n skin of animal. **hiding** n Sl thrashing. **hidebound** adj 1 restricted. 2 narrow-minded.

———— THESAURUS ————

heritage n = **inheritance**, legacy, birthright, tradition, endowment

hero n = **protagonist**, leading man; = **star**, champion, victor, superstar, conqueror

hesitate v = **waver**, delay, pause, wait, doubt ≠ **be decisive**; = **be reluctant**, be unwilling, shrink from, think twice, scruple ≠ **be**

determined

hide¹ v = **conceal**, stash (Inf), secrete, put out of sight ≠ **display**; = **go into hiding**, take cover, keep out of sight, hole up, lie low; = **keep secret**, suppress, withhold, keep quiet about, hush up ≠ **disclose**

hide² n = **skin**, leather, pelt

hideous 🛈 adj repulsive, revolting.
hierarchy 🛈 n, pl **–chies** system of
persons or things arranged in
graded order. **hierarchical** adj
hieroglyphic adj **1** of picture
writing, as used in ancient Egypt.
♦ n **2** symbol representing object,
concept or sound.
hi–fi adj short for HIGH–FIDELITY. ♦ n
high–fidelity equipment.
high 🛈 adj **1** tall, lofty. **2** far up. **3**
(of sound) acute in pitch. **4**
expensive. **5** of great importance,
quality, or rank. **6** Inf in state of
euphoria. ♦ adv **7** at, to a height.
highly adv **highness** n **1** quality of
being high. **2** (with cap.) title of
royal person. **highbrow** n/adj
intellectual. **high–fidelity** adj of
high–quality sound reproducing
equipment. **high–handed** adj
domineering. **highlands** pl n area
of relatively high ground. **highlight**
n **1** outstanding feature. ♦ v **2**
emphasize. **highly strung**
excitable, nervous. **high–rise** adj of
building that has many storeys.

high–tech adj using sophisticated
technology. **high time** latest
possible time. **highwayman** n
formerly, horseman who robbed
travellers.
highway n US and Canad main
road for fast–moving traffic.
hijack 🛈 v divert or wrongfully
take command of a vehicle (esp.
aircraft). **hijacker** n
hike 🛈 v **1** walk a long way (for
pleasure) in country. **2** pull (up),
hitch. **hiker** n
hill 🛈 n **1** natural elevation, small
mountain. **2** mound. **hillock** n little
hill. **hilly** adj
hilt n handle of sword etc.
him pron object of HE. **himself** pron
emphatic form of HE.
hind¹ n female of deer.
hind² adj **hinder, hindmost** at the
back, posterior.
hinder 🛈 v obstruct, impede,
delay. **hindrance** n
hinge n **1** movable joint, as that
on which door hangs. ♦ v **2** attach
with hinge. **3** depend on.

——— THESAURUS ———

hideous adj = **ugly**, revolting,
ghastly, monstrous, grotesque
≠ **beautiful**
hierarchy n = **grading**, ranking,
social order, pecking order, class
system
high adj = **tall**, towering, soaring,
steep, elevated ≠ **short**;
= **extreme**, great, acute, severe,
extraordinary ≠ **low**; = **strong**,
violent, extreme, blustery, squally;
= **important**, chief, powerful,
superior, eminent ≠ **lowly**;

= **high–pitched**, piercing, shrill,
penetrating, strident ≠ **deep** ♦ adv
= **way up**, aloft, far up, to a great
height
hijack v = **seize**, take over,
commandeer, expropriate
hike n = **walk**, march, trek,
ramble, tramp ♦ v = **walk**, march,
trek, ramble, tramp, = **hitch up**,
raise, lift, pull up, jack up
hill n = **mount**, fell, height,
mound, hilltop
hinder v = **obstruct**, stop, check,

hint ⊕ n **1** slight indication. **2** piece of advice. **3** small amount. ♦ v **4** give hint.

hinterland n district lying behind coast, port etc.

hip n **1** either side of body below waist and above thigh. **2** fruit of rose.

hippie n person who rejects conventional dress and lifestyle.

hippopotamus n, pl **-muses**, **-mi** large Afr. animal living in rivers.

hire ⊕ v **1** obtain temporary use of by payment. **2** engage for wage. ♦ n **3** hiring or being hired. **4** payment for use of thing. **hire-purchase** n purchase of goods by instalments.

hirsute adj hairy.

his pron/adj belonging to him.

hiss ⊕ v **1** make sharp sound of letter s. **2** express disapproval thus.

♦ n **3** hissing.

history ⊕ n, pl **-ries 1** (record of) past events. **2** study of these. **historian** n **historic** adj **historical** adj

histrionic adj excessively theatrical, insincere, artificial in manner. **histrionics** pl n behaviour like this.

hit ⊕ v **hitting, hit 1** strike with blow or missile. **2** affect injuriously. **3** find. **4** light (upon). ♦ n **5** blow. **6** success. **hit man** hired assassin.

hitch ⊕ v **1** fasten with loop etc. **2** raise with jerk. **3** be caught or fastened. ♦ n **4** difficulty. **5** knot. **6** jerk. **hitchhike** v travel by begging free rides. **hitchhiker** n

hither adv to this place. **hitherto** adv up to now.

HIV human immunodeficiency

———— THESAURUS ————

block, delay ≠ **help**
hint n = **clue**, suggestion, implication, indication, pointer; (often plural) = **advice**, help, tip(s), suggestion(s), pointer(s); = **trace**, touch, suggestion, dash, suspicion ♦ v (sometimes with **at**) = **suggest**, indicate, imply, intimate, insinuate
hire v = **employ**, commission, take on, engage, appoint; = **rent**, charter, lease, let, engage ♦ n = **rental**, hiring, rent, lease
hiss v = **whistle**, wheeze, whiz, whirr, sibilate; = **jeer**, mock, deride ♦ n = **fizz**, buzz, hissing, fizzing, sibilation
history n = **the past**, antiquity, yesterday, yesteryear, olden days;

= **chronicle**, record, story, account, narrative
hit v = **strike**, beat, knock, bang, slap; = **collide with**, run into, bump into, clash with, smash into; = **affect**, damage, harm, ruin, devastate; = **reach**, gain, achieve, arrive at, accomplish ♦ n = **blow**, knock, stroke, belt (Inf); rap; = **success**, winner, triumph, smash (Inf), sensation; **hit it off** = (Inf) **get on (well) with**, click (Sl), be on good terms, get on like a house on fire (Inf)
hitch n = **problem**, catch, difficulty, hold-up, obstacle ♦ v = (Inf) **hitchhike**, thumb a lift; = **fasten**, join, attach, couple, tie

virus.

hive *n* structure in which bees live. **hive off** transfer.

hives *pl n* eruptive skin disease.

HM His (or Her) Majesty.

HMS His (or Her) Majesty's Service or Ship.

hoard *n* **1** store, esp. hidden. ♦ *v* **2** amass and hide.

hoarding *n* large board for displaying advertisements.

hoarse *adj* sounding husky.

hoary *adj* **hoarier, hoariest 1** grey with age. **2** greyish–white. **3** very old. **hoarfrost** *n* frozen dew.

hoax *n* **1** practical joke. ♦ *v* **2** play trick upon.

hob *n* top area of cooking stove.

hobble *v* **1** walk lamely. **2** tie legs together. ♦ *n* **3** limping gait.

hobby ❶ *n, pl* **–bies** favourite occupation as pastime.

hobbyhorse *n* **1** favourite topic. **2** toy horse.

hobgoblin *n* mischievous fairy.

hobnob *v* **–nobbing, –nobbed 1** drink together. **2** be familiar (with).

hobo *n, pl* **–bos** *US & Canad*

shiftless, wandering person.

hock¹ *n* backward–pointing joint on leg of horse etc.

hock² *n* dry white wine.

hockey *n* **1** team game played on a field with ball and curved sticks. **2** *US & Canad* ice hockey.

hod *n* **1** small trough for carrying bricks etc. **2** coal scuttle.

hoe *n* **1** tool for weeding, breaking ground etc. ♦ *v* **2** work with hoe.

hog *n* **1** pig. **2** greedy person. ♦ *v* **3** *Inf* eat, use (something) selfishly.

hoist ❶ *v* raise aloft, raise with tackle etc.

hold¹ ❶ *v* **holding, held 1** keep in hands. **2** maintain in position. **3** contain. **4** occupy. **5** carry on. **6** detain. **7** be in force. **8** occur. ♦ *n* **9** grasp. **10** influence. **holdall** *n* large travelling bag. **holder** *n* **holding** *n* (*oft. pl*) property. **hold–up** *n* **1** armed robbery. **2** delay.

hold² space in ship or aircraft for cargo.

hole ❶ *n* **1** hollow place. **2** perforation. **3** opening **4** *Inf* unattractive place. **holey** *adj*

hobby *n* = **pastime**, relaxation, leisure pursuit, diversion, avocation

hoist *v* = **raise**, lift, erect, elevate, heave ♦ *n* = **lift**, crane, elevator, winch

hold¹ keep *v* = **embrace**, grasp, clutch, hug, squeeze; = **accommodate**, take, contain, seat, have a capacity for; = **consider**, think, believe, judge,

regard ≠ **deny**; = **occupy**, have, fill, maintain, retain; = **conduct**, convene, call, run, preside over ≠ **cancel** ♦ *n* = **grip**, grasp, clasp; = **foothold**, footing; = **control**, influence, mastery

hole *n* = **cavity**, pit, hollow, chamber, cave; = **opening**, crack, tear, gap, breach; = **burrow**, den, earth, shelter, lair; = (*Inf*) **hovel**, dump (*Inf*), dive (*Sl*), slum; = (*Inf*)

holiday ⊕ n day(s) of rest from work etc., esp. spent away from home.

holistic adj considering the complete person, esp. in treatment of disease.

hollow ⊕ adj 1 having a cavity, not solid. 2 empty. 3 insincere. ◆ n 4 cavity, hole, valley. ◆ v 5 make hollow. 6 excavate.

holly n evergreen shrub with prickly leaves and red berries.

hollyhock n tall plant bearing many large flowers.

holocaust ⊕ n great destruction of life, esp. by fire.

hologram n three-dimensional photographic image.

holster n leather case for pistol, hung from belt etc.

holy ⊕ adj –lier, –liest 1 belonging, devoted to God. 2 free from sin. 3 divine. 4 consecrated. **holily** adv **holiness** n

homage ⊕ n tribute, respect.

home ⊕ n 1 dwelling-place. 2 residence. ◆ adj 3 of home. 4 native. 5 in home. ◆ adv 6 to, at one's home. 7 to the point. ◆ v 8 direct or be directed onto a point or target. **homeless** adj **homelessness** n **homely** adv 1 unpretentious. 2 domesticated. **homeward** adj/adv **homewards** adv **home-made** adj **homesick** adj depressed by absence from home. **homesickness** n **homespun** adj 1 domestic. 2 simple. **homework** n school work done at home.

homeopathy n treatment of disease by small doses of drug that produces symptoms of the disease in healthy people. **homeopathic** adj

homestead n 1 a house or estate and the adjoining land and buildings, esp. on a farm. 2 land assigned to a N American settler.

homicide ⊕ n 1 killing of human being. 2 killer. **homicidal** adj

————— THESAURUS —————

predicament, spot (Inf), fix (Inf), mess, jam (Inf)

holiday n = vacation, leave, break, time off, recess; = festival, fête, celebration, feast, gala

hollow adj = empty, vacant, void, unfilled ≠ solid; = worthless, useless, vain, meaningless, pointless ≠ meaningful; = dull, low, deep, muted, toneless ≠ vibrant ◆ n = cavity, hole, bowl, depression, pit ≠ mound; = valley, dale, glen, dell, dingle ≠ hill ◆ v (often followed by out) = scoop out, dig out, excavate, gouge out

holocaust n = devastation, destruction, genocide, annihilation, conflagration

holy adj = sacred, blessed, hallowed, venerable, consecrated ≠ unsanctified; = devout, godly, religious, pure, righteous ≠ sinful

homage n = respect, honour, worship, devotion, reverence ≠ contempt

home n = dwelling, house, residence, abode, habitation; = birthplace, homeland, home town, native land ◆ adj = domestic, local, internal, native

homily n, pl **-lies** sermon.

homogeneous adj **1** formed of uniform parts. **2** similar.
homogeneity n **homogenize** v break up fat globules in milk and cream to distribute them evenly.

homonym n word of same form as another, but of different sense.

homosexual n/adj (person) sexually attracted to members of the same sex. **homosexuality** n

hone ⊕ v sharpen (on whetstone).

honest ⊕ adj **1** not cheating, lying, stealing etc. **2** genuine.
honestly adv **honesty** n

honey n sweet fluid made by bees. **honeycomb** n **1** wax structure in hexagonal cells. ◆ v **2** fill with cells or perforations.
honeymoon n holiday taken by newly wedded pair. **honeysuckle** n climbing plant.

honk n **1** call of wild goose. **2** sound of motor-horn. ◆ v **3** make this sound.

honour ⊕ n **1** personal integrity. **2** renown. **3** reputation. ◆ v **4** respect highly. **5** confer honour on. **6** accept or pay (bill etc.) when due. **honourable** adj
honorary adj conferred for the sake of honour only.

hood n **1** covering for head and neck. **2** hoodlike thing. **hoodwink** v deceive.

hoodlum n gangster.

hoof n, pl **hooves, hoofs** horny casing of foot of horse etc.

hook ⊕ n **1** bent piece of metal etc., for catching hold, hanging up etc. **2** something resembling hook in shape or function. ◆ v **3** grasp, catch, hold, as with hook.
hooked adj **1** shaped like hook. **2** caught. **3** Sl addicted.

hooligan ⊕ n violent, irresponsible (young) person.
hooliganism n

hoon n Aust & NZ slang loutish youth who drives irresponsibly.

————— THESAURUS —————

homicide n = **murder**, killing, manslaughter, slaying, bloodshed

hone v = **improve**, better, enhance, upgrade, refine

honest adj = **trustworthy**, upright, ethical, honourable, reputable ≠ **dishonest**; = **open**, direct, frank, plain, sincere ≠ **secretive**

honour n = **integrity**, morality, honesty, goodness, fairness ≠ **dishonour**; = **prestige**, credit, reputation, glory, fame ≠ **disgrace**; = **reputation**, standing, prestige, image, status;

= acclaim, praise, recognition, compliments, homage
≠ **contempt** ◆ v = **acclaim**, praise, decorate, commemorate, commend; = **respect**, value, esteem, prize, appreciate ≠ **scorn**; = **fulfil**, keep, carry out, observe, discharge; = **pay**, take, accept, pass, acknowledge ≠ **refuse**

hook n = **fastener**, catch, link, peg, clasp ◆ v = **fasten**, fix, secure, clasp; = **catch**, land, trap, entrap

hooligan n = **delinquent**, vandal, ruffian, lager lout, yob or yobbo (Brit sl)

hoop ⊕ n rigid circular band of metal, wood etc.

hooray interj exclamation of joy or applause.

hoot n 1 owl's cry or similar sound. 2 cry of derision 3 Inf funny person or thing. ◆ v 4 utter hoot.

hooter n device (e.g. horn) to emit hooting sound.

Hoover ® n 1 vacuum cleaner. ◆ v 2 (without cap.) vacuum.

hop¹ ⊕ v hopping, hopped 1 spring on one foot. ◆ n 2 leap, skip.

hop² n 1 climbing plant with bitter cones used to flavour beer etc. ◆ pl 2 the cones.

hope ⊕ n 1 expectation of something desired. 2 thing that gives, or object of, this feeling. ◆ v 3 feel hope (for). **hopeful** adj **hopefully** adv **hopeless** adj

hopper n 1 one who hops. 2 device for feeding material into mill.

hopscotch n children's game of hopping in pattern drawn on ground.

horde ⊕ n large crowd.

horizon ⊕ n line where earth and sky seem to meet. **horizontal** adj parallel with horizon, level.

hormone n substance secreted from gland which stimulates organs of the body.

horn n 1 hard projection on heads of certain animals. 2 various things made of, or resembling it. 3 wind instrument. 4 device (esp. in car) emitting sound. **horny** adj

hornpipe n sailor's lively dance.

hornet n large insect of wasp family.

horoscope n telling of person's fortune by studying positions of planets etc. at his or her birth.

horrendous adj horrific.

horror ⊕ n 1 terror. 2 loathing, fear of. 3 its cause. **horrible** adj 1 exciting horror, hideous, shocking. 2 disagreeable. **horribly** adv **horrid** adj 1 unpleasant, repulsive 2 Inf unkind. **horrific** adj particularly horrible. **horrify** v 1 cause horror (in). 2 shock.

hors d'oeuvre n small dish served before main meal.

horse ⊕ n 1 four-footed animal used for riding. 2 cavalry. 3 frame for support etc. **horsy** adj 1 devoted to horses. 2 like a horse.

horse chestnut tree with white or pink flowers and large nuts.

horsefly n large bloodsucking fly.

horseman n rider on horse.

horsepower n unit of power of

——— THESAURUS ———

hoop n = **ring**, band, loop, wheel, round

hop¹ v = **jump**, spring, bound, leap, skip ◆ n = **jump**, step, spring, bound, leap

hope v = **believe**, look forward to, cross your fingers ◆ n = **belief**, confidence, expectation, longing, dream ≠ despair

horde n = **crowd**, mob, swarm, host, band

horizon n = **skyline**, view, vista

horror n = **terror**, fear, alarm, panic, dread

engine etc. **horseradish** n plant with pungent root. **horseshoe** n protective U–shaped piece of iron nailed to horse's hoof.

horticulture n art or science of gardening.

hose n 1 flexible tube for conveying liquid or gas. 2 stockings. ◆ v 3 water with hose.

hosiery n stockings.

hoser n 1 US sl a person who swindles or deceives others. 2 Canad sl an unsophisticated, esp. rural, person.

hospice n home for care of the terminally ill.

hospital n institution for care of sick. **hospitalize** v send or admit to hospital.

hospitality 🟊 n friendly and liberal reception of strangers or guests. **hospitable** adj

host¹ 🟊 n 1 one who entertains another. 2 innkeeper. 3 compere of show. ◆ v 4 act as a host.

host² 🟊 n large number.

hostage 🟊 n person taken or given as pledge or security.

hostel n building providing accommodation at low cost for students etc.

hostile 🟊 adj 1 antagonistic. 2 warlike. 3 of an enemy. **hostility** n, pl –ties 1 enmity. ◆ pl 2 acts of warfare.

hot 🟊 adj **hotter, hottest** 1 of high temperature. 2 angry. 3 new. 4 spicy. **hotly** adv **hot air** Inf empty talk. **hotbed** n 1 bed of heated earth for young plants. 2 any place encouraging growth. **hot–blooded** adj excitable. **hot dog** hot sausage in split bread roll. **hotfoot** v/adv (go) quickly. **hothead** n intemperate person. **hothouse** n heated greenhouse. **hotline** n direct telephone link for emergency use. **hotplate** n heated plate on electric cooker. **hotchpotch** n 1 medley. 2 dish of many ingredients.

hotel n commercial establishment

— THESAURUS —

horse n = **nag**, mount, mare, colt, filly

hospitality n = **welcome**, warmth, kindness, friendliness, sociability

host¹, hostess n = **master of ceremonies**, proprietor, innkeeper, landlord or landlady; = **presenter**, compere (Brit), anchorman or anchorwoman ◆ v = **present**, introduce, compere (Brit), front (Inf)

host² n = **multitude**, lot, load (Inf), wealth, array

hostage n = **captive**, prisoner,

pawn

hostile adj = **antagonistic**, opposed, contrary, ill–disposed; = **unfriendly**, belligerent, antagonistic, rancorous, ill–disposed ≠ friendly

hot adj = **heated**, boiling, steaming, roasting, searing; = **warm**, close, stifling, humid, torrid ≠ cold; = **spicy**, pungent, peppery, piquant, biting ≠ mild; = **intense**, passionate, heated, spirited, fierce; = **new**, latest, fresh, recent, up to date ≠ old

providing lodging and meals.
hotelier n

hound ❼ n 1 hunting dog. ◆ v 2 chase, urge, pursue.

hour n 1 twenty–fourth part of day. 2 sixty minutes. 3 appointed time. ◆ pl 4 fixed periods for work etc. **hourly** adv/adj **hourglass** n timing device in which sand trickles between two glass compartments.

house ❼ n 1 building for human habitation. 2 legislative assembly. 3 family. 4 business firm. ◆ v 5 give or receive shelter, lodging, or storage. 6 cover or contain.
housing n 1 (providing of) houses. 2 part designed to cover, protect, contain. **houseboat** n boat used as home. **household** n inmates of house collectively. **housekeeper** n person managing affairs of household. **housekeeping** n (money for) running household. **housewife** n woman who runs her own household.

hovel n lowly dwelling.

hover ❼ v 1 hang in the air. 2 loiter. 3 be in state of indecision. **hovercraft** n type of craft which can travel over both land and sea on a cushion of air.

how adv 1 in what way. 2 by what means. 3 in what condition. 4 to what degree. **however** conj 1 nevertheless. ◆ adv 2 in whatever way, degree. 3 all the same.

howl ❼ v/n (utter) long loud cry. **howler** n Inf stupid mistake.

HP, h.p. hire–purchase.

HQ headquarters.

HRH His (or Her) Royal Highness.

hub ❼ n 1 middle part of wheel. 2 central point of activity.

hubbub n confused noise.

huddle ❼ n 1 crowded mass 2 Inf impromptu conference. ◆ v 3 heap, crowd together. 4 hunch.

hue ❼ n colour.

huff n 1 passing mood of anger. ◆

———— THESAURUS ————

hound v = **harass**, harry, bother, provoke, annoy **collective noun** pack

house n = **home**, residence, dwelling, pad (Sl), homestead; = **household**, family; = **firm**, company, business, organization, outfit (Inf); = **assembly**, parliament, Commons, legislative body ◆ v = **accommodate**, quarter, take in, put up, lodge; = **contain**, keep, hold, cover, store; = **take**, accommodate, sleep, provide shelter for, give a bed to
hover v = **float**, fly, hang, drift,

flutter; = **linger**, loiter, hang about or around (Inf); = **waver**, fluctuate, dither (Chiefly Brit), oscillate, vacillate

howl v = **cry**, scream, roar, weep, yell ◆ n = **baying**, cry, bay, bark, barking

hub n = **centre**, heart, focus, core, middle

huddle v = **curl up**, crouch, hunch up; = **crowd**, press, gather, collect, squeeze ◆ n = (Inf) **discussion**, conference, meeting, powwow, confab (Inf)

hue n = **colour**, tone, shade, dye,

v **2** make or become angry. **3** blow.

hug ⊕ *v* **hugging, hugged 1** clasp tightly in the arms. **2** keep close to. ♦ *n* fond embrace.

huge ⊕ *adj* very big. **hugely** *adv* very much.

hulk *n* **1** body of abandoned vessel. **2** large, unwieldy person or thing. **hulking** *adj*

hull ⊕ *n* **1** frame, body of ship. **2** calyx of strawberry etc. ♦ *v* **3** remove shell, hull from (fruit, seeds).

hullabaloo *n, pl* **–loos 1** uproar. **2** clamour.

hum ⊕ *v* **humming, hummed 1** make low continuous sound. **2** sing with closed lips. ♦ *n* **3** humming sound. **hummingbird** *n* very small Amer. bird whose wings make humming noise.

human ⊕ *adj* **1** of man. **2** relating to, characteristic of, man's nature. **humane** *adj* **1** kind. **2** merciful. **humanism** *n* belief in human effort rather than religion. **humanitarian**

n **1** philanthropist. ♦ *adj* **2** philanthropic. **humanity** *n* **1** human nature. **2** human race. **3** kindliness. ♦ *pl* **4** study of literature, philosophy, the arts. **humanize** *v*

humble ⊕ *adj* **1** lowly, modest. ♦ *v* **2** humiliate. **humbly** *adv*

humbug *n* **1** imposter. **2** sham, nonsense. **3** sweet of boiled sugar.

humdrum *adj* commonplace, dull.

humid *adj* moist, damp.

humidifier *n* device for increasing amount of water vapour in air in room etc. **humidity** *n*

humiliate ⊕ *v* lower dignity of, abase, mortify. **humiliation** *n*

humility *n* **1** state of being humble. **2** meekness.

hummock *n* low knoll, hillock.

humour ⊕ *n* **1** faculty of saying or perceiving what excites amusement. **2** amusing speech, writing etc. **3** state of mind, mood. ♦ *v* **4** gratify, indulge.

humorist *n* person who acts, speaks, writes humorously.

tint

hug *v* = **embrace**, cuddle, squeeze, clasp, enfold ♦ *n* = **embrace**, squeeze, bear hug, clinch (*Sl*), clasp

huge *adj* = **enormous**, large, massive, vast, tremendous ≠ **tiny**

hull *n* = **framework**, casing, body, covering, frame

hum *v* = **drone**, buzz, murmur, throb, vibrate; = (*Inf*) **be busy**, buzz, bustle, stir, pulse

human *adj* = **mortal**, manlike

≠ **nonhuman** ♦ *n* = **human being**, person, individual, creature, mortal ≠ **nonhuman**

humble *adj* = **modest**, meek, unassuming, unpretentious, self-effacing ≠ **proud**; = **lowly**, poor, mean, simple, ordinary

≠ **distinguished** ♦ *v* = **humiliate**, disgrace, crush, subdue, chasten ≠ **exalt**

humiliate *v* = **embarrass**, shame, humble, crush, put down

≠ **honour**

humorous *adj*

hump *n* 1 normal or deforming lump, esp. on back. ♦ *v* 2 make hump–shaped. 3 *Sl* carry or heave. **humpback** *n* person with hump. **humus** *n* decayed vegetable and animal mould.

hunch ❶ *n* 1 *Inf* intuition. 2 hump. ♦ *v* 3 bend into hump. **hunchback** *n* humpback.

hundred *n/adj* cardinal number, ten times ten. **hundredth** *adj* ordinal number. **hundredweight** *n* weight of 112 lbs (50.8 kg), 20th part of ton.

hunger ❶ *n/v* 1 (have) discomfort from lack of food. 2 (have) strong desire. **hungrily** *adv* **hungry** *adj* having keen appetite.

hunk ❶ *n* thick piece.

hunt ❶ *v* 1 seek out to kill or capture for sport or food. 2 search

(for). ♦ *n* 3 chase, search. 4 (party organized for) hunting. **hunter** *n*

hurdle ❶ *n* 1 portable frame of bars for temporary fences or for jumping over. 2 obstacle. ♦ *v* 3 race over hurdles.

hurdy–gurdy *n, pl* **–dies** mechanical musical instrument.

hurl ❶ *v* throw violently.

hurly–burly *n* loud confusion.

hurrah, hurray *interj* exclamation of joy or applause.

hurricane ❶ *n* very strong, violent wind or storm.

hurry ❶ *v* **–rying, –ried** 1 (cause to) move or act in great haste. ♦ *n* 2 undue haste. 3 eagerness. **hurriedly** *adv*

hurt ❶ *v* **hurting, hurt** 1 injure, damage, give pain to. 2 feel pain. ♦ *n* 3 wound, injury, harm. **hurtful** *adj*

——————— THESAURUS ———————

humour *n* = **comedy**, funniness, fun, amusement, funny side ≠ **seriousness**; = **mood**, spirits, temper, disposition, frame of mind ♦ *v* = **indulge**, accommodate, go along with, flatter, gratify ≠ **oppose**

hunch *n* = **feeling**, idea, impression, suspicion, intuition ♦ *v* = **crouch**, bend, curve, arch, draw in

hunger *n* = **appetite**, emptiness, hungriness, ravenousness; = **starvation**, famine, malnutrition, undernourishment; = **desire**, appetite, craving, ache, lust

hunk *n* = **lump**, piece, chunk, block, mass

hunt *v* = **stalk**, track, chase, pursue, trail ♦ *v* = **search**, hunting, investigation, chase, pursuit

hurdle *n* = **obstacle**, difficulty, barrier, handicap, hazard; = **fence**, barrier, barricade

hurl *v* = **throw**, fling, launch, cast, pitch

hurricane *n* = **storm**, gale, tornado, cyclone, typhoon

hurry *v* = **rush**, fly, dash, scurry, scoot ≠ **dawdle** ♦ *n* = **rush**, haste, speed, urgency, flurry ≠ **slowness**

hurt *v* = **injure**, damage, wound, cut, disable ≠ **heal**; = **ache**, be sore, be painful, burn, smart; = **harm**, injure, ill–treat, maltreat ♦ *n* = **distress**, suffering, pain, grief,

hurtle ⊕ v rush violently.

husband ⊕ n 1 married man. ♦ v 2 economize. 3 use to best advantage. **husbandry** n 1 farming. 2 economy.

hush ⊕ v 1 make or be silent. ♦ n 2 stillness. 3 quietness.

husk n 1 dry covering of certain seeds and fruits. ♦ v 2 remove husk from. **husky** adj 1 rough in tone. 2 hoarse, throaty.

husky n pl **huskies** Arctic sledge dog.

hussy n, pl –**sies** cheeky young woman.

hustings pl n political campaigning.

hustle v 1 push about, jostle, hurry. ♦ n 2 lively activity.

hut ⊕ n small house or shelter.

hutch n cage for rabbits etc.

hyacinth n bulbous plant with bell-shaped flowers.

hybrid ⊕ n 1 offspring of two plants or animals of different species. ♦ adj 2 crossbred.

hydrangea n ornamental shrub.

hydrant n water-pipe with nozzle for hose.

hydraulic adj concerned with, operated by, pressure transmitted through liquid in pipe.

hydro adj Canad electricity as supplied to a residence, business, institution, etc.

hydrochloric acid strong colourless acid.

hydroelectric adj pert. to generation of electricity by use of water.

hydrofoil n fast, light vessel with hull raised out of water at speed.

hydrogen n colourless gas which combines with oxygen to form water. **hydrogen bomb** atom bomb of enormous power.

hydrogen peroxide colourless liquid used as antiseptic and bleach.

hydrophobia n aversion to water, esp. as symptom of rabies.

hyena n wild animal related to dog.

hygiene ⊕ n (study of) principles and practice of health and cleanliness. **hygienic** adj

hymen n membrane partly covering vagina of virgin.

hymn ⊕ n 1 song of praise, esp. to God. ♦ v 2 praise in song.

———— THESAURUS ————

misery ≠ happiness ♦ adj
= **injured**, wounded, damaged, harmed, cut ≠ healed; = **upset**, wounded, crushed, offended, aggrieved ≠ calmed
hurtle v = **rush**, charge, race, shoot, fly
husband n = **partner**, spouse, mate, better half (humorous) ♦ v
= **conserve**, budget, save, store,

hoard ≠ squander
hush v = **quieten**, silence, mute, muzzle, shush ♦ n = **quiet**, silence, calm, peace, tranquillity
hut n = **cabin**, shack, shanty, hovel
hybrid n = **crossbreed**, cross, mixture, compound, composite;
= **mixture**, compound, composite, amalgam
hygiene n = **cleanliness**,

hype ❶ *n* **1** intensive publicity. ♦ *v* **2** publicize.

hyperbole *n* rhetorical exaggeration.

hypermarket *n* huge self-service store.

hypertension *n* abnormally high blood pressure.

hyphen *n* short line (–) indicating that two words or syllables are to be connected. **hyphenate** *v* **hyphenated** *adj*

hypnosis *n* induced state like deep sleep in which subject acts on external suggestion. **hypnotic** *adj* **hypnotism** *n* **hypnotize** *v* affect with hypnosis.

hypochondria *n* morbid depression without cause, about one's own health. **hypochondriac** *adj/n*

hypocrisy ❶ *n, pl* –**sies 1**

assuming of false appearance of virtue. **2** insincerity. **hypocrite** *n* **hypocritical** *adj*

hypodermic *adj* **1** introduced, injected beneath the skin. ♦ *n* **2** hypodermic syringe or needle.

hypotenuse *n* side of right–angled triangle opposite the right angle.

hypothermia *n* condition of having body temperature reduced to dangerously low level.

hypothesis ❶ *n, pl* –**ses 1** suggested explanation of something. **2** assumption as basis of reasoning. **hypothetical** *adj*

hysterectomy *n, pl* –**mies** surgical operation for removing uterus.

hysteria ❶ *n* **1** mental disorder with emotional outbursts. **2** fit of crying or laughing. **hysterical** *adj* **hysterics** *pl n* fits of hysteria.

———— THESAURUS ————

sanitation, disinfection, sterility

hymn *n* = **religious song**, song of praise, carol, chant, anthem

hype *n* = (*Sl*) **publicity**, promotion, plugging (*Inf*), razzmatazz (*Sl*), brouhaha

hypocrisy *n* = **insincerity**,

pretence, deception, cant, duplicity ≠ **sincerity**

hypothesis *n* = **theory**, premise, proposition, assumption, thesis

hysteria *n* = **frenzy**, panic, madness, agitation, delirium

I i

I pron the pronoun of the first person singular.

ibis n storklike bird.

ice n 1 frozen water. 2 ice cream. ♦ v 3 cover, become covered with ice. 4 cool with ice. 5 cover with icing. **icicle** n hanging spike of ice. **icing** n mixture of sugar and water etc. used to decorate cakes. **icy** adj **icier, iciest** 1 covered with ice. 2 cold. 3 unfriendly. **iceberg** n large floating mass of ice. **ice cream** sweet creamy frozen dessert. **ice hockey** team game played on ice with puck. **ice skate** boot with steel blade for gliding over ice. **ice-skate** v

icon n religious image. **iconoclast** n one who attacks established ideas.

idea ❶ n 1 notion. 2 conception. 3 plan, aim. **ideal** n 1 idea of perfection. 2 perfect person or thing. ♦ adj 3 perfect. **idealism** n tendency to seek perfection in everything. **idealist** n 1 one who strives after the ideal. 2 impractical person. **idealistic** adj **idealization** n

idealize v portray as ideal. **ideally** adv

identity ❶ n, pl **-ties** 1 individuality. 2 state of being exactly alike. **identical** adj very same. **identifiable** adj **identification** n 1 recognition. 2 identifying document. **identify** v 1 establish identity of. 2 associate (oneself) with. 3 treat as identical.

ideology n, pl **-gies** body of ideas, beliefs of group, nation etc. **ideological** adj

idiom n expression peculiar to a language or group. **idiomatic** adj **idiosyncrasy** n, pl **-sies** peculiarity of mind.

idiot ❶ n 1 mentally deficient person. 2 stupid person. **idiocy** n **idiotic** adj utterly stupid.

idle ❶ adj 1 unemployed. 2 lazy. 3 useless. 4 groundless. ♦ v 5 be idle. 6 run slowly in neutral gear. **idleness** n **idler** n **idly** adv

idol ❶ n 1 image worshipped as deity. 2 object of excessive devotion. **idolatry** n **idolize** v love or admire to excess.

THESAURUS
---

idea n = **notion**, thought, view, teaching, opinion; = **intention**, aim, purpose, object, plan

identity n = **individuality**, self, character, personality, existence

idiot n = **fool**, moron, twit (*Inf*, *chiefly Brit*), chump, imbecile

idle adj = **unoccupied**, unemployed, redundant, inactive ≠ occupied; = **unused**, inactive, out of order, out of service; = **lazy**, slow, slack, sluggish, lax ≠ busy; = **useless**, vain, pointless, unsuccessful, ineffective ≠ useful

idyll n (poem describing) picturesque or charming scene or episode. **idyllic** adj delightful.

i.e. that is.

if 🖝 conj **1** on condition or supposition that. **2** whether. **3** although.

igloo n, pl **-loos** domed house made of snow.

ignite 🖝 v (cause to) burn.

ignition n **1** act of kindling or setting on fire. **2** car's electrical firing system.

ignoble adj **1** mean, base. **2** of low birth.

ignominy n **1** public disgrace. **2** shameful act. **ignominious** adj

ignoramus n ignorant person.

ignore 🖝 v disregard, leave out of account. **ignorance** n lack of knowledge. **ignorant** adj **1** lacking knowledge. **2** uneducated.

iguana n large tropical American lizard.

ill 🖝 adj **1** not in good health. **2** bad, evil. **3** harmful. ◆ n **4** evil, harm. ◆ adv **5** badly. **6** hardly.

illness n **ill-advised** adj imprudent. **ill-disposed** adj unsympathetic. **ill-fated** adj unfortunate. **ill-gotten** adj obtained dishonestly. **ill-treat** v treat cruelly. **ill will** hostility.

illegal 🖝 adj against the law.

illegible adj unable to be read.

illegitimate adj **1** born to unmarried parents. **2** irregular. **illegitimacy** n

illicit 🖝 adj **1** illegal. **2** prohibited, forbidden.

illiterate adj **1** unable to read or write. ◆ n **2** illiterate person. **illiteracy** n

illogical adj not logical.

illuminate 🖝 v **1** light up. **2** clarify. **3** decorate with lights or colours. **illumination** n

illusion 🖝 n deceptive appearance

——————— THESAURUS ———————

idol n = **hero**, pin-up, favourite, pet, darling; = **graven image**, god, deity

if conj = **provided**, assuming, given that, providing, supposing

ignite v = **catch fire**, burn, burst into flames, inflame, flare up; = **set fire to**, light, set alight, torch, kindle

ignore v = **pay no attention to**, neglect, disregard, slight, overlook ≠ **pay attention to**

ill adj = **unwell**, sick, poorly (Inf), diseased, weak ≠ **healthy**; = **harmful**, bad, damaging, evil, foul ≠ **favourable** ◆ n = **problem**,

trouble, suffering, worry, injury ◆ adv = **badly**, unfortunately, unfavourably, inauspiciously; = **hardly**, barely, scarcely, just, only just ≠ **well**

illegal adj = **unlawful**, banned, forbidden, prohibited, criminal ≠ **legal**

illicit adj = **illegal**, criminal, prohibited, unlawful, illegitimate ≠ **legal**; = **forbidden**, improper, immoral, guilty, clandestine

illuminate v = **light up**, brighten ≠ **darken**; = **explain**, interpret, make clear, clarify, clear up ≠ **obscure**

or belief. **illusionist** n conjuror.
illusory adj
illustrate ❶ v 1 provide with
pictures or examples. 2 explain by
examples. **illustration** n 1 picture,
diagram. 2 example.
illustrious adj 1 famous. 2
glorious.
image ❶ n 1 likeness. 2 optical
counterpart. 3 double, copy. 4
general impression. 5 word
picture. **imagery** n images
collectively.
imagine ❶ v 1 picture to oneself.
2 think. 3 conjecture. **imaginable**
adj **imaginary** adj existing only in
fantasy. **imagination** n 1 faculty of
making mental images of things
not present. 2 fancy. **imaginative**
adj
imbalance n lack of balance in
emphasis or proportion.
imbecile n 1 idiot. ◆ adj 2 idiotic.
imbibe v drink (in).

imbue v –buing, –bued instil, fill.
imitate ❶ v 1 take as model. 2
copy. **imitation** n 1 act of
imitating. 2 copy. 3 counterfeit. ◆
adj 4 synthetic. **imitative** adj
immaculate ❶ adj 1 spotless. 2
pure.
immaterial adj 1 unimportant. 2
not consisting of matter.
immature adj 1 not fully
developed. 2 lacking wisdom
because of youth.
immediate ❶ adj 1 occurring at
once. 2 closest. **immediately** adv
immense ❶ adj huge, vast.
immensely adv **immensity** n
immerse ❶ v 1 submerge in
liquid. 2 involve. 3 engross.
immersion n
immigrant n settler in foreign
country.
imminent ❶ adj liable to happen
soon. **imminence** n
immobile adj unable to move.

——————— THESAURUS ———————

illusion n = **delusion**,
misconception, misapprehension,
fancy, fallacy; = **fantasy**, vision,
hallucination, trick, spectre
illustrate v = **demonstrate**,
emphasize
image n = **thought**, idea, vision,
concept, impression; likeness,
mirror image; = **figure**, idol, icon,
fetish, talisman
imagine v = **envisage**, see,
picture, plan, think of; = **believe**,
think, suppose, assume, suspect
imitate v = **copy**, follow, repeat,
echo, emulate
immaculate adj = **clean**, spotless,

neat, spruce, squeaky–clean
≠ dirty; = **pure**, perfect,
impeccable, flawless, faultless
≠ corrupt
immediate adj = **instant**, prompt,
instantaneous, quick, on–the–spot
≠ later; = **nearest**, next, direct,
close, near ≠ far
immense adj = **huge**, great,
massive, vast, enormous ≠ tiny
immerse v = **engross**, involve,
absorb, busy, occupy; = **plunge**,
dip, submerge, sink, duck
imminent adj = **near**, coming,
close, approaching, gathering
≠ remote

immobility n **immobilize** v
immolate v kill, sacrifice.
immoral ❶ adj 1 corrupt. 2
promiscuous. **immorality** n
immortal ❶ adj 1 deathless. 2
famed for all time. ♦ n 3 person
living forever. **immortality** n
immortalize v
immune adj 1 protected (against a
disease etc.). 2 exempt. **immunity**
n, pl **–ties. immunization** n process
of making immune to disease.
immunize v
imp n 1 little devil. 2 mischievous
child.
impact ❶ n 1 collision. 2 profound
effect. **impacted** adj wedged.
impair ❶ v weaken, damage.
impairment n
impala n S Afr. antelope.
impale v pierce with sharp
instrument.
impart v 1 communicate. 2 give.
impartial adj 1 unbiased. 2 fair.
impartiality n
impassable adj blocked.
impasse ❶ n deadlock.

impassioned adj full of feeling,
ardent.
impassive adj 1 showing no
emotion. 2 calm.
impatient adj 1 irritable. 2
restless. **impatience** n
impeach v 1 charge, esp. with
treason or crime in office. 2
denounce. **impeachable** adj
impeachment n
impeccable ❶ adj faultless.
impede v hinder. **impediment** n 1
obstruction. 2 defect.
impel v **–pelling, –pelled** 1 induce.
2 drive.
impending ❶ adj imminent.
imperative ❶ adj 1 necessary. 2
peremptory. 3 Grammar
expressing command. ♦ n 4
Grammar imperative mood.
imperfect adj 1 having faults. 2
not complete. **imperfection** n
imperial ❶ adj 1 of empire, or
emperor. 2 majestic. 3 denoting
weights and measures formerly
official in Brit. **imperialism** n policy
of acquiring empire.

──────── THESAURUS ────────

immoral adj = **wicked**, bad,
wrong, corrupt, indecent ≠ **moral**
immortal adj = **timeless**, eternal,
everlasting, lasting, traditional
≠ **ephemeral** ♦ n = **hero**, genius,
great; = **god**, goddess, deity,
divine being, immortal being
impact n = **effect**, influence,
consequences, impression,
repercussions; = **collision**, contact,
crash, knock, stroke
impair v = **worsen**, reduce,
damage, injure, harm ≠ **improve**

impasse n = **deadlock**, stalemate,
standstill, dead end, standoff
impeccable adj = **faultless**,
perfect, immaculate, flawless,
squeaky-clean ≠ **flawed**
impending adj = **looming**,
coming, approaching, near,
forthcoming
imperative adj = **urgent**,
essential, pressing, vital, crucial
≠ **unnecessary**
imperial adj = **royal**, regal, kingly,
queenly, princely

imperil v -illing, -illed endanger.
imperious adj domineering.
impersonal adj objective.
impersonate v pretend to be.
impersonation n impersonator n
impertinent adj insolent, rude.
impertinence n
imperturbable adj calm, not
excitable.
impervious adj 1 impossible to
penetrate. 2 unaffected by.
impetigo n contagious skin
disease.
impetuous adj rash.
impetuosity n
impetus ⊙ n, pl -tuses 1
incentive. 2 momentum.
impinge v encroach (upon).
impious adj irreverent.
implacable adj not to be
placated.
implant ⊙ v insert firmly.
implement ⊙ n 1 tool,
instrument. ♦ v 2 carry out.
implore v entreat earnestly.

imply ⊙ v -plying, -plied 1 hint. 2
mean. implicate v involve.
implication n something implied.
implicit adj 1 implied. 2 absolute.
import ⊙ v 1 bring in. ♦ n 2 thing
imported. 3 meaning. importation
n importer n
important ⊙ adj 1 of great
consequence. 2 eminent,
powerful. importance n
impose v 1 place (upon). 2 take
advantage (of). imposing adj
impressive. imposition n
impossible ⊙ adj 1 not possible. 2
unreasonable. impossibility n, pl
-ties. impossibly adv
impotent adj 1 powerless. 2 (of
males) incapable of sexual
intercourse. impotence n
impound v seize legally.
impoverish ⊙ v make poor or
weak.
impractical adj not sensible.
impregnable adj proof against
attack.

———————— THESAURUS ————————

impetus n = incentive, push, spur,
motivation, impulse; = force,
power, energy, momentum
implant v = insert, fix, graft;
= instil, infuse, inculcate
implement v = carry out, effect,
carry through, complete, apply
≠ hinder ♦ n = tool, machine,
device, instrument, appliance
imply v = suggest, hint, insinuate,
indicate, intimate; = involve,
mean, entail, require, indicate
import v = bring in, buy in, ship
in, introduce ♦ n = (Formal)
significance, concern, value,

weight, consequence; = meaning,
implication, significance, sense,
intention
important adj = significant,
critical, substantial, urgent, serious
≠ unimportant; = powerful,
prominent, commanding,
dominant, influential, skookum
(US & Canad)
impossible adj = not possible, out
of the question, impracticable,
unfeasible; = unachievable, out of
the question, vain, unthinkable,
inconceivable ≠ possible
impoverish v = bankrupt, ruin,

impregnate v 1 saturate. 2 make pregnant.

impresario n, pl -ios 1 organizer of public entertainment. 2 manager of opera, ballet etc.

impress ❶ v 1 affect deeply, usu. favourably. 2 imprint, stamp.

impression n 1 effect. 2 notion, belief. 3 imprint. 4 comic impersonation. **impressionable** adj susceptible. **impressive** adj making deep impression.

imprint ❶ n 1 mark made by pressure. ♦ v 2 stamp. 3 fix in mind.

imprison ❶ v put in prison. **imprisonment** n

improbable ❶ adj unlikely.

impromptu adv/adj 1 without preparation. ♦ n 2 improvisation.

improper ❶ adj 1 indecent. 2 incorrect. **impropriety** n

improve ❶ v make or become better. **improvement** n

improvident adj thriftless.

improvise ❶ v 1 make use of materials at hand. 2 perform,

speak without preparation. **improvisation** n

impudent adj impertinent. **impudence** n

impugn v call in question, challenge.

impulse ❶ n 1 sudden inclination to act. 2 impetus. **impulsive** adj rash.

impunity n **with impunity** without punishment.

impure adj 1 having unwanted substances mixed in. 2 immoral, obscene. **impurity** n

impute v attribute to. **imputation** n reproach.

in prep 1 expresses inclusion within limits of space, time, circumstance, sphere etc. ♦ adv 2 in or into some state, place etc. 3 Inf in vogue etc. ♦ adj 4 Inf fashionable.

inability n lack of means or skill to do something.

inaccurate ❶ adj not correct. **inaccuracy** n, pl -cies

inadequate ❶ adj 1 not enough.

—————— THESAURUS ——————

beggar, break

impress v = **excite**, move, strike, touch, affect

imprint n = **mark**, impression, stamp, indentation ♦ v = **engrave**, print, stamp, impress, etch

imprison v = **jail**, confine, detain, lock up, put away ≠ **free**

improbable adj = **doubtful**, unlikely, dubious, questionable, fanciful ≠ **probable**

improper adj = **inappropriate**, unfit, unsuitable, out of place,

unwarranted ≠ **appropriate**; = **indecent**, vulgar, suggestive, unseemly, untoward ≠ **decent**

improve v = **enhance**, better, add to, upgrade, touch up ≠ **worsen**; = **get better**, pick up, develop, advance, rally

improvise v = **devise**, contrive, concoct, throw together; = **ad-lib**, invent, busk, wing it (Inf), play it by ear (Inf)

impulse n = **urge**, longing, wish, notion, yearning

2 incapable. **inadequacy** n

inane adj foolish.

inanimate adj lifeless.

inappropriate adj not suitable.

inarticulate adj unable to express oneself clearly.

inaugurate v 1 initiate. 2 admit to office. **inaugural** adj **inauguration** n formal initiation (to office etc.).

inauspicious adj unlucky.

inborn adj existing from birth.

incalculable adj 1 beyond calculation. 2 very great.

incandescent adj 1 glowing. 2 produced by glowing filament.

incantation n magic spell.

incapable adj helpless.

incapacitate v 1 disable. 2 disqualify.

incarcerate v imprison.

incarnate adj 1 in human form. 2 typified. **incarnation** n

incendiary adj 1 designed to cause fires. 2 inflammatory. ◆ n 3 fire–bomb.

incense¹ ❶ v enrage.

incense² n 1 gum, spice giving perfume when burned. 2 its smoke.

incentive ❶ n something that

stimulates effort.

inception n beginning.

incessant adj unceasing.

incest n sexual intercourse between close relatives. **incestuous** adj

inch n 1 one twelfth of a foot, or 0.0254 metre. ◆ v 2 move very slowly.

incident ❶ n 1 event, occurrence. 2 public disturbance. **incidence** n extent or frequency of occurrence.

incidental adj occurring as a minor, inevitable, or chance accompaniment. **incidentally** adv 1 by chance. 2 by the way.

incidentals pl n accompanying items.

incinerate v burn up completely. **incinerator** n

incipient adj beginning.

incise v cut into. **incision** n **incisive** adj sharp. **incisor** n cutting tooth.

incite ❶ v urge, stir up.

inclement adj severe.

incline ❶ v 1 lean, slope. 2 (cause to) be disposed. ◆ n 3 slope. **inclination** n 1 liking, tendency. 2 degree of deviation.

include ❶ v 1 have as (part of)

inaccurate adj = **incorrect**, wrong, mistaken, faulty, unreliable ≠ **accurate**

inadequate adj = **insufficient**, meagre, poor, lacking, scant ≠ **adequate**; = **incapable**, incompetent, faulty, deficient, unqualified ≠ **capable**

incense¹ v = **anger**, infuriate, enrage, irritate, madden

incentive n = **inducement**, encouragement, spur, lure, bait ≠ **disincentive**

incident n = **disturbance**, scene, clash, disorder, confrontation; = **adventure**, drama, excitement, crisis, spectacle

incline v = **predispose**, influence, persuade, prejudice, sway ◆ n = **slope**, rise, dip, grade, descent

contents. **2** add in. **inclusion** n
inclusive adj including
(everything).
incognito adv/adj **1** under an
assumed identity. ◆ n **2** assumed
identity.
incoherent adj **1** lacking clarity. **2**
inarticulate. **incoherence** n
income ● n money received from
salary, investments etc.
incoming ● adj **1** coming in. **2**
about to come into office. **3** next.
incomparable adj beyond
comparison.
incompatible ● adj inconsistent,
conflicting.
incompetent ● adj lacking
necessary ability. **incompetence** n
inconceivable adj impossible to
imagine.
inconclusive adj not giving a final
decision.
incongruous adj not appropriate.
incongruity n, pl **-ties**

inconsequential adj **1** trivial. **2**
haphazard.
incontinent adj not able to
control bladder or bowels.
incontrovertible adj undeniable.
inconvenience ● n trouble,
difficulty. **inconvenient** adj
incorporate ● v **1** include. **2** form
into corporation.
incorrigible adj beyond
correction or reform.
increase ● v **1** make or become
greater in size, number etc. ◆ n **2**
growth, enlargement. **increasingly**
adv more and more.
incredible ● adj **1** unbelievable. **2**
Inf amazing. **incredibly** adv
incredulous adj unbelieving.
incredulity n
increment n increase.
incriminate v imply guilt of.
incubate v **1** provide eggs,
bacteria etc. with heat for
development. **2** develop in this

——————— THESAURUS ———————

include v = **contain**, involve,
incorporate, cover, consist of
≠ **exclude**; = **add**, enter, put in,
insert
income n = **revenue**, earnings,
pay, returns, profits
incoming adj = **arriving**, landing,
approaching, entering, returning
≠ **departing**
incompatible adj = **inconsistent**,
conflicting, contradictory,
incongruous, unsuited
≠ **compatible**
incompetent adj = **inept**, useless,
incapable, floundering, bungling
≠ **competent**

inconvenience n = **trouble**,
difficulty, bother, fuss,
disadvantage ◆ v = **trouble**,
bother, disturb, upset, disrupt
incorporate v = **include**, contain,
take in, embrace, integrate
increase v = **raise**, extend, boost,
expand, develop ≠ **decrease** ◆ n
= **growth**, rise, development, gain,
expansion
incredible adj = (Inf) **amazing**,
wonderful, stunning,
extraordinary, overwhelming;
= **unbelievable**, unthinkable,
improbable, inconceivable,
preposterous

way. **incubation** n **incubator** n
apparatus for hatching eggs or
rearing premature babies.
inculcate v fix in the mind.
incumbent n holder of office.
incur ❶ v **–curring, –curred** bring
upon oneself. **incursion** n invasion.
indebted adj owing gratitude or
money.
indecent ❶ adj 1 offensive. 2
unseemly.
indeed ❶ adv 1 really. 2 in fact. ◆
interj 3 denoting surprise, doubt
etc.
indefatigable adj untiring.
indefensible adj not justifiable.
indefinite adj without exact
limits.
indelible adj that cannot be
blotted out. **indelibly** adv
indelicate adj coarse,
embarrassing.
indemnity n, pl **–ties** 1
compensation. 2 security against
loss. **indemnify** v give indemnity
to.
indent v 1 set in (from margin
etc.). 2 notch. 3 order by indent.

◆ n 4 notch. 5 requisition.
indentation n
independent ❶ adj 1 not subject
to others. 2 self-reliant. 3 free. 4
valid in itself. **independence** n 1
being independent. 2 self-
reliance. 3 self-support.
indescribable adj beyond
description.
indeterminate adj uncertain.
index n, pl **indices** 1 alphabetical
list of references. 2 indicator 3
Maths exponent. 4 forefinger. ◆ v
5 provide with, insert in index.
indicate ❶ v 1 point out. 2 state
briefly. 3 signify. **indication** n
indicative adj 1 pointing to. 2
Grammar stating fact. **indicator** n
indict ❶ v accuse, esp. by legal
process. **indictment** n
indifferent ❶ adj 1 uninterested.
2 mediocre. **indifference** n
indigenous adj native.
indigent adj poor, needy.
indigestion n (discomfort caused
by) poor digestion.
indigo n 1 blue dye obtained from
plant. 2 the plant. ◆ adj 3 deep

——————— THESAURUS ———————

incur v = **sustain**, experience,
suffer, gain, earn
indecent adj = **obscene**, lewd,
dirty, inappropriate, rude
≠ **decent**; = **unbecoming**,
unsuitable, vulgar, unseemly,
undignified ≠ **proper**
indeed adv = **certainly**, yes,
definitely, surely, truly
independent adj = **separate**,
unattached, uncontrolled,
unconstrained ≠ **controlled**;

= **self-sufficient**, free, liberated,
self-contained, self-reliant
indicate v = **imply**, suggest, hint,
intimate, signify; = **register**, show,
record, read, express
indict v = **charge**, accuse,
prosecute, summon, impeach
indifferent adj = **unconcerned**,
detached, cold, cool, callous
≠ **concerned**; = **mediocre**,
ordinary, moderate, so-so (Inf),
passable ≠ **excellent**

blue.

indirect ⊕ *adj* **1** done, caused by someone or something else. **2** not by straight route.

indiscreet *adj* tactless in revealing secrets. **indiscretion** *n*

indiscriminate *adj* **1** lacking discrimination. **2** jumbled.

indispensable ⊕ *adj* essential.

indisposed *adj* **1** unwell. **2** disinclined.

indisputable *adj* without doubt.

indissoluble *adj* permanent.

individual ⊕ *adj* **1** single. **2** distinctive. ♦ *n* **3** single person or thing. **individuality** *n* distinctive personality. **individually** *adv* singly.

indoctrinate *v* implant beliefs in the mind of.

indolent *adj* lazy. **indolence** *n*

indoor *adj* **1** within doors. **2** under cover. **indoors** *adv*

indubitable *adj* beyond doubt.

induce ⊕ *v* **1** persuade. **2** bring on. **inducement** *n* incentive.

induct *v* install in office. **induction** *n* **1** inducting. **2** general inference from particular inferences. **3**

production of electric or magnetic state by proximity.

indulge ⊕ *v* **1** gratify. **2** pamper.

indulgence *n* **1** indulging. **2** extravagance. **3** favour, privilege.

indulgent *adj*

industry ⊕ *n*, *pl* –**tries 1** manufacture, processing etc. of goods. **2** branch of this. **3** diligence. **industrial** *adj* of industries, trades. **industrialize** *v* **industrious** *adj* diligent.

inedible *adj* not eatable.

ineffable *adj* unutterable.

ineligible *adj* not fit or qualified (for something).

inept *adj* **1** absurd. **2** out of place. **3** clumsy. **ineptitude** *n*

inert *adj* **1** without power of motion. **2** sluggish. **3** unreactive. **inertia** *n* **1** inactivity. **2** tendency to continue at rest or in uniform motion.

inescapable *adj* unavoidable.

inestimable *adj* immeasurable.

inevitable ⊕ *adj* **1** unavoidable. **2** sure to happen. **inevitability** *n*

inexorable *adj* relentless.

——————— THESAURUS ———————

indirect *adj* = **related**, secondary, subsidiary, incidental, unintended; = **circuitous**, roundabout, curving, wandering, rambling ≠ **direct**

indispensable *adj* = **essential**, necessary, needed, key, vital ≠ **dispensable**

individual *adj* = **separate**, independent, isolated, lone, solitary ≠ **collective**; = **unique**, special, fresh, novel, exclusive ≠ **conventional** ♦ *n* = **person**,

being, human, unit, character

induce *v* = **cause**, produce, create, effect, lead to ≠ **prevent**; = **persuade**, encourage, influence, convince, urge ≠ **dissuade**

indulge *v* = **gratify**, satisfy, feed, give way to, yield to; = **spoil**, pamper, cosset, humour, give in to

industry *n* = **business**, production, manufacturing, trade, commerce; = **trade**, world,

inexplicable *adj* impossible to explain.

infallible *adj* not liable to fail or err.

infamous ☉ *adj* 1 notorious. 2 shocking. **infamy** *n*

infant ☉ *n* very young child. **infancy** *n* 1 babyhood. 2 early stage of development. **infantile** *adj* childish.

infantry *n* foot soldiers.

infect ☉ *v* 1 affect (with disease). 2 contaminate. **infection** *n*

infectious *adj* catching.

infer *v* –ferring, –ferred deduce, conclude. **inference** *n*

inferior ☉ *adj* 1 of poor quality. 2 lower. ♦ *n* 3 one lower (in rank etc.). **inferiority** *n*

infernal *adj* 1 devilish. 2 hellish. 3 *Inf* irritating, confounded.

inferno *n, pl* –nos 1 intense, raging fire. 2 hell.

infertile *adj* barren, not productive.

infest *v* inhabit or overrun in dangerously or unpleasantly large numbers.

infidelity *n, pl* –ties 1 unfaithfulness. 2 religious disbelief. **infidel** *n* unbeliever.

infiltrate ☉ *v* 1 trickle through. 2 gain access surreptitiously.

infinite ☉ *adj* boundless. **infinitely** *adv* exceedingly. **infinitesimal** *adj* extremely small. **infinity** *n* unlimited extent.

infinitive *n* form of verb without tense, person, or number.

infirm *adj* physically or mentally weak. **infirmary** *n* hospital, sick quarters. **infirmity** *n, pl* –ties

inflame ☉ *v* 1 rouse to anger, excitement. 2 cause inflammation in. **inflammable** *adj* 1 easily set on fire. 2 excitable. **inflammation** *n* painful infected swelling. **inflammatory** *adj*

inflate ☉ *v* 1 blow up with air, gas. 2 swell. 3 raise price, esp. artificially. **inflatable** *adj* **inflation** *n* increase in prices and fall in value of money.

inflection, inflexion *n* 1

——— THESAURUS ———

business, service, line

inevitable *adj* = **unavoidable**, inescapable, inexorable, sure, certain ≠ **avoidable**

infamous *adj* = **notorious**, ignominious, disreputable, ill–famed ≠ **esteemed**

infant *n* = **baby**, child, babe, toddler, tot

infect *v* = **pollute**, poison, corrupt, contaminate, taint

inferior *adj* = **lower**, minor, secondary, subsidiary, lesser

≠ **superior** (*Aust sl*) ♦ *n*
= **underling**, junior, subordinate, lesser, menial

infiltrate *v* = **penetrate**, pervade, permeate, percolate, filter through to

infinite *adj* = **limitless**, endless, unlimited, eternal, never–ending ≠ **finite**

inflame *v* = **enrage**, stimulate, provoke, excite, anger ≠ **calm**

inflate *v* = **blow up**, pump up, swell, dilate, distend ≠ **deflate**;

modification of word. **2** modulation of voice.

inflexible *adj* **1** incapable of being bent. **2** stubborn.

inflict ❶ *v* impose, deliver forcibly. **infliction** *n*

influence ❶ *n* **1** power to affect other people, events etc. **2** person, thing possessing such power. ♦ *v* **3** sway. **4** induce. **5** affect. **influential** *adj*

influenza *n* contagious viral disease.

influx ❶ *n* **1** flowing in. **2** inflow.

inform ❶ *v* give information (about). **informant** *n* one who tells. **information** *n* what is told, knowledge. **informative** *adj* **informer** *n*

informal ❶ *adj* **1** relaxed and friendly. **2** appropriate for everyday use. **informally** *adv* **informality** *n*

infrared *adj* below visible spectrum.

infrastructure *n* basic structure or fixed capital items of an

organization or economic system.

infringe *v* transgress, break.

infuriate ❶ *v* enrage.

infuse *v* **1** soak to extract flavour etc. **2** instil. **infusion** *n* **1** infusing. **2** extract obtained.

ingenious ❶ *adj* **1** clever at contriving. **2** cleverly contrived. **ingenuity** *n*

ingenuous *adj* **1** frank. **2** innocent.

ingot *n* block of cast metal, esp. gold.

ingrained *adj* **1** deep-rooted. **2** inveterate.

ingratiate *v* get (oneself) into favour.

ingredient ❶ *n* component part of a mixture.

inhabit ❶ *v* –habiting, –habited dwell in. **inhabitant** *n*

inhale ❶ *v* breathe in (air etc.). **inhalation** *n* **inhaler** *n* container with medical preparation inhaled to help breathing.

inherent ❶ *adj* existing as an inseparable part.

———————— THESAURUS ————————

embroider, embellish

inflict *v* = **impose**, administer, visit, apply, deliver

influence *n* = **control**, power, authority, direction, command; = **power**, authority, pull (*Inf*), importance, prestige ♦ *v* = **affect**, have an effect on, have an impact on, control, concern

influx *n* = **arrival**, rush, invasion, incursion, inundation

inform *v* = **tell**, advise, notify, instruct, enlighten

informal *adj* = **natural**, relaxed, casual, familiar, unofficial

infuriate *v* = **enrage**, anger, provoke, irritate, incense ≠ **soothe**

ingenious *adj* = **creative**, original, brilliant, clever, bright ≠ **unimaginative**

ingredient *n* = **component**, part, element, feature, piece

inhabit *v* = **live in**, occupy, populate, reside in, dwell in

inhale *v* = **breathe in**, gasp, draw in, suck in, respire ≠ **exhale**

inherit ⊕ v -heriting, -herited 1 receive, succeed as heir. 2 derive from parents. **inheritance** n

inhibit ⊕ v -hibiting, -hibited 1 restrain. 2 hinder. **inhibition** n repression of emotion, instinct.

inhospitable adj 1 unfriendly. 2 harsh.

inhuman adj 1 cruel, brutal. 2 not human.

inhumane adj cruel, brutal. **inhumanity** n

inimical adj unfavourable, hostile.

inimitable adj defying imitation.

iniquity n, pl -ties 1 gross injustice. 2 sin. **iniquitous** adj

initial ⊕ adj 1 of, occurring at the beginning. ♦ n 2 initial letter, esp. of person's name. ♦ v 3 mark, sign with one's initials. **initially** adv

initiate ⊕ v 1 originate. 2 admit into closed society. 3 instruct. **initiation** n **initiative** n 1 lead. 2 ability to act independently.

inject ⊕ v 1 put (fluid, medicine etc.) into body with syringe. 2 introduce (new element).

injection n

injunction ⊕ n (judicial) order.

injustice ⊕ n 1 want of justice. 2 wrong. 3 unjust act.

ink n 1 fluid used for writing or printing. ♦ v 2 mark, cover with ink. **inky** adj

inkling n hint, vague idea.

inland ⊕ adj/adv 1 in, towards the interior. 2 away from the sea.

inlay v 1 embed. 2 decorate with inset pattern. ♦ n 3 inlaid piece or pattern.

inlet n 1 entrance. 2 mouth of creek. 3 piece inserted.

inmate n occupant, esp. of prison, hospital, etc.

inmost adj most inward, deepest.

inn n 1 public house providing food and accommodation. 2 hotel. **innkeeper** n

innards pl n Inf internal parts, esp. of body.

innate adj 1 inborn. 2 inherent.

inner ⊕ adj lying within. **innermost** adj

innings n 1 Sport player's or side's

───────── THESAURUS ─────────

inherent adj = **intrinsic**, natural, essential, native, fundamental ≠ **extraneous**

inherit v = **be left**, come into, be willed, succeed to, fall heir to

inhibit v = **hinder**, check, frustrate, curb, restrain ≠ **further**

initial adj = **opening**, first, earliest, beginning, primary ≠ **final**

initiate v = **begin**, start, open, launch, kick off (Inf); = **introduce**, admit, enlist, enrol, launch ♦ n = **novice**, member, pupil, convert,

amateur

inject v = **vaccinate**, administer, inoculate; = **introduce**, bring in, insert, instil, infuse

injunction n = **order**, ruling, command, instruction, mandate

injustice n = **unfairness**, discrimination, prejudice, bias, inequality ≠ **justice**

inland adj = **interior**, internal, upcountry

inner adj = **inside**, internal, interior, inward ≠ **outer**; = **central**,

turn of batting. **2** turn.

innocent 🛈 *adj* **1** guiltless. **2** without experience of evil. ♦ *n* **3** innocent person. **innocence** *n*

innocuous *adj* harmless.

innuendo *n, pl* **–does** indirect accusation.

innumerable *adj* countless.

inoculate *v* immunize by injecting vaccine. **inoculation** *n*

inoperable *adj Med* not able to be operated on. **inoperative** *adj* not operative.

inordinate *adj* excessive.

inorganic *adj* **1** not organic. **2** not containing carbon.

input *n* material, data, current etc. fed into a system.

inquest 🛈 *n* **1** coroner's inquiry into cause of death. **2** detailed inquiry.

inquire 🛈, **enquire** *v* seek information. **inquirer, enquirer** *n* **inquiry, enquiry** *n* **1** question. **2** investigation.

inquisition *n* **1** searching investigation. **2** (*with cap.*) *Hist* tribunal for suppression of heresy. **inquisitor** *n*

inquisitive *adj* **1** curious. **2** prying.

insane 🛈 *adj* **1** mentally deranged. **2** crazy. **insanely** *adv* **1** madly. **2** excessively. **insanity** *n*

insatiable *adj* incapable of being satisfied.

inscribe *v* write, engrave (in or on something). **inscription** *n* words inscribed.

inscrutable *adj* **1** enigmatic. **2** incomprehensible.

insect *n* small, usu. winged animal with six legs. **insecticide** *n* preparation for killing insects.

insecure 🛈 *adj* **1** not safe or firm. **2** anxious.

insensible *adj* **1** unconscious. **2** without feeling. **3** not aware. **insensibly** *adv* imperceptibly.

insensitive *adj* unaware of other people's feelings.

insert 🛈 *v* **1** put into or between. ♦ *n* **2** something inserted. **insertion** *n*

inset *n* something extra inserted. **inset** *v*

inshore *adv/adj* near shore.

inside 🛈 *n* **1** inner part. ♦ *pl* **2** *Inf* stomach, entrails. ♦ *adj/adv/prep* **3**

———————— THESAURUS ————————

middle, internal, interior, personal

innocent *adj* = **not guilty**, in the clear, blameless, clean, honest ≠ **guilty**; = **naive**, open, trusting, simple, childlike ≠ **worldly**; = **harmless**, innocuous, inoffensive, well-meant, unobjectionable

inquest *n* = **inquiry**, investigation, probe, inquisition

inquire *v* = **ask**, question, query, quiz

insane *adj* = **mad**, crazy, mentally ill, crazed, demented ≠ **sane**; = **stupid**, foolish, daft (*Inf*), irresponsible, irrational ≠ **reasonable**

insecure *adj* worried, anxious, afraid ≠ **confident**; = **unsafe**, exposed, vulnerable, wide-open, unprotected ≠ **safe**

insert *v* = **put**, place, position,

in, on, into the inside.

insidious *adj* unseen but deadly.

insight ⊕ *n* discernment.

insignia *pl n*, *pl* **–nias**, **–nia** badges, emblems.

insignificant ⊕ *adj* not important. **insignificance** *n*

insincere *adj* pretending what one does not feel. **insincerity** *n*, *pl* **–ties**

insinuate *v* 1 hint. 2 introduce subtly. **insinuation** *n*

insipid *adj* dull, tasteless.

insist ⊕ *v* 1 demand persistently. 2 maintain. 3 emphasize. **insistence** *n* **insistent** *adj*

insole *n* inner sole of shoe or boot.

insolent *adj* impudent. **insolence** *n*

insoluble *adj* 1 incapable of being solved. 2 incapable of being dissolved.

insolvent *adj* unable to pay one's debts. **insolvency** *n*

insomnia *n* inability to sleep. **insomniac** *adj/n*

inspect ⊕ *v* examine (closely or officially). **inspection** *n* **inspector** *n*

inspire ⊕ *v* 1 arouse creatively. 2 give rise to. **inspiration** *n* 1 good idea. 2 creative influence.

install ⊕ *v* 1 place in position. 2 formally place (person) in position or rank. **installation** *n* 1 act of installing. 2 equipment installed.

instalment ⊕ *n* 1 part payment. 2 one of a series of parts.

instance ⊕ *n* 1 example. ♦ *v* 2 cite.

instant ⊕ *n* 1 moment. ♦ *adj* 2 immediate. 3 (of foods) requiring little preparation. **instantaneous** *adj* happening in an instant.

instantly *adv* at once.

instead ⊕ *adv* in place (of).

slip, slide

inside *n* = **interior**, contents, core, nucleus ♦ *adj* = **inner**, internal, interior, inward ≠ **outside**; = **confidential**, private, secret, internal, exclusive ♦ *adv* = **indoors**, in, within, under cover

insight *n* (*with* **into**) = **understanding**, perception, sense, knowledge, vision

insignificant *adj* = **unimportant**, minor, irrelevant, petty, trivial ≠ **important**

insist *v* = **demand**, order, require, command, dictate; = **assert**, state, maintain, claim, declare

inspect *v* = **examine**, check, look

at, view, survey

inspire *v* stimulate ≠ **discourage**; = **give rise to**, produce, result in, engender

install *v* = **set up**, put in, place, position, station; = **institute**, establish, introduce, invest, ordain

instalment *n* = **payment**, repayment, part payment

instance *n* = **example**, case, occurrence, occasion, sample ♦ *v* = **name**, mention, identify, point out, advance

instant *n* = **moment**, second, flash, split second, jiffy (*Inf*); = **time**, point, hour, moment, stage ♦ *adj* = **immediate**, prompt,

instep n top of foot between toes and ankle.

instigate v incite, urge. **instigation** n **instigator** n

instil v **-stilling, -stilled 1** implant. **2** inculcate.

instinct ⊕ n **1** inborn impulse. **2** unconscious skill. **instinctive** adj

institute ⊕ v **1** establish. **2** set going. ◆ n **3** society for promoting science etc. **institution** n **1** setting up. **2** establishment for care or education. **3** established custom, law etc. **institutional** adj **1** of institutions. **2** routine.

instruct ⊕ v **1** teach. **2** inform. **3** order. **instruction** n **1** teaching, order. ◆ pl **2** directions. **instructive** adj informative. **instructor** n

instrument ⊕ n **1** thing used to make, do, measure etc. **2** mechanism for producing musical sound. **instrumental** adj **1** acting as instrument or means. **2** produced by musical instruments.

insubordinate adj mutinous, rebellious. **insubordination** n

insufferable adj unbearable.

insular adj **1** of an island. **2** narrow-minded.

insulate ⊕ v **1** prevent or reduce transfer of electricity, heat, sound etc. **2** isolate, detach. **insulation** n **insulator** n

insulin n hormone used in treatment of diabetes.

insult ⊕ v **1** behave rudely to. **2** offend. ◆ n **3** affront. **insulting** adj

insuperable adj not able to be overcome.

insurrection n revolt.

intact ⊕ adj **1** untouched. **2** uninjured.

intake n **1** thing, amount taken in. **2** opening.

integer n whole number.

integral ⊕ adj essential. **integrate** v combine into one whole. **integration** n

integrity ⊕ n honesty.

———————— THESAURUS ————————

instantaneous, direct, quick; **= ready-made**, fast, convenience, ready-mixed, ready-cooked

instead adv **= rather**, alternatively, preferably, in preference, in lieu

instinct n **= talent**, skill, gift, capacity, bent

institute v **= establish**, start, found, launch, set up ≠ **end**

instruct v **= order**, tell, direct, charge, bid; **= teach**, school, train, coach, educate

instrument n **= tool**, device, implement, mechanism, appliance; **= agent**, means,

medium, agency, vehicle (SI)

insulate v **= isolate**, protect, screen, defend, shelter

insult v **= offend**, abuse, wound, slight, put down ≠ **praise** ◆ n **= jibe**, slight, put-down, abuse, snub

intact adj **= undamaged**, whole, complete, sound, perfect ≠ **damaged**

integral adj **= essential**, basic, fundamental, necessary, component ≠ **inessential**

integrity n **= honesty**, principle, honour, virtue, goodness

intellect ● n power of thinking and reasoning. **intellectual** adj **1** of, appealing to intellect. **2** having good intellect. ◆ n **3** intellectual person.

intelligent ● adj clever.

intelligence n **1** intellect. **2** information, esp. military.

intelligible adj understandable.

intemperate adj **1** drinking alcohol to excess. **2** immoderate.

intend ● v propose, mean.

intense ● adj **1** very strong or acute. **2** emotional. **intensify** v **-fying, -fied** increase. **intensity** n **intensive** adj

intent ● n **1** purpose. ◆ adj **2** concentrating (on). **3** resolved. **intention** n purpose, aim. **intentional** adj

inter ● v **-terring, -terred** bury. **interment** n

inter- comb. form between, among, mutually, as in interglacial, interrelation.

interact v act on each other.

interaction n **interactive** adj

intercede v plead in favour of, mediate. **intercession** n

intercept ● v **1** cut off. **2** seize, stop in transit. **interception** n

interchange v **1** (cause to) exchange places. ◆ n **2** motorway junction. **interchangeable** adj able to be exchanged in position or use.

intercom n internal communication system.

intercontinental adj **1** connecting continents. **2** (of missile) able to reach one continent from another.

intercourse ● n **1** act of having sex. **2** communications or dealings between individuals or groups.

interest ● n **1** concern, curiosity. **2** thing exciting this. **3** sum paid for borrowed money. **4** advantage. **5** right, share. ◆ v **6** excite, cause to feel interest. **interested** adj **interesting** adj

≠ **dishonesty**; = **unity**, unification, cohesion, coherence, wholeness
intellect n = **intelligence**, mind, reason, understanding, sense
intelligent adj = **clever**, bright, smart, sharp, enlightened ≠ **stupid**
intend v = **plan**, mean, aim, propose, purpose
intense adj = **extreme**, great, severe, fierce, deep ≠ **mild**; = **fierce**, tough
intent adj = **absorbed**, intense, fascinated, preoccupied, enthralled ≠ **indifferent** ◆ n = **intention**, aim, purpose,

meaning, end ≠ **chance**
inter v = **bury**, lay to rest, entomb, consign to the grave
intercept v = **catch**, stop, block, seize, cut off
intercourse n = **sexual intercourse**, sex (Inf), copulation, coitus, carnal knowledge; = **contact**, communication, commerce, dealings
interest n (often plural) = **hobby**, activity, pursuit, entertainment, recreation; (often plural) = **advantage**, good, benefit, profit; = **stake**, investment ◆ v

interface ❶ *adj* area, surface, boundary linking two systems.
interfere ❶ *v* 1 meddle, intervene. 2 clash. **interference** *n* 1 act of interfering 2 *Radio* atmospherics.
interim ❶ *n* 1 meantime. ♦ *adj* 2 temporary.
interior ❶ *adj* 1 inner. 2 inland. 3 indoors. ♦ *n* 4 inside. 5 inland region.
interject *v* interpose (remark etc.). **interjection** *n* 1 exclamation. 2 interjected remark.
interlock *v* lock together firmly.
interloper *n* intruder.
interlude *n* 1 interval. 2 something filling an interval.
intermarry *v* 1 (of families, races, religions) become linked by marriage. 2 marry within one's family. **intermarriage** *n*
intermediate ❶ *adj* 1 coming between. 2 interposed.
intermediary *n*
interminable *adj* endless.
intermission *n* interval.

intermittent *adj* occurring at intervals.
intern *v* confine to special area or camp. **internment** *n*
internal ❶ *adj* 1 inward. 2 interior. 3 within (a country, organization).
international ❶ *adj* 1 of relations between nations. ♦ *n* 2 game or match between teams of different countries.
internecine *adj* 1 mutually destructive. 2 deadly.
interplanetary *adj* of, linking planets.
interplay *n* action and reaction of things upon each other.
interpolate *v* 1 insert new matter. 2 interject.
interpose *v* 1 insert. 2 say as interruption.
interpret ❶ *v* 1 explain. 2 translate, esp. orally. 3 represent. **interpretation** *n* **interpreter** *n*
interrogate *v* question, esp. closely or officially. **interrogation** *n* **interrogative** *n* word used in asking question. **interrogator** *n*

———— THESAURUS ————

= **arouse your curiosity**, fascinate, attract, grip, entertain ≠ **bore**
interface *n* = **connection**, link, boundary, border, frontier
interfere *v* = **meddle**, intervene, intrude, butt in, tamper
interim *adj* = **temporary**, provisional, makeshift, acting, caretaker
interior *n* = **inside**, centre, heart, middle, depths ♦ *adj* = **inside**, internal, inner ≠ **exterior**; = **mental**, emotional,

psychological, private, personal
intermediate *adj* = **middle**, mid, halfway, in–between (*Inf*), midway
internal *adj* = **domestic**, home, national, local, civic; = **inner**, inside, interior ≠ **external**
international *adj* = **global**, world, worldwide, universal, cosmopolitan
interpret *v* = **take**, understand, explain, construe; = **translate**, transliterate; = **explain**, make sense of, decode, decipher,

interrupt ⓿ v 1 break in (upon). 2 stop. 3 block. **interruption** n
intersect v 1 divide by passing across or through. 2 meet and cross. **intersection** n
interstellar adj between stars.
interstice n slit, crevice.
intertwine v twist together.
interval ⓿ n 1 intervening time or space. 2 pause, break. 3 difference (of pitch).
intervene ⓿ v 1 come into a situation in order to change it. 2 be, come between or among. 3 occur in the meantime. 4 interpose. **intervention** n
interview ⓿ n 1 meeting, esp. one involving questioning. ◆ v 2 have interview with. **interviewee** n **interviewer** n
intestate adj not having made a will.
intestine n (usu. pl) lower part of alimentary canal between stomach and anus. **intestinal** adj
intimate[1] ⓿ adj 1 closely

acquainted, familiar. 2 private. 3 having cosy atmosphere. ◆ n 4 intimate friend. **intimacy** n
intimate[2] ⓿ v 1 announce. 2 imply in indirect way. **intimation** n
intimidate ⓿ v frighten into submission. **intimidation** n
into prep 1 expresses motion to a point within. 2 indicates change of state. 3 indicates coming up against, encountering. 4 indicates arithmetical division.
intolerable adj more than can be endured.
intolerant adj narrow-minded.
intone v chant. **intonation** n accent.
intoxicate v make drunk.
intractable adj difficult.
intransigent adj uncompromising.
intravenous adj into a vein.
intrepid adj fearless, undaunted.
intricate ⓿ adj complex. **intricacy** n, pl –cies
intrigue ⓿ n 1 underhand plot. 2

elucidate
interrupt v = **intrude**, disturb, intervene, interfere (with), break in; = **suspend**, stop, end, delay, cease
interval n spell, space; = **break**, interlude, intermission, rest, gap; = **delay**, gap, hold-up, stoppage
intervene v = **step in** (Inf), interfere, mediate, intrude, intercede; = **interrupt**, involve yourself
interview v = **examine**, talk to
intimate[1] adj = **close**, dear, loving,

near, familiar ≠ **distant**; = **private**, personal, confidential, special, individual ≠ **public**; = **detailed**, minute, full, deep, particular; = **cosy**, relaxed, friendly, informal, harmonious ◆ n = **friend**, close friend, crony, confidant or confidante (constant) companion ≠ **stranger**
intimate[2] v = **suggest**, indicate, hint, imply, insinuate; = **announce**, state, declare, communicate, make known
intimidate v = **frighten**, pressure,

secret love affair. ◆ v 3 carry on intrigue. 4 interest, puzzle.

intrinsic adj inherent, essential.

introduce ❶ v 1 make acquainted. 2 present. 3 bring in. 4 insert. **introduction** n 1 introducing. 2 preliminary part of book etc. **introductory** adj preliminary.

introvert n Psychiatry one who looks inward. **introverted** adj

intrude v thrust (oneself) in. **intruder** n **intrusion** n **intrusive** adj

intuition ❶ n spontaneous insight. **intuitive** adj

Inuit n Eskimo of North America or Greenland.

Inuk n a member of any Inuit people.

Inuktitut n Canad the language of the Inuit.

inundate v 1 flood. 2 overwhelm. **inundation** n

inured adj hardened.

invade ❶ v 1 enter by force. 2 overrun. **invader** n **invasion** n

invalid[1] ❶ n 1 one suffering from ill health. ◆ v 2 retire because of illness etc.

invalid[2] ❶ adj having no legal force. **invalidate** v

invaluable ❶ adj priceless.

invasion n see INVADE.

invective n bitter verbal attack.

inveigle v entice.

invent ❶ v 1 devise, originate. 2 fabricate. **invention** n 1 that which is invented. 2 ability to invent. **inventive** adj 1 resourceful. 2 creative. **inventor** n

inventory ❶ n, pl **–tories** detailed list.

——————— THESAURUS ———————

threaten, scare, bully

intricate adj = **complicated**, involved, complex, fancy, elaborate ≠ **simple**

intrigue n = **plot**, scheme, conspiracy, manoeuvre, collusion; = **affair**, romance, intimacy, liaison, amour ◆ v = **interest**, fascinate, attract, rivet, titillate; = **plot**, scheme, manoeuvre, conspire, connive

introduce v = **bring in**, establish, set up, start, found; = **present**, acquaint, make known, familiarize; air; = **add**, insert, inject, throw in (Inf), infuse

intuition n = **instinct**, perception, insight, sixth sense

invade v = **attack**, storm, assault,

capture, occupy; = **infest**, swarm, overrun, ravage, beset

invalid[1] n = **patient**, sufferer, convalescent, valetudinarian ◆ adj = **disabled**, ill, sick, ailing, frail

invalid[2] adj = **null and void**, void, worthless, inoperative ≠ **valid**; = **unfounded**, false, illogical, irrational, unsound ≠ **sound**

invaluable adj = **precious**, valuable, priceless, inestimable, worth your or its weight in gold ≠ **worthless**

invasion n = **attack**, assault, capture, takeover, raid; = **intrusion**, breach, violation, disturbance, disruption

invent v = **create**, make, produce, design, discover; = **make up**,

invert v **1** turn upside down. **2** reverse. **inverse** adj **1** inverted. **2** opposite. **inversion** n

invertebrate n/adj (animal) without backbone.

invest ❶ v **1** lay out (money, time, effort etc.) for profit or advantage. **2** install. **3** endow. **investiture** n formal installation in office or rank. **investment** n **1** investing. **2** money invested. **3** stocks and shares bought. **investor** n

investigate ❶ v **1** inquire into. **2** examine. **investigation** n **investigative** adj **investigator** n

inveterate adj **1** deep-rooted. **2** confirmed.

invidious adj likely to cause ill will.

invigilate v supervise examination candidates. **invigilator** n

invigorate v give vigour to.

invincible adj unconquerable.

inviolable adj not to be violated.

inviolate adj not violated.

invisible ❶ adj not able to be seen.

invite ❶ v **1** request the company of. **2** ask courteously. **3** ask for. **4** attract, call forth. **invitation** n

invoice n **1** list of goods or services sold, with prices. ♦ v **2** make, present an invoice.

invoke ❶ v **1** call on. **2** appeal to. **3** ask earnestly for. **4** summon. **invocation** n

involuntary adj **1** unintentional. **2** instinctive.

involve ❶ v **1** include. **2** entail. **3** implicate (person). **4** concern. **5** entangle. **involved** adj **1** complicated. **2** concerned (in).

inward adj **1** internal. **2** situated within. **3** mental. ♦ adv (also **inwards**) **4** towards the inside. **5** into the mind. **inwardly** adv **1** in the mind. **2** internally.

iodine n nonmetallic element found in seaweed.

ion n electrically charged atom.

IOU n signed paper acknowledging debt.

IQ intelligence quotient.

ire n anger. **irascible** adj hot-tempered. **irate** adj angry.

iridescent adj exhibiting changing colours.

iris n **1** circular membrane of eye containing pupil. **2** plant with sword-shaped leaves and showy flowers.

———— THESAURUS ————

devise, concoct, forge, fake

inventory n = **list**, record, catalogue, listing, account

invest v = **spend**, expend, advance, venture, put in; = **empower**, provide, charge, sanction, license

investigate v = **examine**, study, research, go into, explore

invisible adj = **unseen**, imperceptible, indiscernible, unseeable ≠ **visible**

invite v = **request**, look for, bid for, appeal for; = **encourage**, attract, cause, court, ask for (Inf)

invoke v = **apply**, use, implement, initiate, resort to; = **call upon**, appeal to, pray to, petition, beseech

involve v = **entail**, mean, require,

irk v irritate, vex. **irksome** adj tiresome.

iron ❶ n 1 common metallic element. 2 tool etc. of this metal. 3 appliance used to smooth cloth. 4 metal-headed golf club. ◆ pl 5 fetters. ◆ adj 6 of, like, iron. 7 unyielding. 8 robust. ◆ v 9 press.

ironmonger n dealer in hardware.

irony ❶ n, pl -nies 1 use of words to mean the opposite of what is said. 2 event, situation opposite of that expected. **ironic, ironical** adj of, using, irony.

irradiate v 1 treat with light or beams of particles. 2 shine upon. **irradiation** n

irrational ❶ adj not based on logic.

irregular ❶ adj 1 not regular or even. 2 unconventional. **irregularity** n, pl -ties

irrelevant ❶ adj not connected with the matter in hand. **irrelevance** n

irreparable adj not able to be repaired or remedied.

irresistible ❶ adj 1 too strong to resist. 2 enchanting, seductive.

irrevocable adj not able to be changed.

irrigate v water by artificial channels, pipes etc. **irrigation** n

irritate ❶ v 1 annoy. 2 inflame. **irritable** adj easily annoyed. **irritant** adj/n (person or thing) causing irritation. **irritation** n

is third person sing. of BE.

Islam n Muslim faith or world. **Islamic** adj

island ❶ n 1 piece of land surrounded by water. 2 anything like this. **islander** n inhabitant of island.

isle n island. **islet** n little island.

isobar n line on map connecting places of equal mean barometric pressure.

isolate ❶ v place apart or alone. **isolation** n

—————— THESAURUS ——————

occasion, imply

iron adj = **ferrous**, ferric; = **inflexible**, hard, strong, tough, rigid ≠ **weak**

irony n = **sarcasm**, mockery, ridicule, satire, cynicism; = **paradox**, incongruity

irrational adj = **illogical**, crazy, absurd, unreasonable, preposterous ≠ **rational**

irregular adj = **variable**, erratic, occasional, random, casual ≠ **steady**; = **uneven**, rough, ragged, crooked, jagged ≠ **even**; = **inappropriate**, unconventional,

unethical, unusual, extraordinary

irrelevant adj = **unconnected**, unrelated, unimportant, inappropriate, peripheral ≠ **relevant**

irresistible adj = **overwhelming**, compelling, overpowering, urgent, compulsive

irritate v = **annoy**, anger, bother, needle (Inf), infuriate ≠ **placate**; = **inflame**, pain, rub, scratch, scrape

island n = **isle**, atoll, islet, ait or eyot (dialect), cay or key

isolate v = **separate**, break up, cut

isomer *n* substance with same molecules as another but different atomic arrangement.

isometric *adj* **1** having equal dimensions. **2** relating to muscular contraction without movement.

isometrics *pl n* system of isometric exercises.

isotope *n* atom having different atomic weight from other atoms of same element.

issue ❶ *n* **1** topic of discussion or dispute. **2** edition of newspaper etc. **3** offspring. **4** outcome. ♦ *v* **5** go out. **6** result in. **7** arise (from). **8** give, send out. **9** publish.

isthmus *n, pl* **-muses** neck of land between two seas.

it *pron* neuter pronoun of the third person. **its** *adj* belonging to it. **it's** it is. **itself** *pron* emphatic form of IT.

italic *adj* (of type) sloping. **italics** *pl n* this type, used for emphasis etc. **italicize** *v* put in italics.

itch ❶ *v/n* (feel) irritation in the skin. **itchy** *adj*

item ❶ *n* **1** single thing. **2** piece of information. **3** entry. **itemize** *v*

itinerant *adj* travelling from place to place. **itinerary** *n* **1** plan of journey. **2** route.

ivory *n* hard white substance of the tusks of elephants etc.

ivy *n, pl* **ivies** climbing evergreen plant.

——————————— THESAURUS ———————————

off, detach, split up

issue *n* = **topic**, point, matter, problem, question; = **point**, question, bone of contention; = **edition**, printing, copy, publication, number; = **children**, offspring, babies, kids (*Inf*), heirs ≠ **parent** ♦ *v* = **give out**, release, publish, announce, deliver **take issue with something** or someone

= **disagree with**, question, challenge, oppose, dispute

itch *v* = **prickle**, tickle, tingle; = **long**, ache, crave, pine, hunger ♦ *n* = **irritation**, tingling, prickling, itchiness; = **desire**, longing, craving, passion, yen (*Inf*)

item *n* = **article**, thing, object, piece, unit; = **matter**, point, issue, case, question

J j

jab ⊕ v **jabbing, jabbed 1** poke roughly. **2** thrust, stab. ♦ n **3** poke **4** Inf injection.

jabber v **1** chatter. **2** talk incoherently.

jack n **1** device for lifting heavy weight, esp. motorcar. **2** lowest court card. **3** Bowls ball aimed at. **4** socket and plug connection in electronic equipment. **5** small flag, esp. national, at sea. ♦ v **6** lift with a jack.

jackal n doglike scavenging animal of Asia and Africa.

jackass n **1** male ass. **2** blockhead.

jackboot n large military boot.

jackdaw n small kind of crow.

jacket ⊕ n **1** outer garment, short coat. **2** outer casing, cover.

jackknife n **1** clasp knife. ♦ v **2** angle sharply, esp. the parts of an articulated lorry.

jackpot ⊕ n **1** large prize, accumulated stake, as pool in poker.

Jacuzzi ® n bath with device that swirls water.

jade n **1** ornamental semiprecious stone, usu. dark green. **2** this colour. ♦ adj **3** of this colour.

jaded adj **1** tired. **2** off colour.

jaguar n large S Amer. cat.

jail ⊕ n **1** building for confinement of criminals or suspects. ♦ v **2** send to, confine in prison. **jailer** n

jam ⊕ v **jamming, jammed 1** pack together. **2** (cause to) stick and become unworkable. **3** Radio block (another station). ♦ n **4** fruit preserved by boiling with sugar. **5** crush. **6** hold-up of traffic. **7** awkward situation.

jamb n side post of door, fireplace etc.

jamboree n large gathering or rally of Scouts.

Jan. January.

jangle v **1** (cause to) sound harshly, as bell. **2** (of nerves) be irritated.

janitor n caretaker.

January n first month.

jar¹ ⊕ n **1** round vessel of glass, earthenware etc. **2** Inf glass of esp.

——————— THESAURUS ———————

jab v = **poke**, dig, punch, thrust, tap ♦ n = **poke**, dig, punch, thrust, tap

jacket n = **covering**, casing, case, cover, skin

jackpot n = **prize**, winnings, award, reward, bonanza

jail n = **prison**, penitentiary (US),

confinement, dungeon, nick (Brit sl) ♦ v = **imprison**, confine, detain, lock up, put away

jam n = **predicament**, tight spot, situation, trouble, hole (SI) ♦ v = **pack**, force, press, stuff, squeeze; = **crowd**, throng, crush, mass, surge; = **congest**, block, clog,

beer.

jar² 🔊 v **jarring, jarred** 1 grate, jolt. 2 have distressing effect on. ♦ n 3 jarring sound. 4 shock etc.

jargon n 1 special vocabulary for particular subject. 2 pretentious language.

jasmine n shrub with sweet–smelling flowers.

jaundice n disease marked by yellowness of skin. **jaundiced** adj prejudiced, bitter etc.

jaunt n/v (make) short pleasure excursion.

jaunty adj **–tier, –tiest** 1 sprightly. 2 brisk.

javelin n spear, esp. for throwing in sporting events.

jaw 🔊 n 1 one of bones in which teeth are set. ♦ pl 2 mouth. 3 gripping part of vice etc.

jay n noisy bird of brilliant plumage.

jazz n 1 syncopated music and dance. ♦ v 2 (with up) make more lively. **jazzy** adj flashy, showy.

jealous 🔊 adj 1 envious. 2 suspiciously watchful. **jealousy** n,

pl **–sies**

jeans pl n casual trousers, esp. of denim.

Jeep ® n light four–wheel–drive motor vehicle.

jeer 🔊 v/n scoff, taunt.

jell v 1 congeal 2 Inf assume definite form.

jelly n, pl **–lies** 1 sweet, preserve etc. becoming softly stiff as it cools. 2 anything of similar consistency. **jellyfish** n small jelly–like sea animal.

jemmy n, pl **–mies** short steel crowbar.

jeopardy 🔊 n danger. **jeopardize** v endanger.

jerk 🔊 n 1 sharp push or pull. 2 Sl stupid person. ♦ v 3 move or throw with a jerk. **jerky** adj 1 uneven. 2 spasmodic.

jerkin n sleeveless jacket.

jersey n 1 knitted jumper. 2 machine–knitted fabric.

jest n/v joke. **jester** n 1 joker. 2 Hist professional fool at court.

jet¹ 🔊 n 1 aircraft driven by jet propulsion. 2 stream of liquid, gas

—————— THESAURUS ——————

stick, stall

jar¹ n = **pot**, container, drum, vase, jug

jar² v usually with on = **irritate**, annoy, offend, nettle, irk; = **jolt**, rock, shake, bump, rattle

jargon n = **parlance**, idiom, usage, argot

jaw v = (Inf) **talk**, chat, gossip, chatter, spout

jealous adj = **suspicious**, protective, wary, doubtful,

sceptical ≠ **trusting**; = **envious**, grudging, resentful, green, green with envy ≠ **satisfied**

jeer v = **mock**, deride, heckle, barrack, ridicule ≠ **cheer** ♦ n = **mockery**, abuse, ridicule, taunt, boo ≠ **applause**

jeopardy n = **danger**, risk, peril, vulnerability, insecurity

jerk v = **jolt**, bang, bump, lurch ♦ n = **lurch**, movement, thrust, twitch, jolt

etc. **3** spout, nozzle. ♦ *v* **4** throw out. **5** shoot forth. **jet lag** fatigue caused by crossing time zones in aircraft. **jet propulsion** propulsion by jet of gas or liquid. **jet-propelled** *adj*

jet² *n* hard black mineral. **jet-black** *adj* glossy black.

jetsam *n* goods thrown overboard. **jettison** *v* **1** abandon. **2** throw overboard.

jetty *n, pl* **-ties** small pier, wharf.

Jew *n* one of Hebrew religion or ancestry. **Jewish** *adj*

jewel ⓓ *n* **1** precious stone. **2** ornament containing one. **3** precious thing. **jeweller** *n* dealer in jewels. **jewellery** *n*

jib *n* **1** triangular sail set forward of mast. **2** arm of crane. ♦ *v* **3** (of horse, person) stop and refuse to go on.

jibe see GIBE.

jig *n* **1** lively dance. **2** music for it. **3** guide for cutting etc. ♦ *v* **4** dance jig. **5** make jerky up-and-down movements. **jigsaw** *n* machine fret saw. **jigsaw puzzle** picture cut into pieces, which the user tries to fit together again.

jilt *v* reject (lover).

jingle *n* **1** light metallic noise. **2** catchy rhythmic verse, song etc. ♦ *v* **3** (cause to) make jingling sound.

jingoism *n* aggressive nationalism.

jinks *pl n* **high jinks** boisterous merrymaking.

jinx *n* **1** force, person, thing bringing bad luck. ♦ *v* **2** cause bad luck.

jitters *pl n* worried nervousness, anxiety. **jittery** *adj* nervous.

jive *n* **1** (dance performed to) popular music, esp. of 1950s. ♦ *v* do this dance.

job ⓓ *n* **1** piece of work, task. **2** post **3** *Inf* difficult task. **jobbing** *adj* doing single, particular jobs for payment. **jobless** *adj/pl n* unemployed (people).

jockey *n* **1** rider in horse races. ♦ *v* (*esp. with*) **2** manoeuvre.

jockstrap *n* belt with pouch to support genitals.

jocular *adj* **1** joking. **2** given to joking. **jocularity** *n*

jodhpurs *pl n* tight-legged riding breeches.

jog ⓓ *v* **jogging, jogged 1** run slowly, trot, esp. for exercise. **2** nudge. **3** stimulate. ♦ *n* **4** jogging. **jogger** *n* jogging

Johnny Canuck *n Canad* **1** an informal name for a Canadian. **2** a personification of Canada.

join ⓓ *v* **1** fasten, unite. **2** become a member (of). **3** become connected. **4** (*with* up) enlist. **5** take part (in). ♦ *n* **6** (place of)

———————— THESAURUS ————————

jet¹ *n* = **stream**, current, spring, flow, rush ♦ *v* = **fly**, wing, cruise, soar, zoom

jewel *n* = **gemstone**, gem, ornament, sparkler (*Inf*), rock (*Sl*);

= **treasure**, wonder, darling, pearl, gem

job *n* = **task**, duty, work, venture, enterprise

jog *v* = **run**, trot, canter, lope;

joining. **joiner** n maker of finished woodwork. **joinery** n

joint ❶ n 1 arrangement by which two things fit together. 2 place of this. 3 meat for roasting, oft. with bone 4 Sl disreputable bar or nightclub. 5 Sl marijuana cigarette. ◆ adj 6 shared. ◆ v 7 connect by joints. 8 divide at the joints. **jointly** adv **out of joint 1** dislocated. **2** disorganized.

joist n beam supporting floor or ceiling.

joke ❶ n 1 thing said or done to cause laughter. 2 ridiculous thing. ◆ v 3 make jokes. **joker** n 1 one who jokes. 2 Sl fellow. 3 extra card in pack. **jokey** adj

jolly ❶ adj **–lier, –liest 1** jovial. **2** merry. ◆ v 3 make person, occasion happier. **jollification** n **jollity** n

jolt ❶ n/v 1 jerk. 2 jar. 3 shock. **joss stick** incense stick. **jostle** v knock or push. **jot** n 1 small amount. ◆ v 2 note.

jotter n notebook.

joual n nonstandard Canadian French dialect, esp. as associated with ill-educated speakers.

joule n Electricity unit of work or energy.

journal ❶ n 1 newspaper or other periodical. 2 daily record. **journalism** n editing, writing in periodicals. **journalist** n

journey ❶ n 1 going to a place, excursion. 2 distance travelled. ◆ v 3 travel.

journeyman n qualified craftsman.

jovial adj convivial, merry. **joviality** n

joy ❶ n 1 gladness, pleasure, delight. 2 cause of this. **joyful** adj **joyous** adj extremely happy. **joy ride** trip, esp. in stolen car. **joystick** n 1 control column of aircraft. 2 control device for video game.

JP Justice of the Peace.

jubilant adj exultant. **jubilation** n

——————— THESAURUS ———————

= **nudge**, push, shake, prod; stir

join v = **enrol in**, enter, sign up for, enlist in; = **connect**, unite, couple, link, combine ≠ **detach**

joint adj = **shared**, mutual, collective, communal, united ◆ n = **junction**, connection, brace, bracket, hinge

joke n = **jest**, gag (Inf), wisecrack (Inf), witticism, crack (Inf); = **laugh**, jest, jape, trick, practical joke ◆ v = **jest**, kid (Inf), mock, tease, taunt

jolly adj = **happy**, cheerful, merry, upbeat (Inf), playful ≠ **miserable**

jolt v = **jerk**, push, shake, knock, jar; = **surprise**, stun, disturb, stagger, startle ◆ n = **jerk**, start, jump, shake, bump; = **surprise**, blow, shock, setback, bombshell

journal n = **magazine**, publication, gazette, periodical; = **newspaper**, paper, daily, weekly, monthly

journey n = **trip**, drive, tour, flight, excursion ◆ v = **travel**, go, move, tour, progress

joy n = **delight**, pleasure, satisfaction, ecstasy, enjoyment ≠ **sorrow**

jubilee ❶ *n* time of rejoicing, esp. 25th or 50th anniversary.

judder *v* 1 shake, vibrate. ◆ *n* 2 vibration.

judge ❶ *n* 1 officer appointed to try cases in law courts. 2 one who decides in a dispute, contest etc. 3 one able to form a reliable opinion. ◆ *v* 4 act as judge (of, for). **judgment, judgement** *n* 1 faculty of judging. 2 sentence of court. 3 opinion. **judgmental, judgemental** *adj*

judicial ❶ *adj* of, by a court or judge. **judiciary** *n* judges collectively. **judicious** *adj* well-judged, sensible.

judo *n* modern sport derived from jujitsu.

jug ❶ *n* 1 vessel for liquids, with handle and small spout. 2 its contents.

juggernaut *n* 1 large heavy lorry. 2 irresistible, destructive force.

juggle ❶ *v* 1 keep several objects in the air simultaneously. 2

manipulate to deceive. **juggler** *n*

juice ❶ *n* 1 liquid part of vegetable, fruit or meat. 2 *Inf* electric current. 3 *Inf* petrol. **juicy** *adj* 1 succulent. 2 interesting.

jujitsu *n* Japanese art of wrestling and self-defence.

jukebox *n* automatic, coin-operated record player.

July *n* seventh month.

jumble ❶ *v* 1 mix in confused heap. ◆ *n* 2 confused heap or state. **jumble sale** sale of miscellaneous, usu. second-hand, items.

jumbo ❶ *n* 1 *Inf* elephant. 2 anything very large.

jump ❶ *v* 1 (cause to) spring, leap (over). 2 move hastily. 3 pass or skip (over). 4 rise steeply. 5 start (with astonishment etc.). ◆ *n* 6 act of jumping. 7 obstacle to be jumped. 8 distance, height jumped. 9 sudden rise. **jumper** *n* sweater, pullover. **jumpy** *adj* nervous.

jubilee *n* = **celebration**, holiday, festival, festivity

judge *n* = **magistrate**, justice, beak (*Brit sl*), His, Her *or* Your Honour; = **critic**, assessor, arbiter ◆ *v* = **adjudicate**, referee, umpire, mediate, officiate; = **evaluate**, rate, consider, view, value

judicial *adj* = **legal**, official

jug *n* = **container**, pitcher, urn, carafe, creamer (*US & Canad*)

juggle *v* = **manipulate**, change,

alter, modify, manoeuvre

juice *n* = **liquid**, extract, fluid, liquor, sap

jumble *n* = **muddle**, mixture, mess, disorder, confusion ◆ *v* = **mix**, mistake, confuse, disorder, shuffle

jumbo *adj* = **giant**, large, huge, immense, gigantic ≠ **tiny**

jump *v* = **leap**, spring, bound, bounce, hop; = **recoil**, start, jolt, flinch, shake; = **increase**, rise, climb, escalate, advance; = **miss**, avoid, skip, omit, evade ◆ *n*

junction n 1 place where routes meet. 2 point of connection.

juncture n state of affairs.

June n sixth month.

jungle n 1 equatorial forest. 2 tangled mass. 3 condition of intense competition.

junior ⊕ adj 1 younger. 2 of lower standing. ◆ n 3 junior person.

juniper n evergreen shrub.

junk ⊕ n useless objects. **junkie** n Sl drug addict. **junk food** food of low nutritional value. **junk mail** unsolicited mail.

junket n 1 flavoured curdled milk. 2 excursion.

junta n group holding power in country.

jurisdiction ⊕ n 1 authority. 2 territory covered by it.

jury n, pl **-ries** 1 body of persons sworn to render verdict in court of law. 2 judges of competition.

juror n

just ⊕ adj 1 fair. 2 upright, honest. 3 right, equitable. ◆ adv 4 exactly. 5 barely. 6 at this instant. 7 merely. 8 really. **justice** n 1 moral or legal fairness. 2 judge, magistrate. **justice of the peace** person who can act as judge in local court. **justify** v 1 prove right. 2 vindicate. **justifiable** adj **justification** n

jut v **jutting, jutted** project, stick out, protrude.

jute n plant fibre used for rope, canvas etc.

juvenile ⊕ adj 1 of, for young children. 2 immature. ◆ n 3 young person, child.

juxtapose v put side by side. **juxtaposition** n

——————— THESAURUS ———————

= **leap**, spring, skip, bound, hop;
= **rise**, increase, upswing, advance, upsurge

junior adj = **minor**, lower, secondary, lesser, subordinate

junk n = **rubbish**, refuse, waste, scrap, litter

jurisdiction n = **authority**, power, control, rule, influence; = **range**, area, field, bounds, province

just adv = **recently**, lately, only

now; = **merely**, only, simply, solely; = **barely**, hardly, by a whisker, by the skin of your teeth ◆ adj = **fair**, good, legitimate, upright, honest ≠ **unfair**; = **fitting**, due, correct, deserved, appropriate ≠ **inappropriate**

juvenile n = **child**, youth, minor, girl, boy ≠ **adult** ◆ adj = **immature**, childish, infantile, puerile, young

K k

Kabloona *n* a person who is not of Inuit ancestry, esp. a White person.

kaftan *n* woman's long, loose dress with sleeves.

kak *n S Afr slang* **1** faeces. **2** rubbish.

kaleidoscope *n* **1** optical toy producing changing patterns. **2** any complex pattern.

kaleidoscopic *adj*

kamik *n Canad* a traditional Inuit boot made of caribou hide or sealskin.

kamikaze *n* **1** Japanese suicide pilot. ♦ *adj* **2** (of action) certain to kill or injure the doer.

kangaroo *n, pl* **–roos** Aust. marsupial with strong hind legs for jumping.

karate *n* Japanese system of unarmed combat.

karma *n* person's actions affecting fate for next incarnation.

kayak *n* **1** Inuit canoe. **2** any similar canoe.

kebab *n* **1** dish of small pieces of meat, tomatoes etc. grilled on skewers. **2** grilled minced lamb served in split slice of unleavened bread.

kedgeree *n* dish of fish cooked with rice, eggs etc.

keel *n* lowest longitudinal support on which ship is built. **keel over 1** turn upside down **2** *Inf* collapse suddenly.

keen ➊ *adj* **1** sharp. **2** acute. **3** eager. **4** shrewd. **5** (of price) competitive.

keep ➊ *v* **keeping, kept 1** retain possession of, not lose. **2** hold. **3** (cause to) remain. **4** maintain. **5** remain good. **6** continue. ♦ *n* **7** maintenance. **8** central tower of castle. **keeper** *n* **keeping** *n* **1** harmony. **2** care, charge.

keepsake *n* gift treasured for sake of the giver.

keg *n* **1** small barrel. **2** container for beer.

kelp *n* large seaweed.

ken *n* range of knowledge.

kennel *n* shelter for dog.

—————— THESAURUS ——————

keen *adj* = eager, intense, enthusiastic, passionate, ardent ≠ **unenthusiastic**; = sharp, incisive, cutting, edged, razor–like ≠ **dull**; = perceptive, quick, sharp, acute, smart ≠ **obtuse**; = intense, strong, fierce, relentless, cut–throat

keep *v* (usually with **from**) = prevent, restrain, hinder, keep back; = hold on to, maintain, retain, save, preserve ≠ **lose**; = store, put, place, house, hold; = carry, stock, sell, supply, handle; = support, maintain, sustain, provide for, mind ♦ *n* = board, food, maintenance, living, hold

kerb n stone edging to footpath.

kernel n 1 inner seed of nut or fruit stone. 2 central, essential part.

kerosene n US and Canad another name for PARAFFIN.

kestrel n small falcon.

ketchup n sauce of vinegar, tomatoes etc.

kettle n metal vessel with spout and handle, esp. for boiling water. **kettledrum** n musical instrument made of membrane stretched over copper hemisphere.

key ❶ n 1 instrument for operating lock, winding clock etc. 2 explanation, means of achieving an end etc. 3 Mus set of related notes. ◆ adj 5 most important. **keyboard** n set of keys on piano, computer etc. **keyhole** n opening for key. **keynote** n dominant idea.

kg kilogram.

khaki adj 1 dull, yellowish-brown. ◆ n 2 khaki cloth. 3 military uniform.

kibbutz n, pl **kibbutzim** communal agricultural settlement in Israel.

kick ❶ v 1 strike (out) with foot. 2 recoil. 3 resist 4 Inf free oneself of (habit etc.). ◆ n 5 blow with foot. 6 thrill. 7 strength (of flavour, alcoholic drink etc.). 8 recoil. **kick off** start (a game of football). **kick out** dismiss or expel forcibly.

kid ❶ n 1 young goat. 2 leather of its skin. 3 Inf child. ◆ v 4 Inf tease, deceive. 5 behave, speak in fun.

kidnap ❶ v –napping, –napped seize and hold to ransom.

kidnapper n

kidney n 1 either of the pair of organs which secrete urine. 2 animal kidney used as food.

kill ❶ v 1 deprive of life. 2 put an end to. 3 pass (time). ◆ n 4 act of killing. 5 animals etc. killed. **killer** n

killing adj 1 Inf very tiring. 2 very funny.

kiln furnace, oven.

kilo n short for KILOGRAM.

kilo– comb. form one thousand, as in kilometre, kilowatt.

kilobyte n Comp 1024 bytes.

kilogram, kilogramme n 1000 grams.

kilohertz n 1000 cycles per second.

kilt n pleated tartan skirt worn orig. by Scottish Highlanders.

kimono n, pl **–nos** loose Japanese

———— THESAURUS ————

key n = **opener**, door key, latchkey ◆ adj = **essential**, leading, major, main, important ≠ minor

kick v = **boot**, knock, punt; = (Inf) **give up**, break, stop, abandon, quit ◆ n = (Inf) **thrill**, buzz (Sl), tingle, high (Sl)

kid n = (Inf) **child**, baby, teenager, youngster, infant, ankle–biter (Aust sl) ◆ v = **tease**, joke, trick, fool, pretend

kidnap v = **abduct**, capture, seize, snatch (Sl), hijack

kill v = **slay**, murder, execute, slaughter, destroy; = (Inf) **destroy**, crush, scotch, stop, halt

robe.

kin, kinsfolk n relatives. **kindred**
1 relatives. ◆ adj 2 similar. 3
related. **kinsman** n

kind ❶ n 1 sort, type, class. ◆ adj
2 considerate. 3 gentle. **kindly** adj
–lier, –liest 1 kind, genial. ◆ adv 2
gently. **kindness** n **kind–hearted**
adj

kindergarten n class, school for
children of about four to six years
old.

kindle v 1 set alight. 2 arouse. 3
catch fire. **kindling** n small wood
to kindle fires.

kindy, kindie n, pl –dies Aust & NZ
informal kindergarten.

kinetic adj relating to motion.

king ❶ n 1 male ruler. 2 chess
piece. 3 highest court card 4
Draughts crowned piece. **kingdom**
n 1 state ruled by king. 2 realm. 3
sphere. **kingpin** n Inf chief thing or
person. **king–size** adj Inf very large.
kingfisher n small brightly–
coloured bird.

kink n 1 tight twist in rope, wire,
hair etc. ◆ v 2 make, become
kinked. **kinky** adj 1 full of kinks 2
Inf deviant.

kiosk n 1 small, sometimes
movable booth. 2 public
telephone box.

kip v Inf sleep.

kipper n smoked herring.

kirk n in Scotland, church.

kismet n fate, destiny.

kiss ❶ n 1 touch or caress with
lips. 2 light touch. ◆ v 3 touch
with lips. **kiss of life** mouth–to–
mouth resuscitation.

kist n S Afr large wooden chest.

kit ❶ n 1 outfit, equipment. 2
personal effects, esp. of traveller. 3
set of pieces of equipment sold
ready to be assembled. ◆ v (with
out) 4 provide with kit. **kitbag** n
bag for soldier's kit.

kitchen n room used for cooking.

kite n 1 light papered frame flown
in wind. 2 large hawk.

kitsch n vulgarized, pretentious
art.

kitten n young cat. **kittenish** adj
playful.

kitty n, pl –ties 1 in some card
games, pool. 2 communal fund.

kiwi n 1 NZ flightless bird 2 Inf
New Zealander. **kiwi fruit** edible
fruit with green flesh.

klaxon n loud horn.

kleptomania n compulsion to
steal. **kleptomaniac** n

kloof n S Afr mountain pass or
gorge.

km kilometre.

knack ❶ n 1 acquired facility or
dexterity. 2 trick. 3 habit.

———— THESAURUS ————

kind n = class, sort, type, variety,
brand

king n = ruler, monarch,
sovereign, leader, lord

kiss v = peck (Inf), osculate, neck
(Inf) ◆ n = peck (Inf), snog,

smacker (Sl), French kiss,
osculation

kit n = equipment, materials,
tackle, tools, apparatus

knack n = skill, art, ability, facility,
talent ≠ ineptitude

knacker n buyer of worn-out horses etc. for killing. **knackered** adj Sl exhausted.

knapsack n haversack.

knave n 1 jack at cards. 2 Obs rogue. **knavish** adj

knead v 1 work into dough. 2 massage.

knee n joint between thigh and lower leg. **kneecap** n bone in front of knee. **kneejerk** adj (of reaction) automatic and predictable.

knees-up n Inf party.

kneel ❶ v kneeling, kneeled fall, rest on knees.

knell n/v (ring) death bell.

knickers ❶ pl n woman's undergarment for lower half of body.

knick-knack n trinket.

knife ❶ n, pl knives 1 cutting blade, esp. one in handle, used as implement or weapon. ◆ v 2 cut or stab with knife.

knight n 1 man of rank below baronet. 2 member of medieval order of chivalry. 3 piece in chess. ◆ v 4 confer knighthood on. **knighthood** n

knit ❶ v knitting, knitted 1 form (garment etc.) by linking loops of yarn. 2 draw together. 3 unite.

knob n rounded lump. **knobbly** adj

knock ❶ v 1 strike, hit 2 Inf disparage. 3 rap audibly. 4 (of engine) make metallic noise. ◆ n 5 blow, rap. **knocker** n appliance for knocking on door. **knock back** 1 Inf drink quickly. 2 reject. **knock-kneed** adj having incurved legs. **knock out** 1 render unconscious 2 Inf overwhelm, amaze. **knockout** n

knoll n small hill.

knot ❶ n 1 fastening of strands by looping and pulling tight. 2 cluster. 3 hard lump, esp. in timber. 4 nautical miles per hour. ◆ v 5 tie with knot, in knots. **knotty** adj 1 full of knots. 2 puzzling, difficult.

know ❶ v knowing, knew, known 1 be aware (of), have information (about). 2 be acquainted with. 3 understand. 4 feel certain. **knowing** adj shrewd. **knowingly** adv 1 shrewdly. 2 deliberately. **knowledge** n 1 knowing. 2 what one knows. 3 learning. **knowledgable, knowledgeable** adj well-informed.

———— THESAURUS ————

kneel v = genuflect, stoop

knickers pl n = underwear, smalls, briefs, drawers, panties

knife n = blade, carver, cutter ◆ v = cut, wound, stab, slash, thrust

knit v = join, unite, link, tie, bond; = furrow, tighten, knot, wrinkle, crease

knock v = bang, strike, tap, rap, thump; = hit, strike, punch, belt (Inf), smack; = (Inf) criticize, condemn, put down, run down, abuse ◆ n = knocking, pounding, beating, tap, bang; = bang, blow, impact, jar, collision

knot n = connection, tie, bond, joint, loop ◆ v = tie, secure, bind, loop, tether

knuckle n bone at finger joint.

knuckle down get down (to work).

knuckle–duster n metal appliance on knuckles to add force to blow.

knuckle under submit.

KO knockout.

koala n marsupial Aust. animal, native bear.

kohl n cosmetic powder.

Koran n sacred book of Muslims.

kosher adj **1** conforming to Jewish dietary law **2** Inf legitimate, authentic.

kowtow v **1** prostrate oneself. **2** be obsequious.

krypton n rare atmospheric gas.

kudos n **1** fame. **2** credit.

kugel [**koog**–el] n S Afr rich, fashion–conscious, materialistic young woman.

kung fu n Chinese martial art.

——————————— THESAURUS ———————————

know v = **have knowledge of**, see, understand, recognize, perceive; = **be acquainted with**, recognize, be familiar with, be friends with, be friendly with ≠ **be unfamiliar with**

K

L l

l litre.

lab n Inf short for LABORATORY.

label ❶ n 1 slip of paper, metal etc., giving information. 2 descriptive phrase. ♦ v 3 give label.

laboratory n, pl –ries place for scientific investigations or for manufacture of chemicals.

labour n 1 exertion of body or mind. 2 workers collectively.

labrador n breed of large, smooth–coated retriever dog.

laburnum n tree with yellow hanging flowers.

labyrinth n 1 maze. 2 perplexity.

lace ❶ n 1 patterned openwork fabric. 2 cord, usu. one of pair, to draw edges together. ♦ v 3 fasten with laces. 4 flavour with spirit.

lacy adj fine, like lace.

lacerate v tear, mangle.

lachrymose adj tearful.

lack ❶ n 1 deficiency. ♦ v 2 need, be short of.

lackadaisical adj languid.

lackey n 1 servile follower. 2 footman.

lacklustre adj lacking brilliance or vitality.

laconic adj terse.

lacquer n 1 hard varnish. ♦ v 2 coat with this.

lacrosse n ball game played with long–handled racket.

lad ❶ n boy, young fellow.

ladder n 1 frame with rungs, for climbing. 2 line of torn stitches, esp. in stockings.

laden ❶ adj heavily loaded.

ladle n 1 spoon with long handle and large bowl. ♦ v 2 serve out liquid with a ladle.

lady ❶ n, pl –dies 1 female counterpart of gentleman. 2 polite term for a woman. 3 title of some women of rank. **ladybird** n small beetle, usu. red with black spots.

ladylike adj gracious.

lag¹ ❶ v go too slowly, fall behind

THESAURUS

label n = **tag**, ticket, tab, marker, sticker ♦ v = **tag**, mark, stamp, ticket, tab

lace n = **netting**, net, filigree, meshwork, openwork; = **cord**, tie, string, lacing, shoelace ♦ v = **fasten**, tie, tie up, do up, secure; = **mix**, drug, doctor, add to, spike; = **intertwine**, interweave, entwine, twine, interlink

lack n = **shortage**, want, absence, deficiency, need ≠ **abundance** ♦ v = **miss**, want, need, require, not have ≠ **have**

lad n = **boy**, kid (Inf), guy (Inf), youth, fellow

laden adj = **loaded**, burdened, full, charged, weighed down

lady n = **gentlewoman**, duchess, noble, dame, baroness; = **woman**,

laggard *n* one who lags.

lag² *v* wrap boiler, pipes etc. with insulating material. **lagging** *n* this material.

lag³ *n* Sl convict.

lager *n* light–bodied beer.

lagoon *n* saltwater lake, enclosed by atoll or sandbank.

laid see LAY¹. **laid–back** *adj Inf* relaxed.

lair *n* den of animal.

laird *n* Scottish landowner.

laissez–faire *n* principle of nonintervention.

laity *n* people not belonging to clergy.

lake ⊙ *n* expanse of inland water.

lama *n* Buddhist priest in Tibet or Mongolia.

lamb 1 young of the sheep. **2** its meat. **3** innocent or helpless creature. ♦ *v* **4** give birth to lamb.

lambast, lambaste *v* **1** beat, thrash. **2** reprimand severely.

lame ⊙ *adj* **1** crippled in leg. **2** limping. **3** unconvincing. ♦ *v* **4** cripple.

lamé *n/adj* (fabric) interwoven with gold or silver thread.

lament ⊙ *v* **1** express sorrow (for). ♦ *n* **2** expression of grief. **3** song of grief. **lamentable** *adj* deplorable, disappointing. **lamentation** *n*

laminate *v* **1** make (sheet of material) by bonding together two or more thin sheets. **2** cover with thin sheet. ♦ *n* **3** laminated sheet. **lamination** *n*

lamington *n Aust & NZ* sponge cake coated with a sweet frosting.

lamp *n* appliance (esp. electrical) that produces, light, heat etc. **lamppost** *n* post supporting lamp in street.

lampoon *n/v* (make subject of) a satire.

lamprey *n* fish like an eel.

lance *n* **1** horseman's spear. ♦ *v* **2** pierce with lance or lancet. **lancet** *n* pointed two–edged surgical knife.

land ⊙ *n* **1** solid part of earth's surface. **2** ground. **3** country. **4** estate. ♦ *v* **5** come to land. **6** disembark. **7** arrive on ground. **8** bring to land. **9** *Inf* obtain. **10** catch. **11** *Inf* strike. **landed** *adj* possessing, consisting of lands. **landing** *n* **1** act of landing. **2** platform between flights of stairs. **landlocked** *adj* completely surrounded by land. **landlord** *n* **1** person who lets land or houses etc. **2** master or mistress of inn, boarding house etc. **landlubber** *n* person ignorant of the sea and

———— THESAURUS ————

female, girl, damsel

lag¹ *v* = **hang back**, delay, trail, linger, loiter

lake *n* = **pond**, pool, reservoir, loch (*Scot*), lagoon

lame *adj* = **disabled**, handicapped, crippled, limping,

hobbling; = **unconvincing**, poor, pathetic, inadequate, thin

lament *v* = **bemoan**, grieve, mourn, weep over, complain about ♦ *n* = **complaint**, moan, wailing, lamentation; = **dirge**, requiem, elegy, threnody

ships. **landmark** n **1** conspicuous object. **2** event, decision etc. considered as important stage in development of something.

landscape n **1** piece of inland scenery. **2** picture of this. ◆ v **3** create, arrange garden, park etc.

landslide n **1** falling of soil, rock etc. down mountainside. **2** overwhelming election victory.

lane ❶ n **1** narrow road or street. **2** specified air, sea route. **3** area of road for one stream of traffic.

language ❶ n **1** system of sounds, symbols etc. for communicating thought. **2** style of speech or expression.

languish ❶ v **1** be or become weak or faint. **2** droop, pine.

languid adj lacking energy, spiritless. **languor** n **1** lack of energy. **2** tender mood.

languorous adj

lank adj **1** lean. **2** limp. **lanky** adj

lantern n transparent case for lamp or candle.

lap[1] ❶ n **1** the part between waist and knees of a person when sitting. **2** single circuit of track. **3** stage or part of journey. ◆ v **4** enfold, wrap round. **5** overtake opponent to be one or more circuits ahead.

lap[2] ❶ v **1** drink by scooping up with tongue. **2** (of waves etc.) beat softly.

lapel n part of front of coat folded back towards shoulders.

lapwing n type of plover.

larceny n, pl **-nies** theft.

larch n deciduous conifer tree.

lard n **1** prepared pig's fat. ◆ v **2** insert strips of bacon in (meat). **3** intersperse.

larder n storeroom for food.

large ❶ adj **1** great in size, number etc. ◆ adv **2** in a big way. **largely** adv **largesse** n **1** generosity. **2** gift. **at large 1** free. **2** in general. **large-scale** adj wide-ranging, extensive.

largo adv, pl **-gos**, n Mus (passage

——————— THESAURUS ———————

land n = **ground**, earth, dry land, terra firma; = **soil**, ground, earth, clay, dirt; = **countryside**, farmland; = (Law) **property**, grounds, estate, real estate, realty; = **country**, nation, region, state, district ◆ v = **arrive**, dock, put down, moor, alight; = (Inf) **gain**, get, win, secure, acquire

lane n = **road**, street, track, path, way

language n = **tongue**, dialect, vernacular, patois; = **speech**, communication, expression,

speaking, talk

languish v = **decline**, fade away, wither away, flag, weaken ≠ **flourish**; = (Lit) **waste away**, suffer, rot, be abandoned, be neglected ≠ **thrive**; (often with **for**) = **pine**, long, desire, hunger, yearn

lap[1] n = **circuit**, tour, leg, stretch, circle

lap[2] v = **ripple**, wash, splash, swish, gurgle; = **drink**, sip, lick, swallow, gulp

large adj = **big**, great, huge, heavy, massive ≠ **small**; = **massive**,

played) in slow and dignified manner.

lariat n US and Canad another word for LASSO.

lark¹ n 1 small, brown singing bird. 2 skylark.

lark² n 1 frolic, spree. ♦ v 2 indulge in lark.

larrikin n Aust or NZ old–fashioned slang mischievous or unruly person.

larva n, pl **–vae** immature insect. **larval** adj

larynx n, pl **larynges** part of throat containing vocal cords. **laryngitis** n inflammation of this.

lasagne, lasagna n pasta formed in wide, flat sheets.

lascivious adj lustful.

laser n device for concentrating electromagnetic radiation in an intense, narrow beam.

lash¹ n 1 stroke with whip. 2 flexible part of whip. 3 eyelash. ♦ v 4 strike with whip etc. 5 dash against. 6 attack verbally, ridicule. 7 flick, wave sharply to and fro (with) 8 hit, kick.

lash² ❶ v fasten or bind tightly.

lashings pl n Inf abundance.

lass, lassie n girl.

lassitude n weariness.

lasso n, pl **–sos, –soes** 1 rope with noose for catching cattle etc. ♦ v 2 catch with this.

last¹ ❶ adj/adv 1 after all others. 2 most recent(ly). ♦ adj 3 only remaining. ♦ n 4 last person or thing. **lastly** adv finally. **last–ditch** adj done as final resort. **last straw** small irritation that, coming after others, is too much to bear. **last word** 1 final comment in argument. 2 most recent or best example.

last² ❶ v continue, hold out.

latch ❶ n 1 fastening for door. ♦ v 2 fasten with latch 3 (with onto) become attached to.

late ❶ adj 1 coming after the appointed time. 2 recent. 3 recently dead. ♦ adv 4 after proper time. 5 recently. 6 at, till late hour. **lately** adv not long since.

———————— THESAURUS ————————

great, big, huge, vast ≠ small = **plentiful**, comprehensive, lavish, bountiful, profuse

lash¹ v = **pound**, beat, strike, hammer, drum; = **censure**, attack, blast, put down, criticize; = **whip**, beat, thrash, birch, flog ♦ n = **blow**, hit, strike, stroke, stripe

lash² v = **fasten**, tie, secure, bind, strap

last¹ adj = **most recent**, latest, previous; = **hindmost**, final, at the end, remotest, furthest behind

≠ foremost

last² v = **continue**, remain, survive, carry on, endure ≠ end

latch n = **fastening**, catch, bar, lock, hook ♦ v = **fasten**, bar, secure, bolt, make fast

late adj = **overdue**, delayed, last-minute, belated, tardy ≠ early; = **dead**, deceased, departed, passed on, former ≠ alive; = **recent**, new, advanced, fresh ≠ old ♦ adv = **behind time**, belatedly, tardily, behindhand,

latent *adj* 1 existing but not developed. 2 hidden.
lateral *adj* of, at, from the side.
latex *n* sap or fluid of plants, esp. of rubber tree.
lath *n* thin strip of wood.
lathe *n* machine for turning and shaping.
lather *n* 1 soapy froth. 2 frothy sweat. ◆ *v* 3 make frothy.
Latin *n* 1 language of ancient Romans. ◆ *adj* 2 of ancient Romans or their language.
latitude ❶ *n* 1 angular distance in degrees N or S of equator. 2 scope. ◆ *pl* 3 regions.
latrine *n* in army etc., lavatory.
latter ❶ *adj* 1 second of two. 2 later. 3 more recent. **latterly** *adv*
latter-day *adj* modern.
lattice *n* 1 network of strips of wood, metal etc. 2 window so made.
laud *v* praise. **laudable** *adj* praiseworthy.
laudanum *n* sedative from opium.
laugh ❶ *v/n* (make) sound of amusement, merriment or scorn.

laughable *adj* ludicrous. **laughter** *n*
laughing stock object of general derision.
launch[1] ❶ *v* 1 set afloat. 2 set in motion. 3 begin. 4 propel (missile, spacecraft) into space.
launch[2] *n* large power-driven boat.
laureate *adj* crowned with laurels. **poet laureate** poet with appointment to Royal Household.
laurel *n* 1 glossy-leaved shrub, bay tree. ◆ *pl* 2 its leaves, emblem of victory or merit.
lava *n* molten matter thrown out by volcano.
lavatory ❶ *n, pl* **–ries** toilet, water closet.
lavender *n* 1 shrub with fragrant, pale-lilac flowers. 2 this colour.
lavish ❶ *adj* 1 plentiful, rich. 2 very generous. ◆ *v* 3 spend, bestow, profusely.
law ❶ *n* 1 rule binding on community. 2 system of such rules. 3 legal science. 4 general principle deduced from facts.
lawful *adj* allowed by law. **lawless**

—— THESAURUS[1] ——

dilatorily ≠ **early**
latitude *n* = **scope**, liberty, freedom, room, space
latter *adj* = **last**, ending, closing, final, concluding ≠ **earlier**
laugh *v* = **chuckle**, giggle, snigger, cackle, chortle ◆ *n* = **chortle**, giggle, chuckle, snigger, guffaw; = (*Inf*) **joke**, scream (*Inf*), hoot (*Inf*), lark, prank; = (*Inf*) **clown**, character (*Inf*), scream (*Inf*), entertainer, card (*Inf*)

launch[1] *v* = **propel**, fire, dispatch, discharge, project; = **begin**, start, open, initiate, introduce
lavatory *n* = **toilet**, bathroom, loo (*Brit inf*), privy, cloakroom (*Brit*)
lavish *adj* = **grand**, magnificent, splendid, abundant, copious ≠ **stingy**; = **extravagant**, wild, excessive, exaggerated, wasteful ≠ **thrifty**; = **generous**, free, liberal, bountiful, open-handed ≠ **stingy**
◆ *v* = **shower**, pour, heap, deluge,

adj **1** ignoring laws. **2** violent.
lawyer *n* professional expert in
law. **lawsuit** *n* prosecution of claim
in court.

lawn *n* tended turf in garden etc.
lawyer ⊕ see LAW.

lax *adj* **1** not strict. **2** slack.

laxative *adj/n* (substance) having
loosening effect on bowels. **laxity,
laxness** *n*

lay¹ ⊕ *v* **laying, laid 1** deposit, set,
cause to lie. **2** devise (plan). **3**
attribute (blame). **4** place (bet). **5**
(of animal) produce eggs. **layer** *n*
1 single thickness as stratum or
coating. ◆ *v* **2** form layer. **lay-by** *n*
stopping place for traffic beside
road. **lay off** *v* dismiss staff during
slack period. **lay-off** *n* layout or
arrangement.

lay² ⊕ *adj* not clerical or
professional. **layman** *n* ordinary
person.

lay³ past tense of LIE. **layabout** *n*

lazy person, loafer.

layette *n* clothes for newborn
child.

lazy ⊕ *adj* **lazier, laziest** averse to
work. **laze** *v* be lazy. **lazily** *adv*
lbw *Cricket* leg before wicket.

lead¹ ⊕ *v* **leading, led 1** guide,
conduct. **2** persuade. **3** direct. **4**
be, go, play first. **5** spend (one's
life). **6** result. **7** give access to. ◆ *n*
8 that which leads or is used to
lead. **9** example. **10** front or
principal place, role etc. **11** cable
bringing current to electrical
instrument. **leader** *n* **1** one who
leads. **2** editorial article in
newspaper. **leadership** *n*

lead² *n* **1** soft, heavy grey metal. **2**
graphite in pencil. **3** plummet.
leaded *adj* (of windows) made
from small panes held together by
lead strips. **leaden** *adj* **1** sluggish. **2**
dull grey. **3** made from lead.

leaf ⊕ *n, pl* **leaves 1** organ of

dissipate ≠ **stint**

law *n* = **constitution**, code,
legislation, charter; = **statute**, act,
bill, rule, order; = **principle**, code,
canon, precept, axiom

lawyer *n* = **legal adviser**,
attorney, solicitor, counsel,
advocate

lay¹ *v* = **place**, put, set, spread,
plant; = **devise**, plan, design,
prepare, work out; = **produce**,
bear, deposit; = **arrange**, prepare,
make, organize, position;
= **attribute**, assign, allocate, allot,
ascribe; = **put forward**, offer,
present, advance, lodge; = **bet**,

stake, venture, gamble, chance

lay² *adj* = **nonclerical**, secular,
non-ordained; = **nonspecialist**,
amateur, unqualified, untrained,
inexpert

lazy *adj* = **idle**, inactive, indolent,
slack, negligent ≠ **industrious**;
= **lethargic**, languorous, slow-
moving, languid, sleepy ≠ **quick**

lead¹ *v* = **go in front (of)**, head, be
in front, be at the head (of), walk
in front (of); = **guide**, conduct,
steer, escort, precede; = **connect
to**, link, open onto; = **be ahead
(of)**, be first, exceed, be winning,
excel; = **command**, rule, govern,

photosynthesis in plants, consisting of a flat, usu. green blade on stem. **2** two pages of book etc. **3** thin sheet. ♦ v **4** turn through (pages etc.) cursorily. **leaflet** n **1** small leaf. **2** single printed and folded sheet, handbill. **leafy** adj

league¹ 🛈 n **1** agreement for mutual help. **2** parties to it. **3** federation of clubs etc. **4** Inf class, level.

league² n former measure of distance, about 3 miles.

leak 🛈 n **1** defect that allows escape or entrance of liquid, gas, radiation etc. **2** disclosure. ♦ v **3** let fluid etc. in or out. **4** (of fluid etc.) find its way through leak. **5** (allow to) become known little by

little. **leakage** n **1** leaking. **2** gradual escape or loss. **leaky** adj

lean¹ 🛈 v **leaning, leaned 1** rest against. **2** incline. **3** tend (towards). **4** rely (on). **leaning** n tendency. **lean-to** n room, shed built against existing wall.

lean² adj **1** lacking fat. **2** thin. meagre. ♦ n **4** lean part of meat.

leap 🛈 v **leaping, leapt 1** spring, jump. **2** spring over. ♦ n **3** jump. **leapfrog** n/v vault over person bending down. **leap year** year with extra day.

learn 🛈 v **learning, learned 1** gain skill, knowledge. **2** memorize. **3** find out. **learned** adj showing much learning. **learner** n **learning** n knowledge got by study.

lease 🛈 n **1** contract by which

——————— THESAURUS ———————

preside over, head; **= live**, have, spend, experience, pass ♦ n **= first place**, winning position, primary position, vanguard; **= advantage**, start, edge, margin, winning margin; **= example**, direction, leadership, guidance, model; **= clue**, suggestion, hint, indication, pointer; **= leading role**, principal, protagonist, title role, principal part ♦ adj **= main**, prime, top, leading, first

leaf n **= frond**, blade, cotyledon; **= page**, sheet, folio

league¹ n **= association**, union, alliance, coalition, group; **= (Inf) class**, group, level, category, conspiring with

leak v **= escape**, pass, spill, release, drip; **= disclose**, tell,

reveal, pass on, give away ♦ n **= leakage**, discharge, drip, seepage, percolation; **= hole**, opening, crack, puncture, aperture; **= disclosure**, exposé, exposure, admission, revelation

lean¹ = **bend**, tip, slope, incline, tilt; **= rest**, prop, be supported, recline, repose; **= tend**, prefer, favour, incline, be prone to

lean² adj **= thin**, slim, slender, skinny, angular ≠ **fat**

leap v **= jump**, spring, bound, bounce, hop ♦ n **= jump**, spring, bound, vault; **= rise**, change, increase, soaring, surge

learn v **= master**, grasp, pick up, take in, familiarize yourself with; **= discover**, hear, understand, find out about, become aware;

land or property is rented. ♦ v 2 let, rent by lease. **leasehold** adj held on lease.

leash n lead for dog.

least adj 1 smallest: superlative of LITTLE. ♦ n 2 smallest one. ♦ adv 3 in smallest degree.

leather n prepared skin of animal.

leathery adj like leather, tough.

leave¹ 🟕 v leaving, left 1 go away. 2 allow to remain. 3 entrust. 4 bequeath.

leave² n 1 permission, esp. to be absent from duty. 2 period of such absence. 3 formal parting.

leaven n 1 yeast. ♦ v 2 raise with leaven.

lecherous adj 1 full of lust. 2 lascivious. **lecher** n lecherous man. **lechery** n

lectern n reading desk.

lecture 🟕 n 1 instructive discourse. 2 speech of reproof. ♦ v 3 deliver discourse. 4 reprove.

lecturer n

ledge n 1 narrow shelf sticking out from wall, cliff etc. 2 ridge below surface of sea.

ledger n book of debit and credit accounts.

lee n 1 shelter. 2 side, esp. of ship, away from wind. **leeward** adj/adv/n (on, towards) lee side. **leeway** n 1 leeward drift of ship. 2 room for movement within limits.

leech n species of bloodsucking worm.

leek n plant like onion with long bulb and thick stem.

leer v/n glance with malign or lascivious expression.

lees 🟕 pl n 1 sediment. 2 dregs.

left¹ 🟕 adj 1 on or to the west. 2 opposite to the right. 3 radical, socialist. ♦ adv 4 on or towards the left. ♦ n 5 the left hand or part. 6 Politics reforming or radical party.

leftist n/adj (person) of the political left (also **left–wing**).

left² past tense and past participle

——————— THESAURUS ———————

= **memorize**, commit to memory, learn by heart, learn by rote, learn parrot–fashion

lease v = **hire**, rent, let, loan, charter

leave v = **depart from**, withdraw from, go from, escape from, quit ≠ **arrive**; = **quit**, give up, get out of, resign from, drop out of; = **give up**, abandon, dump (Inf), drop, surrender ≠ **stay with**; = **entrust**, commit, delegate, refer, hand over; = **bequeath**, will, transfer, endow, confer; = **forget**, leave behind, mislay ♦ n

= **holiday**, break, vacation, time off, sabbatical; = **permission**, freedom, sanction, liberty, concession ≠ **refusal**; = **departure**, parting, withdrawal, goodbye, farewell ≠ **arrival**

lecture n = **talk**, address, speech, lesson, instruction; = **telling–off** (Inf), rebuke, reprimand, talking– to (Inf), scolding ♦ v = **talk**, speak, teach, address, discourse; = **tell off** (Inf), berate, scold, reprimand, censure

lees pl n = **sediment**, grounds, deposit, dregs

of LEAVE[1].

leg ❶ n 1 one of limbs on which person or animal walks, runs, stands. 2 part of garment covering leg. 3 support, as leg of table. 4 stage. **leggings** pl n covering of leather or other material (for legs). **leggy** adj long–legged. **legless** adj 1 without leg. 2 Sl very drunk.

legacy ❷ n, pl –cies 1 bequest. 2 thing handed down to successor.

legal ❸ adj in accordance with law. **legality** n **legalize** v make legal. **legally** adv

legate n messenger, representative.

legatee n recipient of legacy.

legato adv, pl –tos Mus smoothly.

legend ❹ n 1 traditional story. 2 notable person or event. 3 inscription. **legendary** adj

legible adj readable. **legibility** n

legion ❺ n 1 various military bodies. 2 association of veterans. 3 large number. ◆ adj 4 countless.

legionary adj/n **legionnaire** n member of legion. **legionnaire's disease** serious bacterial disease similar to pneumonia.

legislate v make laws. **legislation** n 1 act of legislating. 2 laws which are made. **legislative** adj

legitimate ❻ adj 1 born in wedlock. 2 lawful, regular. ◆ v make lawful. **legitimacy** n **legitimize** v

legume n pod.

leisure ❼ n spare time. **leisurely** adj 1 unhurried. ◆ adv 2 slowly.

lekker adj S Afr slang 1 attractive or nice. 2 tasty.

lemming n rodent of arctic regions.

lemon n 1 pale yellow fruit. 2 its colour. 3 Sl useless person or thing. **lemonade** n drink made from lemon juice. **lemon curd** creamy spread made of lemons, butter etc.

lemur n nocturnal animal like

——————— THESAURUS ———————

left¹ adj = **left-hand**, port, larboard (Naut)

leg n = **limb**, member, shank, lower limb, pin (Inf); = **support**, prop, brace, upright; = **stage**, part, section, stretch, lap **pull someone's leg** = (Inf) **tease**, trick, fool, kid (Inf), wind up (Brit sl)

legacy n = **bequest**, inheritance, gift, estate, heirloom

legal adj = **judicial**, judiciary, forensic, juridical, jurisdictive; = **lawful**, allowed, sanctioned, constitutional, valid

legend n = **myth**, story, tale,

fiction, saga; = **celebrity**, star, phenomenon, genius, prodigy; = **inscription**, title, caption, device, motto

legion n = **army**, company, force, division, troop; = **multitude**, host, mass, drove, number

legitimate adj = **lawful**, legal, genuine, authentic, authorized ≠ **unlawful**; = **reasonable**, correct, sensible, valid, warranted ≠ **unreasonable** ◆ v = **legitimize**, allow, permit, sanction, authorize

leisure n = **spare**, free, rest, ease, relaxation ≠ **work**

monkey.

lend v 1 give temporary use of. 2 let out at interest. 3 bestow.

length 🚯 n 1 measurement from end to end. 2 duration. 3 extent. 4 piece of a certain length. **lengthen** v make, become, longer. **lengthy** adj very long.

lenient adj not strict. **leniency** n

lens n, pl **lenses** glass etc. shaped to converge or diverge light rays.

lent see LEND.

Lent n period of fasting from Ash Wednesday to Easter Eve.

lentil n edible seed of leguminous plant.

leopard n large, spotted, carnivorous cat.

leotard n tight–fitting garment covering most of body.

leper n 1 one ill with leprosy. 2 person shunned. **leprosy** n ulcerous skin disease.

leprechaun n mischievous Irish elf.

lesbian 🚯 n 1 homosexual woman. ◆ adj 2 (of woman) homosexual.

lesion n harmful sore on bodily organ.

less 🚯 adj comparative of LITTLE. 1 not so much. ◆ n 2 smaller part, quantity. 3 a lesser amount. ◆ adv 4 to a smaller extent. ◆ prep 5 minus. **lessen** v 1 diminish. 2 reduce. **lesser** adj 1 smaller. 2 minor.

lesson 🚯 n 1 instalment of course of instruction. 2 content of this. 3 experience that teaches. 4 portion of Scripture read in church.

lest conj for fear that.

let[1] 🚯 v letting, let 1 allow, enable, cause. 2 rent. 3 be leased. **let down** 1 disappoint. 2 deflate. **let off** 1 excuse. 2 fire, explode. 3 emit. **let up** v diminish, stop.

let[2] n 1 hindrance. 2 in some games, minor infringement or obstruction.

lethal 🚯 adj deadly.

lethargy n apathy, lack of energy. **lethargic** adj

letter 🚯 n 1 alphabetical symbol. 2 written message. 3 strict meaning, interpretation. ◆ pl 4 literature. ◆ v 5 mark with, in, letters.

lettuce n salad plant.

——— THESAURUS ———

length n = **distance**, reach, measure, extent, span; = **duration**, term, period, space, stretch; = **piece**, measure, section, segment, portion

lesbian adj = **homosexual**, gay, les (Sl), sapphic, lesbo (Sl)

less prep = **minus**, without, lacking, excepting, subtracting

lesson n = **class**, schooling, period, teaching, coaching; = **example**, warning, message, moral, deterrent

let[1] v = **allow**, permit, authorize, give the go–ahead, give permission; = **lease**, hire, rent, rent out, hire out

lethal adj = **deadly**, terminal, fatal, dangerous, devastating ≠ **harmless**

leukaemia n progressive blood disease.

level ⊕ adj **1** horizontal. **2** even, flat. ◆ n **3** horizontal line or surface. **4** instrument for establishing horizontal plane. **5** position on scale. **6** grade. ◆ v **7** make, become level. **8** knock down. **9** aim (gun, accusation etc.). **level crossing** point where railway and road cross. **level-headed** adj not apt to be carried away by emotion.

lever ⊕ n **1** rigid bar pivoted about a fulcrum to transfer a force with mechanical advantage. **2** operating handle. ◆ v **3** prise, move, with lever. **leverage** n **1** action, power of lever. **2** influence.

leveret n young hare.

leviathan n **1** sea monster. **2** anything huge or formidable.

levitation n raising of solid body into the air supernaturally. **levitate** v (cause to) do this.

levity n, pl **-ties** (undue) frivolity.

levy ⊕ v **levying, levied 1** impose (tax). **2** raise (troops). ◆ n **3** imposition or collection of taxes.

lewd adj **1** lustful. **2** indecent.

lexicon n dictionary.

liable ⊕ adj **1** answerable. **2** exposed (to). **3** subject (to). **4** likely (to). **liability** n **1** state of being liable. **2** debt. **3** hindrance, disadvantage. ◆ pl **4** debts.

liar ⊕ n see LIE[1].

lib n Inf short for LIBERATION.

libel ⊕ n **1** published statement falsely damaging person's reputation. ◆ v **2** defame falsely. **libellous** adj defamatory.

liberal ⊕ adj **1** (also with cap.) of political party favouring democratic reforms and individual freedom. **2** generous. **3** tolerant. **4** abundant. ◆ n **5** one who has liberal ideas or opinions. **liberality** n generosity. **liberalize** v make (laws etc.) less restrictive. **liberally**

———— THESAURUS ————

letter n = **message**, line, note, communication, dispatch; = **character**, mark, sign, symbol, education

level n = **position**, standard, degree, grade, standing ◆ adj = **equal**, balanced, at the same height; = **horizontal**, even, flat, smooth, uniform ≠ slanted; = **even**, tied, equal, drawn, neck and neck ◆ v = **equalize**, balance, even up; = **destroy**, devastate, demolish, flatten, knock down ≠ build; = **direct**, point, turn, train, aim; = **flatten**, plane, smooth,

even off or out

lever n = **handle**, bar ◆ v = **prise**, force

levy n = **tax**, fee, toll, tariff, duty ◆ v = **impose**, charge, collect, demand, exact

liable adj = **likely**, tending, inclined, disposed, prone; = **vulnerable**, subject, exposed, prone, susceptible

liar n = **falsifier**, perjurer, fibber, fabricator

libel n = **defamation**, misrepresentation, denigration, smear, calumny ◆ v = **defame**,

adv
liberate ❶ *v* set free. **liberation** *n*
liberator *n*
libertine *n* 1 morally dissolute person. ♦ *adj* 2 dissolute.
liberty ❶ *n, pl* **–ties** freedom. **libertarian** *n/adj* (person) believing in freedom of thought and action. **at liberty 1** free. **2** having the right. **take liberties** be presumptuous.
libido *n, pl* **–dos 1** psychic energy. **2** sexual drive. **libidinous** *adj* lustful.
library *n, pl* **–braries 1** room, building where books are kept. **2** collection of books, records etc. **librarian** *n* keeper of library.
libretto *n, pl* **–tos, –ti** words of opera. **librettist** *n*
lice *n pl* of LOUSE.
licence ❶ *n* 1 permit. **2** permission. **3** excessive liberty. **4** dissoluteness. **license** *v* grant

licence to. **licensee** *n* holder of licence.
license plate *n* the US and Canadian term for NUMBERPLATE.
licentious *adj* dissolute.
lichen *n* small flowerless plants on rocks, trees etc.
licit *adj* lawful.
lick ❶ *v* 1 pass tongue over. **2** touch slightly. **3** *Sl* defeat. ♦ *n* **4** act of licking. **5** small amount (esp. of paint etc.). **6** *Sl* speed. **licking** *n Sl* beating.
licorice *n* see LIQUORICE.
lid *n* 1 movable cover. **2** eyelid.
lido *n, pl* **–dos** pleasure centre with swimming and boating.
lie¹ ❶ *v* **lying, lied** 1 make false statement. ♦ *n* **2** deliberate falsehood. **liar** *n* person who tells lies.
lie² ❶ *v* 1 be horizontal, at rest. **2** be situated. **3** be in certain state. **4** exist. ♦ *n* **5** state (of affairs etc.).

———————— THESAURUS ————————

smear, slur, blacken, malign
liberal *adj* = **tolerant**, open-minded, permissive, indulgent, easy–going ≠ **intolerant**; = **progressive**, radical, reformist, libertarian, forward–looking ≠ **conservative**; = **abundant**, generous, handsome, lavish, ample ≠ **limited**; = **generous**, kind, charitable, extravagant, open-hearted ≠ **stingy**
liberate *v* = **free**, release, rescue, save, deliver ≠ **imprison**
liberty *n* = **independence**, sovereignty, liberation, autonomy, immunity, = **freedom**, liberation,

emancipation, deliverance ≠ **restraint**
licence *n* = **certificate**, document, permit, charter, warrant; = **permission**, the right, authority, leave, sanction ≠ **denial**; = **freedom**, creativity, latitude, independence, liberty ≠ **restraint**; = **laxity**, excess, indulgence, irresponsibility, licentiousness ≠ **moderation**
lick *v* = **taste**, lap, tongue; = (*Inf*) **beat**, defeat, overcome, rout, outstrip; = (*of flames*) **flicker**, touch, flick, dart, ripple ♦ *n* = **dab**, bit, touch, stroke; = (*Inf*) **pace**,

lie in remain in bed late. **lie–in** n
lieu n **in lieu of** in place of.
lieutenant n **1** deputy. **2** junior
army or navy officer.
life ❶ n, pl **lives 1** active principle
of existence. **2** time that it lasts. **3**
story of a person's life. **4** way of
living. **5** vigour, vivacity. **lifeless**
adj **1** dead. **2** insensible. **3** dull.
lifelike adj **lifelong** adj lasting a
lifetime. **life belt, jacket** buoyant
device to keep person afloat.
lifeline n **1** means of help. **2** rope
thrown to person in danger. **life
preserver** n buoyant device to
keep afloat a person in danger of
drowning. **lifestyle** n particular
habits, attitudes etc. of person or
group. **lifetime** n time person,
animal or object lives or functions.
lift ❶ v **1** move upwards in
position, status, mood, volume
etc. **2** take up and remove. **3** Inf
steal. **4** disappear. ◆ n **5** cage in
vertical shaft for raising and
lowering people or goods. **6** act of
lifting. **7** ride in car etc., as

passenger. **8** boost. **liftoff** n
moment rocket leaves the ground.
ligament n band of tissue joining
bones. **ligature** n **1** anything
which binds. **2** thread for tying up
artery.
light¹ ❶ n **1** electromagnetic
radiation by which things are
visible. **2** source of this, lamp. **3**
window. **4** means or act of setting
fire to. **5** understanding. ◆ pl **6**
traffic lights. ◆ adj **7** bright. **8** pale,
not dark. ◆ v **9** set on fire. **10** give
light to. **11** brighten. **lighten** v
give light to. **lighting** n apparatus
for supplying artificial light.
lightning n visible discharge of
electricity in atmosphere.
lighthouse n tower with a light to
guide ships. **light year** distance
light travels in one year.
light² ❶ adj **1** of, or bearing, little
weight. **2** not severe. **3** easy. **4**
trivial. **5** not clumsy. **6** not serious
or profound. **7** (of industry)
producing small, usu. consumer
goods, using light machinery. ◆

—————— THESAURUS ——————

rate, speed, clip (Inf)
lie¹ n = **falsehood**, deceit,
fabrication, fib, fiction ◆ v = **fib**,
fabricate, falsify, prevaricate, not
tell the truth
lie² v = **recline**, rest, lounge,
sprawl, stretch out; = **be placed**,
be, rest, exist, be situated; = **be
situated**, sit, be located, be
positioned, reside
life n = **being**, existence, vitality,
sentience; = **existence**, being,
lifetime, time, days; = **way of life**,

situation, conduct, behaviour, life
style; = **liveliness**, energy, spirit,
vitality, animation; = **biography**,
story, history, profile, confessions
lift v = **raise**, pick up, hoist, draw
up, elevate ≠ lower; = **revoke**,
end, remove, withdraw, stop
≠ impose; = **disappear**, clear,
vanish, disperse, dissipate ◆ n
= **boost**, encouragement,
stimulus, pick–me–up, fillip
≠ blow; = **elevator** (Chiefly US),
hoist, paternoster; = **ride**, run,

adv **8** in light manner. ♦ *v* **9** come by chance (upon). **lighten** *v* reduce, remove (load etc.). **lightly** *adv* **lights** *pl n* lungs of animal.
light-fingered *adj* likely to steal.
light-headed *adj* dizzy, delirious.
light-hearted *adj* carefree.
lightweight *n/adj* (person) of little weight or importance.
lighter *n* **1** device for lighting cigarettes etc. **2** flat-bottomed boat for unloading ships.
like¹ ❶ *adj* **1** resembling. **2** similar. **3** characteristic of. ♦ *adv* **4** in the manner of. ♦ *pron* **5** similar thing.
likelihood *n* probability. **likely** *adj* **1** probable. **2** promising. ♦ *adv* **3** probably. **liken** *v* compare.
likeness *n* **1** resemblance. **2** portrait. **likewise** *adv* in like manner.
like² ❶ *v* find agreeable, enjoy,

love. **likeable** *adj* **liking** *n* **1** fondness. **2** inclination, taste.
lilac *n* shrub bearing pale mauve or white flowers.
lilt *n* rhythmical swing. **lilting** *adj*
lily *n, pl* **lilies** bulbous flowering plant. **lily of the valley** small garden plant with fragrant white flowers.
limb ❶ *n* **1** arm or leg. **2** wing. **3** branch of tree.
limber *adj* pliant, lithe. **limber up** loosen stiff muscles by exercise.
limbo¹ *n* **1** region between Heaven and Hell for the unbaptized. **2** indeterminate place or state.
limbo² *n* West Indian dance in which dancers lean backwards to pass under a bar.
lime¹ *n* **1** calcium compound used in fertilizer, cement. ♦ *v* **2** treat

——— THESAURUS ———

drive, hitch (*Inf*)
light¹ *n* = **brightness**, illumination, luminosity, shining, glow ≠ **dark**;
= **lamp**, torch, candle, flare, beacon; = **match**, spark, flame, lighter; = **aspect**, context, angle, point of view, interpretation ♦ *adj*
= **bright**, brilliant, shining, illuminated, luminous ≠ **dark**;
= **pale**, fair, faded, blonde, blond ≠ **dark** ♦ *v* = **illuminate**, light up, brighten ≠ **darken**; = **ignite**, inflame, kindle, touch off, set alight ≠ **put out**
light² *adj* = **insubstantial**, thin, slight, portable, buoyant ≠ **heavy**;
= **weak**, soft, gentle, moderate, slight ≠ **strong**; = **digestible**,

modest, frugal ≠ **substantial**;
= **insignificant**, small, slight, petty, trivial ≠ **serious**; = **light-hearted**, funny, entertaining, amusing, witty ≠ **serious**; = **nimble**, graceful, deft, agile, sprightly ≠ **clumsy**
like¹ *adj* = **similar to**, same as, equivalent to, parallel to, identical to ≠ **different**
like² *v* = **enjoy**, love, delight in, go for, relish ≠ **dislike**; = **admire**, approve of, appreciate, prize, take to ≠ **dislike**; = **wish**, want, choose, prefer, desire
limb *n* = **part**, member, arm, leg, wing; = **branch**, spur, projection, offshoot, bough

(land) with lime. **limelight** n glare of publicity. **limestone** n sedimentary rock used in building.

lime² n small acid fruit like lemon.

lime–green adj greenish–yellow.

lime³ n tree.

limerick n humorous verse of five lines.

limit ❶ n 1 utmost extent or duration. 2 boundary. ◆ v 3 restrict, restrain, bound. **limitation** n limited company one whose shareholders' liability is restricted.

limousine n large, luxurious car.

limp¹ ❶ v 1 walk lamely. ◆ n 2 limping walk.

limp² ❶ adj without firmness or stiffness.

limpet n shellfish that sticks tightly to rocks.

limpid adj 1 clear. 2 translucent.

linchpin, lynchpin n 1 pin to hold wheel on its axle. 2 essential person or thing.

linctus n, pl **-tuses** syrupy cough medicine.

line ❶ n 1 long narrow mark. 2 row. 3 series, course. 4 telephone connection. 5 progeny. 6 province of activity. 7 shipping company. 8 railway track. 9 any class of goods. 10 cord. 11 approach, policy. ◆ v 12 cover inside. 13 mark with lines. 14 bring into line. **lineage** n descent from, descendants of an ancestor. **lineament** n feature.

linear adj of, in lines. **liner** n large ship or aircraft of passenger line.

linesman n sporting official who helps referee. **line–up** n people or things assembled for particular purpose.

linen adj 1 made of flax. ◆ n 2 linen cloth. 3 linen articles collectively.

linger ❶ v 1 delay, loiter. 2 remain long.

lingerie n women's underwear or nightwear.

linguist n one skilled in languages or language study. **linguistic** adj of languages or their study.

linguistics pl n study, science of language.

liniment n embrocation.

lining n covering for inside of

limit n = **end**, ultimate, deadline, breaking point, extremity; = **boundary**, edge, border, frontier, perimeter ◆ v = **restrict**, control, check, bound, confine

limp¹ v = **hobble**, stagger, stumble, shuffle, hop ◆ n = **lameness**, hobble

limp² adj = **floppy**, soft, slack, drooping, flabby ≠ **stiff**

line n = **stroke**, mark, score, band, scratch; = **wrinkle**, mark, crease,

furrow, crow's foot; = **row**, queue, rank, file, column; = **string**, cable, wire, rope, thread; = **trajectory**, way, course, track, channel; = **boundary**, limit, edge, border, frontier; = **occupation**, work, calling, business, job ◆ v = **border**, edge, bound, fringe; = **mark**, crease, furrow, rule, score; = **under control**, in order, in check

linger v = **stay**, remain, stop, wait, delay

garment etc.
link ⊕ n **1** ring of chain. **2** connection. ♦ v **3** join with, as with, link. **4** intertwine. **linkage** n
links pl n golf course.
linnet n songbird of finch family.
lino n short for LINOLEUM.
linoleum n floor covering of powdered cork, linseed oil etc. backed with hessian.
linseed n seed of flax plant.
lint n soft material for dressing wounds.
lintel n top piece of door or window.
lion ⊕ n large animal of cat family.
lip ⊕ n **1** either edge of the mouth. **2** edge or margin. **3** Sl impudence. **lip-reading** n method of understanding speech by interpreting lip movements. **lip service** insincere tribute or respect. **lipstick** n cosmetic for colouring lips.
liqueur n alcoholic liquor flavoured and sweetened.
liquid ⊕ adj **1** fluid, not solid or gaseous. **2** flowing smoothly. **3** (of

assets) easily converted into money. ♦ n **4** substance in liquid form. **liquefy** v make or become liquid. **liquidity** n state of being able to meet debts. **liquidize** v **liquidizer** n
liquidate v **1** pay (debt). **2** arrange affairs of, and dissolve (company). **3** wipe out, kill.
liquidation n **1** clearing up of financial affairs. **2** bankruptcy.
liquidator n official appointed to liquidate business.
liquor ⊕ n alcoholic liquid.
liquorice n black substance used in medicine and as a sweet.
lira n, pl -re, -ras **1** a former monetary unit of Italy. **2** the standard monetary unit of Turkey.
lisp v/n (speak with) faulty pronunciation of s and z.
lissom, lissome adj supple, agile.
list¹ ⊕ n **1** inventory, register. **2** catalogue. ♦ v **3** place on list.
list² ⊕ v **1** (of ship) lean to one side. ♦ n **2** inclination of ship.
listen ⊕ v try to hear, attend to.
listener n

——— THESAURUS ———

link n = **connection**, relationship, association, tie-up, affinity ♦ v = **associate**, relate, identify, connect, bracket; = **connect**, join, unite, couple, tie ≠ separate
lip n = **edge**, rim, brim, margin, brink; = (Sl) **impudence**, insolence, impertinence, cheek (Inf), effrontery
liquid n = **fluid**, solution, juice, sap ♦ adj = **fluid**, running, flowing, melted, watery; = (of assets)

convertible, disposable, negotiable, realizable
liquor n = **alcohol**, drink, spirits, booze (Inf), hard stuff (Inf); = **juice**, stock, liquid, extract, broth
list¹ n = **inventory**, record, series, roll, index ♦ v = **itemize**, record, enter, register, catalogue
list² v = **lean**, tip, incline, tilt, heel over ♦ n = **tilt**, leaning, slant, cant
listen v = **hear**, attend, pay attention, lend an ear, prick up

listless adj indifferent, languid.

litany n, pl **-nies** prayer with responses.

literal ❶ adj 1 according to the strict meaning of the words, not figurative. 2 actual, true. **literally** adv

literate ❶ adj 1 able to read and write. 2 educated. **literacy** n

literature ❶ n books and writings of a country, period or subject. **literary** adj

lithe adj supple, pliant.

lithium n metallic chemical element.

lithography n method of printing using the antipathy of grease and water. **lithograph** n 1 print so produced. ♦ v 2 print thus.

litmus n blue dye turned red by acids and restored to blue by alkali.

litre n measure of volume of fluid, one cubic decimetre, about 1.75 pints.

litter ❶ n 1 untidy refuse. 2 young of animal produced at one birth. 3 kind of stretcher for wounded. ♦ v 4 strew with litter. 5 give birth to young.

little ❶ adj 1 small, not much. 2 young. ♦ n 3 small quantity. ♦ adv 4 slightly.

liturgy n, pl **-gies** prescribed form of public worship. **liturgical** adj

live¹ ❶ v 1 have life. 2 pass one's life. 3 continue in life. 4 continue, last. 5 dwell. **living** n 1 action of being in life. 2 people now alive. 3 means of living. 4 church benefice. ♦ adj 5 alive. **living room** room in house for relaxation and entertainment.

live² ❶ adj 1 living, alive, active, vital. 2 flaming. 3 (of electrical conductor) carrying current. 4 (of broadcast) transmitted during the actual performance. **liveliness** n **lively** adj brisk, active, vivid. **liven** v (esp. with **up**) make (more) lively.

———————— THESAURUS ————————

your ears; **= pay attention**, observe, obey, mind, heed

literal adj **= exact**, close, strict, accurate, faithful; **= actual**, real, true, simple, plain

literate adj **= educated**, informed, knowledgeable

literature n **= writings**, letters, compositions, lore, creative writing

litter n **= rubbish**, refuse, waste, junk, debris; **= brood**, young, offspring, progeny ♦ v **= clutter**, mess up, clutter up, be scattered about, disorder; **= scatter**, spread,

shower, strew

little adj **= small**, minute, short, tiny, wee ≠ **big**; **= young**, small, junior, infant, immature ♦ adv **= hardly**, barely, scarcely ≠ **much**; **= rarely**, seldom, scarcely, not often, infrequently ≠ **always** ♦ n **= bit**, touch, spot, trace, hint ≠ **lot**

live¹ v **= dwell**, board, settle, lodge, occupy; **= exist**, last, prevail, be, have being; **= survive**, get along, make a living, make ends meet, subsist; **= thrive**, flourish, prosper, have fun, enjoy yourself

livelihood ⊙ n means of living.
liver n 1 organ secreting bile. 2 animal liver as food. **liverish** adj 1 unwell, as from liver upset. 2 touchy, irritable.
livery n, pl **-eries** distinctive dress, esp. servant's.
livestock n farm animals.
livid adj 1 Inf angry, furious. 2 discoloured, as by bruising.
lizard n four-footed reptile.
llama n woolly animal of S America.
load ⊙ n 1 something carried. 2 quantity carried. 3 burden. 4 amount of power used. ◆ v 5 put load on or into. 6 charge (gun). 7 weigh down. **loaded** adj 1 carrying a load. 2 (of dice) dishonestly weighted. 3 (of question) containing hidden trap or implication. 4 (of weapon) charged with ammunition 5 Sl wealthy 6 Sl drunk.
loaf¹ ⊙ n, pl **loaves** 1 mass of baked bread. 2 shaped mass of food.
loaf² ⊙ v idle, loiter. **loafer** n idler.
loam n fertile soil.

loan ⊙ n 1 act of lending. 2 thing lent. 3 money borrowed at interest. ◆ v 4 lend.
loath, loth adj unwilling. **loathe** v feel strong disgust for. **loathing** n disgust. **loathsome** adj
lob n 1 in tennis etc., shot pitched high in air. ◆ v 2 throw, pitch shots thus.
lobby ⊙ n, pl **-bies** 1 corridor into which rooms open. 2 group which tries to influence legislature. ◆ v 3 try to enlist support (of).
lobe n 1 soft, hanging part of ear. 2 rounded segment. **lobotomy** n surgical incision into lobe of brain.
lobelia n garden plant with lobed flowers.
lobster n shellfish with long tail and claws, turning red when boiled.
local ⊙ adj 1 of, existing in particular place. 2 confined to particular place. ◆ n 3 person from district. 4 Inf (nearby) pub. **locale** n scene of event. **locality** n neighbourhood. **localize** v assign, restrict to definite place. **locally** adv

———— THESAURUS ————

live² adj = **living**, alive, breathing, animate; = **active**, unexploded; = **topical**, important, pressing, current, hot
livelihood n = **occupation**, work, employment, living, job
load v = **fill**, stuff, pack, pile, stack; = **make ready**, charge, prime ◆ n = **cargo**, delivery, haul, shipment, batch
loaf¹ n = **lump**, block, cake, cube,

slab; = (Sl) **head**, mind, sense, common sense, nous (Brit sl)
loaf² v = **idle**, hang around, take it easy, lie around, loiter
loan n = **advance**, credit, overdraft ◆ v = **lend**, advance, let out
lobby v = **campaign**, press, pressure, push, influence ◆ n = **pressure group**, group, camp, faction, lobbyists; = **corridor**, passage, entrance, porch, hallway

locate ❶ v **1** find. **2** situate.

location n **1** placing. **2** situation. **3** site of film production away from studio.

loch n Scottish lake or long narrow bay.

lock¹ ❶ n **1** appliance for fastening door, lid etc. **2** arrangement for moving boats from one level of canal to another. **3** extent to which vehicle's front wheels will turn. **4** block, jam. ◆ v **5** fasten, make secure with lock. **6** place in locked container. **7** join firmly. **8** jam. **9** embrace closely. **locker** n small cupboard with lock. **lockjaw** n tetanus. **lockout** n exclusion of workers by employers as means of coercion. **locksmith** n one who makes and mends locks. **lockup** n garage, storage area away from main premises.

lock² n tress of hair.

locket n small hinged pendant for portrait etc.

locomotive n engine for pulling carriages on railway tracks.

locomotion n action, power of moving.

locum Lat substitute, esp. for doctor or clergyman.

locus n, pl **loci** curve traced by all points satisfying specified mathematical condition.

locust n destructive winged insect.

lodge ❶ n **1** house, cabin used seasonally or occasionally, e.g. for hunting, skiing. **2** gatekeeper's house. **3** branch of Freemasons etc. ◆ v **4** house. **5** deposit. **6** bring (a charge etc.). **7** live in another's house at fixed charge. **8** come to rest (in, on). **lodger** n **lodgings** pl n rented accommodation in another person's house.

loft n space under roof. **loftily** adv haughtily. **lofty** adj **1** of great height. **2** elevated. **3** haughty.

log¹ ❶ n **1** trimmed portion of felled tree. **2** record of voyages of ship, aircraft etc. ◆ v **3** enter in a log. **4** record. **5** cut logs.

logbook n

log² n logarithm.

———— THESAURUS ————

local adj = **community**, regional; = **confined**, limited, restricted ◆ n = **resident**, native, inhabitant

locate v = **find**, discover, detect, come across, track down; = **place**, put, set, position, seat

lock¹ v = **fasten**, close, secure, shut, bar; = **unite**, join, link, engage, clench; = **embrace**, press, grasp, clutch, hug ◆ n = **fastening**, catch, bolt, clasp, padlock

lodge n = **cabin**, shelter, cottage, hut, chalet; = **society**, group, club, section, wing ◆ v = **register**, enter, file, submit, put on record; = **stay**, room, board, reside, house; = **stick**, remain, implant, come to rest, imbed

log¹ n = **stump**, block, branch, chunk, trunk; = **record**, account, register, journal, diary ◆ v = **record**, enter, note, register, chart

L

loganberry n purplish–red fruit.

logarithm n one of series of arithmetical functions tabulated for use in calculation.

loggerheads pl n **at loggerheads** quarrelling, disputing.

logic ❼ n 1 science of reasoning. 2 reasoned thought or argument. 3 coherence of various facts, events etc. **logical** adj 1 of logic. 2 according to reason. 3 reasonable. 4 apt to reason correctly.

logistics pl n (with sing or pl v) the handling of supplies and personnel. **logistical** adj

logo n, pl **–os** company emblem or similar device.

loin n 1 part of body between ribs and hip. 2 cut of meat from this. ◆ pl 3 hips and lower abdomen. **loincloth** n garment covering loins only.

loiter v 1 dawdle, hang about. 2 idle. **loiterer** n

loll v 1 sit, lie lazily. 2 (esp. of the tongue) hang out.

lollipop n sweet on small wooden stick.

lolly n, pl **–ies** 1 Inf lollipop or ice lolly 2 Sl money.

lone ❼ adj solitary. **loneliness** n

lonely adj 1 sad because alone. 2 unfrequented. 3 solitary. **loner** n one who prefers to be alone.

lonesome adj Chiefly US and Canad

another word for LONELY.

long[1] ❼ adj 1 having length, esp. great length, in space or time. 2 extensive. 3 protracted. ◆ adv 4 for a long time. **long–distance** adj going between places far apart. **longhand** n words written in full. **long–range** adj 1 into the future. 2 able to travel long distances without refuelling. 3 (of weapons) designed to hit distant target. **long shot** competitor, undertaking, bet etc. with small chance of success. **long–sighted** adj able to see distant objects in focus but not nearby ones. **long–standing** adj existing for a long time. **long–suffering** adj enduring trouble or unhappiness without complaint. **long–winded** adj tediously loquacious.

long[2] ❼ v have keen desire, yearn (for). **longing** n yearning.

longevity n long life.

longitude n distance east or west from standard meridian.

longshoreman n a man employed in the loading or unloading of ships.

loo n Inf lavatory.

look ❼ v 1 direct eyes (at). 2 face. 3 seem. 4 search (for). 5 hope (for) (with) ◆ n 7 looking. 8 view. 9 search (oft. pl) 10 appearance. **lookalike** n person

--- THESAURUS ---

logic n = **reason**, reasoning, sense, good sense

lone adj = **solitary**, single, one, only, sole

long[1] adj = **elongated**, extended, stretched, expanded, extensive ≠ **short**; = **prolonged**, sustained, lengthy, lingering, protracted ≠ **brief**

long[2] v = **desire**, want, wish, burn,

who is double of another. **lookout**
n 1 watchman. 2 place for
watching. 3 prospect.
loom ❶ v 1 appear dimly. 2 seem
ominously close.
loonie n Canad 1 sl a Canadian
dollar coin with a loon bird on one
of its faces. 2 the Canadian
currency.
loony n/adj Sl foolish or insane
(person).
loop ❶ n 1 figure made by curved
line crossing itself. ♦ v 2 form
loop. **loophole** n means of evading
rule without infringing it.
loose ❶ adj 1 slack. 2 not fixed or
restrained. 3 vague. 4 dissolute. ♦
v 5 free. 6 unfasten. 7 slacken. 8
shoot, let fly. **loosen** v make loose.
loose–leaf adj allowing addition or
removal of pages.
loot ❶ n/v plunder.
lop v lopping, lopped 1 cut away

twigs and branches. 2 chop off.
lope v run with long, easy strides.
lopsided adj with one side lower
than the other.
loquacious adj talkative.
lord ❶ n 1 British nobleman. 2
ruler. 3 (with cap.) God. ♦ v 4
domineer. **lordly** adj 1 imperious.
2 fit for a lord. **lordship** n
lore n 1 learning. 2 body of facts
and traditions.
lorry n, pl –ries motor vehicle for
heavy loads, truck.
lose ❶ v losing, lost 1 be deprived
of, fail to retain or use. 2 fail to
get. 3 (of clock etc.) run slow. 4 be
defeated in. **loser** n **loss** n 1 act of
losing. 2 what is lost. **lost** adj 1
unable to be found. 2 unable to
find one's way. 3 bewildered. 4
not won. 5 not utilized.
lot ❶ pron 1 great number. ♦ n 2
collection. 3 large quantity. 4

————— THESAURUS —————

pine
look v = **see**, view, consider,
watch, eye; = **search**, seek, hunt,
forage; = **consider**, contemplate;
= **face**, overlook; = **hope**, expect,
await, anticipate, reckon on ♦ n
= **glimpse**, view, glance,
observation, sight; = **appearance**,
bearing, air, style, aspect
loom v = **appear**, emerge, hover,
take shape, threaten
loop n = **curve**, ring, circle, twist,
curl ♦ v = **twist**, turn, roll, knot,
curl
loose adj = **free**, detached,
insecure, unfettered, unrestricted;
= **slack**, easy, relaxed, sloppy,

loose–fitting ≠ **tight**; = (Old–
fashioned) **promiscuous**, fast,
abandoned, immoral, dissipated
≠ **chaste**; = **vague**, random,
inaccurate, rambling, imprecise
≠ **precise** ♦ v = **free**, release,
liberate, detach, unleash ≠ **fasten**
loot v = **plunder**, rob, raid, sack,
rifle ♦ n = **plunder**, goods, prize,
haul, spoils
lord n = **peer**, nobleman, count,
duke, gentleman; = **ruler**, leader,
chief, master, governor
lose v = **be defeated**, be beaten,
lose out, come to grief; = **mislay**,
drop, forget, be deprived of, lose
track of; = **forfeit**, miss, yield, be

share. **5** fate. **6** item at auction. **7** object used to make decision by chance. **8** area of land. ♦ *pl* **9** *Inf* great numbers or quantity. **a lot** *Inf* a great deal.

lotion 🔊 *n* liquid for washing wounds, improving skin etc.

lottery 🔊 *n, pl* **-teries 1** method of raising funds by selling tickets that win prizes by chance. **2** gamble.

lotus *n* legendary plant whose fruits induce forgetfulness.

loud 🔊 *adj* **1** strongly audible. **2** noisy. **3** *Fig* garish. **loudly** *adv* **loudspeaker** *n* instrument for converting electrical signals into sound audible at a distance.

lounge 🔊 *v* **1** recline, move at ease. ♦ *n* **2** living room of house. **3** public room, area for sitting. **lounge suit** man's suit for daytime wear.

lour see LOWER.

louse *n* parasitic insect. **lousy** *adj* **1** *Sl* bad. **2** *Sl* nasty. **3** having lice.

lout *n* crude, oafish person.

louvre *n* one of set of slats slanted to admit air but not rain.

love 🔊 *n* **1** warm affection. **2** benevolence. **3** sexual passion. **4** sweetheart. **5** *Tennis* score of nothing. ♦ *v* **6** admire passionately. **7** delight in. **lovable** *adj* **lovelorn** *adj* pining for a lover. **lovely** *adj* beautiful, delightful. **lover** *n* **loving** *adj* **1** affectionate. **2** tender. **make love (to)** have sexual intercourse (with).

low 🔊 *adj* **1** not tall, high or elevated. **2** humble. **3** vulgar. **4** unwell. **5** below what is usual. **6** not loud. **lower** *v* **1** cause, allow to move down. **2** diminish, degrade. ♦ *adj* **3** below. **4** at an early stage, period. **lowly** *adj* modest, humble. **lowbrow** *n/adj* nonintellectual (person). **lowdown** *n Inf* inside information. **low-down** *adj Inf* mean, shabby. **lower case** small letters. **low-key** *adj* not intense. **lowland** *n* low-lying country.

————————— THESAURUS —————————

deprived of, pass up (*Inf*)
lot *n* = **bunch** (*Inf*), group, crowd, crew, set; = **destiny**, situation, circumstances, fortune, chance
lotion *n* = **cream**, solution, balm, salve, liniment
lottery *n* = **raffle**, draw, lotto (*Brit, NZ & S Afr*), sweepstake; = **gamble**, chance, risk, hazard, toss-up (*Inf*)
loud *adj* = **noisy**, booming, roaring, thundering, forte (*Mus*) ≠ quiet; = **garish**, bold, glaring, flamboyant, brash ≠ **sombre**
lounge *v* = **relax**, loaf, sprawl, lie

about, take it easy
love *v* = **adore**, care for, treasure, cherish, prize ≠ **hate**; = **enjoy**, like, appreciate, relish, delight in ≠ **dislike** ♦ *n* = **passion**, affection, warmth, attachment, intimacy ≠ **hatred**; = **liking**, taste, bent for, weakness for, relish for; = **beloved**, dear, dearest, lover, darling ≠ **enemy**; = **sympathy**, understanding, pity, humanity, warmth, = **enamoured**, charmed, captivated, smitten, wild (*Inf*)
low *adj* = **small**, little, short,

lower ❶ lour v **1** (of sky) look threatening. **2** scowl.

loyal ❶ adj faithful, true to allegiance. **loyalist** n **loyalty** n

lozenge n **1** small sweet or tablet of medicine. **2** diamond shape.

LP long-playing record.

L–plate n sign on car driven by learner driver.

LSD 1 lysergic acid diethylamide (hallucinogenic drug). **2** pounds, shillings, and pence.

lubricate v **1** oil, grease. **2** make slippery. **lubricant** n substance used for this. **lubrication** n

lucerne n fodder plant.

lucid adj **1** clear. **2** easily understood. **3** sane. **lucidity** n

luck ❶ n **1** chance, whether good or bad. **2** good fortune. **luckily** adv fortunately. **luckless** adj having bad luck. **lucky** adj having good luck.

lucrative ❶ adj very profitable.

ludicrous ❶ adj ridiculous.

lug¹ v drag with effort.

lug² n **1** projection, serving as handle or support. **2** Inf ear.

luggage ❶ n traveller's baggage.

lugubrious adj doleful.

lukewarm adj **1** tepid. **2** indifferent.

lull ❶ v **1** soothe, sing to sleep. **2** calm. **3** subside. ◆ n **4** quiet spell. **lullaby** n lulling song, esp. for children.

lumbago n rheumatism of the lower part of the back.

lumber¹ ❶ n **1** disused articles, useless rubbish. **2** sawn timber. ◆ v **3** Inf burden with something unpleasant. **lumberjack** n US & Canad man who fells trees and prepares logs.

lumber² ❶ v move heavily.

luminous adj **1** shedding light. **2**

stunted, squat ≠ **tall**; = **inferior**, bad, poor, inadequate, unsatisfactory; = **quiet**, soft, gentle, whispered, muted ≠ **loud**; = **dejected**, depressed, miserable, fed up, moody ≠ **happy**; = **coarse**, common, rough, crude, rude; = **ill**, weak, frail, stricken, debilitated ≠ **strong**

lower adj = **subordinate**, under, smaller, junior, minor; = **reduced**, cut, diminished, decreased, lessened ≠ **increased** ◆ v = **drop**, sink, depress, let down, submerge ≠ **raise**; = **lessen**, cut, reduce, diminish, slash ≠ **increase**

loyal adj = **faithful**, true, devoted, dependable, constant ≠ **disloyal**

luck n = **good fortune**, success, advantage, prosperity, blessing; = **fortune**, lot, stars, chance, accident

lucrative adj = **profitable**, rewarding, productive, fruitful, well-paid

ludicrous adj = **ridiculous**, crazy, absurd, preposterous, silly ≠ **sensible**

luggage n = **baggage**, things, cases, bags, gear

lull n = **respite**, pause, quiet, silence, calm ◆ v = **calm**, soothe, subdue, quell, allay

lumber¹ v = (Brit inf) **burden**, land,

glowing. **luminary** n famous person. **luminescence** n emission of light without heat.

lump¹ ❶ n **1** shapeless piece or mass. **2** swelling. **3** large sum. ◆ v **4** throw together. **lumpy** adj **1** full of lumps. **2** uneven.

lump² v Inf tolerate.

lunar adj relating to the moon.

lunatic ❶ adj/n **1** foolish or irresponsible (person). **2** insane (person). **lunacy** n

lunch n **1** meal taken in middle of day. ◆ v **2** eat, entertain to lunch.

luncheon n lunch. **luncheon meat** tinned ground mixture of meat and cereal.

lung n one of the two organs of respiration in vertebrates.

lunge ❶ v **1** thrust with sword etc. ◆ n **2** thrust. **3** sudden movement of body, plunge.

lupin n leguminous plant with spikes of flowers.

lurch ❶ n **1** sudden roll to one side. ◆ v **2** stagger. **leave in the lurch** leave in difficulties.

lure ❶ n **1** bait. **2** power to attract. ◆ v **3** entice. **4** attract.

lurid adj **1** sensational. **2** garish.

lurk ❶ v lie hidden. **lurking** adj (of suspicion) not definite.

luscious adj **1** sweet, juicy. **2** extremely attractive.

lush ❶ adj **1** (of plant growth) luxuriant. **2** luxurious.

lust ❶ n **1** strong desire for sexual gratification. **2** any strong desire. ◆ v **3** have passionate desire. **lustful** adj **lusty** adj vigorous, healthy.

lustre n **1** gloss, sheen. **2** renown. **3** metallic pottery glaze. **lustrous** adj shining.

lute n old stringed musical instrument played like a guitar.

luxury ❶ n, pl **-ries 1** possession and use of costly, choice things for enjoyment. **2** enjoyable, comfortable surroundings. **3**

—————— THESAURUS ——————

load, saddle, encumber ◆ n = (Brit) junk, refuse, rubbish, trash, clutter

lumber² v = **plod**, shuffle, shamble, trudge, stump

lump¹ n = **piece**, ball, block, mass, chunk; = **swelling**, growth, bump, tumour, bulge ◆ v = **group**, throw, mass, combine, collect

lunatic n = **madman**, maniac, psychopath, nutcase (Sl) ◆ adj = **mad**, crazy, insane, irrational, daft

lunge v = **pounce**, charge, dive, leap, plunge ◆ n = **thrust**, charge, pounce, spring, swing

lurch v = **tilt**, roll, pitch, list, rock; = **stagger**, reel, stumble, weave, sway

lure v = **tempt**, draw, attract, invite, trick ◆ n = **temptation**, attraction, incentive, bait, carrot (Inf)

lurk v = **hide**, sneak, prowl, lie in wait, slink

lush adj = **abundant**, green, flourishing, dense, rank; = **luxurious**, grand, elaborate, lavish, extravagant

lust n = **lechery**, sensuality, lewdness, lasciviousness; = **desire**,

enjoyable but not essential thing.
luxuriance n abundance. **luxuriant**
adj **1** growing thickly. **2** abundant.
luxuriate v **1** indulge in luxury. **2**
flourish profusely. **3** take delight
(in). **luxurious** adj **1** fond of luxury.
2 self-indulgent. **3** sumptuous.
lychee n Chinese fruit.
Lycra ® n fabric used for tight-
fitting garments.
lymph n colourless body fluid,
mainly white blood cells.
lymphatic adj
lynch v put to death without trial.
lynx n animal of cat family.
lyre n instrument like harp.
lyric n **1** songlike poem expressing
personal feelings. ♦ pl **2** words of
popular song. **lyrical** adj **1**
expressed in this style. **2**
enthusiastic. **lyricist** n

———— THESAURUS ————

longing, passion, appetite, craving
luxury n = **opulence**, splendour,
richness, extravagance, affluence
≠ **poverty**; = **extravagance**, treat,
extra, indulgence, frill ≠ **necessity**

M m

m metre.
MA Master of Arts.
mac n Inf mackintosh.
macabre adj gruesome, ghastly.
macaroni n pasta in thin tubes.
macaroon n biscuit containing almonds.
macaw n kind of parrot.
mace¹ n staff of office.
mace² n spice made of nutmeg shell.
machete n broad, heavy knife.
Machiavellian adj (politically) unprincipled, crafty.
machine 🛈 n 1 apparatus with several parts to apply mechanical force. 2 controlling organization. 3 mechanical appliance. ♦ v 4 shape etc. with machine. **machinery** n 1 machines or machine parts. 2 procedures by which system functions. **machinist** n **machine gun** automatic gun firing repeatedly.
macho 🛈 adj exhibiting exaggerated pride in masculinity.
machismo n strong, exaggerated masculinity.

mackerel n edible sea fish.
mackintosh n waterproof raincoat.
macramé n ornamental work of knotted cord.
macrocosm n 1 the universe. 2 any large system.
mad 🛈 adj madder, maddest 1 suffering from mental disease, foolish. 2 enthusiastic (about). 3 excited. 4 Inf furious. **madden** v make mad. **madness** n
madam n polite title for a woman.
madcap adj/n reckless (person).
made past tense and past participle of MAKE.
Madonna n Virgin Mary.
madrigal n unaccompanied part song.
maelstrom n great whirlpool.
maestro n, pl –tri, –tros 1 outstanding musician, conductor. 2 master of any art.
magazine 🛈 n 1 periodical publication. 2 appliance for supplying cartridges to gun. 3 storehouse for arms etc.
magenta adj/n (of) deep

--- THESAURUS ---

machine n = **appliance**, device, apparatus, engine, tool; = **system**, structure, organization, machinery, setup (Inf)
macho adj = **manly**, masculine, chauvinist, virile
mad adj = **insane**, crazy (Inf), nuts

(SI), raving, unstable ≠ **sane**; = **foolish**, absurd, wild, stupid, daft (Inf) ≠ **sensible**; = (Inf) **angry**, furious, incensed, enraged, livid (Inf) ≠ **calm**; = **enthusiastic**, wild, crazy (Inf), ardent, fanatical ≠ **nonchalant**; = **frenzied**, wild,

purplish–red.

maggot n grub, larva. **maggoty** adj

magic ❶ n 1 art of supposedly invoking supernatural powers to influence events etc. 2 witchcraft, conjuring. 3 fascinating quality or power. ◆ adj 4 of, using magic.

magical adj **magician** n wizard, conjuror.

magistrate ❶ n civil officer administering law. **magisterial** adj 1 of magistrate. 2 authoritative.

magnanimous adj generous, not petty. **magnanimity** n

magnate n influential person.

magnesium n metallic element. **magnesia** n white powder used in medicine.

magnet n piece of iron, steel having properties of attracting iron, steel. **magnetic** adj 1 of magnet. 2 exerting powerful attraction. **magnetism** n

magnetize v **magneto** n apparatus for ignition in internal–combustion engine. **magnetic tape** coated plastic strip for recording sound or video signals.

magnificent ❶ adj 1 splendid. 2 imposing. 3 excellent. **magnificence** n

magnify ❶ v –fying, –fied 1 increase apparent size of, as with lens. 2 exaggerate. **magnification** n

magnitude ❶ n 1 importance. 2 size.

magnolia n tree with white, sweet–scented flowers.

magnum n large wine bottle.

magpie n black–and–white bird.

maharajah n former title of some Indian princes.

mahogany n tree yielding reddish–brown wood.

maiden ❶ n 1 Lit young unmarried woman. ◆ adj 2 unmarried. 3 first. **maid** n 1 woman servant. 2 Lit maiden. **maiden name** woman's surname before marriage.

——— THESAURUS ———

excited, frenetic, uncontrolled

magazine n = **journal**, publication, supplement, rag (Inf), issue

magic n = **sorcery**, wizardry, witchcraft, enchantment, black art; = **conjuring**, illusion, trickery, sleight of hand, legerdemain; = **charm**, power, glamour, fascination, magnetism ◆ adj = **miraculous**, entrancing, charming, fascinating, marvellous

magistrate n = **judge**, justice, justice of the peace, J.P.

magnificent adj = **splendid**, impressive, imposing, glorious, gorgeous ≠ ordinary; = **brilliant**, fine, excellent, outstanding, superb

magnify v = **enlarge**, increase, boost, expand, intensify ≠ reduce; = **make worse**, exaggerate, intensify, worsen, exacerbate

magnitude n = **importance**, consequence, significance, moment, note ≠ unimportance; = **immensity**, size, extent, enormity, volume ≠ smallness

mail¹ ❶ *n* **1** letters etc. transported and delivered by the post office. **2** postal system. **3** train etc. carrying mail. ◆ *v* **4** send by mail.

mail² *n* armour of interlaced rings.

mailbox *n US and Canad* **1** public box into which letters are put for collection and delivery. **2** private box outside house where occupant's mail is delivered.

mailman *n* person who collects or delivers mail.

maim *v* cripple, mutilate.

main ❶ *adj* **1** chief, principal. ◆ *n* **2** principal pipe, line carrying water etc. **3** *Obs* sea. **mainframe** *n* **1** high-speed general–purpose computer. **2** central processing unit of computer. **mainland** *n* stretch of land which forms main part of a country. **mainstay** *n* chief support. **mainstream** *n* prevailing cultural trend.

maintain ❶ *v* **1** carry on. **2** support. **3** assert. **4** support by argument. **maintenance** *n* **1** maintaining. **2** means of support.

3 upkeep of buildings etc.

maisonette *n* part of house fitted as self-contained dwelling.

maize *n* type of corn.

majesty ❶ *n, pl* **-ties 1** stateliness. **2** sovereignty. **majestic** *adj*

major ❶ *n* **1** army officer above captain. **2** scale in music. **3** *US and Canad* an academic subject chosen as a field of specialization. ◆ *adj* **4** greater in number, extent etc.

majority *n* **1** greater number. **2** coming of age.

make ❶ *v* making, made **1** construct. **2** produce. **3** create. **4** establish. **5** appoint. **6** amount to. **7** cause to do. **8** reach. **9** earn. **10** tend. **11** contribute. ◆ *n* **12** brand, type. **maker** *n* making *n* **make-believe** *n* fantasy, pretence. **make do** manage with inferior alternative. **make it** *Inf* be successful. **makeshift** *adj* serving as temporary substitute. **make-up** *n* **1** cosmetics. **2** characteristics. **3** layout.

mal– *comb. form* ill, badly, as in

———— THESAURUS ————

maiden *n* = (*Lit*) **girl**, maid, lass, damsel, virgin ◆ *adj* = **first**, initial, inaugural, introductory; = **unmarried**, unwed

mail¹ *n* = **letters**, post, correspondence ◆ *v* = **post**, send, forward, e-mail, dispatch

main *adj* = **chief**, leading, head, central, essential ≠ **minor**

maintain *v* = **continue**, retain, preserve, sustain, carry on ≠ **end**; = **assert**, state, claim, insist, declare ≠ **disavow**; = **look after**,

care for, take care of, conserve, keep in good condition

majesty *n* = **grandeur**, glory, splendour, magnificence, nobility ≠ **triviality**

major *adj* = **important**, critical, significant, great, serious; = **main**, higher, greater, bigger, leading ≠ **minor**

make *v* = **produce**, cause, create, effect, lead to; = **perform**, do, effect, carry out, execute; = **force**, cause, compel, drive, require;

malformation, malfunction.

maladjusted *adj* badly adjusted, as to society.

malady *n, pl* **-dies** disease.

malaise *n* vague feeling of discomfort.

malapropism *n* ludicrous misuse of word.

malaria *n* infectious disease transmitted by mosquitoes. **malarial** *adj*

malcontent *adj/n* discontented (person).

male ⊕ *adj* 1 of sex that fertilizes female. 2 of men or male animals. ♦ *n* 3 male person or animal.

malevolent *adj* full of ill will. **malevolence** *n*

malice *n* 1 ill will. 2 spite. **malicious** *adj* spiteful.

malign *adj* 1 causing evil. ♦ *v* 2 slander. **malignancy** *n* **malignant** *adj* 1 feeling ill will. 2 (of disease) resistant to therapy.

malinger *v* feign illness to escape duty.

mall *n* shopping centre.

mallard *n* wild duck.

malleable *adj* 1 capable of being hammered into shape. 2 adaptable.

mallet *n* (wooden) hammer.

malnutrition *n* inadequate nutrition.

malodorous *adj* evil-smelling.

malpractice *n* immoral, illegal or unethical conduct.

malt *n* grain used for brewing.

maltreat *v* treat badly.

mammal *n* animal of type that suckles its young. **mammalian** *adj*

mammary *adj* of, relating to breast.

mammon *n* wealth regarded as source of evil.

mammoth ⊕ *n* 1 extinct animal like an elephant. ♦ *adj* 2 colossal.

man ⊕ *n, pl* **men** 1 human being. 2 human race. 3 adult male. 4 piece used in chess etc. ♦ *v* 5 supply with men. **manful** *adj* brave. **manly** *adj* **manhandle** *v* treat roughly. **manhole** *n* opening through which man may pass to a sewer etc. **mankind** *n* human beings. **manslaughter** *n* unintentional homicide.

mana *n NZ* authority, influence.

manacle *n/v* fetter.

manage ⊕ *v* 1 be in charge of. 2 succeed in doing. 3 control. 4 handle. **manageable** *adj* **management** *n* 1 those who manage. 2 administration.

—— THESAURUS ——

= **create**, build, produce, manufacture, form; = **earn**, get, gain, net, win; = **amount to**, total, constitute, add up to, count as ♦ *n* = **brand**, sort, style, model, kind
male *adj* = **masculine**, manly, macho, virile ≠ **female**
mammoth *adj* = **colossal**, huge,

giant, massive, enormous ≠ **tiny**
man *n* = **male**, guy (*Inf*), fellow (*Inf*), gentleman, bloke (*Brit inf*); = **human**, human being, person, individual, soul; = **mankind**, humanity, people, human race, humankind ♦ *v* = **staff**, people, crew, occupy, garrison

manager n **managerial** adj
mandarin n **1** small orange. **2** high-ranking bureaucrat.
mandate ❶ n **1** command of, or commission to act for, another. **2** instruction from electorate to representative or government.
mandatory adj compulsory.
mandible n lower jawbone.
mandolin n stringed musical instrument.
mane n long hair on neck of horse, lion etc.
manganese n metallic element.
mange n skin disease of dogs etc. **mangy** adj
manger n eating trough in stable.
mangle¹ n **1** machine for rolling clothes etc. to remove water. ◆ v **2** press in mangle.
mangle² v mutilate.
mango n, pl **–goes, –gos** tropical fruit.
mangrove n tropical tree which grows on muddy river banks.
mania n **1** madness. **2** prevailing craze. **maniac** adj/n **1** mad (person). **maniacal, manic** adj affected by mania.

manicure n **1** treatment and care of fingernails and hands. ◆ v **2** treat, care for hands.
manifest ❶ adj **1** clear, undoubted. ◆ v **2** make manifest. **manifestation** n **manifesto** n declaration of policy by political party etc.
manifold adj **1** numerous and varied. ◆ n **2** in engine, pipe with several outlets.
manila, manilla n **1** fibre used for ropes. **2** tough paper.
manipulate ❶ v **1** handle skilfully. **2** manage. **3** falsify. **manipulation** n
manna n **1** nourishment. **2** unexpected gift.
mannequin n woman who models clothes.
manner ❶ n **1** way, style. **2** bearing. **3** sort, kind. ◆ pl **4** social behaviour. **mannered** adj affected. **mannerism** n person's distinctive habit.
manoeuvre ❶ n **1** complicated, perhaps deceptive plan or action. ◆ v **2** employ stratagems. **3** (cause to) perform manoeuvres.
manor n large country house with

——————————— THESAURUS ———————————

manage v = **be in charge of**, run, handle, direct, conduct; = **organize**, use, handle, regulate; = **cope**, survive, succeed, carry on, make do; = **perform**, do, achieve, carry out, undertake; operate
mandate n = **command**, order, commission, instruction, decree
manifest adj = **obvious**, apparent, patent, evident, clear ≠ **concealed** ◆ v = **display**, show, reveal,

express, demonstrate ≠ **conceal**
manipulate v = **influence**, control, direct, negotiate, exploit; = **work**, use, operate, handle
manner n = **style**, way, fashion, method, custom; = **behaviour**, air, bearing, conduct, aspect; = **type**, form, sort, kind, variety
manoeuvre v = **scheme**, wangle (Inf), machinate ◆ n = **stratagem**, scheme, trick, tactic, intrigue; often

land.

manse n house of minister in some religious denominations.

mansion ⊕ n large house.

mantle ⊕ n 1 loose cloak. 2 covering. ♦ v 3 cover.

mantra n sacred word or syllable in Hinduism and Buddhism.

manual ⊕ adj 1 done with the hands. 2 by human labour, not automatic. ♦ n 3 handbook.

manufacture ⊕ v 1 make (materials) into finished articles. 2 concoct. ♦ n 3 making of articles, esp. in large quantities.

manufacturer n

manure n dung or chemical fertilizer used to enrich land.

manuscript n 1 book etc. written by hand. 2 copy for printing.

many adj more, most 1 numerous. ♦ n 2 large number.

map n 1 flat representation of the earth. ♦ v 2 make map of (with) 3 plan.

maple n tree of sycamore family.

maple sugar n US and Canad

sugar made from the sap of the sugar maple.

mar ⊕ v marring, marred spoil.

Mar. March.

maraca n shaken percussion instrument.

marathon n 1 long–distance race. 2 endurance contest.

marble n 1 kind of limestone. 2 small ball used in children's game.

march ⊕ v 1 walk with military step. 2 go, progress. ♦ n 3 action of marching. 4 distance marched. 5 marching tune.

March n third month.

marchioness n wife, widow of marquis.

mare n female horse.

margarine n butter substitute made from vegetable fats.

margin ⊕ n 1 border, edge. 2 space round printed page. 3 amount allowed beyond what is necessary. **marginal** adj

marigold n plant with yellow flowers.

marijuana ⊕ n dried flowers and

plural = **movement**, operation, exercise, war game

mansion n = **residence**, manor, hall, villa, seat

mantle n = **covering**, screen, curtain, blanket, veil; = **cloak**, wrap, cape, hood, shawl

manual adj = **physical**, human; = **hand–operated**, hand, non–automatic ♦ n = **handbook**, guide, instructions, bible

manufacture v = **make**, build, produce, construct, create;

= **concoct**, make up, invent, devise, fabricate ♦ n = **making**, production, construction, assembly, creation

mar v = **ruin**, spoil, scar, flaw, impair ≠ **improve**

march v = **parade**, walk, file, pace, stride; = **walk**, strut, storm, sweep, stride ♦ n = **walk**, trek, slog, yomp (*Brit inf*), routemarch; = **progress**, development, advance, evolution, progression

margin n = **edge**, side, border,

leaves of hemp plant, used as narcotic.

marina n mooring facility for pleasure boats.

marinade n liquid in which food is soaked before cooking. **marinate** v soak in marinade.

marine ⊕ adj **1** of the sea or shipping. ♦ n **2** soldier trained for land or sea combat. **3** fleet.

mariner n sailor.

marionette n puppet.

marital ⊕ adj of marriage.

maritime ⊕ adj **1** of seafaring. **2** near the sea.

mark ⊕ n **1** dot, scar etc. **2** sign, token. **3** letter, number showing evaluation of schoolwork etc. **4** indication. **5** target. ♦ v **6** make mark on. **7** distinguish. **8** notice. **9** assess. **10** stay close to sporting opponent. **marked** adj noticeable. **marker** n **marksman** n skilled shot.

market ⊕ n **1** place for buying and selling. **2** demand for goods.

♦ v **3** offer for sale. **marketable** adj

market garden place where fruit and vegetables are grown for sale.

marmalade n preserve made of oranges, lemons etc.

marmoset n small bushy-tailed monkey.

maroon¹ v **1** leave on deserted island etc. **2** isolate.

maroon² ⊕ adj/n (of) brownish-crimson colour.

marquee n large tent.

marquetry n inlaid work, wood mosaic.

marquis n nobleman of rank below duke.

marrow n **1** fatty substance inside bones. **2** vital part. **3** plant with long, green-striped fruit, eaten as vegetable.

marry ⊕ v **-rying, -ried 1** join as husband and wife. **2** unite closely.

marriage n **1** being married. **2** wedding.

marsh ⊕ n low-lying wet land.

boundary, verge

marijuana n = **cannabis**, pot (Sl), dope (Sl), grass (Sl), hemp

marine adj = **nautical**, maritime, naval, seafaring, seagoing

marital adj = **matrimonial**, nuptial, conjugal, connubial

maritime adj = **nautical**, marine, naval, oceanic, seafaring;
= **coastal**, seaside, littoral

mark n = **spot**, stain, streak, smudge, line; = **characteristic**, feature, standard, quality, measure; = **brand**, impression, label, device, flag; = **target**, goal,

aim, purpose, object ♦ v = **scar**, scratch, stain, streak, blot; = **label**, identify, brand, flag, stamp;
= **grade**, correct, assess, evaluate, appraise; = **distinguish**, show, illustrate, exemplify, denote;
= **observe**, mind, note, notice, attend to

market n = **fair**, mart, bazaar, souk (Arabic) ♦ v = **sell**, promote, retail, peddle, vend

maroon v = **abandon**, leave, desert, strand, leave high and dry (Inf)

marry v = **tie the knot** (Inf), wed,

marshy adj

marshal 🛈 n 1 high officer of state. 2 US law enforcement officer. 3 high-ranking officer in the army, air force. ♦ v 4 arrange. 5 conduct with ceremony.

marshmallow n spongy pink or white sweet.

marsupial n animal that carries its young in pouch.

marten n weasel-like animal.

martial 🛈 adj 1 of war. 2 warlike.

martin n species of swallow.

martinet n strict disciplinarian.

martyr n 1 one who suffers or dies for his beliefs. ♦ v 2 make martyr of.

marvel 🛈 v -velling, -velled 1 wonder. ♦ n 2 wonderful thing.

marvellous adj

marzipan n paste of almonds, sugar etc.

mascara n cosmetic for darkening eyelashes.

mascot n thing supposed to bring luck.

masculine 🛈 adj 1 relating to males. 2 manly.

mash n/v (crush into) soft mass or pulp.

mask 🛈 n 1 covering for face. 2 disguise, pretence. ♦ v 3 disguise.

masochism n abnormal condition where pleasure (esp. sexual) is derived from pain. **masochist** n

mason n worker in stone.

masonry n stonework.

masquerade n 1 masked ball. ♦ v 2 appear in disguise.

mass 🛈 n 1 quantity of matter 2 Physics amount of matter in body. 3 large quantity. ♦ v 4 form into mass. **massive** adj large and heavy.

mass-market adj appealing to many people. **mass-produce** v produce standardized articles in large quantities.

Mass n service in R.C. Church.

massacre 🛈 n 1 indiscriminate, large-scale killing. ♦ v 2 kill indiscriminately.

massage 🛈 n 1 rubbing and

——————— THESAURUS ———————

get hitched (Sl); = **unite**, join, link, bond, ally

marsh n = **swamp**, bog, slough, fen, quagmire

marshal v = **conduct**, take, lead, guide, steer; = **arrange**, group, order, line up, organize

martial adj = **military**, belligerent, warlike, bellicose

marvel v = **be amazed**, wonder, gape, be awed ♦ n = **wonder**, phenomenon, miracle, portent

masculine adj = **male**, manly, mannish, manlike, virile

mask n = **façade**, disguise, front, cover, screen ♦ v = **disguise**, hide, conceal, obscure, cover (up)

mass n = **lot**, collection, load, pile, quantity; = **piece**, block, lump, chunk, hunk; = **size**, matter, weight, extent, bulk ♦ adj = **large-scale**, general, widespread, extensive, universal ♦ v = **gather**, assemble, accumulate, collect, rally

massacre n = **slaughter**, murder, holocaust, carnage, extermination ♦ v = **slaughter**, kill, murder,

kneading of muscles etc. as curative treatment. **masseur** n one who practises massage.

mast n 1 pole for supporting ship's sails. 2 tall support for aerial etc.

mastectomy n, pl **–mies** surgical removal of breast.

master ❶ n 1 one in control. 2 employer. 3 owner. 4 document etc. from which copies are made. 5 expert. 6 teacher. ♦ adj 7 expert, skilled. ♦ v 8 overcome. 9 acquire skill in. **masterful** adj 1 expert, skilled. 2 domineering. **masterly** adj showing great skill. **mastery** n 1 understanding (of). 2 expertise. 3 victory. **mastermind** v 1 plan, direct. ♦ n 2 one who directs complex operation. **masterpiece** n outstanding work.

masticate v chew.

mastiff n large dog.

masturbate v fondle genital organs. **masturbation** n

mat¹ n 1 small rug. 2 piece of fabric to protect another surface. 3 thick tangled mass. ♦ v 4 form into such mass.

mat² adj dull, lustreless.

matador n man who kills bull in bullfights.

match¹ ❶ n 1 contest, game. 2 equal. 3 person, thing corresponding to another. 4 marriage. ♦ v 5 get something corresponding to. 6 oppose, put in competition (with). 7 correspond. **matchmaker** n person who schemes to bring about marriage.

match² n small stick with head which ignites when rubbed. **matchbox** n **matchstick** n

mate ❶ n 1 comrade. 2 husband, wife. 3 one of pair. 4 officer in merchant ship. ♦ v 5 marry. 6 pair. **matey** adj Inf friendly.

material ❶ n 1 substance from

——————— THESAURUS ———————

butcher, wipe out

massage n = **rub-down**, manipulation ♦ v = **rub down**, manipulate, knead

master n = **lord**, ruler, commander, chief, director ≠ **servant**; = **expert**, maestro, ace (Inf), genius, wizard ≠ **amateur**; = **teacher**, tutor, instructor ≠ **student** ♦ adj = **main**, principal, chief, prime, foremost ≠ **lesser** ♦ v = **learn**, understand, pick up, grasp, get the hang of (Inf); = **overcome**, defeat, conquer, tame, triumph over ≠ **give in to**

match¹ n = **game**, test, competition, trial, tie; = **marriage**, pairing, alliance, partnership; = **equal**, rival, peer, counterpart ♦ v = **correspond with**, go with, fit with, harmonize with; = **correspond**, agree, accord, square, coincide

mate ❶ n = (Inf) **friend**, pal (Inf), companion, buddy (Inf), comrade; = **partner**, lover, companion, spouse, consort; = **assistant**, subordinate, apprentice, helper, accomplice ♦ v = **pair**, couple, breed

which thing is made. 2 cloth. 3 information on which piece of work is based. ♦ adj 4 of body. 5 affecting physical wellbeing. 6 important. **materialism** n 1 excessive interest in money and possessions. 2 doctrine that nothing but matter exists. **materialistic** adj **materialize** v come into existence or view. **materially** adv appreciably.
maternal ⊕ adj of mother.
maternity n motherhood.
math n US and Canad mathematics.
mathematics pl n science of number, quantity, shape and space. **mathematical** adj **mathematician** n
maths n Inf mathematics.
matinée n afternoon performance in theatre.
matins pl n morning service.
matriarch n mother as head of family. **matriarchal** adj
matriculate v enrol, be enrolled in college or university.

matrimony n marriage.
matrimonial adj
matrix n, pl **matrices** 1 substance, situation in which something originates, is enclosed. 2 mould.
matron n 1 married woman. 2 woman who superintends domestic arrangements of public institution. 3 former name for NURSING OFFICER.
matter ⊕ n 1 substance of which thing is made. 2 affair. 3 business. 4 trouble. 5 pus. ♦ v 6 be of importance.
mattress n stuffed flat (sprung) case used as part of bed.
mature ⊕ adj 1 ripe, completely developed. 2 grown-up. ♦ v 3 bring, come to maturity. **maturity** n
maudlin adj weakly sentimental.
maul ⊕ v handle roughly.
mausoleum n stately building as a tomb.
mauve adj/n pale purple.
maverick ⊕ n independent, unorthodox person.

——————— THESAURUS ———————

material n = **substance**, matter, stuff; = **cloth**, fabric, textile; = **information**, details, facts, notes, evidence ♦ adj = **physical**, solid, substantial, concrete, bodily; = **relevant**, important, significant, essential, vital
maternal adj = **motherly**, protective, nurturing, maternalistic
matter n = **situation**, concern, business, question, event; = **substance**, material, body, stuff ♦ v = **be important**, make a

difference, count, be relevant, make any difference
mature v = **develop**, grow up, bloom, blossom, come of age ♦ adj = **matured**, seasoned, ripe, mellow; = **grown-up**, adult, of age, fully fledged, full-grown ≠ **immature**
maul v = **mangle**, claw, lacerate, tear; = **ill-treat**, abuse, batter, molest, manhandle
maverick n = **rebel**, radical, dissenter, individualist, protester

maw n stomach.

mawkish adj 1 maudlin. 2 sickly.

maxim n 1 general truth. 2 rule of conduct.

maximum 🟊 adj/n, pl –**mums**, –**ma** greatest (size or number).

maximize v increase to maximum.

may v, past tense **might** expresses possibility, permission, opportunity etc. **maybe** adv 1 perhaps. 2 possibly.

May n fifth month 2 (without cap.) hawthorn or its flowers.

mayfly n short–lived aquatic insect.

Mayday n international distress signal.

mayhem 🟊 n violent destruction.

mayonnaise n creamy sauce, esp. for salads.

mayor n head of municipality.

mayoress n 1 mayor's wife. 2 lady mayor.

maze 🟊 n 1 labyrinth. 2 network of paths, lines. 3 state of confusion.

MBE Member of the Order of the British Empire.

MD Doctor of Medicine.

me pron object of I.

mead n alcoholic drink made from honey.

meadow 🟊 n piece of grassland.

meagre adj lean, scanty.

meal¹ n 1 occasion when food is served and eaten. 2 the food.

meal² n grain ground to powder.

mealy–mouthed adj not outspoken enough.

mean¹ 🟊 v meaning, meant 1 intend. 2 signify. 3 have a meaning. 4 have the intention of behaving. **meaning** n **meaningful** adj of great significance.

mean² 🟊 adj 1 ungenerous, petty. 2 miserly. 3 callous. 4 shabby.

mean³ 🟊 n 1 middle point. ◆ pl 2 that by which thing is done. 3 money. 4 resources. ◆ adj 5 intermediate. 6 average.

meantime, meanwhile adv/n (during) time between one happening and another.

meander v 1 flow windingly. 2 wander aimlessly. ◆ n 3 wandering course.

M

———————— THESAURUS ————————

≠ **traditionalist** ◆ adj = **rebel**, radical, dissenting, individualistic, eccentric

maximum adj = **greatest**, highest, supreme, paramount, utmost ≠ **minimal** ◆ n = **top**, peak, ceiling, utmost, upper limit ≠ **minimum**

mayhem n = **chaos**, trouble, violence, disorder, destruction

maze n = **web**, confusion, tangle, labyrinth, imbroglio

meadow n = **field**, pasture,

grassland, lea (Poet)

mean¹ v = **signify**, indicate, represent, express, stand for; = **intend**, want, plan, expect, design

mean² adj = **miserly**, stingy, parsimonious, niggardly, mercenary ≠ **generous**; = **dishonourable**, petty, shameful, shabby, vile ≠ **honourable**

mean³ n = **average**, middle, balance, norm, midpoint ◆ adj

measles n infectious disease producing rash of red spots.
measly adj Inf meagre.
measure ⚫ n 1 size, quantity. 2 unit, system of measuring. 3 course of action. 4 law. ◆ v 5 ascertain size, quantity of. 6 be (so much) in size or quantity. 7 indicate measurement of.
measurable adj **measured** adj 1 slow and steady. 2 carefully considered. **measurement** n 1 measuring. 2 size.
meat ⚫ n 1 animal flesh as food. 2 food. **meaty** adj
mechanic n 1 one who works with machinery. ◆ pl 2 scientific theory of motion. **mechanical** adj 1 of, by machine. 2 acting without thought.
mechanism ⚫ n 1 structure of machine. 2 piece of machinery. 3 process, technique. **mechanization** n **mechanize** v 1 equip with machinery. 2 make automatic.
medal n piece of metal with inscription etc. used as reward or memento. **medallion** n (design like) large medal.
meddle v interfere.

media n pl of MEDIUM: used esp. of the mass media, radio, television etc.
median adj/n middle (point or line).
mediate ⚫ v intervene to reconcile. **mediation** n **mediator** n
medic n Inf doctor or medical student.
medicine ⚫ n 1 drug or remedy for treating disease. 2 science of preventing, curing disease. **medical** adj **medicate** v impregnate with medicinal substances. **medication** n (treatment with) medicinal substance. **medicinal** adj curative. **medieval** adj of Middle Ages.
mediocre ⚫ adj 1 ordinary, middling. 2 second–rate.
mediocrity n 1 state of being mediocre. 2 mediocre person.
meditate v 1 reflect deeply, esp. on spiritual matters. 2 think about, plan. **meditation** n
medium ⚫ adj 1 between two qualities, degrees etc. ◆ n 2 middle quality. 3 means. 4 agency of communicating news etc. to public. 5 surroundings.

————— THESAURUS —————

= **average**, middle, standard
measure v = **quantify**, determine, assess, weigh, calculate ◆ n
= **quantity**, share, amount, allowance, portion; = **action**, act, step, procedure, means; = **gauge**, rule, scale, metre, ruler; = **law**, act, bill, legislation, resolution
meat n = **food**, flesh
mechanism n = **process**, way,

means, system, operation;
= **machine**, device, tool, instrument, appliance
mediate v = **intervene**, step in (Inf), intercede, referee, umpire
medicine n = **remedy**, drug, cure, prescription, medication
mediocre adj = **second–rate**, average, ordinary, indifferent, middling ≠ **excellent**

medley *n* mixture.

meek *adj* submissive, humble.

meet ❶ *v* **meeting, met 1** come face to face (with). **2** satisfy. **3** pay. **4** converge. **5** assemble. **6** come into contact. **meeting** *n*

megabyte *n* Comp 1 048 576 bytes.

megalith *n* great stone.

megalomania *n* desire for, delusions of grandeur, power etc. **megalomaniac** *adj/n*

megaphone *n* cone–shaped instrument to amplify voice.

megaton *n* explosive power of 1 000 000 tons of TNT.

melancholy ❶ *n* **1** sadness, dejection. ◆ *adj* **2** gloomy, dejected.

melanin *n* dark pigment found in hair, skin etc.

mêlée *n* confused fight.

mellifluous *adj* (of sound)

smooth, sweet.

mellow ❶ *adj* **1** ripe. **2** softened by age, experience. **3** not harsh. **4** genial. ◆ *v* **5** make, become mellow.

melodrama *n* play full of sensational situations. **melodramatic** *adj*

melody ❶ *n, pl* **–dies 1** series of musical notes which make tune. **2** sweet sound. **melodic** *adj* **melodious** *adj*

melon *n* large, fleshy, juicy fruit.

melt ❶ *v* **1** (cause to) become liquid by heat. **2** dissolve. **3** soften. **4** disappear.

member ❶ *n* **1** individual making up body or society. **2** limb. **3** any part of complex whole. **membership** *n*

membrane *n* thin flexible tissue in plant or animal body.

memento *n, pl* **–tos, –toes**

—————— THESAURUS ——————

medium *adj* = **average**, mean, middle, middling, fair ≠ **extraordinary** ◆ *n* = **spiritualist**, seer, clairvoyant, fortune teller, channeller; = **middle**, mean, centre, average, compromise

meet *v* = **encounter**, come across, run into, happen on, find ≠ **avoid**; = **gather**, collect, assemble, get together, come together ≠ **disperse**; = **fulfil**, match (up to), answer, satisfy, discharge ≠ **fall short of**; = **experience**, face, suffer, bear, go through

melancholy *adj* = **sad**, depressed, miserable, gloomy, glum ≠ **happy** ◆ *n* = **sadness**, depression, misery,

gloom, sorrow ≠ **happiness**

mellow *adj* = **full-flavoured**, rich, sweet, delicate; = **ripe**, mature, ripened ≠ **unripe** ◆ *v* = **relax**, improve, settle, calm, mature

melody *n* = **tune**, song, theme, air, music; = **tunefulness**, harmony, musicality, euphony, melodiousness

melt *v* = **dissolve**, run, soften, fuse, thaw; *often with* **away** = **disappear**, fade, vanish, dissolve, disperse; = **soften**, relax, disarm, mollify

member *n* = **representative**, associate, supporter, fellow, subscriber

reminder, souvenir.

memo n, pl **memos** short for MEMORANDUM.

memoir ❶ n autobiography, personal history.

memory ❶ n, pl **–ries** 1 faculty of recalling to mind. 2 recollection. 3 thing remembered. 4 commemoration. **memorable** adj worthy of remembrance. **memorandum** n 1 note to help the memory etc. 2 informal letter. **memorial** n 1 thing which serves to keep in memory. ♦ adj 2 serving as a memorial. **memorize** v commit to memory.

men n pl of MAN.

menace ❶ n 1 threat. ♦ v 2 threaten.

menagerie n collection of wild animals.

mend ❶ v 1 repair. 2 correct, put right. 3 improve. ♦ n 4 repaired breakage.

menial adj 1 requiring little skill. 2 servile. ♦ n 3 servant.

meningitis n inflammation of the membranes of the brain.

menopause n final cessation of menstruation.

menstruation n monthly discharge of blood from womb. **menstrual** adj **menstruate** v

mensuration n measuring.

mental ❶ adj 1 of, by the mind. 2 Inf mad. **mentality** n way of thinking.

menthol n substance found in peppermint.

mention ❶ v 1 refer to briefly. ♦ n 2 acknowledgment. 3 reference to.

mentor ❶ n wise adviser.

menu ❶ n list of dishes served.

——— THESAURUS ———

memoir n = **account**, life, record, journal, essay

memory n = **recall**, mind, retention, ability to remember, powers of recall; = **recollection**, reminder, reminiscence, impression, echo; = **commemoration**, respect, honour, recognition, tribute

menace n = (Inf) **nuisance**, plague, pest, annoyance, troublemaker; = **threat**, warning, intimidation, ill–omen, ominousness ♦ v = **bully**, threaten, intimidate, terrorize, frighten

mend v = **repair**, fix, restore, renew, patch up; = **darn**, repair, patch, stitch, sew; = **heal**, improve, recover, get better, be all right

mental adj = **intellectual**, rational, theoretical, cognitive, brain; = (Inf) **insane**, mad, disturbed, unstable, mentally ill

mention v = **refer to**, point out, bring up, state, reveal ♦ n (often with **of**) = **reference to**, observation, indication, remark on, allusion to; = **acknowledgment**, recognition, tribute, citation, honourable mention

mentor n = **guide**, teacher, coach, adviser, tutor

menu n = **bill of fare**, tariff (Chiefly Brit), set menu, table d'hôte, carte

mercantile adj of trade.

mercenary adj 1 influenced by greed. 2 working merely for reward. ◆ n 3 hired soldier.

merchant ❶ n 1 one engaged in trade. 2 wholesale trader.

merchandise n trader's wares.

merchant navy ships engaged in a nation's commerce.

mercury n silvery metal, liquid at ordinary temperature. **mercurial** adj lively, changeable.

mercy ❶ n, pl –cies 1 refraining from infliction of suffering by one who has right, power to inflict it. 2 fortunate occurrence. **merciful** adj **mere** ❶ adj 1 only. 2 nothing but. **merely** adv

merge ❶ v (cause to) lose identity or be absorbed. **merger** n combination esp. of business firms.

meridian n 1 circle of the earth passing through poles. 2 highest point.

meringue n baked mixture of white of eggs and sugar.

merit ❶ n 1 excellence, worth. 2 quality of deserving reward. ◆ v 3 deserve.

mermaid n imaginary sea creature half woman, half fish.

merry ❶ adj –rier, –riest joyous, cheerful. **merriment** n **merry–go–round** n roundabout.

mesh ❶ n 1 (one of the open spaces of, or wires etc. forming) network, net. ◆ v 2 (cause to) entangle, engage.

mesmerize v hypnotize.

mess ❶ n 1 untidy confusion. 2 trouble. 3 (place where) group regularly eat together. ◆ v 4 potter (about). 5 muddle. **messy** adj

message ❶ n 1 communication sent. 2 meaning, moral. **messenger** n

Messiah n 1 promised saviour. 2 Christ.

met past tense and past participle

M

——— THESAURUS ———

du jour (Fr)

merchant n = **tradesman**, dealer, trader, broker, retailer

mercy n = **compassion**, pity, forgiveness, grace, kindness ≠ **cruelty**; = **blessing**, boon, godsend

mere adj = **simple**, nothing more than, common, plain, pure

merge v = **combine**, blend, fuse, amalgamate, unite ≠ **separate**

merit n = **advantage**, value, quality, worth, strength ◆ v = **deserve**, warrant, be entitled to, earn, have a right to

merry adj = **cheerful**, happy, carefree, jolly, festive ≠ **gloomy**; = (Brit inf) **tipsy**, happy, mellow, tiddly (slang, chiefly Brit.), squiffy (Brit inf)

mesh n = **net**, netting, network, web, tracery ◆ v = **engage**, combine, connect, knit, coordinate

mess n = **untidiness**, disorder, confusion, chaos, litter

message n = **communication**, note, bulletin, word, letter; = **point**, meaning, idea, moral, theme

of MEET.

metabolism n chemical process of living body. **metabolic** adj

metal n mineral substance, malleable and capable of conducting heat and electricity. **metallic** adj **metallurgist** n **metallurgy** n scientific study of metals.

metamorphosis n, pl **–phoses** change of shape, character etc.

metaphor ❶ n figure of speech in which term is transferred to something it does not literally apply to. **metaphorical** adj

mete v mete out 1 distribute. 2 allot.

meteor n small, fast–moving celestial body, visible as streak of incandescence if it enters earth's atmosphere. **meteoric** adj 1 of meteor. 2 brilliant but short–lived. **meteorite** n fallen meteor.

meteorology n study of climate, weather. **meteorological** adj **meteorologist** n

meter n instrument for recording, measuring.

methane n flammable gas, compound of carbon and hydrogen.

method ❶ n 1 way, manner. 2 technique. 3 orderliness. **methodical** adj orderly.

meths n Inf methylated spirits.

methylated spirits alcoholic mixture used as fuel etc.

meticulous adj particular about details.

metre n 1 unit of length in decimal system. 2 SI unit of length. 3 rhythm of poem. **metric** adj of system of weights and measures in which metre is a unit. **metrical** adj 1 of measurement. 2 of poetic metre.

metronome n instrument which marks musical time by means of ticking pendulum.

metropolis n chief city of a region. **metropolitan** adj

mettle n courage, spirit.

mew n/v (utter) cry of cat.

mews pl n (with sing or pl v) yard, street orig. of stables, now oft. converted to houses.

mezzanine n intermediate storey, balcony between two main storeys.

mezzo–soprano n voice, singer between soprano and contralto.

mg milligram.

miasma n unwholesome atmosphere.

mica n mineral found as glittering scales, plates.

microbe n 1 minute organism. 2 disease germ.

microchip n small wafer of silicon containing electronic circuits.

microcosm n miniature representation of larger system.

microfiche n microfilm in sheet form.

—— THESAURUS ——

metaphor n = **figure of speech**, image, symbol, analogy, conceit (Lit)

method n = **manner**, process, approach, technique, way; = **orderliness**, planning, order,

microfilm n miniaturized recording of manuscript, book on roll of film.

microphone n instrument for amplifying, transmitting sounds.

microprocessor n integrated circuit acting as central processing unit in small computer.

microscope n instrument by which very small body is magnified. **microscopic** adj very small.

microwave n 1 electromagnetic wave with wavelength of a few centimetres, used in radar, cooking etc. 2 oven using microwaves.

mid adj intermediate. **midday** n noon. **midnight** n twelve o'clock at night. **midway** adj/adv halfway.

middle ⊕ adj 1 equidistant from two extremes. ♦ n 2 middle point or part. **middling** adj 1 mediocre. 2 moderate. **middle age** period of life between youth and old age. **middle class** social class of businessmen, professional people etc. **middleman** n trader between producer and consumer. **middle–of–the–road** adj moderate.

midge n gnat or similar insect.

midget n very small person or thing.

midriff n middle part of body.

midst n **in the midst of 1** surrounded by. **2** at a point during.

midtown n US and Canad the centre of a town.

midwife n trained person who assists at childbirth. **midwifery** n

mien n person's manner or appearance.

might[1] ⊕ n power, strength. **mightily** adv **mighty** adj

might[2] past tense of MAY.

migraine n severe headache.

migrate ⊕ v move from one place to another. **migrant** n/adj **migration** n

mike n Inf microphone.

mild ⊕ adj 1 not strongly flavoured. 2 gentle. 3 temperate. **mildly** adv

mildew n destructive fungus on plants or things exposed to damp.

mile n measure of length, 1760 yards, 1.609 km. **mileage** n 1 travelling expenses per mile. 2 miles travelled (per gallon of petrol). **mileometer** n device that records miles travelled by vehicle.

———————— THESAURUS ————————

system, purpose

middle n = **centre**, heart, midst, halfway point, midpoint ♦ adj = **central**, medium, mid, intervening, halfway;
= **intermediate**, intervening

might[1] n = **power**, force, energy, strength, vigour **with all your might** = **forcefully**, vigorously,

mightily, manfully, lustily

migrate v = **move**, travel, journey, wander, trek

mild adj = **gentle**, calm, easy–going, meek, placid ≠ harsh;
= **temperate**, warm, calm, moderate, tranquil ≠ cold;
= **bland**, thin, smooth, tasteless, insipid

M

milestone n significant event.
milieu n, pl **milieux**, **milieus** environment.
militant ❶ adj 1 aggressive, vigorous in support of cause. 2 prepared to fight. **militancy** n
military ❶ adj 1 of, for, soldiers, armies or war. ♦ n 2 armed forces.
militarism n enthusiasm for military force and methods. **militia** n military force of citizens for home service.
militate v (esp. with **against**) have strong influence, effect on.
milk ❶ n 1 white fluid with which mammals feed their young. 2 fluid in some plants. ♦ v 3 draw milk from. **milky** adj
mill ❶ n 1 factory. 2 machine for grinding, pulverizing corn, paper etc. ♦ v 3 put through mill. 4 cut fine grooves across edges of (e.g. coins). 5 move in confused manner. **miller** n **millstone** n flat circular stone for grinding.
millennium n, pl **–nia**, **–niums** 1 period of a thousand years. 2 period of peace, happiness.
millet n cereal grass.
milli– comb. form thousandth part of, as in milligram, millilitre, millimetre.

milliner n maker of women's hats.
million n 1000 thousands.
millionaire n owner of a million pounds, dollars etc. **millionth** adj/n
millipede n small animal with many pairs of legs.
mime n 1 acting without words. ♦ v 2 perform mime.
mimic ❶ v **–icking**, **–icked** 1 imitate, esp. for satirical effect. ♦ n 2 one who does this. **mimicry** n act of imitating closely.
mimosa n plant with fluffy, yellow flowers.
minaret n tall slender tower of mosque.
mince ❶ v 1 cut, chop small. 2 soften (words etc.). ♦ n 3 minced meat. **mincer** n mincing adj affected in manner. **mincemeat** n mixture of currants, spices, suet etc. **mince pie** pie containing mincemeat.
mind ❶ n 1 intellectual faculties. 2 memory. 3 intention. 4 taste. 5 sanity. ♦ v 6 take offence at. 7 care for. 8 attend to. 9 heed. **minder** n Sl bodyguard. **mindful** adj heedful.
mindless adj 1 stupid. 2 requiring no thought. 3 careless.

———— THESAURUS ————

militant adj = **aggressive**, active, vigorous, assertive, combative ≠ peaceful
military adj = **warlike**, armed, soldierly, martial ♦ n = **armed forces**, forces, services, army
milk v = **exploit**, pump, take advantage of
mill n = **grinder**, crusher, quern;

= **factory**, works, plant, workshop, foundry ♦ v = **grind**, pound, crush, powder, grate
mimic v = **imitate**, do (Inf), take off (Inf), ape, parody ♦ n = **imitator**, impressionist, copycat (Inf), impersonator, caricaturist
mince v = **cut**, grind, crumble, dice, hash; = **tone down**, spare,

mine[1] ❶ n 1 deep hole for digging out coal, metals etc. 2 hidden deposit of explosive to blow up ship etc. 3 profitable source. ♦ v 4 dig from mines. 5 place explosive mines in, on. **miner** n **minefield** n area of land or sea containing mines. **minesweeper** n ship for clearing mines.

mine[2] pron belonging to me.

mineral n/adj (of) naturally occurring inorganic substance. **mineralogy** n science of minerals. **mineral water** water containing dissolved mineral salts.

minestrone n soup containing vegetables and pasta.

mingle ❶ v 1 mix, blend. 2 mix socially.

mini n 1 something small or miniature. 2 short skirt. ♦ adj 3 small.

miniature ❶ n 1 small painted portrait. 2 anything on small scale. ♦ adj 3 on small scale. **miniaturize** v make to very small scale.

minim n Mus note half the length of semibreve.

minimum ❶ n, pl –mums, –ma 1 lowest point or quantity. ♦ adj 2 least possible. **minimal** adj **minimize** v reduce to minimum.

minion n servile dependant.

minister ❶ n 1 person in charge of department of State. 2 diplomatic representative. 3 clergyman. ♦ v 4 take care of. **ministerial** adj **ministration** n rendering help. **ministry** n, pl –tries 1 office of clergyman. 2 government department.

mink n 1 variety of weasel. 2 its fur.

minnow n small freshwater fish.

M

——————— THESAURUS ———————

moderate, weaken, soften

mind n = **memory**, recollection, remembrance, powers of recollection; = **intelligence**, reason, reasoning, understanding, sense; = **intention**, wish, desire, urge, fancy; = **sanity**, reason, senses, judgment, wits ♦ v = **take offence at**, dislike, care about, object to, resent; = **be careful**, watch, take care, be wary, be cautious; = **look after**, watch, protect, tend, guard; = **pay attention to**, mark, note, listen to, observe; **make up your mind** = **decide**, choose, determine, resolve

mine[1] n = **pit**, deposit, shaft,

colliery, excavation; = **source**, store, fund, stock, supply ♦ v = **dig up**, extract, quarry, unearth, excavate

mingle v = **mix**, combine, blend, merge, unite ≠ **separate**; = **associate**, consort, socialize, rub shoulders (Inf), hobnob ≠ **dissociate**

miniature adj = **small**, little, minute, tiny, toy ≠ **giant**

minimum adj = **lowest**, smallest, least, slightest, minimal ≠ **maximum** ♦ n = **lowest**, least, lowest level, nadir

minister n = **clergyman**, priest, vicar, parson, preacher ♦ v often with **to** = **attend**, serve, tend, take

minor ❶ *adj* **1** lesser. **2** under age.
♦ *n* **3** person below age of legal majority. **4** scale in music. **minority** *n* **1** lesser number, group. **2** state of being a minor.

minster *n* cathedral, large church.

minstrel *n* medieval singer, musician, poet.

mint¹ ❶ *n* **1** place where money is coined. ♦ *adj* **2** brand-new. ♦ *v* **3** coin, invent.

mint² *n* aromatic plant.

minuet *n* stately dance.

minus *prep/adj* **1** less. **2** lacking. **3** negative. ♦ *n* **4** the sign of subtraction (−).

minuscule *adj* very small.

minute¹ ❶ *n* **1** 60th part of hour or degree. ♦ *pl* **2** record of proceedings of meeting etc.

minute² ❶ *adj* **1** very small. **2** precise.

minx *n* bold, flirtatious woman.

miracle ❶ *n* **1** supernatural event. **2** marvel. **miraculous** *adj*

mirage *n* deceptive image in atmosphere.

mire *n* swampy ground, mud.

mirror ❶ *n* **1** glass or polished surface reflecting images. ♦ *v* **2** reflect in or as if in mirror.

mirth *n* merriment, gaiety.

mis– *comb. form* wrong, bad.

misadventure *n* unlucky chance.

misanthrope *n* hater of mankind.

misapprehension *n* misunderstanding.

misappropriate *v* **1** put to dishonest use. **2** embezzle.

miscellaneous *adj* mixed.

miscellany *n* medley.

mischief *n* **1** annoying behaviour. **2** inclination to tease. **3** harm, annoyance. **mischievous** *adj*

misconception *n* wrong idea.

misconduct ❶ *n* unethical behaviour.

miscreant *n* evildoer.

misdemeanour *n* minor offence.

miser *n* hoarder of money.

miserable ❶ *adj* **1** very unhappy. **2** causing misery. **3** worthless. **4** squalid. **misery** *n, pl* **-eries**

misfire *v* fail to fire, start etc.

misfit *n* person not suited to environment.

misfortune ❶ *n* (piece of) bad luck.

——— THESAURUS ———

care of, cater to

minor *adj* = **small**, lesser, slight, petty, trivial ≠ **major**

mint¹ *v* = **make**, produce, strike, cast, stamp

minute¹ *n* = **moment**, second, bit, flash, instant

minute² *adj* = **small**, little, tiny, miniature, microscopic ≠ **huge**;
= **precise**, close, detailed, critical, exact ≠ **imprecise**

miracle *n* = **wonder**, phenomenon, sensation, marvel, amazing achievement

mirror *n* = **looking-glass**, glass (*Brit*), reflector ♦ *v* = **reflect**, follow, copy, echo, emulate

misconduct *n* = **immorality**, wrongdoing, mismanagement, malpractice, impropriety

miserable *adj* = **pathetic**, sorry, shameful, despicable, deplorable

misgiving n (oft. pl) feeling of fear, doubt etc.

misguided ⊕ adj foolish.

mishap n minor accident.

misjudge v judge wrongly.

mislay v put in place which cannot later be remembered.

mislead ⊕ v give false information to.

mismanage v organize badly.

misnomer n wrong name or term.

misogyny n hatred of women.

misogynist n

misprint n printing error.

miss v 1 fail to hit, reach, catch etc. 2 not be in time for. 3 notice or regret absence of. 4 avoid. 5 omit. ◆ n 6 fact, instance of missing. **missing** adj lost, absent.

Miss n 1 title of unmarried woman 2 (without cap.) girl.

missal n book containing prayers, rites etc.

missile ⊕ n that which may be thrown, shot etc. to damage or destroy.

mission ⊕ n 1 specific duty. 2 delegation. 3 those sent.

missionary n, pl –aries one sent to a place, society to spread religion.

missive n letter.

mist ⊕ n water vapour in fine drops. **misty** adj

mistake ⊕ n 1 error. ◆ v 2 fail to understand. 3 take (person or thing) for another. **mistaken** adj

mistletoe n evergreen parasitic plant.

mistress ⊕ n 1 illicit lover of married man. 2 woman with mastery or control. 3 title formerly given to married woman.

mistrust v 1 not trust. ◆ n 2 lack of trust.

misunderstand ⊕ v fail to understand properly.

misunderstanding n

misuse ⊕ n 1 incorrect use. ◆ v 2 use wrongly. 3 treat badly.

mite n 1 very small insect. 2 anything very small.

mitigate v make less severe.

—————————— THESAURUS ——————————

≠ **respectable**

misfortune n often plural = **bad luck**, adversity, hard luck, ill luck, infelicity

misguided adj = **unwise**, mistaken, misplaced, deluded, ill–advised

mislead v = **deceive**, fool, delude, take someone in (Inf), misdirect

missile n = **projectile**, weapon, shell, rocket

mission n = **task**, job, commission, duty, undertaking

mist n = **fog**, cloud, steam, spray, film

mistake n = **error**, blunder, oversight, slip, gaffe ◆ v = **confuse with**, take for, mix up with; = **misunderstand**, misinterpret, misjudge, misread, misconstrue

mistress n = **lover**, girlfriend, concubine, kept woman, paramour

misunderstand v = **misinterpret**, misread, mistake, misjudge, misconstrue

misuse n = **waste**, squandering; desecration ◆ v = **abuse**, misapply,

mitigation n

mitre n 1 bishop's headdress. 2 right-angled joint.

mitt n covering for hand.

mitten n glove with two compartments for thumb and fingers.

mix ❶ v 1 put together, combine, blend. 2 be mixed. 3 associate. **mixed** adj of different elements, races etc. **mixer** n **mixture** n **mix-up** n confused situation.

mm millimetre.

mnemonic n something to help the memory.

moan ❶ v/n (utter) low murmur, usually of pain.

moat n deep wide ditch, esp. round castle.

mob ❶ n 1 disorderly crowd. ◆ v 2 attack in mob, hustle.

mobile ❶ adj 1 capable of movement. 2 easily changed. ◆ n 3 hanging structure designed to move in air currents. **mobility** n

mobilize ❶ v prepare, esp. for military service. **mobilization** n

moccasin n Amer. Indian soft shoe, usu. of deerskin.

mocha n 1 strong dark coffee. 2 flavouring of coffee and chocolate.

mock ❶ v 1 ridicule. 2 mimic. ◆ adj 3 sham. **mockery** n 1 derision. 2 travesty.

mode ❶ n 1 manner. 2 prevailing fashion. **modish** adj fashionable.

model ❶ n 1 miniature representation. 2 pattern. 3 one worthy of imitation. 4 person employed to pose, or display clothing. ◆ adj 5 made as (miniature) copy. 6 exemplary. ◆ v 7 make model of. 8 mould. 9 display (clothing).

———— THESAURUS ————

prostitute

mix v = **combine**, blend, merge, join, cross; = **socialize**, associate, hang out (Inf), mingle, circulate ◆ n = **mixture**, combination, blend, fusion, compound

moan v = **groan**, sigh, sob, whine, lament; = (Inf) **grumble**, complain, groan, whine, carp ◆ n = **groan**, sigh, sob, lament, wail; = (Inf) **complaint**, protest, grumble, whine, grouse

mob n = **crowd**, pack, mass, host, drove; = (Sl) **gang**, group, set, lot, crew (Inf) ◆ v = **surround**, besiege, jostle, fall on, set upon

mobile adj = **movable**, moving, travelling, wandering, portable

mobilize v = **rally**, organize, stimulate, excite, prompt; = **deploy**, prepare, ready, rally, assemble

mock v = **laugh at**, tease, ridicule, taunt, scorn ≠ **respect** ◆ adj = **imitation**, pretended, artificial, fake, false ≠ **genuine**

mode n = **method**, way, system, form, process; = **fashion**, style, trend, rage, vogue

model n = **representation**, image, copy, miniature, dummy; = **pattern**, example, standard, original, ideal; = **sitter**, subject, poser ◆ v = wear, display, sport; = **shape**, form, design, fashion, carve

M

modem n device for connecting two computers by telephone line.

moderate ❶ adj **1** not going to extremes. ♦ n **2** person of moderate views. ♦ v **3** make, become less excessive. **4** preside over. **moderation** n **moderator** n arbitrator.

modern ❶ adj **1** of present or recent times. **2** in, of current fashion. **modernity** n **modernize** v bring up to date.

modest ❶ adj **1** not overrating one's qualities or achievements. **2** moderate, decent. **modesty** n

modicum n small quantity.

modify ❶ v –fying, –fied change slightly. **modification** n

modulate v **1** regulate. **2** vary in tone. **modulation** n

module n (detachable) component with specific function.

mogul ❶ n powerful person.

mohair n cloth of goat's hair.

moist ❶ adj slightly wet. **moisten** v **moisture** n liquid, esp. diffused or in drops.

molar n/adj (tooth) for grinding.

molasses n syrup, by–product of sugar refining.

mole¹ n small dark spot on skin.

mole² n small burrowing animal.

molecule ❶ n simplest freely existing chemical unit. **molecular** adj

molest v pester, interfere with so as to annoy or injure.

moll n Sl gangster's female accomplice.

mollify v –fying, –fied calm down, placate. **mollification** n

mollusc n soft–bodied, usu. hard–shelled animal, e.g. snail.

mollycoddle v pamper.

molten see MELT.

mom n Chiefly US and Canad an informal word for MOTHER.

moment ❶ n short space of, (present) point in, time. **momentarily** adv **momentary** adj lasting only a moment.

momentous ❶ adj of great

———— THESAURUS ————

moderate adj = **mild**, reasonable, controlled, limited, steady ≠ **extreme**; = **average**, middling, fair, ordinary, indifferent ♦ v = **soften**, control, temper, regulate, curb

modern adj = **current**, contemporary, recent, present-day, latter-day; = **up-to-date**, fresh, new, novel, newfangled ≠ **old-fashioned**

modest adj = **moderate**, small, limited, fair, ordinary; = **unpretentious**, reserved, retiring, shy, coy

modify v = **change**, reform, convert, alter, adjust; = **tone down**, lower, qualify, ease, moderate

mogul n = **tycoon**, baron, magnate, big shot (Inf), big noise (Inf)

moist adj = **damp**, wet, soggy, humid, clammy

molecule n = **particle**, jot, speck

moment n = **instant**, second, flash, twinkling, split second; = **time**, point, stage, juncture

importance.

momentum ❶ n 1 force of a moving body. 2 impetus gained from motion.

monarch ❶ n sovereign ruler.

monarchist n supporter of monarchy. **monarchy** n 1 state ruled by sovereign. 2 government by sovereign.

monastery ❶ n, pl **-teries** house occupied by religious order.

monastic adj

Monday n second day of the week.

money ❶ n banknotes, coins etc., used as medium of exchange.

monetary adj **moneyed, monied** adj rich.

mongoose n, pl **-gooses** small animal of Asia and Africa.

mongrel n/adj 1 (animal) of mixed breed. 2 hybrid.

monitor ❶ n 1 person or device which checks, controls, warns, records. 2 pupil assisting teacher with odd jobs. 3 type of large lizard. ◆ v 4 watch, check on.

monk ❶ n one of a religious community of men living apart under vows.

monkey ❶ n 1 long-tailed

primate. 2 mischievous child. ◆ v 3 meddle with.

mono- comb. form single, as in monosyllabic.

monochrome adj of one colour.

monocle n single eyeglass.

monogamy n custom of being married to one person at a time.

monogram n design of letters interwoven.

monograph n short book on single subject.

monolith n large upright block of stone. **monolithic** adj

monologue n long speech by one person.

monopoly n exclusive possession of trade, privilege etc. **monopolize** v claim, take exclusive possession of.

monotone n speech on one note. **monotonous** adj lacking variety, dull. **monotony** n

monsoon n 1 seasonal wind of SE Asia. 2 very heavy rainfall season.

monster n 1 fantastic imaginary beast. 2 huge or misshapen person, animal or thing. ◆ adj 3 huge. **monstrosity** n 1 monstrous being. 2 deformity. **monstrous** adj 1 horrible. 2 shocking. 3

——— THESAURUS ———

momentous adj = **significant**, important, vital, critical, crucial ≠ unimportant

momentum n = **impetus**, force, power, drive, push

monarch n = **ruler**, king or queen sovereign, tsar, potentate

monastery n = **abbey**, convent, priory, cloister, nunnery

money n = **cash**, capital, currency, hard cash, readies (Inf)

monitor v = **check**, follow, watch, survey, observe ◆ n = **guide**, observer, supervisor, invigilator; = **prefect** (Brit), head girl, head boy, senior boy, senior girl

monk n = (Loosely) **friar**, brother

monkey n = **simian**, ape, primate;

enormous.

month *n* one of twelve periods into which the year is divided. **monthly** *adj/adv* once a month.

monument 🛈 *n* anything that commemorates, esp. a building or statue. **monumental** *adj*

mooch *v Sl* loaf, slouch.

mood¹ 🛈 *n* **1** state of mind and feelings. **2** sulk. **moody** *adj* **1** gloomy. **2** changeable in mood.

mood² *n Grammar* form indicating function of verb.

moon 🛈 *n* **1** satellite which revolves round earth. **2** any secondary planet. ◆ *v* **3** go about dreamily. **moonlight** *n*

moor¹ 🛈 *n* tract of open uncultivated land. **moorhen** *n* small black water bird.

moor² 🛈 *v* secure (ship) with chains or ropes. **moorings** *pl n* ropes etc. for mooring.

moose *n* N Amer. deer.

moot *adj* debatable.

mop 🛈 *n* **1** yarn, cloth etc. on end of stick, used for cleaning. **2** tangle (of hair etc.). ◆ *v* **3** clean, wipe as with mop.

mope *v* be gloomy, apathetic.

moped *n* light motorized bicycle.

moral 🛈 *adj* **1** pert. to right and wrong conduct. **2** of good conduct. ◆ *n* **3** practical lesson, e.g. of fable. ◆ *pl* **4** habits with respect to right and wrong. **morality** *n* **1** good moral conduct. **2** moral goodness or badness. **moralize** *v* write, think about moral aspect of things.

morale 🛈 *n* degree of confidence, hope.

morass *n* **1** marsh. **2** mess.

moratorium 🛈 *n, pl* **-ria, -riums** authorized postponement of payments etc.

morbid *adj* **1** unduly interested in death. **2** gruesome. **3** diseased.

mordant *adj* **1** biting. **2** corrosive.

more 🛈 *adj/pron* **1** greater or additional (amount or number): comparative of MANY and MUCH. ◆ *adv* **2** to a greater extent. **3** in addition. **moreover** *adv* besides.

M

——————— THESAURUS ———————

= rascal, horror, devil, rogue, imp

monster *n* = **giant**, mammoth, titan, colossus, monstrosity; = **brute**, devil, beast, demon, villain ◆ *adj* = **huge**, massive, enormous, tremendous, immense

monument *n* = **memorial**, cairn, marker, shrine, tombstone

mood¹ *n* = **state of mind**, spirit, humour, temper, disposition

moon *v* = **idle**, drift, loaf, languish, waste time

moor¹ *n* = **moorland**, fell (*Brit*),

heath

moor² *v* = **tie up**, secure, anchor, dock, lash

mop *n* = **squeegee**, sponge, swab; = **mane**, shock, mass, tangle, mat

moral *adj* = **good**, just, right, principled, decent ≠ **immoral** ◆ *n* = **lesson**, meaning, point, message, teaching

morale *n* = **confidence**, heart, spirit, self-esteem, team spirit

moratorium *n* = **postponement**,

mores *pl n* customs and conventions of society.

morgue *n* mortuary.

moribund *adj* **1** dying. **2** without force or vitality.

morning *n* early part of day until noon. **morn** *n Poet* morning.

moron *n* mentally deficient person.

morose *adj* sullen, moody.

morphine, morphia *n* extract of opium used to relieve pain.

morrow *n Poet* next day.

Morse *n* telegraphic signalling in which letters are represented by dots and dashes.

morsel *n* small piece.

mortal *n adj* **1** subject to death. **2** causing death. ♦ *n* **3** mortal creature. **mortality** *n* **1** state of being mortal. **2** death rate. **3** great loss of life.

mortar *n* **1** mixture of lime, sand and water for holding bricks together. **2** small cannon. **3** vessel in which substances are pounded. **mortarboard** *n* square academic cap.

mortgage *n* **1** conveyance of property as security for debt. ♦ *v* **2** pledge as security.

mortify *v* **-fying, -fied 1** humiliate. **2** subdue by self-denial. **3** (of flesh) be affected with gangrene. **mortification** *n*

mortuary *n, pl* **-aries** building where corpses are kept before burial.

mosaic *n* picture or pattern of small bits of coloured stone, glass etc.

mosque *n* Muslim temple.

mosquito *n, pl* **-toes, -tos** flying, biting insect.

moss *n* small plant growing in masses on moist surfaces. **mossy** *adj*

most *adj/n* **1** (of) greatest number, amount or degree: superlative of MUCH and MANY. ♦ *adv* **2** in the greatest degree.

mostly *adv* generally.

motel *n* roadside hotel for motorists.

moth *n* usu. nocturnal insect like butterfly. **mothball** *n* **1** small ball of chemical to repel moths from stored clothing etc. ♦ *v* **2** store, postpone. **moth-eaten** *adj* **1** damaged by grub of moth. **2** scruffy.

mother *n* **1** female parent. **2** head of religious community of women. ♦ *adj* **3** inborn. ♦ *v* **4** act as mother to. **motherhood** *n* **motherly** *adj* **mother-in-law** *n* mother of one's wife or husband. **mother of pearl** iridescent lining

freeze, halt, suspension, standstill

more *adj* = **extra**, additional, new, other, added ♦ *adv* = **to a greater extent**, longer, better, further, some more

morning *n* = **before noon**, forenoon, morn (*Poet*), a.m.

mortal *adj* = **human**, worldly, passing, fleshly, temporal; = **fatal**, killing, terminal, deadly, destructive ♦ *n* = **human being**, being, man, woman, person

of certain shells.

motif ⓘ n dominating theme.

motion ⓘ n 1 process or action or way of moving. 2 proposal in meeting. ♦ v 3 direct by sign.

motive ⓘ n that which makes person act in particular way. **motivate** v incite. **motivation** n

motley adj 1 varied. 2 multicoloured.

motocross n motorcycle race over rough course.

motor n 1 that which imparts movement. 2 machine to supply power to move. ♦ v 3 travel by car. **motorist** n **motorize** v equip with a motor or motor transport. **motorbike**, **motorcycle** n **motorcar** n **motorway** n main road for fast–moving traffic.

mottled adj marked with blotches.

motto ⓘ n, pl **-toes**, **-tos** saying adopted as rule of conduct.

mould¹ ⓘ n 1 hollow object in which metal etc. is cast. 2 character. 3 shape. ♦ v 4 shape.

moulding n ornamental edging.

mould² ⓘ n fungoid growth caused by dampness. **mouldy** adj

mould³ n loose or surface earth.

moulder v decay.

moult v 1 cast or shed fur, feathers etc. ♦ n 2 moulting.

mound ⓘ n 1 heap. 2 small hill.

mount ⓘ v 1 rise. 2 increase. 3 get on (horse). 4 frame (picture). 5 set up. ♦ v 6 support. 7 horse. 8 hill.

mountain ⓘ n hill of great size. **mountaineer** n one who lives among or climbs mountains. **mountainous** adj **mountain bike** bicycle with straight handlebars and heavy–duty tyres.

M

—————— THESAURUS ——————

mother n = **female parent**, mum (Brit inf), ma (Inf), mater, dam ♦ v = **nurture**, raise, protect, tend, nurse ♦ adj = **native**, natural, innate, inborn

motif n = **design**, shape, decoration, ornament; = **theme**, idea, subject, concept, leitmotif

motion n = **movement**, mobility, travel, progress, flow; = **proposal**, suggestion, recommendation, proposition, submission ♦ v = **gesture**, direct, wave, signal, nod

motive n = **reason**, ground(s), purpose, object, incentive

motto n = **saying**, slogan, maxim, rule, adage

mould¹ n = **cast**, shape, pattern; = **design**, style, fashion, build, form; = **nature**, character, sort, kind, quality ♦ v = **shape**, make, work, form, create; = **influence**, make, form, control, direct

mould² n = **fungus**, blight, mildew

mound n = **heap**, pile, drift, stack, rick; = **hill**, bank, rise, dune, embankment

mount v = **increase**, build, grow, swell, intensify ≠ **decrease**; = **accumulate**, increase, collect, gather, build up; = **ascend**, scale, climb (up), go up, clamber up ≠ **descend** ♦ n = **horse**, steed (Lit); = **backing**, setting, support, stand, base

mountebank n charlatan, fake.

Mountie n Inf a member of the Royal Canadian Mounted Police.

mourn ⊕ v feel, show sorrow (for). **mourner** n **mournful** adj 1 sad. 2 dismal. **mourning** n 1 grieving. 2 clothes of mourner.

mouse n, pl **mice** small rodent. **mousy** adj like mouse, esp. in colour.

mousse n dish of flavoured cream.

moustache n hair on upper lip.

mouth ⊕ n 1 opening in head for eating, speaking etc. 2 opening, entrance. ♦ v 3 form (words) with lips without speaking. **mouth organ** small musical instrument. **mouthpiece** n end of anything placed between lips.

move ⊕ v 1 change position, place. 2 (cause to) be in motion. 3 stir emotions of. 4 incite. 5 propose. 6 change one's dwelling etc. ♦ n 7 a moving. 8 motion.

movement n 1 moving. 2 moving parts. 3 group with common aim. 4 division of piece of music. **movie** n Inf film.

mow ⊕ v **mowing, mowed, mowed** or **mown** cut (grass etc.). **mower** n

MP 1 Member of Parliament. 2 Military Police.

mph miles per hour.

much ⊕ adj **more, most** 1 existing in quantity. ♦ n 2 large amount. 3 important matter. ♦ adv 4 in a great degree. 5 nearly.

muck ⊕ n 1 dung. 2 dirt. **mucky** adj

mucus n fluid secreted by mucous membranes.

mud ⊕ n wet and soft earth. **muddy** adj **mudguard** n cover over wheel. **mudpack** n cosmetic paste to improve complexion.

muddle ⊕ v (esp. with) 1 confuse. 2 bewilder. 3 mismanage. ♦ n 4 confusion.

—— THESAURUS ——

mountain n = **peak**, mount, horn, ridge, fell (Brit); = **heap**, mass, masses, pile, a great deal

mourn v (often with **for**) = **grieve for**, lament, weep for, wail for

mouth n = **lips**, jaws, gob (slang, esp. Brit.), maw, cakehole (Brit sl); = **entrance**, opening, gateway, door, aperture; = **inlet**, outlet, estuary, firth, outfall

move v = **transfer**, change, switch, shift, transpose; = **go**, advance, progress, shift, proceed; = **relocate**, leave, remove, quit, migrate; = **drive**, cause, influence,

persuade, shift ≠ **discourage**; = **touch**, affect, excite, impress, stir; = **propose**, suggest, urge, recommend, request ♦ n = **action**, step, manoeuvre; = **ploy**, action, measure, step, initiative

mow v = **cut**, crop, trim, shear, scythe

much adv = **greatly**, a lot, considerably, decidedly, exceedingly ≠ **hardly**

muck n = **dirt**, mud, filth, ooze, sludge; = **manure**, dung, ordure

mud n = **dirt**, clay, ooze, silt, sludge

muesli n mixture of grain, nuts, dried fruit etc.

muff¹ n tube–shaped covering to keep hands warm.

muff² v bungle, fail in.

muffin n light round yeast cake.

muffle v wrap up, esp. to deaden sound. **muffler** n scarf.

mug¹ ❶ n drinking cup.

mug² ❶ n 1 Sl face. 2 Sl fool, simpleton. ♦ v 3 rob violently. **mugger** n

mug³ v **mugging, mugged** Inf (esp. with **up**) study hard.

muggy adj **–gier, –giest** damp and stifling.

mulberry n tree whose leaves are used to feed silkworms.

mulch n 1 straw, leaves etc. spread as protection for roots of plants. ♦ v 2 protect thus.

mule n 1 cross between horse and ass. 2 hybrid. **mulish** adj obstinate.

mull v 1 heat (wine) with sugar and spices. 2 think (over).

multi– comb. form many, as in multistorey.

multifarious adj of various kinds or parts.

multiple ❶ adj 1 having many parts. ♦ n 2 quantity which contains another an exact number of times. **multiplication** n **multiplicity** n variety, greatness in number. **multiply** v 1 (cause to) increase. 2 combine (two numbers) by multiplication. 3 increase by reproduction.

multitude ❶ n great number.

mum n Inf mother.

mumble v speak indistinctly.

mummy¹ pl **–mies** n embalmed body. **mummify** v

mummy² n Inf mother.

mumps pl n infectious disease marked by swelling in neck.

munch v chew vigorously.

mundane ❶ adj 1 ordinary, everyday. 2 earthly.

municipal ❶ adj belonging to affairs of city or town. **municipality** n city or town with local self–government.

munificent adj very generous. **munificence** n

munted adj NZ slang 1 destroyed or ruined. 2 abnormal or peculiar.

mural n painting on wall.

— THESAURUS —

muddle n = **confusion**, mess, disorder, chaos, tangle ♦ v = **jumble**, disorder, scramble, tangle, mix up; = **confuse**, bewilder, daze, confound, perplex

mug¹ n = **cup**, pot, beaker, tankard

mug² n = **face**, features, countenance, visage; = **fool**, sucker (Sl), chump (Inf), simpleton, easy or soft touch (Sl)

multiple adj = **many**, several, various, numerous, sundry

multitude n = **great number**, host, army, mass, horde

mundane adj = **ordinary**, routine, commonplace, banal, everyday ≠ **extraordinary**; = **earthly**, worldly, secular, mortal, terrestrial ≠ **spiritual**

municipal adj = **civic**, public, local, council, district

M

murder ❶ n 1 unlawful premeditated killing of human being. ♦ v 2 kill thus. **murderer** n **murderous** adj

murk n darkness. **murky** adj

murmur ❶ n –muring, –mured 1 low, indistinct sound. ♦ v 2 make, utter such a sound. 3 complain.

muscle ❶ n 1 part of body which produces movement by contracting. 2 system of muscles. **muscular** adj 1 strong. 2 of muscle.

muse ❶ v 1 ponder. 2 be lost in thought. ♦ n 3 musing. 4 reverie. 5 goddess inspiring creative artist.

museum n (place housing) collection of historical etc. objects.

mush¹ n soft pulpy mass. **mushy** adj

mush² interj order to dogs in sled team to advance.

mushroom n 1 fungoid growth, typically with stem and cap. ♦ v 2 shoot up rapidly.

music n 1 art form using harmonious combination of notes. 2 composition in this art. **musical** adj 1 of, like, interested in music. ♦ n 2 show, film in which music plays essential part. **musician** n

musk n scent obtained from gland

of deer. **musky** adj **muskrat** n 1 N Amer. rodent found near water. 2 its fur.

muskeg n Canad bog or swamp.

musket n Hist infantryman's gun.

Muslim, Moslem n 1 follower of religion of Islam. ♦ adj 2 of Islam.

muslin n fine cotton fabric.

muss v US and Canad inf to make untidy.

mussel n bivalve shellfish.

must ❶ v 1 be obliged to, or certain to. ♦ n 2 necessity.

mustang n wild horse.

mustard n powder made from the seeds of a plant, used in paste as a condiment.

muster ❶ v 1 assemble. ♦ n 2 assembly, esp. for exercise, inspection.

musty adj **mustier, mustiest** mouldy, stale.

mute ❶ adj 1 dumb. 2 silent. ♦ n 3 dumb person 4 Mus contrivance to soften tone of instruments. **muted** adj 1 muffled. 2 subdued.

mutilate v 1 deprive of a limb etc. 2 damage.

mutiny n, pl –nies 1 rebellion against authority, esp. against officers of disciplined body. ♦ v 2

murder n = **killing**, homicide, massacre, assassination, slaying ♦ v = **kill**, massacre, slaughter, assassinate, eliminate (Sl)

murmur v = **mumble**, whisper, mutter ♦ n = **whisper**, drone, purr

muscle n = **tendon**, sinew; = **strength**, might, power, weight, stamina

muse v = **ponder**, consider, reflect, contemplate, deliberate

must n = **necessity**, essential, requirement, fundamental, imperative

muster v = **summon up**, marshal ♦ n = **assembly**, meeting, collection, gathering, rally

mute adj = **silent**, dumb,

commit mutiny. **mutineer** n
mutinous adj
mutter 🛈 v **1** speak, utter
indistinctly. **2** grumble. ♦ n **3**
muttered sound.
mutton n flesh of sheep used as
food.
mutual 🛈 adj **1** done, possessed
etc. by each of two with respect to
the other **2** Inf common.
muzzle n **1** mouth and nose of
animal. **2** cover for these to
prevent biting. **3** open end of gun.
♦ v **4** put muzzle on.
muzzy adj **–zier, –ziest** indistinct,
confused.
my adj belonging to me. **myself**
pron emphatic or reflexive form
of I.
mynah n Indian bird related to
starling.
myopia n short–sightedness.
myopic adj
myriad 🛈 adj **1** innumerable. ♦ n

2 large number.
myrrh n aromatic gum, formerly
used as incense.
myrtle n flowering evergreen
shrub.
myself see MY.
mystery 🛈 n, pl **–teries 1** obscure
or secret thing. **2** anything strange
or inexplicable. **mysterious** adj
mystic 🛈 n one who seeks divine,
spiritual knowledge, esp. by
prayer, contemplation etc.
mystical adj
mystify v **–fying, –fied** bewilder,
puzzle.
mystique n aura of mystery,
power etc.
myth 🛈 n **1** tale with supernatural
characters or events. **2** imaginary
person or object. **mythical** adj
mythology n myths collectively.
myxomatosis n contagious, fatal
disease of rabbits.

M

———————— THESAURUS ————————

unspoken, tacit, wordless
mutter v = **grumble**, complain,
murmur, rumble, whine
mutual adj = **shared**, common,
joint, returned, reciprocal
myriad n = **multitude**, host, army,
swarm, horde ♦ adj
= **innumerable**, countless, untold,
incalculable, immeasurable

mystery n = **puzzle**, problem,
question, secret, riddle
mystical adj = **supernatural**,
mysterious, transcendental, occult,
metaphysical
myth n = **legend**, story, fiction,
saga, fable; = **illusion**, story, fancy,
fantasy, imagination

N n

nab ⊕ v **nabbing, nabbed** Inf **1** arrest (someone). **2** catch (someone) in wrongdoing. ♦ n **2**

nadir n lowest point.

naff adj Sl inferior or useless.

nag¹ ⊕ v **nagging, nagged 1** scold or trouble constantly. ♦ n **2** nagging. **3** one who nags.

nag² ⊕ n Inf horse.

nail ⊕ n **1** horny shield at ends of fingers, toes. **2** small metal spike for fixing wood etc. ♦ v **3** fix with nails.

naive ⊕ adj simple, unaffected, ingenuous. **naiveté, naivety** n

naked ⊕ adj **1** without clothes. **2** exposed, bare. **3** undisguised.

name ⊕ n **1** word by which person, thing etc. is denoted. **2** reputation. ♦ v **3** give name to. **4** call by name. **5** appoint. **6** mention. **nameless** adj **1** without a

name. **2** unknown. **3** indescribable.

namely adv that is to say. **namesake** n person with same name as another.

nanny n, pl **-nies** child's nurse. **nanny goat** she–goat.

nap¹ ⊕ v **1** take short sleep. ♦ n **2** short sleep.

nap² ⊕ n downy surface on cloth made by projecting fibres.

nape n back of neck.

napkin ⊕ n **1** cloth, paper for wiping fingers or lips at table. **2** nappy.

nappy n, pl **-pies** towelling cloth to absorb baby's excrement.

narcissism n abnormal admiration for oneself.

narcissus n, pl **-cissi** genus of bulbous plants including daffodil, esp. one with white flowers.

narcotic ⊕ n/adj (drug) producing

THESAURUS

nab v = **catch**, arrest, apprehend, seize, grab

nag¹ v = **scold**, harass, badger, pester, worry ♦ n = **scold**, complainer, grumbler, virago, shrew

nag² n = **horse** (US), hack

nail v = **fasten**, fix, secure, attach, pin

naive adj = **gullible**, trusting, credulous, unsuspicious, green ≠ **worldly**

naked adj = **nude**, stripped,

exposed, bare, undressed ≠ **dressed**

name n = **title**, nickname, designation, term, handle (Sl) ♦ v = **call**, christen, baptize, dub, term; = **nominate**, choose, select, appoint, specify

nap¹ n = **sleep**, rest, kip (Brit sl), siesta, catnap ♦ v = **sleep**, rest, drop off (Inf), doze, kip (Brit sl)

nap² n = **pile**, down, fibre, weave, grain

napkin n = **serviette**, cloth

numbness and stupor.

nark v Sl annoy, irritate.

narrate v tell (story). **narration** n

narrative n account, story.

narrator n

narrow ⊕ adj 1 of little breadth. 2 limited. ◆ v 3 make, become narrow. **narrow–minded** adj 1 illiberal. 2 bigoted.

nasal adj 1 of nose. ◆ n 2 sound partly produced in nose.

nasturtium n garden plant with red or orange flowers.

nasty ⊕ adj –tier, –tiest 1 foul, unpleasant. 2 spiteful.

nation ⊕ n people or race organized as a state. **national** adj 1 of, characteristic of, a nation. ◆ n 2 citizen. **nationalism** n 1 devotion to one's country. 2 movement for independence. **nationalist** n/adj **nationality** n fact of belonging to a particular nation. **nationalization** n acquisition and management of industries by the state. **nationalize** v **National Health Service** system of medical services financed mainly by taxation. **national service** compulsory military service.

native ⊕ adj 1 inborn. 2 born in particular place. ◆ n 3 native person, animal or plant.

NATO North Atlantic Treaty Organization.

natter Inf ◆ v 1 talk idly. ◆ n 2 idle talk.

natty adj –tier, –tiest neat and smart.

nature ⊕ n 1 innate qualities of person or thing. 2 class, sort 3 (oft. with cap.) power underlying all phenomena. 4 natural unspoilt scenery. **natural** adj 1 of nature. 2 inborn. 3 normal. 4 unaffected. ◆ n 5 something, somebody well suited for something. 6 Mus character used to remove effect of sharp or flat preceding it. **naturalist** n one who studies animals and plants. **naturalize** v admit to citizenship. **naturally** adv **naturism** n nudism.

naughty ⊕ adj –tier, –tiest 1

N

———— THESAURUS ————

narcotic adj = **sedative**, calming, hypnotic, analgesic, soporific

narrow adj = **thin**, fine, slim, slender, tapering ≠ **broad**; = **limited**, restricted, confined, tight, close ≠ **wide**; = **insular**, prejudiced, partial, dogmatic, intolerant ≠ **broad-minded** ◆ v = **restrict**, limit, reduce, constrict

nasty adj = **unpleasant**, ugly, disagreeable ≠ **pleasant**; = **spiteful**, mean, offensive, vicious, unpleasant ≠ **pleasant**; = **disgusting**, unpleasant, offensive, vile, distasteful

nation n = **country**, state, realm

native adj = **mother**, indigenous, vernacular; = **domestic**, local, indigenous, home ◆ n = **inhabitant**, national, resident, citizen, countryman

nature n = **creation**, world, earth, environment, universe; = **quality**, character, make-up, constitution, essence; = **temperament**, character, personality, disposition,

disobedient. **2** *Inf* mildly indecent.

nausea ⏺ *n* feeling that precedes vomiting. **nauseate** *v* sicken. **nauseous** *adj*

nautical *adj* of seamen or ships.

nautical mile 1852 metres.

nave *n* main part of church.

navel *n* small depression in abdomen where umbilical cord was attached.

navigate *v* **1** direct, plot path of ship etc. **2** travel. **navigable** *adj* **navigation** *n* **navigator** *n*

navvy *n, pl* **-vies** labourer employed on roads, railways etc.

navy ⏺ *n, pl* **-vies 1** fleet. **2** warships of country with their crews. ◆ *adj* **3** navy–blue. **naval** *adj* of the navy.

navy–blue *adj* very dark blue.

nay *adv Obs* no.

NB note well.

near ⏺ *prep* **1** close to. ◆ *adv* **2** at or to a short distance. ◆ *adj* **3** close at hand. **4** closely related. **5** stingy. ◆ *v* **6** approach. **nearby** *adj* adjacent. **nearly** *adv* **1** closely. **2** almost. **nearside** *n* side of vehicle

nearer kerb.

neat ⏺ *adj* **1** tidy, orderly. **2** deft. **3** undiluted. **4** *US and Canad* good or pleasing.

nebulous *adj* vague.

necessary ⏺ *adj* **1** that must be done. **2** inevitable. ◆ *n* **3** what is needed. **necessarily** *adv*

necessitate *v* make necessary.

necessity *n* **1** something needed. **2** constraining power. **3** compulsion. **4** poverty.

neck *n* **1** part of body joining head to shoulders. **2** narrow part of anything. **neckerchief** *n* cloth tied round the neck. **necklace** *n* ornament round the neck.

nectar *n* honey of flowers.

nectarine *n* variety of peach.

née *adj* indicating maiden name of married woman.

need ⏺ *v* **1** want, require. ◆ *n* **2** (state, instance of) want. **3** requirement. **4** necessity. **5** poverty. **needful** *adj* necessary. **needless** *adj* unnecessary. **needy** *adj* poor, in want.

———— THESAURUS ————

outlook

naughty *adj* = **disobedient**, bad, mischievous, badly behaved, wayward ≠ **good**; = **obscene**, vulgar, improper, lewd, risqué ≠ **clean**

nausea *n* = **sickness**, vomiting, retching, squeamishness, queasiness

navy *n* = **fleet**, flotilla, armada

near *adj* = **close**, neighbouring, nearby, adjacent, adjoining ≠ **far**; = **imminent**, forthcoming,

approaching, looming, impending ≠ **far-off**

neat *adj* = **tidy**, trim, orderly, spruce, shipshape ≠ **untidy**; = **methodical**, tidy, systematic, fastidious ≠ **disorganized**; = **smart**, trim, tidy, spruce, dapper

necessary *adj* = **needed**, required, essential, vital, compulsory ≠ **unnecessary**; = **inevitable**, certain, unavoidable, inescapable ≠ **avoidable**

need *v* = **want**, miss, require, lack,

needle ⓘ *n* 1 thin pointed piece of metal for sewing, knitting. 2 stylus for record player. 3 leaf of fir tree. ◆ *v* 4 *Inf* goad, provoke. **needlework** *n* sewing, embroidery.

nefarious *adj* wicked.

negate *v* deny, nullify. **negation** *n*

negative ⓘ *adj* 1 expressing denial or refusal. 2 lacking enthusiasm. 3 not positive. 4 of electrical charge having the same polarity as the charge of an electron. ◆ *n* 5 negative word or statement 6 *Photog* picture in which lights and shades are reversed.

neglect ⓘ *v* 1 take no care of. 2 fail to do. ◆ *n* 3 fact of neglecting or being neglected.

negligee *v* woman's light dressing gown.

negligence ⓘ *n* carelessness.

negligent *adj* **negligible** *adj* very small or unimportant.

negotiate ⓘ *v* 1 discuss with view to mutual settlement. 2 arrange by conference. 3 transfer (bill, cheque etc.). 4 get over (obstacle). **negotiable** *adj* **negotiation** *n* **negotiator** *n*

neigh *n/v* (utter) cry of horse.

neighbour *n* one who lives near another. **neighbourhood** *n* 1 district. 2 people of district. **neighbouring** *adj* nearby. **neighbourly** *adj* 1 friendly. 2 helpful.

neither *adj/pron* 1 not the one or the other. ◆ *adv* 2 not on the one hand. 3 not either. ◆ *conj* 4 nor yet.

nemesis *n*, *pl* –**ses** retribution, vengeance.

neologism *n* newly–coined word or phrase.

neon *n* inert gas in the atmosphere, used to illuminate signs and lights.

nephew *n* brother's or sister's son.

nepotism *n* undue favouritism towards one's relations.

nerve ⓘ *n* 1 bundle of fibres carrying feeling, impulses to motion etc. to and from brain. 2

N

———— THESAURUS ————

have to have ◆ *n* = **requirement**, demand, essential, necessity, requisite; = **necessity**, call, demand, obligation; = **emergency**, want, necessity, urgency, exigency

needle *v* = **irritate**, provoke, annoy, harass, taunt

negative *adj* = **pessimistic**, cynical, unwilling, gloomy, jaundiced ≠ **optimistic**; = **dissenting**, contradictory, refusing, denying, rejecting ≠ assenting ◆ *n* = **denial**, no, refusal, rejection, contradiction

neglect *v* = **disregard**, ignore, fail to look after ≠ **look after**; = **shirk**, forget, overlook, omit, evade ◆ *n* = **negligence**, inattention ≠ **care**

negligence *n* = **carelessness**, neglect, disregard, dereliction, slackness

negotiate *v* = **bargain**, deal, discuss, debate, mediate; = **arrange**, work out, bring about, transact

assurance. **3** coolness in danger. **4** audacity. ♦ *pl* **5** sensitiveness to fear, annoyance etc. ♦ *v* **6** give courage to. **nervous** *adj* **1** excitable. **2** apprehensive. **nervy** *adj* nervous, jumpy. **nerve–racking** *adj* very distressing.

nestle ❶ *v* settle comfortably close to something.

net¹ ❶ *n* **1** openwork fabric of meshes of cord etc. ♦ *v* **2** cover with, or catch in, net. **netting** *n* string or wire net. **netball** *n* game in which ball has to be thrown through high net.

net² ❶, **nett** *adj* **1** left after all deductions. ♦ *v* **2** gain, yield as clear profit.

nether *adj* lower.

nettle *n* **1** plant with stinging hairs. ♦ *v* **2** irritate.

network ❶ *n* **1** system of intersecting lines, roads etc. **2** interconnecting group. **3** linked broadcasting stations.

neural *adj* of the nerves.

neuralgia *n* pain in, along nerves.

neurosis *n, pl* **–ses** relatively mild mental disorder. **neurotic** *adj/n*

neuter *adj* **1** neither masculine nor feminine. ♦ *v* **2** castrate (animals).

neutral ❶ *adj* **1** taking neither side in war, dispute etc. **2** without marked qualities. ♦ *n* **3** neutral nation or subject of one. **4** position of disengaged gears. **neutrality** *n* **neutralize** *v* make ineffective.

neutron *n* electrically neutral particle of nucleus of an atom.

never ❶ *adv* at no time.

nevertheless *adv* for all that.

new ❶ *adj* **1** not existing before, fresh. **2** unfamiliar. ♦ *adv* **3** newly. **newly** *adv* recently, freshly. **newcomer** *n* recent arrival. **newfangled** *adj* objectionably or unnecessarily modern.

news ❶ *n* **1** report of recent happenings. **2** interesting fact not previously known. **newsagent** *n* shopkeeper selling newspapers, magazines etc. **newsflash** *n* brief

———— THESAURUS ————

nerve *n* = **bravery**, courage, bottle (*Brit sl*), resolution, daring; = (*Inf*) **impudence**, cheek (*Inf*), audacity, boldness, temerity

nestle *v* = **snuggle**, cuddle, huddle, curl up, nuzzle

net¹ *n* = **mesh**, netting, network, web, lattice ♦ *v* = **catch**, bag, capture, trap, entangle

net², **nett** *adj* = **after taxes**, final, clear, take–home, ultimate ♦ *v* = **earn**, make, clear, gain, realize

network *n* = **web**, system,

arrangement, grid, lattice; = **maze**, warren, labyrinth

neutral *adj* = **unbiased**, impartial, disinterested, even–handed, uninvolved ≠ **biased**; = **expressionless**, dull

never *adv* = **at no time**, not once, not ever ≠ **always**

new *adj* = **modern**, recent, contemporary, up–to–date, latest ≠ **old–fashioned**; = **extra**, more, added, new–found, supplementary

news item, oft. interrupting programme. **newspaper** *n* periodical publication containing news. **newsprint** *n* inexpensive paper. **newsreel** *n* film giving news.

newt *n* small, tailed amphibian.

newton *n* unit of force.

next ❶ *adj/adv* **1** nearest. **2** immediately following. **next-of-kin** *n* closest relative.

NF Newfoundland.

NHS National Health Service.

nib *n* (split) pen point.

nibble *v* **1** take little bites of. ♦ *n* **2** little bite.

nice ❶ *adj* **1** pleasant. **2** friendly. **3** kind. **4** subtle, fine. **5** careful, exact. **nicely** *adv* **nicety** *n* minute distinction or detail.

niche ❶ *n* recess in wall.

nick ❶ *v* **1** make notch in, indent. **2** *Sl* steal. ♦ *n* **3** notch. **4** *Inf* condition. **5** *Sl* prison.

nickel *n* **1** silver-white metal much used in alloys and plating. **2** *US & Canad* five cent piece.

nickname ❶ *n* familiar name.

nicotine *n* poisonous oily liquid in tobacco.

niece *n* brother's or sister's daughter.

nifty *adj* **-tier, -tiest 1** *Inf* smart. **2** quick.

niggard *n* mean, stingy person. **niggardly** *adj/adv*

niggle *v* **1** find fault continually. **2** annoy.

nigh *adj/adv/prep Obs* near.

night ❶ *n* time of darkness between sunset and sunrise. **nightie, nighty** *n* nightdress. **nightly** *adj/adv* (happening, done) every night. **nightcap** *n* drink taken before bedtime. **nightclub** *n* place for dancing, music etc., open late at night. **nightdress** *n* woman's loose robe worn in bed. **nightingale** *n* small bird which sings at night. **nightmare** *n* **1** very bad dream. **2** terrifying experience. **nightshade** *n* various plants of potato family, some with very poisonous berries. **night-time** *n*

nil ❶ *n* nothing, zero.

———————— THESAURUS ————————

news *n* = **information**, latest (*Inf*), report, story, exposé
next *adj* = **following**, later, succeeding, subsequent; = **adjacent**, closest, nearest, neighbouring, adjoining ♦ *adv* = **afterwards**, then, later, following, subsequently
nice *adj* = **pleasant**, delightful, agreeable, good, attractive ≠ **unpleasant**; = **kind**, helpful, obliging, considerate ≠ **unkind**;

= **likable** or likeable friendly, engaging, charming, pleasant; = **polite**, courteous, well-mannered ≠ **vulgar**
niche *n* = **recess**, opening, corner, hollow, nook; = **position**, calling, place, slot (*Inf*), vocation
nick *v* = (*Sl*) **steal**, pinch (*Inf*), swipe (*Sl*), pilfer; = **cut**, mark, score, chip, scratch ♦ *n* = **cut**, mark, scratch, chip, scar
nickname *n* = **pet name**, label,

N

nimble adj agile, quick, dexterous.

nimbus n, pl **-bi, -buses 1** rain or storm cloud. **2** halo.

nincompoop n Inf stupid person.

nine adj/n cardinal number next above eight. **ninth** adj ordinal number. **nineteen** adj/n nine more than ten. **nineteenth** adj/n **ninetieth** adj **ninety** adj/n nine tens.

nip ❶ v **nipping, nipped 1** pinch sharply. **2** detach by pinching, bite. **3** check growth (of plants) thus. **4** Inf hurry. ♦ n **5** pinch. **6** sharp coldness of weather. **7** short drink. **nipper** n **1** thing that nips. **2** Inf small child. **nippy** adj **-pier, -piest 1** Inf cold. **2** quick.

nipple n **1** point of breast, teat. **2** anything like this.

nit n **1** egg of louse or other parasite. **2** Inf nitwit. **nit-picking** adj Inf overconcerned with insignificant detail. **nitwit** n Inf fool.

nitrogen n one of the gases making up air. **nitrate** n compound of nitric acid and an alkali. **nitric** adj **nitroglycerine** n explosive liquid.

no ❶ adj **1** not any, not a. **2** not at all. ♦ adv **3** expresses negative reply. ♦ n **4** refusal. **5** denial. **6** negative vote or voter. **no-one, no one** nobody.

no. number.

noble ❶ adj **1** of the nobility. **2** having high moral qualities. **3** impressive. ♦ n **4** member of the nobility. **nobility** n **1** class holding special rank. **2** being noble. **nobleman** n **nobly** adv

nobody ❶ n **1** no person. **2** person of no importance.

nocturnal adj of, in, by, night.

nod ❶ v **nodding, nodded 1** bow head slightly and quickly in assent, command etc. **2** let head droop with sleep. ♦ n **3** act of nodding. **node** n knot or knob. **nodule** n **1** little knot. **2** rounded irregular mineral mass.

noise ❶ n **1** any sound, esp. disturbing one. ♦ v **2** rumour. **noisy** adj

———— THESAURUS ————

diminutive, epithet, sobriquet
night n = **darkness**, dark, night-time
nil n = **nothing**, love, zero
nip v = **pop**, go, run, rush, dash
no interj = **not at all**, certainly not, of course not, absolutely not, never ≠ **yes** ♦ n = **refusal**, rejection, denial, negation ≠ **consent**
noble adj = **worthy**, generous, upright, honourable, virtuous ≠ **despicable**; = **dignified**, great,

imposing, impressive, distinguished ≠ **lowly**; = **aristocratic**, lordly, titled, patrician, blue-blooded ≠ **humble** ♦ n = **lord**, peer, aristocrat, nobleman ≠ **commoner**
nobody n = **nonentity**, lightweight (Inf), zero, cipher ≠ **celebrity**
nod v = **signal**, indicate, motion, gesture; = **salute**, acknowledge ♦ n = **signal**, sign, motion, gesture, indication

nomad n 1 member of wandering tribe. 2 wanderer. **nomadic** adj
nomenclature n system of names.
nominal ⊕ adj 1 in name only. 2 (of fee etc.) small.
nominate ⊕ v 1 propose as candidate. 2 appoint to office. **nomination** n **nominee** n candidate.
non- comb. form indicates the negative of a word.
nonchalant adj casually unconcerned, indifferent.
noncommissioned officer Mil subordinate officer, risen from the ranks.
noncommittal adj avoiding definite preference or pledge.
nonconformist n dissenter, esp. from Established Church.
nondescript adj lacking distinctive characteristics.
none ⊕ pron 1 no-one, not any. ◆ adv 2 in no way. **nonetheless** adv despite that, however.
nonentity n, pl –ties insignificant person, thing.
nonevent n disappointing or insignificant occurrence.

nonflammable adj not easily set on fire.
nonpareil n/adj (person or thing) unequalled or unrivalled.
nonplussed adj disconcerted.
nonsense ⊕ n 1 absurd language. 2 absurdity. 3 silly conduct.
non sequitur statement with little relation to what preceded it.
nook n sheltered corner.
noon ⊕ n midday, twelve o'clock.
noose n 1 loop on end of rope. 2 snare.
nor conj and not.
norm ⊕ n 1 average level. 2 standard. **normal** adj 1 ordinary. 2 usual. 3 conforming to type. **normality** n **normally** adv
north ⊕ n 1 direction to the right of person facing the sunset. ◆ adv/adj 2 from, towards or in the north. **northerly** adj/n wind from the north. **northern** adj **northwards** adv
nose ⊕ n 1 organ of smell, used also in breathing. 2 any projection resembling a nose. ◆ v 3 (cause to) move forward slowly and carefully. 4 touch with nose. 5

N

——————————— THESAURUS ———————————

noise n = **sound**, row, racket, clamour, din ≠ **silence**
nominal adj = **titular**, formal, purported, in name only, supposed; = **token**, small, symbolic, minimal, trivial
nominate v = **propose**, suggest, recommend, put forward; = **appoint**, name, choose, select, elect
none pron = **not any**, nothing,

zero, not one, nil
nonsense n = **rubbish**, hot air (Inf), twaddle, drivel, tripe (Inf) ≠ **sense**
noon n = **midday**, high noon, noonday, twelve noon, noontide
norm n = **standard**, rule, pattern, average, par
north adj = **northern**, polar, arctic, boreal, northerly ◆ adv = **northward(s)**, in a northerly

smell, sniff. **6** pry. **nosy** *adj Inf* inquisitive. **nose dive** sudden drop.

nosh *Sl* ◆ *n* **1** food. ◆ *v* **2** eat.

nostalgia ⊕ *n* longing for past events. **nostalgic** *adj*

nostril *n* one of the two external openings of the nose.

not *adv* expressing negation, refusal, denial.

notable ⊕ *adj/n* remarkable (person). **notably** *adv*

notary *n, pl* **-ries** person authorized to draw up deeds, contracts.

notation *n* representation of numbers, quantities by symbols.

notch ⊕ *n/v* (make) V-shaped cut.

note ⊕ *n* **1** brief comment or record. **2** short letter. **3** banknote.

4 symbol for musical sound. **5** single tone. **6** fame. **7** notice. ◆ *v* **8** observe, record. **9** heed. **noted** *adj* well-known. **notebook** *n* small book with blank pages for writing.

nothing *n* **1** no thing. **2** not anything, nought. ◆ *adv* **3** not at all, in no way.

notice ⊕ *n* **1** observation. **2** attention. **3** warning, announcement. ◆ *v* **4** observe, mention. **5** give attention to.

notify ⊕ *v* **-fying, -fied** give notice of or to.

notion ⊕ *n* **1** concept. **2** opinion. **3** whim.

notorious ⊕ *adj* known for something bad. **notoriety** *n*

notwithstanding ⊕ *prep* **1** in spite of. ◆ *adv* **2** all the same. ◆

————— THESAURUS —————

direction

nose *n* = **snout**, bill, beak, hooter (*Sl*), proboscis ◆ *v* = **ease forward**, push, edge, shove, nudge; **poke** or **stick your nose into something** = **pry**, interfere, meddle, intrude, snoop (*Inf*)

nostalgia *n* = **reminiscence**, longing, pining, yearning, remembrance

notable *adj* = **remarkable**, striking, unusual, extraordinary, outstanding ≠ **imperceptible**; ◆ *n* = **celebrity**, big name, dignitary, luminary, personage

notch *n* = (*Inf*) **level**, step, degree, grade; = **cut**, nick, incision, indentation, mark ◆ *v* = **cut**, mark, score, nick, scratch

note *n* = **message**, letter,

communication, memo, memorandum ◆ *v* = **notice**, see, observe, perceive; = **bear in mind**, be aware, take into account; = **mention**, record, mark, indicate, register

notice *v* = **observe**, see, note, spot, distinguish ≠ **overlook** ◆ *n* = **notification**, warning, advice, intimation, news; = **attention**, interest, note, regard, consideration ≠ **oversight**

noticeable *adj* = **obvious**, clear, striking, plain, evident

notify *v* = **inform**, tell, advise, alert to, announce

notion *n* = **idea**, view, opinion, belief, concept; = **whim**, wish, desire, fancy, impulse

notorious *adj* = **infamous**,

conj **3** although.

nougat *n* chewy sweet containing nuts, fruit etc.

nought *n* **1** nothing. **2** figure 0.

noun *n* word used as name of person, idea or thing.

nourish ❶ *v* **1** feed. **2** nurture. **nourishment** *n*

Nov. November.

novel[1] ❶ *n* fictitious tale in book form. **novelist** *n*

novel[2] *adj* **1** new, recent. **2** strange. **novelty** *n* **1** newness. **2** something new. **3** small trinket.

November *n* eleventh month.

novice ❶ *n* beginner.

now ❶ *adv* **1** at the present time. **2** immediately. **3** recently. ♦ *conj* **4** seeing that, since. **nowadays** *adv* in these times.

nowhere *adv* not in any place or state.

noxious *adj* poisonous, harmful.

nozzle *n* pointed spout, esp. at end of hose.

NS Nova Scotia.

NSW New South Wales.

nuance *n* delicate shade of difference.

nub *n* **1** small lump. **2** main point.

nubile *adj* **1** sexually attractive. **2** marriageable.

nucleus ❶ *n, pl* **–clei 1** centre, kernel. **2** core of atom. **nuclear** *adj* of, pert. to atomic nucleus. **nuclear energy** energy released by nuclear fission. **nuclear fission** disintegration of atom.

nude ❶ *n/adj* naked (person). **nudism** *n* practice of nudity. **nudist** *n* **nudity** *n*

nudge ❶ *v* **1** touch slightly with elbow. ♦ *n* **2** such touch.

nugget *n* lump of gold.

nuisance ❶ *n* something or someone annoying.

nuke *v Sl* attack or destroy with nuclear weapons.

null *adj* of no effect, void. **nullify** *v* **1** cancel. **2** make useless.

numb ❶ *adj* **1** deprived of feeling. ♦ *v* **2** make numb.

——— THESAURUS ———

disreputable, opprobrious

notwithstanding *prep* = **despite**, in spite of, regardless of

nourish *v* = **feed**, supply, sustain, nurture; = **encourage**, support, maintain, promote, sustain

novel[1] *n* = **story**, tale, fiction, romance, narrative

novel[2] *adj* = **new**, different, original, fresh, unusual ≠ **ordinary**

novice *n* = **beginner**, pupil, amateur, newcomer, trainee ≠ **expert**

now *adv* = **nowadays**, at the

moment; = **immediately**, promptly, instantly, at once, straightaway; **now and then** or **again** = **occasionally**, sometimes, from time to time, on and off, intermittently

nucleus *n* = **centre**, heart, focus, basis, core

nude *adj* = **naked**, stripped, bare, undressed, stark-naked ≠ **dressed**

nudge *n* = **push**, touch, dig, elbow, bump

nuisance *n* = **trouble**, problem, trial, drag (*Inf*), bother (*Inf*)

number ❶ *n* **1** sum or aggregate. **2** word or symbol saying how many. **3** single issue of a paper etc. **4** company, collection. **5** identifying number. ◆ *v* **6** count. **7** class, reckon. **8** give a number to.
numberless *adj* countless.
numeral *n* sign or word denoting a number. **numeracy** *n* ability to use numbers in calculations.
numerate *adj* **numerator** *n* top part of fraction. **numerical** *adj* of numbers. **numerous** *adj* many.
numskull *n* dolt, dunce.
nun *n* woman living (in convent) under religious vows. **nunnery** *n* convent of nuns.
nuptial *adj* of marriage. **nuptials** *pl n* wedding.
nurse ❶ *n* **1** person trained for care of sick or injured. ◆ *v* **2** act as nurse to. **3** suckle. **nursery** *n* **1** room for children. **2** rearing place for plants. **nursing home** private hospital or home for old people. **nursing officer** administrative

head of nursing staff of hospital.
nurture ❶ *n* **1** bringing up. **2** rearing. ◆ *v* **3** bring up. **4** educate. **5** nourish.
nut ❶ *n* **1** fruit consisting of hard shell and kernel. **2** hollow metal collar into which a screw fits. **3** *Inf* head. **4** *Sl* crank, maniac. **nutty** *adj*
nutmeg *n* aromatic seed of Indian tree.
nutrient *adj* **1** nourishing. ◆ *n* **2** something nutritious.
nutrition ❶ *n* **1** receiving foods. **2** act of nourishing. **nutritional, nutritious, nutritive** *adj*
nuzzle *v* **1** burrow, press with nose. **2** nestle.
NWT Northwest Territories.
nylon *n* **1** synthetic material used for fabrics etc. ◆ *pl* **2** stockings of this.
nymph *n* legendary spirit of sea, woods etc.
nymphomaniac *n* woman with abnormally intense sexual desire.

——— THESAURUS ———

≠ **benefit**
numb *adj* = **unfeeling**, dead, frozen, paralysed, insensitive ≠ **sensitive** ◆ *v* knock out, paralyse; = **deaden**, freeze, dull, paralyse, immobilize
number *n* = **numeral**, figure, character, digit, integer; = **amount**, quantity, collection, aggregate ≠ **shortage**; = **crowd**, horde, multitude, throng; = **group**, set, band, crowd, gang ◆ *v* = **amount to**, come to, total, add up to

nurse *v* = **look after**, treat, tend, care for, take care of; = **harbour**, have, maintain, preserve, entertain; = **breast-feed**, feed, nurture, nourish, suckle
nurture *v* = **bring up**, raise, look after, rear, care for ≠ **neglect** ◆ *n* = **upbringing**, training, education, instruction, rearing
nut *n* = (*Sl*) **madman**, psycho (*Sl*), crank (*Inf*), lunatic, maniac; = (*Sl*) **head**, skull
nutrition *n* = **food**, nourishment, sustenance, nutriment

O o

oaf n 1 lout. 2 dolt.

oak n common deciduous tree.

OAP old age pensioner.

oar n wooden lever with broad blade worked by the hands to propel boat.

oasis n, pl **-ses** fertile spot in desert.

oat n (usu. pl) 1 grain of cereal plant. 2 the plant. **oatmeal** n

oath ⊕ n 1 confirmation of truth of statement by naming something sacred. 2 curse.

obdurate adj stubborn, unyielding.

OBE Officer of the Order of the British Empire.

obelisk n tapering rectangular stone column.

obese adj very fat. **obesity** n

obey ⊕ v 1 do the bidding of. 2 do as ordered.

obituary n, pl **-aries** 1 notice, record of death. 2 biographical sketch of deceased person.

object¹ ⊕ n 1 material thing. 2

that to which feeling or action is directed. 3 end or aim. 4 Grammar word dependent on verb or preposition.

object² ⊕ v express or feel dislike or reluctance to something. **objection** n **objectionable** adj

objective ⊕ adj 1 external to the mind. 2 impartial. ♦ n 3 thing or place aimed at.

oblige ⊕ v 1 compel. 2 do favour for (someone). **obligate** v bind, esp. by legal contract. **obligation** n 1 binding duty, promise. 2 debt of gratitude. **obligatory** adj 1 required. 2 binding. **obliging** adj ready to serve others, helpful.

oblique adj 1 slanting. 2 indirect.

obliterate v 1 blot out, efface. 2 destroy completely.

oblong adj 1 rectangular, with adjacent sides unequal. ♦ n 2 oblong figure.

obnoxious adj offensive, odious.

oboe n woodwind instrument.

obscene ⊕ adj indecent,

THESAURUS

oath n = **promise**, bond, pledge, vow, word; = **swear word**, curse, obscenity, blasphemy, expletive

obey v = **carry out**, follow, implement, act upon, carry through ≠ **disregard**

object¹ n = **thing**, article, body, item, entity; = **purpose**, aim, end, point, plan; = **target**, victim,

focus, recipient

object² v with **to** = **protest against**, oppose, argue against, draw the line at, take exception to ≠ **accept**

objective n = **purpose**, aim, goal, end, plan ♦ adj = **factual**, real

oblige v = **compel**, make, force, require, bind; = **help**, assist,

repulsive. **obscenity** n

obscure ❶ adj 1 unclear, indistinct. ♦ v 2 make unintelligible. 3 dim. 4 conceal.

obscurity n 1 indistinctness. 2 lack of intelligibility. 3 obscure place or position.

obsequious adj servile, fawning.

observe ❶ v 1 notice, remark. 2 watch. 3 note systematically. 4 keep, follow. **observance** n 1 keeping of custom. 2 ritual, ceremony. **observant** adj quick to notice. **observation** n **observatory** n place for watching stars etc. **observer** n

obsess v haunt, fill the mind. **obsession** n

obsolete ❶ adj disused, out of date. **obsolescent** adj going out of use.

obstacle ❶ n obstruction.

obstetrics pl n branch of medicine concerned with childbirth. **obstetrician** n

obstinate adj 1 stubborn. 2 hard to overcome or cure. **obstinacy** n

obstreperous adj unruly, noisy.

obstruct ❶ v 1 block up. 2 hinder. 3 impede. **obstruction** n **obstructive** adj

obtain ❶ v 1 get. 2 acquire. 3 be customary. **obtainable** adj

obtrude v thrust forward unduly. **obtrusive** adj

obtuse adj 1 dull of perception. 2 stupid. 3 greater than right angle. 4 not pointed.

obverse n 1 complement. 2 principal side of coin, medal etc.

obviate v remove, make unnecessary.

obvious ❶ adj clear, evident. **obviously** adv

occasion ❶ n 1 time when thing happens. 2 reason, need. 3 opportunity. 4 special event. ♦ v 5 cause. **occasional** adj happening,

benefit, please, humour ≠ **bother**

obscene adj = **indecent**, dirty, offensive, filthy, improper ≠ **decent**; = **offensive**, shocking, evil, disgusting, outrageous

obscure adj = **unknown**, little-known, humble, unfamiliar, out-of-the-way ≠ **famous**; = **abstruse**, complex, confusing, mysterious, vague ≠ **straightforward**; = **unclear**, uncertain, confused, mysterious, doubtful ≠ **well-known** ♦ v = **obstruct**, hinder

observe v = **watch**, study, view, look at, check; = **notice**, see, note, discover, spot; = **remark**, say,

comment, state, note; = **comply with**, keep, follow, respect, carry out ≠ **disregard**

obsolete adj = **outdated**, old, passé, old-fashioned, discarded ≠ **up-to-date**

obstacle n = **obstruction**, block, barrier, hurdle, snag

obstruct v = **block**, close, bar, plug, barricade; = **hold up**, stop, check, block, restrict

obtain v = **get**, gain, acquire, land, net ≠ **lose**; = **achieve**, get, gain, accomplish, attain

obvious adj = **clear**, plain, apparent, evident, distinct

found now and then. **occasionally** adv

Occident n the West.

occult adj 1 secret, mysterious. 2 supernatural.

occupy ❶ v –pying, –pied 1 inhabit, fill. 2 employ. 3 take possession of. **occupancy** n fact of occupying. **occupant** n **occupation** n 1 employment, pursuit. 2 tenancy. 3 military control of country by foreign power. **occupational** adj **occupier** n

occur ❶ v –curring, –curred 1 happen. 2 come to mind. **occurrence** n happening.

ocean n 1 great body of water. 2 large division of this. 3 the sea.

ochre n earth used as yellow or brown pigment.

o'clock adv by the clock.

Oct. October.

octagon n figure with eight angles. **octagonal** adj

octane n chemical found in petrol.

octave n 1 Mus eighth note above or below given note. 2 this space.

octet n (music for) group of eight.

October n tenth month.

octopus n, pl –puses mollusc with eight arms covered with suckers.

odd ❶ adj 1 strange, queer. 2 incidental, random. 3 left over or additional. 4 not even. 5 not part of a set. **oddity** n 1 odd person or thing. 2 quality of being odd.

oddments pl n things left over.

odds pl n 1 advantage conceded in betting. 2 likelihood. **odds and ends** odd fragments or scraps.

ode n lyric poem.

odium n hatred, widespread dislike. **odious** adj

odour ❶ n smell. **odorous** adj 1 fragrant. 2 scented.

odyssey ❶ n long eventful journey.

———————— THESAURUS ————————

≠ **unclear**

occasion n = **time**, moment, point, stage, instance; = **function**, event, affair, do (Inf), happening; = **opportunity**, chance, time, opening, window; = **reason**, cause, call, ground(s), excuse ♦ v = (Formal) **cause**, produce, lead to, inspire, result in

occupy v = **inhabit**, own, live in, dwell in, reside in ≠ **vacate**; = **invade**, take over, capture, seize, conquer ≠ **withdraw**; = **hold**, control, dominate, possess; = **take up**, consume, tie up, use up, monopolize

occur v = **happen**, take place, come about, turn up (Inf), crop up (Inf); = **exist**, appear, be found, develop, turn up

odd adj = **peculiar**, strange, unusual, extraordinary, bizarre; = **unusual**, strange, rare, extraordinary, remarkable ≠ **normal**; = **occasional**, various, random, casual, irregular ≠ **regular**; = **spare**, remaining, extra, surplus, solitary ≠ **matched**

odour n = **smell**, scent, perfume, fragrance, stink

odyssey n = **journey**, tour, trip, quest, trek

oesophagus n, pl **-gi** passage between mouth and stomach.
of prep denotes removal, separation, ownership, attribute, material, quality.
off ❶ adv 1 away. ◆ prep 2 away from. ◆ adj 3 not operative. 4 cancelled or postponed. 5 bad, sour etc. **offhand** adj/adv 1 without previous thought. 2 curt.
off-licence n place where alcoholic drinks are sold for consumption elsewhere. **offset** v counterbalance, compensate.
offspring n children, issue.
offal n 1 edible entrails of animal. 2 refuse.
offend ❶ v 1 hurt feelings of, displease. 2 do wrong. 3 disgust.
offence n 1 wrong. 2 crime. 3 insult. **offender** n **offensive** adj 1 causing displeasure. 2 aggressive. ◆ n 3 position or movement of attack.
offer ❶ v 1 present for acceptance or refusal. 2 tender. 3 propose. 4 attempt. ◆ n 5 offering, bid.

office ❶ n 1 room(s), building, in which business, clerical work etc. is done. 2 commercial or professional organization. 3 official position. 4 service. 5 duty. 6 form of worship. ◆ pl 7 task. 8 service.
officer n 1 one in command in army, navy, ship etc. 2 official.
official ❶ adj 1 with, by, authority. ◆ n 2 one holding office.
officiate v perform duties of office, ceremony.
officious adj 1 importunate in offering service. 2 interfering.
offside adj/adv Sport illegally forward.
often ❶ adv many times.
ogle v 1 stare, look (at) amorously. ◆ n 2 this look.
ogre n 1 man-eating giant. 2 monster.
oh interj exclamation of surprise, pain etc.
ohm n unit of electrical resistance.
oil ❶ n 1 any viscous liquid with smooth, sticky feel. 2 petroleum.

——— THESAURUS ———

off adv = **away**, out, apart, elsewhere, aside ◆ adj = **absent**, gone, unavailable; = **cancelled**, abandoned, postponed, shelved
offend v = **distress**, upset, outrage, wound, slight ≠ **please**
offer v = **provide**, present, furnish, afford ≠ **withhold**; = **volunteer**, come forward, offer your services; = **propose**, suggest, advance, submit; = **give**, show, bring, provide, render ◆ n = **proposal**, suggestion,

proposition, submission; = **bid**, tender, bidding price
office n = **place of work**, workplace, base, workroom, place of business
official adj = **authorized**, formal, sanctioned, licensed, proper ≠ **unofficial**; = **formal**, bureaucratic, ceremonial, solemn, ritualistic ◆ n = **officer**, executive, agent, representative, bureaucrat
often adv = **frequently**, generally, commonly, repeatedly, time and

♦ v 3 lubricate with oil. **oily** adj

oilskin n cloth treated with oil to make it waterproof.

ointment n greasy preparation for healing or beautifying the skin.

O.K., okay Inf ♦ adj/adv/interj 1 all right. ♦ v 2 agree to, endorse.

old ❶ adj 1 aged, having lived or existed long. 2 belonging to earlier period. **olden** adj old. **old-fashioned** adj 1 in style of earlier period, out of date. 2 fond of old ways.

olfactory adj of smelling.

oligarchy n, pl **-chies** government by small group.

olive n 1 evergreen tree. 2 its oil-yielding fruit. 3 its wood. ♦ adj 4 greyish-green.

ombudsman n official who investigates complaints against government organizations.

omelette n dish of eggs beaten and fried.

omen n prophetic happening.

ominous adj boding evil, threatening.

omit ❶ v omitting, omitted leave out, leave undone. **omission** n

omnibus n 1 book etc. containing several works. 2 bus. ♦ adj 3 serving, containing several objects.

omnipotent adj all-powerful.

omniscient adj knowing everything.

omnivorous adj eating both animals and plants. **omnivore** n

on prep 1 above and touching, at, near, towards etc. 2 attached to. 3 concerning. 4 performed upon. 5 during. 6 taking regularly. ♦ adj 7 operating. 8 taking place. ♦ adv 9 so as to be on. 10 forwards. 11 continuously etc. 12 in progress.

oncoming adj approaching from the front. **ongoing** adj in progress, continuing.

once ❶ adv 1 one time. 2 formerly. 3 ever. **at once 1** immediately. 2 simultaneously. **once-over** n Inf quick examination.

one adj 1 lowest cardinal number. 2 single. 3 united. 4 only, without others. 5 identical. ♦ n 6 number or figure 1. 7 unity. 8 single specimen. ♦ pron 9 particular but not stated person. 10 any person. **oneself** pron **one-sided** adj 1 partial. 2 uneven.

onerous adj burdensome.

onion n edible bulb of pungent flavour.

onlooker ❶ n person who watches without taking part.

only ❶ adj 1 being the one

again ≠ **never**

oil v = **lubricate**, grease

old adj = **aged**, elderly, ancient, mature, venerable ≠ **young**; = **out of date**, dated, antique, obsolete, archaic ≠ **up-to-date**

omit ≠ **= leave out**, drop, exclude,

eliminate, skip ≠ **include**; = **forget**, overlook, neglect, pass over, lose sight of

once adv = **on one occasion**, one time, one single time; = **at one time**, previously, formerly, long ago, once upon a time

specimen. ♦ adv 2 solely, merely, exclusively. ♦ conj 3 but then. 4 excepting that.

onset 🟊 n beginning.

onslaught 🟊 n attack.

onto prep on top of.

onus n, pl **onuses** responsibility, burden.

onward 🟊 adj 1 advanced or advancing. ♦ adv 2 in advance, ahead, forward. **onwards** adv

onyx n variety of quartz.

ooze 🟊 v 1 pass slowly out, exude. ♦ n 2 sluggish flow. 3 wet mud.

opal n glassy gemstone displaying variegated colours.

opaque adj not transparent.

open 🟊 adj 1 not shut or blocked up. 2 without lid or door. 3 bare. 4 undisguised. 5 not enclosed, covered or exclusive. 6 spread out, accessible. 7 frank. ♦ v 8 make or become open. 9 begin. ♦ n 10 clear space, unenclosed country.

opening n 1 hole, gap. 2 beginning. 3 opportunity. ♦ adj 4 first. 5 initial. **openly** adv without concealment. **open-minded** adj unprejudiced.

opera n musical drama. **operatic** adj **operetta** n light opera.

operation n 1 the act or method of operating. 2 the condition of being in action. 3 a surgical procedure carried out to remove, replace or repair a diseased or damaged part of the body.

ophthalmic adj of eyes.

opinion 🟊 n 1 what one thinks about something. 2 belief, judgment. **opinionated** adj stubborn in one's opinions.

opium n narcotic drug made from poppy. **opiate** n drug containing opium.

opossum n small Amer. and Aust. marsupial.

opponent 🟊 n adversary, antagonist.

———— THESAURUS ————

onlooker n = **spectator**, witness, observer, viewer, looker-on

only adj = **sole**, one, single, individual, exclusive ♦ adv = **just**, simply, purely, merely

onset n = **beginning**, start, birth, outbreak, inception ≠ **end**

onslaught n = **attack**, charge, campaign, strike, assault ≠ **retreat**

onward adv = **forward**, on, forwards, ahead, beyond

ooze v = **seep**, well, escape, leak, drain

open v = **unfasten**, unlock ≠ **close**; = **unwrap**, uncover, undo,

unravel, untie ≠ **wrap**; ♦ adj = **unclosed**, unlocked, ajar, unfastened, yawning ≠ **closed**; = **unsealed**, unstoppered ≠ **unopened**; = **extended**, unfolded, stretched out, unfurled, straightened out ≠ **shut**; = **frank**, direct, straightforward, sincere, transparent ≠ **sly**; = **receptive**, sympathetic, responsive, amenable, subject; = **unresolved**, unsettled, undecided, debatable, moot

opinion n = **belief**, feeling, view, idea, theory

opportunity ❶ n 1 favourable time or condition. 2 good chance.
opportunity shop Aust & NZ shop selling second–hand clothes, sometimes for charity.
oppose ❶ v resist, set against.
opposite adj 1 contrary. 2 facing. ♦ n 3 the contrary. ♦ prep/adv 4 facing. 5 on the other side.
opposition n 1 resistance. 2 hostility. 3 group opposing another.
oppress ❶ v 1 govern by tyranny. 2 weigh down. **oppression** n
oppressive adj 1 tyrannical. 2 hard to bear. 3 (of weather) hot and tiring.
opt ❶ v make a choice.
optic adj of eye or sight. **optical** adj **optician** n maker of, dealer in spectacles, optical instruments.
optimism n disposition to look on the bright side. **optimist** n **optimistic** adj
optimum ❶ adj/n, pl **-ma, –mums** the best, the most favourable.
option ❶ n 1 choice. 2 thing chosen. **optional** adj leaving to choice.

optometrist n person testing eyesight, prescribing corrective lenses.
opulent adj 1 rich. 2 copious.
opulence n
opus ❶ n, pl **opuses, opera** 1 work. 2 musical composition.
or conj 1 introducing alternatives. 2 if not.
oracle n 1 divine utterance, prophecy given at shrine of god. 2 the shrine. 3 wise adviser.
oral ❶ adj 1 spoken. 2 by mouth. ♦ n 3 spoken examination.
orange adj 1 reddish–yellow. ♦ n 2 reddish–yellow citrus fruit.
orang–utan, orang-utang n large reddish–brown ape.
orator n 1 maker of speech. 2 skilful speaker. **oration** n formal speech. **oratory** n 1 speeches. 2 eloquence.
orb n globe.
orbit ❶ n 1 track of planet, satellite, comet etc. around another heavenly body. 2 field of influence. ♦ v 3 move in, or put into, an orbit.
orchard n (area for) fruit trees.

——————— THESAURUS ———————

opponent n = **adversary**, rival, enemy, competitor, challenger ≠ **ally**
opportunity n = **chance**, opening, time, turn, moment
oppose v = **be against**, fight (against), block, take on, counter ≠ **support**
oppress v = **subjugate**, abuse, suppress, wrong, master ≠ **liberate**; = **depress**, burden,

discourage, torment, harass
opt v = **choose**, decide, prefer, select, elect ≠ **reject**
optimum adj = **ideal**, best, highest, finest, perfect ≠ **worst**
option n = **choice**, alternative, selection, preference, freedom of choice
opus n = **work**, piece, production, creation, composition
oral adj = **spoken**, vocal, verbal,

orchestra n 1 band of musicians. 2 place for such band in theatre etc. **orchestral** adj **orchestrate** v 1 arrange (music) for orchestra. 2 organize (something) to particular effect.

orchid n genus of various flowering plants.

ordain ⊙ v 1 confer holy orders upon. 2 decree, enact.

ordeal ⊙ n severe, trying experience.

order n 1 regular, proper or peaceful arrangement or condition. 2 command.

ordinal number number showing position in series.

ordinance n decree, rule.

ordinary ⊙ adj 1 usual, normal. 2 commonplace. **ordinarily** adv

ordnance n 1 artillery. 2 military stores. **ordnance survey** official geographical survey of Britain.

ore n mineral which yields metal.

oregano n aromatic herb.

organ ⊙ n 1 musical wind instrument of pipes and stops, played with keys. 2 member of animal or plant with particular function. 3 medium of information. **organist** n organ player.

organism ⊙ n plant, animal.

organic adj 1 of, derived from, living organisms. 2 of bodily organs. 3 Chem of compounds formed from carbon. 4 organized, systematic.

organize ⊙ v 1 give definite structure. 2 arrange. 3 unite in a society. **organization** n 1 act of organizing. 2 structure. 3 association, group. **organizer** n

orgasm n sexual climax.

orgy n, pl –gies 1 drunken or licentious revel. 2 unrestrained bout.

orient ⊙, **orientate** n 1 (with cap.) East. ♦ v 2 determine (one's) position (also) **oriental** adj/n **orientation** n

orifice n opening, mouth.

———— THESAURUS ————

unwritten

orbit n = **path**, course, cycle, circle, revolution; = **sphere of influence**, reach, range, influence, province ♦ v = **circle**, ring, go round, revolve around, encircle

ordain v = **appoint**, name, commission, select, invest; = (Formal) **order**, will, rule, demand, require

ordeal n = **hardship**, trial, difficulty, test, suffering ≠ **pleasure**

ordinary adj = **usual**, standard, normal, common, regular;

= **commonplace**, plain, modest, humble, mundane ≠ **extraordinary**

organ n = **body part**, part of the body, element, biological structure; = **newspaper**, medium, voice, vehicle, gazette

organism n = **creature**, being, thing, body, animal

organize v = **arrange**, run, plan, prepare, set up ≠ **disrupt**; = **put in order**, arrange, group, list, file ≠ **muddle**

orient, orientate v = **adjust**,

origami n art of paper folding.
origin ⓣ n 1 beginning. 2 source. 3 parentage. **original** adj 1 earliest. 2 new, not copied. 3 thinking or acting for oneself. ◆ n 4 thing from which another is copied. **originality** n **originally** adv
originate v 1 come or bring into existence, begin. 2 create, pioneer.
ornament ⓣ n 1 any object used to adorn or decorate. ◆ v 2 adorn. **ornamental** adj
ornate adj highly decorated or elaborate.
ornithology n science of birds.
orphan n child whose parents are dead. **orphanage** n institution for care of orphans.
orthodox ⓣ adj 1 holding accepted views. 2 conventional. **orthodoxy** n
oscillate v 1 swing to and fro. 2 waver.
osmosis n movement of liquid through membrane from higher to lower concentration.
osprey n fishing hawk.

ossify v –fying, –fied 1 turn into bone. 2 grow rigid.
ostensible adj 1 apparent. 2 professed.
ostentation n show, pretentious display. **ostentatious** adj
osteopathy n art of treating disease by manipulation of bones. **osteopath** n
ostracize v exclude, banish from society. **ostracism** n
ostrich n large flightless bird.
other ⓣ adj 1 not this. 2 not the same. 3 alternative. ◆ pron 4 other person or thing. **otherwise** adv 1 differently. ◆ conj 2 or else, if not.
otter n furry aquatic fish–eating mammal.
ouch interj exclamation of sudden pain.
ought v expressing obligation or advisability or probability.
ounce ⓣ n unit of weight, sixteenth of pound (28.4 grams).
our adj belonging to us. **ours** pron
ourselves pron emphatic or reflexive form of WE.
oust ⓣ v put out, expel.

———————— THESAURUS ————————

adapt, alter, accustom, align; **= get your bearings**, establish your location
origin n **= beginning**, start, birth, launch, foundation ≠ **end**; **= root**, source, basis, base, seed
ornament n **= decoration**, trimming, accessory, festoon, trinket; **= embellishment**, decoration, embroidery, elaboration, adornment ◆ v **= decorate**, adorn, array, do up

(Inf), embellish
orthodox adj **= established**, official, accepted, received, common ≠ **unorthodox**
other adj **= additional**, more, further, new, added; **= different**, alternative, contrasting, distinct, diverse
ounce n **= shred**, bit, drop, trace, scrap
oust v **= expel**, turn out, dismiss, exclude, exile

out **①** adv/adj **1** from within, away. **2** wrong. **3** not burning. **4** not allowed. **5** Sport dismissed.

outer adj away from the inside.

outermost, outmost adj on extreme outside. **outing** n pleasure excursion. **outward** adj/adv

outbreak ① n sudden occurrence.

outburst ① n sudden expression of emotion.

outcast n rejected person.

outcome ① n result.

outcry ① n, pl **–cries** expression of widespread protest.

outdoors adv in the open air. **outdoor** adj

outfit ① n **1** equipment. **2** clothes and accessories. **3** Inf group or association regarded as a unit.

outgoing ① adj **1** leaving. **2** sociable. **outgoings** pl n expenses.

outlandish adj queer,

extravagantly strange.

outlaw ① n **1** one beyond protection of the law. ◆ v **2** make (someone) an outlaw. **3** ban.

outlay n expenditure.

outline ① n **1** rough sketch. **2** general plan. **3** lines enclosing visible figure. ◆ v **4** sketch. **5** summarize.

outlook ① n **1** point of view. **2** probable outcome.

outlying adj remote.

outmoded adj no longer fashionable or accepted.

outpatient n patient who does not stay in hospital overnight.

outport n Canad isolated fishing village, esp. in Newfoundland.

outpost n outlying settlement.

output ① n **1** quantity produced **2** Comp information produced.

outrage ① n **1** violation of others'

out adj = **not in**, away, elsewhere, outside, gone; = **extinguished**, ended, finished, dead, exhausted

outbreak n = **eruption**, burst, explosion, epidemic, rash

outburst n = **explosion**, fit, surge, outbreak, flare-up

outcome n = **result**, end, consequence, conclusion, payoff (Inf)

outcry n = **protest**, complaint, objection, dissent, outburst

outfit n = **costume**, dress, clothes, clothing, suit; = (Inf) **group**, company, team, party, unit

outgoing adj = **leaving**, former, previous, retiring, withdrawing ≠ **incoming**; = **sociable**, open,

social, warm, friendly ≠ **reserved**

outlaw v = **ban**, bar, veto, forbid, exclude ≠ **legalise**; = **banish**, put a price on (someone's) head ◆ n = (Hist) **bandit**, criminal, thief, robber, fugitive

outline v = **summarize**, draft, plan, trace, sketch (in); = **silhouette**, etch ◆ n = **summary**, review, résumé, rundown, synopsis; = **shape**, lines, form, figure, profile

outlook n = **attitude**, opinion, position, approach, mood; = **prospect(s)**, future, expectations, forecast, prediction

output n = **production**, manufacture, manufacturing,

rights. **2** shocking act. **3** anger arising from this. ◆ *v* **4** commit outrage. **outrageous** *adj* **1** shocking. **2** offensive.

outright ⊕ *adj* **1** complete. **2** definite. ◆ *adv* **3** completely.

outset ⊕ *n* beginning.

outside ⊕ *n* **1** exterior. ◆ *adv* **2** not inside. ◆ *adj* **3** on exterior. **4** unlikely. **5** greatest possible.

outsider *n* **1** person outside specific group. **2** contestant thought unlikely to win.

outsize, outsized *adj* larger than normal.

outskirts ⊕ *pl n* outer areas, districts, esp. of city.

outspan *v S Afr* relax.

outspoken ⊕ *adj* frank, candid.

outstanding ⊕ *adj* **1** excellent. **2** remarkable. **3** unsettled, unpaid.

outweigh ⊕ *v* be more important than.

outwit *v* **–witting, –witted** get the better of by cunning.

oval ⊕ *adj/n* egg–shaped, elliptical (thing).

ovary *n, pl* **–ries** female egg– producing organ. **ovarian** *adj*

ovation ⊕ *n* enthusiastic burst of applause.

oven *n* heated chamber for baking.

over ⊕ *adv* **1** above. **2** beyond. **3** in excess. **4** finished. **5** in repetition. **6** across. **7** downwards. ◆ *prep* **8** above. **9** upon. **10** more than. **11** along. ◆ *n* **12** *Cricket* delivery of six balls from one end.

over– *comb. form* too, too much, in excess, above.

overall ⊕ *n* (also *pl*) **1** loose

——————— THESAURUS ———————

yield, productivity

outrage *v* = **offend**, shock, upset, wound, insult ◆ *n* = **indignation**, shock, anger, rage, fury

outright *adj* = **absolute**, complete, total, perfect, sheer; = **definite**, clear, certain, flat, absolute ◆ *adv* = **openly**, frankly, plainly, overtly, candidly; = **absolutely**, completely, totally, fully, entirely

outset *n* = **beginning**, start, opening, onset, inauguration ≠ **finish**

outside *n* = **exterior**, face, front, covering, skin ◆ *adj* = **external**, outer, exterior, outward, extraneous ≠ **inner**; = **remote**, small, unlikely, slight, slim

outskirts *pl n* = **edge**, boundary, suburbs, fringe, perimeter

outspoken *adj* = **forthright**, open, frank, straightforward, blunt ≠ **reserved**

outstanding *adj* = **excellent**, good, great, important, special ≠ **mediocre**; = **unpaid**, remaining, due, pending, payable

outweigh *v* = **override**, cancel (out), eclipse, offset, compensate for

oval *adj* = **elliptical**, egg–shaped, ovoid

ovation *n* = **applause**, hand, cheers, praise, tribute ≠ **derision**

over *prep* = **above**, on top of; = **on top of**, on, across, upon ◆ *adv* = **above**, overhead, in the sky,

garment worn as protection against dirt etc. ◆ adj 2 total.
overbearing adj domineering.
overboard adv from a boat into water. **go overboard** go to extremes.
overcast adj cloudy.
overcome 𝕋 v 1 conquer. 2 surmount. 3 make incapable or powerless.
overdose n/v (take) excessive dose of drug.
overdraft n withdrawal of more money than is in bank account.
overdrive n very high gear in motor vehicle.
overgrown adj thickly covered with plants.
overhaul 𝕋 v 1 examine and set in order. ◆ n 2 examination and

repair.
overhead 𝕋 adj/adv over one's head, above.
overland adj/adv by land.
overlap v 1 share part of same space or period of time. ◆ n 2 area overlapping.
overlook v 1 fail to notice. 2 disregard.
overseas adj/adv 1 foreign. 2 from or to a place over the sea.
overshadow 𝕋 v reduce significance of.
oversight n 1 failure to notice. 2 mistake.
overt 𝕋 adj open, unconcealed.
overtake 𝕋 v 1 move past. 2 catch up.
overthrow 𝕋 v 1 overturn. 2 defeat. ◆ n 3 ruin. 4 fall.

—— THESAURUS ——

on high, aloft; **= extra**, more, further, beyond, additional ◆ adj **= finished**, done (with), through, ended, closed
overall adj **= total**, full, whole, general, complete ◆ adv **= in general**, generally, mostly, all things considered, on average
overcome v **= defeat**, beat, conquer, master, overwhelm; **= conquer**, beat, master, subdue, triumph over ◆ adj **= overwhelmed**, moved, affected, emotional, choked
overhaul v **= check**, service, maintain, examine, restore; **= overtake**, pass, leave behind, catch up with, get past ◆ n **= check**, service, examination, going-over (Inf), inspection

overhead adj **= raised**, suspended, elevated, aerial, overhanging ◆ adv **= above**, in the sky, on high, aloft, up above ≠ **underneath**
overlook v **= look over** or out on have a view of; **= miss**, forget, neglect, omit, disregard; **= ignore**, excuse, forgive, pardon, disregard
overshadow v **= spoil**, ruin, mar, wreck, blight; **= outshine**, eclipse, surpass, dwarf, tower above
overt adj **= open**, obvious, plain, public, manifest ≠ **hidden**
overtake v **= pass**, leave behind, overhaul, catch up with, get past; **= outdo**, top, exceed, eclipse, surpass
overthrow v **= defeat**, overcome,

overtime n 1 time at work, outside normal working hours. 2 payment for this time. 3 US and Canad period of extra time in a contest or game.

overtone n additional meaning.

overture n 1 Mus orchestral introduction. 2 opening of negotiations.

overwhelm ❶ v 1 crush. 2 submerge. **overwhelming** adj irresistible.

overwrought adj overexcited.

owe ❶ v be bound to repay, be indebted for. **owing** adj owed, due. **owing to** caused by,

as result of.

owl n night bird of prey.

own ❶ adj 1 emphasizes possession. ♦ v 2 possess. 3 acknowledge. 4 confess. **owner** n **ownership** n possession.

ox n, pl **oxen** castrated bull.

oxide n compound of oxygen and one other element.

oxygen n gas in atmosphere essential to life.

oyster n edible mollusc.

Oz n Slang Australia.

oz. ounce.

ozone n form of oxygen with pungent odour.

——————— THESAURUS ———————

conquer, bring down, oust ≠ **uphold** ♦ n = **downfall**, fall, defeat, collapse, destruction ≠ **preservation**

overwhelm v = **overcome**, devastate, stagger, bowl over (Inf), knock (someone) for six (Inf); = **destroy**, defeat, overcome, crush, massacre

owe v = **be in debt (to)**, be in arrears (to), be overdrawn (by), be

obligated or indebted (to)

own adj = **personal**, special, private, individual, particular ♦ v = **possess**, have, keep, hold, enjoy **hold your own** = **keep going**, compete, get on, get along, stand your ground **on your own** = **alone**, by yourself, all alone, unaccompanied; = **independently**, alone, singly, single–handedly, by yourself

P p

p 1 page. **2** pence. **3** penny. **4** *Mus* piano (softly).

pace ⊕ *n* **1** step. **2** rate of movement. ◆ *v* **3** step. **4** set speed for. **5** measure. **pacemaker** *n* **1** electronic device to regulate heartbeat. **2** person who sets speed for race.

pacifier *n US and Canad* a baby's dummy or teething ring.

pacify *v* –**fying**, –**fied** calm.

pacifism *n* **pacifist** *n* **1** advocate of abolition of war. **2** one who refuses to help in war.

pack ⊕ *n* **1** bundle. **2** band of animals. **3** large set of people or things. **4** put together in suitcase etc. **5** make into a bundle. **6** cram. **7** fill. **package** *n* **1** parcel. **2** set of items offered together. ◆ *v* **3** put into packages. **packet** *n* **1** small parcel. **2** small container (and contents).

packsack *n* a US and Canadian word for HAVERSACK.

pact ⊕ *n* covenant, agreement.

pad ⊕ *n* **1** soft stuff used as a cushion, protection etc. **2** block of sheets of paper. **3** foot or sole of various animals. ◆ *v* **4** make soft, fill in, protect etc., with pad. **5** walk with soft step.

paddle¹ ⊕ *n* **1** short oar with broad blade. ◆ *v* **2** move by, as with, paddles.

paddle² ⊕ *v* walk with bare feet in shallow water.

paddock *n* small grass enclosure.

paddy field field where rice is grown.

pademelon, paddymelon [pad-ee-mel-an] *n* small Australian wallaby.

padlock *n/v* (fasten with) detachable lock with hinged hoop.

THESAURUS

pace *n* = **speed**, rate, tempo, velocity; = **step**, walk, stride, tread, gait ◆ *v* = **stride**, walk, pound, patrol, march up and down

pack *v* = **package**, load, store, bundle, stow; = **cram**, crowd, press, fill, stuff ◆ *n* = **packet**, box, package, carton; = **bundle**, parcel, load, burden, rucksack

pact *n* = **agreement**, alliance, treaty, deal, understanding

pad *n* = **wad**, dressing, pack, padding, compress; = **cushion**, filling, stuffing, pillow, bolster; = **notepad**, block, notebook, jotter, writing pad; = (*Sl*) **home**, flat, apartment, place ◆ *v* = **pack**, fill, protect, stuff, cushion; = **lengthen**, stretch, elaborate, fill out, spin out

paddle¹ *n* = **oar**, scull ◆ *v* = **row**, pull, scull

paddle² *v* = **wade**, splash (about),

paediatrics *pl n* branch of medicine dealing with diseases of children. **paediatrician** *n*

paella *n* Spanish dish of rice, chicken, shellfish etc.

pagan ⊕ *adj/n* heathen.

page¹ ⊕ *n* one side of leaf of book etc.

page² ⊕ *n* **1** boy attendant. ♦ *v* **2** summon by loudspeaker announcement or electronic device. **pager** *n* small portable electronic signalling device.

pageant *n* show of persons in costume in procession, dramatic scenes etc.

pagoda *n* pyramidal temple of Chinese or Indian type.

pail *n* bucket.

pain ⊕ *n* **1** bodily or mental suffering. ♦ *pl* **2** trouble. ♦ *v* **3** inflict pain upon. **painful** *adj* **painkiller** *n* drug that reduces pain. **painstaking** *adj* careful.

paint ⊕ *n* **1** colouring matter spread on a surface. ♦ *v* **2** colour, coat, or make picture of, with paint. **painter** *n* **painting** *n*

pair ⊕ *n* **1** set of two. ♦ *v* **2** arrange in twos.

pal ⊕ *n Inf* friend.

palace *n* **1** residence of king, bishop etc. **2** stately mansion.

palatial *adj*

palate *n* **1** roof of mouth. **2** sense of taste. **palatable** *adj* agreeable to eat.

palaver *n* fuss.

pale ⊕ *adj* **1** wan, whitish. ♦ *v* **2** whiten. **3** lose superiority.

palette *n* artist's flat board for mixing colours on.

palindrome *n* word etc., that is the same when read backwards or forwards.

paling *n* upright plank in fence.

pall¹ *n* cloth spread over a coffin. **pallbearer** *n* one carrying coffin at funeral.

pall² *v* **1** become tiresome. **2** cloy.

pallet *n* portable platform for storing and moving goods.

————— THESAURUS —————

slop

pagan *adj* = **heathen**, infidel, polytheistic, idolatrous ♦ *n* = **heathen**, infidel, polytheist, idolater

page¹ *n* = **folio**, side, leaf, sheet

page² *v* = **call**, summon, send for ♦ *n* = **attendant**, pageboy; = **servant**, attendant, squire, pageboy

pain *n* = **suffering**, discomfort, hurt, irritation, tenderness; = **ache**, stinging, aching, cramp, throb ♦ *v* = **distress**, hurt, torture, grieve, torment

paint *n* = **colouring**, colour, stain, dye, tint ♦ *v* = **colour**, cover, coat, stain, whitewash; = **depict**, draw, portray, picture, represent

pair *v* = **team**, match (up), join, couple, twin

pal *n* = (*Inf*) **friend**, companion, mate (*Inf*), buddy (*Inf*), comrade

pale *adj* = **light**, soft, faded, subtle, muted; = **dim**, weak, faint, feeble, thin ♦ *v* = **become pale**, blanch, whiten, go white, lose colour

P

palliate v 1 relieve without curing. 2 excuse. **palliative** adj/n

pallid adj pale. **pallor** n

palm n 1 inner surface of hand. 2 tropical tree. 3 its leaf as symbol of victory. **palmistry** n fortune-telling from lines on palm of hand.

palomino n, pl **-nos** golden horse with white mane and tail.

palpable adj obvious.

palpitate v throb.

palsy n paralysis.

paltry adj **-trier, -triest** worthless.

pamper ⓣ v overindulge, spoil.

pamphlet ⓣ n thin unbound book.

pan[1] ⓣ n 1 broad, shallow vessel. 2 bowl of lavatory. 3 depression in ground. ◆ v 4 Inf criticize harshly.

pan[2] ⓣ v panning, panned move film camera slowly while filming.

pan- comb. form all, as in pan-American.

panacea n universal remedy.

panache n dashing style.

pancake n thin cake of batter fried in pan.

pancreas n digestive gland behind stomach.

panda n large black and white bearlike mammal of China.

pandemonium n din and uproar.

pander v 1 give gratification to. ◆ n 2 pimp.

pane n sheet of glass.

panegyric n speech of praise.

panel n 1 compartment of surface, usu. raised or sunk, e.g. in door. 2 team in quiz game etc. 3 list of jurors, doctors etc. ◆ v 4 adorn with panels.

pang n sudden pain.

panic ⓣ n 1 sudden and infectious fear. ◆ v 2 (cause to) feel panic. **panicky** adj

pannier n basket carried by beast of burden, bicycle etc.

panoply n magnificent array.

panorama ⓣ n wide view.

pansy n, pl **-sies** 1 flower, species of violet. 2 Inf effeminate man.

pant ⓣ v/n gasp.

pantechnicon n large van, esp. for carrying furniture.

panther n variety of leopard.

pantomime n theatrical show, usu. at Christmas time, often founded on a fairy tale.

pantry n, pl **-tries** room for storing food or utensils.

pants ⓣ pl n 1 undergarment for lower trunk 2 US and Canad

pamper v = **spoil**, indulge, pet, cosset, coddle

pamphlet n = **booklet**, leaflet, brochure, circular, tract

pan[1] n = **pot**, container, saucepan ◆ v = (Inf) **criticize**, knock, slam (Sl), censure, tear into (Inf); = **sift out**, look for, search for

pan[2] v = **move along** or **across**, follow, track, sweep

panic n = **fear**, alarm, terror, anxiety, hysteria ◆ v = **go to pieces**, become hysterical, lose your nerve

panorama n = **view**, prospect, vista

pant v = **puff**, blow, breathe, gasp, wheeze

trousers.

pap n soft food.

papacy n, pl **–cies** office of Pope.

papal adj of the Pope.

paper ❶ n 1 material made by pressing pulp of rags, wood etc., into thin sheets. 2 sheet of paper. 3 newspaper. 4 essay. ◆ pl 5 documents etc. ◆ v 6 cover with paper. **paperback** n book with flexible covers.

papier-mâché n paper pulp mixed with paste, shaped and dried hard.

paprika n red pepper.

papyrus n, pl **–ri, –ruses** 1 species of reed. 2 paper made from this.

par n 1 equality of value or standing. 2 Golf estimated standard score. **parity** n 1 equality. 2 analogy.

parable n allegory, story with moral lesson.

parachute n 1 apparatus extending like umbrella used to slow the descent of falling body. ◆ v 2 drop by parachute.

parade ❶ n 1 display. 2 muster of troops. ◆ v 3 march. 4 display.

paradise ❶ n 1 Heaven. 2 state of bliss. 3 Garden of Eden.

paradox ❶ n statement that seems self-contradictory. **paradoxical** adj

paraffin n waxlike or liquid hydrocarbon mixture used as fuel, solvent, etc.

paragon n pattern or model of excellence.

paragraph ❶ n 1 section of chapter or book. ◆ v 2 arrange in paragraphs.

parakeet n small parrot.

parallel ❶ adj/n 1 (line or lines) continuously at equal distances. 2 (thing) precisely corresponding. ◆ v 3 represent as similar.

parallelogram n four-sided figure with opposite sides parallel.

paralysis ❶ n incapacity to move or feel. **paralyse** v 1 affect with paralysis. 2 make immobile. **paralytic** adj/n

paramedic n person working in

——————— THESAURUS ———————

pants pl n = (Brit) **underpants**, briefs, drawers, knickers, panties; = (US) **trousers**, slacks

paper n = **newspaper**, daily, journal, gazette; = **essay**, article, treatise, dissertation ◆ v = **wallpaper**, hang

parade n = **procession**, march, pageant, cavalcade ◆ v = **march**, process, promenade; = **flaunt**, display, exhibit, show off (Inf)

paradise n = **heaven**, Promised Land, Happy Valley (Islam), Elysian fields; = **bliss**, delight, heaven, felicity, utopia

paradox n = **contradiction**, puzzle, anomaly, enigma, oddity

paragraph n = **section**, part, item, passage, clause

parallel n = **equivalent**, counterpart, match, equal, twin ≠ **opposite** ◆ adj = **matching**, corresponding, like, similar, resembling ≠ **different**; = **equidistant**, alongside, side by side ≠ **divergent**

support of medical profession.

parameter 🛈 *n* limiting factor.

paramilitary *adj* organized on military lines.

paramount 🛈 *adj* supreme.

paranoia *n* mental disease with delusions of persecution etc.

paranoid *adj*/*n*

parapet *n* low wall along edge of bridge etc.

paraphernalia *pl n* (*used as sing*) **1** belongings. **2** equipment.

paraphrase *v* express in other words.

paraplegia *n* paralysis of lower body. **paraplegic** *n*/*adj*

parasite 🛈 *n* animal or plant living in or on another. **parasitic** *adj*

parasol *n* sunshade.

paratroops *pl n* troops trained to descend by parachute.

parboil *v* boil until partly cooked.

parcel 🛈 *n* **1** packet. ◆ *v* **2** wrap up. **3** divide into parts.

parch *v* make, become hot and dry.

parchment *n* sheep, goat, calf skin prepared for writing.

pardon 🛈 *v* **1** forgive, excuse. ◆ *n* **2** forgiveness. **3** release from punishment.

pare *v* **1** peel, trim. **2** decrease.

parent 🛈 *n* father or mother.

parentage *n* descent, extraction.

parental *adj*/**parenthood** *n*

parenthesis *n*, *pl* -ses word(s) inserted in passage. **parentheses** *pl n* round brackets, (), used to mark this.

pariah *n* social outcast.

parish 🛈 *n* district under one clergyman. **parishioner** *n* inhabitant of parish.

parity see PAR.

park 🛈 *n* **1** large area of land in natural state for recreational use. ◆ *v* **2** leave for short time. **3** manoeuvre (car) into suitable space.

parka *n* warm waterproof coat.

parkade *n Canad* a building used as a car park.

parkette *n Canad* a small public park.

parking lot *n US and Canad* area

paralysis *n* = **immobility**, palsy

parameter *n* (*Inf*) usually plural = **limit**, restriction, framework, limitation, specification

paramount *adj* = **principal**, prime, first, chief, main ≠ **secondary**

parasite *n* = **sponger** (*Inf*), leech, hanger-on, scrounger (*Inf*), bloodsucker (*Inf*)

parcel *n* = **package**, case, box, pack, bundle ◆ *v often with* **up** = **wrap**, pack, package, tie up, do up

pardon *v* = **forgive**, excuse ≠ **condemn**; ◆ *n* = **forgiveness**, absolution ≠ **condemnation**; = **acquittal**, amnesty, exoneration ≠ **punishment**

parent *n* = **father** or mother, sire, progenitor, procreator, old (*Aust & NZ inf*)

parish *n* = **district**, community

park *n* = **recreation ground**, garden, playground, pleasure

or building where vehicles may be left for a time.

parlance n particular way of speaking.

parley v/n (hold) discussion about terms.

parliament ❶ n law–making assembly of country.

parliamentary adj

parlour ❶ n sitting room.

parochial adj **1** narrow, provincial. **2** of a parish.

parody ❶ n/v, pl **–dies** (write) satirical, amusing imitation of a work.

parole n **1** release of prisoner on condition of good behaviour. ◆ v **2** release on parole.

paroxysm n sudden attack of pain, rage, laughter.

parquet n flooring of wooden blocks.

parrot ❶ n **1** brightly coloured

bird which can imitate speaking. ◆ v **2** repeat words without thinking.

parry ❶ v **–rying, –ried** ward off, turn aside.

parsimony n stinginess.

parsimonious adj

parsley n herb used for seasoning, garnish etc.

parsnip n root vegetable.

parson ❶ n clergyman.

part ❶ n **1** portion. **2** role. **3** duty. **4** region. **5** component. ◆ v **6** divide. **7** separate. **parting** n **1** division of hair on head. **2** separation. **3** leave–taking. **partly** adv in part.

partake v **–taking, –took, –taken** **1** take or have share in. **2** take food or drink.

partial ❶ adj **1** not complete. **2** prejudiced. **3** fond of. **partially** adv partly.

participate ❶ v **1** share in. **2** take

—————————— THESAURUS ——————————

garden, playpark

parliament n = **assembly**, council, congress, senate, convention

parlour n = (Old–fashioned) **sitting room**, lounge, living room, drawing room, front room

parody n = **takeoff** (Inf), satire, caricature, send–up (Brit inf), spoof (Inf) ◆ v = **take off** (Inf), caricature, send up (Brit inf), burlesque, satirize

parrot v = **repeat**, echo, imitate, copy, mimic

parry v = **evade**, avoid, dodge, sidestep; = **ward off**, block, deflect, repel, rebuff

parson n = **clergyman**, minister,

priest, vicar, preacher

part n = **piece**, share, proportion, percentage, bit ≠ **entirety**; often plural = **region**, area, district, neighbourhood, quarter; = **component**, bit, unit, constituent; = **branch**, division, office, section, wing ◆ v = **divide**, separate, break, tear, split ≠ **join**; = **part company**, separate, split up ≠ **meet in good part**

partial adj = **incomplete**, unfinished, imperfect, uncompleted ≠ **complete**; = **biased**, prejudiced, discriminatory, partisan, unfair ≠ **unbiased**

part. **participant** *n* **participation** *n*
participle *n* *Grammar* verbal adjective.
particle 🛈 *n* minute portion.
particular 🛈 *adj* 1 relating to one. 2 distinct. 3 fussy. ♦ *n* 4 detail, item. ♦ *pl* 5 items of information. **particularly** *adv*
partisan 🛈 *n* 1 adherent of a party. 2 guerilla. ♦ *adj* 3 adhering to faction. 4 prejudiced.
partition 🛈 *n* 1 division. 2 interior dividing wall. ♦ *v* 3 divide into sections.
partner 🛈 *n* 1 ally or companion. 2 spouse. **partnership** *n*
partridge *n* game bird.

party 🛈 *n, pl* **-ties** 1 social assembly. 2 group of persons organized together, esp. with common political aim. 3 person.
pass 🛈 *v* 1 go by, beyond, through etc. 2 exceed. 3 transfer. 4 spend. 5 elapse. 6 undergo examination successfully. 7 bring a law into force. ♦ *n* 8 way, esp. through mountains. 9 permit. 10 successful result. **passable** *adj* (just) acceptable. **passing** *adj* 1 transitory. 2 casual. **pass away** die. **pass out** faint.
passage 🛈 *n* 1 opening. 2 corridor. 3 part of book etc. 4 voyage, fare.

———— THESAURUS ————

participate *v* = **take part**, be involved, perform, join, partake ≠ **refrain from**
particle *n* = **bit**, piece, scrap, grain, shred
particular *adj* = **specific**, special, exact, precise, distinct ≠ **general**; = **special**, exceptional, notable, uncommon, marked; = **fussy**, demanding, fastidious, choosy (*Inf*), picky (*Inf*) ≠ **indiscriminate** ♦ *n usually plural* = **detail**, fact, feature, item, circumstance
partisan *adj* = **prejudiced**, one-sided, biased, partial, sectarian ≠ **unbiased** ♦ *n* = **supporter**, devotee, adherent, upholder ≠ **opponent**; = **underground fighter**, guerrilla, freedom fighter, resistance fighter
partition *n* = **screen**, wall, barrier; = **division**, separation, segregation ♦ *v* = **separate**, screen, divide

partner *n* = **spouse**, consort, significant other (*US inf*), mate, husband or wife; = **companion**, ally, colleague, associate, mate
party *n* = **faction**, set, side, league, camp; = **get-together** (*Inf*), celebration, do (*Inf*), gathering, function; = **group**, team, band, company, unit
pass *v* = **go by** or **past**, overtake, drive past, lap, leave behind ≠ **stop**; = **go**, move, travel, progress, flow; = **run**, move, stroke; = **give**, hand, send, transfer, deliver; = **be left**, come, be bequeathed, be inherited by; = **kick**, hit, loft, head, lob; = **elapse**, progress, go by, lapse, wear on ♦ *n* = **licence**, ticket, permit, passport, warrant; = **gap**, route, canyon, gorge, ravine
passage *n* = **corridor**, hall, lobby, vestibule; = **alley**, way, close (*Brit*),

passé adj out–of–date.

passenger 🛈 n traveller, esp. by public conveyance.

passion 🛈 n 1 ardent desire. 2 any strong emotion. 3 great enthusiasm. **passionate** adj

passive 🛈 adj 1 submissive. 2 inactive.

passport n official document granting permission to travel abroad etc.

password n secret word to ensure admission etc.

past 🛈 adj 1 ended. 2 gone by. 3 elapsed. ♦ n 4 bygone times. ♦ adv 5 by. 6 along. ♦ prep 7 beyond. 8 after.

pasta n any of several preparations of dough, e.g. spaghetti.

paste 🛈 n 1 soft mixture. 2 adhesive. ♦ v 3 fasten with paste.

pasting n 1 Sl defeat. 2 strong criticism. **pasty** adj 1 like paste. 2 white. 3 sickly.

pastel 🛈 n 1 coloured crayon. 2 drawing with crayons. 3 pale, delicate colour. ♦ adj 4 (of colour) pale.

pasteurize v sterilize by heat.

pastiche n work of art that mixes or copies styles.

pastille n lozenge.

pastime 🛈 n recreation.

pastor 🛈 n clergyman. **pastoral** adj 1 of rural life. 2 of pastor.

pastry n, pl –ries article of food made chiefly of flour, fat and water.

pasture 🛈 n 1 ground on which cattle graze. ♦ v 2 (cause to) graze.

pasty n pastier, pastiest. pl pasties small pie of meat and

———————— THESAURUS ————————

course, road; **= extract**, reading, piece, section, text; **= journey**, crossing, trip, trek, voyage; **= safe–conduct**, right to travel, freedom to travel, permission to travel

passenger n **= traveller**, rider, fare, commuter, fare payer

passion n **= love**, desire, lust, infatuation, ardour; **= emotion**, feeling, fire, heat, excitement ≠ **indifference**; **= mania**, enthusiasm, obsession, bug (Inf), craving

passive adj **= submissive**, compliant, receptive, docile, quiescent ≠ **spirited**

past n **= former times**, long ago,

days gone by, the olden days ≠ **future**; **= background**, life, history, past life, life story ♦ adj **= former**, early, previous, ancient, bygone ≠ **future**; **= previous**, former, one–time, ex– ♦ prep **= after**, beyond, later than

paste n **= adhesive**, glue, cement, gum ♦ v **= stick**, glue, cement, gum

pastel adj **= pale**, light, soft, delicate, muted ≠ **bright**

pastime n **= activity**, game, entertainment, hobby, recreation

pastor n **= clergyman**, minister, priest, vicar, parson

pasture n **= grassland**, grass, meadow, grazing

crust, baked without a dish.

pat¹ ❶ *v* **patting, patted 1** tap. ♦ *n* **2** tap. **3** small mass, as of butter.

pat² *adv* **1** exactly. **2** fluently. **3** thoroughly learned.

patch ❶ *n* **1** piece of cloth sewed on garment. **2** spot. **3** plot of ground. ♦ *v* **4** mend. **5** repair clumsily. **patchy** *adj* of uneven quality. **patchwork** *n* needlework of different pieces sewn together.

pate *n* **1** head. **2** top of head.

pâté *n* spread of finely minced liver etc.

patent ❶ *n* **1** exclusive right to invention. ♦ *adj* **2** open. **3** evident. ♦ *v* **4** secure a patent. **patently** *adv* obviously.

paternal *adj* **1** fatherly. **2** of a father. **paternity** *n* fatherhood.

path ❶ *n* **1** way, track. **2** course of action.

pathetic ❶ *adj* moving to pity.

pathology *n* science of diseases. **pathological** *adj* **pathologist** *n*

pathos *n* power of exciting tender emotions.

patient ❶ *adj* **1** bearing troubles calmly. ♦ *n* **2** person under medical treatment. **patience** *n*

patio *n, pl* **–tios** paved area adjoining house.

patriarch *n* father and ruler of family.

patrician *n/adj* (one) of noble birth.

patriot ❶ *n* person that loves his or her country. **patriotic** *adj* **patriotism** *n*

patrol ❶ *n* **1** regular circuit by guard. **2** person, small group patrolling. ♦ *v* **3** go round on guard.

patron ❶ *n* **1** one who aids artists, charities etc. **2** regular customer. **3** guardian saint. **patronage** *n* support given by patron. **patronize** *v* **1** assume air of superiority towards. **2** be regular customer.

pat¹ *v* = **stroke**, touch, tap, pet, caress ♦ *n* = **tap**, stroke, clap

patch *n* = **spot**, bit, scrap, shred, small piece; = **plot**, area, ground, land, tract; = **reinforcement**, piece of fabric, piece of cloth, piece of material, piece sewn on ♦ *v often with* **up** = **mend**, cover, repair, reinforce, stitch (up)

patent *n* = **copyright**, licence, franchise, registered trademark ♦ *adj* = **obvious**, apparent, evident, clear, glaring

path *n* = **way**, road, walk, track, trail; = **route**, way, course, direction

pathetic *adj* = **sad**, moving, touching, affecting, distressing ≠ **funny**

patient *n* = **sick person**, case, sufferer, invalid ♦ *adj* = **forbearing**, understanding, forgiving, mild, tolerant ≠ **impatient**

patriot *n* = **nationalist**, loyalist, chauvinist

patrol *v* = **police**, guard, keep watch (on), inspect, safeguard ♦ *n* = **guard**, watch, watchman, sentinel, patrolman

patron *n* = **supporter**, friend,

patter n 1 quick succession of taps 2 *Inf* glib, rapid speech. ♦ v 3 make quick tapping noise.

pattern ⊕ n 1 arrangement of repeated parts. 2 design. 3 plan for cutting cloth etc. 4 model. ♦ v (with on or after) 5 model.

paunch n belly.

pauper n very poor person.

pause ⊕ v/n stop, rest.

pave ⊕ v form surface with stone.

pavement n paved footpath.

pavilion n 1 clubhouse on playing field etc. 2 building for exhibition etc. 3 large tent.

paw ⊕ n 1 foot of animal. ♦ v 2 scrape with forefoot. 3 maul.

pawn¹ v deposit (article) as security for money borrowed.

pawnbroker n lender of money on goods deposited.

pawn² n 1 piece in chess. 2 person used as mere tool.

pay ⊕ v paying, paid 1 give money etc., for goods or services. 2 give. 3 be profitable to. 4 spend. ♦ n 5 wages. **payable** adj justly due. **payee** n person to whom money is paid or due.

payment n

PC 1 personal computer. 2 Police Constable. 3 Privy Councillor.

PE physical education.

pea n 1 edible seed, growing in pods, of climbing plant. 2 the plant.

peace ⊕ n 1 freedom from war. 2 harmony. 3 calm. **peaceable** adj disposed to peace. **peaceful** adj

peach n fruit of delicate flavour.

peacock n male bird with fanlike tail.

peak ⊕ n 1 pointed end of anything, esp. hilltop. 2 highest point.

peal n 1 (succession of) loud sound(s). ♦ v 2 sound loudly.

peanut n 1 pea-shaped nut. ♦ pl

———————— THESAURUS ————————

champion, sponsor, backer; = **customer**, client, buyer, frequenter, shopper

pattern n = **order**, plan, system, method, sequence; = **design**, arrangement, motif, figure, device; = **plan**, design, original, guide, diagram

pause v = **stop briefly**, delay, break, wait, rest ≠ **continue** ♦ n = **stop**, break, interval, rest, gap ≠ **continuance**

pave v = **cover**, floor, surface, concrete, tile

paw v = (*Inf*) **manhandle**, grab, maul, molest, handle roughly

pay v = **reward**, compensate, reimburse, recompense, requite; = **spend**, give, fork out (*Inf*), remit, shell out (*Inf*); = **bring in**, earn, return, net, yield ♦ n = **wages**, income, payment, earnings, fee

peace n = **truce**, ceasefire, treaty, armistice ≠ **war**; = **stillness**, rest, quiet, silence, calm; = **serenity**, calm, composure, contentment, repose; = **harmony**, accord, agreement, concord

peak n = **high point**, crown, climax, culmination, zenith; = **point**, top, tip, summit, brow ♦ v = **culminate**, climax, come to a

P

2 *Inf* trifling amount of money.
pear *n* **1** tree yielding sweet, juicy fruit. **2** the fruit. **pear-shaped** *adj* shaped like a pear, heavier at the bottom than the top.

pearl *n* hard, lustrous structure found esp. in oyster and used as jewel.

peasant ❶ *n* member of low social class, esp. in rural district.

peat *n* decomposed vegetable substance.

pebble *n* small roundish stone.

peccadillo *n, pl* **–loes, –los 1** slight offence. **2** petty crime.

peck ❶ *v* **1** strike with or as with beak. **2** nibble at **3** *Inf* kiss quickly. ♦ *n* **4** pecking movement. **peckish** *adj Inf* hungry.

pectoral *adj* of the breast.

peculiar ❶ *adj* **1** strange. **2** particular. **3** belonging to. **peculiarity** *n, pl* **–ties 1** oddity. **2** characteristic. **3** distinguishing feature.

pedal *n* **1** foot lever. ♦ *v* **2** propel bicycle by using its pedals. **3** use pedal.

pedant *n* one who insists on petty details of book–learning, grammatical rules etc. **pedantic** *adj*

peddle *v* go round selling goods.

pedestal *n* base of column.

pedestrian ❶ *n* **1** one who walks on foot. ♦ *adj* **2** going on foot. **3** commonplace. **4** dull. **pedestrian crossing** place marked where pedestrians may cross road.

pedigree ❶ *n* **1** register of ancestors. **2** genealogy.

pedlar *n* **1** one who sells. **2** hawker.

peek *v/n* peep, glance.

peel ❶ *v* **1** strip off skin, rind or covering. **2** flake off, as skin, rind. ♦ *n* **3** rind, skin.

peep ❶ *v* **1** look slyly or quickly. ♦ *n* **2** such a look.

peer¹ ❶ *v* look closely.

peer² ❶ *n* **1** nobleman. **2** one of the same rank. **peerage** *n* **peerless** *adj* without match or equal. **peer group** group of people of similar age, status etc.

peeved *adj Inf* sulky, irritated.

——————————— THESAURUS ———————————

head

peasant *n* = **rustic**, countryman

peck *v* = **pick**, hit, strike, tap, poke

peculiar *adj* = **odd**, strange, unusual, bizarre, funny ≠ **ordinary**; = **special**, particular, unique, characteristic ≠ **common**

pedestrian *n* = **walker**, foot-traveller ≠ **driver** ♦ *adj* = **dull**, ordinary, boring, commonplace, mundane ≠ **exciting**

pedigree *n* = **lineage**, family, line,

race, stock

peel *n* = **rind**, skin, peeling ♦ *v* = **skin**, scale, strip, pare, shuck

peep *v* = **peek**, look, eyeball (*Sl*), sneak a look, steal a look ♦ *n* = **look**, glimpse, peek, look–see (*Sl*)

peer¹ *v* = **squint**, look, spy, gaze, scan

peer² *n* = **noble**, lord, aristocrat, nobleman; = **equal**, like, fellow, contemporary, compeer

peevish adj 1 fretful. 2 irritable.

peewit n lapwing.

peg ❶ n 1 pin for joining, fastening, marking etc. 2 (mark of) level, standard etc. ◆ v 3 fasten with pegs. 4 stabilize (prices) 5 (with away) persevere.

pejorative adj (of words etc.) with disparaging connotation.

pelican n waterfowl with large pouch beneath its bill. **pelican crossing** road crossing with pedestrian–operated traffic lights.

pellet n little ball.

pelmet n ornamental drapery or board, concealing curtain rail.

pelt¹ v 1 throw missiles. 2 rain persistently. 3 rush.

pelt² n raw hide or skin.

pelvis n bony cavity at base of human trunk. **pelvic** adj

pen¹ **❶** n 1 instrument for writing. ◆ v 2 compose. 3 write. **pen friend** friend with whom one corresponds without meeting.

penknife n small knife with folding blade.

pen² **❶** n/v (put in) enclosure.

penal adj of punishment. **penalize** v impose penalty on. **penalty** n, pl –ties 1 punishment. 2 forfeit 3 Sport handicap.

penance n suffering submitted to as expression of penitence.

pence n pl of PENNY.

penchant n inclination, decided taste.

pencil n 1 instrument, esp. of graphite, for writing etc. ◆ v 2 draw. 3 mark with pencil.

pendant n hanging ornament.

pendent adj hanging.

pending ❶ prep 1 during, until. ◆ adj 2 awaiting settlement. 3 imminent.

pendulous adj hanging, swinging. **pendulum** n suspended weight swinging to and fro.

penetrate ❶ v 1 enter into. 2 pierce. 3 arrive at meaning of. **penetrating** adj 1 sharp. 2 easily heard. 3 quick to understand. **penetration** n

penguin n flightless bird.

penicillin n antibiotic drug.

peninsula n portion of land nearly surrounded by water. **peninsular** adj

penis n male organ of copulation and urination.

penitent adj 1 affected by sense of guilt. ◆ n 2 one that repents. **penitence** n sorrow for sin. **penitentiary** adj, pl –ries, n US prison.

pennant n long narrow flag.

———— THESAURUS ————

peg v = **fasten**, join, fix, secure, attach

pen¹ v = **write (down)**, draft, compose, pencil, draw up

pen² n = **enclosure**, pound, fold, cage, coop ◆ v = **enclose**, confine, cage, fence in, coop up

pending adj = **undecided**, unsettled, in the balance, undetermined

penetrate v = **pierce**, enter, go through, bore, stab (Inf); = **grasp**, work out, figure out (Inf), comprehend, fathom

penny n, pl **pence, pennies** Brit. bronze coin, 100th part of pound.
penniless adj having no money.
pension ❶ n **1** regular payment to old people, soldiers etc. ♦ v **2** grant pension to. **pensioner** n
pensive adj thoughtful.
pentagon n figure with five angles.
penthouse n apartment, flat on top of building.
penultimate adj next before the last.
penury n extreme poverty.
peony n, pl **–nies** plant with showy red, pink, or white flowers.
people ❶ pl n **1** persons generally, nation. **2** race. **3** family. ♦ v **4** populate.
pep n **1** Inf vigour. **2** energy. ♦ v **3** give energy, enthusiasm. **pep talk** Inf talk designed to increase confidence, enthusiasm etc.
pepper ❶ n **1** pungent aromatic spice. **2** slightly pungent vegetable. ♦ v **3** season with pepper. **4** sprinkle. **5** pelt with missiles. **peppermint** n **1** plant noted for aromatic pungent liquor distilled from it. **2** sweet flavoured with this.

per prep **1** for each. **2** by. **3** in manner of.
perambulate v **1** walk through or over. **2** walk about. **perambulator** n pram.
per annum Lat by the year.
per capita Lat for each person.
perceive ❶ v **1** obtain knowledge of through senses. **2** understand.
perceptible adj **perception** n **perceptive** adj
percentage n proportion or rate per hundred. **per cent** in each hundred.
perch¹ ❶ n **1** resting place, as for bird. ♦ v **2** place, as on perch. **3** alight on branch etc. **4** balance on.
perch² n freshwater fish.
perchance adv Obs perhaps.
percolate v **1** pass through fine mesh as liquor. **2** filter. **percolator** n coffeepot with filter.
percussion n striking of one thing against another.
peremptory adj imperious.
perennial ❶ adj **1** lasting through the years. **2** perpetual. ♦ n **3** plant lasting more than two years.

————— THESAURUS —————

pension n = **allowance**, benefit, welfare, annuity, superannuation
people pl n = **persons**, individuals, folk (Inf), men and women, humanity; = **nation**, public, community, subjects, population; = **race**, tribe ♦ v = **inhabit**, occupy, settle, populate, colonize
pepper n = **seasoning**, flavour, spice ♦ v = **pelt**, hit, shower, blitz,

rake; = **sprinkle**, spot, scatter, dot, fleck
perceive v = **see**, notice, note, identify, discover; = **understand**, gather, see, learn, realize
perch¹ v = **sit**, rest, balance, settle ♦ n = **resting place**, post, branch, pole
perennial adj = **continual**, lasting, constant, enduring, persistent

perfect ⓐ *adj* **1** complete. **2** unspoilt. **3** correct, precise. **4** excellent. ◆ *v* **5** improve. **6** make skilful. **perfection** *n* **perfectionist** *n* one who demands highest standards. **perfectly** *adv*

perforate *v* make holes in, penetrate. **perforation** *n*

perform ⓐ *v* **1** fulfil. **2** function. **3** act part. **4** play, as on musical instrument. **performance** *n*

perfume ⓐ *n* **1** agreeable scent. ◆ *v* **2** imbue with an agreeable odour.

perfunctory *adj* done indifferently.

perhaps ⓐ *adv* possibly.

peril ⓐ *n* **1** danger. **2** exposure to injury. **perilous** *adj*

perimeter ⓐ *n* **1** outer boundary of area. **2** length of this.

period ⓐ *n* **1** particular portion of time. **2** series of years. **3** single occurrence of menstruation. **4** full stop. ◆ *adj* **5** (of furniture, dress etc.) belonging to a particular time in history. **periodic** *adj* recurring at regular intervals. **periodical** *adj* **1** periodic. ◆ *n* **2** publication issued at regular intervals. **periodic table** *Chem* chart showing relationship of elements to each other.

peripatetic *adj* travelling about.

periphery *n, pl* **-eries 1** circumference. **2** outside. **peripheral** *adj* unimportant.

periscope *n* instrument used for giving view of objects on different level.

perish ⓐ *v* **1** die. **2** rot. **perishable** *adj* that will not last long. **perishing** *adj Inf* very cold.

perk ⓐ *n* incidental benefit from employment.

perm *n* **1** long-lasting curly hairstyle. ◆ *v* **2** give a perm.

permanent ⓐ *adj* **1** continuing in same state. **2** lasting. **permanence** *n*

P

———— THESAURUS ————

perfect *adj* = **faultless**, correct, pure, impeccable, exemplary ≠ **deficient**; = **excellent**, ideal, supreme, superb, splendid; = **immaculate**, impeccable, flawless, spotless, unblemished ≠ **flawed**; = **complete**, absolute, sheer, utter, consummate ≠ **partial** ◆ *v* = **improve**, develop, polish, refine ≠ **mar**

perform *v* = **do**, achieve, carry out, complete, fulfil; = **fulfil**, carry out, execute, discharge

perfume *n* = **fragrance**, scent

perhaps *adv* = **maybe**, possibly, it may be, it is possible (that), conceivably

peril *n* = **danger**, risk, threat, hazard, menace

perimeter *n* = **boundary**, edge, border, bounds, limit ≠ **centre**

period *n* = **time**, term, season, space, run

perish *v* = **die**, be killed, expire, pass away, lose your life; = **be destroyed**, fall, decline, collapse, disappear; = **rot**, waste away, decay, disintegrate, decompose

perk *n* = (*Brit inf*) **bonus**, benefit, extra, plus, fringe benefit

permeate v 1 pervade. 2 pass through pores of. **permeable** adj

permit ⊕ v –mitting, –mitted 1 allow. 2 give leave to. ♦ n 3 warrant or licence to do something. **permissible** adj **permission** n **permissive** adj (too) tolerant, esp. sexually.

permutation n Maths arrangement of a number of quantities in every possible order.

pernicious adj 1 wicked. 2 harmful.

pernickety adj Inf fussy.

peroxide n short for HYDROGEN PEROXIDE.

perpendicular adj/n 1 (line) at right angles to another. 2 (something) exactly upright.

perpetrate v perform or be responsible for (something bad).

perpetual ⊕ adj 1 continuous. 2 lasting forever. **perpetuate** v 1 make perpetual. 2 not to allow to be forgotten. **perpetuity** n

perplex v 1 puzzle. 2 bewilder. **perplexity** n, pl –ties

persecute ⊕ v oppress because of race, religion etc. **persecution** n

persevere v persist, maintain effort. **perseverance** n

persist ⊕ v continue in spite of obstacles or objections. **persistence** n **persistent** adj

person ⊕ n 1 individual (human) being. 2 body of human being 3 Grammar classification of pronouns and verb forms according to the person speaking, spoken to, or of. **personable** adj pleasant in looks and personality. **personal** adj 1 individual, private. 2 of grammatical person. **personality** n 1 distinctive character. 2 celebrity. **personally** adv 1 independently. 2 in one's own opinion. **personal computer** small computer for word processing or computer games. **personal stereo** portable cassette player with headphones.

persona n, pl –nae someone's personality as presented to others.

personify v –fying, –fied 1 represent as person. 2 typify. **personification** n

personnel ⊕ n staff employed in organization.

perspective ⊕ n 1 mental view. 2

permanent adj = lasting, constant, enduring, persistent, eternal ≠ temporary

permit v = allow, grant, sanction, let, entitle ≠ forbid ♦ n = licence, pass, document, certificate, passport ≠ prohibition

perpetual adj = everlasting, permanent, endless, eternal, lasting ≠ temporary; = continual, repeated, constant, endless,

continuous ≠ brief

persecute v = victimize, torture, torment, oppress, pick on ≠ mollycoddle; = harass, bother, annoy, tease, hassle (Inf) ≠ leave alone

persist v = continue, last, remain, carry on, keep up; = persevere, continue, go on, carry on, keep on

person n = individual, being, body, human, soul

method of drawing on flat surface to give effect of relative distances and sizes.

Perspex ® *n* transparent acrylic substitute for glass.

perspicacious *adj* having quick mental insight.

perspire *v* sweat. **perspiration** *n*

persuade ❿ *v* 1 make (one) do something by argument, charm etc. 2 convince. **persuasion** *n* 1 art, act of persuading. 2 belief. **persuasive** *adj*

pert *adj* forward, saucy.

pertain *v* belong, relate, have reference (to).

pertinacious *adj* persistent.

pertinent *adj* to the point. **pertinence** *n* relevance.

perturb *v* 1 disturb. 2 alarm.

peruse *v* read in careful or leisurely manner. **perusal** *n*

pervade *v* spread through. **pervasive** *adj*

pervert ❿ *v* 1 turn to wrong use. 2 lead astray. ◆ *n* 3 one who practises sexual perversion.

perverse *adj* 1 obstinately or unreasonably wrong. 2 wayward. **perversion** *n* 1 sexual act considered abnormal. 2 corruption. **perversity** *n*

pessimism *n* tendency to see worst side of things. **pessimist** *n* **pessimistic** *adj*

pest ❿ *n* troublesome or harmful thing, person or insect. **pesticide** *n* chemical for killing pests, esp. insects.

pester *v* 1 vex. 2 harass.

pestilence *n* epidemic disease.

pestle *n* instrument with which things are pounded.

pet ❿ *n* 1 animal or person kept or regarded with affection. ◆ *adj* 2 favourite. ◆ *v* 3 make pet of. 4 *Inf* fondle.

petal *n* white or coloured leaflike part of flower.

petite *adj* small, dainty.

petition ❿ *n* 1 request, esp. to sovereign or parliament. ◆ *v* 2 present petition to.

petrel *n* sea bird.

——————— THESAURUS ———————

personnel *n* = **employees**, people, staff, workers, workforce

perspective *n* = **outlook**, attitude, context, angle, frame of reference

persuade *v* = **talk (someone) into**, urge, influence, win (someone) over, induce ≠ **dissuade**; = **cause**, lead, move, influence, motivate

pervert *v* = **distort**, abuse, twist, misuse, warp; = **corrupt**, degrade, deprave, debase, debauch ◆ *n* = **deviant**, degenerate, sicko (*Inf*),

weirdo or weirdie (*Inf*)

pest *n* = **infection**, bug, insect, plague, epidemic; = **nuisance**, trial, pain (*Inf*), drag (*Inf*), bother

pet *adj* = **favourite**, favoured, dearest, cherished, fave (*Inf*) ◆ *n* = **favourite**, treasure, darling, jewel, idol ◆ *v* = **fondle**, pat, stroke, caress; = **pamper**, spoil, indulge, cosset, baby; = (*Inf*) **cuddle**, kiss, snog (*Brit sl*), smooch (*Inf*), neck (*Inf*)

petition *n* = **appeal**, round robin,

petrify v **-fying, -fied 1** turn to stone. **2** make motionless with fear.

petroleum n mineral oil. **petrol** n refined petroleum as used in motorcars etc.

petticoat n woman's underskirt.

pettifogging adj overconcerned with unimportant detail.

petty ① adj **-tier, -tiest 1** unimportant. **2** small-minded.

petty cash cash kept to pay minor expenses. **petty officer** noncommissioned officer in navy.

petulant adj **1** irritable. **2** peevish.

petunia n garden plant.

pew n fixed seat in church.

pewter n greyish alloy of tin and lead.

phallus n, pl **-luses, -li 1** penis. **2** symbol of it used in primitive rites. **phallic** adj

phantom ① n **1** apparition. **2** ghost.

Pharaoh n title of ancient Egyptian kings.

pharmaceutical adj of drugs or pharmacy. **pharmacist** n person qualified to dispense drugs.

pharmacology n study of drugs.

pharmacy n **1** preparation and

dispensing of drugs. **2** dispensary.

phase ① n distinct stage in development. **phase in, out** introduce or discontinue gradually.

PhD Doctor of Philosophy.

pheasant n game bird.

phenomenon ① n, pl **-ena 1** anything observed. **2** remarkable person or thing. **phenomenal** adj

phial n small bottle.

philanthropy n practice of doing good to one's fellow men. **philanthropic** adj **philanthropist** n

philately n stamp collecting. **philatelist** n

philistine n/adj ignorant (person).

philosophy ① n, pl **-phies 1** study of realities and general principles. **2** system of theories on nature of things or on conduct. **philosopher** n **philosophical** adj **1** of, like philosophy. **2** wise, learned. **3** calm, stoical.

phlegm n thick yellowish substance formed in throat.

phlegmatic adj not easily agitated.

phobia n fear or aversion.

phoenix n legendary bird.

phone ① n **1** telephone. **2** telephone message. ◆ v **3** telephone.

phonecard n card used to operate

list of signatures ◆ v = appeal, plead, ask, pray, beg

petty adj = trivial, insignificant, little, small, slight ≠ important; = small-minded, mean, shabby, spiteful, ungenerous ≠ broad-minded

phantom n = spectre, ghost, spirit, shade (Lit), spook (Inf)

phase n = stage, time, point, position, step

phenomenon n = occurrence, happening, fact, event, incident; = wonder, sensation, exception, miracle, marvel

philosophy n = thought, knowledge, thinking, reasoning, wisdom; = outlook, values,

some public telephones.
phonetic *adj* of vocal sounds.
phonetics *pl n* science of vocal sounds.
phoney, phony *Inf* ♦ *adj* **1** sham. **2** suspect. ♦ *n* **3** phoney person or thing.
phosphorus *n* nonmetallic element which appears luminous in the dark. **phosphate** *n* compound of phosphorus.
phosphorescence *n* faint glow in the dark.
photo *n, pl* **photos** *Inf* photograph.
photocopy *n, pl* –**copies 1** photographic reproduction. ♦ *v* **2** make photocopy of.
photogenic *adj* tending to look attractive when photographed.
photograph ❶ *n* **1** picture made by chemical action of light on sensitive film. ♦ *v* **2** take photograph of. **photographer** *n* **photographic** *adj* **photography** *n*
photosynthesis *n* process by which green plant uses sun's energy to make carbohydrates.
phrase ❶ *n* **1** group of words. **2** expression. ♦ *v* **3** express in words.
phraseology *n* choice of words.

physical ❶ *adj* **1** of the body, as contrasted with the mind or spirit. **2** of material things or nature.
physics ❶ *pl n* science of properties of matter and energy. **physical** *adj* **1** bodily, as opposed to mental. **2** material. **physician** *n* qualified medical practitioner.
physicist *n* one skilled in, or student of, physics.
physiognomy *n* face.
physiology *n* science of living things.
physiotherapy *n* therapeutic use of physical means, as massage etc. **physiotherapist** *n*
physique *n* bodily structure, constitution.
pi *n Maths* ratio of circumference of circle to its diameter.
piano *n, pl* **pianos 1** musical instrument with keyboard. ♦ *adj/adv* **2** *Mus* softly. **pianist** *n* performer on piano.
picador *n* mounted bullfighter with lance.
piccalilli *n* pickle of vegetables in mustard sauce.
piccolo *n, pl* –**los** small flute.
pick¹ ❶ *v* **1** choose, select carefully. **2** pluck, gather. **3** find

————————— THESAURUS —————————

principles, convictions, thinking
phone *n* = **telephone**, blower (*Inf*) ♦ *v* = **call**, telephone, ring (up) (*Inf, chiefly Brit*), give someone a call, give someone a ring (*Inf, chiefly Brit*)
photograph *n* = **picture**, photo (*Inf*), shot, print, snap (*Inf*) ♦ *v* = **take a picture of**, record, film,

shoot, snap (*Inf*)
phrase *n* = **expression**, saying, remark, construction, quotation ♦ *v* = **express**, say, word, put, voice
physical *adj* = **corporal**, fleshly, bodily, corporeal; = **earthly**, fleshly, mortal, incarnate
physician *n* = **doctor**, doc (*Inf*), medic (*Inf*), general practitioner,

occasion for. ♦ *n* **4** act of picking. **5** choicest part. **pick on** find fault with. **pickpocket** *n* thief who steals from someone's pocket. **pick up 1** lift. **2** obtain. **3** collect. **4** get better. **5** accelerate. **pick–up** *n* **1** small truck. **2** device for conversion of mechanical energy into electric signals.

pick² *n* tool with curved iron crossbar. **pickaxe** *n* pick.

picket ⓣ *n* **1** pointed stake. **2** party of trade unionists posted to deter would–be workers during strike. ♦ *v* **3** post as picket.

pickle ⓣ *n* **1** food preserved in brine, vinegar etc. **2** awkward situation. ♦ *v* **3** preserve in pickle.

picnic ⓣ *n* **1** pleasure excursion including meal out of doors. ♦ *v* **2** take part in picnic.

picture ⓣ *n* **1** drawing or painting. **2** mental image. **3** film, movie. ♦ *pl* **4** cinema. ♦ *v* **5** represent in, or as in, a picture.

pictorial *adj* **1** of, in, with pictures. ♦ *n* **2** newspaper with pictures.

picturesque *adj* visually striking, vivid.

pidgin *n* language made up of two or more other languages.

pie *n* baked dish of meat, fruit etc. usu. with pastry crust.

piebald *adj* irregularly marked with black and white. **pied** *adj* **1** piebald. **2** variegated.

piece ⓣ *n* **1** bit, part, fragment. **2** single object. **3** literary or musical composition etc. ♦ *v* **4** mend, put together. **piecemeal** *adv* by, in, or into pieces, a bit at a time.

pier ⓣ *n* **1** structure running into sea. **2** piece of solid upright masonry.

———— THESAURUS ————

medical practitioner

pick¹ *v* = **select**, choose, identify, elect, nominate ≠ **reject**; = **gather**, pull, collect, take in, harvest; = **provoke**, start, cause, stir up, incite; = **open**, force, crack (*Inf*), break into, break open ♦ *n* = **choice**, decision, option, selection, preference; = **best**, prime, finest, elect, elite

picket *v* = **blockade**, boycott, demonstrate outside ♦ *n* = **demonstration**, strike, blockade; = **protester**, demonstrator, picketer; = **lookout**, watch, guard, patrol, sentry

pickle *v* = **preserve**, marinade, steep ♦ *n* = **chutney**, relish,

piccalilli

picnic *n* = **excursion**, barbecue, barbie (*Inf*), cookout (*US & Canad*), alfresco meal

picture *n* = **representation**, drawing, painting, portrait, image; = **photograph**, photo, still, shot, image ♦ *v* = **imagine**, see, envision, visualize, conceive of; = **represent**, show, draw, paint, illustrate

piece *n* = **bit**, slice, part, block, quantity; = **component**, part, section, bit, unit

pier *n* = **jetty**, wharf, quay, promenade, landing place; = **pillar**, support, post, column, pile

pierce ⓥ v 1 make hole in. 2 make a way through. **piercing** adj 1 shrill. 2 alert, probing.

piety n, pl –ties 1 godliness. 2 devoutness.

pig ⓝ n 1 wild or domesticated mammal killed for pork, ham, bacon 2 Inf greedy, dirty person. **piggish, piggy** adj **pig-headed** adj obstinate.

pigeon n bird of wild and domesticated varieties. **pigeonhole** n 1 compartment for papers in desk etc. ◆ v 2 defer. 3 classify.

piggyback n ride on the back.

pigment ⓝ n colouring matter, paint or dye.

pigtail n plait of hair on either side of head.

pike¹ n predatory freshwater fish.

pike² n long-handled spear.

pikelet n Aust & NZ small thick pancake.

piker n Aust & NZ slang shirker.

pilau, pilaf, pilaff n Oriental dish of meat or fowl boiled with rice, spices etc.

pilchard n small sea fish like herring.

pile¹ ⓝ n 1 heap. ◆ v 2 heap (up) 3 (with in or out) crowd. ◆ n 4 heap.

pile-up n Inf traffic accident with several vehicles.

pile² ⓝ n beam driven into the ground, esp. as foundation.

pile³ ⓝ n nap of cloth.

piles pl n haemorrhoids.

pilfer v steal small items.

pilgrim ⓝ n one who journeys to sacred place. **pilgrimage** n

pill ⓝ n small ball of medicine swallowed whole. **the pill** oral contraceptive.

pillage v/n plunder.

pillar ⓝ n 1 upright support. 2 strong supporter. **pillar box** red pillar-shaped letter box.

pillion n seat behind rider of motorcycle or horse.

pillory n, pl –ries 1 frame with holes for head and hands in which offender was confined. ◆ v 2 expose to ridicule and abuse.

pillow n cushion for the head, esp. in bed. **pillowcase** n removable cover for pillow.

——————— THESAURUS ———————

pierce v = **penetrate**, stab, spike, enter, bore

pig n = **hog**, sow, boar, swine, porker; = **slob** (Inf) (Sl), glutton

pigment n = **colour**, colouring, paint, stain, dye

pile¹ n = **heap**, collection, mountain, mass, stack; (Inf) often plural = **lot(s)**, mountain(s), load(s) (Inf), oceans, wealth; = **mansion**, building, residence, manor, country house ◆ v = **load**, stuff, pack, stack, charge; = **crowd**, pack, rush, climb, flood

pile² n = **foundation**, support, post, column, beam

pile³ n = **nap**, fibre, down, hair, fur

pilgrim n = **traveller**, wanderer, devotee, wayfarer

pill n = **tablet**, capsule, pellet

pillar n = **support**, post, column, prop, shaft; = **supporter**, leader, mainstay, leading light (Inf), upholder

pilot ❶ n 1 person qualified to fly an aircraft or spacecraft. 2 one qualified to take charge of ship entering or leaving harbour etc. 3 guide. ♦ adj 4 experimental and preliminary. ♦ v 5 act as pilot to. 6 steer. **pilot light** small flame lighting main one in gas appliance.

pimento pl -tos n 1 allspice. 2 sweet red pepper.

pimp n 1 one who solicits for prostitute. ♦ v 2 act as pimp.

pimpernel n plant with small scarlet, blue, or white flowers.

pimple n small pus–filled spot on skin. **pimply** adj

pin ❶ n 1 piece of stiff wire with point and head, for fastening. 2 wooden or metal peg or rivet. ♦ v 3 fasten with pin. 4 seize and hold fast. **pinpoint** v identify exactly. **pinstripe** n very narrow stripe in fabric. **pin-up** n picture of sexually attractive person.

pinafore n 1 apron. 2 dress with bib top.

pincers pl n 1 tool for gripping. 2 claws of lobster etc.

pinch ❶ v 1 nip, squeeze. 2 stint 3 Inf steal 4 Inf arrest. ♦ n 5 nip. 6 small amount. 7 emergency.

pine¹ ❶ v 1 yearn. 2 waste away with grief etc.

pine² n 1 evergreen coniferous tree. 2 its wood.

pineapple n tropical plant bearing large edible fruit.

pinion n 1 bird's wing. ♦ v 2 confine by binding wings, arms etc.

pink ❶ n 1 pale red colour. 2 garden plant. 3 best condition. ♦ adj 4 of the colour pink. ♦ v 5 pierce. 6 cut indented edge. 7 (of engine) knock.

pinnacle ❶ n 1 highest point. 2 mountain peak. 3 pointed turret.

pint n 1 liquid measure. 2 ⅛ gallon (.568 litre).

pioneer ❶ n 1 explorer. 2 early settler. 3 originator. ♦ v 4 act as pioneer.

pious adj 1 devout. 2 self–righteous.

pip¹ n seed in fruit.

——————— THESAURUS ———————

pilot n = **airman**, flyer, aviator, aeronaut; = **helmsman**, navigator, steersman ♦ v = **fly**, operate, be at the controls of ♦ adj = **trial**, test, model, sample, experimental

pin v = **fasten**, stick, attach, join, fix; = **hold fast**, hold down, constrain, immobilize, pinion

pinch v = **nip**, press, squeeze, grasp, compress; = **hurt**, crush, squeeze, pain, cramp; = (Brit inf) **steal**, lift (Inf), nick (slang, chiefly

Brit.), swipe (Sl), knock off (Sl) ♦ n = **nip**, squeeze

pine¹ v = **waste**, decline, sicken, fade, languish

pink adj = **rosy**, rose, salmon, flushed, reddish

pinnacle n = **summit**, top, height, peak

pioneer n = **founder**, leader, developer, innovator, trailblazer; = **settler**, explorer, colonist ♦ v = **develop**, create, establish, start,

pip² n 1 high–pitched sound as time signal on radio. 2 spot on cards, dice etc. 3 *Inf* star on junior officer's shoulder showing rank.
pipe ⊕ n 1 tube of metal or other material. 2 tube with small bowl at end for smoking tobacco. 3 musical instrument. ♦ *pl* 4 bagpipes. ♦ *v* 5 play on pipe. 6 utter in shrill tone. 7 convey by pipe. 8 ornament with piping. **piper** n **piping** n 1 system of pipes. 2 decoration of icing on cake. 3 fancy edging on clothes. **pipeline** n long pipe for transporting oil, water etc.
piquant adj pungent.
pique n 1 feeling of injury. ♦ *v* 2 hurt pride of. 3 irritate.
piranha n fierce tropical Amer. fish.
pirate ⊕ n 1 sea robber. 2 publisher etc. who infringes copyright. 3 person broadcasting illegally. ♦ *v* 4 use or reproduce (artistic work etc.) illicitly. **piracy** n
pirouette n/v (perform) act of spinning round on toe.
pistachio n, *pl* **–chios** small hard–shelled, sweet–tasting nut.

piste n ski slope.
pistol n small firearm for one hand.
piston n in engine, cylindrical part propelled to and fro in hollow cylinder.
pit ⊕ n 1 deep hole in ground. 2 mine or its shaft. 3 depression. 4 part of theatre occupied by orchestra. 5 servicing area on motor–racing track. ♦ *v* 6 set to fight, match. 7 mark with small dents. **pitfall** n hidden danger.
pitch¹ ⊕ v 1 throw. 2 set up. 3 set the key of (a tune). 4 fall headlong. ♦ *n* 5 act of pitching. 6 degree, height, intensity. 7 slope. 8 degree of highness or lowness of sound 9 *Sport* field of play.
pitchfork n 1 fork for lifting hay etc. ♦ *v* 2 throw with, as with, pitchfork.
pitch² n dark sticky substance obtained from tar or turpentine.
pitcher n large jug.
pith n 1 tissue in stems and branches of certain plants. 2 essential part. **pithy** adj 1 terse, concise. 2 consisting of pith.
pittance n small amount of

————— THESAURUS —————

discover
pipe n = **tube**, drain, canal, pipeline, line ♦ *v* = **convey**, channel, conduct
pirate n = **buccaneer**, raider, marauder, corsair, freebooter ♦ *v* = **copy**, steal, reproduce, bootleg, appropriate
pit n = **coal mine**, mine, shaft, colliery, mine shaft ♦ *v* = **scar**,

mark, dent, indent, pockmark
pitch¹ n = **sports field**, ground, stadium, arena, park; = **tone**, sound, key, frequency, timbre; = **level**, point, degree, summit, extent; = **talk**, patter, spiel (*Inf*) ♦ *v* = **throw**, cast, toss, hurl, fling; = **fall**, drop, plunge, dive, tumble; = **set up**, raise, settle, put up, erect; = **toss (about)**, roll, plunge,

money.

pituitary *adj, pl* **-taries** of, pert. to, endocrine gland at base of brain.

pity ❶ *n, pl* **pities 1** sympathy for others' suffering. **2** regrettable fact. ♦ *v* **3** feel pity for. **piteous** *adj*

pitiful *adj* **1** woeful. **2** contemptible. **pitiless** *adj* **1** feeling no pity. **2** hard, merciless.

pivot *n* **1** shaft or pin on which thing turns. ♦ *v* **2** furnish with pivot. **3** hinge on one.

pixie *n* fairy.

pizza *n* baked disc of dough covered with savoury topping.

pizzicato *adv/adj Mus* played by plucking strings with finger.

placard *n* notice for posting up or carrying poster.

placate *v* pacify, appease.

place ❶ *n* **1** locality, spot. **2** position. **3** duty. **4** town, village, residence, buildings. **5**

employment. **6** seat, space. ♦ *v* **7** put in particular place. **8** identify. **9** make (order, bet etc.).

placebo *n, pl* **-bos**, **-boes** inactive substance given to patient in place of active drug.

placenta *n, pl* **-tas**, **-tae 1** organ formed in uterus during pregnancy, providing nutrients for fetus. **2** afterbirth.

placid *adj* calm.

plague ❶ *n* **1** highly contagious disease. **2** *Inf* nuisance. ♦ *v* **3** trouble, annoy.

plaice *n* flat fish.

plaid *n* **1** long Highland cloak or shawl. **2** tartan pattern.

plain ❶ *adj* **1** flat, level. **2** not intricate. **3** clear, simple. **4** candid, forthright. **5** ordinary. **6** without decoration. **7** not beautiful. ♦ *n* **8** tract of level country. ♦ *adv* **9** clearly.

plaintiff *n Law* one who sues in

lurch

pity *n* = **compassion**, charity, sympathy, kindness, fellow feeling ≠ **mercilessness**; = **shame**, sin (*Inf*), misfortune, bummer (*Sl*), crying shame ♦ *v* = **feel sorry for**, feel for, sympathize with, grieve for, weep for

place *n* = **spot**, point, position, site, area; = **region**, quarter, district, neighbourhood, vicinity; = **position**, point, spot, location; = **space**, position, seat, chair ♦ *v* = **lay** (down), put (down), set (down), stand, position; = **put**, lay, set, invest, pin; = **classify**, class,

group, put, order; go down (*US & Canad*)

plague *n* = **disease**, infection, epidemic, pestilence; = **infestation**, invasion, epidemic, influx, host ♦ *v* = **torment**, trouble, torture (*Inf*)

plain *adj* = **unadorned**, simple, basic, severe, bare ≠ **ornate**; = **clear**, obvious, patent, evident, visible ≠ **hidden**; = **straightforward**, open, direct, frank, blunt ≠ **roundabout**; = **ugly**, unattractive, homely (*US & Canad*), unlovely, unprepossessing ≠ **attractive**; = **ordinary**, common,

court.

plaintive adj sad, mournful.

plait n 1 braid of hair, straw etc. ◆ v 2 weave into plaits.

plan ❶ n 1 scheme. 2 way of proceeding. 3 project. 4 drawing. 5 map. ◆ v 6 make plan of. 7 arrange beforehand.

plane¹ ❶ n aeroplane.

plane² ❶ n 1 smooth surface. 2 level. 3 tool for smoothing wood. ◆ v 4 make smooth with plane. ◆ adj 5 perfectly flat or level.

plane³ n tree with broad leaves.

planet n heavenly body revolving round sun. **planetary** adj

planetarium n, pl –iums, –ia apparatus that shows movement of sun, moon, stars and planets by projecting lights on inside of dome.

plank n long flat piece of timber.

plankton n minute animal and vegetable organisms floating in ocean.

plant ❶ n 1 living organism without power of locomotion. 2 building and equipment for manufacturing purposes. ◆ v 3 set in ground to grow. 4 establish 5 Sl hide.

plantation n 1 estate for cultivation of tea, tobacco etc. 2 wood of planted trees.

plaque n 1 ornamental tablet. 2 plate of brooch. 3 deposit on teeth.

plasma n clear, fluid portion of blood.

plaster ❶ n 1 mixture of lime, sand etc. for coating walls etc. 2 adhesive dressing for cut, wound etc. ◆ v 3 apply plaster to. 4 apply like plaster. **plastered** adj Sl drunk.

plastic ❶ n 1 synthetic substance, easily moulded and extremely durable. ◆ adj 2 made of plastic. 3 easily moulded. **plastic surgery** repair, reconstruction of part of body for medical or cosmetic reasons.

Plasticine ® n modelling

——————— THESAURUS ———————

simple, everyday, commonplace ≠ sophisticated ◆ n = flatland, plateau, prairie, grassland, steppe

plan n = scheme, system, design, programme, proposal; = diagram, map, drawing, chart, representation ◆ v = devise, arrange, scheme, plot, draft

plane¹ n = aeroplane, aircraft, jet, airliner, jumbo jet

plane² = flat surface, the flat, horizontal, level surface; = level, position, stage, condition, standard ◆ adj = level, even, flat, regular, smooth ◆ v = skim, sail, skate, glide

plant n = flower, bush, vegetable, herb, weed ◆ v = sow, scatter, transplant, implant, put in the ground; = seed, sow, implant

plaster n = mortar, stucco, gypsum, plaster of Paris; = bandage, dressing, sticking plaster, Elastoplast ®, adhesive plaster ◆ v = cover, spread, coat, smear, overlay

plastic adj = pliant, soft, flexible, supple, pliable ≠ rigid

P

material like clay.
plate ⊕ *n* 1 shallow round dish. 2 flat thin sheet of metal, glass etc. 3 utensils of gold or silver. 4 device for printing illustration in book. 5 device to straighten children's teeth. 6 *Inf* denture. ♦ *v* 7 cover with thin coating of metal.
plateau ⊕ *n, pl* **-teaus, -teaux** 1 tract of level high land. 2 period of stability.
platform ⊕ *n* 1 raised level surface, stage. 2 raised area in station from which passengers board trains.
platinum *n* white heavy malleable metal.
platitude *n* commonplace remark.
platonic *adj* (of love) purely spiritual, friendly.
platoon *n* body of soldiers employed as unit.
platter *n* flat dish.
platypus, duck-billed platypus

n Aust. egg-laying amphibious mammal.
plausible ⊕ *adj* 1 apparently reasonable. 2 persuasive.
play ⊕ *v* 1 amuse oneself. 2 contend with in game. 3 take part in (game). 4 trifle. 5 act the part of. 6 perform (music). 7 perform on (instrument). ♦ *n* 8 dramatic piece or performance. 9 sport. 10 amusement. 11 activity. 12 free movement. 13 gambling. **player** *n* **playful** *adj* lively. **playboy** *n* rich man who lives for pleasure.
playing card one of set of 52 cards. **playing fields** extensive piece of ground for open-air games. **playwright** *n* author of plays.
plaza *n* open space or square.
plea ⊕ *n* 1 entreaty. 2 statement of prisoner or defendant. 3 excuse.
plead *v* 1 make earnest appeal. 2 address court of law. 3 bring forward as excuse or plea.

——————— THESAURUS ———————

plate *n* = **platter**, dish, dinner plate, salver, trencher (*Arch*); = **helping**, course, serving, dish, portion; = **layer**, panel, sheet, slab ♦ *v* = **coat**, gild, laminate, cover, overlay
plateau *n* = **upland**, table, highland, tableland; = **levelling off**, level, stage, stability
platform *n* = **stage**, stand, podium, rostrum, dais; = **policy**, programme, principle, objective(s), manifesto
plausible *adj* = **believable**, possible, likely, reasonable,

credible ≠ **unbelievable**; = **glib**, smooth, specious, smooth-talking, smooth-tongued
play *v* = **amuse yourself**, have fun, sport, fool, romp; = **take part in**, be involved in, engage in, participate in, compete in; = **compete against**, challenge, take on, oppose, contend against ♦ *n* = **amusement**, pleasure, leisure, games, sport; = **drama**, show, piece, comedy, tragedy
plea *n* = **appeal**, request, suit, prayer, petition; = **excuse**, defence, explanation, justification

please ⊕ v **1** be agreeable to. **2** gratify. **3** delight. **4** be willing. ♦ adv **5** word of request. **pleasant** adj pleasing, agreeable. **pleasantry** n joke, humour. **pleased** adj **pleasing** adj **pleasurable** adj giving pleasure. **pleasure** n **1** enjoyment. **2** satisfaction.

pleat n **1** fold made by doubling material. ♦ v **2** make into pleats.

plebeian adj/n (one) of the common people.

plectrum n, pl **–trums**, **–tra** small implement for plucking strings of guitar etc.

pledge ⊕ n **1** solemn promise. **2** thing given as security. ♦ v **3** promise, swear.

plenary adj complete.

plenipotentiary adj/n (envoy) having full powers.

plenitude n abundance.

plenty ⊕ n **1** abundance. **2** quite enough. **plenteous** adj ample. **plentiful** adj

plethora n oversupply.

pleurisy n inflammation of membrane lining chest and covering lungs.

pliable adj easily bent or influenced. **pliant** adj pliable.

pliers pl n tool with hinged arms and jaws for gripping.

plight¹ ⊕ n distressing state.

plight² v promise.

plimsolls pl n rubber-soled canvas shoes.

plinth n slab as base of column etc.

plod v **plodding**, **plodded** walk or work doggedly.

plonk¹ v put down heavily and carelessly.

plonk² n Inf cheap inferior wine.

plop n **1** sound of object falling into water without splash. ♦ v **2** fall with this sound.

plot¹ ⊕ n **1** secret plan, conspiracy. **2** essence of story, play etc. ♦ v **3** plan secretly. **4** mark position of. **5** make map of.

plot² ⊕ n small piece of land.

plough ⊕ n **1** implement for turning up soil. ♦ v **2** turn up with plough, furrow. **3** work at slowly. **ploughman** n

plover n shore bird with straight bill and long pointed wings.

——————— THESAURUS ———————

please v = **delight**, entertain, humour, amuse, suit ≠ **annoy**

pledge n = **promise**, vow, assurance, word, undertaking; = **guarantee**, security, deposit, bail, collateral ♦ v = **promise**, vow, swear, contract, engage

plenty n = **abundance**, wealth, prosperity, fertility, profusion; usually with **of** = **lots of**, enough

plight¹ n = **difficulty**, condition, state, situation, trouble

plot¹ n = **plan**, scheme, intrigue, conspiracy, cabal; = **story**, action, subject, theme, outline ♦ v = **plan**, scheme, conspire, intrigue, manoeuvre; = **devise**, design, lay, conceive, hatch

plot² n = **patch**, lot, area, ground, parcel

plough v = **turn over**, dig, till, cultivate

ploy ⊙ *n* manoeuvre designed to gain advantage.

pluck ⊙ *v* 1 pull, pick off. 2 strip from. 3 sound strings of (guitar etc.) with fingers, plectrum. ♦ *n* 4 courage. 5 sudden pull or tug. **plucky** *adj* brave.

plug ⊙ *n* 1 thing fitting into and filling hole. 2 *Electricity* device connecting appliance to electricity supply. 3 *Inf* favourable mention of product etc. intended to promote it. ♦ *v* 4 stop with plug. 5 *Inf* advertise product etc. by frequently mentioning it.

plum ⊙ *n* 1 fruit with stone. 2 tree bearing it. 3 choicest part, piece, position etc. ♦ *adj* 4 choice.

plumb ⊙ *n* 1 ball of lead attached to string used for sounding, finding the perpendicular etc. ♦ *adj* 2 perpendicular. ♦ *adv* 3 exactly. 4 perpendicularly. ♦ *v* 5 find depth of. 6 equip with, connect to plumbing system. **plumber** *n* worker who attends to water and sewage systems. **plumbing** *n* 1 trade of plumber. 2 system of water and sewage pipes. **plumb line** cord with plumb attached.

plume *n* 1 feather. 2 ornament of feathers etc. ♦ *v* 3 furnish with plumes. 4 pride oneself. **plumage** *n* bird's feathers.

plummet ⊙ *v* –meting, –meted 1 plunge headlong. ♦ *n* 2 plumb line.

plump¹ ⊙ *adj* 1 fat, rounded. ♦ *v* 2 make, become plump.

plump² *v* 1 drop, fall abruptly. 2 choose.

plunder ⊙ *v* 1 take by force. 2 rob. ♦ *n* 3 booty, spoils.

plunge ⊙ *v* 1 put forcibly, throw (into). 2 descend suddenly. ♦ *n* 3 dive. **plunger** *n* suction cap to unblock drains. **plunging** *adj* (of neckline) cut low.

plural *adj* 1 of, denoting more than one. ♦ *n* 2 word in its plural form. **plurality** *n* majority.

ploy *n* = **tactic**, move, trick, device, scheme

pluck *v* = **pull out** *or* off pick, draw, collect, gather; = **tug**, catch, snatch, clutch, jerk ♦ *n* = **courage**, nerve, bottle (*Brit sl*), guts (*Inf*), grit

plug *n* = **stopper**, cork, bung, spigot; = (*Inf*) **mention**, advertisement, advert (*Brit inf*), push, publicity ♦ *v* = **seal**, close, stop, fill, block; = (*Inf*) **mention**, push, promote, publicize, advertise

plum *adj* = **choice**, prize, first-class

plumb *v* = **delve into**, explore, probe, go into, penetrate ♦ *adv* = **exactly**, precisely, bang, slap, spot-on (*Brit inf*)

plummet *v* = **drop**, fall, crash, nose-dive, descend rapidly

plump¹ *adj* = **chubby**, fat, stout, round, tubby ≠ **scrawny**

plunder *v* = **loot**, strip, sack, rob, raid

plunge *v* = **descend**, fall, drop, crash, pitch; = **hurtle**, charge, career, jump, tear ♦ *n* = **dive**,

plus ⚊ *prep* **1** with addition of (usu. indicated by the sign +). ◆ *adj* **2** positive.

plush ⚊ *n* **1** fabric with long nap. ◆ *adj* **2** luxurious.

ply¹ ⚊ *v* **plying, plied 1** wield. **2** work at. **3** supply insistently. **4** go to and fro regularly.

ply² *n* **1** fold or thickness. **2** strand of yarn. **plywood** *n* board of thin layers of wood glued together.

PM prime minister.

p.m. after noon.

pneumatic *adj* of, worked by, inflated with wind or air.

pneumonia *n* inflammation of the lungs.

PO Post Office.

poach¹ *v* **1** take (game) illegally. **2** encroach. **poacher** *n*

poach² *v* simmer (eggs, fish etc.) gently in water etc.

pocket ⚊ *n* **1** small bag inserted in garment. **2** cavity, pouch or hollow. **3** isolated group or area. ◆ *v* **4** put into one's pocket. **5** appropriate. ◆ *adj* **6** small. **pocket**

money small allowance, esp. for children.

pod ⚊ *n* long seed vessel, as of peas, beans etc.

podgy *adj* **podgier, podgiest** short and fat.

podium ⚊ *n*, *pl* **-diums, -dia** small raised platform.

poem ⚊ *n* imaginative composition in rhythmic lines.

poet *n* writer of poems. **poetic** *adj*

poetry *n* art or work of poet, verse.

poep *n* Aust & NZ slang emission of gas from the anus.

poet *n* writer of poems.

pogey *n* Canad sl money received from the state while out of work.

poignant ⚊ *adj* **1** moving. **2** keen. **poignancy** *n*

point ⚊ *n* **1** dot. **2** punctuation mark. **3** detail. **4** unit of value, scoring. **5** degree, stage. **6** moment. **7** gist. **8** purpose. **9** special quality. **10** sharp end. **11** headland. **12** direction mark on compass. **13** movable rail changing train to other rails. **14**

——————— THESAURUS ———————

jump, duck, descent

plus *prep* = **and**, with, added to, coupled with ◆ *n* = (*Inf*)

advantage, benefit, asset, gain, extra

plush *adj* = **luxurious**, luxury, lavish, rich, sumptuous ≠ **cheap**

ply¹ *v* = **work at**, follow, exercise, pursue, carry on

pocket *n* = **pouch**, bag, sack, compartment, receptacle ◆ *adj* = **small**, compact, miniature,

portable, little ◆ *v* = **steal**, take, lift (*Inf*), appropriate, pilfer

pod *n* = **shell**, case, hull, husk, shuck

podium *n* = **platform**, stand, stage, rostrum, dais

poem *n* = **verse**, song, lyric, rhyme, sonnet

poet *n* = **bard**, rhymer, lyricist, lyric poet, versifier

poignant *adj* = **moving**, touching, sad, bitter, intense

power point. ♦ v 15 show direction or position by extending finger. 16 direct. 17 sharpen. 18 fill up joints with mortar. **pointed** adj 1 sharp. 2 direct. **pointer** n 1 indicating rod etc. used for pointing. 2 indication. 3 breed of gun dog. **pointless** adj futile. **point–blank** adj 1 at short range. 2 blunt, direct. ♦ adv 3 bluntly.

poise ⊕ n 1 composure. 2 self–possession. 3 balance. **poised** adj 1 ready. 2 showing poise.

poison ⊕ n 1 substance harmful or fatal to living organism. ♦ v 2 give poison to. 3 infect. **poisonous** adj

poke ⊕ v 1 push, thrust with finger, stick etc. 2 thrust forward. 3 pry. ♦ n 4 act of poking. **poker** n metal rod for poking fire. **poky** adj small, confined, cramped.

poker n card game.

pole¹ ⊕ n long, rounded piece of wood etc.

pole² n 1 each of the ends of axis of earth or celestial sphere. 2 each of opposite ends of magnet, electric cell etc. **polar** adj **polarize** v (cause to) form into groups with opposite views. **polar bear** white bear that lives around North Pole.

poleaxe v stun with heavy blow.

polecat n small animal of weasel family.

police ⊕ n 1 civil force which maintains public order. ♦ v 2 keep in order. **policeman** n member of police force.

policy¹ ⊕ n course of action adopted, esp. in state affairs.

policy² n insurance contract.

polio, poliomyelitis n disease affecting spinal cord, often causing paralysis.

polish ⊕ v 1 make smooth and glossy. 2 refine. ♦ n 3 shine. 4 polishing. 5 substance for polishing. 6 refinement.

polite ⊕ adj 1 showing regard for

point n = **essence**, meaning, subject, question, heart; = **purpose**, aim, object, end, reason; = **aspect**, detail, feature, quality, particular; = **place**, area, position, site, spot; = **moment**, time, stage, period, phase; = **stage**, level, position, condition, degree; = **end**, tip, sharp end, top, spur; = **score**, tally, mark, = **headland**, head, cape, promontory ♦ v = **aim**, level, train, direct; = **indicate**, show, signal, point to, gesture towards

poison n = **toxin**, venom, bane

(Arch) ♦ v = **murder**, kill, give someone poison, administer poison to; = **contaminate**, foul, infect, spoil, pollute

poke v = **jab**, push, stick, dig, stab ♦ n = **jab**, dig, thrust, nudge, prod

pole¹ n = **rod**, post, support, staff, bar

police n = **the law** (Inf), police force, constabulary, fuzz (Sl), boys in blue (Inf) ♦ v = **control**, patrol, guard, watch, protect

policy¹ n = **procedure**, plan, action, practice, scheme

polish n = **varnish**, wax, glaze,

others in manners, speech etc. **2** refined, cultured.

politics ❶ *pl n* **1** art of government. **2** political affairs. **politic** *adj* wise, shrewd. **political** *adj* of the state or its affairs. **politician** *n* one engaged in politics.

polka *n* **1** lively dance. **2** music for it. **polka dot** one of pattern of bold spots on fabric etc.

poll ❶ *n* **1** voting. **2** counting of votes. **3** number of votes recorded. **4** survey of opinion. ♦ *v* **5** receive (votes). **6** take votes of. **7** vote. **polling booth** voting place.

pollen *n* fertilizing dust of flower. **pollinate** *v*

pollute *v* **1** make foul. **2** corrupt. **pollution** *n*

polo *n* game like hockey played on horseback. **polo neck** (sweater with) tight turned-over collar.

poltergeist *n* spirit believed to move furniture, throw objects around etc.

polyester *n* synthetic material. **polygamy** *n* custom of being married to several persons at a time. **polygamist** *n*

polygon *n* figure with many angles or sides.

polystyrene *n* synthetic material used esp. as rigid foam for packing etc.

polythene *n* tough light plastic material.

polyunsaturated *adj* pert. to fats that do not form cholesterol in blood.

polyurethane *n* synthetic material used esp. in paints.

pom *n Aust & NZ slang* person from England (also **pommy**).

pomegranate *n* **1** tree. **2** its fruit with thick rind containing many seeds in red pulp.

pommel *n* **1** front of saddle. **2** knob of sword hilt.

pomp *n* splendid display or ceremony.

pompom *n* decorative tuft of ribbon, wool, feathers etc.

pompous *adj* **1** self-important. **2** ostentatious. **3** (of language) inflated, stilted.

pond ❶ *n* small body of still water.

ponder ❶ *v* muse, think over.

ponderous *adj* **1** heavy, unwieldy.

——— THESAURUS ———

lacquer, japan; **= sheen**, finish, glaze, gloss, brightness; **= style**, class (*Inf*), finish, breeding, grace ♦ *v* **= shine**, wax, smooth, rub, buff; *often with* **up = perfect**, improve, enhance, refine, finish
polite *adj* **= mannerly**, civil, courteous, gracious, respectful ≠ **rude**: **= refined**, cultured, civilized, polished, sophisticated

≠ **uncultured**
politics *n* **= affairs of state**, government, public affairs, civics
poll *n* **= survey**, figures, count, sampling, returns; **= election**, vote, voting, referendum, ballot ♦ *v* **= question**, interview, survey, sample, ballot; **= gain**, return, record, register, tally
pond *n* **= pool**, tarn, small lake,

2 boring.

pong n/v Inf (give off) strong unpleasant smell.

pontiff n 1 Pope. 2 bishop.

pontificate v speak dogmatically.

pontoon¹ n flat-bottomed boat or metal drum for use in supporting temporary bridge.

pontoon² n gambling card game.

pony n, pl **ponies** horse of small breed. **ponytail** n long hair tied at back of head.

poodle n pet dog with long curly hair.

pool¹ ❶ n 1 small body of still water. 2 deep place in river or stream. 3 puddle. 4 swimming pool.

pool² ❶ n 1 common fund or resources. 2 group of people, e.g. typists, shared by several employers. 3 collective stakes in various games. ♦ v 4 put in common fund.

poop n ship's stern.

poor ❶ adj 1 having little money.

2 unproductive. 3 inadequate. 4 inferior. 5 miserable, pitiful. **poorly** adj 1 not in good health. ♦ adv 2 in poor manner.

pop ❶ v **popping, popped** 1 (cause to) make small explosive sound. 2 put or place suddenly. ♦ n 3 small explosive sound.

popcorn n maize that puffs up when roasted.

Pope n bishop of Rome and head of R.C. Church.

poplar n tall slender tree.

poplin n corded fabric, usu. of cotton.

poppadom n thin round crisp Indian bread.

poppy n, pl **-pies** bright-flowered plant yielding opium.

Popsicle n US and Canad an ice lolly.

populace n the common people.

popular ❶ adj 1 finding general favour. 2 of, by the people.
popularity n **popularize** v

populate ❶ v fill with inhabitants.

——————— THESAURUS ———————

fish pond, duck pond
ponder v = **think about**, consider, reflect on, contemplate, deliberate about
pool¹ n = **swimming pool**, lido, swimming bath(s) (Brit), bathing pool (Arch); = **pond**, lake, mere, tarn; = **puddle**, drop, patch
pool² n = **supply**, reserve, fallback ♦ v = **combine**, share, merge, put together, amalgamate
poor adj = **impoverished**, broke (Inf), hard up (Inf), short, needy ≠ **rich**; = **unfortunate**, unlucky,

hapless, pitiful, luckless
≠ **fortunate**; = **inferior**, unsatisfactory, mediocre, second-rate, rotten (Inf) ≠ **excellent**;
= **meagre**, inadequate, insufficient, lacking, incomplete ≠ **ample**
pop n = **bang**, report, crack, noise, burst ♦ v = **burst**, crack, snap, bang, explode
popular adj = **well-liked**, liked, in, accepted, favourite ≠ **unpopular**;
= **common**, general, prevailing, current, conventional ≠ **rare**

population *n* (number of) inhabitants. **populous** *adj* thickly populated.

porcelain *n* fine earthenware, china.

porch *n* covered approach to entrance of building.

porcupine *n* rodent covered with long, pointed quills.

pore¹ ❶ *n* minute opening, esp. in skin. **porous** *adj* 1 allowing liquid to soak through. 2 full of pores.

pore² *v* study closely.

pork *n* pig's flesh as food.

pornography ❶ *n* indecent literature, films etc. **pornographic** *adj*

porpoise *n* blunt-nosed sea mammal like dolphin.

porridge *n* soft food of oatmeal etc. boiled in water.

port¹ ❶ *n* (town with) harbour.

port² *n* left side of ship.

port³ *n* strong red wine.

port⁴ *n* opening in side of ship.

porthole *n* small opening or window in side of ship.

portable ❶ *adj* easily carried.

portcullis *n* grating above gateway that can be lowered to block entrance.

portend *v* 1 foretell. 2 be an omen of. **portent** *n* omen.

porter ❶ *n* 1 person employed to carry luggage etc. 2 doorkeeper.

portfolio *n, pl* **–os** 1 flat portable case for loose papers. 2 collection of work, shares etc.

portico *n, pl* **–coes, –cos** porch, covered walkway.

portion ❶ *n* 1 part, share, helping. 2 destiny, lot. ♦ *v* 3 divide into shares.

portly *adj* **–lier, –liest** bulky, stout.

portmanteau *n, pl* **–teaus, –teaux** leather suitcase, esp. one opening into two compartments.

portray ❶ *v* make pictures of, describe. **portrait** *n* likeness of (face of) individual. **portraiture** *n* **portrayal** *n* act of portraying.

pose ❶ *v* 1 place in attitude. 2 put forward. 3 assume attitude. 4 affect or pretend to be a certain character. ♦ *n* 5 attitude, esp. one assumed for effect.

———— THESAURUS ————

populate *v* = **inhabit**, people, live in, occupy, reside in

pore¹ *n* = **opening**, hole, outlet, orifice

pornography *n* = **obscenity**, porn (*Inf*), dirt, filth, indecency

port¹ *n* = **harbour**, haven, anchorage, seaport

portable *adj* = **light**, compact, convenient, handy, manageable

porter *n* = (*Chiefly Brit*) **doorman**, caretaker, janitor, concierge,

gatekeeper

portion *n* = **part**, bit, piece, section, scrap; = **helping**, serving, piece, plateful; = **share**, allowance, lot, measure, quantity

portray *v* = **play**, take the role of, act the part of, represent, personate (*rare*); = **describe**, present, depict, evoke, delineate; = **represent**, draw, paint, illustrate, sketch

pose *v* = **position yourself**, sit,

posh 🟊 *adj* 1 luxurious. 2 upper–class.

position 🟊 *n* 1 place. 2 situation. 3 attitude. 4 status. 5 employment. ♦ *v* 6 place in position.

positive 🟊 *adj* 1 sure. 2 definite. 3 assertive. 4 constructive. 5 not negative. ♦ *n* 6 something positive.

possess 🟊 *v* 1 own. 2 have mastery of. **possession** *n* 1 act of possessing. 2 ownership. ♦ *pl* 3 things a person possesses.

possessive *adj* 1 of, indicating possession. 2 with excessive desire to possess, control.

possible 🟊 *adj* 1 that can, or may, be, exist, happen or be done. 2 worthy of consideration.

possibility *n*, *pl* **-ties** 1 feasibility. 2 chance. **possibly** *adv* perhaps.

possum see OPOSSUM.

post[1] 🟊 *n* 1 upright pole to support or mark something. ♦ *v* 2 display. 3 stick up (on notice board etc.). **poster** *n* large advertisement.

post[2] 🟊 *n* 1 official carrying of letters or parcels. 2 collection or delivery of these. 3 office. 4 situation. 5 place of duty. 6 fort. ♦ *v* 7 put into official box for carriage by post. 8 station (soldiers etc.) in particular spot. **postage** *n* charge for carrying letter. **postal** *adj* **postal order** written order for payment of sum of money. **postcard** *n* stamped card sent by post. **postman** *n* person who collects and delivers post. **postmark** *n* official mark stamped on letters. **post office** place where postal business is conducted. **post–** *comb. form* 1 after, later than, as in *postwar*. 2 after, later

model, arrange yourself; = **put on airs**, posture, show off (*Inf*) ♦ *n* = **posture**, position, bearing, attitude, stance; = **act**, façade, air, front, posturing

posh *adj* (*Inf, chiefly Brit*) = **smart**, grand, stylish, luxurious, classy (*Sl*); = **upper–class**, high–class

position *n* = **location**, place, point, area, post; = **posture**, attitude, arrangement, pose, stance; = **status**, place, standing, footing, station; = **job**, place, post, opening, office; = **place**, standing, rank, status ♦ *v* = **place**, put, set, stand, arrange

positive *adj* = **beneficial**, useful,

practical, helpful, progressive ≠ **harmful**; = **certain**, sure, convinced, confident, satisfied ≠ **uncertain**; = **definite**, real, clear, firm, certain ≠ **inconclusive**; = (*Inf*) **absolute**, complete, perfect, right (*Brit inf*), real

possess *v* = **own**, have, hold, be in possession of, be the owner of; = **be endowed with**, have, enjoy, benefit from, be possessed of

possible *adj* = **feasible**, viable, workable, achievable, practicable ≠ **unfeasible**; = **likely**, potential, anticipated, probable, odds–on ≠ **improbable**; = **conceivable**, likely, credible, plausible,

than.

posterior *adj* **1** later, hind. ♦ *n* **2** buttocks.

posterity *n* **1** later generations. **2** descendants.

posthaste *adv* with great speed.

posthumous *adj* occurring after death.

postmortem *n* medical examination of dead body.

postpone 🔁 *v* put off to later time, defer.

postscript *n* addition to letter, book.

postulate *v* **1** take for granted. ♦ *n* **2** something postulated.

posture 🔁 *n* **1** attitude, position of body. ♦ *v* **2** pose.

posy *n, pl* **-sies** bunch of flowers.

pot 🔁 *n* **1** round vessel. **2** cooking vessel. ♦ *v* **3** put into, preserve in pot. **potluck** *n* whatever is available.

potassium *n* white metallic element.

potato *n, pl* **-toes 1** plant with

tubers grown for food. **2** one of these tubers.

potato chip *n* the US and Canadian term for CRISP.

potent 🔁 *adj* powerful, influential.

potency *n*

potentate *n* ruler.

potential 🔁 *adj* **1** that might exist or act but does not now. ♦ *n* **2** possibility.

pothole *n* **1** hole in surface of road. **2** underground cave.

potion *n* dose of medicine or poison.

potpourri *n* **1** fragrant mixture of dried flower petals. **2** medley.

potter¹ 🔁 *v* work, act in unsystematic way.

potter² *n* maker of earthenware vessel. **pottery** *n* **1** earthenware. **2** where it is made. **3** art of making it.

potty¹ *adj* *Inf* crazy, silly.

potty² *n* bowl used by small child as toilet.

pouch *n* **1** small bag. **2** pocket. ♦

—————— THESAURUS ——————

hypothetical ≠ **inconceivable**

post¹ *v* = **put something up**, display, affix, pin something up

post² *n* = **mail**, collection, delivery, postal service, snail mail (*Inf*); = **correspondence**, letters, cards, mail ♦ *v* = **send (off)**, forward, mail, get off, transmit; **keep someone posted** = **notify**, brief, advise, inform, report to

postpone *v* = **put off**, delay, suspend, adjourn, shelve ≠ **go ahead with**

posture *n* = **bearing**, set, attitude,

stance, carriage ♦ *v* = **show off** (*Inf*), pose, affect, put on airs

pot *n* = **container**, bowl, pan, vessel, basin

potent *adj* = **powerful**, commanding, dynamic, dominant, influential, skookum (*US & Canad*)

potential *adj* = **possible**, future, likely, promising, probable; ♦ *n* = **ability**, possibilities, capacity, capability, aptitude

potter¹ *v usually with* **around** *or* **about** = **mess about**, tinker,

v **3** put into pouch.

poultice *n* soft composition of mustard, kaolin etc., applied hot to sore or inflamed parts of body.

poultry *n* domestic fowls.

pounce ⚫ *v* **1** spring (upon) suddenly, swoop (upon). ◆ *n* **2** swoop, sudden descent.

pound[1] ⚫ *n* enclosure for stray animals or officially removed vehicles.

pound[2] ⚫ *v* **1** beat, thump. **2** crush to pieces or powder. **3** walk, run heavily.

pound[3] *n* **1** British monetary unit. **2** unit of weight equal to 0.454 kg.

pour ⚫ *v* **1** come out in a stream, crowd etc. **2** flow freely. **3** rain heavily. ◆ *v* **4** give out thus.

pout ⚫ *v* **1** thrust out lips to look sulky. ◆ *n* **2** act of pouting.

poverty ⚫ *n* **1** state of being poor. **2** lack of, scarcity.

powder ⚫ *n* **1** solid matter in fine dry particles. **2** medicine in this form. **3** gunpowder. **4** face powder etc. ◆ *v* **5** apply powder to. **6** reduce to powder. **powdery** *adj*

power ⚫ *n* **1** ability to do or act. **2** strength. **3** authority. **4** control. **5** person or thing having authority. **6** mechanical energy. **7** electricity supply. **powerful** *adj* **powerless** *adj*

pp pages.

PQ Quebec.

PR 1 proportional representation. **2** public relations.

practical ⚫ *adj* **1** given to action rather than theory. **2** sensible, realistic. **3** skilled. **practicable** *adj* that can be done, used etc. **practically** *adv* **1** all but. **2** sensibly. **practical joke** trick intended to make someone look foolish.

——————— THESAURUS ———————

dabble, footle (*Inf*)

pounce *v* = **attack**, strike, jump, leap, swoop

pound[1] *n* = **enclosure**, yard, pen, compound, kennels

pound[2] *v* *sometimes with* **on** = **beat**, strike, hammer, batter, thrash; = **crush**, powder, pulverize; = **pulsate**, beat, pulse, throb, palpitate; = **stomp**, tramp, march, thunder (*Inf*)

pour *v* = **let flow**, spill, splash, dribble, drizzle; = **flow**, stream, run, course, rush; = **rain**, pelt (down), teem, bucket down (*Inf*)

pout *v* = **sulk**, glower, look petulant, pull a long face ◆ *n*

= **sullen look**, glower, long face

poverty *n* = **pennilessness**, want, need, hardship, insolvency ≠ **wealth**; = **scarcity**, lack, absence, want, deficit ≠ **abundance**

powder *n* = **dust**, talc, fine grains, loose particles ◆ *v* = **dust**, cover, scatter, sprinkle, strew

power *n* = **control**, authority, influence, command, dominance; = **ability**, capacity, faculty, property, potential ≠ **inability**; = **authority**, right, licence, privilege, warrant

practical *adj* = **functional**, realistic, pragmatic ≠ **impractical**;

practise ⊕ v 1 do repeatedly, work at to gain skill. 2 do habitually. 3 put into action. 4 exercise profession. **practice** n 1 habit. 2 exercise of art or profession. 3 action, not theory.

pragmatic ⊕ adj concerned with practical consequences.

prairie n a treeless grassy plain of the central US and S Canada.

praise ⊕ n 1 commendation. 2 fact of praising. 3 expression of thanks to God. ♦ v 4 express approval, admiration of. 5 express thanks to God. **praiseworthy** adj

pram n carriage for baby.

prance v/n 1 swagger. 2 caper.

prank n mischievous trick.

prattle v talk like child.

prawn n edible sea shellfish like shrimp.

pray ⊕ v 1 ask earnestly. 2

entreat. 3 offer prayers, esp. to God. **prayer** n 1 action, practice of praying to God. 2 earnest entreaty.

pre– comb. form before, as in prerecord, preshrunk.

preach ⊕ v 1 deliver sermon. 2 give moral, religious advice. 3 advocate. **preacher** n

preamble n introductory part of story etc.

precarious ⊕ adj insecure, unstable, perilous.

precaution ⊕ n previous care to prevent evil or secure good.

precede ⊕ v go, come before in rank, order, time etc. **precedence** n priority in position, rank, time etc. **precedent** n previous case or occurrence taken as rule.

precept n rule for conduct.

precinct ⊕ n 1 enclosed, limited

———————— THESAURUS ————————

= **empirical**, real, applied, actual, hands–on ≠ **theoretical**;
= **sensible**, ordinary, realistic, down–to–earth, matter–of–fact ≠ **impractical**; = **feasible**, possible, viable, workable, practicable ≠ **impractical**

practise v = **rehearse**, study, prepare, perfect, repeat; = **do**, train, exercise, drill; = **carry out**, follow, apply, perform, observe

pragmatic adj = **practical**, sensible, realistic, down–to–earth, utilitarian ≠ **idealistic**

praise v = **acclaim**, approve of, honour, cheer, admire ≠ **criticize**; = **give thanks to**, bless, worship, adore, glorify ♦ n = **approval**,

acclaim, tribute, compliment, congratulations ≠ **criticism**;
= **thanks**, glory, worship, homage, adoration

pray v = **say your prayers**, offer a prayer, recite the rosary; = **beg**, ask, plead, petition, request

preach v often with **to** = **deliver a sermon**, address, evangelize, preach a sermon; = **urge**, teach, champion, recommend, advise

precarious adj = **insecure**, dangerous, tricky, risky, dodgy (Brit, Aust & NZ inf) ≠ **secure**

precaution n = **safeguard**, insurance, protection, provision, safety measure

precede v = **go before**, antedate

area. ♦ *pl* **2** environs.
precious ⊕ *adj* **1** beloved, cherished. **2** of great value.
precipice *n* very steep cliff or rock face.
precipitate ⊕ *v* **1** hasten happening of. **2** throw headlong. **3** *Chem* cause to be deposited in solid form from solution. ♦ *adj* **4** too sudden. **5** rash. ♦ *n* **6** substance chemically precipitated. **precipitation** *n* rain, snow etc.
précis *n, pl* **précis 1** summary. ♦ *v* **2** summarize.
precise ⊕ *adj* **1** definite. **2** exact. **3** careful in observance. **precisely** *adv* **precision** *n*
preclude *v* prevent.
precocious *adj* developed, matured early or too soon.
precursor *n* forerunner.
predatory *adj* preying on other animals. **predator** *n*
predecessor ⊕ *n* one who precedes another in office or position.
predicament ⊕ *n* difficult situation.
predict ⊕ *v* foretell, prophesy. **predictable** *adj* **prediction** *n*
predispose *v* **1** incline, influence. **2** make susceptible.
predominate *v* be main or controlling element. **predominance** *n* **predominant** *adj*
pre-eminent *adj* excelling all others. **pre-eminence** *n*
pre-empt *v* do in advance of or to exclusion of others.
preen *v* **1** trim (feather) with beak. **2** smarten oneself.
prefabricated *adj* (of building) manufactured in shaped sections for rapid assembly.
preface *n* **1** introduction to book etc. ♦ *v* **2** introduce.
prefect *n* **1** person put in authority. **2** schoolchild in position of limited authority over others.
prefer ⊕ *v* **-ferring, -ferred 1** like better. **2** promote. **preferable** *adj* more desirable. **preference** *n* **preferential** *adj* special, privileged. **preferment** *n* promotion.

——————— THESAURUS ———————

precinct *n* = **area**, quarter, section, sector, district
precious *adj* = **valuable**, expensive, fine, prized, dear ≠ **worthless**; = **loved**, prized, dear, treasured, darling; = **affected**, artificial, twee (*Brit inf*), overrefined, overnice
precipitate *v* = **quicken**, trigger, accelerate, advance, hurry; = **throw**, launch, cast, hurl, fling ♦ *adj* = **hasty**, rash, reckless, impulsive, precipitous

precise *adj* = **exact**, specific, particular, express, correct ≠ **vague**; = **strict**, particular, exact, formal, careful ≠ **inexact**
predecessor *n* = **previous job holder**, precursor, forerunner, antecedent; = **ancestor**, forebear, antecedent, forefather
predicament *n* = **fix** (*Inf*), situation, spot (*Inf*), hole (*Sl*), mess
predict *v* = **foretell**, forecast, divine, prophesy, augur
prefer *v* = **like better**, favour, go

prefix n **1** group of letters put at beginning of word. ◆ v **2** put as introduction. **3** put as prefix.

pregnant ❶ adj **1** carrying fetus in womb. **2** full of meaning, significant. **pregnancy** n, pl –**cies**

prehistoric adj before period in which written history begins.

prejudice ❶ n **1** preconceived opinion. **2** unreasonable or unfair dislike. ◆ v **3** influence. **4** bias. **5** injure. **prejudicial** adj

preliminary ❶ adj/n preparatory, introductory (action, statement).

prelude ❶ n **1** Mus introductory movement. **2** performance, event etc. serving as introduction.

premature ❶ adj happening, done before proper time.

premeditated adj planned beforehand.

premier ❶ n **1** prime minister. ◆ adj **2** chief, foremost. **3** first.

première n first performance of play etc.

premise ❶, premiss n Logic proposition from which inference is drawn.

premises ❶ pl n house, building with its belongings.

premium ❶ n **1** bonus. **2** sum paid for insurance. **3** excess over nominal value. **4** great value or regard.

premonition n presentiment.

preoccupy v –**pying**, –**pied** occupy to exclusion of other things. **preoccupation** n

preordained adj determined in advance.

prepare ❶ v **1** make, get ready. **2** concoct, make. **preparation** n **1**

——————— THESAURUS ———————

for, pick, fancy

pregnant adj = **expectant**, expecting (Inf), with child, in the club (Brit sl), big or heavy with child; = **meaningful**, pointed, charged, significant, telling

prejudice n = **discrimination**, injustice, intolerance, bigotry, unfairness; = **bias**, preconception, partiality, preconceived notion, prejudgment ◆ v = **bias**, influence, colour, poison, distort; = **harm**, damage, hurt, injure, mar

preliminary adj = **first**, opening, trial, initial, test ◆ n = **introduction**, opening, beginning, start, prelude

prelude n = **introduction**, beginning, start; = **overture**,

opening, introduction, introductory movement

premature adj = **early**, untimely, before time, unseasonable; = **hasty**, rash, too soon, untimely, ill-timed

premier n = **head of government**, prime minister, chancellor, chief minister, P.M. ◆ adj = **chief**, leading, first, highest, head

premise n = **assumption**, proposition, argument, hypothesis, assertion

premises pl n = **building(s)**, place, office, property, site

premium n = **fee**, charge, payment, instalment; = **surcharge**, extra charge, additional fee or charge

P

making ready beforehand. **2** something prepared, as a medicine. **preparatory** *adj* **1** serving to prepare. **2** introductory.
prepared *adj* **1** ready. **2** willing.
preposition *n* word marking relation between noun or pronoun and other words.
prepossessing *v* impressive.
preposterous *adj* utterly absurd, foolish.
prerequisite *n/adj* (something) required as prior condition.
prerogative *n* peculiar power or right, esp. as vested in sovereign.
prescribe ⊕ *v* **1** set out rules for. **2** order use of (medicine).
prescription *n* **1** prescribing. **2** thing prescribed. **3** written statement of it.
present[1] ⊕ *adj* **1** that is here. **2** now existing or happening. ♦ *n* **3** present time or tense. **presence** *n* **1** being present. **2** appearance, bearing. **presently** *adv* **1** soon **2** *US* at present.

present[2] ⊕ *v* **1** introduce formally. **2** show. **3** give. ♦ *n* **4** gift.
presentable *adj* fit to be seen.
presentation *n* **presenter** *n*
presentiment *n* sense of something about to happen.
preserve ⊕ *v* **1** keep from harm, injury or decay. ♦ *n* **2** special area. **3** fruit preserved by cooking in sugar. **4** place where game is kept for private fishing, shooting. **preservation** *n* **preservative** *n* **1** preserving agent. ♦ *adj* **2** preserving.
preside ⊕ *v* be in charge.
presidency *n* **president** *n* head of society, company, republic etc.
presidential *adj*
press ⊕ *v* **1** subject to push or squeeze. **2** smooth. **3** urge. **4** throng. **5** hasten. ♦ *n* **6** machine for pressing, esp. printing machine. **7** printing house. **8** newspapers and journalists collectively. **9** crowd. **pressing** *adj* **1** urgent. **2** persistent.

——— THESAURUS ———

prepare *v* = **make** *or* **get ready**, arrange, adapt, adjust
prescribe *v* = **specify**, order, direct, stipulate, write a prescription for
present[1] *adj* = **current**, existing, immediate, contemporary, present–day; = **here**, there, near, ready, nearby ≠ **absent**
present[2] *n* = **gift**, offering, grant, donation, hand–out ♦ *v* = **give**, award, hand over, grant, hand out; = **put on**, stage, perform, give, show; = **launch**, display,

parade, exhibit, unveil
preserve *v* = **maintain**, keep, continue, sustain, keep up ≠ **end**; = **protect**, keep, save, maintain, defend ≠ **attack** ♦ *n* = **area**, department, field, territory, province
preside *v* = **officiate**, chair, moderate, be chairperson
press *v* = **push (down)**, depress, lean on, press down, force down; = **push**, squeeze, jam, thrust, ram; = **hug**, squeeze, embrace, clasp, crush; = **urge**, beg, petition,

pressure ⊕ n 1 act of pressing. 2 compelling force 3 *Physics* thrust per unit area.

prestige ⊕ n 1 reputation. 2 influence depending on it. **prestigious** *adj*

presto *adv Mus* very quickly.

presume ⊕ v 1 take for granted. 2 take liberties. **presumably** *adv*

presumption n 1 forward, arrogant opinion or conduct. 2 strong probability. **presumptive** *adj* that may be assumed is true or valid until contrary is proved. **presumptuous** *adj* forward, impudent.

presuppose v assume or take for granted beforehand. **presupposition** n

pretend ⊕ v 1 claim or allege (something untrue). 2 make believe. 3 lay claim (to). **pretence** n simulation. **pretender** n claimant

(to throne). **pretension** n

pretentious *adj* 1 making claim to special merit or importance. 2 given to outward show.

pretext n 1 excuse. 2 pretence.

pretty ⊕ *adj* –tier, –tiest 1 appealing in a delicate way. ♦ *adv* 2 moderately.

prevail ⊕ v 1 gain mastery. 2 be generally established. **prevalent** *adj* 1 widespread. 2 predominant.

prevaricate v tell lies or speak evasively. **prevaricator** n

prevent ⊕ v stop, hinder. **prevention** n **preventive** *adj/n*

preview ⊕ n advance showing.

previous ⊕ *adj* 1 preceding. 2 happening before. **previously** *adv*

prey ⊕ n 1 animal hunted by another for food. 2 victim. ♦ v 3 treat as prey. 4 worry, obsess.

price ⊕ n 1 that for which thing is

———————— THESAURUS ————————

exhort, implore; **= plead**, present, lodge, submit, tender; **= compress**, grind, reduce, mill, crush; **= crowd**, push, gather, surge, flock

pressure n **= force**, crushing, squeezing, compressing, weight; **= power**, influence, force, constraint, sway; **= stress**, demands, strain, heat, load

prestige n **= status**, standing, credit, reputation, honour

presume v **= believe**, think, suppose, assume, guess (*informal, chiefly US & Canad*); **= dare**, venture, go so far as, take the liberty, make so bold as

pretend v **= feign**, affect, assume, allege, fake; **= make believe**, suppose, imagine, act, make up

pretty *adj* **= attractive**, beautiful, lovely, charming, fair ≠ **plain** ♦ *adv* **= (Inf) fairly**, rather, quite, kind of (*Inf*), somewhat

prevail v **= win**, succeed, triumph, overcome, overrule; **= be widespread**, abound, predominate, be current, be prevalent

prevent v **= stop**, avoid, frustrate, hamper, foil ≠ **help**

preview n **= sample**, sneak preview, trailer, taster, foretaste

previous *adj* **= earlier**, former,

P

bought or sold. **2** cost. ◆ v **3** fix, ask price for. **priceless** adj invaluable. **pricey** adj **pricier**, **priciest** Inf expensive.

prick 🟶 v **1** pierce slightly. **2** cause to feel sharp pain. ◆ n **3** slight hole made by pricking. **4** sting. **prickle** n **1** thorn, spike. ◆ v **2** feel pricking sensation. **prickly** adj **1** thorny. **2** stinging. **3** touchy.

pride 🟶 n **1** too high an opinion of oneself. **2** worthy self-esteem. **3** great satisfaction. **4** something causing this. **5** best part of something. **pride oneself** take pride.

priest 🟶 n official minister of religion. **priesthood** n

prig n smug self-righteous person. **priggish** adj

prim adj **primmer**, **primmest** formal and prudish.

primacy n, pl **-cies** supremacy. **prima donna** female opera singer.

primary 🟶 adj **1** chief. **2** earliest. **3** elementary.

primate¹ n one of order of mammals including monkeys and man.

primate² n archbishop.

prime 🟶 adj **1** fundamental. **2** original. **3** chief. **4** best. ◆ n **5** first, best part of anything. ◆ v **6** prepare for use. **primer** n paint for preliminary coating. **Prime Minister** leader of government.

primeval adj of earliest age of the world.

primitive 🟶 adj **1** of an early undeveloped kind. **2** crude.

primrose n **1** pale yellow spring flower. **2** this colour. ◆ adj **3** of this colour.

prince 🟶 n **1** male member of royal family. **2** ruler, chief. **princely** adj **1** generous. **2** magnificent. **princess** n female member of royal family.

past, prior, preceding ≠ **later**
prey n = **quarry**, game, kill; = **victim**, target, mug (Brit sl), dupe, fall guy (Inf)
price n = **cost**, value, rate, charge, figure; = **consequences**, penalty, cost, result, toll ◆ v = **evaluate**, value, estimate, rate, cost
prick v = **pierce**, stab, puncture, punch, lance ◆ n = **puncture**, hole, wound, perforation, pinhole
pride n = **satisfaction**, achievement, fulfilment, delight, content; = **self-respect**, honour, ego, dignity, self-esteem; = **conceit**, vanity, arrogance,

pretension, hubris ≠ **humility**
priest n = **clergyman**, minister, father, divine, vicar
primary adj = **chief**, main, first, highest, greatest ≠ **subordinate**
prime adj = **main**, leading, chief, central, major; = **best**, top, select, highest, quality ◆ n = **peak**, flower, bloom, height, heyday ◆ v = **inform**, tell, train, coach, brief
primitive adj = **early**, first, earliest, original, primary ≠ **modern**; = **crude**, simple, rough, rudimentary, unrefined ≠ **elaborate**
prince n = **ruler**, lord, monarch,

principal 🛈 *adj* **1** chief in importance. ♦ *n* **2** person for whom another is agent. **3** head of institution, esp. school or college. **4** sum of money lent and yielding interest. **principality** *n* territory of prince.

principle 🛈 *n* **1** moral rule. **2** settled reason of action. **3** uprightness. **4** fundamental truth.

print 🛈 *v* **1** reproduce (words, pictures etc.) by pressing inked types on blocks of paper etc. **2** write in imitation of this. **3** *Photog* produce pictures from negatives. **4** stamp (fabric) with design. ♦ *n* **5** printed matter. **6** photograph. **7** impression left by something pressing. **8** printed cotton fabric. **printer** *n*

prior 🛈 *adj* **1** earlier. ♦ *n* **2** leader of religious house or order. **priority** *n* precedence, something given special attention. **priory** *n, pl* –**ries** monastery, nunnery under

prior, prioress. **prior to** before.

prise *v* force open by levering.

prism *n* transparent solid, usu. with triangular ends and rectangular sides, used to disperse light into spectrum.

prison 🛈 *n* jail. **prisoner** *n* **1** one kept in prison. **2** captive.

pristine *adj* completely new and pure.

private 🛈 *adj* **1** secret, not public. **2** not general, individual. **3** personal. **4** secluded. **5** denoting soldier of lowest rank. ♦ *n* **6** private soldier. **privacy** *n* **privatize** *v* transfer (service etc.) from public to private ownership.

privation *n* lack of comforts or necessities.

privet *n* bushy evergreen shrub used for hedges.

privilege *n* right, advantage granted or belonging only to few. **privileged** *adj* enjoying privilege.

privy *adj* **1** admitted to

——————— THESAURUS ———————

sovereign, crown prince

principal *adj* = **main**, leading, chief, prime, first ≠ **minor** ♦ *n* = **headmaster** *or* headmistress head (*Inf*), dean, head teacher, rector; = **star**, lead, leader, prima ballerina, leading man *or* lady; = **capital**, money, assets, working capital

principle *n* = **morals**, standards, ideals, honour, virtue; = **rule**, law, truth, canon

print *v* = **run off**, publish, copy, reproduce, issue; = **publish**, release, circulate, issue,

disseminate; ♦ *n* = **photograph**, photo, snap; = **picture**, plate, etching, engraving, lithograph; = **copy**, photo (*Inf*), picture, reproduction, replica

prior *adj* = **earlier**, previous, former, preceding, foregoing

prison *n* = **jail**, confinement, nick (*Brit sl*), cooler (*Sl*), jug (*Sl*)

private *adj* = **exclusive**, individual, privately owned, own, special ≠ **public**; = **secret**, confidential, covert, unofficial, clandestine ≠ **public**; = **personal**, individual, secret, intimate, undisclosed

knowledge of secret. ♦ n 2 lavatory.

prize ❶ n 1 reward given for success in competition. 2 thing striven for. 3 thing won, e.g. in lottery etc. ♦ adj 4 winning or likely to win prize. ♦ v 5 value highly.

pro¹ adj/adv in favour of. **pros and cons** arguments for and against.

pro² n professional.

pro– comb. form 1 in favour of. 2 instead of.

probable ❶ adj likely. **probability** n, pl **–ties** 1 likelihood. 2 anything probable. **probably** adv

probate n 1 proving of authenticity of will. 2 certificate of this.

probation ❶ n 1 system of dealing with lawbreakers by placing them under supervision. 2 trial period. **probationer** n person on probation.

probe ❶ v 1 search into, examine, question closely. ♦ n 2 that which

probes, or is used to probe. 3 thorough inquiry.

probity n honesty, integrity.

problem ❶ n 1 matter etc. difficult to deal with or solve. 2 question set for solution. **problematical** adj

proceed ❶ v 1 go forward, continue. 2 be carried on. 3 arise from. 4 go to law. **procedure** n act, manner of proceeding. **proceeding** n 1 act or course of action. ♦ pl 2 minutes of meeting. 3 legal action. **proceeds** pl n profit.

process ❶ n 1 series of actions or changes. 2 method of operation. 3 state of going on. 4 action of law. ♦ v 5 handle, treat, prepare by special method of manufacture etc. **procession** n train of persons in formal order.

proclaim ❶ v announce publicly, declare. **proclamation** n

procrastinate v put off, delay. **procrastination** n

procreate v produce offspring.

prize n = **reward**, cup, award, honour, medal ♦ adj = **champion**, best, winning, top, outstanding

probable adj = **likely**, possible, apparent, reasonable to think, credible ≠ **unlikely**

probation n = **trial period**, trial, apprenticeship

probe v often with **into** = **examine**, go into, investigate, explore, search; = **explore**, examine, poke, prod, feel around ♦ n = **investigation**, study, inquiry, analysis, examination

problem n = **difficulty**, trouble, dispute, plight, obstacle; = **puzzle**, question, riddle, enigma, conundrum

proceed v = **begin**, go ahead; = **continue**, go on, progress, carry on, go ahead ≠ **discontinue**

process n = **procedure**, means, course, system, action; = **development**, growth, progress, movement, advance ♦ v = **handle**, manage, action, deal with, fulfil

proclaim v = **announce**, declare, advertise, publish, indicate ≠ **keep**

procreation n

procure v 1 obtain, acquire. 2 bring about. 3 act as pimp. **procurement** n **procurer** n 1 one who procures. 2 pimp.

prod ⊕ v **prodding, prodded** 1 poke. ♦ n 2 prodding. 3 pointed instrument.

prodigal adj 1 wasteful. ♦ n 2 spendthrift.

prodigy ⊕ n, pl **-gies** 1 person with most marvellous gift. 2 thing causing wonder. **prodigious** adj 1 very great. 2 extraordinary.

produce ⊕ v 1 bring into existence. 2 yield. 3 bring forward. 4 manufacture. 5 present on stage, film, television. ♦ n 6 that which is yielded or made. **producer** n **product** n 1 thing produced. 2 consequence. **production** n 1 producing. 2 staging of play etc. **productive** adj 1 fertile. 2 creative. **productivity** n

profane adj 1 irreverent, blasphemous. 2 not sacred. ♦ v 3 treat irreverently. **profanity** n, pl **-ties** profane talk.

profess ⊕ v 1 affirm belief in. 2 claim, pretend. **profession** n 1 calling or occupation, esp. learned, scientific or artistic. 2 professing. **professional** adj 1 engaged in a profession. 2 taking part in sport, music etc. for money. 3 skilled. ♦ n 4 paid player. **professor** n teacher of highest rank in university.

proffer v offer.

proficient adj 1 skilled. 2 expert. **proficiency** n

profile ⊕ n 1 outline, esp. of face, as seen from side. 2 brief biographical sketch.

profit ⊕ n 1 money gained. 2 benefit obtained. ♦ v 3 benefit. 4 earn. **profitable** adj **profiteer** n 1 one who makes excessive profits at public's expense. ♦ v 2 profit thus.

profligate adj 1 recklessly extravagant. 2 depraved, immoral.

secret

prod v = **poke**, push, dig, shove, nudge; = **prompt**, move, urge, motivate, spur ♦ n = **poke**, push, dig, shove, nudge; = **prompt**, signal, cue, reminder, stimulus

prodigy n = **genius**, talent, wizard, mastermind, whizz (Inf)

produce v = **cause**, effect, generate, bring about, give rise to; = **make**, create, develop, manufacture, construct; = **create**, develop, write, turn out, compose; = **yield**, provide, grow, bear, give

♦ n = **fruit and vegetables**, goods, food, products, crops

profess v = **claim**, allege, pretend, fake, make out; = **state**, admit, announce, declare, confess

profile n = **outline**, lines, form, figure, silhouette; = **biography**, sketch, vignette, characterization, thumbnail sketch

profit n often plural = **earnings**, return, revenue, gain, yield ≠ **loss**; = **benefit**, good, use, value, gain ≠ **disadvantage** ♦ v = **make money**, gain, earn; = **benefit**,

profound ⓘ *adj* 1 very learned. 2 deep. 3 heartfelt. **profundity** *n*, *pl* –ties

profuse *adj* abundant. **profusion** *n*

progeny *n*, *pl* –nies children. **progenitor** *n* ancestor.

prognosis *n*, *pl* –noses forecast.

programme ⓘ *n* 1 plan of intended proceedings. 2 broadcast on radio or television. **program** *n* 1 instructions for computer. ◆ *v* 2 feed program into (computer). 3 arrange program.

progress ⓘ *n* 1 onward movement. 2 sequence. ◆ *v* 3 go forward. 4 improve. **progression** *n* 1 moving forward. 2 improvement. **progressive** *adj* 1 progressing by degrees. 2 favouring political or social reform.

prohibit ⓘ *v* forbid. **prohibition** *n* 1 act of forbidding. 2 ban on sale or drinking of alcohol. **prohibitive**

adj 1 tending to forbid or exclude. 2 (of cost) too high to be afforded.

project ⓘ *n* 1 plan, scheme. ◆ *v* 2 plan. 3 throw. 4 cause to appear on distant background. 5 stick out. **projectile** *n* heavy missile.

projection *n* 1 bulge. 2 forecast. **projector** *n* apparatus for projecting photographic images.

proletariat *n* working class. **proletarian** *adj*/*n*

proliferate *v* grow or reproduce rapidly. **proliferation** *n*

prolific ⓘ *adj* 1 fruitful. 2 producing much.

prologue *n* preface.

prolong ⓘ *v* lengthen.

promenade *n* 1 leisurely walk. 2 place made or used for this. ◆ *v* 3 take leisurely walk.

prominent ⓘ *adj* 1 sticking out. 2 conspicuous. 3 distinguished. **prominence** *n*

promiscuous *adj* indiscriminate,

———— THESAURUS ————

help, serve, gain, promote
profound *adj* = **sincere**, acute, intense, great, keen ≠ **insincere**; = **wise**, learned, deep, penetrating, philosophical ≠ **uninformed**

programme *n* = **schedule**, plan, agenda, timetable, listing; = **course**, curriculum, syllabus

progress *n* = **development**, growth, advance, gain, improvement ≠ **regression**; = **movement forward**, passage, advancement, course, advance ≠ **movement backward** ◆ *v* = **move on**, continue, travel,

advance, proceed ≠ **move back**; = **develop**, improve, advance, grow, gain ≠ **get behind**

prohibit *v* = **forbid**, ban, veto, outlaw, disallow ≠ **permit**; = **prevent**, restrict, stop, hamper, hinder ≠ **allow**

project *n* = **scheme**, plan, job, idea, campaign ◆ *v* = **forecast**, expect, estimate, predict, reckon; = **stick out**, extend, stand out, bulge, protrude

prolific *adj* = **productive**, creative, fertile, inventive, copious

prolong *v* = **lengthen**, continue, perpetuate, draw out, extend

esp. in sexual relations.
promiscuity n
promise ❶ v 1 give undertaking or assurance. 2 be likely to. ◆ n 3 undertaking to do or not to do something. 4 potential. **promising** adj 1 showing good signs, hopeful. 2 likely to succeed.
promontory n, pl **–ries** high land jutting out into sea.
promote ❶ v 1 help forward. 2 move up to higher rank or position. 3 encourage sale of. **promoter** n **promotion** n
prompt ❶ adj 1 done at once. 2 punctual. ◆ adv 3 punctually. ◆ v 4 urge, suggest. 5 help (actor or speaker) by suggesting next words. ◆ n 6 cue, reminder. **promulgate** v proclaim, publish.
prone ❶ adj 1 lying face

downwards. 2 inclined (to).
prong n one spike of fork or similar instrument.
pronoun n word used to replace noun.
pronounce ❶ v 1 utter (formally). 2 give opinion. **pronounced** adj strongly marked. **pronouncement** n declaration. **pronunciation** n way word etc. is pronounced.
proof ❶ n 1 evidence. 2 thing which proves. 3 test, demonstration. 4 trial impression from type or engraved plate. 5 standard of strength of alcoholic drink. ◆ adj 6 giving impenetrable defence against.
prop¹ ❶ n/v support.
prop² n object used on set of film, play etc.
propaganda ❶ n organized

————————— THESAURUS —————————

≠ **shorten**

prominent adj = **famous**, leading, top, important, main ≠ **unknown**; = **noticeable**, obvious, outstanding, pronounced, conspicuous ≠ **inconspicuous**
promise v = **guarantee**, pledge, vow, swear, contract; = **seem likely**, look like, show signs of, augur, betoken ◆ n = **guarantee**, word, bond, vow, commitment; = **potential**, ability, talent, capacity, capability
promote v = **help**, back, support, aid, forward ≠ **impede**; = **advertise**, sell, hype, publicize, push; = **raise**, upgrade, elevate, exalt ≠ **demote**
prompt v = **cause**, occasion,

provoke, give rise to, elicit; = **remind**, assist, cue, help out ◆ adj = **immediate**, quick, rapid, instant, timely ≠ **slow** ◆ adv = (Inf) **exactly**, sharp, promptly, on the dot, punctually
prone adj = **liable**, given, subject, inclined, tending ≠ **disinclined**; = **face down**, flat, horizontal, prostrate, recumbent ≠ **face up**
pronounce v = **say**, speak, sound, articulate, enunciate; = **declare**, announce, deliver, proclaim, decree
proof n = **evidence**, demonstration, testimony, confirmation, verification ◆ adj = **impervious**, strong, resistant, impenetrable, repellent

P

dissemination of information to assist or damage political cause etc.

propagate v **1** reproduce, breed. **2** spread. **propagation** n

propel v **–pelling, –pelled** cause to move forward. **propeller** n revolving shaft with blades for driving ship or aircraft. **propulsion** n act of driving forward.

propensity n, pl **–ties 1** inclination. **2** tendency.

proper ⓘ adj **1** appropriate. **2** correct. **3** conforming to etiquette. **4** strict. **5** (of noun) denoting individual person or place. **properly** adv

property ⓘ n, pl **–ties 1** that which is owned. **2** land, real estate. **3** quality, attribute.

prophet ⓘ n **1** inspired teacher or revealer of God's word. **2** foreteller of future. **prophecy** n, pl **–cies** prediction, prophetic utterance.

prophesy v **–sying, –sied** foretell. **prophetic** adj

proponent n one who argues in favour of something.

proportion ⓘ n **1** relative size or number. **2** due relation between connected things or parts. **3** share. ◆ pl **4** dimensions. ◆ v **5** arrange proportions of. **proportional, proportionate** adj in due proportion.

propose ⓘ v **1** put forward for consideration. **2** intend. **3** offer marriage. **proposal** n **proposition** n **1** offer. **2** statement.

propound v put forward for consideration.

proprietor n owner.

propriety n, pl **–ties** properness, correct conduct.

propulsion see PROPEL.

prosaic adj commonplace, unromantic.

proscribe v outlaw, condemn.

———— THESAURUS ————

prop[1] v = **lean**, place, set, stand, position ◆ n = **support**, stay, brace, mainstay, buttress

propaganda n = **information**, advertising, promotion, publicity, hype

proper adj = **real**, actual, genuine, true, bona fide; = **correct**, accepted, established, appropriate, right ≠ **improper**; = **polite**, right, becoming, seemly, fitting ≠ **unseemly**

property n = **possessions**, goods, effects, holdings, capital; = **land**, holding, estate, real estate, freehold; = **quality**, feature,

characteristic, attribute, trait

prophet n = **soothsayer**, forecaster, diviner, oracle, seer

proportion n = **part**, share, amount, division, percentage; = **relative amount**, relationship, ratio; = **balance**, harmony, correspondence, symmetry, concord ◆ pl n = **dimensions**, size, volume, capacity, extent

propose v = **put forward**, present, suggest, advance, submit; = **intend**, mean, plan, aim, design; = **nominate**, name, present, recommend; = **offer marriage**, pop the question (Inf), ask for

prose n speech or writing not in verse.

prosecute ⓣ v carry on, bring legal proceedings against. **prosecution** n **prosecutor** n

prospect ⓣ n 1 expectation, chance for success. 2 view. **prospective** adj 1 anticipated. 2 future. **prospector** n **prospectus** n booklet giving details of university, company etc.

prosper v be successful. **prosperity** n **prosperous** adj 1 successful. 2 well-off.

prostate n gland around neck of male bladder.

prostitute ⓣ n 1 one who offers sexual intercourse in return for payment. ◆ v 2 make a prostitute of. 3 put to unworthy use. **prostitution** n

prostrate adj 1 lying flat. 2 overcome. ◆ v 3 throw flat on ground. 4 reduce to exhaustion.

protagonist ⓣ n 1 leading

character in story. 2 proponent.

protect ⓣ v keep from harm. **protection** n **protective** adj **protector** n

protégé n one under another's patronage.

protein n any of group of organic compounds which form essential part of food of living creatures.

protest ⓣ n 1 declaration or demonstration of objection. ◆ v 2 object. 3 make declaration against. 4 assert formally. **protestation** n strong declaration.

Protestant adj 1 relating to Christian church split from R.C. church. ◆ n 2 member of Protestant church.

protocol ⓣ n diplomatic etiquette.

proton n positively charged particle in nucleus of atom.

prototype ⓣ n original, model, after which thing is copied.

protract v 1 lengthen. 2 prolong.

————————— THESAURUS —————————

someone's hand (in marriage)

prosecute v = (Law) **take someone to court**, try, sue, indict, arraign

prospect n = **likelihood**, chance, possibility, hope, promise; = **idea**, outlook ◆ pl n = **possibilities**, chances, future, potential, expectations ◆ v = **look**, search, seek, dowse

prosper v = **succeed**, advance, progress, thrive, get on

prostitute n = **whore**, hooker (US sl), pro (Sl), tart (Inf), call girl ◆ v = **cheapen**, sell out, pervert,

degrade, devalue

protagonist n = **supporter**, champion, advocate, exponent; = **leading character**, principal, central character, hero or heroine

protect v = **keep someone safe**, defend, support, save, guard ≠ endanger

protest v = **object**, demonstrate, oppose, complain, disagree; = **assert**, insist, maintain, declare, affirm ◆ n = **demonstration**, march, rally, sit-in, demo (Inf)

protocol n = **code of behaviour**, manners, conventions, customs,

protractor n instrument for measuring angles.
protrude v stick out, project.
protrusion n
protuberant adj bulging out.
proud ❶ adj 1 pleased, satisfied. 2 arrogant, haughty.
prove ❶ v proving, proved, proved 1 establish validity of. 2 demonstrate, test. 3 turn out to be. **proven** adj proved.
proverb n short, pithy saying in common use. **proverbial** adj
provide ❶ v 1 make preparation. 2 supply, equip. **provided that** on condition that.
province ❶ n 1 division of country. 2 sphere of action. ◆ pl 3 any part of country outside capital. **provincial** adj 1 of a province. 2 narrow in outlook. ◆ n 3 unsophisticated person. 4 inhabitant of province.

provision ❶ n 1 providing, esp. for the future. 2 thing provided. ◆ pl 3 food. ◆ v 4 supply with food.
provisional adj temporary.
proviso n, pl –sos, –soes condition.
provoke ❶ v 1 anger. 2 arouse. 3 cause. **provocation** n **provocative** adj
prow n bow of vessel.
prowess ❶ n 1 bravery. 2 skill.
prowl v 1 roam stealthily, esp. in search of prey or booty. ◆ n 2 prowling. **prowler** n
proximity ❶ n nearness.
proxy n, pl proxies 1 authorized agent or substitute. 2 writing authorizing one to act as this.
prude n one who is excessively modest or proper. **prudish** adj
prudent ❶ adj 1 careful, discreet. 2 sensible. 3 thrifty. **prudence** n
prune[1] n dried plum.

etiquette
prototype n = **original**, model, first, example, standard
proud adj = **satisfied**, pleased, content, thrilled, glad ≠ **dissatisfied**; = **conceited**, arrogant, lordly, imperious, overbearing ≠ **humble**
prove v = **turn out**, come out, end up; = **verify**, establish, determine, show, confirm ≠ **disprove**
provide v = **supply**, give, distribute, outfit, equip ≠ **withhold**; = **give**, bring, add, produce, present
province n = **region**, section,

district, zone, patch; = **area**, business, concern, responsibility, line
provision n = **supplying**, giving, providing, supply, delivery; = **condition**, term, requirement, demand, rider
provoke v = **anger**, annoy, irritate, infuriate, hassle (Inf) ≠ **pacify**; = **rouse**, cause, produce, promote, occasion ≠ **curb**
prowess n = **skill**, ability, talent, expertise, genius ≠ **inability**; = **bravery**, daring, courage, heroism, mettle ≠ **cowardice**
proximity n = **nearness**, closeness
proxy n = **representative**, agent,

prune² ⊕ v 1 cut out dead parts, excessive branches etc. 2 shorten, reduce.

pry v **prying, pried** make furtive or impertinent inquiries.

PS postscript.

psalm n sacred song.

pseudo– comb. form false.

pseudonym n 1 false, fictitious name. 2 pen name.

psychic ⊕ adj 1 of soul or mind. 2 sensitive to phenomena lying outside range of normal experience. **psychiatric** adj of psychiatry. **psychiatrist** n **psychiatry** n medical treatment of mental diseases. **psychoanalysis** n method of studying and treating mental disorders. **psychoanalyse** v **psychoanalyst** n psychological adj 1 of psychology. 2 of the mind. **psychologist** n **psychology** n 1 study of mind. 2 person's mental make–up. **psychopath** n person afflicted with severe mental disorder. **psychopathic** adj **psychosis** n severe mental disorder. **psychosomatic** adj (of a physical disorder) thought to have psychological causes.

psychotherapy n treatment of disease by psychological, not physical, means.

PTO please turn over.

pub ⊕ n public house, building with bar and licence to sell alcoholic drinks.

puberty n sexual maturity.

pubic adj of the lower abdomen.

public ⊕ adj 1 of or concerning the community as a whole. 2 not private. ♦ n 3 the community or its members. **publican** n keeper of public house. **public house** see PUB. **public school** Brit private fee–paying school.

publicity ⊕ n 1 process of attracting public attention. 2 attention thus gained. **publicize** v advertise.

publish ⊕ v 1 prepare and issue for sale (books, music etc.). 2 make generally known. 3 proclaim. **publication** n **publisher** n

———— THESAURUS ————

deputy, substitute, factor

prudent adj = **cautious**, careful, wary, discreet, vigilant ≠ careless; = **wise**, politic, sensible, shrewd, discerning ≠ unwise; = **thrifty**, economical, sparing, careful, canny ≠ extravagant

prune² v = **cut**, trim, clip, dock, shape; = **reduce**, cut, cut back, trim, cut down

psychic adj = **supernatural**, mystic, occult; = **mystical**, spiritual, magical, other–worldly, paranormal

pub n = **tavern**, bar, inn, saloon

public n = **people**, society, community, nation, everyone ♦ adj = **civic**, government, state, national, local; = **general**, popular, national, shared, common; = **open**, accessible, communal, unrestricted ≠ private; = **well–known**, leading, important, respected, famous

publicity n = **advertising**, press, promotion, hype, boost

P

puck n rubber disc used instead of ball in ice hockey.

pucker v **1** gather into wrinkles. ♦ n **2** crease, fold.

pudding ⊕ n **1** sweet, cooked dessert, often made from suet, flour etc. **2** sweet course of meal. **3** soft savoury dish with pastry or batter. **4** kind of sausage.

puddle n small muddy pool.

puerile adj childish.

puff ⊕ n **1** short blast of breath, wind etc. **2** type of pastry. **3** laudatory notice or advertisement. ♦ v **4** blow abruptly. **5** breathe hard. **6** send out in a puff. **7** inflate. **8** advertise. **9** smoke hard.

puffy adj swollen.

puffin n sea bird with large brightly-coloured beak.

pug n small snub-nosed dog.

pugnacious adj given to fighting.

pugnacity n

pull ⊕ v **1** exert force on object to move it towards source of force. **2** remove. **3** strain or stretch. **4** attract. ♦ n **5** act of pulling. **6**

force exerted by this. **7** Inf influence.

pulley n wheel with groove in rim for cord, used to raise weights.

pullover n jersey, sweater without fastening, to be pulled over head.

pulmonary adj of lungs.

pulp ⊕ n **1** soft, moist, vegetable or animal matter. **2** flesh of fruit. **3** any soft soggy mass. ♦ v **4** reduce to pulp.

pulpit n (enclosed) platform for preacher.

pulse[1] ⊕ n **1** movement of blood in arteries corresponding to heartbeat, discernible to touch, e.g. in wrist. **2** any regular beat or vibration. **pulsate** v throb, quiver. **pulsation** n

pulse[2] n edible seed of pod-bearing plant.

pulverize v reduce to powder.

puma n large Amer. feline carnivore, cougar.

pumice n light porous variety of lava.

pummel v **-melling, -melled** strike

publish v = **put out**, issue, produce, print; = **announce**, reveal, spread, advertise, broadcast

pudding n = **dessert**, afters (Brit inf), sweet, pud (Inf)

puff v = **smoke**, draw, drag (SI), suck, inhale; = **breathe heavily**, pant, exhale, blow, gasp ♦ n = **drag**, pull (SI), moke; = **blast**, breath, whiff, draught, gust

pull v = **draw**, haul, drag, trail, tow ≠ push; = **extract**, pick,

remove, gather, take out ≠ insert; = (Inf) **attract**, draw, bring in, tempt, lure ≠ repel; = **strain**, tear, stretch, rip, wrench ≠ tug ♦ n = **tug**, jerk, yank, twitch, heave ≠ shove; = **puff**, drag (SI), inhalation; = (Inf) **influence**, power, weight, muscle, clout (Inf)

pulp n = **paste**, mash, mush; = **flesh**, meat, soft part ♦ v = **crush**, squash, mash, pulverize

pulse[1] n = **beat**, rhythm, vibration, beating, throb

repeatedly.

pump[1] ⓘ *n* 1 appliance for raising water, or putting in or taking out air or liquid etc. ◆ *v* 2 raise, put in, take out etc. with pump. 3 work like pump.

pump[2] *n* light shoe.

pumpkin *n* edible gourd.

pun *n* 1 play on words. ◆ *v* 2 make pun.

punch[1] ⓘ *n* 1 tool for perforating or stamping. 2 blow with fists. 3 *Inf* vigour. ◆ *v* 4 stamp, perforate with punch. 5 strike with fist.

punch[2] *n* drink of spirits or wine with fruit juice etc.

punctilious *adj* 1 making much of details of etiquette. 2 very exact, particular.

punctual *adj* in good time, not late. **punctuality** *n*

punctuate ⓘ *v* 1 put in punctuation marks. 2 interrupt at intervals. **punctuation** *n* marks put in writing to assist in making sense clear.

puncture ⓘ *n* 1 small hole made by sharp object, esp. in tyre. ◆ *v* 2 prick hole in, perforate.

pundit *n* expert who speaks publicly on subject.

pungent *adj* acrid, bitter.

punish ⓘ *v* 1 cause to suffer for offence. 2 inflict penalty on. 3 use or treat roughly. **punishable** *adj* **punishing** *adj* harsh, difficult. **punishment** *n* **punitive** *adj* inflicting or intending to inflict punishment.

punnet *n* small basket for fruit.

punter ⓘ *n* 1 person who bets. 2 member of public.

puny *adj* **–nier, –niest** small and feeble.

pup *n* young of certain animals, e.g. dog, seal.

pupa *n*, *pl* **–pae, –pas** stage between larva and adult in metamorphosis of insect.

pupil ⓘ *n* 1 person being taught. 2 opening in iris of eye.

puppet ⓘ *n* 1 small doll controlled by operator's hand. 2 *Fig* stooge, pawn.

————— THESAURUS —————

pump[1] *v* = **supply**, send, pour, inject; = **interrogate**, probe, quiz, cross–examine; = **fire**, shoot, discharge, let off

punch[1] *v* = **hit**, strike, box, smash, belt (*Inf*) ◆ *n* = **blow**, hit, sock (*Sl*), jab, swipe (*Inf*); = (*Inf*) **effectiveness**, bite, impact, drive, vigour

punctuate *v* = **interrupt**, break, pepper, sprinkle, intersperse

puncture *n* = **flat tyre**, flat; = **hole**, opening, break, cut, nick ◆

v = **pierce**, cut, nick, penetrate, prick

punish *v* = **discipline**, correct, castigate, chastise, sentence

punitive *adj* = **retaliatory**, in reprisal, retaliative

punter *n* = **gambler**, better, backer; = (*Inf*) **person**, man in the street

pupil *n* = **student**, schoolboy or schoolgirl, schoolchild ≠ **teacher**

puppet *n* = **marionette**, doll, glove puppet, finger puppet;

puppy *n, pl* **-pies** young dog.
purchase ⊕ *v* **1** buy. ◆ *n* **2** buying. **3** what is bought. **4** leverage, grip.
pure ⊕ *adj* **1** unmixed, untainted. **2** simple. **3** faultless. **4** innocent. **5** concerned with theory only.
purely *adv* **purification** *n* **purify** *v* **-fying, -fied** make, become pure, clear or clean. **purist** *n* person obsessed with strict obedience to tradition. **purity** *n* state of being pure.
purée *n* **1** pulp of cooked fruit or vegetables. ◆ *v* **2** reduce to pulp.
purgatory *n* place or state of torment, pain or distress, esp. temporary.
purge ⊕ *v* **1** make clean, purify. **2** remove, get rid of. **3** clear out. ◆ *n* **4** act, process of purging.
purgative *adj/n*
purl *n* **1** stitch that forms ridge in knitting. ◆ *v* **2** knit in purl.
purloin *v* **1** steal. **2** pilfer.
purple *n/adj* (of) colour between crimson and violet.
purport ⊕ *v* **1** claim to be (true etc.). **2** signify, imply. ◆ *n* **3** meaning. **4** apparent meaning.
purpose ⊕ *n* **1** reason, object. **2** design. **3** aim, intention. **4** determination. ◆ *v* **5** intend. **on purpose** intentionally. **purposely** *adv*
purr *n* **1** pleased noise which cat makes. ◆ *v* **2** utter this.
purse ⊕ *n* **1** small bag for money. **2** resources. **3** money as prize. **4** *US and Canad* handbag. ◆ *v* **5** pucker. **purser** *n* ship's officer who keeps accounts.
pursue ⊕ *v* **1** chase. **2** engage in. **3** continue. **pursuer** *n* **pursuit** *n* **1** pursuing. **2** occupation.
purvey *v* supply (provisions).

= **pawn**, tool, instrument, mouthpiece, stooge
purchase *v* = **buy**, pay for, obtain, get, score (*Sl*) ≠ **sell** ◆ *n* = **acquisition**, buy, investment, property, gain; = **grip**, hold, support, leverage, foothold
pure *adj* = **unmixed**, real, simple, natural, straight ≠ **adulterated**; = **clean**, wholesome, sanitary, spotless, sterilized ≠ **contaminated**; = **complete**, total, perfect, absolute, sheer ≠ **qualified**; = **innocent**, modest, good, moral, impeccable ≠ **corrupt**
purge *v* = **rid**, clear, cleanse, strip,

empty ◆ *n* = **removal**, elimination, expulsion, eradication, ejection
purport *v* = **claim**, allege, assert, profess
purpose *n* = **reason**, point, idea, aim, object; = **aim**, end, plan, hope, goal; = **determination**, resolve, will, resolution, ambition
purse *n* = **pouch**, wallet, money-bag; = (*US*) **handbag**, bag, shoulder bag, pocket book, clutch bag ◆ *v* = **pucker**, contract, tighten, pout, press together
pursue *v* = **engage in**, perform, conduct, carry on, practise; = **try for**, seek, desire, search for, aim for; = **continue**, maintain, carry

pus n yellowish matter produced by suppuration.

push ⊙ v 1 move, try to move away by pressure. 2 drive or impel. 3 make thrust. 4 advance with steady effort. ♦ n 5 thrust. 6 persevering self–assertion. 7 big military advance. **pusher** n seller of illegal drugs. **pushy** adj assertive, ambitious. **pushchair** n collapsible chair–shaped carriage for baby.

puss, pussy pl **pusses, pussies** n cat.

pustule n pimple containing pus.

put ⊙ v putting, put 1 place. 2 set. 3 express. 4 throw (esp. shot). ♦ n 5 throw. **put off** 1 postpone. 2 disconcert. 3 repel. **put up** 1 erect. 2 accommodate.

putrid adj 1 decomposed. 2 rotten. **putrefy** v –fying, –fied make or become rotten.

putt v strike (golf ball) along ground. **putter** n golf club for putting.

putty n paste used by glaziers.

puzzle ⊙ v 1 perplex or be perplexed. ♦ n 2 bewildering, perplexing question, problem or toy.

PVC polyvinyl chloride.

pygmy n 1 abnormally undersized person 2 (with cap.) member of one of dwarf peoples of Equatorial Africa. ♦ adj 3 very small.

pyjamas pl n sleeping suit of trousers and jacket.

pylon n tower–like erection, esp. to carry electric cables.

pyramid n solid figure or structure with sloping sides meeting at apex, esp. in ancient Egypt.

pyre n pile of wood for burning dead body.

pyromania n urge to set things on fire. **pyromaniac** n

pyrotechnics n manufacture, display of fireworks.

python n large nonpoisonous snake that crushes its prey.

———— THESAURUS ————

on, keep on, persist in; = **follow**, track, hunt, chase, dog ≠ **flee**; = **court**, woo ≠ **fight shy of**

push v = **shove**, force, press, thrust, drive ≠ **pull**; = **press**, operate, depress, squeeze, activate ♦ n = **shove**, thrust, butt, elbow, nudge ≠ **pull**; = (Inf) **drive**, go

(Inf), energy, initiative, enterprise

put v = **place**, leave, set, position, rest; = **express**, state, word, phrase, utter

puzzle v = **perplex**, confuse, baffle, stump, bewilder ♦ n = **problem**, riddle, question, conundrum, poser

P

Q q

QC *Brit* Queen's Counsel.

QLD Queensland.

quack *n* 1 harsh cry of duck. 2 pretender to medical or other skill. ♦ *v* 3 (of duck) utter cry.

quadrangle *n* 1 four-sided figure. 2 four-sided courtyard in a building.

quadrant *n* quarter of circle.

quadrilateral *adj/n* four-sided (figure).

quadruped *n* four-footed animal.

quadruple *adj* 1 fourfold. ♦ *v* 2 make, become four times as much.

quadruplet *n* one of four offspring born at one birth.

quaff *v* drink heartily or in one draught.

quagmire *n* bog, swamp.

quail[1] *n* small bird of partridge family.

quail[2] *v* 1 flinch. 2 cower.

quaint *adj* 1 interestingly old-fashioned or odd. 2 curious.

quake ⊙ *v* shake, tremble.

qualify ⊙ *v* –fying, –fied 1 make (oneself) competent. 2 moderate. 3 ascribe quality to. **qualification** *n* 1 skill needed for activity. 2 modifying or limiting condition. **qualified** *adj* 1 fully trained. 2 conditional, restricted.

quality ⊙ *n, pl* –ties 1 attribute. 2 (degree of) excellence.

qualm *n* 1 misgiving. 2 sudden feeling of sickness.

quandary *n, pl* –ries state of perplexity, dilemma.

quango *n, pl* –gos partly independent official body, set up by government.

quantify *v* –fying, –fied discover or express the quantity of.

quantity ⊙ *n, pl* –ties (specified or considerable) amount.

quarantine *n/v* (place in) isolation to prevent spreading of infection.

quarrel ⊙ *n* 1 angry dispute. 2 argument. ♦ *v* 3 argue. 4 find fault with. **quarrelsome** *adj*

quarry[1] ⊙ *n* 1 object of hunt or

THESAURUS

quake *v* = **shake**, tremble, quiver, move, rock

qualify *v* = **certify**, equip, empower, train, prepare ≠ **disqualify**; = **restrict**, limit, reduce, ease, moderate

quality *n* = **standard**, standing, class, condition, rank; = **excellence**, status, merit,

position, value; = **characteristic**, feature, attribute, point, side

quantity *n* = **amount**, lot, total, sum, part; = **size**, measure, mass, volume, length

quarrel *n* = **disagreement**, fight, row, argument, dispute ≠ **accord** ♦ *v* = **disagree**, fight, argue, row, clash ≠ **get on** or **along** (with)

pursuit. **2** prey.

quarry² n **1** excavation where stone etc. is dug for building etc.
♦ v **2** get from quarry.

quart n liquid measure, quarter of gallon.

quarter ❶ n **1** fourth part. **2** region, district. **3** mercy. ♦ pl **4** lodgings. ♦ v **5** divide into quarters. **6** lodge. **quarterly** adj happening, due etc. each quarter of year. **quartermaster** n officer responsible for stores.

quartet n (music for) group of four musicians.

quartz n hard glossy mineral.

quash ❶ v **1** annul. **2** reject.

quasi– comb. form **1** not really, as in quasi-religious. **2** not really.

quaver v **1** say or sing in quavering tones. **2** tremble, shake, vibrate. ♦ n **3** musical note half length of crotchet.

quay n **1** solid, fixed landing stage. **2** wharf.

queasy adj **–sier, –siest** inclined to, or causing, sickness.

queen n **1** female sovereign. **2** king's wife. **3** piece in chess. **4** fertile female bee, wasp etc. **5** court card.

queer ❶ adj odd, strange.

quell v **1** crush, put down. **2** allay.

quench v **1** slake. **2** extinguish.

querulous adj peevish, whining.

query ❶ n/v, pl **–ries** question.

quest ❶ n/v search.

question ❶ n **1** sentence seeking for answer. **2** problem. **3** point at issue. **4** doubt. ♦ v **5** ask questions of. **6** dispute. **7** doubt.

questionable adj doubtful.

questionnaire n formal list of questions. **question mark** punctuation mark (?) written at end of questions.

———— THESAURUS ————

quarry¹ n **= prey**, victim, game, goal, aim

quarter n **= district**, region, neighbourhood, place, part; **= mercy**, pity, compassion, charity, sympathy ♦ v **= accommodate**, house, lodge, place, board

quash v **= annul**, overturn, reverse, cancel, overthrow; **= suppress**, crush, put down, beat, overthrow

queen n **= sovereign**, ruler, monarch, leader, Crown; **= leading light**, star, favourite, celebrity, darling

queer adj **= strange**, odd, funny, unusual, extraordinary ≠ **normal**; **= faint**, dizzy, giddy, queasy, light–headed

query n **= question**, inquiry, problem ♦ v **= question**, challenge, doubt, suspect, dispute

quest n **= search**, hunt, mission, enterprise, crusade

question n **= inquiry**, enquiry, query, investigation, examination ≠ **answer**; **= difficulty**, problem, doubt, argument, dispute ♦ v **= interrogate**, cross–examine, interview, examine, probe; **= dispute**, challenge, doubt, suspect, oppose ≠ **accept**; **= under discussion**, at issue, under

Q

queue ❶ n **1** line of waiting persons, vehicles. ◆ v **2** wait in queue.

quibble n/v (make) trivial objection.

quiche n savoury flan.

quick ❶ adj **1** fast. **2** lively. **3** hasty. ◆ n **4** sensitive flesh. ◆ adv **5** rapidly. **quicken** v make, become faster or more lively. **quickly** adj **quicksand** n loose wet sand that engulfs heavy objects. **quicksilver** n mercury. **quickstep** n fast ballroom dance.

quiet ❶ adj **1** with little noise. **2** undisturbed. **3** not showy or obtrusive. ◆ n **4** quietness. ◆ v **5** make, become quiet. **quieten** v

quiff n tuft of brushed–up hair.

quill n **1** large feather. **2** pen made from feather. **3** spine of porcupine.

quilt ❶ n **1** padded coverlet. ◆ v **2** stitch (two pieces of cloth) with pad between.

quinine n drug used to treat fever and as tonic.

quintessence n most perfect representation of a quality. **quintessential** adj

quintet n (music for) group of five musicians.

quintuplet n one of five offspring born at one birth.

quip ❶ n/v (utter) witty saying.

quirk n **1** individual peculiarity of character. **2** unexpected twist.

quit ❶ v **quitting, quit 1** stop doing (something). **2** leave. **3** give up.

quite ❶ adv **1** completely. **2** somewhat. ◆ interj **3** expression of agreement.

quiver¹ v/n shake, tremble.

quiver² n case for arrows.

———— THESAURUS ————

consideration, in doubt, on the agenda; **out of the question = impossible**, unthinkable, inconceivable, not on (Inf), hopeless

queue n = **line**, row, file, train, series

quick adj = **fast**, swift, speedy, express, cracking (Brit inf) ≠ **slow**; = **brief**, passing, hurried, flying, fleeting ≠ **long**; = **immediate**, instant, prompt, sudden, abrupt; = **excitable**, passionate, irritable, touchy, irascible ≠ **calm**

quiet adj = **soft**, low, muted, lowered, whispered ≠ **loud**; = **peaceful**, silent, hushed, soundless, noiseless ≠ **noisy**;

= **calm**, peaceful, tranquil, mild, serene ≠ **exciting** ◆ n = **peace**, rest, tranquillity, ease, silence ≠ **noise**

quilt n = **bedspread**, duvet, coverlet, eiderdown, counterpane

quip n = **joke**, sally, jest, riposte, wisecrack (Inf)

quit v = **resign (from)**, leave, retire (from), pull out (of), step down (from) (Inf); = **stop**, give up, cease, end, drop ≠ **continue**; = **leave**, depart from, go out of, go away from, pull out from

quite adv = **somewhat**, rather, fairly, reasonably, relatively; = **absolutely**, perfectly, completely, totally, fully

quiz ❶ *n, pl* **quizzes 1**
entertainment in which
knowledge of players is tested by
questions. **2** examination,
interrogation. ◆ *v* **3** question,
interrogate. **quizzical** *adj* **1**
questioning. **2** mocking.
quoit *n* **1** ring for throwing at peg
as a game. ◆ *pl* **2** this game.

quorum *n* least number that must
be present to make meeting valid.
quorate *adj*
quota ❶ *n* share to be contributed
or received.
quote ❶ *v* **1** repeat passages
from. **2** state price for. **quotation** *n*
quotient *n* number resulting from
dividing one number by another.

———— THESAURUS ————

quiz *n* = **examination**,
questioning, interrogation,
interview, investigation ◆ *v*
= **question**, ask, interrogate,

examine, investigate
quota *n* = **share**, allowance,
ration, part, limit
quote *v* = **repeat**, recite, recall

R r

R 1 King. 2 Queen. 3 river.

rabbi *n, pl* **-bis** Jewish learned man, spiritual leader.

rabbit *n* small burrowing mammal.

rabble *n* crowd of vulgar, noisy people.

rabid *adj* 1 of, having rabies. 2 fanatical.

rabies *n* infectious disease transmitted by dogs etc.

raccoon *n* small N Amer. mammal.

race¹ ❶ *n* 1 contest of speed. 2 rivalry. 3 strong current. ♦ *pl* 4 meeting for horse racing. ♦ *v* 5 (cause to) run, move swiftly. **racer** *n*

race² *n* 1 group of people of common ancestry with distinguishing physical features. 2 species. **racial** *adj* **racism, racialism** *n* 1 belief in superiority of particular race. 2 antagonism towards members of different race based on this. **racist, racialist** *adj/n*

rack ❶ *n* 1 framework for displaying or holding things. 2 instrument of torture. ♦ *v* 3 torture.

racket¹ ❶ *n* 1 uproar. 2 occupation by which money is made illegally. **racketeer** *n*

racket², racquet *n* 1 bat used in tennis etc. ♦ *pl* 2 ball game.

raconteur *n* skilled storyteller.

racy *adj* **racier, raciest** 1 lively. 2 piquant.

radar *n* device for locating objects by radio waves, which reflect back to their source.

radial see RADIUS.

radiate ❶ *v* 1 emit, be emitted in rays. 2 spread out from centre. **radiance** *n* 1 brightness. 2 splendour. **radiation** *n* 1 transmission of heat, light etc. from one body to another. 2 particles, rays emitted in nuclear decay. **radiator** *n* 1 heating apparatus for rooms. 2 cooling apparatus of car engine.

radical ❶ *adj* 1 fundamental. 2 extreme. 3 of root. ♦ *n* 4 person of extreme (political) views.

radio *n, pl* **-dios** 1 use of

─────────── THESAURUS ───────────

race¹ *n* = **competition**, contest, chase, dash, pursuit; = **contest**, competition, rivalry ♦ *v* = **compete against**, run against; = **compete**, run, contend, take part in a race

rack *n* = **frame**, stand, structure, framework ♦ *v* = **torture**, torment, afflict, oppress, harrow

racket¹ *n* = **noise**, row, fuss, disturbance, outcry; = **fraud**, scheme

radiate *v* = **emit**, spread, send out, pour, shed; = **show**, display, demonstrate, exhibit, emanate

electromagnetic waves for broadcasting, communication etc. **2** device for receiving, amplifying radio signals. **3** broadcasting of radio programmes. ◆ v **4** transmit message etc. by radio.

radioactive adj emitting invisible rays that penetrate matter. **radioactivity** n

radiography n production of image on film by radiation.

radiology n science of use of rays in medicine.

radiotherapy n diagnosis and treatment of disease by X-rays.

radish n pungent root vegetable.

radium n radioactive metallic element.

radius n, pl **radii, radiuses** straight line from centre to circumference of circle. **radial** adj

RAF Royal Air Force.

raffia n prepared palm fibre for making mats etc.

raffle n **1** lottery in which article is won by one of those buying tickets. ◆ v **2** dispose of by raffle.

raft n floating structure of logs, planks etc.

rafter n main beam of roof.

rag n **1** fragment of cloth. **2** torn piece. ◆ pl **3** tattered clothing.

ragged adj **ragtime** n style of jazz piano music.

ragamuffin n ragged, dirty person, esp. child.

rage ⊕ n **1** violent anger. **2** fury. ◆ v **3** speak, act with fury. **4** proceed violently, as storm.

raglan adj (of sleeve) continuing in one piece to the neck.

raid ⊕ n **1** attack. **2** foray. ◆ v **3** make raid on.

rail¹ n horizontal bar. **railing** n fence, barrier made of rails supported by posts. **railway** n track of iron rails on which trains run.

rail² v **1** utter abuse. **2** scold.

rain ⊕ n **1** moisture falling in drops from clouds. ◆ v **2** pour down as, like rain. **rainy** adj **rainbow** n arch of colours in sky. **rainforest** n dense forest in tropics.

raise ⊕ v **1** lift up. **2** set up. **3** build. **4** increase. **5** heighten, as voice. **6** breed. **7** collect. **8** propose, suggest. ◆ n US and Canad pay rise.

raisin n dried grape.

—————— THESAURUS ——————

radical adj = **extreme**, complete, entire, sweeping, severe; = **revolutionary**, extremist, fanatical; = **fundamental**, natural, basic, profound, innate ≠ **superficial** ◆ n = **extremist**, revolutionary, militant, fanatic ≠ **conservative**

rage n = **fury**, temper, frenzy, rampage, tantrum ≠ **calmness** ◆ v = **be furious**, blow up (Inf), fume, lose it (Inf), seethe ≠ **stay calm**

raid v = **steal from**, plunder, pillage, sack ◆ n = **attack**, invasion, foray, sortie, incursion

rain n = **rainfall**, fall, showers, deluge, drizzle ◆ v = **pour**, pelt (down), teem, bucket down (Inf), drizzle; = **fall**, shower, be dropped, sprinkle, be deposited

rake¹ ❶ n 1 tool with long handle and teeth for gathering leaves etc. ♦ v 2 gather, smooth with rake. 3 search over. 4 sweep with shot.

rake² n dissolute man.

rakish adj 1 dashing. 2 speedy.

rally ❶ v, pl –lies 1 bring together, esp. what has been scattered. 2 come together. 3 regain health or strength. ♦ n 4 assembly, esp. outdoor. 5 Tennis lively exchange of strokes.

ram ❶ n 1 male sheep. 2 hydraulic machine. 3 battering engine. ♦ v 4 force, drive. 5 strike against with force. 6 stuff.

ramble ❶ v 1 walk without definite route. 2 talk incoherently. ♦ n 3 rambling walk.

ramp ❶ n gradual slope joining two level surfaces.

rampage ❶ v 1 dash about violently. ♦ n 2 angry or destructive behaviour.

rampant ❶ adj 1 violent. 2 rife. 3 rearing.

rampart n wall for defence.

ramshackle adj rickety.

ran past tense of RUN.

ranch n Amer. cattle farm.

rancid adj smelling or tasting offensively, like stale fat.

rancour n bitter hate.

random ❶ adj by chance, without plan.

randy ❶ adj randier, randiest Sl sexually aroused.

rang past tense of RING¹.

———— THESAURUS ————

raise v = **lift**, elevate, uplift, heave; = **set upright**, lift, elevate; = **increase**, intensify, heighten, advance, boost ≠ reduce; = **make louder**, heighten, amplify, louden; = **collect**, gather, obtain; form, mass; = **cause**, start, produce, create, occasion; = **put forward**, suggest, introduce, advance, broach

rake¹ v = **gather**, collect, remove; = **search**, comb, scour, scrutinize

rake² n = **libertine**, playboy, swinger (Sl), lecher, roué ≠ puritan

rally n = **gathering**, convention, meeting, congress, assembly; = **recovery**, improvement, revival, recuperation ≠ relapse ♦ v unite; = **recover**, improve, revive, get better, recuperate ≠ get worse

ram v = **hit**, force, drive into, crash, impact; = **cram**, force, stuff, jam, thrust

ramble n = **walk**, tour, stroll, hike, roaming ♦ v = **walk**, range, wander, stroll, stray; often with on = **babble**, rabbit (on) (Brit inf), waffle (Inf, chiefly Brit), witter on (Inf)

ramp n = **slope**, incline, gradient, rise

rampage v = **go berserk**, storm, rage, run riot, run amok

rampant adj = **widespread**, prevalent, rife, uncontrolled, unchecked; = (Heraldry) **upright**, standing, rearing, erect

random adj = **chance**, casual, accidental, incidental, haphazard ≠ planned

randy adj = (Inf) **lustful**, hot,

range ❶ *n* **1** limits. **2** row. **3** scope, distance missile can travel. **4** place for shooting practice. **5** kitchen stove. ♦ *v* **6** set in row. **7** extend. **8** roam. **9** fluctuate. **ranger** *n* official patrolling park etc. **rangy** *adj* with long, slender limbs.

rank[1] ❶ *n* **1** row, line. **2** place where taxis wait. **3** order. **4** status. **5** relative position. ♦ *pl* (*also* **rank and file**) **6** common soldiers. **7** great mass of people. ♦ *v* **8** draw up in rank. **9** have rank, place.

rank[2] ❶ *adj* **1** growing too thickly. **2** rancid. **3** flagrant.

rankle *v* continue to cause anger or bitterness.

ransack *v* **1** search thoroughly. **2** pillage.

ransom ❶ *n* **1** release from captivity by payment. **2** amount paid. ♦ *v* **3** pay ransom for.

rant ❶ *v* rave in violent language.

rap ❶ *v* **rapping, rapped 1** give smart slight blow to. **2** utter abruptly. **3** perform monologue to music. ♦ *n* **4** smart slight blow. **5** punishment. **6** monologue set to music.

rapacious *adj* **1** greedy. **2** grasping.

rape[1] ❶ *v* **1** force (woman) to submit to sexual intercourse. ♦ *n* **2** act of raping. **rapist** *n*

rape[2] *n* plant with oil-yielding seeds.

rapid ❶ *adj* **1** quick, swift. ♦ *n* (*esp. pl*) **2** part of river with fast, turbulent current.

rapier *n* fine-bladed sword.

rapport *n* harmony, agreement.

rapt *adj* engrossed. **rapture** *n* ecstasy.

rare[1] ❶ *adj* **1** uncommon. **2** of exceptionally high quality. **rarely** *adv* seldom. **rarity** *n*

rare[2] *adj* (of meat) lightly cooked.

—————— THESAURUS ——————

turned-on (*Sl*), aroused, horny (*Sl*)

range *n* = **series**, variety, selection, assortment, lot; = **limits**, reach ♦ *v* = **vary**, run, reach, extend, stretch; = **roam**, wander, rove, ramble, traverse

rank[1] *n* = **status**, level, position, grade, order; = **class**, caste; = **row**, line, file, column, group ♦ *v* = **order**, dispose; = **arrange**, sort, line up, array, align

rank[2] *adj* = **absolute**, complete, total, gross, sheer; = **foul**, bad, offensive, disgusting, revolting; = **abundant**, lush, luxuriant, dense, profuse

ransom *n* = **payment**, money, price, payoff

rant *v* = **shout**, roar, yell, rave, cry

rap *v* = **hit**, strike, knock, crack, tap ♦ *n* = **blow**, knock, crack, tap, clout (*Inf*); = (*Sl*) **rebuke**, blame, responsibility, punishment

rape[1] *v* = **sexually assault**, violate, abuse, ravish, force ♦ *n* = **sexual assault**, violation, ravishment, outrage

rapid *adj* = **sudden**, prompt, speedy, express, swift ≠ **gradual**

rare[1] *adj* = **uncommon**, unusual, few, strange, scarce ≠ **common**;

R

raring ⊕ *adj* **raring to** enthusiastically willing, ready.

rascal *n* 1 rogue. 2 naughty (young) person.

rash¹ ⊕ *adj* hasty, reckless.

rash² ⊕ *n* 1 skin eruption. 2 outbreak.

rasher *n* slice of bacon.

rasp *n* 1 harsh, grating noise. 2 coarse file. ♦ *v* 3 scrape with rasp. 4 make scraping noise. 5 irritate.

raspberry *n* 1 red, edible berry. 2 plant which bears it.

Rastafarian *n* (*oft. shortened to* **Rasta**) 1 member of Jamaican cult. ♦ *adj* 2 of this cult.

rat *n* 1 small rodent. ♦ *v* 2 inform (on). 3 betray. 4 desert. **ratty** *adj Inf* irritable. **rat race** continual hectic competitive activity.

ratchet *n* set of teeth on bar or wheel allowing motion in one direction only.

rate ⊕ *n* 1 proportion between two things. 2 charge. 3 degree of speed etc. ♦ *pl* 4 local rax on business property. ♦ *v* 5 value.

rather ⊕ *adv* 1 to some extent. 2 preferably. 3 more willingly.

ratify ⊕ *v* **–fying, –fied** confirm. **ratification** *n*

rating ⊕ *n* 1 valuing. 2 classification. 3 sailor.

ratio ⊕ *n, pl* **–tios** 1 proportion. 2 relation.

ration ⊕ *n* 1 fixed allowance of food etc. ♦ *v* 2 supply with, limit to certain amount.

rational ⊕ *adj* reasonable, capable of reasoning. **rationale** *n* reason for decision. **rationalize** *v* 1 justify by plausible reasoning. 2 reorganize to improve efficiency etc.

= **superb**, great, fine, excellent, superlative

raring *adj* in construction *raring to do something* = **eager**, impatient, longing, ready, keen

rash¹ *adj* = **reckless**, hasty, impulsive, imprudent, careless ≠ **cautious**

rash² *n* = **outbreak of spots**, (skin) eruption; = **spate**, series, wave, flood, plague

rate *n* = **speed**, pace, tempo, velocity, frequency; = **degree**, standard, scale, proportion, ratio; = **charge**, price, cost, fee, figure ♦ *v* = **evaluate**, consider, rank, reckon, value; = **deserve**, merit, be entitled to, be worthy of; at

any rate = **in any case**, anyway, anyhow, at all events

rather *adv* = **preferably**, sooner, more readily, more willingly; = **to some extent**, quite, a little, fairly, relatively

ratify *v* = **approve**, establish, confirm, sanction, endorse ≠ **annul**

rating *n* = **position**, placing, rate, order, class

ratio *n* = **proportion**, rate, relation, percentage, fraction

ration *n* = **allowance**, quota, allotment, helping, part ♦ *v* = **limit**, control, restrict, budget

rational *adj* = **sensible**, sound, wise, reasonable, intelligent ≠ **insane**

rattle ⊕ v **1** (cause to) give out succession of short sharp sounds. ♦ n **2** such sound. **3** instrument for making it. **4** set of horny rings in rattlesnake's tail. **rattlesnake** n poisonous snake.

raucous adj hoarse.

raunchy adj **–chier, –chiest** Sl earthy, sexy.

ravage ⊕ v **1** plunder. ♦ n **2** destruction.

rave ⊕ v **1** talk wildly in delirium or enthusiasm. ♦ n **2** wild talk. **3** large–scale party with electronic music. **raving** adj **1** delirious. **2** Inf exceptional.

raven n **1** black bird. ♦ adj **2** jet–black.

ravenous adj very hungry.

ravine n narrow steep–sided valley.

ravioli pl n small squares of pasta with filling.

ravish v **1** enrapture. **2** rape.

ravishing adj lovely.

raw ⊕ adj **1** uncooked. **2** not manufactured or refined. **3** skinned. **4** inexperienced. **5** chilly.

ray[1] ⊕ n **1** narrow beam of light, heat etc. **2** any of set of radiating lines.

ray[2] n marine flatfish.

rayon n synthetic fibre.

raze v destroy completely.

razor n sharp instrument for shaving.

razzle–dazzle, razzmatazz, n showy activity.

RC Roman Catholic.

re ⊕ prep concerning.

RE religious education.

re– comb. form again.

reach ⊕ v **1** arrive at. **2** extend. **3** touch. ♦ n **4** act of reaching. **5** grasp. **6** range.

react ⊕ v act in return, opposition or towards former state. **reaction** n **1** counter or backward tendency. **2** response. **3** chemical or nuclear change. **reactionary** n/adj (person) opposed to change, esp. in politics etc. **reactive** adj chemically active.

———————— THESAURUS ————————

rattle v = **clatter**, bang, jangle; = **shake**, jolt, vibrate, bounce, jar; = (Inf) **fluster**, shake, upset, disturb, disconcert

ravage v = **destroy**, ruin, devastate, spoil, demolish

rave v = **rant**, rage, roar, go mad (Inf) babble; = (Inf) **enthuse**, praise, gush, be mad about (Inf), be wild about (Inf)

raw adj = **unrefined**, natural, crude, unprocessed, basic ≠ **refined**; = **uncooked**, natural, fresh ≠ **cooked**; = **inexperienced**,

new, green, immature, callow ≠ **experienced**; = **chilly**, biting, cold, freezing, bitter

ray[1] n = **beam**, bar, flash, shaft, gleam

re prep = **concerning**, about, regarding, with regard to, with reference to

reach v = **arrive at**, get to, make, attain; = **attain**, get to; = **touch**, grasp, extend to, stretch to, contact ♦ n = **grasp**, range, distance, stretch, capacity; = **jurisdiction**, power, influence

R

reactor *n* apparatus to produce nuclear energy.

read ⊕ *v* **reading, read 1** understand written matter. **2** learn by reading. **3** read and utter. **4** study. **5** understand any indicating instrument. **reader** *n* **1** one who reads. **2** university lecturer. **3** school textbook. **reading** *n*

ready ⊕ *adj* **readier, readiest 1** prepared for action. **2** willing. **readiness** *n*

real ⊕ *adj* **1** happening. **2** actual. **3** genuine. **realism** *n* regarding things as they are. **realist** *n* **realistic** *adj* **reality** *n* real existence. **really** *adv* **real estate** landed property.

realize *v* **1** grasp significance of. **2** make real. **3** convert into money.

realm ⊕ *n* kingdom.

realtor *n US and Canad* agent, esp. accredited one who sells houses, etc. for others.

ream *n* **1** twenty quires of paper. ◆ *pl* **2** *Inf* large quantity of written matter.

reap ⊕ *v* cut and gather harvest.

rear¹ ⊕ *n* back part. **rear admiral** high-ranking naval officer.

rear² ⊕ *v* **1** care for and educate (children). **2** breed. **3** rise on hind feet.

reason ⊕ *n* **1** motive. **2** ability to think. **3** sanity. **4** sensible thought. ◆ *v* **5** think logically. **6** persuade by logical argument. **reasonable** *adj* **1** sensible. **2** suitable. **3** logical.

reassure ⊕ *v* restore confidence to.

rebate ⊕ *n* discount, refund.

rebel ⊕ *v* **–belling, –belled 1** resist lawful authority. ◆ *n* **2** one who

———— THESAURUS ————

react *v* = **respond**, act, proceed, behave

read *v* = **scan**, study, look at, pore over, peruse; = **understand**, interpret, comprehend, construe, decipher; = **register**, show, record, display, indicate

ready *adj* = **prepared**, set, primed, organized ≠ **unprepared**; = **completed**, arranged

real *adj* = **true**, genuine, sincere, factual, unfeigned

realize *v* = **become aware of**, understand, take in, grasp, comprehend; = **fulfil**, achieve, accomplish, make real

realm *n* = **field**, world, area, province, sphere; = **kingdom**,

country, empire, land, domain

reap *v* = **get**, gain, obtain, acquire, derive; = **collect**, gather, bring in, harvest, garner

rear¹ *n* = **back part**, back ≠ **front**

rear² *v* = **bring up**, raise, educate, train, foster; = **breed**, keep; = **rise**, tower, soar, loom

reason *n* = **cause**, grounds, purpose, motive, goal; = **sense**, mind, understanding, judgment, logic ≠ **emotion** ◆ *v* = **deduce**, conclude, work out, make out, infer

reassure *v* = **encourage**, comfort, hearten, gee up, restore confidence to

rebate *n* = **refund**, discount,

rebels. ♦ adj **3** rebelling. **rebellion** n organized open resistance to authority. **rebellious** adj

rebound ⊕ v **1** spring back. **2** misfire, esp. so as to hurt perpetrator. ♦ n **3** recoiling.

rebuff ⊕ n/v repulse, snub.

rebuke ⊕ n/v reprimand.

rebut v –butting, –butted refute, disprove. **rebuttal** n

recalcitrant adj wilfully disobedient.

recall ⊕ v **1** remember. **2** call back. **3** restore. ♦ n **4** summons. **5** ability to remember.

recant v withdraw statement, opinion etc.

recap v **1** recapitulate. ♦ n **2** recapitulation.

recapitulate v state again briefly. **recapitulation** n

recede ⊕ v **1** go back. **2** slope backward.

receipt ⊕ n **1** written acknowledgment of money received. **2** receiving.

receive ⊕ v **1** accept, experience. **2** greet (guests). **receiver** n **1** officer appointed to take public money. **2** one who knowingly takes stolen goods. **3** equipment in telephone etc. to convert electrical signals into sound etc.

recent ⊕ adj **1** lately happened. **2** new. **recently** adv

receptacle n vessel to contain anything.

reception ⊕ n **1** receiving. **2** formal party. **3** area for receiving guests etc. **4** in broadcasting, quality of signals received. **receptionist** n person who receives clients etc.

receptive adj quick, willing to

———————— THESAURUS ————————

reduction, bonus, allowance

rebel n = **revolutionary**, insurgent, secessionist, revolutionist ♦ v = **revolt**, resist, rise up in, mutiny; = **defy**, dissent, disobey

rebound v = **bounce**, ricochet, recoil; = **misfire**, backfire, recoil, boomerang

rebuff v = **reject**, refuse, turn down, cut, slight ≠ **encourage** ♦ n = **rejection**, snub, knock–back, slight, refusal (Sl) ≠ **encouragement**

rebuke v = **scold**, censure, reprimand, castigate, chide ≠ **praise** ♦ n = **scolding**, censure, reprimand, row, dressing down

(Inf) ≠ **praise**

recall v = **recollect**, remember, evoke, call to mind ♦ n = **recollection**, memory, remembrance; = **annulment**, withdrawal, repeal, cancellation, retraction

recede v = **fall back**, withdraw, retreat, return, retire

receipt n = **sales slip**, proof of purchase, counterfoil; = **receiving**, delivery, reception, acceptance

receive v = **get**, accept, be given, pick up, collect; = **experience**, suffer, bear, encounter, sustain; = **greet**, meet, admit, welcome, entertain

recent adj = **new**, modern, up–

receive new ideas.

recess ⊙ n 1 alcove. 2 hollow. 3 suspension of business.

recession ⊙ n 1 period of reduction in trade. 2 act of receding. **recessive** adj receding.

recipe ⊙ n directions for cooking food.

recipient n one that receives.

reciprocal adj 1 complementary. 2 mutual. 3 moving backwards and forwards. **reciprocate** v give and receive mutually.

recite ⊙ v repeat aloud, esp. to audience. **recital** n 1 musical performance, usu. by one person. 2 narration. **recitation** n

reckless ⊙ adj incautious.

reckon ⊙ v 1 count. 2 include. 3 think.

reclaim ⊙ v 1 make fit for

cultivation. 2 bring back. 3 reform. 4 demand the return of.

recline v sit, lie back.

recluse n hermit.

recognize ⊙ v 1 identify again. 2 treat as valid. 3 notice.

recognition n

recoil v 1 draw back in horror. 2 rebound. ♦ n 3 recoiling.

recollect v remember.

recollection n

recommend ⊙ v 1 advise. 2 praise. 3 make acceptable.

recommendation n

recompense v 1 reward. 2 compensate. ♦ n 3 reward. 4 compensation.

reconcile ⊙ v 1 bring back into friendship. 2 adjust, harmonize. **reconciliation** n

reconnoitre v make survey of.

——————— THESAURUS ———————

to-date, late, current ≠ old

reception n = party, gathering, get-together, social gathering, function (Inf); = response, reaction, acknowledgment, treatment, welcome

recess n = break, rest, holiday, interval, vacation; = alcove, corner, bay, hollow, niche

recession n = depression, drop, decline, slump ≠ boom

recipe n = directions, instructions, ingredients; a recipe for something = method, formula, prescription, process, technique

recite v = perform, deliver, repeat, declaim

reckless adj = careless, wild, rash, precipitate, hasty ≠ cautious

reckon v = (Inf) think, believe, suppose, imagine, assume; = consider, rate, account, judge, regard

reclaim v = retrieve, regain; = regain, salvage, recapture, reform, redeem

recognize v = identify, know, place, remember, spot; = acknowledge, allow, accept, admit, grant ≠ ignore; = appreciate, respect, notice

recommend v = advocate, suggest, propose, approve, endorse ≠ disapprove of; = put forward, approve, endorse, commend, praise

reconcile v = resolve, settle, square, adjust, compose;

reconnaissance n survey, esp. for military purposes.

reconstitute v restore (food) to former state, esp. by addition of water.

record ⊕ n 1 document that records. 2 disc with indentations which can be transformed into sound. 3 best achievement. 4 known facts. ♦ v 5 put in writing. 6 preserve (sound etc.) on magnetic tape etc. for reproduction on playback device. **recorder** n 1 one that records. 2 type of flute. 3 judge in certain courts. **record player** instrument for reproducing sound on records.

recount ⊕ v tell in detail.

recoup v recover what has been expended or lost.

recourse n (resorting to) source of help.

recover ⊕ v 1 get back. 2 become healthy again. **recovery** n

recreation ⊕ n agreeable relaxation, amusement.

recrimination n mutual abuse and blame.

recruit ⊕ n 1 newly–enlisted soldier. 2 one newly joining. ♦ v 3 enlist. **recruitment** n

rectangle n oblong four–sided figure with four right angles. **rectangular** adj

rectify v –fying, –fied correct.

rectitude n honesty.

rector n 1 clergyman with care of parish. 2 head of academic institution. **rectory** n rector's house.

rectum n, pl –tums, –ta final section of large intestine.

recumbent adj lying down.

recuperate v restore, be restored from illness etc.

recur ⊕ v –curring, –curred 1 happen again. 2 go or come back in mind. **recurrence** n **recurrent** adj

recycle ⊕ v reprocess substance for use again.

red ⊕ adj/n redder, reddest 1 (of)

——————— THESAURUS ———————

= **reunite**, bring back together, conciliate; = **make peace between**, reunite, propitiate
record n = **document**, file, register, log, report; = **evidence**, trace, documentation, testimony, witness; = **disc**, single, album, LP, vinyl ♦ v = **set down**, minute, note, enter, document; = **make a recording of**, video, tape, video–tape, tape–record; = **register**, show, indicate, give evidence of; = **confidential**, private, unofficial, not for publication

recount v = **tell**, report, describe, relate, repeat
recover v = **get better**, improve, get well, recuperate, heal ≠ **relapse**
recreation n = **leisure**, play, sport, fun, entertainment
recruit v = **assemble**, raise, levy, muster, mobilize ♦ n = **beginner**, trainee, apprentice, novice, convert
recur v = **happen again**, return, repeat, persist, revert
recycle v = **reprocess**, reuse,

R

colour of blood. **2** *Inf* communist.
redden *v* **reddish** *adj* **red-blooded**
adj **1** *Inf* vigorous. **2** virile. **red
carpet** special welcome for
important guest. **red-handed** *adj*
Inf (caught) in the act. **red herring**
topic introduced to divert
attention. **red-hot** *adj* **1** extremely
hot. **2** very keen. **red tape**
excessive adherence to rules.
redwood *n* giant coniferous tree of
California.
redeem ❶ *v* **1** buy back. **2** set
free. **3** free from sin. **4** make up
for. **redemption** *n*
redolent *adj* **1** smelling strongly.
2 reminiscent (of).
redouble *v* increase, intensify.
redoubtable *adj* dreaded,
formidable.
redress ❶ *v* **1** make amends for.
♦ *n* **2** compensation.
reduce ❶ *v* **1** lower. **2** lessen. **3**
bring by necessity to some state. **4**
slim. **5** simplify. **reduction** *n*
redundant ❶ *adj* **1** superfluous. **2**

(of worker) deprived of job
because no longer needed.
redundancy *n*
reed *n* **1** various water plants. **2**
tall straight stem of one. **3** *Mus*
vibrating strip of certain wind
instruments.
reef *n* **1** ridge of rock or coral near
surface of sea. **2** part of sail which
can be rolled up to reduce area.
reek *v/n* (emit) strong unpleasant
smell.
reel ❶ *n* **1** spool on which film,
thread etc. is wound. **2** *Cinema*
portion of film. **3** lively dance. ♦ *v*
4 wind on reel. **5** draw (in) by
means of reel. **6** stagger.
refectory *n*, *pl* **–tories** room for
meals in college etc.
refer ❶ *v* **–ferring**, **–ferred 1** relate
(to). **2** send to for information. **3**
ascribe to. **4** submit for decision.
reference *n* **1** act of referring. **2**
citation. **3** appeal to judgment of
another. **4** testimonial. **5** one to
whom inquiries as to character

salvage, reclaim, save
red *adj* = **crimson**, scarlet, ruby,
vermilion, cherry; = **flushed**,
embarrassed, blushing, florid,
shamefaced; = (*of hair*) **chestnut**,
reddish, flame–coloured, sandy,
Titian; **in the red** = (*Inf*) **in debt**,
insolvent, in arrears, overdrawn
redeem *v* = **reinstate**, absolve,
restore to favour; = **make up for**,
compensate for, atone for, make
amends for; = **buy back**, recover,
regain, retrieve, reclaim; = **save**,
free, deliver, liberate, ransom

redress *v* = **make amends for**,
make up for, compensate for ♦ *n*
= **amends**, payment,
compensation, reparation,
atonement
reduce *v* = **lessen**, cut, lower,
moderate, weaken ≠ **increase**;
= **degrade**, downgrade, break,
humble, bring low ≠ **promote** (*Inf*)
(*Brit sl*)
redundant *adj* = **superfluous**,
extra, surplus, unnecessary,
unwanted ≠ **essential**
reel *v* = **stagger**, rock, roll, pitch,

etc. may be made.

referee ❶ n 1 arbitrator. 2 umpire. ♦ v 3 act as referee.

referendum ❶ n, pl **–dums, –da** submitting of question to electorate.

refill v 1 fill again. ♦ n 2 subsequent filling. 3 replacement supply.

refine ❶ v purify. **refined** adj 1 cultured, polite. 2 purified. **refinement** n 1 subtlety. 2 elaboration. 3 fineness of taste or manners. **refinery** n place where sugar, oil etc. is refined.

reflect ❶ v 1 throw back, esp. light. 2 cast (discredit etc.) upon. 3 meditate. **reflection** n 1 reflecting. 2 image of object given back by mirror etc. 3 thought. 4 expression of thought. **reflective** adj **reflector** n

reflex n 1 involuntary action. ♦ adj 2 (of muscular action) involuntary. 3 bent back. **reflexive** adj Grammar describes verb denoting agent's action on himself.

reform ❶ v 1 improve. 2 abandon evil practices. ♦ n 3 improvement. **reformation** n

refract v change course of light etc. passing from one medium to another. **refraction** n

refractory adj unmanageable.

refrain¹ ❶ v **refrain from** abstain (from).

refrain² ❶ n chorus.

refresh ❶ v 1 revive. 2 renew. 3 brighten. **refreshment** n that which refreshes, esp. food, drink.

refrigerate v 1 freeze. 2 cool. **refrigerant** n/adj **refrigeration** n **refrigerator** n apparatus in which foods, drinks are kept cool.

refuge ❶ n shelter, sanctuary. **refugee** n one who seeks refuge, esp. in foreign country.

———————— THESAURUS ————————

sway

refer v = **direct**, point, send, guide

referee n = **umpire**, judge, ref (Inf), arbiter, arbitrator ♦ v = **umpire**, judge, mediate, adjudicate, arbitrate

referendum n = **public vote**, popular vote, plebiscite

refine v = **purify**, process, filter, cleanse, clarify; = **improve**, perfect, polish, hone

reflect v = **show**, reveal, display, indicate, demonstrate; = **throw back**, return, mirror, echo, reproduce; = **consider**, think,

muse, ponder, meditate

reform n = **improvement**, amendment, rehabilitation, betterment ♦ v = **improve**, correct, restore, amend, mend; = **mend your ways**, go straight (Inf), shape up (Inf), turn over a new leaf, clean up your act (Inf)

refrain¹ v = **stop**, avoid, cease, renounce, abstain

refrain² n = **chorus**, tune, melody

refresh v = **revive**, freshen, revitalize, stimulate, brace; = **stimulate**, prompt, renew, jog

refuge n = **protection**, shelter, asylum

R

refund ① v 1 pay back. ♦ n 2 repayment.

refurbish ① v renovate and brighten up.

refuse¹ ① v decline, deny, reject. **refusal** n

refuse² ① n rubbish.

refute v disprove. **refutation** n

regain ① v 1 get back, recover. 2 reach again.

regal ① adj of, like a king. **regalia** pl n 1 insignia of royalty. 2 emblems of high office.

regale v 1 give pleasure to. 2 feast.

regard ① v 1 look at. 2 consider. 3 relate to. ♦ n 4 look. 5 attention. 6 particular respect. 7 esteem. ♦ pl 8 expression of good will.

regardless adj 1 heedless. ♦ adv 2 in spite of everything.

regatta n meeting for boat races.

regenerate v 1 reform. 2 re-create. 3 reorganize. **regeneration** n

regent n ruler of kingdom during absence, minority etc. of its monarch. **regency** n

reggae n popular music with strong beat.

regime ① n system of government.

regiment n 1 organized body of troops. ♦ v 2 discipline (too) strictly. **regimental** adj

region ① n 1 area, district. 2 part. 3 sphere. **regional** adj

register ① n 1 list. 2 catalogue. 3 device for registering. 4 range of voice or instrument. ♦ v 5 show, be shown on meter, face etc. 6 enter in register. 7 record.

registrar n 1 keeper of a register. 2 senior hospital doctor. **registration** n **registry** n 1 registering. 2 place where registers are kept.

regress v revert to former place, condition etc. **regression** n

regret ① v –gretting, –gretted 1 feel sorry, distressed for loss of or

refund n = repayment, reimbursement, return ♦ v = repay, return, restore, pay back, reimburse

refurbish v = renovate, restore, repair, clean up, overhaul

refuse¹ v = decline, reject, turn down, say no to

refuse² n = rubbish, waste, junk (Inf), litter, garbage

regain v = recover, get back, retrieve, recapture, win back; = get back to, return to, reach again

regal adj = royal, majestic, kingly

or queenly noble, princely

regard v = consider, see, rate, view, judge; = look at, view, eye, watch, observe ♦ n = respect, esteem, thought, concern, care; = look, gaze, scrutiny, stare, glance

regime n = government, rule, management, leadership, reign

region n = area, place, part, quarter, section

register n = list, record, roll, file, diary ♦ v = enrol, enlist, list, note, enter; = record, catalogue, chronicle; mark, indicate, manifest

on account of. ♦ n 2 feeling of sorrow. **regretful** adj **regrettable** adj

regular ⓣ adj 1 normal. 2 habitual. 3 according to rule. 4 periodical. 5 straight. ♦ n 6 soldier in standing army. **regularity** n

regulate ⓣ v 1 adjust. 2 arrange. 3 govern. **regulation** n

regurgitate v 1 vomit. 2 bring back (swallowed food) into mouth.

rehabilitate v 1 help (person) to readjust to society after illness, imprisonment etc. 2 restore to former position. **rehabilitation** n

rehash n 1 old materials presented in new form. ♦ v 2 rework.

rehearse ⓣ v 1 practise (play etc.). 2 repeat. 3 train. **rehearsal** n

reign ⓣ n 1 period of sovereign's rule. ♦ v 2 rule.

reimburse v pay back.

rein n 1 strap attached to bit to guide horse. 2 instrument for governing.

reincarnation n rebirth of soul in successive bodies.

reindeer n, pl **-deer, -deers** deer of cold regions.

reinforce ⓣ v strengthen with new support, material, force. **reinforcement** n

reinstate ⓣ v replace, restore.

reiterate ⓣ v repeat again.

reject ⓣ v 1 refuse to accept. 2 put aside. 3 discard. 4 renounce. ♦ n 5 person or thing rejected. **rejection** n

rejig v **-jigging, -jigged** 1 re-equip. 2 rearrange.

rejoice ⓣ v make or be joyful.

rejoin ⓣ v reply. **rejoinder** n

——————— THESAURUS ———————

regret v = **be** or **feel sorry about**, rue, deplore, bemoan, repent (of) ≠ **satisfied with**; = **mourn**, miss, grieve for or over ♦ n = **remorse**, compunction, bitterness, repentance, contrition

regular adj = **normal**, common, usual, ordinary, typical ≠ **infrequent**; = **steady**, consistent

regulate v = **control**, run, rule, manage, direct; = **moderate**, control, modulate, fit, balance

rehearse v = **practise**, prepare, run through, go over, train

reign v = **be supreme**, prevail, predominate, hold sway; = **rule**, govern, be in power, influence, command ♦ n = **rule**, power,

control, command, monarchy

reinforce v = **support**, strengthen, fortify, toughen, stress

reinstate v = **restore**, recall, re-establish, return

reiterate v = (Formal) **repeat**, restate, say again, do again

reject v = **rebuff**, jilt, turn down, spurn, refuse ≠ **accept**; = **deny**, exclude, veto, relinquish, renounce ≠ **approve**; = **discard**, decline, eliminate, scrap, jettison ≠ **accept** ♦ n = **castoff**, second, discard ≠ **treasure**

rejoice v = **be glad**, celebrate, be happy, glory, be overjoyed ≠ **lament**

rejoin v = **reply**, answer, respond,

R

rejuvenate v restore to youth.

relapse v 1 fall back into evil, illness etc. ♦ n 2 relapsing.

relate ❶ v 1 narrate. 2 establish relation between. 3 have reference to. 4 form sympathetic relationship.

relation ❶ n 1 relative condition. 2 connection by blood or marriage. 3 connection between things. 4 narrative. **relationship** n

relative adj 1 dependent on relation to something else. 2 having reference (to). ♦ n 3 one connected by blood or marriage.

relax ❶ v 1 make, become loose or slack. 2 ease up. 3 make, become less strict. **relaxation** n 1 recreation. 2 abatement.

relay ❶ n 1 fresh set of people or animals relieving others. 2 Radio, TV broadcasting station receiving programmes from another station.

♦ v 3 pass on, as message. **relay race** race between teams of which each runner races part of distance.

release ❶ v 1 set free. 2 permit showing of (film etc.). ♦ n 3 releasing. 4 permission to show publicly. 5 film, record etc. newly issued.

relegate ❶ v 1 put in less important position. 2 demote. **relegation** n

relent v become less severe. **relentless** adj

relevant ❶ adj having to do with the matter in hand. **relevance** n

reliable ❶ see RELY.

relic ❶ n thing remaining.

relief ❶ n 1 alleviation of pain etc. 2 money, food given to victims of disaster. 3 release from duty. 4 one who relieves another. 5 bus, plane etc. operating when a scheduled service is full. 6 freeing

retort, riposte

relate v = **tell**, recount, report, detail, describe

relation n = **similarity**, link, bearing, bond, comparison; = **relative**, kin, kinsman or kinswoman

relax v = **be** or **feel at ease**, chill out (slang, chiefly U.S.), take it easy, lighten up (Sl) ≠ **be alarmed**; = **calm down**, calm, unwind; = **make less tense**, rest

relay v = **broadcast**, carry, spread, communicate, transmit

release v = **set free**, free, discharge, liberate, drop ≠ **imprison**; = **acquit**, let go, let

off, exonerate, absolve ♦ n = **liberation**, freedom, liberty, discharge, emancipation ≠ **imprisonment**; = **acquittal**, exemption, absolution, exoneration; = **issue**, publication, proclamation

relegate v = **demote**, degrade, downgrade

relevant adj = **significant**, appropriate, related, fitting, to the point ≠ **irrelevant**

reliable adj = **dependable**, trustworthy, sure, sound, true ≠ **unreliable**

relic n = **remnant**, vestige, memento, trace, fragment

of besieged city. **7** projection of
carved design from surface. **8**
prominence. **relieve** v
religion n system of belief in,
worship of a supernatural power
or god. **religious** adj **1** of religion.
2 pious. **3** scrupulous.
relinquish ❶ v give up.
relish ❶ v **1** enjoy. ◆ n **2** liking.
3 savoury taste. **4** sauce. **5** pickle.
relocate v move to new place,
esp. to work.
reluctant ❶ adj unwilling.
reluctance n
rely v –lying, –lied **1** depend (on).
2 trust. **reliability** n **reliable** adj
reliance n **1** trust. **2** confidence.
remain ❶ v **1** be left behind. **2**
continue. **3** last. **remainder** n
remains pl n **1** relics. **2** dead body.
remand v send back, esp. into
custody. **on remand** in custody.
remark ❶ v/n (make) casual

comment (on). **remarkable** adj
unusual.
remedy ❶ n, pl –edies **1** means of
curing. ◆ v **2** put right. **remedial**
adj
remember ❶ v retain in, recall to
memory. **remembrance** n
remind ❶ v cause to remember.
reminder n
reminisce v talk, write of past
times, experiences etc.
reminiscence n **reminiscent** adj
remiss adj careless.
remit v –mitting, –mitted **1** send
money for goods etc. **2** refrain
from exacting. **3** give up. **4** return.
5 slacken. ◆ n **6** area of authority.
remission n **1** abatement. **2**
reduction of prison term. **3**
pardon. **remittance** n **1** sending of
money. **2** money sent.
remnant ❶ n fragment.
remonstrate v protest.

———————— THESAURUS ——————————

relief n = **ease**, release, comfort,
cure, remedy; = **rest**, respite,
relaxation, break, breather (Inf);
= **aid**, help, support, assistance,
succour
relinquish v = (Formal) **give up**,
leave, drop, abandon, surrender
relish v = **enjoy**, like, savour, revel
in ≠ **dislike**; = **look forward to**,
fancy ◆ n = **enjoyment**, liking,
love, taste, fancy ≠ **distaste**;
= **condiment**, seasoning, sauce
reluctant adj = **unwilling**, hesitant,
loath, disinclined, unenthusiastic
≠ **willing**
remain v = **stay**, continue, go on,
stand, dwell; = **stay behind**, wait,

delay ≠ **go**; be left, linger
remark v = **comment**, say, state,
reflect, mention; = **notice**, note,
observe, perceive, see ◆ n
= **comment**, observation,
reflection, statement, utterance
remedy n = **cure**, treatment,
medicine, nostrum ◆ v = **put
right**, rectify, fix, correct, set to
rights
remember v = **recall**, think back
to, recollect, reminisce about, call
to mind ≠ **forget**; = **bear in mind**,
keep in mind
remind v = **jog your memory**,
prompt, make you remember
remnant n = **remainder**, remains,

R

remorse ⊕ *n* regret and repentance.
remorseful *adj*
remorseless *adj* pitiless.
remote ⊕ *adj* 1 distant. 2 aloof. 3 slight. **remote control** control of apparatus from distance by electrical device.
remove ⊕ *v* 1 take, go away. 2 transfer. 3 withdraw. **removal** *n*
remunerate ⊕ *v* reward, pay.
remuneration *n* **remunerative** *adj*
renaissance ⊕ *n* revival, rebirth.
renal *adj* of the kidneys.
rend ⊕ *v* **rending, rent** 1 tear apart. 2 burst.
render ⊕ *v* 1 submit. 2 give in return. 3 cause to become. 4 represent. 5 melt down. 6 plaster.
rendezvous *n, pl* –**vous** 1 meeting place. 2 appointment.
rendition *n* 1 performance. 2

translation.
renegade *n* deserter.
renege *v* go back on (promise etc.).
renew ⊕ *v* 1 begin again. 2 make valid again. 3 make new. 4 restore. 5 replenish. **renewal** *n*
renounce ⊕ *v* 1 give up, disown. 2 resign, as claim. **renunciation** *n*
renovate ⊕ *v* restore, repair. **renovation** *n*
renown ⊕ *n* fame.
rent¹ ⊕ *n* 1 payment for use of land, buildings etc. ♦ *v* 2 hire.
rent² ⊕ *n* tear.
reorganize *v* organize in new, more efficient way.
repair¹ ⊕ *v* 1 make whole again. 2 mend. ♦ *n* 3 repaired part. **reparation** *n* compensation.
repair² *v* go (to).

———— THESAURUS ————

trace, fragment, end
remorse *n* = **regret**, shame, guilt, grief, sorrow
remote *adj* = **distant**, far, isolated, out-of-the-way, secluded ≠ **nearby**; = **far**, distant; = **slight**, small, outside, unlikely, slim ≠ **strong**
remove *v* = **take out**, withdraw, extract ≠ **insert**
renaissance, renascence *n* = **rebirth**, revival, restoration, renewal, resurgence
rend *v* = (*Lit*) **tear**, rip, separate, wrench, rupture
render *v* = **make**, cause to become, leave; = **provide**, give, pay, present, supply; = **represent**, portray, depict, do, give

renew *v* = **recommence**, continue, extend, repeat, resume;
= **reaffirm**, resume, recommence;
= **replace**, refresh, replenish, restock; = **restore**, repair, overhaul, mend, refurbish
renounce *v* = **disown**, quit, forsake, recant, forswear
renovate ⊕ *v* = **restore**, repair, refurbish, do up (*Inf*), renew
rent¹ *v* = **hire**, lease ♦ *n* = **hire**, rental, lease, fee, payment
rent² *n* = **tear**, split, rip, slash, slit
repair¹ *v* = **mend**, fix, restore, heal, patch ≠ **damage**; = **put right**, make up for, compensate for, rectify, redress ♦ *n* = **mend**, restoration, overhaul; = **darn**, mend, patch

repartee *n* witty retort. **2** interchange of them.

repatriate *v* send (someone) back to his or her own country. **repatriation** *n*

repay ⊕ *v* **repaying, repaid 1** pay back. **2** make return for. **repayment** *n*

repeal ⊕ *v* revoke, cancel. ♦ *n* **2** cancellation.

repeat ⊕ *v* **1** say, do again. **2** recur. ♦ *n* **3** act, instance of repeating. **repetition** *n* **1** act of repeating. **2** thing repeated. **repetitive** *adj*

repel ⊕ *v* –**pelling**, –**pelled 1** drive back. **2** be repulsive to. **repellent** *adj/n*

repent *v* feel regret for deed or omission. **repentance** *v* **repentant** *adj*

repertoire ⊕ *n* stock of plays, songs etc. that player or company

can give. **repertory** *n* repertoire.

repetition ⊕ see REPEAT.

replace ⊕ *v* **1** substitute for. **2** put back. **replacement** *n*

replay *n* **1** reshowing on TV of sporting incident, esp. in slow motion. **2** second sports match, esp. following earlier draw. ♦ *v* **3** play (match, recording etc.) again.

replenish *v* fill up again.

replete *adj* filled, gorged.

replica ⊕ *n* exact copy. **replicate** *v* make or be copy of.

reply ⊕ *n/v* –**plying**, –**plied** answer.

report ⊕ *n* **1** account. **2** written statement of child's progress at school. **3** rumour. **4** repute. **5** bang. ♦ *v* **6** announce. **7** give account of. **8** complain about. **9** make report. **10** present oneself (to). **reporter** *n*

repose 1 *n*. **2** peace. **3**

— THESAURUS —

repay *v* = **pay back**, refund, settle up, return, square

repeal *v* = **abolish**, reverse, revoke, annul, recall ≠ **pass** ♦ *n* = **abolition**, cancellation, annulment, invalidation, rescindment ≠ **passing**

repeat *v* = **reiterate**, restate ♦ *n* = **repetition**, echo, reiteration

repel *v* = **drive off**, fight, resist, parry, hold off ≠ **submit to**; = **disgust**, offend, revolt, sicken, nauseate ≠ **delight**

repertoire *n* = **range**, list, stock, supply, store

repetition *n* = **recurrence**, repeating, echo

replace *v* = **take the place of**, follow, succeed, oust, take over from; = **substitute**, change, exchange, switch, swap

replica *n* = **reproduction**, model, copy, imitation, facsimile ≠ **original**

reply *v* = **answer**, respond, retort, counter, rejoin ♦ *n* = **answer**, response, reaction, counter, retort

report *v* = **inform of**, communicate, recount; *often with* **on** = **communicate**, tell, state, detail, describe ♦ *n* = **article**, story, piece, write–up; = **account**, record, statement, communication, description; *often*

R

composure. **4** sleep. ♦ v **5** rest.

repository n place where valuables are deposited for safekeeping.

repossess v take back property from one who is behind with payments.

reprehensible adj **1** deserving censure. **2** unworthy.

represent ❶ v **1** stand for. **2** deputize for. **3** act. **4** symbolize. **5** make out to be. **6** describe. **representation** n **representative** n **1** one chosen to stand for group. **2** salesman. ♦ adj **3** typical.

repress ❶ v keep down or under. **repression** n **repressive** adj

reprieve ❶ v **1** suspend execution of (condemned person). ♦ n **2** postponement or cancellation of punishment. **3** respite.

reprimand n/v rebuke.

reprisal n retaliation.

reproach v **1** blame, rebuke. ♦ n **2** scolding. **3** thing bringing discredit. **reproachful** adj

reprobate adj/n depraved (person).

reproduce ❶ v **1** produce copy of. **2** bring new individuals into existence. **reproduction** n **reproductive** adj

reprove v censure, rebuke. **reproof** n

reptile n cold–blooded, air breathing vertebrate, as snake.

republic n state without monarch governed by elected representatives. **republican** adj/n

repudiate v reject authority or validity of.

repugnant adj **1** offensive. **2** distasteful. **3** contrary.

repulse v **1** drive back. **2** rebuff. **3** repel. **repulsion** n **repulsive** adj disgusting.

reputation ❶ n estimation in which a person is held.

request ❶ n **1** asking. **2** thing asked for. ♦ v **3** ask.

Requiem n Mass for the dead.

require ❶ v **1** need. **2** demand. **requirement** n

requisite adj/n essential.

requisition n **1** formal demand,

plural = **news**, word

represent v = **act for**, speak for; = **stand for**, serve as; symbolize, mean, betoken; = **exemplify**, embody, symbolize, typify, personify

repress v = **control**, suppress, hold back, bottle up, check ≠ **release**; = **hold back**, suppress, stifle

reprieve v = **grant a stay of execution to**, pardon, let off the hook (Sl) ♦ n = **stay of execution**,

amnesty, pardon, remission, deferment

reproduce v = **copy**, recreate, replicate, duplicate, match; = **print**, copy

reputation n = **name**, standing, character, esteem, stature

request v = **ask for**, appeal for, put in for, desire ♦ n = **appeal**, call, demand, plea, desire

require v = **need**, crave, want, miss, lack; = **order**, demand,

e.g. for materials. ♦ v 2 demand (supplies). 3 press into service.

requite v repay.

rescind v cancel.

rescue ❶ v –cuing, –cued 1 save, extricate. ♦ n 2 rescuing.

research ❶ n 1 investigation to gather or discover facts. ♦ v 2 investigate.

resemble ❶ v 1 be like. 2 look like. **resemblance** n

resent ❶ v show, feel indignation at. **resentful** adj **resentment** n

reserve ❶ v 1 hold back, set aside. ♦ n (also pl) 2 something, esp. troops, kept for emergencies (also **reservation**). 3 area of land reserved for particular purpose or group. 4 reticence. ♦ adj 5 auxiliary, substitute. **reservation** n 1 reserving. 2 thing reserved. 3 doubt. 4 limitation. **reserved** adj 1 booked. 2 not showing one's

feelings.

reservoir ❶ n 1 enclosed area for storage of water. 2 receptacle for liquid, gas etc.

reshuffle n 1 reorganization. ♦ v 2 reorganize.

reside ❶ v dwell permanently. **residence** n home. **resident** adj/n **residential** adj

residue ❶ n remainder. **residual** adj

resign ❶ v 1 give up (esp. office, job). 2 reconcile (oneself) to. **resignation** n

resilient adj 1 elastic. 2 (of person) recovering quickly from shock etc. **resilience** n

resin n sticky substance from plants, esp. firs and pines.

resist ❶ v withstand, oppose. **resistance** n 1 resisting. 2 opposition. **resistant** adj **resistor** n component of electrical circuit

———— THESAURUS ————

command, compel, exact

rescue v = **save**, get out, release, deliver, recover ≠ **desert** ♦ n = **saving**, salvage, deliverance, release, recovery

research n = **investigation**, study, analysis, examination, probe ♦ v = **investigate**, study, examine, explore, probe

resemble v = **be like**, look like, mirror, parallel, be similar to

resent v = **be bitter about**, object to, grudge, begrudge, take exception to ≠ **be content with**

reserve v = **book**, prearrange, engage; = **put by**, secure ♦ n = **store**, fund, savings, stock,

supply; = **park**, reservation, preserve, sanctuary, tract; = **shyness**, silence, restraint, constraint, reticence; = **reservation**, doubt, delay, uncertainty, indecision

reservoir n = **lake**, pond, basin; = **store**, stock, source, supply, reserves

reside v = (Formal) **live**, lodge, dwell, stay, abide ≠ **visit**

residue n = **remainder**, remains, remnant, leftovers, rest

resign v = **quit**, leave, step down (Inf), vacate, abdicate; = **give up**, abandon, yield, surrender, relinquish

producing resistance to current.
resit v 1 retake (exam). ♦ n 2
exam to be retaken.
resolute adj determined.
resolution n 1 resolving. 2
firmness. 3 thing resolved. 4
decision. 5 vote.
resolve ⊕ v 1 decide. 2 vote. 3
separate component parts of. 4
make clear. ♦ n 5 absolute
determination.
resonance n echoing, esp. in
deep tone. **resonant** adj **resonate** v
resort ⊕ v 1 have recourse. ♦ n 2
place of recreation, e.g. beach. 3
recourse.
resound ⊕ v echo, go on
sounding.
resource ⊕ n 1 ingenuity. 2 that
to which one resorts for support. 3
expedient. ♦ pl 4 stock that can be
drawn on. 5 funds. **resourceful** adj
respect ⊕ n 1 esteem. 2 aspect. 3

reference. ♦ v 4 treat with esteem.
5 show consideration for.
respectability n **respectable** adj 1
worthy of respect. 2 fairly good.
respectful adj **respecting** prep
concerning. **respective** adj 1
relating separately to each. 2
separate. **respectively** adv
respiration n breathing.
respirator n apparatus worn over
mouth and breathed through.
respiratory adj
respite ⊕ n 1 pause, interval. 2
reprieve.
resplendent adj brilliant, shining.
respond ⊕ v 1 answer. 2 react.
respondent adj 1 replying. ♦ n 2
one who answers. 3 defendant.
response n **responsive** adj readily
reacting.
responsible ⊕ adj 1 in charge. 2
liable to answer for. 3 dependable.
4 involving responsibility.

resist v = **oppose**, battle against,
combat, defy, stand up to
≠ **accept**; = **refrain from**, avoid,
keep from, forgo, abstain from
≠ **indulge in**; = **withstand**, be
proof against
resolve v = **work out**, answer,
clear up, crack, fathom; = **decide**,
determine, agree, purpose, intend
♦ n = **determination**, resolution,
willpower, firmness, steadfastness
≠ **indecision**
resort n = **holiday centre**, spot,
retreat, haunt, tourist centre;
= **recourse to**, reference to
resound v = **echo**, resonate,
reverberate, re–echo

resource n = **means**, course,
resort, device, expedient
respect v = **think highly of**, value,
honour, admire, esteem; = **show
consideration for**, honour,
observe, heed ♦ n = **regard**,
honour, recognition, esteem,
admiration ≠ **contempt**;
= **consideration**, kindness,
deference, tact, thoughtfulness;
= **particular**, way, point, matter,
sense
respite n = **pause**, break, rest,
relief, halt
respond v = **answer**, return,
reply, counter, retort ≠ **remain
silent**; often with **to** = **reply to**,

responsibility n, pl –**ties**
rest[1] ⓣ n 1 repose. 2 freedom from exertion etc. 3 pause. 4 support. ◆ v 5 take, give rest. 6 support, be supported. **restful** adj **restless** adj unable to rest or be still.
rest[2] n 1 remainder. ◆ v 2 remain.
restaurant ⓣ n commercial establishment serving food.
restitution n 1 giving back. 2 compensation.
restive adj restless.
restore ⓣ v 1 repair, renew. 2 give back. **restoration** n

restorative adj/n
restrain ⓣ v 1 hold back. 2 prevent. **restraint** n 1 self-control. 2 anything that restrains.
restrict ⓣ v limit. **restriction** n **restrictive** adj
result ⓣ v 1 follow as consequence. 2 happen. 3 end. ◆ n 4 outcome. **resultant** adj
resume ⓣ v begin again. **résumé** n summary. **resumption** n
resurgence ⓣ n rising again. **resurgent** adj
resurrect ⓣ v restore to life, use. **resurrection** n

——————— THESAURUS ———————

answer
responsible adj **= to blame**, guilty, at fault, culpable; **= in charge**, in control, in authority; **= accountable**, liable, answerable ≠ **unaccountable**; **= sensible**, reliable, rational, dependable, trustworthy ≠ **unreliable**
rest[1] v **= relax**, take it easy, sit down, be at ease, put your feet up ≠ **work**; **= stop**, have a break, break off, take a breather (Inf), halt ≠ **keep going**; **= place**, repose, sit, lean, prop; **= be placed**, sit, lie, be supported, recline ◆ n **= relaxation**, repose, leisure ≠ **work**; **= pause**, break, stop, halt, interval; **= refreshment**, release, relief, ease, comfort; **= support**, stand, base, holder, prop; **= calm**, tranquillity, stillness, still, quiet
restaurant n **= café**, diner (Chiefly US & Canad), bistro, cafeteria, tearoom
restore v **= reinstate**, re–

establish, reintroduce ≠ **abolish**; **= revive**, build up, strengthen, refresh, revitalize ≠ **make worse**; **= re-establish**, replace, reinstate, give back; **= repair**, refurbish, renovate, reconstruct, fix (up) ≠ **demolish**
restrain v **= hold back**, control, check, contain, restrict ≠ **encourage**
restrict v **= limit**, regulate, curb, ration ≠ **widen**
result n **= consequence**, effect, outcome, end result, product ≠ **cause** ◆ v **= arise**, follow, issue, happen, appear; **= end in**, bring about, cause, lead to, finish with
resume v **= begin again**, continue, go on with, proceed with, carry on ≠ **discontinue**
resurgence n **= revival**, return, renaissance, resurrection, resumption
resurrect v **= revive**, renew, bring back, reintroduce; **= restore to**

R

resuscitate v restore to consciousness. **resuscitation** n

retail n 1 sale in small quantities. ♦ adv 2 by retail. ♦ v 3 sell, be sold, retail. 4 recount. **retailer** n

retain ⊕ v 1 keep. 2 engage services of. **retainer** n 1 fee to retain esp. barrister. 2 Hist follower of nobleman etc. **retention** n **retentive** adj

retaliate ⊕ v repay in kind. **retaliation** n

retard ⊕ v 1 make slow. 2 impede development of. **retarded** adj

retch v try to vomit.

reticent adj 1 reserved. 2 uncommunicative. **reticence** n

retina n, pl –nas, –nae light– sensitive membrane at back of eye.

retinue n band of followers.

retire ⊕ v 1 give up office or work. 2 go away. 3 go to bed. **retirement** n **retiring** adj unobtrusive, shy.

retort ⊕ v 1 reply. 2 retaliate. ♦ n

3 vigorous reply. 4 vessel with bent neck used for distilling.

retrace v go back over.

retract v 1 draw in or back. 2 withdraw statement. **retraction** n

retreat ⊕ v 1 move back. ♦ n 2 withdrawal. 3 place to which anyone retires. 4 refuge.

retrench v reduce expenditure.

retribution n recompense, esp. for evil.

retrieve ⊕ v 1 fetch back again. 2 regain. **retrieval** n **retriever** n dog trained to retrieve game.

retroactive adj applying to the past.

retrograde adj going backwards, reverting.

retrospect n survey of past. **retrospective** adj

return ⊕ v 1 go, come back. 2 give, send back. 3 report officially. 4 elect. ♦ n 5 returning. 6 profit. 7 report. **returning officer** one conducting election.

reunion n gathering of people

life, raise from the dead

retain v = **maintain**, reserve, preserve, keep up, continue to have; = **keep**, save ≠ **let go**

retaliate v = **pay someone back**, hit back, strike back, reciprocate, take revenge ≠ **turn the other cheek**

retard v = **slow down**, check, arrest, delay, handicap ≠ **speed up**

retire v = **stop working**, give up work; = **withdraw**, leave, exit, go away, depart; = **go to bed**,

turn in (Inf), hit the sack (Sl), hit the hay (Sl)

retort v = **reply**, return, answer, respond, counter ♦ n = **reply**, answer, response (Inf), comeback, riposte

retreat v = **withdraw**, back off, draw back, leave, go back ≠ **advance** ♦ n = **flight**, retirement, departure, withdrawal, evacuation ≠ **advance**; = **refuge**, haven, shelter, sanctuary, hideaway

retrieve v = **get back**, regain, recover, restore, recapture

who have been apart. **reunite** v bring, come together again.

Rev., Revd. Reverend.

rev n Inf revolution (of engine).

revalue v adjust exchange value of currency upwards.

revamp ⊕ v renovate, restore.

reveal ⊕ v 1 make known. 2 show. **revelation** n

reveille n morning bugle call etc. to waken soldiers.

revel ⊕ v –elling, –elled 1 take pleasure (in). 2 make merry. ♦ n (usu. pl) 3 merrymaking. **revelry** n

revenge ⊕ n 1 retaliation for wrong done. ♦ v 2 avenge. 3 make retaliation for.

revenue ⊕ n income, esp. of state.

reverberate v echo, resound. **reverberation** n

revere ⊕ v hold in great regard or religious respect. **reverence** n **reverend** adj (esp. as prefix to clergyman's name) worthy of reverence. **reverent** adj

reverie n daydream.

reverse ⊕ v 1 move (vehicle) backwards. 2 turn other way round. 3 change completely. ♦ n 4 opposite. 5 side opposite. 6 defeat. ♦ adj 7 opposite. **reversal** n

revert ⊕ v return to former state, subject. **reversion** n

review ⊕ v 1 examine. 2 reconsider. 3 hold, make, write review of. ♦ n 4 survey. 5 critical notice of book etc. 6 periodical

——————— THESAURUS ———————

return v = **come back**, go back, retreat, turn back, revert ≠ **depart**; = **put back**, replace, restore, reinstate ≠ **keep**; = **give back**, repay, refund, pay back, reimburse ≠ **keep**; = **recur**, repeat, persist, revert, happen again; = **elect**, choose, vote in ♦ n = **restoration**, reinstatement, re-establishment ≠ **removal**

revamp v = **renovate**, restore, overhaul, refurbish, do up (Inf)

reveal v = **make known**, disclose, give away, make public, tell ≠ **keep secret**; = **show**, display, exhibit, unveil, uncover ≠ **hide**

revel v = **celebrate**, carouse, live it up (Inf), make merry

revenge n = **retaliation**, vengeance, reprisal, retribution, an eye for an eye ♦ v = **avenge**,

repay, take revenge for, get your own back for (Inf)

revenue n = **income**, returns, profits, gain, yield ≠ **expenditure**

revere v = **be in awe of**, respect, honour, worship, reverence ≠ **despise**

reverse v = (Law) **change**, cancel, overturn, overthrow, undo ≠ **implement**; = **turn round**, turn over, turn upside down, upend; = **transpose**, change, move, exchange, transfer ♦ n = **opposite**, contrary, converse, inverse; = **misfortune**, blow, failure, disappointment, setback; = **back**, rear, other side, wrong side, underside ≠ **front** ♦ adj = **opposite**, contrary, converse

revert v = **go back**, return, come back, resume

R

revile v abuse viciously.
revise ● v 1 look over and correct. 2 study again (work done previously). 3 change. revision n
revive ● v bring, come back to life, vigour, use etc. revival n
revoke v 1 withdraw. 2 cancel. revocation n
revolt ● n 1 rebellion. ♦ v 2 rise in rebellion. 3 feel disgust. 4 affect with disgust. revolting adj disgusting.
revolve ● v 1 turn round. 2 be centred on. 3 rotate. revolution n 1 violent overthrow of government. 2 great change. 3 complete rotation. revolutionary adj/n revolutionize v
revue n entertainment with sketches and songs.
revulsion n repugnance or abhorrence.
reward ● n 1 thing given in return for service, conduct etc.

♦ v 2 give reward. rewarding adj
rewind v run (tape, film etc.) back to earlier point.
rewire v provide (house, engine etc.) with new wiring.
rhapsody n, pl –dies 1 freely structured, emotional musical piece. 2 expression of enthusiasm. rhapsodic adj rhapsodize v
rhesus n small, long-tailed monkey. rhesus factor feature distinguishing different types of human blood.
rhetoric ● n 1 art of effective speaking or writing. 2 exaggerated language. rhetorical adj (of question) not requiring an answer.
rheumatism n painful inflammation of joints or muscles. rheumatic adj/n
rhinoceros n, pl –oses, –os large animal with one or two horns on nose.
rhododendron n evergreen flowering shrub.

———— THESAURUS ————

review n = survey, study, analysis, examination, scrutiny; = critique, commentary, evaluation, notice, criticism; = inspection, parade, march past; = magazine, journal, periodical, zine (Inf) ♦ v = reconsider, revise, rethink, reassess, re-examine; = assess, study, judge, evaluate, criticize
revise v = change, review; = edit, correct, alter, update, amend
revive v = revitalize, restore, renew, rekindle, invigorate
revolt n = uprising, rising,

revolution, rebellion, mutiny ♦ v = rebel, rise up, resist, mutiny; = disgust, sicken, repel, repulse, nauseate
revolve v = go round, circle, orbit
reward n = punishment, retribution, comeuppance (Sl), just deserts ♦ v = compensate, pay, repay, recompense, remunerate ≠ penalize
rhetoric n = hyperbole, bombast, wordiness, verbosity, grandiloquence; = oratory, eloquence, public speaking,

rhombus n, pl **–buses, –bi** diamond–shaped figure.

rhubarb n garden plant with edible fleshy stalks.

rhyme ❶ n 1 identity of final sounds in words. 2 word or syllable identical in final sound to another. 3 verse marked by rhyme. ♦ v 4 (of words) have identical final sounds.

rhythm ❶ n measured beat of words, music etc. **rhythmic, –ical** adj

rib n 1 one of curved bones springing from spine and forming framework of upper part of body. 2 raised series of rows in knitting etc. ♦ v 3 mark with ribs. 4 knit to form a rib pattern.

ribald adj irreverent, scurrilous.

ribbon n 1 narrow band of fabric. 2 long strip of anything.

rice n 1 Eastern cereal plant. 2 its seeds as food.

rich ❶ adj 1 wealthy. 2 fertile. 3 abounding. 4 valuable. 5 containing much fat or sugar. 6 mellow. 7 amusing. **riches** pl n wealth. **richly** adv 1 elaborately. 2

fully.

rick¹ n stack of hay etc.

rick² v/n sprain, wrench.

rickets n disease of children marked by softening of bones.

rickety adj shaky, unstable.

rickshaw n two–wheeled man–drawn Asian vehicle.

ricochet v 1 (of bullet) rebound or be deflected. ♦ n 2 rebound.

rid ❶ v ridding, rid 1 relieve of. 2 free. **riddance** n

ridden past participle of RIDE. ♦ adj 1 afflicted, as in disease–ridden. 2 afflicted.

riddle¹ ❶ n 1 question made puzzling to test one's ingenuity. 2 puzzling thing, person.

riddle² ❶ v 1 pierce with many holes. ♦ n 2 coarse sieve.

ride ❶ v riding, rode, ridden 1 sit on and control or propel. 2 be carried on or across. 3 go on horseback or in vehicle. 4 lie at anchor. ♦ n 5 journey on horse, in vehicle. **rider** n 1 one who rides. 2 supplementary clause. 3 addition to document.

ridge n 1 long narrow hill. 2 line

———— THESAURUS ————

speech–making, elocution

rhyme n = **poem**, song, verse, ode, planning

rhythm n = **beat**, swing, accent, pulse, tempo

rich adj = **wealthy**, affluent, well–off, loaded (Sl), prosperous ≠ **poor**; = **well–stocked**, full, productive, ample, abundant ≠ **scarce**; = **full–bodied**, sweet, fatty, tasty, creamy ≠ **bland**;

= **fruitful**, productive, fertile, prolific ≠ **barren**

rid v = **free**, clear, deliver, relieve, purge; **get rid of something** or **someone** = **dispose of**, throw away or out, dump, remove, eliminate

riddle¹ n = **puzzle**, problem, conundrum, poser; = **enigma**, question, secret, mystery, puzzle

riddle² v = **pierce**, pepper,

R

of meeting of two sloping surfaces. ♦ v 3 form into ridges.

ridiculous ⊕ adj deserving to be laughed at, absurd. **ridicule** v 1 laugh at, deride. ♦ n 2 derision.

rife ⊕ adj prevalent, common.

riff n short repeated musical phrase.

riffraff n rabble.

rifle ⊕ v 1 search and rob. ♦ n 2 firearm with long barrel.

rift ⊕ n crack, split.

rig ⊕ v **rigging, rigged** 1 provide (ship) with ropes etc. 2 equip. 3 arrange in dishonest way. ♦ n 4 apparatus for drilling for oil.

rigging n ship's spars and ropes.

right ⊕ adj 1 just. 2 in accordance with truth and duty. 3 true. 4 correct. 5 proper. 6 of side that faces east when front is turned to north. 7 Politics conservative. 8 straight. ♦ v 9 make, become right. ♦ n 10 claim, title etc. allowed or due. 11 what is right. 12 conservative political party. ♦ adv 13 straight. 14 properly. 15 very. 16 on or to right side.

rightful adj **right angle** angle of 90 degrees. **right-hand man** most valuable assistant.

righteous ⊕ adj 1 virtuous. 2 good. **righteousness** n

rigid ⊕ adj 1 inflexible. 2 stiff. **rigidity** n

rigmarole n 1 long, complicated procedure. 2 nonsense.

rigor mortis stiffening of body after death.

rigour n 1 severity. 2 hardship. **rigorous** adj

rile v anger.

——— THESAURUS ———

puncture, perforate, honeycomb

ride v = **control**, handle, manage; = **travel**, be carried, go, move ♦ n = **journey**, drive, trip, lift, outing

ridiculous adj = **laughable**, stupid, silly, absurd, ludicrous ≠ **sensible**

rife adj = **widespread**, rampant, general, common, universal

rifle v = **ransack**, rob, burgle, loot, strip

rift n = **breach**, division, split, separation, falling out (Inf) = **split**, opening, crack, gap, break

rig v = **fix**, engineer (Inf), arrange, manipulate, tamper with; = (Naut) **equip**, fit out, kit out, outfit, supply

right adj = **correct**, true, genuine, accurate, exact ≠ **wrong**; = **proper**, done, becoming, seemly, fitting ≠ **inappropriate**; = **just**, good, fair, moral, proper ≠ **unfair** ♦ adv = **correctly**, truly, precisely, exactly, genuinely ≠ **wrongly**; = **suitably**, fittingly, appropriately, properly, aptly ≠ **improperly**; = **exactly**, squarely, precisely; = **directly**, straight, precisely, exactly, unswervingly ♦ n = **prerogative**, business, power, claim, authority; = **justice**, truth, fairness, legality, righteousness ≠ **injustice** ♦ v = **rectify**, settle, fix, correct, sort out

righteous adj = **virtuous**, good, just, fair, moral ≠ **wicked**

rigid adj = **strict**, set, fixed, exact, rigorous ≠ **flexible**; = **inflexible**,

rim ❶ *n* edge.

rind *n* outer coating of fruits etc.

ring¹ ❶ *v* ringing, rang, rung 1 (cause to) give out resonant sound like bell. **2** telephone. ♦ *n* **3** resonant sound.

ring² ❶ *n* **1** circular band, esp. for finger. **2** circle of persons. **3** enclosed area. ♦ *v* **4** put ring round. **ringer** *n Inf* identical thing or person. **ringleader** *n* instigator of mutiny, riot etc. **ringlet** *n* curly lock of hair. **ring road** main road that bypasses a town (centre). **ringworm** *n* skin disease.

rink *n* sheet of ice for skating.

rinse ❶ *v* **1** remove soap from by applying water. **2** wash lightly. ♦ *n* **3** rinsing. **4** liquid to tint hair.

riot ❶ *n/v* (engage in) tumult,

disorder. **riotous** *adj*

RIP rest in peace.

rip ❶ *v/n* ripping, ripped cut, slash. **ripcord** *n* cord pulled to open parachute. **rip off** *Sl* cheat by overcharging.

ripe ❶ *adj* ready to be harvested, eaten etc. **ripen** *v*

riposte *n* **1** verbal retort. **2** counterattack. ♦ *v* **3** make riposte.

ripple *n* **1** slight wave. **2** soft sound. ♦ *v* **3** form into little waves. **4** (of sounds) rise and fall gently.

rise ❶ *v* rising, rose, risen **1** get up. **2** move upwards. **3** reach higher level. **4** increase. **5** rebel. **6** have its source. ♦ *n* **7** rising. **8** upslope. **9** increase. **rising** *n* revolt.

risk ❶ *n* **1** chance of disaster or loss. ♦ *v* **2** put in jeopardy. **3** take

————— THESAURUS —————

uncompromising, unbending

rim *n* = **edge**, lip, brim

ring¹ *v* = **phone**, call, telephone, buzz (*Inf, chiefly Brit*); = **chime**, sound, toll, reverberate, clang ♦ *n* = **call**, phone call, buzz (*Inf, chiefly Brit*); = **chime**, knell, peal

ring² *n* = **circle**, round, band, circuit, loop; = **arena**, enclosure, circus, rink; = **gang**, group, association, band, circle

rinse *v* = **wash**, clean, dip, splash, cleanse ♦ *n* = **wash**, dip, splash, bath

riot *n* = **disturbance**, disorder, confusion, turmoil, upheaval; = **display**, show, splash, extravaganza, profusion; = **laugh**, joke, scream (*Inf*), hoot (*Inf*), lark ♦ *v* = **rampage**, run riot, go on the

rampage; **run riot** = **rampage**, go wild, be out of control; = **grow profusely**, spread like wildfire

rip *v* = **tear**, cut, split, burst, rend ♦ *n* = **tear**, cut, hole, split, rent

ripe *adj* = **ripened**, seasoned, ready, mature, mellow ≠ **unripe**; = **right**, suitable

rise *v* = **get up**, stand up, get to your feet; = **go up**, climb, ascend ≠ **descend**; = **loom**, tower; = **get steeper**, ascend, go uphill, slope upwards ≠ **drop**; = **increase**, mount ≠ **decrease** ♦ *n* = **upward slope**, incline, elevation, ascent, kopje *or* koppie (*S Afr*); = **increase**, upturn, upswing, upsurge ≠ **decrease**; = **pay increase**, raise (*US*), increment; = **advancement**, progress, climb, promotion

R

chance of. **risky** adj

risotto n, pl **-tos** dish of rice with vegetables, meat etc.

risqué adj suggestive of indecency.

rissole n cake of minced meat coated with breadcrumbs.

rite 🛈 n formal practice or custom, esp. religious. **ritual** n 1 prescribed order of rites. 2 stereotyped behaviour. ♦ adj 3 concerning rites.

rival 🛈 n 1 one that competes with another. ♦ adj 2 in position of rival. ♦ v 3 vie with. **rivalry** n

river 🛈 n large natural stream of water.

rivet n 1 bolt for fastening metal plates, the end being put through holes and then beaten flat. ♦ v 2 fasten firmly. **riveting** adj very interesting.

rivulet n small stream.

RN Royal Navy.

road 🛈 n 1 track, way prepared for passengers, vehicles etc. 2 direction, way. 3 street. **roadblock** n barricade across road to stop traffic for inspection. **roadworks** pl n repairs to road.

roam 🛈 v wander about, rove.

roar 🛈 v/n (utter) loud deep hoarse sound.

roast v 1 cook in oven or over open fire. 2 make, be very hot. ♦ n 3 roasted joint. ♦ adj 4 roasted.

rob 🛈 v robbing, robbed steal from. **robber** n **robbery** n

robe 🛈 n 1 long outer garment. ♦ v 2 dress. 3 put on robes.

robin n small brown bird with red breast.

robot 🛈 n automated machine, esp. performing functions in human manner.

robust 🛈 adj 1 sturdy. 2 strong.

rock¹ 🛈 n 1 stone. 2 mass of stone. 3 hard sweet in sticks. **rockery** n mound of stones in garden. **rocky** adj

———— THESAURUS ————

risk n = **danger**, chance, possibility, hazard ♦ v = **dare**, endanger, jeopardize

rite n = **ceremony**, custom, ritual, practice, procedure

rival n = **opponent**, competitor, contender, contestant, adversary ≠ **supporter** ♦ v = **compete with**, match, equal, compare with, come up to ♦ adj = **competing**, conflicting, opposing

river n = **stream**, brook, creek, waterway, tributary; = **flow**, rush, flood, spate, torrent

road n = **roadway**, highway, motorway, track, route

roam v = **wander**, walk, range, travel, stray

roar v = **guffaw**, laugh heartily, hoot, split your sides (Inf); = **cry**, shout, yell, howl, bellow ♦ n = **guffaw**, hoot

rob v = **steal from**, hold up, mug (Inf); = **raid**, hold up, loot, plunder, burgle

robe n = **gown**, costume, habit

robot n = **machine**, automaton, android, mechanical man

robust adj = **strong**, tough, powerful, fit, healthy ≠ **weak**

rock² ⊕ v 1 (cause to) sway to and fro. ♦ n 2 popular music with heavy beat. **rocker** n 1 curved piece of wood etc. on which thing may rock. 2 rocking chair. **rock and roll** style of popular music. **rocket** n 1 self-propelling device powered by burning of explosive contents. ♦ v 2 move fast, esp. upwards, as rocket.

rock melon n Aust, NZ & US type of melon with sweet orange flesh.

rod ⊕ n 1 slender straight bar, stick. 2 cane.

rodent n gnawing animal.

rodeo n, pl -deos US & Canad display of bareback riding, cattle handling etc.

roe¹ n small species of deer.

roe² n mass of eggs in fish.

rogue ⊕ n 1 scoundrel. 2 mischief-loving person or child.

role ⊕, **rôle** n 1 actor's part. 2 specific task or function.

roll ⊕ v 1 move by turning over and over. 2 wind round. 3 smooth out with roller. 4 move, sweep along. 5 undulate. ♦ n 6 act of rolling. 7 anything rolled up. 8 list.

9 small round piece of baked bread. 10 continuous sound, as of drums, thunder etc. **roller** n 1 cylinder of wood, stone, metal etc. 2 long wave of sea. **roller coaster** narrow undulating railway at funfair. **roller skate** skate with wheels instead of runner. **rolling pin** cylindrical roller for pastry. **rolling stock** locomotives, carriages etc. of railway.

rollicking adj boisterously jovial and merry.

roly-poly n 1 pudding of suet pastry. ♦ adj 2 round, plump.

ROM Comp read only memory.

Roman adj of Rome or Church of Rome. **Roman Catholic** member of that section of Christian Church which acknowledges supremacy of the Pope. **Roman numerals** letters used to represent numbers.

romance ⊕ n 1 love affair. 2 mysterious or exciting quality. 3 tale of chivalry. 4 tale remote from ordinary life. ♦ v 5 exaggerate, fantasize. **romantic** adj 1 characterized by romance. 2 of love. 3 (of literature etc.)

R

——————— THESAURUS ———————

rock¹ n = **stone**, boulder

rock² v = **sway**, pitch, swing, reel, toss; = **shock**, surprise, shake, stun, astonish

rod n = **stick**, bar, pole, shaft, cane

rogue n = **scoundrel**, crook (Inf), villain, fraud, blackguard; = **scamp**, rascal, scally (Northwest English dialect)

role n = **job**, part, position, post,

task; = **part**, character, representation, portrayal

roll v = **turn**, wheel, spin, go round, revolve; = **trundle**, go, move; = **flow**, run, course; = **wind**, bind, wrap, swathe, envelop; = **level**, even, press, smooth, flatten ♦ n = **rumble**, boom, roar, thunder, reverberation; = **register**, record, list, index, census; = **turn**, spin, rotation, cycle, wheel

displaying passion and imagination. ◆ *n* **4** romantic person.

Romany *n, pl* **-nies**, *adj* Gypsy.

romp **①** *v* **1** run, play wildly. ◆ *v* **2** spell of romping. **rompers** *pl n* child's overalls.

roof *n, pl* **roofs 1** outside upper covering of building. ◆ *v* **2** put roof on, over.

rooibos *n S Afr* tea prepared from the dried leaves of an African plant.

rook *n* bird of crow family.

rookie *n Inf* new recruit.

room **①** *n* **1** space. **2** division of house. **3** scope. ◆ *pl* **4** lodgings. **roomy** *adj* spacious.

roost *n/v* perch.

rooster *n US and Canad* domestic cock.

root **①** *n* **1** underground part of plant. **2** source, origin **3** *Anat* embedded portion of tooth, hair etc. ◆ *pl* **4** person's sense of belonging. ◆ *v* **5** (cause to) take root. **6** pull by roots. **7** dig, burrow.

rope **①** *n* **1** thick cord. ◆ *v* **2** secure, mark off with rope.

rort *n Aust informal* dishonest scheme.

rosary *n, pl* **-saries 1** series of prayers. **2** string of beads for counting these prayers.

rose *n* **1** shrub usu. with prickly stems and fragrant flowers. **2** the flower. **3** pink colour. **rosette** *n* rose-shaped bunch of ribbon.

rosy *adj* **1** flushed. **2** promising.

rose-coloured *adj* **1** having colour of rose. **2** unjustifiably optimistic.

rosehip *n* berry-like fruit of rose plant.

rosé *n* pink wine.

rosemary *n* evergreen fragrant flowering shrub.

roster *n* list of turns of duty.

rostrum *n, pl* **-trums, -tra** platform, stage.

rot **①** *v* rotting, rotted **1** decompose, decay. **2** deteriorate physically or mentally. ◆ *n* **3** decay. **4** any disease producing decomposition of tissue. **5** *Inf* nonsense. **rotten** *adj* **1** decomposed. **2** very bad. **3** corrupt. **rotter** *n Inf* despicable

———— THESAURUS ————

romance *n* = **love affair**, relationship, affair, attachment, liaison; = **excitement**, colour, charm, mystery, glamour; = **story**, tale, fantasy, legend, fairy tale

romp *v* = **frolic**, sport, have fun, caper, cavort ◆ *n* = **frolic**, lark (*Inf*), caper; **romp home** = **win easily**, walk it (*Inf*), win hands down, win by a mile (*Inf*)

room *n* = **chamber**, office,

apartment; = **space**, area, capacity, extent, expanse; = **opportunity**, scope, leeway, chance, range

root *n* = **stem**, tuber, rhizome; = **source**, cause, heart, bottom, base

rope *n* = **cord**, line, cable, strand, hawser; **know the ropes** = **be experienced**, be knowledgeable, be an old hand

person.

rota n roster, list.

rotary adj (of movement). circular.

rotate v 1 (cause to) move round centre. 2 (cause to) follow set sequence. **rotation** n

rote n mechanical repetition.

rotor n revolving portion of dynamo motor or turbine.

rotund adj 1 round. 2 plump.

rouge n red powder, cream used to colour cheeks.

rough ⊕ adj 1 not smooth. 2 violent, stormy. 3 rude. 4 approximate. 5 in preliminary form. ♦ v 6 make rough. 7 plan. ♦ n 8 rough state or area. 9 sketch. **roughen** v **roughage** n unassimilated portion of food. **rough it** live without usual comforts etc.

roulette n gambling game played with revolving wheel.

round ⊕ adj 1 spherical, circular, curved. 2 plump. 3 complete. 4

roughly correct. 5 considerable. ♦ adv 6 with circular course. ♦ n 7 thing round in shape. 8 recurrent duties. 9 stage in competition. 10 customary course. 11 game (of golf). 12 period in boxing match etc. 13 cartridge for firearm. ♦ prep 14 about. 15 on all sides of. ♦ v 16 make, become round. 17 move round. **rounders** pl n ball game. **roundly** adv thoroughly. **roundabout** n 1 revolving circular platform on which people ride for amusement. 2 road junction at which traffic passes round central island. ♦ adj 3 not straightforward. **round trip** journey out and back again. **round up** drive (cattle) together.

rouse ⊕ v 1 wake up, stir up, excite. 2 waken.

rout ⊕ n 1 overwhelming defeat, disorderly retreat. ♦ v 2 put to flight.

route ⊕ n road, chosen way.

——————— THESAURUS ———————

rot v = decay, spoil, deteriorate, perish, decompose ♦ n = decay, decomposition, corruption, mould, blight; (Inf) nonsense, rubbish, drivel, twaddle, garbage (Chiefly US)

rough adj = uneven, broken, rocky, irregular, jagged ≠ even; = boisterous, hard, tough, arduous; = ungracious, blunt, rude, coarse, brusque ≠ refined; = unpleasant, hard, difficult, tough, uncomfortable ≠ easy; = approximate, estimated ≠ exact; = vague, general, sketchy,

imprecise, inexact; = basic, crude, unfinished, incomplete, imperfect ≠ complete ♦ n = outline, draft, mock-up, preliminary sketch, bogan (Aust sl)

round n = series, session, cycle, sequence, succession; = stage, turn, level, period, division; = sphere, ball, band, ring, circle ♦ adj = spherical, rounded, curved, circular, cylindrical ♦ v = go round, circle, skirt, flank, bypass

rouse v = wake up, call, wake, awaken; = excite, move, stir, provoke, anger

R

routine 🛈 n 1 regularity of procedure. ♦ adj 2 ordinary, regular.

rove v wander, roam.

row¹ 🛈 n number of things in a straight line.

row² 🛈 Inf ♦ n 1 dispute. 2 disturbance. ♦ v 3 quarrel noisily.

rowan n tree producing bright red berries, mountain ash.

rowdy adj/n –dier, –diest disorderly, noisy (person).

rowlock n device to hold oar on gunwale of boat.

royal 🛈 adj of king or queen.

royalist n supporter of monarchy.

royalty n 1 royal power. 2 royal persons. 3 payment for right, use of invention or copyright.

rpm revolutions per minute.

RSVP please reply.

rub 🛈 v rubbing, rubbed 1 apply pressure to with circular or backwards-and-forwards movement. 2 clean, polish, dry

thus. 3 abrade, chafe. 4 remove by friction. 5 become frayed or worn by friction. ♦ n 6 rubbing.

rubber n 1 elastic dried sap of certain tropical trees. 2 synthetic material resembling this. 3 piece of rubber etc. used for erasing. ♦ adj 4 made of rubber. **rubbery** adj

rubbish 🛈 n 1 refuse. 2 anything worthless. 3 nonsense. ♦ v 4 Inf criticize.

rubble n fragments of stone.

rubella n mild contagious viral disease, German measles.

ruby n, pl –bies 1 precious red gem. 2 its colour. ♦ adj 3 of this colour.

ruck¹ n 1 crowd. 2 common herd.

ruck² n/v crease.

rucksack n pack carried on back, knapsack.

rudder n steering device for boat, aircraft.

ruddy adj –dier, –diest of healthy red colour.

———— THESAURUS ————

rout v = **defeat**, beat, overthrow, thrash, destroy ♦ n = **defeat**, beating, overthrow, thrashing, pasting (Sl)

route n = **way**, course, road, direction, path

routine n = **procedure**, programme, order, practice, method ♦ adj = **usual**, standard, normal, customary, ordinary ≠ **unusual**

row¹ n = **line**, bank, range, series, file

row² n (Inf) = **quarrel**, dispute, argument, squabble, tiff;

= **disturbance**, noise, racket, uproar, commotion ♦ v = **quarrel**, fight, argue, dispute, squabble

royal adj = **regal**, kingly, queenly, princely, imperial; = **splendid**, grand, impressive, magnificent, majestic

rub v = **stroke**, massage, caress; = **polish**, clean, shine, wipe, scour; = **chafe**, scrape, grate, abrade ♦ n = **massage**, caress, kneading

rubbish n = **waste**, refuse, scrap, junk (Inf), litter; = **nonsense**, garbage (Chiefly US), twaddle, rot, trash

R

rude ⊕ *adj* 1 impolite. 2 coarse. 3 vulgar. 4 roughly made.

rudiments *pl n* elements, first principles. **rudimentary** *adj*

rue ⊕ *v* **ruing, rued** 1 grieve for. 2 regret. **rueful** *adj*

ruff *n* 1 frilled collar. 2 natural collar of feathers, fur etc. on some birds and animals. **ruffle** *v* 1 rumple, annoy, frill. ◆ *n* 2 frilled trimming.

ruffian *n* violent, lawless person.

rug *n* 1 small floor mat. 2 woollen coverlet.

rugby *n* form of football in which the ball may be carried.

rugged ⊕ *adj* 1 rough. 2 strong-featured.

ruin ⊕ *n* 1 destruction. 2 downfall. 3 fallen or broken state. 4 loss of wealth etc. ◆ *pl* 5 ruined buildings etc. ◆ *v* 6 bring or come to ruin.

ruinous *adj*

rule ⊕ *n* 1 principle. 2 government. 3 what is usual. 4 measuring stick. ◆ *v* 5 govern. 6 decide. 7 mark with straight lines.

ruler *n* 1 one who governs. 2 stick for measuring or ruling lines.

ruling *n* formal decision.

rum *n* spirit distilled from sugar cane.

rumba *n* lively ballroom dance.

rumble *v/n* (make) noise as of distant thunder.

ruminate *v* 1 chew cud. 2 ponder over. **ruminant** *adj/n* cud-chewing (animal).

rummage *v* search thoroughly.

rummy *n* card game.

rumour ⊕ *n* 1 hearsay, unproved statement. ◆ *v* 2 put around as rumour.

rump *n* 1 tail end. 2 buttocks.

————————— THESAURUS —————————

rude *adj* = **impolite**, insulting, cheeky, abusive, disrespectful ≠ **polite**; = **uncivilized**, rough, coarse, brutish, boorish; = **unpleasant**, sharp, sudden, harsh, startling

rue *v* = (*Lit*) **regret**, mourn, lament, repent, be sorry for

rugged *adj* = **rocky**, broken, rough, craggy, difficult ≠ **even**; = **strong-featured**, rough–hewn, weather-beaten ≠ **delicate**; = **well-built**, strong, tough, robust, sturdy; = **tough**, strong, robust, muscular, sturdy ≠ **delicate**

ruin *v* = **destroy**, devastate, wreck, defeat, smash ≠ **create**;

= **bankrupt**, break, impoverish, beggar, pauperize ◆ *n* = **bankruptcy**, insolvency, destitution; = **disrepair**, decay, disintegration, ruination, wreckage; = **destruction**, fall, breakdown, defeat, collapse ≠ **preservation**

rule *n* = **regulation**, law, direction, guideline, decree; = **precept**, principle, canon, maxim, tenet; = **custom**, procedure, practice, routine, tradition ◆ *v* = **govern**, control, direct, have power over, command over; = **reign**, govern, be in power, be in authority; = **control**, monopolize, tyrannize

rumour *n* = **story**, news, report,

R

rumple v make untidy, dishevelled.

rumpus n, pl **-puses** disturbance.

run ⊕ v **running, ran, run 1** move with more rapid gait than walking. **2** go quickly. **3** flow. **4** flee. **5** compete in race, contest, election. **6** cross by running. **7** expose oneself (to risk etc.). **8** cause to run. **9** manage. **10** operate. ◆ n **11** act, spell of running. **12** rush. **13** tendency, course. **14** enclosure for domestic fowls. **15** ride in car. **16** unravelled stitches. **17** score of one at cricket. **runner** n **1** racer. **2** messenger. **3** curved piece of wood on which sleigh slides. **4** stem of plant forming new roots. **5** strip of cloth, carpet. **running** adj **1** continuous. **2** consecutive. **3** flowing. ◆ n **4** act of moving or flowing quickly. **5** ride in car. **6** continuous period or sequence. **runny** adj **rundown** n summary. **run-down** adj **1** exhausted. **2**

decrepit, broken-down. **run down 1** stop working. **2** reduce. **3** exhaust. **4** denigrate. **run-of-the-mill** adj ordinary. **run out** be completely used up. **runway** n level stretch where aircraft take off and land.

rune n character of old Germanic alphabet.

rung n crossbar in ladder.

runt n unusually small animal.

rupture ⊕ n **1** breaking, breach. **2** hernia. ◆ v **3** break. **4** burst, sever.

rural ⊕ adj **1** of the country. **2** rustic.

ruse n stratagem, trick.

rush[1] ⊕ v **1** hurry or cause to hurry. **2** move violently or rapidly. ◆ n **3** rushing. ◆ adj **4** done with speed. **rush hour** period when many people travel to or from work.

rush[2] n marsh plant with slender pithy stem.

rusk n kind of biscuit.

———— THESAURUS ————

talk, word

run v = **race**, rush, dash, hurry, sprint ≠ **dawdle**; = **flee**, escape, take off (Inf), bolt, beat it (Sl) ≠ **stay**; = **take part**, compete; = **continue**, go, stretch, reach, extend ≠ **stop**; = (Chiefly US & Canad) **compete**, stand, contend, be a candidate, put yourself up for; = **manage**, lead, direct, be in charge of, head; = **go**, work, operate, perform, function; = **perform**, carry out = **work**, go, operate, function; = **pass**, go, move, roll, glide ◆ n = **race**, rush,

dash, sprint, gallop; = **ride**, drive, trip, spin (Inf), outing; = **sequence**, period, stretch, spell, course; = **enclosure**, pen, coop; **in the long run** = **in the end**, eventually

rupture n = **break**, tear, split, crack, rent ◆ v = **break**, separate, tear, split, crack

rural adj = **agricultural**, country

rush[1] v = **hurry**, run, race, shoot, fly ≠ **dawdle**; = **push**, hurry, press, hustle; = **attack**, storm, charge at ◆ n = **dash**, charge, race, scramble, stampede; = **hurry**, haste, hustle ◆ adj = **hasty**, fast,

russet *n/adj* reddish–brown (colour).

rust ❶ *n* 1 reddish–brown coating formed on iron. 2 disease of plants. ◆ *v* 3 affect with rust. **rusty** *adj* 1 corroded. 2 reddish–brown. 3 out of practice.

rustic *adj* 1 simple, homespun. 2 rural. 3 uncouth. boorish. ◆ *n* 4 countryman.

rustle¹ *v/n* (make) sound as of blown dead leaves etc.

rustle² *v US* steal (cattle). **rustler** *n*

rut *n* 1 furrow made by wheel. 2 settled habit.

rutabaga *n* the US and Canadian name for SWEDE.

ruthless ❶ *adj* merciless.

rye *n* grain plant bearing it.

——————— THESAURUS ———————

quick, hurried, rapid ≠ leisurely
rust *n* = **corrosion**, oxidation;
= **mildew**, must, mould, rot, blight

◆ *v* = **corrode**, oxidize
ruthless *adj* = **merciless**, harsh,
cruel, brutal, relentless ≠ **merciful**

R

S s

Sabbath n day of worship and rest, observed on Saturday in Judaism, on Sunday by Christians.

sabbatical adj/n (pert. to) leave for study.

sabotage ⊕ n 1 intentional damage done to roads, machines etc., esp. secretly in war. ♦ v 2 damage intentionally. **saboteur** n

sabre n curved cavalry sword.

sac n pouchlike structure in animal or plant.

saccharin n artificial sweetener.

sachet n small envelope or bag, esp. one holding liquid.

sack ⊕ n 1 large bag, esp. of coarse material. 2 pillaging. 3 Inf dismissal. ♦ v 4 pillage (captured town). 5 Inf dismiss. **sackcloth** n coarse fabric used for sacks.

sacrament n one of certain ceremonies of Christian Church.

sacred ⊕ adj 1 dedicated, regarded as holy. 2 revered. 3 inviolable.

sacrifice ⊕ n 1 giving something up for sake of something else. 2 thing so given up. 3 making of offering to a god. 4 thing offered. ♦ v 5 offer as sacrifice. 6 give up. **sacrificial** adj

sacrilege n misuse, desecration of something sacred. **sacrilegious** adj

sacrosanct adj preserved by religious fear against desecration or violence.

sad ⊕ adj **sadder, saddest 1** sorrowful. 2 unsatisfactory, deplorable. **sadden** v make sad. **sadness** n

saddle ⊕ n 1 rider's seat on horse, bicycle etc. 2 joint of meat. ♦ v 3 put saddle on. 4 lay burden on.

sadism n love of inflicting pain.

--- THESAURUS ---

sabotage v = **damage**, destroy, wreck, disable, disrupt ♦ n = **damage**, destruction, wrecking

sack n = **bag**, pocket, sac, pouch, receptacle; = **dismissal**, discharge, the boot (Sl), the axe (Inf), the push (Sl) ♦ v = (Inf) **dismiss**, fire (Inf), axe (Inf), discharge, give (someone) the push (Inf)

sacred adj = **holy**, hallowed, blessed, divine, revered ≠ **secular**; = **religious**, holy, ecclesiastical, hallowed ≠ **unconsecrated**;

= **inviolable**, protected, sacrosanct, hallowed, inalienable

sacrifice v = **offer**, offer up, immolate; = **give up**, abandon, relinquish, lose, surrender ♦ n = **offering**, oblation; = **surrender**, loss, giving up, rejection, abdication /

sad adj = **unhappy**, down, low, blue, depressed ≠ **happy**; = **tragic**, moving, upsetting, depressing, dismal; = **deplorable**, bad, sorry, terrible, unfortunate ≠ **good**

sadist n **sadistic** adj

safari n, pl –**ris** expedition to hunt or observe wild animals, esp. in Africa.

safe ❶ adj **1** secure, protected. **2** uninjured, out of danger. **3** not involving risk. **4** trustworthy. **5** sure. ♦ n **6** strong lockable container. **safely** adv **safety** n

safeguard n **1** protection. ♦ v **2** protect. **safety pin** pin with guard over the point when closed.

saffron n **1** crocus. **2** orange–coloured flavouring obtained from it. **3** orange colour. ♦ adj **4** orange.

sag ❶ v **sagging, sagged 1** sink in middle. **2** curve downwards under pressure. **3** hang loosely. ♦ n **4** droop.

saga ❶ n **1** legend of Norse heroes. **2** any long (heroic) story.

sage ❶ n **1** very wise man. ♦ adj **2** wise.

sago n starchy cereal from powdered pith of palm tree.

said past tense and past participle of SAY.

sail ❶ n **1** piece of fabric stretched to catch wind for propelling ship etc. **2** act of sailing. **3** arm of windmill. ♦ v **4** travel by water. **5** move smoothly. **6** begin voyage.

sailor n **1** seaman. **2** one who sails.

saint n **1** person recognized as having gained a special place in heaven. **2** exceptionally good person.

sake ❶ n **1** cause, account. **2** end, purpose. **for the sake of 1** on behalf of. **2** to please or benefit.

salad n mixed raw vegetables or fruit used as food.

salami n variety of highly–spiced sausage.

salary ❶ n, pl –**ries** fixed regular payment to persons employed usu. in nonmanual work.

sale ❶ n **1** selling. **2** selling of goods at unusually low prices. **3** auction. **salesman** n **1** shop assistant. **2** one travelling to sell

————— THESAURUS —————

saddle v = **burden**, load, lumber (Brit inf), encumber

safe adj = **protected**, secure, impregnable, out of danger, safe and sound ≠ **endangered**; = **all right**, intact, unscathed, unhurt, unharmed; = **risk–free**, sound, secure, certain, impregnable ♦ n = **strongbox**, vault, coffer, repository, deposit box

sag v = **sink**, bag, droop, fall, slump; = **drop**, sink, slump, flop, droop

saga n = **carry–on** (Inf, chiefly Brit),

performance (Inf), pantomime (Inf)

sage n = **wise man**, philosopher, guru, master, elder ♦ adj = **wise**, sensible, judicious, sagacious, sapient

sail v = **go by water**, cruise, voyage, ride the waves, go by sea; = **set sail**, embark, get under way, put to sea, put off; = **pilot**, steer

sake n = **purpose**, interest, reason, end, aim

salary n = **pay**, income, wage, fee, payment

S

goods.

salient adj 1 prominent, noticeable. 2 jutting out.

saline adj 1 containing, consisting of a chemical salt, esp. common salt. 2 salty.

saliva n liquid which forms in mouth, spittle.

sallow adj of unhealthy pale or yellowish colour.

sally n, pl –lies 1 rushing out, esp. by troops. 2 witty remark. ♦ v 3 rush. 4 set out.

salmon n 1 large silvery fish with orange–pink flesh valued as food. 2 colour of its flesh. ♦ adj 3 of this colour.

salmonella n, pl –lae bacterium causing food poisoning.

salon n 1 (reception room for) guests in fashionable household. 2 commercial premises of hairdressers, beauticians etc.

saloon n 1 public room, esp. on passenger ship. 2 car with fixed roof. **saloon bar** first–class bar in hotel etc.

salt 🟊 n 1 white powdery or crystalline substance consisting mainly of sodium chloride, used to season or preserve food. 2 chemical compound of acid and metal. ♦ v 3 season, sprinkle with, preserve with salt. ♦ adj 4 preserved in salt. **salty** adj of, like salt. **saltcellar** n small vessel for salt at table.

salubrious adj favourable to health, beneficial.

salutary adj producing beneficial result.

salute 🟊 v 1 greet with words or sign. 2 acknowledge with praise. 3 perform military salute. ♦ n 4 word, sign by which one greets another. 5 motion of arm as mark of respect to military superior. 6 firing of guns as military greeting of honour.

salvation 🟊 n fact or state of being saved, esp. of soul.

salve n 1 healing ointment. ♦ v 2 anoint with such, soothe.

salver n (silver) tray for presentation of food, letters etc.

salvo n, pl –vos, –voes simultaneous discharge of guns etc.

same 🟊 adj 1 identical, not different, unchanged. 2 uniform. 3 just mentioned previously.

sample 🟊 n 1 specimen. ♦ v 2 take, give sample of. 3 try.

sampler n beginner's exercise in

———— THESAURUS ————

sale n = **selling**, marketing, dealing, transaction, disposal

salt n marine, seafarer

salute v = **greet**, welcome, acknowledge, address, hail; = **honour**, acknowledge, recognize, pay tribute or homage to ♦ n = **greeting**, recognition, salutation, address

salvation n = **saving**, rescue, recovery, salvage, redemption ≠ **ruin**

same adj = **identical**, similar, alike, equal, twin ≠ **different**; = **the very same**, one and the same, selfsame; = **aforementioned**, aforesaid

embroidery.

sanatorium *n, pl* **–riums, –ria 1** hospital, esp. for chronically ill. **2** health resort.

sanctify *v* **–fying, –fied 1** set apart as holy. **2** free from sin. **sanctity** *n* sacredness. **sanctuary** *n* **1** holy place. **2** place of refuge. **3** nature reserve.

sanctimonious *adj* making affected show of piety.

sanction ⓣ *n* **1** permission, authorization. **2** penalty for breaking law. ◆ *pl* **3** boycott or other coercive measure, esp. by one state against another. ◆ *v* **4** allow, authorize.

sand *n* **1** substance consisting of small grains of rock or mineral, esp. on beach or in desert. ◆ *pl* **2** stretches or banks of this. ◆ *v* **3** polish, smooth with sandpaper. **4** cover, mix with sand. **sandy** *adj* **1** like sand. **2** sand-coloured. **3** consisting of, covered with sand. **sandbag** *n* **1** bag filled with sand or earth as protection against gunfire, floodwater etc. and as weapon. ◆ *v* **2** beat, hit with

sandbag. **sandpaper** *n* paper with sand stuck on it for scraping or polishing. **sandpiper** *n* shore bird with long bill. **sandstone** *n* rock composed of sand.

sandal *n* shoe consisting of sole attached by straps.

sandwich *n* **1** two slices of bread with meat or other substance between. ◆ *v* **2** insert between two other things.

sane ⓣ *adj* **1** of sound mind. **2** sensible, rational. **sanity** *n*

sang past tense of SING.

sanguine *adj* **1** cheerful, confident. **2** ruddy in complexion.

sanitary *adj* helping protection of health against dirt etc. **sanitation** *n* measures, apparatus for preservation of public health.

sap¹ ⓣ *n* **1** moisture which circulates in plants. **2** *Inf* foolish person. **sapling** *n* young tree.

sap² ⓣ *v* **sapping, sapped 1** undermine. **2** weaken.

sapphire *n* **1** (usu. blue) precious stone. **2** deep blue. ◆ *adj* **3** of deep blue colour.

sarcasm *n* **1** bitter or wounding

——————— THESAURUS ———————

sample *n* = **specimen**, example, model, pattern, instance ◆ *v* = **test**, try, experience, taste, inspect

sanction *v* = **permit**, allow, approve, endorse, authorize ≠ **forbid** ◆ *n often plural* = **ban**, boycott, embargo, exclusion, penalty ≠ **permission**; = **permission**, backing, authority, approval, authorization ≠ **ban**

sane *adj* = **rational**, all there (*Inf*), of sound mind, compos mentis (*Lat*), in your right mind ≠ **insane**; = **sensible**, sound, reasonable, balanced, judicious ≠ **foolish**

sap¹ *n* = **juice**, essence, vital fluid, lifeblood; = (*Sl*) **fool**, jerk (*slang, chiefly US & Canad*), idiot, wally (*Sl*), twit (*Inf*)

sap² *v* = **weaken**, drain, undermine, exhaust, deplete

S

ironic remark. **2** (use of) such remarks. **sarcastic** adj

sarcophagus n, pl **-gi**, **-guses** stone coffin.

sardine n small fish of herring family.

sardonic adj characterized by irony, mockery or derision.

sari, saree n long garment worn by Hindu women.

sarmie n S Afr slang sandwich.

sartorial adj of tailor, tailoring, or men's clothes.

sash n decorative belt, ribbon, wound around the body.

Satan n the devil. **satanic** adj devilish.

satchel n small bag, esp. for school books.

satellite n **1** celestial body or man-made projectile orbiting planet. **2** person, country etc. dependent on another.

satin n fabric (of silk, rayon etc.) with glossy surface on one side.

satire ⊕ n use of ridicule or sarcasm to expose vice and folly.

satirical adj **satirize** v make object of satire.

satisfy ⊕ v **-fying, -fied 1** please, meet wishes of. **2** fulfil, supply

adequately. **3** convince.

satisfaction n **satisfactory** adj

satsuma n kind of small orange.

saturate ⊕ v soak thoroughly.

saturation n act, result of saturating.

Saturday n seventh day of the week.

satyr n **1** woodland deity, part man, part goat. **2** lustful man.

sauce n **1** liquid added to food to enhance flavour. ◆ v **2** add sauce to. **saucy** adj impudent. **saucepan** n cooking pot with long handle.

saucer n **1** curved plate put under cup. **2** shallow depression.

sauerkraut n dish of shredded cabbage fermented in brine.

sauna n steam bath.

saunter v **1** walk in leisurely manner, stroll. ◆ n **2** leisurely walk or stroll.

sausage n minced meat enclosed in thin tube of animal intestine or synthetic material. **sausage roll** pastry cylinder filled with sausage.

sauté v **-téing** fry quickly.

savage ⊕ adj **1** wild. **2** ferocious. **3** brutal. **4** uncivilized, primitive. ◆ n **5** member of savage tribe, barbarian. ◆ v **6** attack ferociously.

—— THESAURUS ——

satire n = **mockery**, irony, ridicule; = **parody**, mockery, caricature, lampoon, burlesque

satisfy v = **content**, please, indulge, gratify, pander to ≠ **dissatisfy**; = **convince**, persuade, assure, reassure ≠ **dissuade**; = **comply with**, meet, fulfil, answer, serve ≠ **fail to meet**

saturate v = **flood**, overwhelm, swamp, overrun

savage adj = **cruel**, brutal, vicious, fierce, harsh ≠ **gentle**; = **wild**, fierce, ferocious, unbroken, feral ≠ **tame**; = **primitive**, undeveloped, uncultivated, uncivilized ◆ n = **lout**, yob (Brit sl), barbarian, yahoo, boor ◆ v = **maul**, tear,

save ⓿ *v* 1 rescue, preserve. 2 keep for future. 3 prevent need of. 4 lay by money. ♦ *v* 5 *Sport* act of preventing goal etc. ♦ *prep* 6 except. **saving** *adj* 1 redeeming. ♦ *prep* 2 excepting. ♦ *n* 3 economy. ♦ *pl* 4 money put by for future use.

saviour ⓿ *n* 1 person who rescues another 2 (*with cap.*) Christ.

savour ⓿ *n* 1 characteristic taste or smell. ♦ *v* 2 have particular taste or smell. 3 give flavour to. 4 have flavour of. 5 enjoy. **savoury** *adj* 1 attractive to taste or smell. 2 not sweet.

saw¹ *n* 1 tool with toothed edge for cutting wood etc. ♦ *v* 2 cut with saw. 3 make movements of sawing. **sawdust** *n* fine wood fragments made in sawing.

saw² past tense of SEE.

saxophone *n* keyed wind instrument.

say ⓿ *v* **saying, said** 1 speak. 2 pronounce. 3 state. 4 express. 5 take as example or as near enough. 6 form and deliver opinion. ♦ *n* 7 what one has to say. 8 chance of saying it. 9 share in decision. **saying** *n* maxim, proverb.

scab *n* 1 crust formed over wound. 2 skin disease. 3 disease of plants.

scabbard *n* sheath for sword or dagger.

scaffold *n* 1 temporary platform for workmen. 2 gallows.

scaffolding *n* (material for building) scaffold.

scald *v* 1 burn with hot liquid or steam. 2 heat (liquid) almost to boiling point. ♦ *n* 3 injury by scalding.

scale¹ ⓿ *n* 1 one of the thin, overlapping plates covering fishes and reptiles. 2 thin flake. 3 crust which forms in kettles etc. ♦ *v* 4 remove scales from. 5 come off in scales.

scale² ⓿ *n* 1 graduated table or sequence of marks at regular intervals used as reference in making measurements. 2 series of musical notes. 3 ratio of size between a thing and a model or map of it. 4 (relative) degree,

———————— THESAURUS ————————

claw, attack, mangle (*Inf*)

save *v* = **rescue**, free, release, deliver, recover ≠ **endanger**; = **keep**, reserve, set aside, store, collect ≠ **spend**; = **protect**, keep, guard, preserve, look after

saviour *n* = **rescuer**, deliverer, defender, protector, liberator

savour *v* = **relish**, delight in, revel in, luxuriate in; = **enjoy**, appreciate, relish, delight in, revel

in ♦ *n* = **flavour**, taste, smell, relish, smack

say *v* = **state**, declare, remark, announce, maintain; = **speak**, utter, voice, express, pronounce; = **suggest**, express, imply, communicate, disclose; = **suppose**, supposing, imagine, assume, presume ♦ *n* = **influence**, power, control, authority, weight; = **chance to speak**, vote, voice

extent. ◆ v 5 climb. ◆ adj 6 proportionate.

scale³ n (usu. pl) weighing instrument.

scallop n 1 edible shellfish. 2 edging in small curves like scallop shell. ◆ v 3 shape like scallop shell.

scalp n 1 skin and hair of top of head. ◆ v 2 cut off scalp of.

scalpel n small surgical knife.

scamp n mischievous person.

scamper v 1 run about. 2 run hastily. ◆ n 3 scampering.

scampi pl n large prawns.

scan ❶ v scanning, scanned 1 look at carefully. 2 examine, search using radar or sonar beam. 3 glance over quickly. 4 (of verse) conform to metrical rules. ◆ n 5 scanning. **scanner** n device, esp. electronic, which scans.

scandal ❶ n 1 something disgraceful. 2 malicious gossip. **scandalize** v shock. **scandalous** adj

scant ❶ adj barely sufficient or not sufficient. **scanty** adj

scapegoat ❶ n person bearing blame due to others.

scar ❶ n 1 mark left by healed wound, burn or sore. 2 change resulting from emotional distress. ◆ v 3 mark, heal with scar.

scarce ❶ adj 1 hard to find. 2 existing or available in insufficient quantity. 3 uncommon. **scarcely** adv 1 only just. 2 not quite. 3 definitely or probably not. **scarcity, scarceness** n

scare ❶ v 1 frighten. ◆ n 2 fright, sudden panic. **scary** adj **scarecrow** n 1 thing set up to frighten birds from crops. 2 badly dressed person.

scarf n, pl **scarves, scarfs** long narrow strip of material to put round neck, head etc.

scarlet n 1 brilliant red colour. ◆ adj 2 of this colour. 3 immoral, esp. unchaste. **scarlet fever** infectious fever with scarlet rash.

———— THESAURUS ————

scale¹ n = **flake**, plate, layer, lamina

scale² n = **degree**, size, range, extent, dimensions; measuring system; = **ranking**, ladder, hierarchy, series, sequence ◆ v = **climb up**, mount, ascend, surmount, clamber up

scan v = **glance over**, skim, look over, eye, check; = **survey**, search, investigate, sweep, scour

scandal n = **disgrace**, crime, offence, sin, embarrassment; = **gossip**, talk, rumours, dirt, slander; = **shame**, disgrace,

stigma, infamy, opprobrium

scant adj = **inadequate**, meagre, sparse, little, minimal ≠ **adequate**

scapegoat n = **fall guy** (Inf), whipping boy

scar n = **mark**, injury, wound, blemish ◆ v = **mark**, disfigure, damage, mar, mutilate

scarce adj = **in short supply**, insufficient ≠ **plentiful**; = **rare**, few, uncommon, few and far between, infrequent ≠ **common**

scare v = **frighten**, alarm, terrify, panic, shock ◆ n = **fright**, shock, start

scathing adj harshly critical.

scatter ⊕ v 1 throw in various directions. 2 put here and there. 3 sprinkle. 4 disperse. **scatterbrain** n empty-headed person.

scavenge v search for (anything usable), esp. among discarded material. **scavenger** n 1 person who scavenges. 2 animal, bird which feeds on refuse.

scenario n, pl **–rios** 1 summary of plot of play or film. 2 imagined sequence of future events.

scene ⊕ n 1 place of action of novel, play etc. 2 place of any action. 3 subdivision of play. 4 view. 5 episode. 6 display of strong emotion. **scenery** n 1 natural features of district. 2 constructions used on stage to represent scene of action. **scenic** adj picturesque.

scent ⊕ n 1 distinctive smell, esp. pleasant one. 2 trail. 3 perfume. ♦ v 4 detect or track (by smell). 5 sense. 6 fill with fragrance.

sceptic ⊕ n one who maintains doubt or disbelief. **sceptical** adj **scepticism** n

sceptre n ornamental staff as symbol of royal power.

schedule ⊕ n 1 plan of procedure for project. 2 list. 3 timetable. ♦ v 4 enter into schedule. 5 plan to occur at certain time.

scheme ⊕ n 1 plan, design. 2 project. 3 outline. ♦ v 4 devise, plan, esp. in underhand manner. **scheming** adj

schism n (group resulting from) division in political party, church etc.

schizophrenia n mental disorder involving deterioration of, confusion about personality. **schizophrenic** adj/n

school[1] ⊕ n 1 institution for teaching children or for giving instruction in any subject. 2 buildings of such institution. 3 group of thinkers, writers, artists etc. with principles or methods in

——————— THESAURUS ———————

scatter v = **throw about**, spread, sprinkle, strew, shower ≠ **gather**; = **disperse**, dispel, disband, dissipate ≠ **assemble**

scene n = **act**, part, division, episode; = **setting**, set, background, location, backdrop; = **site**, place, setting, area, position; = (Inf) **world**, business, environment, arena; = **view**, prospect, panorama, vista, landscape; = **fuss**, to-do, row, performance, exhibition

scent n = **fragrance**, smell,

perfume, bouquet, aroma; = **trail**, track, spoor ♦ v = **smell**, sense, detect, sniff, discern

sceptic n = **doubter**, cynic, disbeliever

schedule n = **plan**, programme, agenda, calendar, timetable ♦ v = **plan**, set up, book, programme, arrange

scheme n = **plan**, programme, strategy, system, project; = **plot**, ploy, ruse, intrigue, conspiracy ♦ v = **plot**, plan, intrigue, manoeuvre, conspire

S

common. ♦ v 4 educate. 5 bring under control, train. **scholar** n 1 learned person. 2 one taught in school. **scholarly** adj learned. **scholarship** n 1 learning. 2 prize, grant to student for payment of school or college fees. **scholastic** adj of schools or scholars.

school² n shoal (of fish, whales etc.).

schooner n 1 fore–and–aft rigged vessel with two or more masts. 2 tall glass.

science 🛈 n 1 systematic study and knowledge of natural or physical phenomena. 2 any branch of study concerned with observed material facts. 3 skill, technique. **scientific** adj 1 of the principles of science. 2 systematic. **scientist** n **science fiction** stories making imaginative use of scientific knowledge.

scimitar n curved oriental sword. **scintillating** adj 1 sparkling. 2 animated, witty, clever.

scissors pl n (esp. pair of scissors) cutting instrument of two blades pivoted together.

scoff¹ 🛈 v express derision for. **scoff²** 🛈 v Sl eat rapidly. **scold** v 1 find fault. 2 reprimand. **scone** n small plain cake baked on griddle or in oven.

scope 🛈 n 1 range of activity or application. 2 room, opportunity. **scorch** 🛈 v 1 burn, be burnt, on surface. ♦ n 2 slight burn.

score 🛈 n 1 points gained in game, competition. 2 group of 20 (esp. pl) 3 a lot. 4 musical notation. 5 mark or notch, esp. to keep tally. 6 reason, account. 7 grievance. ♦ v 8 gain points in game. 9 mark. 10 cross out. 11 arrange music (for). 12 keep tally of points.

scorn 🛈 n 1 contempt, derision. ♦ v 2 despise. **scornful** adj **scorpion** n small lobster–shaped animal with sting at end of jointed tail.

scotch v put an end to.

———— THESAURUS ————

school¹ n = **academy**, college, institution, institute, seminary; = **group**, set, circle, faction, followers ♦ v = **train**, coach, discipline, educate, drill
science n = **discipline**, body of knowledge, branch of knowledge
scoff¹ v = **scorn**, mock, laugh at, ridicule, knock (Inf)
scoff² v = **gobble (up)**, wolf, devour, bolt, guzzle
scope n = **opportunity**, room, freedom, space, liberty; = **range**, capacity, reach, area, outlook

scorch v = **burn**, sear, roast, wither, shrivel
score v = **gain**, win, achieve, make, get; = (Mus) **arrange**, set, orchestrate, adapt; = **cut**, scratch, mark, slash, scrape ♦ n = **rating**, mark, grade, percentage; = **points**, result, total, outcome; = **composition**, soundtrack, arrangement, orchestration
scorn n = **contempt**, disdain, mockery, derision, sarcasm ≠ respect ♦ v = **despise**, reject, disdain, slight, be above ≠ respect

scot–free *adj* without harm or loss.

scoundrel *n* villain, blackguard.

scour¹ ❶ *v* **1** clean, polish by rubbing. **2** clean or flush out.

scourer *n* rough pad for cleaning pots and pans.

scour² ❶ *v* move rapidly along or over (territory) in search of something.

scourge *n* **1** whip, lash. **2** severe affliction. ◆ *v* **3** flog. **4** punish severely.

scout ❶ *n* **1** one sent out to reconnoitre. ◆ *v* **2** act as scout.

scowl *v/n* (make) gloomy or sullen frown.

scrabble *v* scrape with hands, claws in disorderly manner.

scrag *n* **1** lean person or animal. **2** lean end of a neck of mutton.

scraggy *adj* thin, bony.

scram *v* **scramming, scrammed** *Inf* go away hastily.

scramble ❶ *v* **1** move along or up by crawling, climbing etc. **2** struggle with others (for). **3** mix up. **4** cook (eggs) beaten up with milk. ◆ *n* **5** scrambling. **6** rough climb. **7** disorderly proceeding.

scrap ❶ *n* **scrapping, scrapped 1** small piece or fragment. **2** leftover material. **3** *Inf* fight. ◆ *pl* **4** leftover food. ◆ *v* **5** break up, discard as useless. **6** *Inf* fight. **scrappy** *adj* **1** unequal in quality. **2** badly finished. **scrapbook** *n* book in which newspaper cuttings or pictures are stuck.

scrape ❶ *v* **1** rub with something sharp. **2** clean, smooth thus. **3** grate. **4** scratch. **5** rub with harsh noise. ◆ *n* **6** act, sound of scraping. **scraper** *n* instrument for scraping.

scratch ❶ *v* **1** score, make narrow surface mark or wound with something sharp. **2** scrape (skin) with nails to relieve itching. **3** remove, withdraw from list, race etc. ◆ *n* **4** wound, mark or sound made by scratching.

———— THESAURUS ————

scour¹ *v* = **scrub**, clean, polish, rub, buff

scour² *v* = **search**, hunt, comb, ransack

scout *n* = **vanguard**, lookout, precursor, outrider, reconnoitrer ◆ *v* = **reconnoitre**, investigate, watch, survey, observe

scramble *v* = **struggle**, climb, crawl, swarm, scrabble; = **strive**, rush, contend, vie, run ◆ *n* = **clamber**, ascent; = **race**, competition, struggle, rush, confusion

scrap *n* = **piece**, fragment, bit, grain, particle; = **waste**, junk, off cuts ◆ *v* = **get rid of**, drop, abandon, ditch (*Sl*), discard ≠ **bring back**

scrape *v* = **rake**, sweep, drag, brush; = **grate**, grind, scratch, squeak, rasp; = **graze**, skin, scratch, bark, scuff; = **clean**, remove, scour ◆ *n* = (*Inf*) **predicament**, difficulty, fix (*Inf*), mess, dilemma

scratch *v* = **rub**, scrape, claw at; = **mark**, cut, score, damage, grate

scrawl v **1** write, draw untidily. ◆ n **2** thing scrawled.

scrawny adj **scrawnier, scrawniest** thin, bony.

scream 🛈 v **1** utter piercing cry, esp. of fear, pain etc. **2** utter in a scream. ◆ n **3** shrill, piercing cry.

screech v/n scream.

screed n long (tedious) letter, passage or speech.

screen 🛈 n **1** device to shelter from heat, light, draught, observation etc. **2** blank surface on which photographic images are projected. **3** windscreen. ◆ v **4** shelter, hide. **5** show (film). **6** examine (group of people) for political motives or for presence of disease, weapons etc.

screw 🛈 n **1** metal pin with spiral thread, twisted into materials to pin or fasten. **2** anything resembling a screw in shape. ◆ v **3** fasten with screw. **4** twist around.

screwdriver n tool for turning screws.

scribble 🛈 v **1** write, draw carelessly. **2** make meaningless marks with pen or pencil. ◆ n **3** something scribbled.

scribe n **1** writer. **2** copyist. ◆ v **3** scratch a line with pointed instrument.

scrimp v **1** make too small or short. **2** treat meanly.

script 🛈 n **1** (system or style of) handwriting. **2** written text of film, play, radio or television programme.

scripture n **1** sacred writings. **2** the Bible.

scroll n **1** roll of parchment or paper. **2** ornament shaped thus.

scrotum n, pl **–ta, –tums** pouch of skin containing testicles.

scrounge v Inf get without cost, by begging. **scrounger** n

scrub¹ 🛈 v **scrubbing, scrubbed 1** clean with hard brush and water. **2** scour. **3** Inf delete, cancel. ◆ n **4** scrubbing.

scrub² n **scrubbing, scrubbed 1** stunted trees. **2** brushwood.

scruff n nape of neck.

scrum, scrummage n **1** Rugby restarting of play in which

——————— THESAURUS ———————

◆ n = **mark**, scrape, graze, blemish, gash

scream v = **cry**, yell, shriek, screech, bawl ◆ n = **cry**, yell, howl, shriek, screech

screen n = **cover**, guard, shade, shelter, shield ◆ v = **broadcast**, show, put on, present, air; = **cover**, hide, conceal, shade, mask; = **investigate**, test, check, examine, scan; = **process**, sort, examine, filter, scan

screw v = **fasten**, fix, attach, bolt, clamp; = **turn**, twist, tighten; = (Inf) **cheat**, do (Sl), rip (someone) off (Sl), skin (Sl), trick

scribble v = **scrawl**, write, jot, dash off

script n = **text**, lines, words, book, copy; = **handwriting**, writing, calligraphy, penmanship

scrub¹ v = **scour**, clean, polish, rub, wash; = (Inf) **cancel**, drop, give up, abolish, forget about

opposing packs of forwards push against each other to gain possession of the ball. **2** disorderly struggle.

scruple n **1** doubt or hesitation about what is morally right. ♦ v **2** hesitate. **scrupulous** adj **1** extremely conscientious. **2** thorough.

scrutiny ⊕ n, pl -nies **1** close examination. **2** critical investigation. **scrutinize** v examine closely.

scuba diving sport of swimming under water using self–contained breathing apparatus.

scud v scudding, scudded **1** run fast. **2** run before wind.

scuff v **1** drag, scrape with feet in walking. **2** graze. ♦ n **3** act, sound of scuffing.

scuffle v **1** fight in disorderly manner. **2** shuffle. ♦ n **3** scuffling.

scull n **1** oar used in stern of boat. **2** short oar used in pairs. ♦ v **3** propel, move by means of sculls.

scullery n, pl -leries place for washing dishes etc.

sculpture ⊕ n **1** art of forming solid figures. **2** product of this art. ♦ v **3** represent by sculpture. **sculptor** n

scum n **1** froth or other floating matter on liquid. **2** waste part of anything. **3** vile people. **scummy** adj

scungy adj -ier, -iest Aust & NZ informal sordid or dirty.

scurrilous adj coarse, indecently abusive.

scurry v -rying, -ried **1** run hastily. ♦ n **2** bustling haste. **3** flurry.

scurvy n disease caused by lack of vitamin C.

scuttle[1] n fireside container for coal.

scuttle[2] v **1** rush away. **2** run hurriedly. ♦ n **3** hurried run.

scuttle[3] v make hole in ship to sink it.

scythe n **1** manual implement with long curved blade for cutting grass. ♦ v **2** cut with scythe.

sea ⊕ n **1** mass of salt water covering greater part of earth. **2** broad tract of this. **3** waves. **4** vast expanse. ♦ adj **5** of the sea. **seagull** n gull. **sea horse** fish with bony–plated body and horselike head. **sea lion** kind of large seal. **seaman** n sailor. **seasick** adj **seasickness** n nausea caused by motion of ship. **seaweed** n plant growing in sea. **seaworthy** adj in fit condition to put to sea.

seal[1] ⊕ n **1** piece of metal or stone engraved with device for impression on wax etc. **2** impression thus made (on letters etc.). **3** device, material preventing passage of water, air, oil etc. ♦ v **4** affix seal to ratify, authorize. **5** mark with stamp as evidence of

S

———————— THESAURUS ————————

scrutiny n = **examination**, study, investigation, search, analysis
sculpture v = **carve**, form, model,

fashion, shape
sea n = **ocean**, the deep, the waves, main; = **mass**, army, host,

some quality. **6** keep close or secret. **7** settle. **8** make watertight, airtight etc.

seal² *n* amphibious furred carnivorous mammal with flippers as limbs.

seam ❶ *n* **1** line of junction of two edges, e.g. of two pieces of cloth. **2** thin layer, stratum. ◆ *v* **3** mark with furrows or wrinkles. **seamless** *adj* **seamy** *adj* sordid.

seance *n* meeting at which people attempt to communicate with the dead.

sear ❶ *v* scorch.

search ❶ *v* **1** look over or through to find something. ◆ *n* **2** act of searching. **3** quest. **searching** *adj* thorough.

season ❶ *n* **1** one of four divisions of year. **2** period during which thing happens etc. ◆ *v* **3** flavour with salt, herbs etc. **4** make reliable or ready for use. **5** make experienced. **seasonable** *adj* **1** appropriate for the season. **2** opportune. **seasonal** *adj* varying with seasons. **seasoning** *n* flavouring.

seat ❶ *n* **1** thing for sitting on. **2** buttocks. **3** base. **4** right to sit (e.g. in council etc.). **5** place where something is located, centred. **6** locality of disease, trouble etc. **7** country house. ◆ *v* **8** make to sit. **9** provide sitting accommodation for. **seat belt** belt worn in vehicle to prevent injury in crash.

secateurs *pl n* small pruning shears.

secede *v* withdraw formally from federation, Church etc. **secession** *n*

seclude *v* guard from, remove from sight, view, contact with others. **secluded** *adj* **1** remote. **2** private. **seclusion** *n*

second¹ ❶ *adj* **1** next after first. **2** alternate, additional. **3** of lower quality. ◆ *n* **4** person or thing coming second. **5** attendant. **6** sixtieth part of minute. ◆ *v* **7** support. **second–class** *adj* inferior. **second–hand** *adj* **1** bought after use by another. **2** not original. **second sight** supposed ability to predict events.

crowd, mob

seal¹ *v* = **settle**, clinch, conclude, consummate, finalize ◆ *n* = **sealant**, sealer, adhesive

seam *n* = **joint**, closure; = **layer**, vein, stratum, lode

sear *v* = **wither**, burn, scorch, sizzle

search *v* = **examine**, investigate, explore, inspect, comb ◆ *n* = **hunt**, look, investigation, examination,

pursuit

season *n* = **period**, time, term, spell ◆ *v* = **flavour**, salt, spice, enliven, pep up

seat *n* = **chair**, bench, stall, stool, pew; = **membership**, place, constituency, chair, incumbency; = **centre**, place, site, heart, capital; = **mansion**, house, residence, abode, ancestral hall ◆ *v* = **sit**, place, settle, set, fix; = **hold**, take,

second² v transfer (employee, officer) temporarily.

secondary ⊕ adj **1** of less importance. **2** developed from something else. **3** *Education* after primary stage.

secret ⊕ adj **1** kept, meant to be kept from knowledge of others. **2** hidden. ♦ n **3** thing kept secret. **secrecy** n keeping or being kept secret. **secretive** adj given to having secrets.

secretary n, pl **-ries 1** one employed to deal with papers and correspondence, keep records etc. **2** head of a state department. **secretariat** n body of secretaries.

secrete v **1** hide. **2** conceal. **3** (of gland etc.) collect and supply particular substance in body. **secretion** n

sect ⊕ n **1** group of people (within religious body etc.) with common interest. **2** faction. **sectarian** adj

section ⊕ n **1** division. **2** portion. **3** distinct part. **4** cutting. **5** drawing of anything as if cut through.

sector ⊕ n part or subdivision.

secular ⊕ adj **1** worldly. **2** lay, not religious.

secure ⊕ adj **1** safe. **2** firmly fixed. **3** certain. ♦ v **4** gain possession of. **5** make safe. **6** make firm. **security** n, pl **-ties 1** state of safety. **2** protection. **3** anything given as bond or pledge.

sedate¹ adj calm, serious.

sedate² v make calm by sedative. **sedation** n **sedative** adj **1** having soothing or calming effect. ♦ n **2** sedative drug.

sediment ⊕ n matter which

———————— THESAURUS ————————

accommodate, sit, contain

second¹ adj **= next**, following, succeeding, subsequent; **= additional**, other, further, extra, alternative; **= inferior**, secondary, subordinate, lower, lesser ♦ n **= supporter**, assistant, aide, colleague, backer ♦ v **= support**, back, endorse, approve, go along with

secondary adj **= subordinate**, minor, lesser, lower, inferior ≠ **main**; **= resultant**, contingent, derived, indirect ≠ **original**

secret adj **= undisclosed**, unknown, confidential, underground, undercover; **= concealed**, hidden, disguised

≠ **unconcealed**

sect n **= group**, division, faction, party, camp

section n **= part**, piece, portion, division, slice; **= district**, area, region, sector, zone

sector n **= part**, division; **= area**, part, region, district, zone

secular adj **= worldly**, lay, earthly, civil, temporal ≠ **religious**

secure v **= obtain**, get, acquire, score (*Sl*), gain ≠ **lose**; **= attach**, stick, fix, bind, fasten ≠ **detach** ♦ adj **= safe**, protected, immune, unassailable ≠ **unprotected**; **= fast**, firm, fixed, stable, steady ≠ **insecure**; **= confident**, sure, easy, certain, assured ≠ **uneasy**

S

settles to the bottom of liquid.
sedition n stirring up of rebellion.
seduce ❶ v persuade to commit some (wrong) deed, esp. sexual intercourse. **seducer** n **seduction** n **seductive** adj alluring.
see¹ ❶ v **seeing, saw, seen 1** perceive with eyes or mentally. **2** watch. **3** find out. **4** interview. **5** make sure. **6** accompany. **7** consider. **seeing** conj in view of the fact that.
see² n diocese, office of bishop.
seed ❶ n **1** reproductive germs of plants. **2** one grain of this. **3** such grains saved or used for sowing. **4** sperm. **5** origin. ♦ v **6** sow with seed. **7** produce seed. **seedling** n young plant raised from seed.

seedy adj **1** shabby. **2** full of seed.
seek ❶ v **seeking, sought** make search or enquiry (for).
seem ❶ v appear (to be or to do).
seemly adj becoming and proper.
seep ❶ v trickle through slowly.
seesaw n **1** plank on which children sit at opposite ends and swing up and down. ♦ v **2** move up and down.
seethe ❶ v **seething, seethed 1** boil, foam. **2** be very agitated. **3** be in constant movement (as large crowd etc.).
segment n **1** piece cut off. **2** section. ♦ v **3** divide into segments.
segregate ❶ v set apart from rest. **segregation** n

———————————— THESAURUS ————————————

sediment n = **dregs**, grounds, residue, lees, deposit
seduce v = **tempt**, lure, entice, mislead, deceive; = **corrupt**, deprave, dishonour, debauch, deflower
see¹ v = **perceive**, spot, notice, sight, witness; = **understand**, get, follow, realize, appreciate; = **find out**, learn, discover, determine, verify; = **consider**, decide, reflect, deliberate, think over; = **make sure**, ensure, guarantee, make certain, see to it; = **accompany**, show, escort, lead, walk; = **speak to**, receive, interview, consult, confer with; = **meet**, come across, happen on, bump into, run across; = **go out with**, court, date (informal, chiefly US), go steady with (Inf)

seed n = **grain**, pip, germ, kernel, egg; = **beginning**, start, germ; = **origin**, source, nucleus; = (Chiefly Bible) **offspring**, children, descendants, issue, progeny; **go or run to seed** = **decline**, deteriorate
seek v = **look for**, pursue, search for, be after, hunt; = **try**, attempt, aim, strive, endeavour
seem v = **appear**, give the impression of being, look
seep v = **ooze**, well, leak, soak, trickle
seethe v = **be furious**, rage, fume, simmer, see red (Inf); = **boil**, bubble, foam, fizz, froth
segment n = **section**, part, piece, division, slice
segregate v = **set apart**, divide, separate, isolate, discriminate against ≠ **unite**

seize ● v 1 grasp. 2 lay hold of. 3 capture. 4 (of machine part) stick tightly through overheating.

seizure n 1 act of taking. 2 sudden onset of disease.

seldom ● adv not often, rarely.

select ● v 1 pick out, choose. ◆ adj 2 choice, picked. 3 exclusive.

selection n 1 option. 2 assortment.

selective adj **selector** n

self n, pl **selves** one's own person or individuality. **selfish** adj 1 unduly concerned with personal profit or pleasure. 2 greedy. **selfless** adj unselfish.

self– comb. form of oneself or itself.

sell ● v **selling**, **sold** 1 hand over for a price. 2 stock, have for sale. 3 make someone accept 4 Inf betray, cheat. 5 find purchasers. **seller** n

Sellotape ® n 1 type of adhesive tape. ◆ v 2 (without cap.) stick with Sellotape.

semaphore n system of signalling by human or mechanical arms.

semblance n 1 (false) appearance. 2 image, likeness.

semen n 1 fluid carrying sperm of male animals. 2 sperm.

semi– comb. form 1 half, partly, not completely, as in semicircle. 2 half, partly, not completely.

semibreve n musical note equal to four crotchets.

semicolon n punctuation mark (;).

semiconductor n substance whose electrical conductivity increases with temperature, used in transistors, circuits etc.

semidetached adj (of house) joined to another by one side only.

semifinal n match, round etc. before final.

seminal adj 1 capable of developing. 2 influential. 3 of semen or seed.

seminar n meeting of group (of students) for discussion.

semiprecious adj (of gemstones) having less value than precious stones.

semolina n hard grains left after sifting of flour, used for puddings etc.

send ● v **sending**, **sent** 1 cause to go or be conveyed. 2 despatch. 3 transmit (by radio).

senile adj showing weakness of old age. **senility** n

senior ● adj 1 superior in rank or standing. 2 older. ◆ n 3 superior. 4

———— THESAURUS ————

seize v = **grab**, grip, grasp, take, snatch ≠ let go; = **take by storm**, take over, acquire, occupy, conquer

seldom adv = **rarely**, not often, infrequently, hardly ever ≠ often

select v = **choose**, take, pick, opt for, decide on ≠ reject ◆ adj = **choice**, special, excellent, superior, first-class ≠ ordinary; = **exclusive**, elite, privileged, cliquish ≠ indiscriminate

sell v = **trade**, exchange, barter ≠ buy; = **deal in**, market, trade in, stock, handle ≠ buy

send v = **dispatch**, forward, direct, convey, remit, = **transmit**, broadcast, communicate

elder person. **seniority** n

sensation ⊕ n 1 operation of sense, feeling, awareness. 2 excited feeling, state of excitement. 3 exciting event. **sensational** adj producing great excitement. **sensationalism** n deliberate use of sensational material.

sense ⊕ n 1 any of bodily faculties of perception or feeling. 2 ability to perceive. 3 consciousness. 4 meaning. 5 coherence. 6 sound practical judgment. ♦ v 7 perceive. **senseless** adj

sensible ⊕ adj 1 reasonable, wise. 2 aware. **sensibility** n ability to feel, esp. emotional or moral feelings.

sensitive ⊕ adj 1 open to, acutely affected by, external impressions. 2 easily affected or altered. 3 easily upset by criticism. 4 responsive to slight changes. **sensitivity**, **sensitiveness** n **sensitize** v make sensitive.

sensor n device that detects or measures the presence of something.

sensory adj relating to senses.

sensual ⊕ adj 1 of senses only and not of mind. 2 given to pursuit of pleasures of sense.

sensuous adj stimulating, or apprehended by, senses, esp. in aesthetic manner.

sentence ⊕ n 1 combination of words expressing a thought. 2 judgment passed on criminal by court or judge. ♦ v 3 pass sentence on, condemn.

sentient adj capable of feeling.

sentiment ⊕ n 1 tendency to be moved by feeling rather than

———— THESAURUS ————

senior adj = **higher ranking**, superior ≠ **subordinate**; = **the elder**, major (Brit) ≠ **junior**
sensation n = **feeling**, sense, impression, perception, awareness; = **excitement**, thrill, stir, furore, commotion
sense n = **feeling**, impression, perception, awareness, consciousness; = **understanding**, awareness; sometimes plural = **intelligence**, reason, understanding, brains (Inf), judgment ≠ **foolishness**; = **meaning**, significance, import, implication, drift ♦ v = **perceive**, feel, understand, pick up, realize ≠ **be unaware of**

sensible adj = **wise**, practical, prudent, shrewd, judicious ≠ **foolish**; = **intelligent**, practical, rational, sound, realistic ≠ **senseless**
sensitive adj = **thoughtful**, kindly, concerned, patient, attentive; = **susceptible to**, responsive to, easily affected by; = **touchy**, oversensitive, easily upset, easily offended, easily hurt ≠ **insensitive**
sensual adj = **sexual**, erotic, raunchy (Sl), lewd, lascivious; = **physical**, bodily, voluptuous, animal, luxurious
sentence n = **punishment**, condemnation ♦ v = **condemn**, doom

reason. **2** mental feeling. **3** opinion. **sentimental** *adj* given to indulgence in sentiment and in its expression. **sentimentality** *n*

sentinel *n* sentry.

sentry *n, pl* **–tries** soldier on watch.

separate ❶ *v* **1** part. **2** divide. ◆ *adj* **3** disconnected, distinct, individual. **separable** *adj* **separation** *n* **1** disconnection. **2** living apart of married couple.

sepia *n* **1** reddish–brown pigment. ◆ *adj* **2** of this colour.

Sept. September.

September *n* ninth month.

septet *n* (music for) group of seven musicians.

septic *adj* **1** (of wound) infected. **2** of, caused by pus–forming bacteria.

septicaemia *n* blood poisoning.

sepulchre *n* **1** tomb. **2** burial vault.

sequel ❶ *n* **1** consequence. **2** continuation, e.g. of story.

sequence ❶ *n* arrangement of things in successive order.

sequin *n* small ornamental metal disc on dresses etc.

seraph *n, pl* **–aphs, –aphim** angel.

serenade *n* **1** sentimental song addressed to woman by lover, esp. at evening. ◆ *v* **2** sing serenade (to)

serendipity *n* gift of making fortunate discoveries by accident.

serene *adj* **1** calm, tranquil. **2** unclouded. **serenity** *n*

serf *n* one of class of medieval labourers bound to, and transferred with, land.

sergeant *n* **1** noncommissioned officer in army. **2** police officer above constable. **sergeant major** highest noncommissioned officer in regiment.

series ❶ *n, pl* **–ries 1** sequence. **2** succession, set (e.g. of radio, TV programmes). **serial** *n* story or play produced in successive episodes. **serialize** *v*

serious ❶ *adj* **1** thoughtful, solemn. **2** earnest, sincere. **3** of importance. **4** giving cause for concern.

——————— THESAURUS ———————

sentiment *n* = **feeling**, idea, view, opinion, attitude; = **sentimentality**, emotion, tenderness, romanticism, sensibility

separate *adj* = **unconnected**, individual, particular, divided, divorced ≠ **connected**; = **individual**, independent, apart, distinct ≠ **joined** ◆ *v* = **divide**, detach, disconnect, disjoin ≠ **combine**; = **come apart**, split,

come away ≠ **connect**; = **sever**, break apart, split in two, divide in two ≠ **join**; = **split up**, part, divorce, break up, part company

sequel *n* = **follow–up**, continuation, development; = **consequence**, result, outcome, conclusion, end

sequence *n* = **succession**, course, series, order, chain

series *n* = **sequence**, course, chain, succession

sermon ① n 1 discourse of religious instruction or exhortation. 2 any similar discourse.

serpent n snake. **serpentine** adj twisting, winding like a snake.

serrated adj having notched, sawlike edge.

serum n watery animal fluid, esp. thin part of blood as used for inoculation or vaccination.

serve ① v 1 work for, under another. 2 attend (to customers) in shop etc. 3 provide. 4 help to (food etc.). 5 present (food etc.) in particular way. 6 be member of military unit. 7 spend time doing. 8 be useful, suitable enough. **servant** n personal or domestic attendant. **service** n 1 act of serving. 2 system organized to provide for needs of public. 3 maintenance of vehicle. 4 use. 5 department of State employment. 6 set of dishes etc. 7 form, session of public worship. ◆ pl 8 armed forces. ◆ v 9 overhaul. **serviceable** adj 1 in working order, usable. 2 durable. **serviceman** n member of

armed forced. **service station** place supplying fuel, oil, maintenance for motor vehicles.

serviette n table napkin.

servile adj 1 slavish, without independence. 2 fawning.

servitude n bondage, slavery.

sesame n plant whose seeds and oil are used in cooking.

session ① n 1 meeting of court etc. 2 continuous series of such meetings. 3 any period devoted to an activity.

set ① v setting, set 1 put or place in specified position or condition. 2 make ready. 3 become firm or fixed. 4 establish. 5 prescribe, allot. 6 put to music. 7 (of sun) go down. ◆ adj 8 fixed, established. 9 deliberate. 10 unvarying. ◆ n 11 act or state of being set. 12 bearing, posture. 13 Radio, TV complete apparatus for reception or transmission. 14 Theatre, Cinema organized settings and equipment to form ensemble of scene. 15 number of associated things, persons. **setback** n anything that hinders or impedes. **set up**

serious adj = **grave**, bad, critical, dangerous, acute; = **important**, crucial, urgent, pressing, worrying ≠ unimportant; = **thoughtful**, detailed, careful, deep, profound; = **deep**, sophisticated

sermon n = **homily**, address

serve v = **work for**, help, aid, assist, be in the service of; = **perform**, do, complete, fulfil, discharge; = **be adequate**, do,

suffice, suit, satisfy; = **present**, provide, supply, deliver, set out

service n = **facility**, system, resource, utility, amenity; = **ceremony**, worship, rite, observance; = **work**, labour, employment, business, office; = **check**, maintenance check ◆ v = **overhaul**, check, maintain, tune (up), go over

session n = **meeting**, hearing,

establish.

sett n badger's burrow.

settee n couch.

setting ❶ n 1 background. 2 surroundings. 3 scenery and other stage accessories. 4 decorative metalwork holding precious stone etc. in position. 5 tableware and cutlery for (single place) at table. 6 music for song.

settle ❶ v 1 arrange. 2 establish. 3 decide upon. 4 end (dispute etc.). 5 pay. 6 make calm or stable. 7 come to rest. 8 subside. 9 become clear. 10 take up residence.

settlement n 1 act of settling. 2 place newly inhabited. 3 money bestowed legally. **settler** n

colonist.

seven adj/n cardinal number next after six. **seventh** adj ordinal number. **seventeen** adj/n ten plus seven. **seventeenth** adj **seventieth** adj **seventy** adj/n ten times seven.

sever ❶ v 1 separate, divide. 2 cut off. **severance** n

several ❶ adj 1 some, a few. 2 separate. 3 individual. ♦ pron 4 indefinite small number.

severe ❶ adj 1 strict. 2 harsh. 3 austere. 4 extreme. **severity** n

sew v sewing, sewed, sewn 1 join with needle and thread. 2 make by sewing. **sewing** n

sewage n refuse, waste matter, excrement conveyed in sewer.

———— THESAURUS ————

sitting, period, conference

set v = **put**, place, lay, position, rest; = **arrange**, decide (upon), settle, establish, determine; = **assign**, give, allot, prescribe; = **harden**, stiffen, solidify, cake, thicken; = **go down**, sink, dip, decline, disappear; = **prepare**, lay, spread, arrange, make ready ♦ adj = **established**, planned, decided, agreed, arranged; = **strict**, rigid, stubborn, inflexible ≠ **flexible**; = **conventional**, traditional, stereotyped, unspontaneous ♦ n = **scenery**, setting, scene, stage set; = **position**, bearing, attitude, carriage, posture; **be set on** or **upon something** = **be determined to**, be intent on, be bent on, be resolute about

setting n = **surroundings**, site, location, set, scene

settle v = **resolve**, work out, put an end to, straighten out; = **pay**, clear, square (up), discharge; = **move to**, take up residence in, live in, dwell in, inhabit; = **colonize**, populate, people, pioneer; = **land**, alight, descend, light, come to rest; = **calm**, quiet, relax, reassure ≠ **disturb**

sever v = **cut**, separate, split, part, divide ≠ **join**; = **discontinue**, terminate, break off, put an end to, dissociate ≠ **continue**

several adj = **some**, a few, a number of, a handful of

severe adj = **serious**, critical, terrible, desperate, extreme; = **acute**, intense, violent, piercing, harrowing; = **strict**, hard, harsh, cruel, rigid ≠ **lenient**; = **grim**, serious, grave, forbidding, stern ≠ **genial**

S

sewer n underground drain.

sex ⊕ n 1 state of being male or female. 2 males or females collectively. 3 sexual intercourse. ♦ adj 4 concerning sex. ♦ v 5 ascertain sex of. **sexism** n discrimination on basis of sex. **sexist** n/adj **sexual** adj **sexy** adj **sexual intercourse** act of procreation in which male's penis is inserted into female's vagina.

sextet n (composition for) six musicians.

shabby ⊕ adj –bier, –biest 1 faded, worn. 2 poorly dressed. 3 mean, dishonourable.

shack ⊕ n rough hut.

shackle n 1 metal ring or fastening for prisoner's wrist or ankle. ♦ v 2 fasten with shackles. 3 hamper.

shade ⊕ n 1 partial darkness. 2 shelter, place sheltered from light, heat etc. 3 darker part of anything. 4 depth of colour. 5 screen 6 US window blind. ♦ v 7 screen from light, darken. 8

represent shades in drawing.

shady adj 1 shielded from sun. 2 Inf dishonest.

shadow ⊕ n 1 dark figure projected by anything that intercepts rays of light. 2 patch of shade. 3 slight trace. ♦ v 4 cast shadow over. 5 follow and watch closely. **shadowy** adj

shaft ⊕ n 1 straight rod, stem, handle. 2 arrow. 3 ray, beam (of light). 4 revolving rod for transmitting power.

shag n 1 long–napped cloth. 2 coarse shredded tobacco. **shaggy** adj 1 covered with rough hair. 2 unkempt.

shake ⊕ v shaking, shook, shaken 1 (cause to) move with quick vibrations. 2 tremble. 3 grasp the hand (of another) in greeting. 4 upset. 5 wave, brandish. ♦ n 6 act of shaking. 7 vibration. 8 jolt. 9 Inf short period of time. **shaky** adj 1 unsteady, insecure. 2 questionable.

shale n flaky fine–grained rock.

——————— THESAURUS ———————

sex n = (Inf) **lovemaking**, sexual relations, copulation, fornication, coitus

shabby adj = **tatty**, worn, ragged, scruffy, tattered ≠ **smart**; = **run-down**, seedy, mean, dilapidated

shack n = **hut**, cabin, shanty

shade n = **hue**, tone, colour, tint; = **dash**, trace, hint, suggestion; = **screen**, covering, cover, blind, curtain; = (Lit) **ghost**, spirit, phantom, spectre, apparition ♦ v = **darken**, shadow, cloud, dim;

= **cover**, protect, screen, hide, shield

shadow n = **silhouette**, shape, outline, profile; = **shade**, dimness, darkness, gloom, cover ♦ v = **shade**, screen, shield, darken, overhang; = **follow**, tail (Inf), trail, stalk

shaft n = **tunnel**, hole, passage, burrow, passageway; = **handle**, staff, pole, rod, stem

shake v = **jiggle**, agitate; = **tremble**, shiver, quake, quiver;

shall *v, past tense* **should** makes compound tenses or moods to express obligation, command, condition or intention.

shallow **ⓘ** *adj* **1** not deep. **2** superficial. ♦ *n* **3** shallow place.

sham **ⓘ** *adj/n* **1** imitation, counterfeit. ♦ *v* **2** pretend, feign.

shamble *v* walk in shuffling, awkward way.

shambles **ⓘ** *pl n* messy, disorderly thing or place.

shame **ⓘ** *n* **1** emotion caused by consciousness of guilt or dishonour in one's conduct or state. **2** cause of disgrace. **3** pity, hard luck. ♦ *v* **4** cause to feel shame. **5** disgrace. **6** force by shame (into). **shameful** *adj* **shameless** *adj* **1** with no sense of shame. **2** indecent. **shamefaced** *adj* ashamed.

shampoo *n* **1** preparation of liquid soap for washing hair, carpets etc.

2 this process. ♦ *v* **3** use shampoo to wash.

shamrock *n* clover leaf, esp. as Irish emblem.

shandy *n, pl* **–dies** drink of beer and lemonade.

shanty¹ *n* **1** temporary wooden building. **2** crude dwelling.

shanty² *n* sailor's song.

shape **ⓘ** *n* **1** external form or appearance. **2** mould, pattern. **3** *Inf* condition. ♦ *v* **4** form, mould. **5** develop. **shapeless** *adj* **shapely** *adj* well–proportioned.

shard *n* broken piece of pottery.

share **ⓘ** *n* **1** portion. **2** quota. **3** lot. **4** unit of ownership in public company. ♦ *v* **5** give, take a share. **6** join with others in doing, using, something. **shareholder** *n*

shark *n* **1** large usu. predatory sea fish. **2** person who cheats others.

sharp **ⓘ** *adj* **1** having keen cutting edge or fine point. **2** not gradual

———— THESAURUS ————

= **rock**, totter; = **wave**, wield, flourish, brandish ♦ *n* = **vibration**, trembling, quaking, jerk, shiver

shallow *adj* = **superficial**, surface, empty, slight, foolish ≠ **deep**

sham *n* = **fraud**, imitation, hoax, pretence, forgery ≠ **the real thing** ♦ *adj* = **false**, artificial, bogus, pretended, mock ≠ **real**

shambles *n* = **chaos**, mess, disorder, confusion, muddle

shame *n* = **embarrassment**, humiliation, ignominy, mortification, abashment ≠ **shamelessness**; = **disgrace**, scandal, discredit, smear,

disrepute ≠ **honour** ♦ *v* = **embarrass**, disgrace, humiliate, humble, mortify ≠ **make proud**; = **dishonour**, degrade, stain, smear, blot ≠ **honour**

shape *n* = **appearance**, form, aspect, guise, likeness; = **form**, profile, outline, lines, build; = **pattern**, model, frame, mould; = **condition**, state, health, trim, fettle ♦ *v* = **form**, make, produce, create, model; = **mould**, form, make, fashion, model

share *n* = **part**, portion, quota, ration, lot ♦ *v* = **divide**, split, distribute, assign; = **go halves on**,

S

or gentle. **3** brisk. **4** clever. **5** harsh. **6** dealing cleverly but unfairly. **7** shrill. **8** strongly marked, esp. in outline. **9** sour. ◆ *adv* **10** promptly. **sharpen** *v* make sharp. **sharpshooter** *n* marksman.

shatter ⊕ *v* **1** break in pieces. **2** ruin (plans etc.). **3** disturb (person) greatly. **shattered** *adj Inf* completely exhausted.

shave ⊕ *v* **shaving, shaved 1** cut close, esp. hair of face or head. **2** pare away. **3** graze. **4** reduce. ◆ *n* **5** shaving. **shavings** *pl n* parings.

shawl *n* piece of fabric to cover woman's shoulders or wrap baby.

she *pron* (*third person fem*) **1** person, animal already referred to. ◆ *comb. form* **2** female, as in *she-wolf*. **3** female.

sheaf *n, pl* **sheaves 1** bundle, esp. of corn. **2** loose leaves of paper.

shear *v* **shearing, sheared 1** clip hair, wool from. **2**

cut through. **3** fracture. **shears** *pl n* large pair of scissors.

sheath *n* close-fitting cover, esp. for knife or sword. **sheathe** *v* put into sheath.

shebeen *n Irish, S Afr & Scot* place where alcohol is sold illegally.

shed¹ ⊕ *n* roofed shelter used as store or workshop.

shed² ⊕ *v* **shedding, shed 1** (cause to) pour forth (e.g. tears, blood). **2** cast off.

sheen ⊕ *n* gloss.

sheep *n, pl* **sheep** ruminant animal bred for wool or meat.

sheepish *adj* embarrassed, shy.

sheepdog *n* dog used for herding sheep.

sheer ⊕ *adj* **1** perpendicular. **2** (of material) very thin, transparent. **3** absolute, unmitigated.

sheet ⊕ *n* **1** large piece of cotton etc. to cover bed. **2** broad piece of any thin material. **3** large expanse.

sheikh, sheik *n* Arab chief.

——————— THESAURUS ———————

go fifty-fifty on (*Inf*)

sharp *adj* = **keen**, jagged, serrated ≠ **blunt**; = **quick-witted**, clever, astute, knowing, quick ≠ **dim**; = **cutting**, biting, bitter, harsh, barbed ≠ **gentle**; = **sudden**, marked, abrupt, extreme, distinct ≠ **gradual**; = **clear**, distinct, well-defined, crisp ≠ **indistinct**; = **sour**, tart, pungent, hot, acid ≠ **bland** ◆ *adv* = **promptly**, precisely, exactly, on time, on the dot ≠ **approximately**

shatter *v* = **smash**, break, burst, crack, crush; = **destroy**, ruin,

wreck, demolish, torpedo

shave *v* = **trim**, crop

shed¹ *n* = **hut**, shack, outhouse

shed² *v* = **drop**, spill, scatter; = **cast off**, discard, moult, slough off; = **give out**, cast, emit, give, radiate

sheen *n* = **shine**, gleam, gloss, polish, brightness

sheer *adj* = **total**, complete, absolute, utter, pure ≠ **moderate**; = **steep**, abrupt, precipitous ≠ **gradual**; = **fine**, thin, transparent, see-through, gossamer ≠ **thick**

shelf *n, pl* **shelves 1** board fixed horizontally (on wall etc.) for holding things. **2** ledge.

shell ❶ *n* **1** hard outer case (esp. of egg, nut etc.). **2** explosive projectile. **3** outer part of structure left when interior is removed. ◆ *v* **4** take shell from. **5** take out of shell. **6** fire at with shells. **shellfish** *n* **1** mollusc. **2** crustacean.

shelter ❶ *n* **1** place, structure giving protection. **2** refuge. ◆ *v* **3** give protection to. **4** take shelter.

shelve ❶ *v* **1** put on a shelf. **2** put off. **3** slope gradually.

shepherd ❶ *n* **1** one who tends sheep. ◆ *v* **2** guide, watch over.

shepherd's pie dish of minced meat and potato.

sherbet *n* fruit-flavoured effervescent powder.

sheriff *n* **1** US law enforcement officer. **2** in England and Wales, chief executive officer of the crown in a county. **3** in Scotland, chief judge of a district. **4** *Canad*

municipal officer who enforces court orders etc.

sherry *n, pl* **-ries** fortified wine.

shield ❶ *n* **1** piece of armour carried on arm. **2** any protection used to stop blows, missiles etc. ◆ *v* **3** cover, protect.

shift ❶ *v* **1** move, change position. ◆ *n* **2** move, change of position. **3** relay of workers. **4** time of their working. **5** woman's underskirt or dress. **shiftless** *adj* lacking in resource or character. **shifty** *adj* evasive, of dubious character.

shilling *n* former Brit. coin, now 5p.

shimmer ❶ *v* **1** shine with quivering light. ◆ *n* **2** such light.

shin *n* **1** front of lower leg. ◆ *v* **2** climb with arms and legs.

shine ❶ *v* **shining, shone 1** give out, reflect light. **2** excel. **3** polish. ◆ *n* **4** brightness, lustre. **5** polishing. **shiny** *adj*

shingle *n* **1** mass of pebbles.

THESAURUS

sheet *n* = **page**, leaf, folio, piece of paper; = **plate**, piece, panel, slab

shell *n* = **husk**, case, pod ◆ *v* = **bomb**, bombard, attack, blitz, strafe

shelter *n* = **cover**, screen; = **protection**, safety, refuge, cover ◆ *v* = **take shelter**, hide, seek refuge, take cover; = **protect**, shield, harbour, safeguard, cover ≠ **endanger**

shelve *v* = **postpone**, defer, freeze, suspend, put aside

shepherd *n* = **drover**, stockman, herdsman, grazier ◆ *v* = **guide**, conduct, steer, herd, usher

shield *n* = **protection**, cover, defence, screen, guard ◆ *v* = **protect**, cover, screen, guard, defend

shift *v* = **move**, move around, budge ◆ *n* = **change**, shifting, displacement

shimmer *v* = **gleam**, twinkle, glisten, scintillate ◆ *n* = **gleam**, iridescence

shine *v* = **gleam**, flash, beam,

shingles n disease causing rash of small blisters.

ship ❶ n 1 large seagoing vessel. ◆ v 2 put on or send (esp. by ship). **shipment** n 1 act of shipping. 2 goods shipped. **shipping** n 1 freight transport business. 2 ships collectively. **shipshape** adj orderly, neat. **shipwreck** n 1 destruction of ship. ◆ v 2 cause shipwreck of. **shipyard** n place for building and repair of ships.

shire n county. **shire horse** large powerful breed of horse.

shirk v evade, try to avoid (duty etc.).

shirt n garment with sleeves and collar for upper part of body.

shirty adj –tier, –tiest Inf annoyed.

shiver¹ ❶ v 1 tremble, usu. with cold or fear. ◆ n 2 act, state of shivering.

shiver² v/n splinter.

shoal¹ n large number of fish swimming together.

shoal² n 1 stretch of shallow water. 2 sandbank.

shock¹ ❶ v 1 horrify, scandalize. ◆ n 2 violent or damaging blow. 3 emotional disturbance. 4 state of weakness, illness, caused by physical or mental shock. 5 paralytic stroke. 6 collision. 7 effect on sensory nerves of electric discharge. **shocking** adj 1 causing horror, disgust or astonishment 2 Inf very bad.

shock² n mass of hair.

shoddy adj –dier, –diest worthless, trashy.

shoe n 1 covering for foot, not enclosing ankle. 2 metal rim put on horse's hoof. 3 various protective plates or undercoverings. ◆ v 4 protect, furnish with shoe(s).

shonky adj –kier, –kiest Aust & NZ inf unreliable or unsound.

shoo interj go away!

shoot ❶ v shooting, shot 1 wound, kill with missile fired from weapon. 2 discharge weapon. 3 send, slide, push rapidly. 4 photograph, film. 5 hunt. 6 sprout. ◆ n 7 young branch, sprout. 8 hunting expedition.

shop ❶ n 1 place for retail sale of goods and services. 2 workshop, works building. ◆ v 3 visit shops to

glow, sparkle; = **polish**, buff, burnish, brush; = **be outstanding**, stand out, excel, be conspicuous ◆ n = **polish**, gloss, sheen, lustre

ship n = **vessel**, boat, craft

shiver¹ v = **shudder**, shake, tremble, quake, quiver ◆ n = **tremble**, shudder, quiver, trembling, flutter

shock¹ n = **upset**, blow, trauma, bombshell, turn (Inf); = **impact**, blow, clash, collision ◆ v = **shake**, stun, stagger, jolt, stupefy; = **horrify**, appal, disgust, revolt, sicken

shoot v = **open fire on**, blast (Sl), hit, kill, plug (Sl); = **fire**, launch, discharge, project, hurl; = **speed**, race, rush, charge, fly ◆ n = **sprout**, branch, bud, sprig,

buy. **shoplifter** n one who steals from shop. **shopsoiled** adj damaged from being displayed in shop.

shore¹ ❶ n edge of sea or lake.

shore² v prop (up).

short ❶ adj 1 not long. 2 not tall. 3 brief. 4 not enough. 5 lacking. 6 abrupt. ◆ adv 7 abruptly. 8 without reaching end. ◆ n 9 drink of spirits. 10 short film. ◆ pl 11 short trousers. **shortage** n deficiency. **shorten** v **shortly** adv 1 soon. 2 briefly. **shortbread, shortcake** n crumbly biscuit made with butter. **short circuit** Electricity connection, often accidental, of low resistance between two parts of circuit. **shortcoming** n failing. **short cut** quicker route or method. **shorthand** n method of rapid writing. **short list** list of candidates from which final choice will be made. **short-sighted** adj 1 unable

to see faraway things clearly. 2 lacking in foresight.

shot ❶ n 1 act of shooting. 2 small lead pellets. 3 marksman. 4 Inf attempt. 5 photograph. 6 dose. 7 Inf injection. **shotgun** n gun for firing shot at short range. **shot put** contest in which athletes throw heavy metal ball.

should past tense of SHALL.

shoulder ❶ n 1 part of body to which arm or foreleg is attached. 2 anything resembling shoulder. 3 side of road. ◆ v 4 undertake. 5 put on one's shoulder. 6 make way by pushing.

shout ❶ n/v (utter) loud cry.

shove ❶ v/n push.

shovel ❶ n 1 instrument for scooping earth etc. ◆ v 2 lift, move (as) with shovel.

show ❶ v **showing, showed, shown** 1 expose to view. 2 point out. 3 explain. 4 prove. 5 guide. 6

——————— THESAURUS ———————

offshoot

shop n = **store**, supermarket, boutique, emporium, hypermarket

shore¹ n = **beach**, coast, sands, strand (Poet), seashore

short adj = **brief**, fleeting, momentary ≠ **long**; = **concise**, brief, succinct, summary, compressed ≠ **lengthy**; = **small**, little, squat, diminutive, petite ≠ **tall**; = **abrupt**, sharp, terse, curt, brusque ≠ **polite**; = **scarce**, wanting, low, limited, lacking ≠ **plentiful** ◆ adv = **abruptly**, suddenly, without warning ≠ **gradually**

shot n = **discharge**, gunfire, crack, blast, explosion; = **ammunition**, bullet, slug, pellet, projectile; = **marksman**, shooter, markswoman; = (Inf) **strike**, throw, lob

shoulder v = **bear**, carry, take on, accept, assume; = **push**, elbow, shove, jostle, press

shout v = **cry (out)**, call (out), yell, scream, roar ◆ n = **cry**, call, yell, scream, roar

shove v = **push**, thrust, elbow, drive, press

shovel v = **move**, scoop, dredge, load, heap

S

appear. **7** be noticeable. ◆ *n* **8** display. **9** entertainment. **10** ostentation. **11** pretence. **showy** *adj* **1** gaudy. **2** ostentatious. **show business** the entertainment industry. **showcase** *n* **1** glass case to display objects. **2** situation in which thing is displayed to best advantage. **showdown** *n* confrontation. **showman** *n* one skilled at presenting anything effectively. **show off** **1** exhibit to invite admiration. **2** behave in this way. **show-off** *n* **showroom** *n* room in which goods for sale are displayed.

shower 🛈 *n* **1** short fall of rain. **2** anything falling like rain. **3** kind of bath in which person stands under water spray. ◆ *v* **4** bestow liberally. **5** take bath in shower.

shrapnel *n* shell splinters.

shred *n* **1** fragment, torn strip. ◆ *v* **2** cut, tear to shreds.

shrew *n* **1** animal like mouse. **2** bad-tempered woman.

shrewd 🛈 *adj* **1** astute. **2** crafty.

shriek 🛈 *n/v* (utter) piercing cry.

shrill *adj* piercing, sharp in tone.

shrimp *n* **1** small edible crustacean. **2** *Inf* undersized person.

shrine *n* place of worship, usu. associated with saint.

shrink 🛈 *v* **shrinking, shrank 1** become smaller. **2** recoil. **3** make smaller. **shrinkage** *n*

shrivel *v* **-elling, -elled** shrink and wither.

shroud 🛈 *n* **1** wrapping for corpse. **2** anything which envelops like a shroud. ◆ *v* **3** put shroud on. **4** veil.

shrub *n* bush. **shrubbery** *n, pl* **-beries**

shrug *v* **shrugging, shrugged 1** raise (shoulders) as sign of indifference, ignorance etc. ◆ *n* **2** shrugging.

shudder 🛈 *v* **1** shake, tremble violently. ◆ *n* **2** shuddering.

shuffle 🛈 *v* **1** move feet without

———— THESAURUS ————

show *v* = **indicate**, demonstrate, prove, reveal, display ≠ **disprove**; = **display**, exhibit; = **guide**, lead, conduct, accompany, direct; = **demonstrate**, describe, explain, teach, illustrate; = **express**, display, reveal, indicate, register ≠ **hide** ◆ *n* = **display**, sight, spectacle, array; = **exhibition**, fair, display, parade, pageant; = **appearance**, display, pose, parade

shower *v* = **cover**, dust, spray, sprinkle

shred *n* = **strip**, bit, piece, scrap, fragment; = **particle**, trace, scrap, grain, atom

shrewd *adj* = **astute**, clever, sharp, keen, smart ≠ **naive**

shriek *n* = **scream**, cry, yell, screech, squeal

shrink *v* = **decrease**, dwindle, lessen, grow or get smaller, contract ≠ **grow**

shroud *n* = **winding sheet**, grave clothes; = **covering**, veil, mantle, screen, pall ◆ *v* = **conceal**, cover, screen, hide, blanket

lifting them. **2** mix (cards). ♦ *n* **3** shuffling. **4** rearrangement.

shun 🛈 *v* shunning, shunned keep away from.

shunt *v* **1** push aside. **2** move (train) from one line to another.

shut 🛈 *v* shutting, shut **1** close. **2** forbid entrance to. **shutter** *n* **1** movable window screen. **2** device in camera admitting light as required.

shuttle 🛈 *n* **1** bobbin-like device to hold thread in weaving, sewing etc. **2** plane, bus etc. travelling to and fro.

shuttlecock *n* cone with feathers, struck to and fro in badminton.

shy¹ 🛈 *adj* **1** timid, bashful. **2** lacking. ♦ *v* **3** start back in fear. **4** show sudden reluctance. ♦ *n* **5** start of fear by horse.

shy² *n/v* throw.

sibilant *adj/n* hissing (sound).

sibling *n* brother or sister.

sick 🛈 *adj* **1** inclined to vomit. **2** not well or healthy. **3** *Inf* macabre. **4** *Inf* bored. **5** *Inf* disgusted. **sicken** *v* **1** make, become sick. **2** disgust. **sickly** *adj* **1** unhealthy. **2** inducing nausea. **sickness** *n*

sickle *n* reaping hook.

side 🛈 *n* **1** one of the surfaces of object that is to right or left. **2** aspect. **3** faction. ♦ *adj* **4** at, in the side. **5** subordinate. ♦ *v* **6** take up cause of. **siding** *n* short line of rails from main line. **sideboard** *n* piece of dining room furniture. **sideburns** *pl n* man's side whiskers. **side effect** additional undesirable effect. **sidekick** *n Inf* close associate. **sidelong** *adj* **1** not directly forward. ♦ *adv* **2** obliquely. **sidestep** *v* avoid. **sidetrack** *v* divert from main topic. **sideways** *adv* to or from the side.

——————— THESAURUS ———————

shudder *v* = **shiver**, shake, tremble, quake, quiver ♦ *n* = **shiver**, tremor, quiver, spasm

shuffle *v* = **shamble**, stagger, stumble, dodder; = **scuffle**, drag, scrape; = **rearrange**, jumble, mix, disorder, disarrange

shun *v* = **avoid**, steer clear of, keep away from

shut *v* = **close**, secure, fasten, seal, slam ≠ **open**

shuttle *v* = **go back and forth**, commute, go to and fro, alternate

shy¹ *adj* = **timid**, self-conscious, bashful, retiring, shrinking ≠ **confident**; = **cautious**, wary, hesitant, suspicious, distrustful

≠ **reckless** ♦ *v* sometimes with **off** or **away** = **recoil**, flinch, draw back, start, balk

sick *adj* = **unwell**, ill, poorly (*Inf*), diseased, ailing ≠ **well**; = **nauseous**, ill, queasy, nauseated; = **tired**, bored, fed up, weary, jaded; = (*Inf*) **morbid**, sadistic, black, macabre, ghoulish

side *n* = **border**, margin, boundary, verge, flank ≠ **middle**; = **face**, surface, facet; = **party**, camp, faction, cause; = **point of view**, viewpoint, position, opinion, angle; = **team**, squad, line-up ♦ *adj* = **subordinate**, minor, secondary, subsidiary, lesser

sidewalk *n US and Canad* paved path for pedestrians.

sidle *v* 1 move in furtive or stealthy manner. 2 move sideways.

siege *n* besieging of town.

siesta *n* rest, sleep in afternoon.

sieve *n* 1 device with perforated bottom. ◆ *v* 2 sift. 3 strain.

sift ❶ *v* separate coarser portion from finer.

sigh *v/n* (utter) long audible breath.

sight ❶ *n* 1 faculty of seeing. 2 thing seen. 3 glimpse. 4 device for guiding by eye. 5 spectacle. ◆ *v* 6 catch sight of. 7 adjust sights on gun etc. **sightseeing** *n* visiting places of interest.

sign ❶ *n* 1 mark, gesture etc. to convey some meaning. 2 (board bearing) notice etc. 3 symbol. 4 omen. ◆ *v* 5 put one's signature to. 6 make sign or gesture.

signal ❶ *n* 1 sign to convey order or information. 2 *Radio* sequence of electrical impulses transmitted or received. ◆ *adj* 3 remarkable. ◆ *v* 4 make signals to. 5 give orders etc. by signals.

signatory *n, pl* **-ries** one of those who signs agreements, treaties.

signature *n* person's name written by himself. **signature tune** tune used to introduce television or radio programme.

signet *n* small seal.

significant ❶ *adj* 1 revealing. 2 designed to make something known. 3 important. **significance** *n*

signify ❶ *v* **-fying, -fied** 1 mean. 2 indicate. 3 imply. 4 be of importance.

silage *n* fodder crop stored in state of partial fermentation.

silence ❶ *n* 1 absence of noise. 2 refraining from speech. ◆ *v* 3 make silent. 4 put a stop to.

silencer *n* device to reduce noise of engine exhaust, gun etc. **silent** *adj*

silhouette ❶ *n* 1 outline of object

———— THESAURUS ————

≠ main

sift *v* = **part**, filter, strain, separate, sieve; = **examine**, investigate, go through, research, analyse

sight *n* = **vision**, eyes, eyesight, seeing, eye; = **spectacle**, show, scene, display, exhibition, vista, pageant; = **view**, field of vision, range of vision, viewing, visibility; = (*Inf*) **eyesore**, mess, monstrosity ◆ *v* = **spot**, see, observe, distinguish, perceive.

sign *n* = **symbol**, mark, device, logo, badge; = **notice**, board,

warning, placard; = **indication**, evidence, mark, signal, symptom ◆ *v* = **gesture**, indicate, signal, beckon, gesticulate; = **autograph**, initial, inscribe

signal *n* = **flare**, beam, beacon ◆ *v* = **gesture**, sign, wave, indicate, motion

significant *adj* = **important**, serious, material, vital, critical ≠ **insignificant**; = **meaningful**, expressive, eloquent, indicative, suggestive ≠ **meaningless**

signify *v* = **indicate**, mean,

seen against light. ♦ v 2 show in silhouette.

silica n naturally occurring dioxide of silicon.

silicon n brittle metal–like element found in sand, clay, stone. **silicon chip** tiny wafer of silicon used in electronics.

silk n 1 fibre made by silkworms. 2 thread, fabric made from this. **silky** adj **silkworm** n larva of certain moth.

sill n ledge beneath window.

silly 🟊 adj –lier, –liest 1 foolish. 2 trivial.

silo n, pl –los pit, tower for storing fodder.

silt n 1 mud deposited by water. ♦ v 2 fill, be choked with silt.

silver n 1 white precious metal. 2 silver coins. 3 cutlery. ♦ adj 4 made of silver. 5 resembling silver or its colour. **silvery** adj

similar 🟊 adj resembling, like.

similarity n likeness.

simile n comparison of one thing with another.

simmer 🟊 v 1 keep or be just below boiling point. 2 be in state of suppressed rage.

simper v smile, utter in silly or affected way.

simple 🟊 adj 1 not complicated. 2 plain. 3 not complex. 4 ordinary. 5 stupid. **simpleton** n foolish person. **simplicity** n **simplify** v make simple, plain or easy. **simply** adv

simulate 🟊 v 1 make pretence of. 2 reproduce. **simulation** n

simultaneous 🟊 adj occurring at the same time.

sin 🟊 n 1 breaking of divine or moral law. ♦ v 2 commit sin. **sinful** adj **sinner** n

since prep 1 during period of time after. ♦ conj 2 from time when. 3 because. ♦ adv 4 from that time.

sincere 🟊 adj 1 not hypocritical. 2

———— THESAURUS ————

suggest, imply, intimate

silence n = **quiet**, peace, calm, hush, lull ≠ **noise**; = **reticence**, dumbness, taciturnity, muteness ≠ **speech** ♦ v = **quieten**, still, quiet, cut off, stifle ≠ **make louder**

silhouette n = **outline**, form, shape, profile ♦ v = **outline**, etch

silly adj = **stupid**, ridiculous, absurd, daft, inane ≠ **clever**

similar adj = **alike**, resembling, comparable ≠ **different**

simmer v = **fume**, seethe, smoulder, rage, be angry

simple adj = **uncomplicated**, clear, plain, understandable, lucid

≠ **complicated**; = **easy**, straightforward, not difficult, effortless, painless; = **plain**, natural, classic, unfussy, unembellished ≠ **elaborate**; = **pure**, mere, sheer, unalloyed; = **artless**, innocent, naive, natural, sincere ≠ **sophisticated**

simulate v = **pretend**, act, feign, affect, put on

simultaneous adj = **coinciding**, concurrent, contemporaneous, coincident, synchronous

sin n = **wickedness**, evil, crime, error, transgression ♦ v = **transgress**, offend, lapse, err, go

genuine. **sincerity** n

sine n in a right-angled triangle, ratio of opposite side to hypotenuse.

sinew n tough, fibrous cord joining muscle to bone.

sing ⊕ v **singing, sang, sung 1** utter (sounds, words) with musical modulation. **2** hum, ring. **3** celebrate in song. **singer** n

singe v **singeing, singed** burn surface of.

single ⊕ adj **1** one only. **2** unmarried. **3** for one. **4** denoting ticket for outward journey only. ◆ n **5** single thing. ◆ v **6** pick (out).

single file persons in one line.

single-handed adj without assistance. **single-minded** adj having one aim only.

singlet n sleeveless undervest.

singular ⊕ adj **1** remarkable. **2** unique. **3** denoting one person or thing.

sinister ⊕ adj **1** threatening. **2** evil-looking. **3** wicked.

sink ⊕ v **sinking, sank, sunk 1** become submerged. **2** drop. **3** decline. **4** penetrate (into). **5** cause to sink. **6** make by digging out. **7** invest. ◆ n **8** fixed basin with waste pipe.

sinuous adj curving.

sinus n cavity in bone, esp. of skull.

sip ⊕ v **sipping, sipped 1** drink in very small portions. ◆ n **2** amount sipped.

siphon n/v (device to) draw liquid from container.

sir n polite term of address for man.

sire n **1** male parent, esp. of horse or domestic animal. ◆ v **2** father.

siren n device making loud wailing noise.

sirloin n prime cut of beef.

sis interj S Afr informal exclamation of disgust.

sissy adj/n, pl **-sies** weak, cowardly (person).

sister n **1** daughter of same

astray

sincere adj = **honest**, genuine, real, true, serious ≠ **false**

sing v = **croon**, carol, chant, warble, yodel; = **trill**, chirp, warble

single adj = **one**, sole, lone, solitary, only; = **individual**, separate, distinct; = **unmarried**, free, unattached, unwed; = **separate**, individual, exclusive, undivided, unshared

singular adj = **single**, individual; = **remarkable**, outstanding, exceptional, notable, eminent

≠ **ordinary**; = **unusual**, odd, strange, extraordinary, curious ≠ **conventional**

sinister adj = **threatening**, evil, menacing, dire, ominous ≠ **reassuring**

sink v = **go down**, founder, go under, submerge, capsize; = **slump**, drop; = **fall**, drop, slip, plunge, subside; = **drop**, fall; = **stoop**, be reduced to, lower yourself

sip v = **drink**, taste, sample, sup ◆ n = **swallow**, drop, taste,

parents. **2** woman fellow–member. **3** senior nurse. **sister-in-law** *n, pl* **sisters-in-law 1** sister of husband or wife. **2** brother's wife.

sit ⊕ *v* **sitting, sat 1** rest on buttocks, thighs. **2** perch. **3** pose for portrait. **4** hold session. **5** remain. **6** take examination. **7** keep watch over baby etc.

sitar *n* stringed musical instrument of India.

site ⊕ *n* **1** place, space for building. ♦ *v* **2** provide with site.

situate *v* place. **situation** *n* **1** position. **2** state of affairs. **3** employment.

six *adj/n* cardinal number one more than five. **sixth** *adj* ordinal number. **sixteen** *n/adj* six and ten. **sixteenth** *adj* **sixtieth** *adj* **sixty** *n/adj* six times ten.

size ⊕ *n* **1** dimensions. **2** one of series of standard measurements. ♦ *v* **3** arrange according to size. **sizable** *adj* quite large. **size up** *v Inf* assess.

sizzle ⊕ *v/n* (make) hissing, spluttering sound as of frying.

skate¹ *n* **1** steel blade attached to boot. ♦ *v* **2** glide as on skates.

skateboard *n* small board mounted on roller–skate wheels.

skate² *n* large marine ray.

skein *n* quantity of yarn, wool etc. in loose knot.

skeleton ⊕ *n* **1** bones of animal. **2** framework. ♦ *adj* **3** reduced to a minimum.

sketch ⊕ *n* **1** rough drawing. **2** short humorous play. ♦ *v* **3** make sketch (of). **sketchy** *adj*

skew *adj/v* (make) slanting or crooked.

skewer *n* pin to fasten meat.

ski *n* **1** long runner fastened to foot for sliding over snow or water. ♦ *v* **2** slide on skis.

skid *v* **skidding, skidded 1** slide (sideways). ♦ *n* **2** instance of this.

skill ⊕ *n* practical ability, cleverness, dexterity. **skilful** *adj* **skilled** *adj*

skim ⊕ *v* **skimming, skimmed 1** remove floating matter from surface of liquid. **2** glide over lightly and rapidly. **3** read quickly. **skimp** *v* **1** give short measure. **2** do imperfectly. **skimpy** *adj* scanty.

skin ⊕ *n* **1** outer covering of body.

S

———————— THESAURUS ————————

thimbleful

sit *v* **= take a seat**, perch, settle down; **= place**, set, put, position, rest; **= be a member of**, serve on, have a seat on, preside on

site *n* **= area**, plot ♦ *v* **= locate**, put, place, set, position

size *n* **= dimensions**, extent, range, amount, mass

sizzle *v* **= hiss**, spit, crackle, fry,

frizzle

skeleton *n* **= bones**, bare bones

sketch *n* **= drawing**, design, draft, delineation ♦ *v* **= draw**, outline, represent, draft, depict

skill *n* **= expertise**, ability, proficiency, art, technique ≠ **clumsiness**

skim *v* **= remove**, separate, cream; **= glide**, fly, coast, sail, float;

2 animal hide. **3** fruit rind. ♦ *v* **4** remove skin of. **skinless** *adj* **skinny** *adj* thin. **skinflint** *n* miser.

skint *adj Sl* having no money.

skip[1] **☎** *v* **skipping, skipped 1** leap lightly. **2** jump over rope. **3** pass over, omit. ♦ *n* **4** act of skipping.

skip[2] *n* large open container for builders' rubbish etc.

skipper *n* captain of ship.

skirmish *n* **1** small battle. ♦ *v* **2** fight briefly.

skirt ☎ *n* **1** woman's garment hanging from waist. **2** lower part of dress, coat etc. ♦ *v* **3** border. **4** go round. **skirting board** narrow board round bottom of wall.

skit *n* satire, esp. theatrical.

skite *v/n Aust & NZ* boast.

skittish *adj* frisky, frivolous.

skive *v* evade work.

skivvy *n, pl* **–vies** servant who does menial work.

skookum *adj Canad* powerful or big.

skulduggery *n Inf* trickery.

skulk *v* sneak out of the way.

skull *n* bony case enclosing brain.

skunk *n* small N Amer. animal which emits evil-smelling fluid.

sky ☎ *n, pl* **skies 1** expanse extending upwards from the horizon. **2** outer space. **skylark** *n* bird that sings while soaring at great height. **skylight** *n* window in roof or ceiling. **skyscraper** *n* very tall building.

slab ☎ *n* thick, broad piece.

slack ☎ *adj* **1** loose. **2** careless. **3** not busy. ♦ *n* **4** loose part. ♦ *v* **5** be idle or lazy. **slacken** *v* **1** become looser. **2** become slower.

slag *n* refuse of smelted metal.

slake *v* satisfy (thirst).

slalom *n* skiing race over winding course.

slam ☎ *v* **slamming, slammed 1** shut noisily. **2** bang. ♦ *n* **3** (noise of) this action.

slang *n* colloquial language.

slant ☎ *v* **1** slope. **2** write, present (news etc.) with bias. ♦ *n* **3** slope. **4** point of view. **slanting** *adj*

slap ☎ *n* **1** blow with open hand

———————— THESAURUS ————————

= scan, glance, run your eye over

skin *n* = **hide**, pelt, fell; = **peel**, rind, husk, casing, outside

skip[1] *v* = **hop**, dance, bob, trip, bounce; = **miss out**, omit, leave out, overlook, pass over

skirt *n* = **border**, edge, flank; *often with* **around** *or* **round** = **go round**, circumvent

sky *n* = **heavens**, firmament

slab *n* = **piece**, slice, lump, chunk, wedge

slack *adj* = **limp**, relaxed, loose,

lax; = **loose**, baggy ≠ **taut**; = **slow**, quiet, inactive, dull, sluggish ≠ **busy**; = **negligent**, lazy, lax, idle, inactive ≠ **strict** *v* = **shirk**, dodge, skive (*Brit sl*) ♦ *n* = **surplus**, excess, glut, surfeit, superabundance

slam *v* = **bang**, crash, smash; = **throw**, dash, hurl, fling

slant *v* = **slope**, incline, tilt, list, bend; = **bias**, colour, twist, angle, distort ♦ *n* = **slope**, incline, tilt, gradient, camber; = **bias**,

or flat instrument. ◆ v **2** strike thus **3** *Inf* put down carelessly. **slapdash** *adj* careless, hasty. **slapstick** *n* boisterous knockabout comedy.

slash 🛈 v/n **1** gash. **2** cut.

slat *n* narrow strip.

slate 🛈 n **1** stone which splits easily in flat sheets. **2** piece of this for covering roof. ◆ v **3** cover with slates. **4** abuse.

slaughter 🛈 n **1** killing. ◆ v **2** kill. **slaughterhouse** *n* place where animals are killed for food.

slave 🛈 n **1** captive, person without freedom or personal rights. ◆ v **2** work like slave. **slavery** *n* **slavish** *adj* servile.

slaver v/n (dribble) saliva from mouth.

slay 🛈 v **slaying, slew, slain** kill.

sleazy *adj* **–zier, –ziest** sordid.

sledge[1] *n* **1** carriage on runners for sliding on snow. **2** toboggan. ◆ v **3** move on sledge.

sledge[2] *n* heavy hammer with long handle.

sleek 🛈 adj glossy, smooth, shiny.

sleep 🛈 n **1** unconscious state regularly occurring in man and animals. **2** slumber, repose. ◆ v **3** take rest in sleep. **sleeper** *n* **1** one who sleeps. **2** beam supporting rails. **3** railway sleeping car. **sleepless** *adj* **sleepy** *adj*

sleet *n* rain and snow falling together.

sleeve *n* part of garment which covers arm.

sleigh *n* sledge.

slender 🛈 adj **1** slim, slight. **2** small in amount.

sleuth *n* detective.

slice 🛈 n **1** thin flat piece cut off. **2** share. ◆ v **3** cut into slices.

slick 🛈 adj **1** smooth. **2** glib. **3** skilful. ◆ v **4** make glossy, smooth. ◆ n **5** slippery area. **6** patch of oil on water.

———————— THESAURUS ————————

emphasis, prejudice, angle, point of view

slap v = **smack**, beat, clap, cuff, swipe ◆ n = **smack**, blow, cuff, swipe, spank

slash v = **smack**, slit, gash, lacerate, score; = **reduce**, cut, decrease, drop, lower ◆ n = **cut**, slit, gash, rent, rip

slate v = (*Inf, chiefly Brit*) **criticize**, censure, rebuke, scold, tear into (*Inf*)

slaughter v = **kill**, murder, massacre, destroy, execute ◆ n = **slaying**, killing, murder, massacre, bloodshed

slave n = **servant**, serf, vassal; = **drudge**, skivvy (*Chiefly Brit*) ◆ v = **toil**, drudge, slog

slay v = (*Arch or Lit*) **kill**, slaughter, massacre, butcher

sleek adj = **glossy**, shiny, lustrous, smooth ≠ **shaggy**

sleep n = **slumber(s)**, nap, doze, snooze (*Inf*), hibernation ◆ v = **slumber**, doze, snooze (*Inf*), hibernate, take a nap

slender adj = **slim**, narrow, slight, lean, willowy ≠ **chubby**; = **faint**, slight, remote, slim, thin ≠ **strong**

slice n = **piece**, segment, portion, wedge, sliver ◆ v = **cut**, divide,

S

slide ⊕ v **sliding, slid 1** slip smoothly along. **2** glide. **3** pass. ◆ n **4** sliding. **5** track for sliding. **6** glass mount for object to be viewed under microscope. **7** photographic transparency.
slight ⊕ adj **1** small, trifling. **2** slim. ◆ v **3** disregard. ◆ n **4** act of discourtesy. **slightly** adv
slim ⊕ adj **slimmer, slimmest 1** thin. **2** slight. ◆ v **3** reduce weight by diet and exercise.
slime n thick, liquid mud. **slimy** adj **1** of, like, covered in slime. **2** insincerely pleasant.
sling ⊕ n **1** loop for hurling stone. **2** bandage for supporting wounded limb. **3** rope for hoisting weights. ◆ v **4** throw.
slink v **slinking, slunk** move stealthily, sneak.
slip ⊕ v **slipping, slipped 1** (cause

to) move smoothly. **2** pass out of (mind etc.). **3** lose balance by sliding. **4** fall from person's grasp. **5** make mistake. **6** put on or take off easily, quickly. ◆ n **7** act or occasion of slipping. **8** mistake. **9** petticoat. **10** small piece of paper. **slipshod** adj slovenly, careless. **slipstream** n stream of air forced backwards by fast-moving object.
slipper n light shoe for indoors.
slippery ⊕ adj **1** so smooth as to cause slipping or to be difficult to hold. **2** unreliable.
slit ⊕ v **1** make long straight cut in. ◆ n **2** long straight cut.
slither v slide unsteadily (down slope etc.).
sliver n splinter.
slob n Inf lazy, untidy person.
slobber v/n slaver.

————————— THESAURUS —————————

carve, sever, dissect
slick adj = skilful, deft, adroit, dexterous, professional ≠ **clumsy**; = **glib**, smooth, plausible, polished, specious ◆ v = **smooth**, sleek, plaster down
slide v = **slip**, slither, glide, skim, coast
slight adj = **small**, minor, insignificant, trivial, feeble ≠ **large**; = **slim**, small, delicate, spare, fragile ≠ **sturdy** ◆ n = **insult**, snub, affront, rebuff, slap in the face (Inf) ≠ **compliment**
slim adj = **slender**, slight, trim, thin, narrow ≠ **chubby**; = **slight**, remote, faint, slender ≠ **strong** ◆ v = **lose weight**, diet ≠ **put on**

weight
sling v = (Inf) **throw**, cast, toss, hurl, fling; = **hang**, suspend
slip v = **fall**, skid; = **slide**, slither; = **sneak**, creep, steal ◆ n = **mistake**, failure, error, blunder, lapse **give someone the slip** = **escape from**, get away from, evade, elude, lose (someone); **let something slip** = **give away**, reveal, disclose, divulge, leak
slippery adj = **smooth**, icy, greasy, glassy, slippy (informal or dialect); = **untrustworthy**, tricky, cunning, dishonest, devious
slit v = **cut (open)**, rip, slash, knife, pierce ◆ n = **cut**, gash, incision, tear, rent

slog v **slogging, slogged 1** hit vigorously. **2** work doggedly. ♦ n **3** struggle.

slogan ⊕ n distinctive phrase.

slop v **slopping, slopped 1** spill, splash. ♦ n **2** liquid spilt. **3** liquid food. ♦ pl **4** liquid refuse. **sloppy** adj careless, untidy.

slope ⊕ v **1** be, place at slant. ♦ n **2** slant.

slot ⊕ n **1** narrow hole. **2** slit for coins. **3** place in series. ♦ v **4** put in slot. **5** Inf place in series.

sloth n **1** S Amer. animal. **2** sluggishness. **slothful** adj

slouch v **1** walk, sit etc. in drooping manner. ♦ n **2** drooping posture.

slovenly adj dirty, untidy.

slow ⊕ adj **1** lasting a long time. **2** moving at low speed. **3** dull. ♦ v **4** slacken speed (of). **slowly** adv

sludge n thick mud.

slug[1] n **1** land snail with no shell. **2** bullet. **sluggish** adj **1** slow, inert. **2** not functioning well.

slug[2] v **1** hit, slog. ♦ n **2** heavy blow. **3** portion of spirits.

sluice n gate, door to control flow of water.

slum ⊕ n squalid street or neighbourhood.

slumber v/n sleep.

slump ⊕ v **1** fall heavily. **2** relax ungracefully. **3** decline suddenly. ♦ n **4** sudden decline.

slur ⊕ v **slurring, slurred 1** pass over lightly. **2** run together (words). **3** disparage. ♦ n **4** slight.

slurp Inf ♦ v **1** eat or drink noisily. ♦ n **2** slurping sound.

slurry n, pl **-ries** muddy liquid mixture.

slush n watery, muddy substance.

slut n dirty (immoral) woman.

sly ⊕ adj **slyer, slyest 1** cunning. **2** deceitful.

smack[1] ⊕ v **1** slap. **2** open and close (lips) loudly. ♦ n **3** slap. **4** such sound. **5** loud kiss. ♦ adv **6** Inf squarely.

smack[2] n **1** taste, flavour. ♦ v **2**

——————— THESAURUS ———————

slogan n = **catch phrase**, motto, tag-line, catchword

slope n = **inclination**, rise, incline, tilt, slant ♦ v = **slant**, incline, drop away, fall, rise

slot n = **opening**, hole, groove, vent, slit; = (Inf) **place**, time, space, opening, position ♦ v = **fit**, insert

slow adj = **unhurried**, sluggish, leisurely, lazy, ponderous ≠ **quick**; = **prolonged**, protracted, long-drawn-out, lingering, gradual; = **late**, behind, tardy ♦ v often with **down** = **decelerate**, brake

slum n = **hovel**, ghetto, shanty

slump v = **fall**, sink, plunge, crash, collapse ≠ **increase**; = **sag**, hunch, droop, slouch, loll ♦ n = **fall**, drop, decline, crash, collapse ≠ **increase**; = **recession**, depression, stagnation, inactivity, hard or bad times

slur n = **insult**, stain, smear, affront, innuendo

sly adj = **roguish**, knowing, arch, mischievous, impish; = **cunning**, scheming, devious, secret, clever ≠ **open** = **secret**, furtive, stealthy,

taste (of). **3** suggest.

small ⊕ *adj* **1** little, unimportant. **2** short. ♦ *n* **3** small slender part, esp. of the back. **smallholding** *n* small area of farmland. **smallpox** *n* contagious disease.

smart ⊕ *adj* **1** astute. **2** clever. **3** well–dressed. ♦ *v* **4** feel, cause pain. ♦ *n* **5** sharp pain. **smarten** *v* make or become smart.

smash ⊕ *v* **1** break. **2** ruin. **3** destroy. ♦ *n* **4** heavy blow. **5** collision. **smashing** *adj Inf* excellent.

smattering *n* slight superficial knowledge.

smear ⊕ *v* **1** rub with grease etc. **2** smudge. **3** slander. ♦ *n* **4** greasy mark. **5** slander.

smell ⊕ *v* **smelling, smelt 1** perceive by nose. **2** give out odour. ♦ *n* **3** faculty of perceiving odours. **4** anything detected by sense of smell. **smelly** *adj* having

nasty smell.

smelt *v* extract metal from ore.

smile *n* **1** curving or parting of lips in pleased or amused expression. ♦ *v* **2** give smile.

smirk *n* **1** smile expressing scorn, smugness. ♦ *v* **2** give smirk.

smite *v* **smiting, smote, smitten 1** strike. **2** afflict.

smith *n* worker in iron, gold etc.

smithy *n* blacksmith's workshop.

smithereens *pl n* shattered fragments.

smock *n* loose, outer garment.

smog *n* mixture of smoke and fog.

smoke *n* **1** cloudy mass that rises from fire etc. ♦ *v* **2** give off smoke. **3** inhale and expel tobacco smoke. **4** expose to smoke. **smoker** *n*

smoky *adj* **smoke screen** thing intended to hide truth.

smooth ⊕ *adj* **1** not rough, even. **2** calm. **3** unctuous. ♦ *v* **4** make

——————— THESAURUS ———————

covert **on the sly**

smack[1] *v* = **slap**, hit, strike, clap, cuff ♦ *n* = **slap**, blow, cuff, swipe, spank ♦ *adv* = (*Inf*) **directly**, right, straight, squarely, precisely

small *adj* = **little**, minute, tiny, mini, miniature ≠ **big**; = **unimportant**, minor, trivial, insignificant, little ≠ **important**; = **modest**, humble, unpretentious ≠ **grand**

smart *adj* = **chic**, trim, neat, stylish, elegant ≠ **scruffy**; = **clever**, bright, intelligent, quick, sharp ≠ **stupid**; = **brisk**, quick, lively, vigorous ♦ *v* = **sting**, burn, hurt

smash *v* = **break**, crush, shatter, crack, demolish; = **shatter**, break, disintegrate, crack, splinter; = **collide**, crash, meet head–on, clash, come into collision ♦ *n* = **collision**, crash, accident

smear *v* = **spread over**, daub, rub on, cover, coat; = **slander**, malign, blacken, besmirch; = **smudge**, soil, dirty, stain, sully ♦ *n* = **smudge**, daub, streak, blot, blotch; = **slander**, libel, defamation, calumny

smell *n* = **odour**, scent, fragrance, perfume, bouquet ♦ *v* = **stink**, reek, pong (*Brit inf*); = **sniff**, scent

smooth.

smother ⊕ v suffocate.

smoulder v 1 burn slowly. 2 (of feelings) be suppressed.

smudge v/n (make) smear, stain (on).

smug ⊕ adj smugger, smuggest self-satisfied, complacent.

smuggle v import, export without paying customs duties. **smuggler** n

smut n 1 piece of soot. 2 obscene talk etc. **smutty** adj

snack ⊕ n light, hasty meal.

snag ⊕ n 1 difficulty. 2 sharp protuberance. 3 hole, loop in fabric. ◆ v 4 catch, damage on snag.

snail n slow-moving mollusc with shell.

snake n 1 long scaly limbless reptile. ◆ v 2 move like snake.

snap ⊕ v snapping, snapped 1 break suddenly. 2 make cracking sound. 3 bite (at) suddenly. 4 speak suddenly, angrily. ◆ n 5 act of snapping. 6 fastener. 7 card game. 8 Inf snapshot. ◆ adj 9 sudden, unplanned. **snappy** adj 1 irritable. 2 Sl quick. 3 Sl fashionable. **snapshot** n photograph.

snare ⊕ n/v trap.

snarl n 1 growl of angry dog. 2 tangle. ◆ v 3 utter snarl.

snatch ⊕ v 1 make quick grab (at). 2 seize, catch. ◆ n 3 grab. 4 fragment.

sneak ⊕ v 1 move about furtively. 2 act in underhand manner. ◆ n 3 petty informer. **sneaking** adj 1 secret. 2 slight but persistent.

sneakers pl n US and Canad canvas shoes with rubber soles.

———— THESAURUS ————

smooth adj = **even**, level, flat, plane, flush ≠ **uneven**; = **sleek**, polished, shiny, glossy, silky ≠ **rough**; = **mellow**, pleasant, mild, agreeable; = **flowing**, steady, regular, uniform, rhythmic; = **easy**, effortless, well-ordered ◆ v = **flatten**, level, press, plane, iron; = **ease**, facilitate ≠ **hinder**

smother v = **extinguish**, put out, stifle, snuff; = **suffocate**, choke, strangle, stifle; = **suppress**, stifle, repress, hide, conceal

smug adj = **self-satisfied**, superior, complacent, conceited

snack n = **light meal**, bite, refreshment(s)

snag n = **difficulty**, hitch, problem, obstacle, catch ◆ v

= **catch**, tear, rip

snap v = **break**, crack, separate; = **pop**, click, crackle; = **speak sharply**, bark, lash out at, jump down (someone's) throat (Inf); = **bite at**, bite, nip ◆ adj = **instant**, immediate, sudden, spur-of-the-moment

snare n = **trap**, net, wire, gin, noose ◆ v = **trap**, catch, net, wire, seize

snatch v = **grab**, grip, grasp, clutch; = **steal**, take, nick (slang, chiefly Brit), pinch (Inf), lift (Inf) ◆ n = **bit**, part, fragment, piece, snippet

sneak v = **slink**, slip, steal, pad, skulk; = **slip**, smuggle, spirit ◆ n = **informer**, betrayer, telltale,

S

sneer 🛈 n 1 scornful, contemptuous expression or remark. ◆ v 2 give sneer.

sneeze v 1 emit breath through nose with sudden involuntary spasm and noise. ◆ n 2 act of sneezing.

snide adj malicious, supercilious.

sniff 🛈 v 1 inhale through nose with sharp hiss. 2 smell 3 (with at) express disapproval etc. ◆ n 4 act of sniffing. **sniffle** v sniff noisily, esp. when suffering from a cold.

snigger n 1 sly, disrespectful laugh, esp. partly stifled. ◆ v 2 produce snigger.

snip v **snipping, snipped** 1 cut with quick stroke. ◆ n 2 quick cut. 3 Inf bargain. **snippet** n small piece.

snipe n 1 wading bird. ◆ v 2 shoot at enemy from cover 3 (with at) criticize. **sniper** n

snivel v –**elling,** –**elled** 1 sniffle to show distress. 2 whine.

snob n one who pretentiously judges others by social rank etc. **snobbery** n **snobbish** adj

snooker n game played on table with balls and cues.

snoop v 1 pry, meddle. 2 peer into.

snooty adj **snootier, snootiest** Sl haughty.

snooze v/n (take) nap.

snore v 1 breathe noisily when asleep. ◆ n 2 sound of snoring.

snorkel n tube for breathing underwater.

snort v 1 make (contemptuous) noise by driving breath through nostrils. ◆ n 2 act of snorting.

snout n animal's nose.

snow n 1 frozen vapour which falls in flakes. ◆ v 2 fall, sprinkle as snow. **snowy** adj **snowball** n 1 snow pressed into hard ball for throwing. ◆ v 2 increase rapidly. **snowdrift** n bank of deep snow. **snowdrop** n small, white, bell-shaped spring flower. **snowman** n figure shaped out of snow. **snowplough** n vehicle for clearing away snow. **snowshoes** pl n racket-shaped shoes for travelling on snow.

snub 🛈 v **snubbing, snubbed** 1 insult (esp. by ignoring) intentionally. ◆ n 2 snubbing. ◆ adj 3 short and blunt. **snub-nosed** adj

snuff¹ n powdered tobacco.

snuff² v extinguish (esp. candle).

snuffle v breathe noisily.

snug adj **snugger, snuggest** warm, comfortable.

snuggle v lie close to, nestle.

so adv 1 to such an extent. 2 in such a manner. 3 very. ◆ conj 4 therefore. 5 in order that. 6 with the result that. ◆ interj 7 well! **so-and-so** n 1 Inf person whose name

—————————— THESAURUS ——————————

Judas, accuser

sneer v = **scorn**, mock, ridicule, laugh, jeer ◆ n = **scorn**, ridicule, mockery, derision, jeer

sniff v = **breathe in**, inhale

snub v = **insult**, slight, put down, humiliate, cut (Inf) ◆ n = **insult**, put-down, affront, slap in the face

is not specified. **2** unpleasant person. **so-called** adj called by but doubtfully deserving that name.

soak ❶ v **1** steep. **2** absorb. **3** drench. **soaking** n/adj

soap n **1** compound of alkali and oil used in washing. ◆ v **2** apply soap to. **soapy** adj **soap opera** television, radio serial dealing with domestic themes.

soar ❶ v **1** fly high. **2** increase rapidly.

sob ❶ v **sobbing, sobbed 1** catch breath, esp. in weeping. ◆ n **2** sobbing.

sober ❶ adj **1** not drunk. **2** temperate. **3** subdued. **4** dull. **5** solemn. ◆ v **6** make, become sober. **sobriety** n

soccer n game of football, with spherical ball.

sociable adj **1** friendly. **2** convivial.

social ❶ adj **1** living in communities. **2** relating to society. **3** sociable. ◆ n **4** informal gathering. **socialize** v

socialism n political system which advocates public ownership of means of production. **socialist** n/adj

society ❶ n, pl **-ties 1** living associated with others. **2** those so living. **3** companionship. **4** association. **5** fashionable people collectively.

sociology n study of societies. **sociological** adj

sock[1] n cloth covering for foot.

sock[2] Sl ◆ v **1** hit. ◆ n **2** blow.

socket n hole or recess for something to fit into.

sod n lump of earth with grass.

soda n **1** compound of sodium. **2** soda water. **soda water** water charged with carbon dioxide.

sodden adj soaked.

sodium n metallic alkaline element. **sodium bicarbonate** compound used in baking powder.

sodomy n anal intercourse.

sofa ❶ n upholstered seat with back and arms.

soft ❶ adj **1** yielding easily to

————— THESAURUS —————

soak v = **wet**, damp, saturate, drench, moisten; = **penetrate**, permeate, seep

soar v = **rise**, increase, grow, mount, climb; = **fly**, wing, climb, ascend ≠ plunge

sob v = **cry**, weep, howl, shed tears

sober adj = **abstinent**, temperate, abstemious, moderate ≠ drunk; = **serious**, cool, grave, reasonable, steady ≠ frivolous; = **plain**, dark, sombre, quiet, subdued ≠ bright

social adj = **communal**, community, collective, group, public ◆ n = **get-together** (Inf), party, gathering, function, reception

society n = **the community**, people, the public, humanity, civilization; = **culture**, community, population; = **organization**, group, club, union, league; = **upper classes**, gentry, elite, high society, beau monde

sofa n = **couch**, settee, divan,

pressure. **2** not hard. **3** mild. **4** easy. **5** subdued. **6** quiet. **7** gentle. **8** (too) lenient. **soften** v make, become soft or softer. **softly** adv

soft drink nonalcoholic drink.

software n computer programs.

soggy adj **–gier, –giest** damp and heavy.

soil[1] ⊕ n earth, ground.

soil[2] ⊕ v make, become dirty.

solace n/v comfort in distress.

solar adj of the sun.

solarium n, pl **–lariums, –laria** place with beds and ultraviolet lights for acquiring artificial suntan.

solder n **1** easily–melted alloy used for joining metal. ◆ v **2** join with it.

soldier ⊕ n **1** one serving in army. ◆ v **2** serve in army **3** (with on) persist doggedly.

sole[1] ⊕ adj one and only. **solely** adv **1** alone. **2** only. **3** entirely.

sole[2] n **1** underside of foot. **2**

underpart of boot etc. ◆ v **3** fit with sole.

sole[3] n small edible flatfish.

solemn ⊕ adj **1** serious. **2** formal. **solemnity** n **solemnize** v celebrate, perform.

solicit v **–iting, –ited 1** request. **2** accost. **solicitor** n lawyer who prepares documents, advises clients. **solicitous** adj **1** anxious. **2** eager. **solicitude** n

solid ⊕ adj **1** not hollow. **2** composed of one substance. **3** firm. **4** reliable. ◆ n **5** body of three dimensions. **6** substance not liquid or gas. **solidarity** n unity. **solidify** v harden.

soliloquy n, pl **–quies** (esp. in drama) thoughts spoken by person while alone.

solitary ⊕ adj alone, single. **solitaire** n **1** game for one person. **2** single precious stone set by itself. **solitude** n state of being alone.

chaise longue

soft adj = **velvety**, smooth, silky, feathery, downy ≠ **rough**; = **yielding**, elastic ≠ **hard**; = **soggy**, swampy, marshy, boggy; = **squashy**, sloppy, mushy, spongy, gelatinous; = **pliable**, flexible, supple, malleable, plastic

soil[1] n = **earth**, ground, clay, dust, dirt; = **territory**, country, land

soil[2] v = **dirty**, foul, stain, pollute, tarnish ≠ **clean**

soldier n = **fighter**, serviceman, trooper, warrior, man–at–arms

sole[1] adj = **only**, one, single,

individual, alone

solemn adj = **serious**, earnest, grave, sober, sedate ≠ **cheerful**; = **formal**, grand, grave, dignified, ceremonial ≠ **informal**

solid adj = **firm**, hard, compact, dense, concrete ≠ **unsubstantial**; = **strong**, stable, sturdy, substantial, unshakable ≠ **unstable**; = **reliable**, dependable, upstanding, worthy, upright ≠ **unreliable**

solitary adj = **unsociable**, reclusive, unsocial, isolated, lonely ≠ **sociable**; = **lone**, alone

solo n, pl **-los 1** music for one performer. ♦ adj **2** unaccompanied, alone. **soloist** n

solstice n shortest (winter) or longest (summer) day.

solve ☉ v **1** work out. **2** find answer to. **soluble** adj **1** capable of being dissolved in liquid. **2** able to be solved. **solution** n **1** answer. **2** dissolving. **3** liquid with something dissolved in it. **solvable** adj **solvency** n **solvent** adj **1** able to meet financial obligations. ♦ n **2** liquid with power of dissolving.

sombre ☉ adj dark, gloomy.

sombrero n, pl **-ros** wide-brimmed hat.

some adj **1** denoting an indefinite number, amount or extent. **2** one or another. **3** certain. ♦ pron **4** portion, quantity. **somebody** pron **1** some person. ♦ n **2** important person. **somehow** adv by some means. **someone** pron somebody. **something** pron thing not clearly defined. **sometime** adv **1** at some unspecified time. ♦ adj **2** former. **sometimes** adv occasionally. **somewhat** adv rather. **somewhere** adv at some unspecified place.

somersault n tumbling head over heels.

son n male child. **son-in-law** n, pl **sons-in-law** daughter's husband.

sonar n device for detecting underwater objects.

sonata n piece of music in several movements.

song ☉ n **1** singing. **2** poem etc. for singing.

sonic adj pert. to sound waves.

sonnet n fourteen-line poem with definite rhyme scheme.

sonorous adj giving out (deep) sound, resonant.

soon ☉ adv **1** in a short time. **2** before long. **3** early, quickly.

soot n black powdery substance formed by burning of coal etc. **sooty** adj

soothe ☉ v **1** make calm, tranquil. **2** relieve (pain etc.).

sop n **1** piece of bread etc. soaked in liquid. **2** bribe. ♦ v **3** steep in water etc. **4** soak (up). **soppy** adj Inf oversentimental.

soporific adj causing sleep.

soprano n, pl **-nos** highest voice in women and boys.

sorbet n (fruit-flavoured) water ice.

sorcerer n magician. **sorcery** n

sordid adj **1** mean, squalid. **2** base.

sore ☉ adj **1** painful. **2** causing annoyance. ♦ n **3** sore place. **sorely** adv greatly.

sorrow ☉ n/v (feel) grief, sadness.

——— THESAURUS ———

solve v = **answer**, work out, resolve, crack, clear up

sombre adj = **gloomy**, sad, sober, grave, dismal ≠ cheerful

song n = **ballad**, air, tune, carol, chant

soon adv = **before long**, shortly, in the near future

soothe v = **calm**, still, quiet, hush, appease ≠ upset; = **relieve**, ease, alleviate, assuage ≠ irritate

sore adj = **painful**, smarting, raw,

sorrowful adj

sorry ⊙ adj **–rier, –riest 1** feeling pity or regret. **2** miserable, wretched.

sort ⊙ n **1** kind, class. ♦ v **2** classify.

sortie n sally by besieged forces.

SOS n **1** international code signal of distress. **2** call for help.

so–so adj Inf mediocre.

soufflé n dish of eggs beaten to froth, flavoured and baked.

soul ⊙ n **1** spiritual and immortal part of human being. **2** person. **3** sensitivity. **4** type of Black music. **soulful** adj

sound[1] ⊙ n **1** what is heard. **2** noise. ♦ v **3** make sound. **4** give

impression of. **5** utter. **soundproof** adj

sound[2] ⊙ adj **1** in good condition. **2** solid. **3** of good judgment. **4** thorough. **5** deep. **soundly** adv thoroughly.

sound[3] v **1** find depth of, as water. **2** ascertain views of. **3** probe.

sound[4] n **1** channel. **2** strait.

soup n liquid food made by boiling meat, vegetables etc.

sour ⊙ adj **1** acid. **2** gone bad. **3** peevish. **4** disagreeable. ♦ v **5** make, become sour.

source ⊙ n **1** origin, starting point. **2** spring.

south n **1** point opposite north. **2** region, part of country etc. lying

———— THESAURUS ————

tender, burning; **= annoyed**, cross, angry, pained, hurt; **= annoying**, troublesome; **= (**Lit**) urgent**, desperate, extreme, dire, pressing

sorrow n **= grief**, sadness, woe, regret, distress ≠ **joy**; **= hardship**, trial, tribulation, affliction, trouble ≠ **good fortune** ♦ v **= grieve**, mourn, lament, be sad, bemoan ≠ **rejoice**

sorry adj **= regretful**, apologetic, contrite, repentant, remorseful ≠ **unapologetic**; **= sympathetic**, moved, full of pity, compassionate, commiserative ≠ **unsympathetic**; **= wretched**, miserable, pathetic, mean, poor

sort n **= kind**, type, class, make, order ♦ v **= arrange**, group, order, rank, divide

soul n **= spirit**, essence, life, vital force; **= embodiment**, essence,

epitome, personification, quintessence; **= person**, being, individual, body, creature

sound[1] n **= noise**, din, report, tone, reverberation; **= idea**, impression, drift ♦ v **= toll**, set off; **= resound**, echo, go off, toll, set off; **= seem**, seem to be, appear to be

sound[2] adj **= fit**, healthy, perfect, intact, unhurt ≠ **frail**; **= sturdy**, strong, solid, stable; **= sensible**, wise, reasonable, right, correct ≠ **irresponsible**

sour adj **= sharp**, acid, tart, bitter, pungent ≠ **sweet**; **= rancid**, turned, gone off, curdled, gone bad ≠ **fresh**; **= bitter**, tart, acrimonious, embittered, disagreeable ≠ **good–natured**

source n **= cause**, origin, derivation, beginning, author;

to that side. ♦ *adj/adv* **3** from, towards or in the south. **southerly** *adj/n* wind from the south. **southern** *adj* **southward** *adj* **southwards** *adv*

souvenir ❶ *n* keepsake, memento.

sou'wester *n* seaman's waterproof headgear.

sovereign ❶ *n* **1** king, queen. **2** former gold coin worth 20 shillings. ♦ *adj* **3** supreme. **4** efficacious. **sovereignty** *n*

sow¹ ❶ *v* **sowing, sowed, sown** scatter, plant seed.

sow² *n* female adult pig.

soya *n* plant yielding edible beans. **soya bean** edible bean used for food and oil. **soy sauce** sauce made from fermented soya beans.

spa *n* **1** medicinal spring. **2** place, resort with one.

space ❶ *n* **1** extent. **2** room. **3** period. **4** empty place. **5** area. **6** expanse. **7** region beyond earth's atmosphere. ♦ *v* **8** place at intervals. **spacious** *adj* roomy.

extensive. **spacecraft, spaceship** *n* vehicle for travel beyond earth's atmosphere. **spaceman** *n* astronaut.

spade¹ *n* tool for digging.

spade² *n* suit at cards.

spaghetti *n* pasta in long strings.

span ❶ *n* **1** extent, space. **2** stretch of arch etc. **3** space from thumb to little finger. ♦ *v* **4** stretch over. **5** measure with hand.

spangle *n* **1** small shiny metallic ornament. ♦ *v* **2** decorate with spangles.

spaniel *n* breed of dog with long ears and silky hair.

spank *v* **1** slap with flat of hand, esp. on buttocks. ♦ *n* **2** spanking.

spanner *n* tool for gripping nut or bolt head.

spar ❶ *v* **sparring, sparred 1** box. **2** dispute, esp. in fun. ♦ *n* **3** sparring.

spare ❶ *v* **1** leave unhurt. **2** show mercy. **3** do without. **4** give away. ♦ *adj* **5** additional. **6** in reserve. **7** thin. ♦ *n* **9** reserve copy. **sparing** *adj* economical, careful.

———————— THESAURUS ————————

= **informant**, authority

souvenir *n* = **keepsake**, reminder, memento

sovereign *adj* = **supreme**, ruling, absolute, royal, principal; = **excellent**, efficient, effectual ♦ *n* = **monarch**, ruler, king or queen chief, potentate

sow¹ *v* = **scatter**, plant, seed, implant

space *n* = **room**, capacity, extent, margin, scope; = **period**, interval,

time, while, span; = **outer space**, the universe, the galaxy, the solar system, the cosmos

spacious *adj* = **roomy**, large, huge, broad, extensive ≠ **limited**

span *n* = **period**, term, duration, spell; = **extent**, reach, spread, length, distance ♦ *v* = **extend across**, cross, bridge, cover, link

spar *v* = **argue**, row, squabble, scrap (*Inf*), wrangle

spare *adj* = **back-up**, reserve,

spark ❶ n 1 small glowing or burning particle. 2 flash of light produced by electrical discharge. 3 trace. ◆ v 4 emit sparks. 5 kindle.

sparkle ❶ v 1 glitter. 2 effervesce. ◆ n 3 glitter. 4 vitality. **sparkling** adj 1 glittering. 2 (of wines) effervescent.

sparrow n small brownish bird.

sparrowhawk n hawk that hunts small birds.

sparse adj thinly scattered.

spartan adj strict, austere.

spasm n 1 sudden convulsive (muscular) contraction. 2 sudden burst of activity etc. **spasmodic** adj

spastic adj 1 affected by spasms. 2 suffering cerebral palsy. ◆ n 3 person with cerebral palsy.

spate ❶ n 1 rush, outpouring. 2 flood.

spatial adj of, in space.

spatter v 1 splash, cast drops over. 2 be scattered in drops. ◆ n 3 spattering.

spatula n utensil with broad, flat

blade for various purposes.

spawn n 1 eggs of fish or frog. ◆ v 2 (of fish or frog) cast eggs.

spay v remove ovaries from (female animal).

speak ❶ v speaking, spoke, spoken 1 utter words. 2 converse. 3 express. 4 communicate in. 5 give speech. **speaker** n 1 one who speaks. 2 speech maker. 3 loudspeaker.

spear n 1 long pointed weapon. ◆ v 2 pierce with spear. **spearhead** n 1 leading force in attack. ◆ v 2 lead attack.

spearmint n type of mint.

special ❶ adj 1 beyond the usual. 2 particular. **specialist** n one who devotes himself to special subject. **speciality** n special product, skill, characteristic etc. **specialization** n **specialize** v 1 be specialist. 2 make special.

species ❶ n, pl –cies group of plants or animals that are closely related.

second, extra, additional; = **extra**, surplus, leftover, over, free ≠ **necessary** ◆ v = **afford**, give, grant, do without, part with; = **have mercy on**, pardon, leave, let off (Inf), go easy on (Inf) ≠ **show no mercy to**

spark n = **flicker**, flash, gleam, glint, flare; = **trace**, hint, scrap, atom, jot ◆ v often with **off** = **start**, stimulate, provoke, inspire, trigger (off)

sparkle v = **glitter**, flash, shine, gleam, shimmer ◆ n = **glitter**,

flash, gleam, flicker, brilliance; = **vivacity**, life, spirit, dash, vitality

spate n = **flood**, flow, torrent, rush, deluge

speak v = **talk**, say something; = **articulate**, say, pronounce, utter, tell

special adj = **exceptional**, important, significant, particular, unique ≠ **ordinary**; = **specific**, particular, distinctive, individual, appropriate ≠ **general**

species n = **kind**, sort, type, group, class

specific ⊕ adj 1 exact in detail. 2 characteristic. **specification** n detailed description of something.

specify v state definitely or in detail.

specimen ⊕ n 1 part typifying whole. 2 individual example.

specious adj deceptively plausible, but false.

speck n 1 small spot, particle. ♦ v 2 mark with spots. **speckle** n/v speck.

spectacle ⊕ n 1 show. 2 thing exhibited. 3 strange, interesting, or ridiculous sight. ♦ pl 4 pair of lenses for correcting defective sight. **spectacular** adj 1 impressive. 2 showy. **spectate** v **spectator** n one who looks on.

spectre ⊕ n 1 ghost. 2 image of something unpleasant.

spectrum n, pl –tra band of colours into which light can be decomposed, e.g. by prism.

speculate ⊕ v 1 guess, conjecture. 2 engage in (risky)

commercial transactions. **speculation** n **speculative** adj **speculator** n

speech ⊕ n 1 act, faculty of speaking. 2 words, language. 3 (formal) talk given before audience. **speechless** adj 1 dumb. 2 at a loss for words.

speed ⊕ n 1 swiftness. 2 rate of progress. ♦ v 3 move quickly. 4 drive vehicle at high speed. 5 further. **speeding** n driving at high speed, esp. over legal limit.

speedy adj **speedometer** n instrument to show speed of vehicle. **speedwell** n plant with small blue flowers.

spell[1] ⊕ v **spelling, spelt** 1 give letters of in order. 2 indicate, result in. **spelling** n

spell[2] ⊕ n 1 magic formula. 2 enchantment. **spellbound** adj 1 enchanted. 2 entranced.

spell[3] ⊕ n (short) period of time, work.

spend ⊕ v **spending, spent** 1 pay

————————— THESAURUS —————————

specific adj = **particular**, special, characteristic, distinguishing ≠ **general**

specimen n = **sample**, example, model, type, pattern; = **example**, model, type

spectacle n = **show**, display, exhibition, event, performance; = **sight**, wonder, scene, phenomenon, curiosity

spectre n = **ghost**, spirit, phantom, vision, apparition

speculate v = **conjecture**, consider, wonder, guess, surmise;

= **gamble**, risk, venture, hazard

speech n = **communication**, talk, conversation, discussion, dialogue; = **diction**, pronunciation, articulation, delivery, fluency; = **language**, tongue, jargon, dialect, idiom

speed n = **rate**, pace ♦ v = **race**, rush, hurry, zoom, career ≠ **crawl**

spell[1] v = **indicate**, mean, signify, point to, imply

spell[2] n = **incantation**, charm; = **enchantment**, magic, fascination, glamour, allure

out. **2** pass (time). **3** use up completely. **spendthrift** *n* wasteful person.

sperm *n* **sperms 1** male reproductive cell. **2** semen.

spew *v* vomit.

sphere ⊕ *n* **1** ball, globe. **2** field of action. **spherical** *adj*

spice ⊕ *n* **1** aromatic or pungent vegetable substance. **2 spices** collectively. **3** anything that adds relish, interest etc. ♦ *v* **4** season with spices. **spicy** *adj*

spick–and–span *adj* neat, smart, new-looking.

spider *n* small eight-legged creature which spins web to catch prey. **spidery** *adj* thin and angular.

spike ⊕ *n* **1** sharp point. **2** long cluster with flowers attached directly to stalk. ♦ *v* **3** pierce, fasten with spike. **4** render ineffective. **spiky** *adj*

spill ⊕ *v* **spilling, spilt 1** (cause to) pour from, flow over, fall out, esp. unintentionally. ♦ *n* **2** fall. **3**

amount spilt. **spillage** *n*

spin ⊕ *v* **spinning, spun 1** (cause to) revolve rapidly. **2** twist into thread. **3** prolong. ♦ *n* **4** spinning.

spinning *n* act, process of drawing out and twisting into threads.

spin–dryer *n* machine in which clothes are spun to remove excess water. **spin–off** *n* incidental benefit.

spinach *n* dark green leafy vegetable.

spindle *n* rod, axis for spinning. **spindly** *adj* long and slender.

spine ⊕ *n* **1** backbone. **2** thin spike, esp. on fish etc. **3** ridge. **4** back of book. **spinal** *adj* **spineless** *adj* **1** lacking in spine. **2** cowardly.

spinster *n* unmarried woman.

spiral ⊕ *n* **1** continuous curve drawn at ever increasing distance from fixed point. **2** anything resembling this. ♦ *adj* **3** shaped like spiral.

spire *n* pointed part of steeple.

spirit ⊕ *n* **1** life principle

——————— THESAURUS ———————

spell² *n* = **period**, time, term, stretch, course

spend *v* = **pay out**, fork out (*Sl*), expend, disburse ≠ **save**; = **pass**, fill, occupy, while away; = **use up**, waste, squander, empty, drain ≠ **save**

sphere *n* = **ball**, globe, orb, globule, circle; = **field**, department, function, territory, capacity

spice *n* = **excitement**, zest, colour, pep, zing (*Inf*)

spike *n* = **point**, stake, spine,

barb, prong ♦ *v* = **impale**, spit, spear, stick

spill *v* = **tip over**, overturn, capsize, knock over; discharge

spin *v* = **revolve**, turn, rotate, reel, whirl; = **reel**, swim, whirl ♦ *n* = (*Inf*) **drive**, ride, joy ride (*Inf*); = **revolution**, roll, whirl, gyration

spine *n* = **backbone**, vertebrae, spinal column, vertebral column; = **barb**, spur, needle, spike, ray

spiral *adj* = **coiled**, winding, whorled, helical ♦ *n* = **coil**, helix, corkscrew, whorl

animating body. **2** disposition. **3** liveliness. **4** courage. **5** essential character or meaning. **6** soul. **7** ghost. ◆ *pl* **8** emotional state. **9** strong alcoholic drink. ◆ *v* **10** carry away mysteriously. **spirited** *adj* lively. **spiritual** *adj* **1** given to, interested in things of the spirit. ◆ *n* **2** sacred song orig. sung by Black slaves in America.

spiritualism *n* belief that spirits of the dead communicate with the living. **spiritualist** *n* **spirituality** *n*

spit¹ 𝗢 *v* **spitting, spat 1** eject saliva (from mouth). ◆ *n* **2** spitting, saliva. **spittle** *n* saliva.

spit² *n* **1** sharp rod to put through meat for roasting. **2** sandy point projecting into the sea. ◆ *v* **3** thrust through.

spite 𝗢 *n* **1** malice. ◆ *v* **2** thwart spitefully. **spiteful** *adj* **in spite of** *prep* **1** regardless of. **2** notwithstanding.

splash 𝗢 *v* **1** scatter liquid about

or on, over something. **2** print (story, photo) prominently in newspaper. ◆ *n* **3** sound of splashing liquid. **4** patch, esp. of colour. **5** (effect of) extravagant display.

splatter *v/n* spatter.

splay *adj* **1** spread out. **2** turned outwards. ◆ *v* **3** spread out. **4** twist outwards.

spleen *n* organ in the abdomen. **splenetic** *adj* spiteful, irritable.

splendid 𝗢 *adj* magnificent, excellent. **splendour** *n*

splice *v* **1** join by interweaving strands. ◆ *n* **2** spliced joint.

splint *n* rigid support for broken limb etc.

splinter 𝗢 *n* **1** thin fragment. ◆ *v* **2** break into fragments.

split 𝗢 *v* **splitting, split 1** break asunder. **2** separate. **3** divide. ◆ *n* **4** crack. **5** division. **split second** very short period of time.

splutter *v* **1** make hissing, spitting

spirit *n* = **soul**, life; = **life force**, vital spark; = **ghost**, phantom, spectre, apparition; = **courage**, guts (*Inf*), grit, backbone, spunk (*Inf*); = **liveliness**, energy, vigour, life, force; = **attitude**, character, temper, outlook, temperament; = **heart**, sense, nature, soul, core

spit¹ *v* = **eject**, throw out ◆ *n* = **saliva**, dribble, spittle, drool, slaver

spite *n* = **malice**, malevolence, ill will, hatred, animosity ≠ **kindness** ◆ *v* = **annoy**, hurt, injure, harm, vex ≠ **benefit**

splash *v* = **paddle**, plunge, bathe, dabble, wade; = **scatter**, shower, spray, sprinkle, wet ◆ *n* = **dash**, touch, spattering; = **spot**, burst, patch, spurt

splendid *adj* = **excellent**, wonderful, marvellous, great (*Inf*), cracking (*Brit inf*) ≠ **poor**; = **magnificent**, grand, impressive, rich, superb ≠ **squalid**

splinter *n* = **sliver**, fragment, chip, flake ◆ *v* = **shatter**, split, fracture, disintegrate

split *v* = **break**, crack, burst, open, give way; = **cut**, break, crack,

sounds. **2** utter incoherently with spitting sounds. ♦ *n* **3** spluttering.

spoil ⊙ *v* spoiling, spoilt **1** damage, injure. **2** damage manners or behaviour of (esp. child) by indulgence. **3** go bad. **spoils** *pl n* booty. **spoilsport** *n* person who spoils others' enjoyment.

spoke *n* radial bar of a wheel.

spokesman, spokeswoman, spokesperson *n* one deputed to speak for others.

sponge *n* **1** marine animal. **2** its skeleton, or a synthetic substance like it, used to absorb liquids. **3** type of light cake. ♦ *v* **4** wipe with sponge. **5** live at the expense of others. **spongy** *adj* **1** spongelike. **2** wet and soft.

sponsor ⊙ *n* **1** one promoting something. **2** one who agrees to give money to charity on completion of a specified activity by another. **3** godparent. ♦ *v* **4** act as sponsor. **sponsorship** *n*

spontaneous ⊙ *adj* **1** voluntary. **2** natural. **spontaneity** *n*

spoof *n* mildly satirical parody.

spook *n Inf* ghost. **spooky** *adj*

spool *n* reel, bobbin.

spoon *n* **1** implement with shallow bowl at end of handle for carrying food to mouth etc. ♦ *v* **2** lift with spoon. **spoonful** *n* **spoon-feed** *v* give (someone) too much help.

sporadic *adj* **1** intermittent. **2** scattered.

spore *n* minute reproductive body of some plants.

sporran *n* pouch worn in front of kilt.

sport ⊙ *n* **1** game, activity for pleasure, competition, exercise. **2** enjoyment. **3** cheerful person, good loser. ♦ *v* **4** wear (esp. ostentatiously). **5** frolic. **6** play (sport). **sporting** *adj* **1** of sport. **2** behaving with fairness, generosity. **sports car** fast low–built car. **sportsman** *n* **1** one who engages in sport. **2** good loser.

spot ⊙ *n* **1** small mark, stain. **2** blemish. **3** pimple. **4** place. **5** (difficult) situation. **6** *Inf* small quantity. ♦ *v* **7** mark with spots. **8** detect. **9** observe. **spotless** *adj* **1**

snap, chop; = **divide**, separate, disunite, disband, cleave;
= **diverge**, separate, branch, fork, part ♦ *n* = **division**, breach, rift, rupture, discord; = **separation**, break-up, split-up

spoil *v* = **ruin**, destroy, wreck, damage, injure ≠ **improve**;
= **overindulge**, indulge, pamper, cosset, coddle ≠ **deprive**;
= **indulge**, pamper, satisfy, gratify,

pander to

sponsor *v* = **back**, fund, finance, promote, subsidize ♦ *n* = **backer**, patron, promoter

spontaneous *adj* = **unplanned**, impromptu, unprompted, willing, natural ≠ **planned**

sport *n* = **game**, exercise, recreation, play, amusement;
= **fun**, joking, teasing, banter, jest
♦ *v* = (*Inf*) **wear**, display, flaunt,

unblemished. **2** pure. **spotty** adj **1** with spots. **2** uneven. **spotlight** n **1** powerful light illuminating small area. **2** centre of attention.

spouse n husband or wife.

spout v **1** pour out. ◆ n **2** projecting tube or lip for pouring liquids. **2** copious discharge.

sprain v/n wrench, twist.

sprat n small sea fish.

sprawl v **1** lie or sit about awkwardly. **2** spread in rambling, unplanned way. ◆ n **3** sprawling.

spray¹ n **1** (device for producing) fine drops of liquid. ◆ v **2** sprinkle with shower of fine drops.

spray² n **1** branch, twig with buds, flowers etc. **2** ornament like this.

spread v spreading, spread **1** extend. **2** stretch out. **3** open out. **4** scatter. **5** distribute. **6** unfold. **7** cover. ◆ n **8** extent. **9** increase. **10**

ample meal. **11** food which can be spread on bread etc. **spread-eagled** adj with arms and legs outstretched.

spree n **1** session of overindulgence. **2** romp.

sprig n small twig.

sprightly adj –lier, –liest lively, brisk.

spring v springing, sprang **1** leap. **2** shoot up or forth. **3** come into being. **4** appear. **5** grow. **6** become bent or spilt. **7** produce unexpectedly. **8** set off (trap). ◆ n **9** leap. **10** recoil. **11** piece of coiled or bent metal with much resilience. **12** flow of water from earth. **13** first season of year.

springy adj elastic. **spring-clean** v clean (house) thoroughly.

springbok n S Afr. antelope.

sprinkle v scatter small drops on, strew. **sprinkler** n **sprinkling** n small quantity or number.

exhibit, flourish

spot n = **mark**, stain, speck, scar, blot; = **pimple**, pustule, zit (Sl); = **place**, site, point, position, scene; = (Inf) **predicament**, trouble, difficulty, mess, plight ◆ v = **see**, observe, catch sight of, sight, recognize; = **mark**, stain, soil, dirty, fleck

spouse n = **partner**, mate, husband or wife, consort, significant other (US inf)

spray¹ n = **droplets**, fine mist, drizzle; = **aerosol**, sprinkler, atomizer ◆ v = **scatter**, shower, sprinkle, diffuse

spray² n = **sprig**, floral arrangement, branch, corsage

spread v = **open** (out), extend, stretch, unfold, sprawl; = **extend**, open, stretch ◆ n = **increase**, development, advance, expansion, proliferation; = **extent**, span, stretch, sweep

spree n = **fling**, binge (Inf), orgy

spring n = **flexibility**, bounce, resilience, elasticity, buoyancy ◆ v = **jump**, bound, leap, bounce, vault; = **originate**, come, derive, start, issue

sprinkle v = **scatter**, dust, strew, pepper, shower

S

sprint ⓘ v 1 run short distance at great speed. ♦ n 2 such run, race.
sprinter n
sprite n elf.
sprocket n toothed wheel, attached to chain.
sprout ⓘ v 1 put forth shoots, spring up. ♦ n 2 shoot.
spruce¹ n variety of fir.
spruce² adj neat in dress. **spruce up** make neat and smart.
spry adj **spryer, spryest** nimble, vigorous.
spur ⓘ n 1 pricking instrument attached to horseman's heel. 2 incitement. 3 stimulus. ♦ v 4 urge on.
spurious adj not genuine.
spurn ⓘ v reject with scorn.
spurt v 1 send, come out in jet. 2 rush suddenly. ♦ n 3 jet. 4 short sudden effort.
spy ⓘ n, pl **spies** 1 one who watches (esp. in rival countries, companies etc.) and reports secretly. ♦ v 2 act as spy. 3 catch

sight of.
squabble ⓘ v/n (engage in) petty, noisy quarrel.
squad ⓘ n small party, esp. of soldiers. **squadron** n division of cavalry regiment, fleet or air force.
squalid adj mean and dirty. **squalor** n
squall n 1 harsh cry. 2 sudden gust of wind. 3 short storm. ♦ v 4 yell.
squander ⓘ v spend wastefully.
square ⓘ n 1 equilateral rectangle. 2 area of this shape. 3 in town, open space (of this shape). 4 product of a number multiplied by itself. 5 instrument for drawing right angles. ♦ adj 6 square in form. 7 honest. 8 straight, even. 9 level, equal. ♦ v 10 make square. 11 find square of. 12 pay. 13 fit, suit.
squash ⓘ v 1 crush flat. 2 pulp. 3 suppress. ♦ n 4 juice of crushed fruit. 5 crowd. 6 game played with rackets and ball in walled court.

———— THESAURUS ————

sprint v = **run**, race, shoot, tear, dash
sprout v = **germinate**, bud, shoot, spring
spur v = **incite**, drive, prompt, urge, stimulate ♦ n = **stimulus**, incentive, impetus, motive, impulse; **on the spur of the moment** = **on impulse**, impulsively, on the spot, impromptu, without planning
spurn v = **reject**, slight, scorn, rebuff, snub ≠ **accept**
spy n = **undercover agent**, mole,

nark (Brit, Aust & NZ sl) ♦ v = **catch sight of**, spot, notice, observe, glimpse
squabble v = **quarrel**, fight, argue, row, dispute ♦ n = **quarrel**, fight, row, argument, dispute
squad n = **team**, group, band, company, force
squander v = **waste**, spend, fritter away, blow (sl), misuse ≠ **save**
square adj = **fair**, straight, genuine, ethical, honest ♦ v often with **with** = **agree**, match, fit, correspond, tally

squat v **squatting, squatted 1** sit on heels. **2** occupy unused premises illegally. ♦ adj **3** short and thick. **squatter** n

squawk n **1** short harsh cry, esp. of bird. ♦ v **2** utter this.

squeak v/n (make) short shrill sound.

squeal n **1** long piercing squeak. ♦ v **2** make one.

squeamish adj **1** easily made sick. **2** easily shocked.

squeeze ⊕ v **1** press. **2** wring. **3** force. **4** hug. ♦ n **5** act of squeezing.

squelch v/n (make) wet sucking sound.

squid n type of cuttlefish.

squiggle n wavy line.

squint v **1** have the eyes turn in different directions. **2** glance sideways. ♦ n **3** this eye disorder. **4** glance.

squire n country gentleman.

squirm v **1** wriggle. **2** be embarrassed. ♦ n **3** squirming.

squirrel n small graceful bushy–tailed tree animal.

squirt v **1** (of liquid) force, be forced through narrow opening. ♦

n **2** jet of liquid.

st. stone (weight).

stab ⊕ v **stabbing, stabbed 1** pierce, strike (at) with pointed weapon. ♦ n **2** blow, wound so inflicted. **3** sudden sensation, e.g. of fear. **4** attempt.

stabilize v make or become stable. **stabilizer** n device to maintain stability of ship, aircraft etc.

stable¹ n **1** building for horses. **2** racehorses of particular owner, establishment. **3** such establishment. ♦ v **4** put into stable.

stable² ⊕ adj **1** firmly fixed. **2** steadfast, resolute. **stability** n **1** steadiness. **2** ability to resist change.

staccato adj/adv Mus with the notes sharply separated.

stack ⊕ n **1** ordered pile, heap. **2** chimney. ♦ v **3** pile in stack.

stadium n, pl **–diums, –dia** open-air arena for athletics etc.

staff ⊕ n **1** body of officers or workers. **2** pole. ♦ v **3** supply with personnel.

stag n male deer.

S

———— THESAURUS ————

squash v = **crush**, press, flatten, mash, smash; = **suppress**, quell, silence, crush, annihilate

squeeze v = **press**, crush, squash, pinch; = **clutch**, press, grip, crush, pinch; = **cram**, press, crowd, force, stuff; = **hug**, embrace, cuddle, clasp, enfold ♦ n = **press**, grip, clasp, crush, pinch; = **crush**, jam, squash, press, crowd

stab v = **pierce**, stick, wound, knife, thrust ♦ n = (Inf) **attempt**, go, try, endeavour; = **twinge**, prick, pang, ache

stable² adj = **secure**, lasting, strong, sound, fast ≠ **insecure**; = **well-balanced**, balanced, sensible, reasonable, rational

stack n = **pile**, heap, mountain, mass, load ♦ v = **pile**, heap up,

stage ⊕ *n* 1 period, division of development. 2 (platform of) theatre. 3 stopping–place on road, distance between two of them. ◆ *v* 4 put (play) on stage. 5 arrange, bring about.

stagger ⊕ *v* 1 walk unsteadily. 2 astound. 3 arrange in overlapping or alternating positions, times. 4 distribute over a period.

staid *adj* of sober and quiet character, sedate.

stain ⊕ *v* 1 spot, mark. 2 apply liquid colouring to (wood etc.). ◆ *n* 3 discoloration or mark. 4 moral blemish. **stainless** *adj* **stainless steel** rustless steel alloy.

stairs *pl n* set of steps, esp. as part of house. **staircase, stairway** *n* 1 structure enclosing stairs. 2 stairs.

stake ⊕ *n* 1 sharpened stick or post. 2 bet. 3 investment. ◆ *v* 4 secure, mark out with stakes. 5 wager, risk.

stalactite *n* lime deposit hanging from roof of cave.

stalagmite *n* lime deposit sticking up from floor of cave.

stale ⊕ *adj* 1 old, lacking freshness. 2 lacking energy, interest through monotony.

stalemate *n* deadlock.

stalk¹ ⊕ *v* 1 follow stealthily. 2 walk in stiff and stately manner.

stalk² *n* 1 plant's stem. 2 anything like this.

stall ⊕ *n* 1 compartment in stable etc. 2 erection for display and sale of goods. 3 front seat in theatre etc. ◆ *v* 4 (of motor engine) unintentionally stop. 5 delay.

stallion *n* uncastrated male horse, esp. for breeding.

stalwart ⊕ *adj* 1 strong, brave. 2 staunch. ◆ *n* 3 stalwart person.

stamina ⊕ *n* power of endurance.

stammer ⊕ *v* 1 speak, say with repetition of syllables. ◆ *n* 2 habit of so speaking.

stamp ⊕ *v* 1 put down foot with

load, assemble, accumulate
staff *n* = **workers**, employees, personnel, workforce, team; = **stick**, pole, rod, crook, cane
stage *n* = **step**, leg, phase, point, level
stagger *v* = **totter**, reel, sway, lurch, wobble; = **astound**, amaze, stun, shock, shake
stain *n* = **mark**, spot, blot, blemish, discoloration; = **stigma**, shame, disgrace, slur, dishonour; = **dye**, colour, tint ◆ *v* = **mark**, soil, discolour, dirty, tinge; = **dye**, colour, tint

stake *n* = **pole**, post, stick, pale, paling
stale *adj* = **old**, hard, dry, decayed ≠ **fresh**; = **musty**, fusty
stalk¹ *v* = **pursue**, follow, track, hunt, shadow
stall *v* = **play for time**, delay, hedge, temporize
stalwart *adj* = **loyal**, faithful, firm, true, dependable; = **strong**, strapping, sturdy, stout ≠ **puny**
stamina *n* = **staying power**, endurance, resilience, force, power
stammer *v* = **stutter**, falter,

force. **2** impress mark on. **3** affix postage stamp. ♦ *n* **4** stamping with foot. **5** imprinted mark. **6** appliance for marking. **7** piece of gummed paper printed with device as evidence of postage etc.

stampede *n* **1** sudden frightened rush, esp. of herd of cattle, crowd. ♦ *v* **2** rush.

stance ❶ *n* **1** manner, position of standing. **2** attitude.

stanchion *n* upright bar used as support.

stand ❶ *v* **standing, stood 1** have, take, set in upright position. **2** be situated. **3** remain firm or stationary. **4** endure. **5** offer oneself as a candidate. **6** be symbol etc. of. **7** *Inf* provide free, treat to. ♦ *n* **8** holding firm. **9** position. **10** something on which thing may be placed. **11** structure from which spectators can watch sport etc. **standing 1** reputation, status. **2** duration. ♦ *adj* **3** erect. **4**

lasting. **5** stagnant. **standoffish** *adj* reserved or haughty.

standard ❶ *n* **1** accepted example of something against which others are judged. **2** degree, quality. **3** flag. ♦ *adj* **4** usual. **5** of recognized authority, accepted as correct. **standardize** *v* regulate by a standard.

standpipe *n* tap attached to water main to provide public water supply.

standpoint *n* point of view.

standstill *n* complete halt.

stanza *n* group of lines of verse.

staple *n* **1** U-shaped piece of metal used to fasten. **2** main product. ♦ *adj* **3** principal. ♦ *v* **4** fasten with staple. **stapler** *n*

star ❶ *n* **1** celestial body, seen as twinkling point of light. **2** asterisk (*). **3** celebrated player, actor. ♦ *v* **4** adorn with stars. **5** mark (with asterisk). **6** feature as star performer. ♦ *adj* **7** most

pause, hesitate, stumble over your words

stamp *n* = **imprint**, mark, brand, signature, earmark ♦ *v* = **print**, mark, impress; = **trample**, step, tread, crush; = **identify**, mark, brand, label, reveal

stance *n* = **attitude**, stand, position, viewpoint, standpoint; = **posture**, carriage, bearing, deportment

stand *v* = **be upright**, be erect, be vertical; = **get to your feet**, rise, stand up, straighten up; = **be located**, be, sit, be positioned, be

situated *or* located; = **be valid**, continue, exist, prevail, remain valid ♦ *n* = **position**, attitude, stance, opinion, determination; = **stall**, booth, kiosk, table, rack; = **support**, base, platform, stage, rack

standard *n* = **level**, grade; = **criterion**, measure, guideline, example, model; *often plural* = **principles**, ideals, morals, ethics; = **flag**, banner, ensign ♦ *adj* = **usual**, normal, customary, average, basic ≠ unusual; = **accepted**, official, established,

important. **stardom** n **starry** adj covered with stars. **starfish** n small star-shaped sea creature.

starboard n right-hand side of ship.

starch n 1 substance forming the main food element in bread, potatoes etc., and used mixed with water, for stiffening linen etc. ◆ v 2 stiffen thus. **starchy** adj 1 containing starch. 2 stiff.

stare ❶ v 1 look fixedly (at). ◆ n 2 staring gaze.

stark ❶ adj 1 blunt, bare. 2 desolate. 3 absolute. ◆ adv 4 completely.

starling n glossy black speckled songbird.

start ❶ v 1 begin. 2 set going. 3 make sudden movement. ◆ n 4 beginning. 5 abrupt movement. 6 advantage of a lead in a race.

starter n 1 first course of meal. 2 electric motor starting car engine. 3 competitor in race. 4 supervisor of start of race.

startle ❶ v give a fright to.

starve v (cause to) suffer or die from hunger. **starvation** n

stash v Inf store in secret place.

state ❶ n 1 condition. 2 politically organized people. 3 government. 4 pomp. ◆ v 5 express in words.

stately adj dignified, lofty.

statement n 1 expression in words. 2 account. **statesman** n respected political leader. **statesmanship** n

static ❶ adj 1 motionless, inactive. ◆ n 2 electrical interference in radio reception.

station ❶ n 1 place where thing stops or is placed. 2 stopping place for railway trains. 3 local office for police force, fire brigade etc. 4 place equipped for radio or

approved, recognized ≠ **unofficial**

star n = **heavenly body**, celestial body; = **celebrity**, big name, megastar (Inf), name, luminary ◆ adj = **leading**, major, celebrated, brilliant, well-known

stare v = **gaze**, look, goggle, watch, gape

stark adj = **plain**, harsh, basic, grim, straightforward; = **sharp**, clear, striking, distinct, clear-cut ◆ adv = **absolutely**, quite, completely, entirely, altogether

start v = **set about**, begin, proceed, embark upon, take the first step ≠ **stop**; = **begin**, arise, originate, issue, appear ≠ **end**;

= **set in motion**, initiate, instigate, open, trigger ≠ **stop**; = **establish**, begin, found, create, launch ≠ **terminate** ◆ n = **beginning**, outset, opening, birth, foundation ≠ **end**; = **jump**, spasm, convulsion

startle v = **surprise**, shock, frighten, scare, make (someone) jump

state n = **country**, nation, land, republic, territory; = **government**, ministry, administration, executive, regime; = **condition**, shape ◆ v = **say**, declare, specify, present, voice

static adj = **stationary**, still, motionless, fixed, immobile

television transmission. **5** bus garage. **6** post. **7** position in life. ◆ v **8** put in position. **stationary** adj **1** not moving. **2** not changing.

station wagon n US and Canad automobile with a rear door and luggage space behind the rear seats.

statue n solid carved or cast image. **statuesque** adj **1** like statue. **2** dignified. **statuette** n small statue.

stature ❶ n **1** bodily height. **2** greatness.

status ❶ n **1** position, rank. **2** prestige. **3** relation to others. **status quo** existing state of affairs. **statute** n law. **statutory** adj **staunch** ❶ adj trustworthy, loyal. **stave** n **1** strip of wood in barrel. ◆ v **2** break hole in. **3** ward (off). **stay**¹ ❶ v **1** remain. **2** reside. **3** endure. **4** stop. **5** postpone. ◆ n **6** remaining, residing. **7** postponement.

stay² n support, prop.

stead n place. **in stead** in place (of).

steady ❶ adj steadier, steadiest **1** firm. **2** regular. **3** temperate. ◆ v **4** make steady. **steadily** adv

steadfast adj firm, unyielding.

steak n thick slice of meat.

steal ❶ v stealing, stole, stolen **1** take without right or permission. **2** move silently.

stealth ❶ n secret or underhand procedure, behaviour. **stealthy** adj

steam n **1** vapour of boiling water. ◆ v **2** give off steam. **3** move by steam power. **4** cook or treat with steam. **steamer** n **1** steam-propelled ship. **steam engine** engine worked by steam. **steamroller** n steam-powered vehicle with heavy rollers, used to level road surfaces.

steed n Lit horse.

steel n **1** hard and malleable metal made by mixing carbon in iron. ◆ v **2** harden.

steep¹ ❶ adj **1** sloping abruptly. **2**

—————— THESAURUS ——————

≠ **moving**

station n = **railway station**, stop, stage, halt, terminal;
= **headquarters**, base, depot;
= **position**, rank, status, standing, post ◆ v = **assign**, post, locate, set, establish

stature n = **height**, build, size

status n = **position**, rank, grade

staunch adj = **loyal**, faithful, stalwart, firm, sound

stay¹ v = **remain**, continue to be, linger, stop, wait ≠ **go** ◆ n = **visit**, stop, holiday, stopover, sojourn;

= **postponement**, delay, suspension, stopping, halt

steady adj = **continuous**, regular, constant, consistent, persistent
≠ **irregular**; = **stable**, fixed, secure, firm, safe ≠ **unstable**; = **regular**, established

steal v = **take**, nick (slang, chiefly Brit.), pinch (Inf), lift (Inf), embezzle; = **copy**, take, appropriate, pinch (Inf)

stealth n = **secrecy**, furtiveness, slyness, sneakiness, unobtrusiveness

(of prices) very high.

steep² v soak, saturate.

steeple n church tower with spire. **steeplechase** n race with obstacles to jump. **steeplejack** n one who builds, repairs chimneys etc.

steer¹ ❶ v 1 guide, direct course of vessel, motor vehicle etc. **2** direct one's course.

steer² n castrated male ox.

stellar adj of stars.

stem¹ ❶ n 1 stalk, trunk. **2** part of word to which inflections are added.

stem² v stemming, stemmed check, dam up.

stench n foul smell.

stencil n 1 thin sheet pierced with pattern which is brushed over with paint or ink, leaving pattern on surface under it. **2** the pattern. ♦ v **3** make pattern thus.

step ❶ v stepping, stepped **1** move and set down foot. **2** proceed (in this way). **3** measure in paces. ♦ n **4** stepping. **5** series of foot movements forming part of dance. **6** measure, act, stage in

proceeding. **7** board, rung etc. to put foot on. **8** degree in scale.

stepladder n folding portable ladder with supporting frame.

stereophonic adj (of sound) giving effect of coming from many directions. **stereo** n 1 stereophonic sound, record player etc. ♦ adj **2** stereophonic.

stereotype ❶ n 1 something (monotonously) familiar, conventional. ♦ v **2** form stereotype of.

sterile ❶ adj 1 unable to produce fruit, crops, young etc. **2** free from (harmful) germs. **sterility** n **sterilize** v render sterile.

sterling ❶ adj 1 genuine, true. **2** of solid worth. **3** in British money. ♦ n **4** British money.

stern¹ adj severe, strict.

stern² n rear part of ship.

sternum n, pl **–na, –nums** breast bone.

steroid n organic compound, oft. used to increase body strength.

stethoscope n instrument for listening to action of heart, lungs etc.

——————— THESAURUS ———————

steep¹ adj = **sheer**, precipitous, abrupt, vertical ≠ **gradual**;
= **sharp**, sudden, abrupt, marked, extreme

steer¹ v = **drive**, control, direct, handle, pilot

stem¹ n = **stalk**, branch, trunk, shoot, axis

stem² v = **stop**, hold back, staunch, check, dam

step n = **pace**, stride, footstep;

= **move**, measure, action, means, act ♦ v = **walk**, pace, tread, move

stereotype n = **formula**, pattern
♦ v = **categorize**, typecast, pigeonhole, standardize

sterile adj = **germ-free**, sterilized, disinfected, aseptic ≠ **unhygienic**;
= **barren**, infertile, unproductive, childless ≠ **fertile**

sterling adj = **excellent**, sound, fine, superlative

stew n **1** food cooked slowly in closed vessel. ◆ v **2** cook slowly.

steward n **1** one who manages another's property. **2** official managing race meeting, assembly etc. **3** attendant on ship or aircraft.

stick ⊕ n sticking, stuck **1** long, thin piece of wood. **2** anything shaped like a stick. ◆ v **3** pierce, stab. **4** place, fasten, as by pins, glue. **5** protrude. **6** adhere. **7** come to stop. **8** jam. **9** remain.

sticker n adhesive label, poster.

sticky adj **1** covered with, like adhesive substance. **2** (of weather) warm, humid. **3** Inf awkward, tricky.

stickleback n small fish with sharp spines on back.

stickler n person who insists on something.

stiff ⊕ adj **1** not easily bent or moved. **2** difficult. **3** thick, not fluid. **4** formal. **5** strong or fresh, as breeze. **stiffen** v **stiffness** n

stifle ⊕ v smother, suppress.

stigma ⊕ n, pl **-mas**, **-mata** mark of disgrace. **stigmatize** v

stile n arrangement of steps for climbing a fence.

still[1] ⊕ adj **1** motionless, noiseless. ◆ v **2** quiet. ◆ adv **3** to this time. **4** yet. **5** even. ◆ n **6** photograph, esp. of film scene. **stillness** n **stillborn** adj born dead.

still[2] n apparatus for distilling.

stimulus ⊕ n, pl **-li 1** something that rouses to activity. **2** incentive. **stimulant** n drug etc. acting as stimulus. **stimulate** v rouse up, spur. **stimulation** n

sting ⊕ v stinging, stung **1** thrust sting into. **2** cause sharp pain to. **3** feel sharp pain. ◆ n **4** (wound, pain, caused by) sharp pointed organ, often poisonous, of certain creatures.

stingy adj **-gier**, **-giest 1** mean. **2** niggardly.

stink ⊕ v **1** give out strongly

———————— THESAURUS ————————

stick n = **twig**, branch; = **cane**, staff, pole, rod, crook ◆ v = (Inf) **put**, place, set, lay, deposit; = **poke**, dig, stab, thrust, pierce; = **fasten**, fix, bind, hold, bond; = **adhere**, cling, become joined, become welded; = **stay**, remain, linger, persist; = (Sl) **tolerate**, take, stand, stomach, abide

stiff adj = **inflexible**, rigid, unyielding, hard, firm ≠ **flexible**; = **formal**, constrained, forced, unnatural, stilted ≠ **informal**; = **vigorous**, great, strong; = **severe**, strict, harsh, hard, heavy

stifle v = **suppress**, repress, stop, check, silence; = **restrain**, suppress, repress, smother

stigma n = **disgrace**, shame, dishonour, stain, slur

still[1] adj = **motionless**, stationary, calm, peaceful, serene ≠ **moving**; = **silent**, quiet, hushed ≠ **noisy** ◆ v = **quieten**, calm, settle, quiet, silence ≠ **get louder**

stimulus n = **incentive**, spur, encouragement, impetus, inducement

sting v = **hurt**, burn, wound; = **smart**, burn, pain, hurt, tingle

S

offensive smell **2** *Sl* be abhorrent.
stint ❶ *v* **1** be frugal, miserly. ◆ *n*
2 allotted amount of work or time.
3 limitation, restriction.
stipulate ❶ *v* specify in making a
bargain. **stipulation** *n* **1** proviso. **2**
condition.
stir ❶ *v* stirring, stirred **1** (begin
to) move. **2** rouse. **3** excite. ◆ *n* **4**
commotion, disturbance.
stirrup *n* loop for supporting foot
of rider on horse.
stitch *n* **1** movement of needle in
sewing etc. **2** its result in the work.
3 sharp pain in side. **4** least
fragment (of clothing). ◆ *v* **5** sew.
stoat *n* small mammal with
brown coat and black–tipped tail.
stock ❶ *n* **1** goods, material
stored, esp. for later use. **2**
financial shares in, or capital of,
company etc. **3** standing,
reputation. **4** farm animals,
livestock. **5** plant, stem from
which cuttings are taken. **6** handle
of gun, tool etc. **7** liquid broth
produced by boiling meat etc. **8**
flowering plant. **9** lineage. ◆ *adj*

10 kept in stock. **11** standard. **12**
hackneyed. ◆ *v* **13** keep, store. **14**
supply with livestock, fish etc.
stockist *n* dealer who stocks a
particular product. **stocky** *adj*
thickset. **stockbroker** *n* agent for
buying, selling shares in
companies. **stock exchange**
institution for buying and selling
shares. **stockpile** *v* acquire and
store large quantity of
(something). **stocktaking** *n*
examination, counting and
valuing of goods in a shop etc.
stockade *n* enclosure of stakes,
barrier.
stocking *n* close–fitting covering
for leg and foot.
stodgy *adj* stodgier, stodgiest
heavy, dull.
stoep *n* *S Afr* verandah.
stoic *adj* **1** capable of much self–
control, great endurance without
complaint. ◆ *n* **2** stoical person.
stoical *adj* **stoicism** *n*
stoke *v* feed, tend fire or furnace.
stoker *n*
stole *n* long scarf or shawl.

stink *v* = **reek**, pong (*Brit inf*) ◆ *v*
= **stench**, pong (*Brit inf*), foul smell,
fetor
stint *n* = **term**, time, turn, period,
share ◆ *v* = **be mean**, hold back,
be sparing, skimp on, be frugal
stipulate *v* = **specify**, agree,
require, contract, settle
stir *v* = **mix**, beat, agitate;
= **stimulate**, move, excite, spur,
provoke ≠ **inhibit** ◆ *n*
= **commotion**, excitement, activity,

disorder, fuss
stock *n* = **shares**, holdings,
securities, investments, bonds;
= **property**, capital, assets, funds;
= **goods**, merchandise, wares,
range, choice; = **supply**, store,
reserve, fund, stockpile ◆ *v* = **sell**,
supply, handle, keep, trade in;
= **fill**, supply, provide with, equip,
furnish ◆ *adj* = **hackneyed**,
routine, banal, trite, overused;
= **regular**, usual, ordinary,

stolid *adj* hard to excite.

stomach **⊕** *n* 1 sac forming chief digestive organ in any animal. 2 appetite. ◆ *v* 3 put up with.

stomp *v* tread heavily.

stone *n* 1 (piece of) rock. 2 gem. 3 hard seed of fruit. 4 hard deposit formed in kidneys, bladder. 5 unit of weight, 14 pounds. ◆ *v* 6 throw stones at. 7 free (fruit) from stones. **stony** *adj* 1 of, like stone. 2 hard. 3 cold. **stone–deaf** *adj* completely deaf.

stooge *n* person taken advantage of.

stool *n* backless chair.

stoop **⊕** *v* 1 lean forward or down. 2 abase, degrade oneself. ◆ *n* 3 stooping posture.

stop **⊕** *v* **stopping, stopped** 1 bring, come to halt. 2 prevent. 3 desist from. 4 fill up an opening. 5 cease. 6 stay. ◆ *n* 7 place where something stops. 8 stopping or

becoming stopped. 9 punctuation mark, esp. full stop. 10 set of pipes in organ having tones of a distinct quality. **stoppage** *n* **stopper** *n* plug for closing bottle etc.

stopcock *n* valve to control flow of fluid in pipe. **stopwatch** *n* watch which can be stopped for exact timing of race.

store **⊕** *v* 1 stock, keep. ◆ *n* 2 shop. 3 abundance. 4 stock. 5 place for keeping goods. 6 warehouse. ◆ *pl* 7 stocks of goods, provisions. **storage** *n*

storey *n* horizontal division of a building.

stork *n* large wading bird.

storm **⊕** *n* 1 violent weather with wind, rain etc. 2 assault on fortress. 3 violent outbreak. ◆ *v* 4 assault. 5 take by storm. 6 rage. **stormy** *adj* like storm.

story **⊕** *n, pl* **–ries** 1 account, tale. 2 newspaper report.

conventional, customary
stomach *n* = **belly**, gut (*Inf*), abdomen, tummy (*Inf*), puku (*NZ*); = **tummy**, pot ◆ *v* = **bear**, take, tolerate, endure, swallow
stoop *v* = **bend**, lean, bow, duck, crouch ◆ *n* = **slouch**, bad posture, round–shoulderedness, sink to, descend to
stop *v* = **quit**, cease, refrain, put an end to, discontinue ≠ **start**; = **prevent**, cut short, arrest, restrain, hold back ≠ **facilitate**; = **end**, conclude, finish, terminate ≠ **continue**; = **cease**, shut down, discontinue, desist ≠ **continue** ◆ *n*

= **halt**, standstill; = **station**, stage, depot, terminus
store *n* = **shop**, outlet, market, mart; = **supply**, stock, reserve, fund, quantity; = **repository**, warehouse, depository, storeroom ◆ *v often with* **away** *or* **up** = **put by**, save, hoard, keep, reserve
storm *n* = **tempest**, hurricane, gale, blizzard, squall; = **outburst**, row, outcry, furore, outbreak ◆ *v* = **rush**, stamp, flounce, fly; = **rage**, rant, thunder, rave, bluster; = **attack**, charge, rush, assault, assail
story *n* = **tale**, romance, narrative,

stout ❶ *adj* **1** fat. **2** sturdy, resolute. ♦ *n* **3** strong dark beer.

stove *n* apparatus for cooking, heating etc.

stow *v* pack away. **stowaway** *n* person who hides in ship to obtain free passage.

straddle *v* **1** bestride. **2** spread legs wide.

straggle *v* stray, get dispersed, linger. **straggler** *n*

straight ❶ *adj* **1** without bend. **2** honest. **3** level. **4** in order. **5** in continuous succession. **6** (of spirits) undiluted. **7** (of face) expressionless. ♦ *n* **8** straight state or part. ♦ *adv* **9** direct. **straighten** *v* **straightaway** *adv* immediately. **straightforward** *adj* **1** open, frank. **2** simple.

strain¹ ❶ *v* **1** stretch tightly. **2** stretch to excess. **3** filter. **4** make

great effort. ♦ *n* **5** stretching force. **6** violent effort. **7** injury from being strained. **8** great demand. **9** (condition caused by) overwork, worry etc. **strained** *adj* **strainer** *n* filter, sieve.

strain² *n* **1** breed or race. **2** trace.

strait ❶ *n* **1** channel of water connecting two larger areas of water. ♦ *pl* **2** position of difficulty or distress. **straitjacket** *n* jacket to confine arms of violent person. **strait-laced** *adj* prudish.

strand¹ *v* **1** run aground. **2** leave, be left in difficulties.

strand² ❶ *n* single thread of string, wire etc.

strange ❶ *adj* **1** odd. **2** unaccustomed. **3** foreign. **strangeness** *n* **stranger** *n* **1** unknown person. **2** foreigner. **3** one unaccustomed (to).

history, legend; **= anecdote**, account, tale, report

stout *adj* **= fat**, big, heavy, overweight, plump **≠ slim**; **= strong**, strapping, muscular, robust, sturdy **≠ puny**; **= brave**, bold, courageous, fearless, resolute **≠ timid**

straight *adj* **= level**, even, right, square, true **≠ crooked**; **= frank**, plain, straightforward, blunt, outright **≠ evasive**; **= successive**, consecutive, continuous, running, solid **≠ discontinuous**; **=** (*Sl*) **conventional**, conservative, bourgeois **≠ fashionable**; **= honest**, just, fair, reliable, respectable **≠ dishonest**;

= undiluted, pure, neat, unadulterated, unmixed; **= in order**, organized, arranged, neat, tidy **≠ untidy** ♦ *adv* **= directly**, precisely, exactly, unswervingly, by the shortest route

strain¹ *n* **= pressure**, stress, demands, burden; **= stress**, anxiety; **= worry**, effort, struggle **≠ ease**; **= burden**, tension; **= injury**, wrench, sprain, pull ♦ *v* **= stretch**, tax, overtax; **= strive**, struggle, endeavour, labour, go for it (*Inf*) **≠ relax**; **= sieve**, filter, sift, purify

strait *n often plural* **= channel**, sound, narrows

strand² *n* **= filament**, fibre, thread,

strangle v 1 kill by squeezing windpipe. 2 suppress.
strangulation n strangling.
stranglehold n
strap n 1 strip, esp. of leather. ◆ v 2 fasten, beat with strap.
strapping adj tall and well-made.
strategy n, pl **-gies** 1 overall plan. 2 art of war. **stratagem** n plan, trick. **strategic** adj **strategist** n
stratosphere n layer of atmosphere high above the earth.
stratum n, pl **strata** 1 layer, esp. of rock. 2 class in society.
stratification n **stratify** v form, deposit in layers.
straw n 1 stalks of grain. 2 long, narrow tube used to suck up liquid. **strawberry** n 1 creeping plant producing red, juicy fruit. 2 the fruit.
stray v 1 wander. 2 digress. 3 get lost. ◆ adj 4 strayed. 5

occasional. 6 scattered. ◆ n 7 stray animal.
streak n 1 long line or band. 2 element. ◆ v 3 mark with streaks. 4 move fast. 5 run naked in public. **streaker** n **streaky** adj
stream n 1 flowing body of water or other liquid. 2 steady flow. ◆ v 3 flow. 4 run with liquid. **streamer** n (paper) ribbon, narrow flag.
street n road in town or village, usu. lined with houses. **streetwise** adj adept at surviving in dangerous environment.
streetcar n US and Canad public transport vehicle powered by an overhead wire and running on rails laid in the road.
strength n 1 quality of being strong. 2 power. **strengthen** v **strenuous** adj 1 energetic. 2 earnest.
stress n 1 emphasis. 2 tension.

———————— THESAURUS ————————

string
strange adj = **odd**, curious, weird, wonderful, extraordinary ≠ **ordinary**; = **unfamiliar**, new, unknown, foreign, novel ≠ **familiar**
strangle v = **throttle**, choke, asphyxiate, strangulate; = **suppress**, inhibit, subdue, stifle, repress
strap n = **tie**, thong, belt ◆ v = **fasten**, tie, secure, bind, lash
strategy n = **policy**, procedure, approach, scheme
stray v = **wander**, go astray, drift; = **drift**, wander, roam, meander, rove ◆ adj = **lost**, abandoned,

homeless, roaming, vagrant; = **random**, chance, accidental
streak n = **band**, line, strip, stroke, layer; = **trace**, touch, element, strain, dash ◆ v = **speed**, fly, tear, flash, sprint
stream n = **river**, brook, burn (Scot), beck, tributary; = **flow**, current, rush, run, course ◆ v = **flow**, run, pour, issue, flood
street n = **road**, lane, avenue, terrace, row
strength n = **might**, muscle, brawn ≠ **weakness**; = **will**, resolution, courage, character, nerve; = **health**, fitness, vigour

S

♦ v 3 emphasize.

stretch ⓣ v 1 extend. 2 exert to utmost. 3 tighten, pull out. 4 reach. 5 have elasticity. ♦ n 6 stretching, being stretched. 7 expanse. 8 spell. **stretcher** n 1 person, thing that stretches. 2 appliance on which disabled person is carried.

strew v strewing, strewed, strewed scatter over surface, spread.

stricken adj seriously affected by disease, grief etc.

strict adj 1 stern, not lax or indulgent. 2 precisely defined. **stricture** n critical remark.

stride v striding, strode, stridden 1 walk with long steps. ♦ n 2 single step. 3 length of step.

strident adj harsh, loud. **stridently** adv **stridency** n

strife ⓣ n 1 conflict. 2 quarrelling.

strike ⓣ v striking, struck 1 hit (against). 2 ignite. 3 attack. 4 sound (time), as bell in clock etc. 5 affect. 6 enter mind of. 7 cease work as protest or to make demands. ♦ v 8 act of striking. **striker** n striking adj noteworthy, impressive.

string ⓣ n 1 (length of) thin cord or other material. 2 series. 3 fibre in plants. ♦ pl 4 conditions. ♦ v 5 provide with, thread on string. 6 form in line, series. **stringed** adj (of musical instruments) furnished with strings. **stringy** adj 1 like string. 2 fibrous.

stringent ⓣ adj strict, binding. **stringency** n

strip ⓣ v stripping, stripped 1 lay bare, take covering off. 2 undress. ♦ n 3 long, narrow piece. **stripper** n **striptease** n cabaret or theatre in which person undresses.

stripe n narrow mark, band. **striped, stripy** adj marked with stripes.

strive ⓣ v striving, strove, striven try hard, struggle.

stroke ⓣ n 1 blow. 2 sudden

stress v = **emphasize**, underline, dwell on ♦ n = **emphasis**, significance, force, weight; = **strain**, pressure, worry, tension, burden; = **accent**, beat, emphasis, accentuation

stretch v = **extend**, cover, spread, reach, put forth; = **last**, continue, go on, carry on, reach; = **pull**, distend, strain, tighten, draw out ♦ n = **expanse**, area, tract, spread, distance; = **period**, time, spell, stint, term

strife n = **conflict**, battle, clash, quarrel, friction

strike v = **walk out**, down tools, revolt, mutiny; = **hit**, smack, thump, beat, knock; = **drive**, hit, smack, wallop (Inf); = **collide with**, hit, run into, bump into; = **knock**, smack, thump, beat

string n = **cord**, twine, fibre; = **series**, line, row, file, sequence

stringent adj = **strict**, tough, rigorous, tight, severe ≠ **lax**

strip v = **undress**, disrobe, unclothe; = **plunder**, rob, loot, empty, sack

action, occurrence. **3** apoplexy. **4** chime of clock. **5** mark made by pen, brush etc. **6** style, method of swimming. **7** act of stroking. ◆ *v* **8** pass hand lightly over.

stroll 🛈 *v* **1** walk in leisurely or idle manner. ◆ *n* **2** leisurely walk.

stroller *n* US and Canad chair-shaped carriage for a baby.

strong 🛈 *adj* **1** powerful, robust, healthy. **2** difficult to break. **3** noticeable. **4** intense. **5** emphatic. **6** not diluted. **7** having a certain number. **strongly** *adv* **stronghold** *n* fortress. **strongroom** *n* room for keeping valuables.

stroppy *adj* **–pier, –piest** *Sl* angry or awkward.

structure 🛈 *n* **1** (arrangement of parts in) construction, building etc. **2** form. ◆ *v* **3** give structure to. **structural** *adj*

struggle 🛈 *v* **1** contend. **2** fight. **3** proceed, work, move with difficulty and effort. ◆ *n* **4** struggling.

strum *v* **strumming, strummed** strike notes of guitar etc.

strut 🛈 *v* **strutting, strutted 1** walk affectedly or pompously. ◆ *n* **2** rigid support. **3** strutting walk.

strychnine *n* poisonous drug.

stub *n* **1** remnant of anything, e.g. pencil. **2** counterfoil. ◆ *v* **3** strike (toes) against fixed object. **4** extinguish by pressing against surface. **stubby** *adj* short, broad.

stubble *n* **1** stumps of cut grain after reaping. **2** short growth of beard.

stubborn 🛈 *adj* unyielding, obstinate.

stucco *n* plaster.

stud¹ *n* **1** nail with large head. **2** removable double-headed button. ◆ *v* **3** set with studs.

——————— THESAURUS ———————

strive *v* = **try**, labour, struggle, attempt, toil

stroke *v* = **caress**, rub, fondle, pet ◆ *n* = **apoplexy**, fit, seizure, attack, collapse; = **blow**, hit, knock, pat, rap

stroll *v* = **walk**, ramble, amble, promenade, saunter ◆ *n* = **walk**, promenade, constitutional, ramble, breath of air

strong *adj* = **powerful**, muscular, tough, athletic, strapping, skookum (*US & Canad*) ≠ **weak**; = **fit**, robust, lusty; = **durable**, substantial, sturdy, heavy-duty, well-built ≠ **flimsy**; = **extreme**, radical, drastic, strict, harsh;

= **decisive**, firm, forceful, decided, determined

structure *n* = **arrangement**, form, make-up, design, organization; = **building**, construction, erection, edifice ◆ *v* = **arrange**, organize, design, shape, build up

struggle *v* = **strive**, labour, toil, work, strain; = **fight**, battle, wrestle, grapple, compete ◆ *n* = **effort**, labour, toil, work, pains; = **fight**, battle, conflict, clash, contest

strut *v* = **swagger**, parade, peacock, prance

stubborn *adj* = **obstinate**, dogged, inflexible, persistent,

stud² *n* set of horses kept for breeding.

studio ❶ *n, pl* **-dios 1** workroom of artist, photographer etc. **2** building, room where film, television or radio shows are made, broadcast.

study ❶ *v* **studying, studied 1** be engaged in learning. **2** make study of. **3** scrutinize. ♦ *n* **4** effort to acquire knowledge. **5** subject of this. **6** room to study in. **7** book, report etc. produced as result of study. **8** sketch. **student** *n* one who studies. **studied** *adj* carefully designed, premeditated. **studious** *adj* **1** fond of study. **2** painstaking. **3** deliberate.

stuff ❶ *v* **1** pack, cram, fill (completely). **2** eat large amount. **3** fill with seasoned mixture. **4** fill (animal's skin) with material to preserve lifelike form. ♦ *n* **5** material. **6** any substance. **7**

belongings. **stuffing** *n* material for stuffing. **stuffy** *adj* **1** lacking fresh air. **2** *Inf* dull, conventional.

stumble ❶ *v* **1** trip and nearly fall. **2** falter. ♦ *n* **3** stumbling.

stump ❶ *n* **1** remnant of tree, tooth etc., when main part has been cut away. **2** one of uprights of wicket in cricket. ♦ *v* **3** confuse, puzzle. **4** walk heavily, noisily. **stumpy** *adj* short and thickset.

stun ❶ *v* **stunning, stunned 1** knock senseless. **2** amaze. **stunning** *adj*

stunt¹ ❶ *n* feat of dexterity or daring.

stunt² *v* stop growth of.

stupefy *v* **-fying, -fied 1** make insensitive, lethargic. **2** astound. **stupefaction** *n*

stupendous *adj* **1** astonishing. **2** amazing. **3** huge.

stupid ❶ *adj* **1** slow-witted. **2** silly. **stupidity** *n*

———— THESAURUS ————

intractable ≠ **compliant**

studio *n* = **workshop**, workroom, atelier

study *v* = **learn**, cram (*Inf*), swot (up) (*Brit inf*), read up, mug up (*Brit sl*); = **examine**, survey, look at, scrutinize; = **contemplate**, read, examine, consider, go into ♦ *n* = **examination**, investigation, analysis, consideration, inspection; = **piece of research**, survey, report, paper, review

stuff *n* = **things**, gear, possessions, effects, equipment; = **substance**, material, essence, matter ♦ *v* = **shove**, force, push, squeeze, jam

stumble *v* = **trip**, fall, slip, reel, stagger; = **totter**, reel, lurch, wobble

stump *v* = **baffle**, confuse, puzzle, bewilder, perplex

stun *v* = **overcome**, shock, confuse, astonish, stagger; = **daze**, knock out, stupefy, numb, benumb

stunt¹ *n* = **feat**, act, trick, exploit, deed

stupid *adj* = **unintelligent**, thick, simple, slow, dim ≠ **intelligent**; = **silly**, foolish, daft (*Inf*), rash, pointless ≠ **sensible**; = **senseless**, dazed, groggy, insensate,

stupor *n* dazed state.

sturdy 🔒 *adj* **–dier, –diest 1** robust, strongly built. **2** vigorous.

sturgeon *n* fish yielding caviare.

stutter *v* **1** speak with difficulty. **2** stammer. ♦ *n* **3** tendency to stutter.

sty *n, pl* **sties** place to keep pigs in.

stye *n, pl* **styes** inflammation on eyelid.

style 🔒 *n* **1** design. **2** manner of writing, doing etc. **3** fashion. **4** elegance. ♦ *v* **5** design. **stylish** *adj* fashionable. **stylist** *n* one cultivating style. **2** designer.

stylus *n* (in record player) tiny point running in groove of record.

suave *adj* smoothly polite.

sub *n* short for SUBMARINE, SUBSCRIPTION, SUBSTITUTE.

subconscious *adj* **1** acting, existing without one's awareness. ♦ *n* **2** *Psychology* part of human mind unknown, or only partly known, to possessor.

subdivide *v* divide again.

subdivision *n*

subdue 🔒 *v* **–duing, –dued** overcome. **subdued** *adj* **1** cowed, quiet. **2** not bright.

subject 🔒 *n* **1** person or thing being dealt with or studied. **2** person under rule of government or monarch. ♦ *adj* **3** owing allegiance. **4** dependent. **5** liable (to). ♦ *v* **6** cause to undergo. **7** subdue. **subjection** *n* act of bringing, or state of being, under control. **subjective** *adj* **1** based on personal feelings, not impartial. **2** existing in the mind. **subjectivity** *n*

subjugate *v* **1** force to submit. **2** conquer. **subjugation** *n*

sublet *v* **–letting, –let** rent out property rented from someone else.

sublime 🔒 *adj* **1** elevated. **2** inspiring awe. **3** exalted.

subliminal *adj* relating to mental processes of which the individual is not aware.

submarine *n* **1** craft which can travel below surface of sea and

————— THESAURUS —————

semiconscious

sturdy *adj* = **robust**, hardy, powerful, athletic, muscular ≠ **puny**; = **substantial**, solid, durable, well-made, well-built ≠ **flimsy**

style *n* = **manner**, way, method, approach, technique; = **elegance**, taste, chic, flair, polish; = **design**, form, cut; = **type**, sort, kind, variety, category ♦ *v* = **design**, cut, tailor, fashion, shape; = **call**, name, term, label, entitle

subdue *v* = **overcome**, defeat, master, break, control; = **moderate**, suppress, soften, mellow, tone down ≠ **arouse**

subject *n* = **topic**, question, issue, matter, point; = **citizen**, resident, native, inhabitant, national ♦ *adj* = **subordinate**, dependent, satellite, inferior, obedient ♦ *v* = **put through**, expose, submit, lay open

sublime *adj* = **noble**, glorious, high, great, grand ≠ **lowly**

S

remain submerged for long periods. ◆ adj 2 below surface of sea.

submerge ❶ v place, go under water. **submersion** n

subordinate ❶ n/adj 1 (one) of lower rank or less importance. ◆ v 2 make, treat as subordinate. **subordination** n

subscribe ❶ v 1 pay, promise to pay (contribution). 2 give support, approval. **subscription** n money paid.

subsequent ❶ adj later, following or coming after in time.

subservient adj submissive, servile.

subside ❶ v 1 abate. 2 sink. **subsidence** n

subsidiary ❶ adj/n secondary (person or thing).

subsidize v 1 help financially. 2 pay grant to. **subsidy** n, pl –dies money granted.

subsist v exist, sustain life.

subsistence n the means by which one supports life.

substance ❶ n 1 (particular kind of) matter. 2 essence. 3 wealth.

substantial adj 1 considerable. 2 of real value. 3 really existing.

substantiate v bring evidence for, prove.

substitute ❶ v 1 put, serve in place of. ◆ n 2 thing, person put in place of another. ◆ adj 3 serving as a substitute. **substitution** n

subsume v incorporate in larger group.

subterfuge n trick, lying excuse used to evade something.

subterranean adj underground.

subtitle n 1 secondary title of book. ◆ pl 2 translation superimposed on foreign film. ◆ v 3 provide with subtitle or subtitles.

subtle ❶ adj 1 not immediately obvious. 2 ingenious. 3 crafty. 4 making fine distinctions. **subtlety** n **subtly** adv

——— THESAURUS ———

submerge v = **flood**, swamp, engulf, overflow, inundate

subordinate n = **inferior**, junior, assistant, aide, second ≠ superior ◆ adj = **inferior**, lesser, lower, junior, subject ≠ superior

subscribe v = **support**, advocate, endorse; = **contribute**, give, donate

subsequent adj = **following**, later, succeeding, after, successive ≠ previous

subside v = **decrease**, diminish, lessen, ease, wane ≠ increase; = **collapse**, sink, cave in, drop, lower

subsidiary adj = **secondary**, lesser, subordinate, minor, supplementary ≠ main

substance n = **material**, body, stuff, fabric; = **importance**, significance, concreteness; = **meaning**, main point, gist, import, significance; = **wealth**, means, property, assets, resources

substitute v = **replace**, exchange, swap, change, switch ◆ n = **replacement**, reserve, surrogate, deputy, sub

subtle adj = **faint**, slight, implied,

subtract v take away, deduct.
subtraction n
suburb n residential area on outskirts of city. **suburban** adj **suburbia** n suburbs and their inhabitants.
subvert v 1 overthrow. 2 corrupt. **subversion** n **subversive** adj
subway n 1 underground passage. 2 US and Canad underground railway.
succeed ⊙ v 1 accomplish purpose. 2 turn out satisfactorily. 3 follow. 4 take place of. **success** n 1 favourable accomplishment, attainment, issue or outcome. 2 successful person or thing. **successful** adj **succession** n 1 following. 2 series. 3 succeeding. **successive** adj 1 following in order. 2 consecutive. **successor** n
succinct adj brief and clear.
succour v/n help in distress.
succulent adj 1 juicy. 2 (of plant) having thick, fleshy leaves. ♦ n 3 such plant. **succulence** n
succumb ⊙ v give way.
such adj 1 of the kind or degree

mentioned. 2 so great, so much.
suck v 1 draw into mouth. 2 hold in mouth. 3 draw in. ♦ n 4 sucking. **sucker** n 1 person, thing that sucks. 2 shoot coming from root or base of stem of plant. 3 Inf one who is easily deceived.
suckle v feed from the breast.
suckling n unweaned infant.
suction n 1 drawing or sucking of air or fluid. 2 force produced by difference in pressure.
sudden ⊙ adj 1 done, occurring unexpectedly. 2 abrupt. **suddenly** adv
suds pl n froth of soap and water.
sue ⊙ v suing, sued 1 prosecute. 2 seek justice from. 3 make application or entreaty.
suede n leather with soft, velvety finish.
suet n hard animal fat.
suffer ⊙ v 1 undergo. 2 tolerate.
suffering n
suffice ⊙ v be adequate, satisfactory (for). **sufficiency** n adequate amount. **sufficient** adj enough, adequate.

——————— THESAURUS ———————

delicate, understated ≠ **obvious**;
= **crafty**, cunning, sly, shrewd, ingenious ≠ **straightforward**;
= **muted**, soft, subdued, low–key, toned down
succeed v = **triumph**, win, prevail;
= **work out**, work, be successful;
= **make it** (Inf), do well, be successful, triumph, thrive ≠ **fail**
succumb v often with **to**
= **surrender**, yield, submit, give in, cave in (Inf) ≠ **beat**; with **to**

= **catch**, fall ill with
sudden adj = **quick**, rapid, unexpected, swift, hurried ≠ **gradual**
sue v = (Law) **take (someone) to court**, prosecute, charge, summon, indict
suffer v = **be in pain**, hurt, ache;
= **be affected**, have trouble with, be afflicted, be troubled with
suffice v = **be enough**, do, be sufficient, be adequate, serve

suffix n group of letters added to end of word.

suffocate v 1 kill, be killed by deprivation of oxygen. 2 smother. **suffocation** n

suffrage n vote or right of voting.

suffuse v well up and spread over.

sugar n 1 sweet crystalline substance. ◆ v 2 sweeten, make pleasant (with sugar). **sugary** adj

suggest ⓣ v 1 propose. 2 call up the idea of. **suggestible** adj easily influenced. **suggestion** n 1 hint. 2 proposal. 3 insinuation of impression, belief etc. into mind. **suggestive** adj containing suggestions, esp. of something indecent.

suicide n 1 act of killing oneself. 2 one who does this. **suicidal** adj

suit ⓣ n 1 set of clothing. 2 garment worn for particular event, purpose. 3 one of four sets in pack of cards. 4 action at law. ◆ v 5 make, be fit or appropriate for. 6 be acceptable to (someone). **suitability** n **suitable** adj fitting, convenient. **suitcase** n flat rectangular travelling case. **suite** ⓣ n 1 matched set of furniture. 2 set of rooms. 3 retinue.

suitor n 1 wooer. 2 one who sues.

sulk v 1 be silent, resentful. ◆ n 2 this mood. **sulky** adj

sullen adj unwilling to talk or be sociable, morose.

sully v –lying, –lied stain, tarnish.

sulphur n pale yellow nonmetallic element. **sulphuric** adj **sulphurous** adj

sultan n ruler of Muslim country.

sultry adj –trier, –triest 1 (of weather) hot, humid. 2 (of person) looking sensual.

sum ⓣ n 1 amount, total. 2 problem in arithmetic. ◆ v 3 add up. 4 make summary of main parts.

summary ⓣ n, pl –ries 1 brief statement of chief points of something. ◆ adj 2 done quickly. **summarily** adv 1 speedily. 2 abruptly. **summarize** v make summary of.

summer n second, warmest season.

summit ⓣ n top, peak.

summon ⓣ v 1 demand attendance of. 2 bid witness appear in court. 3 gather up (energies etc.). **summons** n 1 call. 2 authoritative demand.

sumo n Japanese style of

———— THESAURUS ————

suggest v = **recommend**, propose, advise, advocate, prescribe; = **hint at**, imply, intimate

suit n = **outfit**, costume, ensemble, dress, clothing; = **lawsuit**, case, trial, proceeding, cause ◆ v = **be acceptable to**, please, satisfy, do, gratify; = **agree with**, become, match, go with, harmonize with

suite n = **rooms**, apartment

sum n = **amount**, quantity, volume

summary n = **synopsis**, résumé, précis, review, outline

summit n = **peak**, top, tip,

wrestling.

sumptuous ⊙ *adj* lavish, magnificent. **sumptuousness** *n*

sun *n* **1** luminous body round which earth and other planets revolve. **2** its rays. ♦ *v* **3** expose to sun's rays. **sunless** *adj* **sunny** *adj* **1** like the sun. **2** warm. **3** cheerful. **sunbathe** *v* lie in sunshine. **sunbeam** *n* ray of sun. **sunburn** *n* inflammation of skin due to excessive exposure to sun. **sundown** *n* sunset. **sunflower** *n* plant with large golden flowers. **sunrise** *n* appearance of sun above the horizon. **sunset** *n* disappearance of sun below the horizon. **sunshine** *n* light and warmth from sun. **sunstroke** *n* illness caused by prolonged exposure to hot sun.

sundae *n* ice cream topped with fruit etc.

Sunday *n* first day of the week. **Sunday school** school for religious instruction of children.

sundry *adj* several, various. **sundries** *pl n* odd items, not mentioned in detail.

sup *v* **supping, supped 1** take by sips. **2** take supper. ♦ *n* **3** mouthful of liquid.

super *adj Inf* very good.

super– *comb. form* above, greater, exceedingly, as in *superhuman, supertanker.*

superannuation *n* **1** pension given on retirement. **2** contribution by employee to pension.

superb ⊙ *adj* extremely good or impressive.

supercilious *adj* displaying arrogant pride, scorn.

superficial ⊙ *adj* **1** of or on surface. **2** not careful or thorough. **3** without depth, shallow.

superfluous *adj* extra, unnecessary. **superfluity** *n*

superhuman *adj* beyond normal human ability or experience.

superimpose *v* place on or over something else.

superintend *v* **1** have charge of. **2** overlook. **3** supervise.

superintendent *n* senior police officer.

superior ⊙ *adj* **1** greater in quality or quantity. **2** upper, higher in position, rank or quality. **3** showing consciousness of being so. ♦ *n* **4** supervisor, manager. **superiority** *n*

superlative *adj* **1** of, in highest

———— THESAURUS ————

pinnacle, apex ≠ **base**
summon *v* = **send for**, call, bid, invite; *often with* **up** = **gather**, muster, draw on
sumptuous *adj* = **luxurious**, grand, superb, splendid, gorgeous ≠ **plain**
superb *adj* = **splendid**, excellent,

magnificent, fine, grand ≠ **inferior**
superficial *adj* = **shallow**, frivolous, empty–headed, silly, trivial ≠ **serious**; = **hasty**, cursory, perfunctory, hurried, casual ≠ **thorough**; = **slight**, surface, external, on the surface, exterior ≠ **profound**

degree or quality. **2** surpassing **3** *Grammar* denoting form of adjective, adverb meaning *most*.

supermarket *n* large self–service store.

supernatural ⊕ *adj* **1** being beyond the powers or laws of nature. **2** miraculous.

supernumerary *adj* exceeding the required or regular number.

superpower *n* extremely powerful nation.

supersede *v* take the place of.

supersonic *adj* denoting speed greater than that of sound.

superstition *n* religion, opinion or magic. **superstitious** *adj*

superstructure *n* **1** structure above foundations. **2** part of ship above deck.

supervise ⊕ *v* **1** oversee. **2** direct. **3** inspect and control. **supervision** *n* **supervisor** *n* **supervisory** *adj*

supine *adj* lying on back with face upwards.

supper *n* (light) evening meal.

supplant *v* take the place of.

supple *adj* **1** pliable. **2** flexible.

supply *adv*

supplement ⊕ *n* **1** thing added to fill up, supply deficiency, esp. extra part added to book etc. ♦ *v* **2** add to. **3** supply deficiency. **supplementary** *adj*

supply ⊕ *v* **–plying, –plied 1** furnish. **2** make available. **3** provide. ♦ *n* **4** stock, store. **5** food, materials needed for journey etc.

support ⊕ *v* **1** hold up. **2** sustain. **3** assist. ♦ *n* **4** supporting, being supported. **5** means of support. **supporter** *n* adherent. **supporting** *adj* (of role in film etc.) less important. **supportive** *adj*

suppose ⊕ *v* **1** assume as theory. **2** take for granted. **3** accept as likely. **supposed** *adj* **1** assumed. **2**

——— THESAURUS ———

superior *adj* = **better**, higher, greater, grander, surpassing ≠ **inferior**; = **first–class**, excellent, first–rate, choice, exclusive ≠ **average**; = **supercilious**, patronizing, condescending, haughty, disdainful ♦ *n* = **boss**, senior, director, manager, chief (*Inf*) ≠ **subordinate**

supernatural *adj* = **paranormal**, unearthly, uncanny, ghostly, psychic

supervise *v* = **observe**, guide, monitor, oversee, keep an eye on

supplement *v* = **add to**, reinforce, augment, extend ♦ *n* = **pull–out**,

insert; = **appendix**, add–on, postscript; = **addition**, extra

supply *v* = **provide**, give, furnish, produce, stock ♦ *n* = **store**, fund, stock, source, reserve

support *v* = **help**, back, champion, second, aid ≠ **oppose**; = **provide for**, maintain, look after, keep, fund ≠ **live off**; = **bear out**, confirm, verify, substantiate, corroborate ≠ **refute**; = **bear**, carry, sustain, prop (up), reinforce ♦ *n* = **furtherance**, backing, promotion, assistance, encouragement; = **help**, loyalty ≠ **opposition**

expected, obliged. **3** permitted.
supposedly adv **supposition** n **1** assumption. **2** belief without proof. **3** conjecture.
suppress ⊕ v **1** put down, restrain. **2** keep or withdraw from publication. **suppression** n
suppurate v fester, form pus.
supreme adj **1** highest in authority or rank. **2** utmost.
supremacy n position of being supreme. **supremo** n person in overall authority.
surcharge v/n (make) additional charge.
sure ⊕ adj **1** certain. **2** trustworthy. **3** without doubt. ◆ adv **4** Inf certainly. **surely** adv
surety n person, thing acting as guarantee for another's obligations.
surf n **1** waves breaking on shore. ◆ v **2** ride surf. **surfer** n **surfing** n sport of riding over surf. **surfboard** n board used in surfing.
surface ⊕ n **1** outside face of

object. **2** plane. **3** top. **4** superficial appearance. ◆ adj **5** involving the surface only. ◆ v **6** come to surface.
surfeit n **1** excess. **2** disgust caused by excess. ◆ v **3** feed to excess.
surge ⊕ n **1** wave. **2** sudden increase. ◆ v **3** move in large waves. **4** swell.
surgeon n medical expert who performs operations. **surgery** n **1** medical treatment by operation. **2** doctor's, dentist's consulting room. **surgical** adj
surly adj **–lier, –liest** cross and rude.
surmise v/n guess, conjecture.
surmount v get over, overcome.
surname n family name.
surpass ⊕ v **1** go beyond. **2** excel. **3** outstrip. **surpassing** adj excellent.
surplus ⊕ n **1** what remains over in excess. ◆ adj **2** spare, superfluous.

——————— THESAURUS ———————

suppose v = **imagine**, consider, conjecture, postulate, hypothesize; = **think**, imagine, expect, assume, guess (informal, chiefly US & Canad) presume, infer
suppress v = **stamp out**, stop, check, crush, conquer ≠ **encourage**; = **check**, inhibit, subdue, stop, quell
sure adj = **certain**, positive, decided, convinced, confident ≠ **uncertain**; = **inevitable**, guaranteed, bound, assured, inescapable ≠ **unsure**; = **reliable**,

accurate, dependable, undoubted, undeniable ≠ **unreliable**
surface n = **covering**, face, exterior, side, top ◆ v = **emerge**, come up, come to the surface
surge n = **rush**, flood; = **flow**, wave, rush, roller, gush ◆ v = **rush**, pour, rise, gush; = **roll**, rush, heave
surpass v = **outdo**, beat, exceed, eclipse, excel
surplus n = **excess**, surfeit ≠ **shortage** ◆ adj = **extra**, spare, excess, remaining, odd ≠ **insufficient**

surprise ⊕ n 1 something unexpected. 2 emotion aroused by being taken unawares. ♦ v 3 cause surprise to. 4 astonish. 5 take, come upon unexpectedly.
surrealism n incongruous combination of images. **surreal** adj
surrender ⊕ v 1 hand over, give up. 2 yield. 3 cease resistance. ♦ n 4 act of surrendering.
surreptitious adj 1 done secretly or stealthily. 2 furtive.
surrogate n substitute. **surrogate mother** woman who bears child on behalf of childless couple.
surround ⊕ v 1 be, come all round, encompass. 2 encircle. ♦ n 3 border, edging. **surroundings** pl n conditions, scenery etc. around a person, place, environment.
surveillance ⊕ n close watch, supervision.
survey ⊕ v 1 view, scrutinize. 2 inspect, examine. 3 measure, map (land). ♦ n 4 act of surveying. 5 inspection. 6 report incorporating results of survey. **surveyor** n
survive ⊕ v 1 continue to live or exist. 2 outlive. **survival** n continuation of existence. **survivor** n one who survives.
susceptible ⊕ adj 1 yielding readily (to). 2 capable (of). 3 impressionable. **susceptibility** n
suspect ⊕ v 1 doubt innocence of. 2 have impression of existence or presence of. 3 be inclined to believe that. ♦ adj 4 of suspicious character. ♦ n 5 suspected person.
suspend ⊕ v 1 hang up. 2 cause to cease for a time. 3 keep inoperative. 4 sustain in fluid.

——————— THESAURUS ———————

surprise n = **shock**, revelation, jolt, bombshell, eye–opener (Inf); = **amazement**, astonishment, wonder, incredulity ♦ v = **amaze**, astonish, stun, startle, stagger; = **catch unawares** or **off–guard**, spring upon
surrender v = **give in**, yield, submit, give way, succumb ≠ **resist**; = **give up**, abandon, relinquish, yield, concede ♦ n = **submission**, cave–in (Inf), capitulation, resignation, renunciation
surround v = **enclose**, ring, encircle, encompass, envelop
surveillance n = **observation**, watch, scrutiny, supervision, inspection
survey n = **poll**, study, research, review, inquiry; = **examination**, inspection, scrutiny ♦ v = **interview**, question, poll, research, investigate; = **look over**, view, examine, observe, contemplate; = **measure**, estimate, assess, appraise
survive v = **remain alive**, last, live on, endure
susceptible adj = **responsive**, sensitive, receptive, impressionable, suggestible ≠ **unresponsive**
suspect v = **believe**, feel, guess, consider, suppose ≠ **know**; = **distrust**, doubt, mistrust ≠ **trust** ♦ adj = **dubious**, doubtful, questionable, iffy (Inf) ≠ **innocent**

suspenders pl n straps for supporting stockings.
suspense n 1 state of uncertainty, esp. while awaiting news, an event etc. 2 anxiety, worry. **suspension** n 1 state of being suspended. 2 springs on axle of body of vehicle.
suspicion ⊙ n 1 suspecting, being suspected. 2 slight trace.
suspicious adj
sustain ⊙ v 1 keep, hold up. 2 endure. 3 keep alive. 4 confirm.
sustenance n food.
svelte adj gracefully slim.
swab n 1 mop. 2 pad of surgical wool etc. for cleaning. 3 taking specimen etc. ◆ v 4 clean with swab.
swag n Sl stolen property.
swagger v 1 strut. 2 boast. ◆ n 3 strutting gait. 4 boastful manner.
swallow¹ ⊙ v 1 cause, allow to pass down gullet. 2 suppress. ◆ n 3 act of swallowing.
swallow² n migratory bird with

forked tail.
swamp ⊙ n 1 bog. ◆ v 2 entangle in swamp. 3 overwhelm. 4 flood.
swan n large, web-footed water bird with curved neck.
swap ⊙ v swapping, swapped 1 exchange. 2 barter. ◆ n 3 exchange.
swarm ⊙ n 1 large cluster of insects. 2 vast crowd. ◆ v 3 (of bees) be on the move in swarm. 4 gather in large numbers.
swarthy adj -thier, -thiest dark-complexioned.
swastika n symbol of cross with arms bent at right angles.
swat v swatting, swatted 1 hit smartly. 2 kill, esp. insects.
swathe ⊙ v cover with wraps or bandages.
sway ⊙ v 1 swing unsteadily. 2 (cause to) vacillate in opinion etc. ◆ n 3 control. 4 power. 5 swaying motion.
swear ⊙ v swearing, swore,

————— THESAURUS —————

suspend v = **postpone**, put off, cease, interrupt, shelve ≠ **continue**; = **hang**, attach, dangle
suspicion n = **distrust**, scepticism, mistrust, doubt, misgiving; = **idea**, notion, hunch, guess, impression; = **trace**, touch, hint, suggestion, shade
sustain v = **maintain**, continue, keep up, prolong, protract; = **suffer**, experience, undergo, feel, bear; = **help**, aid, assist; = **keep alive**, nourish, provide for
swallow¹ v = **eat**, consume, devour, swig (Inf)

swamp n = **bog**, marsh, quagmire, slough, fen ◆ v = **flood**, engulf, submerge, inundate; = **overload**, overwhelm, inundate
swap v = **exchange**, trade, switch, interchange, barter
swarm n = **multitude**, crowd, mass, army, host ◆ v = **crowd**, flock, throng, mass, stream; = **teem**, crawl, abound, bristle
swathe v = **wrap**, drape, envelop, cloak, shroud
sway v = **move from side to side**, rock, roll, swing, bend; = **influence**, affect, guide,

sworn 1 promise on oath. **2** cause to take an oath. **3** declare. **4** curse.
swearword n word considered obscene or blasphemous.
sweat ⊕ n **1** moisture oozing from, forming on skin. **2** *Inf* state of anxiety. ♦ v **3** (cause to) exude sweat. **4** toil. **sweaty** *adj*
sweatshirt n long-sleeved cotton jersey.
sweater n woollen jersey.
swede n variety of turnip.
sweep ⊕ v **sweeping, swept 1** clean with broom. **2** pass quickly or magnificently. **3** extend in continuous curve. **4** carry away suddenly. ♦ n **5** act of cleaning with broom. **6** sweeping motion. **7** wide curve. **8** one who cleans chimneys. **sweeping** *adj* **1** wide-ranging. **2** without limitations.
sweepstake n lottery with stakes of participants as prize.
sweet ⊕ *adj* **1** tasting like sugar. **2** agreeable. **3** kind, charming. **4** fragrant. **5** tuneful. **6** dear,

beloved. ♦ n **7** small piece of sweet food. **8** sweet course served at end of meal. **sweeten** v
sweetener n **1** sweetening agent **2** *Sl* bribe. **sweetness** n **sweet corn** type of maize with sweet yellow kernels. **sweetheart** n lover. **sweet pea** plant of pea family with bright flowers. **sweet-talk** v *Inf* coax, flatter.
swell ⊕ v **swelling, swelled, swollen 1** expand. **2** be greatly filled with pride, emotion. ♦ n **3** act of swelling or being swollen. **4** wave of sea. **swelling** n enlargement of part of body, caused by injury or infection.
swerve v **1** swing round, change direction during motion. **2** turn aside (from duty etc.). ♦ n **3** swerving.
swift ⊕ *adj* **1** rapid, quick. ♦ n **2** bird like a swallow.
swig n **1** large swallow of drink. ♦ v **2** drink thus.
swill v **1** drink greedily. **2** pour

———— THESAURUS ————

persuade, induce ♦ n = **power**, control, influence, authority, clout (*Inf*)
swear v = **curse**, blaspheme, be foul-mouthed; = **vow**, promise, testify, attest; = **declare**, assert, affirm
sweat n = (*Inf*) **panic**, anxiety, worry, distress, agitation ♦ v = **perspire**, glow; = (*Inf*) **worry**, fret, agonize, torture yourself
sweep v = **brush**, clean; = **clear**, remove, brush, clean ♦ n = **movement**, move, swing, stroke;

= **extent**, range, stretch, scope
sweet *adj* = **sugary**, cloying, saccharine, icky (*Inf*) ≠ **sour**;
= **fragrant**, aromatic ≠ **stinking**;
= **fresh**, pure ♦ n *usually plural* = **confectionery**, candy (*US*), lolly (*Aust & NZ*), bonbon; = (*Brit*) **dessert**, pudding
swell v = **increase**, rise, grow, mount, expand ≠ **decrease**;
= **expand**, increase, grow, rise, balloon ≠ **shrink** ♦ n = **wave**, surge, billow
swift *adj* = **quick**, prompt, rapid

water over or through. ♦ n 3 liquid pig food. 4 rinsing.

swim v **swimming, swam, swum** 1 support and move oneself in water. 2 float. 3 be flooded. 4 have feeling of dizziness. ♦ n 5 spell of swimming. **swimmer** n **swimmingly** adv successfully.

swindle n/v cheat. **swindler** n

swine n 1 pig. 2 contemptible person.

swing ⊕ v **swinging, swung** 1 (cause to) move to and fro. 2 (cause to) pivot, turn. 3 hang. 4 be hanged. 5 hit out (at). ♦ n 6 act, instance of swinging. 7 seat hung to swing on. 8 fluctuation (esp. in voting pattern).

swingeing adj punishing, severe.

swipe v strike with wide, sweeping or glancing blow.

swirl ⊕ v 1 (cause to) move with eddying motion. ♦ n 2 such motion.

swish v 1 (cause to) move with hissing sound. ♦ n 2 the sound.

switch ⊕ n 1 mechanism to complete or interrupt electric circuit etc. 2 abrupt change. 3 flexible stick or twig. 4 tress of false hair. ♦ v 5 change abruptly. 6 exchange. 7 affect (current etc.) with switch. **switchboard** n installation for connecting telephone calls.

swivel n –**elling,** –**elled** 1 mechanism of two parts which can revolve the one on the other. ♦ v 2 turn (on swivel).

swoop ⊕ v 1 dive, as hawk. ♦ n 2 act of swooping.

sword n weapon with long blade.

swordfish n fish with elongated sharp upper jaw.

swot Inf ♦ v 1 study hard. ♦ n 2 one who works hard at lessons.

sycamore n tree related to maple.

sycophant n one using flattery to gain favours. **sycophantic** adj

syllable n division of word as unit for pronunciation.

syllabus n, pl –**buses,** –**bi** outline of course of study.

syllogism n form of logical reasoning consisting of two premises and conclusion.

symbol ⊕ n 1 sign. 2 thing representing or typifying something. **symbolic** adj **symbolism** n **symbolize** v

symmetry n proportion between parts. **symmetrical** adj

————————— THESAURUS —————————

swing v = **brandish**, wave, shake, flourish, wield; = **sway**, rock, wave, veer, oscillate; usually with **round** = **turn**, swivel, curve, rotate, pivot; = **hit out**, strike, swipe, lash out at, slap ♦ n = **swaying**, sway

swirl v = **whirl**, churn, spin, twist, eddy

switch n = **control**, button, lever, on/off device; = **change**, shift, reversal ♦ v = **change**, shift, divert, deviate; = **exchange**, swap, substitute

swoop v = **pounce**, attack, charge, rush, descend

symbol n = **metaphor**, image, sign, representation, token

sympathy ❶ *n, pl* **–thies 1** feeling for another in pain etc. **2** compassion, pity. **3** sharing of emotion etc. **sympathetic** *adj* **sympathize** *v*

symphony *n, pl* **–nies** composition for full orchestra.

symposium *n, pl* **–siums, –sia** conference.

symptom ❶ *n* **1** change in body indicating disease. **2** sign. **symptomatic** *adj*

synagogue *n* Jewish place of worship.

sync, synch *n Inf* synchronization.

synchromesh *adj* (of gearbox) having device that synchronizes speeds of gears before they engage.

synchronize *v* **1** make agree in time. **2** happen at same time. **synchronization** *n*

syncopate *v* accentuate weak beat in bar of music. **syncopation** *n*

syndicate *n* **1** body of persons associated for some enterprise. ◆ *v* **2** form syndicate. **3** publish in many newspapers at the same time.

syndrome *n* combination of several symptoms in disease.

synod *n* church council.

synonym *n* word with same meaning as another. **synonymous** *adj*

synopsis *n, pl* **–ses** summary, outline.

syntax *n* arrangement of words in sentence.

synthesis *n, pl* **–ses** putting together, combination. **synthesize** *v* make artificially. **synthesizer** *n* electronic keyboard instrument reproducing wide range of musical sounds. **synthetic** *adj* **1** artificial. **2** of synthesis.

syphilis *n* contagious venereal disease.

syringe *n* **1** instrument for drawing in liquid and forcing it out in fine spray. ◆ *v* **2** spray, cleanse with syringe.

syrup *n* **1** thick solution obtained in process of refining sugar. **2** any liquid like this.

system ❶ *n* **1** complex whole. **2** method. **3** classification. **systematic** *adj* methodical.

————— THESAURUS —————

sympathy *n* = **compassion**, understanding, pity, commiseration ≠ **indifference**; = **affinity**, agreement, rapport, fellow feeling ≠ **opposition**

symptom *n* = **sign**, mark,

indication, warning

system *n* = **arrangement**, structure, organization, scheme, classification; = **method**, practice, technique, procedure, routine

T t

ta *interj Inf* thank you.

tab *n* tag, label, short strap.

Tabasco ® *n* hot red pepper sauce.

tabby *n, pl* **–bies,** *adj* (cat) with stripes on lighter background.

table ⊕ *n* **1** flat board supported by legs. **2** facts, figures arranged in lines or columns. ♦ *v* **3** submit (motion etc.) for discussion.

tablespoon *n* spoon for serving food.

tableau *n, pl* **–leaux** group of persons representing some scene.

tablet *n* **1** pill of compressed powdered medicine. **2** cake of soap etc. **3** inscribed slab of stone, wood etc.

tabloid *n* small–sized newspaper with many photographs and usu. sensational style.

taboo ⊕ *adj* **1** forbidden. ♦ *n, pl* **–boos 2** prohibition resulting from social conventions etc.

tacit *adj* implied but not spoken.

taciturn *adj* habitually silent.

tack¹ ⊕ *n* **1** small nail. **2** long loose stitch. **3** *Naut* course of ship obliquely to windward. **4** approach, method. ♦ *v* **5** nail with tacks. **6** stitch lightly. **7** append. **8** sail to windward.

tack² *n* riding harness for horses.

tackies, takkies *pl n, sing* **tacky** *S Afr informal* tennis shoes or plimsolls.

tackle ⊕ *n* **1** equipment, esp. for lifting. **2** *Sport* physical challenge of opponent. ♦ *v* **3** undertake. **4** challenge.

tacky¹ *adj* **tackier, tackiest 1** sticky. **2** not quite dry.

tacky² *adj* **tackier, tackiest** vulgar, tasteless.

tact *n* skill in dealing with people or situations. **tactful** *adj* **tactless** *adj*

tactics *pl n* **1** art of handling troops, ships in battle. **2** methods, plans. **tactical** *adj* **tactician** *n*

─────────── THESAURUS ───────────

table *n* = **counter**, bench, stand, board, surface; = **list**, chart, tabulation, record, roll ♦ *v* = (*Brit*) **submit**, propose, put forward, move, suggest

taboo *n* = **prohibition**, ban, restriction, anathema, interdict ♦ *adj* = **forbidden**, banned, prohibited, unacceptable, outlawed ≠ **permitted**

tack¹ *n* = **nail**, pin, drawing pin ♦ *v* = **fasten**, fix, attach, pin, nail; = (*Brit*) **stitch**, sew, hem, bind, baste

tackle *v* = **deal with**, set about, get stuck into (*Inf*), come or get to grips with; = **undertake**, attempt, embark upon, get stuck into (*Inf*), have a go or stab at (*Inf*) ♦ *n* = **block**, challenge; apparatus

tactile adj of sense of touch.

tadpole n immature frog.

taffeta n stiff silk fabric.

tag¹ ❶ n 1 label identifying or showing price of (something). 2 hanging end. ♦ v 3 add (on).

tag² n 1 children's game where one chaser becomes the chaser upon being touched. ♦ v 2 touch.

tail ❶ n 1 flexible appendage at animal's rear. 2 hindmost, lower or inferior part of anything. ♦ pl 3 reverse side of coin. ♦ v 4 remove tail of. 5 Inf follow closely. **tailback** n queue of traffic stretching back from obstruction. **tailboard** n hinged rear board on lorry etc. **tail coat** man's evening dress jacket. **tail off** diminish gradually. **tailspin** n spinning dive of aircraft. **tailwind** n wind coming from rear.

tailor ❶ n maker of clothing, esp. for men. **tailor-made** adj well-fitting.

taint ❶ v 1 affect or be affected by pollution etc. ♦ n 2 defect. 3 contamination.

take ❶ v taking, took, taken 1 grasp. 2 get. 3 receive. 4 understand. 5 consider. 6 use. 7 capture. 8 steal. 9 accept. 10 bear. 11 consume. 12 assume. 13 carry. 14 accompany. 15 subtract. 16 require. 17 contain, hold. 18 be effective. 19 please. ♦ n 20 (recording of) scene filmed without break. **takings** pl n earnings, receipts. **take after** resemble in face or character. **takeaway** n 1 shop, restaurant selling meals for eating elsewhere. 2 meal bought at this place. **take in** 1 understand. 2 include. 3 make (garment etc.) smaller. 4 deceive. **take off** 1 remove. 2 (of aircraft) leave ground. 3 Inf go away. 4 Inf mimic. **take-off** n **takeover** n act of taking control of company by buying large number of its shares.

talc, talcum powder n powder, usu. scented, to absorb body moisture.

tale ❶ n story, narrative.

talent ❶ n natural ability. **talented**

tag¹ n = **label**, tab, note, ticket, slip ♦ v = **label**, mark

tail n = **extremity**, appendage, brush, rear end, hindquarters ♦ v = (Inf) **follow**, track, shadow, trail, stalk; **turn tail** = **run away**, flee, run off, retreat, cut and run

tailor n = **outfitter**, couturier, dressmaker, seamstress, clothier ♦ v = **adapt**, adjust, modify, style, fashion

taint v = **spoil**, ruin, contaminate, damage, stain ≠ **purify**

take v = **grip**, grab, seize, catch, grasp; = **carry**, bring, bear, transport, ferry ≠ **send**; = **accompany**, lead, bring, guide, conduct; = **remove**, draw, pull, fish, withdraw; = **steal**, appropriate, pocket, pinch (Inf), misappropriate ≠ **return**; = **capture**, seize, take into custody, lay hold of ≠ **release**; = **tolerate**, stand, bear, stomach, endure ≠ **avoid**

tale n = **story**, narrative,

adj gifted.

talisman *n*, *pl* **–mans** object supposed to have magic power.

talk ➊ *v* 1 express, exchange ideas etc. in words. 2 discuss. ◆ *n* 3 lecture. 4 conversation. 5 rumour. 6 discussion. **talkative** *adj*

tall ➊ *adj* 1 high. 2 of great stature.

tally ➊ *v* **–lying, –lied** 1 correspond one with the other. 2 count. ◆ *n* 3 record, account.

talon *n* claw.

tambourine *n* flat half-drum with jingling discs of metal attached.

tame ➊ *adj* 1 not wild, domesticated. 2 uninteresting. ◆ *v* 3 make tame.

tamper *v* interfere (with).

tampon *n* plug of cotton wool inserted into vagina during menstruation.

tan *adj/n* 1 (of) brown colour of skin after exposure to sun etc. ◆ *v* 2 (cause to) go brown. 3 (of animal hide) convert to leather.

tannin *n* vegetable substance used as tanning agent.

tandem *n* bicycle for two.

tandoori *adj* (of Indian food) cooked in a clay oven.

tang *n* strong pungent taste or smell. **tangy** *adj*

tangent *n* line that touches a curve. **tangential** *adj*

tangerine *n* (fruit of) Asian citrus tree.

tangible ➊ *adj* 1 that can be touched. 2 real. **tangibility** *n*

tangle ➊ *n* 1 confused mass or situation. ◆ *v* 2 confuse.

tango *n*, *pl* **–gos** dance of S Amer.

anecdote, account, legend

talent *n* = **ability**, gift, aptitude, capacity, genius

talk *v* = **speak**, chat, chatter, converse, communicate; = **discuss**, confer, negotiate, parley, confabulate; = **inform**, grass (*Brit sl*), tell all, give the game away, blab ◆ *n* = **speech**, lecture, presentation, report, address

tall *adj* = **lofty**, big, giant, long-legged, lanky; = **high**, towering, soaring, steep, elevated ≠ **short**; = (*Inf*) **implausible**, incredible, far-fetched, exaggerated, absurd ≠ **plausible**

tally *n* = **record**, score, total, count, reckoning ◆ *v* = **agree**,

match, accord, fit, square ≠ **disagree**

tame *adj* = **domesticated**, docile, broken, gentle, obedient ≠ **wild**; = **submissive**, meek, compliant, subdued, manageable ≠ **stubborn**; = **unexciting**, boring, dull, bland, uninspiring ≠ **exciting** ◆ *v* = **domesticate**, train, break in, house-train ≠ **make fiercer**; = **subdue**, suppress, master, discipline, humble ≠ **arouse**

tangible *adj* = **definite**, real, positive, material, actual ≠ **intangible**

tangle *n* = **knot**, twist, web, jungle, coil; = **mess**, jam, fix (*Inf*), confusion, complication ◆ *v* = **twist**, knot, mat, coil, mesh

origin.

tank n **1** storage vessel for liquids or gases. **2** armoured motor vehicle on tracks. **tanker** n ship, lorry for carrying liquid.

tankard n large drinking cup.

Tannoy ® n type of public-address system.

tantalize v torment by appearing to offer something.

tantamount adj **tantamount to** equivalent in effect to.

tantrum ❶ n outburst of temper.

tap¹ ❶ v **tapping, tapped 1** strike lightly but with some noise. ♦ n **2** tapping. **tap dance** dance in which the feet beat out elaborate rhythms.

tap² ❶ n **1** valve with handle, plug etc. to regulate or stop flow of fluid. ♦ v **2** draw off with tap. **3** use, draw on. **4** make secret connection to telephone wire to overhear conversation on it.

tape n **1** narrow strip of fabric, paper etc. **2** magnetic recording. ♦ v **3** record (speech, music etc.). **tape measure** tape marked off in centimetres, inches etc. **tape**

recorder apparatus for recording sound on magnetized tape.

tapeworm n long flat parasitic worm.

taper v **1** become gradually thinner. ♦ n **2** thin candle.

tapestry n, pl **–tries** fabric decorated with woven designs.

tapioca n beadlike starch made from cassava root.

tar n **1** thick black liquid distilled from coal etc. ♦ v **2** coat, treat with tar.

tarantula n large (poisonous) hairy spider.

tardy adj **tardier, tardiest** slow, late.

target ❶ n **1** thing aimed at. **2** victim.

tariff ❶ n **1** tax levied on imports etc. **2** list of charges.

Tarmac ® n mixture of tar etc. giving hard, smooth surface to road.

tarn n small mountain lake.

tarnish ❶ v **1** (cause to) become stained or sullied. ♦ n **2** discoloration, blemish.

tarot n pack of cards used in

————— THESAURUS —————

≠ disentangle

tantrum n = **outburst**, temper, hysterics, fit, flare–up

tap¹ v = **knock**, strike, pat, rap, beat ♦ n = **knock**, pat, rap, touch, drumming

tap² n = **valve**, stopcock ♦ v = **listen in on**, monitor, bug (Inf), spy on, eavesdrop on

tape n = **binding**, strip, band, string, ribbon ♦ v = **record**, video,

tape–record, make a recording of; sometimes with **up** = **bind**, secure, stick, seal, wrap

target n = **mark**, goal; = **goal**, aim, objective, end, mark

tariff n = **tax**, duty, toll, levy, excise; = **price list**, schedule

tarnish v = **damage**, taint, blacken, sully, smirch ≠ **enhance**; = **stain**, discolour, darken, blot, blemish ≠ **brighten** ♦ n = **stain**,

fortune–telling.

tarpaulin n (sheet of) heavy hard–wearing waterproof fabric.

tarragon n aromatic herb.

tarry v **–rying, –ried 1** linger, delay. **2** stay behind.

tart¹ ❶ n **1** small pie or flan filled with fruit, jam etc. **2** loose woman.

tart² ❶ adj **1** sour. **2** sharp. **3** bitter.

tartan n woollen cloth woven in pattern of coloured checks.

tartar n crust deposited on teeth.

task ❶ n piece of work (esp. unpleasant or difficult) set or undertaken. **taskmaster** n overseer.

tassel n **1** ornament of fringed knot of threads etc. **2** tuft.

taste ❶ n **1** sense by which flavour, quality of substance is detected by the tongue. **2** (brief) experience of something. **3** small amount. **4** liking. **5** power of discerning, judging. ♦ v **6** observe or distinguish the taste of a substance. **7** take small amount into mouth. **8** experience. **9** have specific flavour. **tasteful** adj with, showing good taste. **tasteless** adj **1** bland, insipid. **2** showing bad taste. **tasty** adj pleasantly flavoured. **taste bud** small organ of taste on tongue.

tattered adj ragged. **tatters** pl n ragged pieces.

tattle v/n gossip, chatter.

tattletale n Chiefly US and Canad a scandalmonger or gossip.

tattoo¹ n **1** beat of drum and bugle call. **2** military spectacle.

tattoo² v **1** mark skin in coloured patterns etc. by pricking. ♦ n **2** pattern made thus.

tatty adj **–tier, –tiest** shabby, worn out.

taunt ❶ v **1** provoke with insults etc. ♦ n **2** scornful remark.

taupe adj brownish–grey.

taut adj **1** drawn tight. **2** under strain.

tavern ❶ n inn, public house.

tawdry adj **–drier, –driest** showy,

————————— THESAURUS —————————

taint, discoloration, spot, blot

tart¹ n = pie, pastry, pasty, tartlet, patty

tart² adj = sharp, acid, sour, bitter, pungent ≠ sweet

task n = job, duty, assignment, exercise, mission; **take someone to task = criticize**, blame, censure, rebuke, reprimand (Inf)

taste n = flavour, savour, relish, smack, tang ≠ **blandness**; = bit, bite, mouthful, sample, dash; = liking, preference, penchant, fondness, partiality ≠ dislike; = **refinement**, style, judgment, discrimination, appreciation ≠ lack of judgment ♦ v = have a flavour of, smack of, savour of; = sample, try, test, sip, savour; = distinguish, perceive, discern, differentiate; = experience, know, undergo, partake of, encounter ≠ miss

taunt v = jeer, mock, tease, ridicule, provoke ♦ n = jeer, dig, insult, ridicule, teasing

tavern n = inn, bar, pub (Inf,

but cheap.

tawny adj **–nier, –niest,** n (of) light yellowish–brown colour.

tax ❶ n **1** compulsory payments imposed by government to raise revenue. **2** heavy demand on something. ♦ v **3** impose tax on. **4** strain. **taxation** n levying of taxes.

tax return statement of income for tax purposes.

taxi, taxicab n **1** motor vehicle for hire with driver. ♦ v **2** (of aircraft) run along ground.

taxidermy n art of stuffing animal skins. **taxidermist** n

TB tuberculosis.

tea n **1** dried leaves of plant cultivated esp. in Asia. **2** infusion of it as beverage. **3** meal eaten in afternoon or early evening. **tea bag** small porous bag of tea leaves. **teapot** n container for making and serving tea. **teaspoon** n small spoon for stirring tea etc. **tea towel** towel for drying dishes.

teach ❶ v **teaching, taught 1** instruct. **2** educate. **3** train. **teacher** n

teak n (hard wood from) E Indian tree.

team ❶ n **1** set of animals, players of game etc. ♦ v **2** (usu. with **up**) (cause to) make a team.

teamwork n cooperative work by team.

tear¹ ❶ v **tearing, tore, torn 1** pull apart. **2** become torn. **3** rush. ♦ n **4** hole or split. **tearaway** n wild or unruly person.

tear² n drop of fluid falling from eye. **tearful** adj **1** inclined to weep. **2** involving tears. **teardrop** n tear **gas** irritant gas causing temporary blindness.

tease ❶ v **1** tantalize, torment, irritate. ♦ n **2** one who teases.

teat n **1** nipple of breast. **2** rubber nipple of baby's bottle.

technical ❶ adj **1** of, specializing in industrial, practical or mechanical arts. **2** belonging to particular art or science. **3** according to letter of the law. **technicality** n point of procedure. **technician** n one skilled in technique of an art. **technique** n **1** method of performance in an art. **2** skill required for mastery of subject.

Technicolor ® n colour photography, esp. in cinema.

technology n **1** application of

chiefly Brit), public house, hostelry

tax n = **charge,** duty, toll, levy, tariff ♦ v = **charge,** rate, assess; = **strain,** stretch, try, test, load

teach v = **instruct,** train, coach, inform, educate

team n = **side,** squad; = **group,** company, set, body, band

tear¹ v = **rip,** split, rend, shred, rupture; = **scratch,** cut (open), gash, lacerate, injure; = **pull apart,** claw, lacerate, mutilate, mangle ♦ n = **hole,** split, rip, rent, snag

tease v = **mock,** provoke, torment, taunt, goad

technical adj = **scientific,** technological, skilled, specialist, specialized

practical, mechanical sciences. **2** technical skills, knowledge. **technological** adj

tedious ⊕ adj causing fatigue or boredom. **tedium** n monotony.

tee n **1** Golf place from which first stroke of hole is made. **2** small peg supporting ball for first stroke.

teem v **1** abound with. **2** swarm. **3** rain heavily.

teens pl n years of life from 13 to 19. **teenage** adj **teenager** n young person between 13 and 19.

teeter v seesaw, wobble.

teeth n pl of TOOTH.

teethe v (of baby) grow first teeth. **teething troubles** problems, difficulties at first stage of something.

teetotal adj pledged to abstain from alcohol. **teetotaller** n

Teflon ® n substance used for nonstick coatings on saucepans etc.

telecommunications pl n communications by telephone, television etc.

telegram n formerly, message sent by telegraph.

telegraph n **1** formerly, electrical apparatus for transmitting messages over distance. ◆ v **2** send by telegraph.

telepathy n action of one mind on another at a distance. **telepathic** adj

telephone ⊕ n **1** apparatus for communicating sound to hearer at a distance. ◆ v **2** communicate, speak by telephone. **telephonist** n person operating telephone switchboard.

teleprinter n apparatus for sending and receiving typed messages by wire.

telescope ⊕ n **1** optical instrument for magnifying distant objects. ◆ v **2** slide together. **telescopic** adj

television ⊕ n **1** system of producing on screen images of distant objects, events etc. by electromagnetic radiation. **2** device for receiving this. **3** programmes etc. viewed on television set. **televise** v **1** transmit by television. **2** make, produce as television programme.

telex n **1** international communication service. ◆ v **2** send by telex.

tell ⊕ v telling, told **1** let know. **2** order. **3** narrate, make known. **4** discern. **5** distinguish. **6** give account. **7** be of weight, importance. **teller** n **1** narrator. **2** bank cashier. **telling** adj effective, striking. **tell off** reprimand. **telltale**

— THESAURUS —

tedious adj = **boring**, dull, dreary, monotonous, drab ≠ **exciting**

telephone n = **phone**, mobile (phone), handset, dog and bone (Sl) ◆ v = **call**, phone, ring (Chiefly Brit), dial

telescope n = **glass**, scope (Inf), spyglass ◆ v = **shorten**, contract, compress, shrink, condense ≠ **lengthen**

television n = **TV**, telly (Brit inf), small screen (Inf), the box (Brit inf),

n 1 sneak. ♦ *adj* 2 revealing.

telly *n, pl* **–lies** *Inf* television (set).

temerity *n* boldness, audacity.

temp *n Inf* one employed on temporary basis.

temper ⊕ *n* 1 frame of mind. 2 angry state. 3 calmness, composure. ♦ *v* 4 restrain, moderate. 5 harden (metal).

temperament ⊕ *n* 1 natural disposition. 2 emotional mood. **temperamental** *adj* 1 moody. 2 erratic.

temperate *adj* 1 (of climate) mild. 2 not extreme. 3 showing moderation. **temperance** *n* 1 moderation. 2 abstinence, esp. from alcohol.

temperature *n* 1 degree of heat or coldness 2 *Inf* high body temperature.

tempest *n* violent storm. **tempestuous** *adj* 1 stormy. 2 violent.

template *n* pattern used to cut out shapes accurately.

temple ⊕ *n* building for worship.

tempo *n, pl* **–pi, –pos** rate, rhythm.

temporal *adj* 1 of time. 2 of this life or world.

temporary ⊕ *adj* lasting only a short time.

tempt ⊕ *v* try to persuade, entice, esp. to something wrong or unwise. **temptation** *n* **tempter** *n* **tempting** *adj* attractive, inviting.

ten *n/adj* cardinal number after nine. **tenth** *adj* ordinal number.

tenable *adj* able to be held, defended, maintained.

tenacious *adj* 1 holding fast. 2 retentive. 3 stubborn. **tenacity** *n*

tenant ⊕ *n* one who holds lands, house etc. on rent or lease. **tenancy** *n*

tench *n, pl* **tench** freshwater fish.

tend¹ ⊕ *v* 1 be inclined. 2 be

——————— THESAURUS ———————

the tube (*Sl*)

tell *v* = **inform**, notify, state to, reveal to, express to; = **describe**, relate, recount, report, portray; = **instruct**, order, command, direct, bid; = **distinguish**, discriminate, discern, differentiate, identify; = **have** *or* **take effect**, register, weigh, count, take its toll **temper** *n* = **irritability**, irascibility, passion, resentment, petulance ≠ **good humour**; = **frame of mind**, nature, mind, mood, constitution; = **rage**, fury, bad mood, passion, tantrum; = **self-control**, composure, cool (*Sl*), calmness,

equanimity ≠ **anger** ♦ *v* = **moderate**, restrain, tone down, soften, soothe ≠ **intensify**; = **strengthen**, harden, toughen, anneal ≠ **soften**

temperament *n* = **nature**, character, personality, make-up, constitution

temple *n* = **shrine**, church, sanctuary, house of God

temporary *adj* = **impermanent**, transitory, brief, fleeting, interim ≠ **permanent**

tempt *v* = **attract**, allure

tenant *n* = **leaseholder**, resident, renter, occupant, inhabitant

conducive. **3** make in direction of.

tendency *n* inclination.

tendentious *adj* controversial.

tend² ⊕ *v* take care of.

tender¹ ⊕ *adj* **1** not tough. **2** easily injured. **3** gentle, loving. **4** delicate.

tender² ⊕ *v* **1** offer. **2** make offer or estimate. ♦ *n* **3** offer or estimate for contract to undertake specific work. **legal tender** currency that must, by law, be accepted as payment.

tendon *n* sinew attaching muscle to bone etc.

tendril *n* slender curling stem by which climbing plant clings.

tenement *n* building divided into separate flats.

tenet *n* belief.

tennis *n* game in which ball is struck with racket by players on opposite sides of net.

tenor *n* **1** male voice between alto and bass. **2** general course, meaning.

tenpin bowling game in which players try to knock over ten skittles with ball.

tense ⊕ *adj* **1** stretched tight. **2** taut. **3** emotionally strained. ♦ *v* **4** make, become tense. **tensile** *adj* of, relating to tension. **tension** *n* **1** stretching. **2** strain when stretched. **3** emotional strain. **4** *Electricity* voltage.

tent *n* portable shelter of canvas.

tentacle *n* flexible organ of some animals (e.g. octopus) used for grasping, feeding etc.

tentative ⊕ *adj* **1** experimental. **2** cautious.

tenterhooks *pl n* **on tenterhooks** in anxious suspense.

tenuous *adj* **1** flimsy. **2** thin.

tenure *n* (length of time of) possession of office etc.

tepee *n* N Amer. Indian cone–shaped tent.

tepid *adj* moderately warm.

tequila *n* Mexican alcoholic drink.

term ⊕ *n* **1** word, expression. **2** limited period of time. **3** period during which schools are open. ♦ *pl* **4** conditions. **5** relationship. ♦ *v* **6** name.

——————— THESAURUS ———————

tend¹ *v* = **be inclined**, be liable, have a tendency, be apt, be prone

tend² *v* = **take care of**, look after, keep, attend, nurture ≠ **neglect**; = **maintain**, take care of, nurture, cultivate, manage ≠ **neglect**

tender¹ *adj* = **gentle**, loving, kind, caring, sympathetic ≠ **harsh**; = **vulnerable**, young, sensitive, raw, youthful ≠ **experienced**

tender² *n* = **offer**, bid, estimate, proposal, submission ♦ *v* = **offer**,

present, submit, give, propose

tense *adj* = **strained**, uneasy, stressful, fraught, charged; = **nervous**, edgy, strained, anxious, apprehensive ≠ **calm** ♦ *v* = **tighten**, strain, brace, stretch, flex ≠ **relax**

tentative *adj* = **unconfirmed**, provisional, indefinite, test, trial ≠ **confirmed**; = **hesitant**, cautious, uncertain, doubtful, faltering ≠ **confident**

terminal ⊕ *adj* **1** at, forming an end. **2** (of disease) ending in death. ♦ *n* **3** terminal part or structure. **4** point where current enters, leaves battery etc. **5** device permitting operation of computer at distance.

terminate ⊕ *v* bring, come to an end. **termination** *n*

terminology *n* set of technical terms or vocabulary.

terminus *n, pl* **-ni, -nuses 1** finishing point. **2** railway station etc. at end of line.

termite *n* wood-eating insect.

tern *n* sea bird like gull.

terrace *n* **1** raised level place. **2** row of houses built as one block (*oft. pl*) **3** unroofed tiers for spectators at sports stadium. ♦ *v* **4** form into terrace.

terracotta *n/adj* **1** (made of) hard unglazed pottery. **2** (of) brownish-red colour.

terrain ⊕ *n* area of ground, esp.

with reference to its physical character.

terrapin *n* type of aquatic tortoise.

terrestrial ⊕ *adj* **1** of the earth. **2** of, living on land.

terrible ⊕ *adj* **1** serious. **2** *Inf* very bad. **3** causing fear. **terribly** *adv*

terrier *n* small dog of various breeds.

terrific ⊕ *adj* **1** very great. **2** *Inf* good. **3** awe-inspiring.

terrify ⊕ *v* **-fying, -fied** frighten greatly. **terrifying** *adj*

territory ⊕ *n, pl* **-ries 1** region. **2** geographical area, esp. a sovereign state. **territorial** *adj* **Territorial Army** reserve army.

terror ⊕ *n* **1** great fear. **2** *Inf* troublesome person or thing.

terrorism *n* use of violence to achieve ends. **terrorist** *n/adj*

terrorize *v* **1** oppress by violence. **2** terrify.

terse *adj* **1** concise. **2** abrupt.

——————— THESAURUS ———————

term *n* = **word**, name, expression, title, label; = **period**, time, spell, while, season ♦ *v* = **call**, name, label, style, entitle

terminal *adj* = **fatal**, deadly, lethal, killing, mortal; = **final**, last, closing, finishing, concluding ≠ **initial** ♦ *n* = **terminus**, station, depot, end of the line

terminate *v* = **end**, stop, conclude, finish, complete ≠ **begin**

terrain *n* = **ground**, country, land, landscape, topography

terrestrial *adj* = **earthly**, worldly, global

terrible *adj* = **awful**, shocking, terrifying, horrible, dreadful; = (*Inf*) **bad**, awful, dreadful, dire, abysmal ≠ **wonderful**; = **serious**, desperate, severe, extreme, dangerous ≠ **mild**

terrific *adj* = (*Inf*) **excellent**, wonderful, brilliant, amazing, outstanding ≠ **awful**; = **intense**, great, huge, enormous, tremendous

terrify *v* = **frighten**, scare, alarm, terrorize, make your hair stand on end

territory *n* = **district**, area, land,

tertiary *adj* third in degree, order etc.

Terylene ® *n* **1** synthetic yarn. **2** fabric made of it.

test ❶ *v* **1** try, put to the proof. **2** carry out examination on. ◆ *n* **3** examination. **4** means of trial.

testing *adj* difficult. **test case** lawsuit viewed as means of establishing precedent. **test match** international sports contest, esp. one of series. **test tube** tubelike glass vessel.

testament ❶ *n* **1** *Law* will **2** (with cap.) one of the two main divisions of the Bible.

testate *adj* (of dead person) having left a valid will.

testicle, **testis** *n* either of two male reproductive glands.

testify ❶ *v* –**fying**, –**fied 1** declare. **2** bear witness (to).

testimony ❶ *n*, *pl* –**nies 1** affirmation. **2** evidence.

testimonial *n* **1** certificate of character etc. **2** gift expressing regard for recipient.

testy *adj* –**tier**, –**tiest** irritable.

tetanus *n* (also called **lockjaw**) acute infectious disease.

tête-à-tête *n*, *pl* –**têtes**, –**tête** private conversation.

tether *n* **1** rope for fastening (grazing) animal. ◆ *v* **2** tie up with rope.

tetrahedron *n*, *pl* –**drons**, –**dra** solid contained by four plane faces.

text ❶ *n* **1** (actual words of) book, passage etc. **2** passage of Bible.

textual *adj* **textbook** *n* book of instruction on particular subject.

textile *n* any fabric or cloth, esp. woven.

texture ❶ *n* **1** structure, appearance. **2** consistency.

than *conj* introduces second part of comparison.

thank ❶ *v* **1** express gratitude to. **2** say thanks. **thankful** *adj* grateful. **thankless** *adj* unrewarding or unappreciated. **thanks** *pl n* words of gratitude.

that *adj* **1** refers to thing already mentioned. **2** refers to thing further away. ◆ *pron* **3** refers to

———————— THESAURUS ————————

region, country

terror *n* = **fear**, alarm, dread, fright, panic; = **nightmare**, monster, bogeyman, devil, fiend

test *v* = **check**, investigate, assess, research, analyse; = **examine**, put someone to the test ◆ *n* = **trial**, research, check, investigation, analysis

testament *n* = **proof**, evidence, testimony, witness, demonstration; = **will**, last wishes

testify *v* = **bear witness**, state, swear, certify, assert ≠ **disprove**

testimony *n* = **evidence**, statement, submission, affidavit, deposition; = **proof**, evidence, demonstration, indication, support

text *n* = **contents**, words, content, wording, body; = **words**, wording

texture *n* = **feel**, consistency, structure, surface, tissue

thank *v* = **say thank you to**, show

particular thing. **4** introduces relative clause. ◆ *conj* **5** introduces noun or adverbial clause.

thatch *n* **1** reeds, straw etc. used as roofing material. ◆ *v* **2** build roof with this.

thaw ❶ *v* **1** melt. **2** (cause to) unfreeze. ◆ *n* **3** melting (of frost etc.).

the *adj* the definite article.

theatre *n* **1** place where plays etc. are performed. **2** dramatic works generally. **3** hospital operating room. **theatrical** *adj* **1** of, for the theatre. **2** exaggerated.

thee *pron Obs* object of THOU.

theft ❶ *n* stealing.

their *adj* of, belonging to them. **theirs** *pron* belonging to them.

them *pron* object of THEY.

themselves *pron* emphatic or reflexive form of THEY.

theme ❶ *n* **1** main topic of book etc. **2** subject of composition. **3** recurring melody. **thematic** *adj*

theme park leisure area designed round one subject.

then *adv* **1** at that time. **2** next. **3** that being so.

thence *adv Obs* from that place or time.

theology *n, pl* **–gies** systematic study of religion and religious beliefs. **theologian** *n* **theological**

adj

theorem *n* proposition which can be demonstrated.

theory ❶ *n, pl* **–ries** **1** supposition to account for something. **2** system of rules and principles, esp. distinguished from practice. **3** an idea or opinion. **theoretical** *adj* **1** based on theory. **2** speculative.

therapy ❶ *n, pl* **–pies** healing treatment. **therapeutic** *adj* **1** of healing. **2** serving to improve health. **therapist** *n*

there *adv* **1** in that place. **2** to that point. **thereby** *adv* by that means. **therefore** *adv* that being so. **thereupon** *adv* immediately.

therm *n* unit of measurement of heat. **thermal** *adj*

thermodynamics *pl n* science that deals with interrelationship of different forms of energy.

thermometer *n* instrument to measure temperature.

Thermos ® *n* vacuum flask.

thermostat *n* apparatus for regulating temperature.

thesaurus *n, pl* **–ruses** book containing lists of synonyms.

these *pron* pl of THIS.

thesis ❶ *n, pl* **theses** **1** written work submitted for degree, diploma. **2** theory maintained in

———— THESAURUS ————

your appreciation to

thaw *v* = **melt**, dissolve, soften, defrost, warm ≠ **freeze**

theft *n* = **stealing**, robbery, thieving, fraud, embezzlement

theme *n* = **motif**, leitmotif;

= **subject**, idea, topic, essence, subject matter

theory *n* = **belief**, feeling, speculation, assumption, hunch

therapy *n* = **remedy**, treatment, cure, healing, method of healing

argument.

thespian adj 1 of the theatre. ♦ n 2 actor, actress.

they pron pronoun of the third person plural.

thick ① adj 1 fat, broad, not thin. 2 dense. 3 crowded. 4 viscous. 5 (of voice) throaty. 6 Inf stupid. ♦ n 7 busiest part. **thicken** v 1 make, become thick. 2 become complicated. **thickness** n 1 dimension through an object. 2 layer. **thickset** adj sturdy, stocky.

thicket n thick growth of trees.

thief ① n, pl **thieves** one who steals. **thieve** v steal.

thigh n upper part of leg.

thimble n cap protecting end of finger when sewing.

thin ① adj **thinner, thinnest** 1 of little thickness. 2 slim. 3 of little density. 4 sparse. 5 fine. 6 not close-packed. ♦ v 7 make, become thin.

thing ① n 1 (material) object. 2 fact, idea.

think ① v **thinking, thought** 1 have one's mind at work. 2 reflect, meditate. 3 reason. 4 deliberate. 5 believe.

third adj 1 of number three in a series. 2 third part. **third degree** violent interrogation. **third party** Law person involved by chance in legal proceedings etc.

thirst ① n 1 desire to drink. 2 feeling caused by lack of drink. 3 craving. ♦ v 4 have thirst. **thirsty** adj

thirteen adj/n three plus ten. **thirteenth** adj

thirty adj/n three times ten. **thirtieth** adj

this adj/pron denotes thing, person near or just mentioned.

thistle n prickly plant.

thither adv Obs to or towards that place.

———————— THESAURUS ————————

thesis n = **proposition**, theory, hypothesis, idea, view; = **dissertation**, paper, treatise, essay, monograph

thick adj = **bulky**, broad, big, large, fat ≠ **thin**; = **wide**, across, deep, broad, in extent or diameter; = **dense**, close, heavy, compact, impenetrable; = **heavy**, heavyweight, dense, chunky, bulky; = **opaque**, heavy, dense, impenetrable

thief n = **robber**, burglar, stealer, plunderer, shoplifter

thin adj = **narrow**, fine, attenuated ≠ **thick**; = **slim**, spare, lean, slight, slender ≠ **fat**; = **meagre**, sparse, scanty, poor, scattered ≠ **plentiful**; = **fine**, delicate, flimsy, sheer, skimpy ≠ **thick**; = **unconvincing**, inadequate, feeble, poor, weak ≠ **convincing**

thing n = **substance**, stuff, being, body, material ♦ pl n = **possessions**, stuff, gear, belongings, effects

think v = **believe**, be of the opinion, be of the view; = **judge**, consider, estimate, reckon, deem

thirst n = **dryness**, thirstiness, drought; = **craving**, appetite, longing, desire, passion ≠ **aversion**

T

thong n narrow strip of leather, strap.

thorax n, pl **thoraxes**, **thoraces** part of body between neck and belly.

thorn ❶ n 1 prickle on plant. 2 bush noted for its thorns. **thorny** adj

thorough ❶ adj 1 careful, methodical. 2 complete.

thoroughly adv **thoroughbred** n pure-bred animal, esp. horse.

thoroughfare n 1 road or passage. 2 right of way.

those pron pl of THAT.

thou pron Obs the second person singular pronoun.

though ❶ conj 1 even if. ◆ adv 2 nevertheless.

thought ❶ n 1 process, product of thinking. 2 what one thinks. 3 meditation. **thoughtful** adj 1 considerate. 2 showing careful

thought. 3 reflective. **thoughtless** adj 1 inconsiderate. 2 careless.

thousand n/adj ten hundred. **thousandth** adj

thrash ❶ v 1 beat. 2 defeat soundly. 3 move in wild manner.

thread ❶ n 1 yarn. 2 ridge cut on screw. 3 theme. ◆ v 4 put thread into. 5 fit film etc. into machine. 6 put on thread. 7 pick (one's way etc.). **threadbare** adj 1 worn, shabby. 2 hackneyed.

threat ❶ n 1 declaration of intention to harm, injure etc. 2 dangerous person or thing.

threaten v make or be threat to.

three adj/n one more than two. **three-dimensional** adj having height, width and depth. **three-ply** adj having three layers or strands. **threesome** n group of three.

thresh v 1 beat to separate grain

thorn n = **prickle**, spike, spine, barb

thorough adj = **comprehensive**, full, complete, sweeping, intensive ≠ cursory; = **careful**, conscientious, painstaking, efficient, meticulous ≠ careless

though conj = **although**, while, even if, even though, notwithstanding ◆ adv = **nevertheless**, still, however, yet, nonetheless

thought n = **thinking**, consideration, reflection, deliberation, musing; = **opinion**, view, idea, concept, notion; = **consideration**, study, attention,

care, regard; = **intention**, plan, idea, design, aim; = **hope**, expectation, prospect, aspiration, anticipation

thrash v = **defeat**, beat, crush, slaughter (Inf), rout; = **beat**, wallop, whip, belt (Inf), cane; = **thresh**, flail, jerk, writhe, toss and turn

thread n = **strand**, fibre, yarn, filament, line; = **theme**, train of thought, direction, plot, drift ◆ v = **move**, pass, ease, thrust, squeeze through

threat n = **danger**, risk, hazard, menace, peril; = **threatening remark**, menace; = **warning**,

from husks. **2** thrash.

threshold ❶ *n* **1** bar of stone forming bottom of doorway. **2** entrance. **3** starting point.

thrice *adv* three times.

thrift ❶ *n* saving, economy.

thrifty *adj* economical.

thrill ❶ *n* **1** sudden sensation of excitement and pleasure. ◆ *v* **2** (cause to) feel a thrill. **3** tremble.

thriller *n* suspenseful book, film etc. **thrilling** *adj*

thrive ❶ *v* **thriving, thrived 1** grow well. **2** prosper.

throat *n* **1** front of neck. **2** passage from mouth to stomach.

throaty *adj* **1** hoarse. **2** deep, guttural.

throb ❶ *v* **throbbing, throbbed 1** quiver strongly, pulsate. ◆ *n* **2** pulsation.

throes *pl n* violent pangs, pain etc. **in the throes of** in the process of.

thrombosis *n, pl* –**ses** clot in blood vessel or heart.

throne *n* **1** ceremonial seat. **2** power of sovereign.

throng ❶ *n/v* crowd.

throttle ❶ *n* **1** device controlling amount of fuel entering engine. ◆ *v* **2** strangle. **3** restrict.

through ❶ *prep* **1** from end to end. **2** in consequence of. **3** by means of. ◆ *adv* **4** from end to end. **5** to the end. ◆ *adj* **6** completed. **7** *Inf* finished. **8** continuous. **9** (of transport, traffic) not stopping. **throughout** *adv/prep* in every part (of). **throughput** *n* quantity of material processed.

throw ❶ *v* **throwing, threw, thrown 1** fling, cast. **2** move, put abruptly, carelessly. **3** cause to fall. ◆ *n* **4** act or distance of throwing. **throwaway** *adj* **1** designed to be discarded after use. **2** done casually. **throwback** *n* person,

———————— THESAURUS ————————

foreshadowing, foreboding

threshold *n* = **entrance**, doorway, door, doorstep; = **start**, beginning, opening, dawn, verge ≠ **end**; = **limit**, margin, starting point, minimum

thrift *n* = **economy**, prudence, frugality, saving, parsimony ≠ **extravagance**

thrill *n* = **pleasure**, kick (*Inf*), buzz (*Sl*), high, stimulation ≠ **tedium** ◆ *v* = **excite**, stimulate, arouse, move, stir

thrive *v* = **prosper**, do well, flourish, increase, grow ≠ **decline**

throb *v* = **pulsate**, pound, beat,

pulse, thump; = **vibrate**, pulsate, reverberate, shake, judder (*Inf*) ◆ *n* = **pulse**, pounding, beat, thump, thumping

throng *v* = **crowd**, flock, congregate, converge, mill around ≠ **disperse**

throttle *v* = **strangle**, choke, garrotte, strangulate

through *prep* = **via**, by way of, by, between, past; = **because of**, by way of, by means of; = **using**, via, by way of, by means of, by virtue of ◆ *adj* = **completed**, done, finished, ended; **through and through** = **completely**, totally,

thing that reverts to earlier type.
thrush n songbird.

thrust ❶ v thrusting, thrust 1
push, drive. **2** stab. ♦ n **3** lunge,
stab. **4** propulsive force or power.

thud n **1** dull heavy sound. ♦ v **2**
make thud.

thug ❶ n violent person.

thumb n **1** shortest, thickest finger
of hand. ♦ v **2** handle with thumb.
3 signal for lift in vehicle.

thumbtack n the US and
Canadian name for DRAWING PIN.

thump ❶ n **1** (sound of) dull
heavy blow. ♦ v **2** strike heavily.

thunder ❶ n **1** loud noise
accompanying lightning. ♦ v **2**
make noise of or like thunder.

thunderbolt, thunderclap n **1**
lightning followed by thunder. **2**
anything unexpected.

Thursday n fifth day of the week.

thus ❶ adv **1** in this way. **2**
therefore.

thwart ❶ v foil, frustrate.

thy adj Obs of or associated with
you. **thyself** pron emphatic or
reflexive form of THOU.

thyme n aromatic herb.

tiara n coronet.

tibia n, pl **tibiae, tibias** shinbone.

tic n spasmodic twitch in muscles,
esp. of face.

tick¹ ❶ n **1** slight tapping sound,
as of watch movement. **2** small
mark (✓) **3** Inf moment. ♦ v **4**
mark with tick. **5** make slight
tapping sound.

tick² n small insect–like parasite
living on blood.

ticket ❶ n **1** card, paper entitling
holder to admission, travel etc. **2**
label. ♦ v **3** attach label to.

tickle v **1** touch, stroke (person
etc.) to produce laughter etc. **2**
amuse. **3** itch. ♦ n **4** act, instance
of this. **ticklish** adj **1** sensitive to
tickling. **2** requiring care.

tiddlywinks pl n game of trying
to flip small plastic discs into cup.

———————— THESAURUS ————————

fully, thoroughly, entirely
throw v = **hurl**, toss, fling, send,
launch; = **toss**, fling, chuck (Inf),
cast, hurl ♦ n = **toss**, pitch, fling,
sling, lob (Inf)
thrust v = **push**, force, shove,
drive, plunge ♦ n = **stab**, pierce,
lunge; = **push**, shove, poke, prod
thug n = **ruffian**, hooligan, tough,
heavy (Sl), gangster
thump v = **strike**, hit, punch,
pound, beat ♦ n = **blow**, knock,
punch, rap, smack; = **thud**, crash,
bang, clunk, thwack
thunder n = **rumble**, crash, boom,

explosion ♦ v = **rumble**, crash,
boom, roar, resound; = **shout**,
roar, yell, bark, bellow
thus adv = **therefore**, so, hence,
consequently, accordingly; = **in
this way**, so, like this, as follows
thwart v = **frustrate**, foil, prevent,
snooker, hinder ≠ **assist**
tick¹ n = **check mark**, mark, line,
stroke, dash; = (Brit inf) **moment**,
second, minute, flash, instant ♦ v
= **mark**, indicate, check off; = **click**,
tap, ticktock
ticket n = **voucher**, pass, coupon,
card, slip; = **label**, tag, marker,

tide ❶ n rise and fall of sea happening twice each day. **tidal** adj **tidal wave** great wave, esp. produced by earthquake. **tide over** help someone for a while.

tidings pl n news.

tidy ❶ adj **–dier, –diest 1** orderly, neat. ♦ v **2** put in order.

tie ❶ v **tying, tied 1** fasten, bind. **2** restrict. **3** equal (score of). ♦ n **4** that with which anything is bound. **5** restraint. **6** piece of material worn knotted round neck. **7** connecting link. **8** contest with equal scores. **9** match, game in eliminating competition. **tied** adj **1** (of public house) selling beer etc. of only one brewer. **2** (of cottage etc.) rented to tenant employed by owner.

tier ❶ n row, rank, layer.

tiff n petty quarrel.

tiger n large carnivorous feline animal.

tight ❶ adj **1** taut, tense. **2** closely fitting. **3** secure, firm. **4** not allowing passage of water etc. **5** cramped. **6** Inf mean. **7** Inf drunk. **tighten** v **tights** pl n one-piece clinging garment covering body from waist to feet. **tightrope** n taut rope on which acrobats perform.

tile n **1** flat piece of ceramic, plastic etc. used for roofs, floors etc. ♦ v **2** cover with tiles.

till¹ ❶ v cultivate.

till² ❶ n **1** drawer for money in shop counter. **2** cash register.

tiller n lever to move rudder of boat.

tilt ❶ v **1** slope, slant. **2** take part in medieval combat with lances. **3** thrust (at). ♦ n **4** slope. **5** Hist combat with mounted men with lances.

———— THESAURUS ————

sticker, card

tide n = **current**, flow, stream, ebb, undertow

tidy adj = **neat**, orderly, clean, spruce, well-kept ≠ **untidy**; = (Inf) **considerable**, large, substantial, goodly, healthy ≠ **small** ♦ v = **neaten**, straighten, order, clean, groom ≠ **disorder**

tie v = **fasten**, bind, join, link, connect ≠ **unfasten**; = **tether**, secure; = **restrict**, limit, confine, bind, restrain ≠ **free** ♦ n = **fastening**, binding, link, bond, knot; = **bond**, relationship, connection, commitment, liaison; = **draw**, dead heat, deadlock,

stalemate

tier n = **row**, bank, layer, line, level

tight adj = **close-fitting**, narrow, cramped, snug, constricted ≠ **loose**; = **secure**, firm, fast, fixed; = **taut**, stretched, rigid ≠ **slack**; = **close**, even, well-matched, hard-fought, evenly-balanced ≠ **uneven**; = (Inf) **miserly**, mean, stingy, grasping, parsimonious ≠ **generous**; = (Inf) **drunk**, intoxicated, plastered (Sl), under the influence (Inf), tipsy ≠ **sober**

till¹ v = **cultivate**, dig, plough, work

till² n = **cash register**, cash box

timber ⓘ *n* 1 wood for building etc. 2 trees.

timbre *n* distinctive quality of voice or sound.

time ⓘ *n* 1 past, present and future as continuous whole. 2 hour. 3 duration. 4 period. 5 point in duration. 6 opportunity. 7 occasion. 8 leisure. ♦ *v* 9 choose time for. 10 note time taken by. **timeless** *adj* changeless, everlasting. **timely** *adj* at appropriate time. **timer** *n* person, device for recording or indicating time. **time bomb** bomb designed to explode at prearranged time. **time–lag** *n* period between cause and effect. **timetable** *n* plan showing times of arrival and departure etc.

timid *adj* 1 easily frightened. 2 shy. **timorous** *adj* 1 timid. 2 indicating fear.

timpani *pl n* set of kettledrums.

tin *n* 1 malleable metal. 2 container made of tin. ♦ *v* 3 put in tin, esp. for preserving. **tinny** *adj* (of sound) thin, metallic. **tinpot** *adj Inf* worthless.

tinder *n* dry easily–burning material used to start fire.

tinge ⓘ *n* 1 slight trace. ♦ *v* 2 colour, flavour slightly.

tingle *v/n* (feel) thrill or pricking sensation.

tinker ⓘ *n* 1 formerly, travelling mender of pots and pans. ♦ *v* 2 fiddle, meddle (with).

tinkle *v* 1 (cause to) give out sounds like small bell. ♦ *n* 2 this sound or action.

tinsel *n* glittering decorative metallic substance.

tint ⓘ *n* 1 (shade of) colour. 2 tinge. ♦ *v* 3 give tint to.

tiny ⓘ *adj* tinier, tiniest very small, minute.

tip¹ ⓘ *n* 1 slender or pointed end of anything. 2 small piece forming an extremity. ♦ *v* 3 put a tip on.

tip² ⓘ *n* 1 small present of money given for service rendered. 2 helpful piece of information. **tip–off** 3 warning, hint. ♦ *v* 4 reward with money **tip off** 5 give tip to.

tip³ ⓘ *v* tipping, tipped 1 tilt, upset. 2 touch lightly. 3 topple over. ♦ *n* 4 place where rubbish is

---
THESAURUS
---

tilt *v* = slant, tip, slope, list, lean ♦ *n* = slope, angle, inclination, list, pitch; = (*Medieval history*) joust, fight, tournament, lists, combat

timber *n* = beams, boards, planks; = wood, logs

time *n* = period, term, space, stretch, spell; = occasion, point, moment, stage, instance; = tempo, beat, rhythm, measure ♦ *v* = schedule, set, plan, book, programme

tinge *n* = tint, colour, shade; = trace, bit, drop, touch, suggestion ♦ *v* = tint, colour

tinker *v* = meddle, play, potter, fiddle (*Inf*), dabble

tint *n* = shade, colour, tone, hue; = dye, wash, rinse, tinge, tincture ♦ *v* = dye, colour

tiny *adj* = small, little, minute, slight, miniature ≠ huge

dumped.

tipple v 1 drink (alcohol) habitually. ♦ n 2 drink.

tipsy adj –sier, –siest (slightly) drunk.

tiptoe v –toeing, –toed 1 walk on ball of foot and toes. 2 walk softly.

tiptop adj of the best quality or condition.

tirade n long angry speech or denunciation.

tire ❶ v 1 reduce energy of, weary. 2 bore. 3 become tired, bored. **tired** adj 1 weary. 2 hackneyed. **tireless** adj not tiring easily. **tiresome** adj irritating, tedious. **tiring** adj

tissue n 1 substance of animal body, plant. 2 soft paper handkerchief.

tit n small bird.

titanic adj huge, epic.

titanium n light metallic element.

titbit n 1 tasty morsel of food. 2 scrap (of scandal etc.).

tithe n 1 (esp. formerly) tenth part of income, paid to church as tax. ♦ v 2 exact tithes from.

titillate v stimulate agreeably.

title ❶ n 1 name of book. 2 heading. 3 name, esp. denoting rank. 4 legal right or document proving it. 5 Sport championship.

titter v/n snigger, giggle.

titular adj 1 pert. to title. 2 nominal.

TNT see TRINITROTOLUENE.

to prep 1 denoting direction, destination. 2 introducing comparison, indirect object, infinitive etc. ♦ adv 3 to fixed position. **to and fro** back and forth.

toad n animal like large frog.

toady n 1 servile flatterer. ♦ v 2 be ingratiating. **toadstool** n fungus like mushroom.

toast ❶ n 1 slice of bread browned on both sides by heat. 2 tribute, proposal of health etc. marked by people drinking together. 3 person or thing so toasted. ♦ v 4 make (bread etc.) crisp and brown. 5 drink toast to. 6 warm at fire. **toaster** n electrical device for toasting bread.

———————— THESAURUS ————————

tip¹ n = **end**, point, head, extremity, sharp end; = **peak**, top, summit, pinnacle, zenith ♦ v = **cap**, top, crown, surmount, finish

tip² v = **reward**, remunerate, give a tip to, sweeten (Inf); = **predict**, back, recommend, think of ♦ n = **gratuity**, gift, reward, present, sweetener (Inf); = **hint**, suggestion, piece of advice, pointer

tip³ v = **pour**, drop, empty, dump,

drain; = (Brit) **dump**, empty, unload, pour out

tire v = **exhaust**, drain, fatigue, weary, wear out ≠ **refresh**; = **flag**, become tired, fail

title n = **name**, designation, term, handle (Sl), moniker or monicker (Sl); = (Sport) **championship**, trophy, bays, crown, honour; = (Law) **ownership**, right, claim, privilege, entitlement

toast v = **brown**, grill, crisp, roast;

tobacco n, pl **-cos**, **-coes** plant with leaves used for smoking.

tobacconist n one who sells tobacco products.

toboggan n sledge for sliding down slope of snow.

today n 1 this day. ♦ adv 2 on this day. 3 nowadays.

toddle v walk with unsteady short steps. **toddler** n young child beginning to walk.

to–do n, pl **–dos** Inf fuss, commotion.

toe n 1 digit of foot. 2 anything resembling this. **toe the line** conform.

toffee n chewy sweet made of boiled sugar etc.

toga n garment worn in ancient Rome.

together ⊕ adv 1 in company. 2 simultaneously.

toggle n small peg fixed crosswise on cord etc. and used for fastening.

toil ⊕ n 1 heavy work or task. ♦ v 2 labour.

toilet ⊕ n 1 lavatory. 2 process of washing, dressing. 3 articles used for this. **toiletries** pl n objects, cosmetics used for cleaning or grooming.

token ⊕ n 1 sign, symbol. 2 disc used as money. 3 gift card, voucher exchangeable for goods. ♦ adj 4 nominal.

tolerate ⊕ v 1 put up with. 2 permit. **tolerable** adj bearable. 2 fair. **tolerance** n **tolerant** adj 1 forbearing. 2 broad–minded. **toleration** n

toll¹ ⊕ v 1 ring (bell) slowly at regular intervals. ♦ n 2 ringing.

toll² ⊕ n 1 tax, esp. for use of bridge or road. 2 loss, damage.

tom n male cat.

———— THESAURUS ————

= **warm (up)**, heat (up), thaw, bring back to life ♦ n = **tribute**, compliment, salute, health, pledge; = **favourite**, celebrity, darling, talk, pet ♦ v = **drink to**, honour, salute, drink (to) the health of

together adv = **collectively**, jointly, as one, with each other, in conjunction ≠ **separately**; = **at the same time**, simultaneously, concurrently, contemporaneously, at one fell swoop ♦ adj = (Inf) **self-possessed**, composed, well-balanced, well-adjusted

toil v = **labour**, work, struggle, strive, sweat (Inf) ♦ n = **hard work**,

effort, application, sweat, graft (Inf) ≠ **idleness**

toilet n = **lavatory**, bathroom, loo (Brit inf), privy, cloakroom (Brit)

token n = **symbol**, mark, sign, note, expression ♦ adj = **nominal**, symbolic, minimal, hollow, superficial

tolerate v = **endure**, stand, take, stomach, put up with (Inf); = **allow**, accept, take, brook ≠ **forbid**

toll¹ v = **ring**, sound, strike, chime, knell ♦ n = **ringing**, chime, knell, clang, peal

toll² n = **charge**, tax, fee, duty, payment; = **damage**, cost, loss,

tomahawk n fighting axe of N Amer. Indians.

tomato n, pl **-toes 1** plant with red fruit. **2** the fruit.

tomb 🔊 n **1** grave. **2** monument over one. **tombstone** n

tombola n lottery with tickets drawn from revolving drum.

tomboy n girl who acts, dresses like boy.

tome n large book.

tomfoolery n foolish behaviour.

tomorrow adv/n (on) the day after today.

tom-tom n drum beaten with hands.

ton n (also **long ton**) **1** measure of weight, 1016 kg (2240 lbs.) (also **short ton**) **2** US measure of weight, 907 kg (2000 lbs.)

tonnage n carrying capacity of ship.

tone 🔊 n **1** quality of musical sound, voice, colour etc. **2** general character. ♦ v **3** blend, harmonize (with). **tone-deaf** adj unable to perceive subtle differences in pitch.

tongs pl n apparatus for handling coal, sugar etc.

tongue 🔊 n **1** organ inside mouth, used for speech, taste etc. **2** language, speech.

tonic 🔊 n **1** medicine etc. with invigorating effect. **2** Mus first note of scale. ♦ adj **3** invigorating, restorative. **tonic water** mineral water oft. containing quinine.

tonight n **1** this (coming) night. ♦ adv **2** on this night.

tonne n metric ton, 1000 kg.

tonsil n gland in throat. **tonsillitis** n inflammation of tonsils.

tonsure n **1** shaving of part of head as religious practice. **2** part shaved.

too 🔊 adv **1** also, in addition. **2** overmuch.

tool 🔊 n **1** implement or appliance for mechanical operations. **2** means to an end. ♦ v **3** work on with tool.

toonie, twonie n Inf Canadian two-dollar coin.

toot n short sound of horn, trumpet etc.

tooth n, pl **teeth 1** bonelike projection in gums of upper and lower jaws of vertebrates. **2** prong, cog. **toothless** adj **toothpaste** n

———— THESAURUS ————

roll, penalty

tomb n = **grave**, vault, crypt, mausoleum, sarcophagus

tone n = **pitch**, inflection, intonation, timbre, modulation; = **volume**, timbre; = **character**, style, feel, air, spirit ♦ v = **harmonize**, match, blend, suit, go well with

tongue n = **language**, speech,

dialect, parlance

tonic n = **stimulant**, boost, pick-me-up (Inf), fillip, shot in the arm (Inf)

too adv = **also**, as well, further, in addition, moreover; = **excessively**, very, extremely, overly, unduly

tool n = **implement**, device, appliance, machine, instrument; = **puppet**, creature, pawn, stooge

paste used to clean teeth.

toothpick *n* small stick for removing food from between teeth.

top ❶ *n* **1** highest part, summit. **2** highest rank. **3** first in merit. **4** garment for upper part of body. **5** lid, stopper of bottle etc. ♦ *adj* **6** highest in position, rank. ♦ *v* **7** cut off, pass, reach, surpass top. **8** provide top for. **topmost** *adj* highest. **topping** *n* sauce or garnish for food. **top brass** important officials. **top hat** man's tall cylindrical hat. **top-heavy** *adj* unbalanced. **top-notch** *adj* excellent, first-class. **topsoil** *n* surface layer of soil.

topaz *n* precious stone of various colours.

topiary *n* trimming trees, bushes into decorative shapes.

topic ❶ *n* subject of discourse, conversation etc. **topical** *adj* up-to-date, having news value.

topography *n, pl* **-phies** (description of) surface features of a place. **topographic** *adj*

topple ❶ *v* (cause to) fall over.

topsy-turvy *adj* in confusion.

tor *n* high rocky hill.

torch *n* **1** portable hand light containing electric battery. **2** burning wooden shaft. **3** any apparatus burning with hot flame.

toreador *n* bullfighter.

torment ❶ *v* **1** torture in body or mind. **2** afflict. **3** tease. ♦ *n* **4** suffering, agony of body or mind. **5** pest. **tormentor, -er** *n*

tornado ❶ *n, pl* **-dos, -does 1** whirlwind. **2** violent storm.

torpedo *n, pl* **-does 1** self-propelled underwater missile with explosive warhead. ♦ *v* **2** strike with torpedo.

torpid *adj* sluggish, apathetic.

torpor *n* torpid state.

torrent *n* **1** rushing stream. **2** downpour. **torrential** *adj*

torrid *adj* **1** parched. **2** highly emotional.

torsion *n* twist, twisting.

torso *n, pl* **-sos** (statue of) body without head or limbs.

tortilla *n* thin Mexican pancake.

tortoise *n* four-footed reptile covered with shell of horny plates.

———— THESAURUS ————

(*Sl*), minion

top *n* = **peak**, summit, head, crown, height ≠ **bottom**; = **lid**, cover, cap, plug, stopper; = **first place**, head, peak, lead, high point ♦ *adj* = **highest**, loftiest, furthest up, uppermost ♦ *v* = **lead**, head, be at the top of, be first in; = **cover**, garnish, finish, crown, cap; = **surpass**, better, beat, improve on, cap ≠ **not be as**

good as

topic *n* = **subject**, point, question, issue, matter

topple *v* = **fall over**, fall, collapse, tumble, overturn

torment *n* = **suffering**, distress, misery, pain, hell ≠ **bliss** ♦ *v* = **torture**, distress, rack, crucify ≠ **comfort**; = **tease**, annoy, bother, irritate, harass

tornado *n* = **whirlwind**, storm,

tortoiseshell n mottled brown shell of turtle.

tortuous adj 1 winding, twisting. 2 involved, not straightforward.

torture ❶ n 1 infliction of severe pain. ♦ v 2 inflict severe pain.

Tory n, pl **Tories** member of conservative political party.

toss ❶ v 1 throw up, about. 2 be thrown, fling oneself about. ♦ n 3 tossing.

tot¹ **❶** n 1 very small child. 2 small quantity, esp. of drink.

tot² v **totting, totted** 1 add (up). 2 amount to.

total ❶ n 1 whole amount. 2 sum. ♦ adj 3 complete, absolute. ♦ v 4 amount to. 5 add up. **totality** n **totally** adv

totalitarian adj of dictatorial, one-party government.

totem n tribal badge or emblem.

totem pole carved post of Amer. Indians.

totter v 1 walk unsteadily. 2 begin to fall.

toucan n large-billed tropical Amer. bird.

touch ❶ v 1 come into contact with. 2 put hand on. 3 reach. 4 affect emotions of. 5 deal with. 6 (with **on**) refer to. ♦ n 7 sense by which qualities of object etc. are perceived by touching. 8 touching. 9 characteristic manner or ability. 10 slight contact, amount etc. **touching** adj 1 emotionally moving. ♦ prep 2 concerning. **touchy** adj easily offended. **touch down** (of aircraft) land. **touchline** n side line of pitch in some games. **touchstone** n criterion.

touché interj acknowledgment that remark or blow has struck target.

tough ❶ adj 1 strong. 2 able to bear hardship, strain. 3 strict. 4

———— THESAURUS ————

hurricane, gale, cyclone

torture v = **torment**, abuse, persecute, afflict, scourge ≠ **comfort** ♦ n = **ill-treatment**, abuse, torment, persecution, maltreatment

toss v = **throw**, pitch, hurl, fling, launch; rock ♦ n = **throw**, pitch, lob (Inf)

tot¹ n = **infant**, child, baby, toddler, mite; = **measure**, shot (Inf), finger, nip, slug

total n = **sum**, entirety, grand total, whole, aggregate ≠ **part** ♦ adj = **complete**, absolute, utter, whole, entire ≠ **partial** ♦ v

= **amount to**, make, come to, reach, equal; = **add up**, work out, compute, reckon, tot up ≠ **subtract**

touch v = **feel**, handle, finger, stroke, brush; = **come into contact**, meet, contact, border, graze; = **affect**, influence, inspire, impress; = **consume**, take, drink, eat, partake of; = **move**, stir, disturb ♦ n = **contact**, push, stroke, brush, press; = **feeling**, handling, physical contact; = **bit**, spot, trace, drop, dash; = **style**, method, technique, way, manner; **touch and go** = **risky**, close, near,

difficult. 5 needing effort to chew.
6 violent. ♦ n 7 *Inf* rough, violent
person. **toughen** v

toupee n wig.

tour 🛈 n 1 travelling round. 2
journey to one place after another.
♦ v 3 make tour. **tourism** n
tourist n

tournament 🛈 n competition,
contest usu. with several stages.

tourniquet n bandage, surgical
instrument to stop bleeding.

tousled adj ruffled.

tout v 1 solicit custom. ♦ n 2
person who sells tickets at inflated
prices.

tow 🛈 v 1 drag along behind, esp.
at end of rope. ♦ n 2 towing or
being towed. **towpath** n path
beside canal or river.

towards 🛈, **toward** prep 1 in
direction of. 2 with regard to. 3 as
contribution to.

towel n cloth for wiping off
moisture after washing.

tower 🛈 n 1 tall strong structure,
esp. part of church etc. 2 fortress.
♦ v 3 stand very high. 4 loom
(over).

town n collection of dwellings etc.
larger than village and smaller
than city. **township** n small town.

toxic 🛈 adj 1 poisonous. 2 due to
poison. **toxicity** n strength of a
poison. **toxin** n poison.

toy 🛈 n 1 something designed to
be played with. ♦ adj 2 very small.
♦ v 3 trifle. **toy boy** much younger
lover of older woman.

toy-toy S Afr ♦ n 1 dance of
political protest. ♦ v 2 perform this
dance.

trace 🛈 n 1 track left by anything.
2 indication. 3 minute quantity. ♦
v 4 follow course of. 5 find out. 6
make plan of. 7 draw or copy
exactly. **tracing paper** transparent
paper placed over drawing, map
etc. to enable exact copy to be
taken.

————— THESAURUS —————

critical, precarious

tough adj = **hardy**, strong,
seasoned, strapping, vigorous;
= **violent**, rough, ruthless,
pugnacious, hard–bitten; = **strict**,
severe, stern, hard, firm ≠ **lenient**;
= **hard**, difficult, troublesome,
uphill, strenuous ♦ n = **ruffian**,
bully, thug, hooligan, bruiser (*Inf*)

tour n = **journey**, expedition,
excursion, trip, outing ♦ v = **visit**,
explore, go round, inspect, walk
round

tournament n = **competition**,
meeting, event, series, contest

tow v = **drag**, draw, pull, haul,
tug

towards prep = **in the direction
of**, to, for, on the way to, en route
for; = **regarding**, about,
concerning, respecting, in relation
to

tower n = **column**, pillar, turret,
belfry, steeple

toxic adj = **poisonous**, deadly,
lethal, harmful, pernicious
≠ **harmless**

toy n = **plaything**, game, doll

trace v = **find**, track (down),
discover, detect, unearth;

trachea n, pl **tracheae** windpipe.

track ● n 1 mark left by passage of anything. 2 path. 3 rough road. 4 course. 5 railway line. 6 jointed metal band as on tank etc. 7 separate song, piece on record. ♦ v 8 follow trail or path of. **track events** athletic sports held on running track. **track record** past accomplishments. **tracksuit** n loose-fitting suit worn by athletes etc.

tract¹ ● n wide expanse, area.

tract² ● n pamphlet, esp. religious one.

traction n action of pulling.

tractor n motor vehicle for hauling, pulling etc.

trade ● n 1 commerce, business. 2 skilled craft. 3 exchange. ♦ v 4 engage in trade. **trader** n **trade–in** n used article given in part payment for new. **trademark**, **trade name** n distinctive legal mark on maker's goods. **trade–off** n exchange made as compromise.

tradesman n 1 dealer. 2 skilled worker. **trade union** society of workers for protection of their interests.

tradition ● n 1 unwritten body of beliefs, facts etc. handed down from generation to generation. 2 custom, practice of long standing. **traditional** adj

traffic ● n 1 vehicles passing to and fro in street, town etc. 2 (illicit) trade. ♦ v 3 trade. **traffic lights** set of coloured lights at road junctions etc.

tragedy ● n, pl **–dies** 1 sad event. 2 dramatic, literary work dealing with serious, sad topic. **tragedian** n actor in, writer of tragedies. **tragic** adj 1 of, in manner of tragedy. 2 disastrous. 3 appalling.

trail ● v 1 drag behind one. 2 lag behind. 3 track, pursue. ♦ n 4

———————— THESAURUS ————————

= **outline**, sketch, draw; = **copy**, map, draft, outline, sketch ♦ n = **bit**, drop, touch, shadow, suggestion; = **remnant**, sign, record, mark, evidence; = **track**, trail, footstep, path, footprint

track n = **path**, way, road, route, trail; = **course**, line, path, orbit, trajectory; = **line**, tramline, marks, traces ♦ v = **follow**, pursue, chase, trace, tail (Inf)

tract¹ n = **area**, region, district, stretch, territory

tract² n = **treatise**, essay, booklet, pamphlet, dissertation

trade n = **commerce**, business, transactions, dealing, exchange; = **job**, employment, business, craft, profession ♦ v = **deal**, do business, traffic, truck, bargain; = **exchange**, switch, swap, barter

tradition n institution; = **established practice**, custom, convention, habit, ritual

traffic n = **transport**, vehicles, transportation, freight; = **trade**, commerce, business, exchange, truck ♦ v = **trade**, deal, exchange, bargain, do business

tragedy n = **disaster**, catastrophe, misfortune, adversity, calamity ≠ **fortune**

track or trace. **5** rough path.
trailer *n* vehicle towed by another vehicle.
train ❶ *v* **1** educate, instruct, cause to grow in particular way. **2** follow course of training. **3** aim (gun etc.). ◆ *n* **4** line of railway vehicles joined to locomotive. **5** succession, esp. of thoughts etc. **6** procession. **7** trailing part of dress.
trainee *n* one training to be skilled worker. **trainer** *n* **training** *n*
traipse *v* walk wearily.
trait ❶ *n* characteristic feature.
traitor ❶ *n* one who is guilty of treason. **traitorous** *adj*
trajectory *n*, *pl* **-ries** line of flight.
tram *n* vehicle running on rails laid on roadway.
tramp ❶ *v* **1** travel on foot. **2** walk heavily. ◆ *n* **3** (homeless) person who travels about on foot. **4** walk. **5** cargo ship without fixed route.
trample ❶ *v* tread on and crush under foot.
trampoline *n* tough canvas sheet

stretched horizontally with elastic cords etc. to frame.
trance ❶ *n* **1** unconscious or dazed state. **2** state of ecstasy or total absorption.
tranche *n* portion.
tranquil *adj* **1** calm, quiet. **2** serene. **tranquillity** *n* **tranquillize** *v* make calm. **tranquillizer** *n* drug which induces calm state.
trans- *comb. form* across, through, beyond.
transact *v* **1** carry through. **2** negotiate. **transaction** *n* **1** performing of business. **2** single sale or purchase. ◆ *pl* **3** proceedings.
transcend ❶ *v* **1** rise above. **2** surpass. **transcendence** *n*
transcendent *adj* **transcendental** *adj* **1** surpassing experience. **2** supernatural. **3** abstruse.
transcendentalism *n*
transcribe *v* **1** copy out. **2** record for later broadcast. **transcript** *n* copy.

————— THESAURUS —————

trail *n* = **path**, track, route, way, course; = **tracks**, path, marks, wake, trace ◆ *v* = **follow**, track, chase, pursue, dog; = **drag**, draw, pull, sweep, haul; = **lag**, follow, drift, wander, linger
train *v* = **instruct**, school, prepare, coach, teach; = **exercise**, prepare, work out, practise, do exercise; = **aim**, point, level, position, direct ◆ *n* = **sequence**, series, chain, string, set
trait *n* = **characteristic**, feature, quality, attribute, quirk

traitor *n* = **betrayer**, deserter, turncoat, renegade, defector ≠ **loyalist**
tramp *v* = **trudge**, stump, toil, plod, traipse (*Inf*); = **hike**, walk, trek, roam, march ◆ *n* = **vagrant**, derelict, drifter, down-and-out; = **tread**, stamp, footstep, footfall; = **hike**, march, trek, ramble, slog
trample *v often with* **on** = **stamp**, crush, squash, tread, flatten
trance *n* = **daze**, dream, abstraction, rapture, reverie
transcend *v* = **surpass**, exceed,

transfer ❶ v **–ferring, –ferred 1**
move, send from one person,
place etc. to another. ◆ n **2**
removal of person or thing from
one place to another. **transference**
n transfer.

transfigure v alter appearance of.

transfix v **1** astound, stun. **2**
pierce through.

transform ❶ v change shape,
character of. **transformation** n
transformer n Electricity apparatus
for changing voltage.

transgress v **1** break (law). **2** sin.
transgression n

transient adj fleeting, not
permanent.

transistor n **1** Electronics small,
semiconducting device used to
amplify electric currents. **2**
portable radio using transistors.

transit ❶ n passage, crossing.
transition n change from one state
to another. **transitive** adj (of verb)
requiring direct object. **transitory**
adj not lasting long.

translate ❶ v **1** turn from one
language into another. **2** interpret.
translation n **translator** n

translucent adj letting light pass

through, semitransparent.

transmit ❶ v **–mitting, –mitted 1**
send, cause to pass to another
place, person etc. **2** send out
(signals) by means of radio waves.
transmission n **1** transmitting. **2**
gears by which power is
communicated from engine to
road wheels.

transmute v change in form,
properties or nature.

transparent ❶ adj **1** letting light
pass without distortion. **2** that can
be seen through. **transparency** n **1**
quality of being transparent. **2**
photographic slide.

transpire v **1** become known. **2**
Inf happen. **3** (of plants) give off
water vapour through leaves.

transplant ❶ v **1** move and plant
again in another place. **2** transfer
organ surgically. ◆ n **3** surgical
transplanting of organ.

transport ❶ v **1** convey from one
place to another. **2** deport. ◆ n **3**
system of conveyance. **4** vehicle
used for this. **transportation** n **1**
transporting. **2** Hist deportation to
penal colony.

transpose v **1** change order of. **2**

———— THESAURUS ————

go beyond, rise above, eclipse
transfer v = **move**, transport,
shift, relocate, transpose ◆ n
= **transference**, move, handover,
change, shift
transform v = **change**, convert,
alter, transmute, remodel
transit n = **movement**, transfer,
transport, passage, crossing
translate v = **render**, put, change,

convert, interpret
transmit v = **broadcast**, televise,
relay, air, radio; = **pass on**, carry,
spread, send, bear
transparent adj = **clear**, sheer,
see–through, lucid, translucent
≠ **opaque**; = **obvious**, plain,
patent, evident, explicit
≠ **uncertain**
transplant v = **implant**, transfer,

put music into different key.

transverse *adj* 1 lying across. 2 at right angles.

transvestite *n* person who wears clothes of opposite sex.

trap ① *n* 1 device for catching game etc. 2 anything planned to deceive, betray etc. 3 arrangement of pipes to prevent escape of gas. 4 movable opening. ◆ *v* 5 catch. 6 trick. **trapper** *n* one who traps animals for their fur.

trapdoor *n* door in floor or roof.

trapeze *n* horizontal bar suspended from two ropes for acrobatics etc.

trapezium *n*, *pl* **–ziums**, **–zia** four–sided figure with two parallel sides of unequal length.

trappings *pl n* equipment, ornaments.

trash ① *n* 1 rubbish. 2 nonsense. 3 US and Canad anything worthless.

trauma ① *n* 1 emotional shock. 2 injury, wound. **traumatic** *adj* **traumatize** *v*

travail *v/n* labour, toil.

travel ① *v* **–elling**, **–elled** 1 go, move from one place to another. ◆ *n* 2 act of travelling. ◆ *pl* 3 (account of) travelling. **traveller** *n* **travelogue** *n* film etc. about travels.

traverse *v* 1 cross, go through or over. ◆ *n* 2 traversing. 3 path across.

travesty *n*, *pl* **–ties** 1 grotesque imitation. ◆ *v* 2 make, be a travesty of.

trawl *v* fish at deep levels with net dragged behind boat. **trawler** *n* trawling boat.

tray *n* flat board, usu. with rim, for carrying things.

treachery *n*, *pl* **–eries** deceit, betrayal. **treacherous** *adj* 1 disloyal. 2 unsafe.

treacle *n* thick syrup produced when sugar is refined.

tread ① *v* **treading**, **trod**, **trodden** 1 walk. 2 trample (on). ◆ *n* 3 treading. 4 fashion of walking. 5 upper fashion of step. 6 part of tyre which makes contact with ground. **treadmill** *n* dreary routine.

——————— THESAURUS ———————

graft

transport *n* = **vehicle**, transportation, conveyance; = **transference**, carrying, delivery, distribution, transportation; *often plural* = **ecstasy**, delight, heaven, bliss, euphoria ≠ despondency ◆ *v* = **convey**, take, move, bring, send; = **enrapture**, move, delight, entrance, enchant; = (*Hist*) **exile**, banish, deport

trap *n* = **snare**, net, gin, pitfall,

noose; = **ambush**, set-up (*Inf*) ◆ *v* = **catch**, snare, ensnare, entrap, take; = **trick**, fool, cheat, lure, seduce

trash *n* = **nonsense**, rubbish, rot, drivel, twaddle ≠ sense; = (*Chiefly US & Canad*) **litter**, refuse, waste, rubbish, junk (*Inf*)

trauma *n* = **shock**, suffering, pain, torture, ordeal; = **injury**, damage, hurt, wound, agony

travel *v* = **go**, journey, move,

treadle n lever worked by foot to turn wheel.

treason ❶ n 1 violation by subject of allegiance to sovereign or state. 2 treachery.

treasure ❶ n 1 riches. 2 valued person or thing. ◆ v 3 prize, cherish. **treasurer** n official in charge of funds. **treasury** n 1 place for treasure. 2 government department in charge of finance. **treasure-trove** n treasure found with no evidence of ownership.

treat ❶ n 1 pleasure, entertainment given. ◆ v 2 deal with, act towards. 3 give medical treatment to. 4 provide with treat. **treatment** n 1 method of counteracting disease. 2 act or mode of treating.

treatise n formal essay.

treaty ❶ n, pl -ties signed contract between states etc.

treble adj 1 threefold. 2 Mus high-pitched. ◆ n 3 soprano voice. ◆ v 4 increase threefold.

tree n large perennial plant with woody trunk.

trek ❶ n 1 long difficult journey. ◆ v 2 make trek.

trellis n lattice or grating of light bars.

tremble ❶ v 1 quiver, shake. 2 feel fear. ◆ n 3 involuntary shaking.

tremendous ❶ adj 1 vast, immense. 2 Inf exciting. 3 Inf excellent.

tremor n 1 quiver. 2 shaking.

tremulous adj quivering slightly.

trench ❶ n long narrow ditch. **trench coat** double-breasted waterproof coat.

trenchant adj cutting, incisive.

trend ❶ n 1 direction, tendency. 2 fashion. **trendy** adj Inf consciously

—————— THESAURUS ——————

tour, progress

tread v = **step**, walk, march, pace, stamp ◆ n = **step**, walk, pace, stride, footstep

treason n = **disloyalty**, mutiny, treachery, duplicity, sedition ≠ **loyalty**

treasure n = **riches**, money, gold, fortune, wealth; = (Inf) **angel**, darling, jewel, gem, paragon ◆ v = **prize**, value, esteem, adore, cherish

treat v = **behave towards**, deal with, handle, act towards, use; = **take care of**, minister to, attend to, give medical treatment to, doctor (Inf); = **provide**, stand (Inf),

entertain, lay on, regale ◆ n = **entertainment**, party, surprise, gift, celebration; = **pleasure**, delight, joy, thrill, satisfaction

treaty n = **agreement**, pact, contract, alliance, convention

trek v = **journey**, march, hike, tramp, rove ◆ n = **slog**, tramp

tremble v = **shake**, shiver, quake, shudder, quiver ◆ n = **shake**, shiver, quake, shudder, wobble

tremendous adj = **huge**, great, enormous, terrific, formidable ≠ **tiny**; = **excellent**, great, wonderful, brilliant, amazing ≠ **terrible**

trench n = **ditch**, channel, drain,

fashionable.

trepidation n fear, anxiety.

trespass v 1 intrude on property etc. of another. ♦ n 2 wrongful entering on another's land. 3 wrongdoing. **trespasser** n

trestle n board fixed on pairs of spreading legs.

trevally n, pl **-lies** Aust & NZ any of various food and game fishes.

trews pl n close–fitting tartan trousers.

tri– comb. form three.

trial ❶ n 1 test, examination. 2 Law investigation of case before judge. 3 thing, person that strains endurance or patience.

triangle n figure with three angles. **triangular** adj

tribe ❶ n 1 race. 2 subdivision of race of people. **tribal** adj

tribulation n trouble, affliction.

tribunal ❶ n 1 lawcourt. 2 body appointed to inquire into specific matter.

tributary n, pl **-taries** stream

flowing into another.

tribute ❶ n 1 sign of honour. 2 tax paid by one state to another.

trice n moment, instant.

trick ❶ n 1 deception. 2 prank. 3 feat of skill or cunning. 4 knack. 5 cards played in one round. ♦ v 6 deceive, cheat. **trickery** n **trickster** n **tricky** adj difficult.

trickle ❶ v 1 (cause to) run, flow, move in thin stream or drops. ♦ n 2 trickling flow.

tricolour n three–coloured striped flag.

tricycle n three–wheeled cycle.

trident n three–pronged spear.

trifle ❶ n 1 insignificant thing or matter. 2 small amount. 3 pudding of sponge cake, whipped cream etc. ♦ v 4 toy (with).

trigger ❶ n 1 catch which releases spring, esp. to fire gun. ♦ v 2 set in action etc. **trigger-happy** adj tending to be irresponsible.

trigonometry n branch of

——— THESAURUS ———

gutter, trough

trend n = **tendency**, swing, drift, inclination, current; = **fashion**, craze, fad (Inf), mode, thing

trial n = (Law) **hearing**, case, court case, inquiry, tribunal; = **test**, experiment, evaluation, audition, dry run (Inf); = **hardship**, suffering, trouble, distress, ordeal

tribe n = **race**, people, family, clan

tribunal n = **hearing**, court, trial

tribute n = **accolade**, testimonial, eulogy, recognition, compliment ≠ **criticism**

trick n = **joke**, stunt, spoof (Inf), prank, practical joke; = **deception**, trap, fraud, manoeuvre, ploy; = **sleight of hand**, stunt, legerdemain; = **secret**, skill, knack, hang (Inf), technique; = **mannerism**, habit, characteristic, trait, quirk ♦ v = **deceive**, trap, take someone in (Inf), fool, cheat

trickle v = **dribble**, run, drop, stream, drip ♦ n = **dribble**, drip, seepage, thin stream

trifle n = **knick-knack**, toy, plaything, bauble, bagatelle

mathematics dealing with relations of sides and angles of triangles.

trilby n, pl **-bies** man's soft felt hat.

trill v/n (sing, play with) rapid alternation between two close notes.

trillion n **1** one million million, 10^{12}. **2** Obs one million million million, 10^{18}.

trilogy n, pl **-gies** series of three related (literary) works.

trim ❶ adj **trimmer**, **trimmest 1** neat, smart. **2** slender. **3** in good order. ◆ v **4** shorten slightly by cutting. **5** prune. **6** decorate. **7** adjust. ◆ n **8** decoration. **9** order, state of being trim. **trimming** n (oft. pl) decoration, addition.

trinitrotoluene n powerful explosive.

trinity n, pl **-ties 1** the state of being threefold **2** (with cap.) state of God as three persons, Father, Son and Holy Spirit.

trinket n small ornament.

trio ❶ n, pl **trios 1** group of three. **2** music for three parts.

trip ❶ n **1** (short) journey for pleasure. **2** stumble. **3** Inf hallucinatory experience caused by drug. ◆ v **4** (cause to) stumble. **5** (cause to) make mistake. **6** run lightly.

tripe n **1** stomach of cow as food. **2** Inf nonsense.

triple ❶ adj **1** threefold. ◆ v **2** treble. **triplet** n one of three offspring born at one birth.

triplicate adj **1** threefold. ◆ n **2** state of being triplicate. **3** one of set of three copies.

tripod n stool, stand etc. with three feet.

trite adj hackneyed, banal.

triumph ❶ n **1** great success. **2** victory. **3** exultation. ◆ v **4** achieve great success or victory. **5** rejoice over victory. **triumphal** adj **triumphant** adj

troll n giant or dwarf in

————— THESAURUS —————

trigger v = **bring about**, start, cause, produce, generate ≠ **prevent**

trim adj = **neat**, smart, tidy, spruce, dapper ≠ **untidy**; = **slender**, fit, slim, sleek, streamlined ◆ v = **cut**, crop, clip, shave, tidy; = **decorate**, dress, array, adorn, ornament ◆ n = **decoration**, edging, border, piping, trimming; = **condition**, health, shape (Inf), fitness, wellness; = **cut**, crop, clipping, shave, pruning

trio n = **threesome**, trinity, trilogy, triad, triumvirate

trip n = **journey**, outing, excursion, day out, run; = **stumble**, fall, slip, misstep ◆ v = **stumble**, fall, fall over, slip, tumble; = **skip**, dance, hop, gambol

triple adj = **treble**, three times ◆ v = **treble**, increase threefold

triumph n = **success**, victory, accomplishment, achievement, coup ≠ **failure**; = **joy**, pride, happiness, rejoicing, elation ◆ v

T

Scandinavian mythology and folklore.

trolley n **1** small wheeled table for food and drink. **2** wheeled cart for moving goods etc. **3** US tram.

trollop n promiscuous woman.

trombone n deep–toned brass instrument. **trombonist** n

troop ❶ n **1** group of persons. ◆ pl **2** soldiers. ◆ v **3** move in troop.

trooper n cavalry soldier.

trophy ❶ n, pl **–phies** prize, award.

tropic n **1** either of two lines of latitude N and S of equator. ◆ pl **2** area of earth's surface between these lines. **tropical** adj **1** pert. to, within tropics. **2** (of climate) very hot.

trot ❶ v **trotting, trotted 1** (of horse) move at medium pace. **2** (of person) run easily with short strides. ◆ n **3** trotting, jog. **trotter** n **1** horse trained to trot in race. **2** foot of pig etc.

troubadour n medieval travelling poet and singer.

trouble ❶ n **1** state or cause of mental distress, pain, inconvenience etc. **2** care. ◆ v **3** be trouble to. **4** be inconvenienced, be agitated. **5** take pains.

troublesome adj **troubleshooter** n person employed to deal with problems.

trough ❶ n **1** long open vessel, esp. for animals' food or water. **2** hollow between waves.

trounce v beat thoroughly, thrash.

troupe n company of performers. **trouper** n

trousers pl n garment covering legs.

trousseau n, pl **–seaux, –seaus** bride's outfit of clothing.

trout n freshwater fish.

trowel n small tool like spade.

truant n one absent without leave. **truancy** n

truce ❶ n temporary cessation of fighting.

———————— THESAURUS ————————

often with **over** = succeed, win, overcome, prevail, prosper ≠ **fail**; = **rejoice**, celebrate, glory, revel, gloat

troop n = **group**, company, team, body, unit ◆ v = **flock**, march, stream, swarm, throng

trophy n = **prize**, cup, award, laurels; = **souvenir**, spoils, relic, memento, booty

trot v = **run**, jog, scamper, lope, canter ◆ n = **run**, jog, lope, canter

trouble n = **bother**, problems, concern, worry, stress; usually

plural = **distress**, problem, worry, pain, anxiety ≠ **pleasure**; = **ailment**, disease, failure, complaint, illness; = **disorder**, fighting, conflict, bother, unrest ≠ **peace** ◆ v = **bother**, worry, upset, disturb, distress ≠ **please**; = **afflict**, hurt, bother, cause discomfort to, pain;

= **inconvenience**, disturb, burden, put out, impose upon ≠ **relieve**

trough n = **manger**, water trough

truce n = **ceasefire**, peace, moratorium, respite, lull

truck[1] *n* wheeled (motor) vehicle for moving goods.

truck[2] *n* dealing, esp. in **have no truck with.**

trucker *n US and Canad* truck driver.

truculent *adj* aggressive, defiant.

trudge *v* 1 walk laboriously. ♦ *n* 2 tiring walk.

true ⚊ *adj* **truer, truest** 1 in accordance with facts. 2 faithful. 3 correct. 4 genuine. **truism** *n* self-evident truth. **truly** *adv* **truth** *n* 1 state of being true. 2 something that is true. **truthful** *adj* 1 accustomed to speak the truth. 2 accurate.

truffle *n* 1 edible underground fungus. 2 sweet flavoured with chocolate.

trump *n* 1 card of suit ranking above others. ♦ *v* 2 play trump. **trump up** invent, concoct.

trumpet *n* 1 metal wind instrument like horn. ♦ *v* 2 blow trumpet. 3 make sound like one. 4 proclaim. **trumpeter** *n*

truncate *v* cut short.

truncheon *n* short thick club.

trundle *v* move heavily, as on

small wheels.

trunk ⚊ *n* 1 main stem of tree. 2 person's body excluding head and limbs. 3 box for clothes etc. 4 elephant's snout. ♦ *pl* 5 man's swimming costume. **trunk call** long-distance telephone call. **trunk road** main road.

truss *v* 1 fasten up, tie up. ♦ *n* 2 support. 3 medical supporting device.

trust ⚊ *n* 1 confidence. 2 firm belief. 3 reliance. 4 combination of business firms. 5 care. 6 property held for another. ♦ *v* 7 rely on. 8 believe in. 9 expect, hope. 10 consign for care. **trustee** *n* one legally holding property for another. **trustful, trusting** *adj* **trustworthy** *adj* **trusty** *adj*

try ⚊ *v* **trying, tried** 1 attempt. 2 test, sample. 3 afflict. 4 examine in court of law. ♦ *n* 5 attempt, effort. 6 *Rugby* score gained by touching ball down over opponent's goal line. **tried** *adj* proved. **trying** *adj* troublesome.

tryst *n* arrangement to meet, esp. secretly.

T-shirt *n* informal (short-sleeved)

——————————— THESAURUS ———————————

true *adj* = **correct**, right, accurate, precise, factual ≠ **false**; = **faithful**, loyal, devoted, dedicated, steady ≠ **unfaithful**; = **exact**, perfect, accurate, precise, spot-on (*Brit inf*) ≠ **inaccurate**

trunk *n* = **stem**, stalk, bole; = **chest**, case, box, crate, coffer; = **body**, torso

trust *v* = **believe in**, have faith in,

depend on, count on, bank on ≠ **distrust**; = **entrust**, commit, assign, confide, consign; = **expect**, hope, suppose, assume, presume ♦ *n* = **confidence**, credit, belief, faith, expectation ≠ **distrust**

try *v* = **attempt**, seek, aim, strive, struggle; = **experiment with**, try out, put to the test, test, taste ♦ *n* = **attempt**, go (*Inf*), shot (*Inf*),

sweater.

tub n **1** open wooden vessel like bottom half of barrel. **2** small round container. **3** bath. **tubby** adj short and fat.

tuba n valved brass wind instrument of low pitch.

tube n **1** long, narrow hollow cylinder. **2** flexible cylinder with cap to hold pastes. **3** underground electric railway. **tubular** adj

tuber n fleshy underground stem of some plants.

tuberculosis n communicable disease, esp. of lung. **tubercular** adj **tuberculin** n bacillus used to treat tuberculosis.

tuck ⊕ v **1** push, fold into small space. **2** gather, stitch in folds. ♦ n **3** stitched fold. **4** Inf food.

tucker n Aust & NZ informal food.

Tuesday n third day of the week.

tuft n bunch of feathers etc.

tug ⊕ v tugging, tugged **1** pull hard or violently. ♦ n **2** violent pull. **3** ship used to tow other vessels. **tug–of–war** n contest in which two teams pull against one another on rope.

tuition ⊕ n teaching, esp. private.

tulip n plant with bright cup–shaped flowers.

tumble ⊕ v **1** (cause to) fall or roll, twist etc. **2** rumple. ♦ n **3** fall. **tumbler** n **1** stemless drinking glass. **2** acrobat. **tumbledown** adj dilapidated. **tumble dryer** machine that dries laundry by rotating it in warm air.

tummy n, pl –mies Inf stomach.

tumour ⊕ n abnormal growth in or on body.

tumult n violent uproar, commotion. **tumultuous** adj

tuna n large marine food and game fish.

tundra n vast treeless zone between ice cap and timber line.

tune ⊕ n **1** melody. **2** quality of being in pitch. **3** adjustment of musical instrument. ♦ v **4** put in tune. **5** adjust machine to obtain efficient running. **6** adjust radio to receive broadcast. **tuneful** adj **tuner** n

tungsten n greyish–white metal.

tunic n **1** close–fitting jacket forming part of uniform. **2** loose hip–length garment.

tunnel ⊕ n **1** underground passage, esp. as track for railway line. ♦ v **2** make tunnel (through).

———— THESAURUS ————

effort, crack (Inf)

tuck v = **push**, stick, stuff, slip, ease ♦ n = (Brit inf) **food**, grub (Sl), nosh (Sl); = **fold**, gather, pleat, pinch

tug v = **pull**, pluck, jerk, yank, wrench ♦ n = **pull**, jerk, yank

tuition n = **training**, schooling, education, teaching, lessons

tumble v = **fall**, drop, topple, plummet, stumble ♦ n = **fall**, drop, trip, plunge, spill

tumour n = **growth**, cancer, swelling, lump, carcinoma (Pathol)

tune n = **melody**, air, song, theme, strain(s); = **harmony**, pitch, euphony ♦ v = **tune up**, adjust

tunnel n = **passage**, underpass,

tupik, tupek n Canad (esp. in the Arctic) a tent of animal skins, a traditional type of Inuit dwelling.

turban n headdress made by coiling length of cloth round head.

turbine n rotary engine driven by steam, gas, water or air playing on blades.

turbot n large flatfish.

tureen n serving dish for soup.

turf ⊕ n, pl **turfs**, **turves** 1 short grass with earth bound to it by matted roots. ♦ v 2 lay with turf. **turf accountant** bookmaker. **turf out** Inf throw out.

turgid adj 1 swollen, inflated. 2 bombastic.

turkey n large bird reared for food.

Turkish adj of Turkey. **Turkish bath** steam bath. **Turkish delight** jelly–like sweet coated with icing sugar.

turmoil ⊕ n confusion, commotion.

turn ⊕ v 1 move around, rotate. 2 change, alter position or direction (of) 3 change in nature. 4 make, shape on lathe. ♦ n 5 turning. 6 inclination etc. 7 period. 8 short

walk. 9 (part of) rotation. 10 performance. **turning** n road, path leading off main rout. **turncoat** n person who deserts party, cause etc. to join another. **turn down** 1 reduce volume or brightness of. 2 refuse. **turnout** n number of people appearing for some purpose. **turnover** n 1 total sales made by business. 2 rate at which staff leave and are replaced. **turnstile** n revolving gate for controlling admission of people. **turntable** n revolving platform. **turn up** v appear.

turnip n plant with edible root.

turpentine n oil from certain trees used in paints etc. **turps** n Inf turpentine.

turquoise n 1 bluish–green precious stone. 2 this colour.

turret n 1 small tower. 2 revolving armoured tower on tank etc.

turtle n sea tortoise.

tusk n long pointed side tooth of elephant etc.

tussle n/v fight, wrestle, struggle.

tutor ⊕ n 1 one teaching individuals or small groups. ♦ v 2 teach. **tutorial** n period of instruction.

passageway, subway, channel ♦ v = **dig**, burrow, mine, bore, drill

turf n = **grass**, sward

turmoil n = **confusion**, disorder, chaos, upheaval, disarray ≠ **peace**

turn v = **change course**, swing round, wheel round, veer, move; = **rotate**, spin, go round (and round), revolve, roll; = **change**,

transform, shape, convert, alter; = **shape**, form, fashion, cast, frame; = **go bad**, go off (Brit inf), curdle; spoil, sour ♦ n = **rotation**, cycle, circle, revolution, spin; = **change of direction**, shift, departure, deviation; = **direction**, course, tack, tendency, drift

tutor n = **teacher**, coach,

T

tutu *n* skirt worn by ballerinas.

tuxedo *n* US and Canad dinner jacket.

TV television.

twang *n* **1** vibrating metallic sound. **2** nasal speech. ♦ *v* **3** (cause to) make such sounds.

tweak *v* **1** pinch and twist or pull. ♦ *n* **2** tweaking.

twee *adj Inf* oversentimental.

tweed *n* rough-surfaced cloth used for clothing.

tweet *n/v* chirp.

tweezers *pl n* small forceps or tongs.

twelve *adj/n* two more than ten. **twelfth** *adj* ordinal number.

twenty *adj/n* twice ten. **twentieth** *adj* ordinal number.

twerp *n Inf* stupid person.

twice *adv* two times.

twiddle *v* **1** fiddle. **2** twist.

twig ⓣ *n* small branch, shoot.

twilight ⓣ *n* soft light after sunset.

twill *n* fabric with surface of parallel ridges.

twin ⓣ *n* **1** one of two children born together. ♦ *v* **2** pair, be paired.

twine *v* **1** twist, coil round. ♦ *n* **2** string, cord.

twinge *n* **1** momentary sharp pain. **2** qualm.

twinkle ⓣ *v* **1** shine with dancing light, sparkle. ♦ *n* **2** twinkling. **3** flash.

twirl *v* **1** turn or twist round quickly. **2** whirl. **3** twiddle.

twist ⓣ *v* **1** make, become spiral, by turning with one end fast. **2** distort, change. **3** wind. ♦ *n* **4** twisting.

twit *n* **1** Inf foolish person. ♦ *v* **2** taunt.

twitch ⓣ *v* **1** give momentary sharp pull or jerk (to). ♦ *n* **2** such pull. **3** spasmodic jerk.

twitter *v* **1** (of birds) utter tremulous sounds. ♦ *n* **2** tremulous sound.

two *n/adj* one more than one.

two-faced *adj* deceitful.

tycoon ⓣ *n* powerful, influential

─── THESAURUS ───

instructor, educator, guide ♦ *v* = **teach**, educate, school, train, coach

twig *n* = **branch**, stick, sprig, shoot, spray

twilight *n* = **dusk**, evening, sunset, early evening, nightfall ≠ **dawn**

twin *n* = **double**, counterpart, mate, match, fellow ♦ *v* = **pair**, match, join, couple, link

twinkle *v* = **sparkle**, flash, shine, glitter, gleam ♦ *n* = **sparkle**, flash, spark, gleam, flicker

twist *v* = **coil**, curl, wind, wrap, screw; = **distort**, screw up, contort, mangle ≠ **straighten** ♦ *n* = **surprise**, change, turn, development, revelation; = **development**, emphasis, variation, slant; = **wind**, turn, spin, swivel, twirl; = **curve**, turn, bend, loop, arc

twitch *v* = **jerk**, flutter, jump, squirm; = **pull (at)**, tug (at), pluck (at), yank (at) ♦ *n* = **jerk**, tic,

businessman.

type ❶ n1 class. 2 sort. 3 model. 4 pattern. 5 characteristic build. 6 specimen. 7 block bearing letter used for printing. ♦ v8 print with typewriter. **typecast** v repeatedly cast (actor, actress) in similar roles. **typescript** n typewritten document. **typewriter** n keyed writing machine. **typist** n one who operates typewriter.

typhoid fever acute infectious disease, esp. of intestines.

typhoon n violent tropical storm.

typhus n infectious feverish disease.

typical ❶ adj1 true to type. 2 characteristic. **typically** adv

typography n1 art of printing. 2 style of printing.

tyrant n oppressive or cruel ruler. **tyrannical** adj1 despotic. 2 ruthless. **tyrannize** v exert ruthless or tyrannical authority (over). **tyrannous** adj **tyranny** n despotism.

tyre n (inflated) rubber ring over rim of wheel of road vehicle.

——————— THESAURUS ———————

spasm, jump, flutter

tycoon n = **magnate**, capitalist, baron, industrialist, financier

type n = **kind**, sort, class, variety,

group

typical adj = **archetypal**, standard, model, normal, stock ≠ unusual

U u

ubiquitous 🔊 *adj* everywhere at once.
udder *n* milk–secreting organ of cow etc.
UFO unidentified flying object.
ugly 🔊 *adj* **uglier, ugliest 1** unpleasant to see, hideous. **2** threatening.
ukulele, ukelele *n* small four–stringed guitar.
ulcer 🔊 *n* open sore on skin.
ulterior *adj* lying beneath, beyond what is revealed.
ultimate 🔊 *adj* **1** last. **2** highest. **3** fundamental. **ultimatum** *n* final terms.
ultra– *comb. form* beyond, excessively, as in *ultramodern.*
ultraviolet *adj* (of electromagnetic radiation) beyond limit of visibility at violet end of spectrum.
umbrage *n* offence, resentment.

umbrella *n* folding circular cover of nylon etc. on stick, carried in hand to protect against rain.
umpire 🔊 *n* **1** person chosen to decide question, or to enforce rules in game. ♦ *v* **2** act as umpire.
umpteen *adj Inf* very many.
un– *comb. form* indicating not, reversal of an action.
unaccountable *adj* that cannot be explained.
unanimous 🔊 *adj* in complete agreement. **unanimity** *n*
unassuming *adj* modest.
unaware 🔊 *adj* not aware.
unawares *adv* unexpectedly.
uncanny *adj* weird, mysterious.
unceremonious *adj* **1** without ceremony. **2** abrupt, rude.
uncertain 🔊 *adj* **1** not able to be known. **2** changeable. **uncertainty** *n*
uncle *n* brother of father or

THESAURUS

ubiquitous *adj* = **ever–present**, pervasive, omnipresent, everywhere, universal
ugly *adj* = **unattractive**, homely (*Chiefly US*), plain, unsightly, unlovely ≠ **beautiful**; = **unpleasant**, shocking, terrible, nasty, distasteful ≠ **pleasant**
ulcer *n* = **sore**, abscess, peptic ulcer, gumboil
ultimate *adj* = **final**, last, end; = **supreme**, highest, greatest,

paramount, superlative
umpire *n* = **referee**, judge, arbiter, arbitrator ♦ *v* = **referee**, judge, adjudicate, arbitrate
unanimous *adj* = **agreed**, united, in agreement, harmonious, like–minded ≠ **divided**
unaware *adj* = **ignorant**, unconscious, oblivious, uninformed, unknowing ≠ **aware**
uncertain *adj* = **unsure**, undecided, vague, unclear,

mother, husband of aunt.

unconscious ⊕ *adj* **1** insensible. **2** not aware. ♦ *n* **3** set of thoughts, memories etc. of which one is not normally aware.

uncouth *adj* clumsy, boorish.

unction *n* anointing. **unctuous** *adj* excessively polite.

under ⊕ *prep* **1** below, beneath. **2** included in. **3** less than. **4** subjected to. ♦ *adv* **5** in lower place or condition. ♦ *adj* **6** lower.

under- *comb. form* beneath, below, lower, as in *underground*.

underarm *adj* **1** from armpit to wrist. **2** *Sport* with hand swung below shoulder level.

undercarriage *n* **1** aircraft's landing gear. **2** framework supporting body of vehicle.

undercurrent *n* **1** current that is not apparent at surface. **2** underlying opinion, emotion.

undercut *v* charge less than (another trader).

underdog ⊕ *n* person, team unlikely to win.

undergo ⊕ *v* experience, endure, sustain.

undergraduate *n* student member of university.

underground ⊕ *adj* **1** under the ground. **2** secret. ♦ *adv* **3** secretly. ♦ *n* **4** secret but organized resistance to government in power. **5** railway system under the ground.

undergrowth *n* small trees, bushes growing beneath taller trees.

underhand *adj* secret, sly.

underlie *v* **1** lie, be placed under. **2** be the foundation, cause, or basis of.

underline ⊕ *v* **1** put line under. **2** emphasize.

underling *n* subordinate.

undermine ⊕ *v* **1** wear away base, support of. **2** weaken insidiously.

underneath *adv* **1** below. ♦ *prep* **2**

———— THESAURUS ————

dubious ≠ **sure** = doubtful, questionable, indefinite, unconfirmed, conjectural ≠ **decided**

unconscious *adj* = **senseless**, knocked out, out cold (*Inf*), out, stunned ≠ **awake**; = **unaware**, ignorant, oblivious, unknowing ≠ **aware**; = **unintentional**, unwitting, inadvertent, accidental ≠ **intentional**

under *prep* = **below**, beneath, underneath ≠ **over**; = **subordinate to**, subject to, governed by, secondary to ♦ *adv* = **below**,

down, beneath ≠ **up**

underdog *n* = **weaker party**, little fellow (*Inf*), outsider

undergo *v* = **experience**, go through, stand, suffer, bear

underground *adj* = **subterranean**, basement, lower-level, sunken, covered; = **secret**, covert, hidden, guerrilla, revolutionary

underline *v* = **emphasize**, stress, highlight, accentuate ≠ **minimize**; = **underscore**, mark

undermine *v* = **weaken**, sabotage, subvert, compromise, disable ≠ **reinforce**

U

under. ◆ adj 3 lower. ◆ n 4 lower surface.

underpants pl n man's underwear for lower part of body.

underpass n road that passes under another road or railway line.

underpin v give strength, support to.

understand ❶ v 1 know and comprehend. 2 realize. 3 infer. 4 take for granted.

understudy n 1 one prepared to take over theatrical part. ◆ v 2 act as understudy.

undertake ❶ v 1 make oneself responsible for. 2 enter upon. 3 promise. **undertaker** n one who arranges funerals. **undertaking** n

undertone ❶ n 1 dropped tone of voice. 2 underlying suggestion.

underwear ❶ n (also) garments worn next to skin.

underworld ❶ n 1 criminals and their associates. 2 Myth abode of the dead.

underwrite ❶ v 1 agree to pay. 2 accept liability in insurance policy. **underwriter** n

undo ❶ v 1 untie, unfasten. 2 reverse. 3 cause downfall of.

undulate v move up and down like waves.

unearth ❶ v 1 dig up. 2 discover.

uneasy ❶ adj 1 anxious. 2 uncomfortable.

unemployed ❶ adj having no paid employment, out of work. **unemployment** n

unexceptionable adj beyond criticism.

unfold ❶ v 1 open, spread out. 2 reveal.

ungainly adj –lier, –liest awkward, clumsy.

uni- comb. form one, as in unicycle.

unicorn n mythical horselike animal with single long horn.

uniform ❶ n 1 identifying clothes

——— THESAURUS ———

understand v = **comprehend**, get, take in, perceive, grasp (Inf); = **believe**, gather, think, see, suppose

undertake v = **agree**, promise, contract, guarantee, engage

underwear n = **underclothes**, lingerie, undies (Inf), undergarments, underthings

underworld n = **criminals**, gangsters, organized crime, gangland (Inf); = **nether world**, Hades, nether regions

underwrite v = **finance**, back, fund, guarantee, sponsor

undo v = **open**, unfasten, loose, untie, unbutton; = **reverse**, cancel, offset, neutralize, invalidate; = **ruin**, defeat, destroy, wreck, shatter

unearth v = **discover**, find, reveal, expose, uncover; = **dig up**, excavate, exhume, dredge up

uneasy adj = **anxious**, worried, troubled, nervous, disturbed ≠ **relaxed**; = **precarious**, strained, uncomfortable, tense, awkward

unemployed adj = **out of work**, redundant, laid off, jobless, idle ≠ **working**

unfold v = **reveal**, tell, present, show, disclose; = **open**, spread

worn by members of same group, e.g. soldiers, nurses etc. ♦ *adj* **2** not changing. **3** regular. **uniformity** *n*

unify ♥ *v* –**fying,** –**fied** make or become one. **unification** *n*

unilateral *adj* **1** one-sided. **2** (of contract) binding one party only.

union ♥ *n* **1** joining into one. **2** state, result of being joined. **3** federation. **4** trade union. **unionize** *v* organize (workers) into trade union.

unique ♥ *adj* **1** being only one of its kind. **2** unparalleled.

unison *n* **1** *Mus* singing etc. of same notes as others. **2** agreement.

unit ♥ *n* **1** single thing or person. **2** group or individual being part of larger whole. **3** standard quantity.

unite ♥ *v* **1** join into one. **2** associate. **3** become one. **4** combine. **unity** *n* **1** state of being

one. **2** harmony. **3** agreement.

universe ♥ *n* **1** all existing things considered as constituting systematic whole. **2** the world.

universal *adj* relating to all things or all people.

university *n, pl* –**ties** educational institution that awards degrees.

unkempt *adj* untidy.

unless *conj* if not, except.

unlike *adj* **1** dissimilar, different. ♦ *prep* **2** not typical of. **unlikely** *adj* improbable.

unravel ♥ *v* –**elling,** –**elled** undo, untangle.

unrest ♥ *n* discontent.

unruly *adj* –**lier,** –**liest** badly behaved, disorderly.

unsavoury *adj* distasteful.

unscathed *adj* not harmed.

unsightly *adj* ugly.

unthinkable ♥ *adj* **1** out of the question. **2** inconceivable. **3** unreasonable.

—————— THESAURUS ——————

out, undo, expand, unfurl

uniform *n* = **regalia**, suit, livery, colours, habit ♦ *adj* = **consistent**, unvarying, similar, even, same ≠ **varying**; = **alike**, similar, like, same, equal

unify *v* = **unite**, join, combine, merge, consolidate ≠ **divide**

union *n* = **joining**, uniting, unification, combination, coalition; = **alliance**, league, association, coalition, federation

unique *adj* = **distinct**, special, exclusive, peculiar, only; = **unparalleled**, unmatched, unequalled, matchless, without

equal

unit *n* = **entity**, whole, item, feature; = **section**, company, group, force, detail; = **measure**, quantity, measurement

unite *v* = **join**, link, combine, couple, blend ≠ **separate**; = **cooperate**, ally, join forces, band, pool ≠ **split**

universe *n* = **cosmos**, space, creation, nature, heavens

unravel *v* = **solve**, explain, work out, resolve, figure out (*Inf*); = **undo**, separate, disentangle, free, unwind

unrest *n* = **discontent**, rebellion,

until conj 1 to the time that. 2 (with a negative) before. ♦ prep 3 up to the time of.

unto prep Obs to.

untoward adj awkward, inconvenient.

unwieldy adj 1 awkward. 2 bulky.

unwind v 1 slacken, undo, unravel. 2 become relaxed.

unwitting adj 1 not knowing. 2 not intentional.

up prep 1 from lower to higher position. 2 along. ♦ adv 3 in or to higher position, source, activity etc. 4 indicating completion.

upward adj/adv **upwards** adv

upbeat adj Inf cheerful. **up-to-date** adj modern, fashionable.

upbringing 𝟏 n rearing and education of children.

update 𝟏 v bring up to date.

upfront adj Inf open, frank.

upgrade 𝟏 v 1 promote to higher position. 2 improve.

upheaval 𝟏 n sudden or violent disturbance.

uphold 𝟏 v maintain, support etc.

upholster v fit springs, coverings on chairs etc. **upholstery** n

upkeep n act, cost of keeping something in good repair.

upon prep on.

upper 𝟏 adj 1 situated above. 2 of superior quality, status etc. ♦ n 3 upper part of boot or shoe. **upper case** capital letters. **upper hand** position of control.

upright 𝟏 adj 1 erect. 2 honest, just. ♦ adv 3 vertically. ♦ n 4 thing standing upright, e.g. post in framework.

uprising 𝟏 n rebellion, revolt.

uproar 𝟏 n tumult, disturbance.

uproot v 1 pull up, as by roots. 2 displace from usual surroundings.

upset 𝟏 v 1 overturn. 2 distress. 3 disrupt. ♦ n 4 unexpected defeat. 5 confusion. ♦ adj 6 disturbed. 7 emotionally troubled.

upshot n outcome, end.

——— THESAURUS ———

protest, strife, agitation ≠ **peace**

unthinkable adj = **impossible**, out of the question, inconceivable, absurd, unreasonable; = **inconceivable**, incredible, unimaginable

upbringing n = **education**, training, breeding, rearing, raising

update v = **bring up to date**, improve, correct, renew, revise

upgrade v = **improve**, better, update, reform, add to

upheaval n = **disturbance**, revolution, disorder, turmoil, disruption

uphold v = **support**, back, defend, aid, champion

upper adj = **topmost**, top ≠ **bottom**; = **higher**, high ≠ **lower**

upright adj = **vertical**, straight, standing up, erect, perpendicular ≠ **horizontal**; = **honest**, good, principled, just, ethical ≠ **dishonourable**

uprising n = **rebellion**, rising, revolution, revolt, disturbance

uproar n = **commotion**, noise, racket, riot, turmoil

upset adj = **distressed**, shaken, disturbed, worried, troubled;

upside down ❶ 1 turned over completely. **2** *Inf* confused.
upstage *v* overshadow.
upstart *n* one suddenly raised to wealth, power etc.
uptight *adj* **1** *Inf* tense. **2** repressed.
uptown *US and Canad* ♦ *adj/adv* towards, in, or relating to some part of a town that is away from the centre. ♦ *n* such a part of a town, esp. a residential part.
uranium *n* white radioactive metallic element.
urban ❶ *adj* relating to town or city.
urbane *adj* elegant, sophisticated.
urchin *n* mischievous, unkempt child.
urge ❶ *v* **1** exhort earnestly. **2** entreat. **3** drive on. ♦ *n* **4** strong desire. **urgency** *n* **urgent** *adj* needing attention at once.

urine *n* fluid excreted by kidneys to bladder and passed as waste from body. **urinal** *n* place for urinating. **urinate** *v* discharge urine.
urn *n* **1** vessel like vase. **2** large container with tap.
us *pron* object of WE.
use ❶ *v* **1** employ. **2** exercise. **3** exploit. **4** consume. ♦ *n* **5** employment. **6** need to employ. **7** serviceableness. **8** profit. **9** habit.
usable *adj* fit for use. **usage** *n* **1** act of using. **2** custom. **used** *adj* **1** second–hand. **2** accustomed.
useful *adj* **useless** *adj* **1** having no practical use. **2** *Inf* inept.
usher ❶ *n* **1** doorkeeper, one showing people to seats etc. ♦ *v* **2** introduce, announce.
usual ❶ *adj* habitual, ordinary. **usually** *adv* as a rule.
usurp *v* seize wrongfully.

——————— THESAURUS ———————

= **sick**, queasy, bad, ill ♦ *v*
= **distress**, trouble, disturb, worry, alarm; = **tip over**, overturn, capsize, knock over, spill; = **mess up**, spoil, disturb, change, confuse ♦ *n* = **distress**, worry, trouble, shock, bother; = **reversal**, shake–up (*Inf*), defeat; = **illness**, complaint, disorder, bug (*Inf*), sickness
upside down *adj* = **inverted**, overturned, upturned; = (*Inf*) **confused**, disordered, chaotic, muddled, topsy–turvy
urban *adj* = **civic**, city, town, metropolitan, municipal
urge *v* = **beg**, exhort, plead,

implore, beseech; = **advocate**, recommend, advise, support, counsel ≠ **discourage** ♦ *n* = **impulse**, longing, wish, desire, drive ≠ **reluctance**
use *v* = **employ**, utilize, work, apply, operate; *sometimes with up* = **consume**, exhaust, spend, run through, expend; = **take advantage of**, exploit, manipulate ♦ *n* = **usage**, employment, operation, application, = **service**, handling, practice, exercise; = **purpose**, end, reason, object
usher *v* = **escort**, lead, direct, guide, conduct ♦ *n* = **attendant**, guide, doorman, escort,

utensil n vessel, implement, esp. in domestic use.
uterus n womb.
utility ❶ n 1 usefulness. 2 benefit. 3 useful thing. ◆ adj 4 made for practical purposes. **utilitarian** adj useful rather than beautiful.
utilize v

utmost ❶ adj 1 to the highest degree. 2 extreme, furthest. ◆ n 3 greatest possible amount.
Utopia n imaginary ideal state.
utter¹ ❶ v express, say.
utterance n
utter² ❶ adj complete, total.
utterly adv

———————— THESAURUS ————————

doorkeeper
usual adj = **normal**, customary, regular, general, common
≠ **unusual**
utility n = **usefulness**, benefit, convenience, practicality, efficacy
utmost adj = **greatest**, highest, maximum, supreme, paramount;

= **farthest**, extreme, last, final ◆ n
= **best**, greatest, maximum, highest, hardest
utter¹ v = **say**, state, speak, voice, express
utter² adj = **absolute**, complete, total, sheer, outright

U

V v

vacant ❶ *adj* empty, unoccupied.
vacancy *n, pl* **–cies** untaken job, room etc.
vacate *v* quit, leave empty.
vacation *n* 1 time when universities and law courts are closed 2 *US and Canad* holidays.
vaccinate *v* inoculate with vaccine. **vaccination** *n* **vaccine** *n* any substance used for inoculation against disease.
vacillate *v* 1 waver. 2 move to and fro. **vacillation** *n*
vacuous *adj* not expressing intelligent thought.
vacuum ❶ *n, pl* **vacuums, vacua** place, region containing no matter and from which all or most air, gas has been removed. **vacuum cleaner** apparatus for removing dust by suction. **vacuum flask** double-walled flask with vacuum between walls, for keeping contents hot or cold.
vagabond *n* 1 person with no fixed home. 2 wandering beggar or thief.
vagina *n* passage from womb to exterior.
vagrant *n* vagabond, tramp.
vagrancy *n*
vague ❶ *adj* 1 indefinite or uncertain. 2 indistinct. 3 not clearly expressed.
vain ❶ *adj* 1 conceited. 2 worthless. 3 unavailing.
vale *n Poet* valley.
valentine *n* (one receiving) card, gift, expressing affection, on Saint Valentine's day.
valet *n* gentleman's personal servant.
valiant *adj* brave, courageous.
valid ❶ *adj* 1 sound. 2 of binding force in law. **validate** *v* make valid. **validity** *n*
Valium ® *n* drug used as tranquillizer.
valley ❶ *n* 1 low area between hills. 2 river basin.

--- THESAURUS ---

vacant *adj* = **empty**, free, available, abandoned, deserted ≠ **occupied**; = **unfilled**, unoccupied ≠ **taken**
vacuum *n* = **gap**, lack, absence, space, deficiency
vague *adj* = **unclear**, indefinite, hazy, confused, loose ≠ **clear**; = **imprecise**, unspecified, generalized, rough, loose

vain *adj* = **futile**, useless, pointless, unsuccessful, idle ≠ **successful**; = **conceited**, narcissistic, proud, arrogant, swaggering ≠ **modest**
valid *adj* = **sound**, good, reasonable, telling, convincing ≠ **unfounded**; = **legal**, official, legitimate, genuine, authentic ≠ **invalid**
valley *n* = **hollow**, dale, glen, vale,

valour n bravery.
value ⊕ n 1 cost. 2 worth. 3 usefulness. 4 importance. ♦ pl 5 principles, standards. ♦ v 6 estimate value of. 7 prize. **valuable** adj 1 precious. 2 worthy. ♦ n (usu. pl) 3 valuable thing. **valuation** n estimated worth. **value–added tax** tax on difference between cost of basic materials and cost of article made from them.
valve n 1 device to control passage of fluid etc. through pipe. 2 Anat part of body allowing one-way passage of fluids.
vampire n (in folklore) corpse that rises from dead to drink blood of the living. **vampire bat** bat that sucks blood of animals.
van¹ n 1 covered vehicle, esp. for goods. 2 railway carriage for goods and use of guard.
van² n short for VANGUARD.
vandal n one who wantonly and deliberately damages or destroys. **vandalism** n **vandalize** v

vane n 1 weathercock. 2 blade of propeller.
vanguard n leading, foremost group, position etc.
vanilla n 1 tropical climbing orchid. 2 its seed pod. 3 essence of this for flavouring.
vanish ⊕ v disappear.
vanity ⊕ n, pl –ties excessive pride or conceit.
vanquish v conquer, overcome.
vantage n advantage. **vantage point** position that gives overall view.
vapid adj flat, dull, insipid.
vapour n 1 gaseous form of a substance. 2 steam, mist. **vaporize** v convert into, pass off in, vapour. **vaporizer** n
variable ⊕ n see VARY.
variegated adj having patches of different colours.
variety ⊕ n, pl –ties 1 state of being varied or various. 2 diversity. 3 varied assortment. 4 sort or kind.
various ⊕ adj diverse, of several kinds.
varnish ⊕ n 1 resinous solution

depression
value n = **importance**, benefit, worth, merit, point ≠ **worthlessness**; = **cost**, price, worth, rate, market price ♦ v = **appreciate**, rate, prize, regard highly, respect ≠ **undervalue**; = **evaluate**, price, estimate, rate, cost
vanish v = **disappear**, dissolve, evaporate, fade away, melt away ≠ **appear**
vanity n = **pride**, arrogance,

conceit, narcissism, egotism ≠ **modesty**
variable adj = **changeable**, unstable, fluctuating, shifting, flexible ≠ **constant**
variety n = **diversity**, change, variation, difference, diversification ≠ **uniformity**; = **range**, selection, assortment, mix, collection; = **type**, sort, kind, class, brand
various adj = **different**, assorted, miscellaneous, varied, distinct ≠ **similar**

put on surface to make it hard and shiny. ♦ v2 apply varnish to.

vary 🛈 v varying, varied (cause to) change, diversify, differ. **variability** n variable adj 1 changeable. 2 unsteady or fickle. ♦ n 3 something subject to variation. **variance** n state of discord, discrepancy. **variant** adj 1 different. ♦ n 2 alternative form. **variation** n 1 alteration. 2 extent to which thing varies. 3 modification. **varied** adj 1 diverse. 2 modified.

vase n vessel, jar as ornament or for holding flowers.

Vaseline ® n jelly–like petroleum product.

vast 🛈 adj very large.

VAT value–added tax.

vat n large vat, tank.

vault¹ 🛈 n 1 arched roof. 2 cellar. 3 burial chamber. 4 secure room for storing valuables.

vault² 🛈 v 1 spring, jump over with the hands resting on something. ♦ n 2 such jump.

veal n calf flesh as food.

vector n Maths quantity that has size and direction.

veer 🛈 v 1 change direction. 2 change one's mind.

vegan n one who eats no meat, eggs, or dairy products.

vegetable n 1 plant, esp. edible one. ♦ adj 2 of, from, concerned with plants.

vegetarian n 1 one who does not eat meat or fish. ♦ adj 2 suitable for vegetarians.

vegetate v 1 (of plants) grow, develop. 2 (of people) live dull, unproductive life. **vegetation** n plants collectively.

vehement adj marked by intensity of feeling.

vehicle 🛈 n means of conveying.

veil 🛈 n 1 light material to cover face or head. ♦ v 2 cover with, as with, veil.

vein 🛈 n 1 tube in body taking blood to heart. 2 fissure in rock filled with ore. **veined** adj

Velcro ® n fabric with tiny hooked threads that adheres to coarse surface.

velocity 🛈 n, pl –ties 1 rate of motion in given direction. 2 speed.

——————— THESAURUS ———————

varnish v = lacquer, polish, glaze, gloss

vary v = differ, be different, be dissimilar, disagree, diverge; = change, shift, swing, alter, fluctuate

vast adj = huge, massive, enormous, great, wide ≠ tiny

vault¹ n = strongroom, repository, depository; = crypt, tomb, catacomb, cellar, mausoleum

vault² v = jump, spring, leap, clear, bound

veer v = change direction, turn, swerve, shift, sheer

vehicle n = conveyance, machine, motor vehicle

veil n = mask, cover, shroud, film, curtain; ♦ v = cover, screen, hide, mask, shield ≠ reveal

vein n = mood, style, note, tone, mode; = seam, layer, stratum,

velvet n silk or cotton fabric with thick, short pile. **velvety** adj 1 of, like velvet. 2 soft and smooth.

vend v sell. **vendor** n **vending machine** machine that dispenses goods automatically.

vendetta n prolonged quarrel.

veneer n 1 thin layer of fine wood. 2 superficial appearance. ♦ v 3 cover with veneer.

venerable adj worthy of reverence. **venerate** v look up to, respect, revere. **veneration** n

vengeance ① n revenge.

vengeful adj

venison n flesh of deer as food.

venom n 1 poison. 2 spite.

venomous adj

vent ① n 1 small hole or outlet. ♦ v 2 give outlet to. 3 utter.

ventilate v supply with fresh air. **ventilation** n **ventilator** n

ventricle n cavity of heart or brain.

ventriloquist n one who can so speak that the sounds seem to come from some other person or place. **ventriloquism** n

venture ① v 1 expose to hazard. 2 risk. 3 dare. 4 have courage to do something or go somewhere. ♦ n 5 risky undertaking.

venue n 1 meeting place. 2 location.

veracious adj truthful. **veracity** n

verandah, veranda n open or partly enclosed porch on outside of house.

verb n part of speech used to express action or being. **verbal** adj of, by, or relating to words spoken rather than written. **verbatim** adj/adv word for word.

verbose adj long-winded.

verdant adj green and fresh.

verdict ① n 1 decision of jury. 2 opinion reached after examination of facts.

verge ① n 1 edge. 2 brink. 3 grass border along road. ♦ v 4 come close to. 5 be on the border of.

verger n church caretaker.

verify ① v –ifying, –ified 1 prove, confirm truth of. 2 test accuracy of. **verification** n

veritable adj actual, true.

vermilion adj/n (of) bright red colour.

course, current

velocity n = **speed**, pace, rapidity, quickness, swiftness

vengeance n = **revenge**, retaliation, reprisal, retribution, requital ≠ **forgiveness**

vent n = **outlet**, opening, aperture, duct, orifice ♦ v = **express**, release, voice, air, discharge ≠ **hold back**

venture n = **undertaking**, project, enterprise, campaign, risk ♦ v = **go**, travel, journey, set out, wander; = **dare**, presume, have the courage to, be brave enough, hazard; = **put forward**, volunteer

verdict n = **decision**, finding, judgment, opinion, sentence

verge n = **brink**, point, edge, threshold

verify v = **check**, make sure, examine, monitor, inspect

vermin pl n harmful animals, parasites etc.

vernacular n **1** commonly spoken language or dialect of particular country or place. ♦ adj **2** of vernacular. **3** native.

verruca n a wart, esp. on the foot.

versatile 🛈 adj capable of, adapted to many different uses, skills etc. **versatility** n

verse n **1** stanza or short subdivision of poem or the Bible. **2** poetry. **versed in** skilled in.

version 🛈 n **1** description from certain point of view. **2** translation. **3** adaptation.

versus prep against.

vertebra n, pl **vertebrae** single section of backbone. **vertebrate** n/adj (animal) with backbone.

vertical 🛈 adj **1** at right angles to the horizon. **2** upright. **3** overhead.

vertigo n giddiness.

verve n **1** enthusiasm. **2** vigour.

very 🛈 adv **1** extremely, to great extent. ♦ adj **2** exact, ideal. **3** absolute.

vespers pl n evening church service.

vessel 🛈 n **1** any object used as a container, esp. for liquids. **2** ship, large boat. **3** tubular structure conveying liquids (e.g. blood) in body.

vest n **1** undergarment for upper body. ♦ v **2** place. **3** confer.

vestment n robe or official garment.

vestibule n entrance hall, lobby.

vestige n small trace, amount.

vestry n, pl **-tries** room in church for keeping vestments, holding meetings etc.

vet 🛈 n short for VETERINARY SURGEON. ♦ v check suitability of.

veteran 🛈 n **1** one who has served a long time, esp. in fighting services. ♦ adj **2** long-serving.

veterinary adj of, concerning the health of animals. **veterinary surgeon** one qualified to treat animal ailments.

veto 🛈 n, pl **-toes 1** power of rejecting piece of legislation. **2** any prohibition. ♦ v **3** enforce veto

——————— THESAURUS ———————

versatile adj = **adaptable**, flexible, all-round, resourceful, multifaceted ≠ **unadaptable**

version n = **form**, variety, variant, sort, class; = **adaptation**, edition, interpretation, form, copy; = **account**, report, description, record, reading

vertical adj sheer, perpendicular, straight (up and down), erect ≠ **horizontal**

very adv = **extremely**, highly, greatly, really, deeply ♦ adj = **exact**, precise, selfsame

vessel n = **ship**, boat, craft; = **container**, receptacle, can, bowl, tank

vet v = **check**, examine, investigate, review, appraise

veteran n = **old hand**, past master, warhorse (Inf), old stager ≠ **novice** ♦ adj = **long-serving**, seasoned, experienced, old, established

V

against.

vex v 1 annoy. 2 distress. **vexation** n 1 cause of irritation. 2 state of distress.

VHF very high frequency.

VI Vancouver Island.

via prep by way of.

viable ❶ adj 1 practicable. 2 able to live and grow independently.

viaduct n bridge over valley for road or railway.

vibrate v 1 (cause to) move to and fro rapidly and continuously. 2 give off (light or sound) by vibration. 3 oscillate. 4 quiver.

vibrant adj 1 throbbing. 2 vibrating. 3 appearing vigorous.

vibration n

VIC Victoria (Australian state).

vicar n clergyman in charge of parish. **vicarage** n vicar's house.

vicarious adj obtained, enjoyed or undergone by imagining another's experiences.

vice¹ ❶ n 1 evil or immoral habit or practice. 2 criminal immorality, esp. prostitution. 3 fault, imperfection.

vice² n appliance with screw mechanism for holding things while working on them.

vice³ adj serving in place of.

viceroy n ruler acting for king in province or dependency.

vice versa ❶ Lat conversely, the other way round.

vicinity n neighbourhood.

vicious ❶ adj 1 wicked, cruel. 2 ferocious, dangerous. **vicious circle** sequence of problems and solutions which always leads back to original problem.

victim ❶ n 1 person or thing killed, injured etc. as result of another's deed, or accident, circumstances etc. 2 person cheated. 3 sacrifice. **victimization** n **victimize** v 1 punish unfairly. 2 make victim of.

victor ❶ n 1 conqueror. 2 winner. **victorious** adj 1 winning. 2 triumphant. **victory** n winning of battle etc.

video adj, pl –os 1 relating to or used in transmission or production of television image. ◆ n 2 video

──────── THESAURUS ────────

veto v = **ban**, block, reject, rule out, turn down ≠ **pass** ◆ n = **ban**, dismissal, rejection, vetoing, boycott ≠ **ratification**

viable adj = **workable**, practical, feasible, suitable, realistic ≠ **unworkable**

vice¹ n = **fault**, failing, weakness, limitation, defect ≠ **good point**; = **wickedness**, evil, corruption, sin, depravity ≠ **virtue**

vice versa adv = **the other way round**, conversely, in reverse, contrariwise

vicious adj = **savage**, brutal, violent, cruel, ferocious ≠ **gentle**; = **malicious**, vindictive, spiteful, mean, cruel

victim n = **casualty**, sufferer, fatality ≠ **survivor**; = **scapegoat**, sacrifice, martyr

victor n = **winner**, champion, conqueror, vanquisher, prizewinner ≠ **loser**

cassette recorder. **3** cassette containing video tape. ♦ *v* **4** record on video. **video cassette recorder** tape recorder for recording and playing back TV programmes and films on cassette. **video tape** magnetic tape used to record TV programmes.

vie ⊕ *v* vying, vied (*with* with or for) contend, compete against or for someone, something.

view ⊕ *n* **1** survey by eyes or mind. **2** range of vision. **3** picture. **4** scene. **5** opinion. **6** purpose. ♦ *v* **7** look at. **8** survey. **9** consider. **viewer** *n* **1** one who views. **2** one who watches television. **3** optical device to assist viewing of photographic slides. **viewfinder** *n* window on camera showing what will appear in photograph. **viewpoint** *n* **1** way of regarding subject. **2** position commanding view of landscape.

vigil *n* keeping awake, watch. **vigilance** *n* **vigilant** *adj* watchful, alert.

vigilante *n* person who takes it

upon himself or herself to enforce the law.

vignette *n* concise description of typical features.

vigour ⊕ *n* **1** force, strength. **2** energy, activity. **vigorous** *adj* **1** strong. **2** energetic. **3** flourishing.

vile ⊕ *adj* **1** very wicked, shameful. **2** disgusting. **3** despicable.

vilify *v* -ifying, -ified unjustly attack the character of.

villa *n* **1** large, luxurious country house. **2** detached or semidetached suburban house.

village *n* small group of houses in country area.

villain ⊕ *n* wicked person. **villainous** *adj*

vindicate ⊕ *v* **1** clear of charges. **2** justify. **vindication** *n*

vindictive *adj* **1** revengeful. **2** inspired by resentment.

vine *n* climbing plant bearing grapes. **vineyard** *n* plantation of vines.

vinegar *n* acid liquid obtained from wine and other alcoholic liquors.

———————— THESAURUS ————————

vie *v* = **compete**, struggle, contend, strive

view *n* sometimes plural = **opinion**, belief, feeling, attitude, impression; = **scene**, picture, sight, prospect, perspective; = **vision**, sight, visibility, perspective, eyeshot ♦ *v* = **regard**, see, consider, perceive, treat

vigour *n* = **energy**, vitality, power, spirit, strength ≠ **weakness**

vile *adj* = **wicked**, evil, corrupt, perverted, degenerate ≠ **honourable**; = **disgusting**, foul, revolting, offensive, nasty ≠ **pleasant**

villain *n* = **evildoer**, criminal, rogue, scoundrel, wretch; = **baddy** (*Inf*), antihero ≠ **hero**

vindicate *v* = **clear**, acquit, exonerate, absolve, let off the hook ≠ **condemn**

V

vintage ⊕ n 1 gathering of the grapes. 2 the yield. 3 wine of particular year. 4 time of origin. ◆ adj 5 best and most typical.

vintner n dealer in wine.

vinyl n 1 plastic material with variety of domestic and industrial uses. 2 record made of vinyl.

viola n see VIOLIN.

violate ⊕ v 1 break (law, agreement etc.). 2 rape. 3 outrage, desecrate. **violation** n

violence ⊕ n 1 use of physical force, usu. intended to cause injury or destruction. 2 great force or strength in action, feeling or expression. **violent** adj

violet n 1 plant with small bluish-purple or white flowers. 2 bluish-purple colour. ◆ adj 3 of this colour.

violin n small four-stringed musical instrument. **viola** n large violin with lower range. **violinist** n

VIP ⊕ very important person.

viper n poisonous snake.

viral adj see VIRUS.

virgin ⊕ n 1 one who has not had sexual intercourse. ◆ adj 2 without

experience of sexual intercourse. 3 uncorrupted. 4 (of land) untilled.

virginal adj **virginity** n

virile adj 1 (of male) capable of copulation or procreation. 2 strong, forceful. **virility** n

virtual adj so in effect, though not in appearance or name.

virtue ⊕ n 1 moral goodness. 2 good quality. 3 merit. **virtuous** adj morally good.

virtuoso n, pl -sos, -si 1 one with special skill, esp. in music. ◆ adj 2 showing great skill. **virtuosity** n

virulent adj 1 very infectious, poisonous etc. 2 malicious.

virus n infecting agent that causes disease. **viral** adj

visa n endorsement on passport permitting bearer to travel into country of issuing government.

visage n face.

vis-à-vis prep in relation to, regarding.

viscount n Brit. nobleman ranking below earl and above baron.

viscous adj thick and sticky.

visible ⊕ adj that can be seen. **visibility** n degree of clarity of

———— THESAURUS ————

vintage adj = high-quality, best, prime, quality, choice

violate v = break, infringe, disobey, transgress, ignore ≠ obey; = invade, infringe on, disturb, upset, shatter; = desecrate, profane, defile, abuse, pollute ≠ honour; = rape, molest, sexually assault, ravish, abuse

violence n = brutality, bloodshed,

savagery, fighting, terrorism; = force, power, strength, might, ferocity

VIP n = celebrity, big name, star, somebody, luminary

virgin n = maiden, girl (Arch) ◆ adj = pure, chaste, immaculate, virginal, vestal ≠ corrupted

virtue n = goodness, integrity, worth, morality, righteousness ≠ vice; = merit, strength, asset,

vision.

vision ❶ n 1 sight. 2 insight. 3 dream. 4 hallucination. **visionary** adj 1 marked by vision. 2 impractical. ♦ n 3 mystic. 4 impractical person.

visit ❶ v -iting, -ited 1 go, come and see. 2 stay temporarily with (someone). 3 call at person's home etc. **visitation** n 1 formal visit or inspection. 2 affliction or plague. **visitor** n

visor n 1 movable front part of helmet. 2 eyeshade, esp. on car. 3 peak on cap.

vista ❶ n extensive view.

visual ❶ adj 1 of sight. 2 visible. **visualize** v form mental image of.

vital ❶ adj 1 necessary to, affecting life. 2 lively. 3 animated. 4 essential. **vitality** n life, vigour.

vitamin n any of group of substances occurring in foodstuffs and essential to health.

viva interj long live.

vivacious adj lively, sprightly. **vivacity** n

vivid ❶ adj 1 bright, intense. 2 true to life.

vivisection n dissection of, or operating on, living animals.

vixen n female fox.

vizor see VISOR.

vocabulary ❶ n, pl -aries 1 list of words, usu. in alphabetical order. 2 stock of words used in particular language or subject.

vocal ❶ adj 1 of, with, or giving out voice. 2 outspoken, articulate. **vocalist** n singer. **vocals** pl n singing part.

vocation ❶ n (urge, inclination, predisposition to) particular career, profession etc. **vocational** adj

vociferous adj shouting, noisy.

plus (Inf), attribute ≠ **failing**

visible adj = **perceptible**, observable, clear, apparent, evident ≠ **invisible**

vision n = **image**, idea, dream, plans, hopes; = **hallucination**, illusion, apparition, revelation, delusion; = **sight**, seeing, eyesight, view, perception; = **foresight**, imagination, perception, insight, awareness

visit v = **call on**, drop in on (Inf), stay at, stay with, stop by; ♦ n = **call**, social call

vista n = **view**, scene, prospect, landscape, panorama

visual adj = **optical**, optic, ocular;

= **observable**, visible, perceptible, discernible ≠ **imperceptible**

vital adj = **essential**, important, necessary, key, basic ≠ **unnecessary**; = **lively**, vigorous, energetic, spirited, dynamic, feisty (US & Canad) ≠ **lethargic**

vivid adj = **clear**, detailed, realistic, telling, moving ≠ **vague**; = **bright**, brilliant, intense, clear, rich ≠ **dull**

vocabulary n = **language**, words, lexicon

vocal adj = **outspoken**, frank, forthright, strident, vociferous ≠ **quiet**; = **spoken**, voiced, uttered, oral, said

vocation n = **profession**, calling,

V

vodka n spirit distilled from potatoes or grain.

vogue ⊕ n 1 fashion, style. 2 popularity.

voice ⊕ n 1 sound given out by person in speaking, singing etc. 2 quality of the sound. 3 expressed opinion. 4 (right to) share in discussion. ♦ v 5 give utterance to, express.

void ⊕ adj 1 empty. 2 destitute. 3 not legally binding. ♦ n 4 empty space. ♦ v 5 make ineffectual or invalid. 6 empty out.

vol. volume.

volatile ⊕ adj 1 evaporating quickly. 2 lively. 3 changeable.

volcano n, pl **-noes, -nos** 1 hole in earth's crust through which lava, ashes, smoke etc. are discharged. 2 mountain so formed. **volcanic** adj

vole n small rodent.

volition n exercise of will.

volley ⊕ n 1 simultaneous discharge of weapons or missiles.

2 rush of oaths, questions etc. 3 Sport kick, stroke etc. at moving ball before it touches ground. ♦ v 4 discharge. 5 kick, strike etc. in volley. **volleyball** n game where ball is hit over high net.

volt n unit of electric potential.

voltage n electric potential difference expressed in volts.

voluble adj talking easily and at length.

volume ⊕ n 1 space occupied. 2 mass. 3 amount. 4 power, fullness of voice or sound. 5 book. 6 part of book bound in one cover.

voluminous adj bulky, copious.

voluntary ⊕ adj 1 having, done by free will. 2 done without payment. 3 supported by free-will contributions. **volunteer** n 1 one who offers service, joins force etc. of his or her own free will. ♦ v 2 offer oneself or one's services.

voluptuous adj 1 of, contributing to pleasures of the senses. 2 sexually alluring because of full,

——————— THESAURUS ———————

vogue n = **fashion**, trend, craze, style, mode

voice n = **tone**, sound, articulation ♦ v = **express**, declare, air, raise, reveal

void n = **emptiness**, space, vacuum, oblivion, blankness ♦ adj = **invalid**, null and void, inoperative, useless, ineffective ♦ v = **invalidate**, nullify, cancel, withdraw, reverse

volatile adj = **changeable**, shifting, variable, unsettled,

unstable ≠ **stable**;
= **temperamental**, erratic, mercurial, up and down (Inf), fickle ≠ **calm**

volley n = **barrage**, blast, burst, shower, hail

volume n = **amount**, quantity, level, body, total; = **capacity**, size, mass, extent, proportions; = **book**, work, title, opus, publication

voluntary adj = **intentional**, deliberate, planned, calculated, wilful ≠ **unintentional**; = **optional**, discretionary, up to the individual,

shapely figure.

vomit 🟊 v –iting, –ited **1** eject (contents of stomach) through mouth. ◆ n **2** matter vomited.

voodoo n religion involving ancestor worship and witchcraft.

voracious adj greedy, ravenous. **voracity** n

vortex n, pl –texes, –tices **1** whirlpool. **2** whirling motion.

vote 🟊 n **1** formal expression of choice. **2** individual pronouncement. **3** right to give it. **4** result of voting. ◆ v **5** express, declare opinion, choice, preference etc. by vote.

vouch v (usu. with for) guarantee. **voucher** n **1** document to establish facts. **2** ticket as substitute for cash.

vow 🟊 n **1** solemn promise, esp. religious one. ◆ v **2** promise,

threaten by vow.

vowel n **1** any speech sound pronounced without stoppage or friction of the breath. **2** letter standing for such sound, as a, e, i, o, u.

voyage 🟊 n **1** journey, esp. long one, by sea or air. ◆ v **2** make voyage.

vulcanize v treat (rubber) with sulphur at high temperature to increase its durability. **vulcanization** n

vulgar 🟊 adj **1** offending against good taste. **2** common. **vulgarity** n

vulnerable 🟊 adj **1** capable of being physically or emotionally wounded or hurt. **2** exposed, open to attack, persuasion etc. **vulnerability** n

vulture n large bird which feeds on carrion.

———— THESAURUS ————

open, unforced ≠ **obligatory**

vomit v = **be sick**, throw up (Inf), spew, heave, retch

vote n = **poll**, election, ballot, referendum, popular vote

vow v = **promise**, pledge, swear, commit, engage ◆ n = **promise**, commitment, pledge, oath, profession

voyage n = **journey**, trip, passage, expedition, crossing

vulgar adj = **tasteless**, common ≠ **tasteful**

vulnerable adj = **susceptible**, helpless, unprotected, defenceless, exposed ≠ **immune**; = **exposed**, open, unprotected, defenceless, accessible ≠ **well-protected**

V

W w

WA 1 Washington. **2** Western Australia.

wacky *adj* **wackier, wackiest** *Inf* eccentric, funny.

wad *n* **1** small pad of fibrous material. **2** thick roll of banknotes. ♦ *v* **3** pad, stuff etc. with wad.

waddle ① *v* **1** walk like duck. ♦ *n* **2** this gait.

wade ① *v* walk through something that hampers movement, esp. water. **wader** *n* person or bird that wades.

wafer *n* thin, crisp biscuit.

waffle[1] *n/v Inf* (use) long–winded and meaningless language.

waffle[2] *n* kind of pancake.

waft *v* **1** convey smoothly through air or water. ♦ *n* **2** breath of wind. **3** odour, whiff.

wag ① *v* **wagging, wagged 1** (cause to) move rapidly from side to side. ♦ *n* **2** instance of wagging **3** *Inf* witty person. **wagtail** *n* small bird with long tail.

wage ① *n* (oft. *pl*) **1** payment for work done. ♦ *v* **2** carry on.

wager *n/v* bet.

waggle *v/n* wag.

wagon, waggon *n* **1** four–wheeled vehicle for heavy loads. **2** railway freight truck.

waif *n* homeless person, esp. child.

wail ① *v/n* cry, lament.

waist *n* **1** part of body between hips and ribs. **2** various narrow central parts. **waistcoat** *n* sleeveless garment worn under jacket or coat.

wait ① *v* **1** stay in one place, remain inactive in expectation (of something). **2** be prepared (for something). **3** delay. **4** serve in restaurant etc. ♦ *n* **5** act or period of waiting. **waiter** *n* attendant on guests at hotel, restaurant etc.

waive ① *v* **1** forgo. **2** not insist on. **waiver** *n* (written statement of) this act.

───── THESAURUS ─────

waddle *v* = **shuffle**, totter, toddle, sway, wobble

wade *v* = **paddle**, splash, splash about, slop; = **walk through**, cross, ford, travel across, pitch in

wag *v* = **wave**, shake, waggle, stir, quiver; ♦ *n* = **wave**, shake, quiver, vibration, wiggle; = **nod**, bob, shake

wage *n* often plural = **payment**, pay, remuneration, fee, reward ♦ *v* = **engage in**, conduct, pursue, carry on, undertake

wail *v* = **cry**, weep, grieve, lament, howl ♦ *n* = **cry**, moan, howl, lament, yowl

wait *v* = **stay**, remain, stop, pause, rest ≠ **go** ♦ *n* = **delay**, gap, pause, interval, stay

waive *v* = **give up**, relinquish,

wake¹ ❶ *v* **waking, woke, woken 1** rouse from sleep. **2** stir up. ♦ *n* **3** vigil. **4** watch beside corpse.
waken *v* wake.
wake² *n* track or path left by anything that has passed.
walk ❶ *v* **1** (cause, assist to) move, travel on foot at ordinary pace. **2** cross, pass through by walking. **3** escort, conduct by walking. ♦ *n* **4** act, instance of walking. **5** path or other place or route for walking.
walking stick stick used as support when walking. **Walkman** ® *n* small portable cassette player with headphones. **walkover** *n Inf* easy victory.
wall ❶ *n* **1** structure of brick, stone etc. serving as fence, side of building etc. **2** surface of one. **3** anything resembling this. ♦ *v* **4** enclose with wall. **5** block up with wall. **wallflower** *n* garden plant.
wallpaper *n* paper, usu. patterned, to cover interior walls.
wallaby *n, pl* **-bies** Aust. marsupial similar to and smaller than kangaroo.

wallet ❶ *n* small folding case, esp. for paper money, documents etc.
wallop *Inf* ♦ *v* **1** beat soundly. **2** strike hard. ♦ *n* **3** stroke or blow.
wallow *v* **1** roll (in liquid or mud). **2** revel (in). ♦ *n* **3** wallowing.
walnut *n* **1** large nut with crinkled shell. **2** tree it grows on. **3** its wood.
walrus *n, pl* **-ruses, -rus** large sea mammal with long tusks.
waltz *n* **1** ballroom dance. **2** music for it. ♦ *v* **3** perform waltz.
wampum *n US and Canad* shells woven together, formerly used by N American Indians for money and ornament.
wan *adj* **wanner, wannest** pale, pallid.
wand *n* stick, esp. as carried by magician etc.
wander ❶ *v* **1** roam, ramble. **2** go astray, deviate. ♦ *n* **3** wandering.
wane ❶ *v/n* **1** decline. **2** (of moon) decrease in size.
wangle *v Inf* get by devious methods.
want ❶ *v* **1** desire. **2** lack. ♦ *n* **3**

——————— THESAURUS ———————

renounce, forsake, drop ≠ **claim**
wake¹ *v* = **awake**, stir, awaken, come to, arise ≠ **fall asleep**; = **awaken**, arouse, rouse, waken; ♦ *n* = **vigil**, watch, funeral, deathwatch
walk *v* = **stride**, stroll, go, move, step; = **escort**, take, see, show, partner ♦ *n* = **stroll**, hike, ramble, march, trek; = **gait**, step, bearing, carriage, tread; = **path**, footpath, track, way, road

wall *n* = **partition**, screen, barrier, enclosure, blockade; = **barrier**, obstacle, barricade, obstruction, check
wallet *n* = **purse**, pocketbook, pouch, case, holder
wander *v* = **roam**, walk, drift, stroll, range ♦ *n* = **excursion**, walk, stroll, cruise, ramble
wane *v* = **decline**, weaken, diminish, fail, fade ≠ **grow**; = **diminish**, decrease, dwindle

W

desire. **4** need. **5** deficiency.
wanted adj being sought, esp. by
police. **wanting** adj **1** lacking. **2**
below standard.
wanton adj **1** dissolute. **2** without
motive. **3** unrestrained.
war ❶ n **1** fighting between
nations. **2** state of hostility. **3**
conflict, contest. ◆ v **4** make war.
warlike adj **1** of, for war. **2** fond of
war. **warfare** n hostilities. **warhead**
n part of missile etc. containing
explosives.
warble v sing with trills. **warbler** n
any of various kinds of small
songbirds.
ward ❶ n **1** division of city,
hospital etc. **2** minor under care of
guardian. **warder** n jailer. **ward off**
avert, repel.
warden ❶ n person in charge of
building, college etc.

wardrobe ❶ n **1** piece of furniture
for hanging clothes in. **2** person's
supply of clothes.
ware n **1** goods. **2** articles
collectively. ◆ pl **3** goods for sale.
warehouse n storehouse for
goods.
warm ❶ adj **1** moderately hot. **2**
serving to maintain heat. **3**
affectionate. **4** enthusiastic. ◆ v **5**
make, become warm. **warmth** n **1**
mild heat. **2** cordiality. **3** intensity
of emotion. **warm up** v **1** make or
become warmer. **2** do preliminary
exercises.
warn ❶ v **1** put on guard. **2**
caution. **3** give advance
information to. **warning** n
warp ❶ v **1** (cause to) twist (out of
shape). **2** pervert or be perverted.
warrant ❶ n **1** authority. **2**
document giving authority. ◆ v **3**

———— THESAURUS ————

≠ **wax**

want v = **wish for**, desire, long for,
crave, covet ≠ **have**; = **need**,
demand, require, call for; ◆ n
= **lack**, need, absence, shortage,
deficiency ≠ **abundance**;
= **poverty**, hardship, privation,
penury, destitution ≠ **wealth**;
= **wish**, will, need, desire,
requirement
war n = **conflict**, drive, attack,
fighting, fight ≠ **peace**; ◆ v
= **fight**, battle, clash, wage war,
campaign ≠ **make peace**
ward n = **room**, department, unit,
quarter, division; = **district**,
constituency, area, division, zone;
= **dependant**, charge, pupil,

minor, protégé
warden n = **jailer**, prison officer,
guard, screw (Sl)
wardrobe n = **clothes cupboard**,
cupboard, closet, cabinet;
= **clothes**, apparel, attire
warm adj = **balmy**, mild,
temperate, pleasant, fine ≠ **cool**;
= **cosy**, snug, toasty (Inf),
comfortable, homely ◆ v = **warm
up**, heat, thaw (out), heat up
≠ **cool down**
warn v = **notify**, tell, remind,
inform, alert; = **advise**, urge,
recommend, counsel, caution
warp v = **distort**, bend, twist,
buckle, deform; ◆ n = **twist**, bend,
defect, flaw, distortion

guarantee. **4** authorize, justify.
warranty n, pl **-ties 1** guarantee of quality of goods. **2** security.
warren n (burrows inhabited by) colony of rabbits.
warrigal Aust ◆ n **1** dingo. ◆ adj **2** wild.
warrior ⊕ n fighter.
wart n small hard growth on skin.
wart hog kind of Afr. wild pig.
wary ⊕ adj **warier, wariest** watchful, cautious, alert.
was past tense, first and third person sing. of BE.
wash ⊕ v **1** clean (oneself, clothes etc.) with water, soap etc. **2** be washable. **3** move, be moved by water. **4** flow, sweep over, against. ◆ n **5** act of washing. **6** clothes washed at one time. **7** sweep of water, esp. set up by moving ship.
washable adj capable of being washed without damage. **washer** n **1** one who, that which, washes. **2** ring put under nut. **washing** n

clothes to be washed. **washout** n Inf complete failure. **wash up** wash dishes and cutlery after meal.
wasp n striped stinging insect resembling bee.
waste ⊕ v **1** expend uselessly. **2** fail to take advantage. **3** dwindle. **4** pine away. ◆ n **5** act of wasting. **6** rubbish. **7** desert. ◆ adj **8** worthless, useless. **9** desert. **10** wasted. **wasteful** adj extravagant.
watch ⊕ v **1** observe closely. **2** guard. **3** wait expectantly (for). **4** be on watch. ◆ n **5** portable timepiece for wrist, pocket etc. **6** state of being on the lookout. **7** spell of duty. **watchful** adj
watchdog n **1** dog kept to guard property. **2** person or group guarding against inefficiency or illegality. **watchman** n man guarding building etc., esp. at night. **watchword** n **1** password. **2** rallying cry.
water ⊕ n **1** transparent,

warrant v = **call for**, demand, require, merit, rate; = **guarantee**, declare, pledge, promise, ensure ◆ n = **authorization**, permit, licence, permission, authority
warrior n = **soldier**, combatant, fighter, gladiator, trooper
wary adj = **suspicious**, sceptical, guarded, distrustful, chary
wash v = **clean**, scrub, sponge, rinse, scour; = **launder**, clean, rinse, dry-clean; = **rinse**, clean, scrub, lather ◆ n = **laundering**, cleaning, clean, cleansing; dip; = **backwash**, slipstream, path, trail,

train; = **splash**, surge, swell, rise and fall, undulation
waste v = **squander**, throw away, blow (Sl), lavish, misuse ≠ **save**; ◆ n = **squandering**, misuse, extravagance, frittering away, dissipation ≠ **saving**; = **rubbish**, refuse, debris, scrap, litter ◆ adj = **unwanted**, useless, worthless, unused, leftover ≠ **necessary**; = **uncultivated**, wild, bare, barren, empty ≠ **cultivated**
watch v = **look at**, observe, regard, eye, see; = **spy on**, follow, track, monitor, keep an eye on ◆ n

colourless, odourless, tasteless liquid, substance of rain, river etc. **2** body of water. **3** urine. ◆ v **4** put water on or into. **5** irrigate or provide with water. **6** salivate. **7** (of eyes) fill with tears. **watery** adj **1** wet. **2** weak. **water closet** sanitary convenience flushed with water. **watercolour** n **1** paint thinned with water. **2** painting in this. **watercress** n plant growing in clear ponds and streams. **waterfall** n vertical descent of waters of river. **water lily** plant that floats on surface of fresh water. **waterlogged** adj saturated, filled with water. **watermark** n faint translucent design in sheet of paper. **watermelon** n melon with green skin and red flesh. **water polo** team game played by swimmers with ball. **waterproof** adj **1** not letting water through. ◆ v **2** make waterproof. ◆ n **3** waterproof garment. **watershed** n **1** line separating two river systems. **2** divide. **water-skiing** n sport of riding over water on skis towed by speedboat. **watertight** adj **1** preventing water from

entering or escaping. **2** with no weak points.

watt n unit of electric power.

wave ⓥ v **1** move to and fro, as hand in greeting or farewell. **2** signal by waving. **3** give, take shape of waves (as hair etc.). ◆ n **4** ridge and trough on water etc. **5** act, gesture of waving. **6** vibration, as in radio waves. **7** prolonged spell. **8** upsurge. **9** wavelike shapes in hair etc. **wavy** adj **wavelength** n distance between the same points of two successive waves.

waver ⓥ v **1** hesitate, be irresolute. **2** be, become unsteady.

wax[1] ⓥ v grow, increase.

wax[2] n **1** yellow, soft, pliable material made by bees. **2** this or similar substance used for sealing, making candles etc. **3** waxy secretion of ear. ◆ v **4** put wax on. **waxy** adj like wax.

way ⓝ n **1** manner. **2** method. **3** direction. **4** path. **5** passage. **6** progress. **7** state or condition. **8** room for activity. **wayfarer** n traveller, esp. on foot. **waylay** v lie in wait for and accost, attack. **wayside** n/adj (by) side or edge of

———————— THESAURUS ————————

= **wristwatch**, timepiece, chronometer; = **guard**, surveillance, observation, vigil, lookout

water n = **liquid**, H₂O ◆ v = **get wet**, cry, weep, become wet, exude water

wave v = **signal**, sign, gesture, gesticulate; = **guide**, point, direct, indicate, signal; = **brandish**, swing,

flourish, wag, shake; ◆ n = **gesture**, sign, signal, indication, gesticulation; = **ripple**, breaker, swell, ridge, roller

waver v = **hesitate**, dither (Chiefly Brit), vacillate, falter, fluctuate ≠ **be decisive**; = **flicker**, shake, tremble, wobble, quiver

wax[1] v = **increase**, grow, develop, expand, swell ≠ **wane**

road. **wayward** *adj* capricious, perverse, wilful.

WC water closet.

we *pron* first person plural pronoun.

weak ⓣ *adj* **1** lacking strength. **2** irresolute. **3** (of sound) faint. **4** (of argument) unconvincing. **5** unprotected, vulnerable. **6** lacking flavour. **weaken** *v* **weakling** *n* feeble creature. **weakly** *adj* **1** weak. **2** sickly. ◆ *adv* **3** in weak manner. **weakness** *n*

weal *n* streak left on flesh by blow of stick or whip.

wealth ⓣ *n* **1** riches. **2** abundance. **wealthy** *adj*

wean *v* **1** accustom to food other than mother's milk. **2** win over, coax away from.

weapon *n* implement to fight with.

wear ⓣ *v* wearing, wore, worn **1** have on the body. **2** show. **3** (cause to) become impaired by use. **4** harass or weaken. **5** last. ◆ *n* **6** act of wearing. **7** things to wear. **8** damage caused by use. **9** ability to resist effect of constant use.

weary ⓣ *adj* **–rier, –riest 1** tired, exhausted, jaded. **2** tiring. **3** tedious. ◆ *v* **4** make, become weary. **weariness** *n*

weasel *n* small carnivorous mammal with long body and short legs.

weather ⓣ *n* **1** day-to-day meteorological conditions, esp. temperature etc. of a place. ◆ *v* **2** affect by weather. **3** endure. **4** resist. **5** come safely through. **weathercock** *n* revolving object to show which way wind blows.

weave ⓣ *v* weaving, wove **1** form

way *n* = **method**, means, system, process, technique; = **manner**, style, fashion, mode; *often plural* = **custom**, manner, habit, style, practice; = **route**, direction, course, road, path; = **journey**, approach, passage; = **distance**, length, stretch

weak *adj* = **feeble**, frail, debilitated, fragile, sickly ≠ **strong**; = **slight**, faint, feeble, pathetic, hollow; = **fragile**, brittle, flimsy, fine, delicate; = **unsafe**, exposed, vulnerable, helpless, unprotected ≠ **secure**

wealth *n* = **riches**, fortune, prosperity, affluence, money ≠ **poverty**; = **property**, capital,

fortune

wear *v* = **be dressed in**, have on, sport (*Inf*), put on; = **show**, present, bear, display, assume; = **deteriorate**, fray, wear thin ◆ *n* = **clothes**, things, dress, gear (*Inf*), attire; = **damage**, wear and tear, erosion, deterioration, attrition ≠ **repair**

weary *adj* = **tired**, exhausted, drained, worn out, done in (*Inf*) ≠ **energetic**; = **tiring**, arduous, tiresome, laborious, wearisome ≠ **refreshing** ◆ *v* = **grow tired**, tire, become bored

weather *n* = **climate**, conditions, temperature, forecast, outlook ◆ *v* = **withstand**, stand, survive,

W

into texture or fabric by interlacing, esp. on loom. **2** construct (*past tense*) **3** make one's way, esp. with side to side motion.

web 🟊 *n* **1** woven fabric. **2** net spun by spider. **3** membrane between toes of waterfowl, frogs etc.

wed 🟊 *v wedding, wedded* **1** marry. **2** unite closely. **wedding** *n* marriage ceremony. **wedlock** *n* marriage.

wedge 🟊 *n* **1** piece of wood, metal etc. tapering to a thin edge. ♦ *v* **2** fasten, split with wedge. **3** stick by compression or crowding.

Wednesday *n* fourth day of the week.

wee *adj* **1** small. **2** little.

weed *n* **1** plant growing where undesired. ♦ *v* **2** clear of weeds.

weedy *adj* **1** full of weeds. **2** weak.

week *n* period of seven days.

weekly *adj/adv* happening, done,

published etc. once a week.

weekday *n* any day of the week except Saturday or Sunday.

weekend *n* Saturday and Sunday.

weep 🟊 *v weeping, wept* **1** shed tears (for). **2** grieve.

weigh 🟊 *v* **1** find weight of. **2** consider. **3** have weight. **4** be burdensome. **weight** *n* **1** measure of the heaviness of an object. **2** quality of heaviness. **3** heavy mass. **4** object of known mass for weighing. **5** importance, influence. ♦ *v* **6** add weight to.

weighting *n* extra allowance paid in special circumstances.

weir *n* river dam.

weird 🟊 *adj* **1** unearthly, uncanny. **2** strange, bizarre.

welcome 🟊 *adj* **1** coming, –comed **1** received gladly. **2** freely permitted. ♦ *n* **3** kindly greeting. ♦ *v* **4** greet with pleasure. **5** receive gladly.

———— THESAURUS ————

overcome, resist ≠ **surrender to**

weave *v* = **knit**, intertwine, plait, braid, entwine; = **zigzag**, wind, crisscross; = **create**, tell, recount, narrate, build

web *n* = **cobweb**, spider's web; = **mesh**, lattice

wed *v* = **get married to**, be united to ≠ **divorce**; = **get married**, marry, be united, tie the knot (*Inf*), take the plunge (*Inf*) ≠ **divorce**

wedge *v* = **squeeze**, force, lodge, jam, crowd ♦ *n* = **block**, lump, chunk

weep *v* = **cry**, shed tears, sob, whimper, mourn ≠ **rejoice**

weigh *v* = **have a weight of**, tip the scales at (*Inf*); = **consider**, examine, contemplate, evaluate, ponder; = **compare**, balance, contrast, juxtapose, place side by side

weird *adj* = **strange**, odd, unusual, bizarre, mysterious ≠ **normal**; = **bizarre**, odd, strange, unusual, queer ≠ **ordinary**

welcome *v* = **greet**, meet, receive, embrace, hail ≠ **reject**; = **accept gladly**, appreciate, embrace, approve of, be pleased by ♦ *n* = **greeting**, welcoming, reception, acceptance, hail

weld ⓣ *v* **1** unite metal by softening with heat. **2** unite closely. ♦ *n* **3** welded joint.
welder *n*
welfare ⓣ *n* wellbeing. **welfare state** system in which government takes responsibility for wellbeing of citizens.
well[1] ⓣ *adv* **better, best 1** in good manner or degree. **2** suitably. **3** intimately. **4** fully. **5** favourably. **6** kindly. **7** to a considerable degree. ♦ *adj* **8** in good health. **9** satisfactory. ♦ *interj* **10** exclamation of surprise, interrogation etc. **wellbeing** *n* state of being well, happy, or prosperous. **well-disposed** *adj* inclined to be friendly. **well-mannered** *adj* having good manners. **well-off** *adj* fairly rich. **well-read** *adj* having read much.
well[2] ⓣ *n* **1** hole sunk into the earth to reach water, gas, oil etc. **2** spring. ♦ *v* **3** spring, gush.
wellies *pl n Inf* wellingtons.
wellingtons *pl n* high waterproof boots.
welter *v* **1** roll or tumble. ♦ *n* **2** turmoil, disorder.
wench *n* young woman.
wend *v* go, travel.
went past tense of GO.
were past tense of BE (*used with you, we and they*)
werewolf *n* in folklore, person who can turn into a wolf.
west *n* **1** part of sky where sun sets. **2** part of country etc. lying to this side. ♦ *adj* **3** that is toward or in this region. ♦ *adv* **4** to the west.
westerly *adj/adv* **western** *adj*
westernize *v* adapt to customs and culture of the West. **westward** *adj/adv* **westwards** *adv*
wet ⓣ *adj* **wetter, wettest 1** having water or other liquid on a surface or being soaked in it. **2** rainy. **3** (of paint, ink etc.) not yet dry. ♦ *v* **4** make wet. ♦ *n* **5** moisture, rain. **wet suit** close-fitting rubber suit worn by divers

THESAURUS

≠ **rejection**
weld *v* = **join**, link, bond, bind, connect; = **unite**, combine, blend, unify, fuse
welfare *n* = **wellbeing**, good, interest, health, security
well[1] *adv* = **skilfully**, expertly, adeptly, professionally, correctly ≠ **badly**; = **satisfactorily**, nicely, smoothly, successfully, pleasantly ≠ **badly**; = **thoroughly**, completely, fully, carefully, effectively; = **intimately**, deeply, fully, profoundly ≠ **slightly**; = **favourably**, highly, kindly, warmly, enthusiastically ≠ **unfavourably**; = **considerably**, easily, very much, significantly, substantially; = **fully**, highly, greatly, amply, very much; = **possibly**, probably, certainly, reasonably, conceivably ♦ *adj* = **healthy**, sound, fit, blooming, in fine fettle ≠ **ill**; = **satisfactory**, right, fine, pleasing, proper ≠ **unsatisfactory**
well[2] *n* = **hole**, bore, pit, shaft ♦ *v* = **flow**, spring, pour, jet, surge

W

etc.

whack ⊙ v **1** strike with sharp resounding sound. ◆ n **2** such blow.

wharf n, pl **wharves, wharfs** platform at harbour, on river etc. for loading and unloading ships.

what pron **1** which thing. **2** that which. **3** request for statement to be repeated. ◆ adj **4** which. **5** as much as. **6** how great, surprising etc. ◆ adv **7** in which way.

whatever pron **1** anything which. **2** of what kind it may be.

whatsoever adj at all.

wheat n cereal plant yielding grain from which bread is chiefly made.

wheedle v coax, cajole.

wheel ⊙ n **1** circular frame or disc revolving on axle. **2** anything like a wheel in shape or function. **3** act of turning. ◆ v **4** (cause to) turn as if on axis. **5** (cause to) move on or as if on wheels. **6** (cause to) change course, esp. in opposite direction. **wheelbarrow** n barrow with one wheel. **wheelchair** n chair mounted on large wheels, used by invalids.

wheeze v **1** breathe with whistling noise. ◆ n **2** this sound.

whelk n edible shellfish.

when adv **1** at what time. ◆ conj **2** at the time that. **3** although. **4** since. ◆ pron **5** at which time.

whenever adj/conj at whatever time.

where adv/conj **1** at what place. **2** at or to the place in which.

whereabouts adv/conj **1** in what, which place. ◆ n **2** present position.

whereas conj **1** considering that. **2** while, on the contrary.

whereby conj by which.

whereupon conj at which point.

wherever adv at whatever place.

wherewithal n necessary funds, resources etc.

whet v **whetting, whetted 1** sharpen. **2** stimulate.

whether conj introduces the first of two alternatives.

whey n watery part of milk left after cheese making.

which adj **1** used in requests for a selection from alternatives. ◆ pron **2** person or thing referred to.

whichever pron

whiff ⊙ n **1** brief smell or

——————— THESAURUS ———————

wet adj = **damp**, soaking, saturated, moist, watery ≠ **dry**; = **rainy**, damp, drizzly, showery, raining ≠ **sunny**; = (Inf) **feeble**, soft, weak, ineffectual, weedy (Inf) ◆ v = **moisten**, spray, dampen, water, soak ≠ **dry** ◆ n = **rain**, drizzle ≠ **fine weather**; = **moisture**, water, liquid, damp, humidity ≠ **dryness**

whack (Inf) v = **strike**, hit, belt (Inf), bang, smack ◆ n = **blow**, hit, stroke, belt (Inf), bang; = (Inf) **share**, part, cut (Inf), bit, portion; = (Inf) **attempt**, go (Inf), try, turn, shot (Inf)

wharf n = **dock**, pier, berth, quay, jetty

wheel n = **disc**, ring, hoop ◆ v = **push**, trundle, roll

suggestion of. **2** puff of air.

while *conj* **1** in the time that. **2** in spite of the fact that, although. **3** whereas. ◆ *v* **4** pass (time) idly. ◆ *n* **5** period of time.

whim ⊕ *n* sudden, passing fancy.

whimsy, whimsey *n* fanciful mood.

whimsical *adj* **1** fanciful. **2** full of whims.

whimper *v* **1** cry or whine softly. **2** complain in this way. ◆ *n* **3** such cry or complaint.

whine ⊕ *n* **1** high-pitched plaintive cry. **2** peevish complaint. ◆ *v* **3** utter this.

whinge *v* **1** complain. ◆ *n* **2** complaint.

whinny *v* **-nying, -nied 1** neigh softly. ◆ *n* **2** soft neigh.

whip ⊕ *n* **1** lash attached to handle for urging or punishing. ◆ *v* **2** strike with whip. **3** beat (cream, eggs) to a froth. **4** pull, move quickly.

whippet *n* dog like small greyhound.

whirl ⊕ *v* **1** swing rapidly round. **2** move rapidly in a circular course. **3** drive at high speed. ◆ *n* **4** whirling movement. **5** confusion, bustle, giddiness. **whirlpool** *n* circular current, eddy. **whirlwind** *n* **1** wind whirling round while moving forwards. ◆ *adj* **2** very quick.

whirr, whir *v* **1** (cause to) fly, spin etc. with buzzing sound. ◆ *n* **2** this sound.

whisk ⊕ *v* **1** brush, sweep, beat lightly. **2** move, remove quickly. **3** beat to a froth. ◆ *n* **4** light brush. **5** egg-beating implement.

whisker *n* **1** any of the long stiff hairs at side of mouth of cat or other animal. ◆ *pl* **2** hair on a man's face.

whisky *n, pl* **-kies** (*Irish, Canad, US* **whiskey**) spirit distilled from fermented cereals.

whisper ⊕ *v* **1** speak in soft, hushed tones, without vibration of vocal cords. **2** rustle. ◆ *n* **3** such speech. **4** trace or suspicion. **5** rustle.

whist *n* card game.

——————— THESAURUS ———————

whiff *n* = **smell**, hint, scent, sniff, aroma

whim *n* = **impulse**, caprice, fancy, urge, notion

whine *v* = **cry**, sob, wail, whimper, sniffle ◆ *n* = **cry**, moan, sob, wail, whimper; = **drone**, note, hum

whip *n* = **lash**, cane, birch, crop, scourge ◆ *v* = **lash**, cane, flog, beat, strap; = (*Inf*) **dash**, shoot, fly, tear, rush; = **whisk**, beat, mix vigorously, stir vigorously; = **incite**, drive, stir, spur, work up

whirl *v* = **spin**, turn, twist, rotate, twirl; = **rotate**, roll, twist, revolve, swirl ◆ *n* = **revolution**, turn, roll, spin, twist; = **bustle**, round, series, succession, flurry; = **confusion**, daze, dither (*Chiefly Brit*), giddiness; spin

whisk *v* = **flick**, whip, sweep, brush; = **beat**, mix vigorously, stir vigorously, whip, fluff up ◆ *n* = **flick**, sweep, brush, whip; = **beater**, mixer, blender

whisper *v* = **murmur**, breathe

W

whistle v 1 produce shrill sound by forcing breath through rounded, nearly closed lips. 2 make similar sound. 3 utter, summon etc. by whistle. ◆ n 4 such sound. 5 any similar sound. 6 instrument to make it.

white ⊕ adj 1 of the colour of snow. 2 pale. 3 light in colour. 4 having a light–coloured skin. ◆ n 5 colour of snow. 6 white pigment. 7 white part. 8 clear fluid round yolk of egg 9 (with cap.) white person. **whiten** v **whitewash** n 1 substance for whitening walls etc. ◆ v 2 apply this. 3 cover up, gloss over.

whither adv 1 Obs to what place. 2 to which.

whittle ⊕ v 1 cut, carve with knife. 2 pare away.

whizz, whiz n **whizzing, whizzed** 1 loud hissing sound. ◆ v 2 move with such sound, or make it.

who pron 1 what or which person or persons. 2 that. **whoever** pron who, any one or every one that.

whodunnit, whodunit n Inf detective story.

whole ⊕ adj 1 containing all elements or parts. 2 not defective or imperfect. 3 healthy. ◆ n 4 complete thing or system. **wholly**

adv **wholehearted** adj 1 sincere. 2 enthusiastic. **wholesale** n 1 sale of goods in large quantities to retailers. ◆ adj 2 dealing by wholesale. 3 extensive.

wholesome adj producing good effect, physically or morally.

whom pron objective form of WHO.

whoop n/v (make) shout or cry expressing excitement etc.

whooping cough infectious disease marked by convulsive coughing with loud whoop or drawing in of breath.

whopper n Inf unusually large thing. **whopping** adj

whore ⊕ n prostitute.

whose pron of whom or which.

why adv for what cause or reason.

wick n strip of thread feeding flame of lamp of candle with oil, grease etc.

wicked adj 1 evil, sinful. 2 very bad.

wicker adj made of woven cane.

wicket n 1 set of cricket stumps. 2 small gate.

wide ⊕ adj 1 having a great extent from side to side, broad. 2 having considerable distance between. 3 spacious. 4 vast. 5 far from the mark. 6 opened fully. ◆ adv 7 to the full extent. 8 far from

———— THESAURUS ————

≠ **shout; =** rustle, sigh, hiss, swish ◆ n = **murmur**, mutter, mumble, undertone; = (Inf) **rumour**, report, gossip, innuendo, insinuation; = **rustle**, sigh, hiss, swish

white adj = **pale**, wan, pasty, pallid, ashen

whittle v = **carve**, cut, hew, shape, trim

whole adj = **complete**, full, total, entire, uncut ≠ **partial**; = **undamaged**, intact, unscathed, unbroken, untouched ≠ **damaged**

whore n = **prostitute**, tart (Inf),

W

the intended target. **widen** *v* **width** *n* breadth. **widespread** *adj* extending over a wide area.

widow *n* **1** woman whose husband is dead and who has not married again. ♦ *v* **2** make a widow of. **widower** *n* man whose wife is dead and who has not married again.

wield ❶ *v* hold and use.

wife ❶ *n, pl* **wives** man's partner in marriage, married woman.

wig *n* artificial hair for the head.

wiggle *v* **1** (cause to) move jerkily from side to side. ♦ *n* **2** wiggling.

wild ❶ *adj* **1** not tamed or domesticated. **2** not cultivated. **3** savage. **4** stormy. **5** uncontrolled. **6** random. **7** excited. **8** rash.

wildcat *n* any of various undomesticated feline animals.

wild–goose chase search that has little chance of success. **wildlife** *n* wild animals and plants

collectively.

wildebeest *n* gnu.

wilderness ❶ *n* desert, waste place.

wildfire *n* **1** raging, uncontrollable fire. **2** anything spreading, moving fast.

wilful *adj* **1** obstinate. **2** self–willed. **3** intentional.

will ❶ *n, past* **would 1** faculty of deciding what one will do. **2** purpose. **3** volition. **4** determination. **5** wish. **6** directions written for disposal of property after death. ♦ *v* **7** wish. **8** intend. **9** leave as legacy. **willing** *adj* **1** ready. **2** given cheerfully. **willingly** *adv* **willingness** *n* **willpower** *n* ability to control oneself, one's actions, impulses.

will² *v, past* **would** forms future tense and indicates intention or conditional result.

will–o'–the–wisp *n* elusive person

—————————— THESAURUS ——————————

streetwalker, call girl

wide *adj* = **spacious**, broad, extensive, roomy, commodious ≠ **confined**; = **baggy**, full, loose, ample, billowing; = **expanded**, dilated, distended ≠ **shut**; = **broad**, extensive, wide-ranging, large, sweeping ≠ **restricted** ♦ *adv* = **fully**, completely ≠ **partly**; = **off target**, astray, off course, off the mark

wield *v* = **brandish**, flourish, manipulate, swing, use; = **exert**, maintain, exercise, have, possess

wife *n* = **spouse**, partner, mate, bride, better half (*humorous*)

wild *adj* = **untamed**, fierce, savage, ferocious, unbroken ≠ **tame**; = **uncultivated**, natural ≠ **cultivated**; = **stormy**, violent, rough, raging, choppy; = **excited**, crazy (*Inf*), enthusiastic, raving, hysterical ≠ **unenthusiastic**; = **uncontrolled**, disorderly, turbulent, wayward, unruly ≠ **calm**; = **mad** (*Inf*), furious, fuming, infuriated, incensed

wilderness *n* = **wilds**, desert, wasteland, uncultivated region

will¹ *n* = **determination**, drive, purpose, commitment, resolution; = **wish**, mind, desire, intention,

W

or thing.

willow n 1 tree with long thin flexible branches. 2 its wood.

willowy adj slender, supple.

willy-nilly adv/adj (occurring) whether desired or not.

wilt ⊕ v (cause to) become limp, lose strength etc.

wimp n Inf feeble person.

wimple n garment framing face, worn by nuns.

win ⊕ v winning, won 1 be successful, victorious. 2 get by labour or effort. ◆ n 3 victory, esp. in games. **winner** n **winning** adj charming. **winnings** pl n sum won in game, betting etc.

wince ⊕ v 1 flinch, draw back, as from pain etc. ◆ n 2 this act.

winch n 1 machine for hoisting or hauling using cable wound round drum. ◆ v 2 move (something) by using a winch.

wind¹ ⊕ n 1 air in motion. 2 breath. 3 flatulence. ◆ v 4 render short of breath, esp. by blow etc.

windward n side against which

wind is blowing. **windy** adj 1 exposed to wind. 2 flatulent.

windfall n 1 unexpected good luck. 2 fallen fruit. **wind instrument** musical instrument played by blowing or air pressure.

windmill n wind-driven apparatus with fanlike sails for raising water, crushing grain etc. **windpipe** n passage from throat to lungs.

windscreen n protective sheet of glass etc. in front of driver or pilot.

windsurfing n sport of sailing standing up on board with single sail.

wind² ⊕ v 1 twine. 2 meander. 3 twist round, coil. 4 wrap. 5 make ready for working by tightening spring. ◆ n 6 act of winding. 7 single turn of something wound.

window n 1 hole in wall (with glass) to admit light, air etc. 2 anything serving in appearance or function. 3 area for display of goods behind glass of shop front.

window-shopping n looking at goods without intending to buy.

———— THESAURUS ————

fancy; **= choice**, prerogative, volition; ◆ v **= wish**, want, prefer, desire, see fit; **= bequeath**, give, leave, transfer, gift

wilt v **= droop**, wither, sag, shrivel; **= weaken**, languish, droop

win v **= be victorious in**, succeed in, prevail in, come first in, be the victor in ≠ **lose**; **= be victorious**, succeed, triumph, overcome, prevail ≠ **lose** ◆ n **= victory**, success, triumph, conquest ≠ **defeat**

wince v **= flinch**, start, shrink, cringe, quail ◆ n **= flinch**, start, cringe

wind¹ n **= air**, blast, hurricane, breeze, draught; **= flatulence**, gas; **= breath**, puff, respiration; **= nonsense**, talk, boasting, hot air, babble; **get wind of something = hear about**, learn of, find out about, become aware of, be told about

wind² v **= meander**, turn, bend, twist, curve; **= wrap**, twist, reel,

windshield n the US and Canadian name for WINDSCREEN.

wine n 1 fermented juice of grape etc. 2 purplish–red colour.

wing ⊕ n 1 feathered limb used by bird in flying. 2 organ of flight of insect or some animals. 3 main lifting surface of aircraft. 4 side area of building, stage etc. 5 group within political party etc. ♦ v 6 fly. 7 move, go very fast. 8 disable, wound slightly. **winger** n Sport player positioned at side of pitch.

wink ⊕ v 1 close and open (one eye) rapidly, esp. to indicate friendliness or as signal. 2 twinkle. ♦ n 3 act of winking.

winkle n edible sea snail. **winkle out** extract, prise out.

winsome adj charming.

winter n 1 coldest season. ♦ v 2 pass, spend the winter. **wintry** adj 1 of, like winter. 2 cold.

wipe ⊕ v 1 rub so as to clean. ♦ n 2 wiping. **wiper** n 1 one that wipes. 2 automatic wiping apparatus. **wipe out** 1 erase. 2 annihilate 3 Sl kill.

wire n 1 metal drawn into thin, flexible strand. 2 something made of wire, e.g. fence. 3 telegram. ♦ v 4 provide, fasten with wire. 5 send by telegraph. **wiring** n system of wires. **wiry** adj 1 like wire. 2 lean and tough. **wire–haired** adj (of various breeds of dog) with short stiff hair.

wise adj 1 having intelligence and knowledge. 2 sensible. **wisdom** n (accumulated) knowledge, learning. **wisdom tooth** large tooth cut usu. after age of twenty.

wish ⊕ v 1 desire. ♦ n 2 expression of desire. 3 thing desired. **wishful** adj too optimistic. **wishy–washy** adj Inf insipid, bland.

wisp n 1 light, delicate streak, as of smoke. 2 twisted handful, usu. of straw etc. 3 stray lock of hair. **wispy** adj

wistful adj 1 longing, yearning. 2 sadly pensive.

wit ⊕ n 1 ability to use words, ideas in clever, amusing way. 2 person with this ability. 3 intellect. 4 understanding. 5 humour. **witticism** n witty remark. **wittingly** adv 1 on purpose. 2 knowingly. **witty** adj

witch ⊕ n 1 person, usu. female,

—————————— THESAURUS ——————————

curl, loop

wing n = **faction**, group, arm, section, branch ♦ v = **fly**, soar, glide, take wing; = **wound**, hit, clip

wink v = **blink**, bat, flutter; = **twinkle**, flash, shine, sparkle, gleam ♦ n = **blink**, flutter, blink, glimmer

wipe v = **clean**, polish, brush, rub, sponge; = **erase**, remove ♦ n = **rub**, brush

wish n = **desire**, want, hope, urge, intention ≠ **aversion** ♦ v = **want**, feel, choose, please, desire

wit n = **humour**, quips, banter, puns, repartee ≠ **seriousness**; = **humorist**, card (Inf), comedian,

W

who practises magic. **2** ugly, wicked woman. **3** fascinating woman. **witchcraft** *n* **witch doctor** in certain societies, man appearing to cure or cause injury, disease by magic.

with *prep* **1** in company or possession of. **2** against. **3** in relation to. **4** through. **5** by means of. **within** *prep/adv* in, inside. **without** *prep* **1** lacking **2** *Obs* outside.

withdraw **⊕** *v* –drawing, –drew, –drawn draw back or out. **withdrawal** *n* **withdrawn** *adj* reserved, unsociable.

wither **⊕** *v* (cause to) wilt, dry up, decline. **withering** *adj* (of glance etc.) scornful.

withhold **⊕** *v* –holding, –held **1** restrain. **2** refrain from giving.

withstand **⊕** *v* –standing, –stood oppose, resist, esp. successfully.

witness **⊕** *n* **1** one who sees something. **2** testimony. **3** one

who gives testimony. ♦ *v* **4** give testimony. **5** see. **6** attest. **7** sign (document) as genuine.

wizard **⊕** *n* **1** sorcerer, magician. *Inf* virtuoso. **wizardry** *n*

wizened *adj* shrivelled, wrinkled.

wobble **⊕** *v* **1** move unsteadily. **2** sway. ♦ *n* **3** unsteady movement. **wobbly** *adj*

woe **⊕** *n* grief. **woebegone** *adj* looking sorrowful. **woeful** *adj* **1** sorrowful. **2** pitiful. **3** wretched.

wok *n* bowl-shaped Chinese cooking pan.

wolf *n, pl* **wolves 1** wild predatory doglike animal. ♦ *v* **2** eat ravenously.

wolverine *n* carnivorous mammal inhabiting Arctic regions.

woman **⊕** *n, pl* **women 1** adult human female. **2** women collectively. **womanish** *adj* effeminate. **womanize** *v* (of man) indulge in many casual affairs. **womanly** *adj* of, proper to woman.

——— THESAURUS ———

wag, joker; **= cleverness**, sense, brains, wisdom, common sense ≠ **stupidity**

witch *n* = **enchantress**, magician, hag, crone, sorceress

withdraw *v* = **remove**, take off, pull out, extract, take away

wither *v* = **wilt**, decline, decay, disintegrate, perish ≠ **flourish**; = **waste**, decline, shrivel

withhold *v* = **keep secret**, refuse, hide, reserve, retain ≠ **reveal**

withstand *v* = **resist**, suffer, bear, oppose, cope with ≠ **give in to**

witness *n* = **observer**, viewer,

spectator, looker-on, watcher ♦ *v* = **see**, view, watch, note, notice; = **countersign**, sign, endorse, validate

wizard *n* = **magician**, witch, shaman, sorcerer, occultist

wobble *v* = **shake**, rock, sway, tremble, teeter; = **tremble**, shake ♦ *n* = **unsteadiness**, shake, tremble

woe *n* = **misery**, distress, grief, agony, gloom ≠ **happiness**

woman *n* = **lady**, girl, female, sheila (*Aust & NZ inf*), vrou (*S Afr*) ≠ **man**

W

womb n female organ in which young develop before birth.

wombat n Aust. burrowing marsupial with heavy body, short legs and dense fur.

won past tense and past participle of WIN.

wonder ❶ n 1 emotion excited by amazing or unusual thing. 2 marvel, miracle. ♦ v 3 be curious about. 4 feel amazement. **wonderful** adj 1 remarkable. 2 very fine. **wondrous** adj 1 inspiring wonder. 2 strange.

wont n 1 custom. ♦ adj 2 accustomed.

woo v court, seek to marry.

wood ❶ n substance of trees, timber. **firewood** tract of land with growing trees. **wooded** adj having many trees. **wooden** adj 1 made of wood. 2 without expression. **woody** adj **woodland** n woods, forest. **woodpecker** n bird which searches tree trunks for insects. **wood pigeon** large pigeon of Europe and Asia. **woodwind** adj/n (of) wind instruments of orchestra. **woodworm** n insect larva that bores into wood.

woof n barking noise.

wool ❶ n 1 soft hair of sheep, goat etc. 2 yarn spun from this. **woollen** adj **woolly** adj 1 of wool. 2 vague, muddled. ♦ n 3 woollen garment.

wop–wops pl n NZ informal remote rural areas.

word ❶ n 1 smallest separate meaningful unit of speech or writing. 2 term. 3 message. 4 brief remark. 5 information. 6 promise. 7 command. ♦ v 8 express in words, esp. in particular way. **wordy** adj using too many words. **word processor** keyboard, computer and VDU for electronic organization and storage of text.

wore past tense of WEAR.

work ❶ n 1 labour. 2 employment. 3 occupation. 4 something made or accomplished. 5 production of art or science. ♦ pl 6 factory. 7 total of person's deeds, writings etc. 8 mechanism of clock etc. ♦ v 9 (cause to)

——————— THESAURUS ———————

wonder v = think, question, puzzle, speculate, query; = be amazed, stare, marvel, be astonished, gape ♦ n = amazement, surprise, admiration, awe, fascination; = phenomenon, sight, miracle, spectacle, curiosity

woo v cultivate; = court, pursue

wood n = timber, planks, planking, lumber (US); (also woods) = woodland, forest, grove, thicket, copse

wool n = fleece, hair, coat

word n = term, name, expression; = chat, tête-à-tête, talk, discussion, consultation; = comment, remark, utterance; = message, news, report, information, notice; = promise, guarantee, pledge, vow, assurance; = command, order, decree, bidding, mandate ♦ v = express, say, state, put

W

operate. **10** make, shape. **11** apply effort. **12** labour. **13** be employed. **14** turn out successfully. **15** ferment. **workable** adj **worker** n **workaholic** n person addicted to work. **working class** social class consisting of wage earners, esp. manual. **working–class** adj **workman** n manual worker **workmanship** n **1** skill of workman. **2** way thing is finished. **workshop** n place where things are made. **world ❶** n **1** the universe. **2** the planet earth. **3** sphere of existence. **4** mankind. **5** any planet. **6** society. **worldly** adj **1** earthly. **2** absorbed in pursuit of material gain.

worm n **1** small limbless creeping snakelike creature. **2** anything resembling worm in shape or movement. ◆ pl **3** (disorder caused by) infestation of worms,

esp. in intestines. ◆ v **4** crawl. **5** insinuate (oneself). **6** extract (secret) craftily. **7** rid of worms.

worn ❶ past participle of WEAR.

worry ❶ v –rying, –ried **1** (be unduly) concerned. **2** trouble, pester, harass. **3** (of dog) seize, shake with teeth. ◆ n **4** (cause of) anxiety, concern. **worried** adj

worse adj/adv comparative of BAD or BADLY. **worsen** v make, grow worse. **worst** adj/adv superlative of BAD or BADLY.

worship ❶ v –shipping, –shipped **1** show religious devotion to. **2** adore. **3** love and admire. ◆ n **4** act of worshipping. **worshipful** adj **worshipper** n

worsted n **1** woollen yarn. ◆ adj **2** made of woollen yarn.

worth ❶ adj **1** having or deserving to have value specified. **2** meriting. ◆ n **3** excellence. **4**

work v = **be employed**, be in work; = **labour**, sweat, slave, toil, slog (away) ≠ relax; = **function**, go, run, operate, be in working order ≠ be out of order; = **succeed**, work out, pay off (Inf), be successful, be effective; = **handle**, move, excite, manipulate, rouse ◆ n = **employment**, business, job, trade, duty ≠ play; = **effort**, industry, labour, sweat, toil ≠ leisure; = **task**, jobs, projects, commissions, duties; = **handiwork**, doing, act, feat, deed **world** n = **earth**, planet, globe; = **mankind**, man, everyone, the

public, everybody; = **sphere**, area, field, environment, realm **worn** adj = **ragged**, frayed, shabby, tattered, tatty **worry** v = **be anxious**, be concerned, be worried, obsess, brood ≠ be unconcerned; = **trouble**, upset, bother, disturb, annoy ≠ soothe ◆ n = **anxiety**, concern, fear, trouble, unease ≠ peace of mind; = **care**, trouble, bother, hassle (Inf) **worship** v = **revere**, praise, honour, adore, glorify ≠ dishonour; = **love**, adore, idolize, put on a pedestal ≠ despise ◆ n = **reverence**, praise,

merit, value. **5** usefulness. **6** quantity to be had for given sum. **worthless** adj **worthwhile** adj worth the time, effort etc. involved. **worthy** adj **1** virtuous. **2** meriting.

would v expressing wish, intention, probability: past tense of WILL. **would–be** adj wishing, pretending to be.

wound¹ ❶ n **1** injury, hurt from cut, stab etc. ◆ v **2** inflict wound on, injure. **3** pain.

wound² past tense and past participle of WIND².

wove past tense of WEAVE. **woven** past participle of WEAVE.

wow interj exclamation of astonishment.

wowser n Aust & NZ slang puritanical person. **2** teetotaller.

wraith n apparition.

wrangle ❶ v **1** quarrel (noisily). **2** dispute. ◆ n **3** noisy quarrel. **4** dispute.

wrap ❶ v **wrapping, wrapped 1** cover, esp. by putting something round. **2** put round. ◆ n **3** loose garment. **wrapper** n covering. **wrapping** n material used to wrap.

wrath ❶ n anger.

wreak v **1** inflict (vengeance). **2** cause.

wreath n something twisted into ring form, esp. band of flowers etc. as memorial or tribute on grave etc. **wreathe** v **1** form into wreath. **2** surround. **3** wind round.

wreck ❶ n **1** destruction of ship. **2** wrecked ship. **3** ruin. ◆ v **4** cause wreck of. **wreckage** n

wren n kind of small songbird.

wrench ❶ v **1** twist. **2** distort. **3** seize forcibly. **4** sprain. ◆ n **5** violent twist. **6** tool for twisting or screwing. **7** spanner.

wrest v **1** take by force. **2** twist violently.

wrestle ❶ v **1** fight (esp. as sport) by grappling and trying to throw down. **2** strive (with). **3** struggle. ◆ n **4** wrestling. **wrestler** n wrestling n

wretch n **1** despicable person. **2**

——————— THESAURUS ———————

regard, respect, honour
worth n = **value**, price, rate, cost, estimate ≠ **worthlessness**; = **merit**, value, quality, importance, excellence ≠ **unworthiness**
wound¹ n = **injury**, cut, hurt, trauma (Pathol), gash ◆ v = **injure**, cut, wing, hurt, pierce; = **offend**, hurt, annoy, sting, mortify
wrangle v = **argue**, fight, row, dispute, disagree ◆ n = **argument**, row, dispute, quarrel, squabble
wrap v = **cover**, enclose, shroud,

swathe, encase; ◆ n = **cloak**, cape, stole, mantle, shawl
wrath n = **anger**, rage, temper, fury, resentment ≠ **satisfaction**
wreck v = **destroy**, break, smash, ruin, devastate ≠ **build**; ◆ n = **shipwreck**, hulk
wrench v = **twist**, force, pull, tear, rip; = **sprain**, strain, rick ◆ n = **twist**, pull, rip, tug, jerk; = **sprain**, strain, twist; = **blow**, shock, upheaval, pang; = **spanner**, adjustable spanner

W

miserable creature. **wretched** *adj* **1** miserable, unhappy. **2** worthless.
wriggle *v* **1** move with twisting action, squirm. ♦ *n* **2** this action.
wring *v* **wringing, wrung 1** twist. **2** extort. **3** squeeze out.
wrinkle ❶ *n* **1** slight ridge or furrow on skin etc. ♦ *v* **2** make, become wrinkled. **wrinkly** *adj*
wrist *n* joint between hand and arm.
writ ❶ *n* written command from law court or other authority.
write ❶ *v* **writing, wrote, written 1** mark paper etc. with symbols or words. **2** compose. **3** send a letter. **4** set down in words. **5** communicate in writing. **writer** *n* **1** one who writes. **2** author.
writing *n* **write-off** *n Inf*

something damaged beyond repair.
writhe *v* twist, squirm in or as in pain etc.
wrong ❶ *adj* **1** not right or good. **2** not suitable. **3** incorrect. **4** mistaken. **5** not functioning properly. ♦ *n* **6** that which is wrong. **7** harm. ♦ *v* **8** do wrong to. **9** think badly of without justification. **wrongful** *adj* **wrongly** *adv*
wrote past tense of WRITE.
wrought *adj* (of metals) shaped by hammering or beating.
wrung past tense and past participle of WRING.
wry *adj* **wrier, wriest** turned to one side, contorted dryly humorous.

————— THESAURUS —————

wrestle *v* = **fight**, battle, struggle, combat, grapple
wrinkle *n* = **line**, fold, crease, furrow, crow's-foot; ♦ *v* = **crease**, gather, fold, crumple, furrow ≠ **smooth**
writ *n* = **summons**, document, decree, indictment, court order
write *v* = **record**, scribble, inscribe, set down, jot down
wrong *adj* = **amiss**, faulty, unsatisfactory, not right, defective;

= **incorrect**, mistaken, false, inaccurate, untrue;
= **inappropriate**, incorrect, unsuitable, unacceptable, undesirable ≠ **correct**; = **bad**, criminal, illegal, evil, unlawful ≠ **moral** ♦ *adv* = **incorrectly**, badly, wrongly, mistakenly, erroneously ≠ **correctly** ♦ *n* = **offence**, injury, crime, error, sin ≠ **good deed** ♦ *v* = **mistreat**, abuse, hurt, harm, cheat ≠ **treat well**

X x Y y Z z

xenophobia *n* hatred, fear, of strangers or aliens.

Xerox *n* **1** machine for copying printed material. ♦ *v* **2** copy with Xerox.

Xmas *n* short for CHRISTMAS.

X-ray, x-ray *n* **1** stream of radiation capable of penetrating solid bodies. ♦ *v* **2** photograph by X-rays.

xylophone *n* musical instrument of wooden bars which sound when struck.

ya *interj S Afr* yes.

yacht *n* vessel propelled by sail or power.

yak *n* ox of Central Asia.

yakka *n Aust & NZ informal* work.

yam *n* sweet potato.

yank 🔁 *v* **1** jerk, tug. **2** pull quickly. ♦ *n* **3** quick tug.

yap *v* **yapping, yapped 1** bark (as small dog). **2** talk idly.

yard[1] *n* unit of length, .915 metre.

yardstick *n* standard of measurement or comparison.

yard[2] *n* piece of enclosed ground, oft. adjoining building and used for some specific purpose.

yarn 🔁 *n* **1** spun thread. **2** tale.

yawn *v* **1** open mouth wide, esp. in sleepiness. **2** gape. ♦ *n* **3** act of yawning.

ye *pron Obs* you.

year *n* **1** time taken by one revolution of earth round sun, about 365 days. **2** twelve months.

yearling *n* animal one year old.

yearly *adv* **1** every year, once a year. ♦ *adj* **2** happening once a year.

yearn 🔁 *v* feel longing, desire.

yeast *n* substance used as fermenting agent, esp. in raising bread.

yebo *interj S Afr informal* yes.

yell *v/n* **1** shout. **2** scream.

yellow *adj* **1** of the colour of lemons, gold etc. **2** *Inf* cowardly. ♦ *n* **3** this colour. **yellow fever** acute infectious tropical disease.

yelp *v/n* (produce) quick, shrill cry.

yen 🔁 *n Inf* longing, craving.

yeoman *n, pl* **-men** *Hist* farmer cultivating his own land.

yes *interj* expresses consent, agreement, or approval.

--- THESAURUS ---

yank *n* = **pull**, tug, jerk, snatch, hitch

yarn *n* = **thread**, fibre, cotton, wool; = (*Inf*) **story**, tale, anecdote, account, narrative

yearn *v* often with **for** = **long**,

desire, hunger, ache, crave

yell *v* = **scream**, shout, cry out, howl, call out ≠ **whisper** ♦ *n* = **scream**, cry, shout, roar, howl ≠ **whisper**

yen *n* = **longing**, desire, craving,

yesterday *n/adv* **1** (on) day before today. **2** (in) recent past.

yet ⊕ *adv* **1** now. **2** still. **3** besides. **4** hitherto. ♦ *conj* **5** but, at the same time, nevertheless.

yeti *n* apelike creature said to inhabit Himalayas.

yew *n* **1** evergreen tree with dark leaves. **2** its wood.

yield ⊕ *v* **1** give or return. **2** produce. **3** give up, surrender. ♦ *n* **4** amount produced.

yob ⊕ yobbo *n Inf* bad–mannered aggressive youth.

yodel *v* **–delling, –delled** warble in falsetto tone.

yoga *n* Hindu system of certain physical and mental exercises.

yogurt, yoghurt *n* thick, custard–like preparation of curdled milk.

yoke *n* **1** wooden bar put across the necks of two animals to hold them together. **2** various objects like a yoke in shape or use. **3** fitted part of garment, esp. round neck, shoulders. **4** bond or tie. **5** domination. ♦ *v* **6** put yoke on. **7** couple, unite.

yokel *n* (old–fashioned) country dweller.

yolk *n* yellow central part of egg.

Yorkshire pudding baked batter made from flour, milk and eggs.

you *pron* (*second person*) **1** refers to person or persons addressed. **2** refers to unspecified person or persons.

young ⊕ *adj* **1** not far advanced in growth, life or existence. **2** not yet old. ♦ *n* **3** offspring. **youngster** *n* child.

your *adj* of, belonging to you.

yours *pron* **yourself** *pron* emphatic or reflexive form of YOU.

youth ⊕ *n* **1** state or time of being young. **2** young man. **3** young people. **youthful** *adj*

YT Yukon Territory.

Yule *n* Christmas season.

yuppie *n* young highly–paid professional person. ♦ *adj* of, like yuppies.

zany *adj* **zanier, zaniest** comical, funny in unusual way.

zap *v* **zapping, zapped** *Sl* attack,

————— THESAURUS —————

yearning, passion

yet *adv* = **so far**, until now, up to now, still, as yet; = **now**, right now, just now, so soon; = **still**, in addition, besides, to boot, into the bargain ♦ *conj* = **nevertheless**, still, however, for all that, notwithstanding

yield *v* = **bow**, submit, give in, surrender, succumb; = **relinquish**, resign, hand over, surrender, turn over ≠ **retain** ♦ *n* = **produce**, crop, harvest, output

yob, yobbo *n* = **thug**, hooligan, lout, hoon (*Aust & NZ sl*), ruffian

young *adj* = **immature**, juvenile, youthful, little, green ≠ **old** ♦ *pl n* = **offspring**, babies, litter, family, issue ≠ **parents**

youth *n* = **immaturity**, adolescence, boyhood *or* girlhood salad days ≠ **old age**; = **boy**, lad, youngster, kid (*Inf*), teenager ≠ **adult**

kill or destroy.

zeal 🛈 n **1** fervour. **2** keenness, enthusiasm. **zealot** n **1** fanatic. **2** enthusiast. **zealous** adj

zebra n striped Afr. animal like a horse.

zenith n **1** point of the heavens directly above an observer. **2** summit. **3** climax.

zephyr n soft, gentle breeze.

zero 🛈 n, pl **-ros, -roes 1** nothing. **2** figure 0. **3** point on graduated instrument from which positive and negative quantities are reckoned. **4** the lowest point.

zest n **1** enjoyment. **2** excitement, interest, flavour. **3** peel of orange or lemon.

zigzag n **1** line or course with sharp turns in alternating directions. ♦ v **2** move along in zigzag course.

zinc n bluish–white metallic element.

zip 🛈 zipper n **1** fastener with two rows of teeth that are closed and opened by a sliding clip. **2** short whizzing sound **3** Inf energy, vigour. ♦ v **4** fasten with zip. **5** move with zip.

zither n flat stringed instrument.

zodiac n imaginary belt of the heavens along which the sun, moon and chief planets appear to move.

zombie, zombi n person appearing lifeless.

zone 🛈 n region with particular characteristics or use.

zoo n, pl **zoos** place where live animals are kept for show.

zoology n study of animals. **zoological** adj **zoologist** n

zoom 🛈 v move, rise very rapidly move with buzzing or humming sound.

zucchini n the US and Canadian name for COURGETTE.

—————— THESAURUS ——————

zeal n = **enthusiasm**, passion, zest, spirit, verve ≠ **apathy**

zero n = **nought**, nothing, nil; = **rock bottom**, the bottom, an all–time low, a nadir, as low as you can get

zip n = (Inf) **energy**, drive, vigour, verve, zest ≠ **lethargy**

zone n = **area**, region, section, sector, district

zoom v = **speed**, shoot, fly, rush, flash

X

Language
In
Action

Supplement

——— TABLE OF CONTENTS ———

INTRODUCTION

Throughout life you often need to communicate your thoughts and feelings in writing. Writing concise and effective letters, speeches, and emails is easy, once you know exactly what you want to say. This supplement covers the basic rules of style and form to follow. The two most important rules for expressing yourself through language are simple, but often ignored:

✔ Be clear
Choose words that occur to you naturally and convey exactly what you mean. If you have a choice between a basic word and a showy one, choose the basic one.

✔ Think of your audience
When writing to or for someone, think of that specific person's position, interests, and relationship to you. When writing to strangers or business contacts, adopt a polite and formal style. When writing to close friends, you are free to use more casual and personal language. People always respond better to letters that show regard for what matters to them.

This guide outlines everything you should need to know to communicate effectively and clearly through writing in all areas of life. It gives answers to frequently asked questions (FAQs), and shows examples of good letters for a variety of situations. It also includes advice for writing and delivering confident and memorable speeches.

Think through what you want to say. Then use this supplement to write it down in a style that will smoothly communicate your message to your audience.

4

—— JOB APPLICATIONS ——

Q. *Should my letter be typed or handwritten?*
A. It should be typed on A4 paper. Only the signature should be handwritten.

Q. *To whom should I address my letter?*
A. If you do not know the name of the person who would deal with your application, call the company to find out their name.

Q. *Is it OK to send out the same letter to all those companies I'm interested in?*
A. No. Try to avoid generalised letters.

Useful phrases

First of all, identify the job you are applying for:
- I would like to inquire as to whether there are any openings for telesales operators in your company.
- I wish to apply for the position of online learning co-ordinator, as advertised on your website.
- I am writing to apply for the above post, as advertised in *The Guardian* of 8 August 2003.

Next, give some examples of career achievements and personal qualities:
- I have gained experience in several major aspects of publishing.
- I have supervised a team of telesales operators on several projects.
- I see myself as systematic and meticulous in my approach to work.
- I get on well with people from all walks of life.

Explain why you want this job:
- I am now keen to find a post with more responsibility.
- I would like to further my career in the field of production.

JOB APPLICATIONS

● Application for an advertised post

45 Fairways
Little Fordnam
Northumberland
N21 3RS
30 June 2003

Mrs F Reid
Recruitment Officer
Affinity Development Projects
3 Albion Court, Newcastle
NE4 7JS

Dear Mrs Reid

re. Community Development Officer post: ref no. 513/6

I am writing in response to your advertisement in *Community Now* magazine, and am enclosing my CV for your review.

As you will see, I have gained valuable experience in working with Black and Asian communities, and I am at present completing a distance-learning course on Equality and Diversity Policy Development.

I am now looking for a post which gives me an opportunity to use my new skills.

I look forward to having the opportunity to discuss this further with you.

Yours sincerely

Brian Hanlan
Brian Hanlan

6

—— JOB APPLICATIONS ——

● A speculative job application

☑ When applying for a job on a speculative basis, try to speak to the person responsible for recruitment in the appropriate department beforehand.

---

34 St Dunstan's Way
Hove BN13 5HY
19 July 2003

Ms D Wallis
Young's Accountancy
19 Lockwood Road
Brighton BN2 6HM

Dear Ms Wallis

Post of Software Development Co-ordinator

Thank you very much for speaking to me yesterday about the possibility of a position as Software Development Co-ordinator.

Please find attached my CV. You will see that I have gained extensive experience in handling large development projects and meeting deadlines.

I am well-organized and self-motivated, and as I am keen to develop my career with Young's Accountancy, I would very much appreciate the opportunity to discuss this position further.

Please feel free to contact me, either by email: dgorman@netserve.com, or by leaving a message on 01783 639012. I look forward to speaking to you.

Yours sincerely

D Gorman
Deborah Gorman

WRITING A CV

Q. *How should a CV be presented?*

A. It should be constructed on a word-processor, well laid out and printed on a good quality printer. Use bullets or similar to start sub-sections or lists.

Q. *I usually send the same CV out to all potential employers. Should I be tailoring it to different jobs?*

A. Yes. Consider carefully how your skills, education, and experience compare with the skills that the job requires. Spend time researching the employer – their structure, products and approach.

Q. *What details do I need to include in my CV?*

A. You should include the following:
personal details: Name, contact details, date of birth.
education: Most recent place of study listed first.
work experience: Again, most recent experience first. Give the name of your employer, job title, and what you actually did and achieved in that job.
skills and interests: Language ability, leadership experience, computing skills or possession of a driving licence should be included.
references: Usually give two names, or if you do not wish to name them on your CV, it is perfectly acceptable to write 'on request'.

Q. *How long should my CV be?*

A. Keep it as short and relevant as possible. One page is ideal. It should not normally be longer than three pages.

—— WRITING A CV ——

● **Basic graduate CV**

Kate Maxwell

DoB   28.02.81
Address   19, The Poplars, Bristol, B10 2JU
Tel   0117 123 4567
Email   katemaxwell@atlantic.net

Education

1999–2003   **BA Hons in Modern Languages, University of Exeter** (final grade 2:1)

1997–99   **Clifton Road Secondary School**: 3 'A' levels: – French (A) German (A) History (B)

1993–97   **Clifton Road Secondary School**: 8 GCSEs

Employment history

2002–03   **Sales Assistant, Langs Bookshop, Bristol**
            I was responsible for training and supervising weekend and holiday staff.

2001–02   **English Assistant, Lycée Benoit, Lyons**
            I taught conversational English to pupils aged 12-18, preparing the older students for both technical and more academic qualifications.

Positions of responsibility held

2000–01   **Entertainments Officer for University Student Social Society**
            I organized and budgeted for entertainment for a student society with over 1000 members.

Other skills: Fluent French and German, Extensive knowledge of Microsoft Word, Excel and Access

References available upon request

9

WRITING A CV

• CV for experienced candidate

Andrew Baird
134 Newton Road, Lincoln, LI5 6HB
tel: 01451 678234 **email:** abaird@coms.net
date of birth: 8 September 1973

Work experience
2000 to present
Coogan and Kidd Web Design Ltd, Lincoln – Website Developer
- Development of company website
- Responsible for team of 8 staff
- Project management: have led several projects providing web design for a number of leading insurance companies

1995–2000
Centaur Software, Cambridge – Computer Programmer
- Programming
- Database design: set up database for network of travel companies
- Software design: assisted in the design of financial management application for use by financial advisers

Programming languages
C, C++, Java, Perl, Visual Basic, VBScript, JavaScript

Applications
Visual Interdev, Dreamweaver

Other skills
clean driving licence held

Education
2001 – Microsoft Certified Systems Engineer
1995 – BSc Computer Science (2:1), University of
        Exeter

References available on request

10

WRITING FOR BUSINESS

● Writing business letters

FAQ

Q. *Is there a particular style I should use?*
A. Most companies have their own 'house style' for layout and punctuation. If you are unsure, look back in the filing to find out what the house style is.

Q. *What do I need to include in a business letter?*
A. You should include: the company letterhead; the letter reference; date; addressee's name and address; salutation (opening); subject heading; body of the letter; subscription (closing); signature or signatory.

 Tips

- Keep letters short and to the point.
- The subject heading indicates the subject of the letter for quick reference and should only be two or three words.
- Avoid using ambiguous terms.
- Remember that the standard method of closing before the signature depends on the opening at the start of the letter. If you opened with 'Dear Sir', you should close with 'Yours faithfully', if you opened with 'Dear Mr…,' you should close with 'Yours sincerely'.
- Always proofread your letters for spelling errors. Don't rely on your computer spell-check facility.
- If the letter has been marked 'Personal', 'Private' or 'Confidential', ensure that the envelope has been marked in the same way. Private means personal, confidential means sensitive.

WRITING FOR BUSINESS

- Thank you for your letter/email …
- With regard to … I am writing to …
- Further to our recent telephone conversation …
- If you require further information please don't hesitate to get in touch.

Ms R. Aitchison
124, Raven Road
HARROGATE HG2 8OP
27th January, 2003

Dear Ms Aitchison

I am writing to thank you for coming down to Oxford yesterday to discuss the possibility of our company taking over responsibility for publishing *The Big Book of Yo-Yos*. This is an exciting opportunity for us and I hope that we are able to reach a mutually beneficial agreement.

I will present this title to my sales and marketing team at our regular meeting midweek. I have sounded my marketing director out already and he is as enthusiastic as I am to publish your book. I am hoping to get a positive response from the sales team also.

I will of course keep you up to date with progress.

Yours sincerely

James Nichols
James Nichols
Publishing Manager

WRITING FOR BUSINESS

● Writing memoranda

FAQ

Q. *What is a memorandum?*
A. A memorandum (or memo) is a short letter or note sent to a particular in-house member of staff or circulated to groups of people.

Q. *Can I send a memo to someone in another company?*
A. Memos are not usually sent out of house.

Q. *What information does a memo usually contain?*
A. A memo usually contains: the sender's name and department; the addressee's name and department; date; and the subject.

Q. *Do I need to keep a copy?*
A. Always keep and file copies of all memoranda, as with other forms of correspondence.

To: Amy Wall   From: Lorna Gilmour
Publishing Production   Editorial Department

23/01/03
THE BIG BOOK OF YO-YOS
TEXT PRINTING COPY

Amy,
With regard to passing the book for press, I enclose the text printing copy.
Please pass this to the printer and request a full set of proofs for checking.
Cover copy for this edition has already passed.

Thanks,
Lorna

WRITING FOR BUSINESS

● Writing business reports

> ### FAQ
>
> **Q.** *How do I start?*
> **A.** Make a note of all the evidence you have amassed and decide on a line of argument. Then group the evidence together under various headings.
> **Q.** *What should a report contain?*
> **A.** A heading; a reason for the report; an argument; and a conclusion or recommendation.
> **Q.** *How do I persuade the reader to accept my proposal?*
> **A.** Find out what the priorities of your reader are, and then write the report from that point of view.

✓ Tips

- Aim to be accurate, concise and brief.
- Keep jargon to a minimum, but use technical words accurately.
- Reports on meetings should be written in the third person: 'It was decided', 'A proposal was put forward'. Individual reports can be written in the first person: 'I looked into the cost of …'
- Think about whether or not you need to include graphics or illustrations (such as pie charts, bar graphs, line graphs or flow charts) and choose the ones that are best suited to your purpose.
- Decide whether you want to use paragraph numbering or headings. Paragraph numbering is often much clearer than using headings and allows you to refer back and forward to specific paragraphs by number. If you do decide to use headings, make sure that the hierarchy is consistent.

WRITING FOR BUSINESS

- To make sure you've included everything, ask yourself three questions:
  - Have I included all the information that may be needed for the reader to make a decision?
  - Have I explained my proposal adequately and proved that it is better than alternatives?
  - Have I successfully put myself in the reader's shoes, and presented the problem and the solutions with his or her priorities in mind?

● **Asking for increased salary**

> **FAQ**
>
> **Q.** *Isn't this usually done verbally?*
> **A.** Yes, but you may be asked to follow up in writing. This gives your supervisor something concrete to use when negotiating with upper management on your behalf.
>
> **Q.** *Whom should I address my letter to?*
> **A.** Check with your supervisor, but it is a good idea to address it to your supervisor, and to copy in his or her manager and the human resource manager if there is one.

 Tips

- Open by telling your recipient how much you enjoy being a part of the team at your company, mentioning specific skills that you have.
- Let your recipient know how valuable you are to them by listing some accomplishments, such as revenue you have brought in to the company or money saved.

WRITING FOR BUSINESS

- Finish off by saying that you would like to continue being a valuable asset to the firm and that you appreciate their serious consideration of your request for an increase.
- Be realistic in the amount that you ask for: find out how much others make in comparable jobs.

Useful phrases

- I am writing to ask if you could consider the question of my salary.
- Since joining PGL, I have greatly enjoyed being a member of the I.T. department.
- During my time with PGL I have made several valuable contributions to the company's success, such as ...
- I am therefore requesting a salary increase of £... per annum.
- I would like to continue being a valuable asset to the firm and I appreciate your serious consideration of my request.
- If you would like to discuss this matter further, please do not hesitate to contact me to arrange a meeting at your convenience.

—— WRITING FOR BUSINESS ——

48 Ashgate Drive
Preston
Lancs PR3 6NZ

14 April 2003

Mr A Williamson
Head of I.T., Planet Insurance Ltd
Henderson Way
Preston, Lancs PR1 4TG

Dear Mr Williamson

Request for increased salary

In the three years that I have been working for Planet Insurance, I have greatly enjoyed being a member of the I.T. department.

I have also made certain accomplishments that have been of benefit to the company. For example, I wrote a computer program which greatly reduced the time spent on certain backup procedures, and was also responsible for the successful introduction of the online account management system.

With these points in mind, I would like to request a salary increase of £2000 per annum.

If you would like to discuss this matter further, please do not hesitate to arrange a meeting at your convenience.

Yours sincerely

Patrick Evans

Patrick Evans

— WRITING FOR BUSINESS —

● Giving notification of maternity leave

☑ You are required by law to give your employer 21 days' notice in writing of your intention to take maternity leave. This protects your right to maternity pay and return to work.

6 Dudley Avenue
Livingston
Edinburgh EH54 5TY

15 July 2003

Mr C McLeod
Cardrona Housing Association
3 Victoria Road
Edinburgh EH3 5WD

Dear Mr McLeod

Maternity leave notification

I am writing to notify you that I am pregnant, the expected date of delivery being 24 September 2003. I plan to begin my maternity leave on 27 August 2003.

I intend to return to work in April 2004, and will give you at least 21 days' notice of the exact date of my return.

Yours sincerely

Linda Allen

Linda Allen

—— WRITING FOR BUSINESS ——

● Asking for holiday entitlement

☑ It may not be necessary to write a letter when asking for holiday entitlement. An email is often considered satisfactory.

Dear George

I would like to take two weeks of my holiday entitlement from 25 April 2003–7 May 2003.

I have checked schedules, and feel confident that my work on the first stage of the current web project will be completed by then.

I hope these dates will be convenient.

Kind regards
Jack Lyons

—— WRITING FOR BUSINESS ——

● Writing a letter of resignation

 Tips

- Keep it simple.
- Try to avoid indirectly criticizing the company or your co-workers: you may wish to use your employer as a reference at a later date.
- Thank the recipient for any help or support they have given you during your time at the company.
- Show that you are willing to make the transfer as easy as possible.

Useful phrases

- This is to inform you that an opportunity has presented itself that will enable me to work in the area of …
- Please accept this letter as my formal resignation as Systems Administrator for DAL Publishing, to become effective as of …
- I am tendering my resignation from your company and wish to advise you that … will be my last day of employment.
- I believe this position will offer me more opportunity for advancement.
- I want to take this opportunity to thank you for your time and efforts in my training and advancement during the past three years.
- The support shown by you and the rest of the management team has been greatly appreciated.
- Please be assured that I will do all I can to assist in the smooth transfer of my responsibilities before leaving.

──── **WRITING FOR BUSINESS** ────

16 Lonsdale Crescent
Betchworth
Surrey RH10 7KM

4 April 2003

Mr K Robertson
Managing Director
Geode Publishing
3-5 Guildford Road
Dorking
Surrey RH7 4GL

Dear Keith
Resignation
I am writing to inform you that I have decided to accept a position at Topline Publishing in Croydon, starting on 2 May 2003. I believe this position will offer me more opportunity for advancement, and allow me to broaden my own experience and knowledge.

I want to take this opportunity to thank you for your time and effort in my training during the past three years, and wish you all the best for continued success in the future.

Please be assured that I will do all I can to assist in the smooth transfer of my responsibilities before leaving.

Yours sincerely

James Payne

James Payne

SCHOOL-RELATED CORRESPONDENCE

FAQ

Q. *Whom should I address my letter to?*
A. For straightforward matters such as homework and absences, write to your child's class teacher. For more serious issues or complaints, address your letter to the headteacher.

Q. *How can I find out about legal issues regarding bullying, truancy, exclusion, etc?*
A. The Advisory Centre for Education (ACE) publishes booklets outlining your rights on these matters. The material can also be read on their website.

● **Explaining a child's absence from school**

> 16 Newstead Road
> Bournemouth
> BO3 6HM
>
> 12 Jan 2004
>
> Dear Mr Dobson
> Stephen was unable to attend school yesterday as he was suffering from a 24-hour stomach bug. He seems to be well enough to come in today.
> Please advise us of any work he should be doing to make up for lost time.
>
> Thank you.
> Yours
> Lesley Allen

SCHOOL-RELATED CORRESPONDENCE

● Excusing a child from school

☑ Your letter is more likely to receive a positive response if you phrase it as a request, and express willingness to make up for any missed work.

---

39 Kayside Cottages
Perth PH2 5GK
16 Jan 2004

Mrs H Ross
Headteacher
St Mary's High School
Perth PH3 5RA

Dear Mrs Ross

Request for absence from school

On 1 Feb 2003, my employer, the NHS, will be observing 'Take your child to work day'. The purpose of this event is to introduce children aged 8–16 to the world of work, and to encourage them to consider a career in medicine.

I am therefore writing to request that my daughter, Isobel, be excused from school that day. She will, of course, make every effort to catch up on any missed work.

I look forward to hearing from you. If you wish to discuss the matter further, please do not hesitate to call me on 01252 568356.

Yours sincerely

Irene Marchant

Irene Marchant

SCHOOL-RELATED CORRESPONDENCE

● Notifying school of bullying

☑ Give details of exactly where and when the incident(s) took place, who was responsible, what happened, and how your child was affected by this. Be sure to ask for details of the school's anti-bullying strategy.

Useful phrases

- I am writing to express my deep concern about …
- My daughter has recently been experiencing …
- I have spoken to … but the situation has not improved.
- He has spoken to his class teacher, who has reprimanded those concerned. However, …
- As you can imagine, this problem is causing him a great deal of anxiety.
- I am anxious to resolve this problem as soon as possible.
- I would like to request a meeting to discuss a resolution to this problem.

SCHOOL-RELATED CORRESPONDENCE

19 Fairfield Drive
Hornslea
Bucks.
RD15 6YS

25 March 2004

Mr D Fitzgerald
Headteacher
Hornslea Primary School
Hornslea
Bucks
RD15 7JA

Dear Mr Fitzgerald

For the last three days my daughter, Helen Moore, has been arriving home in tears, due to continual name-calling from a small group of girls in her class. I have mentioned it to her class teacher, who has spoken to those concerned, but it has only made the problem worse. As you can imagine, this problem is causing Helen great anxiety, and now she is becoming fearful of going to school.

As you have a duty of care towards my child, I would like to request a meeting at your earliest convenience to discuss this.

I look forward to hearing from you.

Yours sincerely,
Katherine Moore
Katherine Moore (Mrs)

SCHOOL-RELATED CORRESPONDENCE

• Excusing a child from religious instruction

67 Langley Avenue
Crawley
W. Sussex
RH8 3FX

12 July 2003

Mrs J Wilson
Langley Green Secondary School
Langley Drive
Crawley
RH8 4WA

Dear Mrs Wilson

Religious instruction

My son, Aashir, will be attending your school from the beginning of next term, and I am writing to ask that he be excused from religious education classes.

He is being raised in the Muslim faith, and receives his religious instruction outside school.

Thank you very much for your understanding.

Yours sincerely

Mahira Pandit

Mahira Pandit (Mrs)

──── DOMESTIC MATTERS ────

● To a landlord concerning domestic repairs

56 Kayside Close
Redditch
Worcs.
RD14 7NX

4 April 2003

Dear Mr Fairchild

I am writing to notify you that the following repairs to 56 Kayside Close require attention:

There are several loose tiles on the roof.
The kitchen tap is leaking.
The sealant round the bath needs replacing.

I would appreciate it if you would contact me as soon as possible to arrange a time to have these problems taken care of.
Thank you very much.

Yours sincerely

Matthew Chalmers

Matthew Chalmers

☑ If repairs are not forthcoming within a reasonable amount of time, write again, reminding the recipient how long you have been waiting. This time you should show your landlord that you are aware of your rights in law.

—— DOMESTIC MATTERS ——

Useful phrases

- Further to my previous correspondence, the following repairs to the above address remain outstanding: …
- I have been waiting for a considerable amount of time to have these repairs completed.
- By law, a landlord is responsible for providing and maintaining residence in a good state of repair.

---

56 Kayside Close
Redditch
Worcs. RD14 7NX

1 May 2003

Dear Mr Fairchild

In my previous correspondence to you I requested repairs to be completed to 56 Kayside Close. The following items remain outstanding:

There are several loose tiles on the roof.
The kitchen tap is leaking.
The sealant round the bath needs replacing.

I have been waiting for a considerable amount of time to have these repairs completed, and would ask you to take care of this matter within one week of receipt of this letter.

May I remind you that by law, a landlord is responsible for providing and maintaining a residence in a good state of repair.

Yours sincerely

Matthew Chalmers

Matthew Chalmers

—— DOMESTIC MATTERS ——

● Letter to a housing advice centre regarding unfair rent

☑ If your landlord/landlady is trying to put the rent up and you don't agree to the increase, it may be worth trying to negotiate with them.

> 45 Victoria Street
> Headley
> Northants. NO3 7FS
>
> 16 April 2003

The Rents Adviser
Headley Housing Advice
4 The Row
Headley, Northants. NO2 4TY

Dear Sir/Madam

Unfair rent query

I am writing to request your advice on an issue regarding an unfair increase in rent.

My landlord has recently increased my rent from £300 a month to £360 a month. Not only do I find this amount unreasonable, but I am also having difficulty sustaining the payments. I would be grateful if you could inform me of my rights in this situation. I look forward to hearing from you.

Yours faithfully

Katherine Gulliver

Katherine Gulliver

——DOMESTIC MATTERS——

• Letter to a housing advice centre regarding eviction

34 Tadworth Court
Ducksbury
Berkshire
RD7 4GN

3 June 2004
Berkshire Housing Assoc.
14 High Road
Ducksbury, Berkshire RD2 3QA

Dear Sir/Madam

Eviction query

I am writing to request advice from you regarding a matter of urgency.

My landlord has just issued me with an eviction notice, due to come into force on 4 July 2003. His justification for this action is that I have not paid my rent for the last two months.

Could you please inform me of my rights, and advise me on how I should proceed?

If you wish to speak to me directly, please call me on 01456 783219.

Thank you in advance.

Yours faithfully

Sally Nettles

Sally Nettles

—— DOMESTIC MATTERS ——

● Letter to a planning authority inquiring as to whether planning permission is needed

☑ Some minor developments may not need express planning permission. However, it is best to consult with the local planning authority before any changes are made.

19 Limes Avenue
Cambridge
CB12 4LA
tel: 01356 721673

17 June 2003

The Planning Department
Cambridge District Council
University Road
Cambridge
CB2 7KS

Dear Sir/Madam
Planning permission inquiry

I am writing to inquire as to whether I will need planning permission for a proposed development I wish to undertake at the above address.

I wish to build a garage at the side of my property, 2.5m high, and with a floor surface area of 6m x 3.5m.

Please let me know if you require further information. I look forward to hearing from you.

Yours faithfully

Harriet Yates

Harriet Yates (Mrs)

——DOMESTIC MATTERS——

● Objecting to planning permission application

> **FAQ**
>
> **Q.** *What sorts of objections are considered valid?*
> **A.** Objections should be confined to such issues as:
> design and appearance, significant overlooking or
> overshadowing, traffic impact and noise, smell or
> other pollutants. Objections which cannot normally
> be considered include the loss of a personal view
> from a particular property, and loss of property
> value.

 Tips

● Write to the Director of Planning at your local
district council.
● Refer to the application number and the site
address.
● Clearly outline the reasons why you wish to object
to the proposal.

DOMESTIC MATTERS

Useful phrases

- I am writing to register my objection to the planning application detailed above.
- The increase in traffic caused by the development would significantly affect the character of the area.
- This building would significantly affect my family's quality of life.
- I urge you to reject this application.

---

7 Fallowfield Terrace
Fordham, Hants SO12 5AZ

19 May 2003
The Director of Planning and Technical Services
Fordham District Council
Fordham, Hants SO13 5HB

Dear Sir/Madam

Planning application no: 00006721 45793
I wish to object to the above planning permission application for 5 Fallowfield Terrace.

This extension, if constructed, would greatly affect the amount of light reaching the back rooms of my house, and compromise my family's privacy.

Please take this into account when considering this application, which I urge you to reject.

Yours faithfully
Malcolm Skinner
Malcolm Skinner

——DOMESTIC MATTERS——

- **Objecting to the proposed erection of a mobile phone mast**

Q. *To whom should I address my letter?*
A. Write to the council's planning department and copy it to your local councillor and the landowner.

Q. *How should I formulate my objection?*
A. Some ideas for formulating your objection are:
  - Have the regulations been followed?
  - Is it necessary?
  - Are there alternative sites available?

✅ *Tips*

- Identify the deadline date for objections.
- Different regions have different policies on the erection of mobile phone masts.
- Find out what your council's policy is before writing your letter.

DOMESTIC MATTERS

45 Hopetoun Gardens
Hopetoun, West Lothian
LV4 7NX

3 April 2003

Mr R. McKinnon
Chief Planning Officer
Hopetoun District Council
Hopetoun, West Lothian
LV2 4GY

Dear Mr McKinnon

Re: planning application no. 39100921/000128
I am writing in objection to the proposed erection
of a telecommunications mast on land situated at
Hopetoun Park, West Lothian. My objection is
based on the following grounds:

The proposed mast would be situated only 30
metres away from a residential area. With no
clear evidence showing that such masts are
safe, particularly with regard to children's
health, I feel that this proximity is
unacceptable.

The mast is unnecessary, since the signal for
the network concerned is adequate in this area.

With these points in mind, I urge you to reject
this application.

Yours sincerely

Roger Hall
Roger Hall

MONEY-RELATED CORRESPONDENCE

- ● **Letter to a lender advising of difficulty in mortgage payment**

 Tips
  - If you are having trouble with your mortgage payments, or if you anticipate problems, contact your lender as soon as possible.
  - In your letter, show that you are willing to negotiate with the lender.
  - Stress that you are keen to keep paying as much as you can afford.

Useful phrases

  - I am writing to inform you that I am anticipating having some difficulty in continuing to meet my mortgage payments.
  - I am currently finding it hard to meet all my financial commitments.
  - I was wondering if it would be possible to reduce my monthly payments.
  - I do hope that you will give sympathetic consideration to my situation.

MONEY-RELATED CORRESPONDENCE

92 Lockwood Avenue
Leadingham GR2 9TN

15 May 2003

Mr J McVee
Senior Credit Controller
Castle Building Society
2 York Road
Leeds, N. Yorks LE3 3RA

Dear Mr McVee

Request for reduction in mortgage payments
I am writing to inform you that, due to my recent redundancy, I anticipate some difficulty in meeting my mortgage payments.

I would therefore like to request that my mortgage payments be temporarily reduced from July, and the terms of my mortgage extended accordingly.

I am keen to continue paying as much as possible, and am currently in consultation with my financial adviser regarding a reasonable figure.

Would it be possible to arrange an interview with you, so that we may come to an arrangement? I do hope that you will give sympathetic consideration to my situation.

Yours sincerely

Jack Everett

Jack Everett

MONEY-RELATED CORRESPONDENCE

- **Letter to an insurance company advising of an accident**

Ken Howland
2 Rowlands Ave
Birmingham B6 7PL

25 July 2003

The Claims Officer
Hotline Insurance
3 Castle Court
London W1 5HT

Dear Sir/Madam
Policy No: 0000931 45621

I am writing to notify you that I wish to make a claim under the above insurance policy.

The insured vehicle was in an accident on 12 July 2003 with another vehicle in Pitlochry, Perthshire, resulting in damage to the rear bumper and lights.

Please contact me at the above address, so that a formal claim may be made.

Thank you for your attention to this matter.

Yours faithfully

Kenneth Howland

Kenneth Howland

MONEY-RELATED CORRESPONDENCE

- ● **Letter to an insurance company advising of a burglary**

> Patrick Norton
> 23 Lucas Rd
> Kingston-Upon-Thames
> Surrey KT6 2PL

25 July 2003
The Claims Officer
UK Assured Ltd
6 West Gorton Rd
Lincoln
LI4 9TZ

Dear Sir/Madam
Policy No: 12409745 000002

I am writing to inform you that I have suffered a loss to the above-named property, and wish to make a claim under the provisions of my insurance policy.

A burglary took place on 23 July 2003, resulting in losses of jewellery worth £2000 and damage to the home which will cost £500 to repair.

I would be grateful if you could contact me at the address shown above, so that a formal claim may be made.

Thank you for your attention to this matter.

Yours faithfully

Patrick Norton

Patrick Norton

LETTERS OF COMPLAINT

FAQ

Q. *To whom should I address the letter?*
A. For a large company, direct your letter to the Customer Relations Manager. For a small company, you should write directly to the Managing Director.

Q. *What is the best way to ensure a speedy reply and get the desired result?*
A. Collect together all the relevant facts, then set them down in a logical sequence. If you have a reference number, quote this in the subject heading of the letter. Specify a time limit within which you expect to hear from the company, and the action you wish to be taken.

Q. *What do I need to know about my legal rights?*
A. It helps if you know the basics of the Sale of Goods Act, and to make this fact known to your recipient.

Useful phrases

- I am writing to express my dissatisfaction with the service I received.
- I have contacted you by telephone three times and each time you have promised to visit and put the faults right.
- To date these problems have not been resolved.
- Under the Goods and Services Act 1982, I am entitled to expect work to be carried out using due care and skill.
- If I do not hear from you within 14 days, I will have no choice but to take the matter further.

—— LETTERS OF COMPLAINT ——

• Letter of complaint regarding unsatisfactory holiday accommodation

16 Hopeside Crescent
Hove
East Sussex
EG13 6HJ

24 August 2003

The Customer Relations Manager
Sunkiss Holidays
58-60 East Preston Street
Manchester
M2 9LP

Dear Sir

Re: booking reference number 61000367

I am writing to express my dissatisfaction at the standard of holiday accommodation at the above holiday apartment in Ibiza last week.

At the time of booking, I requested a three-bedroomed apartment with living room and kitchen. However, we discovered that the third 'bedroom' consisted of a sofa-bed in the living area, and the kitchen was small and dirty.

Under the Supply of Goods and Services Act 1982, I am entitled to expect the accommodation provided to be of a satisfactory standard, as described in your brochure. I look forward to an offer of compensation within 14 days.

Yours faithfully

Charles MacLennan

Charles MacLennan (Mr)

LETTERS OF COMPLAINT

• Letter of complaint regarding a faulty appliance

41 Selwood Avenue
Kingston-upon-Hull
East Yorks HU7 4DS

4 May 2003

Ms Jane Andrews
Customer Relations Officer
Stewarts Electrics
Foxton High Road
London SW3 6BZ

Dear Ms Andrews

Re: faulty appliance

I recently bought a chrome espresso machine
(£129.99) from your store in Middleham. When I
tried to use it, I discovered that due to a faulty
element, the coffee was lukewarm.

I have returned to your store in Middleham on
several occasions, requesting first a replacement,
and subsequently, a refund. The latter has not
been forthcoming, and the shop manager has
now advised me to take my complaint to you.

Under the Sale of Goods Act 1979, purchased
items should be of satisfactory quality and fit for
their purpose. Since neither of these criteria are
met, I would like to request a full
reimbursement of the amount paid. I look
forward to your reply.

Yours sincerely,

A. Fraser

Anne Fraser (Mrs)

LETTERS OF COMPLAINT

● Complaining about public transport

35 Fairways Drive
Penicuik
Midlothian
EH17 4KC

4 October 2003

The Customer Relations Manager, Scotbus
Burns House
McGowan Road
Glasgow G4 7JY

Dear Sir/Madam

I am writing to complain about the bus journey I undertook yesterday on the number 95 bus from Penicuik to Edinburgh. I was dissatisfied with the service in the following ways:

- The bus arrived 20 minutes late.
- The bus finally left the bus station 30 minutes late.
- The temperature inside the bus was about 35 degrees Centigrade.

Being nearly 7 months pregnant, I found this journey very uncomfortable, and by the end, quite distressing.

I would be interested to hear your comments on this, and any offer of compensation you may consider appropriate.

Yours faithfully

P. Holmes

Patricia Holmes

——LETTERS OF COMPLAINT——

• Shoddy workmanship

 Tips

- Discuss the problem with the tradesperson first, and give them a chance to put it right.
- Keep copies of all letters sent and received and make a note of conversations.
- If you choose a contractor that belongs to a trade association, they may offer a conciliation or arbitration service to settle your dispute.

---

77 Bishop Road
Newport
Gwent NP3 5NQ
31 October 2003

Customer Services Manager
L. Smart & Co. Contractors
17 Trevellyan Road
Cardiff CA4 5GT

Dear Sir/Madam
Re: estimate 700003412
I am writing to express my dissatisfaction with the service I received from one of your builders recently. I was originally assured that the work would be completed by 10 October. Three weeks later, the work is still incomplete.

If the problem is not rectified within 14 days, I shall consider our contract to be at an end.

Yours faithfully
Douglas Fairburn
Douglas Fairburn

──LETTERS OF COMPLAINT──

● Complaining to a health authority

✓ *Tips*
- Address your letter to the Complaints Manager of the Local Health Authority.
- Give name of doctor, GP or practitioner concerned.
- State the problem, itemizing any errors clearly and succinctly.

---

7 Oaklands
Horley RH6 2QT

17 November 2003

The Complaints Manager
East Surrey Local Health Authority
5 Market Street
Redhill RH1 4GA

Dear Sir

I am writing to express my concern about the treatment that my elderly mother, Mrs Grace Harding, is currently undergoing. Her GP is Dr Middleton, at Horley Surgery.

My mother, who suffers from shingles, recently received a letter informing her that she could no longer attend the pain clinic at this surgery. She has been given no explanation for this.

Since the NHS claims to be committed to tailoring its services around the needs of individual patients, I look forward to receiving your comments.

Yours faithfully

G. Glover

Gillian Glover

LETTERS OF COMPLAINT

• Complaining about financial services

✓ *Tips*
- You must complain to the firm before you go to the ombudsman.
- Remember to include important details like your customer number or your policy number.
- Remember to enclose copies of any relevant documents.

---

4 Hove Lane
Newhaven
W Sussex BN12 6JL

24 October 2003
The Customer Relations Manager
Castle Building Society
Grove Street, Derby DB5 4FY
Dear Sir/Madam

Complaint: savings acc. no. 9450001992
In August, I opened a savings account with your bank and arranged for a standing order of £150 a month to be made from my current account. However, there has been no credit to my savings account for the previous two months, despite the fact that the money had been debited from my current account. Enclosed are copies of both the relevant statements.

I am appealing for an investigation into this matter, and look forward to hearing from you.

Yours faithfully

Patrick Horton
Patrick Horton

SOCIAL CORRESPONDENCE

● Formal invitations

✓ *Tips*
- Use quality stationery that reflects your own personal style.
- Issue your invitation well in advance of the occasion.
- Include details of the event, the address, date and time, and whether there will be a dress code.

● A wedding invitation

John and Angela Shaw
are delighted to invite

Jeremy Kempton and Kay Whitcroft
to the wedding of their daughter

Catharine

to

Matthew Tibbits

on Saturday 5th April 2004

at 2pm
at Hemel Methodist Church, Bristol
and afterwards to a
Reception at Austen Place, Keynsham

RSVP
Cathy Shaw
89 Caird Drive
Brighton
BN1 9TQ

SOCIAL CORRESPONDENCE

• Refusing invitations

Useful phrases

- Thank you so much for the invitation to …
- Unfortunately I already have something arranged that day.
- It's our 30th wedding anniversary, and we're going out for a meal that night.
- Harry's got his school concert that night.
- I'm really sorry, as I'd have loved to see you all.

• Declining a formal invitation to a wedding

25 Dean Avenue
Yeovil
Somerset
YO3 8LR

23 March 2004

Mr and Mrs K Forbes thank Mr and Mrs O'Neill for their kind invitation to their daughter's wedding, and to the reception afterwards, but regret that a prior engagement prevents them from attending.

—— SOCIAL CORRESPONDENCE ——

• Letters wishing a speedy recovery

FAQ

Q. *What sort of tone should I use?*
A. It is acceptable to use a fairly informal tone if you know that the person will recover quickly. If the illness is serious, you will need to use a slightly more formal tone.
Q. *Should I send a card or a letter?*
A. For informal wishes, a card is most appropriate. For more formal wishes, or if the illness is serious, you may like to write a letter.

• Formal wishes (letter)

Useful phrases

- Hoping you get well very soon.
- Please accept my sympathies …
- … and best wishes for a speedy recovery.
- It must be an anxious time for you.
- Is there any way in which we can help?

SOCIAL CORRESPONDENCE

• Formal letter wishing somebody a speedy recovery

> Upper Steading, 17 June 2003
>
> Dear Mr Grierson
>
> We were very sorry to hear of your wife's sudden illness. Please accept our sympathies and give her our best wishes for a speedy recovery.
>
> If there's anything we can do, please don't hesitate to let us know. In the meantime, we are thinking of you both.
>
> Yours sincerely
>
> *Mary Fawkes*

☑ If the recipient is unlikely to make a full recovery, it is unwise to suggest that this might be the case.

• Letters of condolence

FAQ

Q. *What form should a letter of condolence take?*

A. A letter of condolence should normally be handwritten.

Q. *I never know what to say at such times. Don't letters of condolence require complicated and refined language?*

A. No. Try to express yourself simply, and speak from the heart.

Q. *Should I make reference to God and religion?*

A. Only if you know that your recipient shares your beliefs.

SOCIAL CORRESPONDENCE

✓ *Tips*

- Express your shock or regret at the person's death.
- Briefly point out the deceased's qualities, and any achievements you may want to mention.
- Say how much the deceased will be missed.
- Offer any help that you are genuinely willing to give.

● An informal letter of condolence

Littleton, 24 March 2004

Dear Pat,

We were terribly sad to hear the tragic news of Ken's death. It's been a great shock, and we want you to know that you are in our thoughts.

Everyone who knew Ken found him an exceptional person, with his great talent for painting and his kindness and warmth. We will miss him greatly.

You know that you can call on us any time. Please don't hesitate if there is anything we can do to help.

All our love

Leonie and Andrew

SOCIAL CORRESPONDENCE

● A more formal letter of condolence

Useful phrases

- I was deeply saddened to hear of ...'s death
- It has come to us as a great shock.
- Please accept my sincerest condolences.
- I am sure you know how much he was liked and respected by everyone.
- We will all miss him greatly.

Taunton, 14 April 2004

Dear Mrs Morrison

I was very sad to hear of your husband's death last week, and I write to offer sincere condolences to you and your family.

I am sure you know how much Mr Morrison was liked and respected in the community. We will all miss him greatly.

If there is anything I can do to help, please don't hesitate to get in touch.

Kindest regards

Yvonne Tullis

WRITING SPEECHES

✓ *Tips*

- When writing your speech, look at other people's speeches in books and on websites, to help you decide what's appropriate for you.
- Think about your audience. How formal is the setting? What kind of jokes are likely to go down well?
- Brainstorm on topics.
- Practise your delivery.

• Delivering your speech

> **FAQ**
>
> **Q.** *Is it OK to read my speech or should I memorize it?*
> **A.** It's best not to trust everything to memory. Thoroughly familiarize yourself with your speech and then reduce it to a set of brief notes on cue cards. This way your speech will not sound as if it is being read word for word.
> **Q.** *Should I practise my speech, or might too much practice make it sound contrived?*
> **A.** You should rehearse it thoroughly. Get a friend or family member to help by listening and ask them to tell you honestly how your voice sounds.
> **Q.** *I tend to gabble when I'm nervous. How can I avoid this?*
> **A.** Always take your time, and pause to let your points sink in. Breathe deeply, and don't give in to the urge to speed up.
> **Q.** *How can I give an impression of confidence, even when I'm nervous?*
> **A.** Be conscious of your body language from the start. Look around at your audience for a few seconds before you start to speak, and try to make eye contact with them.

——— WRITING SPEECHES ———

• Wedding speeches

The three main speeches that are usually given at a wedding reception are:
- the bride's father's speech
- the bridegroom's speech
- the best man's speech

 Tips

When drafting your speech, start by considering some of the following points:
- When did you first meet the bride/groom?
- Can you remember anything unusual that happened when you first met?
- What are her/his best qualities?
- Do you have any plans or wishes for your future together? (for bridegroom only)

• The bride's father

> *Useful phrases*

- On behalf of (name of wife) and myself, I would like to start by saying what a pleasure it is to welcome, on this very happy occasion (names of groom's parents), (named close relatives), together with all relatives and friends of both families.
- As father of the bride, it is my privilege to make the first speech, and I would like to start by …
- First I would like to welcome everybody here today to join (bride) and (groom) on this special day.

—— WRITING SPEECHES ——

- I know some people have travelled quite some distance, and I would like to express our gratitude and thanks for the effort they have made.
- (Groom) is attentive, caring, hard-working, intelligent, and informed on most subjects, except football (he supports ……). I am very pleased and proud to welcome him as a son-in-law.
- I would like to welcome my new son-in-law into our family.
- It is now my pleasant duty to propose a toast to the happy couple. Please join me in wishing them a long and happy life together.

● The bridegroom

Useful phrases

- I'd like to thank (bride's father) for those kind words, I am very proud to be your son-in-law; I hope I can live up to your expectations.
- To our parents, thank you for your love and support over the years, for the advice you have given us, for putting up with us and pointing us in the right direction.
- On behalf of my new wife and myself, I would like to say thank you to a few people
- It's been an amazing day and having you all here has helped to make this the most memorable and happiest day of our lives.
- She is beautiful, intelligent, hard-working – the list is endless, but unfortunately I can't read her handwriting …

WRITING SPEECHES

● The best man

Useful phrases

- Firstly on behalf of the bridesmaid(s), (bridesmaids' names), I would like to thank (groom) for his kind words.
- On a serious note, can you all be upstanding and charge your glasses while I propose a toast:
- To the bride – may she share everything with her husband, including the housework!
- Please stay upstanding and join me in a toast to the bride and groom's parents … and those who were sadly unable to be here today.
- It gives me great pleasure to invite you to all stand and raise your glasses in a toast for (bride) and (groom). We wish them well for the future and hope they enjoy a long and happy marriage together.

WRITING SPEECHES

● Writing a eulogy

FAQ

Q. *What sort of tone should I adopt when writing a eulogy?*

A. Generally, a eulogy should be written in an informal, conversational tone. Humour is acceptable if it fits the personality of the deceased.

Q. *Should I just speak about my own experiences of the deceased, or should I try to include other people's experiences?*

A. A eulogy should convey the feelings and experiences of the person giving it. Don't try to speak for all present. However, it can be a good idea to write about memories that the audience can remember, and to get the audience involved in what you are saying.

Q. *How long should I speak for?*

A. Keep it brief. Five to ten minutes is the norm, but it's a good idea to verify that with the officiator.

——— WRITING SPEECHES ———

✓ *Tips*

- Be honest, and focus on the person's positive qualities.
- You may want to include the deceased's favourite poems, book passages, scripture verses, quotes, expressions or lines from songs.
- Is there a humorous or touching event that represents the essence of the deceased?
- What will you miss most about him or her?

Useful phrases

- When I think of …, I think of laughter and love.
- … taught me how to …
- … was involved in so many activities; she/he was very popular.
- I can see her/him now: …ing, …ing and …
- She/he always showed loyalty, courtesy and consideration for others.
- I am so lucky to have had … as a friend.
- I will miss her/him very much.

—— WRITING SPEECHES ——

• Leaving and retirement speeches

✓ *Tips*

- Remember that your approach may be slightly different depending on whether the employee is leaving under happy or more regrettable circumstances.
- Remember that your main aim is to thank the employee and to praise them for any achievements you want to mention.
- Try to think of a humorous anecdote that you can recount about the person who is leaving.

Useful phrases

- When Jack first arrived at the company ...
- Thank you for all your hard work, especially ...
- We respect the decision you have made, and wish you all the best in your future career.
- We are sorry you had to leave under these circumstances, but we wish you every success in the future.
- Your future is looking very exciting, and we wish you great happiness in your new job.
- Please accept this gift as a mark of our respect and gratitude for all you have done.

EMAILS

✓ *Tips*

The rules of polite behaviour for email conversation are known as 'netiquette'. Some of these rules are:

- Do not write in capital letters. This is considered to be the equivalent of shouting in speech.
- Use asterisks (*) before and after a word if you want to emphasize it.
- Be careful about using irony or sarcasm. As readers cannot see you, or hear your tone of voice, statements intended as jokes may be taken seriously.
- Jokes can be shown by using a 'smiley' or 'emoticon' such as :-). On the other hand, do not use too many of these.
- Avoid 'flames'. A flame is an angry response to a message, especially on a newsgroup, which can be very annoying for other newsgroup readers.

• Emoticons

Emoticons or 'smileys' are often used to indicate tone. These symbols are read with the head tilted on the left shoulder. The basic smiley is :-). Tongue-in-cheek remarks might use a winking smiley ;-).

Below is a list of emoticons in common use, both in email and text messaging:

o:-)	angel
;/	confused
>:-)	devil
:-s	I'm not making sense.
:-p	naughty
:-(	sad
:-O	shouting
:o	surprised

——— EMAILS ———

● Net abbreviations

Email abbreviations have developed to shorten messages and speed up typing. Some of the more common ones are:

AFK	away from keyboard	IMHO	in my humble opinion
BAK	back at keyboard	IOW	in other words
BTW	by the way	NRN	no reply necessary
FAQ	frequently asked question(s) (or a web page containing frequently asked questions)	OTOH	on the other hand
		ROFL	rolling on the floor laughing
		RSN	real soon now (often used ironically)
FWIW	for what it's worth		
FYI	for your information	SITD	still in the dark
FUA	frequently used acronym	TIA	thanks in advance
		TIC	tongue in cheek
IAE	in any event	TLA	three letter acronym
IMO	in my opinion		

—— EMAILS ——

● A more formal email

To: edcollins@planet.co.uk, valkaye@planet.co.uk
Cc: robertwestwood@planet.co.uk
Subject: sales review meeting
Attachments: salesfigures_march2003.doc

Dear Ed, Val

I've just been looking at the sales figures for the last quarter, and think it would be beneficial for us all to get together to discuss them.

Attached is a copy of the document, and I'd be grateful for any comments you may have.

Would Thursday afternoon suit you both, say, 2.30pm? Please let me know if this is not convenient.

Regards

Brian

● An informal email *

To: jennymartin@viking.net
Cc:
Subject: Friday night

Hi Jenny

How're things? Hope all's well, and that you had a riveting time last night at the committee meeting ;-)

I was wondering what you and Will are up to on Friday? Do you fancy going out for something to eat? BTW, I've just heard that Kate's taken that new job. IMHO it's not going to be an easy job, but good for her anyway.

Let us know what you think about Friday night.

Lots of love, Tamsin xxx

—— EMAILS ——

• Response to an informal email

To: tforbes@pgl.com
Cc:

Subject: Re: Friday night
Attachments:

Hi Tamsin

You wrote:

>Hope all's well, and that you had a riveting
>time last night at the committee meeting ;-)

I nearly died of boredom, as you can well imagine!

>I was wondering what you and Will are up to
>on Friday? Do you fancy going out for
>something to eat?

Sounds great! I'll have been paid by then, so I'll be up for a big night :-)

>BTW, I've just heard that Kate's taken that new
>job. IMHO it's not going to be an easy job, but
>good for her anyway.

I'm amazed, but I suppose our Kate's always up for a challenge. Rather her than me though …

Looking forward to seeing you. Will give you a ring about meeting up on Friday.

Love

Jenny

xx

TEXT MESSAGING

Text messages sent from mobile phones tend to be short, using a large number of short cuts. Some of the more common abbreviations are listed below:

1CE	once	NO1	no one
2DAY	today	NP	no problem
2MOR	tomorrow	OIC	oh, I see
2NITE	tonight	OMG	oh, my God
ASAP	as soon as	PLS	please
	possible	PPL	people
B	be	R	are
BCNU	be seeing you	RTFM	read the flippin'
BRB	be right back		manual
BTDT	been there, done	RU	are you
that		RUOK	are you okay
BTW	by the way	SOZ	sorry
C	see	STFU	shut up
CID	consider it done	SUM1	someone
COZ	because	THANQ	thank you
CU	see you	THX	thanks
DA	the	TMB	text me back
EZ	easy	TTYL	talk to you later
F2T	free to talk	TXT BAC	text back
FOTFLOL	falling on the	TYVM	thank you very
	floor, laughing		much
	out loud	U	you
GAL	get a life	W/O	without
GR8	great	WAN2	want to
GTG	got to go	WBS	write back soon
H8	hate	WIV	with
K	okay	WKND	weekend
L8	late	WUD?	what you doing?
L8ER	later	XLNT	excellent
LOL	laughing out	Y	why
	loud *or*	YR	your
	loads of love	YYSSW	yeah yeah sure
LV	love		sure whatever
M8	mate		
MMFU	my mate fancies		
	you		
NE	any		
NE1	anyone		
NETHING	anything		